KU-569-936

THE ALL ENGLAND LAW REPORTS 1980

Volume 3

Editor
PETER HUTCHESSON LL M
Barrister, New Zealand

Assistant Editor
BROOK WATSON
of Lincoln's Inn, Barrister
and of the New South Wales Bar

Consulting Editor
WENDY SHOCKETT
of Gray's Inn, Barrister

London
BUTTERWORTHS

ENGLAND:	Butterworth & Co (Publishers) Ltd London: 88 Kingsway, WC2B 6AB
AUSTRALIA:	Butterworths Pty Ltd Sydney: 586 Pacific Highway, Chatswood, NSW 2067 Also at Melbourne, Brisbane, Adelaide and Perth
CANADA:	Butterworth & Co (Canada) Ltd Toronto: 2265 Midland Avenue, Scarborough, M1P 4S1
NEW ZEALAND:	Butterworths of New Zealand Ltd Wellington: 31–35 Cumberland Place
SOUTH AFRICA:	Butterworth & Co (South Africa) (Pty) Ltd Durban: 152–154 Gale Street
USA:	Butterworth & Co (Publishers) Inc Boston: 10 Tower Office Park, Woburn, Mass 01801

ISBN 0 406 85138 7

Typeset by CCC, printed and bound in Great Britain by William Clowes (Beccles) Limited, Beccles and London

REPORTERS

House of Lords

Mary Rose Plummer Barrister

Privy Council

Mary Rose Plummer Barrister

Court of Appeal, Civil Division

Mary Rose Plummer Barrister
Sumra Green Barrister
Frances Rustin Barrister
Avtar S Virdi Esq Barrister
Diana Brahams Barrister
Patricia Hargrove Barrister

Court of Appeal, Criminal Division

N P Metcalfe Esq Barrister
Sepala Munasinghe Esq Barrister
Dilys Tausz Barrister

Courts-Martial Appeals

N P Metcalfe Esq Barrister

Chancery Division

Jacqueline Metcalfe Barrister
Evelyn M C Budd Barrister
Hazel Hartman Barrister
Azza M Abdallah Barrister

Queen's Bench Division

Jacqueline Charles Barrister
M Denise Chorlton Barrister
J M Collins Esq Barrister
Gwynedd Lewis Barrister
Deirdre McKinney Barrister
K Mydeen Esq Barrister
Denise Randall Barrister

Family Division

Bebe Chua Barrister

Revenue Cases

Rengan Krishnan Esq Barrister
Edwina Epstein Barrister

Admiralty

N P Metcalfe Esq Barrister

MANAGER

John W Wilkes Esq

House of Lords

The Lord High Chancellor: Lord Hailsham of St Marylebone

Lords of Appeal in Ordinary

Lord Wilberforce
Lord Diplock
Viscount Dilhorne
(retired 1st August 1980)
Lord Salmon
(retired 30th September 1980)
Lord Edmund-Davies

Lord Fraser of Tullybelton
Lord Russell of Killowen
Lord Keith of Kinkel
Lord Scarman
Lord Roskill
Lord Bridge
(appointed 29th September 1980)

Court of Appeal

The Lord High Chancellor

The Lord Chief Justice of England: Lord Lane

The Master of the Rolls: Lord Denning

The President of the Family Division: Sir John Lewis Arnold

Lords Justices of Appeal

Sir John Megaw
(retired 29th September 1980)
Sir Denys Burton Buckley
Sir John Frederick Eustace Stephenson
Sir Frederick Horace Lawton
Sir Roger Fray Greenwood Ormrod
Sir Nigel Cyprian Bridge
(appointed Lord of Appeal in Ordinary, 29th September 1980)
Sir Sebag Shaw
Sir George Stanley Waller
Sir James Roualeyn Hovell-Thurlow Cumming-Bruce

Sir Edward Walter Eveleigh
Sir Henry Vivian Brandon
Sir Sydney William Templeman
Sir John Francis Donaldson
Sir John Anson Brightman
Sir Desmond James Conrad Ackner
Sir Robin Horace Walford Dunn
Sir Peter Raymond Oliver
Sir Tasker Watkins VC
Sir Patrick McCarthy O'Connor
(appointed 30th September 1980)
Sir William Hugh Griffiths
(appointed 30th September 1980)

Chancery Division

The Lord High Chancellor

The Vice-Chancellor: Sir Robert Edgar Megarry

Sir John Patrick Graham
Sir Peter Harry Batson Woodroffe Foster
Sir John Norman Keates Whitford
Sir Ernest Irvine Goulding
Sir Raymond Henry Walton
Sir Michael John Fox
Sir Christopher John Slade
Sir Nicolas Christopher Henry Browne-Wilkinson
Sir John Evelyn Vinelott
Sir George Brian Hugh Dillon
Sir Martin Charles Nourse

Queen's Bench Division

The Lord Chief Justice of England

Sir Alan Abraham Mocatta
Sir John Thompson
Sir Helenus Patrick Joseph Milmo
Sir Joseph Donaldson Cantley
Sir Hugh Eames Park
Sir Stephen Chapman
Sir Patrick McCarthy O'Connor (appointed Lord Justice of Appeal, 30th September 1980)
Sir Bernard Caulfield
Sir Hilary Gwynne Talbot
Sir William Lloyd Mars-Jones
Sir Ralph Kilner Brown
Sir Phillip Wien
Sir Peter Henry Rowley Bristow
Sir Hugh Harry Valentine Forbes
Sir William Hugh Griffiths (appointed Lord Justice of Appeal, 30th September 1980)
Sir Robert Hugh Mais
Sir Neil Lawson
Sir David Powell Croom-Johnson
Sir John Raymond Phillips
Sir Leslie Kenneth Edward Boreham
Sir John Douglas May
Sir Michael Robert Emanuel Kerr
Sir Alfred William Michael Davies
Sir John Dexter Stocker
Sir Kenneth George Illtyd Jones
Sir Haydn Tudor Evans
Sir Peter Richard Pain
Sir Kenneth Graham Jupp
Sir Robert Lionel Archibald Goff
Sir Stephen Brown
Sir Gordon Slynn
Sir Roger Jocelyn Parker
Sir Ralph Brian Gibson
Sir Walter Derek Thornley Hodgson
Sir James Peter Comyn
Sir Anthony John Leslie Lloyd
Sir Frederick Maurice Drake
Sir Brian Thomas Neill
Sir Roderick Philip Smith
Sir Michael John Mustill
Sir Barry Cross Sheen
Sir David Bruce McNeill
Sir Harry Kenneth Woolf
Sir Thomas Patrick Russell
Sir Peter Edlin Webster
Sir Thomas Henry Bingham
Sir Henry Albert Skinner (appointed 30th September 1980)
Sir Peter Murray Taylor (appointed 30th September 1980)

Family Division

The President of the Family Division

Sir John Brinsmead Latey
Sir Alfred Kenneth Hollings
Sir Charles Trevor Reeve
Sir Francis Brooks Purchas
Dame Rose Heilbron
Sir Brian Drex Bush
Sir Alfred John Balcombe
Sir John Kember Wood
Sir Ronald Gough Waterhouse
Sir John Gervase Kensington Sheldon
Sir Thomas Michael Eastham
Dame Margaret Myfanwy Wood Booth
Sir Christopher James Saunders French
Sir Anthony Leslie Julian Lincoln
Dame Ann Elizabeth Oldfield Butler-Sloss
Sir Anthony Bruce Ewbank

CITATION

These reports are cited thus:

[1980] 3 All ER

REFERENCES

These reports contain references to the following major works of legal reference described in the manner indicated below.

Halsbury's Laws of England

The reference 35 Halsbury's Laws (3rd Edn) 366, para 524, refers to paragraph 524 on page 366 of volume 35 of the third edition, and the reference 26 Halsbury's Laws (4th Edn) 296, para 577 refers to paragraph 577 on page 296 of volume 26 of the fourth edition of Halsbury's Laws of England.

Halsbury's Statutes of England

The reference 5 Halsbury's Statutes (3rd Edn) 302 refers to page 302 of volume 5 of the third edition of Halsbury's Statutes of England.

English and Empire Digest

References are to the replacement volumes (including reissue volumes) of the Digest, and to the continuation volumes of the replacement volumes.

The reference 44 Digest (Repl) 144, *1240*, refers to case number 1240 on page 144 of Digest Replacement Volume 44.

The reference 28(1) Digest (Reissue) 167, *507*, refers to case number 507 on page 167 of Digest Replacement Volume 28(1) Reissue.

The reference Digest (Cont Vol D) 571, *678b*, refers to case number 678b on page 571 of Digest Continuation Volume D.

Halsbury's Statutory Instruments

The reference 12 Halsbury's Statutory Instruments (Third Reissue) 125 refers to page 125 of the third reissue of volume 12 of Halsbury's Statutory Instruments; references to subsequent reissues are similar.

CORRIGENDA

[1980] 2 All ER

p 404. **R v Cuthbertson.** Last line of page: for 's 41 of the Powers of Criminal Courts Act 1973' read 's 43 of the Powers of Criminal Courts Act 1973'.

p 707. **Fothergill v Monarch Airlines Ltd.** Line *g* 5: for 'does not include partial loss of contents' read 'does include partial loss of contents'.

Cases reported in volume 3

Attorney General v Schonfeld and others

b CHANCERY DIVISION
SIR ROBERT MEGARRY V-C
26th, 28th FEBRUARY 1980

*Charity – Receiver and manager – Appointment by court – Powers – Educational charity –
School belonging to charity governed under instrument and articles made under statutory
authority – Instrument vesting power to appoint school governors in charity trustees – Articles
c vesting in governors general conduct of school including appointment of headmaster – Charity in
disarray – Uncertainty as to existing governors of school – Need to appoint new headmaster –
Court appointing receiver and manager of charity 'to manage [its] affairs' – Whether receiver
having power directly to appoint headmaster – Whether trustees having power to appoint
headmaster by virtue of power to appoint governors – Whether receiver entitled to exercise
d trustees' power to remove existing governors and appoint new ones to enable them to appoint
headmaster.*

A boys' grammar school was one of several schools belonging to an educational charity
and was a major asset of the charity. The system of governing the school was provided
for by an instrument of government and articles of government made by the Secretary
of State for Education under the Education Act 1944. The instrument provided that
e there should be eight foundation governors appointed and removable by the trustees of
the charity and four representative governors appointed and removable by the local
education authority. Under the articles the school governors were responsible for the
conduct of the school and the appointment and removal of the headmaster. By 1979 the
charity's affairs were in a state of disarray and controversy, the headmaster of the school
was ill and due to retire, and there was uncertainty about who were the governors of the
f school who would be responsible for appointing a new headmaster. In proceedings
commenced in 1979 by the Attorney General seeking a scheme, the court made an order
appointing a receiver and manager of the charity with power to collect, get in and receive
all the assets, property and effects and 'manage the affairs' of the charity until certain
substantive issues were determined by court proceedings. The charity's affairs consisted
mainly in operating its schools. By a summons in the 1979 proceedings the receiver
g applied for an order that he should be at liberty to advertise for and appoint a new
headmaster of the school, on the ground that a receiver of a charity had the same powers
as the trustees of the charity, and the trustees, by virtue of their power to appoint the
foundation governors whose functions included appointing a headmaster, indirectly had
power to appoint a headmaster. Alternatively, it was contended that the receiver was
entitled to exercise the trustees' direct power to remove the existing foundation
h governors, so far as they could be ascertained, and appoint new governors who could
then, with the representative governors, appoint a new headmaster and exercise the
governors' powers to manage the school.

Held – (1) The power to appoint persons to an office requiring the exercise of skill and
j judgment in the discharge of the functions of that office did not confer on the appointor
a power to do indirectly that which the appointees were appointed to do directly.
Accordingly, the trustees of the charity, though having power to appoint governors who
with other governors could directly appoint a headmaster, did not themselves have
power to appoint a headmaster. It followed that the receiver likewise did not have power
to appoint a headmaster (see p 4 *c* to *e* and p 6 *a* to *c*, post).

(2) However, the remedy of appointing a receiver and manager of a charity was purely equitable and entitled the court to mould the receiver's functions to the needs of *a* the particular case and to give him such powers as the court, within proper limits, considered appropriate. The power 'to manage the affairs' of the charity conferred on the receiver by the court order effectively empowered him to manage the charity's affairs by conducting and controlling directly what could be done by him directly, and making proper provision for others to do what had to be done by others under the system of government relating to the school. On the true construction of the order, therefore, the *b* receiver had power to remove the existing foundation governors and to appoint new ones in their place, and the court would so declare, even though by the instrument of government made under statutory authority the power to appoint and remove governors was conferred on the trustees of the charity. However, in exercising the power the receiver would be required to obtain and consider proper advice on the persons to be appointed governors, to act in the interests of the charity and the school, and to make *c* plain to the existing governors that they were being removed solely to permit the school to function properly and not because of any criticism of them (see p 5 *b* to *g*, post).

Notes

For the appointment of a receiver by the court and the powers and duties of a receiver in general see 32 Halsbury's Laws (3rd Edn) 386–387, 426, paras 617, 618, 700. *d*

For the powers of a person appointed to act as manager, see ibid 460, para 788.

Cases referred to in judgment

Jewish Secondary School Movements Trusts, Re, Attorney General v Schonfeld, 24th October 1979 (unreported).

Johnson (B) & Co (Builders) Ltd, Re [1955] 2 All ER 775, [1955] Ch 634, [1955] 3 WLR 269, *e* CA, 10 Digest (Reissue) 891, 5172.

Summons

In proceedings commenced by the Attorney General for a scheme in relation to the trusts of a charity known as the Jewish Secondary Schools Movement, Mr Bernard Garbacz ('the receiver') was appointed, by an order made by Walton J on 13th July 1979, receiver and *f* manager of the property and affairs of the charity. By a summons dated 4th December the receiver applied for an order that he was entitled and should be at liberty (in consultation with the directorate of educational services of the London Borough of Barnet) to advertise the vacancy of head teacher at the Hasmonean Grammar School for Boys, to invite applications for that position and to make an appointment of such person as he considered fit to be head teacher. The question arose as to the powers of the *g* receiver. The facts are set out in the judgment.

John Mummery for the Attorney General.
Gavin Lightman for the receiver.

Cur adv vult *h*

28th February. **SIR ROBERT MEGARRY V-C** read the following judgment: This summons raises a question on the powers of a receiver and manager appointed by the court. I have not found it altogether easy, particularly as there appears to be no authority anywhere near the point. There is a charity called the Jewish Secondary Schools Movement. Its affairs are in a state of disarray and controversy. In 1978 an originating *j* summons was issued, seeking the determination of a variety of questions relating to the terms of the trusts governing the charity, to who the trustees are, and so on. There seem to be some nine separate instruments executed between 1935 and 1978, each of which may or may not regulate the affairs of the charity. In 1979 another originating summons was issued, seeking, inter alia, a scheme. Both summonses are due to be heard later in this term, with the 1978 summons (the construction summons, as it is called) due to be heard before the 1979 summons. Even if nobody appeals from the decision on these summonses (an assumption that cannot safely be made) it may plainly be some while yet before all is settled, especially if a scheme is directed.

The charity has five schools in the Greater London area, two of them secondary schools and three of them preparatory schools. What is before me is a summons in the 1979 proceedings relating to one of the secondary schools, the Hasmonean Grammar School for Boys. By an order of Walton J made in these proceedings on 13th July 1979, Mr Bernard Garbacz was appointed receiver and manager of the charity. I have not previously encountered the appointment of a receiver of a charity, but I do not doubt the power of the court to make such an order in a suitable case such as this. By the order, the receiver was to 'collect get in and receive all the assets property and effects' belonging to the charity, and also 'to manage the affairs of the said charity' until after the substantive hearing of the originating summons or further order in the meantime. The summons before me seeks an order that the receiver should be at liberty (in consultation with the directorate of educational services of the London Borough of Barnet) to advertise the vacancy of head teacher at the Hasmonean Grammar School for Boys, to invite applications for this position, and in consultation with certain specified persons to make an appointment of such person as the receiver considers fit as such head teacher. I may say that in this judgment I use the term 'receiver' as meaning someone who, like Mr Garbacz, has been appointed by the court to be both receiver and manager.

The status of the school under the Education Act 1944, is that it is a voluntary aided secondary school: see ss 9, 15, and 19. By virtue of s 17 of the Act, there is an instrument of government and articles of government for the school, made by the Minister of Education. The instrument is almost entirely concerned with the governors of the school and their meetings. There are to be eight 'foundation governors' who are to be appointed and be removable by the 'governors for the time being' of the charity, and four 'representative governors' who are to be appointed and be removable by the local education authority. The reference to the 'governors' of the charity must, I think, be read as referring to the trustees of the charity. The articles of government set out detailed provisions for the conduct of the school. The governors have important functions throughout in relation to finance, equipment, the school premises, the appointment and dismissal of the headmaster, the assistant masters and the non-teaching staff, the organisation and curriculum, school holidays, the admission of pupils and so on. The headmaster, of course, has important functions also, but it is abundantly clear that subject to various obligations as to consultation and so on, the general government of the school rests with the governors.

Now the present state of affairs is that the headmaster of the school is unwell and is due to retire at the end of next month. It is highly desirable that a new headmaster should be appointed as soon as is reasonably possible. This may take a little while, since if an applicant from some other school is appointed, he will have to give suitable notice to his present school. If the articles of government which are in evidence provide any guide, the notice will have to be of the order of anything from two to four months in length, expiring at the end of a term, the length depending on the position held and the term in question. If it were known with any certainty who are the governors of the school, they, of course, would be the proper persons to make the appointment. But this is not known: it is far from certain who the present governors are. Hence the present application. In it, counsel appear on behalf of the receiver and on behalf of the Attorney General, who is one of the defendants in the 1978 originating summons and the plaintiff in the 1979 originating summons. None of the other defendants to the summons now before me has appeared or was represented, though the first defendant, Dr Solomon Schonfeld, has from time to time taken part in the proceedings under the originating summons, being sometimes represented and sometimes not. He is or was chairman and principal of the trustees of the charity, and also chairman of the governors of the school. It is plain that he is strongly opposed to any attempt to lessen his control of either the charity or the school, and in particular to any appointment of a headmaster save by his agreement. Though represented before Master Dyson, he has chosen not to appear before me either by counsel or in person.

The relief sought by the summons was supported rather tentatively by counsel for the receiver, and at first rather more enthusiastically by counsel for the Attorney General. By the end, however, counsel for the Attorney General had lost much of his zest for this contention, and it became plain on all hands that, as framed, the application must fail. What was sought was an order that the receiver should make a direct appointment of a headmaster of the school. The receiver, it was said, could do anything that can be done by the trustees of the charity, and so he could appoint a headmaster. When it was objected that the trustees had no power to appoint a headmaster but only power to appoint foundation governors of the school, it was said that the trustees could do directly what they could do indirectly, and as they, through the appointment of governors, could indirectly appoint a headmaster, so the receiver himself could make the appointment directly.

As I have indicated, this contention was impossible to sustain. I cannot see how power to appoint persons to an office which requires those persons to exercise their skill and judgment in discharging their functions can properly be said to confer on the appointor a power to do indirectly what the appointees can do directly. True, if an appointee displeases the appointor, the appointor may be able to remove him and appoint someone else: but what the appointee has previously done has been done, even if it was entirely opposed to the wishes of the appointor. The argument involves the unreality of treating the direct acts of the appointee, however unwelcome, as the indirect acts of the appointor, merely because the appointor has the power of appointment and removal. I have no hesitation in rejecting this argument. In my judgment, the receiver has no power to appoint the headmaster of a school which is subject to the control of governors under a system of government such as there is in the present case. If there were no governors and no such system, but instead the power of appointment were in the trustees, then the position would be entirely different. That, indeed, was the position in relation to the girls' school run by the charity which came before me last October; and in the circumstances of that case I held that the receiver had the power to advertise a vacancy in the post of head teacher of that school and, on taking proper advice, to appoint a suitable person to that post: see *Re Jewish Secondary School Movement's Trusts, Attorney General v Schonfeld* (unreported, 24th October 1979). This appointment, I was told, has now been made. But as I have said, that was an entirely different case. The receiver was doing what the trustees could do, and not what they could not do.

That, however, is not the end of the matter. Counsel for the receiver, supported in due course by counsel for the Attorney General, contended by way of alternative that the receiver could and should exercise the power of the trustees to remove the existing foundation governors of the school, whoever they might be, and appoint new foundation governors in their stead. These new governors could then join with the existing representative governors, and not only take the appropriate steps to appoint a new headmaster but also exercise all or any of the other functions of the governors which at present are clouded by the uncertainty about who the governors are. This, of course, avoids any reliance on any argument about doing directly what can be done indirectly. There would be no indirection at all: the receiver would be doing directly what the trustees of the charity clearly have power to do directly. The question is whether the receiver has power to do this.

In this case, as in many others, it is important to see exactly what the receiver has been appointed to do. A person appointed to be a receiver and manager of a company's property is not thereby appointed to be a manager of the company: see *Re B Johnson & Co (Builders) Ltd* [1955] 2 All ER 775 at 780, 790–791, [1955] Ch 634 at 646, 661–662, an authority which counsel for the receiver helpfully cited. Here, in addition to being appointed to collect, get in and receive all the assets, property and effects of the charity,

the receiver was appointed 'to manage the affairs' of the charity. Those 'affairs' mainly
a consist of the operation of the charity's schools. The girls' school is run directly by the
trustees. The boys' school with which I am now concerned is run by the governors; but
the trustees (in whom, I may say, the school premises are vested) also have important
functions, which include the appointment and removal of the foundation governors.
The boys' school is one of the major assets of the charity, performing important functions
for the charity. Suppose, for instance, that there were no foundation governors, or that
b the foundation governors were in a state of continual deadlock: I should be reluctant to
say that the power 'to manage the affairs' of the charity did not include power to secure
the due management of one of the charity's schools by doing what was necessary to
ensure that there were effective foundation governors. The power 'to manage the affairs'
of the charity must mean the power to manage those affairs effectively, and that must
mean the power of conducting and controlling those affairs according to their nature. It
c means conducting and controlling directly what can be done directly, and making
proper provision for others to conduct and control what has to be done by others.

I have felt considerable hesitation in this case. The appointment and removal of school
governors is not an activity which one is accustomed to associate with receivers. That
hesitation was increased because I lacked the assistance of hearing any argument against
the contentions of counsel for the receiver and for the Attorney General. My hesitation
d has been entirely about the powers of the receiver and manager. I feel no hesitiation
about the need to bring about the proper operation of this charity and its schools in
accordance with the provisions which govern it: that seems to me to be quite plain. My
doubts have been about the power of a receiver and manager of the affairs of a charity to
exercise a power to remove and appoint foundation governors which the instrument of
government, made under statutory authority, confers on the trustees of the charity. In
e the end, however, I have reached the conclusion that I ought to hesitate no more, and
hold that the receiver has the power to remove the existing foundation governors,
whoever they may be, and appoint new foundation governors in their place. I may say
that I see no reason why someone who is or who claims to be an existing foundation
governor should not be removed in this way and then be included in those who are then
appointed to be foundation governors, thereby removing any doubt as to his or her title
f to be a foundation governor.

In holding that the receiver has this power, I bear in mind that the power to appoint
a receiver is purely equitable in its origin; indeed, it was one of the oldest remedies of the
Court of Chancery. The remedy is one to be moulded to the needs of the situation;
within proper limits, a receiver may be given such powers as the court considers to be
appropriate to the particular case. If I am wrong in my conclusion that the order of
g Walton J, on its true construction, authorises the receiver to appoint and remove
foundation governors of the school, then I consider that I can and ought myself now to
give that authority: and this I do. If that means that I am extending the ambit of a
receiver's functions beyond their existing bounds, then I would say that this is only part
of the process of moulding the functions of a receiver to the needs of the case which has
been going on in equity for centuries.

h I must add some caveats. First, I am not deciding that as a matter of routine the
receiver of an educational charity's affairs or assets has the power of appointing and
removing school governors. Much depends on the terms of the appointment, the terms
of the trusts and other provisions governing the charity and its assets, and the
circumstances of the case. Certainly in all ordinary circumstances a receiver would be
well advised, if no more, to seek the directions of the court in such a matter. What I do
j decide is that this receiver in the circumstances of this case has the power in question.
Second, as I suggested to counsel for the receiver in the course of argument, where a
receiver is authorised to exercise such a power, I think that he should do so only after
obtaining and duly considering proper advice about the persons who are to be appointed
as governors. That is particularly important in a case such as this where there is a

considerable degree of controversy as to the operation of the school. Counsel undertook to put before me proposals to this end, and I shall consider them in due course. Let me make it clear that the receiver is not bound to accept all the advice that he is given: indeed, some of it may well be contradictory. What he must do is to obtain the advice, give serious consideration to it all, and then act as he thinks right and proper in the interests of the charity and the school. Third, in exercising his power to remove the existing foundation governors, the receiver must make it plain to them that the power of removal is being exercised solely in order that the school may be properly carried on according to the instrument and articles of government, and that the removal is in no way intended to be any criticism whatever of any of the governors who are being removed. A clean sweep of all who are or claim to be foundation governors is being made so as to remove uncertainties and to put into office eight foundation governors whose title is derived from an order of the court. Subject to that, I hold that the receiver has the power that I have stated.

Declaration accordingly.

Solicitors: *Treasury Solicitor*; *Paisner & Co* (for the receiver).

Azza M Abdallah Barrister.

Yuill v Wilson (Inspector of Taxes)

HOUSE OF LORDS

VISCOUNT DILHORNE, LORD SALMON, LORD EDMUND-DAVIES, LORD RUSSELL OF KILLOWEN AND LORD KEITH OF KINKEL

12th, 13th 14th MAY, 10th JULY 1980

Income tax – Avoidance – Artificial transactions in land – Acquisition of land with sole or main object of realising gain from disposal – Person directly or indirectly providing opportunity of realising gain liable to tax on gain – Land owned by company controlled by English taxpayer – Land sold at full market value to Guernsey company – Land subsequently sold to another company at a profit – Purchase price payable by instalments subject to contingencies – Whether a 'gain' if land sold at full market value – Whether opportunity of realising gain provided 'directly or indirectly' by taxpayer – Whether gain taxable if person realising it not effectively able to enjoy or dispose of it – Income and Corporation Taxes Act 1970, ss 488(2)(3)(8), 489(13).

The taxpayer was the governing director and chairman of Y Ltd, a prosperous building company. He was a substantial shareholder in Y Ltd and his shareholding, together with shares held by English trustees for his family, constituted a controlling interest. Y Ltd owned a parcel of land ('the fen land') which it sold in 1961 for £4,050 to P Ltd, a company in which the shares were held by the taxpayer and English trustees in trust for his family. In 1966 Y Ltd agreed to buy for £194,400 another parcel of land ('the quarry land') comprising 108 acres, the purchase to be completed in stages after March 1972. In May 1972, on the direction of Y Ltd, 27 acres of the quarry land was conveyed for £48,000 by the vendor to D Ltd, a company of which the taxpayer was a director and his children the shareholders. In September 1972 the taxpayer formed a settlement in Guernsey for the benefit of his family and appointed trustees resident in Guernsey, who formed or acquired two Guernsey companies, C Ltd and M Ltd, the shares in which were wholly owned by the Guernsey trustees and held on the trusts of the settlement. In December 1972 C Ltd bought a substantial portion of the fen land from P Ltd for £40,000, and in January 1973 M Ltd bought 27 acres of the quarry land from D Ltd for £81,000. Some months later M Ltd bought a further 54 acres of the quarry land from D Ltd for £97,200. Those prices represented the full undeveloped market value of the land sold, and in each case, as the taxpayer conceded, the land had been 'acquired with the sole or main object of realising a gain' from its disposal within the meaning of s 488(2)[a] of the Income and Corporation Taxes Act 1970. In January 1974 the Guernsey trustees sold all the shares in C Ltd and M Ltd to another Guernsey company, V Ltd, which had been set up by an overseas settlor for overseas beneficiaries who did not include the taxpayer or his family. A week later planning permission to develop the fen land was granted. In March 1974 C Ltd sold the fen land to Y Ltd for £700,000 and M Ltd sold its share of the quarry land to Y Ltd for £648,000. Under the terms of sale of the fen land the only sum C Ltd was immediately entitled to receive on the sale was £45,000, the balance of the purchase price being deposited with a third party to be either paid to C Ltd by instalments or refunded to Y Ltd depending on whether or not certain contingent events occurred. The terms of sale of the quarry land were similar. The taxpayer was assessed to income tax under Sch D, Case VI, for the year 1973–74 on the gains made by C Ltd and M Ltd on the sale of the fen and quarry lands, on the basis that the land had, for the purposes of s 488(2) of the 1970 Act, been acquired with the sole or main object of realising a gain from its disposal and the taxpayer had, for the purposes of s 488(8), provided 'directly or indirectly' an opportunity of realising a capital gain on the disposal and was therefore to be taxed, pursuant to s 488(3), on the gain as income in his hands when the gain was realised. The taxpayer appealed against the assessment but the

a Section 488, so far as material, is set out at p 10 *a* to *h*, post

commissioners upheld it on the grounds that the taxpayer had either directly or through his companies and with the help of his Guernsey trustees obtained the gains for C Ltd *a*
and M Ltd. On appeal, the judge ([1977] 3 All ER 903) affirmed the commissioners' decision. The taxpayer appealed to the Court of Appeal, contending (i) that s 488 did not apply because the land had been sold at the then market value to the person who ultimately realised the gain, (ii) that he had neither directly nor indirectly provided an opportunity for C Ltd and M Ltd to make the gains in question because the shares in those companies had been sold to V Ltd before the gains were made and there had *b*
therefore been a complete break from the taxpayer before the gains were made, and (iii) that in any event s 489(13)[b] applied to gains taxable under s 488 and therefore C Ltd and M Ltd were not to be regarded as having immediately received the full purchase price because they were not in a position effectively to enjoy or dispose of that amount in money or money's worth, having regard to the fact that the purchase price was payable by instalments subject to certain contingencies. The Court of Appeal ([1979] 2 All ER *c*
1205) allowed the taxpayer's appeal, holding that the fact that the land had been acquired at full market value by the person making the capital gain did not exclude the operation of s 488 and that the taxpayer, while not directly providing an opportunity for C Ltd and M Ltd to realise a gain, might have provided such an opportunity 'indirectly', that being dependent on further findings by the commissioners, and in any event the case would have to be reconsidered on the basis that the purchase price was to be received in *d*
instalments. The taxpayer appealed against the remission of the case to the commissioners and the Crown cross-appealed.

Held – (1) The disposal of the land at full market value to C Ltd and M Ltd did not necessarily exclude the application of s 488 of the 1970 Act to the capital gain made on the disposal, since s 488 applied to any gain which fell within the language of the section *e*
and which contained an element of tax avoidance (see p 12 *b* to *d*, p 15 *f*, p 16 *a*, p 21 *g h* and p 25 *d*, post).

(2) The commissioners' finding that the taxpayer 'either directly or through his companies and with the help of Guernsey trustees obtained for those companies the gains which fell within s 488', necessarily implied a finding that the taxpayer 'indirectly' provided C Ltd and M Ltd with the opportunity of realising the gains in question so as *f*
to attract the application of s 488(8). In the circumstances the remission of the case to the commissioners by the Court of Appeal to make further findings of fact was unnecessary and erroneous (see p 12 *b* to p 13 *a*, p 14 *g* to p 15 *a* and *f* to *h*, p 17 *c* to *h*, p 21 *e* to *g*, p 23 *a b*, p 24 *b c* and p 25 *c*).

(3) However, for a capital gain realised by another person to be taxable under s 488(8) as a capital gain realised by the taxpayer, the gain had to be effectively enjoyed or *g*
disposed of by that other person, and accordingly, in computing the gains realised by C Ltd and M Ltd on the sales in 1973–74, the balance of the purchase price which they were required to deposit with a third party were not to be taken into account because they were sums which could not be effectively enjoyed or disposed of by the companies. Furthermore, the gains realised by C Ltd and M Ltd in 1973–74 did not fall to be computed on the basis that the cost of acquisition of the lands and the expenses of *h*
their sale fell to be spread over the years in which C Ltd and M Ltd might have realised the total purchase price; nor, for the purposes of assessing the taxpayer under s 488(3) and (8) did the gains realised by one company fall to be amalgamated with the loss made by the other company, although sale of the shares in C Ltd and M Ltd to V Ltd did not relieve the taxpayer of his liability to tax in respect of gains realised by C Ltd and M Ltd under s 488(8). It followed, therefore, that in the circumstances the gain in respect of *j*
which the taxpayer was chargeable to tax under Sch D of Case VI by virtue of s 488(8) in 1973–74 was the gain of £1,417 realised by M Ltd. The taxpayer's appeal would be

---

b Section 489(13) is set out at p 10 *j*, post

allowed and the Crown's cross-appeal dismissed (see p 14 *b* to *e*, p 15 *a* to *g*, p 16 *a*, p 17 *h*,
a p 21 *h j*, p 22 *d e h j*, p 23 *b* to *e* and p 24 *g* to p 25 *a d*, post).

Decision of the Court of Appeal [1979] 2 All ER 1205 reversed.

Notes

For artificial transactions in land, see 23 Halsbury's Laws (4th Edn) paras 1502–1508.

For the Income and Corporation Taxes Act 1970, ss 488, 489, see 33 Halsbury's Statutes
b (3rd Edn) 634, 637.

Cases referred to in judgment

Bird (RA) & Co v Inland Revenue Comrs 1925 SC 186, 12 Tax Cas 785, 28(1) Digest (Reissue) 602, **1490*.

Bradshaw v Blunden (Inspector of Taxes) (No 2) (1960) 39 Tax Cas 73, 39 ATC 268, [1960]
c TR 147, 53 R & IT 398, 28(1) Digest (Reissue) 563, *2064*.

Foulsham (Inspector of Taxes) v Pickles [1925] AC 458, [1925] All ER Rep 706, 9 Tax Cas 261, 94 LJKB 418, 133 LT 5, HL, 28(1) Digest (Reissue) 358, *1307*.

Leeming v Jones [1930] 1 KB 279, 15 Tax Cas 333, CA; *affd* [1930] AC 415, [1930] All ER Rep 584, 15 Tax Cas 333, 99 LJKB 318, 143 LT 50, 28(1) Digest (Reissue) 25, *94*.

Moriarty (Inspector of Taxes) v Evans Medical Supplies Ltd [1957] 3 All ER 718, [1958] 1
d WLR 66, 37 Tax Cas 540, 36 ATC 277, [1957] TR 297, 51 R & IT 49, HL, 28(1) Digest (Reissue) 31, *121*.

Murphy (Inspector of Taxes) v Australian Machinery and Investment Co Ltd (1948) 30 Tax Cas 244, 41 R & IT 332, CA, 28(1) Digest, (Reissue) 124, *368*.

Sungei Rinching Rubber Co v Inland Revenue Comrs (1925) 94 LJKB 865, CA.

Vestey v Inland Revenue Comrs (Nos 1 and 2) [1979] 3 All ER 976, [1979] 3 WLR 915, HL.

e *Vestey's Executors v Inland Revenue Comrs* [1949] 1 All ER 1108, 31 Tax Cas 1, [1949] TR 149, 42 R & IT 314, HL, 28(1) Digest (Reissue) 443, *1591*.

Appeal and cross-appeal

The taxpayer, Cecil Mortley Yuill, was assessed to income tax for the year 1973–74 on the basis that the capital gains that accrued to two Guernsey companies, owned by trustees
f of a settlement for the benefit of his family, on resale of land to a United Kingdom company, Cecil M Yuill Ltd, controlled by him, his family and his family trusts, fell to be taxed as his income under s 488 of the Income and Corporation Taxes Act 1970. The General Commissioners upheld the assessment. On 29th July 1977, on an appeal by way of case stated, Templeman J affirmed the commissioners' determination ([1977] 3 All ER 903, [1979] 1 WLR 987; for the case stated, see [1977] 3 All ER 903 at 904–914). On 21st
g December 1978, the Court of Appeal (Buckley, Goff and Eveleigh LJJ) ([1979 2 All ER 1205, [1979] 1 WLR 987), allowing the taxpayer's appeal from his decision, set aside the determination of the commissioners and remitted the case to them, with liberty for both the taxpayer and the Crown to adduce further evidence, with the object of allowing the commissioners to make such further findings of fact as, in the light of the judgments of the court and of the evidence as a whole, might seem to them appropriate. The taxpayer
h appealed against the remission and the Crown cross-appealed against the whole order of the Court of Appeal. The facts are set out in the opinion of Viscount Dilhorne.

Leolin Price QC and *C W Koenigsberger* for the taxpayer.
D C Potter QC and *C H McCall* for the Crown.

j Their Lordships took time for consideration.

10th July. The following opinions were delivered.

VISCOUNT DILHORNE. My Lords, the appellant ('the taxpayer') was assessed to income tax under Case VI of Sch D in the sum of £1,129,800 for 1973–74. He appealed to the General Commissioners at Hartlepool and during the hearing of his appeal the Crown contended that that figure should be adjusted to £1,095,853.

The assessment was made under s 488 of the Income and Corporation Taxes Act 1970, the relevant provisions of which read as follows:

> '(1) This section is enacted to prevent the avoidance of tax by persons concerned with land or the development of land.
>
> '(2) This section applies wherever—(*a*) land, or any property deriving its value from land, is acquired with the sole or main object of realising a gain from disposing of the land, or (*b*) land is held as trading stock, or (*c*) land is developed with the sole or main object of realising a gain from disposing of the land when developed, and any gain of a capital nature is obtained from the disposal of the land—(i) by the person acquiring, holding or developing the land, or by any connected person, or (ii) where any arrangement or scheme is effected as respects the land which enables a gain to be realised by any indirect method, or by any series of transactions, by any person who is a party to, or concerned in, the arrangement or scheme; and this subsection applies whether any such person obtains the gain for himself or for any other person.
>
> '(3) Where this section applies, the whole of any such gain shall for all the purposes of the Tax Acts be treated—(*a*) as being income which arises when the gain is realised, and which constitutes profits or gains chargeable to tax under Case VI of Schedule D for the chargeable period in which the gain is realised, and (*b*) subject to the following provisions of this section, as being income of the person by whom the gain is realised.
>
> '(4) For the purposes of this section . . .
>
> '(5) For the said purposes—(*a*) where, whether by a premature sale or otherwise, a person directly or indirectly transmits the opportunity of making a gain to another person, that other person's gain is obtained for him by the first-mentioned person, and (*b*) any number of transactions may be regarded as constituting a single arrangement or scheme if a common purpose can be discerned in them, or if there is other sufficient evidence of a common purpose.
>
> '(6) For the purposes of this section such method of computing a gain shall be adopted as is just and reasonable in the circumstances, taking into account the value of what is obtained for disposing of the land, and allowing only such expenses as are attributable to the land disposed of, and in applying this subsection . . .
>
> '(8) If all or any part of the gain accruing to any person is derived from value, or an opportunity of realising a gain, provided directly or indirectly by some other person, whether or not put at the disposal of the first-mentioned person, subsection (3)(*b*) of this section shall apply to the gain, or that part of it, with the substitution of that other person for the person by whom the gain was realised . . .
>
> '(13) This section shall apply to all persons, whether resident in the United Kingdom or not, if all or any part of the land in question is situated in the United Kingdom.'

This section, which has the marginal note 'Artificial transactions in land' is in Part XVII of the Act which is headed 'Tax Avoidance'.

Section 489 supplements s 487 (which dealt with the sale by an individual of income derived from his personal activities) and s 488. Subsection (13) of that section reads as follows:

> 'For the purposes of the principal sections and this section—"capital amount" means any amount, in money or money's worth . . . "company" includes any body corporate, "share" includes stock, and for the said purposes any amount in money or money's worth shall not be regarded as having become receivable by some person until that person can effectively enjoy or dispose of it.'

Some fifty years ago the taxpayer founded what is now a large and prosperous building business in Hartlepool. For many years the business was carried on by a company called Cecil M Yuill Ltd ('Yuill') and until about 1965 he was its managing director. He was succeeded in that office by a younger man but he continued to take an active interest in the affairs of the company and to play a part in it, and did so at the time of the transactions which led to the assessment being made on him. He is a substantial shareholder in the company and a substantial number of shares in it are held by family trusts for the benefit of his family. The combined shareholdings constitute a controlling interest.

Owton Fens Development Co Ltd ('Development') was formed in 1972 to hold and acquire land for Yuill. The taxpayer's four children were shareholders and the taxpayer and Mr Grieveson, who was also a director of Yuill, were directors.

In 1966 Yuill had agreed to buy 108 acres of land known as Quarry Farm for £194,400. The purchase of a quarter of that land for £48,600 was to be completed by 31st March 1972 and the purchase of the remaining three-quarters was to be completed on later dates.

On 10th May 1972 on the direction of Yuill the first quarter was conveyed to Development for £48,600.

Owton Fens Properties Ltd ('Properties') was another company associated with Yuill. The taxpayer, his wife and the trustees of a family settlement set up by the taxpayer were its shareholders and the taxpayer and his wife were directors with Mr Grieveson its secretary. It was formed to take over from Yuill 67 acres of land at Owton Fens Farm and did so in March 1961 for the sum of £4,050. This case is concerned with 48 acres of this land.

Between 1955 and 1962 the taxpayer created four settlements for the benefit of members of his family, reserving to himself power to appoint new trustees. In 1973 he exercised that power in relation to three of the settlements, appointing as trustees thereof Mr de Putron, Mr M J Wilson and Channel Executor and Trustee Co Ltd (later known as Hillcrest Executor and Trustee Co Ltd). These new trustees have at all times resided in Guernesy. Each trust held a large number of shares in Yuill.

On 20th September 1972 the taxpayer made a fifth settlement for the benefit of members of his family. Its trustees were Mr de Putron and a Mr Bagley, also a resident in Guernsey. These trustees formed two companies in Guernsey named Mayville Ltd and Ceville Ltd. All the shares in those companies were trust property and Mr and Mrs Bagley were directors of the companies of which the trustees had complete control. The commissioners said that the companies 'were merely a legal vehicle to be used by and on behalf of the trustees so as to limit the liability of the trustees should anything go wrong ...'

On 28th December 1972 Properties sold its 48 acres to Ceville Ltd for £40,000 and on 25th March 1974 Ceville sold them to Yuill for £700,000.

On 30th January 1973 Development sold to Mayville Ltd the quarter of the land at Quarry Farm which had been conveyed to it for £81,000 and Mayville bought from Yuill its rights in relation to the remaining three-quarters. On 30th March 1973 and on 25th March 1974 Mayville bought two more quarters, each for £48,600. On 23rd March 1974 Mayville sold three-quarters of that land to Yuill for £648,000 and on 25th March the three-quarters were conveyed to Yuill.

So of the Quarry Farm land which Yuill had agreed to buy for £194,000, the three-quarters of which had been sold to Mayville for £178,200 again became the property of Yuill at a cost of £648,000 and the 48 acres which Yuill had held, again became its property for £700,000.

The Crown contended that by virtue of s 488 the gains made by Ceville and Mayville on the sale of these lands were to be treated as income of the taxpayer. It was not disputed that the taxpayer and the Yuill companies were concerned either directly or indirectly with land and its development and the commissioners found that Ceville and Mayville acquired the lands with the sole or main object of realising a gain from the disposal of them, so s 488(2) applies if any gain was 'obtained' from the disposal either (i) by the person acquiring the land or by any connected person or (ii) where any arrangement or scheme enabled a gain to be realised, by any person who was a party to or concerned in the arrangement or scheme; and the subsection applies whether that person 'obtains' the gain for himself or for any other person.

The commissioners found that there was a scheme or arrangment or a series of transactions which enabled capital gains to be made by Mayville and Ceville on the sale of the lands to Yuill and that the taxpayer 'either directly or through his companies, and with the help of his Guernsey trustees obtained for those companies the said gains . . .'

They thus held that the case came within sub-s (2) (ii) and they upheld the assessment.

The taxpayer's appeal was heard by Templeman J ([1977] 3 All ER 903, [1979] 1 WLR 987). There it was argued for the taxpayer, as it was in the Court of Appeal ([1979] 2 All ER 1205, [1979] 1 WLR 987), on each occasion without success, and it was contended in this House that the sales to Ceville and Mayville were at market value and that this prevented the section from applying. If this submission was well founded, a sale at market value in the chain of transactions leading to a gain being realised would provide an easy method of evading the operation of this section. I am satisfied that it does not do so for the reasons given by Templeman J and by Buckley and Goff LJJ in the Court of Appeal.

Subsection (2) while defining the scope of the section, does not state on whom liability to pay the tax is to fall. That is done by sub-s (3)(*b*) which provides that subject to the following provisions of the section, the gain is to be treated as the income of the person by whom the gain was realised. Those persons were Ceville and Mayville, neither of whom were liable to pay United Kingdom income tax.

So the liability of the taxpayer depends on whether he is caught by sub-s (8) as having provided Ceville and Mayville directly or indirectly with an opportunity of realising a gain.

The taxpayer contends that the assessment should be set aside as, though the commissioners found that he obtained gains for those companies, they did not find that he had provided them with the opportunity of realising those gains.

This contention was rejected by Templeman J but found more favour in the Court of Appeal, Buckley LJ stressing the importance of explicit findings of fact. He thought that if the question of the taxpayer's liability under sub-s (8) was to be pursued, the case should be sent back to the commissioners ([1979] 2 All ER 1205 at 1213, [1979] 1 WLR 987 at 1008)—

> 'with liberty for both the taxpayer and the inspector to adduce further evidence, with the object of allowing the commissioners to make such further findings of fact as in the light of the judgments in this court and of the evidence as a whole may seem to them to be appropriate.'

He deliberately forbore from suggesting on what particular matters they should make findings. Goff LJ agreed that the case should be sent back to the commissioners for them to make such further findings of fact as they might consider appropriate in the light of the judgments and that each side should have liberty to call further evidence. Eveleigh LJ agreed with both judgments. So the Court of Appeal allowed the appeal and set aside the commissioners' determination and sent the case back to the commissioners.

The case stated shows that it was contended for the Crown that the appellant had 'put Ceville and Mayville into a position where they could acquire the land and thereafter make a gain from selling it, so that he provided them with the opportunity of realising the gain' (see [1977] 3 All ER 903 at 909). I, for my part, think it inconceivable that the commissioners failed to appreciate that the taxpayer's liability depended on whether he had provided that opportunity. They found as a fact that he had obtained the gains for these companies. He can hardly have done that without providing them with the opportunity of realising the gains. I cannot conclude that they directed their attention solely to sub-s (2) and ignored sub-s (8). In my view it necessarily follows from their

finding that he obtained the gains for them, that they found that he provided them with
a that opportunity and I see no need to remit the case to the commissioners for them to make a further finding on this point.

Subsection (3) provides that the whole of the gain is to be treated as income which arises when the gain is realised and that it is chargeable to tax under Case VI of Sch D for the chargeable period in which the gain is realised. So the question now to be considered is: was any gain realised by Ceville and Mayville in 1973–74?

b Under the similar and curious agreements for sale entered into by Ceville and Mayville, the sales were conditional on each of those companies arranging loans at 10% interest to Yuill, the loans being secured by mortgages on the lands. Ceville undertook to arrange a loan to Yuill of £655,000 and Mayville to arrange one of £445,000. Each loan was to be available on the date fixed for completion and if there was failure to arrange a loan at that time, the agreement for sale was to be null and void.

c It was also agreed that in partial reimbursement of the interest to be paid by Yuill on the loans, each company would make payments on specified dates to Yuill. Ceville was to pay Yuill £15,000 on 14th July 1974, £30,000 on 14th January 1975 and £15,000 on 14th July 1975, a total of £60,000. Mayville was to pay to Yuill £10,000 on 14th July 1974, £20,000 on 14th January 1975, 14th July 1975, 14th January 1976, 14th July 1976 and 14th January 1977 and £10,000 on the 14th July 1977, a total of £120,000.

d Why these companies should have undertaken to pay to Yuill part of the interest payable by Yuill on the loans was not explained and fortunately is not necessary to understand for the purposes of this case.

The fact that the price to be paid by Yuill was found by borrowing money in no way affects the question whether any, and if so what, gain was realised by these two companies in 1973–74.

e Under each agreement the vendors of the lands, Ceville and Mayville undertook that in the event of nationalisation or compulsory acquisition of the land sold, they would make repayments to Yuill of the purchase price. If nationalisation or compulsory acquisition took place within three years of the agreement, Ceville was to repay £660,000 of the total purchase price of £700,000 and Mayville £460,000 of the total purchase price of £648,000. If that took place after the expiry of the third year and before the expiry
f of the fourth, Ceville was to repay £440,000 and Mayville £345,000, if it took place between the fourth and fifth years Ceville was to repay £220,000 and Mayville £230,000 and if that occurred between the fifth and sixth years Mayville was to repay £115,000.

Ceville undertook to deposit as security for its obligations to repay £655,000 and Mayville to deposit as security for its obligations £445,000. Each sum was to be deposited with a person to be agreed on by the parties or in default of agreement by the auditors
g of the companies. Any interest on the sums deposited was to be the property of Ceville and Mayville. The sums were, it was stated, deposited with Channel Finance Ltd, a Guernsey company which made the loans to Yuill.

If nationalisation or compulsory acquisition did not take place in three years Ceville was to be repaid £215,000 of the sum deposited and Mayville £100,000; if it did not occur in four years Ceville was to be repaid £220,000 and Mayville £115,000; if it did
h not happen in five years Ceville was to be repaid the balance of the £655,000 deposited and Mayville £115,000 and if the land sold by Mayville was not nationalised or so acquired within six years, Mayville was to be repaid the balance of the sum deposited.

If the lands were nationalised or compulsorily acquired within three years, the total sums deposited were to be paid to Yuill. If that happened between the third and the fourth years £435,000 of the sum deposited by Ceville and £330,000 of that deposited
j by Mayville was to be paid to Yuill. If it happened between the fourth and fifth years, £215,000 of the sum deposited by Ceville and £215,000 of that deposited by Mayville were to be paid to Yuill and if between the fifth and sixth years, £100,000 of the sum deposited by Mayville was to be paid to Yuill.

If the lands were nationalised or compulsorily acquired within these periods, Yuill would presumably receive compensation for them and it is not easy to understand why

in that event Ceville and Mayville should have agreed that these repayments should be
made to Yuill. a

Whatever the reason may be, it is apparent that under these agreements only a very
small part of the total purchase prices was at the disposal of Ceville and Mayville on the
completion of the sales and that if there was no nationalisation or compulsory acquisition,
they would get the balance of the purchase price instalments over a period of years. On
the other hand if there was nationalisation or compulsory acquisition within the periods
specified, the whole or part of the sums deposited would never come under their control b
but would be paid to Yuill.

In these circumstances it is, I think, wholly unreal to say that in 1973–74 Ceville and
Mayville realised a gain of the total purchase price less the cost of acquisition of the land
and the expenses of its sale. They only realised a gain in that year if the sums at their
disposal in that year were in excess of the cost of acquisition and those expenses.

The amount of the purchase price which was at the disposal of Ceville in 1973–74 c
appears to have been £45,000. The price paid by that company for the land and the
expenses of its sale appears to have been £50,564 so there does not appear to have been
any gain by that company in that year. The amount of the purchase price which was
then at the disposal of Mayville appears to have been £203,000. The cost of the land and
the expenses of sale appear to have amounted to £201,583 so in that year Mayville appear
to have made a gain of £1,417. d

It was contended for the Crown that as the two companies would only have realised
the total purchase price over a period of years, the cost of acquisition of the land and the
expenses of its sale should be spread over the same period. I can see no justification for
this and I reject this contention. Gains will have been made by these companies as and
when the instalments became repayable to them on demand and the taxpayer will be
chargeable to income tax under Case VI in the years in which those sums became e
payable.

The Crown also contended that to the amounts at the disposal of Ceville and Mayville
in 1973–74, there should be added the value of the rights they had in future years to
receive the sums deposited. Whether those rights were capable of valuation is open to
doubt, bearing in mind that the whole or part of the sums deposited might be returnable
to Yuill. Mr de Putron testified that they could not be valued by actuarial or other f
methods. No finding was made by the commissioners on this and it does not appear that
any evidence on it was given before them on behalf of the Crown. Buckley LJ in the
course of his judgment said that the Crown must be entitled to a finding on this question
of fact if it is so desired, and it would seem that it was thought that this might be one of
the matters with which the commissioners might deal if the case was remitted to them
(see [1979] 2 All ER 1205 at 1217, [1979] 1 WLR 987 at 1012). g

My Lords, it would not in my opinion be right to remit the case to the commissioners
for them to make a finding of fact on this issue when the Crown could at the hearing
before them, if they had thought fit to do so, have put forward the contention as an
alternative to their main contention, that if the two companies had not realised a gain on
the completion of the sales of the full purchase price, they had realised the moneys which
they were able to enjoy and of which they were free to dispose and the value of the h
contingent rights to the balance of the purchase price, and have called evidence with
regard thereto.

I cannot think it right that the Crown should now be given the opportunity of
supplementing the case they presented against the taxpayer and of calling fresh evidence
with regard thereto.

In my opinion the case should not be remitted to the commissioners on this or any j
other point. The power to remit given by the Taxes Management Act 1970, s 56(6) and
(7) is wide but I have not known it exercised so as to enable the Crown to obtain a rehearing and to call fresh evidence in order to obtain a finding on a question which could
have been raised at the first hearing; nor have I known prior to this case of any instance
of a court remitting a case to allow commissioners to make such further findings of fact

and to hear further evidence as they might deem appropriate in the light of the judgment of the court. I do not think that the Court of Appeal was right to remit the case to the commissioners for that purpose.

I have based my conclusions on the meaning which I think should be given to the expression 'the gain is realised'. Section 489 of the Act is as I have said intended to supplement ss 487 and 488. Subsection (13) of s 489 is a definition subsection and, inter alia, states that for the purposes of ss 487 and 488 'any amount in money or money's worth shall not be regarded as having become receivable by some person until that person can effectively enjoy or dispose of it'. The operation of s 488 does not depend on whether money or money's worth is receivable. One does not find in it any reference to money or money's worth being receivable. It depends on whether a gain is obtained or realised. So the operation of this definition is, to say the least, obscure in relation to s 488.

It, however, accords with the meaning which I think should be given to the word 'realised', that is to say, that a gain is not realised until it can be effectively enjoyed or disposed of.

There is one other matter to which I must refer. On 22nd January 1974 the shares in Mayville and Ceville were sold by the trustees for £65,000 and £200 respectively to a Guernsey company called Valnord Investments Ltd, all of whose shares were owned by a trust of which Hillcrest Executor and Trustee Co was a trustee. This sale was rightly described by Templeman J as 'mysterious and unexplained'. It does not in my opinion relieve the taxpayer of liability to be assessed to income tax in respect of gains realised by Ceville and Mayville in respect of the sale of the lands to Yuill.

The Court of Appeal, while remitting the case to the commissioners, discharged their determination that the taxpayer should be assessed to income tax in the sum of £1,095,853. In my opinion that determination should be restored and varied by being reduced to £1,417 being the gain realised in 1973–74 on the sale by Mayville to Yuill of the Quarry Farm land.

As the taxpayer has substantially succeeded in this appeal, I think that the proper order as to costs should be that the Crown should pay his costs on the appeal and cross-appeal here and also below.

LORD SALMON. My Lords, I have had the opportunity of reading in draft the speech prepared by my noble and learned friend Viscount Dilhorne with which I entirely agree. The appeal should be allowed and the cross-appeal allowed to the extent indicated in the speech of my noble and learned friend Viscount Dilhorne.

LORD EDMUND-DAVIES. My Lords, I am in respectful agreement with my noble and learned friends Viscount Dilhorne and Lord Russell, that the General Commissioners sufficiently indicated in para 11(2) of the stated case their clear conclusion that any gains accruing to Mayville and Ceville by selling the Owton Fens and Quarry Farm land to Cecil M Yuill Ltd in 1974 were derived from the opportunity indirectly provided by the taxpayer. I am furthermore satisfied that this was the right conclusion on the evidence. But the Court of Appeal held that the finding was insufficiently definite to justify the taxpayer being mulcted. They accordingly allowed the appeal from the judgment of Templeman J which had upheld the commissioners' determination, and they set aside that determination.

But unfortunately they did not stop there. Instead, and (as we were informed) to the surprise of counsel for both parties, they ordered that the matter be remitted to the commissioners, 'For them to act on in the light of the judgment of this court . . . with liberty to either party to adduce further evidence'. The taxpayer's primary submission to this House is that, the Court of Appeal having set aside the commissioners' determination, there was no point, purpose or propriety in nevertheless remitting the matter back to them. I propose to restrict my remarks solely to a consideration of that submission, prefacing it by saying that I am in respectful agreement with my noble and learned friends Viscount Dilhorne and Lord Russell in the reasons they give for allowing *a* the appeal.

The relevant statutory provisions are in these days to be found in s 56 of the Taxes Management Act 1970, and in particular the following subsections:

> '(6) The High Court shall hear and determine any question or questions of law arising on the case, and shall reverse, affirm or amend the determination in respect *b* of which the case has been stated, or shall remit the matter to the Commissioners with the opinion of the court thereon, or may make such other order in relation to the matter as to the court may seem fit.
>
> '(7) The High Court may cause the case to be sent back for amendment, and thereupon the case shall be amended accordingly, and judgment shall be delivered after it has been amended.' *c*

No question of amendment being involved, we can concentrate on the ambit of sub-s (6). Its terminal words are wide, but, even so, the court ordering remitter is not the final arbiter of the propriety of making such an order. For, as Lord Buckmaster said in *Foulsham (Inspector of Taxes) v Pickles* [1925] AC 458 at 469, [1925] All ER Rep 706 at 712, 'Remission is not a matter of right but of discretion—a discretion to be carefully *d* exercised in each case and dependent upon the special circumstances in which it stands'. So in *Sungei Rinching Rubber Co v Inland Revenue Comrs* (1925) 94 LJKB 865 at 872 Pollock MR said: 'It appears . . . to me impossible to accede to the suggestion of the appellants now made that the case ought to go back before the Commissioners to deal with a *new* contention of the appellants' (emphasis mine). While the court may remit a case to the commissioners for further findings if these be necessary to determine a point of law *e* raised in the case (see *Leeming v Jones* [1930] 1 KB 279 at 284), Lord Denning said in this House in *Moriarty (Inspector of Taxes) v Evans Medical Supplies Ltd* [1957] 3 All ER 718 at 734, [1958] 1 WLR 66 at 88:

> 'The general rule of every appellate court is not to allow a new point to be raised except on a question of law which no evidence could alter; and this applies *f* equally to a Case Stated under a statute worded like s. 64(6) of the Income Tax Act, 1952 . . .'

So it was that in *Vestey's Executors v Inland Revenue Comrs* [1949] 1 All ER 1108 at 1117 Lord Simonds observed:

> 'If it is a condition of the taxpayer's liability that certain facts should be proved, *g* nothing is more necessary, nor anything more easy, than that there should be a clear and explicit finding . . . It may be that they are not found because the Special Commissioners did not feel justified in finding them. Ought the case then to be remitted for further findings? I think not. It was open to the parties, when the case was settled, to obtain a more explicit statement, if indeed the Special Commissioners thought that the circumstances warranted it. After this lapse of time . . . I do think *h* that your Lordships would be justified in remitting the case.'

By way of final reference to the authorities, it is well to recall that Pennycuick J said in *Bradshaw v Blunden (Inspector of Taxes) (No 2)* (1960) 39 Tax Cas 73 at 80:

> 'It is a well-established and salutary rule that the parties to an appeal to the Court *j* should not, in the absence of special circumstances, be enabled to go back to the Commissioners and call fresh evidence on issues which were raised in the original proceedings and as to which they had full opportunity of calling such evidence as they might be advised (see *per* Tucker L.J., in the case of *Murphy* v. *Australian Machinery Investment Co., Ltd.* ((1948) 30 Tax Cas 244 at 260)).'

I would, however, let the Lord President (Clyde) have the last word on the matter of remitter. In *R A Bird & Co v Inland Revenue Comrs* 1925 SC 186 at 191 he said:

> 'It is quite plain from the Case, and from what parties say, that the Appellant did not put before the Commissioners any material other than is reproduced in the Case, bearing on the alleged inadequacy. It seems to me that if we were to send this Case back for further inquiry about this, we might be exposed, as far as I see, in almost any case, to an exactly similar application—whenever, in short, the Appellant has not presented his case to the Commissioners in a way which brings out the point he ultimately desires to make before the Court of Appeal. That would never do. No doubt, if there has been a misunderstanding, we would strain a point to put that right; and if the Commissioners had failed to include or to allude sufficiently to some topic that was brought before them by way of evidence we should remit to put that right. But . . . it is impossible to grant the Appellant the indulgence which he asks in this case.'

My Lords, in the light of these and similar authorities, it is clear that exercise of the power of remitter provided for in s 56(6) of the 1970 Act calls for a cautious approach. I have already indicated that, in my judgment no remitter was here justifiable. But, even had any been called for, I have respectfully to say that it could not properly have given rise to the unrestricted order made by the Court of Appeal in this case. This left unspecified the point or points on which it desired the commissioners to deliberate; these, it seems, were left to be somehow divined 'in the light of the judgment of [the Court of Appeal]'. And the parties were granted wholly unrestricted liberty to adduce further evidence, so that they would not have breached the order even had they called new evidence on new points, and in the result the commissioners could with strict propriety have embarked on a virtual rehearing of the whole case. Counsel for the Crown, while seeking to uphold the remitter, expressly disclaimed any desire to implement that part of it which authorised the calling of further evidence. But that concession need not have been made, for the order, as it stands, permits not only the raising of entirely new contentions but also the adducing of evidence in relation to it.

It is not, I think, relevant to hazard that what the Court of Appeal principally had in mind was the calling of evidence for the Crown before the commissioners with a view to establishing that the contingent rights of Mayville and Ceville in the deposited sums had a realisable value to them in the year 1973–74. But if this was indeed so, my noble and learned friend, Lord Russell, has rightly pointed out that the Crown had argued only for an assessment on the basis of 100% of the purchase price. Furthermore, they had adopted those tactics in the face of evidence called for the taxpayer to the effect that no lesser value could be placed on those contingent interests in March 1974. The taxpayer is therefore entitled to castigate as 'improper and unjust' any liberty extended to the Crown to support the assessment by substituting new figures.

I would therefore hold that the direction to remit cannot stand. The determination of the commissioners should be restored, but the amount thereof should, for the reasons indicated in the speech of my noble and learned friend Viscount Dilhorne, be reduced from £1,095,853 to £1,417, the latter being the amount of the gain realised in the year of assessment 1973–74 by Mayville on the sale of the Quarry Farm land. I would thus allow the appeal and allow the cross-appeal to the extent already indicated in the speech of my noble and learned friend on the Woolsack, and I would award the taxpayer costs here and in the two lower courts.

LORD RUSSELL OF KILLOWEN. My Lords, this appeal concerns an assessment to income tax on Mr Cecil Mortley Yuill ('the taxpayer') on sums said by the Crown to fall to be treated as his income for the year 1973–74 by virtue of s 488 of the Income and Corporation Taxes Act 1970. Subsection (1) of that section states: 'This section is enacted to prevent the avoidance of tax by persons concerned with land or the development of land.' Stated very briefly it was asserted by the Crown that on sales of lands in March 1974 to Cecil M Yuill Ltd ('Yuill') by two Guernsey companies Ceville Ltd and Mayville Ltd those companies made a capital profit of over £1m, and that the taxpayer was liable to income tax on that amount as having, to use a general phrase, put them in the way of making that profit having particular regard to s 488(8).

On appeal to the General Commissioners by the taxpayer the commissioners determined the assessment at a slightly downward adjusted figure still of over £1m. On a case stated Templeman J upheld the determination of the commissioners. On appeal the Court of Appeal set aside the decision of Templeman J and the determination of the commissioners (but not the assessment) but remitted the matter to the commissioners for further consideration on two aspects of the matter with leave to call further evidence.

It is desirable to set out something of the factual background leading to the acquisition by Ceville and Mayville of the lands in England that they sold in March 1974 to Yuill.

The taxpayer was the founder of Yuill which carried on a prosperous business of building land development in North East England. He and the trustees in England of family settlements created by him controlled Yuill of which he was director and chairman, and also an associated company Owton Fens Properties Ltd ('Properties'). There was another company, Owton Fens Development Ltd ('Development') the shares in which were owned by children of the taxpayer.

The settlements made by the taxpayer were the following. (1) January 1955: 999 £1 ordinary shares in Yuill: English trustees: ordinary trusts for three then infant children: statutory power to appoint new trustees in taxpayer. (2) October 1959: 333 of such shares on a recently born daughter: otherwise as above. (3) March 1962: £100 initially: beneficiaries descendants of taxpayer: trusts more sophisticated: similar power to appoint new trustees. (4) September 1972: £5,000: beneficiaries descendants of taxpayer: fairly sophisticated trusts: power in trustees by deed to exclude any class of beneficiaries, a power which was exercised on 21st January 1974 by excluding the taxpayer's four children. The trustees were two Guernsey residents, Mr Putron and Mr Bagley. This was the first step taken by the taxpayer in the direction of Guernsey.

On 29th March 1973 the English trustees of the 1955 settlement retired and the taxpayer appointed in their place Mr de Putron, a Mr M J Wilson also a Guernsey resident (both chartered accountants) and a Guernsey company Channel Executor and Trustee Co Ltd. At that time the trust funds were 1499 £1 ordinary shares and 56,943 'A' £1 ordinary shares in Yuill. On the same day the same Guernsey trustees were appointed of the 1959 settlement, of which the trust funds were then 499 £1 ordinary shares and 18,901 'A' £1 ordinary shares in Yuill. On the same day the same three Guernsey trustees were appointed in place of the English trustees of the 1962 settlement, of which the trust funds were then 65,493 'A' £1 ordinary shares in Yuill and 100 £1 ordinary shares in Development. Thus by then all the relevant family settlements were in the hands of Guernsey trustees.

I return to the history of the lands ultimately sold by Ceville and Mayville to Yuill in March 1974, being respectively Owton Fen lands and Quarry Farm land.

Owton Fen lands, in total some 210 acres, had been bought by Yuill in 1958 and 1959 for a total of £40,000. In 1961 Properties was formed with an issued capital of 300 shares: 60 allotted to the taxpayer, 60 to his wife and 180 to the trustees of a 1961 family settlement not relevant to this appeal. Yuill in 1961 sold 67 acres of the Owton Fen lands to Properties for £4,050. Properties (having sold elsewhere 19 acres thereof) on 28th December 1972 sold the remaining 48 acres of the Owton Fen lands to Ceville for £40,000; it was these 48 acres that Ceville sold in March 1974 to Yuill for a price of £700,000. Ceville had been formed in Guernsey by the Guernsey trustees of the 1972 (£5,000) family settlement, Putron and Bagley.

Quarry Farm lands, 108 acres, were agreed to be bought by Yuill in 1968 for the price of £1,800 per acre, total £194,400. Completion was to be in four quarters by 31st March 1972, 1973, 1974 and 1975, in each case for a payment of £48,600. £5,000 deposit was paid on contract. Development having been formed, the first quarter was in 1972 on the

direction of Yuill conveyed to Development. Mayville, a Guernsey company, was then
a formed by the Guernsey trustees of the 1972 (£5,000) family settlement. On 30th
January 1973 Development sold the first quarter of Quarry Farm lands to Mayville for £81,000. At the same time Mayville bought from Yuill for £100 the right to buy the other three quarters when completion (at £48,600 a quarter) became due. At the same time Mayville orally agreed, subject to conditions, that Yuill (which was after all a development builder) should have the development contract for the Quarry land. In the
b event Mayville on the direction of Yuill acquired the 2nd and 3rd quarters of the Quarry
land (from the original vendor to Yuill) at £48,600 a time in March 1973 and March 1974. It was these three-quarters of the Quarry land that in March 1974 Mayville sold to Yuill at a price of £648,000, having paid £178,200 in acquiring them.

I move now, my Lords, to the two transactions in March 1974 of sale to Yuill by Ceville of 48 acres of Owton Fen for £700,000, and by Mayville of three quarters of the
c Quarry land for £648,000, the capital profits on which sales, though not taxable in the
hands of the Guernsey companies Ceville and Mayville, are claimed by the Crown to be, under s 488 of the Act, assessable as income of the taxpayer in 1973–74 on the ground (in broad terms) that he indirectly procured those capital profits.

By a contract dated 23rd March 1974 Yuill agreed to buy and Ceville agreed to sell 48 acres of land at Owton Fens. The purchase price was stated to be the sum of £700,000
d 'But subject to reductions provided by clause 7 hereof and also subject to the deposit by
the vendor of part of the purchase price as provided by clause 8 hereof'. The sale was also expressed to be conditional on Ceville arranging a loan to Yuill of £655,000 on a first mortgage of the land such loan to be available on the date fixed for completion at interest of 10% per annum. On failure by Ceville to comply with the condition the contract was to be null and void. Clause 6 provided that 'The sale and purchase shall be completed on
e 25th March 1974 when the whole of the purchase money shall be paid. Time shall be of
the essence of the contract'. Clause 7 contained undertakings by Ceville to remain in effect notwithstanding completion. One such undertaking was that Ceville should pay to Yuill £15,000 on 14th July 1974, £30,000 on 14th January 1975, and £15,000 on 14th July 1975, in partial reimbursement of the interest to be paid by Yuill on the said loan during its first year outstanding. The further undertakings by Ceville were that in
f the event of nationalisation or compulsory acquisition of the land within three years
Ceville should repay to Yuill £660,000 of the purchase price of £700,000, that in the event of nationalisation or compulsory acquisition of the land between three and four years Ceville should repay to Yuill £440,000, and that in the event of nationalisation or compulsory acquisition of the land between four and five years Ceville should repay to Yuill £220,000. By clause 8, Ceville undertook that as security for its obligations under
g cl 7 Ceville would deposit £655,000 (part of the purchase price of £700,000) with a
mutually agreed depository (or one nominated by Ceville's auditors) accompanied by an irrevocable letter forbidding the release to Ceville of any part of the sum deposited without the written authority of Yuill. It was further provided that Yuill would authorise release to Ceville as follows: if no nationalisation etc by the end of three years, £215,000; if none by the end of four years, a further £220,000; if none by the end of five
h years, the balance remaining of the deposited £655,000, viz £230,000. Ceville on the
other hand undertook to authorise the depository to release to Yuill sums as follows: if nationalisation etc within three years, the whole £655,000; if between three and four years, £435,000; if between four and five years, £215,000. The other point to be noted is that any interest earned on the deposit was to belong to Ceville.

It appears from an answer on 8th September 1975 to a request for information by the
j Inland Revenue that the lender to Yuill of £655,000 was Channel Finance Ltd of
Guernsey which was also the depository of the £655,000. It is I think to be assumed in the circumstances that at completion the loan and the deposit were simultaneous with payment of the purchase price.

In the result therefore in March 1974 on completion Ceville received in its pocket £45,000, but was unable to get its hands on the £655,000 deposit except in the future

and contingently on the events of nationalisation, etc. If such an event took place in
three years the deposit of £655,000 would never reach Ceville's pocket, and Ceville a
would additionally have to pay £5,000 to Yuill. If the three years passed without such
an event Ceville would have £215,000 in its pocket, but the remaining deposit of
£440,000 could only be claimed by Ceville contingently and in the future at the
expiration of the fourth and fifth years. Ceville however was entitled to the interest
earned from time to time by the deposit, though obliged to contribute to Yuill a total of
some £45,000 over a period to the latter's loan interest obligations. (I do not quite b
understand what was intended as to the £5,000 balance of the deposit that would have
remained had there been nationalisation etc in the fourth year, or in the fifth year, but
I do not think it matters.)

Simultaneously with the sale by Ceville to Yuill of the Owten Fen land, Mayville sold
three quarters of Quarry Farm land to Yuill (completion was on the same day, 25th
March 1974, as completion by Mayville of the purchase of the third quarter from the c
original vendor of Quarry Farm land). The agreement follows the same plan. The price
was £648,000. The loan to be arranged for Yuill by Mayville was £445,000. The
reimbursements of loan interest were to total £120,000. The deposit was to be
£445,000. It is not necessary to spell out the figures for releases to Mayville or Yuill of
the deposit moneys. The lender and depository was also Channel Finance Ltd. My
comments on the outcome of that completion are the same as in the case of the Ceville d
transaction.

A particular point is to be noticed in this connection. In January 1974 the entire
shareholdings in both Ceville and Mayville had been sold by the trustees of the 1972
settlement to another Guernsey company, Valnord Ltd, for £200 and £65,000
respectively. Mr Putron in evidence said that Valnord was trustee of an overseas trust
with overseas beneficiaries who did not include any member of the taxpayer's family. e
In the light of the fact that within two months the purchases at £700,000 and £648,000
from those two companies took place, the transaction appears strange, and an unfortunate
circumstances for the beneficiaries under the 1972 settlement. (It will be recalled that on
21st January 1974 the settlement trustees exercised their power to exclude the taxpayer's
children from all beneficial entitlement under that settlement, and it appears that there
were as yet no remote issue in existence.) However in my clear opinion it would be f
irrelevant for the purposes of the liability of the taxpayer under s 488 of the Act that
profits made by Ceville and Mayville on the sales in March 1974 would not enure to the
benefit of the taxpayer or any member of his family, and accordingly such mystery as
may attend the sale of the shares in Ceville and Mayville by the 1972 settlement trustees
need not be further probed.

I turn now to the statutory provisions. I have already referred to s 488(1): there can be g
no doubt that the events already outlined come within the mischief aimed at, since the
profits of Ceville and Mayville on the March 1974 sales to Yuill are not amenable to
United Kingdom taxation, they being Guernsey companies. By sub-s (2) it is provided
that the section applies 'Wherever—(*a*) land . . . is acquired with the sole or main object
of realising a gain from disposing of the land . . . and any gain of a capital nature is
obtained from the disposal of the land—(i) by the person acquiring . . . the land . . .' It h
is clear that both Ceville and Mayville fall within the description of such a person so
acquiring the lands which they subsequently in March 1974 sold to Yuill. It is also clear
that over the years which have passed without nationalisation etc since then each will
have obtained substantial gains of a capital nature by the disposals, though whether this
is so in respect of the year of the relevant assessment 1973–74 is for later consideration.

Subsection (3) provides that the whole of such gain (of a capital nature) shall for all the j
purposes of the Tax Acts be treated—

> '(*a*) as being income which arises when the gain is realised, and which constitutes profits or gains chargeable to tax under Case VI of Schedule D for the chargeable period in which the gain is realised, and (*b*) subject to the following provisions of this section, as being income of the person by whom the gain is realised.'

Thus far it is to be observed that the provisions cannot be operated against Ceville and Mayville since they are Guernsey companies, and that the taxpayer is not yet touched. However sub-s (8) is in the following terms:

> 'If . . . the gain accruing to any person is derived from . . . an opportunity of realising a gain, provided directly or indirectly by some other person . . . subsection (3)(*b*) of this section shall apply to the gain . . . with the substitution of that other person for the person by whom the gain was realised.'

The General Commissioners clearly in my opinion concluded, in their determination upholding (subject to an agreed downward adjustment) the assessment, that any gains accruing to Ceville and Mayville from their disposal of the lands to Yuill in 1974 were derived from an opportunity of realising it provided indirectly by the taxpayer. It is true that in para 11(2) of the case stated they did not rehearse in its identical terms the language of sub-s (8); they there said ([1977] 3 All ER 903 at 911):

> 'We are satisfied that there was a scheme or arrangement or a series of transactions there which enabled "capital" gains to be made by Mayville and Ceville upon the sale of the Owton Fens land and Quarry Farm land to [Yuill] and that the [taxpayer], either directly or through his Companies, and with the help of his Guernsey Trustees obtained for those Companies the said gains which fall within the provisions of Section 488 . . .'

The Court of Appeal took the view that this finding was, in view of the penal nature of sub-s (8), not sufficiently reliable or definite as a finding against the taxpayer thereunder. I do not, with respect, agree. It may be that there was some elision in the expressions of the commissioners with sub-s (2)(ii) which I have not quoted: but I cannot think that it is other than a fair and obvious reading of para 11(2) of the case stated that the commissioners found that sub-s (8) was satisfied in relation to the taxpayer: indeed that was the crux of the case. On this point the Court of Appeal, being not satisfied that the finding was sufficiently precise, remitted the matter to the commissioners with liberty to call further evidence. I cannot think, in any event, that this was right: if at all they should have remitted the matter with the request that the commissioners should state whether on the evidence already adduced before them they found or did not find that any gain accruing to Ceville or Mayville on the sales in March 1974 to Yuill derived from an opportunity of realising the gain provided directly or indirectly by the taxpayer. Accordingly I would consider the remittal on this point unnecessary and erroneous.

At this stage it is necessary to refer to three points taken on behalf of the taxpayer in disputing liability.

First, it was contended that since according to the evidence the acquisitions of land by Ceville and Mayville were at market value, the section does not bite. Sale, it was said, at market value is not provision or transmission of a relevant opportunity. This contention failed, in my opinion rightly, in both courts below.

Second, it was contended that the relevant avoidance of tax must be at the time tax is avoided; here, by March 1974, there was no question of tax since Ceville and Mayville were Guernsey companies not subject to United Kingdom taxation. This point is, I think, connected with the point earlier mentioned that no benefit could enure to any member of the taxpayer's family having regard to the sales to Valnord Ltd. I reject these contentions.

Third, that if a relevant opportunity was provided to Ceville and Mayville it was *directly* provided by Yuill when it enabled Mayville to acquire the Quarry land (and indeed when it agreed to buy that land in 1974 from Mayville) and was directly provided by Properties when Properties sold the Owton Fens land to Ceville, and indeed by Yuill when Yuill agreed to buy from Ceville. It was contended that if there was a case of a direct provision of an opportunity the Crown could not be entitled to pick and choose between a direct provider and an indirect provider as an administrative choice, and indeed should be required to plump for the direct provider. Hereunder some reliance was placed on the recent case in this House of *Vestey v Inland Revenue Comrs (Nos 1 and 2)* [1979] 3 All ER 976, [1979] 3 WLR 915. I cannot, my Lords, accept these contentions, nor the relevance of the very different case of *Vestey*.

There remains the crucial question whether in respect of the fiscal year 1973–74 the assessment was justified, the assessment being based on the supposition that *on the completion* on 25th March 1974 Ceville and Mayville realised gains measured by the difference between what the lands sold by them to Yuill had cost them (plus expenses in relation to such land) and the stated purchase prices of £700,000 and £648,000. This depends on the language of s 488 coupled in my opinion with the provisions of s 489(13).

I have already analysed the substance of the outcome of the contracts for sale (and their completion) in March 1974 by Ceville and Mayville to Yuill. Section 488(2) speaks of an occasion when '*a gain* of a capital nature is *obtained* from the disposal of the land'. Section 488(3) requires that the *gain* so *obtained* shall be treated as income which arises '*when the gain is realised*', and for the chargeable period '*in which the gain is realised*' and as being income of the person 'by whom *the gain is realised*'. Subsection (8) refers in substituting a person such as the taxpayer also to a person by whom a '*gain was realised*'.

My Lords, I would incline to the view that on the language so far used it would in the circumstances be an exaggeration to say that Ceville and Mayville either obtained or realised on 25th March 1974 a gain calculated by reference to that part of the purchase price which they were obliged to deposit, and in respect of which their ability to demand payment, their entitlement to receive it, was future and contingent. The fact that while the moneys remain on deposit they were entitled to interest earned, subject to a contra obligation to reimburse Yuill certain sums for which Yuill became liable for interest on the loan, does not in my opinion alter that fact.

There is in my opinion a further provision in s 489(13) which supports the view that the whole difference between cost (and expenses) and total purchase prices is not attributable to the year 1973–74. That section is in the following terms:

> '(13) For the purposes of the principal sections and this section—"capital amount" means any amount, in money or money's worth, which, apart from the principal sections, does not fall to be included in any computation of income for purposes of the Tax Acts, and other expressions including the word "capital" shall be construed accordingly, "company" includes any body corporate. "share" includes stock . . . and for the said purposes any amount in money or money's worth shall not be regarded as having become receivable by some person until that person can effectively enjoy or dispose of it.'

It was contended for the Crown that though the principal sections included s 488, the last part of that subsection had not applicability to s 488. I do not accept that: it is as if that last part expressly said 'for the purposes of ss 487, 488, and 489'. Applying in March 1974 the language of that last part to the sums compulsorily deposited, I do not think Ceville and Mayville could then effectively enjoy or dispose of them, and that they are not to be regarded as having then become receivable by them. If that be so, I find it even more difficult to hold that they then realised a gain in the calculation of which the deposited sums should figure.

If that be so, then on the figures of cost and expenses of the lands, compared with such parts of the total purchase price as was not required to be deposited, no capital gain by Ceville and little by Mayville emerges in the year 1973–74.

The Court of Appeal, however, remitted the case to the commissioners, with power to call further evidence, with a view to enabling the Crown to establish if it could that the future and contingent rights of Ceville and Mayville in the deposited sums had a realisable value to Ceville and Mayville in March 1974. Before the commissioners the Crown had argued only for 100% of the purchase price. The Crown made no attempt to adduce evidence in support of some intermediate figure: and evidence was led for the taxpayer to suggest that no such intermediate value could be placed on those future and contingent interests in March 1974. In those circumstances it was in my opinion wrong

to remit the case on this point to the commissioners and oppressive of the taxpayer to
a enable the Crown to reopen an alternative approach on new evidence after deliberately declining to put forward that approach.

I must mention two final points suggested by the Crown. The first was that cost and expenses of the lands should be apportioned to the various 'instalments' and not brought wholly into the calculation of the gains (if any) resulting from what was paid and not deposited. I cannot accept that as a correct method of assessment for 1973–74: in that
b year non constat that any part of the deposits would ever reach Ceville and Mayville; in that event the taxpayer would have been liable in respect of 1973–74 though no capital gain might be made by Ceville and Mayville, without there being any provision for reclaim by him. The other point made was that by the time the case reached this House the full period of five years had run without nationalisation etc and valuation or prophesy was no longer needed. But in my opinion that cannot affect the situation on the
c taxpayer's liability which fell to be assessed in the year of assessment.

On the figures submitted for the taxpayer the Ceville transaction showed a loss for 1973–74 of £5,564 and the Mayville transaction showed a gain for 1973–74 of £1,417. It was suggested for the taxpayer that by amalgamation of these the assessment on the taxpayer should be nil. In my opinion the language of s 488(3) and (8) does not permit such amalgamation, and the figure of £1,417 is the correct basis of assessment on the
d taxpayer in respect of the year 1973–74. I imagine that in the long run it will make little difference.

Accordingly in my opinion the appeal should be allowed and the cross-appeal dealt with on that basis. In some respects I have expressed disagreement with points put forward for the taxpayer, but that should not deprive him of his costs here and in the Court of Appeal and before Templeman J.

e

LORD KEITH OF KINKEL. My Lords, the facts of this case and the circumstances under which it comes before your Lordships' House have been fully stated by my noble and learned friend Viscount Dilhorne, and I need not rehearse them.

The first main point in the appeal is concerned with the significance of the finding
f which, in para 11(1) of the case stated, the commissioners made in these terms ([1977] 3 All ER 903 at 911):

> 'We are satisfied that there was a scheme or arrangement or a series of transactions which enabled "capital" gains to be made by Mayville and Ceville upon the sale of the Owton Fens land and Quarry Farm land to [Yuill] and that the [taxpayer] either directly or through his Companies, and with the help of his Guernsey Trustees
> g obtained for those Companies the said gains which fall within the provisions of Section 488 of the Income and Corporation Taxes Act 1970.'

The question is whether this finding is relevant and sufficiently specific for the purpose of attracting the application to the taxpayer of s 488(8) of the 1970 Act, which provides:

> h 'If . . . the gain accruing to any person is derived from value, or an opportunity of realising a gain, provided directly or indirectly by some other person . . . subsection (3) (*b*) of this section shall apply to the gain . . . with the substitution of that other person for the person by whom the gain was realised.'

It is true that there can be discerned in the commissioners' finding an echo of the
j language of sub-s (2)(ii), which refers to the situation where an arrangement or scheme is effected as respects land which enables a gain to be realised by any series of transactions by any person who is a party to the arrangement or scheme, and of the concluding words of the same subsection, to the effect that it is to apply whether any such person obtains the gain for himself or for any other person. These provisions would not, having regard to the terms of sub-s (3), suffice in themselves to fix the taxpayer with liability to tax. The application of sub-s (8) is essential for that purpose. But the contentions for the

Crown, as set out in the case stated, make it clear the reliance was placed on sub-s (8). There can be no question of the commissioners having overlooked sub-s (8), and in all the *a* circumstances I am of opinion that the passage which I have quoted from para 11(2) of the case stated, read along with their findings of primary fact, necessarily implies a finding that the appellant provided Mayville and Ceville with the opportunity of realising the gains in question, such as to attract the application of sub-s (8).

The Court of Appeal, taking the view that the finding was not sufficiently specific, remitted the case to the commissioners for the purpose, inter alia, of their supplementing *b* the finding, with leave to hear further evidence. In my opinion the remittal for this purpose was unnecessary, and it was in any event inappropriate that the commissioners should be authorised to hear further evidence.

The second main point in the appeal is concerned with the extent, if any, to which Mayville and Ceville realised gains on the completion, on 25th March 1974, of the transactions whereby they disposed of the lands to Yuill. The answer to this point turns *c* on the proper construction of s 488(3), which in my opinion is to be arrived at in the light of s 489(13). Section 488(3), which is the charging provision, is in these terms:

> 'Where this section applies, the whole of any such gain shall for all the purposes of the Tax Acts be treated—(*a*) as being income which arises when the gain is realised, and which constitutes profits or gains chargeable to tax under Case VI of *d* Schedule D for the chargeable period in which the gain is realised, and (*b*) subject to the following provisions of this section, as being income of the person by whom the gain is realised.'

Section 489(13), so far as relevant, provides:

> 'For the purposes of the principal sections [sc sections 487 and 488] and this *e* section . . . any amount in money or money's worth shall not be regarded as having become receivable by some person until that person can effectively enjoy or dispose of it.'

I think there can be no doubt that some content for that provision of s 489(13) must be capable of being found in s 488, and that its application is not, as was contended for the Crown, confined to s 487. In my opinion such content is to be found in the *f* references, in s 488(3) and also elsewhere therein, to a gain being realised. No gain can be realised until some consideration in money or money's worth has at least become receivable. Further, it is to be observed that s 489(8) gives a right of relief, where a person is assessed to tax under either s 487 or s 488 in respect of 'consideration receivable' by another person, against that other person. So far as s 488 is concerned, the relevant liability must be that imposed by sub-s (8). So it is clearly contemplated that a gain *g* realised by another person, under such circumstances as to attract the application of sub-s (8), involves a consideration having 'become receivable' by that other person in the sense of s 489(13).

When the contracts for the sale of the lands were completed in March 1974, Ceville received immediately the sum of £45,000 and Mayville that of £203,000. In each case the balance of the purchase price was tied up under the provisions of the contracts which *h* have been fully set out by my noble and learned friend Viscount Dilhorne, and there was no question of either Mayville or Ceville becoming entitled to receive any further sums in the tax year 1973–74, with which alone this appeal is concerned. In the circumstances I am of opinion that neither Mayville nor Ceville was able during that year effectively to enjoy or dispose of the balance of the purchase price of the lands respectively sold by them. It follows that in neither case is such balance to be taken into computation for the *j* purpose of ascertaining the amount of any gain realised in that year on disposal of the lands. I have not overlooked that Mayville and Ceville were entitled to interest on the sums deposited by them until such time as they might be released. In my opinion that circumstance did not give them effective enjoyment of the deposits, and they certainly could not dispose of them.

It was argued for the Crown that Mayville's and Ceville's contingent future rights to
a receive the deposits should be valued and the resultant figures added to the sums which they actually received in 1973–74. No such contention was advanced before the commissioners, and the Crown led no evidence of such value. There was some evidence from the taxpayer's side that no such valuation could be satisfactorily made. The Court of Appeal took the view that the Crown were entitled to a finding of fact on this matter, and it appears that one of the purposes of the remittal ordered to be made was to enable
b such a finding to be arrived at, in the light, if need be, of further evidence.

In my opinion the remittal for that purpose was misconceived, and it was not at all proper that the Crown should be given the opportunity of opening up a fresh hearing before the commissioners, and leading new evidence on, a point which they had not taken at the original hearing. There is ample authority, to which my noble and learned friend Lord Edmund-Davies has drawn attention, against the propriety of such a course.

c On all the other points argued in the appeal I am in full agreement with the views expressed by my noble and learned friend Viscount Dilhorne. I would accordingly concur in the allowance of the appeal and in the making of an order on the cross-appeal in the terms which he has proposed.

Appeal allowed. Cross-appeal allowed in part.

d

Solicitors: *Sinclair, Roche & Temperley*, agents for *Tilly, Bailey & Irvine*, Hartlepool (for the taxpayer); *Solicitor of Inland Revenue.*

Rengan Krishnan Esq Barrister.

Seamark v Prouse and another a

QUEEN'S BENCH DIVISION
LORD WIDGERY CJ AND WOOLF J
29th JANUARY 1980

Intoxicating liquor – Offences – Drunk in possession of a loaded firearm – Firearm – Whether b
'firearm' includes an air rifle – Licensing Act 1872, s 12.

Informations were preferred against the respondents charging them with being drunk
in possession of a loaded firearm, namely an air rifle, contrary to s 12[a] of the Licensing
Act 1872. The justices dismissed the informations on the ground that, in the absence of
any definition of 'firearm' in the 1872 Act, the word had to be given its ordinary c
meaning and, so construed, did not include an air rifle. The prosecutor appealed.

Held – The appeal would be allowed, and the case remitted to the justices with a
direction to continue the hearing, because the only thing which distinguished an air rifle
from an ordinary rifle was that ammunition was propelled from it by compressed air and
not by cordite, and that difference was not sufficient to prevent it from being a 'firearm' d
within the ordinary meaning of that term as used in s 12 of the 1872 Act (see p 27 *g* to
p 28 *b*, post).

Note
For the offence of being in possession of a loaded firearm when drunk, see 26 Halsbury's
Laws (4th Edn) para 412. e

For the Licensing Act 1872, s 12, see 17 Halsbury's Statutes (3rd Edn) 948.

Case cited
Moore v Gooderham [1960] 3 All ER 575, [1960] 1 WLR 1308.
Ormond Investment Co Ltd v Betts [1928] AC 143, [1928] All ER Rep 709.

f

Case stated
This was a case stated by the justices for the county of Devon in respect of their
adjudication as a magistrates' court sitting at Okehampton on 15th September 1977.
Informations were preferred by the appellant, Christopher Clifford Leslie Seamark,
against each of the respondents, Clifford Cecil Prouse and Romley John Prouse, that at
North Tawton, Devon, on 10th May 1977 he was drunk in possession of a loaded firearm, g
namely, an air rifle, contrary to s 12 of the Licensing Act 1872. Each of the respondents
pleaded not guilty to the charge against him. Prior to hearing evidence, it was agreed
(i) that the two informations should be tried together and (ii) that the justices should first
rule whether the words 'a loaded firearm' in s 12 of the Licensing Act 1872 were capable
of including a loaded air rifle.

The agreed facts were that at approximately 11.15 pm on Tuesday, 10th May 1977, h
each of the respondents was in possession of a BSA ·22 air rifle in the vicinity of their
home in Arundell Road, North Tawton, Devon. On their own admission each respondent
fired one lead pellet at a bottle which they had perched on top of a van parked in
Arundell Road. The respondents, however, were in the garden of their home when they
fired the air rifles at the bottle. Several neighbours were disturbed by the noisy behaviour
of the respondents. The appellant alleged that the respondents, who had been drinking j
intoxicating liquor, were drunk but that particular fact was not admitted on behalf of the
respondents.

---

a Section 12, so far as material, provides: 'Every person ... who is drunk when in possession of any loaded firearms, may be apprehended, and shall be liable to a penalty ...'

It was contended on behalf of the appellant that the expression 'firearm' had the same
a meaning as that contained in s 57 of the Firearms Act 1968, as explained in *Moore v Gooderham* [1960] 3 All ER 575. It was contended on behalf of the respondents that the interpretation of the expression 'firearm' was not governed by s 57 of the Firearms Act 1968, by virtue of the opening three words of that section, namely 'In this Act' which confined any definition therein to the Firearms Act 1968.

The justices came to the following conclusions, namely, (i) that s 57 of the Firearms
b Act 1968 had no effect on the interpretation of the word 'firearm' in the Licensing Act 1872, and (ii) that the words 'loaded firearm' in the Licensing Act 1872 could not in their ordinary meaning be construed to include a loaded air rifle. Accordingly they dismissed both informations. The question stated by the justices for the opinion of the High Court was whether they were right in deciding that a loaded air rifle was not a loaded firearm for the purposes of the Licensing Act 1872.

c

Roger Backhouse for the appellant.
The respondents did not appear and were not represented.

LORD WIDGERY CJ. This is an appeal by case stated by justices for the County of Devon acting for the petty sessional division of Okehampton and sitting at Okehampton
d in September 1977. They there had before them an information preferred by the appellant against the respondents that at North Tawton on 10th May 1977 the respondents were drunk in possession of a loaded firearm, namely, an air rifle, contrary to s 12 of the Licensing Act 1872.

The facts of the case are contained in those three or four lines because the whole issue was whether that which the respondents had in their possession was a loaded firearm.
e One looks naturally enough to the definition clause of the statute creating the offence in the hope of there finding an answer to the problem. We look, therefore, at the Act in question, which is the Licensing Act 1872, and we find there is no statutory definition of a firearm at all. One must work in some other way.

The next thing to do is to inquire whether there is any later legislation which assists us in interpreting this phrase and, if so, to consider to what extent we can take advantage
f of it. But there is, in my judgment, no legislation, contemporary or otherwise, which fills the gap in the 1872 Act.

We have been referred to more than one canon of construction dealing with circumstances in which a later Act within the same subject matter can be used to construe an earlier Act. Putting it bluntly and briefly, such a comparison is allowed where there is an ambiguity in the earlier Act and where it is clear that that ambiguity
g can be resolved by reference to the later Act. But that, in my judgment, does not apply here. I do not think the ambiguity is apparent enough or that there is sufficient similarity between the two subject matters to make it safe and wise to try and obtain guidance from that source. If we reject that, as I think we should, we are left with only one method of approaching the problem, and that is to ask ourselves 'What is the ordinary meaning of the word "firearm"?' and apply that meaning to the terms of the
h Act.

It is not altogether easy to decide how this matter should be dealt with. We have had a reference to the Shorter Oxford Dictionary in which 'firearm' is described as 'a weapon from which missiles are propelled by an explosive, eg gunpowder'. I venture to think that the modern meaning of 'firearm' at all events is somewhat wider than that.

If one compares the air gun, which was the weapon carried by the respondents in this
j case, with a modern rifle, one can say with confidence that the two weapons are substantially identical, save only for the nature of the propellant, i e save only for the fact that the propellant in one case is compressed air and in the other case is cordite.

One puts oneself in the position when an air gun has become part of the modern armoury of sport, and one tries to envisage the discussions which would take place when this new-fangled weapon had been taken into use and Parliament had been accustomed

to it. For my part, I think that the attitude at that time would have been for people to compare the similarity of the two weapons, to observe, as I have observed, that it is only a
the nature of the propellant which distinguishes them, and I do not think that the use of the phrase 'firearm' should be regarded as unsuitable for an air gun merely because of that difference in the propellant. In my judgment, the ordinary meaning of the word requires us to say that the expression 'firearm' does include an air gun. The justices having found in the contrary sense, I think this appeal should be allowed and the case must go back with a direction to continue the hearing on the matters on which a decision b
has not yet been reached.

WOOLF J. I agree.

Appeal allowed. Costs awarded out of central funds.

c

Solicitors: *Sharpe Pritchard & Co*, agents for *N B Jennings*, Exeter (for the appellant).

Jacqueline Charles Barrister.

d

R v Secretary of State for Trade, ex parte Perestrello and another

QUEEN'S BENCH DIVISION
WOOLF J e
28th, 29th, 30th NOVEMBER 1979

*Company – Inspection of company's books and papers – Power of Department of Trade to require production of documents – Exercise of power – Inspectors appointed by department to investigate company controlled by plaintiff – Same inspectors previously investigating another company connected with the plaintiff and now replaced by present company – Notice given by inspectors f
to produce documents – Plaintiff alleging that inspectors biased and acting unfairly – Whether notice reasonable – Whether inspectors biased – Whether power properly exercised – Companies Act 1967, s 109.*

P was the managing director and controller of an overseas company ('the new company') which was incorporated in Antigua and carried on business in Great Britain after a g
similar company ('the old company'), of which P was the chairman, had been wound up following an investigation under s 109[a] of the Companies Act 1967 by inspectors authorised by the Secretary of State. The Secretary of State authorised two of the inspectors who had investigated the old company to investigate the affairs of the new company. A meeting was arranged between the inspectors and P and his solicitor. P co-operated with the inspectors at that meeting and at a further meeting at which his h
solicitor was not present. Nonetheless at the end of the second meeting the inspectors served a notice on him under s 109(2) of the 1967 Act requiring him to produce at their office (i) all accounting records of the new company such as to disclose its financial position, (ii) all files of correspondence relating to the affairs of the new company, including all correspondence with the Antiguan authorities concerning the formation of the company, (iii) copies of all documents or circulars issued by or on behalf of the new j
company to existing or prospective clients, including all documents issued by or on behalf of the new company to clients of the old company, and (iv) copies of all minutes of meetings of directors of the new company. P and the new company claimed that the inspectors were prejudiced against them and were not carrying out their investigation

a Section 109, so far as material, is set out at p 30 *j* to p 31 *c*, post

fairly but in a manner which indicated bias and that this was evidenced by the notice
a served on P. They applied for judicial review seeking, inter alia, an order of certiorari to quash the notice, an order prohibiting the inspectors from continuing their investigation into the affairs of the new company, and a declaration that any investigation into the affairs of the new company under s 109 should be carried out fairly.

Held – (1) The notice was unreasonable and excessive in the circumstances because it was too wide in its scope and did not make clear that the inspectors were in fact merely
b asking P to do no more than he could be required to do under s 109(2) of the 1967 Act, ie to produce documents which were in his possession in the United Kingdom. The notice was also unreasonable and excessive in stipulating that he should produce the documents at the inspectors' office as opposed to the company's office, because that meant that, despite P's co-operation, he and the company would be deprived of the use of the books while they were being examined at the inspectors' office (see p 34 *g* to p 35
c *b*, post).

(2) Nonetheless the application would be dismissed, because on the evidence the applicants had not made out a case of bias or constructive bias on the part of the inspectors and even had they done so, it would not have been a situation where that would be critical, in view of the nature of the power conferred by s 109 of the 1967 Act. Officers carrying out an investigation under s 109 were acting in the role of
d potential prosecutors in so far as their function was to ascertain whether the suspicions which prompted the investigation were justified by what they found. They had to act fairly in the sense of not exceeding or abusing the discretion granted to them under s 109 nor using it for an ulterior purpose, but in the context of s 109 bias was not an appropriate ground on which their actions could be attacked (see p 38 *b* to *g* and p 40 *c*, post); dictum of Lord Parker CJ in *Re K (H) (an infant)* [1967] 1 All ER at 231 applied; *Metropolitan*
e *Properties Co (FGC) v Lannon* [1968] 3 All ER 304 distinguished; *Norwest Holst Ltd v Department of Trade* [1978] 3 All ER 280 explained; *Re Pergamon Press Ltd* [1970] 3 All ER 535, *R v Gaming Board for Great Britain, ex parte Benaim* [1970] 2 All ER 528 considered.

Notes

For investigation of a company's affairs, see 7 Halsbury's Laws (4th Edn) paras 970–976,
f and for cases on the subject, see 9 Digest (Reissue) 649–652, *3897–3909*.

For the rules of natural justice, see 1 Halsbury's Laws (4th Edn) para 64.

For the Companies Act 1967, s 109, see 5 Halsbury's Statutes (3rd Edn) 618.

Cases referred to in judgment

K(H) (an infant), Re [1967] 1 All ER 226, [1967] 2 QB 617, [1967] 2 WLR 962, DC, 2
g Digest (Reissue) 204, *1163*.

Metropolitan Properties Co (FGC) Ltd v Lannon [1968] 3 All ER 304, [1969] 1 QB 577, [1968] 3 WLR 694, 19 P & CR 856, sub nom *R v London Rent Assessment Panel Committee, ex parte Metropolitan Properties Co (FGC) Ltd* [1968] RVR 490, CA; *rvsg in part* [1968] 1 All ER 354, [1968] 1 WLR 815, [1968] RVR 236, DC, 31(2) Digest (Reissue) 1071, *8400*.

h *Norwest Holst Ltd v Department of Trade* [1978] 3 All ER 280, [1978] Ch 201, [1978] 3 WLR 73, CA.

Padfield v Ministry of Agriculture, Fisheries and Food [1968] 1 All ER 694, [1968] AC 997, [1968] 2 WLR 924, HL; *rvsg* [1968] AC 997, [1968] 2 WLR 924, CA, Digest (Cont Vol C) 388, *569a*.

Pearlberg v Varty (Inspector of Taxes) [1972] 2 All ER 6, [1972] 1 WLR 534, 48 Tax Cas 14,
j [1972] TR 5, 51 ATC 4, HL, Digest (Cont Vol D) 505, *2000a*.

Pergamon Press Ltd, Re [1970] 3 All ER 535, [1971] Ch 388, [1970] 3 WLR 792, CA, 9 Digest (Reissue) 651, *3904*.

R v Gaming Board for Great Britain, ex parte Benaim [1970] 2 All ER 528, [1970] 2 QB 417, [1970] 2 WLR 1009, 134 JP 513, CA, Digest (Cont Vol C) 397, *352Aa*.

Ridge v Baldwin [1963] 2 All ER 66, [1964] AC 40, [1963] 2 WLR 935, 127 JP 295, 61 LGR 369, HL, 37 Digest (Repl) 195, *32*.

Cases also cited

Congreve v Home Office [1976] 1 All ER 697, [1976] QB 629, CA.
Hanmann v Bradford Corpn [1970] 2 All ER 690, [1970] 1 WLR 937, CA.
Maxwell v Department of Trade and Industry [1974] 2 All ER 122, [1974] QB 523, CA.
R v Birmingham City Justices, ex parte Chris Foreign Foods (Wholesalers) Ltd [1970] 3 All ER 945, [1970] 1 WLR 1428, DC.
R v St Pancras Vestry (1890) 24 QBD, CA.

Application for judicial review

The applicants, Joao Louis Perestrello and Kendal and Dent Silverbank Ltd ('the company') applied with the leave of the Divisional Court of the Queen's Bench Division for judicial review, seeking against the respondents, the Secretary of State for Trade and two officers of the Board of Trade, Michael Charles Anthony Osborne and Ronald Arthur Terence Stanley ('the officers') (i) an order of prohibition directed to the officers prohibiting them from continuing their inspection into the affairs of the company; (ii) an order of mandamus directed to the officers requiring them to produce to the applicants copies of any reports made by them to the Secretary of State regarding the affairs of the company together with copies of all their notes relating thereto; (iii) a declaration that any inspection into the affairs of the company under s 109 of the Companies Act 1967 carried out by the Secretary of State for Trade or by any other officers other than the respondent officers authorised by the Secretary of State should be carried out fairly; and (iv) an order of certiorari to remove into the High Court and quash the direction served on Mr Perestrello under s 109(2) requiring him to produce (a) all accounting records of the company such as disclosed the financial position of the company, (b) all files of correspondence relating to the affairs of the company, including all correspondence with the Antiguan authorities concerning the formation of the company, and the issue of a licence under the Banking Act 1969, (c) copies of all documents or circulars issued by, or on behalf of, the company to existing or prospective clients, including all documents issued by, or on behalf of, the company to clients of Kendal and Dent Ltd, and (d) copies of all minutes of meetings of directors of the company. The facts are set out in the judgment.

J Hampden Inskip QC and *Jeremy Griggs* for the applicants.
Simon D Brown and *Andrew Collins* for the respondents.

Cur adv vult

WOOLF J. This is an application for judicial review under RSC Ord 53. It has been remitted to a single judge to determine, by the Divisional Court when granting leave.

The application is against the Secretary of State for Trade and two of his officers, a Mr Osborne and Mr Stanley. The applicants are a Mr Perestrello, who describes himself in the application as carrying on business as a silver dealer, and a company, which is called Kendal and Dent Silverbank Ltd, and is registered under s 407 of the Companies Act 1948 for the purposes of carrying on business in Great Britain as KDSB Ltd, as its primary registration is under the laws of Antigua.

The application arises out of s 109 of the Companies Act 1967. That section was incorporated into the 1967 Act, in consequence, no doubt, of a recommendation made by the Jenkins Committee on Company Law ((1962) Cmnd 1749 para 213). I do not propose to read that paragraph, but I do accept that it does provide an insight as to the purpose of s 109.

The provisions of s 109, so far as are relevant to this application, are as follows:

> '(1) The Board of Trade may at any time, if they think there is good reason so to do, give directions to any [of the bodies which are listed and those include] (*e*) a body corporate incorporated outside Great Britain which is carrying on business in Great Britain . . . requiring the body, at such time and place as may be specified in the directions, to produce such books or papers as may be so specified, or may at any

time, if they think there is good reason so to do, authorise any officer of theirs, on
a producing (if required so to do) evidence of his authority, to require any such body as aforesaid to produce to him forthwith any books or papers which the officer may specify.

'(2) Where by virtue of the foregoing subsection the Board of Trade have, or an officer of the Board has, power to require the production of any books or papers from any body, the Board or officer shall have the like power to require production
b of those books or papers from any person who appears to the Board or officer to be in possession of them; but where any such person claims a lien on books or papers produced by him, the production shall be without prejudice to the lien.'

Sub-section 3 gives the officers or the body the right to require an explanation of documents which are produced. Sub-section 4 creates a criminal offence if the requirement is not complied with, subject to the proviso, which states:

c

'... it shall be a defence to prove that they [that is, the documents] were not in his possession or under his control and that it was not reasonably practicable for him to comply with the requirement.'

The reference to 'in his possession' would refer both to the company or to an officer of the
d company.

In addition to s 109, there is also s 111. I do not propose to read that section, but it does provide for security of information.

The background facts can be stated very shortly indeed. The first applicant is the managing director of the company applicant, and it appears very much as though the company is his creature in the sense that he controls that company. The applicant had
e previously been the chairman of another company, which was called Kendal and Dent Ltd, a name very similar to the name of the present applicant.

In the years 1976, 1977 and 1978, the Secretary of State had exercised his powers under the section I have just referred to, and, in 1978, Mr Osborne, one of the respondents, had been authorised to act under s 109. Also, in respect of that year and other years, a Mr Pink and a Mr Howard had been authorised under that section.

f No doubt partly as a result of information gathered from those inspections, on 15th December 1978 a petition was presented by the Secretary of State against Kendal and Dent Ltd, and on 23rd May 1979, after a full hearing, Mr Allan Heyman QC, sitting as a deputy High Court Judge of the Chancery Division, ordered that the company should be wound up. This was on 15th June 1979 and the order was made on the grounds that it was just and equitable that this should happen.

g It is not necessary for me to go into the details of that decision, and I have deliberately not even read the judgment, but Mr Perestrello, in the evidence before me, says of the judgment that it was based on a finding that the company had presented an image of itself to the public which did not disclose the full nature of its business, and a finding that it acted in breach of exchange control regulations. In his evidence, Mr Perestrello contends that the new company, and the business he has established to replace the old
h business, is being carried on in an entirely legitimate and proper manner, and that he has learnt his lesson as a result of his previous experience and there are no grounds of criticism in respect of the new business.

It is the duty of the Department of Trade to supervise businesses which are carried on under a company mantle. Obviously it is of great value that companies can be used for the purposes of commerce, but equally, there are dangers from the public's point of view
j and it is the function of the department, and the Secretary of State who heads that department, to try and prevent abuses.

The Secretary of State has powers under s 165 of the 1948 Act to appoint inspectors, but, as was indicated in the passages from the Jenkins Committee Report, to which I have referred, there were disadvantages in those powers and the s 109 power under the 1967 Act is clearly an important power so far as the Secretary of State is concerned.

In this case he used that power, and the terms in which he used it are set out in the affidavit evidence and are as follows:

> 'The Secretary of State for Trade in pursuance of the powers conferred upon him by Section 109 . . . hereby authorises [and then there is set out the names of Mr Osborne, Mr Stanley and Mr Pink] to require KENDAL AND DENT SILVERBANK LIMITED to produce to them forthwith any books or papers which they may specify.'

Having been armed with those powers, on 6th November 1979 Mr Osborne served a written requirement on Mr Perestrello in his personal capacity, which is in these words:

> 'Take notice that under the authority dated the 12th September 1979 . . . I hereby require you to produce to me at my room at Gavrelle House [and then the address is set out] on the 8th November 1979, the following [and then there are set out four categories of documents]:
>
> '(i) All accounting records of the company such as to disclose the financial position of the company.
>
> '(ii) All files of correspondence relating to the affairs of the company, including all correspondence with the Antiguan authorities concerning the formation of the company, and the issue of a licence under the provisions of the Banking Act 1969.
>
> '(iii) Copies of all documents or circulars issued by, or on behalf of, the company to existing or prospective clients, including all documents issued by, or on behalf of, the company to clients of Kendal and Dent Limited.
>
> '(iv) Copies of all minutes of meetings of directors of the company.'

In relation to that notice I would draw attention, first of all to the fact that the documents are not to be produced at the applicants' premises, but at the Department of Trade's premises, namely Mr Osborne's room at Gavrelle House. Secondly, I would draw attention to the very wide terms of that notice. I have read out the various categories. The second category in particular, seems to me to be in the widest possible terms 'All files of correspondence relating to the affairs of the company', and then it goes on to include certain correspondence with the Antiguan authorities, and that has got to be regarded as in combination with the other requests, and in particular the first request 'All accounting records of the company such as to disclose the financial position of the company'.

It is important in considering that notice that I should say a word or two about its background. That can only be obtained from the evidence which is before me, and it is right that I should say that this case has come on with a great deal of speed. Both the applicants and the respondents have had a limited time in which to prepare their evidence and that should certainly be borne in mind in considering the evidence.

What Mr Perestrello says about the background is as follows. He says that he understood that the Secretary of State had given the authority and that Mr Osborne produced the authority at a meeting at Gavrelle House on 19th September, which was also attended by Mr Perestrello's solicitor. He says that he understood that Mr Osborne had with him another similar notice relating to another company, which, he informed Mr Osborne, was not trading. Mr Perestrello's affidavit continues:

> 'At that meeting and subsequent meetings I made it clear to the officers authorised by the Secretary of State of Trade to conduct the investigation, that I was willing to co-operate with them and make available to them such documentation as I had in my possession regardless of whether the documents related to the business of KDSB Limited or to the business of Silver Exchange, which is an unincorporated business registered under the Registration of Business Names Act 1916, of which I am the proprietor.'

On 30th October, Mr Osborne telephoned him to make arrangements for a further meeting on 6th November, and indicated that he wished to obtain certain further information. Mr Perestrello says that his solicitor was not going to be present and he told

Mr Osborne of that. The meeting duly took place at the offices of the department at 3.15 pm on 6th November. And then Mr Perestrello goes on:

> 'As the meeting was drawing to a close at about 4.45 pm Mr Osborne stated that whilst I had co-operated fully with him on a voluntary basis he now had a further request to make of me with which he anticipated I would be unwilling to comply. He stated that he required access to further documents in order to form a view as to the financial status of the company and he then produced to me a written demand.'

He then refers to the effect of the demand and he says that in his view 'all the documentation referred to therein', applied to 'the four theatres of operation where the company was operating'. He continues:

> 'I immediately protested that it was not possible at such short notice to obtain advice from my legal advisers as to his entitlement to require production of all such documents, as well as to consider with the members of the company the request for the production of such documents, let alone to obtain the very considerable amount of documentation for which he was asking in the time available. He had already been given access to the documents in the United Kingdom which included many details of the business in Antigua as well as all the documents relating to business being done in Great Britain. The additional documentation for the most part related to the business affairs of the company which had no connection at all with the United Kingdom. [Mr Perestrello maintained that] It was clear from the attitude of Mr. Osborne and indeed of Mr. Stanley that they regarded the business in Antigua as a sham: Mr. Osborne [according to Mr Perestrello] asserted that with myself and two other . . . directors of the company . . . "there would be no difficulty in sorting the matter out". I requested an extension of time of Mr. Osborne but he declined to permit it. I then turned to the other . . . officer present . . . whom I understood to be a solicitor, but he adamantly refused to sanction any variation of the demand saying that it had to be complied with fully.'

I have read that passage because in considering the notice it is important to bear in mind that there Mr Perestrello was saying that he had co-operated fully with the department and that contention of Mr Perestrello is not fundamentally disputed by the respondents.

In addition to that evidence there is also evidence which is relevant on this matter from Mr Marson, the applicants' solicitor. I do not think I need read that evidence, but again, it throws a light on the background and does make clear in particular that one of the matters that Mr Marson had very much in mind was whether or not there was any right under s 109 to require the production of documents which were not situated in the United Kingdom.

There is also evidence on behalf of the respondents, and in particular, as one would expect, Mr Osborne deals with this. He says:

> 'At no time has Mr Perestrello made any suggestion of bias or indicated dissatisfaction with the conduct of the inquiry, other than when the formal notice of requirement to produce documents was handed to him on 6 November when he expressed dissatisfaction with the 48 hours specified for compliance. At no time did Mr Perestrello offer access to financial records of his business known as "Silver Exchange" nor did I seek such access. [Here he is disputing something that Mr Perestrello had suggested] On the 30 October I telephoned Mr Perestrello to arrange a meeting. [He then says he produces a note and told Mr Perestrello] quite clearly that he could bring Mr Marson with him if he so wished but Mr Perestrello said it would probably not be necessary. The date of the appointment . . . 6 November was Mr Perestrello's own choice . . . He made no suggestion whatsoever that Mr Marson could not be available [so again there is a dispute] . . . on the contrary he said that he would arrange for Mr Marson to telephone me on 5 November on a particular

> aspect of my inquiry. [Mr Osborne continues:] I was most certainly not made aware that Mr Marson could not attend. Mr Marson did not telephone me himself and Mr Perestrello expressed no desire at any time to have him present. If he had done so, a reasonable postponement of the meeting would have been granted to enable him to have legal representation. At no time have I expressed unwillingness to allow a company officer to be accompanied by a solicitor at any interview. It had been made clear, both at the first meeting on the 19 September while Mr Marson was present, and subsequently by Mr Perestrello, that the company considered that there was doubt over the scope of the provisions of the Companies Act, 1967 in relation to the production of certain books and papers of the company. I examined such books and papers as were made available to me. These did not disclose the company's financial position.'

Now I draw attention to that paragraph and to the fact that Mr Osborne is disputing certain things that Mr Perestrello is saying, but not specifically disputing the contention that there had been general co-operation. And then he goes on:

> 'Section 109 of the Companies Act, 1967 provides that the Board of Trade may "give directions" and require "forthwith" the production of books and papers of the company. In most instances in practice, books and papers are produced "forthwith" on an oral requirement. However, in areas of disagreement, it is considered appropriate to give a written requirement specifying the papers to be produced. This is intended to remove any possible misunderstanding of what it is that the Department seeks, and provides an opportunity for the company and its advisers to make, for example, legal representation as to the Department's powers . . .'

He then goes on to say that he is advised that the Act entitles him to make a requirement 'in so far as those documents appear to be in the possession of Mr Perestrello' and it was stressed before me by counsel on behalf of the Department that the document to which I have referred was only intended to relate to documents in the possession of Mr Perestrello.

In addition to Mr Osborne, Mr Stanley also deposed to an affidavit. Again I do not think it is necessary for me to refer to that affidavit in detail, but it does confirm that Mr Stanley, as well as Mr Osborne, took the view that there was evidence to show that Mr Perestrello was in possession of documents to which the notice refers and then he goes on to say that there are 'cases where it is thought that the documents might be removed or destroyed' and therefore the notice is given forthwith. He says that 'at no time did Mr Perestrello say that he was not in possession of the documents' and that he [Mr Stanley] 'specifically asked him whether there was any problem on item (i) and (ii) in the notice . . . and he did not claim at that meeting that the documents were abroad', and gave no reply to the specific question. He does say that Mr Perestrello objected that 48 hours was not sufficient time.

On the material before me and making the allowances that I have indicated, I regard the notices which were served in this case as being unreasonable and excessive in the circumstances. I can see no justification whatsoever for a notice in these terms being put forward in this particular case on the evidence which is before me. I do not say that that same view would be taken with regard to other cases; I am dealing with this particular case.

First of all I would draw attention to the fact that the notice does not indicate that it only relates to documents in the possession of Mr Perestrello. If it was meant only to refer to documents in Mr Perestrello's possession, then in my view, bearing in mind the nature of the documents, it should have said so; and it should not be a notice which is drawn in a manner which relies on Mr Perestrello ascertaining his rights under the Act, and then reading the notice as being subject to the Act in order to understand what the notice requires.

Secondly, in the circumstances of this case, if the notice was only intended to refer to documents in the United Kingdom, as is contended by the department to be the intention in this case, in my view, it should have said so. It should be borne in mind by the department that this is a case in which, under this very provision of the Act, the notice can lead to criminal proceedings. It is true that if the notice is not complied with, the person concerned has a defence under the Act, but that, in my view, is no justification for a notice being in unreasonably wide terms as I regard this notice as being.

It was contended on behalf of the applicants that the effect of this notice was, if it was fully complied with, to cause them to give up business and although I am not in a position to form a concluded view as to whether it went as far as that, what I do feel is that the notice goes too far, bearing in mind in particular that, as I have already stressed, the documents had to be taken to the Department of Trade's premises; that the applicants would therefore be without the documents for a time; and that it was not a situation where Mr Perestrello, who had been co-operating up until that time, was merely being required to deal with a general request in circumstances where the documents would be produced but remain at his own business premises so that the business could be conducted in the meantime.

What I have said applies to the evidence before me, as I understand that evidence, and the facts of this case, and I stress that there may be other cases where different circumstances apply. It is quite clear on the evidence of Mr Osborne and Mr Stanley that there were particular matters which they were concerned about, but they had already had opportunities to see documents on a voluntary basis and when you are in that sort of situation, in my view, reasonable administration requires you to be much more specific than the notice is in this case.

If the case turned on the question of the validity of the notice, the views that I have already expressed would be enough to achieve a position where that notice could not be relied upon by the department.

However the case which is put forward is not dependent on the notice alone, although the notice is very relevant to the application. The way the matter is put forward is that the notice is evidence in support of the major ground relied on by the applicants in this case and perhaps I should refer to the RSC Ord 53 notice to show the grounds before I proceed further. The notice has been amended more than once. As I understand it in its final form, it reads as follows:

> 'The said M.C.A. Osborne and the said R.A.T. Stanley have demonstrated that in carrying out their investigations they are prejudiced against both the first named and the second named applicants and are not carrying out their inspection fairly; and/or acted capriciously.'

The second ground is no longer relied on. That referred to the requirement of the notice to produce documentation outside the jurisdiction and the applicants are not relying on that because they consider it would not be possible to succeed on that ground. The third ground, which was an amended ground, is that—

> 'The circumstances and manner in which the said M.C.A. Osborne and the said R.A.T. Stanley have carried out their duties indicate bias, alternatively solid grounds upon which right-thinking people would suspect bias.'

and then the fourth ground:

> 'The said M.C.A. Osborne and the said R.A.T. Stanley as officers of the Department of Trade have exceeded their jurisdiction under Section 109 of the Companies Act, 1967.'

and that was said by counsel on behalf of the applicants to relate to asking questions at interviews which went beyond the powers given in s 109, that is the power to provide an explanation as to documents.

The primary matter in respect of which I now have to consider the law, is whether or not allegations of bias or constructive bias on behalf of officers of the department are sufficient to give rise to relief, and if so, whether or not bias or constructive bias, has been shown to arise on the facts which are before me.

Counsel on behalf of the Secretary of State contended that actions of the Secretary of State under s 109 or actions of his officers under the authority of the Secretary of State under s 109, will not be inquired into by the courts unless it is shown that either the Secretary of State or his officers are not acting in good faith. It is the contention of the Secretary of State that that view of the law is supported by the recent decision of the Court of Appeal in *Norwest Holst Ltd v Department of Trade* [1978] 3 All ER 280, [1978] Ch 201.

I regard the contention which I have just referred to, made on behalf of the Secretary of State, as stating the powers of the court in too narrow a manner, and I therefore consider it necessary to go on and consider the contentions of the applicants. Their contention is that this is a stipulation where the authorities establish that the principles of natural justice apply. The first authority on which they rely is the well known case of *Re Pergamon Press Ltd* [1970] 3 All ER 535 at 539, [1971] Ch 388 at 399. In that case Lord Denning MR, having set out the consequences of a report under s 165 of the 1948 Act, goes on to say:

> 'I am clearly of the opinion that the inspectors must act fairly. This is a duty which rests on them, as on many other bodies, even though they are not judicial, nor quasi-judicial, but only administrative.'

He then refers to *R v Gaming Board for Great Britain, ex parte Benaim* [1970] 2 All ER 528, [1970] 2 QB 417 and goes on to say.

> 'The inspectors can obtain information in any way they think best, but before they condemn or criticise a man, they must give him a fair opportunity for correcting or contradicting what is said against him. They need not quote chapter and verse. An outline of the charge will usually suffice.'

In his judgment Sachs LJ says ([1970] 3 All ER 535 at 541, [1971] Ch 338 at 402):

> 'The nature of the proceeding, the purposes for which the reports may be used, the matter which may be found in them and the extent of the publication being respectively as described, it seems to me, as well as to Lord Denning MR, very clear that in the conduct of the proceedings there must be displayed that measure of natural justice which Lord Reid in *Ridge v Baldwin* [1963] 2 All ER 66 at 71, [1964] AC 40 at 65 described as "insusceptible of exact definition, but what a reasonable man would regard as fair procedure in particular circumstances." To come to that conclusion it is, as recent decisions have shown, not necessary to label the proceedings "judicial", "quasi-judicial", "administrative" or "investigatory"; it is the characteristics of the proceeding that matter, not the precise compartment or compartments into which they fall—and one of the principal characteristics of the proceedings under consideration is to be found in the inspectors' duty, in their statutory fact-finding capacity, to produce a report . . .'

Finally there is the following passage in Buckley LJ's judgment ([1970] 3 All ER 535 at 545, [1971] Ch 388 at 407):

> 'The function of an inspector appointed under s 165 of the Companies Act 1948 is an inquisitorial function. His duty is to investigate the affairs of the company and to report on them to the Board of Trade. It is not a judicial function. But having regard to the circumstances which may lead to the appointment of an inspector under s 165 (*b*) . . . and to the fact that under the Act a copy of the report must be furnished to the company, a need for due regard to fair treatment may arise if inspectors propose to report adversely on the conduct of any director or officer. If it is found that a director or officer has made some default or acted improperly in relation to the conduct of the company's affairs, this may well prompt the company

> to institute proceedings against him. In those proceedings the person proceeded against would have the full protection of a judicial process, but, particularly since the company is entitled to a copy of the report, he should not be exposed to the risk of such proceedings without being given a fair opportunity by the inspectors to forestall an adverse report. If inspectors are disposed to report on the conduct of anyone in such a way that he may in consequence be proceeded against, either in criminal or civil proceedings, the inspectors should give him, if he has not already had it, such information of the complaint or criticism which they may make of him in their report and of their reasons for doing so, including such information as to the nature and effect of the evidence which disposes them so to report, as is necessary to give the person concerned a fair opportunity of dealing with the matter, and they should give him such an opportunity.'

The applicants contend that although *Re Pergamon Press Ltd* was based on s 165, a like approach should be taken to the activities of the officers acting under s 109 and it is stated that in particular, Sachs LJ refers to the fact that natural justice is to apply; that Buckley LJ seems to be coming to a similar view, and that, although Lord Denning MR uses a slightly different terminology, it appears that he is of the same view. It is, therefore, the contention of the applicants that the well-known view as to bias which was laid down in the Court of Appeal in *Metropolitan Properties Co (FGC) Ltd v Lannon* [1968] 3 All ER 304 at 310, [1969] 1 QB 577 at 599 should be applied in this case. Lord Denning MR set out the principles which have since been very much accepted into this area of law:

> 'Nevertheless there must appear to be a real likelihood of bias ... There must be circumstances from which a reasonable man would think it likely or probable that the justice, or chairman, as the case may be, would, or did, favour one side unfairly at the expense of the other. The court will not enquire whether he did, in fact, favour one side unfairly. Suffice it that reasonable people might think he did. The reason is plain enough. Justice must be rooted in confidence; and confidence is destroyed when right-minded people go away thinking "The judge was biased".'

An alternative way that the matter is put is based on the equally familiar passage in *Re K (H) (an infant)* [1967] 1 All ER 226 at 231, [1967] 2 QB 617 at 630 in the judgment of Lord Parker CJ. That case was dealing with an immigration officer but what Lord Parker CJ had to say has since been generally applied. It is in these terms:

> '... I myself think that even if an immigration officer is not in a judicial or quasi-judicial capacity, he must at any rate give the immigrant an opportunity of satisfying him of the matters in the subsection, and for that purpose let the immigrant know what his immediate impression is so that the immigrant can disabuse him. That is not, as I see it, a question of acting or being required to act judicially, but of being required to act fairly. Good administration and an honest or *bona fide* decision must, as it seems to me, require not merely impartiality, nor merely bringing one's mind to bear on the problem, but acting fairly, and to the limited extent that the circumstances of any particular case allow, and within the legislative framework under which the administrator is working, only to that limited extent do the so-called rules of natural justice apply, which in a case such as this is merely a duty to act fairly. I appreciate that in saying that it may be said that one is going further than is permitted on the decided cases because heretofore at any rate the decisions of the courts do seem to have drawn a strict line in these matters according to whether there is or is not a duty to act judicially or quasi-judicially.'

I regard it as essential in an area such as this to first of all look at the statutory power. It is only by looking at the statutory power that it is possible to come to a conclusion as to whether the rules of natural justice apply, and if so, the extent to which those rules apply. In the case of s 109, to talk of the rules of natural justice is not really helpful. It is much better to consider the matter as indicated by Lord Parker CJ in *Re K (H) (an infant)*

and ask oneself whether in the situation, what is required by the Act requires a degree of
fairness. In this particular section, the opening words make it clear that the Board of a
Trade, before they exercise their powers, must think there is good reason so to do.
Although this is not specifically stated in the section in relation to their officers, the same
must apply and the officers must also think there is good reason so to do. But although
they must think there is good reason so to do, this does not seem to me to be a situation
where it would be appropriate to read into the Act the requirement of lack of bias which
was enunciated in the *Lannon* case. b

When one considers the functions of those officers, it really is wholly inappropriate to
talk about them not being regarded as biased if they are performing their functions
properly. Take this very case; it is, in my view, almost inevitable that before the powers
under s 109 are exercised, the officers concerned, and through his officers, the Secretary
of State, must regard the situation as one where there are matters to be investigated.
They are acting in a policing role. Their function is to see whether their suspicions are c
justified by what they find, and that being so, it is wholly inappropriate for the case to be
approached in the same way as one would approach a person performing a normal
judicial role or quasi-judicial role; a situation where the person is making a determination.

What is done under s 109 is to ascertain whether there is evidence to support a prima
facie view of a possible undesirable situation in relation to a company, and that being so,
the role of the department is very much the role of the potential prosecutor. The person d
performing that role will of necessity be an inappropriate person to perform the function
which was being considered in the *Lannon* case. So I regard the *Lannon* approach as not
being applicable to these circumstances.

Are there then any limits on the discretion to which I have referred, which is given by
s 109? In my view there certainly are limits. They can be summarised in this way,
although I do not intend this summary to be exhaustive. e

First of all, the persons exercising the power must not exceed or abuse the discretion
which is granted to them by the section; and not acting bona fide and not acting honestly
are examples of that.

Secondly, the person concerned must not use the discretion for some ulterior
purpose. If the person concerned is so prejudiced against someone that he is using the
section, not for the purposes for which the power was given, but, for example, to punish f
someone, then that is using it for an ulterior purpose which would be outside the
statute. It appears to me that it is a requirement of this power that it should be exercised
fairly in the sense that the statutory discretion which it gives should not be abused. I had
cited to me a number of cases which in my view in no way derogate from this approach,
namely such well-established authorities as *Pearlberg v Varty (Inspector of Taxes)* [1972]
2 All ER 6, [1972] 1 WLR 534 and *Padfield v Minister of Agriculture, Fisheries and Food* g
[1968] 1 All ER 694, [1968] AC 997.

The passages in *Norwest Holst Ltd v Department of Trade* to which I have already made
reference must be understood in the light of the situation there being considered. That
case was concerned with the appointment of inspectors under s 165. It was not primarily
concerned with the activities of the inspectors once they had been appointed, and
certainly I do not understand in that case that the Court of Appeal had gone back in any h
way on what they had said in the earlier authority of *Re Pergamon Press Ltd.*

It is true that in the *Norwest Holst* case Lord Denning MR says this ([1978] 3 All ER 280
at 292, [1978] Ch 201 at 224):

> 'Equally, so far as s 109 is concerned, when the officers of the Department of
> Trade are appointed to examine the books, there is no need for the rules of natural j
> justice to be applied. If the company was forewarned and told that the officers were
> coming, what is to happen to the books? In a wicked world, it is not unknown for
> books and papers to be destroyed or lost.'

But, on the facts of this case, the Department of Trade were quite clearly prepared to

give extra time for the solicitor to be present and so it does not appear to be one of the
a cases where the danger that Lord Denning MR had in mind applied.

But quite apart from that, as I understand Lord Denning MR, he is again referring to the question of appointing officers under s 109 to exercise the powers under s 109 and not in fact, to the exercise of those powers. I do regard the passage in the judgment of Geoffrey Lane LJ ([1978] 3 All ER 280 at 296, [1978] Ch 201 at 228–229) as being important. He stresses that fairness demands that the suspect should be given the chance
b of putting his side of the case before the judicial inquiry is over. He says:

> 'That scarcely needs illustration, but if it does it is to be found in *Re Pergamon Press Ltd* in 1971. But on the other side, and the other side are entitled to fairness just as the suspect is, fairness to the inquirer demands that during the administrative period he should be able to investigate without having at every stage to inquire from the suspect what his side of the matter may be.'

c

I naturally of course pay the greatest possible attention to that. I do not seek in any way to dissent from it, but in my view, again, it does not apply to the matters that I am considering and I do not regard it as in any way limiting the proper approach which I have sought to indicate.

So approaching the matter, on the facts of this case, what view do I come to as to the
d conduct of the respondents? First of all it is right that I should say that although I had strong comment to make about the terms of the notice, that does not mean that it helps on the consideration of the present problem. The fact that a department phrases a notice in too wide a terms does not necessarily indicate that the author of that document is biased or capricious. It can merely indicate that the care which should be exercised has not been exercised in the drawing up of the notice and insofar as the applicants rely on
e the terms of the notice in itself as being in support of their case, I am afraid that I do not regard it by itself as being sufficient support of their case in relation to bias or capriciousness.

The second matter which the applicants relied on was the fact that Mr Osborne and Mr Stanley were not only involved in the background of the case, but in fact had played, in the case of Mr Osborne, an active part in the previous proceedings brought by the
f department. Again, in my view, that does not disqualify them in any way from performing the role which they were performing in this case, which, I have indicated, is akin to that of a policeman. Looking at the matter as best I can, I cannot see that there can be anybody more appropriate than Mr Osborne with his background, and Mr Stanley, who had a like background, to continue to carry out this function on behalf of the Secretary of State.

g Mr Perestrello says that he has reformed. In order for that to be judged the best person to make an investigation as to whether or not there is any relevant evidence is someone who is fully familiar with what has happened before; and even if the department had gone to some other officer, in order to perform his function properly he would have had to familiarise himself fully with the background.

The next matter that was relied on by the applicants was that looking at the matter
h from the applicants' point of view, the impression they would get was that 'this is the same old lot again'. Now I can understand that the applicants could take that view, but if I am right in defining the role of the officers and if I am right as to the proper interpretation of the section, it does not seem to me that the fact that the applicants might form that view in any way disentitles the officers from acting. I have not referred to the passages in the evidence, but it is right that I should say that both Mr Stanley and
j Mr Osborne deny that they are biased. They emphasise that they have reached no conclusion and the possible impression in the minds of the applicants must be viewed against those denials.

The third matter on which the applicants relied was the breadth of the questioning which took place, and they say that was certainly outside the powers given by s 109. In my view, this criticism really was a non-starter, because the questioning which took place

was dealt with entirely on a voluntary basis as Mr Perestrello has indicated in his evidence
and, that being so, I can see nothing wrong with the officers using the opportunity which *a*
they had to obtain as much information as Mr Perestrello was prepared voluntarily to
give. The s 109 power is only there to ensure something is done, because of the sanction
of criminal proceedings, which a person is not voluntarily prepared to do. If Mr
Perestrello was not prepared to answer questions, he was quite entitled to refuse to
answer questions. In those circumstances the officers could make use of such powers as
they had under s 109 to compel an answer and no more. But there is nothing to be read *b*
as a limitation on this power of the officers merely because they have an express power
to require explanations in certain limited circumstances.

So really, having listed the matters of criticism relied upon, the conclusion which I
come to is this, that although criticism is justified of the notice which was served, and I
would question the validity of that notice for the reasons that I have indicated, the
applicants have not made out a case, in fact, of bias or constructive bias; and even if they *c*
had made out a case of that nature, bearing in mind the nature of this particular power,
this would not be a situation where that would be critical. In these circumstances, I have
come to the conclusion that the applicants are not entitled to any of the relief they
seek. However, I do take the view that it was proper for them to bring this matter before
the court, and for that reason, and also because this is a case where I am taking a view
different from the department on the law, I propose, subject to counsel persuading me *d*
otherwise, to make no order as to costs. In addition to indicating by that order the merits
of the application to which I have referred, the order will enable the department, if they
wish, to appeal against the reasoning of the judgment which I have just given.

Inskip for the applicants. May I ask your Lordship just to give clarification of one
matter? One of the matters that I was relying on was 'unfairness'. I understand from *e*
your Lordship's judgment that your Lordship, in the circumstances of this case, is saying
there could be no unfairness without bias.

Woolf J. Mr Inskip, I regret that my judgment was so unclear as not to deal specifically
with that point. I will try and clarify the matter in this way. What I have indicated is
that the ground of unfairness on which you were relying, which as I understand it, was *f*
'bias', was not being made out, and although I do regard a duty of fairness as being
applicable within the limits I have indicated, I would say in any event, it would not cover
'bias' as enunciated in the *Lannon* case. So I am finding against you first of all on the basis
that I do not find 'bias' on the evidence before me, and secondly, I am finding against you
because, in my view, as a matter of law, the approach which was indicated by the Court
of Appeal in the *Lannon* case has no application. Does that assist?

g

Inskip. It clarifies your Lordship's reasoning because 'unfairness' and 'bias' were separate
grounds. They were in the notice.

Woolf J. Yes. I do not think it is desirable that I go much further, but I am anxious that
you understand my reasoning and if I can just say this: the 'unfairness' which you refer *h*
to in the grounds which I read out, as I understood it, was based on the fact that the
applicants had acted unfairly on account of the biased activities. I did not understand, in
the way the argument was presented to me, that there was any allegation of 'unfairness'
that went beyond this, apart from the allegation that the respondents were said to have
also acted capriciously, which was again, as I understood it, related to the same matters.
[After counsel addressed the court on costs his Lordship continued:] I fully accept that *j*
you were relying on the notice but you are not still, as I understand it, doing more than
saying that that is evidence of capriciousness or evidence of bias and evidence of
unfairness.

Inskip. Yes, that is absolutely right.

Woolf J. And what I intended my judgment to say was that although I am strongly
a critical of the notice in the way I have indicated, I do not see that it is any evidence which
is sufficient for your purposes to establish a ground of relief.

Inskip. Yes; although unreasonably wide, it was not unfair, if I may say, in the circumstances.

b **Woolf J.** Well, Mr Inskip, I do not think that I can help any more than that. What I am seeking to do is to say that the notice was defectively drawn but that does not mean to say it is necessarily evidence which is conclusive of unfair conduct.

Application refused.

c Solicitors: *Marson & Co* (for the applicants); *Treasury Solicitor* (for the respondents).

K Mydeen Esq Barrister.

Conservative and Unionist Central Office v Burrell (Inspector of Taxes)

CHANCERY DIVISION
VINELOTT J
3rd, 4th, 5th, 6th MARCH, 2nd APRIL 1980

Unincorporated association – Requirements of an unincorporated association – Political party constituted by members of local constituency associations and both Houses of Parliament – Funds raised by party treasurers held by party's central office which provided administrative services to party – Expenditure of funds under control of party leader – Party leader providing link between members of party – Rules for selection of party leader not subject to amendment – Whether rules for selection of party leader constituting contract between members of party – Whether party an unincorporated association – Whether central office holding income from funds on behalf of an unincorporated association – Whether central office liable to corporation tax on income from funds.

The Conservative Party was a political party made up of three elements, namely (i) the Parliamentary Party comprising those members of both Houses of Parliament who took the Conservative whip, (ii) the mass membership represented by the National Union of Conservative and Unionist Associations ('the national union') comprising constituency associations, and (iii) the party headquarters known as the Central Office which operated the party organisation and the party's research department. The party leader linked together the three elements of the party. The formal rules for the selection of the party leader provided for a candidate to be chosen by a ballot of Conservative members of Parliament and presented for election to a party meeting consisting of the Parliamentary Party, Parliamentary candidates and the executive committee of the national union. The rules did not provide for amendment of the selection process. Party treasurers appointed by the party leader and assisted by a board of finance were responsible for raising party funds. The moneys so raised were under the control of the Central Office and the party leader had power to direct how those moneys were to be spent. The Central Office was assessed to corporation tax on investment income and interest over a five year period from 1972 to 1976 on the basis that it was an unincorporated association within s 526(5)[a] of the Income and Corporation Taxes Act 1970 and therefore fell within the meaning of 'company' in s 526(5). The Central Office appealed to the Special Commissioners against the assessment contending (i) that it was not an unincorporated association, (ii) that even if the national union could be said to be an unincorporated association the funds did not belong to the national union since they were administered by the Central Office, and (iii) that in any event, the Conservative Party was an amorphous combination of various elements which lacked the characteristics of an unincorporated association and therefore if the funds were owned by the party the income arising therefrom was not assessable to corporation tax. The Crown accepted that the Central Office was not itself an unincorporated association but contended that the party was, and that the funds held by the Central Office belonged to the party. The Crown based its contention on the submission that the party was linked together both by the powers of the leader and by a contract between the members of the party arising in part out of the rules of the national union, in part out of the rules regulating the party meeting and selection of the leader, and in part out of the rules of the local constituency associations. The Crown further contended that the ownership of the party funds had to be in a body which had legal capacity to own property either as a trustee or as a beneficial owner and that since the moneys contributed to the party's funds were given for a purpose and could not therefore have been given to a non-charitable trust, it followed that there had to be an

a Section 526(5), so far as material, provides: '"company" means . . . any body corporate or unincorporated association . . .'

unincorporated association which was to be treated as the owner of the funds. The
a commissioners found that the funds held by the party treasurers for the use of Central Office were held on behalf of the members of an unincorporated association, which they identified as the Conservative Party, comprising all the members of the local constituency associations together with the members of both Houses taking the party whip, and accordingly upheld the assessments. The Central Office appealed.

b **Held** – Having regard to the fact that the party leader was the only link between the Central Office and the membership of the Conservative Party (consisting of the members of the local constituency associations and the members of both Houses of Parliament taking the Conservative whip), and the fact that the rules for the selection of the party leader (which contained no provision for amendment) could not form any part of any contract between the Parliamentary Party and the mass membership of the local
c constituency associations, it could not be said that the Conservative Party was an unincorporated association. Furthermore, the existence of an unincorporated association was not to be inferred merely because it would be inappropriate to assess some other beneficial owner or trustee to tax in respect of the income. It followed that the funds and the income therefrom held by the Central Office under the control of the party leader were not held on behalf of an unincorporated association. The appeal would therefore
d be allowed (see p 59 *d* to *f* and p 60 *e* to p 61 *b*, post).

Notes

For corporations and unincorporated associations, see 9 Halsbury's Laws (4th Edn) para 1201.

For the Income and Corporation Taxes Act 1970, s 526, see 33 Halsbury's Statutes (3rd
e Edn) 681.

Cases referred to in judgment

Barclays Bank Ltd v Quistclose Investments Ltd [1968] 3 All ER 651, [1970] AC 567, [1968] 3 WLR 1097, HL, 3 Digest (Reissue) 576, *3700*.

Beswick v Beswick [1967] 2 All ER 1197, [1968] AC 58, [1967] 3 WLR 932, HL, 12 Digest
f (Reissue) 49, *256*.

Franklin v Inland Revenue Comrs, Swaythling's Executors v Inland Revenue Comrs (1930) 15 Tax Cas 464, 28(1) Digest (Reissue) 505, *1837*.

Grant's Will Trusts, Re [1979] 3 All ER 359, [1980] 1 WLR 360.

Macaulay's Estate, Re, Macaulay v O'Donnell [1943] Ch 435, HL, 8(1) Digest (Reissue) 275, *1033*.

g *Recher's Will Trusts, Re, National Westminster Bank Ltd v National Anti-Vivisection Society Ltd* [1971] 3 All ER 401, [1972] Ch 526, [1971] 3 WLR 321, 8(1) Digest (Reissue) 297, *398*.

Thackrah, Re, Thackrah v Wilson [1939] 2 All ER 4, 8(1) Digest (Reissue) 278, *265*.

Wells, Re, Swinburne-Hanham v Howard [1933] Ch 29, [1932] All ER Rep 277, 101 LJ Ch 346, 148 LT 5, CA, 35 Digest (Repl) 412, *1072*.

Wood Preservation Ltd v Prior (Inspector of Taxes) [1969] 1 All ER 364, [1969] 1 WLR
h 1077, 45 Tax Cas 112, 47 ATC 364, [1968] TR 353, CA and HL, 28(1) Digest (Reissue) 462, *1664*.

Cases also cited

Astor's Settlement Trusts, Re, Astor v Scholfield [1952] 1 All ER 1067, [1952] Ch 534.

Caledonian Employees' Benevolent Society, Re 1928 SC 633

j *General Assembly of Free Church of Scotland v Lord Overtoun* [1904] AC 515, HL.

Gillingham Bus Disaster Fund, Re [1958] 2 All ER 749, [1959] Ch 62, CA.

Hobourn Aero Components Ltd's Air-Raid Distress Fund, Re, Ryan v Forrest [1946] 1 All ER 501, [1946] Ch 194, CA.

Price, Re, Midland Bank Executor and Trustee Co Ltd v Harwood [1943] 2 All ER 505, [1943] Ch 422.

Reel v Holder [1979] 3 All ER 1041, [1979] 1 WLR 1252.

Saywell v Pope (Inspector of Taxes) [1979] STC 824.
Smith v Anderson (1880) 15 Ch D 247, [1874–80] All ER Rep 1121, CA.
Smith, Re, Johnson v Bright-Smith [1914] 1 Ch 937.

Case stated

1. At a hearing before the Commissioners for the Special Purposes of the Income Tax Acts on 17th, 18th, 19th and 20th July 1978, the Conservative and Unionist Central Office ('the Central Office') appealed against assessments to corporation tax in the sum of £40,000 for each of the accounting periods ended on 31st March 1972 to 31st March 1976 inclusive.

2. The question which the commissioners had to decide is shortly stated in para 1(1) of the decision in para IX below.

3. The following witnesses gave evidence before the commissioners: the Rt Hon Eric, Baron Chelmer and Mr George Gavin Carlyle. Written statements by these witnesses were also submitted to the commissioners which contained helpful summaries of the evidence-in-chief which the witnesses gave before the commissioners. In so far as they related to matters of fact the commissioners accepted them as accurate; in so far as they contained expressions of opinion or views on the question in issue before them the commissioners regarded them as supplementing the submissions made by counsel for the Central Office. Lord Chelmer qualified his statement in one important particular. He corrected the statement that he had been a subscribing member of the Conservative Party for forty years by saying that he had over a period of forty years been a member of several constituency associations. The commissioners summarised in para 2 of their decision their findings of fact based on the evidence of Lord Chelmer and Mr Carlyle and in their written statements and the other documentary evidence which they made available to the commissioners.

[Paragraph 4 listed the documents proved or admitted before the commissioners.]

5. The relevant facts as found by the commissioners on the basis of the evidence submitted were set out in para 2 of their decision.

6. The contentions advanced by counsel for the Central Office were set out in para 4(i) to (iv) of the commissioners' decision.

7. The contentions advanced by counsel for the Crown were set out in para 4(v) of the commissioners' decision.

8. In addition to the cases referred to in para 9.3 the following cases and authority were cited in the course of argument: *Smith v Anderson* (1880) 15 Ch D 247, [1874–80] All ER Rep 1121; *Re Astor's Settlement Trusts, Astor v Scholfield* [1952] 1 All ER 1067, [1952] Ch 534; *Leahy v Attorney General of New South Wales* [1959] 2 All ER 300, [1959] AC 457; *Wood Preservation Ltd v Prior (Inspector of Taxes)* [1969] 1 All ER 364, [1969] 1 WLR 1077; *Re Denley's Trust Deed, Holman v H H Martyn & Co Ltd* [1968] 3 All ER 65, [1969] 1 Ch 373; Snell, the Principles of Equity (27th Edn, 1973, pp 99–100).

9. The commissioners who heard the appeal took time to consider their decision and gave it in writing on 31st August 1978 as follows:

> '1. *The Issue* (1) This appeal relates to corporation tax assessments for each of the five years ending on 31 March 1972 to 1976 inclusive made on the Conservative and Unionist Central Office, commonly and conveniently called "Central Office". No objection is raised to the name used for the purpose of the assessments. No point is taken that the taxpayer has not been correctly identified: the point taken is that there is no taxpayer to identify. Liability for corporation tax is imposed on companies by section 238(1) Income and Corporation Taxes Act 1970. "Company" is defined in section 526(5) of the Act as meaning any body corporate or unincorporated association. In the Income and Expenditure Account of the Central Funds of the Conservative and Unionist Party for each of the relevant years the income which it is sought to tax is identified as investment income and interest. [Counsel for the Central Office] argues that Central Office, whatever else it may be, is not a company within the relevant definition and that there is, as a matter of law,

no unincorporated association in existence to which the Central Office funds belong so as to make that unincorporated association liable to corporation tax on the income. While disposed to accept that Central Office is not an unincorporated association, [counsel for the Crown] argues that there is an unincorporated association, identifiable as the Conservative Party, on behalf of which and subject to the rules of which the Central Office funds are held. The issue in this appeal is whether or not such an unincorporated association exists. If it does not no corporation tax is payable on the income and the assessments must be discharged. If, however, it does, the income must be accurately quantified and the adjusted assessments upheld. (2) At this point one general observation, may, perhaps, usefully be made. Obviously there is a sense in which the Party exists. Central Office is identified as the Party Headquarters. Those who work there, whether in a voluntary or professional capacity, acknowledge their allegiance to the Leader of the Party. The Chairman of the Party is responsible for making the policy of the Party known, the Treasurers for the Party's finance. But those who use these expressions in their day to day work, or to describe the party organisation in Party literature, (Lord Chelmer, for example, the Senior Party Treasurer in the relevant years, or Mr Carlyle, a Central Office "professional" with the title of Comptroller, both of whom gave evidence before us), use them in relation to an organisation with which they are familiar. Their concern is not to analyse that organisation but to make it function effectively. For them it is sufficient that, by historical accident or by design, there is an organisation regulated by a system of checks and balances which works and works well. Questions of ultimate authority, still less questions of identifying legal rights and powers, simply do not arise. The reply of one of the witnesses to the question what would happen to the Central Office funds in an extreme situation, a split in the Party for example, to the effect that one could only wait and see was patently honest, sincere and practical. The question which we have to answer, is a question which does not arise in the day to day running and management of a political party.

'2. *The Evidence* (1) One of the leaflets which is in evidence before us describes the Conservative Party organisation in these terms: "... basically, the structure is very simple and is made up of three elements: (i) the Parliamentary Party which consists of those Members of both Houses who take the Conservative Whip. This is the oldest element and embodies the Party in Parliament; (ii) the mass membership represented by the National Union of which the constituency association is the basic unit; and (iii) the Party headquarters—the Central Office—which with its area offices operates the machinery of Party organisation throughout England and Wales, and the Conservative Research Department. These three elements are complementary. This pattern, parliamentary, National Union and agency, is repeated at three levels, constituency, area and national. At the head stands the Leader of the Party." (2) Members of the Parliamentary Party can readily be identified since they are all Members of one or other House who take the Conservative Whip. The Party literature stresses that selection of a candidate is a matter for the local constituency association "Subject to certain simple Party rules—for example, candidates must be approved by the Standing Advisory Committee and therefore included on the official list—associations have complete freedom in making their choice". The Party rules referred to were put forward in a Report of a Review Committee to the National Union. The Standing Advisory Committee on Candidates includes various officers of the National Union, the Chairman and Deputy Chairman of the Party Organisation and the Chief Whip. (3) The National Union of Conservative and Unionist Associations, the mass membership element in the Party organisation, is the federation of Conservative constituency associations in England and Wales to which each association affiliates. The leaflet on the Party organisation states that its popular description "The National Union" is an apt one since the three elements of the Party, parliamentary Members and candidates, the voluntary subscribing members and the professional executives unite as members of its executive committees. The voluntary subscribing members are those who join their local constituency associations, each in itself a separate autonomous unincorporated association, affiliated to the National Union and capable of being disaffiliated by that body, expected to contribute to central funds but not bound, still less compellable, to do so. The functions of the National Union are expressed to be: (i) To support and encourage the development of the principles and aims of the Conservative Party. (ii) To secure the election of Conservative candidates. (iii) To form and develop Conservative Associations in every Constituency. (iv) To form a centre of united action and to act as a link between the Leader of the Party and all sections of the Party. (v) To work closely in co-ordination with the Conservative Central Office. The objects of a typical local constituency association, allowing for the difference in territorial scope, are not dissimilar and include: (1) To provide an efficient organisation of the Conservative Party in the constituency. (2) To spread the knowledge of Conservative principles and policy, and generally to promote the interests of the Party in the constituency. (3) To secure the return of a Conservative Member of Parliament for the constituency . . . (vii) To co-operate with the area council and with Party headquarters in the common aim of establishing in power a Conservative and Unionist Government. (viii) To contribute to the central funds of the Party. An individual wishing to become "a member of the Conservative Party" who applied to the Party headquarters for membership would be referred to his local constituency association. There is no such thing as membership of the Party obtainable through Central Office. As as matter of history the National Union was formed in 1867 as a federation of local Conservative associations. It was formed before Central Office was established. The National Union has its own rules and elected officers and a full time secretary appointed by its National Executive Committee. Affiliation fees paid by constituent associations are handled by Central Office and are treated as reducing the expenditure incurred in operating the National Union, the balance of such expenditure being met out of central funds. Both Lord Chelmer and Mr Carlyle, (and from the point of view of explaining how the organisation works, no one could be better qualified to explain than they), were emphatic about the separateness of the National Union and Central Office. To them it would be an absurdity to identify the National Union as the owner of the funds administered by Central Office. At one stage Lord Chelmer was chairman of a committee charged with the task of reviewing the constitution of the National Union. A suggestion that the National Union should in some way be enlarged to embrace Central Office was considered and rejected. Lord Chelmer described the main function of the National Union as being to discuss and devise policy. It is for this purpose that it holds the Party Meeting every year, an occasion quite separate from the Party Conference which it is also the function of the National Union to organise. The Annual Conference is specifically referred to in the Rules of the National Union. As we understand the position, no such clear rules are anywhere laid down regarding the Party Meeting but there has, we were told, always been a Party Meeting and it now has a specific function to perform in relation to the selection of the Leader of the Party. The Party Meeting, organised by the National Union and the Chief Whip jointly, consists of Conservative Members of both Houses, Parliamentary Candidates and members of the National Union Executive Committee. The members of this Committee, approximately 180 in all, which is described as covering all sections of the Party, are identified under the Rules of the National Union. They include the Leader of the Party, certain of the officers of the Party Organisation including the Party Chairman and Treasurers, certain officers of Central Office and representatives of each Provisional Area. (4) Central Office was founded in 1870 by Disraeli. As the Leaflet on the Party organisation puts it, "The post of Party Manager was created and the general control and direction of Central Office was in the hands of the Whips until 1911, when the

first Party Chairman was . . . appointed. At first separate offices were maintained
a but since 1872 the National Union and Central Office have occupied the same
building, working closely together, while preserving their separate identities". Lord
Chelmer put it that Central Office has three faces, one towards the National Union
for which it provides services, another towards the Leader of the Party and the
shadow cabinet or cabinet, as the case might be, and the third towards the
Parliamentary Party, Conservative Members of both Houses. At the same time it
b was not directly linked with any of these bodies. Mr Carlyle identified the three
principal functions of Central Office as, being (i) through its area offices to provide
relevant knowledge to constituency associations and to channel money to needy
constituencies and generally to provide the administrative structure which enables
the National Union to discharge its function; (ii) to provide the organisation and
information which enables the Party to fight elections as a national unit; and (iii) to
c make available to constituency associations certain services which it might prove
costly for them to provide for themselves. Historically Central Office was established
to meet the needs of the Leader of the Party. Today the ultimate source of its
authority remains the Party Leader. For all practical purposes, however, the
Chairman of the Party, appointed by and answerable to the Leader of the Party,
controls Central Office. The Party Treasurers are appointed by the Leader of the
d Party and are accountable to him or her. They are responsible for the custody of the
assets of the Party and for administering the income and expenditure. One of their
main functions is to seek donations to the funds which they administer. In cross-
examination both Lord Chelmer and Mr Carlyle were invited to speculate on what
course of action they might adopt if directed by the Leader of the Party, (whose
authority generally to direct how matters within the scope of Central Office's
e activities should be dealt with they acknowledged), to apply Central Office funds in
some totally improper or mistaken way. Their position as we understood it, was
that however unlikely such a situation might be, circumstances could conceivably
arise in which, all resources of reason and persuasion being exhausted, they might
feel bound as a matter of conscience to put, if they could, the funds within their
control out of reach of the Leader of the Party, such course being followed almost
f certainly by resignation and a public explanation of their actions. (5) The position
of the Leader of the Party is that certain rules were laid down in 1965 as to the
procedure to be adopted in selecting a Party Leader. There is to be a ballot, (if
necessary, more than one), of the Party in the House of Commons. It is provided
that thereafter "The Candidate thus elected by the Commons Party will be presented
for election as Party Leader to the Party Meeting constituted as at present." Asked
g whose the rules were which regulated the selection of a Party Leader Lord Chelmer
replied that he was unable to say. In this he was, in our view, wholly sincere and
entirely consistent. The evidence which we have been asked to consider confirms
the impression to which we have already referred, that in relation to the affairs of a
political party there are questions which in practice do not get asked either because
the situations with which they deal are regarded from a practical point of view as so
h remote and unlikely as to be irrelevant, or because as a matter of simple political
prudence they are best not asked or answered before they have to be.

'3. *The Law* We were usefully referred to a number of cases dealing with the
characteristics of unincorporated associations in a variety of contexts. Three of the
cases contain short statements of what are some of the essential features in law of an
unincorporated association. In *Re Thackrah* [1939] 2 All ER 4 at 6 a gift by will to
j the Oxford Group was in question. Bennett J commented: "Before one can find an
association, there must be some rules, either written or oral, by which those who are
supposed to be members of it are tied together. I think that they would probably
be written rules. There must be some constitution." In *Re Price* [1943] 2 All ER
505 at 508, [1943] Ch 422 at 428 Cohen J referred to the comment of Lord
Buckmaster in *Macaulay v O'Donnell* [1943] Ch 435 at 436 referring to a gift to an

unincorporated association: "A group of people defined and bound together by rules
and called by a distinctive name can be the subject of a gift as well as any individual
or incorporated body." In the case of *The Caledonian Employees Benevolent Society* a
1928 SC 633 at 635 absence of any consensual contract among its members was a bar
to the claim that the Society was an unincorporated association. The Lord President,
referring to the Companies (Consolidation) Act, 1908 said: "It is not, I think, open
to doubt that the fundamental and essential characteristic of the whole class of
bodies described in the Act as companies, associations, and partnerships, is that they b
are bodies constituted by some species of contract of society, and founded on the
contractual obligations thus undertaken by the members, or *socii, inter se.* . . . No
doubt the word 'association' is by itself capable of including a wide variety of much
more loosely and irregularly constituted bodies of persons; but looking to the
context in which it appears . . . I see no reason to doubt that what is meant is a
society (whatever its object) based on consensual contract among its constituent c
members whereby their mutual relations *inter se* with regard to some common
object are regulated and enforced." We also derived assistance from what Brightman
J, dealing with a gift to a non-charitable association, said in *In re Recher's Will Trusts*
[1971] 3 All ER 401 at 407–408, [1972] Ch 526 at 538–539: "A trust for non-
charitable purposes, as distinct from a trust for individuals, is clearly void because
there is no beneficiary. It does not, however, follow that persons cannot band d
themselves together as an association or society, pay subscriptions and validly devote
their funds in pursuit of some lawful non-charitable purpose. An obvious example
is a members' social club. But it is not essential that the members should only
intend to secure direct personal advantages to themselves. The association may be
one in which personal advantages to the members are combined with the pursuit of
some outside purpose. Or the association may be one which offers no personal e
benefit at all to the members, the funds of the association being applied exclusively
to the pursuit of some outside purpose. Such an association of persons is bound, I
would think, to have some sort of constitution; that is to say, the rights and
liabilities of the members of the association will inevitably depend on some form of
contract *inter se*, usually evidenced by a set of rules. In the present case it appears to
me clear that the life members, the ordinary members and the associate members f
of the . . . society were bound together by a contract *inter se.* Any such member was
entitled to the rights and subject to the liabilities defined by the rules. If the
committee acted contrary to the rules, an individual member would be entitled to
take proceedings in the courts to compel observance of the rules or to recover
damages for any loss he had suffered as a result of the breach of contract. As and
when a member paid his subscription to the association, he would be subjecting his g
money to the disposition and expenditure thereof laid down by the rules. That is
to say, the member would be bound to permit, and entitled to require, the honorary
trustees and other members of the society to deal with that subscription in
accordance with the lawful directions of the committee. Those directions would
include the expenditure of that subscription as part of the general funds of the
association, in furthering the objects of the association. The resultant situation, on h
analysis, is that the . . . society represented an organisation of individuals bound
together by a contract under which their subscriptions became, as it were, mandated
towards a certain type of expenditure as adumbrated in rule 1. Just as the two
parties to a bi-partite bargain can vary or terminate their contract by mutual
consent, so it must follow that the life members, ordinary members and associate
members of the . . . society could, at any moment of time, by unanimous agreement j
(or by majority vote, if the rules so prescribe), vary or terminate their multi-partite
contract. There would be no limit to the type of variation or termination to which
all might agree. There is no private trust or trust for charitable purposes or other
trust to hinder the process. It follows that if all members agreed, they could decide
to wind up the . . . society and divide the net assets among themselves beneficially.

No one would have any locus standi to stop them so doing. The contract is the same as any other contract and concerns only those who are parties to it, that is to say, the members of the society. The funds of such an association may, of course, be derived not only from the subscriptions of the contracting parties but also from donations from non-contracting parties and legacies from persons who have died. In the case of a donation which is not accompanied by any words which purport to impose a trust, it seems to me that the gift takes effect in favour of the existing members of the association as an accretion to the funds which are the subject-matter of the contract which such members have made *inter se*, and falls to be dealt with in precisely the same way as the funds which the members themselves have subscribed. So, in the case of a legacy. In the absence of words which purport to impose a trust, the legacy is a gift to the members beneficially, not as joint tenants or as tenants in common so as to entitle each member to an immediate distributive share, but as an accretion to the funds which are the subject matter of the contract which the members have made *inter se*." By reference to these and other cases [counsel for the Central Office] identified in argument six characteristics of an unincorporated association: (i) Membership. There must be members, socii, of the association. (ii) Contract. There must be a contract between the members *inter se*. The contract will usually be found in a set of written rules. (iii) Constitution. There must be some constitutional arrangement for meetings of members and for the appointment of committees and officers. (iv) Adherence. A member must be free to join or leave the association at will. (v) Continuity. The association must continue in existence quite independently of any changes which may occur in the composition of the membership. (vi) Formation. There must, as a matter of history, have been a moment of time when a number of persons combined or banded together to form the association. These [counsel for Central Office] identified as essential or normal characteristics of an unincorporated association and submitted by way of summary, a definition in these terms: "An unincorporated association exists whenever persons who lawfully associate together to achieve a common purpose ('the members') bind themselves together by an enforceable contract by the terms of which (i) persons may, by agreeing to the terms of the contract, become members and (ii) persons may, by resiling from the contract, cease to be members and (iii) so far as the law permits, only those persons who are, from time to time, members have a share in the assets, or are burdened by the liabilities of, the association." With reservations [counsel for the Crown] was disposed to accept six characteristics [set out by counsel for Central Office] as relevant and indicative of the existence of an unincorporated association. He referred us to *In re Smith* [1914] 1 Ch 937 in support of the proposition that the "contract" between the members of an unincorporated association might be an agreement or understanding falling short of a legally enforceable contract. We did not find it necessary to go more deeply into this point since it appeared to be the case that [counsel for the Crown's] argument was to the effect that there was indeed an enforceable contractual relationship between the members of the unincorporated association which he said existed. More to the point, perhaps, in relation to the argument generally were some of the passages in the speeches in the *Free Church of Scotland* case [1904] AC 515, to which we were referred. For example Lord Davey referred to that Church as "a voluntary and unincorporated association of Christians united on the basis of agreement in certain religious tenets and principles of worship, discipline and Church government." (See [1904] AC 515 at 643). This was an illustration of an unincorporated association where the basis of the banding together was a commitment to and acceptance of certain ideas and doctrines and where the contract between the members depended not so much on any written rules as on what had to be inferred from all the surrounding circumstances. Clearly no one member of the Church could extract his share of the assets without the consent of all.

'4. *The Contentions* (i) [Counsel for the Central Office's] first contention was to the effect that Central Office is not an unincorporated association. (ii) His second contention was that even if the National Union could be said to be an unincorporated *a* association, the Central funds of the Party, administered by Central Office, are not the funds of the National Union. (iii) His third contention was that the Party is a political movement and that the Revenue's attempt to fit it into the legal framework of an unincorporated association is misguided and misconceived. He referred us to what Lord Chelmer had said about the suggestion that there was an organisation which could be called the Conservative Party and identified as an unincorporated *b* association: "The Conservative Party is a political movement in which I believe profoundly, but organisationally it is the somewhat amorphous combination of the various structures and persons to which I have referred." These last included the National Union, the Central Office, the Constituency Associations and the Party Treasurers. [Counsel's] argument [for the Central Office] was that the amorphous combination lacked the characteristics of an unincorporated association. The *c* various structures have grown and developed independently each from its own separate historical origins. (iv) [Counsel for the Central Office] recognised that his argument leaves unanswered the question who does own the central funds but he submitted that it was sufficient for his argument that they are not owned by an unincorporated association. (v) [Counsel for the Crown] did not dispute that Central Office is not an unincorporated association. As to the National Union he *d* submitted that an unincorporated association of local constituency associations is not a practical possibility as a matter of law, such an association being in law an association of all the individual members of the local associations. His submission was that an unincorporated association exists called the Conservative Party, of which the members are the individual subscribing members of all the local constituency associations and the Members of both Houses taking the Conservative Whip. He *e* pointed to the procedure for the selection of the Leader of the Party. The authority of the Leader is derived from the Party Meeting, being the representatives of the mass membership and the Parliamentary Party. Thus the Conservative Party consists of all those who have declared their support for the common aim either by joining a local constituency association or, being qualified, by taking the Conservative Whip. The contract between the members is to be found in the rules *f* of the local associations, in the terms on which local associations are affiliated to the National Union and in the rules and practices which regulate the Party Meeting, the selection of the Party Leader and the delegation to the Party Leader of the wide powers of control over the affairs and funds of the Party which the Party Leader exercises through Central Office and the officers of the Party. Those who work at Central Office, apart from the honorary officers, are employees, not necessarily *g* members *of* the Party but clearly workers *for* the Party. The contract between the members of the unincorporated association so far as it relates to money is that their money, if not expended locally, will go into the central funds of the Party and will be administered and applied for the purposes of the Party by the Party Treasurers and Central Office under the control and direction of the Party Leader.

'5. *The Conclusion* In our judgment, [counsel for the Crown's] submission is to *h* be preferred: we hold that there is, as a matter of law, an unincorporated association which can accurately be identified as the Conservative Party, a recognisable body more precisely defined and more compact than the wider political movement to which the name Conservative Party is commonly given. Taking the six characteristics of an unincorporated association: (i) The Conservative Party has members. They become members in one of two ways: either they join a local *j* constituency association affiliated to the National Union and pay such subscription as the rules of the local constituency association require; or being eligible, by taking the Conservative Whip, in the case of Members of the House of Commons having first, if necessary, been approved by the Party's Standing Advisory Committee, adopted by a local constituency association and elected. (ii) The contract between

> members of the Conservative Party is to be found in part in the rules of the National Union, in part in the rules which regulate the Party Meeting and the selection of the Leader of the Party and in part in the rules of local constituency associations. Thus, for example, those contracting parties who pay subscriptions to local constituency associations do so on the basis that some part of what they subscribe may be applied as a contribution to the central funds of the Party. If the local constituency association, for example through the quota system, makes a contribution to central funds, the money will be applied by Central Office for Party purposes under the direction of the Party Treasurers subject to such general instructions as the Party Leader may be minded to give. A member having subscribed must be taken to have contracted with his fellow members not to seek to withdraw his money but to permit it to be dealt with and applied for Party purposes as those with responsibility for such matters under the Party's "constitution" decide. (iii) There are "constitutional" arrangements for members to elect representatives and for those representatives to meet in various meetings. Similarly provision is made for the election of committees and appointment of officers. Rules govern the selection of the Leader of the Party. Every member has a right to the extent to which the rules permit to participate in the various decision making and selection processes and a duty to abide by and accept the outcome. There is no single document which can be described as the "constitution" of the unincorporated association. The mutual contract between members has to be found in the rules of several of the constituent elements of the Party's organisation and the constitution in those same rules and in the rules, whether written or customary, which regulate the relationships between the constituent elements. The diagram [not set out in this report] which illustrates the Party Organisation illustrates the extent to which the substantive rules of the constitution are embedded in the interstices of the relationships between the different parts of that organisation. (iv) Subscribing members are clearly free to join or leave the Conservative Party at will. Those who are members by virtue of taking the Conservative Whip are similarly free to forego that particular qualification for membership. (v) History shows and every reasonable expectation supports the continuity of the Conservative Party, however much individual members may come and go. (vi) As to the banding together of the members, that they have banded together in pursuit of a common purpose is, we think, clear beyond doubt. (We are inclined to accept [counsel for the Crown's] argument that if at the material time there is a body of persons bound together by the acceptance of a common purpose and rules designed to provide an organisation for securing that purpose, it is unnecessary to identify the precise point of time at which the banding together occurred.) It is, therefore, our view that the claim for corporation tax succeeds. The Conservative Party, comprising members of local Conservative constituency associations and those members of both Houses who take the Conservative Whip, may properly be described as a voluntary and unincorporated association of individuals united on the basis of agreement in certain political tenets and principles and by acceptance of an established structure for regulating a political party.'

10. The appeals were then adjourned to enable figures to be agreed between the parties. Subsequently figures were agreed between them and on 18th October 1978 the commissioners adjusted the assessments accordingly.

11. Central Office immediately after the determination of the appeals declared its dissatisfaction therewith as being erroneous in point of law and on 6th November 1978 required the commissioners to state a case for the opinion of the High Court pursuant to s 56 of the Taxes Management Act 1970.

12. The case was submitted to the parties in draft form for their comments and for the assistance of the court the commissioners set out the following points to which their attention was directed in reply:

'(a) [Counsel for the Crown's] submissions which we have endeavoured to summarise in paragraph [9.4(v)] were put forward subject to one overriding a
submission to the effect that the notion of an amorphous combination of a character unknown to the law must be rejected. The ownership of the party funds must be in a body having legal capacity to own property. Ruling out alternative concepts such as a trust or individual ownership by a person or company (which possibilities did not fit the facts) it was necessary to consider the possibility of an unincorporated association if the argument was not to arise that the party had no valid claim to the b
funds in issue. (b) In paragraph [9.4(iii)] we referred to what Lord Chelmer had said about the Conservative Party being a political movement. In cross-examination Lord Chelmer also said this: "I would have thought that within the Conservative Party the expression 'the Party'—a very loose one—would mean the Members of both Houses of Parliament who take the Whip, all the Constituency Associations plus those peripheral bodies which form part of the National Union and part of the c
professional experts who support those activities in Central Office and in the areas." (c) In paragraph [9.2(4)] we referred to the Chairman of the Party and to the Party Treasurers. It was not intended to be other than implicit in our references that Chairman and Treasurer held office at the will of the Leader of the Party by whom they could be replaced at a moment's notice. (d) In paragraph [9.2(4)] we referred to what Lord Chelmer and Mr Carlyle said with regard to a possible disposal d
of Central Office funds. Both in fact referred to the possibility of the payment of the funds to the Trustees of the Trust known as the "1949 Conservative and Unionist Trust" which was a trust set up in 1949 with the intention that it should be suggested as the recipient of moneys intended to be bequeathed to the Party should anyone make enquiries at the time of drafting a will how best such a bequest should be effected. (e) Mr Carlyle's oral evidence included the following points:–(i) To e
illustrate the proposition that the quota system whereby the constituency associations are asked to contribute to the central funds is voluntary Mr Carlyle said that in 1976 thirty associations paid nothing, and more than half of the total paid less than their quota. This was typical for a non-election year. (ii) Central Office has no membership. (iii) Neither the constituency associations not the National Union have powers of control over Central Office, nor does Central Office have f
powers of control over the constituency associations. (iv) Historically Central Office was not formed by a number of persons banding together to form it.'

13. The question of law for the opinion of the court was whether there was such an unincorporated association as the commissioners held existed which could accurately be described as the Conservative Party, and which is assessable to corporation tax in respect of the income in question. g

Andrew Park QC and *David Goldberg* for Central Office.
Brian Davenport and *R W Ham* for the Crown.

Cur adv vult

h

2nd April. **VINELOTT J** read the following judgment: The question in this appeal is whether assessments to corporation tax for each of the five years ending on 31st March 1972 to 1976 (both inclusive) which have been made on the Conservative and Unionist Central Office ('the Central Office') were properly so made. That question in turn depends on whether, as the Special Commissioners have found, certain funds held by the j
Central Office, the income of which it is sought to assess to corporation tax, are held by the Central Office or its officials on behalf of or as agents for an unincorporated association.

There are two points which I should make clear at the onset. First of all, there is no question of corporation tax or income tax being payable on donations or subscriptions

made to the Central Office or to the Conservative Party. The question only arises in
a relation to income derived from donations and subscriptions which are accumulated and
invested by the Central Office; the flow of donations and subscriptions is inevitably
erratic and during periods when the inflow is large a surplus is built up and invested in
short term investments which are then available to meet the more easily predictable
outflow. Secondly, the question is not whether the income of these funds attracts tax.
If the income is not assessable to corporation tax it is admittedly liable to income tax
b either by deduction at source or by assessment on the party treasurer or officials of the
Central Office who, in terms of s 114 of the Income and Corporation Taxes Act 1970,
were 'the persons receiving or entitled to the income'. That is why this question arises
only at a late stage in the history of the Conservative Party. Corporation tax was
introduced as recently as 1965. It is chargeable on the income of companies (s 238(1) of
the Income and Corporation Taxes Act 1970 read in conjunction with s 238(4)(*a*) of that
c Act) and the word 'company' is defined in s 526(5) as, subject to an immaterial exception,
'any body corporate or unincorporated association'. When first introduced the rate at
which corporation tax was levied was much the same as the standard rate of income
tax. Thus, it made no practical difference whether the income of funds held by the
Central Office was liable to income tax or corporation tax. Although the two rates did
not long remain the same, there was no significant divergence until with the passing of
d the Finance Act 1971 the classic UK combination of a relatively high standard rate of
income tax with substantial earned income relief up to a given level of total income was
abandoned and the present combination of a lower basic rate with an additional rate of
tax (now 15%) on investment income was substituted. Thereafter, the difference
between the basic rate of income tax (now 30%) and the rate at which corporation tax has
been charged (now 52%) has been significant.

e There is waiting in the wings a question whether, if the income of funds held by the
Central Office attracts income tax but not corporation tax, the income also attracts the
additional rate of tax as income 'arising to trustees' within s 16 of the Finance Act 1973
which is not the income of any settlor of beneficiary. If it does the financial consequences
of the question before me now will be reduced, although the difference between the two
bases of assessment will still be significant.

f As I have said, the question is whether the income of funds held by or under the
control of the Central Office is income of funds held on behalf of an unincorporated
association. The Special Commissioners in answering this question in the affirmative
identified the unincorporated association as the Conservative Party which they found to
be an association 'comprising members of local Conservative Constituency Associations
and those Members of both Houses who take the Conservative whip'.

g The commissioners had before them written statements of two eminent Conservatives,
namely Lord Chelmer, who has held a number of senior positions in the Conservative
Party, including that of chairman of the Conserative Board of Finance and chairman of
the National Union of Conservative and Unionist Associations, and Mr George Gavin
Carlyle, a career member of the Central Office who is now comptroller of the Central
Office. They also had before them documentary evidence comprising (1) the annual
h report of the Central Office for the year 1975–76 and specimen invoices and contracts of
employment, (2) a note explaining the operation of the bank accounts of the Central
Office and the way in which investment and deposit accounts are held and operated, (3)
the constitution and rules of the Conservative Board of Finance, (4) the rules and standing
orders of the National Union of Conservative and Unionist Associations ('the National
Union') as revised in 1972, 1975 and 1978, (5) a booklet entitled 'Notes for Constituency
j Treasurers', (6) a booklet issued by the Central Office in 1971 entitled 'The Party
Organisation' ('the blue book'), (7) specimen rules of a local Conservative Association
with membership forms and (8) an organisational summary dated 15th May 1973 issued
by the Central Office.

The structure of the Conservative party organisation is described in the blue book in
the following terms:

'... basically, the structure is very simple and is made up of three elements:– (i) the Parliamentary Party which consists of those Members of both Houses who take the Conservative Whip. This is the oldest element and embodies the Party in Parliament; (ii) the membership represented by the National Union of which the constituency association is the basic unit; and (iii) the Party headquarters—the Central Office—which with its area offices operates the machinery of Party organisation throughout England and Wales, and the Conservative Research Department. These three elements are complementary. This pattern, parliamentary, National Union and agency, is repeated at three levels, constituency, area and national. At the head stands the Leader of the Party.'

Of these three elements or strands the first requires little explanation. The members of the House of Commons who take the Conservative whip are, of course, normally, if not invariably, selected by their local constituency associations. The blue book stresses that 'Subject to certain simple Party rules—for example, candidates must be approved by the Standing Advisory Committee and therefore included on the official list—associations have complete freedom in making their choice'. The party rules referred to were first put forward in a report of a review committee of the national union. The standing advisory committee on candidates includes various officers of the national union, the chairman and deputy chairman of the party organisation and the chief whip.

The second strand, the national union, was formed in 1867 as a federation of local conservative associations. The blue book explains:

'At first called the National Union of Conservative and Constitutional Associations, its name was changed in 1912, when the Conservative and Liberal Unionist wings of the Party amalgamated, and again in 1924, when its present title, National Union of Conservative and Unionist Associations, was adopted.'

It was formed, following the extension of the franchise, to co-ordinate local constituency parties and to foster conservatism as a national movement. Its functions are expressed to be, in r II—

'(1) To support and encourage the development of the principles and aims of the Conservative Party. (2) To secure the election of Conservative candidates. (3) To form and develop Conservative Associations in every Constituency. (4) To form a centre of united action and to act as a link between the Leader of the Party and all sections of the Party. (5) To work closely in co-ordination with the Conservative Central Office.'

Rule III of the national union defines its membership which is said to 'consist of all those who subscribe annually to any registered Constituency Association or any other recognised Conservative body'. Rule III also provides that:

'(a) A registered Conservative Association shall be a Constituency Association which subscribes annually to the National Union an affiliation fee ... (b) A recognised Conservative body shall be one which has been approved by the Executive Committee of the National Union.'

Each of the local constituency conservative associations is unquestionably an unincorporated association. Clause 2 of the rules of a typical constituency association (draft rules are supplied by the national union, though their adoption is not compulsory) sets out the objects of the association, which include the following:

'(1) To provide an efficient organisation of the Conservative Party in the constituency. (2) To spread the knowledge of Conservative principles and policy, and generally to promote the interests of the Party in the constituency. (3) To secure the return of a Conservative Member of Parliament for the Constituency. (4) To secure the return at local government elections of such councillors as are chosen for support by the Party. (5) To watch the revision of the Constituency

register of electors in the interests of the Party and to take steps to ensure that all
a supporters who are qualified are in a position to record their votes. (6) To keep in touch with the Conservative and Unionist Associations in neighbouring constituencies, and to afford mutual assistance whenever possible. (7) To co-operate with the area council and with Party headquarters in the common aim of establishing in power a Conservative and Unionist Government. (8) To contribute to the central funds of the Party.'

b References in these rules and any other documents to the party headquarters are references to the Central Office.

One of the functions of the local constituency conservative association is to raise money to defray the expenses of the Central Office. A quota is fixed annually by the board of finance (which I shall turn to in a moment), but Lord Chelmer in his written statement made it clear that the payment of this quota was voluntary. There is no means
c by which a local association can be compelled to pay its quota or to make any other contribution to national funds.

All the local constituency associations are affiliated to the national union. I have already cited the rules which set out its functions and membership. Lord Chelmer described its main function as providing a meeting place where representatives of the mass membership of the party come together to dicuss and debate policy. It organises
d the annual party conference. It is controlled by a central council which includes in addition to representatives of local conservative associations representatives of a number of other conservative bodies including, for instance, representatives of the Young Conservatives, the Trade Union Advisory Committee, the Conservative Overseas Bureau, the Association of Conservative Clubs and the Primrose League.

Counsel for the Crown submitted that the national union is itself an unincorporated
e association, its members being all the members of all the local constituency conservative associations. He submitted, rightly I think, that, not being a legal person, an unincorporated association cannot itself be a member of another unincorporated association, and he submitted that r III of the national union can only be given effect if the membership is taken to include all members of the local constituency associations. I doubt whether that conclusion necessarily follows. I can see no reason why an
f unincorporated association should not agree to send representatives to meet representatives from other unincorporated associations having a common purpose in order to discuss matters of common interest, whether informally or in accordance with some formal constitution, without its members thereby becoming members of a wider unincorporated association. The constitution of the Central Council suggests to my mind that it is not an amalgam of the members of the different local constituency
g associations but a meeting place of delegates with an agreed constitution but no members. However, the question does not arise for decision and I express no considered opinion on it. The unincorporated association which the commissioners have found to exist is an amalgam of all the local constituency associations and of the party in Paliament and not an amalgam of the national union and the party in Parliament.

The Central Office had its origins in the appointment by Disraeli of Gorst to be his
h principal agent in 1870. Before then the chief agent of the leader of the party had been a partner in a London firm of solicitors, first Rose and later Spofforth. With the appointment of Gorst, whose post is described in the blue book as that of party manager, the responsibility of the leader's principal agent was much enlarged. He was required to build up the party organisation and to ensure that a candidate was available for every seat offering a hope of success. Mr Carlyle explains in his evidence:

j

> 'For some time after 1870 the whips were closely involved in the work of Central Office and were responsible for controlling central funds, but over the years their involvement decreased and the office is now a separate organisation with officers appointed by the leader managing its funds. It continues however to perform the function of serving the party leader. The office established by Disraeli was created

to serve him and grapple with the effects of the Second Reform Act for which he was widely blamed. Although the office has been much enlarged since Disraeli's time, it still exists to serve the party leader. All the appointment of the principal officers of Central Office are made by the leader, and it is to the leader that they are responsible.'

These are the three main strands. They intertwine not only at national but also at lower levels. The rules of the national union provide for the constitution of provincial area councils and provincial area committees which reflect at a lower level the Central Council and the executive committee of the national union. The Central Office also appoints an agent for each provincial area (11 in all) whose task is to advise and encourage individual constituency associations. But the link is informal. Lord Chelmer explains that the provincial or area agent 'can only offer help and advice which may be accepted or rejected'.

Those are the three strands identified in the blue book. But this description of the three strands is incomplete without an account of the way in which the moneys which provide the life blood of the movement are provided. The persons responsible for raising these moneys are known as party treasurers. They (like the party chairman) are appointed by the leader of the party. The expenditure of the moneys raised is under the control of the Central Office and thus ultimately under the control of the leader of the party. The party treasurers are assisted in their work by a board of finance. The rules governing this board state that it was 'established in pursuance of a resolution of the Executive Committee of the National Union on 20th April 1944 unanimously endorsing a recommendation of its Special Finance Committee that a National Board of Finance should be set up'. The relevant rules provide that:

'3. The Board is responsible to the Chairman of the Party Organisation from whom it derives its authority. 4. The functions of the Board are to organise in co-operation with Provincial Areas and the Treasurers of the Party, the raising of funds for the Party, and to make such agreements with Provincial Areas and other organisations as may be necessary to achieve this purpose. Its functions shall include the duty of advising those concerned on the value or desirability of particular activities of the Central Office in the areas. 5. The Board shall consist of the Party Treasurers, of whom one shall be Chairman, the Area Treasurers and up to a maximum of five co-opted members.'

Thus, again, the links between the party treasurers and the Central Office and the national union at national level are reflected by links at the local area levels.

As I have said, the expenditure of the funds raised by the party treasurers is under the control of the Central Office and thus indirectly under the control of the leader of the party. In the case stated the commissioners record:

'In cross-examination both Lord Chelmer and Mr Carlyle were invited to speculate on what course of action they might adopt if directed by the Leader of the Party, (whose authority generally to direct how matters within the scope of Central Office's activities should be dealt with they acknowledged), to apply Central Office funds in some totally improper or mistaken way. Their position as we understood it, was that however unlikely such a situation might be, circumstances could conceivably arise in which, all resources of reason and persuasion being exhausted, they might feel bound as a matter of conscience to put, if they could, the funds within their control out of reach of the Leader of the Party, such course being followed almost certainly by resignation and a public explanation of their actions.'

There is one other important element in the constitutional arrangements which govern the workings of the Conservative Party. The leader of the party is described in the blue book as—

> 'heading both the Conservative Party in Parliament and the Conservative party
> *a* Organisation in the country, including the Party Headquarters. The Leader thus stands at the apex of the entire structure of the Party, linking together the three elements of the Parliamentary Party, National Union and Party Headquarters.'

Before 1965 the leader of the party emerged following what are conventionally called 'the usual processes of consultation'. Since then the process of electing the leader has been formalised. Appendix A of the blue book sets out the present procedure for the
b selection of the leader of the Conservative and Unionist Party. The selection is made by a three-stage ballot of the party in the House of Commons, the chairman of the 1922 Committee being responsible for the conduct of it. The statement of the procedure in app A concludes with the sentence: 'The candidate thus elected by the Commons Party will be presented for election as Party Leader to the Party Meeting constituted as at present.' The case stated records:

c

> 'Asked whose the rules were which regulated the selection of a Party Leader Lord Chelmer replied that he was unable to say. In this he was, in our view, wholly sincere and entirely consistent. The evidence which we have been asked to consider confirms the impression to which we have already referred, that in relation to the affairs of a political party there are questions which in practice do not get asked
> *d* either because the situations with which they deal are regarded from a practical point of view as so remote and unlikely as to be irrelevant, or because as a matter of simple political prudence they are best not asked or answered before they have to be.'

As I have said, the commissioners found that the funds held by the party treasurers for the use of the Central Office were held on behalf of the members of an unincorporated
e association which they identified as comprising all the members of the local constituency associations together with the members of both Houses who take the party whip. In so doing they accepted the submissions made by counsel for the Crown, which they summarised in the following terms:

> '[Counsel for the Crown] did not dispute that Central Office is not an
> *f* unincorporated association. As to the National Union he submitted that an unincorporated association of local constituency associations is not a practical possibility as a matter of law, such an association being in law an association of all the individual members of the local associations. His submission was that an unincorporated association exists called the Conservative Party, of which the members are the individual subscribing members of all the local constituency
> *g* associations and the Members of both Houses taking the Conservative Whip. He pointed to the procedure for the selection of the leader of the Party. The authority of the Leader is derived from the Party Meeting, being the representatives of the mass membership and the Parliamentary Party. Thus the Conservative Party consists of all those who have declared their support for the common aim either by joining a local constituency association or, being qualified, by taking the
> *h* Conservative Whip. The contract between the members is to be found in the rules of the local associations, in the terms on which local associations are affiliated to the National Union and in the rules and practices which regulate the Party Meeting, the selection of the Party Leader and the delegation to the Party Leader of the wide powers of control over the affairs and funds of the Party which the Party Leader exercises through Central Office and the officers of the Party. Those who work at
> *j* Central Office, apart from the honorary officers, are employees, not necessarily members *of* the Party but clearly workers *for* the Party. The contract between the members of the unincorporated association so far as it relates to money is that their money, if not expended locally, will go into the central funds of the Party and will be administered and applied for the purposes of the Party by the Party Treasurers and Central Office under the control and direction of the Party Leader.'

Counsel for the Central Office had submitted that there are six characteristics which are either essential or normal characteristics of an unincorporated association. They are: (i) there must be members of the association; (ii) there must be a contract binding the members inter se; (iii) there will normally be some constitutional arrangement for meetings of members and for the appointment of committees and officers; (iv) a member will normally be free to join or leave the association at will; (v) the association will normally continue in existence independently of any change that may occur in the composition of the association; and (vi) there must as a matter of history have been a moment in time when a number of persons combined or banded together to form the association.

Counsel for the Central Office made it clear in his argument in this appeal that (iii), (iv) and (v) were not put forward as essential characteristics of an unincorportated association. It is possible to imagine an unincorporated association which lacked at least one of these characteristics. For instance, a members' club might be so exclusive as to make no provision for the admission of new members and the original members might conceivably band themselves together in life membership. But the first two characteristics are put forward, I think rightly, as essential characteristics. Indeed, they seem to me no more than an analysis of the concept of an unincorporated association. The sixth characteristic is, I think, also a necessary characteristic of an unincorporated association. If an unincorporated association is a 'group of people defined and bound together by rules and called by a distinctive name' (see per Lord Buckmaster in *Re Macaulay's Estate, Macaulay v O'Donnell* [1943] Ch 435 at 428) there must have been a moment in time when the first members agreed expressly or impliedly to be bound by the rules. But in practice the task of answering the question whether a body with a distinctive name is an unincorporated association will rarely if ever be much assisted by asking when it came into existence. In many if not most cases an unincorporated association will have been gradually transformed over a period of time into something very different from the unincorporated association from which it grew, and it may well be impossible to ascertain either the date of its formation of the moment in time in this process of change when it assumed its distinctive contemporary character.

The Special Commissioners in summarising their conclusions followed the classification of an unincorporated association submitted by counsel for the Central Office. I shall read their findings as to the first three characteristics in full:

> '(i) The Conservative Party has members. They become members in one of two ways: either they join a local constituency association affiliated to the National Union and pay such subscription as the rules of the local constituency association require; or being eligible, by taking the Conservative Whip, in the case of Members of the House of Commons having first, if necessary, been approved by the Party's Standing Advisory Committee adopted by a local constituency association and elected. (ii) The contract between members of the Conservative party is to be found in part in the rules of the National Union, in part in the rules which regulate the Party Meeting and the selection of the Leader of the Party and in part in the rules of local constituency associations. Thus, for example, those contracting parties who pay subscriptions to local constituency associations do so on the basis that some part of what they subscribe may be applied as a contribution to the central funds of the Party. If the local constituency association, for example through the quota system, makes a contribution to central funds, the money will be applied by Central Office for Party purposes under the direction of the Party Treasurer subject to such general instructions as the Party Leader may be minded to give. A member having subscribed must be taken to have contracted with his fellow members not to seek to withdraw his money but to permit it to be dealt with and applied for Party purposes as those with responsibility for such matters under the Party's "constitution" decide. (iii) There are 'constitutional' arrangements for members to elect representatives and for those representatives to meet in various meetings. Similarly

> provision is made for the election of committees and appointment of officers. Rules govern the selection of the Leader of the Party. Every member has a right to the extent to which the rules permit to participate in the various decision making and selection processes and a duty to abide by and accept the outcome.'

As to the remaining characteristics, they found that members are free to join or leave the party at will, that there is very reasonable expectation of continuity and that—

> '(vi) As to the banding together of the members, that they have banded together in pursuit of a common purpose is, we think, clear beyond doubt. (We are inclined to accept [counsel for the Crown's] argument that if at the material time there is a body of persons bound together by the acceptance of a common purpose and rules designed to provide an organisation for securing that purpose, it is unnecessary to identify the precise point in time at which the banding together occurred.)'

The conclusion that there is such an unincorporated association must, I think, be an inference from the documentary evidence before the commissioners supplemented by the written statements and oral evidence of Lord Chelmer and Mr Carlyle. It is, in my judgment, an inference which it is impossible to found on that material. One element in the contract which the commissioners have found to exist consists of the rules for the selection of the party leader. That must, I think, be an essential element. The evidence shows that the Central Office works under the direction of the party leader and that the party leader can direct how the moneys under the control of the Central Office are to be spent. It is a constant theme throughout the evidence that neither the national union nor the constituency associations have any control over those moneys. Thus if those moneys are to be treated as in any sense belonging to the members of this wide unincorporated association it can only be because of the link provided by the party leader, and by the power of the party leader to direct how the moneys under the control of the Central Office are to be spent. Whilst the origin of the rules for the selection of the party leader is obscure, it is clear that these rules cannot form any part of any contract between the Paliamentary Party and the mass membership of the local constituency associations. In the process of selecting the party leader neither the national union nor the local constituency associations is consulted: the party leader when selected is 'presented for election' at the party meeting. It is inconceivable that these rules which contain in themselves no provision for amendment can now only be amended with the consent of the members of the local constituency associations. Furthermore, the rule only came into existence in 1965. It is absurd to suppose that a new unincorporated association came into existence altering or formalising the constitution of the Conservative Party in 1965 unsuspected by its supposed members when these rules were devised. Faced with these difficulties, counsel for the Crown submitted that an unincorporated association with the same members existed before 1965 and that the rules of that association then included the usual processes of consultation which formerly led to the selection of the party leader. That submission faces at least two insuperable difficulties. First, the process of consultation has never been, and I think probably could not be, recorded in any body of rules. Second, there is nothing to suggest that the members of the local constituency associations played any part in this process of consultation or that the consultation was confined to members of this suggested unincorporated association.

I have so far focused attention on the rules for the election of the party leader. But there are other powerful objections to the existence of the unincorporated association which the commissioners have found to exist. It is in my mind absurd to suppose that a member of parliament who crosses the floor thereby becomes a member of an unincorporated association, of the existence of which he was unaware and the membership of which carries a proprietary interest in funds under the control of the Central Office though with no obligation himself to subscribe to them. The inclusion of peers who accept the Conservative whip as members of such an association appears to me to be no less absurd. They play no part in the election of the party leader, they need not be members of any local constituency association and they are under no obligation to contribute to the funds under the control of the Central Office. As members of this inferred (and previously unsuspected) unincorporated association they have no role, they incur no liabilities and have no rights. In my judgment this evidence shows, and shows conclusively, that the Conservative Party is a political movement with many parts (some of which are unincorporated associations) which in practice work together to a common end. The links between those parts (which are reflected at every level) are, as counsel for the Central Office expressed it, functional and not constitutional. However, it is, I think, apparent from the case stated that the commissioners felt that they were compelled to reject this obvious explanation or description of the practical effect of the arrangements disclosed in the evidence and to construct out of unpromising material an unreal entity because of an argument addressed to them by counsel for the Crown, to which they referred (in an addition to their draft case included at the request of the Crown) as his 'overriding submission'. This overriding submission as elaborated before me by counsel for the Crown is shortly as follows. It is said that, in the words of Romer LJ in *Re Wells, Swinburne-Hanham v Howard* [1933] Ch 29 at 56, [1932] All ER Rep 277 at 287: 'the rule at common law is that property must belong to somebody and where there is no other owner, not where the owner is unknown, that is the distinction, it is the property of the Crown.' Similarly, it is said that once the legal owner is found he must be either a trustee holding on some effective trust (including trusts for a charitable purpose and bare trusts, whether created by express words or by implication or arising by operation of law) or he must be a beneficial owner. In the present case, it is said, a donor to the funds of the Conservative Party clearly intends to divest himself of every proprietary interest in the money he contributes. Therefore, it is said, as there cannot be a trust for a non-charitable purpose, effect can only be given to the donor's intention if it is possible to construct out of the material before the court some unincorporated association which can be said to be the owner of moneys given for the purposes of the Conservative Party. The purpose which the owner wishes to further is then achieved, the argument continues, not by the creation of a trust for the purpose (which is a legal impossibility) but by inferring the existence of an unincorporated association, the members of which can then be treated as the owners of those moneys and the rules of which will in practice ensure that the moneys will be devoted to the intended purpose. The only alternative, it is said, is that the moneys given to the party treasurers must belong beneficially either to the party treasurers or possibly to the party leader (on the footing that the party leader has, albeit indirectly and within the broad limits to which I have referred, a power to direct how the money should be spent, which is the equivalent of beneficial ownership). Counsel for the Crown went further. He submitted that unless an unincorporated association can be found which can be treated as the owner of the funds the income of the funds must form part of the total income for tax purposes of the party treasurers or alternatively the party leader. He made it clear that that last submission was not an argument in terrorem but submitted that the practical inconvenience that would result unless the funds can be said to be the funds of an unincorporated association are so severe and extreme that the court is compelled to discover from the material before it an unincorporated association the members of which can be said to be the owners of the funds and the rules of which can be relied on to give practical effect to the intentions of the parties. It is, as I have said, clear from the case stated that it was this 'overriding submission' which persuaded the commissioners that they must infer the existence of an unincorporated association from material which, as I see it, cannot possibly found that inference. Indeed, as I understand his argument, counsel for the Crown accepts that without that compelling need to avoid the practical inconvenience and absurdity of treating the party funds as being in the beneficial ownership of the party treasurers or the party leader there would be no sufficient ground for inferring the existence of this unincorporated association, for the existence of which he successfully contended before the commissioners.

In my judgment this approach to the question whether there exists an unincorporated

association the members of which own the funds held by or to the order of the
a Central Office is fundamentally misconceived. A taxpayer is not to be taxed on the ground that certain income must be either his or the income of some other taxpayer and that that other taxpayer has either successfully resisted a claim to tax on the same income or that for some other reason it would be unfair or inconvenient that he should pay tax on it. But the dilemma on which this argument rests is, in any event, in my opinion a false one. It is simply not the case that the legal owner of property must always hold the
b property on some effective trust or be the beneficial owner of it. An executor in the course of administering a will is not a trustee of his testator's property; equally, he is not the beneficial owner. Counsel for the Crown said that the position of an executor is for all practical purposes (or at least for the purposes of his argument) the same as that of a trustee because he can be controlled by the court in his dealings with the testator's property and ultimately can be compelled to account to the legatees. But a situation in
c which the beneficial ownership of property which is not held by trustees on some effective trust is left in suspense can also be produced by contract and may possibly arise in other circumstances. In *Wood Preservation Ltd v Prior* [1969] 1 All ER 364, [1969] 1 WLR 1077 a company called the British Ratin Co Ltd offered to buy the whole of the issued share capital of Wood Preservation Ltd. The offer was accepted by all the shareholders of Wood Preservation Ltd including another company, Silexine Paints Ltd,
d which owned 75% of the shares. But the offer was conditional on a German company continuing in favour of Wood Preservation Ltd certain rights previously enjoyed by Silexine Paints Ltd. It was agreed that while the contract remained conditional Wood Preservation Ltd would not declare or pay any dividend or bonus on its shares. Whilst this contract remained conditional Silexine Paints Ltd assigned its business to Wood Preservation Ltd. The question was whether it was at that time the beneficial owner of
e its shares in Wood Preservation Ltd within s 17 of the Finance Act 1954. It was held that it was not. Lord Donovan said ([1969] 1 All ER 364 at 367, [1969] 1 WLR 1077 at 1096):

> 'A number of authorities have been cited to us. I do not discuss them (though it was useful indeed to be referred to them) because none of the cases covers this point, viz., what is "beneficial ownership" within the meaning of that expression in s 17?
> f It would be rash indeed to attempt an exhaustive definition, and I do not do it. I merely say that the facts in the present case do not, in my opinion, satisfy any reasonable interpretation, involving, as they do, that on 15th March 1960, by the contract of sale of the shares, which was accepted shortly afterwards, Silexine, Ltd. ceased to be able to appropriate to itself any of the benefits of ownership. This does not necessarily involve the consequence that British Ratin, Ltd., became the
> g beneficial owner while the condition remained operative. It is possible for property to lack any beneficial owner for a time, for example, property still being administered by an executor which will go eventually to the residuary legatee.'

Of course, that was a decision on the meaning of 'beneficial owner' in a special statutory context. But the observation at the end of the passage I have cited was not directed to the
h particular issue in that case.

The consolidated appeals in *Franklin v Inland Revenue Comrs, Swaythling's Executors v Inland Revenue Comrs* (1930) 15 Tax Cas 464 provide another instance where contractual arrangements may result in income being held in suspense (at least for fiscal purposes) and not part of the total income of any taxpayer. In that case one Samuel Franklin, a partner in a firm of bankers and bullion merchants, had the right under the partnership
j deed to nominate a successor by will. The nominated partner, if he satisfied certain conditions, might be accepted or rejected by the other partners but their acceptance was not to be unreasonably witheld. Samuel who died in 1918, nominated his son Alan who satisfied the conditions for admission in 1920. He was not accepted. There was litigation about the propriety of his rejection. But apart from the uncertainty created by the litigation (which was not material for this purpose inasmuch as the true beneficial

ownership of Samuel's share of profits after 1920 would be resolved in the course of this
litigation) during the two years from 1918 to 1920 Samuel's share of the profits was a
necessarily in suspense because Alan had not qualified for admission. Under the terms
of the partnership deed, during the period until acceptance or rejection Samuel's share of
the profits was to devolve in this way. If Alan was accepted Samuel's share of the profits
was to go to his brother Ernest until Alan's acceptance and thereafter to Alan. If Alan was
rejected Samuel's share of the profits was to devolve on the other partners in proportion
of their respective shares in the partnership profits. Ernest took 25% under the latter b
division, so what was at stake in this appeal was 75% of Samuel's share. The executors of
Lord Swaythling were also entitled under this latter division to 25% of Samuel's share.
Rowlatt J said (15 Tax Cas 464 at 472):

> 'As regards the remaining 75 per cent. in Mr. Ernest Franklin's case, and as
> regards everything in Lord Swaythling's case, during those years, whether he got it
> depended upon what was put down in the future. Under those circumstances, Mr. c
> Latter argues, and I think argues correctly, that those moneys do not form part of
> the shares to which the Appellant, and Lord Swaythling too, are entitled, during the
> year to which the claim relates, in the partnership profits, such profits being
> estimated according to the several rules as is required by Section 20 of the Income
> Tax Act. I think Mr. Latter is correct in putting forward that argument. It entirely
> depends upon a future event whether these two gentlemen will have the money to d
> which I am referring or whether they will not, and I do not see how I can say that,
> speaking in the years of taxation, they are entitled during the year to these
> moneys. This is not a case where they may become entitled by virtue of a future
> ascertainment or on facts on the year, or a future declaration of rights arising upon
> facts in the year—I think that is an entirely different case, and we have had many
> cases like that. This is where the thing is contingent upon a fact which is going to e
> happen in a future year, and I think it is impossible to say that he is entitled to it in
> the years which passed before that event happens. I cannot see myself that there is
> any distinction between this case and the case of contingent interests under a trust
> fund, which creates the position which was of course remedied by the Act which has
> been recently passed giving infants relief as regards reclaiming of income tax; it
> rests upon the same basis.' f

That latter statutory provision was that which subsequently became s 228 of the Income
Tax Act 1952.

In that case the question was whether the income was part of the total income of
Ernest Franklin or of Lord Swaythling. But the conclusion that it was not must I think
also entail the consequence that during the period of suspense nobody was beneficially g
entitled to Samuel's share of the profits.

Further, counsel's submissions for the Crown lead to extravagantly absurd results. An
example will illustrate this. Suppose that an explorer were to invite subscriptions to a
fund to finance an expedition to explore some unexplored area of the world. That would
clearly not be a charitable purpose and there is no unincorporated association which can
be conjured up as the owner of the subscribed fund. Counsel's submission for the h
Crown, if well founded, would lead to the conclusion that either the subscribers would
remain the beneficial owners of the moneys subscribed, the explorer having no more
than a revocable mandate to use them for the stated purpose, or alternatively the
subscribed fund would belong beneficially to the explorer who would be free to abandon
the exploration and spend the moneys on himself. Counsel for the Crown frankly
accepted that this consequence follows from his argument and said that the latter j
alternative is the correct one. The law would be in a very sorry state if it were so, but I
do not think it is. It appears to me that if someone invites subscriptions on the
representation that he will use the fund subscribed for a particular purpose, he undertakes
to use the fund for that purpose and for no other and to keep the subscribed fund and any
accretions to it (including any income earned by investing the fund pending its

application in pursuance of the stated purpose) separate from his own moneys. I can see no reason why if the purpose is sufficiently well defined, and if the order would not necessitate constant and possibly ineffective supervision by the court, the court should not make an order directing him to apply the subscribed fund and any accretions to it for the stated purpose. The example I have given would probably not meet these criteria, but it is not difficult to imagine a case where a fund was subscribed for a purpose which would meet these criteria, for instance, a fund raised by subscription for immediate distribution to a class of persons who were not objects of charity, the subscriptions being invited on terms which did not give rise to any private trust. There appears to me to be a clear analogy between an invitation to subscribe to a fund on a representation that it will be used for a particular purpose and a third party contract of the kind considered in *Beswick v Beswick* [1967] 2 All ER 1197, [1968] AC 58. However, apart from the possible remedy of specific performance I can see no reason why the court should not restrain the recipient of such a fund from applying it (or any accretions to it such as income of investments made with it) otherwise that in pursuance of the stated purpose. If that is so, then it appears to me that the recipient of the fund is clearly not the beneficial owner of it and that the income of it is not part of his total income for tax purposes. Equally, whilst the purpose remains unperformed and capable of performance the subscribers are clearly not the beneficial owners of the fund or of the income (if any) derived from it. If the stated purpose proves impossible to achieve or if there is any surplus remaining after it has been accomplished there will be an implied obligation to return the fund and any accretions thereto to the subscribers in proportion to their original contributions, save that a proportion of the fund representing subscriptions made anonymously or in circumstances in which the subscribers receive some benefit (for instance, by subscription to a whist drive or raffle) might then devolve as bona vacantia.

The answer of counsel for the Crown to the solution I have endeavoured to formulate was that it confused property and contract. He said that the subscriptions are moneys given, not consideration for any contractual undertaking. I do not see why the fact that subscriptions are made for a stated purpose should not found an obligation binding on the recipient to use the moneys subscribed for that purpose, to keep them separate from his own moneys and to return them if this purpose is frustrated or if the funds subscribed are more than is needed to accomplish it. The reply of counsel for the Crown reflects the argument of counsel for the appellant in *Barclays Bank Ltd v Quistclose Investments Ltd* [1968] 3 All ER 651, [1970] AC 567 and invites the answer given by Lord Wilberforce who said ([1968] 3 All ER 651 at 655, [1970] AC 567 at 582): 'I can appreciate no reason why the flexible interplay of law and equity cannot let in these practical arrangements, and other variations if desired: it would be to the discredit of both systems if they could not.'

Counsel for the Crown also relied on a passage in the judgment of Brightman J in *Re Recher's Will Trusts* [1971] 3 All ER 401 at 405, [1972] Ch 526 at 536 where he said: 'It would astonish a layman to be told that there was a difficulty in his giving a legacy to an unincorporated non-charitable society which he had or could have supported without trouble during his lifetime.' In the present case, said counsel for the Crown, a testamentary bequest to the Conservative Party would be void unless it could be construed as a gift to the members of an unincorporated association who could (by resolution if the rules so provide or acting unanimously if they do not) revoke or amend the rules and either distribute the moneys amongst themselves or apply them in any other way they might wish. Similarly, it is said, unless moneys given to the Conservative Party inter vivos can be taken as given to an unincorporated association the gift will either fail or alternatively take effect as a gift to the party treasurers or the party leader. This argument to my mind places too much stress on a single sentence in the judgment of Brightman J. A testamentary gift to a named society which is not an incorporated body must fail unless it can be construed as a gift to the members of an unincorporated association either as joint tenants or as an accretion to the funds of the association to be applied in accordance with its rules (commonly with a view to the furtherance of its objects). But in the case of a testamentary gift there is no room for the implication of any contract between the testator and the persons who are to receive the bequest. In the case of an inter vivos subscription the intention of the subscriber can be given effect by the implication of contractual undertakings of the kind I have described. On further consideration that seems to me to be the proper explanation of the status of the subscriptions made by members of the Chertsey and Walton Constituency Labour Party on which I made some observations in *Re Grant's Will Trusts* [1979] 3 All ER 359, [1980] 1 WLR 360. The right of subscribers to the return of their subscriptions so far as not used for the purposes for which they were subscribed rests on an implied contractual term and not on a resulting trust. The facts in *Re Thackrah* [1939] 2 All ER 4 may provide another analogy. There, a testamentary gift to the secretary of the Oxford Group was held invalid on the ground that the evidence did not establish the existence of 'an association of individuals banded together under the name of the Oxford Group'. Bennett J observed ([1939] 2 All ER 4 at 6): 'Before one can find an association, there must be some rules, either written or oral, by which those who are supposed to be members of it are tied together. I think that they would probably be written rules. There must be some constitution.' But the Oxford Group was the name given to the religious movement and I can see no reason why a donation inter vivos to the secretary of a movement so named to be used for the purposes of the group should not have been contractually enforceable (at least to the extent of preventing the secretary from misapplying it or mixing it with his own moneys) and the facts stated in the report of *Re Thackrah* [1939] 2 All ER 4 suggest that some donations had been so given in order to provide for the maintenance of the offices and staff which the Oxford Group apparently had.

In my judgment, therefore, this appeal succeeds.

Appeal allowed.

Solicitors: *Trower, Still & Keeling* (for the Central Office); *Solicitor of Inland Revenue.*

Edwina Epstein Barrister.

Supplementary Benefits Commission v Jull
Y v Supplementary Benefits Commission

HOUSE OF LORDS

LORD WILBERFORCE, VISCOUNT DILHORNE, LORD SALMON, LORD FRASER OF TULLYBELTON AND LORD RUSSELL OF KILLOWEN

16th, 17th, 18th JUNE, 30th JULY 1980

Supplementary benefit – Entitlement – Aggregation of requirements and resources – Persons having to provide for requirements of another person – Meaning of 'requirements' – Other person child under age of 16 – Mother providing for child – Mother receiving money for support of child from father under court order – Amount payable exceeding normal requirements of child – Whether mother having to provide for 'requirements' – Whether child's resources to be aggregated with mother's for purpose of determining her entitlement to supplementary benefit – Supplementary Benefits Act 1976, s 1, Sch 1, para 3(2).

In the first case the mother obtained an order in the county court against her husband, from whom she was separated, to pay maintenance of £21 a week direct to her and £12 a week to their six year old son who was in her care. The husband paid no maintenance to her under the order but regularly paid their son the £12 per week. The money was taken care of by the mother and held for the son's benefit. Since the husband failed to pay any maintenance to her the mother applied for supplementary benefit to the Supplementary Benefits Commission. In calculating her entitlement to benefit the commission aggregated the weekly requirements and resources of the mother with those of her son, with the result that she received less benefit than that to which she would have otherwise been entitled. The mother appealed to a supplementary benefits appeal tribunal, contending that because the amount payable by the husband exceeded the normal requirements of the child as calculated in accordance with the Supplementary Benefits Act 1976 she did not provide her son's requirements and accordingly it was not necessary for her requirements and resources to be aggregated with those of her son's under para 3(2)[a] of Sch 1 to the 1976 Act in assessing the amount of supplementary benefit. The tribunal allowed her appeal and directed that the child's normal requirements and the child's normal resources of £12 be removed from the assessment on the ground that the obligations of the mother and father under s 17[b] of the Act had been met by the periodical payments to the child and accordingly that the mother had no need to provide for his requirements. The High Court affirmed the tribunal's decision holding that requirements meant monetary requirements. The commission appealed directly to the House of Lords.

In the second case the mother obtained an affiliation order under the Affiliation Proceedings Act 1957 for the payment of £8 a week for the maintenance of her illegitimate child which exceeded the normal requirements of the child as calculated in accordance with the 1976 Act. When she applied for supplementary benefit the commission aggregated her resources and requirements with those of her child. The appeal tribunal affirmed the commission's decision. The mother appealed to the High Court and the judge, following the decision in the first case, allowed her appeal. The commission appealed directly to the House of Lords.

Held – The word 'requirements' in both s 1[c] of and para 3(2) of Sch 1 to the 1976 Act meant the needs of the person, ie a home, food, clothes and the like. In each case the

---

a Paragraph 3(2) is set out at p 67 *h*, post.
b Section 17, so far as material, is set out at p 70 *j*, post.
c Section 1, so far as material, is set out at p 70 *g h*, post.

mother had to and did provide for her child's requirements within para 3(2). Even if she
received money for the support of her child as a result of a court order that did not mean *a*
that she did not, and was not required to, provide for her child's requirements, and the source of the money was irrelevant. It followed therefore that in each case para 3(2) required that the resources of the child were to be aggregated with those of the mother in order to determine the mother's entitlement to supplementary benefit. The appeals would accordingly be allowed (see p 67 *a*, p 68 *j* to p 69 *a f*, p 71 *d h j* and p 72 *a*, post).

Dictum of Cairns LJ in *K v JMP Co Ltd* [1975] 1 All ER at 1036 disapproved. *b*

Per Lord Wilberforce, Viscount Dilhorne, Lord Fraser and Lord Russell. Paragraph 3(2) of Sch 1 to the 1976 Act does not require any calculation of the cost of meeting the requirements of a dependant whose resources are to be aggregated with those of an applicant for supplementary benefit (see p 67 *a*, p 69 *e f*, p 71 *j* and p 72 *a b*, post).

Notes *c*

For aggregation of requirements and resources for the purpose of calculating entitlement to supplementary benefit, see Supplement to 27 Halsbury's Laws (3rd Edn) para 947A.2.

For the Supplementary Benefits Act 1976, ss 1, 17, Sch 1, para 3, see 46 Halsbury's Statutes (3rd Edn) 1048, 1060, 1076.

d

Case referred to in opinions

K v JMP Co Ltd [1975] 1 All ER 1030, [1976] QB 85, [1975] 2 WLR 457, CA, Digest (Cont Vol D) 711, *94Ab*.

Appeals

Supplementary Benefits Commission v Jull *e*

The Supplementary Benefits Commission appealed against a decision of Woolf J dated 20th March 1980 dismissing their appeal against a decision of the Reading Supplementary Benefits Appeal Tribunal dated 17th September 1979 whereby it allowed an appeal by the respondent, Mrs Susan Jull, against a decision of the commission and ordered that her requirements and resources were not to be aggregated with those of her child in
calculating her entitlement to supplementary benefit under the Supplementary Benefits *f*
Act 1976. An Appeal Committee of the House of Lords granted the appellants leave to appeal directly to the House, Woolf J having granted them a certificate pursuant to s 12(3)(*a*) of the Administration of Justice Act 1969 that a point of law of general public importance was involved in the decision. The facts are set out in the opinion of Viscount Dilhorne.

g

Y v Supplementary Benefits Commission

The Supplementary Benefits Commission appealed against a decision of Comyn J dated 17th April 1980 whereby he allowed an appeal by the respondent, Mrs Y, against a decision of the Yeovil Supplementary Benefits Appeal Tribunal dated 14th September 1979 dismissing her appeal against a decision of the commission and ordered that the
requirements and resources of Mrs Y should not be aggregated with those of her child in *h*
determining her entitlement to supplementary benefit under the 1976 Act. An Appeal Committee of the House of Lords granted the appellants leave to appeal directly to the House, Comyn J having granted them a certificate pursuant to s 12(3)(*a*) of the 1969 Act that a point of law of general public importance was involved in the decision. The facts are set out in the opinion of Viscount Dilhorne.

j

Simon Brown and *Andrew Collins* for the appellants.
Ian A Kennedy QC and *Linda Davies* for Mrs Jull.
J Hampden Inskip QC and *Nigel Inglis-Jones* for Mrs Y.

Their Lordships took time for consideration.

30th July. The following opinions were delivered.

a **LORD WILBERFORCE.** My Lords, I agree that these appeals should be allowed for the reasons given by my noble and learned friends Viscount Dilhorne and Lord Salmon, whose speeches I have had the benefit of reading in advance.

VISCOUNT DILHORNE. My Lords, the Supplementary Benefits Act 1976, a
b consolidation Act, by s 1(1) provides that, subject to the provisions of the Act, every
person in Great Britain of or over 16 'whose resources are insufficient to meet his
requirements shall be entitled to benefit . . .' Section 1(2) provides that where, under the
provisions of the Act, the requirements and resources of any person fall to be aggregated
with, and treated as, those of another person, that other person only shall be entitled to
supplementary benefit, and s 1(3), that the requirements of any person to be taken into
c account do not include any medical, surgical, optical, aural or dental requirements.

Although the 1976 Act contains an interpretation section, s 34, that does not contain any definition of the meaning to be given to the words 'requirements' and 'resources', and so, in the absence of any contrary indication, those words must be given their ordinary natural meaning.

'Resources' must mean financial resources, but it does not follow that requirements
d means financial requirements. A child requires to be looked after and cared for, to be
provided with food, clothing and a home. Money will be needed to meet those
requirements; and, while 'requirements' could be interpreted to mean financial
requirements, the presence of s 1(3) is an indication that requirements means the needs
of a child and not the money required to meet those needs. It would indeed be odd if in
sub-s (1) that word had a different meaning to that it has in this subsection.

e Section 2(2) provides that entitlement to, and the amount of, any supplementary benefit is to be determined in accordance with the provisions of Part I of and Sch 1 to the Act and any regulations made by the Secretary of State.

Paragraph 1(1) of that schedule states that the amount of any supplementary benefit to which a person is entitled shall be the amount by which his resources fall short of his requirements; and para 1(2) reads as follows:

> f 'For the purpose of ascertaining that amount—(*a*) the weekly requirements of any person shall be taken to be the aggregate of such of the amounts specified in Part II of this Schedule as are applicable to his case; and (*b*) the resources of any person shall be calculated in accordance with Part III of this Schedule.'

Paragraph 3 of the schedule reads as follows:

> g '(1) Where—(*a*) a husband and wife are members of the same household, their requirements and resources shall be aggregated and treated as the husband's; (*b*) two persons are cohabiting as man and wife, their requirements and resources shall, unless there are exceptional circumstances, be aggregated and treated as the man's.
>
> '(2) Where a person has to provide for the requirements of another person who is
> a member of the same household, not being a person falling within sub-paragraph
> h (1) above—(*a*) the requirements of that other person may, and if he has not attained
> the age of 16 shall, be aggregated with, and treated as, those of the first mentioned
> person; and (*b*) where their requirements are so aggregated, their resources shall be
> similarly aggregated.'

On 30th May 1979 the respondent Mrs Jull obtained an order in Andover County
j Court for the payment to her of maintenance pending suit of £21 a week. At the same
time an order was made for the payment to the child of the marriage of £12 a week, the
order providing that the receipt of the custodial parent, who was Mrs Jull, was to be a
sufficient discharge for the payment ordered to be made to the child. As the child was
then six years old, the payments ordered to be made to him were no doubt received by
Mrs Jull.

As her husband did not comply with the maintenance order, though he regularly paid the £12 a week for his child, Mrs Jull applied for supplementary benefit. The appellents *a* were of the opinion that para 3(2) of the schedule required her resources and requirements to be aggregated with those of her child with the consequence that the amount of benefit to which she was entitled was less by £6·70 a week than that to which she would have been entitled if there had been no aggregation.

She appealed to the Reading Supplementary Benefits Appeal Tribunal who allowed her appeal on the ground that as her husband was paying £12 a week to his child she did *b* not have to provide for his requirements and so aggregation was not required.

The appellants appealed to the High Court and Woolf J dismissed their appeal. They now appeal direct to this House.

The facts in the other appeal are very similar. On 28th June 1979 Mrs Y obtained an order under the Affiliation Proceedings Act 1957 for the payment of £8 a week for the maintenance of her child born on 20th March 1979. She applied for supplementary *c* benefit. The appellants were of the opinion that her resources and requirements must be aggregated with those of her child with the consequence that the amount she received in benefit was less by £3·60 a week than that she would have received if there had not been aggregation. She appealed to the Yeovil Supplementary Benefits Appeal Tribunal who dismissed her appeal. She then appealed to the High Court and Comyn J, following the judgment of Woolf J, allowed her appeal on the ground that in view of the payment of *d* £8 a week she did not have to provide for the requirements of her child. From that decision the appellants appeal direct to this House.

In each appeal the same question has to be decided. Had the mother to provide for the requirements of her child living with her in the same household? If so, in each case there had to be aggregation. To this question, which is one of fact, a layman would, I think, without any hesitation give an affirmative answer. Each mother looked after her child *e* and provided food and clothing for it and attended to its needs. How then can it be said that she did not provide for her child's requirements?

Part II of the schedule is headed 'Calculation of Requirements' and this Part states how the requirements are to be assessed in money terms. The calculation has to be made so that the amount of benefit payable can be determined. Paragraph 7 in this Part is headed 'Normal requirements' and states the amount of money which has for the purpose of the *f* calculation to be taken as the normal requirement of persons other than blind persons. In addition to the sums so stated there may be added an amount for rent and on other grounds. In this paragraph the normal requirements of a child of less than 11 but not less than 5 years were £4·35 and of a child less than 5 years £3·60. These amounts have now been increased to £5·30 and £4·40. So the amount paid by Mr Jull each week exceeded the normal requirements of his child as calculated in accordance with Part II *g* and the amount paid under the affiliation order exceeded the requirements so calculated of Mrs Y's child. In these circumstances it was contended on behalf of the two mothers that they did not provide for the requirements of their children.

These contentions were upheld by Woolf and Comyn JJ.

My Lords, I regret that I cannot agree with their conclusions. It does not, in my opinion, follow, from the fact that for the determination of the amount of benefit the *h* normal requirements of a child are to be assessed at a particular amount of money, that the word 'requirements' where it appears in the Act is to be interpreted as meaning that sum of money and it would be wrong in my view to construe the opening words of para 3(2) as if they were 'Where a person has to provide the calculated requirements of another person . . .'

A child requires food, clothing and a home. He may also require medical, surgical, *j* optical, aural or dental treatment. If he does, those requirements are not to be taken into account. In s 1(3) 'requirements' has its ordinary natural meaning and in my opinion it has the same meaning in para 3(2). I am unable to escape from the conclusion that in each of these cases the mother had to and did provide for the requirements of her young child. If money comes into a mother's hands for the support of her child either as a result of an order such as that made by the Andover County Court or under an affiliation order or in any other way, that does not mean that she does not and does not have to provide for the requirements of her child. If hers are the hands which dispense the money necessary to provide for the child's requirements, it matters not what is the source of the money.

I recognise that aggregation may mean that the amount of benefit a mother may obtain may be less than that which she would obtain if there was no aggregation and that where a child's resources are large and hers are small, she may benefit from the use of the child's resources, but that may happen whenever there is aggregation. A husband who claims benefit may find the benefit reduced in consequence of his wife's resources. A man cohabiting with a woman may find the same and for the purpose of supplementary benefit his and her resources are lumped together even though the man may have no right to the use of the woman's money.

Paragraph 3(1) shows that a husband and wife living together in the same household are to be treated as one unit and that a man and woman cohabiting are also to be treated as one unit. Paragraph 3(2) similarly requires a person and a dependant living in the same household to be treated as one unit. Indeed the opening words of that paragraph provide the test for dependancy.

In *K v JMP Co Ltd* [1975] 1 All ER 1030, [1976] QB 85, a Fatal Accidents Acts case, it was submitted that once damages were awarded to the children to supply their immediate needs in the way of food, lodging, clothing etc the damages would be aggregated with the mother's resources with the result that she would lose her entitlement to supplementary benefit. This was rejected by Cairns and Stephenson LJJ, Cairns LJ saying that 'requirements' must mean 'requirements in respect of payments for the necessaries of life and these are all provided for by the uncontested part of the damages awarded to the children.' (see [1975] 1 All ER 1030 at 1036, [1976] QB 85 at 94).

It will be apparent from what I have said that I do not think that this statement is correct. The provision of the requirements of another will establish that person's dependancy and for the purposes of para 3(2) it is not in my opinion necessary and the 1976 Act does not require any calculation of the cost of meeting those requirements or the assumption that the amount calculated in accordance with Part II is what is meant by requirements in that paragraph.

I would allow these appeals.

LORD SALMON. My Lords, these appeals raise an important point concerning the true construction of para 3(2) of Sch 1 to the Supplementary Benefits Act 1976.

There is no difference of any significance between the facts of these two appeals. I will therefore briefly set out the facts of the first of them. The respondent, Mrs Jull, obtained an order in the Andover County Court on 3rd May 1979 against her husband (from whom she was then living apart and is now divorced) to pay maintenance of £21 a week direct to her and £12 a week to their son who was then six years old. Mr Jull paid no maintenance to Mrs Jull but regularly paid their son £12 a week. The fact that this money went to this young child and belonged to him did not mean that he himself handled it or could have done so. It was taken care of by his mother and used by her for her son's benefit. Since Mr Jull had failed to pay any maintenance to his wife, she applied for supplementary benefit to the Supplementary Benefits Commission, the appellants. The commission aggregated the weekly requirements and resources of Mrs Jull and her son as follows:

Mrs Jull's requirements	£15·55
Her son's requirements	£5·30
Rent requirement	£11·71
	£32·56

and their weekly resources as follows:

Child benefit	£4·00
Maintenance (child's)	£12·00
	£16·00

a

The difference between the weekly requirements and the weekly resources amounted to b £16·56. The commission added onto the £16·56 £1·70 for central heating and paid Mrs Jull a weekly supplementary benefit of £18·26. It follows that had there been no aggregation of requirements and resources Mrs Jull would have received £6·70 more supplementary benefit a week than she in fact received.

Mrs Jull appealed to the appropriate supplementary benefits appeal tribunal on the ground that, owing to her husband's weekly payment of £12 a week to their son, she did c not have to provide for her son's requirements, and that accordingly it was not necessary, under the 1976 Act, for the requirements and the resources of Mrs Jull and her son to be aggregated. The appeal tribunal allowed Mrs Jull's appeal. The commission then appealed to the High Court against the appeal tribunal decision on the ground that it was erroneous in law. This appeal was heard and dismissed by Woolf J who concluded that the decision of the appeal tribunal was correct and that in any event he was bound to d dismiss the appeal by the decision of the Court of Appeal in *K v JMP Co Ltd* [1975] 1 All ER 1030, [1976] QB 85. The learned judge then granted a certificate under s 12 of the Administration of Justice Act 1969 to enable an appeal from this judgment to be brought direct to your Lordships' House.

The facts in the second appeal, as I have already indicated, have no significant difference from the facts of the first appeal with which I have already dealt. The mother in the e second appeal was not married to the father of her child who was one year old when she obtained an order under the Affiliation Proceedings Act 1957 for the weekly payment of £8 for the maintenance of his child. When she applied for supplementary benefit, the commission aggregated the requirements and resources of mother and daughter in assessing the mother's weekly supplementary benefit; and this resulted in the mother receiving £3·60 less than she would otherwise have received in weekly benefit. There f was then an appeal to the supplementary benefits appeal tribunal and from them to the High Court. Comyn J followed the judgment of Woolf J and decided in favour of the mother and granted a certificate enabling an appeal from his judgment to be brought direct to your Lordships' House.

Before considering the points of law raised by these appeals, it is I think necessary to set out the relevant provisions in the Supplementary Benefits Act 1976: g

> '**1.**—(1) Subject to the provisions of this Act, every person in Great Britain of or over the age of 16 whose resources are insufficient to meet his requirements shall be entitled to benefit . . .
>
> '(2) Where, under the provisions of this Act, the requirements and resources of any person fall to be aggregated with, and treated as, those of another person, that h other person only shall be entitled to supplementary benefit . . .
>
> '(3) The requirements of any person to be taken into account for the purposes of this Act do not include any medical, surgical, optical, aural or dental requirements . . .'
>
> '**2** . . . (2) Entitlement to, and the amount of, any supplementary benefit shall be determined in accordance with:—(*a*) the provisions of this Part of this Act and j Schedule 1 to this Act . . .'
>
> '**17.**—(1) For the purposes of this Act—(*a*) a man shall be liable to maintain his wife and his children; and (*b*) a woman shall be liable to maintain her husband and her children . . .'

And Sch 1 provides:

a

> '1.—(1) Subject to the following provisions of this Part of this Schedule, the amount of any supplementary benefit to which a person is entitled shall be the amount by which his resources fall short of his requirements.
>
> '(2) For the purpose of ascertaining that amount—(*a*) the weekly requirements of any person shall be taken to be the aggregate of such of the amounts specified in Part II of this Schedule as are applicable to his case; and (*b*) the resources of any person
> b shall be calculated in accordance with Part III of this Schedule . . .
>
> '3.—(1) Where—(*a*) a husband and wife are members of the same household, their requirements and resources shall be aggregated and treated as the husband's; (*b*) two persons are cohabiting as man and wife, their requirements and resources shall, unless there are exceptional circumstances, be aggregated and treated as the man's.
>
> c
>
> '(2) Where a person has to provide for the requirements of another person who is a member of that same household . . . (*a*) the requirements of that other person may, and if he has not attained the age of 16 shall, be aggregated with, and treated as, those of the first mentioned person; and (*b*) where their requirements are so aggregated, their resources shall be similarly aggregated.'

d Although the interpretation section, s 35, of the Act does not interpret or define the meaning of the words 'requirements' or 'resources', para 3 of Sch 1 does however, in my view, make the meaning of these words reasonably plain. 'Requirements' for persons claiming supplementary benefits means, for example, a home, food, clothes and the like. Paragraph 7 of Sch 1 sets out merely what is considered to be the proper price of such requirements.

e 'Resources' means the money available to pay for the requirements. If the persons concerned have not sufficient resources to provide the necessary requirements, the supplementary benefits will bridge that financial gap.

It seems to me that para 3(1) of Sch 1 is intended to prevent a man and a woman who are cohabiting together, whether married or not, from each obtaining a separate supplementary benefit. Accordingly, for the purpose of assessing a proper supplementary
f benefit for both, the requirements and the resources of the man and woman are aggregated and treated as the man's. One supplementary benefit for both would almost always save the taxpayers' money more than if there were one supplementary benefit for each.

Similarly, a mother has to provide for the requirements for herself and for her child whilst he is under 16 years old and living with her in the same household. These
g requirements and resources of the mother and son are aggregated and treated as those of the mother. The weekly sum for maintenance of the son sent to him by his father are the resources of the son which are aggregated with those of the mother before her weekly supplementary benefit is decided. This seems to me to be absolutely fair and is certainly in accordance with the 1976 Act.

Comyn and Woolf JJ placed considerable reliance on *K v JMP Co Ltd* [1975] 1 All ER
h 1030, [1976] QB 85. This was a Fatal Accidents Acts case, the facts of which were very complicated, and I do not propose to weary your Lordships with them. I agree with my noble and learned friend Viscount Dilhorne when he expresses the view that the statement made by Cairns LJ ([1975] 1 All ER 1030 at 1036, [1976] QB 85 at 94) was incorrect. Neither this statement therefore, nor anything else I can find in the case, can be of any help to the respondents. My Lords, I would allow the appeals.

j

LORD FRASER OF TULLYBELTON. My Lords, I have had the advantage of reading in draft the speeches of my noble and learned friends Viscount Dilhorne and Lord Salmon. I agree with them and for the reasons given by them I would allow these appeals.

LORD RUSSELL OF KILLOWEN. My Lords, I am in agreement with my noble and learned friends Viscount Dilhorne and Lord Salmon that, for the reasons they give, a these appeals succeed.

I would only add one comment. The children as such cannot qualify for supplementary benefit. Accordingly the scale of figures for their 'requirements' does not come into the picture unless and until the decision is made under the statute that the case is one for aggregation. Those figures are not, therefore, to be taken as the basis on which that decision is to be made. b

Appeals allowed.

Solicitors: *Solicitor to the Department of Health and Social Security; C S Ranson & Co,* Andover (for Mrs Jull); *Park Nelson & Doyle Devonshire,* agents for *Clarke, Willmott & Clarke,* Yeovil (for Mrs Y). c

Mary Rose Plummer Barrister.

Castanho v Brown & Root (UK) Ltd and another d

COURT OF APPEAL, CIVIL DIVISION
LORD DENNING MR, SHAW AND BRANDON LJJ
12th, 13th, 14th, 15th, 18th, 19th FEBRUARY, 22nd APRIL 1980 e

Practice – Discontinuance of action – Discontinuance by plaintiff – Action brought in England claiming damages for personal injuries – Defendant ordered to make interim payments on admitting liability – Plaintiff commencing action in America in hope of getting higher damages – Plaintiff purporting to discontinue English action – Defendant applying for order to strike out notice of discontinuance and for injunction to restrain plaintiff continuing proceedings in America f *and commencing other proceedings there or elsewhere – Whether notice of discontinuance should be struck out – Whether injunction should be granted.*

The plaintiff, a Portuguese national residing in Portugal, was employed by the second defendants, a Panamanian company, as an oiler on one of their ships. In February 1977 he sustained severe personal injuries in an accident which occurred on board the ship g when she was at an English port. As a result he brought an action in England against the first defendants, a United Kingdom company which provided shore services for the ship, and the second defendants claiming damages in respect of his injuries. Unknown to the plaintiff's English solicitors, both the first and second defendants were part of a large Texan group of companies. On 22nd March 1978 a consent order was made requiring the second defendants to make an interim payment of £7,250 to the plaintiff, which h they did. In June the second defendants admitted liability by letter. At about that time the plaintiff was approached by a firm of American lawyers, who pressed him to hand over the case to them and to give them authority to enforce his claim in America on a contingency fee basis. He was reluctant to do so. In December there was an order, not by consent, that the second defendants should make a further interim payment of £20,000, which they did. At about that time the plaintiff's English solicitors were j approached by the American lawyers, and, following discussions between the American lawyers, the English solicitors and the plaintiff, the latter were persuaded that the plaintiff was likely to obtain much higher damages in America. On 7th February 1979, while the English action was still pending, process was issued in the plaintiff's name and allegedly on the plaintiff's authority in one of the state courts in Texas claiming, against

the first and second defendants and other companies in the group, damages in respect of
a the plaintiff's accident. The following day the plaintiff signed a power of attorney in
favour of the American lawyers giving them exclusive power to represent him in the
prosecution of his claim in America and providing, inter alia, for them to be paid out of
the amounts received or recovered by the plaintiff, for the action in England not to be
concluded prior to the decision in the American action and that in the event of the
English action being reactivated by the defendants the course to be followed would be
b decided by agreement between the American lawyers and the English solicitors or in
default of agreement by the English solicitors. On 6th April the defendants entered a
special appearance in the American action objecting to the jurisdiction of the Texas
court. On 30th April they delivered their defence in the English action in which they
formally admitted liability. The following day they issued a summons for directions and
applied for an injunction restraining the plaintiff from continuing the American action
c and from commencing further proceedings in America or elsewhere in respect of his
accident. Within 14 days of the service of the defence, the English solicitors, with the
plaintiff's authority, gave notice of discontinuance, pursuant to RSC Ord 21, r 2[a]. Their
purpose in so doing was to improve the plaintiff's position in resisting the defendants'
efforts to stay the American proceedings. On 6th June, on the hearing of the defendants'
summons for directions, it was directed that it should be treated as an application to
d strike out the plaintiff's notice of discontinuance, and was adjourned to a date to be
fixed. On 26th June the defendants filed a notice in Texas calling on the plaintiff's
attorney to show his authority for bringing an action there. On 18th July, while the
action in the Texas state court was still pending, the American lawyers launched an
action in the plaintiff's name in a federal court in Texas claiming, in respect of the same
accident, $US5m compensatory damages and $US10m punitive damages. The following
e day the action in the Texas state court was terminated by the filing of a nonsuit. Service
of the second American action was effected on 22nd August, and on 11th September the
defendants filed motion to dismiss and to show authority for bringing the action in the
federal court. On 2nd October the defendants' applications in the English action for an
order striking out the notice of discontinuance and for an injunction to restrain the
plaintiff from continuing the action in the federal court and from commencing further
f proceedings in America or elsewhere were referred to a judge in chambers. At the
hearing before him it was stated, allegedly by the plaintiff's authority, (i) that the
plaintiff was prepared to submit to orders (a) setting aside the notice of discontinuance if
the £27,250 paid to him was not repaid and (b) restraining the action in the federal court
until the money was repaid, (ii) that the American lawyers proposed to make the
repayment, and (iii) that if the federal court declined jurisdiction the plaintiff would
g consider himself free, and would seek, to commence a fresh action against the defendants
in England. On 19th November the judge ([1980] 1 All ER 689) struck out the notice
of discontinuance, with the result that the English action remained in being, on the
ground that the plaintiff's advisers would be guilty of an abuse of the process of the court
if the plaintiff could discontinue the English action without leave in order to improve his
position in the American proceedings while remaining free to commence a fresh action
h in England if those proceedings failed. He also granted the injunction sought by the
defendants. The plaintiff appealed. On 8th February 1980 the plaintiff issued a second
writ in England against the defendants in case the American courts declined jurisdiction.

Held – (1) (Lord Denning MR dissenting) The appeal would be allowed and the
defendants' application to strike out the notice of discontinuance would be refused
j because—

(a) (per Shaw LJ) having regard to the fact that the only sanction in RSC Ord 21 against
an erstwhile plaintiff commencing another action based on substantially the same cause
was the provision in r 5 that if he did commence another action before he had paid the

a Rule 2, so far as material, is set out at p 86 j, post

defendant's costs in the discontinued action the court might order the proceedings in the second action to be stayed until those costs were paid, it was clear that Ord 21 was a *a* compact code designed to restore the parties to their position before the first action was brought, and, since the right under Ord 21, r 2(1) was explicit and unqualified, and the plaintiff did not require leave to discontinue, it was not an abuse of process to issue such a notice pursuant to the order (see p 87 *b* to *d*, p 88 *c* to *e* and *g* to *j* and p 90 *a b*, post);

(b) (per Brandon LJ) since it had always been open to the plaintiff, if he had been so advised early enough, to sue the defendants in Texas and never to have brought an action *b* against them in England, it was entirely legitimate for him to seek to sue his employers in Texas if, even after allowing for contingency fees, he stood to recover at least five times more by way of damages in Texas, notwithstanding that the determination of the claim in Texas was bound to involve much greater expense and inconvenience; and, provided the interim payments were repaid and the protective action begun by the plaintiff on 8th February 1980 was stayed, justice required that the plaintiff should be left free to *c* continue his proceedings in Texas (see p 92 *e* to *h*, p 93 *f g* and p 94 *a* to *e* and *j* to p 95 *c*, *post*).

(2) The injunction restraining the plaintiff from commencing or continuing proceedings in the United States should be discharged because the jurisdiction or power to compel a plaintiff to sue in England by restraining him from proceeding in another forum elsewhere should be exercised with great caution, since where an injunction was *d* granted to so restrain a person the English court was interferring, albeit indirectly, with proceedings in another jurisdiction (see p 82 *a b*, p 89 *e*, p 90 *a b*, p 91 *j* to p 92 *b* and p 95 *b c*, post).

Decision of Parker J [1980] 1 All ER 689 reversed.

Notes *e*

For the discontinuance of an action, see 30 Halsbury's Laws (3rd Edn) 409, para 770, and for cases on the subject, see 51 Digest (Repl) 570–574, *2036–2080*.

RSC Ord 21, r 2(2A), which was inserted by RSC (Amendment No 2) 1980, SI 1980 No 1010, and which came into force on 1st October 1980, provides that a party in whose favour an interim payment has been ordered, in accordance with RSC Ord 29, r 11 (as substituted by the same amending rules), may not discontinue any action or counterclaim, *f* or withdraw any particular claim therein, except with the leave of the High Court or the consent of all the other parties.

Cases referred to in judgments

Atlantic Star, The, The Atlantic Star (Owners) v The Bona Spes (Owners) [1973] 2 All ER 175, [1974] AC 436, [1973] 2 WLR 795, [1973] 2 Lloyd's Rep 197, HL, 11 Digest (Reissue) *g* 645, *1777*.

Busfield, Re, Whaley v Busfield (1886) 32 Ch D 123, 55 LJ Ch 467, 54 LT 220, CA, 10 Digest (Reissue) 957, *5644*.

Carron Iron Co v Maclaren (1885) 5 HL Cas 416, HL, 28(2) Digest (Reissue) 1152, *1534*.

Christiansborg, The (1885) 10 PD 141, 54 LJP 84, 53 LT 612, 5 Asp MLC 491, CA, 11 Digest (Reissue) 645, *1774*. *h*

Cohen v Rothfield [1919] 1 KB 410, [1918–19] All ER Rep 260, 88 LJKB 468, 120 LT 434, CA, 11 Digest (Reissue) 630, *1728*.

Fox v Star Newspaper Co [1898] 1 QB 636, CA; *affd* [1900] AC 19, 69 LJQB 117, 81 LT 562, HL, 51 Digest (Repl) 572, *2057*.

Goldsmith v Sperrings Ltd [1977] 2 All ER 566, [1977] 1 WLR 478, CA, Digest (Cont Vol E 654, *781b*. *j*

Hess v Labouchere (1898) 14 TLR 350, CA, 51 Digest (Repl) 574, *2071*.

Mackender v Feldia AG [1966] 3 All ER 847, [1967] 2 QB 590, [1967] 2 WLR 119, [1966] 2 Lloyd's Rep 449, CA, 50 Digest (Repl) 341, *689*.

Mackey v James Henry Monks (Preston) Ltd [1918] AC 59, 87 LJPC 28, 118 LT 65, 82 JP 105, HL, 51 Digest (Repl) 1002, *5369*.

MacShannon v Rockware Glass Ltd [1977] 2 All ER 449, [1977] 1 WLR 376, CA; *rvsd*

[1978] 1 All ER 625, [1978] AC 795, [1978] 2 WLR 362, HL, Digest (Cont Vol E) 99, *1691a*.

Newcomen v Coulson (1878) 7 Ch D 764, 47 LJ Ch 429, 38 LT 275, 51 Digest (Repl) 575, *2087*.

Royal Exchange Assurance Co Ltd v Compania Naviera Santi SA,The Tropaioforos (No 2) [1962] 1 Lloyd's Rep 410, 11 Digest (Reissue) 637, *1714*.

Settlement Corpn v Hochschild [1965] 3 All ER 486, [1966] Ch 10, [1965] 2 WLR 1150, 11 Digest (Reissue) 639, *1730*.

United Australia Ltd v Barclays Bank Ltd [1940] 4 All ER 20, [1941] AC 1, 109 LJKB 919, 164 LT 139, 46 Com Cas 1, HL, 3 Digest (Reissue) 607, *3842*.

Unterweser Reederei GmbH v Zapata Offshore Co, The Chaparral [1972] 2 Lloyd's Rep 315, (US SC); *rvsg* [1971] 2 Lloyd's Rep 348 (US CA).

Cases also cited

Acrow (Automation) Ltd v Rex Chainbelt Inc [1971] 3 All ER 1175, [1971] 1 WLR 1676, CA.
Chaplin v Boys [1969] 2 All ER 1085, [1971] AC 356, HL.
Conybeare v Lewis (1880) 13 Ch D 469.
Hartlepool, The (1950) 84 Ll L Rep 145.
Hospital for Sick Children (Board of Governors) v Walt Disney Productions Inc [1967] 1 All ER 1005, [1968] Ch 52, CA.
Hyman v Helm (1883) 24 Ch D 531, CA.
Ionian Bank v Couvreur [1969] 2 All ER 651, [1969] 1 WLR 781, CA.
Kinnaird (Lord) v Field [1905] 2 Ch 306.
Liddell's Settlement Trusts, Re [1936] 1 All ER 239, [1936] Ch 365, CA.
M'Elroy v M'Allister 1949 SC 110.
McHenry v Lewis (1882) 22 Ch D 397, CA.
Metropolitan Bank Ltd v Pooley (1885) 10 App Cas 210, [1881–5] All ER Rep 949, HL.
Mundy v Butterly Co Ltd [1932] 2 Ch 227.
Peruvian Guano Co v Bockwoldt (1883) 23 Ch D 225, CA.
Quo Vadis, The [1951] 1 Lloyd's Rep 425.
Raymond v Tapson (1882) 22 Ch D 430, CA.
Robertson v Purdey [1906] 2 Ch 615.
Sayers v International Drilling Co NV [1971] 3 All ER 163, [1971] 1 WLR 1176, CA.
Senior v Holdsworth [1975] 2 All ER 1009, [1976] QB 23, CA.
Soya Margareta, The, Owners of cargo on board the Soya Louisa v Owners of the Soya Margareta [1960] 2 All ER 756, [1961] 1 WLR 709.

Appeal

Brown & Root (UK) Ltd and Jackson Marine SA of Panama, the first and second defendants in an action commenced by the plaintiff, Inocencio Fernando Castanho, a Portuguese citizen, claiming damages for personal injuries sustained in an accident on 11th February 1977 applied by summons dated 1st May 1979, and amended pursuant to leave of the court, for an injunction restraining the plaintiff (1) from continuing an action in Texas and (2) from commencing, causing to be commenced, continuing or prosecuting further proceedings in the United States of America or elsewhere in respect of his accident against Jackson Marine Inc, Jackson Marine SA, Jackson Marine Services NV, Jackson Marine Nederland BV, Brown & Root Inc, Brown & Root (UK) Ltd or any of them. On 14th May the plaintiff filed a notice of discontinuance of the action pursuant to RSC Ord 21, r 2. On 6th June when the defendants' summons for directions dated 1st May 1979 came on for hearing it was directed that it be treated as an application to strike out the notice of discontinuance, and was adjourned to a date to be fixed. On 2nd October Master Elton referred the defendants' applications to a judge in chambers. On 19th November 1979 Parker J ([1980] 1 All ER 689) struck out the notice of discontinuance and granted the injunction sought. The plaintiff appealed. The facts are set out in the judgments of Lord Denning MR and Shaw LJ.

J Melville Williams QC, George Newman and *John Hendy* for the plaintiff.
Christopher Bathurst QC and *Michael Lerego* for the defendants.

Cur adv vult

22nd April. The following judgments were read. *a*

LORD DENNING MR. 'A Texas-style claim is big business.' That is how the newspapers put it. The managers of the business are two attorneys of Houston, Texas. They keep a look-out for men injured on the North Sea oil rigs. The worse a man is injured, the better for business. Especially when he has been rendered a quadriplegic *b* and his employers have no answer to his claim. Their look-out man tells the Texan attorneys. They come across to England. They see the injured man and say to him: 'Do not bring your action in England or Scotland. You will only get £150,000 there. Let us bring it in Texas. We can get you £2,500,000 in Texas.' If he agrees, they get him to sign a power of attorney which provides for their reward. Under it the attorneys are to get 40% of any damages recovered. That is £1,200,000 for themselves. Big business *c* indeed!

In our present case, however, the Texan attorneys struck a snag. Their look-out man was too late. The injured man had already gone to solicitors in England before the Texan attorneys got to know of it. His English solicitors had already started an action for him against his employers. They had succeeded so well that they had already obtained from the English court orders for interim payments amounting to £27,250. He had spent *d* that sum on buying land and putting a house on it. How were the Texan lawyers to overcome that snag? Could they legitimately start an action in Texas when the English proceedings had got so far?

They devised a plan. They said to the English solicitors: 'Let us arrange things together. You drop the action in England and let us help one another in an action in Texas. We will ourselves pay back the £27,250 out of our own pocket. We will pay him *e* his salary and everything. We will pay you all your proper costs for the actual work you do. We will recoup it out of the £2,500,000 we get in Texas.' So they would get their 40%. The English solicitors would get their proper costs. A clever plan indeed. But will it work? That is the question in this case.

In detail *f*

A motor vessel called the American Moon was engaged in carrying supplies to oil rigs in the North Sea. On 11th February 1977 she was lying at Great Yarmouth in Norfolk. One of her crew was Inocencio Castanho, a Portuguese. He was transferring oil from a drum to a tank, by a pipe with compressed air. A valve flew off and went into his neck. It penetrated his spinal cord. He was completely paralysed in his arms and legs, a quadriplegic. He is completely dependent on others for everything. Both by day and by *g* night.

He was in Stoke Mandeville hospital for nine months from February to November 1977. He was well looked after there. The employers treated him very well. They continued to pay him his full salary of $690 a month. They arranged for members of his family to visit him from Portugal. They paid all their expenses. Their representative visited him regularly once a month to see to his welfare. After nine months, the doctors *h* thought it would be better for him to be with his wife and family in Portugal. So his employers arranged for a specially fitted aeroplane to take him back to Portugal. They also provided special equipment at his home in Portugal, so as to enable him to get about. Their representative in Lisbon visited him at his home, so as to do all they could for him and his family. His wife has been very good. She is doing everything for him. The only thing outstanding is the amount of compensation to be paid to him. *j*

The legal history in England up to June 1978

Soon after the accident his wife and brother came to see him at Stoke Mandeville. They asked the Portuguese Consulate to find a solicitor for him to claim compensation.

The Portuguese Consulate suggested B M Birnberg & Co, solicitors, of London. They
a were instructed on 4th May 1977. They got in touch with the employers' solicitors,
Clyde & Co, of London. No doubt Clyde & Co were aware of the Texas-style claims
made by some injured men. So they were glad the proceedings were started in England
rather than America. They did everything they could to keep them in England. They
said they would willingly make an interim payment on account. This was arranged and
everything done properly. A writ was issued in September 1977. An order by consent
b was made on 22nd March 1978 for £7,500 to be paid as an interim payment. A
statement of claim was delivered on 28th March 1978. But no defence was delivered at
that time. It was deferred by consent till later.

The Texans come on the scene

The Texans came on the scene in June 1978. Someone told them of the accident to the
c plaintiff. They did not know his address in Portugal. So they wrote to Stoke Mandeville
and got them to forward it to him. Then things moved rapidly. No expense was
spared. The Texan lawyers were ready to pay out large sums themselves out of their own
pocket, without security, because of the 40% contingency fee opening up before them.
They were ready to cast their bread upon the waters in the expectancy of the £1,200,000
fee which would be theirs.

d One of their top men, Bob Chaffin (he had been named in the newspapers), went to
Portugal to see the plaintiff. Bob Chaffin was closely associated with the firm of Benton
Musslewhite of Houston, Texas. Bob Chaffin pressed the plaintiff to let their firm take
over the claim. He succeeded so far that on 3rd July 1978 their firm, Benton
Musselwhite, sent the plaintiff a power of attorney to sign authorising them to institute
proceedings in Texas. They told him to sign it where marked 'X' and to return it to
e them.

The plaintiff seems to have been a little uncertain. He did not sign the power of
attorney at that time. Instead, in August 1978, he got in touch with the employers'
representative in Lisbon. He told him 'he would like the case to rest with the people (in
London) who are handling it'.

This made the Texan lawyers very concerned. They had not got the power of attorney
f back signed by the plaintiff. So they took quick action. Early in September 1978 Mr
Benton Musslewhite himself went over to Portugal. He saw the plaintiff, and told him
the advantage of proceedings in the United States. He then went from Portugal over to
London and saw Mrs Margaret Bowden, the managing clerk from Birnberg & Co. He
told her how American law operated. He told her that, if they were permitted to sue in
the United States, they would make advance payments to the plaintiff so as to cover all
g his needs; and that they were confident of success; and that they would expect the
damages to come up to $5,000,000. Mrs Bowden was impressed and asked him to send
her his credentials. He did so. He went back and sent her a batch of papers showing the
successes which Benton Musslewhite and Bob Chaffin had achieved in the cases they had
handled; and in addition a draft claim which they proposed to file on behalf of the
plaintiff in the American court.

h This was followed up by another visit to England by Mr Benton Musslewhite in
December 1978. He had meetings again with Mrs Margaret Bowden; and also with
counsel for the plaintiff, Mr Melville Williams QC. It was then decided that the
American lawyers should be instructed to pursue a claim in the United States of America
where the potential damages were very much greater. Counsel advised that 'the English
action should proceed, though not to judgment, as this would be a bar to the American
j action', that Birnberg & Co should co-operate with the American lawyers in the interests
of the plaintiff, but should only get their proper costs. Benton Musslewhite were to pay
the English lawyers their proper costs for work done, charged in the ordinary way, win
or lose.

That decision was duly implemented. So much so that on 31st January 1979 Mrs
Bowden herself visited the plaintiff at his home in Portugal, taking with her various

papers including a power of attorney in Portuguese for him to sign in favour of Benton Musslewhite, prepared by Benton Musslewhite.

The power of attorney

The power of attorney in Portuguese was executed in the plaintiff's hamlet of Varzim. By it the plaintiff conferred on Benton Musslewhite exclusive powers to represent him judicially in the United States; and promised to pay them, if settled out of court, one-third part of the moneys received, and 40% if the petition were filed in the court. Any expenses that were incurred on behalf of the plaintiff were to come out of the sums he received. If he got nothing, he had to pay nothing. There was an express clause that 'It is understood that the process initiated in England will not be concluded prior to the decision in the United States'. The object of that provision was, no doubt, to keep the English proceedings alive in case the American proceedings were unsuccessful.

The power of attorney also contained a provision by which Benton Musslewhite agreed to pay the plaintiff his salary, if the employers stopped paying it; and also agreed to repay any amounts received by the plaintiff by way of interim payments in the English proceedings; also any extra cost necessary to complete the house etc in Portugal. All these payments were no doubt being made by Benton Musslewhite out of their own pocket, in view of the large contingency fee which they hoped to receive in due course.

To English eyes that power of attorney was champertous in the extreme. The Texan lawyers were maintaining the proceedings in the United States, laying out large sums in support of it, and stipulating in return for 40% of the damages received: if they lost, they were to get nothing. And the English lawyers were helping them, going out to Portugal to get the power of attorney signed, and so forth. If such an agreement was made in regard to English proceedings, it would be invalid as contrary to public policy. But I would assume that it was not invalid by the law of the United States.

The English proceedings still continue

Whilst the American lawyers were pressing the plaintiff to proceed in the United States, the English proceedings were still going on. As I have said, the solicitors had already received an interim payment of £7,250. In October 1978, knowing full well of the American approach, they decided to apply in the English proceedings for a further interim payment of £20,000. On 10th October 1978 they wrote to Clyde & Co:

> '... the cost of building a pre-fabricated bungalow will be £7,000 but the plot of land will cost £19,000 ... it is imperative that our client is re-housed immediately ... we are instructed to ask for a further interim payment of £20,000 to cover these immediate costs.'

Birnberg & Co took out a summons. On 8th December 1978 Master Elton made an order for interim payment of £20,000. That sum was paid. The plot of land was bought. Arrangements were made for the erection of the bungalow.

The two proceedings going on together

For a time proceedings went on in Texas and England together. On 7th February 1979 the plaintiff issued a suit in the Texas State Court. He claimed damages for his injuries on the ground that the employers were guilty of gross negligence. The claim was for $5,000,000.

On 30th April 1979 the defendants delivered a defence in the English action. They admitted that the plaintiff was employed by the defendants, Jackson Marine SA, and that the accident was caused by the negligence of the chief engineer who was their servant. Thus leaving only the question of damages.

On 1st May 1979 the defendants took out two summonses in the English action. One was a summons for an injunction to restrain the plaintiff from continuing with the proceedings in Texas or any other proceedings there. The other was a summons asking for directions as to the trial of the English action. Before these summonses were heard, however, the plaintiff's lawyers took a step which is of crucial importance in the case. They gave notice of discontinuance of the English action.

The notice of discontinuance

Now you will remember that in the Portuguese power of attorney it was stipulated that the English action was not to be concluded prior to the decision of the United States' courts. The lawyers advising the plaintiff seem to have had second thoughts about this. It might give rise to difficulties in the American courts. So long as the English action was alive, the American courts might not let the Texan action go ahead. So they decided to bring the English proceedings to an end. They looked up the Supreme Court Practice and found that under RSC Ord 21, r 2(1), the plaintiff could discontinue the proceedings without leave at any time within 14 days after service of the defence. But after 14 days, leave would be necessary, and the English court might not give leave, so the English action would remain alive.

Now the defence had been served on 30th April 1979. On the very last day, 14th May 1979, the English lawyers served this document:

'NOTICE OF DISCONTINUANCE PURSUANT TO ORDER 21 RULE 2

'TAKE NOTICE that the Plaintiff hereby discontinues this action against the first and second Defendants pursuant to Order 21, rule 2. 14 days have not elapsed since date of service of Defence.

'DATED the 14th day of May 1979.

'B. M. BIRNBERG & CO.'

Was it authorised?

At once the query arises: did the solicitors have authority to give this notice of discontinuance, having regard to the terms of the power of attorney? There is nothing in writing to show that the plaintiff authorised the notice of discontinuance, but it is said that he authorised it over the telephone. Parker J doubted the validity of this. I too doubt it. The agency created by the power of attorney was governed presumably by the law of Portugal: see Dicey and Morris on the Conflict of Laws (9th Edn, 1973, p 869, r 167). If it is the same as English law, I doubt whether parol evidence would be admissible to contradict the express terms of the power of attorney.

So the notice of discontinuance may be invalid on the simple ground that it was not authorised.

The Texan actions

Soon afterwards the employers applied to stay the first Texan action. There was a hearing in Houston on 18th June 1979. English lawyers went over to give evidence about the position in the English action. No doubt Benton Musslewhite paid the costs of their English lawyers. But the application seems to have left some misgivings on the Texan side. At any rate, on 19th July 1979 the Texan lawyers filed a notice of nonsuit in their action and started a fresh action. At the same time they started the second Texan action. This was in the federal court, the United States District Court for Texas. They claimed \$5m compensatory damages and \$10m punitive damages and requested trial by jury. Since that time there have been voluminous proceedings in the federal court, motions for judgment, motions to stay and motions of all sorts. It is not necessary to describe them here. Save to say that there is a vista of prolonged and expensive litigation in the United States before a conclusion is reached.

The English proceedings

Returning now to the English proceedings, the summonses came on for hearing before Master Elton. He thought the notice of discontinuance was open to question. He treated the summons for directions as a summons to set it aside. He referred both summonses to the judge. On 19th November 1979 Parker J ([1980] 1 All ER 689) struck out the notice of discontinuance with the result that the English action remained in being. He also granted an injunction restraining the plaintiff from continuing the proceedings in America. He gave a reasoned judgment which will repay perusal. Now there is an appeal to this court.

Was the notice of discontinuance valid?

The judge held that, in giving the notice of discontinuance, the plaintiff's advisers were guilty of an abuse of process of the court. This was because the plaintiff had received interim payments of £27,250 in the English action. He himself had expended them and could not repay them. But the American lawyers had offered to repay them, out of their own pocket. In the judge's view this offer of repayment did not cure the abuse of process.

In giving the notice of discontinuance, the plaintiff's advisers relied on RSC Ord 21, r 2(1), which says that the plaintiff may, *without* the leave of the court, discontinue the action at any time not later than 14 days after service of the defence. That rule goes back several years, long before interim payments were thought of. Interim payments were introduced in 1970 as a result of the Administration of Justice Act 1969 and RSC Ord 29, rr 12 to 17. Those provisions enable the court, in personal injury cases, where the plaintiff was likely to succeed, to order a defendant to make interim payments on account of any damages for which the defendant may be liable 'if a final judgment is given' for the plaintiff. There is no provision for repayment except that 'on giving or making a final judgment' the court may order the repayment of any sum by which the interim payment exceeds the amount which the defendant is liable to pay to the plaintiff. There is no provision for repayment in the case of discontinuance.

The legislative purpose is clear. It was to enable the plaintiff to receive interim payments, and spend them on his own immediate needs and expenses, rather than have to wait for years until trial. The legislature did not contemplate that he should ever be called on to repay them, on discontinuance or at any other time, except in the unlikely event that he got less at the trial.

How does that legislative purpose fit in with RSC Ord 21, r 2(1) which enables a plaintiff to discontinue, without the leave of the court, within 14 days after defence? I fear that the draftsmen of interim payments forgot all about notices of discontinuance. Interim payments are quite inconsistent with a right to discontinue without leave. It is inconceivable that a plaintiff can be allowed to give notice of discontinuance and walk off with the interim payments, which he has already spent, and then start a fresh action for damages, without so much as a 'by your leave'. The only way of reconciling the provisions is to hold that, once interim payments have been sought and received and spent, the plaintiff can no longer discontinue without the leave of the court.

Another way of reaching the same result is to hold, as Parker J did, that, once interim payments have been sought and received and spent, it is an abuse of the process of the court to discontinue the proceedings without the leave of the court. I summarised the cases on 'abuse of process' in *Goldsmith v Sperrings Ltd* [1977] 2 All ER 566 at 574–575, [1977] 1 WLR 478 at 489–490. I said:

> 'On the face of it, in any particular case, the legal process may appear to be entirely proper and correct. [So here the notice of discontinuance, on the face of it, is in time and correctly done without leave.] What may make it wrongful is the purpose for which it is used.'

If it is used for the purpose of the party obtaining some collateral advantage for himself, and not for the purpose for which such proceedings are properly designed and exist, he will be held guilty of abuse of the process of the court. So here the notice of discontinuance was done without leave, so as to aid the American lawyers in obtaining 40% for themselves out of the American litigation. That was an abuse of the process of the English court.

If I am right in thinking that leave is necessary, then the court can do what is right and
a just. It can insist on repayment, at once in cash, as a condition of giving leave to discontinue; or alternatively it can allow the plaintiff to retain the interim payments (and not repay them) on condition that no other action shall be brought for the same cause: see *Hess v Labouchere* (1898) 14 TLR 350 by A L Smith LJ; or it can refuse leave and insist on the case going to judgment: see *Fox v Star Newspaper Co* [1898] 1 QB 636; [1900] AC 19. There are some words of Chitty LJ which fit this case (see [1898] 1 QB 636 at 639):

b 'The principle of the rule is plain. It is that after the proceedings have reached a certain stage the plaintiff, who has brought his adversary into court, shall not be able to escape by a side door and avoid the contest. He is then to be no longer dominus litis, and it is for the judge to say whether the action shall be discontinued or not and upon what terms.'

c The 'certain stage' in this case is when interim payments have been sought and received and spent.

Counsel for the plaintiff sought to overcome this argument by offering to repay the interim payments. That does not impress me in the least. It is not the plaintiff who is offering to repay them. It is the American lawyers out of their own pocket, looking forward eventually to their 40% of the damages. That very offer of repayment, made in
d an English action, is champertous. It is invalid at any rate in the eyes of an English court. It is the English courts which have jurisdiction over the English action. The cause of action here is situate in England: see Dicey and Morris on the Conflict of Laws (9th Edn, 1973, p 506, r 78). In *Mackender v Feldia AG* [1966] 3 All ER 847 at 851, [1967] 2 QB 590 at 601 Diplock LJ said: 'English courts will not enforce an agreement, whatever be its proper law, if it is contrary to English law, whether statute law or common law.' So they
e will not countenance this champertous offer, which is contrary to English law.

There is yet another way of reaching the same result. It is by the doctrine of election. The plaintiff here had only one cause of action. He had a choice before him: either to litigate it here in England or to pursue it in the United States. At the beginning he did not know of the choice; but in September 1978 he and his advisers knew that it was open to him. Yet in October 1978 they made an application in the English action for
f interim payment of another £20,000. They got it, and he spent it. That was an unequivocal act, deciding to pursue his right of action in England, in lieu of his right of action in America. It comes within the words of Lord Atkin in *United Australia Ltd v Barclays Bank Ltd* [1940] 4 All ER 20 at 37, [1941] AC 1 at 30:

'... if a man is entitled to one of two inconsistent rights, it is fitting that, when, with full knowledge, he has done an unequivocal act showing that he has chosen the
g one, he cannot afterwards pursue the other, which after the first choice, is by reason of the inconsistency, no longer his to choose.'

On all these grounds, therefore, I would support the decision of the judge that the notice of discontinuance was invalid. The defendants were entitled, and are entitled, to insist on the English action going on to judgment. If this be so, then clearly the Texan
h action should no longer be proceeded with.

Injunction

The judge granted an injunction to stop the plaintiff from proceeding further with his action in the United States. At first sight this seemed to me to be an extraordinary thing to do. It looked like an interference with the courts of the United States. But on
j examination I find that these courts can and do grant injunctions of this kind: on the ground that they operate only against the party and not against the court. The authorities are *Carron Iron Co v Maclaren* (1855) 5 HL Cas 416 at 436 by Lord Cranworth LC; *The Christiansborg* (1885) 10 PD 141 at 152–153 by Bagallay LJ; *The Tropaioforos (No 2)* [1962] 1 Lloyd's Rep 410 where Megaw J gave a valuable review of all the cases. And I am interested to see that the Supreme Court of the United States has affirmed an injunction

to restrain proceedings in an English court: see *Unterweser Reederei GmbH v Zapata Offshore Co, The Chaparral* [1972] 2 Lloyd's Rep 315. This jurisdiction, however, should only be granted with great caution so as to avoid even the appearance of undue interference with another court: see *Cohen v Rothfield* [1919] 1 KB 410, [1918–19] All ER Rep 260 and *Settlement Corpn v Hochschild* [1965] 3 All ER 486, [1966] Ch 10. I feel this so strongly that I would not myself do as the judge did. I would not grant an injunction. But, even if it were right to grant an injunction, I think that there would be great difficulty in enforcing it. In our present case the defendants' solicitors applied to a judge in chambers for leave to serve a summons for contempt, on Mr Benton Musslewhite and on Mr Chaffin, in Houston, Texas. The judge granted leave: and in pursuance of it we are told that summonses for contempt of the English court were served in the streets of Houston, Texas, on Mr Benton Musslewhite and Mr Robert Chaffin. They asked for them to be committed to Pentonville Prison here in London, England. That cannot be right. The common law does not permit any service of process out of the jurisdiction on a person out of the jurisdiction, even in the case of the service of a writ claiming damages: see *Re Busfield, Whaley v Busfield* (1886) 32 Ch D 123. A fortiori it does not permit a summons to commit to be served out of the jurisdiction. The only cases in which service can be made out of the jurisdiction are those set out in RSC Ord 11 and they do not apply here.

There is, however, an alternative open. I see no reason why, in lieu of an injunction, the court should not grant a declaration that the notice of discontinuance was invalid; and that the English action was and still is a pending action; that it is open to the plaintiff to proceed to trial and get judgment for the amount of damages assessed by the English court; or, if the plaintiff does not choose to proceed, for the defendants to ask for judgment to be entered for them.

If such a declaration were granted by the English court, I should expect that the courts of the United States would themselves not allow the Texan action to continue. The cause of action arose in England. It was properly cognisable and enforceable in the English courts. The plaintiff sued in the English courts on that cause of action. A final judgment in the English courts on that cause of action would, I should think, be recognised by the courts of the United States; just as we would recognise a final judgment by a court in the United States: see Dicey and Morris on the Conflict of Laws (9th Edn, 1973, p 1018, r 184).

Conclusion

I find myself in substantial agreement with Parker J: save that I would grant a declaration instead of an injunction.

Seeing that Shaw and Brandon LJJ take a diferent view, I would like to state how I see the justice of this case.

Here is a Portuguese citizen who has a cause of action against his employers. The cause of action undoubtedly arose in England. At Great Yarmouth in Norfolk. He was treated for months in an English hospital. The Portuguese Consulate advised him to sue in England. His chose in action is situate in England, because England is the country where it is properly recoverable and can be enforced: see Dicey and Morris on the Conflict of Laws (9th Edn, 1973, p 506, r 78). He brought his action in England and got interim payments of £27,250 in England on account of the damages recoverable here. By so doing he reduced his chose of action into possession in England. If his action had proceeded to trial in England, or been settled, he would soon have recovered compensation amounting to £150,000 or £200,000, a sum which most people in Portugal or England would have considered reasonable, and even generous. Yet that course was interrupted by the lawyers from Texas. They persuaded him to suspend his English action and to bring proceedings in Texas, in the hope that he would get an award of £2,500,000, out of which the Texan lawyers would get £1,200,000. They would finance it at their own cost entirely. They would charge him nothing if they failed in the United States. He could then revert to his action in England. To our English eyes that

arrangement with him savoured of champerty. The Texan lawyers were conducting the
a litigation in the United States, and directing the litigation in England, on the footing that they would get 40% of the spoils if they won and nothing if they lost. In so far as these arrangements affected the chose in action, they are governed by the lex situs: see Dicey and Morris on the Conflict of Laws (9th Edn, 1973, pp 506, 547, rr 78, 83). The lex situs was English law; and by English law they were contrary to public policy, and should not be enforced. This very case is a good example of the evils to which champerty can give
b rise. There has been voluminous and expensive litigation in the United States already; and there is a vista of much more to come, before the plaintiff can get anything there, if he ever does. He would have been better advised to take the bird in the hand in England rather than the dozen in the bush in the United States, where the bush is a thicket full of sharp thorns. Simple justice to him would be for the employers to pay him £200,000 to settle the English action, and for the proceedings in the United States to be dropped.
c That is what the judge felt. It is what I feel too. I would therefore dismiss the appeal and let the plaintiff be compensated here and now by a payment of £200,000. But as Shaw and Brandon LJJ think otherwise, he will have to wait till the proceedings end in the United States; and that may be a very long time. He may be dead by then.

SHAW LJ. This case has a complicated history. I need not recount the detail of it for
d that has been done already. It has also developed some extraordinary features. It is in regard to them that I add my own observations to what has been said in the judgment of Lord Denning MR as I find myself differing from his conclusions and from those of Parker J.

The plaintiff is a Portuguese subject. This fact is not without significance since it makes him a foreigner equally in England and in the United States of America. In the
e course of his employment he suffered a tragic accident which has reduced him to utter helplessness and made him wholly dependent on others. Apart from being paralysed in his upper and lower limbs, almost every bodily function has been impaired. He was little more than thirty years old when this catastrophe befell him, and he has the responsibility of a wife and children to maintain. There can be no true measure of compensation in such a case. The minimum requirement is to provide for his care for
f what life he has still to live; and there must be made good also the loss of earnings resulting from his incapacity. These elements are capable more or less of calculation or estimation; but what of amends for pain and suffering and the loss of enjoyment of life? No process of computation will serve to provide a real answer or an effective one. The response of the courts to the challenge presented by this problem is inevitably imbued with a conventional quality; and in different societies and environments
g different conventions prevail. It cannot be said that any are necessarily more right than others. If someone who has been reduced to a human wreck can seek amends in a more generous environment, his misfortune is the more offset by that fortuitous circumstance. At least the victim will have the satisfaction of knowing that the destruction of his own capacity to derive enjoyment from physical life has had the consequence of augmenting his family's prospects of living securely on a good standard. It must not be
h thought that this is to compensate the dependants of the victim. The satisfaction is *his*, and is an important aspect of the amends he is entitled to receive. The pursuit of that satisfaction is in my opinion to be commended as justifiable and not condemned as avaricious; and the provision of a munificent measure of compensation is to be applauded and should not be denigrated as extravagant or exorbitant. It would in my view be less than human to deny to such a victim the opportunity to pursue his claim for
j compensation wherever it will evoke the most generous response. Yet this is exactly what has been and is being attempted in the course of this litigation in which the unattractive aspects are by no means all on one side.

With these preliminary observations, I turn to the salient features in the history.

The disaster happened on 11th February 1977. The plaintiff was paralysed from the neck downwards. He was given such treatment as medical science can provide at Stoke

Mandeville hospital. The Portuguese Consul took up his case. As the locus of the accident was a vessel in English waters, a firm of solicitors in London was consulted. They ascertained who were the ostensible employers and who might be responsible for any negligence which might be the cause of the plaintiff's appalling injuries. So far as they could ascertain, at any rate superficially, an English company called Brown & Root (UK) Ltd which provided shore services for the American Moon bore the liability. The solicitors retained for the plaintiff can hardly be blamed for not then discovering that Brown & Root (UK) Ltd was part of a vast complex based in Texas and that it, together with a number of other corporate bodies, operated under the aegis of a Texan corporation called Jackson Marine Inc. So on 9th May 1977 they addressed a letter to Brown & Root (UK) Ltd saying that they held that company liable to compensate the plaintiff for his injuries. It has emerged in these proceedings that all the corporations comprised in the Jackson empire are insured with the same insurers. In England Messrs Clyde & Co, whom I shall call 'Clydes', act for those insurers. It is notorious that in the United States the scale of damages for injuries of the magnitude sustained by the plaintiff is something in the region of ten times what is regarded as appropriate by the conventional standards of the courts of this country. One can almost hear the sigh of mingled astonishment and relief breathed by those concerned for the insurers for Jacksons (as I shall call the combination of corporate bodies) when proceedings were proposed in England. No better policy could be pursued from the insurers' point of view than to encourage the issue of those proceedings in this country and to confine them there. In pursuing this policy Clydes were acting in the best interests of their insurer clients, no doubt absolutely correctly in accordance with their professional duty.

On 1st June 1977 they wrote in response to the letter which had been sent to Brown & Root (UK) Ltd by Messrs Birnberg & Co (whom I shall call 'Birnbergs'), the plaintiff's solicitors. That letter read:

> 'Dear Sirs,
>
> *'Mr. I. F. da Costa Castanho.*
>
> 'Your letter of 9th May addressed to Brown & Root (U.K.) Limited has been passed to us for our attention. We are investigating the matter, and in due course shall write to you again. In the meantime, liability is not admitted.'

They followed that letter up by another dated 28th June. I read the full text:

> 'We refer to our letter of 1st June, and write to say that we have now had the opportunity of investigating this matter. We are not, of course, in a position to admit liability, but it would appear that some degree of liability may rest on Jackson Marine Corporation, for whom we act. That being the case, as we expect you are aware, Jackson Marine continue to pay Mr. Castanho's salary, and have paid the expenses incurred by members of his family who have travelled from Portugal to visit him. However, our clients recognise that in the very difficult circumstances now facing Mr. Castanho, further expense of a more general nature is likely to be incurred, and we therefore invite you to suggest a figure by way of interim payment to assist Mr. Castanho and his family, which we shall put to our clients for their consideration. We are, of course, authorised to accept service of proceedings, which in any event must be issued for the purpose of the interim payment. We recognise that it will be a considerable time before you will be in a position accurately to formulate your client's claim, but we are sure that you will keep us informed of all material developments. We expect you know, but we feel that we ought to place on record, that about once a month Mr. Castro, a representative of the Highlands Insurance Co., and of the Brown & Root Group, visits Mr. Castanho in hospital. These visits are purely to enquire after his progress, and to ensure that the welfare of himself and his family is properly looked after. Legal matters are not discussed. We hope that you will have no objection to the continuation of these visits, but if you do, perhaps you will let us know. In the meantime, we await to hear from you on the subject of the interim payment.'

An interesting feature of this early communication from Clydes is the reiterated

reference to the prospect of an interim payment and the indication that the institution
a of proceedings was necessary to make such a payment possible. Birnbergs' reply dated 13th July was not entirely satisfactory for it suggested an interim payment before writ. On the very next day Clydes wrote in answer. Again their letter deserves to be read in full. After acknowledging Birnbergs' letter of the day before, they continued in these terms:

> 'We will accept service on behalf of Jackson Marine Corporation. We do not
> b think that any liability rests upon Brown & Root (U.K.) Limited, and we do not at present have instructions to accept service on their behalf. However, if you will kindly send us the Writ, we expect to have instructions to accept service on behalf of both Defendants. As we said in our letter of 28th June, we shall certainly take instructions on the question of an interim payment, and note that you consider that £7,000 would be a suitable figure. We shall write to you again as soon as we have
> c instructions on this point. We certainly agree with you that there is no bar to our settling an interim payment at this stage, but we should like to have a formal order from the Court in respect of it. We cannot exclude the possibility that at some later stage we may fail to agree on quantum, and in that connection we should like to draw your attention to the notes to Order 29 . . . There, the Editors suggest that a Defendant who makes an interim payment voluntarily, and without an Order of
> d the Court, is not entitled to take that interim payment into account when making a payment into Court. We would wish to avoid this problem, and therefore ask that at the appropriate stage you issue a Summons. Naturally, there will be no opposition to your Summons in respect of the agreed amount. We shall now take our clients' instructions, and look forward to hearing from you with your Writ. We shall also deal with the question of your client's salary, and write to you in more detail.'

e The once more repeated reference to the prospect of an interim payment was again related to a persistent and insistent suggestion as to the issue of a writ. In the light of the ensuing history this assumes a special significance.

The carrot of an interim payment and of the other solicitudes proffered could hardly be resisted when dangled so assiduously. It was seized with avidity. The plaintiff's plight was a desperate one. He had been an ordinary seaman and had few resources to
f cope with his predicament. On 14th October 1977 Birnbergs sent the original writ to Clydes together with a copy. There were now proceedings started in England, and there, if the then and any other prospective defendant had their way, the proceedings would also finish. On 26th October Clydes were writing:

> 'We refer to our conversation with Mrs Bowden on 24th October, and write to confirm what we then told you. According to the information with which our
> g clients have provided us, your client was employed by a company called Jackson Marine S.A. . . . We therefore consider that this company are the proper Defendants to this action, and although we cannot prevent you from suing Brown & Root (U.K.) Limited, we think that you ought to sue Jackson Marine S.A. As arranged, we are returning the Writ to you so that Jackson Marine S.A. may be added as defendants, and so that this amendment can be effected before service, and so with the least
> h expense and trouble. If you will kindly return the amended Writ to us, we will accept service on behalf of both Defendants and will let you have an Appearance as soon as possible. You will thereafter be able to issue the Summons for an interim payment.'

Then it goes on to deal with the visits to the plaintiff in hospital.

j The company suggested as the proper defendant was not a part of Jacksons incorporated in Texas, its registration and its domicile were in Panama. The writ which had been issued on 29th September was amended in accordance with Clydes' suggestion and the added defendant admitted liability. On 22nd March 1978, on the application of the plaintiff and at the invitation if not instigation of Clydes, an order was made by consent against Jackson Marine SA under RSC Ord 29, r 9, for an interim payment by them of £7,250, those defendants having admitted liability.

The action could now be regarded as firmly and irremovably established in the
English jurisdiction. It may be that it was this consideration which caused the defendants a
to oppose a second application made in November 1978 for a further £20,000 which the
plaintiff urgently needed to buy a suitable house in Portugal. As even by English
standards the damages were likely to be many times that sum, it is at least peculiar that
the application should have been resisted by a corporate member of a wealthy complex
such as Jacksons, the more so as liability had been admitted. It permits at least the
surmise that the earlier show of solicitude had not been disinterested and was tactical b
rather than humanitarian. Now that the action was tied (or apparently so) to the courts
of this country, there was no point in providing any more carrots. However the plaintiff
did continue to receive his salary via the second defendants, and his medical expenses
were paid by them.

At that time or soon afterwards (that is, about the end of 1978 and the beginning of
1979) a dramatic change deformed the scene. The plaintiff had been approached by the c
American lawyers. They advised that he could and should pursue his claim not in
England but in the State of Texas, USA. They promised greatly magnified damages.
They offered also pending the recovery of those damages financial support for the
plaintiff on a comprehensive and liberal scale. True, they required as payment for their
services 40% of any damages he would be awarded and the return of their money
advances; but only if he won, as they were confident he would. Even so he would be left d
very substantially better off than he could hope to be at the highest with a judgment in
this country. The practice of exacting payment on a contingency basis for legal services
is not only foreign to English concepts but is viewed here with positive disapproval.
Nonetheless it does not behove English legal institutions, whether solicitors or the Bar or
the judiciary, to adopt a lofty, let alone a pious, attitude in regard to the contingency
system. It is accepted by the legal institutions of the United States and they are entitled e
not only to hold their views on the matter but to apply them in practice, as they regularly
do. It is no business of ours, and we must allow that they know theirs.

Faced with the prospect of vastly adding to the measure of satisfaction he might expect
by pursuing his claim in Texas instead of in England, it seems that the plaintiff may have
hesitated at first. Perhaps that prospect seemed too good to be true. However he did not
hesitate long. Self-interest prevailed and the American lawyers were instructed on his f
behalf to institute proceedings in Texas and to pursue them there. In February 1979 the
plaintiff executed a power of attorney in favour of the American lawyers. Their first act
on his behalf was to issue proceedings in the State Court of Texas which they did during
February. In addition to the defendants in the original action, others of the Jackson
corporations were sued as well.

Meanwhile in England the defendants in the action brought here served their defence g
on 30th April 1979. Brown & Root (UK) Ltd denied liability but it was admitted by
Jackson Marine SA. By this time the action was no longer of interest to the plaintiff. His
English solicitors served a notice of discontinuance on 14th May 1979, just within 14
days of the service of the defence. In view of the suggested doubt as to their authority to
serve that notice, it is pertinent to recall that they were then (and still are) on the record
as the plaintiff's solicitors in whatever proceedings inure in England. However wide the h
terms of the power of attorney given to the American lawyers, they could not be invested
with authority to take any part in those proceedings on behalf of the then plaintiff; and
conversely that power of attorney could not per se divest Birnbergs of their general
authority to do in the English action on behalf of their client what appeared to them at
the time to be in his best interests. I see no real basis for misgiving as to whether the
notice of discontinuance was with Birnbergs' authority at the time it was served. What j
then was its effect?

RSC Ord 21, r 2 (1) provides:

> 'The plaintiff in an action begun by writ may, without the leave of the Court, discontinue the action . . . as against all or any of the defendants at any time not later than 14 days after service of the defence on him . . .'

I have omitted the immaterial parts of the rule. There could ordinarily be no question a but that this notice brought the action to a summary end. All that was left of it is to be found in RSC Ord 62 which deals with costs and nothing else. Rule 10 of that order provides (again I leave out words not relevant in the present context):

> 'Where a plaintiff by notice in writing and without leave . . . discontinues his action against any defendant . . . the defendant may tax his costs of the action . . . and, if the taxed costs are not paid within 4 days after taxation, may sign judgment b for them.'

In this way it is contemplated that the position between the parties will be restored to what it was before the action was started; and there is a sanction against the erstwhile plaintiff starting another action based on substantially the same cause of action. RSC Ord 21 provides that if he does start another action before he has paid the defendant's costs in c the discontinued action the court may order the proceedings in the second action to be stayed until those costs are paid. This is the only sanction to be found in the rules. It seems to me to be clear that this compact code is designed to bring about what can properly be regarded as a restitutio in integrum restoring the respective parties to the positions they occupied before the first action was brought. No other adjustments or redress is contemplated or called for. The first note in the Supreme Court Practice (1979, d vol 1, p 362, para 21/2–5/1) to the rules in Ord 21 says: 'These Rules constitute a complete code on the subject of withdrawal and discontinuance . . . of an action.'

In the present case a complication has been introduced in the form of the interim payments under RSC Ord 29, r 9. That order says nothing about what is to happen to such payments if the action is discontinued without leave within the time limited by Ord 21. Is the right to discontinue without leave in any way affected? The question was e raised in a very odd way.

By the time the defendants came to serve their defence, their advisers had become aware of the institution of proceedings in the State Court of Texas. I dare say they were outraged. All had appeared set for a trial in England with a comparatively moderate assessment of damages. Now all was threatened. It was quite intolerable to the insurers that their expectations should be thus thwarted. On 12th May 1979, ie the day after f serving their defence, the defendants served a summons for directions and asked for an injunction to restrain the proceedings in Texas. The application for directions came before the master on 6th June. The plaintiff had by that date served his notice of discontinuance so he did not attend. The master having been told something of the history of the matter decided that the summons for directions should be treated as an application to strike out the notice of discontinuance as being an abuse of process. It is g questionable whether the defendants were at that stage entitled to take out a summons for directions at all, but in the light of the master's order this has no importance other than showing the state of consternation into which the defendants or their insurers were thrown by the proceedings in Texas. In the state court there strenuous efforts were made to stay the plaintiff's action. His advisers thought it expedient to abandon the action in the state court and to institute fresh proceedings in the Texas federal court. This they did h in July 1979. They considered the federal court would be more ready to accept jurisdiction. The proceedings in that court also provoked an application for a stay; but when it was dealt with some months later it was unsuccessful. There is an appeal pending against the refusal of a stay, but by the rules of procedure in Texas the appeal on the issue of jurisdiction will be heard only after the substantive issues in the action have been resolved. I mention this merely as part of the narrative. In my view, for reasons I j shall seek to explain later, what is happening or may happen in the courts of Texas has nothing to do with us. The material consideration is that since the end of 1979 and up to the present time the federal court of the State of Texas in the United States of America has accepted jurisdiction to try an action at the suit of the plaintiff claiming damages compensatory and punitive against Jacksons for the injuries he sustained on the American Moon.

In England the long vacation had interrupted the progress of events. It was not until

2nd October that the adjourned summons to strike out the notice of discontinuance came again before the master. The application for an injunction to restrain the plaintiff from pursuing his proceedings in Texas was then pending before the judge in chambers. The master therefore adjourned the summons to strike out to the judge so that he might deal with all the matters involved at one and the same time. The matter came before Parker J on 29th October. Both sides were represented by counsel and their argument and submissions occupied some two days. Judgment was reserved and was given in open court on 19th November. In the result it was ordered that the notice of discontinuance be struck out under the inherent jurisdiction of the court as being an abuse of process. The judge also granted an injunction whereby the plaintiff and anyone acting on his behalf, including his American lawyers, were enjoined not to pursue the proceedings in the federal court of Texas or to take any part in them on the plaintiff's behalf.

I have read Parker J's careful and elaborate judgment with respectful admiration; but I find it impossible to agree with his conclusions or to accept the reasons on which they are founded.

I deal first, as did the judge, with the notice of discontinuance. To begin with, it seems an inversion of logic to speak of an act which purports to terminate a process as being an abuse of that process. It may be that to seek to retain or to take advantage of some benefit which accrued while the process was in being would constitute an abuse, but I find it difficult to see how giving a process its quietus can be an abuse of it. The right accorded by RSC Ord 21, r 2(1) is explicit and unqualified. The note in the Supreme Court Practice to Ord 21, r 2 sets out the three conditions which must be fulfilled if the notice of discontinuance is to be effective. There is no hint that there may be circumstances in which, although the specified conditions are satisfied, the discontinuance will be ineffectual or may be declared by the court to be so.

It is of value to recall the corresponding rule before the revision of the Rules of the Supreme Court in 1962. It was then in the following form:

> 'The plaintiff may, at any time before receipt of the defendant's defence, or after the receipt thereof before taking any other proceeding in the action (save any interlocutory application), by notice in writing, wholly discontinue his action . . .'

In those days there was no provision elsewhere in the rules for interim payments. I doubt whether, if there had been one, an application for such payments would have been regarded as other than interlocutory so that the absolute right to discontinue would have prevailed notwithstanding such payments. The rule in the old form had the disadvantage of giving rise to much contention as to what might in a particular case constitute 'taking any other proceedings in the action'. Accordingly the rule was modified by substituting a simple time limit.

It is said in the present case that although the plaintiff complied with the rules he has abused the process of the court. How and why I fail to see. It is true that he obtained two interim payments amounting to a substantial sum. They were paid on the basis that a judgment in favour of the plaintiff was probable and that it would be for a substantially larger amount. The defendant who made the payment could, as I see it, seek to recover the sums so paid as moneys paid to his use for a consideration which has failed. In any case I see no real incipient financial prejudice, for if the plaintiff successfully pursues his claim in Texas, the federal court there will be apprised of and impose the necessary terms of adjustment for the £27,250 already received by the plaintiff, if indeed he has not by then paid it back. We are told by counsel for the plaintiff that he, with the assistance no doubt of his American lawyers, will pay that sum back forthwith. I see no reason to make that repayment a condition of preserving the operation of a regular and valid notice of discontinuance. I do not think the court has any power to impose such a condition where discontinuance is possible without leave under the rules.

Then it is said that the plaintiff has procured the advantage of an admission of liability by Jackson Marine SA. If the admission was honest, it can have done nobody any harm. If it was part of a tactical plan, so much the worse for those who employed such tactics.

Any judicial tribunal that functions in a civilised community will not in its independent jurisdiction do other than form its own judgment on what is admitted or proved before that tribunal and not elsewhere in a foreign jurisdiction.

There remains the injunction. It was in these terms:

> 'It is ordered and directed that the plaintiff by himself his servants or agents or otherwise howsoever be perpetually restrained and an injunction is hereby granted perpetually restraining him from commencing or causing to be commenced or continuing or prosecuting any further or other proceedings in the United States of America or elsewhere against . . .'

and there follow the names of the various Jackson companies made defendants in the proceedings in Texas.

A crop of question marks and not a few exclamation marks spring to the mind on reading the terms of this order. In the first place, it could have no just foundation unless the plaintiff is held by the scruff of his neck to an action in England that he wished to abandon and which he had in my opinion effectively discontinued.

Even, however, if the English action remained alive and a concurrent action in relation to the same subject matter is brought in another jurisdiction, what should the attitude of the English courts be if they are asked to regularise that situation? There is much law as to the principles which should be applied in seeking to preserve the balance of justice. I do not canvass the authorities but seek to apply the result of examining them. There is little doubt that the question for an English court is whether or not to stay the proceedings in this country. It is over *those* proceedings that they have the authority and the power to exercise control. *They* are within its jurisdiction. To attempt in effect to stay proceedings in a foreign jurisdiction is to usurp the function of the courts of that jurisdiction. Whatever moral or ethical considerations may inspire (or cloud) the judgment of an English court, it must not seek to meddle officiously with the jurisdiction of foreign tribunals in regard to matters which they consider to be within the province of that jurisdiction. The only apparent (but not real) exception is where the parties to litigation have contracted to sue only in the courts of this country. In such a case the courts might grant an injunction if proceedings were to be instituted abroad, but this would be no more than the enforcement of an English contract not to sue abroad.

The exclamation marks which I have envisaged come to the mind on many grounds. The plaintiff in the federal court of Texas is a Portuguese subject; he is unlikely, especially having regard to his physical state, ever to be in England. His American lawyers are in duty bound to act in his best interests in pursuing the action in Texas. They must regard an order of an English court which forbids them to do their professional duty in America as an unwarranted and ridiculous charade. They too are outside the jurisdiction. We were told that two of the American attorneys acting for the plaintiff have been served in Texas with a notice of motion for their committal to prison for 'contempt in aiding and abetting [the plaintiff] in prosecuting proceedings in the United States District Court for the Eastern District of Texas'.

I do not permit myself the luxury of conjecturing what they said and are saying about that absurd episode. It was probably derisive. Even if they came to England, I wonder who would dare to pursue such a motion; and I shrink from the contemplation of the proceedings in court, and their inevitable outcome.

In the course of the appeal it was urged on this court that the striking out of the notice of discontinuance and the granting of the injunction were justified as a means of countering improprieties and breaches of professional codes of conduct by the American attorneys. Even if the allegations of misconduct were well founded, and I am in no position to express any opinion on this topic and would not even if I were, what business is it of an English court in relation to matters which have taken place outside England? The courts and the professional bodies of the United States must deal with that if and when it arises. Maintenance and champerty have ugly connotations in English law, but the emotive use of such expressions does not confer on an English court a universal moral supervision of legal institutions in other countries. The allegations of impropriety were

yet another desperate and disingenuous effort to keep the plaintiff's claim within the relatively moderate limits now current in the courts of England. Fortunately American a
corporations, like their insurers, are aware of the scale of damages in the United States and they arrange their policies and the premiums accordingly.

This is a case about money, not morality. I see no warrant for the injunction and I would discharge it.

In my judgment the appeal should be allowed in its entirety.

b

BRANDON LJ (read by Shaw LJ). The detailed history of this case is fully set out in the judgment of Parker J and it is not necessary therefore that I should do more than give a brief outline of it.

In February 1977 the plaintiff, who is Portuguese, was employed as an oiler on board the oil rig service ship American Moon. On the 11th of that month, when the ship was lying alongside in the port of Great Yarmouth, the plaintiff sustained a very serious c
accident which has left him a quadriplegic.

The American Moon was owned and operated by Jackson Marine Corpn ('JMC'), a company incorporated in the State of Texas. JMC carries on its activities, which are worldwide, either directly or indirectly through the medium of various subsidiary companies which are wholly owned and controlled by it. Some of these subsidiary companies are also incorporated in Texas. Others are incorporated in various countries d
outside the United States, including Panama, the Netherlands Antilles, Holland and England.

The plaintiff, acting through English solicitors, began by suing his employers in England, naming as defendants two companies in the JMC group, one Panamanian and the other English. That was in November 1977. Later, in February 1979, after proceeding with his action here for over a year, and obtaining two interim payments e
from the second defendants in the course of doing so, he sued his employers afresh in Texas. He first sued them in a state court, naming as defendants JMC and five other companies in the JMC group, including the two already sued in England. Then in July 1979 he withdrew his action in the state court and began another action in a federal court in the same state, naming as defendants JMC and two only of the five subsidiaries previously sued in the state court. f

The reason why the plaintiff sued his employers afresh in Texas was that, after his action in England had already got under way, he had been informed by US attorneys (who subsequently acted for him) that he would, if successful, recover far higher damages in Texas than in England. The reason why his action in Texas was switched from the state court to the federal court was that his US attorneys thought that the latter court was more likely to accept jurisdiction than the former. g

When the plaintiff had first sued his employers afresh in Texas in February 1979, he had left his action in England alive, though in abeyance. Later, however, after the defendants in the English action had on 1st May 1979 applied for an injunction restraining him from proceeding in Texas, and for directions for trial, the plaintiff on 15th May 1979 discontinued his action here. This was something which, by reason of what I think can fairly be described as a procedural quirk, he was entitled to do without h
leave under the relevant rule of court. The defendants' response to the discontinuance was to convert their application for directions for trial into an application to strike out the notice of discontinuance as an abuse of the process of the court.

In the result the judge had before him in November 1979 two applications by the defendants. The first was for an injunction restraining the plaintiff from proceeding further against his employers in Texas or elsewhere outside England. The second was for j
an order striking out the notice of discontinuance as an abuse of the process of the court. The judge granted both applications and the plaintiff now appeals against his decision.

So far as the jurisdiction of the court generally in matters of this kind is concerned, it has long been established that there may be circumstances in which an English court will (i) compel a plaintiff, who desires to sue in England, to sue in another forum elsewhere

instead, or (ii) compel a plaintiff, who desires to sue in another forum elsewhere, to sue
a in England instead. In case (i) the court achieves its purpose by staying any proceedings which the plaintiff has brought here, so leaving him with the only practical alternative of beginning or continuing proceedings in the other forum. In case (ii) the court achieves its purpose by granting an injunction restraining the plaintiff from beginning or continuing proceedings in the other forum, leaving him with the only practical alternative of beginning or continuing proceedings here.

b It follows that, when on 1st May 1979 the defendants in the action here applied for an injunction restraining the plaintiff from proceeding against his employers in Texas or elsewhere outside England, the court certainly had jurisdiction to intervene in the manner sought. Difficult questions arise, however, as to the effect on that jurisdiction of the discontinuance of the action by the plaintiff on 15th May 1979. Did the discontinuance, by bringing the action to an end, also bring to an end the court's
c jurisdiction to intervene? If so, does the court have power to restore that jurisdiction, as it were, by striking out the notice of discontinuance as an abuse of its process? If so, ought the court to exercise that power in the circumstances of the case?

These questions do not need to be answered unless the court considers that, if it had jurisdiction to intervene by granting the injunction sought, it ought to do so. I propose therefore to leave them on one side for the time being, to assume that the necessary
d jurisdiction exists and to consider whether on that assumption it ought to be exercised.

The circumstances in which an English court will compel a plaintiff, who desires to sue in England, to sue in another forum elsewhere instead were examined in two recent cases in the House of Lords: *The Atlantic Star* [1973] 2 All ER 175, [1974] AC 436 and *MacShannon v Rockware Glass Ltd* [1978] 1 All ER 625, [1978] AC 795.

In the second of these two cases Lord Diplock, stated the criteria applicable in this way
e ([1978] 1 All ER 625 at 630, [1978] AC 795 at 812):

> 'In order to justify a stay, two conditions must be satisfied, one positive and the other negative: (a) the defendant must satisfy the court that there is another forum to whose jurisdiction he is amenable in which justice can be done between the parties at substantially less inconvenience or expense, and (b) the stay must not deprive the plaintiff of a legitimate personal or juridical advantage which would be
> f available to him if he invoked the jurisdiction of the English court.'

It is clear from *The Atlantic Star* that, if the positive condition at (a) above is satisfied, but the negative condition (b) above is not, the court has to carry out a balancing operation. It has to weigh in the one scale the advantage to the plaintiff of suing in England, and in the other scale the disadvantage to the defendant of being sued there,
g and then decide which of the two should, as a matter of justice, prevail. In carrying out that balancing operation the court must have regard to all the relevant circumstances of the particular case.

It was submitted for the defendants on this appeal that there is no difference, in principle, between compelling a plaintiff, who desires to sue in England, to sue in another forum elsewhere (as was done in the two House of Lords cases referred to above),
h and compelling a plaintiff, who desires to sue in another forum elsewhere, to sue or go on suing in England (as it is sought to compel the plaintiff to do in the present case); and that the same criteria should therefore apply, mutatis mutandis, to the exercise of the court's power of compulsion in either case.

I would accept this submission as a broad proposition. In my opinion, however, some qualification of it is necessary for this reason. Where a stay is granted of an action here,
j the English court is doing no more than exercising control over its own proceedings. By contrast, where an injunction is granted restraining a person from suing in another forum elsewhere, the English court is interfering, albeit indirectly, with proceedings in another jurisdiction.

This distinction led Scrutton LJ to say, in *Cohen v Rothfield* [1919] 1 KB 410 at 413, [1918–19] All ER Rep 260 at 261, that the power to grant injunctions in such cases 'should be exercised with great caution to avoid even the appearance of undue interference with another Court'. I agree with that observation and consider that, while the power to compel a plaintiff to sue in another forum elsewhere by staying proceedings here should itself (as the authorities show) be exercised with caution, the power to compel a plaintiff to sue here by restraining him from proceeding in another forum elsewhere should be exercised with ever greater caution.

Bearing this qualification in mind, I propose to consider first whether the criteria laid down by Lord Diplock in *MacShannon v Rockware Glass Ltd* are satisfied, mutatis mutandis, in the present case.

So far as criterion (a) is concerned, the question is whether the English court is a forum to whose jurisdiction the employers are amenable in which justice can be done between the parties at substantially less inconvenience and expense than in Texas. The answer to this question must clearly be in the affirmative. The action in England is well advanced, with liability of one of the two defendants admitted and the amount of damages only in issue. It should be possible to bring it to trial and to obtain a final judgment in it within a comparatively short time and without any further great expense. The action in Texas, on the other hand, is only in its early stages. Issues are raised in it with regard to punitive as well as compensatory damages and a full-dress trial before a jury is contemplated. Witnesses will have to be brought from abroad or depositions obtained from them. From these and other matters, it is clear that the determination of the claim in Texas is bound to involve much greater inconvenience and expense than its determination in England.

So far as criterion (b) is concerned, the question is whether an injunction restraining the plaintiff from proceeding in Texas would deprive him of a legitimate personal or juridical advantage which would be available to him if he continued his action there. The answer to this question must also clearly be in the affirmative: he stands to recover, even after allowing for the contingency fees of his US attorneys, at least five times more by way of damages in Texas than in England, and, if he can get that very great advantage by suing his employers in their own state, it seems to me entirely legitimate for him to seek to do so.

We have a situation, therefore, where criterion (a) is satisfied but criterion (b) is not, so that the balancing operation to which I referred earlier has to be carried out, and carried out with due regard to all the relevant circumstances of the case.

If it were merely a question of weighing in the one scale the advantage to the plaintiff of being able to recover at least five times as large an amount of damages in Texas as in England and in the other scale the much increased inconvenience and expense to the JMC group of having to contest the claim in Texas, I should have no doubt whatever that the advantage to the plaintiff should prevail.

I say that for the following reasons. It would always have been open to the plaintiff, if he had been so advised early enough, to sue the JMC group in Texas first, and never to have brought any action against them in England at all. If he had done so, the JMC group could not, so far as I can see, have compelled him to sue in England, and would have had to incur the inconvenience and expense of contesting the claim in Texas in any event. The only additional expenses which the JMC group will have incurred if the plaintiff is now allowed to go on in Texas after beginning an action in England and later discontinuing it are the costs incurred by the defendants in the English action. These costs, however, are recoverable by the defendants from the plaintiff under RSC Ord 62, r 10, so that they can be disregarded.

It follows that, if the scales are to be tilted in favour of granting an injunction against the plaintiff, it must be by reason of other factors in the case which would make it just that this should happen. A number of such other factors were indeed relied on by the defendants and it is necessary that I should now state what they are and consider what weight, if any, should be given to them.

One matter relied on by the defendants was that England is the natural and proper forum for the determination of the claim. As to this, I would accept that England is a natural and proper forum for two reasons: first, the accident took place in an English port, and, second, much of the medical evidence is to be found, immediately at any rate, in this country. The plaintiff, however, is not English but Portuguese, and the JMC group by which he was employed is based, directly or indirectly, in Texas. In these circumstances I consider that Texas is also a natural and proper forum for the determination of the claim; no more so, perhaps, than England, but no less so either.

A second matter relied on by the defendants was that the second defendants had made an admission of liability in the English action which would prejudice the JMC group in the action in Texas. If this was a case in which the employers had any reasonable prospect of success on the issue of liability for compensatory damages at least, there might be something in the point. On the evidence about the accident, however, it is clear beyond doubt that it was caused by negligence of the ship's chief engineer for which the employers must be vicariously liable, whether the claim is determined in England or Texas. In these circumstances I do not consider that the likelihood of any prejudice to the JMC group arising from the admission has been made out.

A third matter relied on by the defendants, and relied on as being of great weight, was the receipt by the plaintiff of two interim payments in the action in England. With regard to these there is a curious situation. Two interim payments were made under RSC Ord 29, rr 9 to 12. The first payment was for £7,250, made pursuant to an order dated 22nd March 1978. This was a consent order asked for by the plaintiff's solicitors largely at the prompting of the defendants' solicitors. The second payment was for £20,000 made pursuant to an order (not by consent) dated 8th December 1978. The purpose of the second payment was to enable the plaintiff to buy a plot of land and build a suitable prefabricated bungalow on it.

The question arises whether, following the discontinuance of the action on 15th May 1979, these interim payments became repayable. Examination of the relevant rules reveals a strange lacuna in them. RSC Ord 29, r 9 defines an interim payment as meaning a payment on account of damages in respect of personal injuries which a defendant may be held liable to pay to a plaintiff. Rule 12 provides that one situation in which interim payments may be ordered is where a defendant has admitted liability for a plaintiff's claim. Rule 16 provides for adjustment of the amount payable on final judgment or order by taking into account any interim payments previously made. There is, however, no rule covering the situation where interim payments are made by a defendant to a plaintiff, and the plaintiff, being entitled to do so, then discontinues the action without leave, so that the stage of final judgment or order is never reached.

It seems to me that, even though there is no express rule in Ord 29 authorising the court to order repayment in such circumstances, the court must have inherent jurisdiction, in the interests of justice, to do so. The payments are ordered and made on account of a sum to be awarded on final judgment or order. If, by the choice of the plaintiff who has received them, there will never be a final judgment or order, justice requires that he should repay them.

While it follows from what I have just said that I consider that the court has power in the present case to order the plaintiff to repay the interim payments, the question whether it has such power or not does not really matter. This is because counsel for the plaintiff has indicated that his client is willing to repay the interim payments, and will either submit to an order to repay them if the court has power to make it, or else give an undertaking to repay them if the court has no such power.

It is clear that any repayment of the interim payments would in practice be financed not by the plaintiff himself but by his US attorneys by way of advance against his ultimate recovery in Texas. This was objected to as improper by the defendants; but I do not see that, if the interim payments are repaid, it matters from what source the repayment, so long as it is authorised by the plaintiff, is made. The point is one which relates, and relates only to the propriety of the professional conduct of the plaintiff's US attorneys, a matter which, for reasons which I shall develop later, is in my view outside the purview of this court.

The defendants' case with regard to these interim payments was really this. The plaintiff had, it was said, come to the English court and there gained an important advantage which he could not have gained if he had sued his employers only in Texas.

Then, having gained that important advantage, he had abandoned the English court and
gone off to the Texas court in order to recover there much higher final damages than he a
could have got by continuing in the English court. By so acting he was getting, or trying
to get, the best of both worlds, and it was unjust to the employers that he should be
allowed to do so.

I see the force of this argument. The answer to it, however, seems to me to be that, if
the interim payments are repaid, the employers will be no worse off in this respect than
if the English action had never been begun. No injustice to the employers in relation to b
the interim payments will, therefore, inure.

A fourth matter relied on for the defendants was that, following the discontinuance of
the plaintiff's action in England, he would be entitled, if the Texas court declined
jurisdiction, to begin a further action here, and that it was unjust that he should be able
to keep his options open in this way.

The practical position with regard to this matter is as follows. The plaintiff has issued c
a fresh writ here to protect his position in the event of the Texas court declining
jurisdiction. This possibility is, however, extremely remote. The Texas court has, since
the hearing before Parker J in November 1979, dismissed applications by the defendants
there to stay the action on jurisdictional grounds. We have been told that this decision
may be open to review on a final appeal after trial, but there was no evidence to show
that, if such a review took place, a reversal of the decision was at all likely. In these d
circumstances it seems extremely unlikely that the plaintiff would ever wish to prosecute
the further action begun by the protective writ referred to earlier.

In so far, however, as the existence of this further action poses a threat, even if a remote
one, to the defendants, it can, I think, be taken care of by ordering a stay of the action
concerned. I understand counsel for the plaintiff to be willing to submit to such an order
being made forthwith. e

The defendants directed a good deal of criticism at the conduct of the plaintiff's US
attorneys. They were, of course, retained by the plaintiff on a contingency fee basis.
This is normal practice in the United States, and no objection could properly be taken to
it. The US attorneys are, however, helping to finance the plaintiff in other ways, first, by
agreeing to pay his salary if his employers cease doing so, and, second, a point to which
I have already referred earlier, by offering to repay the interim payments if that should f
become necessary.

Evidence was adduced to show that, in acting in these last two ways, the attorneys
might be in breach of one or more of the codes of professional conduct (those of the
American Bar Association and the Texas Bar Association) by which their behaviour
should be governed.

In my opinion, this court is not concerned with, and ought not to inquire into, g
questions of that kind. The plaintiff has done what he has done, in suing his employers
in Texas and in discontinuing his action here, on the combined advice of his English
solicitors and counsel on the one hand and his US attorneys on the other. If the latter
have in some way offended against the professional codes which apply to them in their
own country, it must be left to the courts of that country or the associations concerned
to take such action, if any, as they think fit. h

In this connection it is to be observed that maintenance has never been a ground for
staying an action in England: see *Mackey v James Henry Monks (Preston) Ltd* [1918] AC 59
at 91 per Lord Parker. Even less can it be a ground for restraining proceedings in another
forum elsewhere.

Accordingly I do not consider that the conduct of the plaintiff's attorneys, so far as it
is criticised by the defendants, is a relevant matter to be weighed in the scales against j
him.

Having weighed in one scale the very great advantage to the plaintiff of suing his
employers in Texas rather than in England and in the other scale all the various matters
relied on by the defendants as being disadvantages to them of his being allowed to do so,
or as otherwise making it unjust that he should be allowed to do so, I have reached the
conclusion that the balance comes down clearly in the plaintiff's favour.

I am not persuaded that, provided the interim payments are repaid, and the protective
a action recently begun by the plaintiff here is stayed, there is anything unjust about the plaintiff being allowed to continue his proceedings in Texas. On the contrary I think that justice requires that, subject to these two matters, he should be left free to do so.

Since I should not think it right, assuming the court had jurisdiction to do so, to grant the injunction sought by the defendants, it is unnecessary for me to decide the difficult questions which I posed earlier as to the effect of the discontinuance of the action on that
b jurisdiction. I shall, therefore, express no opinion one way or the other on those questions.

For the reasons which I have given, and subject to the two conditions which I have mentioned, I would allow the appeal and set aside the orders of the judge made on 19th November 1979.

c *Appeal allowed. Injunction discharged. Order striking out the notice of discontinuance set aside. Court order to include terms for stay of plaintiff's second protective writ and repayment by the plaintiff of the interim payments of £27,250 (not to be drawn up for 14 days to allow offer or tender of that amount to be made to defendants). Leave to appeal to the House of Lords.*

Solicitors: *B M Birnberg & Co* (for the plaintiff); *Clyde & Co* (for the defendants).

d Sumra Green Barrister.

Marren (Inspector of Taxes) v Ingles

HOUSE OF LORDS

e LORD WILBERFORCE, VISCOUNT DILHORNE, LORD SALMON, LORD FRASER OF TULLYBELTON AND LORD RUSSELL OF KILLOWEN

18th, 19th, 23rd JUNE, 24th JULY 1980

f *Capital gains tax – Disposal of assets – Capital sum derived from assets notwithstanding no asset acquired by person paying sum – Sale of shares in private company – Consideration to consist of fixed sum payable immediately and further unascertainable sum payable on future contingency by reference to specified formula – Whether right to receive further sum an asset – Whether right a 'debt' – Whether there was a disposal of asset when further sum became payable – Finance Act 1965, s 22(1)(3), Sch 7, para 11(1).*

On 15th September 1970 the taxpayer sold shares in a private company in consideration of an immediate payment of £750 per share plus the right to receive a sum ('half the
g profit') which was one-half of the amount by which the market price of the shares on flotation of the company, should flotation occur, exceeded £750. On 5th December 1972, when the right matured, the taxpayer accordingly received from the purchaser the sum of £2,825 per share. The Crown claimed that the taxpayer's right to receive half the profit was an 'asset' within s 22(1)[a] of the Finance Act 1965, that when it matured a 'capital sum [was] derived from' it within s 22(3)[b] of that Act so as to give rise to a deemed
h disposal under that subsection, and that the taxpayer was chargeable to tax in the year 1972–73 on the gain accruing to him from such a disposal. The taxpayer appealed, contending that, although the value on 15th September 1970 of the right to receive half the profit fell to be included in the computation of the gain on the sale of the shares on that date, the receipt of half the profit on 5th December 1972 did not give rise to a charge to tax in the year 1972–73. The taxpayer contended alternatively that the right to
j receive half the profit was a 'debt' to which para 11[c] of Sch 7 to the 1965 applied, and consequently was exempt from liability to tax. The Special Commissioners allowed the taxpayer's appeal holding that when an asset was sold for a deferred payment the 1965

a Section 22(1), so far as material, is set out at p 100*a*, post
b Section 22(3), so far as material, is set out at p 97*g* and p 98*c*, post
c Paragraph 11, so far as material, is set out at p 101*bc*, post

Act did not treat such consideration as a separate asset, and that such consideration was not a debt within para 11. The judge dismissed the Crown's appeal, holding that the *a* operation of s 22(3) was confined exclusively to cases where no asset was acquired. The Court of Appeal allowed the Crown's appeal, holding that the right to half the profit was an 'asset' within s 22(1), that when the taxpayer became entitled to receive it there was a deemed disposal of that asset giving rise to a chargeable gain by virtue of s 22(3), and that the taxpayer's right to it did not amount to a 'debt' within para 11(1). The taxpayer appealed. *b*

Held – The appeal would be dismissed for the following reasons—

(1) 'Asset' in s 22(1) of the 1965 Act was defined in the widest terms to mean all forms of property and was apt to include the incorporeal right to money's worth which was part of the consideration given for the shares in 1970. Furthermore, that right was properly to be régarded as a separate asset and not simply as a deferred part of the price of the shares. It followed that, since the right was an asset, the sum which the taxpayer received *c* was 'derived from' the asset, and there was therefore, by virtue of s 22(3), a disposal of the asset 'notwithstanding that no asset [was] acquired by the person paying the capital sum', those words being words not of limitation but of extension, the purpose of which was to establish a 'disposal' in cases to which the subsection would not otherwise apply and in which a 'disposal' would not ordinarily be thought to exist, so that s 22(3) could apply whether or not an asset was acquired. Accordingly, the sum received by the taxpayer *d* when his right to half the profit matured represented proceeds on the disposal of an asset liable to capital gains tax (see p 97*j*, p 98*abef*, p 99*bc* and p 100*c* to p 101*b* and *j*, post); dictum of Walton J in *Inland Revenue Comrs v Montgomery* [1975] 1 All ER at 671 disapproved.

(2) The liability in respect of half the profit, being a possible liability to pay an unidentifiable sum at an unascertainable date, was not a 'debt' within para 11(1) of Sch *e* 7 to the 1965 Act (see p 98*g* to p 99*c* and p 101*d* to *j*, post).

Notes

For capital sums derived from assets where no asset is acquired, see 5 Halsbury's Laws (4th Edn) para 38.

For the Finance Act 1965, s 22, Sch 7, para 11, see 34 Halsbury's Statutes (3rd Edn) 877, *f* 956.

With effect from 6th April 1979 s 22(1), (3) of, and para 11 of Sch 7 to, the 1965 Act have been replaced by ss 19(1), 20(1) and 134(1)–(4) of the Capital Gains Tax Act 1979.

Cases referred to in opinions

Inland Revenue Comrs v Montgomery [1975] 1 All ER 664, [1975] Ch 266, [1975] 2 WLR 326, [1975] STC 182, 49 Tax Cas 679, 53 ATC 392, [1974] TR 377, Digest (Cont Vol *g* D) 477, *1452 h*.

Mortimore v Inland Revenue Comrs (1864) 2 H & C 838, 33 LJ Ex 263, 10 LT 655, 159 ER 347, 35 Digest (Repl) 362, *654*.

O'Brien (Inspector of Taxes) v Benson's Hosiery (Holdings) Ltd [1979] 3 All ER 652, [1980] AC 562, [1979] 3 WLR 572, [1979] STC 735, HL, Digest (Cont Vol E) 304, *1452 e(v)*.

O'Driscoll v Manchester Insurance Committee [1915] 3 KB 499, 85 LJKB 83, 113 LT 683, 79 *h* JP 553, 13 LGR 1156, CA, 21 Digest (Repl) 734, *2269*.

Appeal

The taxpayer, James Leslie Ingles, appealed against an order of the Court of Appeal (Ormrod, Templeman LJJ and Sir David Cairns) ([1979] STC 637, [1979] 1 WLR 1131) dated 14th May 1979 allowing an appeal by the Crown against an order of Slade J ([1979] *j* STC 58, [1979] 1 WLR 1131) dated 10th July 1978 dismissing its appeal by way of case stated from the determination of the Commissioners for the Special Purposes of the Income Tax Acts allowing an appeal by the taxpayer against assessments to capital gains tax for the years 1970–71 in the sum of £119,124 and for the year 1972–73 in the sum of £21,000. The facts are set out in the opinion of Lord Wilberforce.

Leolin Price QC and *D J Ritchie* for the taxpayer.
Michael Nolan QC and *C H McCall* for the Crown.

Their Lordships took time for consideration.

24th July. The following opinions were delivered.

LORD WILBERFORCE. My Lords, in this appeal the taxpayer, Mr J L Ingles, is contesting an assessment to capital gains tax which arises out of a contract made in September 1970. He succeeded before the Special Commissioners and in the High Court (Slade J) ([1979] STC 58, [1979] 1 WLR 1131) but lost in the Court of Appeal ([1979] STC 637, [1979] 1 WLR 1131). The transaction giving rise to the claim for tax is comparatively simple; not so the relevant provisions of the Finance Act 1965.

By a contract of 15th September 1970 the taxpayer, as one of several vendors, agreed to sell to the Industrial and Commercial Finance Corpn Ltd ('ICFC') 69 shares in J L Ingles (Holdings) Ltd. For 41 of these shares ICFC agreed to pay a cash price of £1,500 per share. For the remaining 28 shares ICFC agreed to pay an immediate cash price of £750 per share plus a sum to be paid at a future date defined as 'half of the profit'. This was to be one-half of the amount by which the sale price should exceed £750. The sale price was, broadly, to represent the middle market price on the first day of dealings after a flotation of the company, if a flotation should occur. Thus, for the 28 shares in question, there was a consideration consisting of (i) an immediate ascertained cash sum and (ii) a conditional and unquantified amount payable at an unascertained future date.

In fact there was a flotation in November 1972 and dealings commenced on 5th December 1972. On that date (allowing for a subdivision which had occurred of the shares) the 'half of the profit' amounted to £2,825 per (original) share. The question is whether, on that date, or when the money was paid, a charge to capital gains tax arose by reference to the sum receivable by the taxpayer. The exact amount of the tax (if any) remains to be fixed.

The contentions are as follows. The taxpayer focuses attention on 15th September 1970, the date of the agreement. He accepts that there was on that date a 'disposal' of all 69 shares, and agrees that a charge to capital gains tax then arose. As regards the 28 shares, this tax, he contends (and I do not understand the Crown to differ) should be based on the cash sum of £750 plus the value, to be assessed as on that date, of his contingent right to receive the deferred price less, of course, the cost of the shares, apparently £1 per share. This, he says, represents the totality of his liability in respect of the 28 shares. The Crown, on the other hand, while claiming tax for the year 1970–71 on the basis already described, makes an additional claim for 1972–73 based on the deferred consideration received in that year. They base this claim on s 22(3) of the Finance Act 1965, the relevant part of which reads:

> '... there is for the purposes of this Part of this Act a disposal of assets by their owner where any capital sum is derived from assets notwithstanding that no asset is acquired by the person paying the capital sum ...'

The taxpayer contends that this subsection does not apply, briefly because an asset was acquired by ICFC, namely the shares. In the alternative, if the subsection is capable of applying, he says that he is taken out of it by para 11(1) of Sch 7:

> 'Where a person incurs a debt to another ... no chargeable gain shall accrue to that [i e the original] creditor ... on a disposal of the debt, except in the case of the [sic] debt on a security ...'

The first question, that concerning s 22(3), involves consideration of the words 'notwithstanding that no asset is acquired ...', for the rest of the paragraph gives rise to no difficulty. There was an asset in the form of the obligation (a chose in action) to pay the deferred consideration. The deferred consideration when it was paid, in 1972, was, it is difficult to deny, a capital sum derived from that asset. Section 22(1)(*a*) of the 1965 Act expressly provides that incorporeal property, of which a chose in action is an undoubted example, is an asset for the purposes of the tax. I do not think that there is any doubt or problem up to this point. But the question remains whether the taxpayer can succeed in the contention that the words 'notwithstanding that no asset is acquired' introduce a condition of a limiting character, with the result if an asset *is acquired* the subsection does not apply. For the purposes of this argument I shall assume that an asset was acquired by the payer of the capital (viz ICFC), though there is much to be said for the contrary view and indeed the Court of Appeal accepted it. Support for the taxpayer's contention is given by a passage from the judgment of Walton J in *Inland Revenue Comrs v Montgomery* [1975] 1 All ER 664 at 671, [1975] Ch 266 at 271–272, which was followed and applied by Slade J and which led him to accept the taxpayer's contention. But I regret that I am unable to agree. Section 22(3), after the provision which I have quoted, goes on to provide some examples to which in particular the subsection is stated to apply. These are:

> '(*a*) capital sums received by way of compensation for any kind of damage or injury to assets or for the loss, destruction or dissipation of assets or for any depreciation or risk of depreciation of an asset, (*b*) capital sums received under a policy of insurance of the risk of any kind of damage or injury to, or the loss or depreciation of, assets, (*c*) capital sums received in return for forfeiture or surrender of rights, or for refraining from exercising rights, and (*d*) capital sums received as consideration for use or exploitation of assets.'

Now it is obvious that in some, if not most, of these examples there is the possibility that an asset *may* be acquired by the person paying the capital sum. The clearest of these is (*d*), if the sum is paid for the grant of a licence or a profit; but also under (*b*), if the payer of the sum acquires rights by subrogation, or under (*a*) if after payment of damages the property in respect of which they were paid vests in the payer. The observations of Walton J in *Inland Revenue Comrs v Montgomery* do not take account of these possibilities (to which others could be added) and to that extent must be too wide. But, apart from this, I cannot read the words in question ('notwithstanding . . .' etc) as pointing in the direction desired by the taxpayer. In my understanding they are evidently words not of limitation but of extension, the purpose of which is to apply the subsection (so as to establish a 'disposal') to cases to which it would not otherwise apply and in which a 'disposal' would not naturally be thought to exist. In other words they mean, in my opinion, 'Whether or not an asset is acquired'. With this meaning, the examples given in paras (*a*) to (*d*) easily fit.

I therefore consider that, in the absence of a contrary or exempting provision, s 22(3) applies to the case.

Then is the taxpayer exempted by para 11(1) of Sch 7? This is a provision of notable obscurity, the purpose and philosophy of which it is difficult to detect. It has to be examined at two points in time.

First, was there a debt in September 1970? In my opinion there was not. No case was cited, and I should be surprised if one could be found, in which a contingent right (which might never be realised) to receive an unascertainable amount of money at an unknown date has been considered to be a debt; and no meaning however untechnical of that word could, to my satisfaction, include such a right. The legislation does, of course, make provision for debts not immediately payable; it does so by the draconian method of charging them, when a charge arises, without any allowance for deferral (see Sch 6, para 14(5)); and I would, for the purpose of argument, be prepared to agree that a contingent debt might come within the paragraph. In *Mortimore v Inland Revenue Comrs* (1864) 2 H & C 838, 159 ER 347, a case concerned with stamp duty, Martin B so held. But from this it would be a large step to hold to be included an unascertainable sum payable, if a contingency happens, at an unascertainable date, a step which I am unable to take. I adopt in this part of the case, as did the Court of Appeal, the reasoning of the learned judge.

Then, second, was there a debt on 5th December 1972 when the contingency arrived, the date became fixed and the amount became ascertained? I think there was, though I am not so sure that a debt was then 'incurred'. But it remains the fact that the amount of the debt was derived from the asset (the chose in action) created in 1972, and is sought to be charged on that basis, under s 22(3). I cannot accept that the exemption in para 11(1) of Sch 7 applies in such a case. If it were otherwise, and if the taxpayer's contention

were correct, no charge under s 22 could arise in any case where the person making the
a disposal did not receive immediate payment. That would largely nullify the section.
Whatever para 11(1) does mean, it cannot have been intended to have so wide an effect.
I think that the Crown is correct in analysing this transaction into an acquisition of an
asset (viz a chose in action) in 1970 from which a capital sum arose in 1972 and that there
is no question of a debt being disposed of at any time.

I would dismiss the appeal.

b

VISCOUNT DILHORNE. My Lords, as I agree with all that my noble and learned friend Lord Wilberforce has said in his speech which I have seen in draft, there is no point in my writing a speech to the same effect.

For the reasons he gives this appeal should be dismissed.

c **LORD SALMON.** My Lords, I have had the advantage of reading in draft the speech
of my noble and learned friend Lord Wilberforce with which I entirely agree. I would
therefore dismiss the appeal.

LORD FRASER OF TULLYBELTON. My Lords, this appeal raises questions of
construction of the capital gains tax provisions in Part III of the Finance Act 1965. They
d arise out of an agreement made on 15th September 1970 between the taxpayer and two
other persons ('the vendors') on one side and a company, ICFC ('the purchaser'), on the
other. All three vendors were parties to the proceedings in the courts below, but in order
to save costs it has been agreed that this appeal will govern all three cases. Nevertheless,
I find it convenient to refer to the vendors collectively and to the total number of their
shares.

e By the agreement the vendors agreed to sell and the purchaser agreed to purchase 167
'A' ordinary shares of £1 each in a private company, J L Ingles (Holdings) Ltd.
Completion took place on 15th September 1970. As to 107 of the shares the price was
£1,500 per share. It was duly paid and no question arises about it. As to the remaining
60 shares, of which 28 belonged to the taxpayer, the price was agreed at £750 plus 'half
of the profit'. The £750 was paid in cash on completion. The expression 'half of the
f profit' was defined as meaning one-half of the amount by which 'the sale price' exceeded
£750. 'The sale price' was elaborately defined according to various possible future
events, one of which was flotation of the company by the grant of permission to deal in
its shares on a recognised stock exchange in the United Kingdom before 31st December
1975. Flotation did take place on 29th November 1972, and the definition of the sale
price which came into effect in consequence of that event was the middle market price
g of the shares on the first day of dealings after flotation, namely 5th December 1972. By
that date the original shares had been subdivided and a scrip issue had been made, with
the result that the original 'A' ordinary shares had come to be represented by 480,000
shares of 5p each in the company. The middle market price on 5th December 1972 was
equivalent to a price of £6,400 for each of the original shares. 'Half of the profit'
therefore was £2,825, being one-half of the amount by which £6,400 exceeds £750.
h The figures are not in dispute.

The agreement gave rise to immediate disposals of all 167 shares, within the meaning
of the capital gains tax provisions of the 1965 Act. The cost of acquisition by the vendors
had been £1 per share. Accordingly, the vendors were assessed to capital gains tax on the
107 shares sold at £1,500 each on a chargeable gain of £1,499 per share. As to that there
is no dispute. The dispute arises in connection with the other 60 shares (referred to in the
j agreement and hereinafter as 'the shareholdings'). It is agreed that, in respect of the
shareholdings, the vendors ought to have been assessed on the footing that in the fiscal
year 1970–71 they had made a chargeable gain of the difference between the cost price
of £1 and the consideration received for each share, made up of £750 in cash plus the
value on 15th September 1970 of their contingent right to half of the profit. The value
of that right on 15th September 1970 has not yet been assessed; indeed, there is a
suggestion that it may be impossible to assess, and nothing that I say is intended to
indicate any opinion on the valuation of the right as at 15th September 1970.

Capital gains tax was imposed by s 19(1) of the 1965 Act on chargeable gains accruing to a person 'on the disposal of assets'. Section 22(1) of the Act provides, inter alia, as follows: 'All forms of property shall be assets for the purposes of this Part of this Act . . . including—(*a*) options, debts and incorporeal property generally . . .' Section 22(3) is the provision on which the Crown's claim is directly based. The relevant part of it has been quoted by my noble and learned friend Lord Wilberforce.

The Crown has made assessments for the fiscal year 1972–73 in respect of the receipt by the vendors of the capital sum equivalent to £2,825 per original share. The assessment was made on the basis that on 5th December 1972 the vendors made a disposal of a separate asset consisting of the right to receive that sum. The claim by the Crown was negatived by the Special Commissioners and, on appeal by stated case, by Slade J, but the Court of Appeal (Templeman, Ormrod LJJ and Sir David Cairns) reversed that decision and upheld the claim.

The first question is whether the right to half of the profit is properly to be regarded as a separate asset, or simply as a deferred part of the price of the shareholdings. In my opinion, the former view is correct. 'Asset' is defined in s 22(1) in the widest terms to mean all forms of property, and it has been construed accordingly in *O'Brien (Inspector of Taxes) v Benson's Hosiery Ltd* [1979] 3 All ER 652 at 655, [1980] AC 562 at 572 by Lord Russell. It is therefore apt to include the incorporeal right to money's worth which was part of the consideration given for the shareholdings in 1970. The vendors could have disposed of the right at any time after 15th September 1970 by selling it or giving it away and assigning it. If they had done so, there would have been an actual disposal of an asset and the vendors would have been liable for capital gains tax on the amount, if any, by which the price or value of the asset at the date of disposal exceeded its value on 15th September 1970. Of course, if the price or value had been less than the value on 15th September 1970, they would have made a chargeable loss which they could have set off against gains in the same or future fiscal years. So there is nothing unfair in treating it as an asset. In fact, they did not dispose of the right but they held it until it matured on 5th December 1972. If the right was an 'asset', then the sum which the vendors received on that date was 'derived from' the asset. There was therefore, by virtue of s 22(3), a disposal of the asset, notwithstanding that no asset was acquired by the 'person paying the capital sum', the purchaser. The sum was paid to satisfy or extinguish the right and not as any part of the consideration for the shareholdings; full consideration for them had already been given on 15th September 1970. The capital sum is therefore not in any relevant sense derived from the shareholdings, and the taxpayer's complaint that he was being assessed to capital gains tax twice over on the price is misconceived. The position is no different in principle from what it would have been if the vendors had received new shares in another company as part of the consideration for the shareholdings and had later disposed of the new shares.

In my opinion, Slade J was mistaken in treating the receipt of the shareholdings by the purchasers as relevant for the purposes of s 22(3). The reference there to no asset being 'acquired by' the person paying the capital sum must be to an asset acquired in exchange for the capital sum, and the shareholdings were not acquired by the purchaser in exchange for the capital sum paid in December 1972. The material question is not whether acquisition of the asset and payment of the capital sum were contemporaneous or not but whether one was consideration for the other. Moreover Slade J, following a decision of Walton J in *Inland Revenue Comrs v Montgomery* [1975] 1 All ER 664, [1975] Ch 266 held that the words 'notwithstanding that no asset is acquired by the person paying the capital sum' in s 22(3) meant that the application of the subsection was confined to cases where no asset was acquired. I am unable to agree. The ordinary meaning of the word 'notwithstanding' according to the Shorter English Dictionary is 'despite, in spite of'. One might perhaps suggest also 'whether or not'. It is a word of extension, not of limitation, and I see no reason to read it here in a limiting sense. The comprehensive provisions of sub-ss (1) and (2) of s 22 may render it not strictly necessary for sub-s (3) to apply to cases where an asset is acquired by the person paying the capital sum, but, even if there is some overlapping, that is not uncommon in fiscal legislation in order to avoid leaving a loophole. In my opinion sub-s (3) applies whether or not an asset

is acquired by the person paying the capital sum. That construction is, if anything,
a fortified by reference to the examples given in paras (*a*) to (*d*) of sub-s (3), some of which are of cases where payment of the capital sum might well attract corresponding assets. Thus, looking at para (*b*), where a capital sum is paid under a policy of insurance the insurers will often acquire by subrogation an asset consisting of the assured's right of action against a wrongdoer. Accordingly, I consider that the decision in *Inland Revenue Comrs v Montgomery* on this point was erroneous.

b There remains the second question in the case: was the vendor's right to 'half of the profit' a debt in the sense of para 11 of Sch 7 to the 1965 Act, which provides as follows:

> '(1) Where a person incurs a debt to another, whether in sterling or in some other currency, no chargeable gain shall accrue to that (that is the original) creditor or his legatee on a disposal of the debt, except in the case of the debt on a security . . .
>
> c '(2) Subject to the provisions of paragraphs 5 and 6 of this Schedule (and subject to the foregoing sub-paragraph) the satisfaction of a debt or part of it . . . shall be treated as a disposal of the debt or of that part by the creditor made at the time when the debt or that part is satisfied . . .'

If this asset was a 'debt' the vendors were the original creditors and sub-para (1) would therefore apply, so that no chargeable gain would accrue to them. The meaning of the
d word debt depends very much on its context. It is capable of including a contingent debt which may never become payable: see *Mortimore v Inland Revenue Comrs* (1864) 2 H & C 838, 159 ER 347. It is also capable of including a sum of which the amount is not ascertained: see *O'Driscoll v Manchester Insurance Committee* [1915] 3 KB 499. But I agree with Slade J and with Templeman LJ, both of whom held that the word 'debt' in para 11 does not apply to the obligation of the purchaser under this agreement, which was
e described by Templeman LJ as 'a *possible* liability to pay an *unidentifiable* sum at an *unascertainable* date' (see [1979] STC 637 at 639, [1979] 1 WLR 1131 at 1147). The words to which I have added emphasis bring out the three factors of this obligation which cumulatively prevent its being a debt in the sense of para 11. Further, the reference to a person who 'incurs' a debt 'whether in sterling or in some other currency' points, in my opinion, towards the debt being definite, or at least ascertainable, in amount. Similarly,
f para 14 of Sch 6 to the 1965 Act, dealing with consideration payable by instalments which, by para 14(5), is to be brought into account initially without regard to, inter alia, 'a risk of any part of the consideration being irrecoverable', seems clearly to be referring to consideration of an ascertained amount. It is appropriate for dealing with a debt which cannot increase in value but may decrease if it proves to be partly irrecoverable. Both para 11 of Sch 7 and para 14 of Sch 6 are to be contrasted with s 22(3) which applies
g to an asset which might either rise or fall in value.

Finally, it was suggested that, even if the right to receive half of the profits was not a debt at first, it became one when it was quantified and became immediately payable on 5th December 1972. I agree with Slade J and Templeman LJ that that cannot be right because it would lead to absurd results. Every obligation that is ultimately discharged by a money payment must be quantified before payment, and on this argument, capital
h gains tax would always be excluded when a definite price became payable. In my opinion, para 11 of Sch 7 only applies to an obligation which has been a debt from the time it came into existence, or at least from the time when it was acquired by the taxpayer.

I would refuse the appeal.

j **LORD RUSSELL OF KILLOWEN.** My Lords I have had the advantage of reading in draft the speech delivered by my noble and learned friend Lord Fraser. I agree with it and with his conclusion that this appeal should be dismissed.

Appeal dismissed.

Solicitors: *Hancock & Willis*, agents for *Wragge & Co*, Birmingham (for the taxpayer); *Solicitor of Inland Revenue.*

Rengan Krishnan Esq Barrister.

Customs and Excise Commissioners v George Wimpey & Co Ltd

COURT OF APPEAL, CIVIL DIVISION
LORD DENNING MR, WALLER AND DUNN LJJ
12th, 13th MARCH 1980

Customs and excise – Hydrocarbon oils – Rebate – Penalty – Commissioners empowered to recover 'amount equal to rebate' in addition to penalty if rebate wrongly allowed – Whether 'amount equal to rebate' a penalty – Whether commissioners restricted to bringing proceedings in court of summary jurisdiction – Hydrocarbon Oil (Customs & Excise) Act 1971, s 11(1) – Customs and Excise Act 1952, s 283(1).

The provision in s 11(1)[a] of the Hydrocarbon Oil (Customs & Excise) Act 1971 that 'the Commissioners [of Customs and Excise] may recover from [a person who uses heavy oil in contravention of s 10(3)[b] of that Act] an amount equal to the rebate on like oil at the rate in force at the time of the contravention' is not a penalty despite the fact that it is immediately preceded by provision for liability 'to a penalty of three times the value of the oil or £100, whichever is the greater' for contravention and despite also the fact that the marginal note to s 11 refers to 'Penalties for misuse of rebated heavy oil'. Accordingly the commissioners may recover an amount so claimed as wrongly allowed rebate by proceedings in the High Court and are not restricted by s 283(1)[c] of the Customs and Excise Act 1952 to bringing proceedings in a court of summary jurisdiction (see p 104 *f* to p 105 *b* and *d* to *f* and p 107 *a* to *c*, post).

Notes

For the Customs and Excise Act 1952, s 283, see 9 Halsbury's Statutes (3rd Edn) 187.

For the Hydrocarbon Oil (Customs & Excise) Act 1971, ss 10, 11, see 41 ibid 498, 499.

As from 1st April 1979 s 283(1) of the 1952 Act has been replaced by s 147(1) of the Customs and Excise Management Act 1979 and ss 10(3) and 11 of the 1971 Act have been replaced by ss 12(2) and 13 of the Hydrocarbon Oil Duties Act 1979.

Cases referred to in judgments

Barraclough v Brown [1897] AC 615, [1895–9] All ER Rep 239, 66 LJQB 672, 76 LT 797, 62 JP 275, 8 Asp MLC 290, 2 Com Cas 249, HL, 44 Digest (Repl) 345, *1802*.

Pyx Granite Co Ltd v Ministry of Housing and Local Government [1959] 3 All ER 1, [1960] AC 260, [1959] 3 WLR 346, 123 JP 429, 58 LGR 1, 10 P & CR 319, HL, 45 Digest (Repl) 336, *37*.

Cases also cited

Brown v Allweather Mechanical Grouting Co Ltd [1953] 1 All ER 474, [1954] 2 QB 443, DC.

Customs and Excise Comrs v Sokolow's Trustee [1954] 2 All ER 5, [1954] 2 QB 336.

Director of Public Prosecutions v Schildkamp [1969] 3 All ER 1640, [1971] AC 1, HL.

Farrell v Alexander [1976] 2 All ER 721, [1977] AC 59, HL.

Qualter, Hall & Co Ltd v Board of Trade [1961] 3 All ER 389, [1962] Ch 273, CA.

Interlocutory appeal

By writ issued on 18th September 1978, the plaintiffs, the Commissioners of Customs and Excise, claimed against the defendants, George Wimpey & Co Ltd ('Wimpeys') (i) a sum of £1,228·75 being a rebate of duty paid to Wimpeys in respect of the operation by

a Section 11(1), so far as material, is set out at p 104 *b c*, post
b Section 10(3), so far as material, is set out at p 105 *g h*, post
c Section 283(1), so far as material, is set out at p 104 *d*, post

them of tractors engaged in brushing public roads in the Newcastle area from 1971
a onwards and (ii) a declaration that if Wimpeys were using heavy oil in respect of which a rebate of duty had been allowed for the operation of tractors engaged in brushing public roads then an amount equal to the rebate so allowed was repayable to the commissioners under s 11(1) of the Hydrocarbon Oil (Customs & Excise) Act 1971. On 19th March 1979 Master Bickford-Smith ordered that the commissioners be granted leave to enter judgment for a sum to be assessed unless Wimpeys served a defence within
b 21 days. Wimpeys appealed against the order on the ground that the High Court had no jurisdiction to entertain the commissioners' claim. On 18th November 1979 May J dismissed that appeal and Wimpeys appealed to the Court of Appeal. The facts are set out in the judgment of Lord Denning MR.

Patrick Medd QC and *Graham Garner* for Wimpeys.
c *Simon Brown* for the commissioners.

LORD DENNING MR. George Wimpey & Co Ltd ('Wimpeys') are big contractors up and down the country. In the course of their work, they often leave mud and dirt about the roads. It has to be cleared up. For that purpose, they use tractors to brush the roads. Those tractors use what is called 'heavy oil'. Wimpeys have been paying tax at a
d lower rate on that 'heavy oil' on the basis that the tax is only 1p a gallon, whereas on other vehicles used on the road with heavy oil the tax is 22½p a gallon.

The Commissioners of Customs and Excise say that Wimpeys are not entitled to pay tax at a lower rate, and they claim the amount of the rebate which has been paid to them. It was not until February 1976 that the commissioners discovered what Wimpeys were doing. Then, on 19th February 1976 one of their officers went to Brunton Lane in
e Newcastle upon Tyne. He found there a tractor, registration no ELR 299J, brushing the road. He thought that the proper rate of tax had not been paid on the heavy oil used in that tractor. So he got into touch with Wimpeys in order to find out how often they had been using this tractor over the years and other tractors like it. The commissioners then estimated that the rebate of duty in respect of tractors operated in the Newcastle area from 1971 came to £1,228·75. The commissioners discovered that tractors were being
f used in the same way in other areas. They discovered one in Darlington, and another in Scotland.

Being of opinion that the proper duty had not been paid on the heavy oil, on 18th September 1978 the commissioners brought an action in law, claiming a declaration that Wimpeys had not been paying the proper amount for the fuel. That issue having been joined in the High Court, Wimpeys took the point that no such declaration could be
g obtained from the High Court. That point was argued before the judge, and it has been argued before us here today. Wimpeys say that the only remedy is for the commissioners to prosecute them in the magistrates' court, on the ground that that is the only place where the commissioners are entitled to go to recover these sums. If this contention is correct, it is to the advantage of Wimpeys. In the magistrates' court they are not compelled to give discovery, whereas in the High Court they may have to give discovery;
h and a declaration can be made against them.

Counsel for Wimpeys has put forward an interesting argument before us, with his usual care and skill. I will not go through all the numerous statutes to which we have been referred, but the Hydrocarbon Oil (Customs & Excise) Act 1971 provides for differences in tax on oil according to the vehicle in which it is used. A high rate has to be paid on heavy oil used in vehicles which are used on the roads such as motor cars. A
j low rate of tax is payable on vehicles which are used in fields and on land such as farm tractors and digging machines. In this case the eventual issue is: into what category do these tractors fall? Wimpeys say that they are digging machines, and therefore they are only obliged to pay the lower rate of tax, whereas the commissioners say they are used on the roads and ought to pay the higher rate. The issue depends on the use to which the vehicle is put.

The machinery for recovering the tax depends on ss 10 and 11 of the Hydrocarbon Oil (Customs & Excise) Act 1971. Section 10 is very complicated, but the effect of it is, that if a person does use a tractor for brushing roads without paying the proper duty on the heavy oil, he is guilty of an offence: see s 10(1) to (3). The question for us today is whether, in addition to that person being guilty of an offence, proceedings can be brought for the recovery of the amount which should be paid.

Section 11(1) provides:

> 'A person who—(*a*) uses heavy oil in contravention of section 10(3) of this Act . . . shall be liable to a penalty of three times the value of the oil or £100, whichever is the greater; and the Commissioners may recover from him an amount equal to the rebate on like oil at the rate in force at the time of the contravention.'

Counsel for Wimpeys has argued before us that the second part of that subsection, 'may recover from him an amount equal to the rebate on like oil', is hinged onto the first part. He maintains that the second part is really an additional pecuniary penalty. That section is one of the many provisions in the Customs and Excise Act 1952 and the Finance Acts dealing with offences against the Customs and Excise. Section 283(1) of the 1952 Act provides:

> '. . . any proceedings for an offence under the said Acts may be commenced at any time within, and shall not be commenced later than, three years from the date of the commission of the offence.'

And those proceedings are to be commenced before the magistrates. Section 273(1) provides: 'Without prejudice to any other provision of this Act, any amount due by way of customs or excise duty may be recovered as a debt due to the Crown.'

It was urged, and I thought at first that there was something in it, that under the Customs and Excise Acts proceedings can either be taken under s 273 of the 1952 Act for a debt due to the Crown or under s 283 as proceedings before the magistrates. And that those are the only two proceedings available. As a result of the discussion before us, I was satisfied that, although those two sections provide two methods by which money can be dealt with or recovered, nevertheless there is a third method. It is contained in the second part of s 11(1) of the Hydrocarbon Oil (Customs & Excise) Act 1971 that 'the Commissioners may recover from him an amount equal to the rebate on like oil at the rate in force at the time of the contravention.' That is a method of recovery which can be taken by the commissioners in any of the ordinary courts of the land. Indeed, I doubt very much whether they could recover the amount before the magistrates.

Although we have been through all the sections from 1935 onwards, this afternoon counsel for the commissioners drew our attention to a most interesting section. It is s 9(6) of the Finance Act 1960, which provides:

> 'Where a person contravenes the said subsection (2) in respect of any oils, then without prejudice to any penalty of forfeiture the Commissioners may recover from him an amount equal to the rebate on like oils at the rate in force at the time of the contravention.'

That is the predecessor of s 11(2) of the present 1971 consolidation Act. The words 'without prejudice to any penalty of forfeiture' show that this particular provision is not a penalty of forfeiture at all. It is open to the commissioners to recover the amount in any of the courts in the land.

In this context, counsel for the commissioners referred us to *Pyx Granite Co Ltd v Ministry of Housing and Local Government* [1959] 3 All ER 1, [1960] AC 260, and particularly to the observations of Viscount Simonds [1959] 3 All ER 1 at 6, [1960] AC 260 at 286. He distinguished *Barraclough v Brown* [1897] AC 615, [1895–9] All ER Rep 239 on the ground that there the remedy and the right were inextricably bound together: you only got the right by going to the magistrates' court. Whereas here they are not so bound together.

It is quite plain that the commissioners can recover these amounts in proceedings in the High Court. They can obtain a declaration such as they seek. They can, if need be, obtain discovery from Wimpeys as to the number of tractors they have been using and for how long. In that way they can recover the amount of duty which ought to be paid with regard to the heavy oil used in them. I see no objection to the jurisdiction of the High Court.

I would dismiss the appeal accordingly.

WALLER LJ. I agree with the judgment of Lord Denning MR. The provisions relating to hydrocarbon oil appear to be very complicated. It seems that hydrocarbon oil is divided by statute between heavy and light; and the heavy oil, if it is for home use, does not have to pay the full duty. The full duty, as Lord Denning MR has said, is 22½p; but, if it is required and used for home use, there is a rebate which reduces that 22½p to 1p; and the provisions that we are concerned to consider here are the provisions of ss 10 and 11 of the Hydrocarbon Oil (Customs & Excise) Act 1971, and in particular s 11. Lord Denning MR has already read s 11(1), the important part of it being the distinction between the words 'shall be liable to a penalty of three times the value of the oil or £100, whichever is the greater', and the words 'and the Commissioners may recover from him an amount equal to the rebate on like oil at the rate in force at the time of the contravention'.

Counsel for Wimpeys made two other points, apart from his submissions about s 273, which Lord Denning MR has already read. He submitted that this was a penalty, because it was contained in a section, namely s 11, which was headed 'Penalties for misuse of rebated heavy oil'. Secondly he submitted that it was a penalty because it was not exact compensation for the duty which was lost. He relied on the words 'an amount equal to the rebate on like oils at the rate in force at the time of the contravention'. In my judgment, looking at the section without considering the history (the history, incidentally, strengthens this conclusion), sub-s (1) of s 11 deals with the penalties and then, as a completely separate sentence, sets out this provision for recovery. Therefore it seems to me that the latter is probably not a penalty.

But when you go to the second part of the submission of counsel for Wimpeys, that the provision is not being made for exact compensation, in my judgment the conclusion is the exact opposite because, when one looks at s 10(3), which is the section creating the offence the penalties for which are set out in s 11(1), s 10(3) says this: 'No heavy oil on the delivery of which for home use rebate has been allowed . . .'; if I may just interpose there, that means that oil has arrived in this country, it has gone to a refinery, and it has come out of the refinery as a delivery of heavy oil for home use; and, therefore, instead of the 22½p which was due, there was a rebate of 21½p, leaving only 1p to be paid. So that reads:

> 'No heavy oil on the delivery of which for home use rebate has been allowed shall—(*a*) be used as fuel for a vehicle to which this section applies [and I need not worry about para (*b*)] unless an amount equal to the amount for the time being allowable in respect of rebate on like oil has been paid to the Commissioners in accordance with regulations made for the purposes of this section'

and we have been told that the regulations made for the purposes of the section require that the commissioners shall have authorised in writing such a payment to be made. One can see the common sense of the arrangement, because, if the rate of duty varies from year to year, it may be very difficult to ascertain precisely what duty has been paid; and, as counsel for the commissioners pointed out, if there is a large tank, there may be some oil in it which has borne one rate of duty and some which has borne a different rate. So s 10(3) provides that a payment should be made before the vehicle is used, being 'an amount equal to the amount for the time being allowable in respect of rebate on like oil', in other words, a current rebate. That is not only the sensible way of dealing with it, but, when the vehicle is being used without that payment being made, that is what the commissioners have actually lost. So the proviso to the second part of s 11(1) exactly defines the loss which the commissioners have made. So that strengthens the case for saying that this in not a penalty but a provision for ensuring as far as possible that the commissioners may recover that rebate which would have been made at that particular time.

I am quite satisfied that this provision is not a provision for a penalty. Furthermore, when the argument is made that this is a sum which should be recovered as part of the proceedings in a court of summary jurisdiction, there is no provision restricting this to a court of summary jurisdiction. I would reserve my opinion whether or not it is possible to recover in such proceedings. It seems improbable that it is and, in my view, the claim which is made in this case in the High Court is one which is properly made, and I would dismiss this appeal.

DUNN LJ. I agree with both judgments delivered by Lord Denning MR and Waller LJ.

Appeal dismissed. Leave to appeal to the House of Lords refused.

Solicitors: *P J Ward* (for Wimpeys); *Solicitor for the Customs and Excise.*

Sumra Green Barrister.

R v Crown Court at Croydon, ex parte Bernard

QUEEN'S BENCH DIVISION
LORD LANE CJ AND WOOLF J
6th MAY 1980

Crown Court – Appeal to Crown Court – Power of court on appeal – Appeal against conviction by magistrates – Defendant committed to Crown Court for sentence – Sentence passed on understanding that defendant did not wish to appeal against conviction – Defendant subsequently given leave to appeal out of time against conviction – Crown Court judge declining to hear appeal on ground court functus officio – Whether Crown Court having jurisdiction to hear appeal – Whether determination of sentence on committal for sentence rendering court functus officio in regard to appeal against conviction.

On 26th November 1979 the applicant was convicted of two offences by a juvenile court and was committed to the Crown Court for sentence. At the hearing in the Crown Court the judge asked the applicant's counsel whether the applicant was seeking leave to appeal against conviction as counsel had intimated that the applicant questioned the correctness of the convictions. Counsel, who took instructions from his instructing solicitors' clerk but without consulting the applicant himself, said he had no instructions to appeal against conviction. The judge sentenced the applicant to borstal training. In January 1980 the applicant told his solicitors that he wished to appeal against the convictions, and they, having investigated the case history, obtained leave from the Crown Court to appeal out of time against the convictions. The Crown Court judge before whom the matter came for hearing held he had no power to hear the appeal on the ground that, the applicant having been sentenced for the offences, there had been a final adjudication on both conviction and sentence and the court was functus officio. The applicant applied

for an order of mandamus directing the Crown Court to hear the appeal against
a conviction.

Held – The Crown Court had two separate jurisdictions in regard to a decision of justices, namely the jurisdiction to determine sentence where there had been a committal to the court for sentence and the jurisdiction to hear an appeal from the justices' decision. A decision by the Crown Court determining sentence under the jurisdiction
b on committal for sentence did not, therefore, render the court functus officio in regard to the jurisdiction to hear an appeal against conviction. It followed that an order of mandamus would be made directing the Crown Court to hear the applicant's appeal against conviction (see p 109 *e* to *h* and p 110 *a*, post).

Notes
c For the jurisdiction of the Crown Court in regard to committals for sentence and in regard to appeals from magistrates' courts, see 10 Halsbury's Laws (4th Edn) paras 876–877.

Case referred to in judgments
d *R v Faithful* [1950] 2 All ER 1251, 115 JP 20, 49 LGR 141, 34 Cr App R 220, CCA, 14(2) Digest (Repl) 714, 6000.

Application for judicial review
Peter Burchill Bernard applied, pursuant to leave of Booth J given on 9th April 1980, by notice of motion dated 11th April 1980 for an order of certiorari to bring up and quash
e an order for borstal training and a sentence of one day's detention passed on him by the Crown Court at Croydon on 20th December 1979 or alternatively for an order of mandamus directed to the Crown Court at Croydon requiring the court to hear and determine the applicant's appeal against conviction lodged by notice dated 18th January 1980. The grounds of the application were (i) that the sentence had been passed on the applicant after counsel, under a misapprehension of the true position, had informed the
f court that he had instructions not to proceed with an appeal against conviction, and (ii) that on 12th March 1980 the Crown Court had refused to entertain the applicant's appeal against conviction notwithstanding that leave to appeal out of time had been granted on 22nd January 1980. The facts are set out in the judgment of Lord Lane CJ.

David Barnard for the applicant.
g *Charles Byers* for the Metropolitan Police.

LORD LANE CJ. This is an application for judicial review pursuant to leave granted by the vacation judge on 9th April 1980.

There are two alternative remedies which are suggested in this case. One is an order
h of mandamus directed to the Crown Court at Croydon to hear the applicant's appeal. The other remedy suggested in the alternative is an order of certiorari to bring up and quash a sentence passed by a different judge at the Crown Court at Croydon in respect of the offence.

The facts of the case are unusual, but it is necessary to go into them in a little detail in order to explain how this appeal comes about. On 26th November 1979 the applicant was convicted by the Croydon Juvenile Court of two offences: assaulting a police officer
j was the first and attempting to steal a tape recorder was the second. He was committed by the justices to the Crown Court for sentence under s 28 of the Magistrates' Courts Act 1952, which reads as follows:

> '(1) Where a person is convicted by a magistrates' court of an offence punishable on summary conviction with imprisonment, then, if on the day of the conviction

> he is not less than fifteen but under twenty-one years old and is a person who, under subsections (2) and (4) of section one of the Criminal Justice Act, 1961, may be committed for a sentence of borstal training the court may commit him in custody or on bail to the Crown Court for sentence in accordance with the provisions of section twenty of the Criminal Justice Act, 1948 . . .'

That is the section brought up to date by s 56 of the Criminal Justice Act 1967 under which the justices committed him.

Before the justices and throughout the subsequent proceedings he was represented by counsel, not counsel who appears for him today, but a young man of very recent call to the Bar. It seems that after his conviction before the justices the applicant was expressing his wish to appeal against his conviction. That wish was again apparently conveyed to the solicitors who were acting for him. An employee of the solicitors' firm gave the impression to the young member of the Bar that a partner in the firm had advised against an appeal, though it seems that impression was due to a misunderstanding.

The next step in the proceedings was the appearance of the applicant before her Honour Judge Graham Hall on 20th December 1979 at the Crown Court at Croydon. All that was before that court was of course the question of sentence. Nevertheless, in his address to the judge, young counsel alleged and said that his client was still questioning the correctness of the conviction. The judge then very properly, if we may respectfully say so, asked whether the applicant wished to seek leave to appeal against conviction out of time. If everything had gone right, the young member of the Bar would have taken further instructions from his client and asked him what the true situation was. But counsel took instructions only from the solicitors' clerk who was there. He did not take the precaution of seeing the client himself, and the clerk who was attending on counsel gave the impression that the instructions of the firm's partner were that no appeal against conviction should be launched. Thereupon counsel told the judge that he had no instructions to appeal against conviction, so the hearing with regard to sentence continued.

The applicant was sent to borstal for the attempted theft and one day's detention in respect of the charge of assault. So the matter seemed to have ended.

But in January 1980 a letter was sent by the applicant to the solicitors, and in it he maintains his innocence of the offences charged against him and suggests that he still wants to appeal against the conviction because he thinks that he is in borstal for something that he never did.

That letter came to the notice of one of the partners in the firm of solicitors, who made investigations about the history of the matter and at once applied by letter to the court for leave to appeal out of time against conviction. By a letter dated 22nd January 1980 a reply came from the Crown Court saying that the judge who had heard the matter of sentence, Judge Graham Hall, had granted the required extension.

The next scene is the Crown Court at Croydon again when an appeal against conviction was sought to be launched. That was on 12th March 1980 before a recorder. When the matters were explained to the recorder he formed the view that because the applicant had been sentenced in respect of these two offences there had been a final adjudication with regard to conviction and sentence, and accordingly the court was functus officio and had no basis on which to continue.

The matter rests there. The recorder has declined to hear the appeal because he thinks the court has no power to hear it. Counsel for the applicant submits to us as his first proposition that it was the duty of the recorder to hear that appeal and he was mistaken when he came to the conclusion that he had no power.

The case which was cited to the recorder was *R v Faithful* [1950] 2 All ER 1251. The circumstances of that case appear from the headnote, which runs as follows:

> 'On Aug. 30, 1950, the applicant was committed, under the Criminal Justice Act, 1948, s. 29(1), to the County of London Quarter Sessions for sentence on his conviction of larceny by a metropolitan magistrate, and on Sept. 8 he was sentenced

to three years' corrective training. On Sept. 11 he gave notice of appeal to the
a quarter sessions against his conviction, and on Oct. 5 the appeal was dismissed.

'HELD: (i) an appeal committee of quarter sessions which meet frequently, before passing sentence on an offender after a committal under s. 29(1), should satisfy themselves that the time for appealing against the conviction has expired. If the time for appealing has not expired and the offender informs them that he intends to appeal, the committee should adjourn consideration of the sentence.

b '(ii) an appeal committee which do not meet so frequently, before passing sentence in any case in which the time for appealing against conviction has not expired, should ascertain whether the offender intends to appeal. If he informs them he intends to appeal, the committee should offer an adjournment and inform the offender of the possible delay and that he must remain in custody.'

c The passage which apparently was said to be relevant to the present case is as follows (at 1252):

'On Oct. 5 that appeal was heard by the appeal committee of quarter sessions and was dismissed. Thus, it is seen that the applicant's appeal against conviction was heard and disposed of after he had been committed for sentence and had been sentenced. That, in the view of this court, is an undesirable state of affairs.'

d

It does not seem to me that that decision is of any assistance in the present case for determining whether the court at Croydon was functus officio in the circumstances which I have related. What it does make clear, however, is this. The judge who passed the sentence at Croydon, Judge Graham Hall, acted with complete propriety in addressing the questions she did address to the applicant's counsel before passing sentence.

e The way in which the matter is put on behalf of the applicant here is this. The Crown Court has two separate forms of jurisdiction. It has the task of hearing and determining committals for sentence, the task of deciding (having inquired into all the circumstances) what is the proper sentence which should be passed on someone who has been sent from the justices to be sentenced by the Crown Court. The second duty and power which it has is the right to hear appeals from the justices.

f The submission is that a determination made under the first of those powers of duties does not render the court functus officio so far as the second form of power or duty is concerned, that is to say that the passing of a sentence does not mean that the court has finished its functions so far as the right to hear appeals against conviction is concerned. With that contention I would respectfully agree.

The suggestion made by counsel who appears in what he describes as a state of
g benevolent neutrality on behalf of the Metropolitan Police does not seem to me to be attractive, because he suggests that if the answer is as the applicant would have it then one might get a situation where the conviction has been quashed whereas the sentence still remains. He says, as in this case, one might get a person in borstal whose conviction has been quashed. The answer to that rather extraordinary proposition seems to me to be that once a conviction has gone then so has everything which depends on the
h conviction, and one of the things which depends on the conviction is the sentence. When the conviction has gone, then so has the sentence.

Consequently, it seems to me that the proper order in this case is an order of mandamus directed to the Crown Court at Croydon to hear this appeal and determine it.

In those circumstances the other alternative put forward by counsel on behalf of the applicant does not seem to me to fall for decision. He suggests that an order of certiorari
j should be directed to the Crown Court at Croydon in respect of the sentence which was imposed on the applicant by Judge Graham Hall, and that once that order of certiorari has gone and that sentence is quashed, then the applicant would be back in his previous state and could carry on his appeal thenceforward.

Whether that is a correct submission or not I do not propose to say. It is not necessary for the decision of this court. It obviously raises all sorts of difficult problems. In my judgment, the true answer to the present case is an order of mandamus directed in the way I have explained. a

WOOLF J. I agree.

Order of mandamus granted.

Solicitors: *Robert Blackford & Co* (for the applicant); *R E T Birch*. b

Denise Randall Barrister.

c

Perrot v Supplementary Benefits Commission

COURT OF APPEAL, CIVIL DIVISION d
STEPHENSON, BRIGHTMAN LJJ AND DAME ELIZABETH LANE
1st, 23rd MAY 1980

Supplementary benefit – Entitlement – Exclusion of right to benefit – Full-time remunerative work – Remunerative work – Claimant running business from home at a loss and claiming benefit – Whether 'remunerative work' meaning profitable work or merely paid work – Whether e *claimant entitled to benefit – Supplementary Benefits Act 1976, s 6.*

The claimant was entitled to, and received, supplementary benefit. However, while in receipt of benefit she commenced business as a translation agency in her own home. The business was conducted at a net loss and the claimant continued to claim benefit. The Supplementary Benefits Commission then decided that she was 'engaged in remunerative f full-time work' and therefore excluded by s 6[a] of the Supplementary Benefits Act 1976 from entitlement to benefit. The claimant's appeal to a supplementary benefit appeal tribunal was dismissed. The claimant appealed to the High Court contending, inter alia, that because her business was conducted at a loss she was not engaged in 'remunerative' work and was therefore not disqualified by s 6. The judge dismissed her appeal. She appealed to the Court of Appeal. g

Held – Although according to ordinary usage 'remunerative' could mean either 'paid' or 'profitable', in the context of s 6 of the 1976 Act it referred to work which was paid for regardless of whether that resulted in a profit to the recipient, since it would lead to imprecision and anomaly if it had to be determined whether work done by a claimant for supplementary benefit was profitable, particularly as calculations for benefit were h made on a weekly basis. It followed that since the claimant was being paid, she was engaged in remunerative work for the purposes of s 6 and the commission had correctly disallowed her claim for benefit. The claimant's appeal would accordingly be dismissed (see p 114 *j* to p 115 *a* and p 116 *a b* and *j* to p 117 *a* and *c* to *e*, post).

Notes j
For entitlement to supplementary benefit, see 27 Halsbury's Laws (3rd Edn) para 898.

For the Supplementary Benefits Act 1976, s 6, see 46 Halsbury's Statutes (3rd Edn) 1050.

---

a Section 6 is set out at p 112 *a* to *c*, post

Cases referred to in judgments

a *Brutus v Cozens* [1972] 2 All ER 1297, [1973] AC 854, [1972] 3 WLR 521, 136 JP 636, 56 Cr App R 799, HL, Digest (Cont Vol D) 211, *7271a*.

R v Postmaster-General (1876) 1 QBD 658, 45 LJ QB 609, 35 LT 241, DC; *affd* 3 QBD 428, 47 LJ QB 435, 38 LT 89, CA, 45 Digest (Repl) 181, *61*.

Vandyk v Minister of Pensions and National Insurance [1954] 2 All ER 723, [1955] 1 QB 29 [1954] 3 WLR 342, 35 Digest (Repl) 802, *5*.

b

Appeal

Mireille Berthé-Louise Perrot ('the claimant') appealed against the decision of his Honour Judge Stabb QC sitting as a judge of the High Court given on 17th May 1979 dismissing the claimant's appeal by notice of motion under the Tribunal and Inquiries Act 1971 that the South London Supplementary Benefits Appeal Tribunal had erred in law in
c dismissing her appeal against the decision of the Supplementary Benefits Commission that she was not entitled to supplementary benefits under s 1 of the Supplementary Benefits Act 1976. The facts are set out in the judgment of Brightman LJ.

Stephen Sedley for the claimant.
David Latham for the commission.

d

Cur adv vult

23rd May. The following judgments were read.

e **BRIGHTMAN LJ** (delivering the first judgment at the invitation of Stephenson LJ). This is an appeal from a decision of his Honour Judge Stabb QC, sitting as a judge of the High Court, given on 17th May 1979. It concerns the construction of s 6 of the Supplementary Benefits Act 1976. The question is whether the claimant, who was in business on her own account as the proprietor of a translation agency, was engaged in 'remunerative work' notwithstanding that her expenses in conducting the business of
f the agency exceeded the remuneration received in respect of the services provided by the agency.

The claimant was formerly in the employ of a publishing company. She left owing to ill-health. In October 1975, having exhausted her right to payments by way of unemployment benefit, she began to receive supplementary benefit under the 1976 Act. She was the owner of the house in which she lived, and she decided to set up
g business there on her own account as a translation agency. She traded under the name of 'Unimessage', which she changed to 'Unimessage International' when she opened a branch in Paris. In the year 1976 her gross receipts were £1,048, and expenses £2,171, leading to a net loss for the year of £1,123. In 1977 the comparable figures were gross receipts £1,387, expenses £1,696 and net loss £309.

On 5th June 1978 the Supplementary Benefits Commission decided that the claimant
h was not entitled to benefit as from 2nd June 1978 because she was engaged in remunerative full-time work. The claimant appealed from that decision to the South London Supplementary Benefits Appeal Tribunal and thence to the High Court, but before I deal with those appeals I will turn to some of the provisions of the Act and the regulations made thereunder.

Section 1 of the Act provides that, subject to the provisions of the Act, every person in
j Great Britain of or over the age of 16 years whose resources are insufficient to meet his requirements shall be entitled to a supplementary pension if of pensionable age, or to a supplementary allowance if under pensionable age. Under s 2 the Supplementary Benefits Commission determines the right to and the amount of the supplementary benefit. Section 6 excludes certain persons from entitlement to supplementary benefit. The section reads:

'(1) Except as provided in the following provisions of this section and in section 9(1) of this Act (supplementary benefit paid after a return to full-time employment *a* following a trade dispute), for any period during which a person is engaged in remunerative full-time work he shall not be entitled to supplementary benefit.

'(2) The Secretary of State may, by regulations made under this subsection, make provision for postponing the exclusion of persons becoming engaged in remunerative full-time work from a right to supplementary benefit under subsection (1) above for such period from the beginning of their engagement as may be specified *b* in the regulations.

'(3) There is no exclusion from a right to supplementary benefit under subsection (1) above where the earning power of a self-employed person is, by reason of a disability, substantially reduced in comparison with that of other persons similarly occupied. In this subsection "self-employed person" means a person engaged in any work otherwise than under a contract of service.' *c*

A measure of flexibility is introduced by s 4 which provides that s 6 shall not prevent the payment of supplementary benefit in an urgent case. Under Sch 1, para 1 the amount of any supplementary benefit to which a person is entitled shall be the amount by which his resources fall short of his requirements. Requirements are to be calculated on a weekly basis, and the supplementary benefit is a weekly amount. Paragraphs 5 to 16 deal with *d* the method of calculating a person's 'requirements' and paras 17 to 30 deal with the mode of calculating a person's 'resources'. Paragraph 21 reads:

'For the purposes of this Schedule a person's net weekly earnings shall be calculated or estimated in such manner as the Secretary of State may, by regulations made under this paragraph, prescribe.' *e*

The Secretary of State has issued the Supplementary Benefits (General) Regulations 1977, SI 1977 No 1141. Regulation 5 reads as follows:

'(1) For the purposes of Schedule 1 to the Act a person's net weekly earnings shall be the net remuneration or profit, calculated on a weekly basis, derived by him from any occupation or occupations and, in particular, in so far as the earnings *f* consist of salary or wages, there shall be deducted—(*a*) any sum the deduction of which from salary or wages is authorised by statute; and (*b*) any expenses reasonably incurred by him in connection with his employment.

'(2) Where the actual earnings of a person for a week are not immediately ascertainable for the purposes of calculating his net weekly earnings under paragraph (1), his net weekly earnings shall be estimated on the basis of such information as he *g* is able to supply and such other relevant information as is available.'

The question at issue is whether the claimant is disqualified by s 6 of the Act. For the disqualification to apply it must be established that the applicant is, for the period in question, engaged in work which is (a) remunerative and (b) full-time.

The appeal was dismissed by the South London Supplementary Benefits Appeal *h* Tribunal by a majority decision. The three members of the tribunal accepted that the claimant was engaged in remunerative work. But one member considered that she was not engaged in full-time work since the work carried out by her would have taken less than 30 hours a week.

The appellant appealed to the High Court. The only point taken before Judge Stabb was that the tribunal was wrong in law in concluding that 'remunerative work' meant *j* work for which a person was remunerated notwithstanding that it was not 'profitable'. The learned judge decided against the claimant and expressed his conclusion as follows:

'[Counsel for the claimant] contended that the word "remunerative" connotes, or must be shown to connote, some profit element, and that s 6 only takes effect when

> it is shown that the money received overtops the necessary expenses. Quite apart from the practical difficulty or indeed impossibility of administering the provisions of this Act on a weekly basis in a case such as this, if such a contention were right, I am of the opinion that "remunerative employment" means, and can only mean, employment which is gainful in the sense that it is employment where money is paid for the service which is rendered . . . I think that the appeal tribunal quite correctly interpreted s 6 and as the [claimant's] work was undoubtedly paid for, although the business unhappily did not show a net profit at the end of the year, the employment was accordingly remunerative, and s 6 must accordingly apply. In those circumstances I confirm the decision of the appeal tribunal.'

The Oxford English Dictionary gives one obsolete meaning to the word 'remunerative', which I shall ignore, and two current meanings: '2 . . . that remunerates or rewards [The literary illustrations which follow are unhelpful for and I think inappropriate to present purposes]. 3 . . . that brings remuneration; profitable.' The meaning 'brings remuneration' indicates to me that 'remunerative work' can be interpreted, without abuse of language, as work which brings remuneration, i e is paid for.

However, I have no doubt that the sense in which ordinary persons use the word 'remunerative' in ordinary conversation is 'profitable' in a broad and general sense, not just a net profit of £1 a year after deducting expenses, but an appreciable profit appropriate to the context in which the word is used. If the accounts of a business concern show that its receipts exceed its expenditure by the sum of £1, the concern would theoretically be in profit, though infinitesimal. It would not usually be described as a remunerative concern. The word 'remunerative', meaning 'profitable', so used by ordinary people in ordinary conversation, is vague and ambiguous. In the same context it can mean quite different things to different people. The meaning verges on the subjective.

Counsel for the commission described the 'profitable' meaning of the word 'remunerative' as the 'colloquial' meaning, that is to say, belonging to familiar speech as distinct from its meaning in formal or elevated language (as the Concise Oxford Dictionary defines non-colloquial use). But so elevated did that non-colloquial use of the word 'remunerative' prove to be, that counsel was quite unable to conjure up a single example of its use in ordinary speech to indicate payment as distinct from profitability.

In urging on us the meaning 'profitable', counsel for the claimant argued that the object of the Act is to meet cases of actual need and that the Act focuses on the adequacy or inadequacy of a person's resources. As the word 'remunerative' can bear the meaning 'profitable', it should be given that meaning in the Act because one would expect the Act only to be concerned with 'work' which produces 'resources'. 'Work' which does not add to the worker's 'resources', because expenditure overtakes receipts, leaves a person just as much in need as if he were not engaged in any work. One would not therefore expect a person unprofitably engaged in work to be disqualified from benefit. The word 'remunerative' more naturally means 'profitable' than 'paid'. It is the antithesis of 'unremunerative' which means unprofitable and, so far as I am aware, is not confined to 'unpaid'. So ran the argument.

Counsel's argument for the commission was that 'remunerative work' was work which brings 'remuneration'. Section 6 defines the type of work which disqualifies, i e paid work, and is not looking to the commercial result of the work which may vary between profit and loss week by week. It is the character of the work which is being defined, not the economic result of the work. If 'remunerative' means 'profitable', then inevitably the question arises: how profitable? It would be unreal and arbitrary to treat work as 'remunerative' in the sense of 'profitable' if receipts exceed expenses by £1, but not remunerative if expenses exceed receipts by £1. In ordinary parlance the word 'remunerative' would never be attributed to a business which made a profit of £1 in the course of a year. So ran the commission's argument.

It is appropriate to refer, if only to show that it has not been overlooked, to *Vandyk v*

Minister of Pensions and National Insurance [1954] 2 All ER 723, [1955] 1 QB 29. That was concerned with the definition of 'insured persons', who were divided for the purposes of the National Insurance Act 1946 into three classes by s 1(2) as follows:

> '(*a*) employed persons, that is to say persons gainfully occupied in employment in Great Britain, being employed under a contract of service; (*b*) self-employed persons, that is to say persons gainfully occupied in employment in Great Britain who are not employed persons; (*c*) non-employed persons, that is to say persons who are not employed or self-employed persons.'

The appellant, who was physically incapacitated, was employed at a salary with allowances of £375 a year, but incurred necessary expenses in relation to that employment which exceeded £375. It was decided by Slade J that he was nevertheless gainfully employed. In the course of his judgment he said this ([1954] 2 All ER 723 at 726, [1955] 1 QB 29 at 36):

> 'It seems to me that there are many difficulties in accepting the construction contended for by counsel for the appellant and I will deal with those before I put my own construction. First, it is obvious that if "gainfully occupied in employment" means striking a balance between the receipts and the expenditure to see which of the two exceeds the other, the position (as counsel for the Minister put it in argument) might fluctuate de die in diem, that is to say, an insured person would be an "employed person" whenever the receipts exceeded the expenditure by the smallest amount, and would automatically cease to be an "employed person" whenever the expenditure exceeded the receipts. Secondly, it would postulate some means of ascertaining the standard or criterion to be applied in assessing the expenditure alleged to have been incurred. In the present case I am assuming it was all reasonably incurred, but is the test to be reasonableness or must it be not only reasonably but exclusively or necessarily incurred, or what other standard is to be employed?'

The second difficulty adverted to by the judge does not arise in the instant case, because reg 5, to which I have referred, defines deductible expenses as 'expenses reasonably incurred by him in connection with his employment'. The judge came to the conclusion that the question was not whether the employed person was 'getting something out of it' but whether he was 'getting something for it', and the words 'gainfully occupied' were really in contradistinction to a contract of employment in an honorary and unpaid capacity. The reasoning of the case is equally applicable to self-employment.

That decision is useful as illustrative of the problems which can face the court if a statute uses ambiguous words such as 'gainful', but it is not conclusive of the meaning of a different word in a different statute. It also serves to remind us that we are not at liberty to interpret a statute by reference to regulations made under it (see *Vandyk v Minister of Pensions and National Insurance* [1954] 2 All ER 723 at 726, [1955] 1 QB 29 at 37). Counsel for the claimant concedes that he cannot argue, from the reference in reg 5 of the 1977 regulations to 'net remuneration or profit' struck after deduction of 'any expenses reasonably incurred', that s 6 must be looking at profitability rather than payment.

I think that the arguments are finely balanced, but I have come to the conclusion that the argument of the commission is correct. What has weighed most with me is that the claimant's submission inevitably means that £1 net profit is enough to make work 'remunerative' in the sense of 'profitable'. That concession (and it was expressly conceded) is to my mind fatal because it involves the use of the word 'remunerative' in a highly artificial sense in which the word would in fact never be used by anyone. The failure to make the concession would be equally fatal. If 'remunerative' is used in the ordinary sense of 'profitable', meaning 'broadly profitable', it is totally devoid of precision. I

therefore find myself constrained to adopt the permissible, though unusual if not
a pedagogic, meaning of 'work which brings remuneration' or, as I would prefer to put it, 'work which is paid for'.

I would dismiss the appeal.

STEPHENSON LJ. The question raised by this appeal is whether it is an error of law to hold that the claimant was 'engaged in remunerative full-time work' when she was
b denied supplementary benefit by the commission. If she was then engaged in remunerative full-time work, she was not entitled to it because s 6(1) of the Supplementary Benefits Act 1976 says so, and the appeal must be dismissed. If she was not so engaged, she was entitled, and her appeal should be allowed.

It is admitted that she was engaged in full-time work. Was she so engaged in remunerative work on the facts and on the meaning of those words in the subsection?
c She was in fact remunerated for the work by being paid fees for it. But during the relevant period the expenses she incurred in her work exceeded those fees and were used to repay her overdraft with her bank. If work is remunerative when it brings remuneration, she was engaged in remunerative work; if work is not remunerative unless it is profitable, she was not.

The dictionary to which we were referred shows that remunerative can mean 'bringing
d remuneration' or 'profitable'. In my opinion counsel for the commission was right to accept that in ordinary speech (he preferred to call it 'colloquially' but got no support from the dictionary for that adverb) remunerative means profitable. Remunerative work or a remunerative enterprise is one which pays, and pays not simply in the sense that payment is received for it or in the course of it but pays in the sense that it pays enough to make it worth doing or undertaking. 'It pays to advertise' would not be true
e if advertising cost so much that the advertiser was out of pocket at the end of a reasonable time, but it could be true, I suppose, if the resources of the advertiser enabled him to continue advertising until its rewards exceeded its expenses and to wait for the day when it showed a profit. So it is commonly, and I would agree colloquially, said in these days of the welfare state, high taxation and inflation-indexed pensions of an unemployed person or a person who has earned a retirement pension that it pays him *not* to work,
f because though he is in each case paid for the work he would be 'better off' if he drew unemployment benefit or his retirement pension. It is in that sense of 'paying' that work is commonly said to be remunerative (or perhaps lucrative); and it is in that sense, for instance, that the word was used by the Duke of Plaza-Toro when he sang:

> g 'To help unhappy commoners, and add to their enjoyment,
> Affords a man of noble rank congenial employment;
> Of our attempts we offer you examples illustrative:
> The work is light, and, I may add, it's most remunerative.'

And the 'examples illustrative' in the following duet indicate how 'very paying' the work
h was (see W. S. Gilbert, The Gondoliers, Act II).

Supplementary benefit is for those whose resources are insufficient to meet their requirements: see s 1(1) of the 1976 Act. So counsel for the claimant submits that a person unprofitably self-employed like the claimant should be entitled to supplementary benefit and the statute should be construed accordingly to meet her need. He referred us to other provisions in the Act and the regulations the Supplementary Benefits (General)
j Regulations 1977, SI 1977 No 1141, including those in which the same expression is used: s 4(3) and Sch 1, para 22(3); compare also the Family Income Supplements Act 1970, s 1(1)(*a*). But I do not get any help from them in construing the expression. Is anything more needed to support the claimant's interpretation of it than the admission that it is its ordinary meaning and Lord Reid's observation in *Brutus v Cozens* [1972] 2 All ER 1297 at 1299, [1973] AC 854 at 861 that the usual question is 'whether . . . the words

of the statute do or do not as a matter of ordinary usage of the English language cover or apply to facts which have been proved'?

In my judgment, the word 'remunerative' still retains its natural meaning of 'remunerating', 'bringing remuneration' and it is in that sense that it is used in the expression 'remunerative full-time work' in the 1976 and 1970 Acts. Work or employment (the marginal note to s 6 indicates that there is no difference between the two words) may be for a consideration or for nothing, paid or unpaid, for gain or for love or duty. That is a simple dichotomy illustrated by the illuminating judgment of Slade J in *Vandyk v Minister of Pensions and National Insurance* [1954] 2 All ER 723, [1955] 1 QB 29 in construing different words, 'gainfully occupied in employment', in a different statute, the National Insurance Act 1946. But I find that some of the considerations which militate against Parliament limiting gainful occupation to an occupation which shows a net gain or profit before insurance contributions are payable are also apt to defeat the possibility of its intending to limit remunerative full-time work to work which shows a net gain or profit. Parliament has not excluded persons engaged or occupied in *gainful* full-time work from entitlement to supplementary benefit or family income supplement. But in considering the object of the exclusion from entitlement to supplementary benefit Parliament would surely have recognised that persons do not engage in unpaid full-time work unless they have private means, or in paid full-time work unless it fulfils the hope that induced them to do it and really pays them in the sense that they not merely take something for it but make something out of it. *Part-time* work, paid or unpaid, remunerated or unremunerated, may well be more likely to leave resources insufficient to meet requirements. But full-time paid or remunerative work is unlikely to create such a condition of need even for the limited class of self-employed persons clearly contemplated by s 6(3). The 1976 Act does not use the expression *paid* (full-time) work, perhaps because remuneration may take other forms than payment of money: see *R v Postmaster General* (1876) 1 QBD 658 at 663.

I do not think any material distinction could be drawn between remunerative, remunerating and remunerated work. The first two seem to mean the same and the third could be used if you regarded the work as remunerated (or paid) rather than the person who does it as remunerated (or paid) for it. But what I find an impracticable distinction is that between a job which makes a net profit of £1 and a job which makes a net loss of £1 at any particular time. To call the first remunerative and the second not is difficult enough; to suppose that the legislature meant to exclude the first from entitlement to supplementary benefit but the second not is to my mind impossible. Both are, in my opinion, remunerative, regardless of the question whether the weekly, monthly or yearly balance sheet shows a credit or a debit balance, just as the paid worker is engaged in remunerative work regardless of what he would get if he went out of work or into retirement. What the remunerated worker, whether self-employed or employed by others, does with his or her remuneration, whether by choice or under compulsion or by choice determined by the compulsion of economic necessity, is irrelevant to the remunerative character of the work and the commission's statutory duty under s 6(1).

What, it may be asked, of the person whose earnings are all attached by an order of the court, or all paid into his or her bank in reduction of an overdraft, before ever they reach his or her pocket? And what of the person, employed not by himself but by another, whose wages or salary are not paid until after he has spent them (or more or less than them) on outgoings to a greater or lesser extent required for his work? I answer that all those cases are distinguishable from the claimant's on the facts and may or may not be distinguishable in the application of the statutory exclusion to them. They do not enable me to regard the claimant's full-time work as unremunerative. It was, in my judgment, remunerative as the commission, the tribunal and the judge all thought. I agree with them. I agree with Brightman LJ that the claimant's construction of the word 'remunerative' impales her on the horns of the dilemma expounded at the end of his judgment which are fatal to her case. I agree that the appeal should accordingly be dismissed.

DAME ELIZABETH LANE (read by Stephenson LJ). I have had the advantage of
a reading the judgments being given by Stephenson and Brightman LJJ, with which I agree.

It seems that the word 'remunerative' in s 6(1) of the Supplementary Benefits Act 1976 may be interpreted as descriptive either of the financial results of full-time work or alternatively of the work itself. If the former be the correct interpretation, it is difficult to understand why Parliament did not make this clear by the use of some such words as,
b for example, '... remunerative full-time work resulting in a profit'.

I refer to the concession made on behalf of the claimant that, on the existing wording of the subsection, a profit of £1 net would bring into operation the exclusion from supplementary benefit whereas a loss of £1 net would not do so. Surely this would give such an anomalous, not to say absurd, effect to the subsection that Parliament cannot have intended it.

c Further, as supplementary benefit is calculated on a weekly basis, it is difficult to see how payment, or withholding, of benefit could be correctly achieved without weekly accounting in cases where the work done involved incurring expenses. Yet a person might be engaged in full-time work for weeks or months on end without receiving any payment at all, although thereafter entitled to be paid what would amount to a handsome net profit for the period concerned. In the case of a person in the position of the
d claimant, the receipt of supplementary benefit would, no doubt, provide a convenient, interest-free source of money to assist in building up a business, but this would hardly be consonant with the intention of the Act.

I have come to the conclusion that the word 'remunerative' as used in s 6(1) is descriptive of the work itself and not of its financial results.

I would also dismiss this appeal.

e

Appeal dismissed. Leave to appeal to the House of Lords refused.

Solicitors: *Evill & Coleman* (for the claimant); *Solicitor to the Department of Health and Social Security.*

f Patricia Hargrove Barrister.

Pioneer Shipping Ltd and another v BTP Tioxide Ltd
The Nema

g

COURT OF APPEAL, CIVIL DIVISION
LORD DENNING MR, TEMPLEMAN AND WATKINS LJJ
29th, 30th APRIL, 1st, 2nd, 6th, 22nd MAY 1980

h

Shipping – Charterparty – Frustration – Delay – Consecutive voyage charterparty – Shipowners chartering vessel to charterers for six or seven consecutive voyages in 1979 season – Strike starting after completion of first voyage – Only two more voyages likely to be possible before end of 1979 season – Agreement by shipowners to charter vessel to charterers for seven voyages in 1980 season – Whether charterparty frustrated in whole or only in part.

j

Arbitration – Award – Leave to appeal against award – Factors to be considered by court when deciding whether to grant leave – Arbitration Act 1979, s 1.

By a charterparty dated 2nd November 1978 the owners of a vessel chartered her to the charterers for seven consecutive voyages for the carriage of cargo from Sorel in Canada

to ports in Europe between April and December 1979, those being the months when
Sorel was not ice-bound. The charterparty incorporated a Centrocon arbitration clause a
under which any dispute was to be referred to the 'final arbitrament' of an arbitrator or
arbitrators. The owners were to present the vessel for the commencement of each
voyage at Sorel, and the charterers were given the right to cancel her for any voyage for
which she was not presented for loading by 5th December 1979. The charterers were
exempted from any liability to pay freight in respect of time lost in loading on account
of strikes. A strike broke out at Sorel while the vessel was away on the first voyage and b
was still in progress when she arrived back at Sorel on 20th June, thus preventing her
from being loaded for the second voyage. Discussions took place between the owners
and charterers about the effect of the strike and on 28th June they agreed that an
addendum ('addendum 2') be made to the charterparty by which, inter alia, (i) the vessel
was to be released to the owners for one voyage to Glasgow ('the intermediate voyage') at
the end of which she was to return to Sorel, (ii) if the strike was still continuing at the end c
of the intermediate voyage the situation was to be 'discussed without obligation', and (iii)
the owners agreed to carry seven further cargoes in the 1980 season. The owners were
unable to secure a cargo to carry out the intermediate voyage immediately, so, on 11th
July 1979, the charterers by a further addendum ('addendum 3') agreed to pay the
owners compensation at the rate of $2,000 a day until the strike ended or the intermediate
voyage commenced. On 20th July the vessel sailed on the intermediate voyage and on d
10th August finished discharging her cargo at Glasgow. The strike at Sorel was still
continuing, so the owners asked the charterers for permission to carry out an extended
voyage. The charterers refused but the owners nevertheless arranged for the vessel to go
to Brazil and then to Portugal. The parties agreed to submit to arbitration the question
of whether the vessel was free to go on a further intermediate voyage or was obliged to
return to Sorel, the owners requesting a declaration that the charterparty was partly or e
wholly at an end by reason of frustration. By the time the hearing took place on 26th
September the vessel had reached Portugal and the strike at Sorel was still continuing.
The arbitrator decided that the whole of the charterparty had been frustrated by 26th
September and the vessel was therefore not obliged to return to Sorel during the 1979
season. In his award he stated that his decision related only to the seven consecutive
voyages for 1979, that he had disregarded addenda 2 and 3 in arriving at his conclusion, f
that he could not foretell when the strike would end, and that he had decided that the
charterparty had been frustrated because by 26th September the vessel had completed
only one of the seven consecutive voyages and, after taking into account the prospective
delay due to the strike, no more than two further contractual voyages were likely during
the remainder of the 1979 season, and the performance of only three out of seven
contractual voyages constituted something radically different from what had originally g
been agreed by the owners. The strike ended on 5th October. The charterers applied to
a judge for leave to appeal under the Arbitration Act 1979 against the award. The judge
gave leave and allowed the appeal on the grounds that the arbitrator had erred in
considering the 1979 season separately, because the original charterparty of 2nd
November 1978 and the two subsequent addenda constituted one indivisible contract
extending over two seasons, with a necessary break for physical reasons (ie climatic h
conditions) during the winter, and that when the two seasons were taken together under
one contract the delay did not amount to frustration of the contract. He nonetheless
gave the owners leave to appeal under s 1 of the 1979 Act to the Court of Appeal.

Held – The appeal would be allowed and the decision of the arbitrator that the
charterparty in so far as it related to the 1979 season had been frustrated would be upheld j
for the following reasons—

(1) On the true construction of the agreement between the parties the provisions
relating to the 1979 season were in all essentials independent of those relating to the 1980
season and were to be considered separately. The arbitrator had been correct to disregard
addenda 2 and 3 and to decide that the voyages for the 1979 and 1980 seasons were
separate and divisible adventures (see p 125 *j* to p 126 *a*, p 127 *e f*, p 128 *h j* and p 132 *e*,

post); *Larrinaga & Co Ltd v Société Franco-Américaine des Phosphates de Médulla, Paris* [1923] *a* All ER Rep 1 applied.

(2) There were no grounds for interfering with the arbitrator's decision because the arbitrator had properly directed himself on the law and there was no evidence that he had come to a conclusion on the facts which no reasonable arbitrator could have reached (see p 126 *c* to *g* and *j* to p 127 *a e f*, p 128 *j* to p 129 *a*, p 130 *e* to p 131 *a* and p 132 *d e*, post); *Re an arbitration between Comptoir Commercial Anversois and Power, Son & Co* [1918– *b* 19] All ER Rep 661, *Davis Contractors Ltd v Fareham Urban District Council* [1956] 2 All ER 145, dictum of Devlin J in *Universal Cargo Carriers Corpn v Citati* [1957] 2 All ER at 83, *Tsakiroglou & Co v Noblee Thorl GmbH* [1961] 2 All ER 179 and *The Angelia* [1973] 2 All ER 144 considered.

Observations on when the court should grant leave to appeal against an arbitrator's award under the 1979 Act (see p 124 *d* to p 125 *f*, post).

c

Notes

For frustration of contract generally, and the application of the doctrine to charterparties, see 9 Halsbury's Laws (4th Edn) paras 450, 452, and for cases on the subject, see 12 Digest (Reissue) 484–498, *3435–3488*.

For frustration caused by delay, see 9 Halsbury's Laws (4th Edn) para 453 and for cases *d* on the subject relating to charterparties, see 12 Digest (Reissue) 484–49, *3435–3465*.

For the Arbitration Act 1979, s 1, see 49 Halsbury's Statutes (3rd Edn) 59.

Cases referred to in judgments

Angelia, The, Trade and Transport Inc v Iino Kaiun Kaisha Ltd [1973] 2 All ER 144, [1973] 1 WLR 210, [1972] 2 Lloyd's Rep 154, Digest (Cont Vol D) 823, *1355a*.

e *British Launderers' Research Association v Central Middlesex Assessment Committee and Hendon Rating Authority* [1949] 1 All ER 21, [1949] 1 KB 462, [1949] LJR 416, 113 JP 72, 47 LGR 113, CA, 38 Digest (Repl) 583, *627*.

Comptoir Commercial Anversois and Power, Son & Co, Re an arbitration between [1920] 1 KB 868, [1918–19] All ER Rep 661, 89 LJKB 849, 122 LT 567, CA, 39 Digest (Repl) 570, *975*.

f *Davis Contractors Ltd v Fareham Urban District Council* [1956] 2 All ER 145, [1956] AC 696, [1956] 3 WLR 37, 54 LGR 289, HL, 7 Digest (Reissue) 368, *2356*.

Dominion Coal Co v Roberts (1920) 36 TLR 837, 4 Ll L Rep 434, 41 Digest (Repl) 234, *565*.

Edwards (Inspector of Taxes) v Bairstow [1955] 3 All ER 48, [1956] AC 14, [1955] 3 WLR 410, 36 Tax Cas 207, [1955] TR 209, 34 ATC 198, 48 R & IT 534, HL, 28(1) Digest (Reissue) 566, *2089*.

g *Federal Commerce and Navigation Co Ltd v Tradax Export SA, The Maratha Envoy* [1977] 2 All ER 849, [1978] AC 1, [1977] 3 WLR 126, [1977] 2 Lloyd's Rep 301, HL Digest (Cont Vol E) 555, *2543b*.

Halfdan Grieg & Co A/S v Sterling Coal & Navigation Corpn, The Lysland [1973] 2 All ER 1073, [1973] QB 843, [1973] 2 WLR 904, [1973] 1 Lloyd's Rep 296, CA, Digest (Cont Vol D) 42, *1144a*.

h *Jackson v Union Marine Insurance Co Ltd* (1873) LR 8 CP 572; *affd* LR 10 CP 125, [1874–80] All ER Rep 317, 44 LJCP 27, 31 LT 789, 2 Asp MLC 435, Ex Ch, 12 Digest (Reissue) 484, *3435*.

Larrinaga & Co Ltd v Société Franco-Américaine des Phosphates de Médulla, Paris (1922) 28 Com Cas 1, CA; *affd* 92 LJKB 455, [1923] All ER Rep 1, 129 LT 65, 16 Asp MLC 133, 29 Com Cas 1, HL, 41 Digest (Repl) 156, *31*.

j *Mechanical and General Inventions Co Ltd and Lehwess v Austin and Austin Motor Co Ltd* [1935] AC 346, [1935] All ER Rep 22, 104 LJKB 403, 153 LT 153, HL, 12 Digest (Reissue) 227, *1484*.

Metropolitan Railway Co v Wright (1886) 11 App Cas 152, [1886–90] All ER Rep 391, 55 LJQB 401, 54 LT 658, HL, 8(1) Digest (Reissue) 91, *570*.

Pilgrim Shipping Co Ltd v State Trading Corpn of India Ltd, The Hadjitsakos [1975] 1 Lloyd's Rep 356, CA.

Secretary of State for Employment and Productivity v C Maurice & Co Ltd [1969] 2 All ER 37, [1969] 2 AC 346, [1969] 2 WLR 797, [1969] TR 105, 48 ATC 95, HL, Digest (Cont Vol C) 845, *841Af*.

Tsakiroglou & Co v Noblee Thorl GmbH [1961] 2 All ER 179, [1962] AC 93, [1961] 2 WLR 633, [1961] 1 Lloyd's Rep 329, HL, Digest (Cont Vol A) 295, *3390b*.

Universal Cargo Carriers Corpn v Citati [1957] 2 All ER 70, [1957] 2 QB 401, [1957] 2 WLR 713, [1957] 1 Lloyd's Rep 174; *affd* [1957] 3 All ER 234, [1957] 1 WLR 979, [1957] 2 Lloyd's Rep 191, CA, Digest (Cont Vol A) 290, *2979a*.

Cases also cited

Ambatielos (E E) v Grace Brothers & Co Ltd (1922) 13 Ll L Rep 227, HL.

American Cyanamid Co v Ethicon Ltd [1975] 1 All ER 504, [1975] AC 396, HL.

Bank Line Ltd v A Capel & Co [1919] AC 435, [1918–19] All ER Rep 504, HL.

Cehave NV v Bremer Handelsgesellschaft mbH, The Hansa Nord [1975] 3 All ER 739, [1976] QB 44, CA.

Compagnie Primera de Navagaziona de Panama and Compania Arrendataria de Monopolio de Petroleos SA, Re an arbitration between, The Yolanda [1939] 4 All ER 81, [1940] 1 KB 362, CA.

Denny, Mott & Dickson Ltd v James B Fraser & Co Ltd [1944] AC 265, HL.

Dobell & Co v Green & Co [1900] 1 QB 526, 5 Com Cas 161, CA.

Dunford & Co Ltd v Compania Anonima Maritima Union (1911) 16 Com Cas 181.

Embiricos v Sydney Reid & Co [1914] 3 KB 45, [1914–15] All ER Rep 185.

Empresa Cubana de Fletes v Lagonisi Shipping Co Ltd, The Georgios C [1971] 1 All ER 193, [1971] 1 QB 488, CA.

Hong Kong Fir Shipping Co Ltd v Kawasaki Kisen Kaisha Ltd [1962] 1 All ER 474, [1962] 2 QB 26, CA.

Intertradex SA v Lesieur-Tourteaux SARL [1978] 2 Lloyd's Rep 509, CA.

Maple Flock Co Ltd v Universal Furniture Products (Wembley) Ltd [1934] 1 KB 148, [1933] All ER Rep 15, CA.

Mersey Steel and Iron Co v Naylor, Benzon & Co (1884) 9 App Cas 434, [1881–5] All ER Rep 365, HL.

Ocean Tramp Tankers Corpn v V/O Sovfracht, The Eugenia [1964] 1 All ER 161, [1964] 2 QB 226, CA.

Penelope, The [1928] P 180.

Port Line Ltd v Ben Line Steamers Ltd [1958] 1 All ER 787, [1958] 2 QB 146.

Reardon Smith Line Ltd v Ministry of Agriculture, Fisheries and Food [1963] 1 All ER 545, [1963] AC 691, HL.

Smyth (Ross T) & Co Ltd (Liverpool) v W N Lindsay Ltd (Leith) [1953] 2 All ER 1064, [1953] 1 WLR 1280.

Tamplin (FA) Steamship Co Ltd v Anglo-Mexican Petroleum Products Co Ltd [1916] 2 AC 397, [1916–17] All ER Rep 104, HL.

Unitramp v Garnac Grain Co Inc, The Hermine [1979] 1 Lloyd's Rep 212, CA.

Woodhouse AC Israel Cocoa Ltd SA v Nigerian Produce Marketing Co Ltd [1972] 2 All ER 271, [1972] AC 741, HL.

Appeal

Pioneer Shipping Ltd, the owners of the vessel Nema, appealed by leave of and pursuant to the certificate granted under s 1(7) of the Arbitration Act 1979 by Robert Goff J against so much of the judge's judgment dated 21st December 1979 as ordered that an arbitration award of Mr Donald Davies dated 3rd October 1979 be varied by substituting for the declaration in the award a declaration that the charterparty dated 2nd November 1978 whereby the owners of the Nema chartered her to the respondents, BTP Tioxide Ltd, had not been frustrated and that the Nema was and had at all material times since 10th

August 1979 been obliged to return to Sorel. The facts are set out in the judgment of
a Lord Denning MR.

Anthony Diamond QC and *H B Eder* for the owners.
Bernard Rix for the charterers.

Cur adv vult

b 22nd May. The following judgments were read.

LORD DENNING MR. This is the first case under the Arbitration Act 1979. It applies to arbitrations commenced on or after 1st August 1979. Henceforward no case stated. No alternative award. Simply a reasoned decision by the arbitrator. Only to be questioned if the judge gives leave. And then only on a point of law. Usually stopping
c at the judge, with no appeal to the Court of Appeal.

The charter of 2nd November 1978

The Nema flies the Greek flag. She was Liberian owned. On 2nd November 1978 the owners chartered the vessel to a British company on a consecutive voyage charter. Under it she was to proceed to Sorel. That is a port in Quebec on the St Lawrence River. It
d handles mineral traffic. The port of Sorel is open for seagoing vessels during most of the year, but for three or four winter months only for ice-reinforced vessels. The Nema was not ice-reinforced. The Nema on each voyage was to load at Sorel 15,000 tons (5% more or less) of titanium slag in bulk; and proceed across the Atlantic to Calais or Hartlepool and there deliver the same. She was to do six consecutive voyages to Sorel and back. Each voyage was to take a minimum of 30 days and a maximum of 50 days. On the
e return voyages from Europe she was allowed to carry cargo on three voyages but the rest were to be in ballast. The six voyages were to start in April 1979, and end in December 1979. But the charterers had an option to require a seventh voyage which they exercised. So it was for seven voyages.

The 'strike' clauses

f By cl 5 the cargo was to be shipped at the rate of 5,000 tons a working day, except that time lost by the following causes should not be computed in loading or discharging time: these included 'Strikes, lock-outs, stoppages of Miners, Workmen, Lightermen, Tugboatmen or other hands essential to the . . . Discharge of the said Cargo'. By cl 27 in the event of any 'general strike . . . which may prevent the Shipment of Titanium Slag under this Charter, the Owners . . . have the option of cancelling this Charter . . .'

g

The arbitration clause

The charter incorporated the Centrocon arbitration clause which read:

> 'All disputes from time to time arising out of this contract shall, unless the parties agree forthwith on a single Arbitrator, be referred to the final arbitrament of two Arbitrators carrying on business in London, who shall be members of the Baltic and
> h engaged in the shipping and/or mineral trades . . . with power to such Arbitrators to appoint an Umpire.'

Looking ahead, I may say that in this case the parties agreed on a single arbitrator, Mr Donald Davies. The dispute which arose was referred to him under that clause for 'final arbitrament'. Note the word 'final'.

j

The first voyage

The Nema duly performed the first voyage. She crossed the Atlantic and arrived at Sorel on 17th May 1979. She was loaded with titanium slag in three days. She left on 20th May for Europe. She returned to Sorel arriving there on 20th June, and gave notice of readiness for the second voyage.

But the charterers were unable to load her. They were prevented by a strike. It had started a fortnight earlier on 6th June. There was a total shutdown of the titanium plant a
at Sorel. No one could tell how long it would last. A previous strike had lasted for nine months.

In strict law the Nema should have waited there at Sorel, queueing up there, until the strike ended. This would be at the owners' expense, because the charterers were exempt from any liability for time lost by reason of the strike clause.

After waiting for two days, from 20th to 22nd June, the shipowners sought to cancel b
the second voyage. They relied on cl 27, suggesting that the strike was a 'general strike' (a view which afterwards was seen to be untenable). There followed discussions. The upshot was that within a week they agreed on an important addendum to the original charter.

Addendum 2 dated 28th June 1979 c

Note that this addendum was made eight months after the original charter of 2nd November 1978. These were the principal terms:

(1) The second voyage from Sorel was to be postponed. The owners were to be at liberty to take her, for their own benefit, on an intermediate voyage. She was to be at liberty to lift a cargo of iron ore from the St Lawrence to Glasgow. The Nema was then to return in ballast to load her next cargo to Sorel. That intermediate voyage was d
expected to take 30 to 50 days. But, if the strike ended during her absence, and the charterers had to charter another vessel to lift the titanium slag, the owners had to perform a replacement voyage at a later date (in lieu of the second voyage).

(2) On completion of that intermediate voyage, the Nema was to return to Sorel to perform the remaining voyages in 1979, ie voyages two to seven under the charterparty dated 2nd November 1978; and the charterers were to pay an increased freight rate, e
increased by $US1·00 a ton.

(3) The shipowners agreed to lift seven further cargoes in the 1980 season, commencing laydays 1st April 1980, cancelling date 30th April 1980, with freight rate increased by a further $US3·50 a ton.

(4) If the strike at Sorel was still in existence when the Nema had discharged her cargo of iron ore at Glasgow (on the intermediate voyage) 'the situation to be discussed without f
obligation'.

Addendum 3

It so happened, however, that the owners were unable to carry out that proposed intermediate voyage. They were unable to secure a cargo of iron ore at that time. So the Nema remained at Sorel from 20th June until 11th July 1979. The strike was still on, g
and looked like going on indefinitely. So the parties agreed to an addendum 3, under which the charterers agreed to pay the owners compensation at the rate of $US2,000 a day from 1st July 1979 until the vessel could get an intermediate voyage.

The intermediate voyage

Three weeks later, with the strike still on, the owners did manage to fix the Nema for h
an intermediate voyage. On 20th July the Nema sailed from the St Lawrence with a cargo of iron ore. She carried it to Glasgow and completed discharging there on 10th August 1979. This intermediate voyage was done, of course, by the owners for their own account. But even when she had discharged at Glasgow the strike at Sorel was still on. So the question at once arose: was she to go back across the Atlantic to Sorel? That seemed to the owners to be of doubtful value, as there were still no signs of the strike j
ending. So they asked the charterers for permission to carry out a round voyage for 22 days for the British Steel Corpn. The charterers refused. The utmost they would agree to was for the Nema to carry a return cargo across the Atlantic to Sorel, if she could get it. The owners felt this was not good enough, as the strike still looked like going on indefinitely. So on 16th August they fixed the Nema for another intermediate voyage.

She was to go out to Brazil, pick up a cargo there and carry it back to Spain. This voyage was expected to last for 45 to 50 days.

The charterers, however, wanted to get the Nema to go back to Sorel, in case the strike ended. So on 17th August 1979 they went ex parte to Mars-Jones J and got an injunction; but on the next day, 18th August, inter partes the judge lifted that injunction. He only did so, however, on the owners giving an undertaking that, pending an arbitration, they would not fix the vessel for any other voyages, other than that one already fixed on 16th August. So on 16th August the Nema sailed on her second intermediate voyage, to Brazil and back to Spain. It was not expected to be completed before the end of September 1979.

The arbitration

Meanwhile, both parties were anxious to know where they stood. The strike at Sorel was still on and showed no sign of finishing. So the parties agreed to an early arbitration, before a single arbitrator, Mr Donald Davies. They did not make any exclusion agreement under s 4 of the 1979 Act. The arbitration was arranged for the earliest date that could be arranged. It was on Wednesday, 26th September 1979. It so happened that by that time the Nema on her intermediate voyage had done better than expected. She had completed the voyage and discharged her cargo in Spain on 23rd September. She was poised to move westwards depending on the outcome of the arbitration. There was still no prospect of the strike ending. The most optimistic put it as going on for several more weeks.

The hearing took all day on Wednesday, 26th September, both sides being represented by counsel, and not finishing until 8.50 pm. Each side asked for a reasoned award.

On Friday, 28th September, the arbitrator sent a telex to both parties giving his decision:

> 'The whole of the charterparty contract . . . is now frustrated. I intend to publish a reasoned award in respect of the above matter. Also the other contentions [previously] put before me, about the middle of next week.'

That decision meant that the owners were free to fix the Nema at once for another voyage, on their own account. But they were unable to do so at once, because of the undertaking they had given to Mars-Jones J on 17th August not to fix her for another voyage pending the arbitration. So on Tuesday, 2nd October, the owners applied to Mocatta J. They asked to be released from their undertaking. Mocatta J was much influenced by the fact that the parties had asked the arbitrator for a speedy decision, so as to know what to do. He thought that in those circumstances no judge would grant the charterers leave to appeal. So he released the owners from the undertaking. They fixed her for another voyage or voyages in the year 1979 but regarded themselves as still bound by addendum 2 for the 1980 season.

On Wednesday, 3rd October 1979, Mr Donald Davies gave his reasoned award. It was an outstanding piece of work. It covered 19 pages dealing with all the facts and the law in an excellent manner. All within one week. These were his findings:

> 'The whole of the consecutive voyage charterparty dated November 3rd, 1978, was frustrated by September 26th, 1979.
>
> 'For the sake of completeness I should mention that I have disregarded addendums Nos. 2 and 3 while arriving at my conclusions. My decision only adverts to the seven consecutive voyages for 1979. No consideration has been given by me to the part of the addendum relating to the seven voyages contemplated for the 1980 season.'

Later on, at the request of the parties, Mr Donald Davies explained a little more:

> 'When writing up my reasons, it occurred to me that there might, repeat might, be an arguable point that, despite frustration of the obligation entered into by the

> charterparty of November 2nd, there was an agreement of some nature regarding the 1980 season arising from Addendum No. 2. I felt that I had not heard sufficient argument on this aspect to make any decision on the matter and, in any event, thought such was not necessary in view of having come to the decision that the contract, as evidenced by the charterparty of November 2nd, had become frustrated.'

The upshot of it was that the 1979 season was frustrated but the 1980 season remained intact.

The giving of leave

The charterers applied to Robert Goff J for leave to appeal. He gave leave. The owners appealed to this court. We held that we had jurisdiction to entertain an appeal, from a granting or refusal of leave, but that we should not in this case interfere with the judge's grant of leave.

Looking back on it now, with knowledge of all that has happened since, it is, I think, a pity that the judge gave leave, and a pity too that we affirmed his decision. By granting leave, the parties have been involved in much litigation and expense, which they ought to have been spared.

This experience prompts me to make some reflections on the circumstances in which a judge should or should not give leave.

The position under the 1979 Act is very different from that under the 1950 Act. Under that Act we set out guidelines as to the circumstances in which an arbitrator should state his award in the form of a special case. We did it in (*Halfden Grieg & Co A/S v Sterling Coal & Navigation Corpn, The Lysland* [1973] 2 All ER 1073 at 1077, [1973] QB 843 at 862. Those guidelines should be discarded. They are not applicable to the new Act.

The first guideline is given by s 1(4) of the Act. Leave is not to be given unless the point of law could 'substantially affect the rights' of one or both of the parties. In short, it must be a point of practical importance, not an academic point, nor a minor point.

The second guideline is given by s 1(2), (3) and (7). The decision of the arbitrator is final unless the judge gives leave. Once he gives leave, the judge is to hear the appeal. His decision is final unless he certifies that the question is one of general importance, or is one which for some other special reason should be considered by the Court of Appeal. This finality gives rise to these reflections.

Take a case where the sole question is the proper interpretation of a commercial contract. Not a standard form. But a 'one-off' clause in a 'one-off' contract. The interpretation of it is unlikely ever to arise again. The parties agree, as here, to the 'final arbitrament' of an arbitrator carrying on business in the City of London. To my mind, in the ordinary way, once the arbitrator has given his award, containing his interpretation of the clause, the judge should not give leave to appeal. Not even when a large sum of money is involved. For this reason. On such a clause, the arbitrator is just as likely to be right as the judge, probably more likely. Because he, with his expertise, will interpret the clause in its commercial sense, whereas the judge, with no knowledge of the trade, may interpret the clause in its literal sense. And, once the judge has decided it, there is no appeal; because it is not a case for a certificate. Then as between the arbitrator and the judge, whose decision is to be preferred? I should say that in general, in the absence of some special reason, it should be the decision of the arbitrator; because it was he to whom the parties agreed to submit it on the basis that his decision was to be final, and not the judge's. But if the arbitrator intimated that he would welcome an appeal, that would be a special reason for giving leave.

It is different with a clause in a standard form, and a question arises which is likely to come up again and again. The decision on such a question may well be one of general public importance within s 1(8) of the 1979 Act. If a judge is prepared so to certify, he may often consider it desirable to give leave. But, even then, he should hesitate a little before giving it. He must remember that, even in a standard form, a commercial arbitrator is better placed to interpret it in a commercial sense, or in a sense acceptable to the parties, than the judge himself is. He should not give leave unless it is a really debatable point. If the arbitrator has put on the clause the meaning generally accepted in the trade, leave should be refused, because that is what the parties would have expected when they agreed to the arbitration. I would repeat what I said in *Pilgrim Shipping Co Ltd v State Trading Corpn of India Ltd, The Hadjitsakos* [1975] 1 Lloyd's Rep 356 at 360–361 in the hope that the commercial judges will accept it as the correct approach since the 1979 Act.

Take then a case like the present, in which the point is whether a contract was ended by frustration or not. In *Universal Cargo Carriers Corpn v Citati* [1957] 2 All ER 70 at 83, [1957] 2 QB 401 at 435, Devlin J said: '. . . while the application of the doctrine of frustration is a matter of law, the assessment of a period of delay sufficient to constitute frustration is a question of fact': whereas, in *The Angelia, Trade and Transport Inc v Iino Kaiun Kaisha Ltd* [1973] 2 All ER 144 at 154, [1973] 1 WLR 210 at 221 Kerr J said that it was 'an inference of law to be drawn by the court from the facts found in the special case'. I must say that I prefer the approach of Devlin J. It is mixed law and fact. But, whichever way it is put, the decision of the arbitrator on frustration should normally be accepted. He is just as likely to be right as a judge. He is as well able to make the 'assessment' or to draw the 'inference' as a judge. His decision should be accepted unless it is an 'assessment' or an 'inference' which could not reasonably be drawn from the facts: see *British Launderers' Research Association v Central Middlesex Assessment Committee and Hendon Rating Authority* [1949] 1 All ER 21 at 25–26, [1949] 1 KB 462 at 471–472. Leave to appeal should normally be refused. Especially in a case like the present (where the parties sought and obtained a speedy ruling from the arbitrator) so as to know what the vessel was to do on her next voyage. Was she to go across to Sorel under the charterparty? Were the owners at liberty to fix her for a fresh voyage elsewhere? Once the arbitrator gives his decision, the parties should abide by it. Even though both parties asked for a reasoned award, still they should abide by it, unless it is manifest that the arbitrator has gone wrong.

If those guidelines had been followed by Robert Goff J in this case, he would have refused leave. But, as he gave leave, we have to consider the points of law arising on the arbitrator's decision.

Divisible or indivisible

On the findings of the arbitrator, it is plain that he considered the 1979 season (in the original charterparty) separately from the 1980 season (in addendum 2). His finding was that by 26th September 1979 the venture for the 1979 season had become frustrated by the delay due to the strike at Sorel. He gave no finding about the 1980 season, because he had not directed his mind to it.

The judge held that the arbitrator made a mistake in considering the 1979 season separately. He held that the original charterparty and the addenda 'constituted one indivisible contract: it was simply an indivisible consecutive voyage charterparty extending over two seasons, with a necessary break for physical reasons during the winter'. So he held that the two seasons must be considered together as coming under one contract. That whole contract was not frustrated. So the parties remained bound.

This question, divisible or indivisible, is a question of law depending on the true interpretation of the documents. We were referred to two cases on this sort of point. One was a decision of Rowlatt J in 1920, *Dominion Coal Co v Roberts* 4 Ll L Rep 434. The other was a decision of the Court of Appeal and House of Lords in 1922, *Larrinaga & Co Ltd v Société Franco-Américaine des Phosphates de Médulla, Paris* 28 Com Cas 1; *affd* [1923] All ER Rep 1. I think we should be guided by the *Larrinaga* case. Viewing this case broadly, the 1979 season was separate from the 1980 season. There were some connecting features, in that in some circumstances the manner of performing the 1979 season might affect the 1980 season. That impressed the judge. But it does not impress me. In all essentials the two seasons were separate and independent. The 1979 season might be frustrated, but the 1980 season might still remain binding.

So I proceed to consider whether the 1979 season was frustrated.

Frustration

The arbitrator here said that, in the main, 'Arbitrators and judges have a divergency of approach in respect of how much delay is required to frustrate a charterparty'.

This case is an excellent example. The arbitrator found that the 1979 season had been frustrated, owing to the delay caused by the strike. The judge on the same facts found that it had not been frustrated. But he gave leave to appeal.

To my mind the judge was in error in his approach. He asked himself, as if it were a pure question of law: 'On these facts, was the contract (in so far as it concerned the 1979 season) frustrated or not?' Whereas, I think he should have accepted the decision of the arbitrator as final, unless the charterers showed either (i) that the arbitrator misdirected himself in point of law or (ii) the decision was such that no reasonable arbitrator could reach. In short, under the Arbitration Act 1979 the judge should apply the same test in regard to an arbitrator's decision as the courts habitually apply in regard to decisions of magistrates or tribunals, which can be questioned only on points of law. These tests were stated by the House of Lords in *Edwards (Inspector of Taxes) v Bairstow* [1955] 3 All ER 48, [1956] AC 14 and in regard to specialist tribunals in *Secretary of State for Employment and Productivity v C Maurice & Co Ltd* [1969] 2 All ER 37, [1969] 2 AC 347. An arbitrator in the City of London is a specialist tribunal. It is as well to remember that in the great case of *Jackson v Union Marine Insurance Co Ltd* (1873) LR 8 CP 572; *affd* LR 10 CP 125, [1874–80] All ER Rep 317 (which was the foundation of the doctrine of frustration of delay) the jury found that—

> 'the time necessary to get the ship off and repairing her so as to be a cargo-carrying ship was so long as to put an end in a commercial sense to the commercial speculation entered into by the shipowner and charterers' (see LR 10 CP 125 at 141).

The Exchequer Chamber said that the question could not have been left in better terms. No court would have set aside that finding of the jury unless it was 'perverse' in this sense, that it was a finding no reasonable man could reach: see *Metropolitan Railway Co v Wright* (1886) 11 App Cas 152, [1886–90] All ER Rep 391, *Mechanical and General Inventions Co Ltd and Lehwess v Austin and Austin Motor Co Ltd* [1935] AC 346 at 374–375, [1935] All ER Rep 22 at 35 by Lord Wright. Likewise with the finding of the arbitrator appointed by the parties.

Applied to this case

The arbitrator directed himself very properly in point of law. He said:

> 'As I understand it, the general principle relating to frustration is that evinced in *Davis Contractors Ltd v Fareham Urban District Council* [1956] 2 All ER 145, [1956] AC 696, namely, the change of obligation theory; performance, because of the supervening events, must be something radically different from that which was undertaken under the contract; "it was not this that I promised to do".'

Then he applied it to the facts, saying:

> 'I think that the application of the foregoing, to the facts of this case, leads to the conclusion that the whole of the consecutive voyage Charterparty was frustrated by September 26th.'

He goes on at some length to elaborate his reasons for coming to that conclusion. He pointed out that the strike had gone on for over 3½ months and might go on for months more. Even if it ended quickly, it would be impossible to do more than three out of the seven voyages for the 1979 season. That put an end in a commercial sense to the venture for that season. His finding is to my mind eminently reasonable. No one could suggest

that it was unreasonable. It ought to have been accepted. The judge should not have
a interfered with it.

The future

The arbitrator in his award expressed the concern of many in the City of London with the restrictive approach shown by some judges in determining commercial disputes. He said:

b 'There are some in the City of London, and other maritime centres, who think that commercial justice is sometimes sacrificed upon the altar of certainty, and that a slightly more liberal approach, in the application of frustration principles, to supervening events, would be more appropriate to the pace of modern commercial life.'

c I share those sentiments. I hope that, as a result of our decision today, the judges will adopt the 'slightly more liberal approach' besought by the City of London. Not only in frustration cases, but in others, of which a typical example is *Federal Commerce and Navigation Co Ltd v Tradax Export SA, The Maratha Envoy* [1977] 2 All ER 849, [1978] AC 1 in which the House of Lords took a different view from that taken in a similar case by maritime arbitrators in the City of New York.

d This is a good case to show the new approach warranted by the 1979 Act. The judge, for whom we all have the greatest respect, went by the old approach. He treated it as if there had been a case stated, on both points: (i) 'divisible' or 'indivisible' and (ii) frustration by delay. He considered both points afresh, on the facts stated in the award. He came to his own independent conclusion on them. He reversed the arbitrator on both.

Under the new approach, the judge should not have given leave at all. Not on the
e 'divisible or indivisible' point, because it was a 'one-off' point. Not on the 'frustration by delay' point, because the arbitrator had not misdirected himself in law or in fact.

The judge, however, did give leave; and he did certify the case as one of general importance. As such, I have come to the conclusion that the judge was in error. He should have adopted the new approach. He ought not to have reversed the decision of the arbitrator, which the parties had agreed should be 'final', unless it was clearly
f wrong. It was not.

In the result, the owners are relieved from any liability in respect of the 1979 season, but are still liable to perform the 1980 season.

I would allow the appeal, accordingly.

g **TEMPLEMAN LJ.** On 26th September 1979 someone had to decide what was to happen to the Nema. The arbitrator decided that enough was enough; the charterparty had been disrupted by the strike at Sorel, the charterers refused to allow a voyage by voyage solution and there was continuing doubt as to the length of time (if any) which would be available between the end of the strike and the beginning of the ice. The arbitrator, urged to speed his award, promptly declared that the Nema was not obliged
h to return to Sorel during the 1979 season. With some judicial encouragement the vessel plunged away to earn her keep and the owners breathed a sigh of relief. Subsequently, the charterers, with the benefit of hindsight, asked and were given leave to challenge the arbitration award in the courts. The commercial judge held that the arbitrator was wrong. This court is asked to hold that the commercial judge was wrong and, whether we find that the arbitrator was right or the judge was right, the House of Lords may be
j petitioned to say that we are wrong. The arbitration took one long day, the hearing before the commercial judge took $3\frac{1}{2}$ days in addition to the day spent on discussing leave, the hearing in this court has taken over three days and we know not what the future history (if any) of this litigation will unfold. The ultimate loser will have the consolation of establishing yet another distinguishable authority on the subject of frustration at the price of damages or costs or both.

The arbitrator concerned himself with the seven voyages which were due to take place during the 1979 season pursuant to the charterparty dated 2nd November 1978. By *a* addendum 2 dated 28th June 1979 and by addendum 3 dated 11th July 1979 the rights and obligations of the owners and the charterers relating to the 1979 charterparty were varied. In addition, addendum 2 provided for a charterparty of seven voyages to take place during the 1980 season. The question is whether the 1979 charterparty and the 1980 charterparty were, in the words of Lord Atkinson in *Larrinaga & Co Ltd v Société Franco-Américaine des Phosphates de Médulla, Paris*, (1922) 29 Com Cas 1 at 11, [1923] All *b* ER Rep 1 at 8—

> 'wholly distinct, separate, and severable adventures between which there was no interdependence in the sense that the carrying out of any one of them was made to depend in any way upon the carrying out or abandonment of the others.'

Under the 1979 charterparty the Nema was to present herself at Sorel to load the first *c* cargo not earlier than 1st April 1979 nor later than 30th April 1979 without the consent of the charterers. The charterers were entitled to cancel the ship for any voyage for which she was not presented for loading by 5th December 1979. Under the 1980 charterparty the Nema was to present herself at Sorel to load the first cargo not earlier than 1st April 1980 nor later than 30th April 1980 without the consent of the charterers. The charterers were entitled to cancel the ship for any voyage for which she *d* was not presented for loading by 31st December 1980. The gap between the two seasons, 1979 and 1980, was not simply a physical necessity imposed by climatic conditions. If climate was the sole reason for the gap, there was no sense in providing for loading not earlier than 1st April 1980 without the charterers' consent and no reason why the charterers should be allowed to cancel on or after 30th April 1980 in the event of late arrival for the first voyage but not in the event of late arrival for any other voyage. It was *e* argued that cl 8 of addendum 2 might affect the obligations of the parties under the 1980 charterparty. Clause 8 varied the 1979 charterparty by providing that if the Nema, which was then at Sorel after transporting the first 1979 cargo, left Sorel on a voyage for the benefit of the owners, as permitted by cl 2 of addendum 2, and if the strike ended while the Nema was absent, and if the charterers chartered another vessel to lift the charterers' second cargo, then the owners would 'perform a replacement voyage in 1979 *f* if possible, otherwise FOW [first open water] 1980 ...' Refusal to carry out this replacement voyage might have been a breach of the 1979 charterparty but would not have been a breach of the 1980 charterparty. If the Nema was absent from Sorel on the permitted owners' voyage when the strike ended, and if the charterers hired another vessel for their second 1979 cargo, and if the owners did not provide a replacement voyage in 1979, and if the owners attempted to carry out a replacement voyage beginning *g* FOW 1980, and if the Nema did not report back to Sorel before 30th April 1980 for the first voyage of the 1980 charterparty, then the charterers would have been entitled to cancel, just as they would have been entitled to cancel if, for one of a multitude of other reasons, the Nema failed to report to load the first cargo of the 1980 charterparty before 30th April 1980. Neither cl 8 nor any other clause of addendum 2 made the 1980 charterparty dependent on the carrying out or abandonment of the 1979 charterparty. *h* Clause 8 was a dead letter by 26th September 1979 when the arbitrator was obliged to determine frustration. The arbitrator gave no consideration to the seven voyages contemplated for the 1980 season. The charterers and the owners are operating the 1980 charterparty without regard to the débâcle of the 1979 charterparty. I decline to join together the 1979 and 1980 charterparties.

The question which the arbitrator considered was whether the 1979 charterparty was *j* frustrated by 26th September 1979. The arbitrator correctly directed himself that—

> 'the general principle relating to frustration is that evinced in *Davis Contractors Ltd v Fareham Urban District Council* [1956] 2 All ER 145, [1956] AC 696, namely the change of obligation theory; performance, because of supervening events, must be

something radically different from that which was undertaken with the contract;
a "it was not this that I promised to do".'

By the charterparty, dated 2nd November 1978, it was agreed that there should be six or,
at the option of the charterers, seven continuous voyages by the Nema from Sorel to
Calais or Hartlepool carrying titanium slag for the charterers between April 1979 and the
end of the 1979 season. For each voyage the owners were to present the Nema at Sorel
b and thereupon the charterers were to load 15,000 long tons and to pay freight at the rate
of $US12 per ton if the cargo were discharged at Calais or $US13 per ton if the cargo were
discharged at Hartlepool. The vessel was not presented for the first voyage until 17th
May 1979 but the charterers allowed the charterparty to continue. On 20th May the
Nema, having loaded, sailed from Sorel on her first voyage. On 6th June there was a
strike at Sorel and from then onwards no cargo could be loaded at Sorel on the Nema
c until the strike ended. There had been a considerable number of labour disputes at Sorel
over the years. Strikes had been as short as ten days and as long as nine months. On 20th
June the Nema arrived back at Sorel from her first voyage but was unable to load because
of the continuing strike. Nevertheless the charterers on 21st June exercised their option
for a seventh voyage and the charterparty thereupon became a charterparty for seven
consecutive voyages of which one had been completed. On 28th June, by addendum 2,
d the charterers agreed to release the Nema to the owners to undertake one voyage from
the St Lawrence to Glasgow or Birkenhead 'thereafter returning in ballast to load her
next cargo at Sorel'. On 11th July, by addendum 3, the charterers agreed to pay the
owners $US2,000 per day from 1st July 1979 until the strike ended or the charterers
released the Nema to perform a voyage of anticipated maximum 30 days' duration. On
20th July the Nema was released to the owners and sailed on a voyage to Glasgow.
e Compensation amounting to $US40,000 had become payable and was paid. On 10th
August the Nema finished discharging cargo at Glasgow and the charterers insisted that
she should return to Sorel but said that she might carry a cargo from Glasgow to
Canada. On that date, namely 10th August, there were no signs of the strike at Sorel
ending; the local information from Sorel was pessimistic regarding any likely end to the
strike, and, in fact, some doubts were being expressed whether the plant would reopen
f that year. On 16th August the owners defied the charterers and arranged for the Nema
to depart from Glasgow on a voyage anticipated to last between 45 and 50 days to Brazil
and thence to Portugal. On 17th August the charterers applied to the court in this
country for an injunction to restrain the Nema doing anything save return to Sorel. The
injunction was granted and was discharged on the following day, namely 18th August,
only on the owners' undertaking, pending arbitration, not to fix a further voyage after
g the conclusion of the arrangements they had already made for the ship to go to Brazil and
then to Portugal. During the remainder of August, the strike situation at Sorel showed
no signs of improvement. In fact, with the combination of holiday periods, fine weather
and workers not suffering financial pressures, there appeared to be no inclination by the
men to end the strike. Some discussion took place during the last week of August but
did not result in any conclusion. Negotiations continued into the first week of September
h leading to an offer by the employers on 4th September, but the offer was rejected on 5th
September by a 77% majority, after a recommendation for rejection by the union
executive. After this turn of events the feeling in Sorel was that an early return to work
could not be expected. Between 5th September and the date of the arbitration, namely
26th September, the situation at Sorel did not change. No meetings took place between
the employers and the union, and no further meetings were scheduled for the future.
j The Nema on the day of the arbitration was in Portugal poised to move westwards,
depending on the outcome of the arbitration. On 26th September 'there were no
immediate prospects for the ending of the strike. The earliest probable date, for the
resumption of loading of titanium slag is the end of October'.

The arbitrator was asked by the owners for a declaration that the 'consecutive voyage
charterparty was partly or wholly at an end by reason of frustration . . .' The arbitrator

was asked by the charterers for a declaration that the charterparty had not been frustrated by 26th September and for a declaration 'that under the terms of the charterparty the vessel is obliged to return in ballast to Sorel to perform the next voyage'.

Thus on 26th September the arbitrator had to decide whether the charterparty dated 2nd November 1978 as amended by addendum 2 and addendum 3 was frustrated. If so, the owners were free to deal with the Nema as they pleased between 26th September 1979 and the end of the 1979 season. If the charterparty was not frustrated on 26th September, then the Nema must sail from Portugal to Sorel there to wait until the end of the strike or the end of the year. The question for the arbitrator was whether the contemplated continuous seven voyage charter to be carried out between April and the end of December was frustrated by the ascertained delay between 20th June 1979 (when the implementation of the charterparty was interrupted after one voyage) and 26th September 1979 (the date of the arbitration) plus the probable delay until the end of October and the possible delay thereafter.

The arbitrator found that—

> 'By September 26th, the vessel had completed only one of the seven contemplated voyages and after taking the prospective delay into account, no more than two further contractual voyages were likely during the remainder of the open season. The result is, therefore, that the Nema will only perform three of the seven contractual voyages, at most; this, to my mind, constitutes something radically different from that originally undertaken by the owners of the vessel.'

He declared that—

> 'The whole of the consecutive voyage charterparty dated November 2, 1978 became frustrated by September 26, 1979 and the "NEMA" is not obliged to return to Sorel during the 1979 open season.'

I have reached the same conclusion. In any event I am not prepared to substitute the decision of the court for the decision of the arbitrator. Even if frustration by delay is a matter of law which enables the court to interfere with the arbitrator, I do not consider that the court is justified in interfering in the present circumstances unless the arbitrator has misdirected himself or has reached a conclusion which no reasonable arbitrator could reach. There was no misdirection and the arbitrator reached a reasonable conclusion. In deciding whether delay in the circumstances of the present case was sufficient to frustrate the contract, questions of fact, degree and judgment are involved.

The parties had contemplated that the Nema would carry out up to seven continuous voyages between April and the end of 1979 transporting cargo for the charterers and earning for each voyage a predetermined freight for the owners. The arbitrator decided that the parties had not contemplated and the owners had not promised that if, after one voyage, there was an interruption between 20th June and 26th September, and if the interruption looked like continuing until the end of October and might continue thereafter, the Nema would proceed to Sorel on 26th September there to wait, without transporting cargo or earning freight, until a voyage became possible, or until the passage of time revealed that no further voyage would be possible in 1979. That was what the arbitrator thought on 26th September 1979 in the light of the information then available. The charterers have not advanced any good reason for asserting that the arbitrator was wrong save the irrelevant reason that in the event the interruption ended on 5th October.

In the present case there is one circumstance which in my judgment disqualifies the court from insisting that on 26th September the court would have reached a conclusion different from that of the arbitrator. That circumstance is that the court inevitably considers the matter with hindsight, that is to say with knowledge that the strike ended on 5th October. On 26th September the arbitrator was driven by both parties to make a decision without knowing whether or when the strike would end. Until the strike ended the Nema could not be employed for the benefit of either the charterers or the owners but must wait at Sorel with a full crew at great expense to the owners and no good to anybody. If in the circumstances the arbitrator decided that it was really too much to expect the owners to send the Nema back to Sorel on 26th September, I do not consider that the court is in any position to decide that he was wrong.

The owners rely on the passage in *Universal Cargo Carriers Corpn v Citati* [1957] 2 All ER 70 at 83, [1957] 2 QB 401 at 435 where Devlin J said:

> 'I think that, while the application of the doctrine of frustration is a matter of law, the assessment of a period of delay sufficient to constitute frustration is a question of fact. The period has to be measured, no doubt, in the light of the principles that have been laid down in cases as to the sort of thing that amounts to frustration, but it is in the end a finding of fact. As such it can be successfully attacked only if I am satisfied that the arbitrator could only have reached his conclusion of fact by applying some wrong principle of law.'

The charterers rely on *The Angelia, Trade and Transport Inc v Iino Kaiun Kaisha Ltd* [1973] 2 All ER 144 at 153, [1973] 1 WLR 210 at 220, where Kerr J said that he found it difficult to reconcile the cited passage from the *Citati* case with the decision of the Court of Appeal in *Re an arbitration between Comptoir Commercial Anversois and Power Son & Co* [1920] 1 KB 868, [1918–19] All ER Rep 661.

In *Re an arbitration between Comptoir, Commercial Anversois and Power Son & Co* the sellers claimed that a contract for sale was frustrated because the sellers were unable to procure war insurance for the cargo and they were unable to secure payment for the cargo as soon as it was put on board in accordance with the usual practice of selling of exchange because of the outbreak of the 1914–18 war. Neither delay nor anything else made the contract wholly or partly impossible. In *The Angelia* [1973] 2 All ER 144 at 153, [1973] 1 WLR 210 at 220 Kerr J considered that the statement by Devlin J in the *Citati* case which I have quoted was inconsistent also with the speech of Lord Radcliffe in *Davis Contractors Ltd v Fareham Urban District Council* [1956] 2 All ER 145 at 159, [1956] AC 696 at 727 and above all with *Tsakiroglou & Co v Noblee Thorl GmbH* [1961] 2 All ER 179, [1962] AC 93. In *Davis Contractors Ltd v Fareham Urban District Council* a building contract to build 78 houses for a local authority for a fixed sum within a period of 8 months took 22 months to complete owing to unexpected circumstances. Delay did not make the contract wholly or partly impossible. It was a little difficult for the builders to submit that the contract had been frustrated although it had been completed. The argument was presented and rejected. In the present case by 26th September 1979 it was no longer possible to complete the contract of seven voyages. Only one voyage had been completed, it was probable that only two more voyages would be completed and possible that only one or even none would be carried out. In *Davis v Fareham Urban District Council* [1956] 2 All ER 145 at 159, [1956] AC 696 at 727 Lord Radcliffe said:

> '... the theory of frustration ... is represented by a rule which the courts will apply in certain limited circumstances for the purpose of deciding that contractual obligations, ex facie binding, are no longer enforceable against the parties. The description of the circumstances that justify the application of the rule and, consequently, the decision whether, in a particular case, those circumstances exist are, I think, necessarily questions of law.'

I do not think that this passage is in conflict with the passage of Devlin J in *Universal Cargo Carriers Corpn v Citati*, which was dealing with the narrow question of how much delay in a relevant case is sufficient to constitute frustration, and not with the question whether delay was a circumstance which could result in frustration. Kerr J also relied on *Tsakiroglou & Co v Noblee Thorl GmbH*. In that case the sellers agreed to ship goods from the Sudan to Hamburg. After the date of contract the Suez Canal was closed to navigation. It was held that there was no implied term that the goods would be shipped via Suez or by the usual and customary route at the date of the contract and that, although the route via the Cape involved a change in the performance of the contract, it was not such a fundamental change from that undertaken under the contract as to entitle the sellers to say that the contract was frustrated. Again this was a case where delay did not make the contract impossible but made the carrying out of the contract an operation which was both longer and more expensive than had been first contemplated. In *The Angelia* itself, if delay in loading had not taken place, the contract would have been completed by the end of August. The delay meant that the contract could not be completed until about 10th October. That was another case in which the contract originally contemplated could be carried out, but over a longer period. Arbitrators found that the contemplated delay in completion was sufficient to frustrate the contract. Kerr J reversed the arbitrators. He pointed out (see [1973] 2 All ER 144 at 155, [1973] 1 WLR 210 at 222) that the possibility of delay in loading was contemplated by the express terms of the charterparty and that the consequence of any delay was purely financial for one side or the other.

In the present case delay in loading due to strikes was contemplated, but it is conceded that the express clause of the contract which enabled the owners to cancel the charterparty in the event of a general strike (cl 27) and the clause in the charterparty which prevented time running against the charterers if strikes rendered loading impossible (cl 5) were not designed to deal with the situation where delay has taken place sufficient to produce frustration by rendering the contract wholly or partly impossible. The present case, unlike the *Comptoir, Davis* and *Angelia* cases, involves the question whether ascertained delay which has rendered part of the contract impossible of performance and future delay of an unascertainable duration which may render part or all of the remainder of the contract impossible of performance combine to frustrate the contract. Like the arbitrator I have come to the conclusion that by 26th September the contract was frustrated and I would allow the appeal accordingly.

WATKINS LJ (read by Lord Denning MR). I agree that this appeal should be allowed for the reasons which Lord Denning MR and Templeman LJ have stated. There is nothing I can usefully add.

Appeal allowed. Arbitrator's award upheld. Leave to appeal to the House of Lords refused.

Solicitors: *Holman, Fenwick & Willan* (for the owners); *Sinclair, Roche & Temperley* (for the charterers).

Sumra Green Barrister.

O'Brien and others v Sim-Chem Ltd

HOUSE OF LORDS

LORD DIPLOCK, VISCOUNT DILHORNE, LORD SALMON, LORD RUSSELL OF KILLOWEN AND LORD KEITH OF KINKEL

7th, 8th, 30th JULY 1980

Employment – Equality of treatment between men and women – Equivalent work – Job evaluation study – Scheme to remunerate men and women employees for equivalent work according to job evaluation study – Scheme not implemented because of government pay policy – Women and men continuing to be paid unequally – Effect of job evaluation study on remuneration for equivalent work – Whether job evaluation study determining term of women's contracts relating to remuneration even though scheme not implemented – Whether women employees entitled to equal pay even though scheme not implemented – Equal Pay Act 1970 (as amended by the Sex Discrimination Act 1975), s 1(2)(b)(i)).

The employers carried out a job evaluation study on the work done by their male and female clerical employees with a view to introducing a pay structure to provide equal pay

for men and women doing equivalent work. In October 1975, as a result of the study,
a a scheme was formulated grading all clerical jobs into six grades of equivalent work, the
grades being related to the demands of the jobs. The employers and the employees
negotiated and agreed salary ranges for each grade. The employers intended to draw up
a merit assessment scheme to determine individual salaries within each grade but never
did so. By a letter dated 24th March 1976 the employers informed each employee of the
grade of his or her job within the scheme and the salary range within the grade and stated
b that they intended to introduce the scheme with effect from 26th April 1976 but that
salaries could not be adjusted in accordance with the scheme at that time because of the
government's pay policy. Accordingly, the employees continued to be remunerated
under their existing contracts and, because the scheme was never implemented, women
clerical employees continued to be paid less than men. In May 1977 three women
employees applied to an industrial tribunal claiming that the employers had refused to
c give them equal pay since October 1975, but the tribunal dismissed their applications on
the ground that the applicants could not claim, under s 1(2)[a] of the Equal Pay Act 1970,
to be entitled to pay equal to that paid to men whose work had been rated equivalent to
theirs in the scheme because the scheme had never been implemented. The applicants
appealed to the Employment Appeal Tribunal which allowed the appeal, holding that
'the rating of [their] work' in the scheme as equivalent with that of men had 'determined'
d a 'term' of the applicants' contracts, ie the term regulating their remuneration, within
s 1(2)(*b*)(i) of the 1970 Act, and since the applicants were being paid less than the men
they were entitled to an equality clause in regard to pay in their contracts. The Court of
Appeal ([1980] 2 All ER 307) allowed an appeal by the employers on the ground that a
term of a woman's contract could not be 'determined' by the rating of the work in a job
evaluation study until the job evaluation scheme had been implemented and the
e woman's contract modified to give effect to the scheme, because the word 'determined'
denoted a causative effect between the rating of the work in the scheme and the fixing
of the terms of the woman's contract, and since the scheme had never been implemented
the terms of the applicants' contracts relating to remuneration had never been
'determined' by the rating of their work in the scheme. The applicants appealed,
contending that the word 'determined' in s 1(2)(*b*) merely meant measured by, or
f ascertained by reference to, the job evaluation scheme.

Held – For the purpose of determining the effect of the equality clause which by s 1(1)
of the 1970 Act a woman employee's contract of employment was deemed to contain,
once a job evaluation study under s 1(5) of the Act had been carried out enabling a
comparison between the terms and conditions of the respective contracts of men and
women in the same employment to be made and discrimination against a woman to be
g detected, the woman's contract was deemed by the equality clause either to be modified
by virtue of s 1(2)(*a*) in the case of like work to exclude less favourable terms in her
contract and include more favourable terms which were in the man's contract or to be
treated as being so modified by virtue of s 1(2)(*b*) in the case of work rated as
equivalent. Since the employers had carried out a job evaluation study which enabled a
h comparison between male and female employees doing equivalent work to be made and
any discrimination to be detected, the term of the applicants' contracts relating to
remuneration was to be treated, as from the date of the scheme, as being modified so as
to be not less favourable than the similar term in the contracts of men whose job had
been given an equal value in the job evaluation scheme. The appeal would accordingly
be allowed (see p 135 *a* to *c*, p 137 *a* to *c* and *g* to *j* and p 138 *a*, post).
j Decision of the Court of Appeal [1980] 2 All ER 307 reversed.

Notes

For equal treatment of men and women as regards terms and conditions of employment, see 16 Halsbury's Laws (4th Edn) para 767.

---

a Section 1(2), so far as material, is set out at p 135 *g* and p 136 *g*, post

For the Equal Pay Act 1970, s 1 (as amended by the Sex Discrimination Act 1975, s 8),
see 45 Halsbury's Statutes (3rd Edn) 290. a

Case referred to in opinions

Bank of England v Vagliano Brothers [1891] AC 107, [1891–4] All ER Rep 93, 60 LJQB 145,
64 LT 353, 55 JP 676, HL, 44 Digest (Repl) 377, *2177*.

Appeal

On 20th May 1977 Patricia O'Brien, Doris Lloyd Coleman and Isabel Mary Clarkson ('the b
applicants') applied to an industrial tribunal for a decision on the question whether Sim-
Chem Ltd ('the employers') could institute equal pay on their behalf in accordance with
s 1(2)(*b*) of the Equal Pay Act 1970 as a result of a job evaluation study completed on
behalf of the employers in October 1975 and confirmed on 26th April 1976.

The study had been set up by the employers with a view to introducing a pay structure
for female clerical employees who were not doing work of the same or a similar nature c
to any male employee, by providing that men and women who were doing equivalent
work would be paid equally. The study recommended that all clerical jobs with the
employers should be graded into six grades which were to be related solely to the
demands of the jobs, and that provision should be made for the determination of
individual salaries on the basis of how well the job was being performed by the individual
as opposed to what job was being performed. The employers accepted the proposed d
grading of jobs and negotiated a salary range for each grade with the employees' union.
At the time of the study the government operated a policy of pay restraint and the
employers considered that the new graded pay structure infringed that policy and that
if the new pay structure was implemented the employers would be subjected to sanctions
imposed by the government, such as the withdrawal of government contracts and loss of
discretionary grants or loans. The employers therefore wrote to each of the employees e
affected by the new pay structure, including the applicants, on 24th March 1976
informing them of the new grade of their jobs and the salary range and that no salary
adjustments could be made at that time because of the government pay restrictions.
Individual employees continued to be paid in accordance with their existing contracts
rather than by reference to the grading of jobs described in the letter of 24th March.

The applicants applied to an industrial tribunal on the ground that they were employed f
on work rated in the study as equivalent with that of men in respect of grading but were
not receiving equal pay. By a decision dated 4th November 1977 an industrial tribunal
sitting at Manchester on 11th October 1977 (chairman Mr W Ashworth) dismissed the
applications on the ground that the job evaluation scheme giving effect to the job
evaluation study had not been implemented by the employers. The applicants appealed
to the Employment Appeal Tribunal (Phillips J, Mr S C Marley and Mrs A L T Taylor) g
which by a judgment given on 28th July 1978 allowed the appeal and ordered '... that
in the case of each [applicant] the term of her contract of employment relating to
remuneration should be treated as so modified as to be not less favourable than the
similar term in the contract of employment of any man whose job has been given equal
value to her job in the evaluation scheme dated 26th April 1976 in so far as grading is
concerned and that the position within the grade is to be determined by agreement. And h
the tribunal further orders that the aforesaid order be not enforced until 31st October
1978 without prejudice to any agreement being reached to its being enforced at an
earlier date, or as relating back to an earlier date. Liberty to apply as to the form of the
aforesaid order ...' The employers appealed to the Court of Appeal (Stephenson,
Cumming-Bruce and Waller LJJ) ([1980] 2 All ER 307, [1980] 1 WLR 734) which
allowed the appeal on 21st December 1979 and restored the order of the industrial j
tribunal. The court refused leave to appeal to the House of Lords. On 27th March 1980
the Appeal Committee of the House of Lords granted the applicants leave to appeal.

Anthony Lester QC and *Eldred Tabachnik* for the applicants.
Martin Collins QC and *Giles Wingate-Saul* for the employers.

Their Lordships took time for consideration.

a 30th July. The following opinions were delivered.

LORD DIPLOCK. My Lords, I have had the advantage of reading in draft the speech prepared by my noble and learned friend Lord Russell with which I agree, and I too would allow the appeal.

b **VISCOUNT DILHORNE.** My Lords, I agree with the speech of my noble and learned friend Lord Russell which I have seen in draft. I would allow the appeal and restore the order of the Employment Appeal Tribunal with the variations he proposes.

LORD SALMON. My Lords, I have had the advantage of reading in draft the speech
c prepared by my noble and learned friend Lord Russell with which I agree. I too would allow the appeal.

LORD RUSSELL OF KILLOWEN. My Lords, the Equal Pay Act 1970 came into force on 29th December 1975, simultaneously with and as amended by the Sex Discrimination Act 1975. The 1970 Act in its amended form is conveniently set out in
d Part II of Sch 1 to the 1975 Act. The 1970 Act is entitled 'An Act to prevent discrimination, as regards terms and conditions of employment, between men and women'. It deals so far as concerns these appeals with two situations. The first is where a woman is employed on 'like work' with a man in the same employment; the second (with which these appeals are directly concerned) is where a woman is employed on work 'rated as equivalent' with that of a man in the same employment.

e By s 1(1) of the 1970 Act each woman's contract now in question became deemed to include 'an equality clause'. Whether such an equality clause has any and if so what effect depends on the particular circumstances.

It is convenient to consider first the provisions affecting a 'like work' case. A 'like work' case is described in s 1(4) as follows:

> 'A woman is to be regarded as employed on like work with men if, but only if,
> *f* her work and theirs is of the same or a broadly similar nature, and the differences (if any) between the things she does and the things they do are not of practical importance in relation to terms and conditions of employment; and accordingly in comparing her work with theirs regard shall be had to the frequency or otherwise with which any such differences occur in practice as well as to the nature and extent of the differences.'

g Section 1(2) provides:

> 'An equality clause is a provision which relates to terms (whether concerned with pay or not) of a contract under which a woman is employed (the "woman's contract"), and has the effect that—(*a*) where the woman is employed on like work with a man in the same employment—(i) if (apart from the equality clause) any
> *h* term of the woman's contract is or becomes less favourable to the woman than a term of a similar kind in the contract under which that man is employed, that term of the woman's contract shall be treated as so modified as not to be less favourable, and (ii) if (apart from the equality clause) at any time the woman's contract does not include a term corresponding to a term benefiting that man included in the contract under which he is employed, the woman's contract shall be treated as including
> *j* such a term . . .'

It is to be observed that the question whether there is a case of 'like work' is an objective fact which in the case of a woman's contract at the coming into force of the 1970 Act either exists or does not exist. It is for the relevant tribunal to decide that question (if there be dispute), and also to decide whether modification or addition is required under para (*a*)(i) and (ii) as a result of the deemed equality provision. In short, the exercise requires a comparison of the terms and conditions of employment of the *a* woman and of the man in a case of 'like work'.

There is, be it noted, a further possible consideration in a 'like work' case under s 1(3), which provides:

> 'An equality clause shall not operate in relation to a variation between the woman's contract and the man's contract if the employer proves that the variation is genuinely due to a material difference (other than the difference of sex) between *b* her case and his.'

The function of that subsection is to enable the employer to show on what may be called a merit basis that the man in the 'like work' is as one *individual* entitled to preferential treatment; an example might be long service.

I turn now to sub-ss (2)(*b*)(i) and (ii) and (5) which deal with cases where the woman *c* and the man are employed on jobs which, though not 'like work', have been 'rated as equivalent' as a result of a job evaluation study. Section 1(5) provides:

> 'A woman is to be regarded as employed on work rated as equivalent with that of any men if, but only if, her job and their job have been given an equal value, in terms of the demand made on a worker under various headings (for instance effort, skill, decision), on a study undertaken with a view to evaluating in those terms the *d* jobs to be done by all or any of the employees in an undertaking or group of undertakings, or would have been given an equal value but for the evaluation being made on a system setting different values for men and women on the same demand under any heading.'

Job evaluation studies with a view to pinpointing equivalents and differences are not *e* confined to the 1970 Act: they are in more general use in industry in an attempt to achieve a broadly sound pay structure. Reference may be made to a document placed before us, 'ACAS Guide No 1—Job Evaluation'.

It is of importance to note that a job evaluation study cannot be carried out without the agreement of the relevant parties, including of course the employer, that there shall be one. Maybe it was recognised that such a study could not sensibly be made *f* compulsory.

I note at this stage that s 1(3) already quoted, which might be described as providing for permissible merit variation, applies also to a case of equivalent job rating.

I turn finally to the provisions of s 1(2)(*b*) which deals with a case where there is not 'like work' but where work of a woman has by the application of s 1(5) been rated an equivalent with that of a man. Section 1(2)(*b*) provides as follows: *g*

> 'An equality clause is a provision which relates to terms (whether concerned with pay or not) of a contract under which a woman is employed (the "woman's contract"), and has the effect that . . . (*b*) where the woman is employed on work rated as equivalent with that of a man in the same employment—(i) if (apart from the equality clause) any term of the woman's contract determined by the rating of *h* the work is or becomes less favourable to the woman than a term of a similar kind in the contract under which that man is employed, that term of the woman's contract shall be treated as so modified as not to be less favourable, and (ii) if (apart from the equality clause) at any time the woman's contract does not include a term corresponding to a term benefiting that man included in the contract under which he is employed and determined by the rating of the work, the woman's contract *j* shall be treated as including such a term.'

It is to be observed that para (*b*) follows exactly the pattern of para (*a*), but contains additionally in sub-para (i) the words 'determined by the rating of the work' and in sub-para (ii) the words 'and determined by the rating of the work'. It is over the meaning (if any) to be given to those words that argument has ranged.

Taking a general approach to the legislation, I find that the 'like work' provisions operate on a situation in which comparison of terms and conditions, under respectively the woman's and the man's contract, is necessarily feasible, and as soon as that comparison is made it can be decided whether there is a relevant discrimination between the woman and the man, subject of course to the provisions of s 1(3). Once a job evaluation study has been undertaken and has resulted in a conclusion that the job of the woman has been evaluated under s 1(5) as of equal value with the job of the man, then the comparison of the respective terms of their contracts of employment is made feasible and a decision can be made (subject of course to s 1(3)) whether 'modification' under para (*b*)(i) or 'treatment' under para (*b*)(ii) is called for by the equality clause. I would expect that at that stage when comparison becomes first feasible, and discrimination can first be detected, that the provisions of para (*b*) would be intended to bite, and bite at once. Comparison of terms and conditions of employment must be at the heart of the legislation, and I cannot imagine any reason why Parliament should postpone to a later stage the operation of para (*b*).

In the present case the pay structure of the employer was not adjusted as a result of the conclusions of the equivalent jobs value study. (The reason for this is not relevant to the decision of these appeals.) It was in fact anxiety lest a conflict with government pay policy would be involved, with consequences adverse to the commercial interests of the employer. The employers contend that unless and until there is such a resulting adjustment one does not reach the stage of deciding whether para (*b*) is operative, and for this they rely on the presence of the phrases 'term . . . determined by the rating of the work'. They say that some effect must be given to them: that unless the employers' contention is correct no effect is given to them, since without their presence para (*b*) would have exactly the same effect as is contended for by the applicants. That last submission is, I think, correct. The employers argue that 'the rating of the work' in sub-paras (i) and (ii) refers to something different from 'work rated as equivalent' in para (*b*) (and in s 1(5)). This I am wholly unable to accept, despite the suggested element of tautology.

The fact is that the exercise of equivalent work rating pursuant to a study undertaken under s 1(5) does not determine in any sense any term of the woman's contract, nor determine in any sense any term of the man's contract beneficial to him but absent from that of the woman. That is not a function of the exercise.

The employers based an argument on the fact that they were under no statutory obligation to participate in a job evaluation exercise, which is true, and which I have already suggested may be due to an impossibility of enforcing it. Therefore, it is contended, that the employers should not be assumed to be under compulsion just because they have co-operated in a voluntary exercise. I do not agree. It seems to me eminently sensible that Parliament should impose the requirements of para (*b*) at the moment when the evaluation study and exercise has made available a comparison which can show discrimination.

In summary, therefore, I am of opinion that the words in dispute cannot have the result contended for by the employers. We were offered a number of dictionary substitutes for 'determined' none of which appealed to me. The best that I can do is to take the phrase as indicating that the very outcome of the equivalent job rating is to show the term to be less favourable. The next best that I can do is to echo the words of Lord Bramwell in *Bank of England v Vagliano Brothers* [1891] AC 107 at 138, [1891–4] All ER Rep 93 at 110, 'This beats me', and jettison the words in dispute as making no contribution to the manifest intention of Parliament.

I would therefore allow the appeals and restore the order of the Employment Appeal Tribunal with the following variations: (1) add after 'modified' the words 'with effect from 26th April 1976'; (2) add before 'to be determined by agreement' the words 'if possible'; (3) delete '31st October 1978' and substitute 'the expiration of three months after the decision of the appeal in the House of Lords; and (4) delete the words after 'Liberty to apply'.

LORD KEITH OF KINKEL. My Lords, I have had the advantage of reading in draft the speech of my noble and learned friend Lord Russell. I agree entirely with his *a* reasoning and his conclusion that the appeal should be allowed and an order made in the terms which he has proposed.

Appeal allowed; order of Employment Appeal Tribunal varied.

Solicitors: *Pattison & Brewer* (for the applicants); *C G H Mackenzie*, Stockport (for the *b* employers).

Mary Rose Plummer Barrister.

c

Alloway v Phillips (Inspector of Taxes)

COURT OF APPEAL, CIVIL DIVISION
LORD DENNING MR, WALLER AND DUNN LJJ *d*
13th, 14th, 17th MARCH 1980

Income tax – Capital or income receipts – Sale of property – Profits or gains arising from property in United Kingdom – Payment for provision of information – Contract made between newspaper and agent for taxpayer – Contract requiring taxpayer to provide information about her life with her convict husband – Taxpayer resident abroad – Contract governed by English law *e* *and payment to be made to agent on behalf of taxpayer – Whether payment 'profits or gains arising ... from property ... in the United Kingdom' – Whether payment received as capital or income – Whether payment arising from the contract or from the services performed by taxpayer – Income and Corporation Taxes Act 1970, s 108, para 1(a)(iii).*

The taxpayer, who lived in Canada, was the wife of a man who had been convicted and *f* sentenced to imprisonment for robbery, had escaped from prison and had been recaptured. After his recapture a reporter from an English newspaper visited the taxpayer in Canada to get information for writing articles about her for publication in the newspaper. The articles were published in February and March 1968. In March 1968 the newspaper made two payments totalling £39,000 in respect of the articles to a firm of English solicitors. It was common ground that the payments were made by the *g* newspaper to others on the taxpayer's behalf. The Crown, however, claimed that the payments were made in pursuance of a contract between the taxpayer and the newspaper and for that purpose relied on a document dated 10th February 1968 containing an agreement which was expressed to be made between the newspaper, the taxpayer and her husband, the latter two acting through an employee of the solicitors'. The agreement recited that the newspaper desired to publish a series of articles on the taxpayer's life and *h* experiences with her husband, including an account of the robbery, to be written by the reporter in conjunction with the taxpayer. The agreement contained covenants by the taxpayer restricting her from providing material relating to the subject matter of the articles to persons other than the newspaper and granted the newspaper the sole and exclusive world rights to publish her story. In consideration of the agreement the newspaper agreed to pay the taxpayer £39,000, of which £19,000 would be paid on *j* delivery of the approved final transcript and £20,000 on publication of the first article. Under the agreement the money payable to the taxpayer was to be paid to the solicitors' employee for and on behalf of the taxpayer. The taxpayer was assessed to income tax for the year 1967–68 under Sch D, Case VI, on the basis that the £39,000 constituted 'annual profits or gains arising or accruing ... from ... property ... in the United Kingdom', within s 108, para 1(*a*)(iii)[a] of the Income and Corporation Taxes Act 1970. The Special Commissioners, having made the finding that the taxpayer did ratify the agreement purported to have been made on her behalf by the solicitors' employee and that the sum payable under the agreement constituted income, determined that the sum received by the taxpayer accrued from property in the United Kingdom within s 108, para 1(*a*)(iii) and dismissed the taxpayer's appeal. The judge affirmed the commissioners' determination. The taxpayer appealed, contending (i) that the agreement of 10th February 1968 was unenforceable because she had not ratified it (ii) that the consideration received by her was wholly or partly of a capital nature, and (iii) that, even if the agreement had been ratified by her and the money received by her constituted profits or gains of a revenue nature, the payment did not arise or accrue from 'property' in the United Kingdom but arose from services of the taxpayer (as opposed to property) provided outside the jurisdiction, the agreement being no more than incidental machinery for regulating the method of paying the income and having no independent vitality of its own.

Held – The money paid by the newspaper to the taxpayer was a profit or gain arising or accruing to the taxpayer from property in the United Kingdom within s 108, Sch D, para 1(*a*)(iii) of the 1970 Act chargeable to tax under Sch D, Case VI, and the appeal would accordingly be dismissed, for the following reasons—

(1) There was sufficient evidence to justify the commissioners' finding that although the taxpayer did not expressly authorise the agreement of 10th February 1968 she had ratified it. Accordingly, there was a binding contract between the taxpayer and the newspaper and the taxpayer was entitled to seek payment of the sums provided for in the contract (see p 141 *g* to *j*, p 143 *g h*, p 144 *e f*, p 145 *j*, p 146 *d e* and p 147 *e*, post).

(2) The commissioners had found as a fact, on the evidence before them, that the money received by the taxpayer was of an income nature, and there was no ground on which the court could interfere with their finding (see p 141 *j*, p 143 *g h*, p 145 *h j*, p 146 *d e* and p 147 *e*, post).

(3) The source of the income did not lie in the taxpayer's information but in the taxpayer's right to demand from the newspaper payment of the sums agreed under the contract. The right, being a chose in action, was property within s 108, Sch D, para 1(*a*)(iii). Moreover, the newspaper being resident in the United Kingdom, the chose in action was enforceable in the United Kingdom and, therefore, situated in the United Kingdom (see p 143 *c d* and *g h*, p 144 *g*, p 145 *f* to *h* and p 147 *d e*, post); *Gospel v Purchase (Inspector of Taxes)* [1951] 2 All ER 1071, *Firestone Tyre and Rubber Co Ltd v Lewellin (Inspector of Taxes)* [1957] 1 All ER 561, *Carson (Inspector of Taxes) v Peter Cheyney's Executor* [1958] 3 All ER 573 and *Hume (Inspector of Taxes) v Asquith* [1969] 1 All ER 868 distinguished.

Notes

For ratification by a principal of a contract entered into by an agent, see 1 Halsbury's Laws (4th Edn) paras 756–768, and for cases on the subject, see 1(2) Digest (Reissue) 565–591, *3891–4061*.

For the distinction between capital and income, see 23 Halsbury's Laws (4th Edn) paras 10–17.

For the meaning of 'property' in the charge to tax, see ibid para 198.

For the Income and Corporation Taxes Act 1970, s 108, see 33 Halsbury's Statutes (3rd Edn) 150.

Cases referred to in judgments

Byron v Byron (1595) 1 Cro Eliz 472, 78 ER 709.

Carson (Inspector of Taxes) v Peter Cheyney's Executor [1958] 3 All ER 573, [1959] AC 412, [1958] 3 WLR 740, 38 Tax Cas 240, [1958] TR 349, 37 ATC 347, 51 R & IT 824, HL, 28(1) Digest (Reissue) 239, *737*.

a Section 108, so far as material, is set out at p 142 *a b*, post

Edwards (Inspector of Taxes) v Bairstow [1955] 3 All ER 48, [1956] AC 14, [1955] 3 WLR 410, 36 Tax Cas 207, [1955] TR 209, 34 ATC 198, 48 R & IT 534, HL, 28(1) Digest (Reissue) 566, *2089*.
English, Scottish and Australian Bank Ltd v Inland Revenue Comrs [1932] AC 238, [1931] All ER Rep 212, 101 LJKB 193, 146 LT 330, HL, 39 Digest (Repl) 331, *708*.
Firestone Tyre and Rubber Co Ltd v Lewellin (Inspector of Taxes) [1957] 1 All ER 561, 37 Tax Cas 111, HL, 28(1) Digest (Reissue) 374, *1380*.
Gospel v Purchase (Inspector of Taxes) [1951] 2 All ER 1071, 45 R & IT 14, sub nom *Stainer's Executors v Purchase* [1952] AC 280, 32 Tax Cas 367, [1951] TR 353, 30 ATC 291, HL, 28(1) Digest (Reissue) 257, *827*.
Housden (Inspector of Taxes) v Marshall [1958] 3 All ER 639, [1959] 1 WLR 1, 38 Tax Cas 233, [1958] TR 337, 37 ATC 337, 52 R & IT 60, 28(1) Digest (Reissue) 317, *1122*.
Hume (Inspector of Taxes) v Asquith [1969] 1 All ER 868, [1969] 2 Ch 58, 45 Tax Cas 251, [1968] TR 369, 47 ATC 377, sub nom *Home (Inspector of Taxes) v Asquith* [1969] 2 WLR 225, 28(1) Digest (Reissue) 239, *738*.
Marsh v Joseph [1897] 1 Ch 213, [1895–9] All ER Rep 977, 66 LJ Ch 128, 75 LT 558, CA, 43 Digest (Repl) 414, *4386*.
New York Life Insurance Co v Public Trustee [1924] 2 Ch 101, 93 LJ Ch 449, 131 LT 438, CA, 11 Digest (Reissue) 479, *851*.

Cases also cited

Boardman v Phipps [1966] 3 All ER 721, [1967] 2 AC 46, HL.
Craven-Ellis v Canons Ltd [1936] 2 All ER 1066, [1936] 2 KB 403.
Danish Mercantile Co Ltd v Beaumont [1951] 1 All ER 925, [1951] Ch 680, CA.
Evans Medical Supplies Ltd v Moriarty [1957] 3 All ER 718, [1958] 1 WLR 66, 37 Tax Cas 540, HL.
Fitzgerald v Inland Revenue Comrs [1919] 2 KB 154, 88 LJKB 1125, 7 Tax Cas 284.
Gardner, Mountain & D'Ambrumenil Ltd v Inland Revenue Comrs [1947] 1 All ER 650, 177 LT 16, 29 Tax Cas 69, HL.
Heather v Redfern & Sons Ltd (1944) 171 LT 127, 26 Tax Cas 119.
Hobbs v Hussey (Inspector of Taxes) [1942] 1 All ER 445, [1942] 1 KB 491, 24 Tax Cas 153.
Luxor (Eastbourne) Ltd v Cooper [1941] 1 All ER 33, [1941] AC 108, HL.
Ryall v Hoare, Ryall v Honeywill [1923] 2 KB 447, [1923] All ER Rep 528, 8 Tax Cas 521.
Trollope (George) & Sons v Martyr Brothers [1934] 2 KB 436, 40 Com Cas 53, CA.

Appeal

The taxpayer, Mrs Patricia Alloway, appealed against an order of Brightman J ([1979] STC 452, [1979] 1 WLR 564) dated 23rd February 1979 dismissing her appeal by way of case stated from the decision of the Commissioners for the Special Purposes of the Income Tax Acts affirming the assessments made on her under Sch D, Case VI in respect of payments made to her by a company, News of the World Ltd, pursuant to an arrangement purported to have been made on her behalf by one Mr Emanuel Pryde acting as her agent. The facts are set out in the judgment of Lord Denning MR.

Marcus Jones for the taxpayer.
Brian Davenport for the Crown.

LORD DENNING MR. On 8th August 1963 there was the great train robbery. Over £2½m were stolen. The robbers were caught. They were tried in 1964 at the Aylesbury Assizes. One of the gang was Charles Frank Wilson. He was convicted and sentenced to 30 years' imprisonment. But he escaped from prison and went to Canada. His wife joined him there. They hid there living under the names of Mr and Mrs Alloway. In January 1968 the police discovered them. Charles Wilson was arrested, brought back to England, and put back in prison again. (We are told that he has since been released on parole.)

Now his wife remained for a few months in Canada. She was very nervous and taking sleeping pills. But in February 1968, soon after her husband had been taken back to England, someone telephoned her from England and told her that a reporter from the News of the World was coming to see her, that she should speak to him and that she would be paid for doing so. A little later the reporter arrived. He brought a typewriter with him. He stayed in Mrs Alloway's house for about a week. He talked with her and her friends. He saw the papers and photographs that she had with her. He wrote up a story in journalese about Charles Wilson's part in the robbery, of his life 'on the run', and so forth. The first instalment appeared in the News of the World on Sunday, 25th February 1968, and the remaining instalments on the five following Sundays finishing on Sunday, 31st March.

The newspaper paid well for her help. They paid solicitors named Sampson & Co in the City of London two cheques. One for £19,000 and the other for £20,000. The solicitors cashed the cheques and put them, I expect, into their client's account. Charles Wilson made a claim to the money, but they did not pay it to him. His wife came back to England some time in 1968 after 5th April, when the tax year ended. She tried to get the money, but found it very difficult. She asked a friend of her husband to deal with it. Eventually, after four or five years, in 1973 she was paid a lump sum of £28,000 and, in addition, a house at East Horsley in Surrey was purchased in her name.

Now the News of the World had, I expect, in their tax returns included the payment of £39,000 as part of their expenditure for the year 1967–68. I also expect that the Revenue authorities discovered in 1973 that the wife had received payment of that sum or its equivalent. At any rate, in 1974 the Revenue authorities assessed her for income tax on £39,000 just within the six years after it had been paid by the News of the World to her solicitors.

Then there came to light a written agreement. It was dated 10th February 1968 and purported to be made between the News of the World and Charles Wilson and his wife. Her address was given as Rigaud, Quebec, Canada. His was given as 'care of 11 St. Bride Street' in the City of London. That was the address of Sampson & Co, the solicitors. They were presumably, at that time, his solicitors as well as hers. But they were not described as agents. A man called Emanuel Pryde, a South African attorney, was described as the agent of the husband and wife.

Under this agreement the wife agreed to co-operate in the writing of articles for the newspapers; and the newspaper agreed to pay her £19,000 on delivery of the typescript with her approval indorsed thereon, and on publication of the first instalment another £20,000. It also provided that the agreement was to be construed in accordance with English law, and the High Court of Justice in England should be the court having jurisdiction over the matter.

The first question is whether that agreement was binding or not. The Special Commissioners found that the wife did not expressly authorise it; but they found that she ratified it by all that she did in implementing it, namely by receiving the telephone call from London, and acting on it by receiving the newspaper reporter into her home, and seeking payment of the sums provided for in the contract. I wondered at first whether she had sufficient knowledge of the contents of the document to warrant a finding of ratification; but I think the circumstances were such as to warrant the clear inference that she was adopting the supposed agent's acts, whatever they were: see *Marsh v Joseph* [1897] 1 Ch 213 at 247, [1895–99] All ER Rep 977 at 982 by Lord Russell CJ. And on ratification the agreement became just as binding on the parties as if she had previously authorised it.

Next arises the question: was she liable to pay tax on it for the year 1967–68 when it was paid over to Sampsons? Or for the year 1973–74 when they paid it over to her? The answer is, I think, that, if she is liable at all, it is for the year 1967–68. It is a general principle that receipts are to be taken as accruing in the period in which the money is earned, even though it is not paid or received till a later period. These sums were certainly earned in the year 1967–68.

Now here is the point in the case: at that time, in February or March 1968, the wife was not resident in the United Kingdom. She was resident in Canada. In order that she should be made liable for tax on the £39,000, it must be brought within the Income and Corporation Taxes Act 1970, s 108 (being Sch D), para 1(*a*)(iii) as being—

> 'the annual profits or gains arising or accruing . . . (iii) to any person, whether a British subject or not, although not resident in the United Kingdom, from any property whatever in the United Kingdom . . .'

and under Sch D, Case VI (s 109(2)) as being—

> 'tax in respect of any annual profits or gains not falling under any other Case of Schedule D . . .'

The crucial question is whether this £39,000 was an annual profit or gain accruing to her on any property whatever in the United Kingdom.

Counsel for Mrs Alloway submitted two interesting propositions to us. First, he submitted that the wife here had no property in the United Kingdom. She derived her profits from the services that she had rendered in Canada. Second, he submitted that her rights under the contract were not property in the United Kingdom. The contract was only machinery for collecting the reward for her services. It had no independent vitality.

For his first proposition counsel for Mrs Alloway referred us to *Housden (Inspector of Taxes) v Marshall* [1958] 3 All ER 639, [1959] 1 WLR 1. That was a case where a jockey sold his reminiscences to a reporter of the Sunday Chronicle and was paid £750 for an article. Harman J held that he had to pay tax on it as an 'annual profit or gain.' I will read, because it is interesting and typical of Harman J, what he had to say about services of this kind. He said ([1958] 3 All ER 639 at 640, [1959] 1 WLR 1 at 5–6):

> 'This kind of case arises either as a result of something emanating from the famous, e.g., Lord Haig, the soldier, and Steve Donoghue, the jockey, or from the infamous, e.g., William Cooper Hobbs (blackmail, forgery and arson). Either category can produce money, particularly, I think, from the Sunday newspapers, because the public likes to read at its ease before the fireside sensational reminiscences of either of these two categories of persons. Strictly speaking, they are not usually reminiscences of these persons at all; they are written by what are called "ghost" writers. The celebrated or notorious character communicates this or that to the "ghost" and as here, may allow his signature to be used to give an air of reality to an otherwise bald and unconvincing narrative. The issue here is agreed to be capable of a simple statement: Was the transaction on the one side the sale by the taxpayer of some property of his, or was he really agreeing to perform services for the newspaper for a reward?'

As a result, Harman J said, he was paid a sum of money for services rendered; that is a taxable subject matter; and the jockey was held liable to pay tax on the sum. That was the case which counsel for Mrs Alloway submitted for his first proposition that the wife had derived her profits from the services that she had rendered.

For his second proposition counsel for Mrs Alloway submitted that rights under the contract were not property. The contract did not matter because it was mere machinery: it had no independent vitality. For that proposition he referred us to a case concerning Mr Leslie Howard, the actor: see *Gospel v Purchase (Inspector of Taxes)* [1951] 2 All ER 1071, [1952] AC 280. Mr Leslie Howard was a film actor, acting for money. He was paid lump sums, and a share of the profits, under a contract. Lord Asquith said ([1951] 2 All ER 1071 at 1076, [1952] AC 280 at 291):

> 'The contracts in the present case enjoy, in my view, no such independent vitality. The consideration for what Mr Howard was to do—to act or manage—was

> not the grant of a contract or contracts but the payments of money under the terms of those contracts. Mr Howard acted for money: he did not act for contracts. The contracts were mere incidental machinery regulating the measure of the services to be rendered by him, on the one hand, and, on the other, that of the payments to be made by his employers; they were not the source, but the instrument of payment . . .'

Those two propositions seem to carry counsel for Mrs Alloway quite a long way. He cited other cases on his second proposition: see *Carson (Inspector of Taxes) v Peter Cheyney's Executor* [1958] 3 All ER 573 at 576, [1959] AC 412 at 424 and the decision of Pennycuick J in *Hume (Inspector of Taxes) v Asquith* [1969] 1 All ER 868, [1969] 2 Ch 58.

It seems to me that those cases are entirely distinguishable from the present case. They were cases where people were resident in the United Kingdom, rendering services *here* in return for payment *here*. The question was whether the royalties were classified under Case II or Case III of Sch D. It seems to me that they have no application at all to the present case where the wife was resident in Canada, rendering services *there* in return for payment *here*. This case comes under Case VI of Sch D. It seems to me clear that this wife had property in the United Kingdom. She had a chose in action here. She had a right to receive from the News of the World the sum of £39,000. That was situate in England. Dicey and Morris on the Conflict of Laws (9th Edn, 1973, p 506, r 78) says: 'Choses in action generally are situate in the country where they are properly recoverable or can be enforced.' It seems to me that she had her chose of action in this country worth an actual gain of £39,000.

I would have thought the same would apply if there were an implied contract by which, in return for services in Canada, she was to be paid a quantum meruit payable in England.

The truth is that she had a chose in action in England. It was property in England; but she had no property at all in Canada. She had no copyright there. She only had the information in her head which she told to the newspaper reporter. That is not a species of property known to the law of England, nor, I expect, to the law of Canada. If the revenue law of Canada is the same as that of England, she would not be liable to pay tax there on the sum of £39,000. She was not carrying on any profession or vocation there. She would only be liable if she had property there, and she had none.

In conclusion I may say that many people regret the practice of such newspapers in paying money to criminals or their wives, so as to get a sensational story to publish. There is nothing illegal in it, so far as I know. But on one point I am clear: if the criminals or their wives get money by relating their stories to newspapers, they ought to pay tax on their profits and gains. That is this very case. The wife is now in England. She is outside the jurisdiction of the Canadian courts. She received the money here and ought to pay tax here on the sums she received here.

I think that the commissioners and the judge were quite right, and I would dismiss the appeal.

WALLER LJ. I agree. The question which arises in this case is whether or not this sum of £39,000 is taxable in the United Kingdom. Counsel for Mrs Alloway has submitted that it is not because he says the source of the profit arose wholly in Canada during the visit of the News of the World representative with his typewriter in early 1968. He submitted that it is wrong to hold that the contract was property in the United Kingdom. There was also an argument before us as to the nature of the contract and whether it could be said to have been ratified. Finally counsel for Mrs Alloway said that if he was wrong on all these points he would submit that the £39,000 was capital and not income and therefore was not taxable.

So the first question is: was this contract properly ratified? The commissioners found that it was. They were in doubt whether further evidence should have been called from *a* Mrs Alloway's husband, and they decided to deal with the case without him. They said that they accepted Mrs Alloway's evidence subject to qualifications. The qualifications were:

> 'In our view Mrs Alloway was made acquainted at some stage between the re-arrest of her husband and the arrival of the newspaper's reporter (either by letters *b* from her husband or a telephone call from one of his associates) that arrangements were being made on her behalf for the sale of her story and of their general tenor—although she may not have known in detail the terms of the Purported Agreement or of Mr Pryde's participation in it. [Then later in the same passage the commissioners say]: We find therefore that Mr Pryde did not enter into the Purported Agreement with Mrs Alloway's prior authority expressly given. Whether *c* Mr Pryde had her implied authority is a more difficult question which we are unable to determine on the facts before us, since we have heard insufficient evidence of the circumstances which led up to the conclusion of the Purported Agreement. However that may be, we have no doubt that Mrs Alloway adopted the arrangements to which Mr Pryde had put his signature when she acquiesced in these arrangements following the telephone call from London and performed her part of the agreement *d* by receiving the newspaper's representative into her home and providing the services described in the contract. The agency was therefore validated by ratification and Mrs Alloway was in our view entitled to seek, as she subsequently did, payment of the sums provided for in the contract in England.'

e There was also a term in the contract which said that the sum of £19,000 was to be paid on the delivery to the company of the final typescript with the approval in writing of the contributor, the agent and the company indorsed thereon. So she had had to sign her approval on the typescript, no doubt before the representative left Canada. In my opinion there was ample evidence to support the finding of the commissioners that she adopted that contract.

f The next question was whether or not the contract was made in the United Kingdom. Lord Denning MR has already quoted the passage from Dicey and Morris on the Conflict of Laws (9th Edn, 1973, p 506, r 78): 'Choses in action generally are situate in the country where they are properly recoverable or can be enforced', a proposition that was approved by this court in *New York Life Insurance Co v Public Trustee* [1924] 2 Ch 101 at 109. There can be no question but that the debtor was in the United Kingdom. The contract provided that payment be made to Sampson & Co's office in London. The *g* rights under the contract are therefore property situate in the United Kingdom.

Counsel for Mrs Alloway submitted that under the authority of the three cases which Lord Denning MR has already mentioned (*Gospel v Purchase (Inspector of Taxes)* [1951] 2 All ER 1071, [1952] AC 280, *Carson (Inspector of Taxes) v Peter Cheyney's Executor* [1958] 3 All ER 573, [1959] AC 412 and *Hume (Inspector of Taxes) v Asquith* [1969] 1 All ER 868, *h* [1969] 2 Ch 58) that the rights made under such a contract did not represent property for taxation purposes; but consideration of those cases does not support his argument. In the last of those cases, *Hume v Asquith*, Pennycuick J was considering a similar problem. He said in a matter which had given him some perplexity ([1969] 1 All ER 868 at 881–882, [1969] 2 Ch 58 at 78):

j

> 'That is the position which arises where a professional man, having entered into a royalty contract, and while still carrying on his profession, proceeds to assign the benefit of that royalty contract. In such a case it seems clear, at first sight, to say no more, that the royalties could not be treated as part of the professional income of the

> person who has made the disposition, because they are no longer his income. On the other hand, it appears that, representing as they do uncollected income owing to the person carrying on the profession, they could equally not be taxed in the hands of the assignee. [Then later Pennycuick J quoted from the judgment of Jenkins LJ in *Gospel v Purchase* [1951] 2 All ER 1071 at 1077, where Jenkins LJ said:] "It is I think reasonably plain that periodical payments in respect of a contractual right to a share in the receipts or profits of the distribution of a film acquired otherwise than in the course of a trade, profession or vocation falling within Cases I or II of sched. D would be taxable under Case III, r. 1(*a*), as falling within the words: 'any . . . annual payment . . . .'" [Pennycuick J went on to say:] Counsel for the Crown was at first disposed to say that in that passage JENKINS, L.J., was deciding the present case, but I think that when one looks at that passage one sees that what the learned judge was addressing himself to was a contractual right which was acquired on its creation otherwise than in the course of a profession; i.e., where at the date of the contract the contracting party is not carrying on a profession.'

So the distinction which Pennycuick J was making was that between where there is income from a profession or a trade and where there is no profession or trade. It is the difference between assessments made under Case I or Case II and, in this case, Case VI. These cases make it clear that as the law stood at that time a man in a profession was assessed under Case I and the mode of assessment did not change at his death. Accordingly at that time earnings after his death were not taxable and it was not possible to argue that the case should change. They were still professional earnings even though paid after death.

This case is not concerned with professional earnings or with trading profits because Mrs Alloway was not carrying on a trade or profession. Section 108, para 1 of the Income and Corporation Taxes Act 1970 says:

> 'Tax under this Schedule shall be charged in respect of—(*a*) the annual profits or gains arising or accruing . . . (iii) to any person, whether a British subject or not, although not resident in the United Kingdom, from any property whatever in the United Kingdom . . .'

The property in that case is not associated with a trade or profession.

This contract gave to Mrs Alloway a number of rights in which she could have sued in the United Kingdom if necessary. She had no property in Canada capable of producing profits. The information about her husband was not property. It required this contract to convert it into property. This sum of £39,000 was in my opinion a profit or gain arising from property in the United Kingdom. It is entirely within s 108, para 1(*a*)(iii). It does not fall within any other class of Sch D, and therefore is correctly charged under Case VI.

Finally there was counsel for the wife's submission about this being capital and not income. The commissioners found that this was income and not capital. I do not accept the argument of counsel for the wife that once the sum was paid the rights under the contract ceased to exist. The commissioners made a finding of fact that this was income, and there was ample evidence on which they could so find; and, in my view, it is impossible to interfere with their finding.

I agree with the judgment of the judge, and I would dismiss this appeal.

DUNN LJ. I also agree. The Special Commissioners made two important findings of fact: first, the taxpayer ratified the agreement purported to have been made on her behalf on 10th February 1968, and, second, that the sums payable under that agreement constituted income and not capital. The circumstances in which the court will interfere with findings of fact made by Special Commissioners was stated by Lord Radcliffe in *Edwards (Inspector of Taxes) v Bairstow* [1955] 3 All ER 48 at 57–58, [1956] AC 14 at 36 *a* in the following terms:

> 'If the Case contains anything ex facie which is bad law and which bears on the determination, it is, obviously, erroneous in point of law. But, without any such misconception appearing ex facie, it may be that the facts found are such that no person acting judicially and properly instructed as to the relevant law could have *b* come to the determination under appeal. In those circumstances, too, the court must intervene. It has no option but to assume that there has been some misconception of the law, and that this has been responsible for the determination. So there, too, there has been error in point of law. I do not think that it much matters whether this state of affairs is described as one in which there is no evidence to support the determination, or as one in which the evidence is inconsistent with, *c* and contradictory of, the determination, or as one in which the true and only reasonable conclusion contradicts the determination. Rightly understood, each phrase propounds the same test. For my part, I prefer the last of the three, since I think that it is rather misleading to speak of there being no evidence to support a conclusion when, in cases such as these, many of the facts are likely to be neutral in themselves, and only to take their colour from the combination of circumstances in *d* which they are found to occur.'

Applying that test, I agree with the judge that there was no ground for interfering with the finding of fact of the commissioners.

But it is said that, even accepting that the agreement was ratified by the taxpayer and that the moneys payable thereunder were income, yet no tax was chargeable because the *e* source of income was not the agreement but the services provided by the taxpayer in making her knowledge and information available to the News of the World, and those services were provided outside the jurisdiction at a time when she resided in Canada. It was said that the agreement was no more than incidental machinery regulating the method of paying the income and had no independent vitality of its own.

Reliance for this proposition was placed on three House of Lords cases, *Firestone Tyre* *f* *and Rubber Co Ltd v Lewellin (Inspector of Taxes)* [1957] 1 All ER 561, *Gospel v Purchase (Inspector of Taxes)* [1951] 2 All ER 1071, [1952] AC 280 and *Carson (Inspector of Taxes) v Peter Cheyney's Executor* [1958] 3 All ER 573, [1959] AC 412. Special reliance was placed on the speech of Lord Asquith in *Gospel v Purchase* [1951] 2 All ER 1071 at 1076, [1952] AC 280 at 291 at the passage cited by Lord Denning MR. In those cases, however, tax was charged under Cases I and II of s 109 (1) and (2) of the Income and Corporation Taxes *g* Act 1970, being tax in respect of any trade, profession or vocation carried on in the United Kingdom. The limitation of the cases was explained by Pennycuick J in the passage cited by Waller LJ in *Hume (Inspector of Taxes) v Asquith* [1969] 1 All ER 868 at 881–882, [1969] 2 Ch 58 at 78. In my judgment, the principle contended for on behalf of the taxpayer applies only to cases where tax is charged under Cases I and II in respect of profits of any trade, business or profession. In the instant case tax was charged under *h* Case VI, which had been described as a sweeping-up case. The particular provision relied on by the Crown is s 108, Sch D, para 1(*a*)(iii), and I will read the material words:

> '... the annual profits or gains arising or accruing ... (iii) to any person, whether a British subject or not, although not resident in the United Kingdom, from any *j* property whatever in the United Kingdom ...'

Counsel for the Crown in his able argument pointed out that 'the bundle of rights', as he called it, and in particular the right to receive payment arising from the agreement,

constituted a chose in action. Section 205 of the Law of Property Act 1925 includes
a choses in action in the definition of property (see s 205(1)(xx)). Now a chose in action has
a location as much as any other species of property. Dicey and Morris on the Conflict of Laws (9th Edn 1973, p 506, r 78) states the rule in this way: 'Choses in action generally are situate in the country where they are properly recoverable or can be enforced': see *English, Scottish and Australian Bank Ltd v Inland Revenue Comrs* [1932] AC 238, [1931] All ER Rep 212. Lord Buckmaster stated the proposition in this way ([1932] AC 238 at 246,
b [1931] All ER Rep 212 at 215):

> 'If, however, once it be assumed that a debt must have a local situation, as I think it must, it can only be where the debtor or the creditor resides, and the fact that it has for other and similar purposes been assumed to be determined by the residence of the debtor and not the creditor is a sufficient reason for holding that that is its
> c situation for the purpose of the statute.'

And Lord Warrington said ([1932] AC 238 at 248, [1931] All ER Rep 212 at 217):

> 'So far back as the reign of Elizabeth in *Byron* v. *Byron* ((1595) 1 Cro Eliz 472, 78 ER 709) Anderson J. is reported as saying: "The debt" (namely, that in question in that case) "is where the bond is, being upon a specialty; but debt upon a contract
> d follows the person of the debtor; and this difference hath been oftentimes agreed."'

In the instant case the debtor was the News of the World, and the News of the World is resident in England. Moreover the agreement expressly provided that it was to be construed in accordance with English law and the High Court in England should be the court of jurisdiction. In these circumstances, the taxpayer's right to recover the payment
e under the agreement constituted property in the United Kingdom, and she was properly charged to tax on those payments.

For those reasons, and for the reasons given by Lord Denning MR and Waller LJ, I too would dismiss the appeal.

Appeal dismissed.

f

Solicitors: *David Lewis & Co* (for the taxpayer); *Solicitor of Inland Revenue.*

Sumra Green Barrister.

Stone v The Queen a

PRIVY COUNCIL
LORD DIPLOCK, LORD SALMON, LORD ELWYN-JONES, LORD RUSSELL OF KILLOWEN AND LORD
KEITH OF KINKEL
14th JANUARY, 4th MARCH 1980
b

*Jamaica – Constitutional law – Entrenched provisions of Constitution – Trial by jury – Grave
crimes tried by judge with jury when Constitution came into force – Statute enacting that certain
crimes to be tried by judge without a jury – Statute not enacted by special procedure for amending
entrenched provisions – Whether trial by jury entrenched in Constitution – Whether statute
required to be passed by special procedure – Jamaica (Constitution) Order in Council 1962 (SI
1962 No 1550), art 13(1), Sch 2, s 97(1).* c

The appellant was convicted in 1976 of firearms offences by a judge of the Supreme
Court of Jamaica sitting without a jury as a High Court Division of the Gun Court.
Provision was made by the Gun Court Act 1974, as amended in 1976, for such offences
to be tried by a judge without a jury. The appellant appealed to the Court of Appeal of
Jamaica, contending that the 1974 Act and the 1976 amendment were unconstitutional d
and void in so far as they provided for trial by a judge without a jury since the right of
an accused to trial by jury when charged with a grave crime was entrenched in the
Constitution of Jamaica and could only be restricted or dispensed with by legislation
passed in accordance with the special procedure provided by s 49 of the Constitution for
altering entrenched provisions of the Constitution, and that neither the 1974 Act nor the
1976 amendment had been passed in accordance with that procedure. The appellant e
submitted that although trial by jury was not specifically entrenched in the Constitution,
it was impliedly entrenched by virtue of s 97(1)[a] of the Constitution which provided that
the Supreme Court was to have such 'jurisdiction and powers' as were conferred on it by
the Constitution 'or any other law' and s 13(1)[b] of the Jamaica (Constitution) Order in
Council 1962 which provided that the Supreme Court then in existence was to be the
Supreme Court for the purposes of the Constitution, and, since the Supreme Court in f
existence when the 1962 order was made tried grave crimes by a Supreme Court judge
sitting with a jury, the right to trial by jury was consequently part of the 'jurisdiction and
powers' of the Supreme Court entrenched by art 13(1) and s 97(1). The Court of Appeal
refused the appellant leave to appeal, but gave him leave to appeal to the Privy Council.

Held – Trial by a Supreme Court judge without a jury under the 1974 Act or the 1976 g
amendment was a matter of practice and procedure rather than a matter of the
'jurisdiction and powers' of the Supreme Court for the purposes of s 97(1) of the
Constitution which did not, therefore, entrench trial by jury in such cases or render the
1974 Act and the 1976 amendment unconstitutional. In any event, by virtue of s 97(1)
the Supreme Court had such jurisdiction and powers as were conferred on it 'by any
other law' and the 1974 Act and the 1976 amendment were laws which had extended the h
jurisdiction and powers of the court to try grave crimes by a judge with a jury by adding
further jurisdiction or power to try such crimes without a jury. The appeal would
accordingly be dismissed (see p 150 *b* and *e* to *j*, post).

Dictum of Lord Diplock in *Hinds v The Queen* [1976] 1 All ER at 360 applied.

Notes j
For the judicature of Jamaica, see 6 Halsbury's Laws (4th Edn) para 971.

---

a Section 97(1), is set out at p 149 *j*, post
b Article 13(1), so far as material, is set out at p 150 *a*, post

Case referred to in judgment

a *Hinds v The Queen* [1976] 1 All ER 353, [1977] AC 195, [1976] 2 WLR 366, PC, Digest (Cont Vol E) 50, *625a*.

Appeal

Trevor Stone appealed against the decision of the Court of Appeal of Jamaica (Zacca, Henry JJA and Roare AJA given on 29th July 1977 refusing his application for leave to
b appeal against his conviction on 11th May 1976 by the High Court Division of the Gun Court (Melville J sitting without a jury) on two counts of being in illegal possession of a firearm and robbery with aggravation. The Court of Appeal gave the appellant leave to appeal to Her Majesty in Council on 15th March 1978. The facts are set out in the judgment of the Board.

c *Ian Ramsay* (of the Jamaican Bar) and *William Glossop* for the appellant.
The Deputy Director of Public Prosecutions of Jamaica (*Henderson Downer*) for the Crown.

LORD DIPLOCK. The appellant was tried on 11th May 1976 before Melville J, sitting without a jury, as a High Court Division of the Gun Court, on an indictment which charged him (1) with illegal possession of a firearm contrary to s 20(1)(*b*) of the Firearms
d Act, (2) with robbery with aggravation contrary to s 37(1)(*a*) of the Larceny Act, and (3) with shooting with intent to cause grievous bodily harm. All three counts related to offences which fall within the jurisdiction conferred on a High Court Division of the Gun Court under s 5(2) of the Gun Court Act as amended by the Gun Court (Amendment) Act 1976 ('the amended Act'). The judge convicted the appellant on the first two counts and acquitted him on the third. On the first count the judge imposed
e a sentence of imprisonment for life, which is mandatory under s 8(2) of the amended Act; on the second count he imposed a sentence of 20 years' imprisonment and 6 strokes. Against these convictions the appellant applied to the Court of Appeal for leave to appeal on a number of grounds, one of which raised a question of interpretation of the Constitution of Jamaica. His application was refused by the Court of Appeal on 29th July 1977, and leave to appeal to Her Majesty in Council against such refusal was granted by
f the Court of Appeal on 15th March 1978. The only ground of appeal that has been relied on before this Board is that which raises a question as to the interpretation of the Constitution, the constitutional point.

Put in summary form the submission made on behalf of the appellant is: that the right of an accused to trial by jury in the case of grave crimes is entrenched in the Constitution of Jamaica; it can only be withdrawn or restricted by an Act of Parliament passed in
g accordance with the special procedure prescribed by s 49 of the Constitution; neither the Gun Court Act nor the Gun Court (Amendment) Act 1976 was passed in accordance with those procedures; therefore, in so far as ss 4(*b*), 5(2) and 9(*b*) of the amended Act purport to provide for the trial of grave crimes (ie firearm offences) by a Supreme Court judge *sitting without a jury* they are inconsistent with the Constitution and void: see the Constitution, s 2.

h In the reasons for judgment of the Court of Appeal delivered by Rowe AJA the grounds on which this submission must be rejected are set out compendiously. Their Lordships, since they are in full agreement with the reasoning of the Court of Appeal, feel able to deal with the matter briefly.

The entrenched constitutional rights of a person charged with a criminal offence are to be found in s 20 of the Constitution. They entitle him to be tried 'by an independent
j and impartial court established by law'. The section contains no mention of trial by jury; though this is where one would expect to find such a right if it were intended to be entrenched.

The appellant is accordingly driven to rely on s 97(1) of the Constitution: 'There shall be a Supreme Court for Jamaica which shall have such jurisdiction and powers as may be conferred upon it by this Constitution or any other law.'

His submission is that, because at the date of coming into force of the Constitution grave crimes were tried in circuit courts by a judge of the Supreme Court sitting with a jury, the reference in this section to a Supreme Court coupled with the provision in art 13(1) of the Jamaica (Constitution) Order in Council 1962, SI 1962 No 1550, that 'the Supreme Court in existence immediately before the commencement of this Order shall be the Supreme Court for the purposes of the Constitution' by necessary implication entrenched in the Constitution the then existing right to be tried by jury in the Supreme Court in all cases of grave crimes.

Their Lordships see no ground for any such implication. As was pointed out by the Judicial Committee in *Hinds v The Queen* [1976] 1 All ER 353 at 360, [1977] AC 195 at 213, the expression 'Supreme Court' in the Constitution is used as a collective description of all those individual judges who, whether sitting alone or with other judges, or with a jury, are entitled to exercise the jurisdiction which was exercised by the Supreme Court of Judicature of Jamaica before the Constitution came into force. The power of Parliament under s 48(1) to make laws for the peace, order and good government of Jamaica embraces a power to establish new courts, to confer jurisdiction on them and to regulate their practice and procedure and those of courts already in existence at the time the Constitution came into force. This Parliament may do by ordinary law unless either (1) it would be inconsistent with s 20 or s 25 of the Constitution (in which case it must be passed in the manner prescribed by s 50) or (2) it would conflict with what this Board in *Hinds v The Queen* held to be a necessary implication from Chapter VII of the Constitution: that jurisdiction to try crimes of great gravity (as reflected by the sentences which they attract) may not be conferred on a court, by whatever label it is described, unless the individual judges of the court are judges of the Supreme Court or have been appointed in the same manner and on the same terms of tenure as those to which judges of the Supreme Court are entitled under Chapter VII. A High Court Division of the Gun Court does consist of a Supreme Court judge. So there is no conflict with the Constitution under that head.

That when exercising the criminal jurisdiction conferred on him by s 5(2) of the amended Act the Supreme Court judge sits without a jury is, in their Lordships' view, more aptly described as a matter of practice and procedure rather than 'jurisdiction' or 'powers' as those expressions are used in s 97 of the Constitution. The only fetters on Parliament's power to regulate the practice and procedure to be followed by courts of law in exercising their jurisdiction are those contained in ss 20 and 25 of the Constitution; and it is rightly conceded that these provisions do not confer any entrenched right to trial by jury for criminal offences.

Moreover, even if the mode of trial, in the instant case by a Supreme Court judge sitting without a jury, were, on a liberal interpretation, capable of falling within the expressions 'jurisdiction' or 'powers', s 97 would, in their Lordships' view, be of no avail to the appellant; since, if while sitting under the description of a 'High Court Division' of the Gun Court, a Supreme Court judge is in substance exercising the jurisdiction of the Supreme Court, as their Lordships consider he is, s 97(1) by its reference to 'any other law' authorises Parliament to extend the jurisdiction or powers of the Supreme Court, as it existed at the commencement of the Constitution, to try grave crimes by a judge of that court when sitting with a jury, by adding to it jurisdiction or power to try such crimes when sitting without a jury.

In their Lordships' view the constitutional point is without substance. They are in full agreement with the reasons given by the Court of Appeal for refusing the appellant leave to appeal to that court. They will humbly advise Her Majesty that this appeal should be dismissed.

Appeal dismissed.

Solicitors: *Philip Conway, Thomas & Co* (for the appellant); *Charles Russell & Co* (for the Crown).

Sumra Green Barrister.

a

R v Machin

COURT OF APPEAL, CRIMINAL DIVISION
LORD WIDGERY CJ, EVELEIGH LJ AND O'CONNOR J
18th, 28th MARCH 1980

b *Criminal law – Obstructing course of justice – Attempting to pervert course of justice – Attempt – Substantive offence – Ingredients of offence – Appellant fabricating evidence of police assault with intention of showing that statement made by him to police was made involuntarily – Appellant not pursuing plan of showing police assaulted him – Whether appellant's conduct intended and having tendency to pervert course of justice – Whether appellant's conduct required to be assessed by reference to proximity to an ultimate offence.*

c

The appellant made a statement to the police admitting a charge which had been made against him. Later, with the intention of showing that he had been assaulted by the police and that his statement had been made involuntarily, he fabricated evidence of an assault on him by the police. He, decided however, not to pursue his plan. He was subsequently convicted of attempting to pervert the course of public justice by fabricating
d evidence of a false allegation of assault by police officers. He appealed, contending that the acts alleged were not sufficiently proximate to the offence of perverting the course of public justice to amount to an attempt to do so.

Held – The gist of the offence of attempting to pervert the course of public justice was conduct which was intended and had a tendency to lead to a miscarriage of justice,
e regardless of whether a miscarriage actually occurred. The word 'attempt' was misleading to the extent that it suggested that the conduct of the defendant should be assessed in terms of proximity to an ultimate offence. The word was, however, convenient for use in cases where it could not be proved that the course of justice was actually perverted, but it did no more than describe a substantive offence consisting of conduct which had a tendency and was intended to pervert the course of justice. Since the appellant's acts had
f a tendency to pervert the course of justice even though his plan was not pursued to a conclusion, he had been properly convicted and his appeal would be dismissed (see p 154 *a* to *c*, post).

R v Vreones [1891] 1 QB 360, *R v Andrews* [1973] 1 All ER 857 and *R v Rowell* [1978] 1 All ER 665 considered.

g **Notes**

For the offence of perverting the course of justice, see 11 Halsbury's Laws (4th Edn) para 955, and for cases on the subject, see 15 Digest (Reissue) 972, *8397–8401*.

Cases referred to in judgment

R v Andrews [1973] 1 All ER 857, [1973] QB 422, [1973] 2 WLR 116, 57 Cr App R 254,
h [1973] RTR 508, CA, 14(1) Digest (Reissue) 116, *781*.

R v Rowell [1978] 1 All ER 665, [1978] 1 WLR 132, 142 JP 181, 65 Cr App R 174, CA, Digest (Cont Vol E) 152, *8401a*.

R v Vreones [1891] 1 QB 360, 60 LJMC 62, 64 LT 389, 55 JP 536, 17 Cox CC 267, CCR, 15 Digest (Reissue) 974, *8412*.

j **Cases also cited**

R v Britton [1973] RTR 502, CA.

R v Grimes [1968] 3 All ER 179.

R v Kellett [1975] 3 All ER 468, [1976] QB 372, CA.

R v Panayiotou [1973] 3 All ER 112, [1973] 1 WLR 1032, CA.

R v Thomas [1979] 1 All ER 577, [1979] QB 326, CA.

Appeal

Lawrence Machin appealed against his conviction on 5th October 1979 in the Crown Court at Doncaster before his Honour Judge Michael Walker and a jury on a charge of attempting to pervert the course of public justice. The facts are set out in the judgment of the court.

Lionel Scott (assigned by the Registrar of Criminal Appeals) for the appellant.
R M Harrison for the Crown.

Cur adv vult

28th March. **EVELEIGH LJ** read the following judgment of the court: On 5th October 1979 in the Crown Court at Doncaster the appellant was convicted of attempting to pervert the course of public justice and was sentenced to nine months' imprisonment. He now appeals against conviction.

On 10th August 1978 police officers on two separate occasions stopped a motor vehicle belonging to the appellant. On each occasion it was driven by a different man and neither of them held a valid driving licence. On 19th August the appellant made written statements to the police claiming that neither man had permission to use the vehicle. On 10th September he went to the police station in connection with another matter. Two friends, Brian Allen and Keith Shaw, waited outside. In the station the appellant dictated two statements to the effect that he had given the two men permission to drive the vehicle and that he was aware that they did not hold licences and were not covered by insurance.

Thereafter the prosecution case was as follows. When the appellant left the police station he asked Allen to punch him in the eye. This Allen did causing the eye to swell. The appellant told Shaw and Mrs Shaw that the police officers had hit him. He said the same thing to his own wife and told her to telephone the Doncaster police and lodge a complaint. This she did. He made similar allegations to a hospital doctor and to his solicitor. He went to a photographer who photographed the eye. He asked Allen to give evidence that the police had caused his injury and Allen agreed. Later however Allen changed his mind. The appellant did not in fact collect the photograph.

The appellant made a written statement admitting these facts, but in evidence he said that the statement had been composed by the police and that he had signed it because the police had threatened to have his children put into care if he did not sign. He denied the facts alleged by the prosecution.

At the close of the prosecution case counsel submitted to the judge that the facts alleged did not go far enough to amount to an attempt. Before this court he has argued that to charge the offence of attempting to pervert the course of public justice is to charge an inchoate offence and that the jury should be given directions as to how they may decide whether or not an act is sufficiently proximate to amount to an attempt.

The judge addressed the jury as follows:

> 'Now, what is attempting to pervert the course of public justice? It is this. It is the doing of an act or series of acts which have a tendency and are intended to pervert the course of justice. Now, as to the course of justice, members of the jury, nobody disputes in this particular case that the course of justice in relation to the alleged offence of permitting this motor car to be used without insurance, nobody disputes that the course of justice had begun . . .'

He went on to say:

> 'What is perverting the course of public justice? Members of the jury, it is the doing of something; or attempting to pervert the course of justice is doing something which is designed to lead to a false conclusion if the matter goes the whole way, and doing an act or a series of acts which have a tendency to, and are

> intended to pervert the course of public justice is this offence of attempting to pervert the course of public justice.'

Counsel has also submitted that if his primary submission is wrong the acts alleged in any event did not have a tendency to pervert the course of justice.

In directing the jury as he did the judge was following the words of Pollock B in *R v Vreones* [1891] 1 QB 360. There the defendant had tampered with wheat samples taken for submission to arbitrators to be appointed to determine any dispute that might arise as to the quality of the consignment. He was convicted of a common law misdemeanour of attempting by the manufacture of false evidence to mislead a judicial tribunal. Pollock B said (at 369): 'The real offence here is the doing of some act which has a tendency and is intended to pervert the administration of public justice.'

In *R v Andrews* [1973] 1 All ER 857, [1973] QB 422 the accused sought to persuade the defendant in a motor accident prosecution to pay him to give false evidence at the trial. Referring to *R v Vreones*, Lord Widgery CJ said ([1973] 1 All ER 857 at 859, [1973] QB 422 at 425):

> 'So that the question arose whether it was possible to have an attempt to pervert the course of justice. Lord Coleridge CJ said ([1891] 1 QB 360 at 366–367): "The first count of the indictment in substance charges the defendant with the misdemeanour of attempting, by the manufacture of false evidence, to mislead a judicial tribunal which might come into existence. If the act itself of the defendant was completed, I cannot doubt that to manufacture false evidence for the purpose of misleading a judicial tribunal is a misdemeanour . . . I think that an attempt to pervert the course of justice is *in itself* a punishable misdemeanour; and though I should myself have thought so on the grounds of sense and reason, there is also plenty of authority to show that it is a misdemeanour in point of law." Accordingly, to produce false evidence with a view to misleading the court and perverting the course of justice is a substantive offence; an attempt so to act can be charged as such, and in our judgment an incitement so to act is also a charge known to the law and properly to be preferred in appropriate circumstances.'

In *R v Rowell* [1978] 1 All ER 667 at 671, [1978] 1 WLR 132 at 138 Ormrod LJ said:

> 'The remaining grounds of appeal, namely duplicity in the indictment and the lack of sufficiently proximate acts to constitute an attempt, are both based, in our opinion, on the same false premise, which arises from the description of the offence as "Attempting to pervert the course of public justice". The use of the word "attempt" in this context is misleading. The appellant was not charged with an attempt to commit a substantive offence but with the substantive offence itself, which is more accurately, if less compendiously, described in Pollock B's words [in *Vreones* [1891] 1 QB 360 at 369] which we have already quoted, namely the doing of an act (or we would add a series of acts) which has a tendency and is intended to pervert the course of justice. Lord Coleridge CJ said [in *Vreones* (at 367)] "I think that an attempt to pervert the course of justice is in itself a punishable misdemeanour."'

The law is concerned to forbid unlawful conduct which may result in a miscarriage of justice. There are specific common law offences such as embracery and personating a juryman. There are statutory offences, for example, the concealing of information for reward about an arrestable offence contrary to s 5(1) of the Criminal Law Act 1967. On the other hand, as is pointed out in the Law Commission's report on offences relating to interference with the course of justice (Law Com 96 (1980)), the common law recognises a wide general offence variously referred to as perverting or obstructing the course of justice, obstructing or interfering with the administration of justice, and defeating the due course or the ends of justice. The particular acts or conduct in question may take many different forms including conduct that amounts in itself to some other criminal

offence or attempt thereat in the strict sense of an inchoate offence. The gist of the offence is conduct which may lead and is intended to lead to a miscarriage of justice a
whether or not a miscarriage actually occurs. We therefore respectfully agree that the use of the word 'attempt' in the present context is misleading, as was said in *R v Rowell*. The word is convenient for use in the case where it cannot be proved that the course of justice was actually perverted but it does no more than describe a substantive offence which consists of conduct which has the tendency and is intended to pervert the course of justice. To do an act with the intention of perverting the course of justice is not of b
itself enough. The act must also have that tendency.

We are therefore of the opinion that the jury should not be directed to assess the accused's conduct in terms of proximity to an ultimate offence but should be left to consider its tendency and the intention of the accused as was done in this case. In our opinion, the acts alleged did have a tendency to pervert the course of justice even though the accused's plan was not pursued to a final successful conclusion, and the verdict of the c
jury was clearly supported by the evidence.

Appeal dismissed.

Solicitors: *M J Rose*, Sheffield (for the Crown).

d

Sepala Munasinghe Esq Barrister.

Sioux Inc v China Salvage Co, Kwangchow Branch and another e

The American Sioux

COURT OF APPEAL, CIVIL DIVISION
LORD DENNING MR, BRIDGE LJ AND SIR DAVID CAIRNS
10th, 11th, 12th DECEMBER 1979 f

Arbitration – Commencement – Extension of time fixed by agreement – Power of court to extend time – Time limit on claims imposed by Lloyd's standard form of salvage agreement – Salvors requiring shipowner to lodge security with Lloyd's – Shipowner also paying sum in cash in part payment of salvor's award – Shipowner failing to make claim for arbitration within fixed time of completion of security – Shipowner applying for extension of time to claim arbitration to g
determine salvor's proper remuneration – Whether jurisdiction to extend time in favour of shipowner – Whether 'claims' in respect of which court has power to extend time restricted to causes of action – Whether judge entitled to require shipowner to lodge further security and make further part payment based on judge's estimate of likely award as condition of granting extension – Arbitration Act 1950, s 27. h

The salvors agreed to salve a stranded vessel and on 25th September 1978 entered into an agreement with the shipowners on Lloyd's standard form of salvage agreement. In June 1979, before the salvage operation was completed, the salvors required the shipowners to provide security with Lloyd's for the salvors' costs, expenses and interest in the sum of $US2,400,000. The shipowners disputed that sum claiming that it was excessive but j
nevertheless provided the required security, which was completed on 27th July 1979. The shipowners also paid the salvors $US200,000 in cash in part payment of the anticipated amount of the salvage award. By cl 6 of the salvage agreement any 'claim' for arbitration under the agreement had to be received by Lloyd's within 42 days from the date of completion of the security, and, if a claim for arbitration was not made within

that time, Lloyd's was entitled to call on the party providing the security to pay the
a amount of it and, in the event of non-payment, to realise the security and pay the proceeds to the salvors. Lloyd's usual practice was to notify the shipowners as soon as the security was completed of the date when the 42-day period would expire but that practice was, by an oversight, not followed and the shipowners were not notified of the expiry date. In consequence the shipowners failed to make a claim for arbitration within time. The salvors applied to Lloyd's for release to them of the security. On 1st October
b 1979, which was 25 days after the expiry of the 42-day period, the shipowners applied to the court under s 27[a] of the Arbitration Act 1950 for an extension of the time fixed under the agreement for claiming arbitration on the amount of the salvage award. The judge held that the court had no jurisdiction under s 27 to extend the time in favour of the shipowners because the 'claims' to which s 27 applied were limited to claims which were causes of action and the shipowners, being merely indebted to the salvors for the
c amount of their remuneration, had no cause of action against them. The judge went on to hold, however, that, had he had jurisdiction, he would only have granted an extension on condition that the shipowners gave further security of $US500,000 and also paid a further $US200,000 in part payment of the salvage award, because in his estimate the award was not likely to be less than $US400,000. The shipowners appealed against the refusal to grant them an extension of time, and offered to pay a further $US115,000 in
d part payment of the award. On the appeal the salvors conceded that if there was jurisdiction to extend the time a refusal of an extension would cause the shipowners undue hardship and that the proper amount of the salvage award was disputed.

Held – (1) A shipowners' claim to arbitration to determine the proper amount of salvors' remuneration was a 'claim' under cl 6 of the agreement to which s 27 of the 1950 Act
e applied since the word 'claim' in both cl 6 and s 27 was not restricted to causes of action. Accordingly, it being conceded that there was a dispute to which the salvage agreement applied and that there would be undue hardship if time was not extended in the shipowners' favour, there was jurisdiction to grant the shipowners an extension of time (see p 158 *h* to p 159 *b* and *f* to *h* and p 160 *a* to *e* and *h*, post).

(2) The terms imposed by the judge for the grant of an extension of time were wrong
f in principle, and an extension would be granted on the terms of the shipowners' offer to make a further part payment of $115,000, because (a) in the circumstances the judge had been wrong to estimate the lowest amount of the salvage award and on the basis of that estimate require the shipowners to provide further part payment of $200,000, for payments on account were not recoverable by the shipowners, and (b) it was inappropriate to order further security since there was no material before the judge to indicate that
g there had been a change in circumstances affecting the adequacy of the existing security of $2,400,000 and the shipowners' delay of 25 days in claiming arbitration had not been due to any significant fault on their part and had not caused any significant prejudice to the salvors (see p 159 *c* to *f* and *j* to p 160 *b* and *e* to *h*, post).

Per Bridge LJ. Any claim to have determined by arbitration a matter in issue between the parties on which the rights of the party making the claim depend is a 'claim' within
h s 27 of the 1950 Act (see p 159 *g*, post).

Notes

For the statutory power to extend time for commencing an arbitration, see 2 Halsbury's Laws (4th Edn) para 544, and for cases on the subject, see 3 Digest (Reissue) 7–9, *1–15*.

For the Arbitration Act 1950, s 27, see 2 Halsbury's Statutes (3rd Edn) 457.

j

Cases referred to in judgments

Consolidated Investment & Contracting Co v Saponaria, The Virgo [1978] 3 All ER 988, [1978] 1 WLR 986, [1978] 2 Lloyd's Rep 167, CA, Digest (Cont Vol E) 11, *15a*.

a Section 27, so far as material, is set out at p 158 *d e*, post

Liberian Shipping Corpn v A King & Sons Ltd, The Pegasus [1967] 1 All ER 934, [1967] 2 QB 86, [1967] 2 WLR 856, [1967] 1 Lloyd's Rep 302, CA, 3 Digest (Reissue) 7, *10*.
Nea Agrex SA v Baltic Shipping Co Ltd [1976] 2 All ER 842, [1976] QB 933, [1976] 2 WLR 925, [1976] 2 Lloyd's Rep 47, CA, 3 Digest (Reissue) 8, *15*.
Rolimpex (Ch E) Ltd v Avra Shipping Co Ltd, The Angeliki [1973] 1 Lloyd's Rep 226, 3 Digest (Reissue) 8, *13*.
SI Pension Trustees Ltd v Williams Hudson Ltd (1977) 35 P & CR 54.

Cases also cited

Black-Clawson International Ltd v Papierwerke Waldhof-Aschaffenburg AG [1975] 1 All ER 810, [1975] AC 591, HL; *rvsg* [1974] 2 All ER 611, [1974] QB 660, CA.
Bunge SA v Kruse [1979] 1 Lloyd's Rep 279.
Nestlé Co Ltd v E Biggins & Co Ltd [1958] 1 Lloyd's Rep 398, DC.
Richmond Shipping Ltd v Agro Co of Canada Ltd, The Simonburn (*No 2*) [1973] 2 Lloyd's Rep 145.
Shordiche-Churchward v Cordle [1959] 1 All ER 599, [1959] 1 WLR 351, CA.

Appeal

By writ dated 2nd October 1979 the plaintiffs, Sioux Inc, owners of the vessel American Sioux ('the shipowners'), brought an action seeking the following forms of relief: (1) a declaration that the first defendants, the Corporation of Lloyd's, were not entitled to call on the shipowners to pay the amount of the security given to Lloyd's pursuant to a Lloyd's standard form of salvage agreement ('the agreement') dated 25th September 1978 between, inter alios, the shipowners and the second and third defendants, Transpac Marine SA and China Salvage Co, Kwangchow Branch ('the salvors'), or to realise or enforce the security and/or pay the amount thereof to the salvors; (2) an injunction restraining Lloyd's by themselves, their servants or agents or otherwise from calling on the shipowners to pay the amount of the security and from realising or enforcing or taking any step to realise or enforce it and/or from paying the amount thereof to the salvors; and (3) an injunction restraining the salvors by themselves, their servants or agents or otherwise from requesting or otherwise inducing Lloyd's to call on the shipowners to pay the amount of the security or to realise or enforce it and/or pay the amount thereof to the salvors. By an originating summons in the action the shipowners applied for an extension of the time for claiming arbitration under the agreement pursuant to s 27 of the Arbitration Act 1950. By a judgment given on 20th November 1979 Sheen J dismissed the application. The shipowners appealed. The ground of the appeal was that the judge was wrong in law in holding that he had no jurisdiction under s 27 to extend the time unconditionally until 1st October 1979. The facts are set out in the judgment of Lord Denning MR.

Gordon Pollock QC and *Nigel Teare* for the shipowners.
Michael Thomas QC and *David Steel* for the salvors.
Charles Macdonald for Lloyd's.

LORD DENNING MR. The ship American Sioux was newly built in 1978. She was on her first voyage. She was carrying containers. She stranded on a reef near the Paracel Islands in the South China Sea. That was on 24th September 1978. The news soon reached Hong Kong, 300 miles away. Two salvage companies sent out tugs to the rescue at once. Each signed a Lloyd's standard form of salvage agreement on the principle of 'no cure—no pay'.

It turned out to be a big job. The containers had to be taken off to lighten her. After some months, she was got off the reef and towed in her damaged state to Hong Kong. She was redelivered to the owners on 20th August 1979. It took about 11 months. She has not yet been repaired. The salvors claim a reward which they say would be over \$US2m for their work in saving the hull apart from the cargo. The shipowners say that the ship in its damaged state in Hong Kong was only worth $US500,000; and that it is a recognised principle of salvage law that the reward cannot exceed the salvage value, and that at least 10% or 20% should be left for the owners. So the owners say that the award should be even less than $US500,000.

Now for the dispute. In June 1979, before the salvage operation was completed, the salvors notified the Committee of Lloyd's that they required the owners to put up security in the sum of $US2,400,000. This was to cover, according to Lloyd's form, costs, expenses and interest. The shipowners protested that that was excessive. But, nevertheless, they arranged to provide it through the Bank of America in London. At the same time they negotiated with a view to paying $US200,000 cash down to the salvors in part payment in anticipation of the arbitration award.

Now comes the point. On 27th July 1979 the security was completed. The shipowners provided at that date security in the sum of $2,400,000. Thenceforward, under the Lloyd's standard form, the time started running for claiming arbitration. The owners had 42 days in which to claim arbitration. If they did not do so there was a provision in the form that Lloyd's were to pay over the amount to the salvors. It is cl 6 of the standard form. As everything depends on it in this case, I will read it fully:

> 'Where security is given to the Committee of Lloyd's any claim for arbitration must be made in writing or by telegram or by telex and must be received by the Committee of Lloyd's within 42 days from the date of completion of such security. If such a claim is not made by any of the parties entitled or authorised to make a claim for arbitration in respect of the salved property on behalf of which security has been given, the Committee of Lloyd's shall after the expiry of the said 42 days call upon the party or parties concerned to pay the amount thereof and in the event of non-payment shall realize or enforce the security and pay over the amount thereof to the Contractor. The receipt of the Contractor shall be a good discharge to the Committee of Lloyd's for any monies so paid and it shall incur no responsibility to any of the parties concerned for making such payment. No claim for arbitration shall be entertained or acted upon unless received by the Committee of Lloyd's within 42 days from the date of completion of the security.'

The 42 days expired on 6th September 1979. The shipowners did not make their claim within the 42 days. They were 25 days late. Now they seek an extension under s 27 of the Arbitration Act 1950. The salvors say that that section does not apply to a Lloyd's salvage agreement; and that the six weeks are imperative and unalterable; and the shipowners cannot now get any extension of time. Having failed to claim arbitration within the 42 days, they can do nothing more, and the salvors can claim the whole security of $2,400,000.

Before dealing with the law, I must explain why the shipowners were 25 days late. It was not their fault. It was all due to an oversight at Lloyd's. In these cases it is the practice of Lloyd's, as soon as the security is completed, to notify the parties concerned and tell them when the 42-day period would expire. In this case the salvors demanded security of the cargo interest. It was provided. Lloyd's carried out their usual practice with regard to cargo interests, and told them when the 42-day period would expire. So the cargo interests knew all about it. But, by some oversight, Lloyd's did not send the 42-day letter to the shipowners. The clerk at Lloyd's, in an affidavit, explains it in this way:

> 'I did not write any letter to Norton Rose [the solicitors for the shipowners] at this time or send them a copy of the letter I wrote to Constants [they were for the cargo interests]. This was an oversight on my part. If I had followed the usual practice adopted in the department I would have written a 42 day letter to Norton Rose with reference to the ship security.'

We are told that it is also the practice of Lloyd's to telephone the parties about a week or two before the 42 days have expired in order to warn them of that fact. That too was not done in this case, again apparently by an oversight.

The owners were dismayed, of course, when the salvors applied in the circumstances for the security to be released to them. As soon as the shipowners got to know of this, *a* they applied, on 1st October 1979, for an extension of time. This is the telex which they sent:

> 'On Friday the 28th the undersigned spoke to Mr Dollimore [of Lloyd's] to enquire when satisfactory security had in fact been lodged and when 42 day period expired and was told 29th July last and 6th September respectively. We accordingly hereby give late notice of application for arbitration on behalf of shipowners. We *b* also request to be advised name of arbitrator appointed in accordance with the application already made by one of the parties.'

So they applied to the court, 25 days late, for an extension of time under s 27.

Sheen J held that s 27 did not apply to this arbitration clause. He did so because he thought the word 'claim' in cl 6 was to be interpreted as meaning a cause of action; and *c* that it did not apply in favour of the shipowners here because they had no cause of action at all. From that decision, the shipowners have appealed to this court.

It raises a question under s 27. That section was first introduced in 1934 following the report of Mackinnon J's Committee in 1927 (Cmd 2817). Section 27 says:

> 'Where the terms of an agreement to refer future disputes to arbitration provide *d* that any claims to which the agreement applies shall be barred unless notice to appoint an arbitrator is given . . . within a time fixed . . . and a dispute arises to which the agreement applies, the High Court [and these are the important words] if it is of opinion that in the circumstances of the case undue hardship would otherwise be caused, and notwithstanding that the time so fixed has expired, may, on such terms, if any, as the justice of the case may require, but without prejudice to the provisions of any enactment limiting the time for the commencement of *e* arbitration proceedings, extend the time for such period as it thinks proper.'

So the High Court has power to extend the time. In the early days that section was restrictively interpreted. But, ever since *Liberian Shipping Corpn v A King & Sons Ltd, The Pegasus* [1967] 1 All ER 934, [1967] 2 QB 86, it has been construed more liberally. We were taken by counsel for the shipowners through a number of cases since 1967 in which *f* attempts have been made to restrict its application; but all these attempts have failed. Thus in *Ch E Rolimpex Ltd v Avra Shipping Co Ltd, The Angeliki* [1973] 2 Lloyd's Rep 226 Kerr J held that s 27 did not apply to the time limit under the Hague Rules; but we have since held that it does: see *Nea Agrex SA v Baltic Shipping Co Ltd* [1976] 2 All ER 842, [1976] QB 933. In *Consolidated Investment & Contracting Co v Saponaria, The Virgo* [1978] 3 All ER 988, [1978] 1 WLR 986, it was submitted that s 27 did not apply to cases where *g* the right was barred; but we held in this court that it did not matter whether the right or the remedy was barred. In any case the section applied. Then there was a later case before Forbes J, *SI Pension Trustees Ltd v Williams Hudson Ltd* (1977) 35 P & CR 54, where he held that s 27 applied.

I need not go further through the cases because this case is not governed by any of them. It is to be dealt with on the construction of cl 6 itself. It seems to me that the *h* word 'claim' there is not confined to causes of action, as the judge said. It applies to a claim for arbitration so as to fix the amount of the salvage award. Suppose, for instance, in this case that within the 42 days the salvors claimed an award in excess of the amount of the security, in excess of the $2,400,000, clearly they would be entitled to have an arbitration on that matter. Seeing that the salvors could claim arbitration within the 42 days on the ground that the sum should be more, surely the shipowners could claim *j* arbitration within the 42 days on the ground that it should be less. What is sauce for the goose is sauce for the gander! What is sauce for the salvors is sauce for the shipowners too! The word 'claim', in my opinion, here means simply a claim for the salvage award to be assessed by arbitration. The claim which the shipowners make here (that it should be less than the $2,400,000) is a claim for arbitration. It is a claim which, under cl 6 of the agreement, would be barred if not made within six weeks. Then s 27 comes in; and, as I have often said, it is virtually to be regarded as written into all these arbitration agreements. It says that if the court is of opinion that undue hardship would be caused it can extend the time.

The judge found that undue hardship would be caused to the shipowners. His finding on that point is not challenged in this court. That is clearly right. It is no fault of the shipowners that the 25 days elapsed. Those days elapsed because of the oversight of a clerk at Lloyd's. The salvors have suffered no prejudice in any way because of that lapse of 25 days. They are just as well able to contest the case. They know everything about it, as they would have done if the claim had been made within the 42 days. So, on the matter of jurisdiction, I hold that there is jurisdiction to grant the extension of time.

Now I come to the next point: 'on such terms as the justice of the case may require'. The judge did not have to give a decision on it, but he considered the terms. He said that, if he had had jurisdiction, he would only have granted it on the terms that the shipowners should pay a further sum of $200,000 within 28 days—(they have already paid the first $200,000) and also give security in a further sum of $500,000.

He said as to the additional $200,000: 'It is inconceivable that the salvor's award will be fixed at less than $400,000.' I am not sure that that is correct. On the evidence before us, it is arguable that it would be less than $400,000. It must be remembered that a payment would be the equivalent of an unconditional judgment for the amount. It could not be recovered back. So it should not be made a term unless it was unarguably due. For present purposes it is sufficient to accept the offer made on behalf of the owners that they are ready to pay another $115,000 on account of the salvage award. That seems to me to meet the case entirely on that point.

As to the sum of $500,000 as further security, it seems to me that that was incorrect. The salvors put their initial figure at $2,400,000, no doubt on the generous side. They have taken into account the delay in assessing it, the loss of interest, and so forth. It is not appropriate to add a further sum by way of security.

The costs of this application should, of course, be borne by the shipowners because they are applying for an extension of time. They must pay all the costs at all events in the court below. They must also pay the $115,000 which I have mentioned. Those are terms which seem to me would be justified. The extension of time should be allowed.

BRIDGE LJ. The point raised on the construction of s 27 of the Arbitration Act 1950 is a short one. Having regard to the mischief which that section is intended to remedy, I think it is right to give the word 'claim' in the section a wide and liberal interpretation. In my judgment, any claim to have determined by arbitration a matter in issue between the parties on which the rights of the party making the claim depend is a claim within the meaning of the section. So here the determination by arbitration of the proper amount of the salvors' remuneration directly governs the right of the shipowners to recover part of the security they were required to provide for the release of their ship. The shipowners' claim to such a determination is, in my view, clearly one to which the section applies. That being so, I think it is now conceded that the mere fact of the shipowners bringing these proceedings for an extension of time to commence the arbitration is sufficient to satisfy the requirement of the section that a dispute arises to which the agreement applies. I therefore respectfully disagree with the judge's conclusion that we have no jurisdiction to extend the shipowners' time.

On the question of terms, there are in my view far too many imponderables which may affect the eventual outcome of the arbitration to make it appropriate to order the shipowners to make to the salvors a payment on account (which, once made, would be irrecoverable) of any greater sum than they have offered so far.

With regard to security, its amount was fixed by the salvors in June. There can have been no significant change in the circumstances affecting the appropriateness of the figure then fixed between June and October. Moreover the delay of 25 days on the part of the shipowners in claiming arbitration was neither occasioned by any significant fault on their part, nor the cause of any significant prejudice to the salvors. Accordingly, it would in my judgment be inappropriate to order any increase in the amount of the security.

For these reasons, I too would allow the appeal and order that the shipowners' time be extended unconditionally.

SIR DAVID CAIRNS. In my opinion, when the shipowners gave notice of their claim to arbitration, they were in effect making a claim that their liability to salvage was something less than $2,400,000, the total of the security they had given and the sum they had paid on account.

Counsel on behalf of the salvors conceded that, if the salvors had wished to obtain *more* than $2,400,000 from the shipowners and had given notice claiming arbitration after the expiration of the 42 days, they would have been making a claim and could have applied to the court under s 27 of the Arbitration Act 1950 for an extension of time. He could give no ground in common fairness why one party should be able to apply for extra time in order to get *more* money whereas the other party should not be able to apply in order to have to pay less. He simply relied on the language of s 27 which he contended could have no other meaning than that on which he relied.

I, like Lord Denning MR and Bridge LJ, take a different view of the construction of the section. I consider that the word 'claim' is fully capable of bearing the meaning to which I referred at the beginning of this judgment. I accept that the narrower meaning as found by the judge is a possible one, but it would be so unjust that I cannot believe it was the meaning intended by Parliament.

If there was a claim by the shipowners, it was obviously not a claim which the salvors were willing to accede to, and accordingly there was a dispute between them. I therefore conclude that the judge was wrong in holding that he had no jurisdiction to extend the time. It is conceded that he was right in his opinion that the case was one of hardship and that there should be an extension of time if the court had jurisdiction to grant it.

There remains the question of terms. Here, with very great respect to Sheen J, I am satisfied that he erred in principle in respect to both the conditions which he imposed. As to payment on account, it has to be borne in mind that no *order* for payment on account could be made either by an arbitrator or by a judge. If it were admitted that the right figure for a salvage award would be at least £X, it would be reasonable to make the payment of £X on account a *condition* of extending the time under s 27. If an estimate advanced on behalf of the shipowners were plainly bogus, then again such a condition would be appropriate. Otherwise I cannot think that it is right for a judge to form an estimate of what he considers the lowest sum likely to be awarded and to make the condition that the shipowners shall make a payment on account accordingly, a payment which would not be recoverable if the judge's estimate turned out to be too high. I would therefore limit the additional sum to be paid on account to the $115,000 to which the owners agreed.

As to the condition of giving a further $500,000 security, this was something which was not asked for by the salvors and there was no material before the judge to indicate that any change had occurred since they themselves fixed the figure for security at $2,400,000. I would therefore omit that condition altogether.

For those reasons I too would allow the appeal and make the order proposed by Lord Denning MR and Bridge LJ.

Appeal allowed.

Solicitors: *Norton, Rose, Botterell & Roche* (for the shipowners); *William A Crump & Son* and *Constant & Constant* (for the salvors); *Waltons & Morse* (for Lloyd's).

Sumra Green Barrister.

a # Attorney General v British Broadcasting Corporation

HOUSE OF LORDS

VISCOUNT DILHORNE, LORD SALMON, LORD EDMUND-DAVIES, LORD FRASER OF TULLYBELTON AND LORD SCARMAN

b 31st MARCH, 1st, 2nd, 15th APRIL, 12th JUNE 1980

Contempt of court – Publications concerning legal proceedings – Court – Inferior court – Local valuation court – Defendants proposing to broadcast television programme on issue pending before local valuation court – Plaintiffs seeking injunction to restrain broadcast – Whether local valuation court 'an inferior court' – Whether contempt of local valuation court punishable by c *committal – General Rate Act 1967, s 88 – RSC Ord 52, r 1(2)(a)(iii).*

The BBC advertised their intention to show on 19th February 1978 a television programme concerning a religious sect. The programme was extremely critical of the sect and among other things stated that they were not entitled to exemption from liability for rates on their meeting rooms because they were not open to all members of d the public and so were not places of public religious worship within s 39 of the General Rate Act 1967. The sect had applied for exemption from rating of their meeting place at Andover on the ground that it was a place of public religious worship for the purposes of s 39. Both the local authority and the valuation officer had lodged objections. The hearing of the application before the local valuation court at Andover, constituted under s 88[a] of the 1967 Act, was arranged for 10th March. On hearing of the BBC's intention e to broadcast the programme the sect demanded that it be cancelled because they asserted that it would be a contempt of the local valuation court at Andover. When the BBC refused, the Attorney General applied for an injunction against the BBC restraining them from showing the programme. The BBC contended, inter alia, that the local valuation court was not 'an inferior court' for the purposes of RSC Ord 52, r 1(2)(*a*)(iii)[b] and therefore the Divisional Court of the Queen's Bench Division had no power to punish a f contempt committed in connection with its proceedings. The Divisional Court ([1978] 2 All ER 731) held that a local valuation court was an inferior court and in lieu of issuing an injunction accepted an undertaking from the BBC not to broadcast the programme until after 10th March. The Court of Appeal ([1979] 3 All ER 45) dismissed an appeal by the BBC. The BBC appealed to the House of Lords.

Held – A local valuation court constituted under s 88 of the 1967 Act was not an inferior g court for the purposes of RSC Ord 52, r 1(2)(*a*)(iii) because although it was termed a 'court' its functions were essentially administrative and it was not a court of law established to exercise the judicial power of the state. Accordingly the jurisdiction in relation to contempt of the Divisional Court of the Queen's Bench Division did not extend to it and the appeal would therefore be allowed (see p 167 *b* to *g*, p 168 *j* to p 169 *c*, p 170 *b e f*, p 175 *j* to p 176 *c*, p 177 *f*, p 182 *c* to *e* and p 183 *f* to *h*, post).

h Observations on what constitutes a court (see p 166 *b* to *h*, p 172 *j* to p 175 *j*, p 180 *h* to p 181 *b* and *j* to p 182 *c*, post).

Decision of the Court of Appeal [1979] 3 All ER 45 reversed.

Notes

For what constitutes a court, see 10 Halsbury's Laws (4th Edn) paras 701–702, and for cases on the subject, see 16 Digest (Repl) 113–115, *1–20*.

j For the constitution and procedure of local valuation courts, see 32 Halsbury's Laws (3rd Edn) 122–123, paras 167–168.

For the General Rate Act 1967, ss 39, 88, see 27 Halsbury's Statutes (3rd Edn) 130, 182.

a Section 88, so far as material, is set out at p 174 *j*, post

b Rule 1(2), so far as material, is set out at p 164 *f*, post

Cases referred to in opinions

Attorney General v Times Newspapers Ltd [1973] 3 All ER 54, [1974] AC 273, [1973] 3 WLR 298, HL, Digest (Cont Vol D) 254, *204c*. a

Bonnard v Perryman [1891] 2 Ch 269, [1891–4] All ER Rep 965, 60 LJ Ch 617, 65 LT 506, CA, 32 Digest (Reissue) 323, *2686*.

Boulter v Kent Justices [1897] AC 556, 66 LJQB 787, 77 LT 288, 61 JP 532, HL, 16 Digest (Repl) 114, *6*.

Church of Jesus Christ of Latter-Day Saints v Henning [1963] 2 All ER 733, [1964] AC 420, [1963] 3 WLR 88, 127 JP 481, 61 LGR 565, [1963] RVR 422, HL, Digest (Cont Vol A) 1287, *376a*. b

Collins v Henry Whiteway & Co Ltd [1927] 2 KB 378, 90 LJKB 790, 137 LT 297, 32 Digest (Reissue) 218, *1859*.

Helmore v Smith (No 2) (1886) 35 Ch D 449, 56 LJ Ch 145, 56 LT 72, CA, 36(2) Digest (Reissue) 772, *1489*. c

Huddart, Parker & Co Pty Ltd v Moorehead, Appleton v Moorehead (1909) 8 CLR 330, 8(2) Digest (Reissue) 745, *970.

Inland Revenue Comrs v Sneath [1932] 2 KB 362, [1932] All ER Rep 739, 101 LJKB 330, 146 LT 434, 17 Tax Cas 149, CA, 28(1) Digest (Reissue) 522, *1905*.

Lewis v British Broadcasting Corpn [1979] Court of Appeal Transcript 193.

Mersey Docks and Harbour Board v West Derby Assessment Committee and Bottomley [1932] 1 KB 40, [1931] All ER Rep 409, 101 LJKB 8, 145 LT 592, 95 JP 186, 29 LGR 576, [1926–31] 2 BRA 846, CA, 16 Digest (Repl) 114, *12*. d

Morecambe and Heysham Corpn v Robinson (Valuation Officer) [1961] 1 All ER 721, [1961] 1 WLR 373, 125 JP 259, 59 LGR 160, CA, Digest (Cont Vol A) 1294, *887a*.

Post Office v Estuary Radio Ltd [1967] 3 All ER 663, [1968] 2 QB 740, [1967] 1 WLR 1396, [1967] 2 Lloyd's Rep 299, CA, 14(1) Digest (Reissue) 163, *1150*. e

R v Daily Herald, ex parte Bishop of Norwich [1932] 2 KB 402, 101 LJKB 305, 146 LT 485, DC, 16 Digest (Repl) 13, *57*.

R v Daily Mail, ex parte Farnsworth [1921] 2 KB 733, 90 LJKB 871, 125 LT 63, DC, 16 Digest (Repl) 13, *56*.

R v Davies [1906] 1 KB 32, [1904–7] All ER Rep 60, 75 LJKB 104, 93 LT 772, DC, 16 Digest (Repl) 12, *44*. f

R v Electricity Comrs, ex parte London Electricity Joint Committee Co (1920) Ltd [1924] 1 KB 171, [1923] All ER Rep 150, 93 LJ KB 390, 130 LT 164, 88 JP 13, 21 LGR 719, CA, 16 Digest (Repl) 433, *2381*.

R v Paddington Valuation Officer, ex parte Peachey Property Corpn Ltd [1965] 2 All ER 836, [1966] 1 QB 380, [1965] 3 WLR 426, 129 JP 447, 63 LGR 353, [1965] RVR 384, [1965] RA 177, CA, Digest (Cont Vol B) 616, *1327a*. g

R v Parke [1903] 2 KB 432, [1900–3] All ER Rep 721, 89 LT 439, 72 LJKB 839, 67 JP 421, DC, 16 Digest (Repl) 25, *192*.

R v St Mary Abbots, Kensington Assessment Committee [1891] 1 QB 378, 60 LJMC 52, 64 LT 240, 55 JP 502, (1891–93) Ryde Rat App 276, CA, 38 Digest (Repl) 697, *1362*.

R v Westminster Assessment Committee, ex parte Grosvenor House (Park Lane) Ltd [1940] 4 All ER 132, [1941] 1 KB 53, 110 LJKB 6, 165 LT 43, 104 JP 428, CA, 38 Digest (Repl) 768, *1837*. h

Ranaweera v Ramachandran [1970] AC 962, [1970] 2 WLR 500, 45 Tax Cas 423n, [1969] TR 507, PC, 28(1) Digest (Reissue) 545, **1340*.

Ranaweera v Wickramasinghe [1970] AC 951, [1970] 2 WLR 491, sub nom *Ranaweera v Ceylon Inland Revenue Comr* [1969] TR 501, PC, 28(1) Digest (Reissue) 545, *1339.

Royal Aquarium and Summer and Winter Garden Society Ltd v Parkinson [1892] 1 QB 431, [1891–4] All ER Rep 429, 61 LJQB 409, 66 LT 513, 56 JP 404, CA, 16 Digest (Repl) 114, *5*. j

Shell Co of Australia Ltd v Federal Comr of Taxation [1931] AC 275, [1930] All ER Rep 671, 100 LJPC 55, 144 LT 421, 16 Digest (Repl) 115, *20*.

Society of Medical Officers of Health v Hope (Valuation Officer) [1960] 1 All ER 317, [1960]

AC 551, [1960] 2 WLR 404, 124 JP 128, 58 LGR 165, 5 RRC 388, HL, 21 Digest (Repl)
a 249, *333*.
Sunday Times v United Kingdom (1979) 2 EHRR 245, European Court of Human Rights.

Appeal

The British Broadcasting Corporation ('the BBC') appealed against the decision of the Court of Appeal (Eveleigh LJ and Sir Stanley Rees, Lord Denning MR dissenting) ([1979]
b 3 All ER 45, [1979] 3 WLR 312) dated 11th April 1979 dismissing an appeal by the BBC against the judgment of the Divisional Court of the Queen's Bench Division (Lord Widgery CJ, Wien and Kenneth Jones JJ) ([1978] 2 All ER 731, [1978] 1 WLR 477) given on 17th February 1978 declaring that a local valuation court was an inferior court for the purposes of the powers of the Divisional Court under RSC Ord 52, r 1(2) relating to contempt. The facts are set out in the opinion of Viscount Dilhorne.

c

A T Hoolahan QC, Richard Walker and *Harry Sales* for the BBC.
Raymond Kidwell QC, Simon Brown and *John Greenbourne* for the Attorney General.

Their Lordships took time for consideration.

d 12th June. The following opinions were delivered.

VISCOUNT DILHORNE. My Lords, on 9th February 1978 the British Broadcasting Corporation ('the BBC') advertised in the Radio Times their intention to broadcast a television programme about a sect called the 'Exclusive Brethren'. It was a repeat of a television programme broadcast by the BBC on 26th September 1976. Your Lordships
e have not seen the text of the proposed broadcast and have not seen any evidence as to the activities of the sect. Lord Denning MR, at the commencement of his judgment, gave a short account of their tenets and activities which he said 'must be taken with reserve' as their activities had not been proved by evidence. Among other things he said that their doctrine had caused such distress that 'it is said that in Andover it led to two deaths which the coroner described as murder and suicide'. It is not necessary for the purposes
f of this appeal to express any opinion about the Exclusive Brethren. It suffices to say that Lord Denning MR who had seen a transcript of the broadcast, which your Lordships have not, described it as 'extremely hostile to, and critical of' the Exclusive Brethren. Among other things, he said that it stated that they were not entitled to exemption from liability for rates on their meeting rooms by virtue of s 39 of the General Rate Act 1967 as it was said that their meeting rooms were not open to the public and so were not 'places
g of public religious worship' coming within that section.

The Exclusive Brethren had applied for the exemption from rates of their meeting room at Andover. To this both the local authority and the valuation officer objected and the question whether they were entitled to exemption was to come before the local valuation court at Andover on 10th March 1978.

The Exclusive Brethren demanded that the broadcast should not be made on the
h ground that its content would prejudice the hearing of their case before the local valuation court and interfere with the administration of justice. When the BBC refused to accede to this demand, the matter was brought to the attention of the Attorney General who on 17th February, two days before the proposed broadcast, issued a writ claiming an injunction restraining the BBC from making it. The same day an application was made to the Divisional Court for an interlocutory injunction.

j It is sometimes asserted that no judge will be influenced in his judgment by anything said by the media and consequently that the need to prevent the publication of matter prejudicial to the hearing of a case only exists where the decision rests with laymen. This claim to judicial superiority over human frailty is one that I find some difficulty in accepting. Every holder of a judicial office does his utmost not to let his mind be affected by what he has seen or heard or read outside the court and he will not knowingly let himself be influenced in any way by the media, nor in my view will any layman experienced in the discharge of judicial duties. Nevertheless it should, I think, be *a* recognised that a man may not be able to put that which he has seen, heard or read entirely out of his mind and that he may be subconsciously affected by it. As Lord Denning MR said, the stream of justice must be kept clean and pure. It is the law, and it remains the law until it is changed by Parliament, that the publication of matter likely to prejudice the hearing of a case before a court of law will constitute a contempt of court punishable by fine or imprisonment or both. *b*

In this appeal we do not have to pronounce on whether the proposed broadcast would have prejudicially affected the hearing before the local valuation court. Although it clearly was likely to have aroused hostility to the Exclusive Brethren, it by no means follows that it would have prejudiced their claim to relief from rates. The mere assertion in the course of the broadcast that they were not entitled to that relief was in my view unlikely to have affected in any way a decision on whether their meeting room was a *c* place of public religious worship coming within s 39.

As I have said, on 17th February an application was made to the Divisional Court for an interlocutory injunction to prevent the broadcast being made two days later. Unknown to the parties to the action, the Attorney General and the BBC, though presumably not unknown to the Exclusive Brethren, there was then no prospect of the claim to rate relief being heard by the local valuation court on 10th March, the local *d* authority and the valuation officer having withdrawn their objection to the claim on 16th February[1].

Before the Divisional Court, where naturally the matter had to be dealt with in a great hurry, it not being known to that court that there would be no hearing before the local valuation court, it appears to have been assumed that the broadcast would be prejudicial to the hearing and the only question considered was whether the local valuation court *e* was a court coming within RSC Ord 52, r 1, which so far as material reads as follows:

> '(2) Where contempt of court—(*a*) is committed in connection with—(i) any proceedings before a Divisional Court of the Queen's Bench Division, or (ii) criminal proceedings, except where the contempt is committed in the face of the court or consists of disobedience to an order of the court or a breach of an undertaking to the court, or (iii) proceedings in an inferior court ... then ... an order of committal *f* may be made only by a Divisional Court of the Queen's Bench Division ...'

On the Divisional Court holding that it was, the BBC undertook not to broadcast the programme until after 10th March. The Divisional Court consequently made no order save as to costs.

The BBC appealed, asking that the Divisional Court's declaration that a local valuation *g* court is a court for the purposes of the powers of the court relating to contempt should be set aside. The hearing of the appeal commenced on 1st March and ended on the 6th. Judgment was given on 11th April. From Lord Denning MR's judgment it appears that the Court of Appeal in the course of the hearing were informed that there would be no hearing before the local valuation court on 10th March. It follows that there could be no question of contempt of that court being committed by the BBC, and that being so, *h* I must confess to some surprise that the Court of Appeal nevertheless entertained the matter.

They held by a majority, Lord Denning MR dissenting, that a local valuation court was a court coming within the rule. It follows that in their view the Divisional Court's jurisdiction extends to punishing contempt of that court. The Court of Appeal gave leave to appeal to this House, so your Lordships are now called on to decide what is in *j* reality a hypothetical question, namely can the Divisional Court punish as a contempt of

1 His Lordship subsequently acknowledged that the case before the local valuation court had not in fact been withdrawn before the hearing in the Divisional Court

court conduct likely to prejudice a hearing before a local valuation court. If it can, it has
a power to restrain publication of matter likely to have that effect.

It is most unusual for this House to pronounce on hypothetical questions. Ordinarily
we refuse to do so and it is with some reluctance that in this case I am prepared to depart
from our usual practice. I do so for the following reasons. Both parties want us to do
so. The BBC naturally do not wish to commit contempt of court. They want to know
where they stand. If they repeat the broadcast, they want to know if they are liable to be
b proceeded against for contempt should there happen to be an application pending before
one of the many local valuation courts in the country by the Exclusive Brethren for rate
relief. For the Attorney General it was suggested that if a local valuation court is a court
coming within the rule, the following tribunals must also be courts coming within the
rule: agricultural land tribunals, the Commons Commissioners, immigration adjudica-
tors, immigration appeal tribunals, the Lands Tribunal, the Mines and Quarries Tribunal,
c pension appeal tribunals, the Performing Rights Tribunal, the Plant Varieties and Seeds
Tribunal, the Transport Tribunal and VAT tribunals, of which according to the annual
report of the Council on Tribunals for 1978–79 (HC Paper (1979–80) no 359) there are
well over 500 in this country. If this suggestion is well founded, it means that the media
are at risk of being proceeded against for contempt should anything be published which
is likely to affect a hearing before any of these tribunals.

d If the reasoning of the Court of Appeal is accepted, and unless your Lordships deal
with this case it will be, then it means that until the question has been litigated in respect
of each of these tribunals, there will be great and undesirable uncertainty as to the extent
of the Divisional Court's jurisdiction to punish for contempt.

I think the desirability of your Lordships, if possible, removing or diminishing this
uncertainty, justifies the taking of the exceptional course of considering this now
e hypothetical question.

Local valuation courts are a comparatively modern innovation. They were created in
1948 by s 44(1) of the Local Government Act of that year (now replaced by the General
Rate Act 1967, s 88) which stated that:

> 'Local valuation courts constituted as hereinafter provided shall be convened . . .
> f for the purpose of hearing and determining appeals . . . against draft valuation lists
> and against objections to proposals for the alteration of valuation lists.'

Before 1948 it was the task of assessment committees to deal with these matters. The
1948 Act provided, and the 1967 Act now provides, that a local valuation court is to
consist of three persons, a chairman or deputy chairman and two others all drawn from
g a local valuation panel in accordance with a scheme submitted by each county and
county borough council and approved by the minister, that each scheme was to state by
whom the members of the panel were to be appointed, that the court should normally
sit in public, that it could take evidence on oath and for that purpose administer the oath,
that the parties to an appeal should be entitled to examine witnesses and to call witnesses,
that after hearing an appeal the court was to give such directions as to the manner in
h which the hereditament in question was to be dealt with in the valuation list as appeared
necessary and that it was the duty of the valuation officer to give effect to those directions.

Under the 1948 Act an appeal lay from a local valuation court to the county court.
Under the 1967 Act it now lies to the Lands Tribunal.

Under the scheme shown to us, all members of the local valuation panel were to be
appointed by the county council. The Acts do not provide, nor did this scheme, that any
j member of the panel or the clerk to the local valuation court should have any legal
qualification. But for his view that to be a court a member or the clerk must have legal
qualifications, it would seem that Lord Denning MR would have agreed with other
members of the court that a local valuation court was a court.

That in my view is the first question to be decided in this appeal. Despite these
statutory provisions the appellants submit that the local valuation court is not a court but

this is not the only question to be considered. If it is a court, it clearly is an inferior court but is it a court contempt of which the Divisional Court has jurisdiction to punish? a

In my opinion it is a court but my conclusion is based on a different ground from those put forward on behalf of the Attorney General and those accepted by the Court of Appeal. Counsel for the Attorney General submitted that a court must be established by Parliament and must administer public justice in public. Eveleigh LJ in his judgment in the Court of Appeal listed six characteristics which he said a court must have and found those present in a valuation court. b

In my view, when an Act of Parliament provides that a court shall be constituted, no other conclusion is possible than that it is a court. And here the 1948 Act provided that the court to be constituted should have all the features that one associates with a court.

I know of no authority for the view that a tribunal is not a court unless a member or the clerk to the court has legal qualifications. A coroner's court is just one example of a court without any requirements of legal qualifications. c

There is a wide variety of courts; so there is of tribunals as the long list in the appendix to the report of the Council on Tribunals for 1978–79 shows. While every court is a tribunal, the converse is not true. There are many tribunals which are not courts despite the fact that they are charged with dealing with certain matters and have features in common with courts. A distinction is drawn in this country between tribunals which are courts and those which are not. Sometimes that which is called a tribunal is declared d by the Act creating it to be a court. Instances of this are the Iron and Steel Arbitration Tribunal which, by s 44(1) of the Iron and Steel Act 1949, was declared to be a court of record and the Transport Tribunal which also, by the Transport Act 1962, Sch 10, is declared to be a court of record. There are other instances. Generally I would say that just because a tribunal has features resembling those of a court it should not be held to be a court. Tribunals created by or under Acts of Parliament are not as a general rule e courts unless constituted as such by the Act creating them. The only exception to this that I can find is the Lands Tribunal which has a status which singles it out from the rest. Apart from the Lands Tribunal and the Transport Tribunal, I do not regard any of those tribunals which it was suggested were courts if a local valuation court is a court as courts despite their similarity to that court.

In 1958 the Council on Tribunals was created by the Tribunals and Inquiries Act of f that year. One of the tasks of the council was to keep under review the tribunals listed in Sch 1 to that Act. That schedule did not include local valuation courts. That Act has now been replaced by the Tribunals and Inquiries Act 1971 which states that the council is to keep under review the tribunals listed in Sch 1 to that Act and that schedule includes local valuation courts. I do not know why this change was made. Local valuation courts are the only courts named in the list. It may be that in 1971 Parliament thought that, g though called a court, a local valuation court was not a court; but this, in view of the terms of the Local Government Act 1948 and of the General Rate Act 1967, is, I think, most unlikely. I think that the more likely explanation is that Parliament thought them to be courts of such a character (and as I have said, all courts are tribunals) as to make it desirable that they should be subject to the supervision of the council.

However this may be, the inclusion of local valuation courts in the list does not in my h opinion suffice to establish that an Act stating that courts are to be constituted can properly be interpreted as creating something which is not a court.

I now turn to the question whether it is a court contempt of which the Divisional Court has power to punish. This involves consideration of the jurisdiction of that court. It may be limited to protecting inferior courts which are courts of law. It may extend to all courts which have been established as courts by the state or it may extend j beyond that to all tribunals which have the same features as courts. I have come to the conclusion that it does not extend as far as that. It can be argued that it should, but to hold that it does would, in my view, be to trespass on the field of the legislature. As I have pointed out, Parliament has on occasions enacted that a tribunal shall be a court. When it has refrained from doing so, save in the case of the Lands Tribunal, I am not prepared to hold that a tribunal it has created, no matter how much it resembles a court, is a court. And the jurisdiction of the Divisional Court in relation to contempt only extends to courts.

I need not dilate on the uncertainty that would result from the contrary view or on its effect on freedom of speech. This case, when so much argument has been directed to detailed examination of the functions of valuation courts, illustrates the complexities involved in determining whether the similarities are such that a particular tribunal not declared to be a court is nevertheless one.

I do not think that the Divisional Court's jurisdiction extends to all courts created by the state, for I think that a distinction has to be drawn between courts which discharge judicial functions and those which discharge administrative ones, between courts of law which form part of the judicial system of the country on the one hand and courts which are constituted to resolve problems which arise in the course of administration of the government of this country. In my opinion a local valuation court comes within the latter category. It discharges functions formerly performed by assessment committees. It has to resolve disputes as to the valuation of hereditaments. While its decisions will affect an occupier's liability for rates, it does not determine his liability. It is just part of the process of rating. It has to act judicially but that does not make it a court of law. The fact that it has to act judicially means, as Fry LJ said in *Royal Aquarium and Summer and Winter Garden Society Ltd v Parkinson* [1892] 1 QB 431 at 447, [1891–4] All ER Rep 429 at 434, that its proceedings must be 'conducted with the fairness and impartiality which characterise proceedings in Courts of justice, and are proper to the functions of a judge' and not, though established by law, that it is a court of law and part of the judicial system of the country. In *R v St Mary Abbotts, Kensington Assessment Committee* [1891] 1 QB 378 Lord Esher MR said that an assessment committee was not a court or tribunal exercising judicial functions in the legal acceptation of the term. A local valuation court, as I have said, discharges the same functions as an assessment committee did and they have not changed their character. I hold that such a court's functions are administrative, not judicial. No case was cited to us of the law of contempt being applied to tribunals or courts discharging, albeit judicially, administrative functions and I for my part am not prepared to extend the law by applying it to such tribunals or courts.

I recognise that this conclusion still leaves an area of uncertainty. If your Lordships agree with me about this, it will still leave it open to argument whether a court established by Parliament discharges administrative or judicial functions, about whether or not it is a court of law, but the area of uncertainty will be much diminished.

To sum up, my conclusions are as follows: (1) a local valuation court is a court; (2) it is a court which discharges administrative functions and is not a court of law; (3) consequently, the jurisdiction in relation to contempt of the Divisional Court does not extend to it; and (4) that court's jurisdiction only extends to courts of law and RSC Ord 52, r 1 when it refers to 'inferior courts' must be taken to mean inferior courts of law.

For these reasons I would allow the appeal.

LORD SALMON. My Lords, this appeal raises important questions relating to preservation of freedom of speech and prevention of contempt of court, which are sometimes difficult to reconcile with each other.

On 26th September 1976 the BBC broadcast on television what purported to be the habits, teaching and attitudes of a religious sect called 'the Exclusive Brethren' which adhered to the principles laid down by an American called James Taylor Jnr. The broadcast was extremely hostile to the sect; it made it plain that the sect taught that anyone who is not one of its members is necessarily evil, and accordingly decreed that the sect's members must dissociate themselves from any such persons whosoever they may be, husband, wife, father, mother, brother or sister. They must not even talk to them or eat with them. According to the broadcast, this doctrine was applied so strictly that it caused the deepest distress amongst many and led in Andover to two deaths which the coroner described as murder and suicide. The broadcast also quoted the following words of a distinguished Queen's Counsel: 'The doctrine of separation from evil as interpreted and applied under the teachings of James Taylor Jnr was detrimental to the true interests *a* of the community . . .', and also the words of a lady who said in effect that the Exclusive Brethren, up and down the country, had applied for and obtained rate relief for their meeting houses at which their religious services were held but that they were not entitled to any rate relief because their religious services were closed to the public.

In the course of the broadcast, the BBC spokesman said: 'We have given the Brethren the right to reply; they haven't chosen to exercise this. And, in the meantime, the *b* tragedies go on.' After that broadcast a number of actions were brought by the Exclusive Brethren; and these actions are still outstanding. But no action was brought by the Exclusive Brethren against the BBC for libel. I wish to make it plain that there is no evidence whether or not what was said in the broadcast was accurate.

There was a meeting room at Andover in which the Exclusive Brethren's religious worship took place. The trustees of that meeting room made a request to the valuation *c* officer that it should be granted relief from rates on the ground that it was a 'place for public religious worship'. The local authority and the valuation officer objected to that request. These objections were treated as an appeal to the local valuation court which was convened for 10th March 1978 to hear and decide the appeal.

On 9th February 1978 the Radio Times announced that the broadcast of 26th September 1976, to which I have referred, would be repeated on Sunday, 19th February *d* 1978. The London solicitors of the Exclusive Brethren wrote to the BBC on 15th February 1978 asserting that the repeat programme on Sunday, 19th February would be a contempt of the local valuation court when it sat on Friday, 10th March to decide whether or not the objections by the local authority and the valuation officer to the request by the Exclusive Brethren for rate relief should be allowed. Those solicitors got in touch with the Attorney General on Thursday, 16th February, and he apparently took *e* the view that the BBC programme would constitute a contempt of the Andover local valuation court when it sat on 10th March 1978. A writ was issued by the Attorney General against the BBC on 17th February 1978 claiming an injunction to restrain the BBC from broadcasting 'a programme dealing with matters relating to the Exclusive Brethren and the matters pending before the local valuation court at Andover'.

The BBC's broadcast raised matters of great public importance and, if true, was *f* rendering an important service to the public. The broadcast was indubitably defamatory. But, as I have said, the Exclusive Brethren brought no action for libel. Had they done so, and the BBC had raised a defence of justification, it is highly unlikely that the Brethren could have obtained an interim injunction in that action to prevent the BBC from repeating their broadcast of 26th September 1976 (see the judgment of Lord Coleridge CJ with which Lord Esher MR, Lindley, Bowen and Lopes LJJ concurred in *g* *Bonnard v Perryman* [1891] 2 Ch 269 at 284–285, [1891–4] All ER Rep 965 at 968–969, an authority which has never been challenged).

In the Divisional Court it was agreed that the result of the case must depend on whether the local valuation court was an 'inferior court'. The judgment of Lord Widgery CJ, with which Wien and Kenneth Jones JJ concurred, ended with the following words ([1978] 2 All ER 731 at 736, [1978] 1 WLR 477 at 483): *h*

> 'I am quite satisfied, for my own part, that the local valuation court which will sit at Andover on 10th March will be an inferior court for the purposes of RSC Ord 52. Having reached that stage, I understand counsel's concession to be that the BBC will abandon their intention to transmit this programme.'

So, no interim injunction nor any other order was made save that the BBC should pay the *j* costs.

I cannot accept that if the local valuation court is 'an inferior court' this would have enabled an interim injunction to be ordered against the BBC to prevent it from repeating the 26th September 1976 broadcast prior to 10th March.

I agree, for the reasons given by counsel for the Attorney General, which I need not repeat, that a local valuation court has some of the attributes of the long-established 'inferior courts'. There is today a plethora of such tribunals which may well resemble the old 'inferior courts'. In my view, it does not by any means follow that the modern inferior courts need the umbrella of contempt of court or that they come under it. Indeed, in my opinion, public policy requires that most of the principles relating to contempt of court which have for ages necessarily applied to the long-established inferior courts such as county courts, magistrates' courts, courts-martial, coroners' courts and consistory courts shall not apply to valuation courts and the host of other modern tribunals which may be regarded as inferior courts; otherwise the scope of contempt of court would be unnecessarily extended and accordingly freedom of speech and freedom of the press would be unnecessarily contracted.

These two freedoms are two of the pillars of liberty. They should never be diminished unless justice so requires, eg if a man is charged with a criminal offence it would be a gross contempt of court for the press to publish any of his past wrongdoings or indeed to write prejudicial articles about him. There would be a grave danger that such conduct might prevent him from having a fair trial; juries are sometimes seriously prejudiced from what they hear or read. The media however is very careful to avoid these pitfalls whether in criminal trials or civil trials by jury.

Practically every civil action is however tried by judge alone. Some of these cases are of great public importance. Contempt of court in relation to such cases was carefully considered by the Phillimore Committee and its report was published about six years ago (Cmnd 5571 (1974)). Nothing has happened since, although the report contains excellent recommendations and suggestions for much needed reforms. I am and have always been satisfied that no judge would be influenced in his judgment by what may be said by the media. If he were, he would not be fit to be a judge. In my view, this branch of our law is in urgent need of careful consideration by Parliament.

We, however, are directly concerned in this appeal only with local valuation courts which are concerned with disputes between valuation officers and ratepayers as to the amount of rates which a ratepayer should pay, and also as to relief from rates. Practically, none of the business that goes on in local valuation courts is of any interest, except to those directly concerned, and is hardly ever mentioned in the press or any of the media. The present case is a very rare exception. For example, I am convinced that the BBC's proposed repeat attack against the Exclusive Brethren on 19th February 1978 should never have been held to be a contempt of court even if the valuation court had then been about to consider whether the Exclusive Brethren should be relieved of liability to pay rates. The BBC's attack on 26th September 1976, if true, was a very real service to the public; it purported to expose the misery and harm caused by the Brethren to the many young people whom they enlisted and cruelly cut off from their mothers, fathers, brothers, sisters and friends, and indeed from anyone who had not joined the ranks of the Exclusive Brethren. I do not believe that the BBC's attempt to protect the public from the Exclusive Brethren could have prevented the Brethren from being relieved from rates by the valuation court for the following reasons. The right to the Brethren's relief from rates in respect of the meeting houses where their religious services took place depended on whether these were 'places of public religious worship': see the General Rate Act 1967, s 39. Your Lordships' House in considering a similar question relating to the Mormon church in *Church of Jesus Christ of Latter-Day Saints v Henning* [1963] 2 All ER 733, [1964] AC 420 decided that the Mormon chapels in which religious services took place and which were open to the public were relieved from the payment of rates but that the Mormon temple which was open for religious services only to certain distinguished members of the Mormon church enjoyed no such relief. In the present case, if the valuation court had to consider the matter, it would have been for the Brethren to establish that their religious services, held in their meeting houses, were open to the public. Perhaps a difficult task if the BBC broadcast was correct; for if a sect refuses to allow any of its members to have any contact with anyone but themselves it is hardly likely that the public would be allowed to be present during their religious services. If however evidence did establish that the public were allowed by the Brethren to attend their religious services, it seems most probable that the valuation court would *a* have relieved the Brethren from rates whatever the broadcast had said.

If the valuation court had not accepted the Brethren's evidence, the Brethren might have considered that they had not received justice from the valuation court, in which event they would have been entitled to appeal to the Lands Tribunal before whom there would be a complete rehearing. That tribunal is presided over by a professional judge of nearly equal standing to a High Court judge. There is, in my view, no possibility of the *b* Lands Tribunal being prejudiced or influenced by the press or television or any of the media. I entirely agree with Lord Denning MR that for these reasons no publicity affecting a party before a local valuation court should be held to be a contempt of court.

The Exclusive Brethren were completely protected against the original broadcast of 26th February 1976 and would have been equally protected against any repeat broadcast, providing that the broadcasts were untrue. They could have claimed damages for libel *c* which, if they had won the action, would have been very heavy indeed; far, far greater than any of the rates from which they are now relieved. I would only add that if the broadcast was accurate and a defence of justification was established it would have been a shocking blot on the law if it had previously prevented the BBC, by an interim injunction, from republishing the broadcast which would have been of great service to the public. *d*

The description 'contempt of court' no doubt has an historical basis but it is nevertheless most misleading. Its object is not to protect the dignity of the courts or the judges but to protect the administration of justice. Virtually none of the long-standing inferior courts have the power to protect themselves against anyone interfering with their administration of justice. The power to protect them is however exercisable by the Queen's Bench Divisional Court. *e*

For the reasons I have indicated, the host of modern inferior courts and tribunals do not, in my view, require and do not have any protection against comments which may be made by the press and the like in respect of matters which those courts or tribunals have to decide. On the other hand, it may be that if these courts or tribunals, whilst they were sitting, were prevented by obstruction from performing their duties, they could be protected by the Queen's Bench Divisional Court. This point does not however arise in *f* the present case, and I express no concluded view about it.

My Lords, for the reasons I have stated, I would allow the appeal.

LORD EDMUND-DAVIES. My Lords, the sole question arising in this appeal is whether a local valuation court comes within the jurisdiction of the High Court whereby in a proper case its functioning may be protected by contempt proceedings. RSC Ord 52, *g* r 1 provides:

> 'Where contempt of court—(*a*) is committed in connection with ... (iii) proceedings in an inferior court ... then ... an order of committal may be made only by a Divisional Court of the Queen's Bench Division ...'

Is a local valuation court an 'inferior court' for the purposes of the order? *h*

The facts giving rise to the appeal are these. An organisation known as 'The Exclusive Brethren' applied for rating relief for its meeting house at Andover on the ground that it was 'a place of public religious worship' for the purposes of s 39 of the General Rate Act 1967. The application was to be heard by the local valuation court at Andover on 10th March 1978. In the issue of the Radio Times dated 9th February the appellants ('the BBC') announced their intention to televise on 19th February a programme concerning *j* the organisation. It was highly critical and had been previously televised in September 1976. At the instigation of certain Exclusive Brethren, on 17th February Her Majesty's Attorney General instituted proceedings by writ, claiming an injunction to restrain the BBC from again televising the programme on the ground that this would constitute a contempt of the pending proceedings before the local valuation court, as it raised the

very same issue of whether the Andover premises were a place of public religious
a worship.

The matter came before the Divisional Court on the same day as the writ was issued. The question whether the proposed broadcast would constitute a contempt were it to take place was not canvassed, the BBC undertaking that, were the local valuation court held to be an 'inferior court', they would not proceed with the broadcast. The Divisional Court unanimously so held, Lord Widgery CJ saying ([1978] 2 All ER 731 at 736, [1978]
b 1 WLR 477 at 483):

> 'I am bound to say I think that the local valuation court is one of the clearest examples of an inferior court that we meet in the field of administrative justice.'

The Court of Appeal by a majority upheld that decision and dismissed the BBC's appeal, but granted them leave to appeal to your Lordship's House.

c Questions of policy of considerable importance are involved. For, as Lord Denning MR observed extra-judicially many years ago (The Road to Justice, 1955, p 78):

> '... the press play a vital part in the administration of justice. It is the watchdog to see that every trial is conducted fairly, openly and above board... But the watchdog may sometimes break loose and have to be punished for misbehaviour.'

d Counsel for the BBC has strongly argued that it is against the public interest to extend the contempt jurisdiction beyond its established limits and thereby to infringe the freedom of speech. On the other hand, your Lordships were urged on behalf of the Attorney General to attach a liberal meaning to the phrase 'inferior court' and so protect such bodies as the local valuation court from unwarranted interference by public discussion of issues about to be tried by them. The importance of such competing considerations
e was indicated with typical clarity by Lord Morris, who said in *Attorney General v Times Newspapers Ltd* [1973] 3 All ER 54 at 66, [1974] AC 273 at 302:

> 'In the general interests of the community it is imperative that the authority of the courts should not be imperilled and that recourse to them should not be subject to unjustifiable interference... But as the purpose and existence of courts of law is to preserve freedom within the law for all well disposed members of the community,
> f it is manifest that the courts must never impose any limitations on free speech or free discussion or free criticism beyond those which are absolutely necessary.'

Conducting a balancing exercise between these competing considerations can give rise to considerable difficulties, as the present appeal demonstrates. But if I may respectfully say so, the Attorney General appears to regard that exercise with some nonchalance, as is
g evidenced by the following quotations from his printed case to your Lordships' House:

> 'If it is regarded as unclear upon the authorities whether Local Valuation Courts are properly to be regarded as inferior courts, it is submitted that policy requires a liberal approach to be adopted in resolving the issue. The essential object of the law of contempt is to protect the administration of justice at all levels and in all spheres; such protection as it affords should accordingly be available to all bodies which have
> h to administer justice... Given the ample safeguards which exist to ensure that contempt proceedings are not themselves used oppressively or otherwise abused, there is every advantage in recognising a wide contempt jurisdiction of the superior courts... and to adopt if necessary an elastic approach to the determination of the question whether a particular body constitutes an inferior court in the law of contempt... The exercise of the contempt jurisdictions of the High Court is within
> j the discretion and under the control of the court (and in practice the Attorney General) as the guardian of the public interest; it is largely confined to cases where no other adequate or suitable remedy is available, and it must always be considered in the light of, and weighed against, the public interest in the freedom of expression.'

My Lords, in so far as the Attorney General invites the courts to rely on his ipse dixit in the confidence that all holders of that office will always be both wise and just about instituting proceedings for contempt, acceptance of his invitation would involve a denial *a* of justice to those who on occasion are bold enough to challenge that a particular holder has been either wise or just. And it would doom this appeal to failure from the start. In the Court of Appeal, Lord Denning MR said ([1979] 3 All ER 45 at 51, [1979] 3 WLR 312 at 318):

> 'To my mind the courts should not award [the Attorney General] such an injunction except in a clear case where there would manifestly be a contempt of *b* court for the publication to take place. The same reasoning applies here as in the cases where a party seeks to restrain the publication of a libel.'

Equal clarity and certainty should prevail in relation to the question of *jurisdiction* to commit for contempt. It is unacceptable to leave it to the Attorney General ultimately to decide when and where contempt proceedings will lie for, as Sir Stanley Rees *c* pertinently observed in the Court of Appeal ([1979] 3 All ER 45 at 57, [1979] 3 WLR 312 at 324):

> '... it is ... vital to ensure that freedom of expression in the press and in broadcasting should not be unwarrantably fettered. *It is equally important that the press and the broadcasting authorities should be able to know in advance what tribunals are inferior courts within the ambit of RSC Ord 52, r 1.*' (Emphasis mine.) *d*

But, my Lords, it would be misleading to suppose that 'court' and 'inferior court' have any special or particular meaning for the purpose of Ord 52, r 1, which merely provides the committal machinery and has nothing to do with circumscribing or defining the courts in respect of which contempt proceedings may properly be instituted. The power to commit is far more ancient than any rules of court. In *R v Daily Herald, ex parte Bishop* *e* *of Norwich* [1932] 2 KB 402 the submission that a consistory court was not a King's court, but an ecclesiastical court, and that the protective custody of the Divisional Court did not extend to it was rejected, Lord Hewart CJ saying (at 412):

> 'None of us has any doubt that this Court has jurisdiction. The jurisdiction is inherent, and ... by virtue of that jurisdiction this Court may correct an inferior *f* court such as a Consistory Court ...'

So the question is: what is a 'court'? Oswald said (Contempt of Court, 3rd Edn, 1910, p 6):

> 'To speak generally, contempt of court may be said to be constituted by any conduct that tends to bring the authority and administration of the law into *g* disrespect or disregard, or to interfere with or prejudice parties litigant or their witnesses during the litigation.'

But counsel for the Attorney General disputes that contempt proceedings are restricted to 'courts of justice'. He submits that the only desiderata for this purpose are that the body should (i) be set up by Parliament, (ii) sit in public and (iii) administer 'public law', *h* ie statutes and the common law, as opposed to the private 'laws' administered, for example, by a domestic tribunal. Provided it possessed all three characteristics, so the submission went, the body is an 'inferior court' for the purpose of contempt proceedings.

It is abundantly clear that, were this submission accepted, the law of contempt would be extended far beyond its present scope. But learned counsel urged that were this House now to declare that such is the law clarity would result and the public interest *j* would be served. For my part, however, I prefer to inquire what constitutes an 'inferior court' under the present law before considering whether some ampler connotation would advance the public weal.

It is comparatively easy to identify and discard those tests which are *not* sure guides to the true meaning of 'court' for our present purposes. In *Shell Co of Australia v Federal*

Comr of Taxation [1931] AC 275 at 296–297, [1930] All ER Rep 671 at 679–680 Lord Sankey LC said:

> 'The authorities are clear to show that there are tribunals with many of the trappings of a Court which, nevertheless, are not Courts in the strict sense of exercising judicial power . . . In that connection it may be useful to enumerate some negative propositions on this subject: 1. A tribunal is not necessarily a Court in this strict sense because it gives a final decision. 2. Nor because it hears witnesses on oath. 3. Nor because two or more contending parties appear before it between whom it has to decide. 4. Nor because it gives decisions which affect the rights of subjects. 5. Nor because there is an appeal to a Court. 6. Nor because it is a body to which a matter is referred by another body.'

It may, however, be open to doubt if a tribunal which lacks any of those 'trappings' is a court. But, as Lord Diplock rightly observed in *Ranaweera v Ramachadran* [1970] AC 962 at 972, Lord Sankey LC's list of negatives '. . . throws a little light upon what characteristics *are* conclusive either of its exercising judicial functions or of its exercising executive or administrative functions'.

And there are still other features the presence of which is not decisive of the matter. They include the following: (1) the fact that the tribunal is called a 'court', as in the case of the local valuation court; (2) the necessity of sitting in public; (3) the fact that the tribunal has power to administer oaths and hear evidence on oath; (4) the fact that prerogative writs may issue in relation to the tribunal's proceedings; (5) the fact that absolute privilege against an action for defamation protects those participating in its proceedings.

As to these 'non-tests', the following comments may be made. (1) The Court of Referees constituted under the Unemployment Insurance Act 1920 is but one example of a tribunal so entitled which is merely an administrative body: see *Collins v Henry Whiteway & Co Ltd* [1927] 2 KB 378. And in *Society of Medical Officers of Health v Hope (Valuation Officer)* [1960] 1 All ER 317 at 324, [1960] AC 551 at 567 Lord Keith said:

> 'Nor do I find it easy to distinguish the functions performed by assessment committees before the coming into operation of the Local Government Act, 1948, from those now performed by a local valuation court, or to think, because the new body is differently constituted and called a court, that a greater importance and effect should be attached to its decisions.'

(2) Many tribunals which are clearly not 'courts' are required to sit in public: for example, justices at licensing meetings (*Boulter v Kent Justices* [1897] AC 556). And in *Lewis v British Broadcasting Corpn* [1979] Court of Appeal transcript 193 where the magistrates sat in public to hear an appeal against the refusal of a licence under the Pet Animals Act 1951, Lord Denning MR expressed the unanimous view of the Court of Appeal in saying: 'I very much doubt whether the magistrates . . . are an inferior court such as attract the proceedings for contempt of court . . . A licensing body is not normally an inferior court.' (3) Many tribunals which are clearly not 'inferior courts' have such a power; for example, local inquiries relating to the exercise of any statutory function of local authorities (see the Local Government Act 1972, s 250(2)). (4) Although in the court-martial case of *R v Daily Mail, ex parte Farnsworth* [1921] 2 KB 733 and the consistory court case of *R v Daily Herald, ex parte Bishop of Norwich* [1932] 2 KB 402 the view was expressed that jurisdiction to issue a prerogative writ went hand in hand with jurisdiction to commit for contempt, in the light of *Mersey Docks and Harbour Board v West Derby Assessment Committee and Bottomley* [1932] 1 KB 40 at 104, *R v Electricity Comrs, ex parte London Electricity Joint Committee Co (1920) Ltd* [1924] 1 KB 171, [1923] All ER Rep 150 and *R v Paddington Valuation Officer, ex parte Peachey Property Corpn Ltd* [1965] 2 All ER 836, [1966] 1 QB 380 counsel for the Attorney General accepted that this is not

so. (5) Counsel further accepted that the availability of absolute privilege does not also necessarily connote that contempt proceedings will lie. a

For Lord Denning MR there is in the present context a fatal flaw in the constitution of a local valuation court. He said in his dissenting judgment ([1979] 3 All ER 45 at 53–54, [1979] 3 WLR 312 at 321):

> '... to my mind, this body lacks one important characteristic of a court: it has no one on it or connected with it who is legally qualified or experienced. To constitute b a court there should be a chairman who is a lawyer or at any rate have at his elbow a clerk or assistant who is a lawyer qualified by examination or by experience, as a justice's clerk is.'

But it has to be said that it is only comparatively recently that the clerk to a bench of lay magistrates was required to have any formal qualifications and at the earlier stage their c 'experience' was at times of an insubstantial kind. And Eveleigh LJ pointed out ([1979] 3 All ER 45 at 56, [1979] 3 WLR 312 at 323) that a coroner's court and the former quarter sessions were undoubtedly 'courts' though they did not measure up to the test propounded by Lord Denning MR.

Are there, then, *any* identifiable hallmarks of an 'inferior court'? Eveleigh LJ considered that they are six in number, and said ([1979] 3 All ER 45 at 55, [1979] 3 WLR d 312 at 323):

> 'In my opinion, the first is that [the tribunal] should have been created by the state. At one time courts were created or recognised by the monarch. Now they are created by Parliament. Thus, while an arbitration tribunal may contain many of the attributes of a court, it will lack this first essential one. Secondly, it must e conduct its procedure in accordance with the rules of natural justice. Thirdly, that procedure will involve a public hearing with the power at least to receive evidence orally, to permit the oral examination and cross-examination of witnesses and to hear argument on the issues before it. Fourthly, it arrives at a decision which is final and binding as long as it stands. Fifthly, there will be two parties at least before it, one of whom may be the Crown, who are interested in the decision. Sixthly, the f decision will be concerned with legal rights.'

Eveleigh LJ considered that local valuation courts have all those attributes. In assessing the acceptability of his six tests it is necessary to have regard to how they and their predecessors, the local assessment committees, were created, and to consider their functions and how they worked. In the light of several decisions of the Court of Appeal, g it was conceded before your Lordships that local assessment committees, created by the Union Assessment Committee Act 1862, and replaced by the local valuation courts by the Local Government Act 1948, were *not* courts. But that concession was linked with a submission that there were important differences between the functions of the two bodies, and that what was true of the earlier does not apply to the later, and this despite the observations of Lord Keith which I quoted earlier. Indeed, counsel for the Attorney h General listed no less than 14 characteristics which he submitted qualified local valuation courts to be regarded as 'inferior courts' (see [1979] 3 All ER at 53, [1979] 3 WLR 312, at 320–321 per Lord Denning MR). Their function was thus prescribed by s 88(1) of the General Rate Act 1967:

> 'Local valuation courts ... shall be convened as often as may be necessary for the j purpose of hearing and determining appeals ... against objections to proposals for the alteration of valuation lists.'

Having heard and determined such objections, the local valuation court proceeds to give directions as to the manner in which the hereditament in question is to be treated in the valuation list, whereupon the valuation officer must cause the list to be altered accordingly (see s 76(5)).

Bearing in mind the limited scope of the statutory provision, the following respectful comments are called for in relation to such of counsel's 14 'characteristics' as I have not already dealt with. (1) Its members are drawn from a local valuation panel of persons nominated by the county council and approved of by the Secretary of State for the Environment, surely a most unusual method of constituting a 'court': see s 88(2) of the 1967 Act as amended by the Local Government Act 1972, s 172. (5) It is inaccurate to say that 'Its decisions are final, subject to appeal'. On the contrary, (i) a person aggrieved by a current valuation list may at *any* time propose an alteration of the list (see s 69(1) of the 1967 Act) and (b) its decisions do not create an estoppel per rem judicatam or even inter partes: see *Society of Medical Officers of Health v Hope (Valuation Officer)* [1960] 1 All ER 317, [1960] AC 551. (6) The fact that an appeal lies to the Lands Tribunal has no significance, for many bodies which are not themselves 'courts' may appeal to another body that is; for example, an appeal lay under the Union Assessment Committee Act 1862, s 32 to quarter sessions from a local assessment committee which ex concessis was not a court. (7) Save that the applicant begins, a local valuation court has *no* fixed procedure and may itself decide in what order all other persons are heard. (8) Even although it must discharge its duties in a 'judicial' manner, it does not for that reason have the status of a court: see *Royal Aquarium and Summer and Winter Garden Society Ltd v Parkinson* [1892] 1 QB 431, [1891–4] All ER Rep 429 to which I shall revert. (9) It is not correct that the proceedings take the form of a 'lis'. The valuation officer is a neutral, public officer charged with the recurring duty of bringing into existence a valuation list, and he cannot be described as a party so as to make the proceedings a lis inter partes: see *R v Westminster Assessment Committee, ex parte Grosvenor House (Park Lane) Ltd* [1940] 4 All ER 132, [1941] 1 KB 53 and *Society of Medical Officers of Health v Hope (Valuation Officer)*. (12) The fact that '... its decisions ... amount to a declaration which is binding on those concerned' is a 'characteristic' shared with the determination of a valuation officer, a rent officer, a rent assessment committee and other officials, none of whom constitute a 'court'. A similar comment could be made, mutatis mutandis, of Eveleigh LJ's 'characteristics' (13) and (14).

On the other side, it is notable that a local valuation court is not bound by the rules of evidence, that it has no power of itself to summon witnesses or to order the production and inspection of documents, and that its members may rely on their own knowledge, as well as on the evidence and argument (see *Morecambe and Heysham Corpn v Robinson (Valuation Officer)* [1961] 1 All ER 721 at 724, [1961] 1 WLR 373 at 377 per Holroyd Pearce LJ). They are, of course, expected to discharge their functions in accordance with the rules of natural justice. It may thus be said that they must act 'judicially'. But it emphatically does not follow that they are to be classed as a judicial body or a court. The point is important, and in the *Royal Aquarium Society* case [1892] 1 QB 431 at 452, [1891–1894] All ER Rep 429 at 436 Lopes LJ dealt with it by saying:

> 'The word "judicial" has two meanings. It may refer to the discharge of duties exercisable by a judge or by justices in court, or to administrative duties which need not be performed in court, but in respect of which it is necessary to bring to bear a judicial mind—that is, a mind to determine what is fair and just in respect of the matters under consideration. Justices, for instance, act judicially when administering law in court, and they also act judicially when determining in their private room what is right and fair in some administrative matter brought before them ...'

At the end of the day it has unfortunately to be said that there emerges no sure guide, no unmistakable hallmark by which a 'court' or 'inferior court' may unerringly be identified. It is largely a matter of impression. My own firm view is that a local valuation court is not such a body. I would add that, if Parliament had it in mind to

bring local valuation courts within the contempt procedure by which the Divisional
Court is empowered to protect 'inferior courts', it is regrettable that they did not make a
this clear by legislation, as they have already done in several other Acts of Parliament
cited to your Lordships and ranging from the Tribunals of Inquiry (Evidence) Act 1921,
s 1(2) to the Parliamentary Commissioner Act 1967, s 9. Yet nothing of the sort has been
done, and this despite the recurring opportunities of conveniently doing so which have
arisen since the Local Government Act 1948 first created local valuation courts.

My Lords, at the outset of this regrettably long speech I indicated the reasons which b
have led me and others to the conclusion that contempt proceedings should never be
instituted or upheld by the courts unless it is clear beyond doubt that the demands of
justice make them essential. For like reasons, I consider that it should not be left to the
judges to widen the scope of such proceedings, and I have no doubt that to accede to the
Attorney General's submissions in this appeal would in truth involve such a widening.
I would not myself be a party to it. If it is to be done at all, I think the task must be left c
to Parliament. I would therefore allow this appeal.

LORD FRASER OF TULLYBELTON. My Lords, I have had the privilege of
reading in draft the speech prepared by my noble and learned friend Lord Scarman. I
agree that in deciding this appeal the House has to hold a balance between the principle
of freedom of expression and the principle that the administration of justice must be d
kept free from outside interference. Neither principle is more important than the other,
and where they come into conflict, as they do in this case, the boundary has to be drawn
between the spheres in which they respectively operate. That is not the way in which the
European Court of Human Rights would approach the question, as we see from the
following passage in the report of *Sunday Times v United Kingdom* (1979) 2 EHRR 245 at
281: e

> 'Whilst emphasising that it is not its function to pronounce itself on an
> interpretation of English law adopted in the House of Lords, the court points out
> that it has to take a different approach. The court is faced not with a choice between
> two conflicting principles, but with a principle of freedom of expression that is
> subject to a number of exceptions which must be narrowly interpreted.' f

It is, therefore, not to be expected that decisions of this House on questions of this sort
will invariably be consistent with those of the European Court. This House, and other
courts in the United Kingdom, should have regard to the provisions of the Convention
for the Protection of Human Rights and Fundamental Freedoms (Rome, 4th November
1950; TS 71 (1953); Cmd 8969) and to the decisions of the Court of Human Rights in
cases, of which this is one, where our domestic law is not firmly settled. But the g
convention does not form part of our law, and the decision on what that law is is for our
domestic courts and for this House.

RSC Ord 52, r 1 provides that a Divisional Court of the Queen's Bench Division may
punish contempt of court if it is committed in connection with 'proceedings in an
inferior court' and the immediate question for decision is whether a local valuation court
constituted in terms of the General Rate Act 1967 is an inferior court to which that rule h
applies. In order to answer the question satisfactorily it is necessary to find some way of
ascertaining the class of tribunal which is protected by the law against contempt. The
jurisdiction of the Queen's Bench Division to afford protection to inferior courts has
sometimes been regarded as the counterpart of its jurisdiction to correct them if they
made an illegal exercise of arbitrary powers: see *R v Davies* [1906] 1 KB 32, [1904–7] All
ER Rep 60. But liability to correction by prerogative writs applies to bodies which are j
clearly not courts, and these are now so numerous that the fact that a body is liable to
such correction is no indication that it is an inferior court. Another possibility might
have been to define the class as consisting of all tribunals whose proceedings are protected
by absolute privilege, but that also was (rightly) not suggested on behalf of the Attorney
General because it would unduly enlarge the class.

The contention on behalf of the Attorney General was that the class of inferior courts to which RSC Ord 52 applied consisted of all bodies which possess certain characteristics, including having been created by the Crown or by Parliament, and administering justice in public, even though they were not courts of justice in the full sense. But that definition is open to two grave objections: it is too uncertain and it is probably too wide. Uncertainty is a serious objection because of the large number of tribunals set up by modern legislation, many of which might be on the borderline. It is undesirable that anyone intending to publish information in the newspapers or on radio or television relating to proceedings pending before a tribunal should have to examine in detail the functions and constitution of the tribunal in order to ascertain whether it is protected by the law against contempt. The second objection is even more serious, because, if protection is extended widely, the right to freedom of expression would be correspondingly reduced. That objection would have great weight with an English court without reference to the European convention, and it is reinforced by the convention. The contention of the Attorney General cannot therefore be accepted, and, in my opinion, the class of inferior courts protected by the law against contempt should be limited to those which are truly courts of law, exercising the judicial power of the state. Not all bodies which are called courts will be included; for example, a court of referees under the Unemployment Insurance Act 1920 would not qualify (see *Collins v Henry Whiteway & Co Ltd* [1927] 2 KB 378), nor, I think, would a court of inquiry under Part II of the Industrial Courts Act 1919. Both these courts perform administrative acts and are not courts of justice.

I recognise that limiting the protection against contempt in this way is difficult to justify in strict logic. It may well be that the need for protection against interference from newspaper articles or television programmes relating to pending proceedings before a tribunal is greater when the tribunal is not a court of law than when it is, because members of a tribunal which is not a court of law are often laymen who may find more difficulty in excluding irrelevant matter from their minds than the professional lawyers who constitute or preside over most courts of law. Nevertheless, strict logic must give way to the practical convenience of having a test which can be applied with reasonable certainty and of avoiding too great a curtailment of the right of freedom of expression.

For the reasons explained by others of your Lordships I agree that the local valuation court is not a court of law, but a body whose functions are of an administrative character. It is therefore not within the class of inferior courts to which the law of contempt applies.

I would allow the appeal.

LORD SCARMAN. My Lords, this appeal would have been at any time an important one: for it requires the House to consider two interests of great public importance, freedom of speech and the administration of justice, and to decide which in the circumstances should prevail.

But, coming to your Lordships' House so soon after the European Court of Human Rights has held that a decision of this House, upholding at the suit of the Attorney General an injunction prohibiting the publication by The Sunday Times of its thalidomide article, was an interference with the newspaper's right to freedom of expression which could not be justified under art 10(2) of the European Convention on Human Rights as being 'necessary in a democratic society', it has an enhanced importance. Of course, neither the convention nor the European Court's decision in *Sunday Times v United Kingdom* (1979) 2 EHRR 245 is part of our law. This House's decision, even though the European court has held the rule it declares to be an infringement of the convention, is the law. Our courts must continue to look not to the European court's decision reported as *Sunday Times v United Kingdom* but to the House of Lords decision reported in *Attorney General v Times Newspapers Ltd* [1973] 3 All ER 54, [1974] AC 273 for the rule of English law. Yet there is a presumption, albeit rebuttable, that our municipal law will be consistent with our international obligations: for an example see *Post Office v Estuary Radio Ltd* [1967] 3 All ER 663 at 682, [1968] 2 QB 740 at 757 per Diplock LJ. Moreover, under the practice statement of July 1966 (*Note* [1966] 3 All ER 77, [1966] 1 WLR 1234), this House has taken to itself the power to refuse to follow a previous decision of its own if convinced that it is necessary in the interest of justice to depart from it. Though, on its facts, the present case does not provide the House with the opportunity to reconsider its *Sunday Times* decision (and we have heard no argument on the point), I do not doubt that, in considering how far we should extend the application of contempt of court, we must bear in mind the impact of whatever decision we may be minded to make on the international obligations assumed by the United Kingdom under the European convention. If the issue should ultimately be, as I think in this case it is, a question of legal policy, we must have regard to the country's international obligation to observe the European convention as interpreted by the European Court of Human Rights.

The appeal raises two questions: (1) whether a local valuation court is truly a court; and, if it is, (2) does it 'come within the contempt jurisdiction of the High Court, whereby in a proper case its proceedings may be protected by contempt proceedings before the High Court'? (I borrow these words from para 2 of the Attorney General's written case.)

The way in which the case was conducted before the Divisional Court and in the Court of Appeal has left the impression that the decisive question is the first. But it is not. The second is the critical question. And for the reasons which I shall endeavour to explain I have reached the conclusion that, though a local valuation court is a court, it is not one to which the law of contempt of court applies.

Local valuation courts are the successors of 'assessment committees'. By the Union Assessment Committee Act 1862, any person aggrieved by a valuation list could give notice of objection, and the appropriate assessment committee was to hold meetings for hearing and determining such objections. The committee's character, when exercising this function, fell to be considered by the Court of Appeal in *R v St Mary Abbotts, Kensington Assessment Committee* [1891] 1 QB 378. It was a case in which a householder claimed the right to appear by an agent, a right which the court upheld. Lord Esher MR described the committee in these terms (at 382):

> 'The assessment committee have been called a court or tribunal, and spoken of as exercising judicial functions. They are a certain number of persons, in this case selected vestrymen, to whom power has been given by statute to hear objections, which have been made to the valuation list, and to decide whether such objections are well founded. I do not think that they are a court or a tribunal exercising judicial functions in the legal acceptation of the terms.'

One may safely infer from his words that, while recognising the judicial nature of the function, Lord Esher MR would not have extended the law of contempt of court to the committee because he did not think it was 'a court or tribunal exercising judicial functions in the legal acceptation of the terms'. Although assessment committees have disappeared, the case remains important. Assessment committees, while they had other purely administrative functions, did possess judicial functions directly comparable with those now performed by local valuation courts. As Parliament had not put the 'court' label on them, it was not necessary for the judges so to describe them. The Court of Appeal, therefore, in the *St Mary Abbotts* case was not troubled by a label; but it did have to consider the substantial question: the character of the body when it was exercising its judicial function. By refusing to hold that the committee's undoubted judicial functions made it a court or tribunal in legal acceptation, the Court of Appeal recognised that judicial functions may be exercised by a body whose task is administrative, not judicial. Further, it regarded the assessment of values to be entered in a rating valuation list and the hearing of objections to entries in the list as administrative in character, notwithstanding the existence of a judicial function in determining such objections.

In the following year another important case was decided, *Royal Aquarium and Summer and Winter Garden Society Ltd v Parkinson* [1892] 1 QB 431, [1891–4] All ER Rep 429. At a meeting of the London County Council for granting music and dancing licences a county councillor made a defamatory statement with regard to the applicant for a licence. He claimed absolute privilege. The Court of Appeal rejected the claim, holding that the council in such meeting was not a court as that term is understood in the law relating to absolute privilege. In the course of his judgment Fry LJ examined the legislation to determine the character in which the council acted when hearing applications for licences and concluded that the proceeding was administrative, not judicial. He considered that the word 'court' had an ascertainable meaning in this branch of English law, but refrained from telling us what it is (see [1892] 1 QB 431 at 446, [1891–4] All ER Rep 429 at 433). He remarked that Parliament itself was a court, even though its duties as a whole were deliberative and legislative, because the duties of a part of it were judicial. He recognised the existence of courts, which 'though not courts of justice, are nevertheless courts according to our law', eg a court of investigation such as the coroner's court, which is of ancient royal origin. This led him to the view, which is, I think, constitutionally correct and true to the historical origins of our court system, that the existence of immunity from suit for defamation, which participants in a court's proceedings enjoy—

> '... does not depend upon the question whether the subject-matter of consideration is a Court of Justice, but whether it is a Court in law. Wherever you find a Court in law, to that the law attaches certain privileges, among which is the immunity in question.'

(See [1892] 1 QB 431 at 447, [1891–4] All ER Rep 429 at 434.) I would add that, though a court in law will also have the protection of the doctrine of contempt of court, it does not follow that because an institution enjoys the protection for its proceedings of absolute privilege it necessarily follows it has also the protection of the law relating to contempt of court. Nevertheless 'a court in law' will have the two protections. Fry LJ then directed his attention to a submission of the defendant in that case, namely that whenever a body has to decide questions, and in so doing has to act judicially, it must be held that there is a judicial proceeding to which the immunity of absolute privilege ought to attach. He rejected it; and I find his reason for doing so of considerable assistance in reaching a conclusion on this appeal. Fry LJ said ([1892] 1 QB 431 at 447, [1891–4] All ER Rep 429 at 434):

> 'But this argument was used on behalf of the defendant. It was said that the existence of this immunity is based on considerations of public policy, and that, as a matter of public policy, wherever a body has to decide questions, and in so doing has to act judicially, it must be held that there is a judicial proceeding to which this immunity ought to attach. It seems to me that the sense in which the word "judicial" is used in that argument is this: it is used as meaning that the proceedings are such as ought to be conducted with the fairness and impartiality which characterize proceedings in Courts of justice, and are proper to the functions of a judge, not that the members of the supposed body are members of a Court. Consider to what lengths the doctrine would extend, if this immunity were applied to every body which is bound to decide judicially in the sense of deciding fairly and impartially. It would apply to assessment committees, boards of guardians, to the Inns of Court when considering the conduct of one of their members, to the General Medical Council when considering questions affecting the position of a medical man, and to all arbitrators. Is it necessary, on grounds of public policy, that the doctrine of immunity should be carried as far as this? I say not.'

It is an argument based on public policy. Different considerations apply to contempt of court, of course. Nevertheless, the warning of Fry LJ is one to which I shall return when considering the great number of tribunals (some of them described as courts) which Parliament has found necessary to establish in its attempt to secure public acceptability of the activities of modern central and local government. But essentially the Court of

Appeal in the *Royal Aquarium* case was approaching the categorisation of a body entrusted
with a judicial function in the same way as it had done in the *St Mary Abbotts* case. It *a*
considered that the existence of a judicial function did not necessarily make the body to
which it was entrusted 'a court in law'; nor did it necessarily attract 'the privileges'
enjoyed by a court in law. In each case the judges stressed the importance of the purpose
which the judicial function was intended to serve. If it were administrative, the body
would not be a court in law.

The Local Government Act 1948 introduced a new valuation and rating procedure. *b*
Valuations were to be made not by overseers locally appointed but by Inland Revenue
officers. New valuation lists were to be prepared. Any person aggrieved by an entry in
the list could make a proposal for alteration of the list. Assessment committees were
swept away. In their place local valuation courts were constituted by the Act to 'be
convened as often as may be necessary for the purpose of hearing and determining
appeals ... against draft valuation lists and against objections to proposals for the *c*
alteration of valuation lists': see s 44(1). In *Society of Medical Officers of Health v Hope
(Valuation Officer)* [1960] 1 All ER 317, [1960] AC 551 this House had to consider whether
a decision of a local valuation court created an estoppel per rem judicatam when a new
quinquennial valuation list had to be brought into existence. The House held that it did
not. In the course of his speech Lord Radcliffe considered the nature of a local valuation
court. He spoke of it as a court of limited jurisdiction, saying ([1960] 1 All ER 317 at *d*
321–322, [1960] AC 551 at 563–564):

> 'For that limited purpose [ie deciding what is to be the assessment or liability of
> a person for a defined and terminable period] it is a court with a jurisdiction
> competent to produce a final decision between the parties before it; but it is not a
> court of competent jurisdiction to decide general questions of law with that finality
> which is needed to set up the estoppel per rem judicatam that arises in certain *e*
> contexts from legal judgments. It seems to me to be entirely congruous with this
> conception of the functions of a local valuation court and their inherent limitation
> that the Local Government Act, 1948, should express its powers to make decisions
> in the words that I have already quoted from s. 48(4): "... the local valuation court
> shall give such directions with respect to the manner in which the hereditament in
> question is to be treated in the valuation list as appear to them to be necessary to give *f*
> effect to the contention of the appellant if and so far as that contention appears to the
> court to be well founded ..."'

By the 1862 Act Parliament had conferred on a local committee certain judicial
functions but did not describe the committee as a court. By the 1948 Act Parliament
expressly established what it called a court in place of the committee. It ill behoves a
judge to say that what Parliament says is a court is not a court. And I would respectfully *g*
agree with Lord Radcliffe's description of a local valuation court as a court of limited
jurisdiction.

Much of the statutory law relating to rating and valuation in England and Wales was
consolidated in the General Rate Act 1967. The consolidation included the provisions
constituting the local valuation courts (see ss 76 to 93). The language and style of these *h*
provisions are consistent only with an intention by Parliament to create a court, albeit
with a jurisdiction strictly limited by the statute.

But, in my judgment, not every court is a court of judicature, ie a court in law. Nor
am I prepared to assume that Parliament intends to establish a court as part of the
country's judicial system whenever it constitutes a court. The word 'court' does, in
modern English usage, emphasise that the body so described has judicial functions to *j*
exercise; but it is frequently used to describe bodies which, though they exercise judicial
functions, are not part of the judicial system of the kingdom. Fry LJ made the point in
the passage I have quoted, and there is an abundance of modern instances of this usage
of the word. When, therefore, Parliament entrusts a body with a judicial function, it is
necessary to examine the legislation to discover its purpose. The mere application of the

'court' label does not determine the question; nor, I would add, does the absence of the
a label conclude the question the other way. In *Collins v Henry Whiteway & Co Ltd* [1927] 2 KB 278 Horridge J held that the Court of Referees constituted under the Unemployment Insurance Act 1920 had an administrative purpose and that, though it exercised a judicial function, it was not a court of law. He did not consider himself bound by Parliament's label. In the constitutionally complex case of *Shell Co of Australia v Federal Comr of Taxation* [1931] AC 275, [1930] All ER Rep 671 the Privy Council held that the Board of
b Review, created by federal statute to review the decisions of the Commissioner of Taxation, was not a court exercising the judicial power of the Commonwealth but was an administrative tribunal. There are two striking passages in the opinion of the Board delivered by Lord Sankey LC. He said ([1931] AC 275 at 295–296, [1930] All ER Rep 671 at 679):

> 'Starke J., speaking of the Board of Review, describes its position as follows: "It has
> c power to review the assessment of the Commissioner, and its decisions are to be deemed to be assessments, determinations or decisions of the Commissioner (Act No. 28 of 1925, s. 10). Now, the Commissioner causes assessments to be made for the purpose of ascertaining the taxable income upon which income tax shall be levied (Act 1915–21, s. 31; Act of 1922, s. 35). His function is to ascertain the amount of income upon which the tax is imposed. That does not, in my opinion,
> d involve any exercise of the judicial power of a Commonwealth; it is an administrative function. The decision of a Board of Review stands, as we have seen, precisely on the same position. Its functions are in aid of the administrative functions of government. So far, then, a Board does not exercise the judicial power of the Commonwealth. We then come to the right of appeal to this Court from determinations of Boards of Review. That is a right given both to the Commissioner
> e and to the taxpayer. A right of appeal in itself does not establish the vesting of judicial power either in the Commissioner or in a Board of Review. The Parliament may have imposed upon the Courts the duty of reviewing administrative determinations." Is this right? What is "judicial power"? Their Lordships are of opinion that one of the best definitions is that given by Griffith C.J. in *Huddart, Parker & Co. v Moorehead* ((1909) 8 CLR 330 at 357), where he says: "I am of opinion
> f that the words 'judicial power' as used in s. 71 of the Constitution mean the power which every sovereign authority must of necessity have to decide controversies between its subjects, or between itself and its subjects, whether the rights relate to life, liberty or property. The exercise of this power does not begin until some tribunal which has power to give a binding and authoritative decision (whether subject to appeal or not) is called upon to take action."'

g

This affirmation of the positive meaning of the judicial power which characterises a court of law was followed by a catalogue of significant negatives. He said ([1931] AC 275 at 297, [1930] All ER Rep 671 at 680):

> 'In that connection it may be useful to enumerate some negative propositions on this subject: 1. A tribunal is not necessarily a Court in this strict sense because it
> h gives a final decision. 2. Nor because it hears witnesses on oath. 3. Nor because two or more contending parties appear before it between whom it has to decide. 4. Nor because it gives decisions which affect the rights of subjects. Nor because there is an appeal to a Court. 6. Nor because it is a body to which a matter is referred by another body. See *Rex.* v. *Electricity Commissioners* ([1924] 1 KB 171, [1923] All ER Rep 150).'

j

Though the United Kindom has no written constitution comparable with that of Australia, both are common law countries, and in both judicial power is an exercise of sovereign power. I would identify a court in (or 'of') law, ie a court of judicature, as a body established by law to exercise, either generally or subject to defined limits, the judicial power of the state. In this context judicial power is to be contrasted with legislative and executive (ie administrative) power. If the body under review is established for a purely legislative or administrative purpose, it is part of the legislative or administrative system of the state, even though it has to perform duties which are judicial in character. Though the ubiquitous presence of the state makes itself felt in all sorts of situations never envisaged when our law was in its formative stage, the judicial power of the state exercised through judges appointed by the state remains an independent, and recognisably separate, function of government. Unless a body exercising judicial functions can be demonstrated to be part of this judicial system, it is not, in my judgment, a court in law. I would add that the judicial system is not limited to the courts of the civil power. Courts-martial and consistory courts (the latter since 1540) are as truly entrusted with the exercise of the judicial power of the state as are the civil courts; see *R v Daily Mail, ex parte Farnsworth* [1921] 2 KB 733 and *R v Daily Herald, ex parte Bishop of Norwich* [1932] 2 KB 402.

My Lords, a local valuation court fails this test. Its function is essentially administrative, though it must act judicially in discharging it. Its purpose is, on objection being made, to give directions as to the manner in which a hereditament is to be treated in the valuation list: see the General Rate Act 1967, s 76(5). The fact, which is plain on the face of the statute, that it must act judicially in hearing and determining objections does not alter its administrative purpose: compare *Ranaweera v Wickramasinghe* [1970] AC 951. The fact that it is a court (Parliament's description) with an administrative purpose does not make it part of the judicial system of the kingdom. The limits of its jurisdiction, as explored by Lord Radcliffe in *Hope's* case, reinforce the administrative nature of the purpose it serves. At the end of the day its one power is to correct a valuation list. It imposes no tax, no liability on the citizen to pay any money or do any act. It has an important role in the machinery for determining a rate, and must act judicially; but it does not determine the amount of the rate or impose a liability to pay it. Its work is strictly comparable with the judicial responsibility of its predecessor, the assessment committee. I conclude, therefore, that a local valuation court is an administrative court, but not a court of law. Though I rest no part of my argument on the law relating to income tax, I would think it is wholly consistent with the view taken by the courts of the character of the Commissioners of the Income Tax: see *Inland Revenue Comrs v Sneath* [1932] 2 KB 362, [1932] All ER Rep 739.

The second question may now be rephrased. Does a body established for an administrative purpose but required to act judicially in the achievement of that purpose attract to itself the protection of the doctrine of contempt of court?

The High Court has power to punish summarily, ie without trial by jury on indictment, for contempt of its own proceedings. The Court of King's Bench, now a constituent part of the High Court of Justice, has power to punish summarily for contempt of inferior courts: see *R v Parke* [1903] 2 KB 432, [1900–3] All ER Rep 721 and *R v Davies* [1906] 1 KB 32, [1904–7] All ER Rep 60. This jurisdiction is today regulated by RSC Ord 52, r 1. The question for your Lordships is whether this power, which admittedly extends to inferior courts which are part of the judicial system of the kingdom, extends to administrative courts, or to bodies not so described but required in pursuit of their administrative purpose to act judicially.

Historically, there is no reason why it should be so extended. Summary punishment by attachment for contempt of court owes its origin to the fact that the offence was that of interfering with the King's justice administered in his 'aula', ie courtyard, or 'curia', ie council: see Holdsworth, History of English Law (7th Edn, 1956, vol 3, pp 391–393) and Oswald, Law of Contempt (3rd Edn, 1910, p 13). It was an offence against the judicial power of the sovereign. In the nineteenth century the judicial system was developed so as to include courts established not under the royal prerogative of justice but by statute, notably the county court and the courts of summary jurisdiction. The question arose at the beginning of the twentieth century whether the High Court, which clearly could punish for contempt of its own proceedings, could also punish for contempt of inferior courts. In 1906 in *R v Davies*, the King's Bench Divisional Court (Alverstone CJ, Wills

and Darling JJ) decided that it could. The judgment of the court was delivered by Wills
a J. He reviewed the law. He cited with approval a dictum of Bowen LJ in *Helmore v Smith*
(No 2) (1886) 35 Ch D 449 at 455: 'contempt of court is not to vindicate the dignity of the
court . . . but to prevent undue interference with the administration of justice.' Wills J
concluded that the state of the authorities was such as to leave the question entirely open
for the court's decision (see [1906] 1 KB 32 at 47, [1904–7] All ER Rep 60 at 69). He held
that the mischief to be stopped in the case of inferior courts was identical with that in
b superior courts. The inferior court in the case was quarter sessions: and there could be
no doubt that quarter sessions (and, indeed, petty sessions) were part of the judicial
system of the kingdom. The case did not decide, nor did it give, any indication as to the
true answer to the question raised by this appeal.

It is plain that in the present case the Court of Appeal, especially Lord Denning MR,
though he dissented on a specific point, gave great weight to the policy considerations
c which impressed themselves on the mind of Wills J in the *Davies* case. Inferior courts
have no power to protect themselves: some of them have a very extended and important
jurisdiction: 'The danger is perhaps greater to them than it is to the Superior Courts of
having their efficiency impaired by publications' relating to pending proceedings (see *R*
v Davies [1906] 1 KB 32 at 48, [1904–7] All ER Rep 60 at 70). But there are weighty
considerations to be put into the balance on the other side. First, there is freedom of
d speech, i e the right to express opinions and impart information with the complementary
right of the public to hear opinions and receive information. Second, there is the danger
recognised by Fry LJ in the *Royal Aquarium* case: the great number of tribunals and other
bodies exercising judicial functions to which the doctrine of contempt of court could be
applied, if extended beyond courts in law. Appendix C of the annual report of the
Council on Tribunals for 1978–79 reveals the very large number and variety of such
e tribunals. How can a newspaper or broadcasting authority ever be sure that it is not
expressing an opinion or making a report on some matter which is under consideration
by some tribunal or another? And it matters not that the newspaper may have a defence
of innocent publication. For we are considering a policy of law designed to prevent such
publications. The plethora of tribunals results in an absurdity: either the policy is a
nonsense because it can seldom be enforced, or it takes effect, in which event freedom of
f speech may be widely restricted and injustice done.

Neither the meagre authorities available in the books nor the historical origins of
contempt of court require the House to extend the doctrine to administrative courts and
tribunals. Legal policy in today's world would be better served, in my judgment, if we
refused so to extend it. If Parliament wishes to extend the doctrine to a specific
institution which it establishes, it must say so explicitly in its enactment, as it has done
g on occasion, eg the Tribunals of Inquiry (Evidence) Act 1921. I would not think it
desirable to extend the doctrine, which is unknown, and not apparently needed, in most
civilised legal systems, beyond its historical scope, namely the proceedings of courts of
judicature. If we are to make the extension, we have to ask ourselves, if the United
Kingdom is to comply with its international obligations, whether the extension is
necessary in our democratic society. Is there 'a pressing social need' for the extension?
h For that, according to the European Court of Human Rights see *Sunday Times v United*
Kingdom (1979) 2 EHRR 245 at 275. It has not been demonstrated to me that there is.

For these reasons I would allow the appeal.

I would add a few general comments not necessary for the decision in this case but
relevant to the reform of the law. The allegation of contempt with which this case is
concerned is publication of matter alleged to be prejudicial to the fair trial of pending
j proceedings. The Attorney General must have thought it in the public interest to secure
the suppression of the broadcast, an issue on which it is not possible to express an opinion
since we have not seen it. But the prior restraint of publication, though occasionally
necessary in serious cases, is a drastic interference with freedom of speech and should
only be ordered where there is a substantial risk of grave injustice. I understand the test
of 'pressing social need' as being exactly that.

Contempt 'in the face of the court', ie physical interruption or a scandalising of the court, should ordinarily be the subject of criminal proceedings after the event; and the criminal law, if it does not do so already, should cover, in one way or another, the offence of obstructing or interfering with the course of proceedings in administrative courts and tribunals as well as in courts of judicature.

It is high time, I would think, that we rearranged our law so that the ancient but misleading term 'contempt of court' disappeared from the law's vocabulary.

Appeal allowed.

Solicitors: *E A C Bostock* (for the BBC); *Treasury Solicitor.*

Mary Rose Plummer Barrister.

Siddiqui and another v Rashid

COURT OF APPEAL, CIVIL DIVISION
STEPHENSON, DUNN LJJ AND SIR DAVID CAIRNS
22nd MAY 1980

Rent restriction – Alternative accommodation – Suitable to needs of tenant as regards extent and character – Character – Cultural interests and proximity of friends – Tenant living in London and working in Luton offered alternative accommodation in Luton – New accommodation suitable in all respects but removed from tenant's friends, mosque and cultural centre – Whether cultural interests and proximity of friends relevant to suitability to needs of tenant as regards 'character' – Rent Act 1977, s 98(1), Sch 15, para 5(1)(b).

The tenant, a Muslim, occupied a room in a house in London under a protected tenancy and worked in Luton. The landlords of the house were the trustees of an Islamic mission. They wished to sell the house with vacant possession in order to buy a larger property for their charitable work and accordingly offered the tenant alternative accommodation in Luton which was reasonably suitable to the needs of the tenant as regards rental and extent and to his means and was closer to his work. The tenant refused to move and the landlords brought proceedings in the county court for possession. The county court judge granted a possession order on the ground that the Luton premises constituted 'suitable alternative accommodation' for the purposes of s 98(1)(*a*)[a] of the Rent Act 1977 since it fulfilled the conditions as to suitability set out in para 5[b] of Sch 15 to that Act. The tenant appealed, contending that the alternative accommodation was not suitable to his needs as regards 'character' within para 5(1)(*b*) because it would take him away from his friends and his local mosque and cultural centre in London.

Held – In determining for the purposes of para 5(1)(*b*) of Sch 15 to the 1977 Act whether alternative accommodation offered to a tenant was suitable to his needs as regards 'character', environmental or peripheral matters could be taken into account only in so far as they related to the character of the property itself, since the term 'character' did not extend to such matters as the society of friends or cultural interests. On that basis, the alternative accommodation offered was suitable to the tenant's needs, and, having regard to the necessity for the landlords to sell the house for their charitable work, it was

a Section 98(1) set out at p 185 *j* to p 186 *a*, post
b Paragraph 5, so far as material, is set out at p 186 *f*, post

reasonable for the purposes of s 98(1) of the 1977 Act to make an order for possession.
a The tenant's appeal would accordingly be dismissed (see p 188 *j* to p 189 *h*, post).

Redspring v Francis [1973] 1 All ER 640 distinguished.

Notes

For alternative accommodation as a condition for the recovery of possession of a dwelling house subject to a protected tenancy, see 23 Halsbury's Laws (3rd Edn) 815–818, para
b 1594, and for cases on the subject, see 31(2) Digest (Reissue) 1106–1112, *8581–8626*.

For the Rent Act 1977, s 98, Sch 15, para 5, see 47 Halsbury's Statutes (3rd Edn) 504, 614.

Case referred to in judgments

Redspring v Francis [1973] 1 All ER 640, [1973] 1 WLR 134, CA, 31(2) Digest (Reissue)
c 1112, *8624*.

Appeal

Ghulam Rashid, the tenant of a room in premises situated at 148 Liverpool Road, London N1, appealed against an order for possession made against him by his Honour Judge Dow in the Clerkenwell County Court on 8th January 1980 on the application of
d the landlords, Rashid Ahmad Siddiqui and Habib-Ur Rehman. The facts are set out in the judgment of Stephenson LJ.

Paul Morgan for the tenant.
Julian Fulbrook for the landlords.

e **STEPHENSON LJ.** This is an appeal from an order for possession of a flat in London, a first floor rear room at 148 Liverpool Road, London N1, which his Honour Judge Dow made against the tenant, Mr Rashid, at the suit of Mr Siddiqui and Mr Rehman, the landlords, and the trustees of the United Kingdom Islamic Mission. They wanted to sell the property in which this room is, in order to buy a larger property for their charitable work and they were able to offer the tenant alternative accommodation in another room
f in a house not in London but in Luton, at 128 Oak Road. As the judge said in the agreed note of his judgment which we have, but which, by a misunderstanding of the practice, has not been referred to him for approval:

> 'On the face of it this sounds odd; it is a long way from where he lives, quite a long way at any rate, but the whole point is that he works in Luton and so far as I know will continue to do so.'

g That may be an over-simplification of the point of the case and of the point of this appeal, but that is the position: that a tenant, who, according to the evidence, had been living in London since 1964 and had been working in Luton since 1967, is objecting to being compelled by the order of the judge to leave his room in London, far from his work, and take up residence in a room in Luton much nearer to his work.

h As is well known, the relevant statutory provisions require a judge, before he makes an order evicting a protected tenant, as the defendant admittedly was, to be satisfied that it is reasonable to make the order and that suitable alternative accommodation has been offered and is available to the tenant. Those provisions are now contained in the consolidating Rent Act 1977. Part VII of that Act, which deals with security of tenure, opens with s 98, which provides as follows:

j

> '(1) Subject to this Part of this Act, a court shall not make an order for possession of a dwelling-house which is for the time being let on a protected tenancy or subject to a statutory tenancy unless the court considers it reasonable to make such an order and either—(*a*) the court is satisfied that suitable alternative accommodation is available for the tenant or will be available for him when the order in question takes

> effect, or (*b*) the circumstances are as specified in any of the Cases in Part I of Schedule 15 to this Act . . .' a

It is paragraph (*a*) of the subsection which is relevant in this case.

Subsection (4) provides:

> 'Part IV of Schedule 15 shall have effect for determining whether, for the purposes of subsection (1)(*a*) above, suitable alternative accommodation is or will be available for a tenant.' b

Part IV of Sch 15 begins with para 3 and provides:

> '3. For the purposes of section 98(1)(*a*) of this Act, a certificate of the housing authority for the district in which the dwelling-house in question is situated, certifying that the authority will provide suitable alternative accommodation for the tenant by a date specified in the certificate, shall be conclusive evidence that c suitable alternative accommodation will be available for him by that date.
>
> '4. Where no such certificate as is mentioned in paragraph 3 above is produced to the court, accommodation shall be deemed to be suitable for the purposes of section 98(1)(*a*) of this Act if it consists of either—(*a*) premises which are to be let as a separate dwelling such that they will then be let on a protected tenancy, or (*b*) premises to be let as a separate dwelling on terms which will, in the opinion of the d court, afford to the tenant security of tenure reasonably equivalent to the security afforded by Part VII of this Act in the case of a protected tenancy, and, in the opinion of the court, the accommodation fulfils the relevant conditions as defined in paragraph 5 below . . .'

No question arises under para 3; it is a para 4 situation, and sub-paras (*a*) and (*b*) of that paragraph are also immaterial because they are satisfied. But the question is whether the e accommodation which the plaintiff landlords offered fulfilled the relevant conditions as defined in para 5, which I now read:

> '(1) For the purposes of paragraph 4 above, the relevant conditions are that the accommodation is reasonably suitable [that adverb has been introduced] to the needs of the tenant and his family as regards proximity to place of work, and f either—(*a*) similar as regards rental and extent to the accommodation afforded by dwelling-houses provided in the neighbourhood by any housing authority for persons whose needs as regards extent are, in the opinion of the court, similar to those of the tenant and of his family; or (*b*) reasonably suitable to the means of the tenant and to the needs of the tenant and his family as regards extent and character . . .' g

No question arises as to this room in Luton being reasonably suitable to the needs of the tenant as regards proximity to place of work. Equally no dispute arises as to the suitability of this room as regards rental and extent; and no question arises as to its reasonable suitability to the tenant's means. But what is in dispute is whether this room would be reasonably suitable to the needs of the tenant and his family as regards character. The judge, as I said, made an order for possession and was satisfied that it was h reasonably suitable accommodation as regards character to the needs of the tenant, and he has found that it was reasonable for him to make the order.

Counsel for the tenant, in his interesting argument before us, has submitted that the judge was wrong on the first point, but I think he would agree that he is not able any longer to maintain that, if he was right on the first point, he was wrong on the second point, or so plainly wrong, at any rate, that this court could interfere and substitute its j view of what was reasonable for the judge's view.

The judge considered suitability in this way:

> 'The [tenant] did not suggest that the alternative premises were not suitable as regards extent, but has endeavoured to persuade me that "character" must be given

a wide interpretation and that, if you move a person from the place where he carries out his leisure activities and where his friends are, that can be brought under the heading of character. I totally disagree. In *Redspring v Francis* [1973 1 All ER 640, [1973] 1 WLR 134 character was clearly defined in the headnote ([1973] 1 WLR 134) by reference to the premises being "somewhere where the tenant could live in reasonably comfortable conditions suitable to the style of life which he led". This is reflected in the judgment of Buckley LJ ([1973] 1 All ER 640 at 643, [1973] 1 WLR 134 at 138) where he went on to say that "environmental matters must inevitably affect the suitability of offered accommodation to provide him with the sort of conditions in which it is reasonable that he should live." [The judge continued:] Having viewed 128 Oak Road, I am perfectly satisfied that the tenant could lead a perfectly good life in accordance with his present style. I am totally unable to accept the submission that the upsetting effect that the move would have, and that, although he would be near his work, he would be further from the mosque he so often attends and where his friends are, can be included in "character". I cannot be moved. I must follow the words of the statute. The character of the property refers to the property itself. I have had the advantage of seeing both properties and have made notes. [Those notes are before us.] In my view, the alternative premises at Oak Road are preferable; furthermore, another room which has not been let would be available for the [tenant] if he wished it. Furthermore, he will have exclusive use of the kitchen, the sink and a very nice modern bathroom.' (He had had to share in the London premises.)

The judge then went on to consider 'reasonableness', and said:

'That is more arguable, but one must consider the landlords' side. They are trying to help the members of the Muslim community; they are trying to sell 148 Liverpool Road to pay back a loan to buy a larger property in the Euston area. It is obvious that they will get more for the property with vacant possession than with a tenant. I cannot accept the argument that anyone would be prepared to offer as much if the defendant were there. It is perfectly reasonable for the landlords to seek an order for possession so that they can sell the property at the best price available. The plaintiffs have amply proved their case and I make an order for possession in 28 days.'

We are bound by authority not to give a very narrow construction to the word 'character' in para 5(1)(*b*) of Sch 15 to the 1977 Act. The wording of the relevant statutory provisions which this court had to consider in *Redspring v Francis* was the same, and in that case this court rejected the argument that the character to which the court must have regard did not include what the county court judge in that case had called 'environmental aspects or peripheral amenities'. That was a case which in some respects resembled this. Buckley LJ, in the leading judgment, said ([1973] 1 All ER 640 at 642, [1973] 1 WLR 134 at 137):

'So we have to consider whether in the present case the accommodation offered at 108 Fleet Road is reasonably suitable to the needs of the tenant as regards extent and character. No point arises in this case in relation to proximity to the place of work or the means of the tenant. We are concerned only with the question whether the accommodation is reasonably suitable to her needs as regards extent and character. Extent, as I have already stated, is conceded. So the question is whether the accommodation is reasonably suited to her needs in respect of its character.'

That was exactly the same position as in this case. There the county court judge had made an order for possession, because he took the view that equally good accommodation next to a smelly fish and chip shop and a good deal of motor traffic and noise was suitable alternative accommodation to similar premises in a quiet street not far off which the tenant had been occupying for 30 years. He was able to take that view because of the narrow view which he took of the meaning of the word 'character'. In his judgment, quoted by Buckley LJ he had said ([1973] 1 All ER 640 at 642, [1973] WLR 134 at 137):

> 'The "needs" contemplated by [the paragraph], cited in argument, are not the same as tastes and inclinations: they are needs of an urgent, compelling nature—space, transport, a bathroom, etc. Peripheral amenities are of a different category: by this I am not saying that the tenant's objections are fanciful but I find that her needs are met, apart from the environmental aspect. One must look at the whole of the picture, and I have not forgotten the hospital, the fish and chip shop, the public house and the cinema.'

This court held that in spite of that last sentence the judge really had forgotten, or, at any rate, put out of the picture, the hospital, the fish and chip shop, the public house and the cinema and the smells and the noises that all that and the proximity of a busy road provide; and was wrong in excluding from his consideration the question whether the accommodation offered was reasonably suited to the tenants needs in respect of its character. Buckley LJ lists 'environmental matters' ([1973] 1 All ER 640 at 643–644, [1973] 1 WLR 134 at 139):

> 'environmental matters such as the smell from the fish and chip shop, the noise from the public house, noise perhaps from vehicles going to and from the hospital and matters of that kind. In so doing, with respect to the judge I think he misdirected himself. Those, I think, are all matters properly to be taken into consideration in connection with the making of such an order as was sought in this case.'

Orr LJ agreed, and Sachs LJ also agreed, and added some observations to the effect that for there to be a difference in character that must of course normally relate to a difference in kind rather than a difference of lesser degree, and in that case he held that there was a difference in kind between the character of the two premises.

As was pointed out in the course of the argument, the statutory provisions say nothing of difference in character, but counsel for the tenant has submitted that it was only if there could be shown to be some difference in character between the two premises that this question of unsuitability of alternative accommodation to the needs of the tenant as regards character could arise. What he submits (and he did not appear in the county court, but it was submitted in the county court) is that the court must look at environmental aspects, and that means the respective locations of the two premises, and see whether the tenant's needs are satisfied as regards the new location. Those needs are not merely physical needs, it was submitted, but such needs as were given in evidence here, need for a devout Muslim to keep in touch with his local mosque and cultural centre (in this case the mosque and cultural centre in Regent's Park) and need to enjoy the company of friends whom he had made in the course of his many years' residence in London. The judge was not wholly satisfied, according to a note which he made in the course of his notes of the evidence, with the tenant's evidence as to his attendances and need to attend at the Regent's Park mosque, but he ruled that the need of the tenant to visit that mosque and the cultural centre there, and to keep in touch with his London friends, did not relate to the character of the property, as environmental aspects had to relate if they were to be a relevant consideration to the question of the suitability of the alternative accommodation.

The 1977 Act does not say that the alternative accommodation must be reasonably suitable to the needs of the tenant as regards location or, of course, as regards environment, and for my part I would regard the county court judge as right in this case in confining 'character' to the 'character of the property'. I find nothing in the judgment of this court in *Redspring v Francis* to indicate that that is wrong, or to extend the meaning of 'character' beyond character of the property. The character of the property was directly affected by the environmental matters which were the subject of the tenant's objection to her move. I have read them from the judgment of Buckley LJ; noise and smell were matters which would directly affect the tenant in the enjoyment of her property, so they could well be said to relate to the character of the property. I cannot think that Parliament intended to include such matters as the society of friends, or cultural interest, in using the language that it did in the particular word 'character'. Nor can I accept that Buckley LJ had any such considerations in mind when he referred, in the passages which the county court judge quoted from his judgment, to the needs of the tenant to have 'somewhere where the tenant could live in reasonably comfortable conditions suitable to the style of life which he led', and referred to the accommodation providing him with the sort of conditions in which it is reasonable that he should live. To extend the character of the property to cover the two matters on which the defendant relies, namely his friends in London and his mosque and cultural, centre would, in my judgment, be unwarranted. The tenant said he did not want to leave London or to live in Luton, although he worked there, but it is clear that his preference for London and objection to Luton was based on those two considerations.

In my judgment it would be impossible to say that the room in Luton was not one in which he could live in reasonably comfortable conditions suitable to the style of life which he was leading in London, or that it did not provide him with the sort of conditions in which it was reasonable that he should live.

He implied that his workmates in Luton were not as much friends of his as his friends in London, but he agreed that his workmates were friends. However that may be, I do not think that the court is required to go into such questions in considering suitability. I would therefore hold that the judge was right in the conclusion which he reached as to the reasonable suitability of the alternative accommodation in Luton which the landlords offered to the tenant.

That would not conclude the matter if counsel had felt able to challenge the judge's view of what was reasonable. The language of the judge, which I have read, when he went on to consider 'reasonableness' may not be the language in which he would have put his consideration of the matter in a reserved judgment; but I am not satisfied that he was indicating that the leisure activities and the spiritual needs of this tenant, or any tenant, would be irrelevant to the question of overall reasonableness. What he was clearly deciding was that it was perfectly reasonable for the landlords to seek an order for possession and it was reasonable for him to grant it. I need not detail the evidence that was given as to the work of the mission, of the trustees who were seeking possession; but the judge was quite satisfied that they needed to sell these premises to carry on their charitable work, that they had had to borrow money to acquire the larger property which they needed to carry on that work, and that they could repay the loan if they could sell the property in which the tenant was living with vacant possession.

For these reasons, in my judgment, the judge came to the right conclusion and I would dismiss the appeal.

DUNN LJ. I agree.

SIR DAVID CAIRNS. I also agree.

Appeal dismissed.

Solicitors: *J P Malnick & Co* (for the tenant); *Munir & Co* (for the landlords).

Patricia Hargrove Barrister.

Barclay-Johnson v Yuill a

CHANCERY DIVISION
SIR ROBERT MEGARRY V-C
18th, 21st APRIL 1980

Injunction – Interlocutory – Danger that defendant may transfer assets out of jurisdiction – b
Injunction restraining removal of assets out of the jurisdiction – English defendant – Whether jurisdiction to grant Mareva injunction against English national domiciled in England – Whether Mareva jurisdiction restricted to preventing foreigners from removing assets out of jurisdiction.

The plaintiff and defendant were jointly engaged in the purchase, renovation and resale of a flat. The proceeds of the resale, amounting to some £3,300, were paid into a bank c
account in the defendant's name. A dispute arose between the parties over a sum of £2,000 which the plaintiff claimed the defendant owed her, and in the course of negotiations with the defendant's solicitors to agree a statement of account the plaintiff discovered that the defendant had sold his own flat, had gone abroad and was cruising in an ocean-going yacht of which he was a part-owner. The defendant, who was an English national with an English domicile, had previously lived abroad when in financial d
difficulties, and the plaintiff, fearing that he would again do so and transfer his assets out of the jurisdiction, issued a writ claiming the sum of £2,000 and the taking of accounts and obtained a Mareva injunction[a] restraining the defendant from removing the proceeds of the resale of the flat out of the jurisdiction or otherwise dealing with them except by placing them in a deposit account. When the injunction came up for extension the defendant submitted that it should not be continued because the Mareva jurisdiction e
was restricted to preventing foreign nationals from removing assets out of the jurisdiction and the court ought not to grant a Mareva injunction against an English national domiciled in England.

Held – The grant of a Mareva injunction was not barred merely because the defendant was not a foreigner or a foreign-based person, although the defendant's nationality, f
domicile and place of residence could be material to a greater or lesser degree in determining whether there was a real risk that the assets would be removed from the jurisdiction. The essence of the jurisdiction was the existence of a real risk that the defendant would remove his assets from the jurisdiction and thereby stultify the judgment sought by the plaintiff. On the facts, the plaintiff had, on balance, established that there was a real risk of removal of the £3,300 in the bank account and the injunction g
would accordingly be continued, although it would be restricted to the amount claimed by the plaintiff and costs (see p 194 *d* to p 195 *e* and *g* and p 196 *a* to *j*, post).

Third Chandris Shipping Corpn v Unimarine SA [1979] 2 All ER 972 and *Chartered Bank v Daklouche* [1980] 1 All ER 205 applied.

Lister & Co v Stubbs [1886–90] All ER Rep 797, *Mareva Compania Naviera SA v International Bulkcarriers SA* (1975) [1980] 1 All ER 213, *Rasu Maritima SA v Perusahaan* h
Pertambangan Minyak Dan Gas Bumi Negara (Pertamina) and Government of Indonesia (as interveners) [1977] 3 All ER 324, *Siskina (Cargo owners) v Distos Compania Naviera SA* [1977] 3 All ER 803 and *Allen v Jambo Holdings Ltd* [1980] 2 All ER 502 considered.

The Agrabele [1979] 2 Lloyd's Rep 117 not followed.

Notes j
For an injunction restraining disposition of property, see 24 Halsbury's Laws (4th Edn) para 1018, and for cases on the subject, see 28(2) Digest (Reissue) 1091–1094, 918–960.

---

a See *Mareva Compania Naviera SA v International Bulkcarriers SA* [1980] 1 All ER 213

Cases referred to in judgment

a *Allen v Jambo Holdings Ltd* [1980] 2 All ER 502, CA.

Chartered Bank v Daklouche [1980] 1 All ER 205, [1980] 1 WLR 107, CA.

Etablissement Esefka International Anstalt v Central Bank of Nigeria [1979] 1 Lloyd's Rep 445, CA, Digest (Cont Vol E) 334, *79f*.

Gebr Van Weelde Scheepvart Kantoor BV v Homeric Marine Services Ltd, The Agrabele [1979] 2 Lloyd's Rep 117, Digest (Cont Vol E) 334, *79g*.

b *Iraqi Ministry of Defence v Arcepey Shipping Co SA (Gillespie Brothers & Co Ltd intervening), The Angel Bell* [1980] 1 All ER 480, [1980] 1 WLR 488, [1979] 2 Lloyd's Rep 491.

Lister & Co v Stubbs (1890) 45 Ch D 1, [1886–90] All ER Rep 797, 59 LJ Ch 570, 63 LT 75, CA, (2) Digest (Reissue) 659, *4513*.

Mareva Compania Naviera SA v International Bulkcarriers SA, The Mareva (1975) [1980] 1 All ER 213, [1975] 2 Lloyd's Rep 509, CA, Digest (Cont Vol E) 331, *79b*.

c *Montecchi v Shimco (UK) Ltd* [1979] 1 WLR 1180, CA, Digest (Cont Vol E) 334, *79h*.

Nippon Yusen Kaisha v Karageorgis [1975] 3 All ER 282, [1975] 1 WLR 1093, [1975] 2 Lloyd's Rep 137, CA, Digest (Cont Vol D) 534, *79a*.

Rasu Maritima SA v Perusahaan Pertambangan Minyak Dan Gas Bumi Negara (Pertamina) and Government of Indonesia (as interveners) [1977] 3 All ER 324, [1978] QB 644, [1977] 3 WLR 518, [1977] 2 Lloyd's Rep 397, CA, Digest (Cont Vol E) 331, *79c*.

d *Siskina (Cargo owners) v Distos Compania Naviera SA, The Siskina* [1977] 3 All ER 803, [1979] AC 210, [1977] 3 WLR 818, [1978] 1 Lloyd's Rep 1, HL, Digest (Cont Vol E) 660, *782a*.

Third Chandris Shipping Corpn v Unimarine SA, The Pythia, The Angelic Wings, The Genie [1979] 2 All ER 972, [1979] QB 645, [1979] 3 WLR 122, [1979] 2 Lloyd's Rep 184, CA, Digest (Cont Vol E) 333, *79e*.

e

Motion

By a writ dated 15th April 1980 the plaintiff, Patricia Mary Barclay-Johnson, sought against the defendant, Cecil Mortley Yuill, inter alia, (i) a declaration that the sum of £2,000 remained due and owing to the plaintiff from the defendant in respect of the transfer of a leasehold property at 12 St Quintin's Avenue, London, by the plaintiff to the f defendant, (ii) a declaration that money had and received by the defendant to the plaintiff's use and money received by the defendant as agent for the plaintiff was retained by him and converted to his own use, (iii) an account of all money received by the defendant or his agent and the manner in which the defendant applied such money, (iv) an inquiry as to the balance of such money remaining in the defendant's hands or under his control after giving credit for all money properly expended by him for or on behalf g of the plaintiff, and (v) an order that the defendant pay to the plaintiff the sum of £2,000 together with such sums as may be found due on the inquiry and the taking of the account. On 16th April the plaintiff applied by notice of motion for an ex parte injunction restraining the defendant from removing or taking steps to remove out of the jurisdiction or dealing with the net proceeds of sale of the leasehold property at 12 St Quintin's Avenue otherwise than by paying them into a bank deposit account within the h jurisdiction and keeping them separate from any other moneys. The facts are set out in the judgment.

Christopher Semken for the plaintiff.
David Unwin for the defendant.

j

SIR ROBERT MEGARRY V-C. This opposed ex parte motion raises the question whether a Mareva injunction can and should be granted against a defendant who is in no sense a foreigner. The plaintiff and the defendant have been associated for some while in the business of acquiring dilapidated premises, renovating them and then selling them. The plaintiff says that she employed the defendant as her agent and building contractor, whereas the defendant alleges that there was a partnership between them. At the centre of the present dispute there is a penthouse flat which the plaintiff says she transferred to the defendant on 20th October 1977, on the terms that the defendant would carry out building works in the flat to the plaintiff's order to the value of £28,000, and then pay the plaintiff a sum which came to be agreed at £2,000. This sum, she says, was never paid, and on or about 30th August 1978 her then solicitors registered a caution against dealings in respect of the flat. There was litigation between the parties in which attempts were made to agree the state of accounts between them, but progress was slow: the plaintiff says that she paid some £146,000 to the defendant, and that she believes that the defendant's figure of £73,000 expended by him on the plaintiff's behalf is inflated, so that her claim against him will exceed £73,000.

While the negotiations were proceeding, the plaintiff's present solicitors were notified by the defendant's solicitors that their client had either gone abroad or was about to do so: this was on 2nd or 3rd April 1980. The plaintiff promptly made a telephone call to the penthouse flat in order to speak to the defendant, and the call was answered by a lady who said that she had purchased the flat and knew nothing about any caution. The plaintiff says that neither she nor her former or present solicitors ever applied for the cancellation of the caution or received any notice from the Land Registry about its removal. Inquiries of the Land Registry have elicited the information that no caution is now registered in respect of the flat. The way in which the caution vanished is at present mysterious, though it seems to have been removed on 18th September 1978 in connection in some way with a charge to a bank.

I pause there to say that both counsel for the plaintiff and counsel for the defendant were in a position of some difficulty, though for different reasons. A substantial part of the former's papers in this case had gone astray, whereas the latter, though instructed generally by the defendant's solicitors, was unable to obtain any specific instructions from the defendant himself. This was because the defendant was abroad, believed to be cruising in the Mediterranean, and could not be reached by his solicitors, who had accepted service on his behalf. The plaintiff says that the defendant is part-owner of a 54-ft twin-engined diesel yacht. Nevertheless, both counsel did their best to be helpful, and of course I have to deal with the case on the information that is before me. This consists of the writ, issued on 15th April 1980, a notice of motion and an affidavit sworn by the plaintiff on 18th April, the day on which counsel moved before me. The plaintiff had previously, during the vacation, obtained an ex parte injunction from Booth J over 18th April in terms of the notice of motion now before me. Put shortly, this seeks an injunction restraining the defendant from removing or taking steps to remove out of the jurisdiction or dealing with the net proceeds of sale of the penthouse flat otherwise than by paying them into a bank deposit account within the jurisdiction and keeping them separate from any other moneys. What the plaintiff seeks and the defendant opposes is a continuation of the ex parte injunction. Counsel accepts that some £3,300 standing to the credit of the defendant in a bank account in his name represents the balance of the proceeds of sale of the penthouse flat.

The plaintiff's evidence is that she fears that the defendant will remove all his assets from the jurisdiction and so render nugatory the relief that she seeks in her action. This relief includes a claim to the £2,000, the taking of accounts and the payment to the plaintiff of what is found due to her on taking the accounts. The plaintiff says that, when the defendant was previously in financial difficulties, he went to live in the United States for a considerable period; this was in or about 1976. Last summer he told her that he would go abroad again, and she fears that he will sell his interests in the United Kingdom and live on the yacht overseas. He is, of course, out of the jurisdiction on the yacht at present, so far as is known.

Now in those circumstances, counsel for the defendant, in addition to commenting adversely on the plaintiff's evidence, took what in effect is a preliminary point of law. This is simply that no Mareva injunction can be granted against a defendant who is not a foreigner, and that as the defendant cannot in any way be described as a foreigner the injunction ought not to be continued. During his submissions he conceded that in some circumstances a person about to depart from the realm, even though not a foreigner, a might be the subject of a Mareva injunction. But basically his submission was that apart from these circumstances, Mareva injunctions were for foreigners alone. As the argument had not concluded at the normal time for adjournment on 18th April, I continued the injunction over today, and the question is whether it should be further continued or discharged. If counsel for the defendant's point of law is right, then of course the injunction must be discharged. In order to decide this I must, I think, b examine the basis of the Mareva jurisdiction.

The Mareva jurisdiction takes its name from *Mareva Compania Naviera SA v International Bulkcarriers SA* (1975) [1980] 1 All ER 213, [1975] 2 Lloyd's Rep 509, a case which concerned the vessel Mareva: I shall call it 'the *Mareva* case'. Its immediate precursor was *Nippon Yusen Kaisha v Karageorgis* [1975] 3 All ER 282, [1975] 1 WLR 1093. Both are decisions of the Court of Appeal on ex parte applications, and in both c cases injunctions of the type now sought before me were granted against foreign defendants who had assets within the jurisdiction. I think that it is the *Mareva* case which has given its name to the injunction because in the earlier case the court had not been referred to *Lister & Co v Stubbs* (1890) 45 Ch D 1, [1886–90] All ER Rep 797 or any of the other cases in that line which pointed in the opposite direction, and it was in the *Mareva* case that the Court of Appeal held that, notwithstanding those authorities, the d injunction should be granted.

There are thus two lines of authority. First, there is the *Lister v Stubbs* line. In broad terms, this establishes the general proposition that the court will not grant an injunction to restrain a defendant from parting with his assets so that they may be preserved in case the plaintiff's claim succeeds. The plaintiff, like other creditors of the defendant, must obtain his judgment and then enforce it. He cannot prevent the defendant from e disposing of his assets pendente lite merely because he fears that by the time he obtains judgment in his favour the defendant will have no assets against which the judgment can be enforced. Were the law otherwise, the way would lie open to any claimant to paralyse the activities of any person or firm against whom he makes his claim by obtaining an injunction freezing their assets. Of course, the due exercise of the court's discretion would exclude flagrant abuses: but the disruptive peril to commercial activities might be f grave. This refusal to grant injunctions was well-settled law before 1975: see *Siskina (Cargo owners) v Distos Compania Naviera SA* [1977] 3 All ER 803 at 828, [1979] AC 210 at 260 per Lord Hailsham; and see the *Pertamina* case [1977] 3 All ER 324 at 332, [1978] QB 644 at 659 per Lord Denning MR. (The correct name of this case, even omitting the name of the party intervening, is *Rasu Maritima SA v Perusahaan Pertambangan Minyak Dan Gas Bumi Negara*, but in mercy to all I impose a short title by reference to the name g of the company concerned.) Furthermore, this doctrine was established when the statutory jurisdiction to grant an injunction was, as it is now, a power to do so in all cases in which it appeared to the court to be 'just or convenient' to do so: see the Supreme Court of Judicature Act 1873, s 23(8); the Supreme Court of Judicature (Consolidation) Act 1925, s 45(1).

The other line of authority is, of course, the *Mareva* line. This was based on the h statutory language that I have just mentioned, and it shows that in certain circumstances it is 'just or convenient' to grant such an injunction. The question is what those circumstances are. In the *Siskina* case [1977] 2 All ER 803 at 829, [1979] AC 210 at 261 Lord Hailsham referred to 'foreign based defendants with assets in England'. In *The Pertamina* case [1977] 3 All ER 324 at 333, [1978] QB 644 at 659 Lord Denning MR referred to a defendant who is 'out of the jurisdiction but has assets in this country'. The j contrast is with those who 'are within the jurisdiction of the court and have assets here'(see the *Pertamina* case [1977] 3 All ER 324 at 332, [1978] QB 644 at 659 per Lord Denning MR), a phrase which in *Chartered Bank v Daklouche* [1980] 1 All ER 205 at 209, [1980] 1 WLR 107 at 112 Lord Denning MR explained as meaning cases where the defendants 'were permanently settled here and had their assets here'. He added: 'If a defendant is likely to leave England at short notice, a Mareva injunction may well be granted.'

The relevant facts in the *Chartered Bank* case were that the defendants were a Lebanese married couple engaged in business in the Persian Gulf. The wife bought a house in England and their daughters went to school here. The husband then encountered financial difficulties and disappeared, but some of his money was transmitted to a bank account in the wife's name in England. A bank to which the husband owed money then sought and obtained a Mareva injunction in respect of the money in the wife's bank account here. Eveleigh LJ held that the wife was not an 'English based defendant' within Lord Hailsham's phrase, and Lord Denning MR, as I have indicated, did not regard her as being 'permanently settled here'. The case shows that a Mareva injunction may be granted against a defendant who is within the jurisdiction, even if he or she owns a house here, and that the jurisdiction is not confined to those who are outside the realm. I know that in *The Agrabele* [1979] 2 Lloyd's Rep 117 Lloyd J held that there was a settled practice against granting Mareva injunctions against defendants resident within the jurisdiction; but in reaching this conclusion the judge had been loyally applying what Lord Denning MR had said in the *Pertamina* case before, of course, it had been explained in the *Chartered Bank* case. In any case, for reasons which will appear, I would, with all respect, hesitate long before accepting that the place of residence provided any Mareva touchstone.

It seems to me that the heart and core of the Mareva injunction is the risk of the defendant removing his assets from the jurisdiction and so stultifying any judgment given by the courts in the action. If there is no real risk of this, such an injunction should be refused; if there is a real risk, then if the other requirements are satisfied the injunction ought to be granted. If the assets are likely to remain in the jurisdiction, then the plaintiff, like all others with claims against the defendant, must run the risk, common to all, that the defendant may dissipate his assets, or consume them in discharging other liabilities, and so leave nothing with which to satisfy any judgment. On the other hand, if there is a real risk of the assets being removed from the jurisdiction, a Mareva injunction will prevent their removal. It is not enough for such an injunction merely to forbid the defendant to remove them from the jurisdiction, for otherwise he might transfer them to some collaborator who would then remove them; accordingly, the injunction will restrain the defendant from disposing of them even within the jurisdiction. But that does not mean that the assets will remain sterilised for the benefit of the plaintiff, for the court will permit the defendant to use them for paying debts as they fall due: see *Iraqi Ministry of Defence v Arcepey Shipping Co SA* [1980] 1 All ER 480 at 486, [1980] 1 WLR 488 at 494 per Robert Goff J.

If, then, the essence of the jurisdiction is the risk of the assets being removed from the jurisdiction, I cannot see why it should be confined to 'foreigners', in any sense of that term. True, expressions such as 'foreign defendants' (see, for example, *Montecchi v Shimco (UK) Ltd* [1979] 1 WLR 1180 at 1183 and the *Siskina* case [1977] 3 All ER 803 at 822, [1979] AC 210 at 253), and 'foreign based defendants' (see the *Siskina* case [1977] 3 All ER 803 at 829, [1979] AC 210 at 261) appear in the cases, and for the most part the cases have concerned those who may fairly be called foreigners. Indeed, in the *Siskina* case [1977] 2 All ER 803 at 822, [1979] AC 210 at 253, Lord Diplock puts the jurisdiction in terms of a foreign defendant who does not reside or have a place of business within the jurisdiction, though I would read this as being descriptive of the past rather than restrictive of the future. Naturally the risk of removal of assets from the jurisdiction will usually be greater or more obvious in the case of foreign-based defendants, and so the jurisdiction has grown up in relation to them. But I cannot see why this should make some requirement of foreignness a prerequisite of the jurisdiction. If, for example, an Englishman who has lived and worked all his life in England is engaged in making arrangements to emigrate and remove all his assets with him, is the court to say 'He is not a foreigner, nor is he yet foreign-based, and so no Mareva injunction can be granted'? Why should it make all the difference if instead he had been a foreign national with a foreign domicile who, after living and working here for a while, was preparing to leave with his assets? Is it really to be said that in relation to Mareva injunctions, there is one law for the foreigner and another for the English, and that this flows from a statutory power to grant an injunction if it appears to the court to be 'just or convenient' to do so? I cannot see any sensible ground for holding that in this respect there is some privilege or immunity for the English and Welsh.

In saying this, I do not intend to suggest that matters of nationality, domicile, residence and so on are irrelevant in Mareva applications. Any or all of them may be of considerable importance in so far as they bear on the risk of removal. If the defendant has not even come to this country, the risk of his assets here being removed abroad will normally be high. If a foreign national is here, his nationality will often make it easier for him at short notice to go abroad with his assets, and remain there, easier than for a citizen of the United Kingdom; and his foreign domicile would render it more probable that he would do this. At the same time, it must be remembered that since the first Mareva injunction was granted, there has been a significant change, in that within the last year the abolition of exchange control has made it easier for everybody to transfer assets abroad.

In the result, I would hold (1) that it is no bar to the grant of a Mareva injunction that the defendant is not a foreigner, or is not foreign-based, in any sense of those terms, (2) that it is essential that there should be a real risk of the defendant's assets being removed from the jurisdiction in such a way as to stultify any judgment that the plaintiff may obtain, and (3) that, in determining whether there is such a risk, questions of the defendant's nationality, domicile, place of residence and many other matters may be material to a greater or a lesser degree.

In addition to establishing the existence of a sufficient risk of removal of the defendant's assets, the plaintiff must satisfy certain other requirements. I shall not attempt any comprehensive survey, particularly in view of the guidelines laid down by Lord Denning MR in *Third Chandris Shipping Corp v Unimarine SA* [1979] 2 All ER 972 at 984–985, [1979] QB 645 at 668–669. But I may refer to three of them. One is that it must appear that there is a danger of default if the assets are removed from the jurisdiction. Even if the risk of removal is great, no Mareva injunction should be granted unless there is also a danger of default. A reputable foreign company, accustomed to paying its debts, ought not to be prevented from removing its assets from the jurisdiction, especially if it has substantial assets in countries in which English judgments can be enforced. In commercial cases, it suffices if there are facts 'from which the Commercial Court, like a prudent, sensible commercial man, can properly infer a danger of default if assets are removed from the jurisdiction': see the *Third Chandris* case [1979] 2 All ER 972 at 987, [1979] QB 645 at 671 per Lawton LJ. If nothing can be found out about the defendant, that by itself may suffice: see the *Third Chandris* case [1979] 2 All ER 972 at 987, [1979] QB 645 at 672. See also *Etablissement Esefka International Anstalt v Central Bank of Nigeria* [1979] 1 Lloyd's Rep 445.

Second, the plaintiff must establish his claim with sufficient particularity, and show a good arguable case, though he need not demonstrate that his case is strong enough to entitle him to judgment under RSC Ord 14: see the *Pertamina* case [1977] 3 All ER 518, [1978] QB 644. Third, the case must be one in which, on weighing the considerations for and against the grant of an injunction, the balance of convenience is in favour of granting it. In considering this in Mareva cases, I think that some weight must be given to the principle of *Lister & Co v Stubbs* (1890) 45 Ch D 1, [1886–90] All ER Rep 797; I have already mentioned this. The Mareva prohibition against making any disposition of the assets within the country is a normal ancillary of the prohibition against removing the assets from the country, and if this is likely to affect the defendant seriously I think that he is entitled to have this put into the scales against the grant of the injunction. Much may depend on the assets in question. If, as in many of the reported cases, there is merely an isolated asset here, the harm to the defendant may be small. On the other hand, if he is trading here and the injunction would 'freeze' his bank account, the injury may be grave. I think that he should be able to rely on the *Lister* principle except so far as it cannot be fairly reconciled with the needs of the *Mareva* doctrine. I would regard the *Lister* principle as remaining the rule, and the *Mareva* doctrine as constituting a limited exception to it.

I return to the facts of this case. I have already given my reasons for rejecting preliminary objection of counsel for the defendant on the law, and for holding that the *a* defendant's lack of foreignness, if I may so call it, provides no bar to the granting of the injunction sought. The question is thus whether on those facts it ought to be granted. Counsel realistically accepted that the plaintiff had put forward a clearly formulated claim to the £2,000, but he pointed to an almost complete absence of particularity in the remainder of the plaintiff's claim. In this, I agree with him. I think that the plaintiff's claim attains the requisite standard of particularity as regards the £2,000, but not as *b* regards anything else.

As for the risk of removal, it seems clear that the £3,300 in the bank account, like the £70,000 in the *Chartered Bank* case, can, as Lord Denning MR put it, 'be removed at the stroke of a pen from England outside the reach of the creditors' (see [1980] 1 All ER 205 at 210, [1980] 1 WLR 107 at 113. The evidence before me is far from being as cogent as might have been wished, and mainly consists of simple assertions by the plaintiff of what *c* she fears the defendant will do. However, the defendant's previous departure to America, and his present absence on an ocean-going yacht after selling the flat in which he lived seem to me to justify an inference that there is sufficient risk of so easily removable an asset as the bank balance being removed from the jurisdiction; and, in contrast with the Central Bank of Nigeria in the *Etablissement Esefka* case, there does not seem to be any ground on which it could be inferred that the £2,000 would be paid even if the £3,300 *d* is released. There is nothing to indicate that the defendant has other assets of any substance except the part-share in the yacht which is already outside the jurisdiction; and, if he does not return, there is nothing to indicate where he will go, or whether it will be to a jurisdiction in which an English judgment will be enforceable. On the whole, I think that the plaintiff has, by no great margin, made out a sufficient case under this head. The court, like other human institutions, must at times take some risks; and in *e* doing so I think that it should initially err on the side of conservation rather than dispersion.

On the question of discretion, counsel forcefully contended that the defendant, being in ignorance of the existing injunction, might in good faith be issuing cheques drawn on the £3,300 in his bank account, and that his credit would be likely to be gravely impaired if the injunction restrains the bank from honouring those cheques. As Mareva *f* injunctions are normally granted ex parte and without warning to the defendant so as to ensure that the defendant does not remove the assets as soon as he learns of the danger, this must be a risk which flows from many, if not most, of these injunctions, for a greater or lesser time. I do not think that such a risk will normally inhibit the grant of such an injunction. However, in the present case there is a further point. I cannot see that it would be right to continue the injunction against the whole of the £3,300 when the *g* claim on which it can properly be based is only £2,000. Allow a reasonable sum for costs, and there still should be a balance which ought not to be subject to restraint; and this might well suffice for any incidental cheques that have been drawn on the account. I shall hear counsel on the matter of quantum.

Accordingly, I propose to continue the injunction. It is not known when the defendant will return to the jurisdiction, if at all. It was suggested that he might well *h* return in a week's time. In view of the uncertainty, the proper course may be to continue the present ex parte injunction until further order, with liberty to the defendant to apply to vary or discharge it on short notice to the plaintiff. On this, too, I shall hear counsel; and arrangements must also be made as to the inter partes motion.

There is one point that I should add. The *Mareva* doctrine grew up in commercial surroundings, particularly in relation to ships. Much that was said in the judgments *j* reflected that commercial background. On the other hand, I do not think that there is any authority for confining it to commercial matters, even if it were possible to define them at all accurately. The case now before me is in some respects commercial in nature, though it is far from being the sort of case that finds its way into the Commercial Court, the true home of the Mareva injunction. However, if, as I think, the foundation of the doctrine is the need to prevent judgments of the court from being rendered ineffective by the removal of the defendant's assets from the jurisdiction, then on principle I can see no reason for confining it to commercial cases. It seems to me to be a doctrine of general application. The decision of the Court of Appeal in *Allen v Jambo Holdings Ltd* [1980] 2 All ER 502 plainly seems to me to support this proposition. I need therefore say no more about that point. All I shall say is that it seems to be that in the short five years of its life the *Mareva* doctrine has shed all the possible limitations of its origin. It is now a quite general doctrine, free from any possible requirements of foreignness, commerce or anything else; and in a proper case it depends only on the existence of a sufficient risk of the defendant's assets being removed from the jurisdiction with a consequent danger of the plaintiff being deprived of the fruits of the judgment that he is seeking.

Order accordingly.

Solicitors: *Biddle & Co*, agents for *Hepworth & Chadwick*, Leeds (for the plaintiff); *Jay Benning & Co* (for the defendant).

Azza M Abdallah Barrister.

Bankers Trust International Ltd v Todd Shipyard Corporation

The Halcyon Isle

PRIVY COUNCIL

LORD DIPLOCK, LORD SALMON, LORD ELWYN-JONES, LORD SCARMAN AND LORD LANE

11th, 12th, 13th, 14th FEBRUARY, 24th JUNE 1980

Shipping – Maritime lien – Liens recognised by British law – Lien for repairs to ship – Lien given by United States law – Lien not a recognised maritime lien by English or Singapore law – Priority – Mortgagee having priority under law of Singapore over claim of repairer in distribution of proceeds of sale of ship – Claimant with maritime lien under Singapore law having priority over mortgagee – Ranking of claims.

The appellants, an English bank, held a mortgage on a British ship dated 27th April 1973 and registered in London on 8th May 1974. In March 1974 the respondents, who were ship repairers in New York, executed repairs to the ship in New York under a contract made in New York. The repairs were not paid for and under United States law the repairers were entitled to a maritime lien for the price of the repairs to the ship. Following the repairs the ship sailed to Singapore where both the appellants and the respondents brought actions in rem in the High Court against the owners of the ship. The appellants claimed the amount due under their mortgage and the respondents claimed the amount of the repairs. Both obtained judgment on their claims. The ship was arrested in Singapore waters and subsequently sold by order of the court, the sum received being insufficient to meet in full the claims of the creditors of its owners. The appellants sought the determination of the court on the question of priority of payment to the creditors. Under the law of Singapore a claimant who had a maritime lien under the law of Singapore had priority over a mortgagee, but ship repairers did not have a maritime lien for repairs executed in Singapore and could not therefore claim priority over a mortgagee. The respondents contended that they were entitled to priority over the appellants on the ground that the maritime lien conferred on them by United States law was a substantive right in the ship to which the law of Singapore should give effect

in determining the priority of competing judgment debts. The High Court of Singapore
gave judgment for the appellants but the Court of Appeal in Singapore reversed that *a*
decision. The appellants appealed to the Privy Council, contending that the courts of
Singapore, applying the lex fori, should determine the priority of competing judgment
debts in accordance with the nature of the claims and since the claim of the respondents
was that of a necessaries man, which by the lex fori ranked after the claim of a mortgagee,
the appellants' claim had priority over the respondents' claim. The law of Singapore on
this issue was the same as English law. *b*

Held (Lord Salmon and Lord Scarman dissenting) – Questions as to the right to proceed
in rem against a ship as well as priorities between competing claimants in the distribution
of the proceeds of its sale in an action in rem were questions of jurisdiction which in
principle fell to be determined by Singapore law as the lex fori. Since under English
rules of conflict of laws maritime claims were classified as giving rise to maritime liens *c*
which were enforceable in actions in rem in English courts only if the events on which
the claim was founded would have given rise to a maritime lien in English law if those
events had occurred within the territorial jurisdiction of the English court, the question
whether a necessaries man was entitled to priority over a mortgagee in the proceeds of
sale of a ship depended on whether, if the repairs to the ship had been done in Singapore,
the repairer would have been entitled under the law of Singapore to a maritime lien on *d*
the ship for the price of them. Since a ship repairer did not have a maritime lien on a
ship for repairs executed in Singapore it followed that the appellants as mortgagees were
entitled to priority. The appeal would therefore be allowed (see p 203 *j* to p 204 *a*, p 206
e f and p 208 *e* to *g*, post).

Per Lord Diplock, Lord Elwyn-Jones and Lord Lane. A maritime lien continues to be
enforceable by an action in rem against the ship in connection with which the claim that *e*
gave rise to the lien arose, notwithstanding any subsequent sale of the ship to a third
party and notwithstanding that the purchaser had no notice of the lien and no personal
liability on the claim from which the lien arose, this being a characteristic pointing to a
maritime lien partaking of the nature of a proprietary right in the ship (see p 203 *b c*,
post).

f

Notes

For priority of liens, see 35 Halsbury's Laws (3rd Edn) 788, paras 1213–1214, and for
mode of determination of claims, see ibid 793, para 1224.

Cases referred to in judgment and dissenting opinion

Acrux, The, Cassa Nazionale Della Previdenza Marinara v Proceeds of Sale of Italian Steamship Acrux [1965] 2 All ER 323, [1965] P 391, [1965] 3 WLR 80, [1965] 1 Lloyd's Rep 565, 1(1) Digest (Reissue) 262, *1551*. *g*

Christine Isle, The [1974] AMC 331.

Coal Export Corpn v Notias [1962] EA 220.

Colorado, The [1923] P 102, [1923] All ER Rep 531, 92 LJP 100, 128 LT 759, 16 Asp MLC 145, 14 Ll L Rep 251, CA, 42 Digest (Repl) 1108, *9253*. *h*

Dapueto v James Wyllie & Co, The Pieve Superiore (1874) LR 5 PC 482, 43 LJ Adm 20, 30 LT 887, 2 Asp MLC 319, PC, 1(1) Digest (Reissue) 272, *1610*.

Don v Lippmann (1837) 5 Cl & Fin 1, 7 ER 303, HL, 11 Digest (Reissue) 479, *862*.

Golubchick, The (1840) 1 Wm Rob 143, 166 ER 526, 1(1) Digest (Reissue) 260, *1537*.

Hamilton v Baker, The Sara (1889) 14 App Cas 209, 58 LJP 57, 61 LT 26, 6 Asp MLC 413, HL, 42 Digest (Repl) 1093, *9068*. *j*

Harmer v Bell, The Bold Buccleugh (1852) 7 Moo PCC 267, [1843–60] All ER Rep 125, 19 LTOS 235, 13 ER 884, PC, 42 Digest (Repl) 1083, *8956*.

Johnson v Black, The Two Ellens (1872) LR 4 PC 161, 8 Moo PCC NS 398, 41 LJ Adm 33, 26 LT 1, 1 Asp MLC 208, 17 ER 361, PC, 42 Digest (Repl) 1106, *9239*.

Marquis v The Astoria [1931] Ex CR 195, 42 Digest (Repl) 1102, **2448*.

Milford, The (1858) Sw 362, 31 LTOS 42, 4 Jur NS 417, 166 ER 1167, 42 Digest (Repl) 1090, *9025*.

Nestor (Brig), The (1831) 1 Sumner 73, US Circuit Ct, 1st Circuit.

Pacific, The (1864) Brown & Lush 243, 3 New Rep 709, 33 LJPM & A 120, 10 LT 541, 10 Jur NS 1110, 2 Mar LC 21, 167 ER 356, 42 Digest (Repl) 1097, *9112*.

Ripon City, The [1897] P 226, [1895–9] All ER Rep 487, 66 LJP 110, 77 LT 98, 8 Asp MLC 304, 42 Digest (Repl) 1095, *9087*.

Salacia, The (1862) Lush 545, 32 LJPM & A 41, 7 LT 440, 9 Jur NS 27, 1 Mar LC 261, 167 ER 246, 42 Digest (Repl) 1104, *9204*.

Strandhill, The v Walter W Hodder Co Inc [1926] SCR 680, [1926] 4 DLR 801, 1(1) Digest (Reissue) 251, **802*.

Tagus, The [1903] P 44, 72 LJP 4, 87 LT 598, 9 Asp MLC 371, 42 Digest (Repl) 1090, *9026*.

Tervaete, The [1922] P 259, [1922] All ER Rep 387, 91 LJP 213, 128 LT 176, 16 Asp MLC 48, CA, 42 Digest (Repl) 1085, *8977*.

Todd Shipyards Corpn v Altema Compania Maritima SA and the Ship Ioannis Daskalelis, The Ioannis Daskalelis [1974] 1 Lloyd's Rep 174, 32 DLR (3d) 571, [1974] SCR 1248, Digest (Cont Vol D) 838, **2481a*.

United Africa Co Ltd v MV Tolten (Owners), The Tolten [1946] 2 All ER 372, [1946] P 135, [1947] LJR 201, 175 LT 469, CA, 11 Digest (Reissue) 398, *387*.

Zigurds, The [1932] P 113, 101 LJP 75, 148 LT 72, 18 Asp MLC 324, 43 Ll L Rep 156, 11 Digest (Reissue) 631, *1685*.

Appeal

Bankers Trust International Ltd appealed by leave of the Court of Appeal of the Republic of Singapore granted on 22nd March 1978 against a judgment dated 8th December 1977 and two orders dated 9th March 1978 of the Court of Appeal in Singapore (Wee Chong Jin CJ, F A Chua and A P Rajah JJ) allowing an appeal by the respondents, Todd Shipyards Corpn, from a judgment of the High Court of the Republic of Singapore (Kulasekaram J) dated 19th January 1977 by which it was held that the respondents' judgment debt for the execution of repairs carried out and necessaries supplied to the vessel Halcyon Isle should rank in priority to the appellants' judgment debt for sums due under a registered mortgage over the vessel in the distribution of the proceeds of sale of the vessel. In reversing the decision of the High Court the Court of Appeal held that the respondents' maritime lien conferred by United States law was a substantive right to which the law of Singapore would give effect and which in consequence gave the respondents priority over the appellants. The facts are set out in the judgment of the Board.

Michael Thomas QC and *Simon Gault* for the appellants.
Richard Stone QC and *Jervis Kay* for the respondents.

LORD DIPLOCK. The appellants ('the mortgagees') are an English bank. They held a mortgage on a British ship, the Halcyon Isle, registered in London. It was dated 27th April 1973 and registered on 8th May 1974. The respondents ('the necessaries men') are ship repairers carrying on business in New York. They executed repairs to the Halcyon Isle at their Brooklyn yard in New York State in March 1974. Under United States law a ship repairer is entitled to a maritime lien for the price of repairs done to a ship. The Halcyon Isle was arrested in Singapore on 5th September 1974, in an action in rem brought in the High Court of Singapore by the mortgagees. On 6th March 1975, it was sold by order of the court, for a sum insufficient to satisfy in full the claims of all the creditors of its owners. The question of law directly involved in this appeal is whether, in the distribution of the proceeds of sale, the claim of the mortgagees should take priority over the claim of the necessaries men or vice versa.

Although the Admiralty jurisidiction of the High Court of Singapore is statutory, the order of priorities in the distribution of the proceeds of sale of a ship in an action in rem or in a limitation action is not. It is a matter of practice and procedure of that court in the exercise of its Admiralty jurisdiction; and in matters of practice and procedure, as well as the substantive law which it administers, there is no relevant difference between the law of Singapore and the law of England. Since nearly all the cases to be cited will be English cases, their Lordships will for brevity use the expression 'English law' as embracing also the law of Singapore administered by the High Court of Singapore in the exercise of its Admiralty jurisdiction.

At first sight, the answer to the question posed by this appeal seems simple. The priorities as between claimants to a limited fund which is being distributed by a court of law are matters of procedure which under English rules of conflict of laws are governed by the lex fori; so English law is the only relevant law by which the priorities as between the mortgagees and the necessaries men are to be determined; and in English law mortgagees take priority over necessaries men.

In the case of a ship, however, the classification of claims against its former owners for the purpose of determining priorities to participate in the proceeds of its sale may raise a further problem of conflict of laws, since claims may have arisen as a result of events that occurred not only on the high seas but also within the territorial jurisdictions of a number of different foreign states. So the lex causae of one claim may differ from the lex causae of another, even though the events which gave rise to the claim in each of those foreign states are similar in all respects, except their geographical location; the leges causarum of various claims, of which under English conflict rules the 'proper law' is that of different states, may assign different legal consequences to similar events. So the court distributing the limited fund may be faced, as in the instant case, with the problems of classifying the foreign claims arising under differing foreign systems of law in order to assign each of them to the appropriate class in the order of priorities under the lex fori of the distributing court.

The choice would appear to lie between (1) on the one hand classifying by reference to the events on which each claim was founded and giving to it the priority to which it would be entitled under the lex fori if those events had occurred within the territorial jurisdiction of the distributing court, or (2) on the other hand applying a complicated kind of partial renvoi by (i) first ascertaining in respect of each foreign claim the legal consequences, *other than those relating to priorities in the distribution of a limited fund,* that would be attributed under its own lex causae to the events on which the claim is founded; and (ii) then giving to the foreign claim the priority accorded under the lex fori to claims arising from events, however dissimilar, which would have given rise to the same or analogous legal consequences if they had occurred within the territorial jurisdiction of the distributing court. To omit the dissection of the lex causae of the claim that the second choice prescribes and to say instead that if under the lex causae the relevant events would give rise to a maritime lien, the English court must give to those courts all the legal consequences of a maritime lien under English law would, in their Lordships' view, be too simplistic an approach to the questions of conflicts of law that are involved.

Even apart from the merit of simplicity, the choice in favour of the first alternative, classification by reference to events, appears to their Lordships to be preferable in principle. In distributing a limited fund that is insufficient to pay in full all creditors of a debtor whose claims against him have already been quantified and proved, the court is not any longer concerned with enforcing against the debtor himself the individual creditors' original rights against him. It is primarily concerned in doing even-handed justice between competing creditors whose respective claims to be a creditor may have arisen under a whole variety of different and, it may be, conflicting systems of national law. It may be plausibly suggested that the moral and rational justification of the general conflicts of law rule, applied by English courts to claims arising out of foreign contracts, that the contract should be given the same legal consequences as would be accorded to it under its 'proper law', is that the legitimate expectations of the parties to the contract as to their rights against one another, which will result from entering into and carrying out the contract, ought not to be defeated by any change of the forum in which such rights have to be enforced. Rights of priority over other creditors of the defaulting party to

such a contract, in a judicial distribution of a fund which is insufficient to satisfy all the
a creditors in full, are not, however, rights of the parties to the contract against one
another. They are rights as between one party to the contract against strangers to the
contract, the other creditors, who have done nothing to arouse any legitimate expectations
in that party as to the priority to which he will be entitled in the distribution of such a
fund. Every such creditor whose claim is based on contract or quasi-contract must have
known that in so far as the legal consequences of his claim under its own lex causae
b included rights to priority over other classes of creditors in the distribution of a limited
fund resulting from an action in rem against a ship, that particular part of the lex causae
would be compelled to yield to the lex fori of any foreign court in which the action in
rem might be brought.

Counsel for the necessaries men in the instant case, who are experienced litigants in
courts of Admiralty, has not suggested that they were not perfectly well aware of this
c when they allowed the Halcyon Isle to vacate the berth that it was occupying in their
busy repair yard in Brooklyn and thereby relinquished their possessory lien for the
unpaid work that they had done on the ship. They would likewise know that if the
Halcyon Isle were to enter a port in any of the major trading countries of the world while
their bill *remained unpaid* they could have it arrested in an action in rem and in this way
obtain the security of the ship itself for their claim; subject, however, to being postponed
d to any other claimants who might be entitled to priority under the lex fori of the country
in which the action was brought. They, or their lawyers, would know, too, that the
priorities as between various kinds of maritime claims accorded by the lex fori were
subject to considerable variation as between one country and another.

In the case of claimants to a limited fund consisting of the proceeds of sale of a ship in
an action in rem brought in a court which, like the High Court of Singapore, applies
e English Admiralty law and practice, the problems of classifying foreign maritime claims
for the purposes of determining priorities is complicated by the legal concept of
'maritime lien' to which some classes of maritime claims against a shipowner give rise in
English law while other classes do not. This concept, derived as it is from the civil law and
not the common law, may fairly be described as sui generis.

The classic description of a maritime lien in English law is to be found in *Harmer v Bell,*
f *The Bold Buccleugh* (1852) 7 Moo PCC 267 at 284, [1843–60] All ER Rep 125 at 128, a case
decided by the Privy Council at a time when the English Court of Admiralty regarded
itself as applying not so much English law as the 'general law of the sea of the whole of
Europe'. Jervis CJ described the concept as having its origin in the civil law. He adopted
as correct Lord Tenterden's definition of 'maritime lien' in Abbott on Shipping, as
meaning 'a claim or privilege upon a thing to be carried into effect by legal process'; and
g Jervis CJ added (7 Moo PCC 267 at 284–285, [1843–60] All ER Rep 125 at 128):

> 'This claim or privilege travels with the thing, into whosesoever possession it may
> come. It is inchoate from the moment the claim or privilege attaches, and when
> carried into effect by legal process, by a proceeding in rem, relates back to the period
> when it first attached.'

h The expression 'privilege' in this description of a maritime lien is a reference to the
concept of 'privilège' in the civil law from which the French Code Civil is derived.
There, privilège is used in the sense of the right of a creditor of a particular class to be paid
out of a particular fund or the proceeds of sale of a particular thing in priority to other
classes of creditors of the owner or former owner of the fund or thing. In the French
Code Civil it is distinguished from the concept of 'hypothèque', which was the subject of
j detailed analysis by the English Court of Appeal in *The Colorado* [1923] P 102, [1923] All
ER Rep 531.

Jervis CJ, speaking in 1852, said that a maritime lien existed in every case in which the
Court of Admiralty had jurisdiction to entertain an action in rem against a ship.
Jurisdiction in rem and maritime lien went hand in hand. This had been true when the
jurisdiction of the Court of Admiralty was at its lowest ebb in the early years of the
nineteenth century as a result of harassment by the courts of common law. It has

remained true in the law of the United States of America where today all maritime claims enforceable in rem are treated as giving rise to maritime liens; but it was no longer true in English law, even by 1852, after the jurisdiction of the Court of Admiralty had been extended by the Admiralty Court Act 1840 and the Merchant Shipping Act 1854. Subsequent extensions of jurisdiction in rem in respect of maritime claims were made by the Admiralty Court Act 1861 and by later Merchant Shipping Acts until its modern jurisdiction was laid down in the Administration of Justice Act 1956, which is in the same terms as the High Court (Admiralty Jurisdiction) Act of Singapore.

During the period that the English Court of Admiralty regarded itself as applying the 'general law of the sea' four classes of claims only were treated as giving rise to maritime liens on ships, viz (1) salvage, (2) collision damage, (3) seaman's wages and (4) bottomry. Bottomry is now obsolete, but historically it provided a normal means of providing security for the price of goods and services supplied to a ship by necessaries men outside its home port. Two additional classes of claims were added to this list by statute in the nineteenth century. These were: (5) master's wages and (6) master's disbursements.

The ranking for the purpose of priority in the distribution of a limited fund that has been accorded by the English Court of Admiralty to claims within the various classes that were treated as giving rise to maritime liens was complicated. It still is. It can be found conveniently set out in McGaffie, Fugeman and Gray on Admiralty Practice (1964, paras 1574 ff) (British Shipping Laws, vol 1). For present purposes it is sufficient to observe that the priorities, whether between class and class or within one class, bear no relation to the general rule applicable to other charges on property as security for a debt: qui prior est tempore potior est jure. This rule is based on the principle that when the owner of a thing grants a charge on it as security for the payment of a sum of money, he transfers to the grantee part of his own proprietary rights in the thing and so deprives himself of the ability to transfer to a subsequent grantee anything more than such proprietary rights as remain to him.

This principle, based as it is on the concept of a transfer of proprietary rights, cannot explain the priorities accorded to maritime liens. Indeed a later maritime lien for one class of claim may rank in priority to an earlier maritime lien for another class of claim, and even within a single class a later maritime lien may rank in priority to an earlier one.

Thus when Gorrell Barnes P in *The Ripon City* [1897] P 226 at 242, [1895–9] All ER Rep 487 at 498 said of a maritime lien: 'It is a right acquired by one over a thing belonging to another—a jus in re aliena. It is, so to speak, a subtraction from the absolute property of the owner in the thing', the second sentence is inaccurate if it is to be regarded as suggesting that the owner of a ship, once it has become the subject of a maritime lien, can no longer create a charge on the *whole* property in the ship which will rank in priority to the existing lien. This he can do, as for instance by entering into a salvage contract or by signing on a crew.

In English Admiralty law and practice claims of all those six classes that have hitherto been treated as giving rise to a maritime lien take priority over claims under mortgages in the distribution of a limited fund by the court, and mortgages themselves rank in priority to all classes of claims that have not been treated as giving rise to maritime liens.

(In view of the reference hereafter to be made to *The Colorado* it is also relevant to note that for the purpose of priority of ranking inter se mortgages fall into two classes: (1) British registered mortgages (which can only be on British ships) and (2) other mortgages, British or foreign (which can be on either British or foreign ships). British registered mortgages rank in priority to all other mortgages and rank inter se in order of date of registration. All other mortgages regardless of whether they are British or foreign rank inter se in order of date of creation.)

The pattern of priorities, which has been applied by the English Admiralty Court in the distribution of the fund representing the proceeds of sale of a ship in an action in rem, thus affords no logical basis for concluding that, if a new class of claim additional to the six that have hitherto been recognised were treated under its own lex causae as having given rise to a maritime lien, this should have any effect on its ranking for the purpose of priority under the lex fori in the distribution of the fund by the court and, in particular, no logical basis for concluding that this should entitle it to priority over mortgages.

There is, however, an additional legal characteristic of a maritime lien in English law which distinguishes it from maritime claims to which no maritime lien attaches and which is not confined to rights to a particular rank of priority in the distribution by a court of justice of a limited fund among the various classes of creditors of a single debtor. A maritime lien continues to be enforceable by an action in rem against the ship in connection with which the claim that gave rise to the lien arose, notwithstanding any subsequent sale of the ship to a third party and notwithstanding that the purchaser had no notice of the lien and no personal liability on the claim from which the lien arose. This characteristic points in the direction of a maritime lien partaking of the nature of a proprietary right in the ship.

It is true that in the instant case this complication does not in fact arise; there had been no change of ownership since the claim of the necessaries men arose. Nevertheless it would be wrong to overlook this special characteristic of a maritime lien (for which the French expression is 'droit de suite') in any consideration of how a claim, which under its own lex causae would be treated as having the same legal consequences as those of a maritime lien in English law, is to be classified under English rules of conflict of laws for the purpose of distribution of a fund under Singapore law as the lex fori; for a maritime lien does something more than merely affect priorities.

As explained in the passage from *Harmer v Bell, The Bold Buccleugh* that has already been cited, any charge that a maritime lien creates on a ship is initially inchoate only; unlike a mortgage it creates no immediate right of property; it is, and will continue to be, devoid of any legal consequences unless and until it is 'carried into effect by legal process, by a proceeding in rem'. Any proprietary right to which it may give rise is thus dependent on the lienee being recognised as entitled to proceed in rem against the ship in the court in which he is seeking to enforce his maritime lien. Under the domestic law of a number of civil law countries even the inchoate charge to which some classes of maritime claims give rise is evanescent. Unless enforced by legal process within a limited time, for instance within one year or before the commencement of the next voyage, it never comes to life. In English law, while there is no specific time limit to a maritime lien the right to enforce it may be lost by laches.

If and when a maritime lien is carried into effect by legal process, however, the charge dates back to the time that the claim on which it is founded arose. It is only this retrospective consequence of his having been able to enforce the legal process in a court of law that enables a claimant, whose entitlement to a maritime lien is still inchoate and has not yet come into effect, to pursue his claim to the lien, as it were proleptically, in a proceeding in rem against the ship at a time when it no longer belongs to the shipowner who was personally liable to satisfy the claim in respect of which the lien arose.

This characteristic of a maritime lien is one that is unique in English law. It has the result that the recognition of any new class of claim arising under foreign law, as giving rise to a maritime lien in English law because it does so under it own lex causae, may affect not only priorities as between classes of creditors of a particular debtor in the distribution of the proceeds of sale of a particular ship in an action in rem, but such recognition may also extend the classes of persons who are entitled to bring such an action against a particular ship, ie by including among them some who, although they have no claim against the current owner of the ship, have claims against his predecessor in ownership.

But any question as to who is entitled to bring a particular kind of proceeding in an English court, like questions of priorities in distribution of a fund, is a question of jurisdiction. It too, under English rules of conflict of laws, falls to be decided by English law as the lex fori.

Their Lordships therefore conclude that, in principle, the question as to the right to proceed in rem against a ship as well as priorities in the distribution between competing claimants of the proceeds of its sale in an action in rem in the High Court of Singapore *a* falls to be determined by the lex fori, as if the events that gave rise to the claim had occurred in Singapore.

Although in the English cases involving claims to maritime liens, which extend over a period of a century and a half, there is no apparent recognition in the judgments that any hidden problems of conflict of laws might be involved, the English Courts of Admiralty have consistently applied English rules as to what classes of events give rise to *b* maritime liens wherever those events may have occurred. Not one single case has been drawn to their Lordships' attention in which it has been treated as relevant that a transaction or event did or did not give rise to a maritime lien under the law of the country where the transaction or event took place; even though the judges of the Court of Admiralty were fully aware that under the law of many European countries claims falling outside the six classes recognised by English law were treated by those countries' *c* courts as giving rise to maritime liens. Claims for the supply of necessaries provided the most widespread example of foreign recognition of a maritime lien; but, under French law in particular, a wide variety of other maritime claims were treated as giving rise to privilèges, ie maritime liens.

To take an early example in *The Golubchick* (1840) 1 W Rob 143, 166 ER 526, the English rule was applied by Dr Lushington to claims for wages by Spanish seamen *d* engaged on a Russian vessel. In *Dapueto v James Wyllie & Co, The Pieve Superiore* (1874) LR 5 PC 482, the Privy Council in the course of its judgment stated as self-evident that cargo claims against an Italian vessel did not give rise to a maritime lien. *The Milford* (1858) Sw 362, 166 ER 1167, *The Tagus* [1903] P 44, *The Zigurds* [1932] P 113 and *The Acrux* [1965] 2 All ER 323, [1965] P 391 are supporting authorities, spanning a century, in which the court has applied English rules as to the existence and extent of maritime *e* liens and not the differing rules which would have been applicable under the lex causae.

The statutory extensions by the Admiralty Courts Acts 1840 and 1861 of the jurisdiction of the English Court of Admiralty to entertain actions in rem against ships in respect of claims of most of the kinds now listed in the current Singapore and English statutes, including claims by necessaries men, might have been regarded as entitling these new claims to maritime liens. Under Admiralty practice as it then existed this *f* would have given to them that priority over mortgagees to which the necessaries men in the instant case would be entitled under United States law. After some early vacillation by Dr Lushington, however, it was decided by the Privy Council in *Johnson v Black, The Two Ellens* (1872) LR 4 PC 161, that those English statutes did not create a maritime lien for any of the additional classes of claims over which the Court of Admiralty had newly been granted jurisdiction, and that, accordingly, mortgagees had priorities over *g* necessaries men: see also *The Pacific* (1864) Brown & Lush 243, 167 ER 356. It required an express provision of an English statute to create a maritime lien for classes of claims other than those entitled to such liens under what the Court of Admiralty regarded and referred to as the 'general law of the seas'. This was done in the case of masters' wages by the Merchant Shipping Act 1854, *The Salacia* (1862) Lush 545, 167 ER 246, and in the case of masters' disbursements by the Merchant Shipping Act 1889 after the House of *h* Lords in *Hamilton v Baker, The Sara* (1889) 14 App Cas 209 had held that the earlier statutes conferred no such lien.

In coming to the conclusion in the instant case that, because it would have given rise to a maritime lien under its lex causae (United States law) to which effect would be given by an American court applying United States law as the lex fori, the necessaries men's claim was therefore entitled to the same priority over mortgages as maritime liens as a *j* class enjoy over mortgages under the law of Singapore as the lex fori, the Court of Appeal were greatly influenced by the decision of the Supreme Court of Canada in *The Ioannis Daskalelis* [1974] 1 Lloyd's Rep 174 that under Canadian law, which in Admiralty matters is derived from English law, American necessaries men took priority over mortgagees of a Greek ship. There had been a previous decision of the Supreme Court of Canada in

1926, *The Strandhill v Walter W Hodder Co Inc* [1926] SCR 680, in which it had been held
a that American necessaries men could proceed to enforce their claim by an action in rem
against the ship notwithstanding a subsequent change in ownership; but this earlier
decision expressly left open the question whether priorities between competing claims
would be determined by Canadian law. A subsequent decision of the Canadian Court of
Exchequer had determined that priorities were to be determined by Canadian law:
Marquis v The Astoria [1931] Ex CR 195. In overruling *Marquis v The Astoria* the Supreme
b Court of Canada in *The Ioannis Daskalelis* relied strongly on the judgment of the English
Court of Appeal in *The Colorado* [1923] P 102, [1923] All ER Rep 531, a case that was not
concerned with a claim to a maritime lien at all.

The only question in *The Colorado* was whether a hypothèque executed and registered
in France over a French ship created a proprietary right in the ship which the court
would recognise as similar enough in legal character to an English mortgage to justify
c according it the priority over the claim of necessaries men to which a mortgagee would
be entitled in *English* law. This is not a problem that would have troubled the Court of
Admiralty when it was manned by civil lawyers; they would have known all about the
legal concept of hypothèque. An examination of the expert evidence of French law,
which can be found in the report of the case in 16 Asp MLC 145–147, discloses that,
contrary to what Scrutton LJ said ([1923] P 102 at 109, [1923] All ER Rep 531 at 535), a
d hypothèque does constitute a jus in rem or right of property in the ship that is created
consensually to secure a debt; although, unlike an English mortgage, it gives no right to
take possession of the res. There is nothing inchoate about it; it requires registration and
is enforceable by judicial sale. It has different characteristics from a privilège in French
law and, what is significant for present purposes, according to the *French* law of priorities,
it ranks behind and not before the claims of necessaries men.

e In *The Colorado* the court looked at the French law as the 'proper law' of the hypothèque
simply to see what its legal nature was. In describing the right created by hypothèque
in French law as being equivalent to a maritime lien in English law (a passage much
relied on by the Canadian court) Scrutton LJ can only have been speaking loosely. They
have some characteristics in common; but Scrutton LJ could hardly be taken to have
been suggesting that a hypothèque would take priority over a prior English mortgage,
f as it would if it were to be treated by an English court as being a maritime lien. On the
contrary the *French* law as to the priority of maritime liens over hypothèques was said by
all three Lords Justices to be irrelevant; nor did any of the members of the court regard
their decision as inconsistent with *The Milford* or *The Tagus*. Both these cases were cited
by Scrutton and Atkin LJJ in support of their respective judgments.

Moreover the same three Lords Justices had in the previous year decided *The Tervaete*
g [1922] P 259, [1922] All ER Rep 387. Atkin LJ there says in terms: '[The maritime lien]
is confined to a right to take proceedings in a court of law', and: 'The right of maritime
lien appears . . . to be essentially different from a right of property, hypothec or pledge
created by [a] voluntary act.' Scrutton LJ refers to a maritime lien as 'a privilege or lien
. . . in this sense, that *if the vessel comes within English territorial waters* it may be arrested
and the claim or privilege on it will date back to the time of the lien.' (Emphasis
h mine.) Bankes LJ considered that a maritime lien might properly be regarded in one or
other of three ways: 'as a step in the process of enforcing a claim against the owners of a
ship, or as a remedy or partial remedy in itself, or as a means of securing priority of
claim.' The reasoning of all three judgments is consistent only with the characterisation
of a maritime lien in English law as involving rights that are procedural or remedial
only, and accordingly the question whether a particular class of claim gives rise to a
j maritime lien or not as being one to be determined by English law as the lex fori. Their
Lordships, with great respect, consider that in *The Ioannis Daskalelis* the judgments in *The
Colorado* were misunderstood by the Supreme Court.

In the instant case the Court of Appeal in Singapore also relied on statements on the
legal nature of a maritime lien in English law which are to be found in the judgment of
Scott LJ in *United Africa Co Ltd v MV Tolten (Owners), The Tolten* [1946] 2 All ER 372,

[1946] P 135. That was an action brought to enforce a maritime lien for damage caused by a ship in collision with a port installation in Nigeria. Collision damage gives rise to a maritime lien in English law and in the maritime law of the great majority of other Western countries, ie under what Scott LJ repeatedly referred to in his judgment as 'the general law of the sea amongst Western nations' out of which, he said, our own maritime law largely grew. Scott LJ in *The Tolten* was not concerned with the 'proper law' by which the existence or non-existence of a maritime lien was to be determined, but with a question that was purely one of English law as the lex fori, namely a choice between two competing rules of English law as to the jursidiction of English courts, viz the existence of jurisdiction to enforce against a ship which had come within English territorial waters what was unquestionably recognised by English law as a maritime lien and the absence of any jurisdiction to entertain actions concerning foreign land. Scott LJ had participated in the conferences which resulted in the International Convention on Maritime Liens and Mortgages of 1926 which the United Kingdom never ratified because it required member states to create and recognise maritime liens in favour of necessaries men. No one was better aware than Scott LJ of the wide departure from what he called the general law of the sea that had occurred in many western countries as regards the creation of maritime liens under their domestic law for a whole variety of claims against shipowners. France and the United States were conspicuous examples of this. Their domestic laws provided for the enforcement of maritime liens in respect of nearly every kind of maritime claim listed in s 3 of the High Court (Admiralty Jurisdiction) Act of Singapore. Throughout his judgment in *The Tolten* their Lordships think it clear that Scott LJ was treating English law as the only proper law to determine what kind of transaction or event gave rise to a maritime lien that an English court had jurisdiction to enforce as such.

In their Lordships' view the English authorities on close examination support the principle that, in the application of English rules of conflict of laws, maritime claims are classified as giving rise to maritime liens which are enforceable in actions in rem in English courts where *and only where* the events on which the claim is founded would have given rise to a maritime lien in English law, if those events had occurred within the territorial jurisdiction of the English court.

From principle and authority their Lordships turn finally to the language of what is now the statutory source of Admiralty jurisdiction of the High Court of Singapore, the High Court (Admiralty Jurisdiction) Act. It is in the same terms as the corresponding provisions of the English Administration of Justice Act 1956, which confer on the High Court of England its current Admiralty jurisdiction in rem and in personam. The English statute was passed to enable this country to ratify the International Convention relating to the Arrest ['saisi conservatoire'] of Sea-going Ships (Brussels, 10th May 1952; Misc 13 (1952) Cmd 8954) ('the 1952 convention'). The Singapore Act was probably passed for the same purpose although, in the event, it appears that Singapore has not yet ratified the convention. Nevertheless the identical words of the Singapore statute ought also to be construed in the light of the convention to which the English statute was intended to give effect.

The list of claims over which the High Court has Admiralty jurisdiction under the statute ('maritime claims') reproduces, with one addition relating to forfeiture and condemnation, the list of maritime claims to be found in the convention. The list is both exhaustive of the claims in respect of which the courts of one contracting party to the convention may arrest a ship flying the flag of any other contracting party, and is compulsory on the court if invoked by an applicant claiming to be entitled to any of the maritime claims in the list.

The convention deals with what in civil law countries are treated as two separate kinds of 'jurisdiction', viz: (1) jurisdiction to arrest a ship on the application of a person claiming to be a creditor of the present or former owner of the ship in respect of a maritime claim and to release the ship on the provision of bail or security sufficient to satisfy a judgment for the claim rendered by a court of competent jurisdiction (ie saisi conservatoire) and (2) jurisdiction to determine the claim on the merits (ie sur le fond) and to order a judicial sale of the ship to satisfy the claim and any other maritime claims affecting the ship.

The concept of saisi conservatoire is unknown to English law. In civil law countries it is not peculiar to maritime law; it applies to other kinds of moveable property. It is a procedure whereby a court, which has no jurisdiction over a claim ratione causae but within whose geographical area of jurisdiction property of the defendant to the claim is to be found, may arrest that property on the application of the claimant and retain it, or any security provided to obtain its release, in judicial custody to abide the result of the judgment of another court which does have jurisdiction over the claim ratione causae. Although generally exercised by one court having local jurisdiction in aid of another court with local jurisdiction in the same country, it also extends to saisi conservatoire in aid of foreign courts.

In English and Singapore law where saisi conservatoire is unknown, jurisdiction in rem to arrest a ship on the application of a claimant and jurisdiction to adjudicate on the merits of his maritime claim are coextensive. The convention recognises the supremacy of the lex fori in matters of jurisdiction to adjudicate on the merits, by providing in art 7:

> 'The Courts of the country in which the arrest was made shall have jurisdiction to determine the case upon its merits [*ie sur le fond*] *if the domestic law of the country in which the arrest is made gives jurisdiction to such Courts.*' (Emphasis mine.)

Leaving aside questions as to the ownership or possession of ships, the maritime claims appearing in the list contained in the convention and the English and Singapore statutes fall into three classes: (1) claims in respect of mortgages or charges on a ship; (2) maritime claims which in English law give rise to a 'maritime lien' on a ship for the amount claimed; and (3) maritime claims which give rise to a right of arrest of a ship but in English law do *not* give rise to a maritime lien. As has been pointed out, apart from questions of priorities, with which the convention does not deal at all, an essential difference between claims in classes (2) and (3) is that claims which give rise to a maritime lien on a ship may be enforced in rem against that ship notwithstanding that it has subsequently been sold to a bona fide purchaser for value without notice of the claim. This is expressly provided for in art 8 of the International Convention of 1926 on Maritime Liens and Mortgages which says: 'Claims secured by a lien follow the vessel into whatever hands it may pass.' It is this that makes the recognition of types of claims as giving rise to maritime liens of considerable commercial importance to the market for the purchase and sale of ships and in the provision of finance for their construction and acquisition. Article 9 of the 1952 convention is important. Among the maritime nations of the world at the time of the 1952 convention, there was still no uniformity of recognition of what categories of maritime claims gave rise to maritime liens. The United Kingdom policy, reflected in its refusal to ratify the 1926 Convention on Maritime Liens and Mortgages, had been to keep down to a minimum the number of maritime liens that should be recognised, so as to prevent what can be described as 'secret charges' arising and gaining priority over mortgagees and over subsequent purchasers for value of the ship. The United Kingdom stood at one extreme; under its domestic law only six categories of claims, one of which is obsolete, give rise to maritime liens. The United States stood at the other; under its domestic law maritime liens are granted for practically all classes of maritime claims, including even claims for damage to cargo and for damages for breach of charterparty.

Article 2 of the 1952 convention which confers the right of arrest for claims other than those arising under mortgages, hypothecations and other similar charges says nothing about change of ownership of the particular ship between the time the claim arose and the time of the arrest. This is dealt with by art 9 which provides, in the English language version:

> '9. *Nothing in this Convention shall be construed* as creating a right of action which,

> apart from the provisions of this Convention, would not arise under the law applied by the Court which had seisin of the case *nor as creating any maritime liens which do not exist under such law* or under the Convention on Maritime Liens and Mortgages, if the latter is applicable.' (Emphasis mine.)

In the French language version, 'any maritime liens' appears as 'aucun droit de suite', which may be thought to be a clearer expression in the context of arts 2 and 9.

Article 9 of the convention in their Lordships' view points strongly to wide international recognition of the characterisation of 'maritime liens' where this expression is used in the 1926 and 1952 conventions, as procedural or remedial only and governed by the lex fori of the country whose courts have seisin of the case.

The English and Singapore statutes of which the subject matter, be it noted, is the 'jurisdiction' of the court, comply with the requirements of arts 2 and 9 of the 1952 convention by the provisions appearing in s 4(2), (3) and (4) of the Singapore statute. In general sub-ss (2) and (4) confine the jurisdiction of the court to entertain actions in rem, and consequently the right of arrest, to ships belonging to the person who was owner of the ship in respect of which the claim arises at the date when that claim arose; but sub-s (3) extends the jurisdiction of the court to entertain actions in rem against the particular ship in respect of which there is a 'maritime lien or other charge' on it for the amount claimed, regardless of who is currently that ship's owner. 'Maritime lien' as used in s 4(3) should thus be understood in the same sense as the same expression in art 9 of the 1952 convention. If so understood this, in their Lordships' view, lends support to the proper characterisation of its legal nature under Singapore law as procedural or remedial, and thus governed solely by the lex fori.

Their Lordships are accordingly of opinion that in principle, in accordance with long-established English authorities and consistently with international comity as evidenced by the wide acceptance of the 1952 International Convention on the Arrest of Sea-going Ships, the question whether or not in the instant case the necessaries men are entitled to priority over the mortgagees in the proceeds of sale of the Halcyon Isle depends on whether or not if the repairs to the ship had been done in Singapore the repairer would have been entitled under the law of Singapore to a maritime lien on the Halcyon Isle for the price of them. The answer to that question is that they are not. The mortgagees are entitled to priority.

In the instant case, as in the two Canadian cases of *Walter W Hodder Co Inc v The Strandhill* and *The Ioannis Daskalelis*, the claim of the necessaries men is for the price of repairs to the ship. Such a claim, wherever the repairs were done, whether in Singapore or abroad, may well invite sympathy since the repairs may have added to the value of the ship and thus to the value of the security to which the mortgagees can have resort. As a matter of policy such a claim might not unreasonably be given priority over claims by holders of prior mortgages the value of whose security had thereby been enhanced. If this is to be done, however, it will, in their Lordships' view have to be done by the legislature. It is far too late to add, by judicial decision, an additional class of claim to those which have hitherto been recognised as giving rise to maritime liens under the law of Singapore; nor is this what the judgment of the Court of Appeal in the instant case purports to do. The argument for the necessaries men that was accepted by the Court of Appeal was not confined to claims for necessaries. It was that wherever a maritime claim of any of the kinds listed in paras (*d*) to (*q*) of s 3(1) of the High Court (Admiralty Jurisdiction) Act gives rise to a maritime lien under its own lex causae, as could be the case with claims of every kind referred to in the list, even including damages for breach of charterparty if the lex causae was United States law, the High Court of Singapore is required by Singapore law to give the claim priority over earlier and subsequent mortgagees and over all claims for the price of necessaries supplied to the ship in Singapore itself or in any other country under whose domestic law claims for necessaries do not attract a maritime lien.

For the reasons already given their Lordships consider that this argument is unsound, and the appeal must be allowed, the judgment of the Court of Appeal set aside and the

judgment of Kulasekaram J restored. The respondents must pay the costs of the appeal
a to the Court of Appeal and of this appeal.

Dissenting opinion by **LORD SALMON** and **LORD SCARMAN**. In this appeal many questions have to be considered, but only one issue arises for decision. The issue is: when a ship is sold by order of the court in a creditor's action in rem against the ship and the proceeds of sale are insufficient to pay all creditors in full does a ship repairer, who has provided his services and materials abroad and has by the lex loci the benefit of
b a maritime lien, enjoy priority over a mortgagee? Or is his foreign lien to be disregarded in determining his priority? The issue has arisen in Singapore but, so far as this appeal is concerned, the law of Singapore is substantially the same as the law of England. The trial judge ruled in favour of the mortgagee. The Court of Appeal reversed him, ruling in favour of the ship repairer. The mortgagee now appeals to this Board. No question arises as to the jurisdiction of the court: see the High Court (Admiralty Jurisdiction) Act,
c s 3(1) (*l*) and (*m*). The one question is the effect within the jurisdiction of a maritime lien conferred by the lex loci contractus.

In *The Tolten* [1946] 2 All ER 372 at 376, [1946] P 135 at 144 Scott LJ described the maritime lien as 'one of the first principles of the law of the sea, and very far reaching in its effects'. But, if the appellants are right, a maritime lien is in the modern law no more than a procedural remedy. So far from being far reaching, its validity and effect will be
d subject to the domestic law of the forum in which it is sought to be enforced.

If this be the law, we have travelled a great distance from the concept of a universal law of the sea. We have returned to the legal climate which in England prior to 1840 nourished the common law courts by excluding the Admiralty jurisdiction from 'the body of the County', ie the internal waters, ports and dockyards of the country. In the climate of a dominating domestic law the concepts and principles of the law of the sea
e wilt and die.

The Court of Appeal in Singapore, allying itself with the Supreme Court of Canada and accepting the classic description of a maritime lien to be found in the English cases (notably *Harmer v Bell, The Bold Buccleugh* (1852) 7 Moo PC 267, [1843–60] All ER Rep 125 refused to treat a maritime lien as a mere procedural remedy. Delivering the
f judgment of the court, Wee Chong Jin CJ said:

> 'Apart from authority, we are of the opinion that in principle the courts of this country ought to recognise the substantive right acquired under foreign law as a valid right and to give effect to that recognition when determining the question of priorities between the ship repairers and the mortgagees of the res.'

g We agree that the issue in this appeal should be approached on the basis of principle, and we attach great weight to the view of the republic's Court of Appeal as to what the law of Singapore ought in principle to be.

The relevant facts are few and can be shortly stated. The Halcyon Isle is a British ship. The appellants, an English company, were first mortgagees and registered as such on 8th May 1974. The respondents are American ship repairers who in March 1974 did
h repairs and supplied materials to the ship while it was in the port of New York. The ship reached Singapore waters in the summer of that year. While there, it was arrested. The ship repairers had issued a writ in rem against the ship: so also had the mortgagees. After arrest, the ship was sold by order of the court. In due course the ship repairers obtained a judgment for $237,011 and the mortgagees a judgment for $14,413,000. The proceeds of the sale amounted only to $1,380,000. If, therefore, the mortgagees win their appeal,
j they take all (subject to certain admitted preferential claims by other creditors). If the ship repairers are victorious, they will be paid in full, the mortgagees taking what remains after the ship repairers have been paid.

First, certain matters which are not in dispute. Under United States law a ship repairer has a maritime lien against the ship. According to the uncontradicted evidence of a New York 'attorney at law and Proctor in Admiralty' the rendition by the ship repairer of services and repairs to the ship 'gives rise to a valid maritime lien . . . which confers on [him] rights of the same nature and quality as are conferred upon the holder of a maritime lien under English law.' It is equally not in dispute that under the law of Singapore, as of England: (1) 'whatever relates to the remedy to be enforced, must be determined by the lex fori': see Lord Brougham in *Don v Lippmann* (1837) 5 Cl & Fin 1 at 13, 7 ER 303 at 307; (2) the priority of creditors claiming against a fund in court (including the proceeds of the judicial sale of a ship) is governed by the lex fori; (3) the claim of a mortgagee has priority over the claim of a ship repairer for repairs executed in Singapore; (4) ship repairers do not have a maritime lien on a ship for repairs executed in Singapore; (5) a claimant who has a maritime lien recognised by the law has priority over a mortgagee. These propositions are to be found stated in the Court of Appeal's judgment as being not in dispute. They narrow the issue to the question: does the law of Singapore recognise a foreign maritime lien as a substantive right of property vested in a claimant who can show that he enjoys it under the law of the place where he performed his services? The law, admittedly, gives effect to a validly established foreign mortgage, recognising that the mortgage is an essential element of the claim. Is a validly established foreign maritime lien to be treated in the same way, as part of the claim? Or is it a remedy made available by the lex fori?

The law of Singapore follows English law in restricting maritime liens arising under its domestic law to only a few cases; in modern conditions, they are for all practical purposes limited to salvage, wages (or salaries) of the crew, master's disbursements and liabilities incurred on behalf of the ship, and damage done by the ship: see *The Ripon City* [1897] P 226 at 242, [1895–9] All ER Rep 487 at 498. Whether it be put in terms of the law of the sea or of the rules of private international law, the question has to be asked and answered in this appeal: does English and Singapore law recognise a foreign maritime lien, where none would exist, had the claim arisen in England or Singapore? Whatever the answer, the result is unsatisfactory. If in the affirmative, maritime states may be tempted to pass 'chauvinistic' laws conferring liens on a plurality of claims so that the claimants may obtain abroad a preference denied to domestic claimants; if in the negative, claimants who have given the ship credit in reliance on their lien may find themselves sorely deceived. If the law of the sea were a truly universal code, those dangers would disappear. Unfortunately the maritime nations, though they have tried, have failed to secure uniformity in their rules regarding maritime liens: see the fate of the two conventions of 1926 and 1967 (British Shipping Laws, vol 8 (2nd Edn, 1973), pp 1392, 1397) each entitled (optimistically) an International Convention for the Unification of Certain Rules of Law relating to Maritime Liens and Mortgages. Though it signed each of them, the United Kingdom has not ratified either of them; Singapore (fully independent since 1965) has signed neither of them. In such confusion policy is an uncertain guide to the law. Principle offers a better prospect for the future.

Against this background the submissions of the parties have to be considered. The basic submission of the appellants is that in determining priorities the lex fori looks to the nature of the claim, and has no regard to the existence, or absence, of a maritime lien. The nature of the claim determines the priority of the judgment debt founded on it. The claim of the ship repairer is that of a necessaries man and, by the lex fori, ranks after the claim of a mortgagee. The reference in the books to the ranking of maritime liens before mortgage debts means no more than that the claims which under the domestic law have the benefit of a maritime lien, notably salvage, wages and for damage done by the ship, enjoy their priority not because they have the 'privilege' of a maritime lien but because of the nature of the claims themselves.

The respondents submit that a maritime lien is a substantive property right given by the law as a security for the claim and attaching to the claim as soon as the cause of action arises, though it does not take effect until legal proceedings are brought against the ship. They submit that it is as absurd, in characterising a claim to which the law attaches the security of a maritime lien, to ignore the existence of the lien as it would be to characterise a mortgagee's claim as merely one for the repayment of money lent. In each

the security is part of the nature of the claim. They further submit that both principle
a and the weight of authority (which it is conceded is not all one way) support the view, for
which they contend, that English law has regard to the maritime lien in determining the
nature of the claim. If, therefore, the court finds that the claim has under its lex loci a
valid maritime lien, the lex fori will give the claim the priority over a mortgagee which
it accords to a claim having the benefit of an English lien.

In *Harmer v Bell, The Bold Buccleugh* (1852) 7 Moo PCC 267, [1843–60] All ER Rep 125
b Jervis CJ looked at the maritime law to help him towards a decision that English law
recognised damage done by a ship in a collision as creating a maritime lien: and this at
a time when Parliament had already intervened to put Admiralty jurisdiction on a
statutory basis by the Admiralty Court Act 1840. After contrasting a maritime lien with
the possessory lien of the common law, he said that in maritime law the word (ie, lien)
is used 'to express, as if by analogy, the nature of claims which neither presuppose nor
c originate in possession'. He continued (7 Moo PCC 267 at 284, [1843–60] All ER Rep
125 at 128):

> 'This was well understood in the Civil Law, by which there might be a pledge
> with possession, and a hypothecation without possession, and by which in either
> case the right travelled with the thing into whosesoever possession it came. Having
> its origin in this rule of the Civil Law, a maritime lien is well defined by Lord
> d Tenterden, to mean a claim or privilege upon a thing to be carried into effect by
> legal process; and Mr. Justice Story (*The Brig Nestor* (1831) 1 Sumner 73 at 78)
> explains that process to be a proceeding *in rem*, and adds, that wherever a lien or
> claim is given upon the thing, then the Admiralty enforces it by a proceeding *in rem*,
> and indeed is the only Court competent to enforce it.'

e In this passage he clearly identifies the origin of the concept in the maritime law (itself
derived from the Roman and the civil law), compares it with a civil law hypothèque, and
treats it as going to the nature of the claim. A little later, he describes it as a claim or
privilege which 'travels with the thing, into whosesoever possession it may come' and
adds 'when carried into effect by . . . a proceeding in rem, relates back to the period when
it first attached' (7 Moo PCC 267 at 284–285, [1843–60] All ER Rep 125 at 128).

f The subsequent case law has, save in one respect, adopted and developed Jervis CJ's
description of the nature and incidents of the maritime lien. Jervis CJ declared, 'that in
all cases where a proceeding *in rem* is the proper course, there a maritime lien exists' (7
Moo PCC 267 at 284, [1843–60] All ER Rep 125 at 128); but the Admiralty jurisdiction
of the English court has developed otherwise, for an action in rem is available in respect
of claims to which no maritime lien attaches. The history of this development is referred
g to by Scott LJ in *The Tolten* [1946] 2 All ER 372 at 376, [1946] P 135 at 144–145; but he
cites with approval the conclusion of Gorell Barnes J in *The Ripon City* [1897] P 226 at
242, [1895–9] All ER Rep 487 at 498:

> 'It [ie a maritime lien] is a right acquired by one over a thing belonging to
> another—a *jus in re aliena*. It is, so to speak, a subtraction from the absolute property
> of the owner in the thing.'

h

The classic cases, from which these quotations have been taken, do not touch the
question that arises in this appeal. The repairs were carried out by the respondents in the
USA under a contract with the then owners of the ship; this contract was governed by the
lex loci contractus, as both parties to the contract must have known. This law indubitably
conferred a maritime lien on the respondents in respect of their repairs to this ship:
j otherwise the respondents would never have allowed the ship to leave their yard without
payment. It is obvious also that these repairs must have added to the value of the ship
and therefore to the value of the security of the appellant mortgagees.

The law relating to the repair of ships in England under contracts governed by English
law differs, however, from that in the USA. The repairers of a ship in England do not
acquire any maritime lien over a ship which they have repaired; and accordingly they

rarely allow the ship to leave their yard until they are paid, or have arranged other security for the repairs. a

In England, the lex fori decides the priority of the rights which exist against a ship, eg the rights conferred by a maritime lien taking precedence over the rights of a mortgagee. The question is, does English law, in circumstances such as these, recognise the maritime lien created by the law of the USA, ie the lex loci contractus, where no such lien exists by its own internal law? In our view the balance of authorities, the comity of nations, private international law and natural justice all answer this question in the b affirmative. If this be correct then English law (the lex fori) gives the maritime lien created by the lex loci contractus precedence over the appellants' mortgage.

If it were otherwise, injustice would prevail. The respondents would be deprived of their maritime lien, valid as it appeared to be throughout the world, and without which they would obviously never have allowed the ship to sail away without paying a dollar for the important repairs on which the respondents had spent a great deal of time and c money and from which the appellants obtained substantial advantages.

It is suggested in the majority judgment that the respondents were well aware that the lex loci contractus, conferring on them their maritime lien, was likely to be disregarded by overseas lex fori in its determination of priorities. We entirely disagree. The importance which the respondents attached to their maritime lien is clearly shown by the ship repair contract which included the term: 'Nothing herein shall be deemed to d constitute a waiver of our maritime lien.' Moreover, in many countries the lex loci gives priority to maritime liens over mortgages.

In our opinion, the respondents clearly relied on the fact that overseas the lex loci and the maritime lien which it created would both be respected, and the lien would be given the priority which it rightly received from the Court of Appeal in Singapore according to the law of Singapore and of England. e

Finally, on this aspect of the matter, it must be remembered that the nations have failed to introduce a uniform code governing maritime liens. The two international conventions relating to maritime liens, on which the majority places great weight, cannot affect, in our view, the result of this appeal. Neither of them has been signed by Singapore; and neither of them ratified by the United Kingdom.

It is submitted, however, by the appellants that the weight of authority supports their f case. We do not agree: we think that the contrary is true.

In *The Milford* (1858) Sw 362, 166 ER 1167 the question was whether the statute gave a foreign master a remedy against the freight for his wages. Dr Lushington doubted whether he was called on to give any opinion on the foreign law (see Sw 362 at 365, 166 ER 1167 at 1170), and, in the result, gave none, holding that s 191 of the Merchant Shipping Act 1854 gave the master the same right and remedies as seamen have (Sw 362 g at 367, 166 ER 1167 at 1170). The statute gave a remedy; and he applied it. It was not, therefore, necessary to go into the lex loci contractus. The decision is no authority for the proposition that an English court will never have regard to the lex loci contractus in order to determine the nature of the claim for the purpose of determining its priority, or that, in determining its nature, it will disregard the existence of a validly created foreign maritime lien. h

The Tagus [1903] P 44 also turned on the language of the same statutory provision, by now s 167 Merchant Shipping Act 1894. The law of Argentina, the lex loci contractus, gave a privilege on the ship and freight only for wages due for the last voyage. The British statute was not so limited. It was 'perfectly general' in its terms ([1903] P 44 at 53). The question is simply one of remedy, and was recognised as such by Scrutton LJ in *The Colorado* [1923] P 102 at 108, [1923] All ER Rep 531 at 534. *The Tagus* does not j touch on the question any more than does *The Milford*. Both turn on the question of remedy. Nobody doubted in either case that the master had a claim. But in neither case did the court have to consider whether or not he had under the lex loci a maritime lien (in *The Tagus* he plainly had none other than for his last voyage): for he had a remedy under the statute.

Whatever be the true analysis of these two cases, the English law must be seen as
a having been settled in favour of paying regard, in appropriate cases, to the lex loci contractus, if *The Colorado* was correctly decided. It was a decision of the Court of Appeal (Bankes, Scrutton and Atkin LJJ). The court had before it a motion to determine priorities. The competing claimants were Cardiff ship repairers and the holder of a French hypothèque. It was established that the French courts would give a necessaries man priority over a hypothécaire. English courts would, of course, do the reverse; for
b English law postpones a necessaries man to persons who have what is equivalent to a maritime lien. The Court of Appeal applied the priorities of its lex fori, but looked to the French law to determine the nature of the claim based on a hypothèque. Scrutton LJ, described the approach of the courts to the problem in these words ([1923] P 102 at 109, [1923] All ER Rep 531 at 535):

> 'Now the English Court has a claim from an English necessaries man who has no
> c possessory lien or maritime lien, but merely in England a right to arrest the ship in rem to satisfy his claim against the owner of the ship. It has also a claim by a person who has a hypothèque, and it may legitimately consult the foreign law as to what a hypothèque is. It is proved to be, not a right of property in the ship, but a right to arrest the ship in the hands of subsequent owners to satisfy a claim against a previous owner. But such a right is the same as a maritime lien as described by
> d Mellish L.J. in *The Two Ellens* ((1872) LR 4 PC 161, 17 ER 361), by Gorell Barnes J. in *The Ripon City* ([1897] P 226 at 241, [1895–9] All ER Rep 487 at 497), and by this Court in *The Tervaete* ([1922] P 259 at 264, [1922] All ER Rep 387 at 389). And the English Courts administering their own law would give a claim secured by a maritime lien priority over the claim of a necessaries man, who cannot arrest the ship against a subsequent owner. The fallacy of the appellants' argument appears
> e to be that because the French Courts would give a French necessaries man, or a necessaries man suing in the Courts of France, priority over the claimant under a hypothèque, therefore an English Court should give an English necessaries man similar priority. The answer is that the appellants are not asking for French remedies, but English remedies; and the English law postpones them to persons who have what is equivalent to a maritime lien.'

f

Bankes and Atkin LJJ ([1923] P 102 at 107 and 111–12, [1923] All ER Rep 531 at 534 and 535–536) also looked to the French law to establish the nature of the claim. Bankes LJ described it as having 'attributes which entitled it to rank on a question of priorities in the same class as a maritime lien'; and Atkin LJ said it was 'a right closely resembling a maritime lien'. The case is a neat illustration of the application of two principles of the
g law. The court looks to the lex loci to determine the nature of the claim. Having established its nature, the court applies the priorities of its own law, the lex fori. The effect of the decision is succinctly summarised in Cheshire's Private International Law (9th Edn, 1974, p 697): 'French law determined the substance of A's right, English law determined whether a right of that nature ranked before or after an opposing claim.'

Two more recent cases, however, contain obiter dicta which in our opinion are
h inconsistent with the decision in *The Colorado*. In *The Zigurds* [1932] P 113 Langton J had to consider a submission based on *The Colorado*. It was submitted that a German necessaries man had under German law rights equivalent to those of a maritime lien and should, accordingly, enjoy the priority given by English law to a maritime lienor's claim. The judge negatived the submission as to the effect of German law: but, discussing *The Colorado*, he indicated his opinion that English law would not allow its priorities to
j be determined by the existence of a foreign maritime lien where none would be given by English law. However, he concluded ([1932] P 113 at 125) that it was 'idle' to consider debatable questions as to maritime liens in other cases since he had accepted expert evidence that German law gave no analogous rights in the case he had to decide.

Hewson J adopted a similar approach in *The Acrux* [1965] 2 All ER 323, [1965] P 391. Again the point did not arise for decision, the question in the case being whether social insurance contributions required by Italian law to be paid by shipowners in respect of the crews of Italian ships were to be treated as part of the crews' wages for the purpose of determining whether English courts had jurisdiction to entertain a claim for their recovery under s 1(1)(*o*) of the Administration of Justice Act 1956. The question was as to the meaning of 'wages' in the subsection. Nevertheless the judge went on to consider whether Italian law conferred a maritime lien on the claim. He found that it did, but expressed the opinion that it was not one which would be recognised by the English courts ([1965] 2 All ER 323 at 331, [1965] P 391 at 402). He added ([1965] 2 All ER 323 at 331, [1965] P 391 at 403): 'The categories of maritime lien as recognised by this court cannot, in my view, be extended except by the legislature.'

If this expression of opinion be correct, it constitutes a denial of the approach adopted by the Court of Appeal in *The Colorado*. It would deny the courts the opportunity, which was taken in *The Colorado*, to have resort to the rules of private international law. And if it be urged that a better result would be achieved by a new international convention to be accepted by the maritime nations of the world, we would reply that experience suggests that such a convention may be a long time coming. Meanwhile the aid of private international law, slender and inadequate though it is, should not, in our opinion, be rejected.

The difference of approach visible in the English case law is reflected elsewhere. Since *The Colorado* was decided, there have been two notable decisions overseas, which have taken the line, indicated by Langton J in *The Zigurds* and by Hewson J in *The Acrux*, that the existence of a foreign maritime lien is not to be considered in determining the nature of the claim, for which priority is sought. They are *Coal Export Corpn v Notias* [1962] EA 220 (East African Court of Appeal in Aden) and *The Christine Isle* [1974] AMC 331 (Bermuda). But a series of Canadian cases had adopted *The Colorado* approach: see particularly *The Strandhill v Walter W Hodder Co Inc* [1926] SCR 680, and *The Ioannis Daskalelis* [1974] 1 Lloyd's Rep 174. We agree with the Court of Appeal in thinking that the Canadian Supreme Court's reasoning in *The Ioannis Daskalelis* is very persuasive, and would draw attention, as Wee Chong Jin CJ did, to a comment of Ritchie J ([1974] 1 Lloyd's Rep 174 at 178), where he treated *The Colorado* as authority for the contention—

> 'that where a right in the nature of a maritime lien exists under a foreign law which is the proper law of the contract, the English Courts will recognize it and will accord it the priority which a right *of that nature* would be given under English procedure.' (Ritchie J's emphasis.)

In our opinion the English Court of Appeal in *The Colorado* adopted the approach which is correct in principle. A maritime lien is a right of property given by way of security for a maritime claim. If the Admiralty Court has, as in the present case, jurisdiction to entertain the claim, it will not disregard the lien. A maritime lien validly conferred by the lex loci is as much part of the claim as is a mortgage similarly valid by the lex loci. Each is a limited right of property securing the claim. The lien travels with the claim, as does the mortgage: and the claim travels with the ship. It would be a denial of history and principle, in the present chaos of the law of the sea governing the recognition and priority of maritime liens and mortgages, to refuse the aid of private international law.

For these reasons, we think that the Court of Appeal reached the correct conclusion and would dismiss the appeal.

Appeal allowed.

Solicitors: *Linklaters & Paines* (for the appellants); *Thomas Cooper & Stibbard* (for the respondents).

Mary Rose Plummer Barrister.

CSI International Co Ltd v Archway Personnel (Middle East) Ltd

COURT OF APPEAL, CIVIL DIVISION
ROSKILL, EVELEIGH LJJ AND WALTON J
29th FEBRUARY 1980

Pleading – Counterclaim – When counterclaim can be made – Plaintiff obtaining summary judgment against defendant and defendant satisfying judgment – Counterclaim raised but not pleaded prior to summary judgment – Whether defendant entitled to serve counterclaim after judgment obtained and satisfied – Whether power to 'make' counterclaim entitling defendant to plead counterclaim after final judgment obtained – Supreme Court of Judicature (Consolidation) *Act 1925, s 39(1) – RSC Ord 15, r 2.*

The plaintiffs, a foreign company, brought an action against the defendants, an English company, on a dishonoured cheque. There was no defence to the action and the plaintiffs applied by summons for summary judgment under RSC Ord 14. On the hearing of the summons the defendants filed an affidavit in which they asserted a counterclaim against the plaintiffs but they made no request for directions in regard to a counterclaim and did not serve a formal pleading of a counterclaim. On 28th November 1978 the master entered final judgment for the plaintiff on the Ord 14 summons and refused a stay of execution. On 10th April 1979 the defendants fully satisfied the judgment by a bankers' draft sent under cover of a letter with which they enclosed, by way of service, a counterclaim. Subsequently, purporting to comply with RSC Ord 15, r 3(3), the defendants attached the counterclaim to a defence and served both on the plaintiffs. The plaintiffs contended that there was no power to deliver a counterclaim once there was a judgment given under Ord 14 without a stay of execution and thereafter satisfied, and therefore did not serve a defence to the counterclaim. The defendants signed judgment against the plaintiffs in default of defence. On 18th July 1979 the master set aside the default judgment on the ground that service of the counterclaim after the plaintiffs had obtained the summary judgment was irregular. The defendants appealed to the judge in chambers who allowed the appeal to the extent of holding that the counterclaim had been properly served and that the plaintiffs were required to serve a defence to it. The plaintiffs appealed. The defendants contended that the right to 'make' a counterclaim given by RSC Ord 15, r 2[a] entitled them to serve the counterclaim notwithstanding that final judgment had been obtained under Ord 14 and satisfied. Because the plaintiffs were out of the jurisdiction the defendants would have found it difficult to bring a separate action against them.

Held – RSC Ord 15, r 2 only operated within the provisions of s 39(1)[b] of the Supreme Court of Judicature (Consolidation) Act 1925, and, accordingly, for a counterclaim to be validly made within Ord 15, r 2, there had to be still extant a cause or matter in which the defendant could properly claim a counterclaim by his pleading, within s 39(1)(*a*). Although the defendants' counterclaim might have been raised before the summary judgment had been obtained and satisfied, the counterclaim had not been properly made because (i) there had been no summons for directions relating to the counterclaim, (ii) it had not been properly pleaded before the judgment had been obtained and satisfied, and (iii) after the judgment had been obtained and satisfied there had been no action extant in which the counterclaim could properly have been pleaded. Accordingly, the master's order would be restored and the appeal allowed (see p 220 *d* to *g* and *j* to p 221 *b*, post).

a Rule 2, so far as material, is set out at p 219 *c*, post
b Section 39(1), so far as material, is set out at p 218 *h*, post

Per Roskill LJ. There is nothing to stop a defendant making a counterclaim where
there is a judgment against him which has not been stayed, even though he has not *a*
served a defence, provided that the counterclaim falls within the general purview of s 39
of the 1925 Act and the relevant Rules of the Supreme Court (see p 219 *j* to p 220 *a*, post).

Notes

For counterclaim generally and for service of a counterclaim, see 34 Halsbury's Laws (3rd
Edn) 410, 416, paras 719, 737, and for cases on the subject, see 50 Digest (Repl) 184, 185, *b*
1560, 1566.

For the Supreme Court of Judicature (Consolidation) Act 1925, s 39, see 25 Halsbury's
Statutes (3rd Edn) 711.

Appeal

The plaintiffs, CSI International Co Ltd, appealed pursuant to leave against the order of *c*
Sir Douglas Frank QC sitting as a deputy judge of the High Court on 18th January 1980
allowing an appeal by the defendants, Archway Personnel (Middle East) Ltd, from an
order of Master Lubbock made on 18th July 1979 that the judgment entered by the
defendants against the plaintiffs in default of a defence to the defendants' purported
counterclaim be set aside for irregularity on the ground that final judgment in the action
between the plaintiffs and the defendants had been granted to the plaintiffs under RSC *d*
Ord 14 on 29th November 1978. The facts are set out in the judgment of Roskill LJ.

L J Libbert for the plaintiffs.
Isaac Jacob for the defendants.

ROSKILL LJ. This is an appeal from an order of Sir Douglas Frank QC, sitting as a *e*
deputy judge of the High Court in chambers on 18th January 1980. The deputy judge
gave judgment in open court at the request of the parties because he said that the
question raised was important, namely whether a counterclaim could be served after a
final judgment had been obtained by a plaintiff and indeed satisfied.

The facts are a little unusual and raise a curious point under the Rules of the Supreme
Court. The plaintiffs are a company incorporated in Thailand. The defendants are an *f*
English limited company, which seem to be the alter ego of a gentleman called Mr
Paschali. Those two companies apparently worked together to provide manpower for
contracting work in the Middle East and, in particular, Saudi Arabia, and the defendants
made arrangements with another company, called Avco Dallah Ltd, which we are told
was a consortium of a United States company and a Saudi Arabian company under which
the defendants supplied such manpower for Avco. *g*

An agreement was made between the plaintiffs and the defendants under which the
plaintiffs would recruit persons in Thailand for working in the Middle East, and it is
common ground that that agreement between the plaintiffs and the defendants was
made in Thailand.

Various disputes, with the details of which we are not concerned, thereafter arose. On
6th June 1978 a settlement of those disputes was made. The terms do not matter, save *h*
that the defendants would pay the plaintiffs sums totalling £43,816 by three postdated
cheques indorsed personally by three named persons. The first cheque was for £15,000
payable on 6th July, the second was for a like sum payable on 6th August, and the third,
the balance of the sum I have already mentioned, namely £13,816, was payable on 6th
September 1978.

The first postdated cheque was presented on due date and was dishonoured on *j*
presentation. The plaintiffs thereupon issued a writ. At the same time there was
another writ concerning a dispute between the defendants and Avco, with which we are
not concerned.

On the modern authorities, to an action brought in these circumstances on a
dishonoured cheque there was no defence. However the defendants put in an affidavit

by Mr Paschali. That affidavit, with all respect to the draftsman (no doubt he did his best) obviously disclosed no defence. But it did say that there was an action pending by the defendants against Avco and for that reason the defendant sought a stay of execution on any RSC Ord 14 judgment which the plaintiffs were likely to get.

Paragraph 11 of the affidavit reads thus:

> '... it is true that the cheque in the sum of £15,000 has not been paid and that the plaintiffs are entitled to Judgment for this. However I would ask that the Court make an order that this Judgment not be enforced until after the hearing of a Counterclaim to be brought by [the defendants] against the Plaintiffs. The nature of the counterclaim is that the Plaintiffs were agents for [the defendants]. From January 1978 whilst the agency agreement was still in existence they dealt with Avco Dallah directly and in breach of their duty of good faith. They claim commission on workers who were in fact recruited by them as our agents and "stole" our contract with Avco Dallah. It is [the defendants'] intention to bring a counterclaim claiming damages for this breach of duty of good faith. However it will take some time for all counsel's requirements as to this to be satisfied and [the defendants] cannot make [their] counterclaim until certain further research has taken place ...'

That affidavit, if I may be forgiven the colloquialism, did not cut much ice with Master Lubbock. He entered judgment for the plaintiffs for £15,000 and interest, making a total of £15,476·71. He refused a stay of execution. There was, on the occasion of that summons for judgment, no request whatever made for directions in connection with a counterclaim which had been, I avoid the use of the word 'raised', but I will say 'adumbrated' in that paragraph in that affidavit.

That judgment was obtained on 28th November 1978. The plaintiffs were not immediately paid. They took various steps to try and enforce that judgment. On 10th April 1979, the defendants' solicitors wrote a letter to the plaintiffs' solicitors saying that they were glad to tell the plaintiffs solicitors that their clients had put them in funds to discharge the sums due, totalling £16,016·44 which was the amount of the judgment and interest and costs. They sent, under cover of that letter of 10th April, a bankers', draft for that sum, and they added (and one must note that this was some four months after the date of the judgment) that they enclosed a counterclaim by way of service. The letter goes on:

> 'Our client is very concerned that your clients are a Thai company and if our client is successful and we believe they will be there will be no assets in this country against which the counterclaim and costs could be enforced.'

That counterclaim, which has at least the merit of brevity, was settled by counsel for the defendants. That document was not welcomed by the plaintiffs' solicitors. They wrote back on 12th April saying:

> 'The action against [the defendants] is closed, and your Clients have no right to serve a Counterclaim within the context of those proceedings. We accordingly return it herewith ...'.

They suggested that fresh proceedings be brought against the plaintiffs in Thailand.

The defendants' solicitors replied on 18th April:

> 'Prior to serving the Counterclaim upon you we discussed the matter with Counsel who stated we were quite entitled to serve the Counterclaim in this action despite the fact of the judgment. The Counterclaim is therefore returned and we should be obliged to know whether you intend to serve a Defence to Counterlcaim otherwise we will proceed with the Summons for Directions.'

The counterclaim was again sent back, on 24th April, by the plaintiffs' solicitors. On

26th April, the defendants' solicitors, in a succinct letter wrote: 'Order 15, rule 3, sub-
paragraph 3. Counterclaim returned. Yours faithfully . . .' a

On 27th April, the plaintiffs' solicitors acknowledged that letter. Once again they sent
the unhappy counterclaim back and drew attention to one of the rules. Then on 1st May
the defendants' came back yet again, agreeing that they had served a counterclaim but
not a document which was also a defence to which the counterclaim was attached. So the
defendants, at that point, had a second bite at the cherry and wrote: '. . . and we therefore
serve a Defence and Counterclaim and agree that the Counterclaim we have previously b
served was of no effect whatsoever.'

Enclosed with that letter was counsel's second attempt at a pleading; it was in exactly
the same language as before save that it was headed: 'Defence and Counterclaim.' The
'defence' says: 'The Defendant admits the claim and will set off so much of the
Counterclaim as will totally or partially extinguish the Plaintiffs' claim.' One admires
counsel's ingenuity, if he will allow me to say so, since, at that point, judgment had c
already been signed against his clients and satisfied so there was no liability left to
admit. But it was said that the counterclaim was bad unless it was attached to a defence
and so the battle concerning the counterclaim continued.

Ultimately, the defendants signed judgment in default against the plaintiffs on that
counterclaim. The matter then went back to Master Lubbock, who set aside the default
judgment on the ground of irregularity. d

There was an appeal to Sir Douglas Frank QC, sitting as a deputy judge of the High
Court in chambers, and he allowed the appeal to a limited extent. He purported to say
he was setting aside the judgment 'on the merits'. We are told that that phrase was used
by agreement between counsel, and not by the court. With respect it is not a very happy
phrase. But what I think it was intended to convey was that this counterclaim had been
properly served and therefore the plaintiffs should be required to serve a defence to e
counterclaim, for which the deputy judge gave leave.

The deputy judge, as I have said, delivered his judgment in open court. The plaintiffs
appeal saying that the deputy judge's order was wrong and that the master's order was
right. The plaintiffs say that they should not have been required to serve a defence to
that counterclaim.

It will have been observed from the chronology which I have outlined that the so- f
called defence and counterclaim was not served until after the judgment, which the
plaintiffs had obtained against the defendants, had been fully satisfied as to principal,
interest and costs. Nonetheless it is said that the defendants were at that time entitled to
serve that defence and counterclaim.

In order to consider the merits of the rival submissions, it is necessary to start with the
provisions of the Supreme Court of Judicature (Consolidation) Act 1925. The relevant g
sections start at s 39. The most relevant section, for present purposes, on which the
relevant Rules of the Supreme Court are based is s 39(1). This provides:

> 'The court or judge shall have power to grant to any defendant in respect of any
> equitable estate or right or other matter or equity, and also in respect of any legal
> estate, right or title claimed or asserted by him—(*a*) all such relief against any h
> plaintiff or petitioner as the defendant has properly claimed by his pleading, and as
> the court or judge might have granted in any suit instituted for that purpose by that
> defendant against the same plaintiff or petitioner; and (*b*) all such relief relating to
> or connected with the original subject of the cause or matter, claimed in like
> manner against any other person . . .'

I need not read the rest of that. j

It is necessary against the background of that statutory provision, which is the
foundation for the relevant rules, to look for a moment at certain Rules of the Supreme
Court. I need not read RSC Ord 14, rr 1 and 2, but RSC Ord 14, r 3 reads:

> '(1) Unless on the hearing of an application under Rule 1 either the Court

> dismisses the application or the defendant satisfies the Court with respect to the
> a claim, or the part of a claim, to which the application relates that there is an issue or question in dispute which ought to be tried or that there ought for some other reason to be a trial of that claim or part, the Court may give such judgment for the plaintiff against that defendant on that claim or part as may be just having regard to the nature of the remedy or relief claimed.
>
> '(2) The Court may by order and subject to such conditions, if any, as may be just,
> b stay execution of any judgment given against a defendant under this rule until after the trial of any counterclaim made or raised by the defendant in the action.'

I draw attention to that phrase 'made or raised' in contrast to the language of RSC Ord 15, to which I now turn.

RSC Ord 15, r 2, deals with causes of actions and counterclaims against a plaintiff, and
c provides thus:

> '(1) Subject to rule 5(2) a defendant in any action who alleges that he has any claim or is entitled to any relief or remedy against a plaintiff in the action in respect of any matter (whenever and however arising) may, instead of bringing a separate action, make [notice the word is 'make' and not 'make or raise'] a counterclaim in respect of that matter; and where he does so he must add the counterclaim to his
> d defence . . .'

I turn to RSC Ord 18, r 3:

> '(1) A plaintiff on whom a defendant serves a defence must serve a reply on that defendant if it is needed for compliance with Rule 8, and if no reply is served, Rule 14(1) will apply.
>
> e '(2) A plaintiff on whom a defendant serves a counterclaim must, if he intends to defend it, serve on that defendant a defence to counterclaim . . .'

Various points were argued before the deputy judge and have been repeated by counsel for the plaintiffs in this court. Counsel put in the forefront of his argument, as he did before the judge, that it was not possible to have a counterclaim in any
f circumstances unless there was a defence to which that counterclaim could be attached. The deputy judge dealt with that point in his judgment. After setting out the rules and orders to which I have referred, he said:

> 'In my judgment these absurdities and anomalies are not necessary if one gives to the rule the meaning that the counterclaim must be added to the defence where a defence has been delivered and to reject a meaning that a counterclaim must be
> g pursued by a separate action where no defence has been delivered. It seems to me, although it is not necessary to my decision, that the reason for the requirement is to minimise the number of pleadings and that is linked with RSC Ord 18, r 3(3) where a plaintiff is required to serve a defence and reply to a counterclaim in the same document.'

h On that point I find myself, with respect, in complete agreement with the deputy judge, and I have nothing more to say on it.

Then counsel for the plaintiffs said there was no power to deliver a counterclaim once there was a judgment given under RSC Ord 14 and there was no stay of execution on that judgment. Of course, in many cases before the master and the judge in chambers, this would not be a live point, as counsel accepted, for the reason that no useful purpose
j would be served by a plaintiff seeking to take this point against a defendant. But here, plainly, the defendants are in difficulties under RSC Ord 11 in serving the plaintiffs in a separate action, and therefore this point (although it would not arise in the ordinary way) is of particular importance. I am bound to say that, for the reasons the deputy judge gave, I do not think there is anything to stop a defendant serving a counterclaim (and I use the word 'serve' as a neutral word but perhaps I should have said 'making' a

counterclaim) where there is a judgment against him which has not been stayed, provided that the counterclaim falls within the general purview of s 39 of the 1925 Act and other relevant rules to which I have referred.

But what happened here was that nothing was done about the counterclaim on the Ord 14 summons before the master, even if one assumes that para 11 which I have already read from the affidavit can be said to 'raise' a counterclaim for the purposes of the relevant part of Ord 14, r 3(2). Thereafter month after month elapsed and the judgment in favour of the plaintiffs was wholly satisfied before any attempt was made to advance or serve or, to use the wording of the rule, to make a counterclaim.

Walton J asked counsel for the defendant what his submission was regarding any possible time limit on 'making' a counterclaim. Counsel grasped the nettle. He said there was no relevant time limit because there was a lacuna in the rules in the case where a judgment had not been stayed. He claimed that a defendant was at liberty at any time thereafter to deliver a counterclaim. Now in a case such as the present that would have most curious results. A counterclaim may be barred by the Limitation Act 1939 (see the Supreme Court Practice 1979 (vol 1, p 166, para 15/2/2)). Section 28 of the 1939 Act provides that 'a claim by way of set-off or counterclaim is deemed to be a separate action and to have been commenced on the same date as the action in which it is pleaded'.

If counsel's argument is taken to its logical conclusion, then notwithstanding that the plaintiffs had obtained full satisfaction of the judgment, the defendants can, years later, as it were, out of the blue, serve a counterclaim. I do not think that is right. It may be that certain amendments are required and could, with advantage, be made to the rules in order to make clear what the position is. But I rest my decision on this simple point: where a counterclaim, even if it has previously been raised, has not been the subject of a summons for directions, or, when required, of a formal pleading before the time when the plaintiff has received full satisfaction of the judgment which he has obtained against the defendant, I do not think there is still extant any action by the plaintiff in which the defendant could properly counterclaim against him. The action has, for all practical purposes, come to an end when satisfaction of the judgment has been obtained.

I have considerable sympathy for the defendants; it may be that if other steps had been taken at other times other results might have followed. I do not know, and I express no opinion. Suffice it to say that the master was right and, with great respect to the deputy judge, I do not think his order was right. I should perhaps say that many of the points taken in this court were not argued fully or perhaps at all before the deputy judge. It may well be that had they been so argued he would have reached the same conclusion as we have done.

I would allow the appeal to this extent: I would set aside the default judgment which the defendants obtained against the plaintiffs, and the deputy judge's order that a defence to the counterclaim should be filed. It seems to me that the counterclaim was not properly served; there was a material irregularity in its service since the defendants had no right to serve it. Therefore in the result the master's order should stand.

EVELEIGH LJ. Section 36 of the Supreme Court of Judicature (Consolidation) Act 1925 reads:

> 'Subject to the express provisions of any other Act, in every civil cause or matter commenced in the High Court, law and equity shall be administered by the High Court and the Court of Appeal, as the case may be, according to the provisions of the seven sections of this Act next following.'

One such section of course is s 39, which relates to the jurisdiction of the court in relation to a counterclaim. It seems to me that RSC Ord 15 can only operate under s 39, which itself operates under s 36; in other words, there has to be a cause or matter in which a counterclaim has been or can be properly pleaded in accordance with the words of s 39, and in the present case it has not been pleaded even though it may perhaps have been 'raised'. No directions have been given relating to a counterclaim before the

judgment was satisfied and consequently in my opinion there was no cause or matter
a extant that could cover any proceedings in relation to a counterclaim that was not yet properly pleaded.

I agree with the order proposed by Roskill LJ.

WALTON J. I agree with both the judgments which have fallen from Roskill and Eveleigh LJJ and I also agree with the order which should be made.

b

Appeal allowed: order of deputy judge set aside; master's order reinstated.

Solicitors: *Baker & McKenzie* (for the plaintiff); *Eric Cheek & Co*, South Harrow (for the defendants).

Bebe Chua Barrister.

c

Stanton (Inspector of Taxes) v Drayton Commercial Investment Co Ltd

d CHANCERY DIVISION
VINELOTT J
25th, 26th FEBRUARY, 24th MARCH 1980

Capital gains tax – Computation of chargeable gains – Cost of acquisition of asset – Consideration given for acquisition of asset – Value of consideration – Company purchasing securities under
e *conditional contract – Company allotting shares to vendor at agreed price in consideration – Whether value of consideration ascertained by reference to agreed value or to market value of shares when contract became unconditional – Finance Act 1965, Sch 6, para 4(1)(a) – Finance Act 1971, Sch 10, para 10(2).*

By an agreement dated 21st September 1972 the taxpayer company agreed to purchase
f a portfolio of investments from an insurance company at the price of £3,937,962, the price to be satisfied by the allotment of 2,461,226 ordinary shares in the taxpayer company at the issue price of 160p per share. The agreement was conditional on the passing of a resolution by the members of the taxpayer company creating the new shares, and the granting of permission to deal in and a quotation for the new shares on the Stock Exchange before 31st October 1972. The necessary resolution was passed at an
g extraordinary general meeting of the taxpayer company on 9th October and the permission to deal in and a quotation for the shares was given by the Stock Exchange on 11th October. On the same day the agreement was completed when the shares were allotted to the insurance company. The shares were first quoted on the Stock Exchange on 12th October when the middle market price was 125p per share. On the disposal by the taxpayer company during the accounting periods ending 31st December 1972 and
h 31st December 1973 of certain of the investments comprised in the portfolio, assessments to corporation tax were made on the footing that, in ascertaining the chargeable gains accruing to the taxpayer company, the consideration given for the investments by the taxpayer company allowable as a deduction under the Finance Act 1965, Sch 6, para 4(1)(*a*)[a], should be the value of the shares according to their first quotation in the Stock

j a Paragraph 4(1), so far as material, provides: 'Subject to the following provisions of this Schedule, the sums allowable as a deduction from the consideration in the computation under this Schedule of the gain accruing to a person on the disposal of an asset shall be restricted to—(*a*) the amount or value of the consideration, in money or money's worth, given by him or on his behalf wholly and exclusively for the acquisition of the asset, together with the incidental costs to him of the acquisition or, if the asset was not acquired by him, any expenditure wholly and exclusively incurred by him in providing the asset . . .'

Exchange official list on 12th October. The Special Commissioners allowed an appeal by the taxpayer company against the assessment on the ground that the value of the shares a allotted in satisfaction of the price of the investments should be ascertained by reference to the agreed issue price of the shares. The Crown appealed.

Held – The word 'value' in para 4(1)(*a*) of Sch 6 to the 1965 Act meant market value. Accordingly, although the cost entered into the books of the taxpayer company as the price of acquisition of the portfolio of investments could only have been the agreed sum b of £3,937,962, the value of the consideration given by the taxpayer company for the acquisition of the portfolio was the market value of the shares which the taxpayer company was entitled and bound to issue to the insurance company in satisfaction of that price. It followed, therefore, that in computing the chargeable gain arising on the sale of the portfolio the sum allowable as a deduction under Sch 6, para 4(1)(*a*) was the market value of the shares which the taxpayer company allotted to the insurance company on c 11th October when, pursuant to the Finance Act 1971, Sch 10, para 10(2)[b], the agreement became unconditional. The appeal would therefore be allowed (see p 230 *e* to *g* and p 231 *c d*, and *f g*, post).

Notes

For deductions in computing chargeable gains, see 5 Halsbury's Laws (4th Edn) para 147. d

For the Finance Act 1965, Sch 6, para 4, see 34 Halsbury's Statutes (3rd Edn) 931.

For the Finance Act 1971, Sch 10, para 10, see 41 ibid 1534.

With effect from 6th April 1979, Sch 6, para 4 to the 1965 Act and Sch 10, para 10 to the 1971 Act have been replaced by the Capital Gains Tax Act 1979, ss 32, 27.

Cases referred to in judgment e

Aberdeen Construction Group Ltd v Inland Revenue Comrs [1978] 1 All ER 962, [1978] AC 885, [1978] 2 WLR 648, [1978] STC 127, [1978] TR 25, HL, Digest (Cont Vol E) 304, *1452e (iii)*.

British South Africa Co v Varty (Inspector of Taxes) [1965] 2 All ER 395, [1966] AC 381. [1965] 3 WLR 47, 42 Tax Cas 406, HL, 28(1) Digest (Reissue) 28, *112*.

Brooklands Selangor Holdings Ltd v Inland Revenue Comrs [1970] 2 All ER 76, [1970] 1 WLR f 429, 48 ATC 496, [1969] TR 485, 10 Digest (Reissue) 1193, *7425*.

Craddock (Inspector of Taxes) v Zevo Finance Co Ltd [1944] 1 All ER 566, 27 Tax Cas 267, CA; *affd* [1946] 1 All ER 523n, 27 Tax Cas 267, 174 LT 385, HL, 28(1) Digest (Reissue) 124, *367*.

Crane Fruehauf Ltd v Inland Revenue Comrs [1974] 1 All ER 811, [1974] STC 110, [1973] TR 309; *affd* [1975] 1 All ER 429, [1975] STC 51, [1974] TR 389, CA, 10 Digest g (Reissue) 1194, *7429*.

Inland Revenue Comrs v Blott, Inland Revenue Comrs v Greenwood [1921] AC 171, 8 Tax Cas 101, 90 LJKB 1028, 125 LT 497, HL, 28(1) Digest (Reissue) 513, *1865*.

Lowry (Inspector of Taxes) v Consolidated African Selection Trust Ltd [1940] 2 All ER 545, [1940] AC 648, 23 Tax Cas 259, 109 LJKB 539, 164 LT 56, HL, 28(1) Digest (Reissue) 149, *461*. h

Osborne (Inspector of Taxes) v Steel Barrel Co Ltd [1942] 1 All ER 634, 24 Tax Cas 293, CA, 28(1) Digest (Reissue) 121, *357*.

Cases also cited

Battle v Inland Revenue Comrs [1980] STC 86.

Lap Shun Textiles Industrial Co Ltd v Collector of Stamp Revenue [1976] 1 All ER 833, [1976] j AC 530, PC.

Stanyforth v Inland Revenue Comrs [1930] AC 339, [1929] All ER Rep 176, HL.

---

b Paragraph 10(2), so far as material, provides: 'If the contract is conditional . . . the time at which the disposal and acquisition is made is the time when the condition is satisfied.'

Wilkins (Inspector of Taxes) v Rogerson [1961] 1 All ER 358, [1961] Ch 133, CA.
Wragg Ltd, Re [1897] 1 Ch 796, [1895–9] All ER Rep 398, CA.

Case stated

1. At a meeting of the Commissioners for the Special Purposes of the Income Tax Acts held on 3rd November 1977, Drayton Commercial Investment Co Ltd ('Drayton') appealed against the following assessments to corporation tax: accounting period to 31st December 1972, £178,011; accounting period to 31st December 1973, £440,000.

2. Shortly stated the question for the commissioners' decision was whether in ascertaining the chargeable gains accruing to Drayton on the disposal of securities which it had acquired for a price satisfied by the allotment of ordinary shares in Drayton the value of the shares so allotted was, for the purpose of para 4(1)(*a*) of Sch 6 to the Finance Act 1965, equal to the issue price of such shares (ie their par value plus the premium at which they were allotted) or the market value of these shares according to the first quotation in the Stock Exchange official list following the allotment.

3. No witnesses were called by either party.

[Paragraph 4 listed the documents admitted before the commissioners.]

5. The following facts were admitted between the parties: (a) At all times relevant to the appeal Drayton was called Union Commercial Investment Co Ltd. (b) On 21st September 1972 the agreement, which was a conditional agreement, was entered into. Eagle Star Insurance Co Ltd ('Eagle Star') agreed to sell and Drayton agreed to purchase a portfolio of securities at the price of £3,937,962 to be satisfied by the allotment by Drayton to Eagle Star of 2,461,226 ordinary shares of 25p each in Drayton 'the issue price of each such Share for the purpose of satisfying the consideration being one hundred and sixty pence (160p)'. Such ordinary shares ('the consideration shares') were to be issued credited as fully paid up and to rank pari passu in all respects with the existing ordinary shares of Drayton save in respect of any final dividend in respect of the year ending 31st December 1972. The agreement was conditional on (i) the members of Drayton passing the necessary resolution to create the consideration shares and (ii) the Stock Exchange granting permission to deal in and quotation for the consideration shares before 31st October 1972. The price of £3,937,962 was agreed on by reference to the middle market quotations of the securities in the portfolio as at 31st August 1972. (c) On 22nd September 1972 the chairman of Drayton sent a circular letter to each of the members of Drayton giving them particulars of the agreement and informing them that the consideration for the acquisition of the portfolio of investments which had been valued on the basis of middle market quotations on 31st August 1972 at £3,937,962 was to be satisfied by the issue of 2,461,226 ordinary shares of Drayton and that on the basis of the middle market quotation of Drayton's ordinary shares of 25p each at 31st August 1972 the portfolio was effectively being purchased for £3,494,941 at a discount of 11·25% on its market value. (d) On 9th October 1972 at an extraordinary general meeting of Drayton the necessary resolution to create the consideration shares was passed. (e) On 11th October 1972 the Stock Exchange granted permission to deal in and quotation for the consideration shares after allotment. (f) The agreement was completed on 11th October 1972 when (inter alia) the consideration shares were allotted by Drayton to Eagle Star. (g) The middle market quotation based on the daily official list of the ordinary shares of 25p each of Drayton was: (i) 142p on 31st August 1972; (ii) 134p on 21st September 1972; (iii) 125p on 12th October 1972, being the day on which the consideration shares were first quoted. (h) During the accounting periods under appeal Drayton disposed of some of the securities comprised in the portfolio.

6. It was common ground between the parties that the agreement was an arm's length transaction and that the question in issue between them was what was the value of the consideration that had been 'given' by Drayton for the purpose of para 4(1)(*a*) of Sch 6 to the 1965 Act.

7. It was contended on behalf of the Crown: (a) that the value of the consideration shares was equal to the middle market price obtainable for the consideration shares on

the Stock Exchange when they were first quoted on 12th October 1972 at 125p per share ie £3,076,532; (b) that the assessments under appeal should therefore be adjusted by attributing to the consideration shares for the purpose of para 4(1)(*a*) a value of £3,076,532.

8. It was contended on behalf of Drayton: (a) that the value of the consideration was £3,937,962 because that was both the consideration expressed in the agreement (based on the middle market quotations of the securities contained in the portfolio on 31st August 1972) and the amount credited as paid in respect of the consideration shares; (b) that the assessments under appeal should be adjusted accordingly.

9. The commissioners were referred to the following authorities: *Brooklands Selangor Holdings Ltd v Inland Revenue Comrs* [1970] 2 All ER 76, [1970] 1 WLR 429; *Craddock (Inspector of Taxes) v Zevo Finance Co Ltd* [1946] 1 All ER 523n, 27 Tax Cas 267, HL; *Crane Fruehauf Ltd v Inland Revenue Comrs* [1975] 1 All ER 429, CA; *Henry Head & Co Ltd v Ropner Holdings Ltd* [1951] 2 All ER 994, [1952] 1 Ch 124; *Murphy (Inspector of Taxes) v Australian Machinery & Investment Co Ltd* (1948) 30 Tax Cas 244; *Osborne (Inspector of Taxes) v Steel Barrel Co Ltd* [1942] 1 All ER 634, 24 Tax Cas 293, CA.

10. The commissioners who heard the appeal, took time to consider their decision and gave it in writing on 29th November 1977 as follows:

> 'It is common ground that the parties to the Sale Agreement of 21 September 1972 were at arm's length and that the consideration for the acquisition by [Drayton] of the portfolio of investments under the agreement (£3,937,962) was fixed by reference to the middle market prices on 31 August 1972.
>
> 'The Sale Agreement provided that the "price of £3,937,962" was to be satisfied by the issue of 2,461,226 Ordinary Shares of 25p each in [Drayton] at 160p each. It is not disputed by the Crown that there were bona fide commercial reasons for the figure of 160p being somewhat in excess of the price at which [Drayton's] shares were currently being dealt in on the Stock Exchange.
>
> 'The Sale Agreement was a conditional contract. The conditions were satisfied on 11 October 1972 and, by virtue of paragraph 10 of Schedule 10, Finance Act 1971 the time of the disposal of the portfolio to [Drayton] is to be taken as 11 October 1972.
>
> '[Drayton] says that the agreed price was £3,937,962, this was a bargain at arm's length and the consideration was duly satisfied by the issue at a premium of shares to that amount and accordingly £3,937,962 is the figure at which the shares were acquired for capital gains tax purposes. Counsel referred us to the observations in *Craddock v Zevo Finance Co Ltd* [1946] 1 All ER 523n, 27 Tax Cas 267 and *Osborne v Steel Barrel Co Ltd* [1942] 1 All ER 634 to the effect that for Schedule D, Case 1 income tax purposes the cost to the trading taxpayer of acquiring assets for shares issued at par is, in the absence of evidence to the contrary, the nominal value of the consideration shares. Lord Greene MR rejected an argument that consideration in the form of fully paid shares allotted by a company must in all cases be treated as being of the value of the shares, no more and no less (see [1944] 1 All ER 566 at 569). So too in *Brooklands Selangor Holdings Ltd v Inland Revenue Comrs* [1970] 2 All ER 76, [1970] 1 WLR 429 Pennycuick J (obiter) rejected an argument that the consideration for the purpose of section 55(1)(c) Finance Act 1927 was anything other than the consideration which was based on a professional valuation of the assets of the particular existing company and expressed in the agreement for sale.
>
> 'The Crown contends that the tax authorities are distinguishable on the ground that they involved the question of issuing shares at a discount. As to the *Brooklands Selangor* case the Crown contends that dicta in the later case of *Crane Fruehauf Ltd v Inland Revenue Comrs* [1974] 1 All ER 811; *affd* [1975] 1 All ER 429 equating the value of share consideration to the value of assets acquired for that consideration are to be preferred.
>
> 'Gains are computed in accordance with section 22 Finance Act 1965, subsection (9) of which provides that they shall be computed in accordance with Part I of

Schedule 6 to that Act. Paragraph 4(1)(*a*) of Schedule 6 provides that the gain shall be "restricted to the amount or value of the consideration, in money or money's worth, given by him . . . wholly and exclusively for the acquisition of the asset . . ." Consequently one must find the consideration in money's worth "given" by [Drayton]. Is this the consideration received by the vendor or the consideration moving from the purchaser? Clearly, we think, the latter for that is what is "given" in return for the asset acquired.

'Counsel for [Drayton] meets this approach by pointing to the term of the sale agreement which says that the price is £3,937,962 and, as that price was fully satisfied by the issue of 2,461,226 shares in [Drayton] at 160p each, that is the money's worth "given" to the vendor. The Crown on the other hand contends that this approach is not correct. True, says the Crown, the price was £3,937,962 but the agreement goes on to say that it shall be satisfied by the issue of 2,461,226 shares at 160p. Paragraph 4 directs that the value, not the price, of the consideration given is to be ascertained. [Drayton] "gave" (ie parted with) 2,461,226 shares. Their "price" was 160p a share but the best evidence of their "value" was what they were worth on 11 October 1972. It was said that this figure was in the region of 125p a share, that being the middle market figure on the Stock Exchange. The Crown relied on *Crane Fruehauf v Inland Revenue Comrs* and in particular on the observation, obiter, of Russell LJ in the Court of Appeal that in the circumstances of that case the market value of the consideration shares at the moment of their issue would be a good indication of the amount or value of the consideration (see [1975] 1 All ER 429 at 434).

'In our view the approach of [Drayton] is the correct one. *Crane Fruehauf* is not, it seems to us, of assistance because that case was concerned with the valuation, for the purpose of ad valorem "conveyance or transfer on sale" stamp duty, of "the consideration for the sale", in other words the valuation of the consideration received by the vendor (Finance Act 1963, section 55, as amended, and Stamp Act 1891 section 6), whereas in the present case we are concerned with the valuation of the consideration moving from the purchaser. The key to the solution of the present problem is, we think, as Counsel for [Drayton] submitted, to be found in the following extract from the judgment of Lord Greene MR in *Osborne v Steel Barrel Co Ltd* [1942] 1 All ER 634 at 637–638: 'The primary liability of an allottee of shares is to pay for them in cash; but, when shares are allotted credited as fully paid, this primary liability is satisfied by a consideration other than cash passing from the allottee. A company, therefore, when, in pursuance of such a transaction, it agrees to credit the shares as fully paid, is giving up what it would otherwise have had—namely, the right to call on the allottee for payment of the par value in cash . . . when fully-paid shares are properly issued for a consideration other than cash, the consideration moving from the company must be at least equal in value to the par value of the shares and must be based on an honest estimate by the directors of the value of the assets acquired.' Lord Greene MR's remarks are not in terms confined to income tax computations and are expressed in general terms. Although he refers to shares issued at par his reasoning applies equally to shares issued at a premium.

'Paragraph 4 of Schedule 6 does not specify "market value" (cf section 22(4) Finance Act 1965). It is the "value . . . given" which has to be ascertained and the means by which that "value" is to be ascertained are not specified. On Lord Greene MR's analysis [Drayton] has, in pursuance of a perfectly genuine transaction including the issue of its Ordinary Shares at 160p each, "given up" the right to call on Eagle Star Insurance Co Ltd to pay to it the sum of £3,937,962, being the issue price of the shares and the value of the assets acquired by [Drayton]. That sum therefore represents the value of the consideration "given" by [Drayton] within the meaning of Paragraph 4.

'We accordingly decide that the gain is to be computed on the basis that [Drayton] gave value to the extent of £3,937,962 for the acquisition of the portfolio of investments and adjourn the appeal for the figures to be agreed.'

11. Figures were in due course agreed between the parties and on 12th June 1978 the commissioners adjusted the assessments by reducing that for the period to 31st December 1972 to nil and that for the period to 31st December 1973 to £349,429.

12. The Crown immediately after the determination of the appeal declared its dissatisfaction therewith as being erroneous in point of law and on 15th June 1978 required the commissioners to state a case for the opinion of the High Court pursuant to s 56 of the Taxes Management Act 1970.

13. The question for the opinion of the court was whether the commissioners' decision was correct in law.

Peter Gibson for the Crown.
Michael Nolan QC and *Robert Venables* for Drayton.

Cur adv vult

24th March. **VINELOTT J** read the following judgment: By cl 1 of an agreement for sale dated 21st September 1972 and made between Eagle Star Insurance Co Ltd ('Eagle Star)', of the one part, and the respondent, Drayton Commercial Investment Co Ltd (which was then known as Union Commercial Investment Co Ltd, and which I shall call 'Drayton'), of the other part, Eagle Star agreed to sell and Drayton to purchase a portfolio of investments specified in an agreed schedule at the price of £3,937,962—

> 'to be satisfied by the allotment by the Purchaser to the Vendor of 2,461,226 Ordinary Shares of 25 pence each in the Purchaser the issue price of each such Share for the purpose of satisfying the consideration being 160 pence.'

The ordinary shares were to be issued credited as fully paid up, and were to rank pari passu with the then existing ordinary shares of Drayton save that they were not to participate in any final dividend paid on the ordinary shares in respect of the year ending 31st December 1972. The vendor was to be entitled, in lieu of such dividend, to a gross dividend equal to the aggregate of the gross dividends paid to Drayton (or which would have been paid but for any disposal) in respect of the investments comprised in the portfolio during the period from 1st September 1972 to 31st December 1972 after deducting gross dividends received by Drayton but claimed by Eagle Star on investments quoted ex-dividend on 31st August 1972.

It was provided by cl 2 that the agreement was conditional on—

> '(i) the Members of the Purchaser passing the necessary Resolution of the Company in general meeting creating the new shares in the Purchaser required to satisfy the consideration above mentioned; (ii) the Stock Exchange (London) granting permission to deal in and quotation for such new shares subject to allotment before 31st October, 1972.'

Clause 3 provided that the agreement should be completed within seven days after these conditions were both satisfied. In the event, the necessary resolution was passed at an extraordinary general meeting of Drayton on 9th October 1972 and permission to deal in and a quotation for the shares to be issued by Drayton was given by the Stock Exchange on 11th October 1972. The agreement was completed on 11th October 1972 when the shares which Drayton had agreed to issue were allotted to Eagle Star. The shares so allotted were first quoted on the Stock Exchange on 12th October 1972.

Clause 4 provided that, as the portfolio had been valued at mid-market quotations on 31st August 1972, Eagle Star was to be entitled to all the dividends and interest on investments quoted ex-dividend on that day, and Drayton to dividends and interest declared and paid after that day.

Between 11th October 1972 and 31st October 1972, and during 1973, Drayton disposed of certain of the investments comprised in the portfolio. Assessments to corporation tax were made on the footing that, in ascertaining the chargeable gains

accruing to Drayton on the disposal of these investments, the value of the portfolio
a should be taken as equal to the market value of the shares issued by Drayton ascertained in accordance with Stock Exchange quoted prices on the day on which the shares were first quoted in the Stock Exchange official list after the allotment. Drayton successfully appealed against those assessments on the ground that the value of the shares allotted was the price at which they were issued, that is, the par value plus the premium entered into Drayton's books. As I have said, the issue price was ascertained by reference to mid-
b market prices of the investments comprised in the portfolio quoted on the Stock Exchange on 31st August 1972. On that day the mid-market price of Drayton's ordinary shares was 142p. If that price is applied to the shares which Drayton agreed to issue as consideration for the acquisition of the portfolio, the portfolio was effectively purchased for £3,494,941, representing a discount of 11·25% on its value. On 21st September 1972 the mid-market quoted price of shares of Drayton was 134p and on 12th October 125p.

c Corporation tax is chargeable in respect of chargeable gains of companies computed in accordance with the principles applicable to capital gains tax (see the Income and Corporation Taxes Act 1970, ss 238 and 265). Schedule 6 to the Finance Act 1965 contains provisions governing the computation of the amount of a gain accruing on the disposal of an asset. Paragraph 4(1) restricts the sums allowable as a deduction from the consideration for the disposal to sums falling under three heads, one of which (embodied
d in para (*a*)) allows the deduction of the consideration given for the acquisition. It allows the deduction by the taxpayer, in terms of para (*a*), of 'the amount or value of the consideration, in money or money's worth, given by him or on his behalf wholly and exclusively for the acquisition of the asset'. The main issue in this appeal is simply whether the amount or value of the consideration given by Drayton for the portfolio of investments was the price, namely £3,937,950, which under the terms of cl 1 was to be
e satisfied by the allotment of 2,461,226 shares of Drayton or the value of those shares. Although the paragraph does not specifically so provide, 'value' must, I think, mean market value.

There is a subsidiary question whether, if the answer to this question is that 'the amount or value of the consideration' was the market value of the shares of Drayton issued in satisfaction of the sum of £3,937,950, the market value should be ascertained
f at 21st September or at 11th October 1972; and, in the latter event, whether it should be ascertained by reference to prices quoted on the Stock Exchange on 12th October 1972.

The Crown's contention is that under the agreement the consideration for the portfolio given by Drayton consisted of the shares of Drayton which Drayton were contractually bound to issue. As the agreement was conditional, the disposal of the portfolio by Eagle Star and its acquisition by Drayton must both be taken to have been made when the
g conditions in cl 2 were first satisfied (see para 10(2) of Sch 10 to the Finance Act 1971), that is, 11th October. The market value on 11th October must be ascertained by reference to the price at which the shares were first quoted on the Stock Exchange on 12th October, either by analogy to s 44(3) of the 1965 Act or because quoted prices must be taken as the prima facie measure of value, although, of course, as s 44(3) recognises, there may be special circumstances which make it inappropriate as a measure of market
h value.

The argument for Drayton (which, as I have said, persuaded the Special Commissioners) is shortly as follows. It is said that where a company acquires property in return for the issue of its shares then, unless the contract for the acquisition of the property is merely colourable or is illusory or fraudulent, the amount or value of the consideration given by the company is the amount of the credit which it gives to the vendor of the property for
j the value of the property acquired. That amount or value falls to be determined by reference to the terms of the contract. This proposition is said to be established by the decisions of the Court of Appeal in *Osborne (Inspector of Taxes) v Steel Barrel Co Ltd* [1942] 1 All ER 634, 24 Tax Cas 293 and *Craddock (Inspector of Taxes) v Zevo Finance Co Ltd* [1946] 1 All ER 523n, 27 Tax Cas 267 and to these cases I now turn.

In *Osborne (Inspector of Taxes) v Steel Barrel Co Ltd* a Mr Hood Barrs, a well-known figure to those familiar with the Tax Cases, entered into a contract with the receiver of a company in liquidation (which I shall call 'the old company') for the purchase of its business premises, goodwill, stock-in-trade and effects at the price of £10,500. Subsequently, he entered into an agreement with the respondent company under which the respondent company in effect took the benefit of the contract with the receiver, Mr Hood Barrs constituting himself a trustee thereof; and, in consideration therefor and for other services performed by Mr Hood Barrs on its behalf, and of his agreement to serve the respondent company as managing director in the future, the respondent company allotted him 29,997 shares credited as fully paid. On completion of the agreement with the receiver, the business and assets of the old company were entered into the books of the respondent company at £10,500, the price paid to the receiver, which, of course, the respondent company became liable to pay under the original agreement. Of that sum, £2,493 was apportioned to stock. Subsequently, the stock was revalued, and the opening figure of the stock was entered at £21,375 19s 8d. The Special Commissioners found that the value of the stock when the respondent company acquired it was £10,000, and that the profits of the respondent company for the year ended 5th April 1933 and subsequent years should be determined on that footing. An appeal by the Crown was allowed by Macnaghten J on the ground that (to quote the summary in the judgment of Lord Greene MR on the subsequent appeal) 'the issue of the shares did not cost the appellant company anything; that accordingly the shares issued in respect of the stock added nothing to the price, and the only thing that the company paid for the stock was a proportionate part of the cash', that is, of the £10,500 paid under the original agreement.

In relation to this argument Lord Greene MR, in a passage which has often been cited and which I hope I shall be forgiven for citing again, said ([1942] 1 All ER 634 at 637–638):

> 'It was strenuously argued on behalf of the Crown that if a company acquires stock in consideration of the issue of fully-paid shares to the vendor, that stock must, for the purpose of ascertaining the company's profits, be treated as having been acquired for nothing, with the result that, when it comes to be sold, the Revenue is entitled to treat the whole of the purchase price obtained on the sale as a profit. This is a remarkable contention, and it would require conclusive authority before we could accept it. The cases relied on in its support were *Inland Revenue Comrs.* v. *Blott* ([1921] AC 171) and *Lowry* v. *Consolidated African Selection Trust, Ltd.*, ([1940] 2 All ER 545, [1940] AC 648), neither of which, in our view, has any bearing on the point. The argument really rests on a misconception as to what happens when a company issues shares credited as fully paid for a consideration other than cash. The primary liability of an allottee of shares is to pay for them in cash; but, when shares are allotted credited as fully paid, this primary liability is satisfied by a consideration other than cash passing from the allottee. A company, therefore, when, in pursuance of such a transaction, it agrees to credit the shares as fully paid, is giving up what it would otherwise have had—namely, the right to call on the allottee for payment of the par value in cash. A company cannot issue £1,000 nominal worth of shares for stock of the market value of £500, since shares cannot be issued at a discount. Accordingly, when fully-paid shares are properly issued for a consideration other than cash, the consideration moving from the company must be at the least equal in value to the par value of the shares and must be based on an honest estimate by the directors of the value of the assets acquired.'

In retrospect, and with the benefit of Lord Greene MR's analysis, it can be seen that the argument advanced by the Crown was an absurd one. It amounted to saying that whenever a company acquires property (the relevant 'property' being in that case the benefit of the contract with the receiver) in exchange for an issue of its own shares then because it pays nothing in cash it gives nothing for the property. The same fallacy, in a more subtle form, underlay the argument of the Crown in *Craddock (Inspector of Taxes) v Zevo Finance Co Ltd* [1944] 1 All ER 566. In that case, the respondent company, a finance dealing company, was formed to take over a portfolio of investments belonging to another investment dealing company. The investments in the portfolio were purchased by the respondent company at the prices at which they stood in the books of the vendor company though that was a figure far in excess of the value of the portfolio ascertained in accordance with mid-market prices quoted on the Stock Exchange. Under the agreement for the purchase of the portfolio, the agreed price was satisfied in part by the assumption by the respondent company of certain liabilities of the vendor company, and in part by the allotment of shares of the respondent company which were credited as fully paid. It was argued by the Crown that in computing the profits of the respondent company the amount to be debited as the cost of the investments (being stock-in-trade of the respondent company) was their market value and not, as the respondent company contended, the price which the respondent company paid, namely the aggregate of the liabilities which the respondent company took over and the amount credited as paid up on the shares of the company which were issued at par. That, as Lord Greene MR pointed out, necessarily led to the conclusion that the shares issued by the respondent company were issued at a discount, and he said ([1944] 1 All ER 566 at 569–570):

> 'The fallacy, if I may respectfully so call it, which underlies the argument, is to be found in the assertion that where a company issues its own shares as consideration for the acquisition of property, these shares are to be treated as money's worth as though they were shares in another company altogether, transferred by way of consideration for the acquisition. This proposition amounts to saying that consideration in the form of fully-paid shares allotted by a company must be treated as being of the value of the shares, no more and no less. Such a contention will not bear a moment's examination where the transaction is a straightforward one and not a mere device for issuing shares at a discount. In the everyday case of reconstruction, the shares in the new company allotted to the shareholders of the old company as fully-paid will often, if not in most cases, fetch substantially less than their nominal value if sold in the market. But this does not mean that they are to be treated as having been issued at a discount; or that the price paid by the new company for the assets which it acquires from the old company ought to be treated as something less than the nominal value of the fully-paid shares. The Crown in this case is in fact attempting to depart from the rule (the correctness of which it itself admits) that the figure at which stock in trade is to be brought in is its cost to the trader and substitute the alleged market value of the stock for its cost. Of course, in a case where stock which a company proposes to acquire for shares is deliberately overvalued for the purpose of issuing an inflated amount of share capital, very different considerations apply. But nothing of the kind is present in this case which, as I have already pointed out, is a perfectly proper and normal reconstruction. The propriety of the course adopted is manifest when the uncertainty as to the value of the investments, which is pointed out by the commissioners, is borne in mind. It is, I think, true as a general proposition that, where a company acquires property for fully-paid shares of its own, the price paid by the company is, *prima facie*, the nominal value of the shares. It is for those who assert the contrary to establish it, as could be done, for example, in the suggested case of a deliberately inflated valuation. In the present case the Crown has failed to establish the contrary on the facts as found; and there is no justification for the proposition that, on these facts, the commissioners were bound in law to decide the appeal in favour of the Crown.'

The decision of the Court of Appeal was affirmed in the House of Lords. I do not propose to cite extensively from the speeches there. Lord Simon said ((1946) 27 Tax Cas 267 at 287):

> 'The crucial transaction, albeit in a reconstruction, is a transaction of sale and purchase, and the proper figure to be debited in respect of the purchased investments

> is the cost thereof to the Respondent. That cost is set out in the agreement between the Zevo Syndicate and its liquidator of the one part and the Respondent of the *a* other part dated 15th June 1932, and the shares allotted as part of the purchase price are allotted "credited as fully paid". [Then, after citing from the judgment of Lord Greene MR, he continued:] The contrary proposition amounts to saying that consideration in the form of its fully paid shares allotted by a company must be treated as being the value of the shares, no more and no less. I agree with the Master of the Rolls that such a contention will not bear a moment's examination when the *b* transaction is a straightforward one and not a mere device for issuing shares at a discount. To put the matter in its simplest form, the profit or loss to a trader in dealing with his stock in trade is arrived at for Income Tax purposes by comparing what his stock in fact cost him with what he in fact realised on resale. It is unsound to substitute alleged market values for what it in fact cost him.'

Lord Wright said (27 Tax Cas 267 at 289): *c*

> 'It is well established that the issue of shares at a discount is illegal. It has also been held that, if the consideration for the issue of shares is a sum of money which is less than the nominal value of the shares, the shares will be treated as issued at a discount. If, on the other hand, the shares are issued for something other than a money consideration, the position is different because the Court does not inquire *d* into the adequacy of the consideration so long as the transaction is a genuine and honest agreement deliberately entered into between two persons or companies.'

I have set out the facts in the *Steel Barrel* and *Zevo Finance Co* cases, and extracts from the judgments and speeches, at some length because examination of them shows that, far from supporting the proposition for which the taxpayer relies on them, they are in fact inconsistent with it. The cost of the portfolio to Drayton was unquestionably the sum *e* of £3,937,962. It could be nothing else. That was the cost that had to be entered into Drayton's books to balance the sums which were in part applied in paying up shares at par and in part credited to share premium account. If Drayton had been a share dealing company and if the portfolio had been acquired as stock-in-trade, that is the sum that would have been debited against sums realised on subsequent disposals in order to ascertain its trading profit. But in ascertaining the amount of the gain to be computed *f* in accordance with Part III of the Finance Act 1965 the amount to be deducted in respect of the consideration for the acquisition is the amount or value of that consideration. To equate the cost to Drayton of issuing the shares in satisfaction of the agreed price with the 'amount or value' of that consideration is in my judgment to repeat the fallacy which Lord Greene MR found to underly the argument of the Crown in the *Steel Barrel* and *Zevo Finance Co* cases. To repeat what Lord Greene MR said in the *Zevo Finance Co* case *g* [1944] 1 All ER 566 at 569:

> 'In the everyday case of reconstruction, the shares in the new company allotted to the shareholders of the old company as fully paid will often, if not in most cases, fetch substantially less than their nominal value if sold in the market.'

Counsel for Drayton sought support for his submission in the observation of Lord *h* Wilberforce in *Aberdeen Construction Group Ltd v Inland Revenue Comrs* [1978] 1 All ER 962 at 966, [1978] AC 885 at 892–893 where he said:

> 'The capital gains tax is of comparatively recent origin. The legislation imposing it, mainly the Finance Act 1965, is necessarily complicated, and the detailed provisions, as they affect this or any other case, must of course be looked at with *j* care. But a guiding principle must underly any interpretation of the Act, namely, that its purpose is to tax capital gains and to make allowance for capital losses, each of which ought to be arrived at on normal business principles. No doubt anomalies may occur, but in straightforward situations, such as this, the courts should hesitate before accepting results which are paradoxical and contrary to business sense. To

paraphrase a famous cliché, the capital gains tax is a tax on gains: it is not a tax on
a arithmetical differences.'

As the price of £3,937,962 was entered, and admittedly properly entered, into the books of Drayton as the cost of the shares, that figure should, counsel for Drayton said, be taken on proper accounting principles as the base from which the gain to Drayton should be calculated. But in the *Aberdeen Construction Group Ltd v Inland Revenue Comrs*
b the total investment of the appellant company in another company consisted in part of share capital and in part of a loan. It sold the shares at a price in excess of the price it had paid for them (by way of subscription) but on terms that it would 'waive the loan'. The aggregate of the price it had paid for the shares and the loan which was to be waived exceeded the cash price at which it sold the shares. In the House of Lords the opinion of the majority of their Lordships who heard the appeal was that the 'business reality' was
c that the appellant company had made a loss on the disposal of its total investment. Here, it seems to me, the 'business reality' is that, while the cost entered into the books of Drayton as the price of the acquisition of the portfolio was and could only have been the agreed sum of £3,937,962, the value of the consideration which it gave for the portfolio was the value of the shares which it was entitled and bound to issue in satisfaction of that price. That was the value received by Eagle Star, which would of course go into its books
d as arising on the disposal of the portfolio. As I see it, for capital gains tax purposes it is the value of the consideration given by Drayton and not the cost of the consideration to Drayton which is deductible under para 4(1)(*a*).

Counsel for Drayton submitted in the alternative that the amount or value of the consideration should be determined for commercial as well as for tax purposes at the date of the agreement. For this proposition, he relied on the decision of the House of Lords
e in *British South Africa v Varty (Inspector of Taxes)* [1965] 2 All ER 395, [1966] AC 381. That, again, was a Sch D case. The question was whether, when the respondent company, which acquired an option to subscribe for shares of another company, exercised the option, it realised a profit, the profit being the difference between the price at which it was entitled to subscribe for the shares and their market value at the time of the exercise of the option. It paid nothing for the option, which was granted as part of a wider
f transaction. It was held in the House of Lords that it did not. I can see nothing in that decision which in any way supports counsel's submission for Drayton. Paragraph 10 of Sch 10 to the Finance Act 1971 requires that in the case of a conditional contract the contract is to be treated as coming into existence when it became unconditional. Paragraph 4(1)(*a*) requires that the amount to be deducted in respect of consideration be limited to the amount or value of the consideration, and that must be the amount or
g value of the consideration at the date of the contract, that latter date being, in accordance with para 10, the date when it becomes unconditional.

In my judgment, therefore, the Crown's contentions are well founded. I reach that conclusion simply on the language of para 4(1)(*a*) of Sch 6 to the Finance Act 1965 and para 10 of Sch 10 to the Finance Act 1971. But counsel for the Crown referred me to two cases in the field of stamp duty which lend some support to this conclusion. In *Brooklands*
h *Selangor Holdings Ltd v Inland Revenue Comrs* [1970] 2 All ER 76, [1970] 1 WLR 429 the question was whether a very elaborate scheme was 'a scheme for the reconstruction of any company or companies or the amalgamation of any companies' within s 55 of the Finance Act 1927; and, if so, whether it satisfied the conditions for exemption from stamp duty contained in that section. It was held by the commissioners that it was not a scheme of reconstruction or amalgamation within s 55, and that decision was upheld
j by Pennycuick J. The commissioners also decided in favour of the Crown on another ground, namely that one of the conditions in s 55 was not satisfied. That condition, so far as material, required that the consideration for the acquisition of not less than 90% of the share capital of an existing company must consist 'as to not less than 90 per cent. thereof . . . in the issue of shares in the transferee company to the holders of shares in the existing company in exchange for the shares held by them in the existing company'. In

the *Brooklands* case, the 'consideration' that was relevant for the purposes of the condition
consisted of 3,003,991 stock units of £1 each plus £115,593 in cash. The commissioners a
held that the condition was not satisfied on the ground that the market value of the stock
units was £722,835, so that the cash element was more than 10% of the aggregate. In his
judgment Pennycuick J said ([1970] 2 All ER 76 at 88, [1970] 1 WLR 429 at 447):

> 'I am wholly unpersuaded that the contention advanced on behalf of the
> commissioners on this point is well founded. In the first place I am not persuaded
> that the word "consideration" in para (*c*) of s 55(1) means anything other than the b
> expressed consideration. I do not find it necessary to equate, and I do not think I
> would be justified in equating, that word "consideration" there with the expression
> "amount or value of the consideration" in the charge for transfer duty.'

He referred to the passage in the speech of Lord Greene MR in the *Zevo Finance Co* case
which I have cited and commented that 'that passage goes some way towards meeting the c
contention of the commissioners in this case' ([1970] 2 All ER 76 at 90, [1970] 1 WLR
429 at 448).

In the case now before me, the commissioners seem to have taken the view that these
observations by Pennycuick J supported the case advanced by Drayton. But it seems to
me that in that passage Pennycuick J is drawing precisely the distinction between the
'consideration' entered into the books of a company which acquires property in exchange d
for its own shares and the 'amount or value' of the shares so given which is fundamental
to the Crown's case.

The other case is the decision of Templeman J in *Crane Fruehauf Ltd v Inland Revenue
Comrs* [1974] 1 All ER 811 and of the Court of Appeal ([1975] 1 All ER 429) affirming
his decision. That was another case which turned on s 55 of the Finance Act 1927. The
directors of Crane Fruehauf ('Crane') negotiated the acquisition of the entire shareholding e
of Boden Trailers Ltd ('Boden'), the consideration being the issue of 1·8m shares of Crane
and £100,000 cash. But one of the shareholders of Crane was a company called Fruehauf
International Ltd ('FIL'), which held one-third of the shares of Crane and did not want to
see its proportionate shareholding watered down by the issue of shares to the Boden
shareholders. That was something it was in a position to prevent because it had a
shareholding sufficient to stop the necessary increase in the capital of Crane. To satisfy f
FIL, an arrangement was entered into under which the shareholders of Boden agreed to
sell their shares to Crane in exchange for the issue of 1·8m ordinary shares of £1 each and
£100,000 cash, and under which FIL was given an option to acquire from each of the
Boden shareholders one-third of the newly-issued Crane shares (600,000 in all) at £1 per
share. The option was exercised before the shares were issued. The purchase of the
Boden shares by Crane and the purchase of one-third of the new Crane shares by FIL were g
completed on the same day, the new Crane shares being issued to the Boden shareholders,
who then executed transfers of 600,000 of them and delivered the transfers and share
certificates to FIL. The question was whether Crane were entitled to relief under s 55,
and that question turned on whether it could be said that the consideration for the
acquisition of the Boden shares consisted as to not less than 90% in the issue of shares of
Crane. It was held by Templeman J and by the Court of Appeal that it did not so consist h
because, in the words of Russell LJ [1975] 1 All ER 429 at 433, the consideration was—

> '1,200,000 shares plus £100,000, plus 600,000 shares subject to an immediate
> obligation (which the very mechanics of the transaction made inescapable) and right
> to receive £600,000; and this situation was procured by Crane in the bargain
> offered by Crane to the Boden shareholders.'

j

But there was a subsidiary question. On the footing that s 55 did not apply, the
transfers of the Boden shares attracted ad valorem stamp duty, and under s 55 of the
Stamp Act 1891 the value of which ad valorem duty was payable included the value of
the 1·8m shares of Crane, which were part of the consideration for the Boden shares. It
was conceded by the Crown that the 600,000 shares which were subject to FIL's option

fell to be valued at the option price of £600,000. As to the balance of 1·2m shares, it was
a argued that those shares ought to be valued at the price at which they were issued, that
being the cost brought into the accounts of Crane. That argument precisely reflects the
argument advanced on behalf of Drayton in the present case. The *Brooklands* and *Zevo Finance Co* cases were cited to Templeman J, although he does not refer to them in his
judgment. He rejected the argument ([1974] 1 All ER 811 at 822–823) on the ground
that Crane's accounts—

b 'are not decisive of the real value of the Crane shares required to be assessed by
s 55 of the Stamp Act 1891. By s 6 of that Act the value must be assessed as on "the
date of the instrument". The date of the instrument is either the date when each
transfer was signed between 1st and 22nd September, as counsel for Crane contends,
or on 12th October, when the transfers were delivered to Crane. In my judgment
the value is the Stock Exchange value on the correct date, which is 12th October.
c Before that date each instrument was in escrow, conditional on Crane issuing
1,800,000 Crane shares and paying £100,000. On that date each share could have
been sold for the Stock Exchange price.'

That decision was affirmed in the Court of Appeal. Russell LJ said ([1975] 1 All ER
429 at 434):

d 'On the basis that Crane was not entitled to relief under s 55 of the 1927 Act it was
submitted on behalf of Crane, as well in this court as before Templeman J, that the
appropriate dates for valuing the 1,200,000 Crane shares, being part of the
consideration for the transfer of the Boden shares within s 55 of the 1891 Act, were
the respective dates on which the transfers of the Boden shares were signed by the
holders. Section 6 of the Stamp Act 1891 provides that where an instrument is
e chargeable with ad valorem duty in respect of any stock (which includes shares)—
"the duty shall be calculated on the value, on the day of the date of the instrument
... of the stock or security according to the average price thereof." At the respective
dates when the Boden shareholders signed the transfers of their shares the Crane
shares had not been issued and accordingly, so the argument ran, s 6 had no
f application and the value of the Crane shares ought to be taken to be the issue price
attributed to those shares in the books of Crane. Templeman J rejected these
submissions, taking the view that until the issue of the Crane shares on 12th
October 1967 each of the transfers of the Boden shares was in escrow conditional on
the issue of the Crane shares. The date of the several transfers was accordingly 12th
October 1967 on which date each share could have been sold for the stock exchange
g price. In my judgment, Templeman J came to a correct conclusion for the reason
which he gave. I would, however, add this. Where s 6 of the 1891 Act does not
apply, the commissioners must do the best they can and, if it were correct that the
transfers were executed prior to the issue of the Crane shares, the market value of
the latter at the moment of their issue plus the cash payable to the vendors would
in my view be a good indication of the amount or value of the consideration for the
transfers.'

h The Special Commissioners distinguished *Crane Fruehauf* on the ground that—

'*Crane Fruehauf* is not, it seems to us, of assistance because that case was concerned
with the valuation, for the purpose of ad valorem "conveyance or transfer on sale"
stamp duty, of "the consideration for the sale", in other words the valuation of the
consideration received by the vendor (Finance Act 1963, section 55, as amended,
j and Stamp Act 1891, section 6), whereas in the present case we are concerned with
the valuation of the consideration moving from the purchaser.'

I cannot see that that can be a valid ground of distinction. Under the joint effect of s 55
of the Finance Act 1963 and of s 55(1) of the Stamp Act 1891 the ad valorem duty payable
on the transfer of the Boden shares fell to be computed by reference to the value of the

Crane shares, and that in turn fell to be ascertained 'on the value, on the day of the date of the instrument' of the Crane shares 'according to the average price thereof'. The argument before Templeman J and before the Court of Appeal was that the value of the Crane shares ought to be taken as the issue price brought into its books. It may be that in the Court of Appeal, at least, that argument was put forward, not as a general proposition but as an exception founded on the special circumstance that when the Boden shareholders signed their transfers the Crane shares had not been issued, so that (as I envisage the argument) the issue price was the only available measure of value. But, however the argument was put in the *Crane Fruehauf* case, the decision of Templeman J and of the Court of Appeal, as I see it, is inconsistent with the general proposition that, when shares of a company are issued at par or at a premium in consideration for the acquisition of property, the value of the consideration is the cost to the company of the acquisition of the property, that is, the par value of the issued shares plus premium.

Counsel for the Crown also relied on the contrast between the provisions of the now defunct short-term capital gains tax, under which the base for ascertaining capital gains was ascertained in accordance with Sch D principles, that is, the cost to the company, and the very different approach in the 1965 Act. As I have reached the clear conclusion from the language of para 4(1)(*a*) alone that this appeal succeeds, I do not propose to enter into any comparison of the contrast between these two very different fiscal structures.

It is common ground that Drayton is entitled to adduce evidence and argument in favour of its contention that the market value of its shares when issued to Eagle Star was in excess of the value arrived at by mere multiplication of Stock Exchange prices. In these circumstances, I propose to refer the assessments back to the commissioners for the determination of their value; and, unless I hear any argument to the contrary, I shall make the usual order that Drayton pay the commissioners their costs of the appeal.

Appeal allowed. Case remitted to the Special Commissioners.

Solicitors: *Solicitor of Inland Revenue; Ashurst, Morris, Crisp & Co* (for Drayton).

Edwina Epstein Barrister.

a # Elsden and another v Pick

COURT OF APPEAL, CIVIL DIVISION
BUCKLEY, SHAW AND BRIGHTMAN LJJ
3rd, 4th, 5th, 6th, 7th, 28th MARCH 1980

b *Agricultural holding – Notice to quit – Length of notice – Validity of notice – Statutory requirement that at least 12 months' notice be given – Landlord offering to accept shorter notice – Tenant accepting offer but later claiming short notice invalid – Whether landlord entitled to waive right to 12 months' notice – Whether landlord effectively waiving right – Whether notice valid – Agricultural Holdings Act 1948, s 23(1).*

c The plaintiffs were the landlords of two farms of which the defendant was the tenant. Section 23(1)[a] of the Agricultural Holdings Act 1948 provided that a notice to quit an agricultural holding would be invalid if it purported to terminate the tenancy before the expiration of 12 months from the end of the then current year of tenancy. By the terms of the parties' lease the requisite notice was one year's notice in writing expiring on 6th April in any year. In 1977 the tenant got into financial difficulties and on 4th April he
d approached the landlords' agent and warned him that he might have to quit the farms. The agent, being sympathetic to the tenant's plight, suggested that the tenant take some more time to make a final decision and that if the tenant decided within the next five days to terminate either or both tenancies he would accept a notice to quit backdated to 4th April. The tenant agreed and, having reconsidered, decided to quit one farm only. Accordingly on 7th April he gave the agent a notice to quit dated 4th April to expire on
e 5th April 1978. The agent accepted the notice. The tenant later changed his mind and asked that his notice be disregarded. The landlords refused and brought proceedings for possession. At the trial the tenant contended that the notice was invalid since it did not comply with s 23(1) in that it purported 'to terminate the tenancy before the expiration of twelve months from the end of the then current year of [the] tenancy'. The judge upheld that contention on the ground that s 23(1) was a mandatory provision, and
f dismissed the landlords' claim. The landlords appealed.

Held – On the true construction of s 23(1) of the 1948 Act, which merely made notices which did not comply with its provisions 'invalid' and not 'unlawful', a party to a tenancy agreement was not prevented from waiving his strict right to insist on a notice to quit of at least 12 months' duration and accepting the termination of the tenancy before the expiration of that period. The suggestion by the landlords' agent that the notice to quit
g be backdated and his acceptance of the notice despite the fact that the notice thereby given was less than 12 months was an effective waiver by the landlords of the requirements regarding length of notice. It followed that the landlords' appeal would be allowed (see p 240 *f* to p 241 *b* and p 242 *a* to p 243 *c*, post).

Notes
h For length of notice to quit an agricultural holding, see 1 Halsbury's Laws (4th Edn) para 1051, and for cases on the subject, see 2 Digest (Reissue) 18–19, *57–65*.

For the Agricultural Holdings Act 1948, s 23, see 1 Halsbury's Statutes (3rd Edn) 705.

Cases referred to in judgments
Johnstone v Hudlestone (1825) 4 B & C 922, 7 Dow & Ry KB 411, 4 LJOSKB 71, 107 ER
j 1302, 31(2) Digest (Reissue) 758, *6275*.

Steadman v Steadman [1974] 2 All ER 977, [1976] AC 536, [1974] 3 WLR 56, 29 P & CR 249, HL, Digest (Cont Vol D) 795, *81a*.

---

a Section 23(1) is set out at p 238 *f g*, post

Cases also cited

Alan (WJ) & Co Ltd v El Nasr Export & Import Co [1972] 2 All ER 127, [1972] 2 QB 189, CA. a

Beesly v Hallwood Estates Ltd [1960] 2 All ER 314, [1960] 1 WLR 549.

Bremer Handelsgesellschaft v Vanden Avenne-Izegem PVBA [1978] 2 Lloyd's Rep 109, HL.

Buckmaster v Harrop (1802) 7 Ves 341, 32 ER 139.

Clerk v Wright (1737) 1 Atk 12, 26 ER 9, LC.

Crabb v Arun District Coucil [1975] 3 All ER 865, [1976] Ch 179, CA. b

Doe d Murrell v Milward (1838) 3 M & W 328, 150 ER 1170.

Flather v Hood (1928) 44 TLR 698.

Hankey v Clavering [1942] 2 All ER 311, [1942] 2 KB 326, CA.

Hughes v Metropolitan Railway Co (1877) 2 App Cas 439, [1874–80] All ER Rep 187, HL.

Johnson v Moreton [1978] 3 All ER 37, [1980] AC 37, HL.

Kammins Ballroom Co Ltd v Zenith Investments (Torquay) Ltd [1969] 3 All ER 1268, [1971] AC 850, HL. c

Levey & Co v Goldberg [1922] 1 KB 688.

Ogle v Earl Vane (1868) LR 3 QB 272.

O'Reilly v Thompson (1791) 2 Cox Eq Cas 271, 30 ER 126.

Phillips v Edwards (1864) 33 Beav 440, 55 ER 438.

d

Appeal

The plaintiffs, Richard William Hilary Elsden and Charles Michael Watson-Smyth, appealed against the decision of Robert Wright QC, sitting as a deputy judge of the High Court in the Chancery Division, given on 26th February 1979 dismissing the plaintiff's claim against the defendant, John Shelbourn Pick, for a declaration that they were entitled to possession as from 6th April 1978 of Woodside Farm, Newton, Lincolnshire, e of which the plaintiffs were the landlords and the defendant the tenant. The facts are set out in the judgment of Shaw LJ.

J Maurice Price QC and *Henry Harrod* for the plaintiffs.
Jonathan Parker QC for Mr Pick.

f

Cur adv vult

28th March. The following judgments were read.

SHAW LJ (delivering the first judgment at the invitation of Buckley LJ). This is an g appeal by the plaintiffs in the action from a judgment of Robert Wright QC, sitting as a deputy judge of the High Court, given on 26th February 1979 whereby he refused their claim for a declaration that they were entitled to possession of Woodside Farm, Newton, Lincolnshire as on 6th April 1978.

The plaintiffs were at all material times the trustees of a settlement which included the Welby estate. The principal beneficiary under the settlement is Sir Bruno Welby Bt. He h was concerned with the management of the estate, of which a Mr Cawthra was the land agent.

Included in the estate were a number of farms some of which were let to tenant farmers. Two, which were known respectively as Woodside Farm and Welby Warren Farm, were so let to the defendant, Mr Pick, who by 1977 had occupied them for many years. For reasons which are not relevant to the present appeal, the Welby estate had at j some time towards the end of the 1960s adopted the policy of not reletting farms on the estate when they fell vacant. Sir Bruno had formed a family company called D & S Farms Ltd; it took over the tenancies of such farms and farmed them in partnership with a Mr Giles Halfhead under the partnership title Sapperton Farming Co.

At the beginning of 1977 Mr Pick, who had until then farmed Welby Warren Farm and Woodside Farm with reasonable success, found himself surrounded by misfortune, both matrimonial and financial. His wife was in the process of divorcing him. He was confronted by burdensome obligations and liabilities. He was in a state of great mental stress and consulted his solicitor about his various troubles. On 1st April 1977 the solicitor wrote, advising him that from what he had been told there was a real possilibity that Mr Pick might have to cease business. Mr Pick himself foresaw that he might find himself so destitute of resources that he would not be able to pay the rent of his farm, or at any rate the rents of both of them. In that situation he did what an honourable man would do. On 4th April, which was a Monday, he went to see Mr Cawthra, who acted for the landlord trustees, and told him what his position was. Their respective versions of what took place as recounted in their evidence before the deputy judge did not altogether tally. The judge's assessment of them as witnesses was that each was honestly seeking to recall what was arranged between them at that meeting but that Mr Cawthra's recollection was the more reliable. This assessment is not challenged. According to Mr Cawthra he was shown the letter from Mr Pick's solicitor. A half year's rent in respect of each of the two farms held by Mr Pick was to fall due on 14th April. He was concerned whether he should give notice to terminate one or both tenancies. The requisite notice was one year's notice in writing, expiring on 6th April in any year. If, therefore, Mr Pick wished to bring either tenancy to an end by notice he would have to give that notice before 6th April 1977 so as to expire on 6th April 1978.

Mr Cawthra was not then anxious to recover possession of the farms held by Mr Pick, who had been over many years a good tenant as well as a good farmer. He suggested that Mr Pick might bide his time at least for a few days before coming to a final decision as to relinquishing either or both of his tenancies. In pursuance of this suggestion he proposed that Mr Pick should make out notices in respect of each farm, dated 4th April 1977 to expire on 5th April 1978. This latter date was erroneous as it should have been 6th April, but this slip appears to have passed unnoticed even at the trial and has not been the foundation of any of the many submissions addressed to this court. Mr Cawthra's suggestion was that if by the end of the week (that is by Saturday, 9th April 1977) Mr Pick had resolved to give notice to determine one or both of his tenancies he might then give the notice antedated as proposed and it would be accepted. Mr Cawthra, when cross-examined at the trial, said he was not absolutely certain whether or not late service would invalidate the notice. He said: 'I thought if we agreed delayed service it would be valid.' According to the learned deputy judge's findings, Mr Pick accepted Mr Cawthra's proposals and went away to consider them in relation to his own financial circumstances and prospects.

It seems also that Mr Cawthra promised that if later on Mr Pick's position improved and he wished after all to continue as before then Mr Cawthra would recommend to the landlords that Mr Pick be allowed to retract his notice.

On Thursday, 7th April, Mr Pick returned to Mr Cawthra's office. He took with him two letters. Each bore the date stamp '4th April 1977'.

The first letter read:

> 'Dear Mr Cawthra,
>
> 'Following our conversation this morning, after giving more thought to it, and talking to father about it, I enclose a form of words which I hope you will accept as notice on the Newton Farm. The Welby Farm, I think, I should not give up unless I have to. I need a little more time to work out the implications on that one. Many thanks for your sympathy and understanding.
>
> 'Yours sincerely,
> 'John Pick.'

The second document was a notice in respect of Woodside Farm, the body of it was in these terms:

> 'To the Trustees of the Newton Settlement, the Estate Office, Denton.
>
> 'I, John Shelbourne Pick, tenant of the farm known as Woodside Farm, situate at

Newton, near Sleaford in the County of Lincolnshire hereby give you notice of my intention to terminate my tenancy of the above holding on April 5th 1978. a

'Dated April 4th 1977.

'Signed J S Pick, Woodside Farm, Newton, Sleaford.'

Mr Cawthra inquired whether that notice represented Mr Pick's final decision. Mr Pick said it did. He asked for some grace in regard to the payment of rent due for Woodside Farm on 12th April, and was accorded it. In the event the rent for each of the farms was duly paid by Mr Pick. According to his version of the arrangement between b him and Mr Cawthra the notice to quit should then have been torn up. However this assertion was rejected by the deputy judge and it is unnecessary to consider it further. However, when early in the following August he got a letter from Mr Cawthra the contents of which indicated that his tenancy was regarded as coming to an end, he wrote a reproachful reply. It was dated 12th August 1977 and read thus:

'Dear Mr Cawthra, c

'I am very distressed by your letter received this morning. I cannot believe that you would do this, after 40 years here as loyal tenants, because of a hasty, unnecessary act done without any advice. I was very close to a nervous breakdown at the time, a time of extreme stress the reasons for which I discussed with you, and I must appeal to you not to try to hold me to the consequences of such an irrational action. Perhaps we could discuss the matter. Incidentally, I trust that this will now d be treated reasonably confidentially [and he goes on to say why].'

It is evident from the tone and tenor of this missive that Mr Pick believed that he had given a notice which would be effective to determine his tenancy of Woodside Farm if it was to be taken at its face value. Mr Cawthra's response was that matters had progressed too far to allow the notice to quit to be retracted. e

Thereafter Mr Pick, having procured a copy of that notice, consulted his solicitors. He has since maintained that the purported notice was ineffective and did not determine his tenancy. Accordingly he has asserted a right to remain in possession. Hence the claim for a declaration. Mr Pick's basic contention has been that the purported notice to quit Woodside Farm was not an effective notice because it was not in conformity with the requirements of the tenancy agreement and contravened s 23(1) of the Agricultural f Holdings Act 1948, which I now read:

'A notice to quit an agricultural holding or part of an agricultural holding shall (notwithstanding any provision to the contrary in the contract of tenancy of the holding) be invalid if it purports to terminate the tenancy before the expiration of twelve months from the end of the then current year of tenancy.' g

This is the root of the controversy which was ventilated in the court below. The deputy judge came to the conclusion that the effect of that statutory provision was to vitiate a notice which did not conform to the requirement of being a year's notice expiring on 5th April (sic). The judge regarded the provision as mandatory and as permitting of no contractual relaxation in any circumstances. He dismissed the plaintiff's contention that the arrangement or agreement made between Mr Cawthra and Mr Pick h served to validate the notice as and when served in these terms:

'Finally, as a matter of legal analysis, whereas in this case the tenancy agreement provides for 12 months' notice, I find difficulty in seeing how an arrangement to accept short notice can be treated otherwise than as a variation of the tenancy. If so, it falls within the prohibition in s 23 against contracting out.' j

As I have said, this was the primary issue; but the plaintiffs were not without other resources. Apart from any question of due statutory notice, counsel for the plaintiffs contended on their behalf that a tenant could at any time surrender his interest and if that surrender was accepted the interest would thereupon cease. This contention was rejected on the ground that the parties had not got a surrender in contemplation. The judge said:

> 'I am afraid I cannot accept it because as a matter of fact Mr Pick and Mr Cawthra did not intend to enter into a conditional contract of surrender. Mr Cawthra thought he was accepting late service of a notice under the tenancy agreement. This is made clear by the passage from his evidence which I have set out above: "I thought if we agreed delayed service it would be valid." His requirement that the notice should be dated before 5th April points in that direction. So also does his evidence generally. He told me that he considered that this was going to be a termination of the tenancy in the ordinary way. This is also confirmed by Mr Cawthra's attitude when he had written to Mr Pick the letter dated 10th August 1977 and it had become apparent that Mr Pick did not wish to leave. Mr Cawthra wrote in a letter dated 15th August 1977: "... it would appear that you are now asking for the notice to quit Woodside Farm next Lady Day to be withdrawn." In a letter of 7th September 1977 he wrote that Mr Pick on a certain occasion had not even suggested that he might "be regretting giving his notice." The form of the notice to quit which I have already read indicates a notice to quit under the tenancy agreement. That was also Mr Pick's understanding of the position. I find this to be so on the evidence of what took place on this point at the meeting of 4th April. There is really no dispute about this part of what took place. On this basis the notice falls fairly and squarely within the prohibition in s 23. I realise, however, that what the parties may have said is not conclusive. They are not lawyers. It is the duty of the court to ascertain the legal consequences of what has been done. The name parties give to a transaction may not determine its legal nature. Nevertheless, a contract is a matter of the intention of the parties. In this case I am satisfied that the intention was to give a notice under the tenancy agreement but to accept service of it late. I do not think the court can hold the arrangement to be a contract of surrender. That would be to distort what I find to be the agreement which the parties reached. Moreover, I do not think the court ought to be astute to analyse a transaction so as to bring it outside a statutory provision when the consequence would be (a) to distort the true intention of the parties and (b) to drive a coach and four through the statutory provision. Having reached that conclusion it is unnecessary for me to deal with the questions of law which arose on the basis that the contract was one of surrender.'

In this connection there had arisen also problems as to consideration and whether or not there was a sufficient memorandum in writing to satisfy s 40 of the Law of Property Act 1925, since a surrender involved, if only incidentally, the transfer of an interest in land. As to consideration, counsel for the plaintiffs submitted that mutual promises to forgo existing contractual rights constituted consideration passing from each of the parties related as landlord and tenant. The judge accepted this, but was of the view it did not resolve the problem. Counsel conceded that there was no sufficient memorandum in writing. This appeared to me, as to the other members of this court, a somewhat surprising concession since the notice dated 4th April, and the letter which accompanied it, contained all the essential elements of a memorandum for the purposes of s 40. Counsel asked leave to retract his concession and as it was made in relation to the construction of documents, which is a matter of law, that leave was granted. If, therefore, surrender may provide a solution there is no inhibiting evidential factor. This being so, it is unnecessary to pursue the somewhat desperate proposition, as it seems to me, that there was part performance on the part of the plaintiffs which was sufficient to support their claim to specific performance of the agreement between them and Mr Pick, that he would surrender his tenancy on 5th April 1978. The part performance relied on consisted of acts done by the plaintiffs in relation to collateral matters, such as employing the services of a valuer to arrive at figures for the tenant's interest so as to determine compensation and so on. It was contended that these acts done, not in pursuance of the contract of surrender itself, but in reliance on its having been made and fulfilled came within the concept of acts of part performance as delineated in *Steadman v Steadman* [1974] 2 All ER 977, [1976] AC 536. I do not myself read their Lordships' opinions in that case as enlarging the fundamental concept of acts of part performance. Such acts must still be in furtherance of the contract and not merely a recognition of its existence or its contemplation. However it is unnecessary, in the light of the view I have reached as to the primary issue, to dwell further on this aspect. I content myself by saying that I do not regard the speeches in *Steadman v Steadman* as introducing a radical change in the basic concept of what may be regarded as an act of part performance. It must still necessarily be an act in furtherance of the contract alleged to have been made, although it may not go so far as to amount to the discharge of any primary obligation imposed by it.

Another argument for the plaintiffs was founded on estoppel. In this court it was enlarged so as to take in the subtle ramifications of promissory estoppel. Counsel for the defendant, who appeared before the deputy judge as well as on this appeal, met this with the retort that estoppel cannot aid a party to overcome what was a statutory prohibition. This was indeed the essential theme of the defendant's case in refutation of every contrary argument. It was the simple statement that s 23(1) precluded the efficacy of any notice to quit which was of less than 12 months' duration and that was the end of any argument.

I therefore turn back to the section itself in order to examine its language and to deduce its clear tenor. It is clear that it is designed principally to protect the tenant farmer from peremptory or unduly prejudicial ejectment on the part of the landlord. Nonetheless it serves also to protect a landlord from the abandonment of a tenancy in circumstances which may cause a discontinuity in cultivation or a lapse from proper standards of husbandry. Thus the time for the ending of a tenancy is a matter of common interest both to a landlord and to his tenant. It may suit them both to determine a tenancy without waiting for what may be as long as nearly two years to bring it to an end. No statute could have so absurd an intention as to constrain a landlord and a tenant of an agricultural holding to remain bound in that relationship at a time when neither desires that it should endure. If they are in accord, can it matter whether they demonstrate that accord by an agreement to surrender or an agreement to accept short notice?

I have read s 23(1); the first matter to observe is that the subsection uses the word 'invalid' and not 'unlawful'. Thus there is no penal prohibition; it is simply that provision in the tenancy agreement for a shorter notice than 12 months is nugatory. So also any variation of a tenancy agreement in relation to an agricultural holding which purports to make a shorter period of notice than 12 months effective will fail of its purpose. This produces the situation that there can be no operative provision whereby notice can in prospect be made effective if it is less than 12 months; but a notice is of course a unilateral act available to one party or the other without the ad hoc consent of the party to whom the notice is given. There seems to me to be no impediment created by s 23(1) to the party in receipt of a notice to quit to waive his strict right that the notice should expire on a particular day or that it should be of a particular duration. A contractual provision which inures for the benefit of a party can be waived by that party albeit that his right to that benefit is reinforced by statute. There may be circumstances which might qualify this situation, as where an element of public interest is involved, but in such a case one would expect the statutory provision to speak in terms of illegality (thus: 'It shall be unlawful') rather than of mere invalidity.

I would wish to pay respectful tribute to the careful analysis by the deputy judge; but in my judgment he erred in concluding that as between the landlord and the tenant of an agricultural holding there could not be a waiver of the requisite term of notice. The statutory provisions do not extend to a situation such as that which developed between Mr Cawthra, acting on behalf of the plaintiffs, and Mr Pick. The outcome of their discussions on 4th April and the acceptance by Mr Cawthra of the notice and the accompanying letter handed to him on 7th April was that the plaintiffs effectively waived, as I am of the view that they were entitled to do, the requirements of the tenancy agreement as to the term and the expiry of the notice. The plaintiffs were not precluded from such waiver by s 23(1) of the Agricultural Holdings Act 1948 or in any other way. It follows that in my judgment Mr Pick's tenancy was duly determined as at 5th April 1978, and that the plaintiffs were entitled to the declaration claimed in their writ.

I would allow the appeal and make that declaration in their favour.

BRIGHTMAN LJ. On 7th April 1977, in the circumstances outlined by Shaw LJ, the tenant of Woodside Farm, Newton, handed to the landlords' agent his notice of intention to quit, dated 4th April. Accordingly the length of the notice fell short of one year by a matter of three days. The notice was accompanied by a letter from the tenant to the agent: 'I enclose a form of words which I hope you will accept as notice on the Newton Farm. The Welby Farm, I think, I should not give up unless I have to.' Both the landlords' agent and the tenant fully understood that less than one year's notice was being given. The agent agreed with the tenant that he would accept the notice to quit as a valid notice notwithstanding that the length of the notice was short. The landlords' agent also accepted the notice despite another defect, namely, that the notice did not strictly accord with the tenancy agreement in that the date of termination was expressed to be 5th April and not 6th April (a point which was probably not appreciated by either side, and on which nothing turns). It was the intention of the landlords' agent, and also the intention of the tenant, that the tenancy should end on 5th April 1978 by virtue of the defective notice so given.

The tenant now seeks to resile from the mutually intended consequence of the defective notice to quit. To do so the tenant relies on s 23 of the Agricultural Holdings Act 1948. The question is whether he can lawfully do so. The trial judge held that he could.

Section 23(1) provides that a notice to quit an agricultural holding shall be invalid if it purports to terminate the tenancy before the expiration of 12 months from the end of the then current year of the tenancy. If, for example, an agricultural holding is held on a yearly tenancy which is silent as to the length of notice to quit required to terminate the tenancy, the notice will be invalid if it purports to be less than a 12 months' notice, calculated in the specified manner, although only a 6 months' notice is required at common law. Even if the tenancy agreement specifies that a shorter length of notice may be given, a notice of less than 12 months would still be invalid, because the subsection has effect 'notwithstanding any provision to the contrary in the contract of tenancy of the holding'.

In the instant case the tenant's counsel argued that a notice which is defective because it is short is defective in all circumstances and for all purposes, and is incapable of valid acceptance by the recipient. If a notice served by the tenant is short by a day, but the landlord is content to accept it and so agrees with the tenant, nevertheless the notice is waste paper and the agreement of the parties is valueless. It is no good the tenant saying, 'Please accept this notice as a valid notice to quit although it is short by a day' and the landlord saying, 'I am willing to accept it'. They have to go off to their solicitors and ask for a written agreement to be drawn up to end the tenancy. Such an agreement, says counsel, will be perfectly valid. But not an agreement by the recipient of the notice to accept the notice though defective in length.

Take this extreme case. The landlord serves on his tenant notice to quit. The notice is one day short of the statutory 12 months. The tenant spots the defect and informs the landlord of it, but states that he will accept the notice despite the defect. The tenant intends to emigrate and makes all his plans to leave the country. I will assume that the landlord does not know about the tenant's plans, so as to avoid any complications about estoppel. A day before the notice expires the landlord tells the tenant that the notice to quit was indeed invalid, but that the invalidity was not cured by the landlord's express acceptance of the notice and that the tenant is legally liable for another year's rent and performance of the covenants, or more likely two years having regard to the timing which I have assumed in this extreme example. On the argument put forward by the tenant's counsel, the landlord will have a cast-iron case against his tenant.

I ask myself whether this can possibly be the law. I do not think it can be. What s 23 means is that a short notice to quit is invalid as against the recipient. A tenant is not bound to accept less than the statutory 12 months' notice to quit served by his landlord (nor vice versa) even if the tenancy agreement so provides. If the tenant chooses to do so, he can simply ignore a short notice served on him and resist any attempt by the landlord to recover possession on the strength of it. But if the tenant wishes to do so, he can bind himself to accept it. The parties are entitled to agree that the notice shall be treated in all respects as if it were a notice of the statutory length. If the parties so agree, the tenancy will come to an end on the agreed date by virtue of the defective notice to quit which it is agreed shall be treated as valid. Such an agreement could not effectively be made before a notice to quit is served, because the parties cannot agree that the tenancy shall be capable of being terminated by a short notice. Neither the landlord nor the tenant can bind himself in advance to accept a short notice from the other of them. That would be a 'provision to the contrary' in, or supplemental to, the contract of tenancy and would not be effective. But once an invalid notice has been served, which the recipient is entitled to ignore, I see nothing in s 23 to prohibit an agreement between landlord and tenant that the notice shall be followed by the same consequences as if it were valid.

There is an alternative approach, which in my view is equally tenable. Although in the instant case the notice to quit is invalid qua notice to quit, it contains all the ingredients which are needed to constitute a valid written acceptance on 7th April of the oral offer made on 4th April by the landlords' agent, or (if this is the correct interpretation of the events) a valid written offer on 7th April which the landlords' agent accepted orally on the same day. The difference between the two interpretations is of no moment because the legal consequences are the same. On the assumption that the latter interpretation is correct, the defective notice was an expression of the intention, and therefore of the willingness, of the tenant that the tenancy agreement should terminate on 5th April 1978, which intention the tenant communicated to the landlords' agent in the hope or expectation that the agent would accede thereto. The agent did accede thereto, as a result of which there was consensus ad idem between tenant and agent that the tenancy should end on 5th April 1978. Such a course of dealing seems to me on analysis to be indistinguishable in any relevant respect from an offer by the tenant to terminate the tenancy on 5th April 1978, which offer is accepted by the landlords. Such an agreement is clearly outside s 23.

I find support for this approach in the judgment of Bayley J in *Johnstone v Hudlestone*, (1825) 4 B & C 922 at 935, 107 ER 1302 at 1307 to which Buckley LJ invited counsel's attention during the course of the argument.

For myself, I do not mind which way the case is put and I doubt whether there is any substantial difference between the two interpretations of the events.

I would allow the appeal for the reasons which I have endeavoured to express.

BUCKLEY LJ. The Agricultural Holdings Act 1948, s 23 is clearly designed to protect an agricultural tenant against eviction from his holding against his will by shorter notice than the section prescribes. It may also confer advantages on the landlord by ensuring that he will receive at least 12 months' notice from the tenant of termination of the tenancy. It does not, like ss 23 and 24 of the Landlord and Tenant Act 1954, provide that a tenancy shall not come to an end except by being terminated in accordance with the provisions of the Act. It does not, in my judgment, preclude determination of an agricultural tenancy on shorter notice than the 1948 Act requires if both parties agree to this. Counsel for Mr Pick concedes, rightly in my view, that the parties to an agricultural tenancy can bring the tenancy to an end by an agreement that the tenant shall surrender the tenancy to the landlord forthwith or by an agreement that the tenancy shall come to an end at some future date which is less remote than the earliest date at which it could be brought to an end by a notice to quit in accordance with the section.

In a case which is unregulated by any statutory provision, if a tenant gives notice to quit in circumstances which make the notice ineffective (perhaps because it is too short or because it is given for the wrong day) the landlord can, if he chooses, agree to accept the notice as valid notwithstanding the defect in it: he can waive his right to rely on the defect. If he does so in a manner which is legally binding, the notice will take effect as if it were not defective. There is, in my opinion, nothing in s 23 of the 1948 Act to prevent the parties to an agricultural tenancy from waiving any defect in a notice to quit, including a failure to comply with the requirements of the section itself.

It is, in my opinion, clear on the evidence that both Mr Cawthra and Mr Pick thought that the notice to quit handed by Mr Pick to Mr Cawthra on 7th April 1977 was an effective notice, notwithstanding that it was a day late, because Mr Cawthra on the landlords' behalf agreed to accept it as effective. Mr Cawthra in evidence said that he had had some doubts about this, but the judge found that Mr Cawthra believed that the notice would terminate the tenancy. What then occurred cannot, in my judgment, have constituted a surrender of the tenancy, for it is well settled that a tenancy cannot be surrendered in futuro. I agree with the judge that in the circumstances of this case one could not find that there was an agreement for a future surrender of the tenancy. An agreement to surrender a term or to terminate the relation of landlord and tenant on a particular date and an effective notice to terminate the tenancy on that date may have the same legal effect, but they are different transactions; one operates bilaterally by way of contract, the other unilaterally by setting a term to a contract (viz the tenancy) in exercise of a power under that contract.

A contract to render an existing defective notice to quit effective by waiving the defect is not, in my view, a contract to vary the tenancy agreement. An agricultural tenancy could not, consistently with s 23, be modified by agreement between the parties in such a way that either party to it could terminate it by a notice to quit which did not accord with the terms of the section. Such an agreement would conflict with the words of the section which are within brackets. But it does not follow from this that, when a notice to quit has been given which fails to satisfy the requirements of the section, the parties cannot effectually agree that, notwithstanding the defect in the notice, it shall take effect as though it were a valid notice. Such an agreement would not, in my opinion, conflict with any part of the section. It would not alter any of the terms of the tenancy agreement. Its effect is that the parties agree to the tenancy coming to an end on the date specified in the notice, subject to which the tenancy remains in full force and effect. So viewed, and in my opinion rightly so viewed, the agreement comes within counsel's concession.

I therefore agree with the judge that in the present case the intention of the parties was that Mr Pick should give notice under the tenancy agreement and that consequently the acceptance by Mr Cawthra of late service of the notice did not give rise to a contract for the surrender of the tenancy. With deference, however, I do not agree with him that the agreement to accept short notice involved a variation of the tenancy falling within the prohibition in s 23 against contracting out of the section. In my judgment, Mr Cawthra's agreement on the landlord's behalf on 7th April 1977 to accept the notice to quit as a valid notice effectually determining the tenancy on 5th April 1978 had the effect of a binding waiver of any defect in the notice and of a binding agreement that the tenancy should accordingly come to an end on 5th April 1978. Such waiver and such agreement did not, in my judgment, conflict with s 23. It is not contended that, if that transaction can legally take effect, it was not contractually binding and supported by mutual consideration. It is consequently, in my judgment, binding on Mr Pick.

For these reasons and for those contained in the judgments already delivered, with which I agree, I would consequently allow this appeal.

Appeal allowed. Leave to appeal to the House of Lords refused.

Solicitors: *Dawson & Co* (for the plaintiffs); *Roythorne & Co*, Spalding (for Mr Pick.)

Diana Brahams Barrister.

Brown (Inspector of Taxes) v Burnley Football and Athletic Co Ltd a

CHANCERY DIVISION
VINELOTT J
28th, 29th FEBRUARY, 3rd MARCH 1980 b

Income tax – Deduction in computing profits – Capital or revenue expenditure – Repairs – Stand for spectators in football stadium replaced with new stand – Whether replacement of stand constituting 'repairs' – Income and Corporation Taxes Act 1970, s 130(d).

Income tax – Capital allowances – Machinery or plant – Plant – Stand for spectators in football stadium – Whether expenditure on new stand expenditure on provision of 'plant' – Finance Act c
1971, s 41.

In 1969 the directors of a football club were advised that a spectators' stand in the club's
stadium was no longer safe. In the following years the stand was demolished and
replaced with a modern concrete stand in almost the same position and of approximately
the same capacity as the old stand at a cost of £209,365. The stadium consisted of the d
playing field with the surrounding stands and terraces and other facilities such as baths,
changing rooms and a car park. The club claimed that the erection of the new stand
constituted 'repairs' of the premises occupied by the club and, accordingly, the
expenditure was an allowable deduction in computing its taxable profits under s 130(*d*)[a]
of the Income and Corporation Taxes Act 1970, or, alternatively, that the expenditure on
the stand was expenditure incurred on the provision of 'plant' within the meaning of s 41 e
of the Finance Act 1971. The Special Commissioners held that the stadium, defined as
the playing field together with the surrounding stands and terraces, was an entity of
which the stand was physically, commercially and functionally an inseparable part, that
the replacement of the old stand represented repairs, and that, accordingly, the
expenditure was an allowable deduction. They rejected the club's claim that the stand
was 'plant' on the ground that the stand was not part of the apparatus with which the f
club carried on its trade. The Crown appealed.

Held – The appeal would be allowed for the following reasons—
(1) Repair was restoration by renewal or replacement of subsidiary parts of a whole.
The premises occupied by the club comprised a number of distinct parts each of which
had its own distinct function. On the facts, the stand was one such part and, accordingly,
its replacement could not be said to be the repair of a larger entity, whether identified as g
the whole of the premises occupied by the club for the purposes of its business or as the
playing field and the surrounding stands and terraces alone (see p 252 *b* to *f* and p 255 *c*
d and *f* to p 256 *a*, post); dictum of Buckley LJ in *Lurcott v Wakely & Wheeler* [1911–13]
All ER Rep at 49 followed.
(2) The stand was not 'plant' since it did not perform any function, whether passively
or actively, in the actual processes which constituted the club's trade, and, accordingly, h
the expenditure on the erection of the stand was not capital expenditure on the provision
of 'plant' within s 41 of the 1971 Act (see p 256 *h*, post).

Notes
For what constitutes repairs, see 23 Halsbury's Laws (4th Edn) para 322, and for cases on
the subject, see 28(1) Digest (Reissue) 169–171, 515–520. j
For allowances for machinery and plant, see 23 Halsbury's Laws (4th Edn) para 416, and for cases on the meaning of 'plant', see 28(1) Digest (Reissue) 214–216, 637–643.
For the Income and Corporation Taxes Act 1970, s 130, see 33 Halsbury's Statutes (3rd Edn) 182.
For the Finance Act 1971, s 41, see 41 ibid 1459.

a Section 130, so far as material, is set out at p 251 *c*, post

Cases referred to in judgment

a *Hodgins (Inspector of Taxes) v Plunder & Pollak (Ireland) Ltd* [1957] IR 58, CA.
Inland Revenue Comrs v Barclay, Curle & Co Ltd [1969] 1 All ER 732, [1969] 1 WLR 675, 45 Tax Cas 221, [1969] Lloyd's Rep 169, 48 ATC 17, [1969] TR 21, [1969] RVR 102, 1969 SLT 122, HL, 28(1) Digest (Reissue) 465, *1676*.
Jones (Samuel) & Co (Devonvale) Ltd v Inland Revenue Comrs 1952 SC 94, 32 Tax Cas 513, 1952 SLT 144, 30 ATC 412, [1951] TR 411, 28(1) Digest (Reissue) 191, *591*.
b *Lurcott v Wakely & Wheeler* [1911] 1 KB 905, [1911–13] All ER Rep 41, 80 LJKB 713, 104 LT 290, CA, 31(2) Digest (Reissue) 622, *5087*.
Margrett (Inspector of Taxes) v Lowestoft Water & Gas Co (1935) 19 Tax Cas 481, 28(1) Digest (Reissue) 215, *640*.
O'Grady (Inspector of Taxes) v Bullcroft Main Collieries Ltd, O'Grady (Inspector of Taxes) v Markham Main Colliery Ltd (1932) 17 Tax Cas 93, 28(1) Digest (Reissue) 184, *559*.
c *Phillips (Inspector of Taxes) v Whieldon Sanitary Potteries Ltd* (1952) 33 Tax Cas 213, 31 ATC 82, [1952] TR 113, 45 R & IT 269, 28(1) Digest (Reissue) 169, *516*.
Regent Oil Co Ltd v Strick, Regent Oil Co Ltd v Inland Revenue Comrs [1965] 3 All ER 174, [1966] AC 295, [1965] 3 WLR 636, 43 Tax Cas 1, 44 ATC 264, [1965] TR 277, HL, 28(1) Digest (Reissue) 183, *552*.
Van den Berghs Ltd v Clark (Inspector of Taxes) [1935] AC 431, [1935] All ER Rep 874, 19
d Tax Cas 390, 104 LJKB 343, 153 LT 171, HL, 28(1) Digest (Reissue) 185, *564*.
Whimster & Co v Inland Revenue Comrs 1926 SC 20, 12 Tax Cas 813, 28(1) Digest (Reissue) 600, **1484*.
Wynne-Jones (Inspector of Taxes) v Bedale Auction Ltd [1977] STC 50, [1977] TR 293.

Cases also cited

e *Conn (Inspector of Taxes) v Robins Brothers Ltd* (1966) 43 Tax Cas 266.
Lawrie (William P) v Inland Revenue Comrs 1952 SC 394, 34 Tax Cas 20.
Rhodesia Railways Ltd v Bechuanaland Income Tax Collector [1933] AC 368, PC.
St John's School (Mountford and Knibbs) v Ward (Inspector of Taxes) [1975] STC 7, 49 Tax Cas 524.
Yarmouth v France (1887) 19 QBD 647.

f

Case stated

1. At a hearing by the Commissioners for the Special Purposes of the Income Tax Acts which took place in Manchester on 24th and 25th July 1978 the Burnley Football and Athletic Co Ltd ('the club') appealed against an assessment to corporation tax for the accounting period to 31st March 1974 in the sum of £100. It was, however, agreed
g between the parties that in any event the assessment fell to be discharged and that the question in issue was the amount of the loss which the club was entitled to carry forward on a claim made under s 177(1) of the Income and Corporation Taxes Act 1970. The hearing proceeded on that basis.

2. Shortly put the question for decision was whether expenditure on replacing a stand on the club's football ground was allowable expenditure in computing the club's taxable
h profits or allowable losses or must be regarded as non-deductible capital expenditure.

[Paragraphs 3 and 4 listed the witnesses who gave evidence and the documents proved or admitted before the commissioners.]

5. (i) The relevant facts as found by the commissioners on the basis of the evidence agreed or adduced before them are set out in para 9(1) to (5) below. (ii) By way of assistance to the court the commissioners added the following observations on the facts
j as so set out including observations advanced by the parties: (a) *Paragraph* 9(2). To the comment that the new stand was designed to take seats and seats were fitted may be added the comment that the stand would have been unsuitable for use by standing spectators. The seats would have been useless without the stand. (b) *Paragraph* 9(3). To the description of the different parts of the stadium may be added the comment that normally spectators are not permitted to move from one part of the ground to another but there are means of access for officials. (c) *Paragraph* 9(13). With regard to the reference under (a) to the cost of the stadium it may be noted that in the accounts the

'Pavilions, Stands and Property' were included in the balance sheet at cost £414,938 plus
additions during the year of £75,120, £490,058 in total. This figure would not include a
the cost of the new stand which was shown as 'Replacement of Brunshaw Road Stand
£209,365' in the income and expenditure account. The report of the directors included
a note to the effect that: 'In view of the specialised nature of the Land and Buildings at
Turf Moor, Burnley, (and elsewhere) the Directors are not able to place a market value on
these assets.'

6. The contentions advanced by counsel for the club are summarised in para 9(6) and b
(7) below.

7. The contentions advanced by the inspector on behalf of the Crown are summarised
in para 9(8), (9) and (10) below.

8. Cases cited to the commissioners in the course of argument included: *Dixon
(Inspector of Taxes) v Fitch's Garage Ltd* [1975] 3 All ER 455, [1976] 1 WLR 215, [1975]
STC 480; *Hodgins (Inspector of Taxes) v Plunder & Pollak (Ireland) Ltd* [1957] IR 58; *Inland* c
Revenue Comrs v Barclay Curle & Co Ltd [1969] 1 All ER 732, [1969] 1 WLR 675, 45 Tax
Cas 221, HL; *Jones (Samuel) & Co (Devonvale) Ltd v Inland Revenue Comrs* 1952 SC 94, 32
Tax Cas 513; *Lurcott v Wakely & Wheeler* [1911] 1 KB 905, [1911–13] All ER Rep 41, CA;
Phillips (Inspector of Taxes) v Whieldon Sanitary Potteries Ltd (1952) 33 Tax Cas 213;
Rhodesia Railways Ltd v Bechuanaland Income Tax Collector [1933] AC 368, PC; *St John's
School (Mountford and Knibbs) v Ward (Inspector of Taxes)* [1975] STC 7, 49 Tax Cas 524; d
Wynne-Jones (Inspector of Taxes) v Bedale Auction Ltd [1977] STC 50; *Yarmouth v France*
(1887) 19 QBD 647.

9. The commissioners who heard the appeal took time to consider their decision and
gave it in writing on 14th August 1978 as follows:

'1. In 1969 the Directors of the Burnley Football & Athletic Co Ltd, (the Club),
were advised by their architect, Mr James Parker, that the Brunshaw Road stand on e
the Club's football ground at Turf Moor could no longer be regarded as safe. The
stand which was a covered stand of traditional type, had been built in 1912. The
roof was supported at the back by a brick wall and at the front by steel stanchions.
Mr Parker had observed that the roof trusses were becoming distorted and that
cracks were appearing in the brick wall. He suspected trouble at the base of the
stanchions. Subsequent investigation showed his suspicions to be well founded: the f
stanchions were badly corroded. Mr Parker's advice to the Directors was that the
only course to adopt with regard to the stand was to demolish it. In due course Mr
Parker supervised the demolition of the stand.

'2. In 1972 the Directors engaged Mr A D Jenkins' firm [a firm of chartered
architects] to design a replacement stand. Initially the instructions were simply to
design a stand to take the place of the Brunshaw Road Stand which had been g
demolished. At a later stage a building was designed to fit in at the back of and
partly under the stand. Eventually this building housed a directors' suite, office
accommodation and a social club. But the stand itself was described by Mr Jenkins
as a very simple, straightforward stand. It was of modern design. The stanchions
supporting the roof were constructed of reinforced concrete and the terracing units,
designed to take seats, of precast concrete. Under safety and fire regulations a h
replacement stand constructed of steel and timber would not have been
permitted. The old stand had been sited further back from the playing field and
closer to Brunshaw Road. Between the stand and the field there had been concrete
terraces for standing spectators. These terraces went when the replacement stand
was erected. A recent report had drawn attention to the need to provide a safety
reservoir area, space in the open air where people could go in an emergency if it j
became necessary to empty the stand in a hurry. Accordingly the new stand was
closer to the field leaving a space between the stand and Brunshaw Road. Because
the stand was closer to the field and the pitch of the terracing within the stand
steeper than in the old stand, the new stand was lower than the old but of
approximately the same length. The old stand provided seats of a kind for 3,455
spectators. The instruction given to Mr Jenkins' firm was to produce a new stand
with seats for approximately 3,000 spectators. In fact, the new stand provided seats

for 3,162 spectators. The stand was designed to take seats and seats were fitted. It was a matter agreed between the parties to this appeal that for tax purposes these seats would in any event be regarded as "plant" qualifying for capital allowances.

'3. On the side of the playing field opposite to the Brunshaw Road stand are concreted terraces built on an embankment with a roof over. At one end of the playing field is the Cricket Field stand, providing seats for 4,419 spectators, which was completed in 1969. At the other end are open terraces for standing spectators. The covered terraces opposite the Brunshaw Road stand and the open terraces at the end of the playing field opposite the Cricket Field stand can accommodate approximately 28,000 to 30,000 standing spectators so that the capacity of the Turf Moor football ground is of the order of 37,000. Different charges are made for access to the different spectator areas, £1·20 to an adult for admission to the terraces, £2·20 to an adult for a seat in the Cricket Field stand, and £2·90 for a seat in the Brunshaw Road stand. Separate entrances are provided to each part. A part of the terraces on the side of the playing field opposite the Brunshaw Road stand is reserved and fenced off for the supporters of visiting teams.

'4. Dr R D Iven, a director of the Club for fifteen years and the Club Doctor for thirty, told in evidence of the effect on the Club's fortunes of the loss of the Brunshaw Road stand for two and a half seasons, the period during which the demolition of the old stand and the construction of the replacement stand was taking place. He regarded this period as the worst ever in his experience of the Club. He described the players as, in effect, losing their bearings when a green hoarding was erected down the side of the playing field where the stand had been. It was during this period that the Club's team was relegated to the second division in the Football League. Since the new stand had come into use he reckoned that the Club was holding its own in the matter of gates as compared with other second division clubs. Gates went up and down. Currently the general tendency was for gates to go down. The gate was affected by the standing of a visiting club and by the standing of the Club's own team. Seats were provided in the replacement stand because there had been seats in the old stand. The Football League imposed no requirements regarding the provision of stands or seats. Seats were, however, necessary if the Club was to function as a top-rate club. Gates were affected by the facilities provided for spectators at a football ground.

'5. To replace the Brunshaw Road stand cost the Club £209,365.

'6. [Counsel] for the Club, argued that this was a sum expended for repairs of premises occupied for the purposes of the Club's trade within the meaning of paragraph (*d*) of section 130 Income and Corporation Taxes Act 1970 and as such, a sum to be deducted in computing the amount of the Club's taxable profits. He referred us to the familiar passage in the judgment of Buckley LJ in *Lurcott v Wakely & Wheeler* [1911] 1 KB 905 at 924, [1911–13] All ER Rep 41 at 49, where it is pointed out that "Repair is restoration by renewal or replacement of subsidiary parts of a whole". The relevant whole in the present case was, [counsel] argued, the football stadium at Turf Moor, comprising the playing field and the stands and terraces provided for spectators. Just as the replaced chimney in *Samuel Jones & Co (Devonvale) Ltd v Inland Revenue Comrs* 1952 SC 94 was physically, commercially and functionally an inseparable part of an entirety, part of a single profit-earning undertaking, so here the Brunshaw Road stand was physically, commercially and functionally a part of the profit-producing entity, the football stadium at Turf Moor.

'7. If, contrary to his first submission, the replacement of the stand was not covered by the expression "repairs of premises", [counsel] argued that within the meaning of section 41 Finance Act 1971, the cost of replacing the stand must be regarded as capital expenditure on the provision of plant for the purposes of the Club's trade and, as such, qualified for such an allowance as is referred to in that section. (It was common ground that if either of the arguments for the Club succeeded, the effect would be that the £209,365 could be deducted in computing the Club's profits for corporation tax purposes.) On this part of the argument [counsel] referred us to the familiar passage in the judgment of Lindley LJ in

Yarmouth v France (1887) 19 QBD 647 at 658 where "plant" is identified as including
whatever apparatus is used by a business man in carrying on his business, and to the a
decision of the House of Lords in *Inland Revenue Comrs v Barclay Curle & Co Ltd*
[1969] 1 All ER 732, [1969] 1 WLR 675, in which it was held that a structure, in that
case a dry dock, could be plant if it was used in a trade to discharge the function of
plant. The Club's trade is to provide football matches for spectators to watch, and
to provide the spectators with the opportunity to watch them. Seats provided for
spectators must be positioned so that those who watch can see the game. A stand is, b
therefore, not just part of the setting in which the trade is carried on, but is itself
part of the means by which that is supplied to the spectator which it is the trade of
the Club to supply.

'8. [The Crown] argued that the sum expended on the new stand was not a sum
expended for repairs of premises within the meaning of paragraph (*d*) of section 130
Income and Corporation Taxes Act 1970 but it was either capital employed in c
improvements of premises occupied for the purposes of the Club's trade within the
meaning of paragraph (*g*) of that section or was a sum employed as capital in the
trade within the meaning of paragraph (*f*). The costly reconstruction of the stand
had, he argued, left the Club with a new stand, different in size and shape from the
old stand and in a different position. The stand stood in a separate, severable, self-
contained area and was itself the relevant entirety. There was no requirement that d
the Club should provide a stand. It could have continued to trade without replacing
the old stand. The crucial consideration was that at the end of the day the Club had
a new, separate asset, itself a profit-producing entity.

'9. [The Crown] emphasised the relevance of the analysis adopted by Donovan J
in *Phillips v Whieldon Sanitary Potteries Ltd* (1952) 33 Tax Cas 213, when the
conclusion reached on the facts was that it was proper to regard the barrier there in e
question as the premises. He also relied on the alternative conclusion in that case
that the expenditure on the barrier was capital expenditure on account of its size and
importance, and argued that the work of creating the new stand was work of such
size and importance that the cost constituted capital expenditure.

'10. As to the alternative possibility that the new stand was plant [the Crown]
argued that the stand was simply part of the setting in which the Club's trade was f
carried on, not apparatus with which it was carried on. Like the laboratory and the
gymnasium in *St John's School (Mountford and Knibbs) v Ward (Inspector of Taxes)*
[1975] STC 7, which were held to be buildings with no function to perform other
than to shelter the persons who were being educated inside, the stand was simply a
structure in which spectators could be housed while watching a football match.
Like the canopy over the petrol pumps in *Dixon (Inspector of Taxes) v Fitch's Garage* g
Ltd [1975] 3 All ER 455, [1976] 1 WLR 215, which merely made the business of
supplying petrol more comfortable for attendants and motorists, so the stand merely
provided shelter and comfort for spectators. It was an amenity, not an item of
functional apparatus.

'11. We were referred to a number of other cases in addition to those already
mentioned. We noted with respectful sympathy the comment of Foster J in *Wynne-* h
Jones (Inspector of Taxes) v Bedale Auction Ltd [1977] STC 50, that it is difficult, if not
impossible, to spell out any one test from the cases. Support can, however, in our
view, be found for these relevant propositions: 1. Each case has to be decided on its
own particular facts: eg the *Whieldon Sanitary Potteries* case and the *Bedale Auction*
case. 2. Whether work done represents "repairs" turns on identifying "the entirety":
the *Samuel Jones* case and the *Whieldon Sanitary Potteries* case. 3. What constitutes j
"the entirety" is a commercial and business problem. Is there a single profit-earning
undertaking, a single profit-earning entity? See the *Samuel Jones* case 1952 SC 94 at
100 and *Hodgins (Inspector of Taxes) v Plunder & Pollak (Ireland) Ltd* [1957] IR 58 at
70–71. 4. The replacement of a subsidiary unit will be a repair in relation to the
whole profit-earning entity unless what is done goes beyond being the mere
replacement of something that was there before and constitutes an extension and
improvement: see the *Plunder & Pollak* case [1957] IR 58 at 71–72.

'12. On the facts we find the Stadium to have been the profit-earning entity, the premises occupied for the purposes of the Club's trade to which paragraph (*d*) of section 130 refers. The actual playing field together with the surrounding stands and terraces was where, to use a colloquialism, it all happened: the spectators paid their money to occupy the stands and terraces so that they might watch the players on the field and, as spectators and supporters, participate in the matches put on by the Club. We find the stadium, as we have defined it, to be the premises and the stand to be physically, commercially and functionally an inseparable part. On that footing it seems to us that the replacement of the Brunshaw Road stand qualifies as "repairs of premises" and we so hold.

'13. As to the contentions that because of its size and importance the cost of replacing the stand constituted capital expenditure and that because of the differences in the stand the reconstruction amounted to an alteration of and improvement to the premises, the following points appear to us to be relevant: (a) No evidence was before us as to how the cost replacing the Brunshaw Road stand compared with the cost of the whole stadium. What we were told was that the stand occupied approximately 1/15th of the total area occupied by the stadium. (b) The new stand was a substantial structure but its capacity was less than that of the stand which it replaced. (c) Concrete replaced wood and steel but in *Rhodesia Railways Ltd v Bechuanaland Income Tax Collector* [1933] AC 368, once it was established that the renewal of parts of the line constituted repairs, the materials used to renew the parts made no difference—nor the size of the expenditure in relation to the taxpayer's expected income. (d) The position of the stand after the reconstruction was changed but so was the position of the chimney in the *Samuel Jones* case. The critical factor, as it seems to us, is that the new stand discharged precisely the same function as the old. It added nothing to the premises. (e) When the decision to replace the old Brunshaw Road stand was taken, the stand was dangerous. It would not have been safe to use it. Without a stand on the Brunshaw Road side of the playing field, the stadium was patently inadequate and less effective than it had been as premises for the purposes of the Club's trade. Replacement of the stand restored the stadium to its former condition: it left the Club with a stadium the whole of which could be used but it added nothing new to the Club's assets.

'14. On the basis that the cost of replacing the Brunshaw Road stand was expenditure on repairs of premises and that that expenditure, (unlike the expenditure on the buildings erected behind and under the stand), added nothing new to the Club's premises and produced no substantial improvement in the functioning of the stadium as a stadium, the Club's appeal succeeds and the £209,365 falls to be deducted in computing its taxable profits.

'15. It seems to us to follow with reference to the alternative argument that if, as we have found, the stadium constitutes a single entity being premises occupied for the purposes of the Club's trade, the Brunshaw Road stand is essentially part of the setting within which the Club carries on its trade. The stand is not plant functioning, whether passively or actively, in the actual processes which constitute the trade. The football matches take place and the spectators come to watch within, rather than by means of, the stadium.'

10. The commissioners then adjourned the hearing to enable the parties to agree the figures. Figures were agreed between the parties and on 2nd November 1978 the commissioners reduced the assessment to 'nil' accordingly and declared loss relief to be available under s 177 of the Income and Corporation Taxes Act 1970 in the sum of £219,406.

11. The Crown thereupon declared its dissatisfaction therewith as being erroneous in point of law and on 13th November 1978 required the commissioners to state a case for the opinion of the High Court pursuant to s 56 of the Taxes Management Act 1970.

12. The questions of law for the opinion of the court were: (1) did the commissioners make any error of law in holding the replacement of the stand to be a 'repair'?

(2) whether or not the expenditure on replacing the stand was expenditure on a repair, should the commissioners as a matter of law have classified the expenditure on replacing the stand as capital expenditure not allowable as a deduction in computing the profits or losses of the club's trade? and (3) if the expenditure on replacing the stand was capital expenditure was it expenditure on the provision of plant for the purposes of the club's trade so as to qualify for a first year allowance under s 41 of the Finance Act 1971?

J S Hobhouse QC and *Brian Davenport* for the Crown.
Harold Lomas for the club.

Cur adv vult

3rd March. **VINELOTT J** read the following judgment: The taxpayer, the Burnley Football and Athletic Co Ltd ('the club'), is one of the oldest proprietary football clubs in this country. The company was incorporated in 1897. Its football ground, which is known as Turf Moor Football Ground, adjoins Brunshaw Road in Burnley. In 1912 a covered stand was built backing onto Brunshaw Road. In front were open concrete terraces for standing spectators which fronted onto the side of the football pitch. Opposite, on the other side of the pitch, were covered concrete terraces also for standing spectators. A spectator seated in the Brunshaw Road stand immediately before its demolition, and facing the pitch, would have seen on his left, running across the goalmouth end of the pitch, another stand which was then nearing completion and which is now known as the Cricket Field stand. To his right, running behind the other goalmouth, he would have seen further uncovered concrete terraces for standing spectators.

In 1969 it was found that the Brunshaw Road stand was dangerous and unsafe. The roof was supported at the back by a brick wall and at the front by steel stanchions. The roof trusses were becoming distorted, and cracks were appearing in the brick wall. Investigations showed that the stanchions were badly corroded. The directors decided to demolish it. It is not clear from the case whether this decision was made before or during the erection of the Cricket Field stand. The old Brunshaw Road stand was demolished towards the end of 1969. The terraces in front of the demolished stand remained in use for some time.

In 1972 a new stand was designed. It was designed to go nearer the football pitch where the concrete terraces stood, thereby leaving a space between the back of the stand and Brunshaw Road which could be used as a 'safety reservoir' for the crowd of spectators in case of emergency. The concrete terraces were therefore removed, and for a time that side of the pitch was bounded by a green-painted hoarding. During this period the club's fortunes declined. It was relegated to the second division, and gates went down. The directors attributed this to the disorientation of players faced by a hoarding where previously there had been home supporters. Be that as it may, in the latter half of 1974 the new stand was erected. The stanchions supporting the roof are made of reinforced concrete, and the roof and terraces are of precast concrete.

After the new stand had been designed the directors decided to make use of the area under, and part of the area at the back of, the stand to house a directors' suite, office accommodation and a social club. However, it is common ground that this addition is not an integral part of the structure of the stand, which could have been built, and indeed was originally designed to be built, without the added building.

The stand was designed to take seats, and seats were fitted. The expense of fitting the seats has been allowed as a deduction for tax purposes on the ground that they are plant qualifying for capital allowances under the Finance Act 1971, s 41. The old stand provided accommodation for 3,455 spectators; the new stand provides accommodation for 3,162. The Cricket Field stand can accommodate 4,419 seated spectators, and the open terraces opposite the Brunshaw Road stand and opposite the Cricket Field stand together accommodate between 28,000 and 30,000 standing spectators. Different charges are of course made for access to different parts of the ground, ranging from £1·20 for access to the open terraces to £2·90 for access to the Brunshaw Road stand.

There are two main questions in this appeal. The first is whether the erection of the
a new stand was a 'repair' of premises occupied by the club. There is a subsidiary question
whether, if it was a repair, the cost of re-erecting the stand was nonetheless of a capital
rather than a revenue nature. The very experienced Special Commissioners decided
these questions in favour of the club. From their decision the Crown appeals. The
second question, which arises only if the erection of the new stand was either not a
'repair' or was a repair which ought to be charged to capital and not to revenue, is
b whether the expenditure was expenditure on the provision of plant for the club's trade,
attracting a 100% first year allowance under s 41 of the 1971 Act.

The first question

Section 130 of the Income and Corporation Taxes Act 1970 provides that in computing
the amount of profits or gains to be charged under Case I or Case II of Sch D—

c

> 'no sum shall be deducted in respect of . . . (*d*) any sum expended for repairs of
> premises occupied . . . for the purposes of the trade, profession or vocation, beyond
> the sum actually expended for those purposes . . . (*g*) any capital employed in
> improvements of premises occupied for the purposes of the trade, profession or
> vocation . . .'

d These provisions operate negatively; that is to say, they are restrictions on an implicit
right to deduct sums expended for repairs, being, of course, sums which were wholly and
exclusively laid out for the purposes of the trade, profession or vocation. The deduction
is not to exceed 'the sum actually expended for those purposes'. The effect of those
words, as I see it, is to limit the deduction to sums actually expended during the relevant
year of assessment and to exclude apportionment of sums subsequently expended but
e attributable to repairs which may have accrued over a period.

The first question is thus whether the erection of the new Brunshaw Road stand was
a 'repair' within para (*d*). In answering this question it is important to bear in mind the
warning given by Lord Reid in a different but analogous context where the question was
whether lump sum premiums given by the Regent Oil Co Ltd to secure its outlets for the
sale of its products (the premiums being paid for the lease of petrol stations to the
f company, which then sublet them to the retailer at a nominal rent) were chargeable to
revenue. In *Regent Oil Co Ltd v Strick (Inspector of Taxes)* [1965] 3 All ER 174 at 178–179,
[1966] AC 295 at 312–313 Lord Reid said:

> 'Whether a particular outlay by a trader can be set against income or must be
> regarded as a capital outlay has proved to be a difficult question. It may be possible
> g to reconcile all the decisions, but it is certainly not possible to reconcile all the
> reasons given for them. I think that much of the difficulty has arisen from taking
> too literally general statements made in earlier cases and seeking to apply them to
> a different kind of case which their authors almost certainly did not have in mind—
> in seeking to treat expressions of judicial opinion as if they were words in an Act of
> Parliament. Moreover a further source of difficulty has been a tendency in some
> h cases to treat some one criterion as paramount and to press it to its logical conclusion
> without proper regard to other factors in the case. The true view appears to me to
> be that stated by LORD MACMILLAN in *Van den Berghs, Ltd.* v. *Clark* ([1935] AC 431 at
> 438, [1935] All ER Rep 874 at 886): "While each case is found to turn on its own
> facts, and no infallible criterion emerges, nevertheless the decisions are useful as
> illustrations and as affording indications of the kind of considerations which may
> j relevantly be borne in mind in approaching the problem." One must, I think,
> always keep in mind the essential nature of the question. The Income Tax Act,
> 1952 requires the balance of profits and gains to be found. So a profit and loss
> account must be prepared setting on one side income receipts and on the other
> expenses properly chargeable against them. In so far as the Act prohibits a particular
> kind of deduction it must receive effect. Beyond that no one has to my knowledge
> questioned the opinion of the Lord President (LORD CLYDE) in *Whimster & Co.* v.
> *Inland Revenue Comrs.* (1926 SC 20 at 25) where, after stating that profit is the

> difference between receipts and expenditure, he said "... the account of profit and loss to be made up for the purpose of ascertaining that difference must be framed consistently with the ordinary principles of commercial accounting, so far as *a* applicable." So it is not surprising that no one test or principle or rule of thumb is paramount. The question is ultimately a question of law for the court, but it is a question which must be answered in light of all the circumstances which it is reasonable to take into account, and the weight which must be given to a particular circumstance in a particular case must depend rather on common sense than on a *b* strict application of any single legal principle.'

Thus decided cases are of value as illustrations of what in other contexts have been found to be within or without the boundary of what can be considered a 'repair' and as reminders of the factors that have been found to assist the court in reaching a conclusion. But no one factor can be isolated and elevated into a governing criterion. Nor can the same weight be given to any one factor equally in all contexts. However, *c* two general observations can be made. First, in the often-cited words of Buckley LJ in *Lurcott v Wakely & Wheeler* [1911] 1 KB 905 at 924, [1911–13] All ER Rep 41 at 49:

> 'Repair is restoration by renewal or replacement of subsidiary parts of a whole. Renewal, as distinguished from repair, is reconstruction of the entirety, meaning by the entirety not necessarily the whole but substantially the whole subject-matter *d* under discussion.'

The second and related observation is that the question 'Is this a work of repair?' prompts the further question 'A repair of what?'; or, as Buckley LJ expressed it, 'What is "the whole subject-matter" under discussion?' In the case of a covenant in a lease it may be possible to identify the whole as the whole of the demised premises. In the context of s 130(*d*) there is no such guide. The paragraph refers to 'repairs of premises occupied', *e* not to 'the premises occupied', for the purposes of the trade. Reference to the cases cited to the Special Commissioners in which the courts have had to consider whether given work was work of repair the cost of which fell to be allowed in computing the profits or losses of the taxpayer's trade illustrates the paramount importance of correctly identifying the whole which is said to have been repaired.

In *O'Grady (Inspector of Taxes) v Bullcroft Main Collieries Ltd* (1932) 17 Tax Cas 93 a *f* chimney which carried away the fumes of the furnace which provided steam for a colliery was replaced by a new and better one. Counsel for the club stressed that the new chimney was an improvement on the old. But that was not the ground, or at least the only ground, on which Rowlatt J decided the case. He said (17 Tax Cas 93 at 102):

> 'This was a factory chimney to which the gases and fumes, and so on, were led by flues and then went up the chimney. It was unsafe and would not do any more. *g* What they did was simply this: They built a new chimney at a little distance away in another place; they put flues to that chimney and then, when it was finished, they switched the gases from the old flues into the new flues and so up the new chimney. I do not think it is possible to regard that as repairing a subsidiary part of the factory. I think it is simply having a new one. And they had them both. Perhaps they pulled down the old one; perhaps they kept it, because they thought *h* it was an artistic thing to look at. There is no accounting for tastes in manufacturing circles. Anyhow, they simply built a new chimney and started to use that one instead of the old one. I think the chimney is the entirety here and they simply renewed it.'

The decision of the Court of Session in *Samuel Jones & Co (Devonvale) Ltd v Inland* *j* *Revenue Comrs* 1952 SC 94 stands in sharp contrast. There the taxpayer company carried on the business of processing paper in a factory. A chimney which carried away the fumes from furnaces which heated boilers which in turn produced steam for the factory became unsafe and had to be renewed. To avoid interruption in the work of the factory a new chimney was built while the old remained in use. But both the old and new chimneys were part of the structure of the main factory block. The commissioners found ((1951) 32 Tax Cas 513 at 514): 'Seen from inside the building, the bottom part of

the chimney resembles a pillar with the roof running into its sides.' The commissioners
a held that they were bound by the decision of Rowlatt J to hold that the construction of the new chimney was not a repair. In reviewing that decision the Lord President of the Court of Session (Lord Cooper) said (1952 SC 94 at 100):

> 'It is no part of our duty to review the decision of Rowlatt, J., as applied to the facts in the *O'Grady* case, but, so far as this case is concerned, the facts seem to me to demonstrate beyond a doubt that the chimney with which we are concerned is
> b physically, commercially and functionally an inseparable part of an "entirety", which is the factory. It is quite impossible to describe this chimney as being in the words of Rowlatt, J., the "entirety" with which we are concerned. It is doubtless an indispensable part of the factory, doubtless an integral part, but none the less a subsidiary part, and one of many subsidiary parts, of a single industrial profit-earning undertaking.'

c

In *Phillips (Inspector of Taxes) v Whieldon Sanitary Potteries Ltd* (1952) 33 Tax Cas 213 a factory where pottery was manufactured ran alongside a canal. Originally, the factory had been separated from the canal by an embankment, but as a result of subsidence due to underground coal working the embankment sank below the level of the canal. To prevent water seeping into the factory a new barrier was built on the site of the old
d embankment. Donovan J, reversing the decision of the General Commissioners, held that the building of the barrier was not a work of repair. He said (33 Tax Cas 213 at 219):

> 'In my judgment, the "premises" for the purpose of Rule 3(*d*) [of the rules applicable to Sch D, Cases I and II] may sometimes be the whole of the trader's business premises and may sometimes be a specific building forming part of those
> e premises. Thus, if a factory window were blown out and had to be repaired, it would be obviously wrong to argue that as the entirety of the window had been restored it was not a repair to the premises. In such a case the "premises" would be the entire factory, in relation to which the window would be a repair and nothing else. But if, for example, a retort house in a gasworks was destroyed and had to be rebuilt, one would hardly call that a repair to the gasworks. The size of the retort
> f house would compel one to regard that as the premises for the purpose of Rule 3(*d*); and since it had been replaced in full it could not be said to have been repaired. These examples illustrate what I think is the truth, that there is no one line of approach to the problem which is exclusively correct. In some cases it will be right to regard the premises as the entire factory, and in others as some part of the factory. Whichever alternative is the right one to adopt will depend upon the facts
> g of the particular case. Rowlatt, J., took the view in the *O'Grady* case that he must regard the chimney itself as the premises, or, as he described it, the "entirety", and I would respectfully agree with him.'

Then, having referred to the decision of the Court of Session in *Samuel Jones & Co (Devonvale) v Inland Revenue Comrs*, he said (33 Tax Cas 213 at 219):

> h 'In the case now before me [counsel], for the Respondent Company, used the Scottish decision in this way. He says the Commissioners were entitled to regard the factory premises as a whole and must be taken to have done so. On that view, the new barrier was simply a repair to the factory and an allowance of the cost is due under Rule 3(*d*) . . . For myself, I cannot accede to the argument and, indeed, it is difficult to detect its limits. Why, for example, should the retort house in a
> j gasworks not be regarded as part of the premises constituting the entire gasworks, so that the replacement of the retort house would simply be a repair of the gasworks? The only answer suggested is: "Well, that would be an obvious case of something amounting to more than a mere repair." So, I think, is the present case. Having regard to the size and importance of the new barrier in relation to the factory as a whole, I think it is proper to regard the barrier itself as the premises for the purpose of Rule 3(*d*) and as the barrier is a new one I cannot regard it as a repair to the old.'

In *Hodgins v Plunder & Pollak (Ireland) Ltd* [1957] IR 58 the taxpayer company carried on business as leather manufacturers and tanners in a factory within the curtilage of which was a weigh-house which contained machinery for weighing vehicles. The building housing the machinery was larger than needed for that purpose, and the remainder was used as a store. The building having been damaged in a storm, it was demolished. A new store was erected elsewhere in the factory. A smaller structure was built to house the instruments used for weighing the vehicles. In the court of first instance Maguire J reached the conclusion that the erection of the latter building was a work of repair on the ground that the weighbridge itself plus the ramp leading to it plus the instruments and the building housing them were part of a whole which had been repaired in the way I have described. In the Court of Appeal Kingsmill Moore J treated the factory as an entire profit-earning entity. He said ([1957] IR 58 at 71):

> 'In a big undertaking there will be a necessity to do minor repairs every year and also a recurrent necessity to replace units which have fallen into such a state of age or dilapidation that patching is no longer economical. The profit-earning entity is the whole of the premises taken together, and the replacement of a unit, even if such a unit be a separate building, must be viewed in relation to the profit-earning entity.'

There is one other case I should mention as it is referred to in the case. In *Wynne-Jones (Inspector of Taxes) v Bedale Auction Ltd* [1977] STC 50 the taxpayer company carried on business as auctioneers of cattle. It purchased an auction mart comprising livestock pens, stalls, a small office building and a cattle ring. The ring was small in area (1,820 square feet) compared with the whole (some 23,000 square feet), and was largely rebuilt. A roof with a ventilation system was put over the entire ring, which had previously been partly open. Foster J rejected an argument that the whole property occupied by the taxpayer company had been repaired. He said ([1977] STC 50 at 59):

> 'In my judgment, each case must turn on its own facts and no exhaustive test can be found to assist the court. I find the idea that one can have premises within premises a difficult one, though it has behind it the weighty views of both Rowlatt J ((1932) 17 Tax Cas 93) and Donovan J ((1952) 33 Tax Cas 213) judges of the highest repute, particularly in tax matters. I am forced into saying in this case that the ring itself must be considered the premises, for if I take the mart as a whole the ring is the nerve centre where the whole of the business of buying and selling takes place and all the rest of the mart is only ancillary to the ring, permitting the transport and movement of animals to the ring and their exit and removal after the auction. I do not think that the conclusion of the commissioners that the ring, though an integral part, is a subsidiary part of the mart can be sustained.'

In the present case the Special Commissioners reached the conclusion that the erection of the new Brunshaw Road stand was a repair by the following steps. In para 9(11) of the stated case they set out four 'relevant propositions' which they deduce from the cases to which I have referred. They are as follows: '1. Each case has to be decided on its own particular facts'; and they refer to the *Whieldon* and *Bedale Auction* cases. '2. Whether work done represents "repairs" turns on identifying "the entirety"'; and they refer to the *Samuel Jones* and *Whieldon* cases. '3. What constitutes "the entirety" is a commercial and business problem. Is there a single profit-earning undertaking, a single profit-earning entity?'; and they refer to the *Samuel Jones* and *Hodgins v Plunder & Pollak* cases. '4. The replacement of a subsidiary unit will be a repair in relation to the whole profit-earning entity unless what is done goes beyond being the mere replacement of something that was there before and constitutes an extension and improvement'; and they refer to the *Plunder & Pollak* case.

In para 9(12) they state their conclusion in the following terms:

> 'On the facts we find the Stadium to have been the profit-earning entity, the premises occupied for the purposes of the Club's trade to which paragraph (*d*) of section 130 refers. The actual playing field together with the surrounding stands and terraces was where, to use a colloquialism, it all happened: the spectators paid

> their money to occupy the stands and terraces so that they might watch the players on the field and, as spectators and supporters, participate in the matches put on by the Club. We find the stadium, as we have defined it, to be the premises and the stand to be physically, commercially and functionally an inseparable part. On that footing it seems to us that the replacement of the Brunshaw Road stand qualifies as "repairs of premises" and we so hold.'

The central propositions are that the question whether work is work of repair 'turns' on identifying 'the entirety', and that what constitutes the entirety is a commercial problem to be answered by the test: is there a single profit-earning undertaking, a single profit-earning entity? The language in which this test is framed clearly reflects the language used by Lord Cooper in the *Samuel Jones* case 1952 SC 94 at 100, where he said that the chimney there in question was 'physically, commercially and functionally an inseparable part of an "entirety"', and part of 'a single industrial profit-earning undertaking'.

But, in my judgment, in elevating this observation into a general principle capable of being applied to the solution of the question whether given work is a replacement of a part of a whole and so a repair (so long as it does not go beyond mere replacement and constitute an extension and improvement), the Special Commissioners erred. A single profit-earning undertaking or entity may be carried on in premises which consist of several distinct parts. An example will be found in the gas retort instanced in the passage from the judgment of Donovan J in *Phillips v Whieldon Sanitary Potteries Ltd* which I have cited. The profit-earning undertaking may even be carried on in premises which are geographically separate. For instance, the manufacture of a specialised steel product might require the production of high-grade steel in one building, the process of producing the specialised product being carried on in a factory some distance away. The question 'What is the whole, the entirety, the entity which is said to have been repaired by replacement of part?' cannot be answered by any one yardstick or rule of thumb. It must, in the words of Lord Reid, 'be answered in the light of all the circumstances which it is reasonable to take into account' (see *Regent Oil Co Ltd v Strick* [1965] 3 All ER 174 at 179, [1966] AC 295 at 313).

Application of the principle enunciated in para 9(11)(3.) of the case would not, as it seems to me, have pointed to the playing field and the surrounding stands and terraces which the Special Commissioners take in para 9(12) to constitute the 'entity' or 'premises' which were repaired. The profit-earning undertaking comprehended also a car park, changing rooms, baths and, more remotely, a gymnasium. All were, as I see it, equally part of the 'profit-earning entity'. Counsel for the club submitted that in para 9(12) the Special Commissioners departed from the test laid down in para 9(11)(3.) and applied a different and, he said, the correct test. There, he said, the whole was identified as those parts of the profit-earning entity which were in use when the ground was fulfilling its primary function of providing a professional football match for the entertainment of spectators, for whose admission a charge had been made. But in my judgment that test is equally artificial and remote from the facts. It may be that, for instance, a sports stadium designed and built as a single building would constitute separate 'premises', and that replacement or renewal of a part, more or less extensive, would be a repair of the premises as a whole, though it is not easy to see why, in such a case, a car park, baths and changing rooms forming an integral part of the structure should not be as much part of the stadium as the spectators' seats and the ground itself. However, in the present case the premises occupied by the club comprised a number of distinct structures. It was not designed, far less built, in accordance with a single plan. For instance, the Cricket Field stand was added in 1969. Each separate part of the whole had its own distinct function. No part, except the football pitch itself, was necessary to the performance of the club's central activity of arranging professional football matches as a spectacle. The club could have continued its activities without affording covered seats for those of its supporters prepared to pay for that amenity. It could have leased a part of its ground to another prepared to afford that or other amenities, as I believe is sometimes done by racecourse owners.

In my judgment, therefore, the erection of the new Brunshaw Road stand was not a 'repair' of any larger entity, whether identified as the whole premises occupied by the *a* club for the purposes of its business or as the field and surrounding stands and terraces alone. As I have said, in reaching the contrary conclusion the Special Commissioners in my judgment placed too much stress on the passages in the judgments of Lord Cooper in *Samuel Jones* and of Kingsmill Moore J in *Plunder & Pollak* which I have cited. In speaking of the chimney as 'physically, commercially and functionally . . . part of an "entirety", which is the factory', Lord Cooper should not be taken as laying down a *b* principle that the renewal of part of what can be seen as physically, commercially and functionally a profit-earning whole is prima facie a repair. He was concerned to emphasise that on the particular facts of that case the chimney was a necessary and integral part of a larger entity which was repaired.

As I have reached the clear conclusion that the erection of the new stand was not a repair, the further question whether, if it had been a repair, it could nonetheless have *c* been expenditure of a capital nature does not arise for decision. It is also a question which can only be asked on the hypothesis, in my judgment false, that the erection of the new stand was a replacement of part of some larger whole. It would I think be undesirable that I should express any opinion whether, if the hypothesis had been well founded, the expenditure would have been expenditure of a revenue or capital nature, having regard to the interval between the erection of the old stand and the erection of the *d* new stand, and to the enduring nature of the new stand.

The second question

Counsel's alternative submission for the club was that the new Brunshaw Road stand was 'plant' attracting a first year allowance. It was, he said, a structure which discharged the function of plant, like the dry dock considered by the House of Lords in *Inland* *e* *Revenue Comrs v Barclay Curle & Co Ltd* [1969] 1 All ER 732, [1969] 1 WLR 675. The function it discharged was, he said, to position spectators so that they could see the game, that being what they had paid their entrance money for. He relied on the fact that the cost of the seats fitted in the new stand had been agreed to be plant, and likened the stand to the water tower in *Margrett (Inspector of Taxes) v Lowestoft Water and Gas Co* (1935) 19 Tax Cas 481, which the majority of their Lordships who heard the appeal in the *Barclay* *f* *Curle* case considered should have been held to have been plant. He stressed that the Special Commissioners had found that the stand would have been unsuitable for use by standing spectators, and that the seats would have been useless without the stand.

I cannot see that any inference can be drawn from these findings of the Special Commissioners, or from the fact that first year allowances have been agreed on the footing that the seats were plant. It is frequently the case that a building is designed and *g* constructed in such a way that it can conveniently accommodate the plant used in a particular trade, and indeed in some cases in such a way that it will be of little value for any other purpose. That does not mean that it is any the less the setting or place where, rather than the means by which, the trade is carried on. In my judgment the Special Commissioners came to the correct conclusion, namely that 'The stand is not plant functioning, whether passively or actively, in the actual processes which constitute the *h* trade. The football matches take place and the spectators come to watch within, rather than by means of, the stadium'.

I think I must allow the appeal.

Appeal allowed.

j

Solicitors: *Solicitor of Inland Revenue*; *John Sutcliffe & Sons*, Burnley (for the club).

Rengan Krishnan Esq Barrister.

a

Port Jackson Stevedoring Pty Ltd v Salmond & Spraggon (Australia) Pty Ltd
The New York Star

b PRIVY COUNCIL
LORD WILBERFORCE, LORD DIPLOCK, LORD FRASER OF TULLYBELTON, LORD SCARMAN AND LORD ROSKILL
12th, 13th, 14th, 15th MAY, 10th JULY 1980

Shipping – Bill of lading – Limitation of liability – Rights of stranger to contract – Bill of lading
c *extending benefit of defences and liabilities conferred thereby to independent contractors employed*
by carrier – Bill of lading also providing that carrier's responsibility terminating as soon as goods left ship's tackle – Goods discharged and stored by stevedore employed by carrier – Goods stolen from stevedore's store – Whether stevedore entitled to benefit of contractual provisions of bill of lading.

Shipping – Bill of lading – Time for bringing claims – Suit barred unless brought within one year
d *after delivery of goods – Fundamental breach of contract – Loss or misdelivery of consignee's goods – Effect on time bar clause – Whether fundamental breach depriving party in breach of benefit of time bar clause – Water Carriage of Goods Act 1936 (Canada), Sch (Hague Rules), art III, r 6.*

A consignment of razor blades was shipped on board a vessel for transhipment from
e Canada to Australia, the relevant bill of lading naming the respondent as consignee. The appellant company commonly acted as stevedore for the carrier at the port of discharge. The bill of lading was expressed to have effect subject to the provisions of the Water Carriage of Goods Act 1936 of Canada, the schedule to which embodied the text of the Hague Rules. Clause 2 of the bill of lading extended the benefit of defences and immunities conferred by the bill on the carrier to independent contractors employed by
f the carrier. Clause 5 provided that the carrier's responsibility terminated as soon as the goods left the ship's tackle at the port of discharge. Clause 8 provided that the consignee should take delivery of the goods from the ship's rail immediately the ship was ready to discharge or else pay demurrage. Clause 17 barred, in terms similar to the time bar in art III, r 6, of the Hague Rules, any action if not brought within one year after the delivery of the goods or the date when the goods should have been delivered. On the
g ship's arrival in Sydney and in accordance with the normal practice in the port, the consignment was discharged from the ship and placed by the stevedore in a shed on the wharf under its control. When the consignee presented the bill of lading the goods were found to have been stolen from the wharf, having been delivered by servants of the stevedore to persons who had no right to receive them. More than a year after the goods should have been delivered, the consignee brought an action in the Supreme Court of
h New South Wales against the stevedore alleging negligence in failing to take proper care of the goods. The trial judge found that the stevedore had been negligent in the care of the goods and that there had been a misdelivery, but he went on to hold that the stevedore had established that it was the agent of the carrier and accordingly cl 17 of the bill of lading afforded it a defence to the action. The Court of Appeal of New South Wales allowed an appeal by the consignee on the ground that there was no proof of
j consideration moving from the stevedore to entitle it to the defences in the bill of lading. The High Court of Australia dismissed an appeal by the stevedore. The stevedore appealed to the Judicial Committee of the Privy Council. At the hearing of the appeal, the consignee contended, as it had in the courts below, (i) that it had not been shown that the carrier had had authority to act on the stevedore's behalf in accepting the bill of lading and that the stevedore could therefore not avail itself of the defences and

immunities in the bill, and (ii) that the stevedore had been in fundamental breach of its obligations as bailee of the goods and that accordingly the bill of lading had ceased to a
have any operation after the goods had passed over the ship's rail.

Held – The stevedore was entitled to claim exemption from liability under cl 17 of the bill of lading, and the appeal would accordingly be allowed, for the following reasons—

(1) Although there was room in each case for evidence as to the precise relationship of carrier and stevedore and the practice at the port of discharge, it was established law that in the normal situation involving the employment of a stevedore by a carrier, commercial b
practice required the stevedore to enjoy the benefit of contractual provisions in the bill of lading. Shippers, carriers and stevedores knew that such immunity was intended; and in principle a search for the factual ingredients required to confer the benefit was unnecessary. In the particular case, agency had been found as a fact and according to established legal principles consideration had been provided by the stevedore (see p 260 *j* to p 261 *g* and p 264 *j*, post); *New Zealand Shipping Co Ltd v A M Satterthwaite & Co Ltd* c
[1974] 1 All ER 1015 explained; dictum of Lord Reid in *Scruttons Ltd v Midland Silicones Ltd* [1962] 1 All ER at 10 considered.

(2) On its true construction it was quite unreal to equate cl 17 of the bill of lading with those provisions which related to the performance of the contract. Clause 17 was a clause which came into operation when contractual performance had become impossible or been given up; it then regulated the manner in which liability for breach of contract was d
to be established. In that respect it was indistinguishable from an arbitration or a forum clause which, it was clearly established, survived a repudiatory breach (see p 262 *b* and *d* to *g* and p 264 *j*, post); *Heyman v Darwins Ltd* [1942] 1 All ER 337 and *Photo Production Ltd v Securicor Transport Ltd* [1980] 1 All ER 556 considered.

(3) Although the terms of the bill of lading provided that the carrier's responsibility should be limited to the part of the transport performed as a carrier and should terminate e
as soon as the goods left the ship's tackle, the contract contemplated that in circumstances where the consignee failed to take delivery ex ship's rail the carrier might continue to have some responsibility for the goods after discharge, cl 5 of the bill of lading attributing that responsibility to the carrier as bailee. If a carrier acted as his own stevedore and himself stacked and stored the goods, he would be liable for them, as bailee, under the contract; and, if he instead employed a third party to discharge, stack and store, that f
person would be acting in the course of the carrier's employment, performing duties which otherwise the carrier would have had to perform under the bill of lading, and so would be entitled to the same immunity as the carrier would have had (see p 264 *b* to *j*, post).

Notes

For the doctrine of privity of contract and the common law exceptions thereto, see 9 g
Halsbury's Laws (4th Edn) paras 329–331, 336–338, 382–384, and for cases on the subject, see 12 Digest (Reissue) 48–56, *237–291*.

For time limits under the Hague Rules for actions for loss of or damage to goods carried by sea, see 35 Halsbury's Laws (3rd Edn) 523, para 750.

For the Hague Rules, art III, r 6, as set out in the schedule to the Carriage of Goods by h
Sea Act 1924, see 31 Halsbury's Statutes (3rd Edn) 529, and as amended by the Brussels Protocol and set out in the schedule to the Carriage of Goods by Sea Act 1971, see 41 ibid 1321.

Cases referred to in judgments

Heyman v Darwins Ltd [1942] 1 All ER 337, [1942] AC 356, 111 LJKB 241, 166 LT 306, HL, 2 Digest (Repl) 492, *435*. j

Keane v Australian Steamships Pty Ltd (1929) 41 CLR 484, [1929] VLR 116, 2 ALT 367, [1929] ALR 81.

New Zealand Shipping Co Ltd v A M Satterthwaite & Co Ltd, The Eurymedon [1974] 1 All ER 1015, [1975] AC 154, [1974] 2 WLR 865, [1974] 1 Lloyd's Rep 534, [1974] 1 NZLR 505, PC, Digest (Cont Vol D) 114, *99a*.

Photo Production Ltd v Securicor Transport Ltd [1980] 1 All ER 556, [1980] 2 WLR 283, HL; *rvsg* [1978] 3 All ER 146, [1978] 1 WLR 856, [1978] 2 Lloyd's Rep 172, CA, Digest (Cont Vol E) 111, *3407a*.

Scruttons Ltd v Midland Silicones Ltd [1962] 1 All ER 1, [1962] AC 446, [1962] 2 WLR 186, [1961] 2 Lloyd's Rep 365, HL, 12 Digest (Reissue) 53, *275*.

Suisse Atlantique Société d'Armement Maritime SA v NV Rotterdamsche Kolen Centrale [1966] 2 All ER 61, [1967] 1 AC 361, [1966] 2 WLR 944, [1966] 1 Lloyd's Rep 529, HL, Digest (Cont Vol B) 642, *2413a*.

Thomas National Transport (Melbourne) Pty Ltd v May & Baker (Australia) Pty Ltd (1966) 115 CLR 353, [1967] ALR 3, 40 ALJR 189, [1966] 2 Lloyd's Rep 347, HC of Aust.

Appeal

Port Jackson Stevedoring Pty Ltd ('the stevedore') appealed pursuant to special leave granted on 15th November 1978 against the judgment of the High Court of Australia (Stephen, Mason, Jacobs and Murphy JJ, Barwick CJ dissenting) dated 3rd April 1978 dismissing an appeal from the Court of Appeal of the Supreme Court of New South Wales (Hutley, Glass and Mahoney JJA) dated 8th October 1976 allowing an appeal by the respondent, Salmond & Spraggon (Australia) Pty Ltd ('the consignee'), from the decision of Sheppard J given on 14th July 1975 in the Supreme Court of New South Wales (Common Law Division, Commercial List) in an action brought in respect of a shipment of 37 cartons of razor blades shipped from St John, New Brunswick, Canada, to Sydney, Australia, the relevant bill of lading providing in cl 1 that 'This Bill of Lading shall have effect subject to the provisions of the Water Carriage of Goods Act 1936 enacted by the Parliament of the Dominion of Canada, and the said Act shall be deemed to be incorporated herein . . .' The facts are set out in the judgment of the Board.

A M Gleeson QC and *B W Rayment* (both of the New South Wales Bar) for the stevedore.
J S Hobhouse QC, Brian Davenport QC and *Jonathan Gaisman* for the consignee.

LORD WILBERFORCE. This is an appeal, by special leave, from a judgment of the High Court of Australia dated 3rd April 1978 which, by a majority, dismissed an appeal from the Court of Appeal of the Supreme Court of New South Wales. That court had allowed an appeal from a decision of Sheppard J sitting in commercial causes by which he dismissed the action.

The action was brought by the respondent ('the consignee') in respect of a consignment of razor blades in 37 cartons, shipped from Canada to Australia on the New York Star, a ship of the Blue Star Line. The relevant bill of lading dated 27th March 1970 was issued in Montreal, Quebec; the port of loading was St John, New Brunswick; and the port of discharge was Sydney. The shipper named in the bill of lading was Schick Safety Razor Co Division of Eversharp of Canada Ltd; the respondent was named as consignee. The bill of lading was issued to the consignor and was transmitted to and accepted by the consignee.

The appellant ('the stevedore') carried on business as stevedore in the port of Sydney; 49% of its capital was owned by Blue Star Line Australia Ltd and it commonly acted as stevedore in Sydney for the Blue Star Line.

The New York Star arrived at Sydney on 10th May 1970. On her arrival (and there was evidence that this was in accordance with the normal practice in the port) the packages of razor blades were discharged from the ship and placed by the stevedore in part of a shed (called 'the dead house') on the wharf which was under its control. Later the goods were stolen from the wharf, having been delivered by servants of the stevedore to persons who had no right to receive them, so that when the consignee presented the bill of lading they were unavailable. The consignee brought this action against the stevedore and against the ship's agent, Joint Cargo Services Pty Ltd, alleging negligence in failing to take proper care of the goods, delivery of the goods to an unauthorised person and non-delivery to the consignee. The action against the ship's agent failed at first instance and has not been the subject of appeal. The trial judge, however, found that the stevedore had been negligent in the care of the goods and that there had been a misdelivery; these findings have not been disputed.

The bill of lading contained, in cl 2, a Himalaya clause (see *Adler v Dickson* [1954] 3 All ER 397, [1955] 1 QB 158) extending the benefit of defences and immunities conferred by the bill of lading on the carrier to independent contractors employed by the carrier, and also, in cl 17, a time bar (similar to that contained in the Hague Rules) barring any action if not brought within one year after the delivery of the goods or the date when the goods should have been delivered; this action was not so brought. These provisions were in substance identical with those considered by this Board in *New Zealand Shipping Co Ltd v Satterthwaite & Co Ltd* [1974] 1 All ER 1015, [1975] AC 154, an appeal from the Court of Appeal in New Zealand. The stevedore relied on these provisions as affording a defence to this action.

It is now necessary to state in detail the issues which were contested, and the decisions which were given in the three courts in Australia.

Before Sheppard J it was contended by the consignee (i) that there had been a fundamental breach by the stevedore of its obligations as bailee of the goods (the 'fundamental breach' point), (ii) that one of the necessary conditions for applying the Himalaya clause had not been satisfied, in that it had not been shown that the carrier had authority to act on the stevedore's behalf in accepting the bill of lading (the 'agency' point), (iii) that the bill of lading ceased to have any operation after the goods passed over the ship's rail (the 'capacity' point). Sheppard J rejected all these contentions, though he found that the necessary agency was established only by ratification. He gave judgment for the stevedore.

In the Court of Appeal the same three contentions were put forward, and were rejected by the court. The court found that the necessary agency was directly established by the evidence, so that reliance on ratification was not necessary. In addition, however, the consignee was given leave to take a fresh point, namely (iv) that there was no proof of consideration moving from the stevedore so as to entitle it to the benefit of defences and immunity clauses in the bill of lading (the 'consideration' point). The Court of Appeal accepted that contention, allowed the appeal and gave judgment for the consignee for $14,684·98 damages.

In the High Court of Australia the 'agency' point and the 'consideration' point were again argued, but rejected by the majority of the court (Barwick CJ, Mason and Jacobs JJ). There was also argument on the 'fundamental breach' point, but this was not dealt with in the judgments. As to the 'capacity' point, senior counsel for the consignee expressly disclaimed reliance on it (not surprisingly since Glass JA in the Court of Appeal had described it as 'without substance') and argument on it was not heard. However, the majority of the court (Barwick CJ dissenting) decided the appeal in favour of the consignee on this point.

Finally, it should be mentioned that the Board's decision in *Satterthwaite's* case was followed without question by the trial judge and by the Court of Appeal. Their Lordships understand that there was no argument in the High Court on the correctness of this decision. However two members of the majority (Stephen and Murphy JJ) expressed disagreement with it.

It was in this situation that their Lordships decided, exceptionally, to grant special leave to appeal to Her Majesty in Council.

It will be seen from the foregoing that the point which calls for decision by their Lordships is the 'capacity' point. This was fully argued by both sides to the appeal. Before dealing with it, their Lordships must briefly state their position on the other points, on which argument was addressed by the consignee.

First, as to the Board's decision in *Satterthwaite's* case. This was a decision, in principle, that the Himalaya clause is capable of conferring on a third person falling within the description 'servant or agent of the Carrier (including every independent contractor from time to time employed by the Carrier)' defences and immunities conferred by the bill of lading on the carrier as if such persons were parties to the contract contained in or evidenced by the bill of lading. But the decision was not merely a decision on this principle, for it was made clear that in fact stevedores employed by the carrier may come within it, and moreover that they normally and typically will do so. It may indeed be said that the significance of *Satterthwaite's* case lay not so much in the establishment of any new legal principle as in the finding that, in the normal situation involving the employment of stevedores by carriers, accepted principles enable and require the stevedore to enjoy the benefit of contractual provisions in the bill of lading. In the words of Mason and Jacobs JJ in the High Court:

> 'When the circumstances described by Lord Reid [sc in *Scruttons Ltd v Midland Silicones Ltd* [1962] 1 All ER 1 at 10, [1962] AC 446 at 474] exist, the stevedore will on the generally accepted principles of the law of contract be entitled to his personal contractual immunity. The importance of [*Satterthwaite's* case] is the manner in which on the bare facts of the case their Lordships were able to discern a contract between the shipper and the stevedore, and, we would add, to do so in a manner which limited the approach to those commercial contexts in which immunity of the stevedore was clearly intended in form and almost certainly known by both the shipper and the stevedore to be intended.'

Although, in each case, there will be room for evidence as to the precise relationship of carrier and stevedore and as to the practice at the relevant port, the decision does not support, and their Lordships would not encourage, a search for fine distinctions which would diminish the general applicability, in the light of established commercial practice, of the principle. As regards its applicability in Australia, their Lordships are content to leave the matter as it was left by the Australian courts, including the High Court. They are the more satisfied to do so in view of the reasoned analysis of the legal principles involved which appears in the judgment of Barwick CJ. Their Lordships find, as Barwick CJ himself declares, this to be in substantial agreement with and indeed to constitute a powerful reinforcement of one of the two possible bases put forward in the Board's judgment.

The applicability of the decision was accepted in their joint judgment by Mason and Jacobs JJ although they reached a decision adverse to the stevedore on the 'capacity' point.

Second, as to the factual ingredients needed to confer on the stevedore the benefit of the contract. From what has already been said it follows that this issue requires no prolonged discussion. Not only is the factual situation in the present case in all respects typical of that which the Board, in *Satterthwaite's* case, thought sufficient to confer that benefit, but each relevant ingredient has, in fact, been found to exist. Agency has been found, as a fact, by all three courts, with only the qualification as regards the judgment of Sheppard J already mentioned. The provision of consideration by the stevedore was held to follow from this Board's decision in *Satterthwaite's* case and in addition was independently justified through Barwick CJ's analysis.

Third, as to 'fundamental breach'. The proposition that exemption clauses may be held inapplicable to certain breaches of contract as a matter of construction of the contract, as held by the House of Lords in *Suisse Atlantique Société d'Armement Maritime SA v NV Rotterdamsche Kolen Centrale* [1966] 2 All ER 61, [1967] 1 AC 361 and *Photo Production Ltd v Securicor Transport Ltd* [1980] 1 All ER 556, [1980] 2 WLR 283, and indorsed in Australia by Windeyer J in *Thomas National Transport (Melbourne) Pty Ltd v May & Baker (Australia) Pty Ltd* (1966) 115 CLR 353 at 376, was not disputed. But counsel for the consignee put forward a special, and ingenious, argument that, because of the fundamental nature of the breach, the stevedore had deprived itself of the benefit of cl 17 of the bill of lading, the time bar clause. A breach of a repudiatory character, which he contended that the breach in question was, entitles the innocent party, unless he waives the breach, to claim to be released from further performance of his obligations under the contract. So far their Lordships of course agree. One of these obligations, counsel proceeded to argue, was to bring any action on the breach within a period of one year, and the innocent party was released from this obligation. An alternative way of putting it was that the bringing of suit within one year was a condition with which the *a* innocent party was obliged to comply; the repudiatory breach discharged this condition. A further point made was that cl 17 applied at most to actions for breach of contract; the stevedore's negligence as bailee, however, gave rise to an action in tort which was not governed by the time bar.

Their Lordships' opinion on these arguments is clear. However adroitly presented, they are unsound, and indeed unreal. Clause 17 is drafted in general and all-embracing *b* terms:

> 'In any event the Carrier and the ship shall be discharged from all liability in respect of loss or damage unless suit is brought within one year after the delivery of the goods or the date when the goods should have been delivered. Suit shall not be deemed brought until jurisdiction shall have been obtained over the Carrier and/or *c* the ship by service of process or by an agreement to appear.'

The reference to delivery of the goods shows clearly that the clause is directed towards the carrier's obligations as bailee of the goods. It cannot be supposed that it admits of a distinction between obligations in contract and liability in tort; 'all liability' means what it says.

Moreover it is quite unreal to equate this clause with those provisions in the contract *d* which relate to performance. It is a clause which comes into operation when contractual performance has become impossible, or has been given up; then, it regulates the manner in which liability for breach of contract is to be established. In this respect their Lordships found it relevantly indistinguishable from an arbitration clause, or a forum clause, which, on clear authority, survive a repudiatory breach (see *Heyman v Darwins Ltd* [1942] 1 All ER 337, [1942] AC 356; *Photo Production Ltd v Securicor Transport Ltd* [1980] *e* 1 All ER 556 at 567, [1980] 2 WLR 283 at 295). Counsel for the consignee appealed for support to some observations by Lord Diplock in *Photo Production Ltd v Securicor Transport Ltd* [1980] 1 All ER 556 at 566–567, [1980] 2 WLR 283 at 294–295, where reference is made to putting an end 'to all primary obligations . . . remaining unperformed'. But these words were never intended to cover such 'obligations', to use Lord Diplock's word, as arise when primary obligations have been put an end to. There then arise, on his *f* Lordship's analysis, secondary obligations which include an obligation to pay monetary compensation. Whether these have been modified by agreement is a matter of construction of the contract. The analysis, indeed, so far from supporting the consignee's argument, is directly opposed to it. Their Lordships are of opinion that, on construction and analysis, cl 17 plainly operates to exclude the consignee's claim.

Their Lordships now deal with the 'capacity' argument. This rather inapposite word *g* has been used, for convenience, in order to indicate the general nature of the submission. More fully, this was that, at the time when the loss occurred, the goods had been discharged and were no longer in the custody of the carrier. Consequently, the stevedore was acting not as an independent contractor employed by the carrier to perform the carrier's obligations under the bill of lading, but as a bailee. His liability, in that capacity, was independent of and not governed by any of the clauses of the *h* contract. This point enables a distinction to be made with *Satterthwaite's* case, for there, since the goods were damaged in the course of discharge, the capacity of the stevedore as a person acting on behalf of the carrier was not contested.

Their Lordships can at this point dispose of one question of fact. It appears to have been the view both of Stephen J and of Mason and Jacobs JJ in the High Court that the stevedore was remunerated for his services in stacking and storing the goods on the *j* wharf by the consignee; this, if correct, might be an argument for finding that it was not, in respect of these matters, acting in the course of employment by the carrier. In fact, however, the evidence, including the actual account, showed that these charges were paid by the ship's agent on behalf of the carrier, thus, if anything, giving rise to an inference the other way. Their Lordships put this matter aside and proceed to deal with the point on the construction of the relevant provisions of the bill of lading.

On its face, the document stated that delivery would be effected 'by the Carrier or his Agents' in exchange for the bill of lading, and the preamble provided that the goods were—

> 'to be transported subject to all the terms of this bill of lading . . . to the port of discharge . . . and there, to be delivered or transhipped on payment of the charges thereon . . .'

and further—

> 'It is agreed that the custody and carriage of the goods are subject to the following terms on the face and back hereof which shall govern the relations, whatsoever they may be, between the shipper, consignee, and the Carrier, Master and ship in every contingency, wheresoever and whatsoever occuring . . .'

Clause 5 was as follows:

> 'The Carrier's responsibility in respect of the goods as a carrier shall not attach until the goods are actually loaded for transportation upon the ship and shall terminate without notice as soon as the goods leave the ship's tackle at the Port of Discharge from Ship or other place where the Carrier is authorised to make delivery or end its responsibility. Any responsibility of the Carrier in respect of the goods attaching prior to such loading or continuing after leaving the ship's tackle as aforesaid, shall not exceed that of an ordinary bailee, and, in particular, the Carrier shall not be liable for loss or damage to the goods due to—flood: fire, as provided elsewhere in this bill of lading: falling or collapse of wharf, pier or warehouse: robbery, theft or pilferage: strikes, lockouts or stoppage or restraint of labor from whatever cause, whether partial or general: any of the risks or causes mentioned in paragraphs (*a*), (*e*) to (*l*) inclusive and (*k*) to (*p*) inclusive, of subdivision 2 of Section 4 of the Carriage of Goods by Sea Act of the United States; or any risks or causes whatsoever, not included in the foregoing, and whether like or unlike those hereinabove mentioned, where the loss or damage is not due to the fault or neglect of the Carrier. The Carrier shall not be liable in any capacity whatsoever for any non-delivery or mis-delivery, or loss of or damage to the goods occurring while the goods are not in the actual custody of the Carrier.'

Clause 8 was as follows:

> 'Delivery of the goods shall be taken by the consignee or holder of the Bill of Lading from the vessel's rail immediately the vessel is ready to discharge, berthed or not berthed, and continuously as fast as vessel can deliver notwithstanding any custom of the port to the contrary. The Carrier shall be at liberty to discharge continuously day and night, Sundays and holidays included, all extra expenses to be for account of the Consignee or Receiver of the goods notwithstanding any custom of the port to the contrary. If the Consignee or holder of the Bill of Lading does not for any reason take delivery as provided herein, they shall be jointly and severally liable to pay the vessel on demand demurrage at the rate of one shilling and sixpence sterling per gross register ton per day or portion of a day during the delay so caused: such demurrage shall be paid in cash day by day to the Carrier, the Master or Agents. If the Consignee or holder of the Bill of Lading requires delivery before or after usual hours he shall pay any extra expenses incurred in consequence. Delivery ex ship's rail shall constitute due delivery of the goods described herein and the carrier's liability shall cease at that point notwithstanding consignee receiving delivery at some point removed from the ship's side and custom of the port being to the contrary. The Carrier and his Agents shall have the right of nominating the Berth or Berths for loading and discharging at all ports and places whatsoever any custom to the contrary notwithstanding. The Carrier shall not be required to give any notification of disposition or arrival of the goods.'

Clause 14 was as follows:

> 'Neither the carrier nor any corporation owned by, subsidiary to or associated or a affiliated with the Carrier shall be liable to answer for or make good any loss or damage to the goods occurring at any time and even though before loading on or after discharge from the ship, by reason or by means of any fire whatsoever, unless such fire shall be caused by its design or neglect.'

These provisions must be interpreted in the light of the practice that consignees rarely take delivery of goods at the ship's rail but will normally collect them after some period b of storage on or near the wharf. The parties must therefore have contemplated that the carrier, if it did not store the goods itself, would employ some other person to do so. Furthermore a document headed 'Port Jackson Stevedoring Pty. Ltd. Basic Terms and Conditions for Stevedoring at Sydney, N.S.W.' showed that it was contemplated that the stevedore would be so employed. These practical considerations, which are developed in the judgment of Barwick CJ, explain the somewhat intricate interrelation of cll 5 and 8. c

It is convenient to start with cl 8. This, in the first sentence, creates an obligation on the consignee to take delivery from the ship's rail the moment that the ship is ready to discharge; if he does not he must pay demurrage. This provision, which is in line with the decision in *Keane v Australian Steamships Pty Ltd* (1929) 41 CLR 484, is a valuable protection for the carrier, which he may, or may not, insist on. The bill of lading takes account of both possibilities. The first sentence of cl 5, quite consistently, provides that d the carrier's responsibility *as a carrier* terminates as soon as the goods leave the ship's tackle. But, since the carrier may not have insisted that the consignee take delivery at this point, the rest of cl 5 continues by recognising that the carrier may continue to have some responsibility for the goods after discharge. He cannot after all dump them on the wharf and leave them there. So to suppose would be commercially unreal and is not contemplated by the bill of lading. Clause 5 in terms attributes responsibility to the e carrier as bailee and defines the period in express terms as 'continuing after leaving the ship's tackle'. There is nothing in the latter part of cl 8 that is inconsistent with this. It merely provides that *delivery* ex ship's rail shall constitute *due delivery* and that the carrier's liability shall cease at that point. But this leaves open the option not to insist on delivery ex ship's rail, and leaves, to be governed by cl 5, his responsibility if he does not.

The question may be asked: what is the carrier's position if he acts as his own stevedore f and himself stacks and stores the goods? In the High Court, Stephen J did not provide an answer to this, but, in view of the provisions referred to above, their Lordships think that the answer is clear, namely that he would be liable for them, as bailee, under the contract. If that is so, it seems indisputable that if, instead, the carrier employs a third party to discharge, stack and store that person would be acting in the course of his employment, performing duties which otherwise the carrier would perform under the g bill of lading, and so would be entitled to the same immunity as the carrier would have. Their Lordships would add that both cl 5, in references to theft or pilferage (which may be expected to occur, if it does occur, on the wharf) and cl 14, referring to fire occurring after discharge, also recognise that the carrier may have responsibilities after this event. It is made clear by cl 5 that, irrespective of the period of carriage defined by the contract, the immunity of the carrier is not coextensive with this period but extends h both before and after it. The stevedore's immunity extends, by virtue of cl 2, over the same period.

On this point (and indeed on the appeal as a whole) their Lordships are in agreement with the judgment of Barwick CJ. They will humbly advise Her Majesty that the appeal be allowed. The costs order of the High Court of Australia will remain undisturbed and the costs of this appeal will be borne by the stevedore in accordance with the undertaking j which it gave.

Appeal allowed.

Solicitors: *Richards, Butler & Co* (for the stevedore); *Clyde & Co* (for the consignee).

Sumra Green Barrister.

a R v Commission for Racial Equality, ex parte Cottrell & Rothon (a firm)

QUEEN'S BENCH DIVISION
LORD LANE CJ AND WOOLF J
b 7th MAY 1980

Race relations – Investigation of complaint – Commission for Racial Equality – Duty to act fairly – Requirements of fairness – Parties entitled to fair hearing – Evidence of discrimination contained in report submitted by commission's officers – Witnesses not present when person accused of discrimination given opportunity to make oral representations – No opportunity for
c *accused person to cross-examine witnesses – Whether accused person entitled to cross-examine witnesses – Whether denial of opportunity to cross-examine witnesses a breach of natural justice.*

Evidence – Hearsay – Race relations cases – Hearing before Commission for Racial Equality – Allegation of racial discrimination – Commission's decision based on report presented by its officers – Commission entitled to delegate its functions to its officers – Whether report of officers
d *inadmissible as hearsay – Race Relations Act 1976, s 48(3).*

Following her dismissal, a former employee of a firm of estate agents made allegations of racial discrimination against the firm in the way in which it carried on its business. After making some tests which appeared to substantiate the allegations, the Commission for Racial Equality agreed the terms of reference for a possible formal investigation into the
e allegations under the Race Relations Act 1976. The firm was accordingly given notice of the investigation as required by s 49[a] of the 1976 Act and given an opportunity to make representations to the commission. The firm made representations in which they gave an explanation of their conduct. The commission did not accept the explanation and decided to proceed with a formal investigation. Officers of the commission interviewed various clients of the firm and produced a report which they presented to the
f commission. On the basis of the report the commission decided that the firm had contravened certain provisions of the 1976 Act. The firm was notified of that decision, told that the commission was considering issuing a non-discrimination notice under s 58[b] of the 1976 Act and offered an opportunity of making oral and written representations. The firm's solicitors sent written representations to the commission and instructed counsel to make oral representations on the firm's behalf. At the hearing by
g the commission of the oral representations the witnesses on whose evidence the commission relied were not present and counsel had no opportunity to cross-examine them. Following the hearing the commission decided to issue a non-discrimination notice. The firm applied for an order of certiorari to quash the commission's decision on the grounds (i) that the conduct of the hearing before the commission did not accord with the rules for a judicial hearing and the rules of natural justice in that the firm's
h counsel was not able to cross-examine the witnesses on whose evidence the commission had relied and (ii) that the evidence of the witnesses was communicated to the commission in the form of a report from the commission's officers and was therefore hearsay and inadmissible.

Held – The application would be dismissed for the following reasons—

(1) Since there were degrees of judicial hearing, ranging from matters of pure
j administration to a full hearing of a criminal cause or matter in court and each case was different, it was necessary to consider the basic nature of the particular proceeding in deciding whether there had been a breach of the rules of natural justice. A formal

a Section 49, so far as material, is set out at p 267 *e* to *h*, post

b Section 58, so far as material, is set out at p 269 *b* to *e*, post

investigation under the 1976 Act was an administrative function which did not require the formalities of cross-examination of witnesses whom the commission had seen and a
from whom they had taken statements. Accordingly it could not be said that the hearing did not accord with the rules for a judicial hearing. Furthermore, all that the rules of natural justice meant was that the proceedings in question were required to be conducted in a way which was fair in all the circumstances, which in the case of a formal investigation conducted by the commission under the 1976 Act included a consideration of the nature of the provisions of the Act itself and a consideration of any penalty which b
might be imposed thereunder. Since neither s 58 nor any other provision of the 1976 Act gave a right to cross-examine any of the witnesses and since there were no penalties in the form of fines or imprisonment or the like imposed under the Act, it could not be said that the conduct of the hearing before the commission did not accord with the rules of natural justice (see p 271 *a b* and *d* to *g* and p 273 *b c*, post); dictum of Scarman LJ in *Selvarajan v Race Relations Board* [1976] 1 All ER at 24 followed; *R v Hull Prison Board of* c
Visitors, ex parte St Germain (No 2) [1979] 3 All ER 545 distinguished.

(2) Since the commission were entitled, and as a matter of practical politics bound, under s 48(3)[c] of the 1976 Act to delegate their functions in relation to a formal investigation to their servants, it followed that any reports produced by those servants were necessarily hearsay; and, if it was proper for the commission to delegate their functions in that way, it was equally proper to act on the reports which the servants d
produced (see p 273 *b c*, post); dictum of Lawton LJ in *Selvarajan v Race Relations Board* [1976] 1 All ER at 22 applied.

Notes

For the power of the Commission for Racial Equality to conduct formal investigations and to issue non-discrimination notices, see Supplement to 4 Halsbury's Laws (4th Edn) e
paras 1042B. 3, 1042C. 4.

For the rules of natural justice and the duty to act fairly, see 1 Halsbury's Laws (4th Edn) paras 64, 66.

For the rule against hearsay evidence generally, see 17 ibid para 53.

For the Race Relations Act 1976, ss 48, 49, 58, see 46 Halsbury's Statutes (3rd Edn) 429, 437. f

Cases referred to in judgments

R v Deputy Industrial Injuries Comr, ex parte Moore [1965] 1 All ER 81, [1965] 1 QB 456, [1965] 2 WLR 89, CA, Digest (Cont Vol B) 543, *4589a*.

R v Hull Prison Board of Visitors, ex parte St Germain (No 2) [1979] 3 All ER 545, [1979] 1 WLR 1041, DC. g

Selvarajan v Race Relations Board [1976] 1 All ER 12, sub nom *R v Race Relations Board, ex parte Selvarajan* [1975] 1 WLR 1686, CA, 2 Digest (Reissue) 318, *1787*.

Application for judicial review

The applicant, Cottrell & Rothon, a firm of estate agents, applied with the leave of the Divisional Court of the Queen's Bench Division given on 21st November 1979 for h
judicial review, seeking against the respondents, the Commission for Racial Equality, an order of certiorari to remove into the High Court for the purpose of it being quashed a decision of the commission of 11th October 1979 whereby a non-discrimination notice was issued against the firm under s 58 of the Race Relations Act 1976. The facts are set out in the judgment of Lord Lane CJ.

j

Lord Hooson QC and *Jennie Horne* for the firm.
Desmond Browne for the commission.

c Section 48(3) is set out at p 268 *b*, post

LORD LANE CJ. In this case a firm of estate agents applies for judicial review in the shape of an order of certiorari directed to the Commission for Racial Equality, pursuant to leave given by this court on 21st November 1979.

The case concerns an alleged infringement of the provisions of the Race Relations Act 1976, an Act which, we are told, has not previously been the subject of consideration by this court. It arises out of a situation in which it was suggested that the applicants (to whom I shall refer as 'the firm' hereafter) carried out a system of discrimination against coloured people in the course of their business as estate agents. One of the allegations, if not the primary allegation, was that vendors of property who were coloured had their names entered on cards which were pink, whereas white people had their particulars entered on white cards; and certain other discriminatory matters, it is said, were carried on in the way of business by the firm so that, if a coloured purchaser appeared on the scene, the likelihood would be that he would not receive the same number, or possibly the same quality, of properties for his consideration as would a white prospective purchaser.

The chronology of events is as follows, put as briefly as one may. A Miss Prince was employed by the firm in some sort of clerical capacity for a short time between 5th December 1977 and 12th January 1978. She was, it seems, dismissed from her employment, and at the end of January she was making allegations of racial discrimination against the firm. She made those allegations to the commission.

Certain tests were carried out by the commission. I think they sent two white people and two coloured people as pretended prospective clients, and the result of those tests was that to that extent Miss Prince's allegations were substantiated.

On 5th April 1978 the commission, on the strength of those investigations and tests, agreed the terms of reference for a possible formal investigation into these complaints under the 1976 Act.

On the 21st April the firm was informed and the s 49 procedure was instituted. Section 49 reads as follows:

> '(1) The Commission shall not embark on a formal investigation unless the requirements of this section have been complied with.
>
> '(2) Terms of reference for the investigation shall be drawn up by the Commission or, if the Commission were required by the Secretary of State to conduct the investigation, by the Secretary of State after consulting the Commission.
>
> '(3) It shall be the duty of the Commission to give general notice of the holding of the investigation unless the terms of reference confine it to activities of persons named in them, but in such a case the Commission shall in the prescribed manner give those persons notice of the holding of the investigation.
>
> '(4) Where the terms of reference of the investigation confine it to activities of persons named in them and the Commission in the course of it propose to investigate any act made unlawful by this Act which they believe that a person so named may have done, the Commission shall—(*a*) inform that person of their belief and of their proposal to investigate the act in question; and (*b*) offer him an opportunity of making oral or written representations with regard to it (or both oral and written representations if he thinks fit); and a person so named who avails himself of an opportunity under this subsection of making oral representations may be represented—(i) by counsel or a solicitor; or (ii) by some other person of his choice, not being a person to whom the Commission object on the ground that he is unsuitable . . .'

This was an opportunity to make written representations, and those representations were made. The representations contained an explanation of the pink and white card system which I have described, the suggestion by the firm being that that distinction between card colour was not based on any distinction between customer colour but was based on the accent of the person applying or intending to become a customer. In other words, the pink cards indicated, according to this suggestion, that the person whose particulars were entered on that pink card spoke with a foreign accent. So much for that explanation.

On 11th May there was a letter from the firm explaining the system. On 17th May the commission altered the charges which had been drafted and deleted two of them. It is not necessary to give any detail as to that.

On 5th June 1978 the commission decided to proceed with the formal investigation. On 5th July they nominated two persons to carry out that investigation, a Mr Maan and a Mr Campbell-Lee, under the provisions of s 48(3) of the Act. Section 48 has the sidenote 'Power to conduct formal investigations'. Subsection (3) reads:

> 'The Commission may nominate one or more Commissioners, with or without one or more additional Commissioners, to conduct a formal investigation on their behalf, and may delegate any of their functions in relation to the investigation to the person so nominated.'

That is what happened in this case. There were minutes to that effect which are before us, although the minutes are of a slightly later date owing to an administrative error. The nominated commissioners are clearly intended to be an extension of the personality of the whole commission. Their delegated functions are set out in a minute before us which there is no need for me to read.

Then came a slight hiccup in the proceedings because on 18th May 1979 the firm took steps to try and spike the guns of the commission. They issued a writ claiming an injunction to prevent the commission from interviewing clients of the firm on whose cards were certain apparently discriminatory markings. On 25th May, a week later, that matter was heard and the injunction was refused with costs. That was the end of the incident.

On 4th July the commission decided that the firm had contravened certain sections of the 1976 Act, namely s 20(1), which reads as follows:

> 'It is unlawful for any person concerned with the provision (for payment or not) of goods, facilities or services to the public or a section of the public to discriminate against a person who seeks to obtain or use those goods, facilities or services—(*a*) by refusing or deliberately omitting to provide him with any of them; or (*b*) by refusing or deliberately omitting to provide him with goods, facilities or services of the like quality, in the like manner and on the like terms as are normal in the first-mentioned person's case in relation to other members of the public or (where the person so seeking belongs to a section of the public) to other members of that section.'

That has to be read in conjunction with s 1(1)(*a*) of the Act. The side heading is 'Racial discrimination' and it reads as follows:

> 'A person discriminates against another in any circumstances relevant for the purposes of any provision of this Act if—(*a*) on racial grounds he treats that other less favourably than he treats or would treat other persons . . .'

The second infringement alleged was an infringement of s 30, which has the side heading 'Instructions to discriminate'. It reads as follows:

> 'It is unlawful for a person—(*a*) who has authority over another person; or (*b*) in accordance with whose wishes that other person is accustomed to act, to instruct him to do any act which is unlawful by virtue of Part II or III, or procure or attempt to procure the doing by him of any such act.'

That is the instigation to act. That again has to be read in conjunction with s 1, the terms of which I have already set out.

Finally, a breach was alleged of s 33, which is 'Aiding unlawful acts' and which reads as follows:

> '(1) A person who knowingly aids another person to do an act made unlawful by

> this Act shall be treated for the purposes of this Act as himself doing an unlawful act of the like description . . .'

These allegations were, as is necessary under the Act, communicated to the firm and the firm was told that the commission were minded to issue a notice and to act in accordance with s 58(5). Again it is necessary to read that provision:

> 'The Commission shall not serve a non-discrimination notice in respect of any person unless they have first—(*a*) given him notice that they are minded to issue a non-discrimination notice in his case, specifying the grounds on which they contemplate doing so; and (*b*) offered him an opportunity of making oral or written representations in the matter (or both oral and written representations if he thinks fit) within a period of not less than 28 days specified in the notice; and (*c*) taken account of any representations so made by him.'

In order to set the matter in its true light, it is perhaps convenient at this stage to read the other provisions of s 58, namely sub-ss (1) and (2). The section is headed 'Issue of non-discrimination notice' and the subsections read:

> '(1) This section applies to—(*a*) an unlawful discriminatory act; and (*b*) an act contravening section 28; and (*c*) an act contravening section 29, 30 or 31, and so applies whether or not proceedings have been brought in respect of the Act.
>
> '(2) If in the course of a formal investigation the Commission become satisfied that a person is committing, or has committed, any such acts, the Commission may in the prescribed manner serve on him a notice in the prescribed form ("a non-discrimination notice") requiring him—(*a*) not to commit any such acts; and (*b*) where compliance with paragraph (*a*) involves changes in any of his practices or other arrangements—(i) to inform the Commission that he has effected those changes and what those changes are; and (ii) to take such steps as may be reasonably required by the notice for the purpose of affording that information to other persons concerned.'

On 27th July a Mr Graham on behalf of the commission set out the grounds on which the commission had decided to proceed in a full letter. In that letter he sets out in minute detail those charges which have been laid, so to speak, against the firm, and the evidence on which the commission is acting. The commission obviously (and one has only to read the letter to see this) went to great trouble and great pains in order to set out the basis of their allegations against the firm. In the letter the following paragraph appears:

> 'In the light of the above the Commission is minded, subject to any representations the Agency may make, to issue a non-discrimination notice requiring the Agency, its servants and agents not to permit any such act as described in paragraphs (a), (b) and (c) above, or any other act which is an unlawful discriminatory act by virtue of sections 20, 30 and 33 of the Act.'

Following that paragraph the firm are reminded of their rights under s 58(5)(*b*), which I have already read, and they are offered the opportunity of making representations, either oral or written or both, to the two commissioners who have been designated to carry out the investigation.

On 29th August came a reply from the firm's solicitors consisting of eight pages setting out in detail their answers to some of the allegations which are made against them. On 24th September oral representations were made to the commissioners, solicitor and counsel appearing on behalf of the firm before the commissioners and the commissioners having the advantage of the submissions of counsel who was instructed by the firm to put forward their case. It is plain, in fairness to counsel, that no one was au fait with the procedure which was likely to be adopted, and that, in the circumstances, is not altogether surprising because this type of procedure is at this stage at any rate by no means common.

It seems that counsel was expecting, or perhaps half-expecting in the back of her mind, that she might have the opportunity of cross-examining certain of the witnesses on whose evidence the commission were evidently relying. It seems that some such suggestion was made by her at the outset, although it is true that no note of it appears in the very full note which was taken on behalf of the commission by two of their employees, a Miss Smith and a Mr Deutsch. But there is no doubt that in the note of her submissions counsel said there was no evidence other than hearsay evidence and she said that she expected the commission to operate on a judicial standard. She reminded the commissioners that her clients had received no signed statement and had had no opportunity to cross-examine. She said that if the evidence was challenged in a higher court the failure to make witnesses available was a serious step.

It seems to me that what counsel was indicating there was that, although this was at the end of the day, she was making her submission and she was registering a complaint, and if the matter went further, she would rely, so far as she was able, on the fact that she had not been permitted to cross-examine any of the witnesses, as I say, on whose evidence the commission were relying.

That brings me to an examination of the nature of the grounds on which this application for judicial review is based. In the statement filed by the firm pursuant to the Rules of the Supreme Court it is said:

> 'The grounds on which the said relief is sought are as follows:—The conduct of the hearing before the Commission on which the decision of the Commission of the 11th day of October, 1979 was based, did not accord with the rules for a judicial hearing and the rules of natural justice in that; (1) the Applicant was not permitted to cross examine witnesses upon whose evidence the Commission relied in reaching their decision, those witnesses not being produced at the hearing of the case; (2) evidence was heard and admitted which would not be admissible in a Court of law, and upon which the Commission relied in reaching its findings. That such witness evidence as was relied on was not produced in statement or Affidavit form and that such evidence as was relied on was inadmissible hearsay evidence . . .'

There is a third ground based on the identity of the commissioners who carried out the investigation and the fact that they were part of the full commission which came to the ultimate determination. That ground was very properly abandoned by counsel for the firm in the course of argument as being untenable.

But there was a further ground adumbrated, although not expressly set out, with which it will in due course be necessary to deal, and that is, if I can paraphrase the more elegant words which counsel used, that the two investigators appointed to determine did not themselves carry out the investigation but left it very largely to employees or servants or administrators of the commission and they passed on that information to the board at second hand.

It is necessary now to deal with each of those three complaints in turn. First of all, as regards the question that no cross-examination was permitted, it is dealt with in the affidavit in reply by the commission by a Dr Sanders in this form:

> '. . . that as a matter of law those under formal investigation by the Commission have no right to cross-examine the witnesses seen by the Commission. (Furthermore, no application to cross-examine any particular witness was ever made by [the firm's] legal advisers at or prior to the oral representation on 24th September, 1979.)'

As to the second point, I have said enough already to indicate that counsel at the hearing before the commissioners could scarcely have been expected to do more than she did to register her complaint about the matter. This point comes down to the decision whether in these circumstances the commission were, in the light of the rules of natural justice, obliged to allow their witnesses to be cross-examined.

Of course there is a wealth of authority on what are and what are not the rules of natural justice. The rules have been described in various ways, as 'an unruly horse', I

think, in one decision, and there is no doubt that what may be the rules of natural justice
a in one case may very well not be the rules of natural justice in another. As has frequently
been said, and there is no harm in repeating it, all that the rules of natural justice mean
is that the proceedings must be conducted in a way which is fair to the firm in this case,
fair in all the circumstances. All the circumstances include a number of different
considerations. First of all, the penalties, if any. There are no penalties under this Act in
the form of fines or imprisonment or anything like that, but what counsel for the firm
b has drawn to our attention, quite correctly, is that under the terms of the Estate Agents
Act 1979 (and no one has been able to discover whether that has come into operation yet
or not[1]) there is no doubt that a person on whom a non-discriminatory notice has been
served may, if he is an estate agent, suffer, if certain procedural steps are taken, grave
disadvantages, because it is open, subject to a number of safeguards into which I do not
propose to go, for the Director General of Fair Trading to take steps to see that a person
c against whom this action had been taken under the Race Relations Act 1976 does not
practise in business as an estate agent.

Of course it is a very long call from saying that a person who has this non-
discrimination notice served on him is necessarily going to suffer in his business by the
action of the Director General of Fair Trading. Many procedures have to be gone
through before that can take place, but there is that danger there, and that is one of the
d matters which is a circumstance to be taken into account.

The next matter, and possibly the most important matter, is the nature of the
provisions of the 1976 Act itself. I have read sufficient of the contents of s 58 of that Act
to indicate that there is no mention in that section, or indeed in any other section, of any
right to cross-examine any of the witnesses. That perhaps is a surprising omission if it
was the intention of Parliament to allow a person in the position of the firm in this case
e the full panoply of legal rights which would take place at a judicial hearing.

It seems to me that there are degrees of judicial hearing, and those degrees run from
the borders of pure administration to the borders of the full hearing of a criminal cause
or matter in the Crown Court. It does not profit one to try to pigeon-hole the particular
set of circumstances either into the administrative pigeon-hole or into the judicial
pigeon-hole. Each case will inevitably differ, and one must ask oneself what is the basic
f nature of the proceeding which was going on here. It seems to me that basically this was
an investigation being carried out by the commission. It is true that in the course of the
investigation the commission may form a view, but it does not seem to me that that is
a proceeding which requires in the name of fairness any right in the firm in this case to
be able to cross-examine witnesses whom the commission have seen and from whom
they have taken statements. I repeat the wording of s 58(2) in emphasis of that point:
g 'If in the course of a formal investigation the Commission become satisfied that a person
is committing . . .' and so on. It seems to me that that is so near an administrative
function as to make little difference and is the type of investigation or proceeding which
does not require the formalities of cross-examination.

We have been referred to a number of cases, and in particular *Selvarajan v Race
Relations Board* [1976] 1 All ER 12, [1975] 1 WLR 1686. This was a decision under the
h earlier Race Relations Act 1968, and, as counsel for the firm has rightly pointed out, there
are very sharp and material distinctions between the 1968 Act and the 1976 Act. The
1968 Act required the commission to act very largely as a purely investigating and
conciliating body, and any litigation or determination was left to the county court or the
regular courts of the land to determine. But nevertheless there are passages which do cast
some light on the attitude of the courts to this type of situation.

j Scarman LJ says this ([1976] 1 All ER 12 at 24, [1975] 1 WLR 1686 at 1700):

> 'The Race Relations Board does not exercise judicial functions. Part II of the Act

---

1 At 1st October 1980 no day had been appointed under s 36(2) of the Estate Agents Act 1979 for the coming into force of that Act.

is absolutely clear. The board was created so that in the sensitive field of race relations compliance with the law and the resolution of differences could first be *a* sought without recourse to the courts with their necessarily open and formalised judicial process. The board is an administrative agency charged with a number of critically important functions in the administration of the law; but it is not a judicial institution—nor is it the apex of a hierarchy of judicial institutions. The procedures are not adversarial but conciliatory: settlement, not litigation, is the business of the board, and it is left to the board to decide how best to perform the *b* functions which the Act requires it to perform, namely, investigation, the formation of an opinion, conciliation, and, if all else fails, the taking of legal proceedings in the county court.'

R v Deputy Industrial Injuries Comr, ex parte Moore [1965] 1 All ER 81, [1965] 1 QB 456 was cited to us, and a passage in the judgment of Diplock LJ seems to be appropriate *c* ([1965] 1 All ER 81 at 94, [1965] 1 QB 456 at 488):

> '... these technical rules of evidence form no part of the rules of natural justice. The requirement that a person exercising quasi-judicial functions must base his decision on evidence means no more than that it must be based on material which tends logically to show the existence or non-existence of facts relevant to the issue to be determined, or to show the likelihood or unlikelihood of the occurrence of *d* some future event the occurrence of which would be relevant. It means that he must not spin a coin or consult an astrologer; but he may take into account any material which, as a matter of reason, has some probative value in the sense mentioned above. If it is capable of having any probative value, the weight to be attached to it is a matter for the person to whom Parliament has entrusted the responsibility of deciding the issue. The supervisory jurisdiction of the High Court *e* does not entitle it to usurp this responsibility and to substitute its own view for his.'

Counsel for the firm sought to derive assistance from some of the passages of the decision of this court in *R v Hull Prison Board of Visitors, ex parte St Germain (No 2)* [1979] 3 All ER 545, [1979] 1 WLR 1401, but it seems to me that the decision there was based on facts widely differing from those in the present case. That was truly a judicial proceeding carried out by the prison visitors, and the complaint there was that there had *f* been no opportunity to cross-examine prison officers in hotly disputed questions of identity. Speaking for myself, I derive little assistance from any dicta in that case.

We are not here to substitute our view for the view of the commission. They undoubtedly went to very great lengths to investigate and examine all the voluminous evidence which was before them. There is now before us, at a late stage it is true, the report of the formal investigation which was carried out and a copy of which was sent to *g* each member of the commission (60 pages in all). No one can complain that this matter was not thoroughly investigated. It seems to me for the reasons I have endeavoured to set out that in this case there was no breach of the rules of fairness in that cross-examination was not permitted or that the witnesses did not attend.

The next point is the hearsay point, and that is dealt with succinctly by what Lawton LJ said in the *Selvarajan* case [1976] 1 All ER 12 at 22, [1975] 1 WLR 1686 at 1698: *h*

> 'For my part I can see no reason at all why the board should not delegate to its staff the function of collecting information. It would be impractical for the members of the board themselves to make investigations. How the board does what Parliament has entrusted it to do is not a matter for the courts to decide as long as it acts fairly and in good faith. It is for the board, not the courts, to decide how much *j* information each of its members should have when considering a particular case. As long as the board, or one of its constituent committees, has enough information to enable it to make a fair assessment of the case, the court will not interfere.'

Similar passages are to be found in the other two judgments, and it is plain that that was the view of the court.

That answers both questions (2) and (3) posed by counsel for the firm, namely the a hearsay point and the delegation point, because once one reaches the stage of accepting that the commission are not only entitled to but as a matter of practical politics are bound to delegate the investigation to their underlings, or servants, it follows that the reports produced by those servants were necessarily hearsay. But, if it is proper to delegate in that way, then equally it is proper to act on the reports which the servants or subordinates produce. I can see nothing wrong in the commission acting as they did on the evidence b contained in these various reports. I can see nothing wrong in the fact that they delegated to those servants the task of the investigation. In short, none of the three grounds relied on by the firm succeeds and I would accordingly dismiss this application.

WOOLF J. I agree.

c *Application dismissed.*

Solicitors: *Mohabir & Co* (for the firm); *Bindman & Partners* (for the commission).

Denise Randall Barrister.

d

R v Hucklebridge
e Attorney General's Reference (No 3 of 1980)

COURT OF APPEAL, CRIMINAL DIVISION
LORD LANE CJ, BOREHAM AND GIBSON JJ
10th JUNE 1980

f *Firearms – Certificate – Exemption – Shot gun – Smooth-bore gun with barrel not less than 24 inches in length – Rifle altered by removing rifling from barrel – Gun still capable of firing rifle ammunition – Whether gun as altered a 'shot gun' – Whether exempt from requirement of having a certificate – Firearms Act 1968, s 1(3)(a).*

Informations were preferred against the appellant charging him with being in possession g of two rifles without a firearm certificate, contrary to s 1[a] of the Firearms Act 1968. Both guns had originally been Lee-Enfield ·303 rifles but had been converted to smooth-bore guns by having the rifling reamed out. One of the guns had been rechambered to take shot gun cartridges, the other had not. Both guns were still capable of firing a ·303 bullet but with considerably less accuracy and velocity than before. By virtue of s 1(3)(*a*), the 1968 Act did not apply to a 'shot gun' which was defined as 'a smooth-bore gun with a h barrel not less than 24 inches in length'. The appellant was acquitted in respect of the rechambered gun but convicted in respect of the gun which had not been rechambered. He appealed against the conviction and the Attorney General made a reference to the court in respect of the acquittal.

Held – Both guns came within the description of a shot gun in s 1(3)(*a*) of the 1968 Act j since they had a smooth bore and a barrel more than 24 inches in length, and were therefore guns for which a firearm certificate was not required, despite the fact that both guns looked like and had most of the components of a rifle. The appellant's appeal

a Section 1, so far as material, is set out at p 275 *e f*, post would therefore be allowed and the Attorney General's reference determined accordingly (see p 275 *h j*, p 276 *e* to *j* and p 277 *d* and *h*, post).

Dictum of Lord Widgery CJ in *Creaser v Tunnicliffe* [1978] 1 All ER at 573 applied.

Creaser v Tunnicliffe [1978] 1 All ER 569 not followed.

Notes

For restrictions on the possession of firearms and exemptions from the requirement of a firearm certificate, see 11 Halsbury's Laws (4th Edn) paras 875–876, and for cases on firearms, see 15 Digest (Repl) 804, *7645–7648*.

For the Firearms Act 1968, s 1, see 8 Halsbury's Statutes (3rd Edn) 729.

Case referred to in judgment

Creaser v Tunnicliffe [1978] 1 All ER 569, [1977] 1 WLR 1493, 142 JP 245, 66 Cr App R 66, DC, Digest (Cont Vol E) 150, *8040a*.

Cases also cited

Cafferata v Wilson, Reeve v Wilson [1936] 3 All ER 149, DC.

R v Freeman [1970] 2 All ER 413, [1970] 1 WLR 788, CA.

Watson v Herman [1952] 2 All ER 70, DC.

Appeal and Attorney General's reference

David William Hucklebridge appealed against his conviction on 10th July 1979 at the Crown Court at Portsmouth before his Honour Judge Galpin and a jury on a charge of possessing a rifle without a firearm certificate, contrary to s 1 of the Firearms Act 1968. Arising out of the appellant's acquittal on a similar count at the same trial, the Attorney General referred, under s 36 of the Criminal Justice Act 1972, for the opinion of the court the question whether it was possible so to adapt a Lee-Enfield rifle, which had admittedly been a firearm within the definition of s 57(1) of the 1968 Act, requiring a firearm certificate pursuant to s 1(1) of that Act as to exclude the firearm from the necessity for such a certificate by reason of s 1(3)(*a*) of that Act. The appellant consented to the use of his name in the proceedings. The facts are set out in the judgment of the court.

Stephen Parish for the appellant in the appeal and the respondent to the reference.

Brian Leary QC and *James Tabor* for the Crown in the appeal and the Attorney General in the reference.

LORD LANE CJ delivered the following judgment of the court: On 19th July 1979 at the Crown Court at Portsmouth, the appellant (who has indicated his lack of objection to his name being published, this being an Attorney General's reference) was convicted on count 2 in the indictment with which we are concerned, charging him with possessing a rifle no P39869 without a firearm certificate, contrary to s 1 of the Firearms Act 1968. He was, on the judge's direction, found not guilty of count 1 in the indictment, of possessing a rifle no FB20954 without a firearm certificate contrary to the same section. He was sentenced to a fine of £20 or one month's imprisonment in default in respect of the count of which he was found guilty, namely count 2. He had originally pleaded not guilty to that count, but in the light of a direction by the judge he, on advice, changed his plea.

Consequently there is one conviction and one acquittal, with both of which, rather unusually, this court is now concerned. We are concerned with the conviction because on a point of law the appellant appeals against that conviction. We are concerned with the acquittal because there has been a reference by the Attorney General to this court in respect of the acquittal, both of course arising out of the same trial.

It is necessary to describe the two guns with which we are concerned. The gun in count 1 had been a Lee-Enfield rifle, which had been converted to smooth bore by the rifling being reamed out and had been rechambered to take ·410 shot gun cartridges. But it is correct to say that it was still capable of firing ·303 cartridges, though, owing to

the obvious increase in bore, it would no longer be so accurate as it originally was, nor
a would the range of the rifle be the same, it would be very much reduced. The evidence was that it would be lethal up to about 100 yards. It had been reproofed at the Birmingham Proof House.

The gun in count 2 had also been a Lee-Enfield ·303 rifle. It had been converted to smooth bore by the same process as that in respect of the first count, but this gun had not been rechambered to take shot gun cartridges. It was still capable of firing ·303 cartridges
b with the same loss of velocity and accuracy as the other gun. It had been reproofed as a smooth-bore gun, but could not, as I say, fire shot gun cartridges.

The facts were not really in dispute and the judge was called on, as a matter of submission at the close of the expert evidence as to the guns, to decide whether or not the rechambered gun had become a shot gun within the exception of s 1(3)(*a*) of the 1968 Act so that a firearm certificate was not required in respect of it. So far as that gun was
c concerned, the judge ruled in favour of the appellant.

The appellant appeals against his conviction on count 2. He has a certificate of the judge in respect of that appeal, although such a certificate was not necessary, this appeal being on a point of law. The Attorney General refers this matter in respect of count 1 to this court, asking the court to rule on the following:

> 'Whether it is possible so to adapt a Lee Enfield rifle, which has admittedly been
> d a firearm within the definition of Section 57(1) of the Firearms Act 1968 requiring a firearm certificate pursuant to Section 1(1) of the same Act so as to exclude the said firearm from the necessity for such a certificate by reason of Section 1(3)(*a*) of the same Act.'

It is necessary therefore to consider the various statutory provisions which are designed
e to cover this situation. I turn accordingly to the 1968 Act. Section 1 reads as follows:

> '(1) Subject to any exemption under this Act, it is an offence for a person—(*a*) to have in his possession, or to purchase or acquire, a firearm to which this section applies without holding a firearm certificate in force at the time, or otherwise than as authorised by such a certificate . . .
>
> '(3) This section applies to every firearm except—(*a*) a shot gun (that is to say a
> f smooth-bore gun with a barrel not less than 24 inches in length, not being an air gun) . . . '

The question in this case, or put more accurately the two questions in this case, depend entirely on the interpretation to be put on those words in s 1(3)(*a*).

In sub-s (4) of s 57 of the 1968 Act shot gun is interpreted as follows:

> g '"shot gun" has the meaning assigned to it by section 1(3)(*a*) of this Act and, in sections 3(1) and 45(2) of this Act and in the definition of "firearms dealer", includes any component part of a shot gun and any accessory to a shot gun designed or adapted to diminish the noise or flash caused by firing the gun.'

Consequently that interpretation section in a word refers a person desirous of having
h a definition of shot gun back to s 1(3)(*a*), namely 'a shot gun (that is to say a smooth-bore gun with a barrel not less than 24 inches in length, not being an air gun)'.

The contention of counsel for the appellant is simple. He submits that those two sections taken together, namely ss 1 and 57, make it perfectly plain that the words in parenthesis in s 1(3)(*a*) are, for the purposes of this Act, a definition of what the Act means by 'shot gun'. He goes on to submit that these two guns, each of them although
j originally Lee-Enfield rifles properly so called, have ceased to be Lee-Enfield rifles properly so called and have become smooth-bore guns with barrels not less than 24 inches in length. That being the case, says counsel, they are plainly within s 1(3)(*a*) and consequently do not require a firearm certificate. Accordingly, in his submission, the appellant should not only have been acquitted on count 1 but he should have been acquitted on count 2 as well.

This matter has been considered by the Divisional Court in *Creaser v Tunnicliffe* [1978] 1 All ER 569, [1977] 1 WLR 1493. The circumstances in that case are summarised in the *a* headnote to the report as follows ([1977] 1 WLR 1493):

> 'Both the defendants collected firearms and both held a number of firearm certificates for specified guns and a shot gun certificate (which covered all shot guns in the certificate holder's possession). They had in their possession certain rifles without firearm certificates from which they had removed the rifling but the gun could still discharge the same ammunition as before the alteration. In respect of *b* those guns, informations were preferred against the defendants that they were in possession of a firearm otherwise than as authorised by a firearm certificate, contrary to section 1(1) of the Firearms Act 1968. The justices rejected the defendants' contention that the removal of the rifling had the effect of altering the weapon to a smooth-bore gun within the definition of a shot gun in section 1(3) of the Act. They held that, except in the case of certain antique guns, the defendants required *c* firearm certificates and had committed offences under section 1(1) of the Act.'

The defendants appealed against that conviction. The Divisional Court dismissed the appeal, but Lord Widgery CJ dissented and held that in his view the appeal should succeed. It was held by the majority ([1977] 1 WLR 1493)— *d*

> 'that a rifle from which the rifling had been removed could still be used as a rifle, albeit with a lesser degree of accuracy, and it remained a rifle and, therefore, a firearm as defined by section 57 and subject to the provisions of section 1(1) of the Act.'

It seems to this court that what impression the weapon makes on the court, namely does it impress the court as being a rifle or does it impress the court as being a shot gun, *e* is an immaterial consideration. What the court has to consider, and I do not apologise for repeating it, is the definition in s 1(3)(*a*).

This court, with respect to the majority in *Creaser v Tunnicliffe*, finds the reasoning of Lord Widgery CJ compelling. I cite a passage from his judgment ([1978] 1 All ER 569 at 573, [1977] 1 WLR 1493 at 1500): *f*

> 'When one goes back to examine the circumstances in which a firearm may be possessed without a firearm certificate, which means going back to s 1 of the 1968 Act, one is immediately struck by the fact that the broad distinction drawn between one firearm and another firearm is that the smooth-bore weapon (popularly called a shot gun) goes into one class, and all the rest go into another. Thus all the rifles are in a class described by s 1. The reason must be clear enough. It is because the *g* element of risk, danger and lethal quality which a rifle has when compared to a shot gun is very different. Parliament no doubt had in mind that people may have a legitimate excuse for holding shot guns but not have any excuse for saying they required a rifle. One looks again at the matter which has been mentioned several times by Watkins J, s 1(3), which contains the vital definition in these terms: "This section applies to every firearm except—(*a*) a shot gun (that is to say a smooth-bore *h* gun with a barrel not less than 24 inches in length . . .)" In my imagination I pick up one of these weapons and look at it. I say: has it got a smooth bore? Yes, because the rifling has gone. Is the barrel more than 24 inches in length? Yes, it is. Therefore it is a shot gun for the purposes of this Act. How is that approach to be faulted? It is said by some that this cannot be a shot gun. This Lee Enfield with the rifling bored out does not look like a shot gun; one cannot shoot rabbits with it. *j* That may be so. It still seems to me to satisfy the definition of a shot gun in the Act.'

With that passage this court respectfully agrees. As I say, it is not for us to express our view what the particular weapon might look like. That is not the problem. The question is: does it come within the exception as Parliament has set that exception?

Counsel for the Attorney General draws our attention to sub-s (1) of s 57 which reads
a as follows:

> 'In this Act, the expression "firearm" means a lethal barrelled weapon of any description from which any shot, bullet or other missile can be discharged and includes—(*a*) any prohibited weapon, whether it is such a lethal weapon as aforesaid or not; and (*b*) any component part of such a lethal or prohibited weapon; and (*c*) any accessory to any such weapon designed or adapted to diminish the noise or flash
> b caused by firing the weapon ...'

He asks us to pay regard to the fact that the component parts of the Lee-Enfield or most of them are still there. It has only got an adapted barrel and chamber. The rest of the gun remains the same. All the component parts of the gun are the original component parts. Ergo, he says, it is covered by sub-s (1)(*c*).

c But that overlooks the words which follow in that subsection, which read as follows:

> '... and so much of section 1 of this Act as excludes any description of firearm from the category of firearms to which that section applies shall be construed as also excluding component parts of, and accessories to, firearms of that description.'

So that once you have got to the situation, which this court thinks you have, that this is
d within the definition of shot gun, then all the component parts are likewise protected by the exception. That argument is circular and does not avail the Attorney General.

Finally counsel, in his concluding argument, was trying to impress us with the dangerous situation which may result if the Attorney General's reference does not succeed and if the appeal against conviction on the other count does succeed. He was suggesting to us that that might open the floodgate to undesirable possessors of weapons
e which could take ·303 cartridges and might be detrimental to law-abiding citizens. Some of course think that a shot gun is just as lethal a weapon as a rifle. In certain circumstances it would be. In any event if the holder or possessor of one of these modified weapons desires to discharge from the weapon, albeit inefficiently, a round of ·303 ammunition, he will, we understand, have to possess a firearm certificate before he can obtain such ammunition. In any event even if that is not the case, it is not for this
f court to fly in the face of what we consider to be the plain words of an Act of Parliament. If it is required to close up a possible loophole, that is for Parliament to do and not this court.

Finally there is one other matter to which it is desirable to draw attention, and that is the precise wording of the exception. This is a matter to which the court in *Creaser v Tunnicliffe* did not advert. The last words, 'not being an air gun', seem to this court to
g have been unnecessary if the Crown's submission is correct, because an air gun would already have been excluded by virtue of the Act; that was a weapon not capable of firing ordinary shot gun ammunition. That particular point is not necessary, strictly speaking, for the decision of this court, but it is by way of comment.

For these reasons the appeal against conviction on count 2 succeeds and the conviction is quashed. The answer to the Attorney General's reference, namely whether it is
h possible so to adapt a Lee-Enfield rifle, which has admittedly been a firearm within the definition of s 57(1) of the 1968 Act as to exclude the firearm from the necessity for such a certificate by reason of s 1(3)(*a*) of that Act, is Yes.

Appeal in R v Hucklebridge allowed. Determination of Attorney General's reference in accordance with judgment.

j

Solicitors: *Gray, Purdue & Co*, Waterlooville (for the appellant in the appeal and the respondent to the reference); *Director of Public Prosecutions.*

Denise Randall Barrister.

Edwards (Inspector of Taxes) v Clinch a

COURT OF APPEAL, CIVIL DIVISION
BUCKLEY, ACKNER AND OLIVER LJJ
17th, 18th APRIL, 9th MAY 1980

Income tax – Emoluments from office or employment – Office – Inspector appointed to hold a public local inquiry – Whether inspector holding an 'office' – Whether inspector's remuneration taxable under Sch E, Case I – Income and Corporation Taxes Act 1970, s 181(1). b

The taxpayer was one of a panel of persons invited by the Department of the Environment from time to time to act as inspectors at public local inquiries for the Secretary of State for the Environment. The taxpayer would be contacted by an official c of the department, informed of the location and date of the inquiry and the daily fee payable, and invited to undertake the inquiry. The taxpayer could then either accept or refuse the invitation. If he accepted, the taxpayer was sent the relevant papers together with an authority in writing, signed on behalf of the Secretary of State, appointing him to hold the particular inquiry. The taxpayer was solely responsible for the conduct and procedure at the inquiry, subject to the rules governing tribunals and inquiries. The d taxpayer was remunerated by daily fees according to the length of the inquiry and received no retainer or salary. The Crown claimed that the taxpayer's position was a public office capable of being held by persons in succession and therefore an 'office' within s 181(1)[a] of the Income and Corporation Taxes Act 1970, and accordingly the fees received by him were chargeable to tax under Case I of Sch E. The taxpayer appealed to the General Commissioners, contending that his appointment was not an office within e s 181(1) because the holding of each inquiry was an ad hoc appointment of indeterminate length which he was free to accept or refuse. The General Commissioners allowed the appeal but their decision was reversed by the judge ([1979] 1 All ER 648), who held that for the purposes of s 181(1) an inspector at a public local inquiry held a series of offices to which he was appointed from time to time by the person having the power of appointment to such offices. The taxpayer appealed. f

Held – An office was a post which existed independently of the identity of the person who occupied it for the time being and which had a sufficient degree of continuance and permanence to enable it to be held by successive incumbents. Since the taxpayer's appointment to conduct a public local inquiry was an ad hoc appointment for the particular inquiry it lacked the characteristics of an 'office' within s 181(1) of the 1970 Act and the taxpayer was not assessable to tax under Sch E in respect of the fees received g by him for conducting such inquiries. The appeal would therefore be allowed (see p 281 *g* to *j*, p 285 *h* to p 286 *b*, p 289 *g* to p 290 *b*, p 291 *h j*, p 293 *e f* and p 294 *h j*, post).

Dictum of Rowlatt J in *Great Western Railway Co v Bater (Surveyor of Taxes)* [1920] 3 KB at 274 applied.

Decision of Walton J [1979] 1 All ER 648 reversed. h

Notes

For meaning of 'office' and 'employment', see 23 Halsbury's Laws (4th Edn) paras 647–648, and for cases on the subject, see 28(1) Digest (Reissue) 320–323, *1130–1147*.

For the Income and Corporation Taxes Act 1970, s 181, see 33 Halsbury's Statutes (3rd Edn) 255. j

For 1974–75 and subsequent years of assessment, s 181(1) of the 1970 Act has been amended by s 2(1) of the Finance Act 1974.

a Section 181(1), so far as material, provides: 'The Schedule referred to as Schedule E is as follows:— SCHEDULE E 1. Tax under this Schedule shall be charged in respect of any office or employment on emoluments therefrom ...'

Cases referred to in judgments

Dale v Inland Revenue Comrs [1953] 2 All ER 671, [1954] AC 11, [1953] 3 WLR 448, 34 Tax Cas 468, 32 ATC 294, [1953] TR 269, 46 R & IT 513, HL, 28(1) Digest (Reissue) 583, *2163*.

Davies (Inspector of Taxes) v Braithwaite [1931] 2 KB 628, [1931] All ER Rep 792, 18 Tax Cas 198, 100 LJKB 619, 145 LT 693, 28(1) Digest (Reissue) 241, *746*.

Farrell v Alexander [1976] 2 All ER 721, [1977] AC 59, [1976] 3 WLR 145, 32 P & CR 292, HL, Digest (Cont Vol E) 382, *8375b*.

Great Western Railway Co v Bater (Surveyor of Taxes) [1920] 3 KB 266, 90 LJKB 41, 124 LT 92, 8 Tax Cas 231; *affd* [1921] 2 KB 128, 90 LJKB 550, 125 LT 321, 8 Tax Case 231, CA; *rvsd* [1922] 2 AC 1, 91 LJKB 472, 127 LT 170, 8 Tax Cas 231, HL, 28(1) Digest (Reissue) 320, *1132*.

Inland Revenue Comrs v Brander & Cruickshank [1971] 1 All ER 36, [1971] 1 WLR 212, 46 Tax Cas 574, [1970] TR 353, HL; *affg* 1970 SLT 159, 46 Tax Cas 574, 28(1) Digest (Reissue) 46, *193*.

McMillan v Guest (Inspector of Taxes) [1942] 1 All ER 606, [1942] AC 561, 24 Tax Cas 190, 111 LJKB 398, 167 LT 329, HL; *affg* [1940] 4 All ER 452, [1941] 1 KB 258, 24 Tax Cas 190, 110 LJKB 125, CA, 28(1) Digest (Reissue) 337, *1219*.

Mitchell (Inspector of Taxes) v Ross [1961] 3 All ER 49, [1962] AC 813, [1961] 3 WLR 411, 40 Tax Cas 11, 40 ATC 199, [1961] TR 191, HL; *rvsg* [1960] 2 All ER 218, [1960] Ch 498, [1960] 2 WLR 766, 40 Tax Cas 11, 39 ATC 52, [1960] TR 79, CA; *affg* [1959] 3 All ER 341, [1960] Ch 145, [1959] 3 WLR 550, 40 Tax Cas 11, 38 ATC 422, [1959] TR 225, 28(1) Digest (Reissue) 321, *1138*.

Appeal

Frank Howard Clinch ('the taxpayer') appealed against the judgment of Walton J ([1979] 1 All ER 648, [1979] 1 WLR 338) given on 29th November 1978 whereby he allowed an appeal by the Crown from the decision of the Commissioners for the General Purposes of the Income Tax that he was not assessable to income tax under Sch E for the years 1973–74 and 1974–75 in respect of payments for conducting public local inquiries as the holder of an office within s 181(1) of the Income and Corporation Taxes Act 1970. The facts are set out in the judgment of Buckley LJ.

Michael Nolan QC and *John Gardiner* for the taxpayer.
Brian Davenport QC and *Richard Aikens* for the Crown.

Cur adv vult

9th May. The following judgments were read.

BUCKLEY LJ. This is an appeal from a decision of Walton J ([1979] 1 All ER 648, [1979] 1 WLR 338) on 29th November 1978 whereby he allowed an appeal from a decision of the General Commissioners for Income Tax who had held that the taxpayer had been incorrectly assessed to income tax under Sch E for the years 1973–74 and 1974–75 in respect of fees which he had earned in those years by conducting public local inquiries in respect of matters such as compulsory purchases for which the Secretary of State for the Environment was responsible. The question is whether the taxpayer should have been assessed in respect of these fees under Sch E or under Sch D, Case II.

The facts are set out in the case stated and I need not recapitulate them (the case is set out at [1979] 1 All ER 649–650). It is sufficient to say that the taxpayer is a civil engineer by profession and that he was in each of the relevant two years, and had been for some time previously, one of a panel of persons whom the Secretary of State from time to time invited to conduct independent public inquiries and to make reports thereon. When so invited the taxpayer was under no obligation to accept the nomination. He was remunerated for these services exclusively by fees on a daily basis. He was solely responsible for the conduct and procedure at any inquiry which he was appointed to conduct, subject to the rules governing tribunals and inquiries. Until the year 1973–74 the taxpayer was assessed in respect of such fees under Sch D, Case II. In the two years in question, however, he was assessed in respect of such fees (apparently without any previous warning) under Sch E. It seems that assessment under Sch E may prove disadvantageous to the taxpayer on a number of grounds, due in part to the fact that assessments under Sch E are made on the receipts for the current year, whereas assessments under Sch D are made on earnings of the previous year.

The charge to tax under Sch E is now contained in the Income and Corporation Taxes Act 1970, s 181, which provides, so far as relevant to this case, that tax under Sch E shall be charged in respect of any office or employment on emoluments therefrom. The charge to tax under Sch D is to be found in s 108 of the 1970 Act which, so far as presently relevant, provides that tax under Sch D shall be charged in respect of the annual profits or gains arising or accruing to any person residing in the United kingdom from any trade, profession or vocation, whether carried on in the United Kingdom or elsewhere, and all other annual profits or gains not charged under Sch A, B, C or E and not specially exempted from tax. If the fees with which we are concerned are chargeable under Sch E as emoluments of an office or employment they are excluded from Sch D. It is not suggested that they were emoluments of an employment for the purposes of Sch E. Consequently the sole question is whether the fees were emoluments of an office. The answer to this question must depend on the meaning to be attributed to the word 'office'.

We have been referred by counsel to a number of authorities in which over the years the meaning to be given to that word has been considered, starting with *Great Western Railway Co v Bater (Surveyor of Taxes)* [1922] 2 AC 1 and ending with *Inland Revenue Comrs v Brander & Cruickshank* [1971] 1 All ER 36, [1971] 1 WLR 212. These cases have been decided at various stages of the history of legislation relating to income tax. Counsel for the Crown, relying on what was said by Lord Wilberforce in *Farrell v Alexander* [1976] 2 All ER 721 at 726, [1977] AC 59 at 73, has submitted that the 1970 Act should be construed without recourse to legislative antecedents and decisions on earlier Acts. Lord Wilberforce said:

> '... self-contained statutes, whether consolidating previous law, or so doing with amendments, should be interpreted, if reasonably possible, without recourse to antecedents, and ... the recourse should only be had when there is a real and substantial difficulty or ambiguity which classical methods of construction cannot resolve.'

The question for decision in *Farrell v Alexander* was, it seems to me, of a very different character from the question which we have to consider. The question was whether the words 'any person' in the Rent Act 1968, s 85 should be construed as limited to the landlord. To do so was to limit very wide words to a very narrow application. This was sought to be achieved by reliance on decisions on earlier Acts of Parliament. In the present case we are faced with the problem of putting a meaning on an ordinary word in the English language, which has been used over a long period in income tax legislation. The courts have from time to time had to consider the proper meaning to be attributed to that ordinary English word in that legislation. It is not, in my judgment, in conflict with the principle enunciated by Lord Wilberforce to look at past decisions to discover what the courts in the past have thought to be the appropriate meaning to attribute to that ordinary English word. In doing so, however, we should guard ourselves against treating as authoritative decisions which were reached for reasons which may no longer be appropriate.

The word 'office' has a wide variety of meanings in our language and is certainly not a term of art in our law. It is not, in my view, a term which is free from ambiguity. The Income and Corporation Taxes Act 1970 contains, and its predecessors have contained, no definition of 'office'. We have to discover what meaning is most appropriately applied to it in Sch E. Of the meanings attributed by the Oxford English Dictionary to the word the following comes nearest to the sense of the present case:

> 'A position or place to which certain duties are attached, especially one of a more or less public character; a position of trust, authority, or service under constituted authority; a place in the administration of government, the public service, the direction of a corporation, company, society etc.'

This appears to me to indicate, if any such clarification were necessary, that the office is something which is distinct from the holder of the office.

Before proceeding further, it may perhaps be helpful if I say, as shortly as I may, something about the history of the charge under Sch E. The familiar arrangement classifying income under Schs A, B, C, D and E was first adopted in the year 1803. The income tax was abolished in 1816, but revived in 1842 on the same general lines as before 1816. Under Sch E of that Act, that is the 1842 Act, the tax was charged (by r 3) 'on all public offices and employments of profit of the description hereinafter mentioned'. There then followed a long catalogue of public offices, ending with the words 'and every other public office or employment of profit of a public nature'. Under subsequent rules the tax was to be deducted at source, and by r 1 it was provided that assessments should be for a whole year without any new assessment notwithstanding any change in the occupancy of the office. This scheme of assessment, with some verbal alterations, continued in force until 1956. Many amendments followed, year by year, from 1843 until 1918 when the first consolidating Act was passed. By the Income Tax Acts 1918 and 1952 tax was charged under Sch E in respect of 'every public office or employment of profit'. Under Sch D tax was charged in respect of annual profits or gains arising or accruing from (inter alia) 'any trade, profession, employment or vocation'. By the Finance Act 1922, s 18(1), profits or gains arising or accruing from an employment, which under the 1918 Act would have been chargeable to tax under Sch D (i e non-public employment) were transferred to Sch E. By the Finance Act 1956, s 10, Sch E was amended to charge to tax emoluments from 'any office or employment' omitting the word 'public'. That is the language still to be found in s 181 of the 1970 Act. It will be seen that the only change which has taken place in the use of the word 'office' is that, where in the 1842 and 1918 Acts there were references to 'any public office', since 1956 the language has been 'any office'. This is not, in my opinion, a difference of any significance in respect of the meaning to be given to the word 'office'. There have, however, been considerable changes in the context afforded by the provisions of the statutes from time to time in force.

Before considering the authorities which bear on this question, I may perhaps be allowed to say in what sense, unguided by authority and without attempting to formulate a precise definition, I should be inclined to understand the word 'office' as used in Sch E. An 'office' in this context is, in my opinion, a post which can be recognised as existing, whether it be occupied for the time being or vacant, and which, if occupied, does not owe its existence in any way to the identity of the incumbent or his appointment to the post. It follows, I think, that the office must owe its existence to some constituent instrument, whether it be a charter, statute, declaration of trust, contract (other than a contract of personal service) or instrument of some other kind. It also follows, in my view, that the office must have a sufficient degree of continuance to admit of its being held by successive incumbents; it need not be capable of permanent or prolonged or indefinite existence, but it cannot be limited to the tenure of one man, for if it were so it would lack that independent existence which to my mind the word 'office' imports. It may be that it should in some degree possess a public character, but it is unnecessary to decide that point in this case, for the taxpayer's functions in respect of which the fees were received undoubtedly had such a character.

In *Great Western Railway Co v Bater (Surveyor of Taxes)* [1922] 2 AC 1 the question for decision was whether a Mr Hall, who was employed as a clerk by the Great Western Railway Co, could properly be said to hold a public office. Rowlatt J referred to the fact that under r 1 of the 1842 Act the assessment in respect of the emoluments of an office was to be made for a year in respect of the office and that it was to be in force for a whole *a* year and levied without any new assessment notwithstanding that a change of person having or exercising the office or employment had taken place in the course of the year. He expressed his own personal view in the following terms (8 Tax Cas 231 at 235; cf [1920] 3 KB 266 at 274):

> 'Now it is argued, and to my mind argued most forcibly, that that shows that what those who used the language of the Act of 1842 meant, when they spoke of an *b* office or an employment, was an office or employment which was a subsisting, permanent, substantive position, which had an existence independent of the person who filled it, which went on and was filled in succession by successive holders; and if you merely had a man who was engaged on whatever terms, to do duties which were assigned to him, his employment to do those duties did not create an office to which those duties were attached. He merely was employed to do certain things *c* and that is an end of it; and if there was no office or employment existing in the case as a thing, the so-called office or employment was merely an aggregate of the activities of the particular man for the time being. And I think myself that is sound. I am not going to decide that, because I think I ought not to in the state of the authorities, but my own view is that the people in 1842 who used this language meant by an office a substantive thing that existed apart from the holder.' *d*

When the case reached the House of Lords the House adopted Rowlatt J's view. Lord Atkinson said that he fully concurred in the passage which I have read from Rowlatt J's judgment (see [1922] 2 AC 1 at 15). Lord Sumner said that in his opinion Mr Hall's situation was not an office or an employment of profit and that no one would think of calling it so; it enjoyed neither publicity nor continuity; and it was not distinguishable *e* from that of the engine driver in any respect that falls within the meaning of Sch E. It is true that the noble and learned Lords who sat on that case did pay attention in their speeches to the machinery of assessment prescribed by the Sch E of 1842. This was partly due to the fact that they were concerned to decide whether Mr Hall's post could be considered to be a 'public office' within the meaning of the Sch E of 1842, for those were the words to be construed; but I do not think their consideration of that question can be *f* satisfactorily divorced from the views which they expressed about the character of an 'office'. I would consequently accept that that decision should be regarded as coloured by the form of the legislation then in force.

The next case for consideration is *McMillan v Guest (Inspector of Taxes)* [1942] 1 All ER 606, [1942] AC 561, which was a decision on the Sch E of 1918. The question in that case was whether a non-executive director of a private limited company was assessable under *g* Sch E on his remuneration as a director on the footing that he held a 'public office'. Lawrence J held that the taxpayer was not liable under Sch E. His decision was reversed in this court, whose decision was affirmed in the House of Lords. In this case, it seems to me, the House of Lords addressed itself to the question how the word 'office' should be understood in the ordinary sense of language without regard to legislative history. Lord Atkin said ([1942] 1 All ER 606 at 607, [1942] AC 561 at 564): 'It is necessary to *h* consider whether the appellant (1) held an office, (2) held a public office, (3) held a public office within the United Kingdom.' He answered the first question in the following terms:

> 'On the first point there was no dispute. There is no statutory definition of "office". Without adopting the sentence as a complete definition, one may treat the following expression of ROWLATT, J., in *Great Western Ry. Co.* v. *Bater* ([1920] 3 KB *j* 266 at 274) as a generally sufficient statement of the meaning of the word: "an office or employment which was a subsisting, permanent, substantive position, which had an existence independent of the person who filled it, which went on and was filled in succession by successive holders." This statement was adopted by LORD ATKINSON in his judgment in the same case in the House of Lords ([1922] AC 1 at 15). There can be no doubt that the director of a company holds such an office as is described.'

Lord Wright said ([1942] 1 All ER 606 at 608, [1942] AC 561 at 566):

> a 'The word "office" is of indefinite content; its various meanings cover four columns of the NEW ENGLISH DICTIONARY, but I take as the most relevant for the purposes of this case the following: "A position or place to which certain duties are attached, especially one of a more or less public character." This, I think, roughly corresponds with such approaches to a definition as have been attempted in the
> b authorities, in particular *Great Western Ry. Co.* v. *Bater*, where the legal construction of these words which had been in Sched. E since 1803 . . . was discussed.'

Later he said ([1942] 1 All ER 606 at 608–609, [1942] AC 561 at 566–567):

> 'I do not attempt what their Lordships did not attempt in *Bater's Case*, i.e., an exact definition of these words. They are deliberately, I imagine, left vague.
> c Though their true construction is a matter of law, they are to be applied in the facts of the particular case according to the ordinary use of language and the dictates of common sense, with due regard to the requirement that there must be some degree of permanence and publicity in the office.'

On this point Lord Porter contented himself with saying ([1942] 1 All ER 606 at 611, [1942] AC 561 at 570): 'That it is an office is, I think, plain. It has permanancy apart from
d the temporary holder and is held in one of the specified corporations.' Lord Roche agreed with Lord Atkin.

In *Mitchell (Inspector of Taxes) v Ross* [1961] 3 All ER 49, [1962] AC 813, decided under the Income Tax Act 1952, the question was whether a taxpayer who had been appointed to be a part-time consultant with a regional hospital board was assessable in respect of the profits or gains arising from that appointment under Sch D or under Sch E. Upjohn J
e decided that they fell to be assessed under Sch E, and his decision on that point was affirmed by the Court of Appeal. In the course of his judgment Lord Evershed MR placed reliance on the terms of the National Health Service Act 1946 which required the Minister to appoint consultants and on the fact that the taxpayer's appointment as a part-time consultant was made by the regional hospital board under powers delegated to them under that Act by the Minister. He also relied on the terms of the contract between
f the taxpayer and the regional hospital board. He referred to *Great Western Railway Co v Bater (Surveyor of Taxes)* and to *McMillan v Guest (Inspector of Taxes)*, and held that the taxpayer's appointment clearly satisfied the test indicated by those citations. Pearce LJ agreed that it was clear that the taxpayer's appointment was an office. Harman LJ also agreed, saying ([1960] 2 All ER 218 at 230, [1960] Ch 498 at 530): 'An office is a position or post which goes on without regard to the identity of the holder of it from time to time
g as was said, in effect, by ROWLATT, J., in *Great Western Ry. Co.* v. *Bater* and approved by LORD ATKIN in *McMillan v Guest*.' The case went to the House of Lords but on another point. In the House of Lords counsel for the taxpayer conceded that the case fell within Sch E. Viscount Simonds said that in his opinion the concession was rightly made and that the opposite view was not arguable (see [1961] 3 All ER 49 at 51, [1962] AC 813 at 832). Lord Radcliffe said that he entirely agreed with Upjohn J, who had held at first
h instance that the taxpayer's appointment was a public office (see [1961] 3 All ER 49 at 54, [1962] AC).

The last of this series of authorities to which I must refer is *Inland Revenue Comrs v Brander & Cruickshank* [1971] 1 All ER 36, [1971] 1 WLR 212, decided under the Finance Act 1956. That case related to a Scottish firm of advocates who also acted as secretaries and registrars to a number of companies. Two of the companies were taken over and in
j consequence the taxpayers lost their positions as secretaries and registrars with those companies and received a sum of £2,500 by way of compensation. If this sum was a receipt of the taxpayers' profession as advocates it was taxable under Case II of Sch D. If on the other hand it was an emolument of an office which, if taxable at all, would be taxable under Sch E, it was exempt from tax under the Finance Act 1960, s 38(3). The Special Commissioners held that the taxpayers' appointments as registrars were 'offices' and that accordingly the case fell within Sch E and not Sch D, and that consequently the

taxpayers were exempt from tax. The Court of Session upheld that decision and the House of Lords affirmed the decision of the Court of Session. Lord Morris drew attention a to the fact that the Companies Act 1948 made it necessary that the performance of the statutory duty of maintaining a company's register should be assigned to someone. He held that the Special Commissioners were warranted on the facts as found in holding that the appointments in question were appointments to offices. He said ([1971] 1 All ER 36 at 41, [1971] 1 WLR 212 at 215):

> 'Even though the Companies Act 1948 does not require that there should be an b appointment as registrar, a company must arrange that some person or persons should on its behalf perform the statutory duties of maintaining its register. In doing so, it may establish a position which successively will be held by different persons. If it does so the company may have created what could rationally for income tax purposes be called an office.'

c

Lord Guest concurred in the view that the post of registrar was an 'office' within the meaning of Sch E (see [1971] 1 All ER 36 at 43, [1971] 1 WLR 212 at 217), and Lord Donovan said that he did not think it possible to say that as a matter of law the commissioners were disentitled to take the view that each registrarship was an office within the meaning of the schedule (see [1971] 1 All ER 36 at 46, [1971] 1 WLR 212 at 220). In so holding the commissioners had founded themselves on the decision in d *McMillan v Guest (Inspector of Taxes)*.

We were also referred to the decision of Rowlatt J in *Davies (Inspector of Taxes) v Braithwaite* [1931] 2 KB 628, [1931] All ER Rep 792 relating to the theatrical earnings of the late Dame Lilian Braithwaite. For my part I derive little assistance from that decision.

These decisions were, of course, decisions on the particular facts of each case and e related to a variety of statutory provisions in force from time to time. Nevertheless, even if they should not be regarded as binding on us in the present case, they clearly constitute a body of very highly persuasive authority on the sense to be put on the word 'office' in a Sch E context. They appear to me to give strong support to the personal view which I formulated earlier in this judgment on the meaning to be attributed to the word for present purposes, and I find in them nothing to prompt me to qualify that view. In f particular I would draw attention to the frequent references to the characteristic of continuance.

The Crown throughout this case maintained that on each occasion when the taxpayer was invited to conduct a public inquiry he was appointed to a separate office, which continued until his functions in relation to that inquiry were fully discharged, whereupon that office came to an end. g

The learned judge felt impelled to accept that view by four considerations. Although, no doubt, in fairness to the learned judge these four considerations should be considered collectively as cumulative indications of the existence of a series of offices, I will comment on each in turn.

The first of these four considerations is 'that the inspector has no employer'. This must, I think, stem from what was said by Lord Normand in *Dale v Inland Revenue Comrs* h [1953] 2 All ER 671 at 673, [1954] AC 11 at 26. The question in that case was whether the late Sir Henry Dale as a trustee of the will of the late Sir Henry Wellcome, under which he received an annuity for so long as he remained a trustee of the will, held 'an office of profit' within the Income Tax Act 1918, s 14(3). Lord Normand said:

> 'The first point to consider is whether trusteeship is within the ordinary sense of j the word an "office", and on this I can only say that "office" is an apt word to describe a trustee's position, or any position in which services are due by the holder and in which the holder has no employer.'

The holders of innumerable offices, no doubt, owe duties and have no employer, but it cannot, in my opinion, be accurate to say that anyone who owes duties but has no

employer is the holder of an office. All sorts of self-employed persons undertake
a obligations to perform duties in the course of their self-employment without having any employer. For example, many professional men such as accountants, architects or solicitors undertake duties to their clients, but could not properly be said to have any employer or to be the holders of offices. Moreover, the converse also would, I think, be untrue. I feel fairly confident that one could find many holders of what would certainly be accepted as being offices in ordinary parlance who do so under a contract of service.

b The second consideration referred to by the learned judge was the following: 'That the person who conducts the inquiry is the person appointed, the inspector, and not the taxpayer considered as a person. Without the appointment having first been made, his acts would be wholly nugatory.' No doubt the acts of anybody who purported to conduct a public inquiry under the Acquisition of Land (Authorisation Procedure) Act 1946 without having been appointed to do so would be nugatory, but in any case in
c which a person appointed to conduct such an inquiry does so I see no basis for saying that he acts otherwise than in the capacity of an individual so appointed. The title 'inspector' has no countenance under the statute. It is a term of convenience frequently used to describe a person appointed to conduct a public inquiry, but nothing more. The relevant paragraph of Sch 1 to the Act refers merely to 'a person appointed by the confirming authority for the purpose', ie for the purpose of conducting a public local inquiry (see
d Sch 1, para 4(2)). Anyone who is so appointed is invested with authority to conduct the inquiry in such way as he thinks fit subject to the regulations contained in the Compulsory Purchase by Ministers (Inquiries Procedure) Rules 1967, SI 1967 No 720, which describe him merely as 'the appointed person'. With deference to the learned judge, I see no justification for treating the person so appointed as having any status distinct from his status as a person selected by the Minister to carry out the particular
e task.

The third consideration was 'that the duty placed on the inspector was one which was placed by statute'. This is true, and if the other criteria for the existence of an 'office' were present, this might well be a relevant consideration.

The final consideration referred to by the learned judge is this: 'That in the event of the person originally appointed not for any reason carrying out the duties placed on him, the
f only method of procedure (apart from abandoning the proposed enquiry altogether) would be to appoint another inspector.' As I understand the position, in the event of a person appointed to conduct a public inquiry being unable or unwilling for any reason to complete the task, there would be no question of another person being appointed in his place to carry on from the point which the inquiry had reached: it would be necessary to start a new inquiry from the beginning. The second apointment would not take effect
g in any sense in succession to the first.

For these reasons these four points do not have the same persuasive force for me as they had for the learned judge.

Counsel for the Crown pressed on us the public nature of the duties undertaken by anyone who is appointed to conduct a public inquiry. This is in effect the learned judge's third significant consideration. Counsel for the Crown stressed that, although these
h duties stem from the appointment of the individual appointed to conduct the inquiry and relate exclusively to that inquiry, they are statutory duties of a quasi judicial and public character. That the duties are statutory and that they are of a public character cannot be denied. Nevertheless I for my part cannot regard these characteristics alone as sufficient to constitute the appointment an appointment to an 'office'. There was no continuity about the taxpayer's position as a person appointed from time to time to
j conduct public inquiries. Each appointment was distinct from all the others and was effective only for the purpose of the particular inquiry to which it related. So soon as that inquiry was completed by the taxpayer making his report, the appointment was spent. Had the taxpayer for any reason failed to complete his assignment as the person charged with the responsibility of conducting a particular inquiry and reporting on it, the appointment would have lapsed; no one would or could have been appointed to complete

that particular assignment; it would have become necessary to embark on a new inquiry and to appoint a new appointed person for the purpose of that new inquiry. So each appointment was personal to the taxpayer; it lacked the characteristic of independent existence and continuance which, in my judgment, is one of the essential characteristics of an 'office'.

These considerations lead me to a different conclusion from that reached by the learned judge. In my judgment the taxpayer did not hold any 'office' within the meaning of Sch E in respect of any of the public inquiries which he was appointed to conduct. The emoluments which he earned by reason of those appointments fall, in my judgment, to be assessed under Sch D.

I would consequently allow this appeal.

ACKNER LJ. The question which this appeal raises is: what is an 'office' within the meaning of s 181 of the Income and Corporation Taxes Act 1970? For many years the taxpayer and those like him, who were appointed by a Minister to hold from time to time a public local inquiry, were not treated by the Revenue as holding an 'office' within the meaning of that section and thus falling under Sch E, Case I as distinct from carrying on a profession or vocation falling within Case II of Sch D (s 109(2)) of the 1970 Act.

However, suddenly, without any prior warning to the taxpayer, the Revenue, in the words of Walton J, behaving in an extremely insensitive way, changed their practice and subjected the taxpayer to the PAYE provisions of s 204 of the 1970 Act and the regulations made thereunder. This of course is not the only disadvantage resulting from being taxed under Sch E. Without going into any detail, such a basis of taxation, when imposed on a person who is otherwise taxed under Sch D, can give rise to 'peaks and troughs' problems, that is, unreal fluctuations in income with resultant tax disadvantages. It can create anomalies in relation to the charging of expenses, and on retirement it can create added complications to the already complicated situation, resulting from the Sch D basis of taxation being that of the preceding year of assessment.

Was the Crown correct in its second thoughts? The General Commissioners thought that they were wrong and Walton J thought that they were right.

There is no statutory definition of the word 'office' but the courts have time and again treated the words of Rowlatt J in *Great Western Railway Co v Bater (Surveyor of Taxes)* [1920] 3 KB 266 at 274 as a generally sufficient statement of the meaning of the word (see in particular *McMillan v Guest (Inspector of Taxes)* [1942] 1 All ER 606 at 607, [1942] AC 561 at 564 per Lord Atkin). The expression used by Rowlatt J was: '... a subsisting permanent substantive position which had an existence independent of the person who filled it and which went on and was filled in succession by successive holders.' Lord Wright in *McMillan's* case [1942] 1 All ER 606 at 608, [1942] AC 561 at 566, in resisting an exact definition of the word, chose from the four columns of the New English Dictionary the following as the most relevant: '... a position or place to which certain duties are attached especially one of a more or less public character.' He took the view that this roughly corresponded with such approaches to a definition as had been attempted, in particular in *Bater's* case [1922] 2 AC 1. He added however, that the word has to be construed in relation to the facts of the particular case, 'according to the ordinary use of language and dictates of common sense, with due regard to the requirement that there must be some degree of permanence and publicity in the office' (see [1942] 1 All ER 606 at 608–609, [1942] AC 561 at 567).

In the most recent of the cases, *Inland Revenue Comrs v Brander & Cruikshank* [1971] 1 All ER 36, [1971] 1 WLR 212, the Crown contended that the compensation of £2,500 received on termination of the respondent's appointments as registrars of two companies was a trading receipt and therefore should have been included in the firm's profits assessable under Case II of Sch D. The appointments, they contended, were like agencies and not offices or employments under Sch E. Lord Guthrie in the Court of Session, having referred to Rowlatt J's dictum, said (46 Tax Cas 574 at 584):

> 'What the Special Commissioners had to decide was whether in the particular cases of the two companies the Respondents were holders of substantive positions to

> which duties were attached, and which had the quality of permanency irrespective a of the particular holder's tenure, or whether they merely did some work of a particular kind for the companies.'

Lord Migdale, who also referred to the same dictum, observed (46 Tax Cas 574 at 587): 'This work of keeping the registers entailed a position which had an existence of its own. If one holder gave it up someone else had to be appointed to carry it on.' The Court of Session accordingly held that the registrarships were 'offices', and that those b offices were not assets of the respondent's business assessable under Sch D. That decision was upheld by the House of Lords. Lord Morris said ([1971] 1 All ER 36 at 41, [1971] 1 WLR 212 at 215):

> 'A duty is imposed on a company to keep a register of members (Companies Act 1948, s 110). Even though the Companies Act 1948 does not require that there c should be an appointment as registrar, a company must arrange that a person or persons should on its behalf perform the statutory duties of maintaining its register. In doing so, it may establish a position which successively will be held by different persons. If it does so the company may have created what could rationally for income tax purposes be called an office.'

d Lord Morris then referred to *McMillan v Guest (Inspector of Taxes)*, where Lord Atkin was prepared to accept Rowlatt J's dictum in the *Bater* case, as adopted by Lord Atkinson when that case went to appeal as being a generally sufficient statement of the meaning. He also referred to Lord Wright's observations in the selfsame case, to which I have earlier made reference.

The taxpayer was, because of his qualifications and experience as a chartered civil e engineer, invited from time to time by the Department of Environment to hold a public local inquiry where objections had been entered to a proposed compulsory purchase order. The Department was given power under the Acquisition of Land (Authorisation Procedure) Act 1946 to appoint a person to hold such an inquiry. The Compulsory Purchase by Ministers (Inquiries Procedure) Rules 1967 made under the provisions of s 7A of the Tribunal and Inquiries Act 1958 prescribe the procedures to be followed at f such public local inquiries.

When it became necessary to hold such a public local inquiry, the taxpayer would be contacted by telephone by a department official who would inform him of the location and date of the inquiry, and the daily fee payable, and would invite the taxpayer to undertake the inquiry. The taxpayer then had complete discretion whether to accept or refuse the invitation. He was solely remunerated by such daily fees according to the g length of the inquiry, and received no retainer or salary. Payment was made by the department only in response to a fee account submitted by the taxpayer. He did, however, receive travelling and subsistence allowance on Civil Service scales. No statement of 'terms of employment' under the Contracts of Employment Act 1963 was ever served on him and no question of redundancy payments arose on the completion of an inquiry. On acceptance of the invitation, the taxpayer would have forwarded to him h the papers relevant to the inquiry together with an authority in writing, signed on behalf of the Secretary of State, appointing him to hold the particular inquiry. Thereafter he held an independent public inquiry without direction or guidance from the Secretary of State, and always announced his independent status at the commencement of the inquiry. The taxpayer was solely responsible for the conduct and procedure at such an inquiry, subject to the rules governing tribunals and inquiries. If the taxpayer became j ill, or had some urgent business to attend to, during the progress of the inquiry, he could ask to be released from his engagement. The department, if it consented to his release, would then find some other inspector, as it so described the appointment, and a fresh inquiry would have to take place. The taxpayer stamped his own insurance card as a self-employed person.

At the hearing of the taxpayer's appeal before the General Commissioners against the Revenue's decision, the Crown accepted that the 'office', as it so contended was the status

of this engagement, subsisted from the date when the appointment was made to the date when the report of the inquiry was delivered to the Secretary of State. It was contended a
for the Crown that each such office was a separate office within the meaning of s 181(1) of the 1970 Act.

The General Commissioners, whose attention was drawn to the relevant authorities, found that the taxpayer's appointment was a 'transient, indeterminate, once only execution of a task, for which he was peculiarly qualified'. They concluded that the taxpayer's discharge of the duties of an inspector holding a public local inquiry did *not* b
amount to the holding of an office within the meaning of Case I of Sch E. Clearly the General Commissioners reached their conclusions because of the lack of permanence and the lack of continuity of the engagement.

Walton J reversed the General Commissioners' decision. He was of the opinion that the authorities to which his attention was drawn, in particular *Bater's* and *McMillan's* cases, provided only 'slight guidance'. He concluded that there would not be the slightest c
doubt that a person appointed to conduct an inquiry under the 1946 Act holds an office save for two matters to which I shall refer shortly hereafter. The factors which in his view would otherwise make the conclusion inevitable were:

1. 'That the Inspector has no employer.' Counsel for the taxpayer rightly points out that of course neither does a self-employed man, which was undoubtedly the status of the taxpayer. d

2. 'That the person who conducts the inquiry is the person appointed, the inspector, and not the taxpayer considered as a person. Without the appointment having first been made his acts would be wholly nugatory.' But the person who conducts the inquiry is the taxpayer considered as a person. He owes his appointment to the particular skill and/or experience which he has. Of course he would have no locus standi without the formal appointment first being made, but then the same would equally apply to an e
arbitrator, who counsel for the Crown concedes is not appointed to an 'office'.

3. 'That the duty placed on the inspector was one placed by statute.' I take this to mean that, once having accepted the appointment, then the taxpayer's conduct of the public local inquiry was, to some extent, controlled and circumscribed by the statutes to which I have made reference. Again I cannot see any great significance in this point, since equally an arbitrator's conduct of an arbitration is controlled and circumscribed to f
some extent by the Arbitration Acts and by the courts. The obligation to observe statutory requirements cannot in itself create an office.

4. 'That in the event of the person originally appointed not for any reason carrying out the duties placed on him, the only method of procedure (apart from abandoning the proposed enquiry altogether) would be to appoint another inspector.' This statement is not strictly accurate, since if the person originally appointed does not carry out the duties g
placed on him, the proposed inquiry has to be abandoned and another inspector has to be appointed. But this equally applies to any other engagement of a professional character.

The first of the two matters which caused the learned judge some hesitation were as follows ([1979] 1 All ER 648 at 654, [1979] 1 WLR 338 at 345):

> '... that, in complete contradistinction to the description of an office given by h
> Rowlatt J ... the so-called "office" here was of a merely temporary nature: it was the reverse of permanent, in that once his report had been delivered he was functus officio and that was the end of that inquiry.'

The learned judge however concluded that it was not a proper use of authority 'to wrench a statement such as that made by Rowlatt J out of context'. In the learned judge's view j
the context in which he was making that statement was in relation to who might conceivably be, and who might not conceivably be, the holder of a public office in a railway company. But in my judgment there was no wrenching of the words out of context. The learned judge's attention was not directed to *Davies (Inspector of Taxes) v Braithwaite* [1931] 2 KB 628, [1931] All ER Rep 792. The case concerned the question whether Miss Lilian Braithwaite, the well-known actress, ought to have been assessed under Sch D of the Income Tax Act 1918 as following her profession as an actress or

whether she ought to be assessed under Sch E as exercising certain employments under the particular engagement which she made. At the outset of his judgment Rowlatt J explained the requirement of a degree of permanence. He said ([1931] 2 KB 628 at 633–634; cf [1931] All ER Rep 792 at 794):

> 'The scheme of the Income Tax Acts used to be included under Sch. D "profession, employment, or vocation." That was held to be a fairly comprehensible definition of persons who carried on business on their own account. Under Sch. E were public offices. It was recognized that where a person was in a permanent situation it was much better to assess his salary as the salary of the situation than to go to him personally and assess him in respect of his earnings. There were persons, like railway clerks, who were hired for an indefinite period. For the purposes of assessment to income tax they were treated as holders of offices. That was a very convenient method of assessment to income tax. Then a case arose (*Great Western Ry. Co. v. Bater*), in which I pointed out that these railway clerks were not holders of offices at all. I said that my own view was that Parliament in using this language in 1842 meant by an office a substantive thing that existed apart from its holder. It was something which had an existence independent of the person who filled it. It was something which was held by tenure and title rather than by contract and which continued to exist, though the holders of it might change and it was filled in succession by successive holders. The House of Lords decided that my view was right. It was therefore found convenient to put "employment" expressly in Sch. E.'

He further stated in relation to Miss Braithwaite's activities ([1931] 2 KB 628 at 635–636, [1931] All ER Rep 792 at 795):

> 'But I would go further than that and say that it seems to me that where one finds a method of earning a livelihood which does not consist of the obtaining of a post and staying in it, but consists of a series of engagements moving from one to the other—and in the case of an actor's or actress's life it certainly involves going from one to the other and not going on playing one part for the rest of his or her life, but in obtaining first one engagement, then another, and a whole series of them—then each of those engagements cannot be considered an employment, but is a mere engagement in the course of exercising a profession, and every profession and every trade does involve the making of successive engagements and successive contracts and, in one sense of the word, employments.'

Clearly to my mind, the learned judge was stressing, as did Lord Wright, the need for some degree of permanence. This feature is, in my judgment, reflected in the requirement of continuity. Thus an office is a position or post which goes on without regard to the identity of the holder of it from time to time, as Harman LJ summarised the effect of Rowlatt J's observations in the *Bater* case (see *Mitchell (Inspector of Taxes) v Ross* [1961] 3 All ER 49, [1962] AC 813, a case concerning medical specialists who were appointed as part time consultants under the national health service and also had private patients.)

The other point was that in the cases to which the learned judge had made reference the persons found to be holding an office had a steady remuneration therefrom, whereas an inspector was paid by means of fees calculated so as to reflect the time which had been spent on the discharge of his duties after the appointment. I agree with the learned judge that the mere method of calculation of the remuneration has little bearing on the question whether the person receiving it is or is not holding an office.

I return to the character of the appointment by the Minister of the taxpayer. It was a temporary ad hoc appointment confined to the taxpayer. He was not appointed to a position which had an existence of its own. It had no quality of permanency about it. It was conceded that it subsisted only from the date when he was appointed to the date when the report of the inquiry was delivered to the Secretary of State. It was, as the General Commissioners correctly observed, a transient, indeterminate, once-only execution of a task for which the taxpayer was peculiarly qualified.

While I of course accept that Rowlatt J's statement of the meaning of 'office' has not the precision of a definition, the frequency with which it has been approved as a generally sufficient statement, gives it the status of an important guide to the construction of the word. The appointment of the taxpayer fails in virtually every respect to meet its requirements. Moreover, adopting the approach of Lord Wright and construing the word in relation to the facts of the particular case according to the ordinary use of language and the dictates of common sense, with due regard to the requirement that there must be some degree of permanence, I would equally hold that the taxpayer has been wrongly assessed under Sch E. Accordingly I too would allow this appeal.

OLIVER LJ. Section 181 of the Income and Corporation Taxes Act 1970 taxes under Sch E the emoluments from any office or employment. It is common ground that the taxpayer, the respondent to the Crown's appeal from the General Commissioners, was not at any material time, in anybody's employment. The Crown claims, however, that he held an office, or to be exact a series of offices, the office in each case being that of a person appointed by the Secretary of State for the Environment to hold an inquiry into objections made to a particular compulsory purchase order. The taxpayer was, no doubt, engaged to make the inquiry in each case because the Secretary of State considered that his particular professional expertise, that of a civil engineer, made him a person peculiarly suited to conduct such an inquiry and to report to the Secretary of State his opinion as to the validity or otherwise of the objections. The Secretary of State has been in the habit for some years of engaging the services of the taxpayer to carry out inquiries of this nature. The taxpayer is one of a number of suitably qualified people whose names are on a panel kept by the department as persons willing and available to do this type of work. As and when an inquiry requires to be held, an approach is made by the department to one or more persons who are members of the panel and who appear suited to the particular inquiry. The member is asked whether he will be willing to undertake it. He is told the general nature of it, the time it is likely to occupy and the amount of the daily fee. There is, apparently, no fixed or statutory scale, although no doubt the department has its own internal limits on what can be offered. Membership of the panel imports no duty to accept. That is a matter entirely for the member's discretion, but assuming that he is available, is satisfied with the daily fee offered and notifies his acceptance, the necessary papers will be forwarded to him together with a formal notification that the Secretary of State has appointed him, pursuant to the statutory powers, to hold the inquiry. Travelling and subsistence allowances on Civil Service scales are paid to him, but payment of the daily fees for the inquiry will be made by the department only when the person appointed submits his account.

Up to the fiscal year 1973–74 the fees which the taxpayer received in this way were returned by him as part of the receipts of his profession as a civil engineer and were taxed accordingly under Sch D, but the Revenue practice then changed and for the years 1973–74 and 1974–75 the taxpayer's receipts from this source have been assessed to tax under Sch E. The matter is one of very considerable general importance, although it makes, I think, no or very little difference to the amount of tax which the taxpayer will have to pay in respect of the years in question. The taxpayer appealed against the assessments to the General Commissioners, claiming that the fees paid to him did not arise from an employment (which was conceded) and likewise did not arise from any office held by him. There was no question, of course, but that the receipts were taxable, the only question being whether they were properly taxable under Sch E. The General Commissioners upheld the taxpayer's contention that they were not, and from that the Crown appealed by way of case stated to the High Court, where Walton J held that they were.

The statutory provisions under which the inquiries held by the taxpayer were conducted have already been referred to, so far as material, in the judgments already delivered and I will not take up time by reciting them in extenso. It is however worth noting that there is nothing in the 1946 Act itself to indicate the machinery by which inquiries are to be made. There is no office of 'inquirer' or 'inspector' created by the Act but merely a provision authorising the Minister to 'cause to be held' the appropriate inquiries. The way in which the person charged with the function of carrying out the

inquiry is to be selected, engaged or remunerated is again entirely at large, and the
a manner in which he approaches and executes the task of inquiring and reporting is a matter which is left to his discretion except to the extent that he must follow the procedural requirements of the Compulsory Purchase by Ministers (Inquiries Procedure) Rules 1967. It is here that we find the phrase 'the appointed person', used to signify the person who has been requested to undertake and has accepted the task of carrying out the inquiry, but it does not, I think, have any significance beyond that of being a useful
b description. Such a person is commonly referred to as 'the inspector' but again this is not a term of art and it has no statutory foundation.

The Income and Corporation Taxes Act 1970, unlike some of the earlier legislation limiting and defining the income assessable under Sch E, contains no internal guidance on the meaning of the word 'office'. If one looks merely at the dictionary definition of the word (and the New Oxford Dictionary contains some eight senses in which it is used),
c one finds that it is so wide as to cover virtually any position entailing work for which a person is remunerated. That definition which is favoured by counsel for the Crown and by the learned judge is:

> 'A position or place to which certain duties are attached, especially one of a more or less public character; a position of trust, authority or service under constituted
> d authority; a place in the administration of government, the public service, the direction of a corporation, company, society, etc.'

The difficulty about this as a guide to the interpretation of the statute is that, if it is literally applied, it is apt to cover all sorts of posts which nobody in ordinary parlance would describe as 'offices'. Indeed it is difficult to imagine any position, however menial, to which there are not attached certain defined duties. Counsel for the Crown, however,
e attaches great importance to the words 'especially one of a more or less public character', and whilst he disclaims any intention of treating 'public character' as a touchstone (rather than a badge which is commonly, although not universally, found) he stresses that the duty to hold an inquiry is a duty imposed by a public general statute, that it is of the essence of such an inquiry that it should be conducted in public, and that it falls to be conducted, to an extent at least, in accordance with regulations contained in a statutory
f instrument. Whilst, however, these features cannot be ignored, I am not, for my part, convinced that they carry the weight accorded to them by the learned judge in his judgment. Many duties are laid on many bodies by statute and many of them fall to be performed publicly. But it does not at all follow from that that every person engaged to perform them is the holder of an 'office'. A local authority has, for instance, a statutory duty to collect refuse but that does not, as it seems to me, elevate the corporation
g dustman to the status of an 'officer' of the corporation, even though he performs his duties in public. Nothing, after all, could be more public than a dustcart. That the duties undertaken by the propositus are duties the performance of which is required by statute and are duties publicly performed constitutes, no doubt, a common feature of many positions to which, in ordinary parlance, the word 'office' would be applied, but it is not and it cannot be conclusive, as, indeed, counsel for the Crown accepts. The secretary of
h a golf club holds, no doubt, an office in the club, but he performs no public or statutory duties at all.

It seems to me that, as a matter of ordinary language the word 'office' imports the concept (it may be an entirely artificial concept) of a position which exists quite independently of the person who is for the time being filling it. It connotes, I think, a degree of permanence in the sense not (or not necessarily) of something which goes on
j from generation to generation, but at least of not being co-terminous with the life or availability of a particular individual. Certainly this is a feature which is stressed in the cases decided under the predecessors of the 1970 Act.

Counsel for the Crown submits, however, that these earlier cases are of very limited help, for two reasons. In the first place, he refers to the passage in the speech of Lord Wilberforce in *Farrell v Alexander* [1976] 2 All ER 721, [1977] AC 59 which has already been quoted in the judgment of Buckley LJ.

In the instant case, counsel for the Crown submits, the classical method of construction,

that is, to look for the ordinary meaning of the word, does enable the court to arrive at
a solution and there is not only no need but it is not strictly permissible to look at the a
sense in which the word was construed under earlier legislation, which not only was not
in the ipsissima verba of the 1970 Act but which was enacted against the background of
a radically different system of tax collection. But this seems to me to be very much a case
where the classical methods of construction do not, in fact, easily produce a certain result
and I find some difficulty in accepting the Crown's submission that an expression whose
ordinary meaning has given rise to so much debate is free from ambiguity. b

It is fair to say, however, that the earlier cases in which the word has fallen to be
construed do require to be approached with a degree of caution. Prior to 1922 tax under
Sch E was charged 'in respect of every *public* office or employment of profit' and it was
charged on the 'salaries, fees, wages, perquisites or profits . . . therefrom'. Profits or gains
arising from 'any trade, profession, employment or vocation' were taxed under Sch D,
employments chargeable under other schedules being excluded in Case II of Sch D. c
Under s 18 of the Finance Act 1922 profits or gains from an office, employment or
pension previously charged under Sch D ceased to be so chargeable and became
chargeable under Sch E. This has to be borne in mind in considering any decision prior
to 1922 and the more so because the rules applicable to Sch E then in force contained this
important provision, a provision which continued in force until the Finance Act 1956.
The rule was in these terms: d

> 'Every assessment shall be made for one year, and the tax in respect thereof shall
> be levied for that year without any new assessment, notwithstanding any change in
> the holder of any office or employment; but if, during the year of assessment, any
> person chargeable quits the office or employment, or dies, he, or his executors or
> administrators, respectively, shall be liable for tax in respect of the period during
> which he held or exercised the office or employment, and any successor shall in like e
> manner be liable in respect of the period during which he has held or exercised the
> same.'

It seems that similar provisions appeared in the 1842 Act and in *Great Western Railway
Co v Bater* [1922] 2 AC 1, in which the court was called on to decide whether a clerk in
the employment of the Great Western Railway was the holder of a public office or f
employment, Rowlatt J referred to those provisions. He said ([1920] 3 KB 266 at 274):

> 'It is argued . . . that that shows that what those who used the language of the Act
> of 1842 meant when they spoke of an office or an employment of profit was an
> office or employment which was a subsisting, permanent, substantive position,
> which had an existence independent from the person who filled it, which went on
> and was filled in succession by successive holders.' g

He expressed the view, which, for reasons which he then gave, he felt disentitled to hold,
that by an 'office' was meant 'a substantive thing that existed apart from the holder'. His
actual decision was upheld in the Court of Appeal ([1921] 2 KB 128) but reversed in the
House of Lords ([1922] 2 AC 1). The passage to which I have referred in Rowlatt J's
judgment was, however, approved by Lord Atkinson, but again it is significant that this
was in the context of the rule quoted above. He referred particularly to the word h
'successor' and said ([1922] 2 AC 1 at 14): 'It seems to indicate continuity of the office or
employment, and also to indicate the existence of something external to the person who
may hold the one or exercise the other.' A similar emphasis is found in the speech of
Lord Sumner.

The expression of Rowlatt J quoted above was treated by Lord Atkin as generally a
sufficient statement of the meaning of the word 'office' in *McMillan v Guest (Inspector of* j
Taxes) [1942] 1 All ER 606, [1942] AC 561 and in the same case Lord Wright observed
([1942] 1 All ER 606 at 608–609, [1942] AC 561 at 567) that the statutory words
'employment' and 'office' were—

> 'To be applied in the facts of the particular case according to the ordinary use of
> language and the dictates of common sense, with due regard to the requirement
> that there must be some degree of permanence and publicity in the office.'

Again, however, Lord Wright may, in referring to 'the' office rather than 'an' office have
a had in mind that, for the purposes of the statute, the word had to be construed in the light of the particular kind of office referred to in r 2, which clearly does import a degree of permanence. The expression office again fell to be construed in *Mitchell (Inspector of Taxes) v Ross* [1961] 3 All ER 49, [1962] AC 813, a case which also, although decided after the elimination of r 2 in the 1956 Finance Act, was dealing with assessments made under the pre-1956 legislation. Again reference was made both by Upjohn J ([1959] 3 All ER
b 341, [1960] Ch 145) and by the Court of Appeal ([1960] 2 All ER 218, [1960] Ch 498) to *Bater's* case and *McMillan v Guest (Inspector of Taxes)*. It is, however, fair to say that the fact that Rowlatt J had expressed the view which was subsequently approved by the House of Lords with specific reference to r 2 does not seem to have been treated in this case as a matter of significance. Harman LJ for instance, was content simply to say that 'An office is a position or post which goes on without regard to the holder of it from time
c to time, as was said, in effect by ROWLATT, J.' (see [1960] 2 All ER 218 at 230, [1960] Ch 498 at 530).

The same approach can be found in *Inland Revenue Comrs v Brander & Cruikshank* [1971] 1 All ER 36, [1971] 1 WLR 212 which was concerned with an assessment for the year 1967–68 and therefore with legislation in which the expression fell to be construed without reference to r 2 in the form in which it had existed at the time of the earlier
d decisions. Yet, again both in the Court of Session and in the House of Lords what had been said by Rowlatt J in *Bater's* case and by Lord Wright in *McMillan v Guest (Inspector of Taxes)* was adopted and approved. Lord Morris observed that a limited company had to arrange for someone to keep its statutory register and continued ([1971] 1 All ER 36 at 41, [1971] 1 WLR 212 at 215):

> 'In doing so, it may establish a position which successively will be held by
> e different persons. If it does so the company may have created what could rationally for income tax purposes be called an office.'

So here, once again, emphasis is laid on the concept of continuance apart from the individual holder. This, as it seems to me, is something entirely lacking in the instant case. The duty of making the inquiry is one which is offered to and accepted by the individual ad hoc. If he is unable to complete it and to make his report for any reason,
f there is no question of appointing a successor to the office of conducting that inquiry. There has to be a new inquiry by another individual equally appointed ad hoc, and on terms which fall to be separately negotiated with him.

Turning now to the judgment of the learned judge, there were four factors present in the instant case which, in his view, rendered the conclusion that the taxpayer was the holder of an 'office' inevitable. The first of these was that the person appointed to hold
g an inquiry has no employer. Now of course, I agree that the absence of an employer must narrow the field of inquiry where the question is whether the propositus holds an 'office or employment'. But I cannot, speaking for myself, see why the absence of an employer is itself indicative of the holding of an office. It could only be so on the footing that the words 'office or employment' were themselves exhaustive descriptions of every method of earning taxable profits, which they plainly are not. And indeed a great many
h employees hold offices under their employer.

It may be, however, that what the learned judge had in mind here was the statement of Lord Normand in *Dale v Inland Revenue Comrs* [1953] 2 All ER 671 at 673, [1954] AC 11 at 26 that 'office' is an apt word to describe any position in which services are done by the holder and in which the holder has no employer. But Lord Normand's reference to 'any position' has, I think, to be viewed in the context in which he made it, that is to say
j in relation to a position (in that case, that of a trustee) which existed quite apart from the individual appointed to hold it. The second feature to which the learned judge attached critical importance was (and I quote from the judgment ([1979] 1 All ER 648 at 654, [1979] 1 WLR 338 at 344)): 'That the person who conducts the inquiry is the person appointed, the inspector, and not the taxpayer considered as a person. Without the appointment having first been made, his acts would be wholly nugatory.' I am not sure that I follow this. Of course it is true that the taxpayer has no authority to conduct an

inquiry unless the Secretary of State engages him to conduct it, but I do not myself see why this is determinative of the nature of that which he is engaged to do. An agent has no power to bind his principal unless he is authorised to do so, but such authority does not convert him into the holder of an office. Nor indeed does it appear to be entirely accurate to say that the person who conducts the inquiry is not the taxpayer considered as a person. The assumption here seems to be that on appointment the taxpayer dons a sort of Greek mask, that of an 'inspector'. But, as I have already mentioned, the expression 'the inspector' is merely a convenient term which has no statutory foundation and when one examines the form of appointment it is seen that it appoints 'Mr. F. M. Clinch, B.Sc., A.C.G.I., C.Eng., F.I.Mun.E., F.I.C.E., M.R.T.P.I., to hold a Public Local Inquiry for the purpose of hearing objections and representations' and so on. Of course, if he did not appoint the taxpayer, the Secretary of State would find somebody else to perform the same function, because he is charged with the duty of causing an inquiry to be held.

The third matter to which the learned judge attached great importance was the statutory nature of the duties. I agree that this is an important feature, but for reasons already mentioned, I am unable to regard it as conclusive. In *Mitchell (Inspector of Taxes) v Ross* [1961] 3 All ER 49, [1962] AC 813 the critical feature was that a part-time consultant under the national health service was, as it was said, an instrument of the Minister for the carrying out of the general scheme of the National Health Service Act 1946, which imposed on him the duty of providing a general medical service. But that was really quite a different case and it was a case in which the person concerned was remunerated by a regular salary and pension for carrying out the Minister's function. Here the Secretary of State's function is not to hold the inquiry but to cause an inquiry to be held, and it is of the essence of the inquiry that it should be conducted by someone who is quite independent of the Secretary of State. Indeed the notes issued by the Department of the Environment emphasise that those whose names are included on the panel maintained by the department 'have no allegiance to the Department and the Department has no continuing responsibility for them'.

The final matter, which the learned judge found to be compulsive, was the fact that if the person appointed was unable to complete the inquiry, the only course open to the Secretary of State would be to appoint another person. This, however, seems to me to point rather against the Crown's contention or to be at best neutral. It seems to me that it means no more than this, that the Secretary of State would then have to cause a fresh inquiry to be held. I cannot, for my part, find in this any indication that either the person who has failed to complete the first inquiry or the person engaged to carry out the second is the holder of an 'office'.

I do not, therefore, find any of these matters persuasive. Nor, equally, do I find it a persuasive argument that since the person appointed to carry out the inquiry is not carrying on the business or profession of carrying out inquiries the fees earned cannot be taxable under Sch D as part of his professional earnings. The function is one which is frequently fulfilled by professional men, by reason of their peculiar expertise, as a normal part of their professional activities and I would not, for my part, consider it a misdescription to describe the fees received as professional receipts. But whether that is right or wrong they would, in any event, be taxable under Case VI of Sch D. I do not think that the present problem can be answered simply by postulating the question 'If it is not an office, what is it?'

Ultimately the point is very much one of impression and the application of the ordinary meaning of language. I take a different view from that taken by the learned judge. I do not think that in the ordinary use of language it would be appropriate to describe the taxpayer's activity in carrying out an inquiry as the holding of an office.

I agree that the appeal should be allowed.

Appeal allowed. Leave to appeal to House of Lords granted, the Crown undertaking that on any such appeal the order for costs made in the Court of Appeal will not be disturbed and the Crown will not ask for costs in the House of Lords.

Solicitors: *Lovell, White & King* (for the taxpayer); *Solicitor of Inland Revenue.*

Edwina Epstein Barrister.

Shearer (Inspector of Taxes) v Bercain Ltd

CHANCERY DIVISION
WALTON J
19th, 20th FEBRUARY, 7th MARCH 1980

Income tax – Close company – Shortfall in distributions – Calculation of shortfall – Restriction imposed by law as regards making of distributions – Imposed by law – Taxpayer company acquiring two companies by issuing its own shares in exchange for the shares of the two companies – Payment of gross dividends by acquired companies out of their pre-acquisition profits – Whether taxpayer company obliged to create share premium account in respect of excess value of shares acquired over the nominal value of its shares issued in exchange therefor – Whether taxpayer company subject to restrictions imposed by law as regards making of distribution – Companies Act 1948, s 56 – Income and Corporation Taxes Act 1970, s 290(4).

The taxpayer company, incorporated as an investment holding company, acquired the share capital of two limited companies by an issue of its own shares. The values of the shares of the two companies were £84,000 and £12,000. The nominal value of the shares which the taxpayer company issued in exchange was £4,100. The taxpayer company created a share premium account in respect of the excess value of the shares acquired over the nominal value of its shares issued in exchange. In December 1971 the two companies paid gross dividends of £36,050 out of their pre-acquisition profits. On receipt of those dividends, the taxpayer company wrote down the value of its investments in the two companies. The taxpayer company was assessed to tax on the basis that there was a shortfall in its distributions in a sum equal to the amount of the dividends it had received from the companies. It was common ground between the parties that if the taxpayer company was obliged to create a share premium account equal in amount to the excess of the value of the shares acquired over the nominal value of the shares issued in exchange it was subject to a 'restriction imposed by law', within s 290(4)[a] of the Income and Corporation Taxes Act 1970, as regards the distribution of the dividends it had received from the acquired companies and that the shortfall assessment should be discharged. The Crown contended that since the shares were acquired by the taxpayer company in exchange for an issue of its own shares it was not required to enter the shares in its accounts at any value in excess of the nominal value of the shares issued in exchange, and accordingly the distribution of the dividends paid to the taxpayer company by the companies out of their pre-acquisition profits was not subject to any restriction imposed by law. The Special Commissioners discharged the assessments on the ground that, under the Companies Act 1948, s 56[b], the taxpayer company was obliged to create a share premium account in respect of the excess value of the shares of the two acquired companies and that the taxpayer company was accordingly subject to a restriction imposed by law as regards the making of the distribution, within s 290(4) of the 1970 Act. The Crown appealed.

Held – Where shares were issued at a premium, whether for cash or otherwise than for cash, s 56 of the 1948 Act required the premium to be carried into a share premium account in the books of the company issuing the shares, and the premium could only be distributed if the procedure for reduction of capital was carried through. It followed that, under s 56, the taxpayer company was required to create the share premium

a Section 290(4) provides: 'Where a company is subject to any restriction imposed by law as regards the making of distributions, any shortfall in its distributions for an accounting period shall be disregarded to the extent to which the company could not make distributions up to the required standard without contravening that restriction.'

b Section 56 is set out at p 301 *d* to *f*, post

account in respect of the excess value of the shares acquired over the nominal value of its own shares issued in exchange and, accordingly, was subject to a restriction imposed by law within s 290(4) of the 1970 Act on making the distribution. The shortfall assessments made on the taxpayer company were, therefore, not valid. The Crown's appeal would be dismissed (see p 304 to *d* and *g h*, p 310 *d* and p 312 *j* to p 313 *a*, post).

Henry Head & Co Ltd v Ropner Holdings Ltd [1951] 2 All ER 994 followed.

Notes

For legal restrictions on distributions by close companies, see 23 Halsbury's Laws (4th Edn) para 1219, and for cases on distributions by close companies, see 28(1) Digest (Reissue) 406–412, *1481–1499*.

For the issue of shares at a premium, see 7 Halsbury's Laws (4th Edn) para 150 and for cases on the subject, see 9 Digest (Reissue) 319–320, *1892–1893*.

For the Income and Corporation Taxes Act 1970, s 290, see 33 Halsbury's Statutes (3rd Edn) 396.

For the Companies Act 1948, s 56, see 5 ibid 164.

For 1973–74 and subsequent years of assessment s 290(4) of the 1970 Act has been replaced by s 94(1) of, and Sch 16, para 14 to, the Finance Act 1972.

Cases referred to in judgment

Craddock (Inspector of Taxes) v Zevo Finance Co Ltd [1944] 1 All ER 566, 27 Tax Cas 267, CA; *affd* [1946] 1 All ER 523, 27 Tax Cas 267, HL, 28(1) Digest (Reissue) 124, *367*.

Drown v Gaumont-British Picture Corpn Ltd [1937] 2 All ER 609, [1937] Ch 402, 106 LJ Ch 241, 157 LT 543, 9 Digest (Reissue) 655, *3923*.

Head (Henry) & Co Ltd v Ropner Holdings Ltd [1951] 2 All ER 994, [1952] Ch 124, [1951] 2 Lloyd's Rep 348, 9 Digest (Reissue) 319, *1893*.

Hilder v Dexter [1902] AC 474, 71 LJ Ch 781, 87 LT 311, 7 Com Cas 258, 9 Mans 378, HL, 9 Digest (Reissue) 183, *1116*.

Lowry (Inspector of Taxes) v Consolidated African Selection Trust Ltd [1940] 2 All ER 545, [1940] AC 648, 23 Tax Cas 259, 109 LJKB 539, HL, 28(1) Digest (Reissue) 149, *461*.

Noble (Inspector of Taxes) v Laygate Investments Ltd [1978] 2 All ER 1067, [1978] 1 WLR 1457, [1978] STC 430, Digest (Cont Vol E) 305, *1499b*.

Osborne (Inspector of Taxes) v Steel Barrel Co Ltd [1942] 1 All ER 634, 24 Tax Cas 293, CA, 28(1) Digest (Reissue) 121, *357*.

Youde's Billposting Ltd, Re, Clayton's Case, Crowther's Case (1902) 18 TLR 731, CA, 9 Digest (Reissue) 474, *2825*.

Case stated

1. At a meeting of the Commissioners for the Special Purposes of the Income Tax Acts held on 27th, 28th and 31st October 1977, Bercain Ltd ('the taxpayer company') appealed against an assessment to income tax made in respect of the year 1973–74 under s 289 of the Income and Corporation Taxes Act 1970 in the sum of £36,066.

2. Shortly stated, the question for decision was whether the taxpayer company, which had created a share premium account equal in amount to the excess of the value of shares which it had acquired in two limited companies, Lennard and Tracey Ltd ('Lennard') and Alexander Stuart Ltd ('Alexander'), over the nominal value of the shares which it had issued in exchange therefor, was subject to any restriction imposed by law as regards the making of distributions within the meaning of s 290(4) of the 1970 Act.

3. Mr Edward Lawson FCA, principal advisory accountant to the Board of Inland Revenue, gave evidence before the commissioners.

[Paragraph 4 listed the documents proved or admitted before the commissioners.]

5. The facts which as a result of the evidence both oral and documentary the commissioners found proved or admitted are set out in the decision on the appeal.

6. It was contended on behalf of the taxpayer company: (i) that dividends could not be paid out of share capital; (ii) that a share premium account was to be treated under s 56 of the Companies Act 1948 as if it were share capital; (iii) that the taxpayer company was obliged by the provisions of s 56 to create a share premium account; (iv) that there were no assets available out of which a distribution of £36,050 could have been made;

(v) that the pre-acquisition profits of Lennard and Alexander could not be treated as revenue profits of the taxpayer company; (vi) that the taxpayer company was subject to a restriction imposed by law as regards the distribution of the £36,050 in question; (vii) that the provisions of s 290(4) of the 1970 Act applied; and (viii) that the taxpayer company's appeal should be allowed and the shortfall assessment discharged.

7. It was accepted on behalf of the Crown that a company which acquired shares in another company in exchange for shares issued at a premium was obliged to create a share premium account but it was contended on its behalf: (i) that where shares were acquired by a company in exchange for an issue of its own shares there was no rule of law which required the company to enter the shares in its accounts at any value in excess of the nominal value of the shares issued in exchange; (ii) that there was no settled accountancy practice which could be relied on as making it commercially necessary for the acquiring company to value the shares acquired for the purpose of creating a premium; (iii) that if the acquiring company issued shares at nominal value and no share premium account was created there was no rule of law which prevented it from distributing dividends received from the company whose shares it acquired; (iv) that there was no general rule of law which restricted the distribution by the acquiring company of pre-acquisition profits of the company whose shares it acquired; (v) that no such restriction (as described in sub-para (iv) above) was imposed by para 15(5) of Sch 8 (as amended) to the Companies Act 1948 (that sub-paragraph was a rider to para 15(4) of Sch 8 and related to the contents of the statement to be annexed to the balance sheet when group accounts were not submitted); it did not affect the substantive law or declarations of dividends; in any case it was inconceivable that Parliament when empowering (by s 454(1) of the 1948 Act, as amended) the Board of Trade to alter or add to the requirements of Sch 8 should have intended the Board of Trade to have power to alter fundamental principles of law as to what was and what was not distributable); (vi) that there was no settled accountancy practice which restricted the distribution by the acquiring company of pre-acquisition profits of the company whose shares it acquired; (vii) that s 290(4) of the 1970 Act did not apply where, as in the circumstances of the appeal, the restriction on distribution arose as a result of the voluntary act of the directors of the acquiring company; (viii) that the decision in *Henry Head & Co Ltd v Ropner Holdings Ltd* [1951] 2 All ER 994, [1952] Ch 124 applied only where the acquiring company acquired shares at a valuation and was irrelevant to the circumstances of this appeal; and (ix) that the appeal should be dismissed in principle and the assessment reduced to an agreed figure of £36,050 (tax thereon: £10,815).

8. The cases and authorities cited to the commissioners included: *Craddock (Inspector of Taxes) v Zevo Finance Co Ltd* [1944] 1 All ER 566, 27 Tax Cas 267, HL; *Duff's Settlements Trusts, Re, National Provincial Bank Ltd v Gregson* [1951] 2 All ER 534, [1951] Ch 923, CA; *Drown v Gaumont-British Picture Corpn Ltd* [1937] 2 All ER 609, [1937] Ch 402; *Foster v New Trinidad Lake Asphalt Co Ltd* [1901] 1 Ch 208; *Head (Henry) & Co Ltd v Ropner Holdings Ltd* [1951] 2 All ER 994, [1952] Ch 124; *Osborne (Inspector of Taxes) v Steel Barrel Co Ltd* [1942] 1 All ER 634, 42 Tax Cas 293, CA; *Trevor v Whitworth* (1887) 12 App Cas 409, [1886–90] All ER Rep 46.

9. The commissioners who heard the appeal, took time to consider their decision and gave it in writing on 29th November 1977 as follows:

> '1. The [taxpayer company] was incorporated on 2 August 1971 as an investment holding company, to acquire the whole of the issued capital of 2 other companies, Lennard and Tracey Ltd ("Lennard") and Alexander Stuart Ltd ("Alexander"), both of which carried on business as textile manufacturers' agents. At the time of its incorporation its authorised capital was £100 divided into 100 shares of £1 each, which were issued for cash. Shortly afterwards its authorised capital was increased to £4,200, and a further 4,100 shares of £1 each were issued. Since then the 4,200 issued shares have been held as to 4,198 by Mr M Altman and as to the remaining 2 by Mr K J Dessauer as nominee for Mr Altman. Mr Altman and Mr Dessauer are the sole directors of [the taxpayer company] and Mr Altman is its chairman.

'2. Pursuant to an Agreement dated 1 September 1971 [the taxpayer company] acquired the whole of the issued capital of Lennard, then valued at £84,000 and *a* consisting of 3,500 fully paid Ordinary Shares of £1 each, "on the basis of the issue and allotment of one . . . Ordinary Share in its capital in exchange for each Ordinary Share in Lennard transferred to it." Prior to 1 September 1971 the whole of the issued capital of Lennard was beneficially owned by Mr Altman, who was, and remains, a director and chairman of that company.

'3. Pursuant to an Agreement dated 1 October 1971 [the taxpayer company] on *b* that date acquired the whole of the issued capital of Alexander, then valued at £12,000 and consisting of 3,000 fully paid Ordinary Shares of £1 each "on the basis of the issue and allotment of one . . . Ordinary Share in its capital in exchange for each five Ordinary Shares in Alexander transferred to it." Prior to 1 October 1971 the whole of the issued capital of Alexander was beneficially owned by Mr Altman, who was, and remains a director and chairman of that company. *c*

'4. [The taxpayer company] elected under section 256 Income and Corporation Taxes Act 1970 to receive dividends and interest in full from Lennard and from Alexander and the Inspector of Taxes accepted the election as from 11 November 1971.

'5. Mr Altman thus received 4,100 shares in [the taxpayer company] (3,500 for his shares in Lennard and 600 for his shares in Alexander) in exchange for the whole *d* of the issued capitals of Lennard and Alexander, which at the time was valued at £96,000 (Lennard £84,000 and Alexander £12,000). The excess of the value of the shares acquired over the nominal value of the shares which [the taxpayer company] issued in exchange was thus £91,900. [The taxpayer company] created a share premium account in the sum of £91,717 (viz £91,900 less £183, being the cost of formation, increase of capital and acquisition of the shares). *e*

'6. In December 1971 Lennard and Alexander paid gross dividends to [the taxpayer company] amounting in aggregate to £36,050 (Lennard £35,000 and Alexander £1,050) out of pre-acquisition profits. On receipt of the dividends [the taxpayer company] wrote down the value of its investments in Lennard and Alexander to £59,950 (viz £96,000 minus £36,050).

'7. The Inspector of Taxes made a "shortfall" assessment on [the taxpayer *f* company] under section 289 Income and Corporation Taxes Act 1970 for the year 1973–74 in the sum of £36,066 (income tax thereon £10,819·80). The point at issue which we have to decide on [the taxpayer company's] appeal against this assessment is short to state but difficult to resolve. It is whether [the taxpayer company] was, within the meaning of section 290(4) Income and Corporation Taxes Act 1970 "subject to any restrictions imposed by law as regards the making of *g* distributions."

'8. It is common ground between the parties that if, on its purchase of shares in Lennard and Alexander, [the taxpayer company] was obliged (as distinct from being free to do so or not do so, as it wished) to create a share premium account equal in amount to the excess of the value of the shares acquired over the nominal value of the shares issued in exchange therefor then there was such a restriction and the *h* shortfall assessment should be discharged. It is also common ground that if there was no such obligation the assessment should be confirmed.

'9. Mr Edward Lawson FCA, Principal Advisory Accountant to the Board of Inland Revenue gave evidence before us as regards accountancy practice. To put it shortly this was that it was largely a matter of personal opinion whether a company's balance sheet gave "a true and fair view of the state of affairs of the company" as *j* required by section 149(1) Companies Act 1948 and that consequently there was no uniform practice adopted by accountants as regards the creation (or not) of a share premium account where a company (whether public or private) issued shares in exchange for assets (other than cash) which it purchased as an investment. In Mr Lawson's view a further reason for this difference of practice was because accountants knew that lawyers differed in their opinions as to whether in such circumstances the creation of a share premium account was obligatory by law—under section 56 Companies Act 1948. It was therefore Mr Lawson's view that, *if* there was no such legal obligation, accountancy practice left it open to [the taxpayer company] either to draw up accounts in the way it had done or, if it preferred, to draw up accounts without creating a share premium account and to regard the pre-acquisition profit as available for distribution: in Mr Lawson's opinion, however, there was no good commercial, financial or accounting reason for creating a share premium account in the present case. We accepted Mr Lawson's evidence.

'10. A number of reported cases and text books was cited to us. After carefully considering these and fully recognizing that the question is one on which legal opinion has differed, we think that the plain language of section 56 Companies Act 1948 is mandatory and requires the excess of value of assets (whether cash or not) over the nominal value of shares issued in exchange for such assets to be carried to a share premium account in the books of the acquiring company. In our view the decision of Harman J in *Henry Head & Co Ltd v Ropner Holdings Ltd* [1951] 2 All ER 994, [1952] Ch 124 is a direct authority on this precise point. Counsel for the Crown contended that it was irrelevant to the appeal before us because in *Ropner* the valuation which had been made of the assets to be acquired was a vital factor in deciding the basis of acquisition: Harman J had approached the question before him on that footing and those passages in his judgment (see [1951] 2 All ER 994 at 997, [1952] Ch 124 at 128) which in terms might seem to be decisive if applied to the appeal before us were not in point in the circumstances of this appeal. We cannot accept this view. It appears to us that Harman J was considering facts which in essence are indistinguishable from those in the present proceedings. The valuation of the assets to be acquired in *Ropner* was, it seems to us, merely a preliminary step taken before the parties entered upon consideration of how exactly the amalgamation of the two shipping companies should be achieved. It was not until after the value of the assets of each such company had been equalised in the light of the valuation that it was decided, on advice, that the amalgamation should be carried out by the issue by the acquiring company of a pound of its shares for a pound's worth nominal of the shares to be acquired and this decision was taken in the knowledge that the real value of the shares to be acquired far exceeded their nominal value. The amalgamation in the case before us was carried out in precisely the same way. The value of the shares to be acquired by [the taxpayer company] was known and the amalgamation was achieved on the basis of the issue by [the taxpayer company] of shares the nominal value of which fell far short of the value of the shares acquired. In *Ropner* the excess of the value of the shares acquired over the nominal value of the shares issued was carried in the Balance Sheet of the acquiring company to Share Premium Account. The Balance Sheet of [the taxpayer company] was drawn up likewise with a share premium account showing the excess value of the shares acquired. Harman J posed the question which he had to determine as "whether the [acquiring company] were obliged to keep their accounts in that way" and after considering section 56 he concluded that they were (see [1951] 2 All ER 994 at 996, [1952] Ch 124 at 127). We are faced with the same question in like circumstances and on the authority of *Ropner* are, we think, bound to reach the same conclusion.

'11. We hold that [the taxpayer company] was obliged to create the share premium account. From this it follows that [the taxpayer company] was subject to the restrictions imposed by section 56 as regards the making of distributions and its appeal succeeds on these grounds.

'12. We were, however, asked by Counsel for the Crown to make findings of fact on 3 points even though we might be against him on his main contention. In accepting Mr Lawson's evidence we have made the findings for which he asked on 2 of the 3 points. The third finding which Counsel asked for was that Mr Altman's only motive for procuring [the taxpayer company's] acquisition of the shares of

Lennard and Alexander was to impose a restriction on the distribution of the pre-acquisition profits. No direct evidence on this point was adduced before us and we *a* are unable to infer from the facts proved or admitted before us what Mr Altman's motive was.

'13. We discharge the assessment on [the taxpayer company].'

10. The Crown immediately after the determination of the appeal declared to the commissioners its dissatisfaction therewith as being erroneous in point of law and on 7th December 1977 required them to state a case for the opinion of the High Court pursuant *b* to s 56 of the Taxes Management Act 1970. The question of law for the opinion of the court was whether the commissioners' decision was correct.

Leonard Bromley QC and *Peter Gibson* for the Crown.
Richard Sykes as amicus curiae.
The taxpayer company was not represented.

c

Cur adv vult

7th March. **WALTON J** read the following judgment: The difficulty in the present case arises in this wise. Bercain Ltd ('the taxpayer company') was incorporated on the 2nd August 1971 as an investment holding company with an authorised capital of £100 in shares of £1 each, which was shortly thereafter increased to £4,200. The original 100 *d* shares were issued for cash; the additional 4,100 shares were issued in exchange for the issued share capitals of two companies, Lennard and Tracey Ltd ('Lennard') and Alexander Stuart Ltd ('Alexander'). In fact, the values of the shares in these two companies at the time of the issue of the 4,100 shares in the taxpayer company were £84,000 and £12,000 respectively. Accordingly, the taxpayer company acquired assets worth £96,000 in total for an issue of 4,100 shares of a nominal value of £1 each, that is *e* to say, assets worth £91,900 more than the nominal value of these shares. The taxpayer company thereupon created a share premium account in the sum of £91,717, that is to say, the sum of £91,900 less the costs of its formation, increase of capital and acquisition of the shares, amounting in all to some £183. The taxpayer company made group income elections under the Income and Corporation Taxes Act 1970, s 256, in respect of both subsidiaries, and such elections were accepted by the inspector of taxes as from 11th *f* November 1971. In December 1971 the two subsidiaries paid gross dividends to the taxpayer company out of pre-acquisition profits; and, on receipt of such dividends, the taxpayer company wrote down the value of its investments in the two subsidiaries from £96,000 to £59,950. The inspector made a shortfall assessment on the taxpayer company under s 289 of the 1970 Act for the year 1973–74 in the sum of £36,066. To this the taxpayer company replied that it was, within the meaning of s 290(4) of the 1970 Act, *g* subject to a restriction imposed by law as regards the making of distributions, and accordingly the assessment did not lie. On appeal to the Special Commissioners the taxpayer company's contention was upheld, and the assessment discharged. The Crown has now appealed to the High Court.

It has throughout been accepted on behalf of the Crown that, if the taxpayer company was by law obliged to create the share premium account which it did in fact create, then *h* its contentions were unanswerable. Accordingly, the debate in this case has mainly (but, as will hereafter appear, not exclusively) centred round the true construction and effect of s 56 of the Companies Act 1948, a section which was newly introduced into company law by the Companies Act 1947.

The vice which the section was designed to correct was that, under the prior law, there was nothing to prevent a company paying a dividend out of assets representing premiums *j* received on the issue of its shares. This had been established in 1937 in *Drown v Gaumont-British Picture Corpn Ltd* [1937] 2 All ER 609, [1937] Ch 402. A moment or two's thought will show that, however good law this may be, it is pretty poor economics, and very adverse to the interests of any shareholders who have paid a premium for their shares. In substance, in paying a premium they will have paid the full value of their slice of assets of the company, which is then diminished by the payment out of the premium. So it is hardly surprising that the Cohen Committee, on whose work the 1947 Act was based, a recommended that in the cases of the issue of shares at a premium, those premiums should be carried to a share premium account, which was to be distributable only if the procedure for reduction of capital was carried through (see the Report of the Committee on Company Law Amendment, Cmd 6659 (1945)).

Prior to the coming into force of the 1947 Act, I do not think that many company lawyers would have thought of a premium on the issue of shares as being anything other b than a cash payment, a payment of £X plus £Y for a share of the nominal value of £X, £Y being the premium. In the case of the acquisition of valuable assets for shares of a less nominal value, however, precisely the same situation could arise, because in such a case there was nothing to prevent the company from writing up the value of those assets to their true worth, and distributing the resulting surplus over the nominal value of the shares issued in exchange as dividend. Accordingly, when they came to frame the c provisions of s 56, the framers did not simply provide for the issue of shares at a cash premium. Instead, what they provided ran as follows:

> '(1) Where a company issues shares at a premium, whether for cash or otherwise, a sum equal to the aggregate amount or value of the premiums on those shares shall be transferred to an account, to be called "the share premium account", and the d provisions of this Act relating to the reduction of the share capital of a company shall, except as provided in this section, apply as if the share premium account were paid up share capital of the company.
>
> '(2) The share premium account may, notwithstanding anything in the foregoing subsection, be applied by the company in paying up unissued shares of the company to be issued to members of the company as fully paid bonus shares, in writing off— e (*a*) the preliminary expenses of the company; or (*b*) the expenses of, or the commission paid or discount allowed on, any issue of shares or debentures of the company; or in providing for the premium payable on redemption of any redeemable preference shares or of any debentures of the company.
>
> '(3) Where a company has before the commencement of this Act issued any shares at a premium, this section shall apply as if the shares had been issued after the f commencement of this Act: Provided that any part of the premiums which has been so applied that it does not at the commencement of this Act form an identifiable part of the company's reserves within the meaning of the Eighth Schedule to this Act shall be disregarded in determining the sum to be included in the share premium account.'

Concentrating for the moment on sub-s (1) of that section, it would appear as plain as g a pikestaff that it is designed to negative the evils to which I have referred above in both their branches. It caters for a premium being in cash, because the shares are issued for cash, and a premium being otherwise than in cash, because the shares are issued otherwise than for cash; and in both cases these premiums have to be carried to a share premium account. The words 'value of the premiums' point clearly to a case where the premiums h have to be valued, a point which, as I shall explain hereafter, is fatal to one of the arguments proffered on behalf of the Crown on this appeal.

There is, in fact, the shortest possible of all answers to this appeal, which was indeed the one on which the Special Commissioners themselves relied, namely that the matter is covered by authority, authority which is wholly indistinguishable, namely *Henry Head & Co Ltd v Ropner Holdings Ltd* [1951] 2 All ER 994, [1952] Ch 124. Although counsel for the Crown, in his opening submissions, was inclined to consider (as an alternative to j submitting that that case was wrongly decided) that he could distinguish it, I think he came round in his reply to the view, which I think is undoubtedly correct, that it is wholly indistinguishable from the facts of this case. So to that case I now turn, and I propose to read the whole of it ([1952] Ch 124 at 124–128):

> 'In 1948, a holding company was incorporated to acquire, for amalgamation purposes, two shipping companies formerly carried on under the same manage-

ment. The assets of these two companies were of slightly unequal value. There was issued in the aggregate to the shareholders in these two companies the entire a
authorized capital of the amalgamated company, which was £1,759,606. The real value of the shares at par was £5,066,506 in excess of that sum. The balance sheet of the holding company showed that this sum of £5,066,506 was appropriated to the credit of "Capital Reserve—Share Premium Account".—*Held*, that this was a proper appropriation, the transaction being within the provisions of section 56 of the Companies Act, 1948. b

'MOTION (treated as the trial of the action). The material facts are fully set out in the judgment. The plaintiffs, Henry Head & Co. Ld., sought an injunction restraining the defendants, Ropner Holdings Ld., from retaining £5,066,506, standing to the credit of "Capital Reserve—Share Premium Account" in the books and accounts of the defendant company as a sum credited therein to share premium account, or from treating any part thereof (in the books or accounts or otherwise) as c
representing the aggregate amount or value of premium on shares to which s. 56 of the Companies Act, 1948, applies, or from treating that sum otherwise than as constituting a general reserve of the defendant company.

'*Charles Russell K.C.* and *Cecil W. Turner* for the plaintiff company. The holding company had, at the time of the amalgamation, no assets and no shares to which any value could be attached. There was therefore nothing to which this premium could d
be added. It was not the intention of the legislature to extend, under this section, the meaning of the word "premium." No definition can be found showing that the word "premium" included this kind of transaction.

'*Geoffrey Cross K.C.* and *Ian G. H. Campbell* for the defendant, the holding company. The holding company has taken the proper course in making this appropriation. The use of the word "premium" in section 56 is not confined to a e
cash payment. [Counsel referred to *Drown* v. *Gaumont-British Picture Corporation Ltd.*].

'*Russell K.C.* replied.'

Pausing there for one moment, it was in his opening that counsel for the Crown was inclined to submit to that, because there had been (as will appear in a moment) a valuation of the shareholdings in the two companies prior to the amalgamation, that f
valuation somehow formed part of the terms of offer of the shares. There is no such suggestion in the judgment, and no trace of it in the arguments I have just read. Moreover, the most natural way, and, indeed, I think the only way which would assist counsel's argument for the Crown in this matter, would have been if the offer to the shareholders had been to acquire their shares for £X (the real value) to be satisfied by the issue of shares in the new company on a one-for-one basis. If that had been the nature of g
the transaction, it is quite inconceivable that Mr Geoffrey Cross KC would not have added to his argument something along the lines: 'But if it is necessary to find a cash premium, then I rely on the fact that there was a cash price of £X indicated in the offer.' Indeed, I venture to think that if there had been any such possibility open to him he would not have been able to make the point, as there would have been no proceedings h
for him to make it in. The report continues:

'HARMAN J. The defendant company is what is popularly known as a holding company and was incorporated at the end of 1948, having as its first and paramount object the acquisition for amalgamation purposes of two shipping companies formerly carried on separately under the same management. The amalgamation was of the simplest kind. The shareholders in the two companies were willing to j
sell their shares in the two companies in exchange for shares in the holding company. At that point there arose the question of the rate of capitalization. Sometimes this figure is a merely nominal figure; at other times it is designed to reflect the true value of the assets being acquired. In the present case a valuation of the assets of the two companies was procured from a firm of accountants. No doubt those calculations were based on information given by persons having a knowledge

of shipping, a knowledge which accountants would not have, and they merely valued the physical assets of the two companies, leaving out questions of profit-earning capacity, goodwill and so forth. They then apparently arrived at a value of the assets of each of the constituent companies and advised that the one having slightly larger assets than the other should issue by way of capital profit dividend a sufficient sum to its shareholders to reduce the value of the assets to an equality with the other company. At that point it was possible to advise, and the advice was given, that a pound-for-pound capitalization—that is to say, a pound of the new company's shares for a pound's worth, nominal, of the constituent company's shares—was a fair method of performing the amalgamation. Accordingly, there was issued in the aggregate to the shareholders in the two companies the entire authorized capital of the holding company, which was £1,759,606. That did not, however, do anything more than represent the aggregate of the nominal value of the shares of the constituent companies. The real value of the shares was, if the valuation was right, approximately £5,000,000 in excess of that sum. The issuing company has therefore acquired for its shares assets worth between six and seven millions, if that valuation be, as I think I must suppose it to be for these purposes, a true reflection of the value of the assets acquired at the time of their acquisition. When the balance sheet of the holding company appears for the year ended March 31, 1949, one finds on the left-hand side the issued capital set out, and below that, under the words "Capital Reserve, Share Premium Account (less formation expenses)," rather over £5,000,000. On the other side is stated the value of the shares in the subsidiary companies as valued in the way I have mentioned, and they are valued at rather under £7,000,000. When the consolidated balance sheet is looked at, a rather more express statement is found, namely: "Share Premium Account, being the excess of the value of the net assets of subsidiary companies at the date of acquisition over the book value of the investments (less formation expenses)"; and that is what this £5,000,000 figure is. The directors have been advised that they are bound to show their accounts in that way, and, not only they, but the plaintiffs, who are large shareholders, regard that as a very undesirable thing, because it fixes an unfortunate kind of rigidity on the structure of the company, having regard to the fact that an account kept under that name, namely, the Share Premium Account, can only have anything paid out of it by means of a transaction analogous to a reduction of capital. It is, in effect, as if the company had originally been capitalized at approximately £7,000,000 instead of £1,750,000. [Breaking in to comment at that point, it appears to have been a curious feature of this case that everybody concerned, plaintiff, defendants and (to some extent, at any rate) the judge, were anxious to escape from the clutches of s 56, but found themselves unable so to do. Harman J went on:] The question which I have to determine is whether the defendants were obliged to keep their accounts in that way. That depends purely on section 56 of the Companies Act, 1948, which is a new departure in legislation and was, it is said, intended to make compulsory that which had long seemed to be desirable, namely, the practice of putting aside as a reserve and treating in the ordinary way as capital cash premiums received on the issue of shares at a premium. The attention of the public and the legislature was, perhaps, drawn to this by cases such as *Drown* v. *Gaumont-British Picture Corporation Ld.*, where the defendant corporation, notwithstanding that it was making very large trading losses, paid out by way of dividend a large sum, principally drawn from a share premium account. Clauson J. held that there was nothing against that in law. Section 56 set out to remedy that omission in these words [Harman J is reported as having read sub-s (1)]. Consequently, the share premium account can be distributed in the same restricted way and with the same leave of the court as if paid up share capital was being returned to the shareholders. Counsel for the plaintiff company asks who would suppose that a common type of transaction of the sort now under consideration was the issue of shares at a premium and says that nobody in the city or in the commercial world would dream of so describing it. It is with a sense of shock at first that one hears that

> this transaction was the issue of shares at a premium. Everybody, I suppose, who hears those words thinks of a company which, being in a strong trading position, wants further capital and puts forward its shares for the subscription of the public at such a price as the market in those shares justifies, whatever it may be, 30s. a £1 share, £5 a £1 share, or any price obtainable; and the 10s. or £4 above the nominal value of a share which it acquires as a result of that transaction is no doubt a premium. That is what is ordinarily meant by the issue of shares at a premium. The first words of subsection (1) are: "Where a company issues shares at a premium." If the words had stopped there, one might have said that the subsection merely refers to cash transactions of that sort, but it goes on to say "whether for cash or otherwise." What "otherwise" can there be? It must be a consideration other than cash, namely, goods or assets of some physical sort. Continuing, the subsection contains the words "a sum equal to the aggregate amount or value of the premiums on those shares shall be transferred to an account, to be called 'the share premium account'". Apparently, if the shares are issued for a consideration other than cash and the value of the assets acquired is more than the nominal value of the shares issued, you have issued shares at a premium; and I think that counsel for the plaintiff company was constrained to admit that, in the ordinary case, that was so. This subsection at least has that much result; but he says that the line must be drawn somewhere. It cannot apply, he says, where the issuing company has no assets at all other than the assets which it will acquire as the price of the issue of shares. "Premium" (he argues) means something resulting from the excess value of its already existing assets over the nominal value of its shares. I am much attracted by that. I have every desire to reduce the effect of this section to what I cannot help thinking would be more reasonable limits, but I do not see my way to limiting it in that way. It is not stated to be a section which only applies after the company has been in existence a year, or after the company has acquired assets, or when the company is a going concern, or which does not apply on the occasion of a holding company buying shares on an amalgamation. Whether that is an oversight on the part of the legislature, or whether it was intended to produce the effect is seems to have produced, it is not for me to speculate. All I can say is that this transaction seems to me to come within the words of the section, and I do not see my way to holding as a matter of construction that it is outside it. If that is so, the inevitable result is that the action must fail.'

And there was a declaration accordingly.

Counsel for the Crown submitted that when Harman J there used the word 'Apparently . . .' he was expressing doubts about the construction which he was putting on the section. I do not think that this is correct. Nowhere does he express any doubts, and in my view the word 'apparently' merely expresses forensic surprise at finding the somewhat, as he apparently considered, bizarre effect of the section.

As I have already noted, this decision is absolutely indistinguishable in law from the present case, and I could simply decide to follow it without further ado. Strictly, it is not binding on me, being only a decision of a judge of co-ordinate jurisdiction, although, since it has stood now for some 28 years without the slightest breath of adverse comment in the reports, and must have been acted on countless times by companies in the position of the taxpayer company, it would be a bold move not to follow it.

However, it would be discourteous of me to take this simple course having regard to the careful and lucid arguments addressed to me by both counsel for the Crown and by counsel as amicus curiae. The position of counsel as amicus curiae requires a little explanation. The taxpayer company simply does not appear on this appeal, and when the matter first came on for hearing before Fox J he suggested, and counsel for the Crown concurred in the view, that the appeal raised wide and difficult issues on which there ought to be full inter partes argument. Accordingly, the usual steps which have to be taken in such a case (whatever those steps may be) were taken, and counsel took up the cudgels as amicus curiae.

So I now turn to consider counsel's submissions for the Crown. I should perhaps get
a out of the way one matter on which there is no dispute between the parties. It is common ground that the vital words, vital, that is, from the tax point of view, 'imposed by law' in s 290(4) of the 1970 Act indicate a state of affairs in which the company and its directors have no option. They do not apply to any situation which is created by the voluntary act of the company or its directors. If authority for this proposition is required (it appears quite self-evident) it is to be found in *Noble (Inspector of Taxes) v Laygate*
b *Investments Ltd* [1978] 2 All ER 1067, [1978] 1 WLR 1457.

It was counsel's subsmission for the Crown that that was the case here. To use his own exact words, 'The [taxpayer company] chose to put itself within s 56, but did not have to'. I find that a somewhat odd way of putting the point, but I assume that what was meant was that the share premium account which the taxpayer company created was not one which was created pursuant to the requirements of s 56. I cannot help thinking that
c if the taxpayer company did indeed have any real choice in the matter, and chose that s 56 should apply, there would indeed thereafter be a restriction imposed by law on the declaration of a dividend, for the simple reason that, whatever the taxpayer company did thereafter, it would be unable to escape from the requirements of that section; and this would have represented a quick conclusion to the present case.

As a lead in to the crucial point in the case, the true construction of s 56, counsel for
d the Crown made seven submissions as to the pre-1947 Companies Act law, as follows: (1) the cost to a company of assets acquired by an issue of shares was prima facie the nominal value of the shares issued; (2) an issue of shares otherwise than for cash did not require a valuation, provided that the directors honestly estimated that the assets being acquired were worth at least the par value of the shares issues; (3) it was for the company to determine the terms of issue of its shares; (4) the company was entitled to forgo the
e chance of making a profit on an issue of shares; it was not compellable to issue them at a premium; (5) the number of shares to be issued was a matter for the discretion of the company, not governed by the value of the consideration received; (6) the vice in the law at this time was the distribution of a premium obtained on shares as income; (7) the issue of shares at a premium meant an issue, i e, allotment, on terms such that the amount of the premium was ascertainable from the terms of issue. In my judgment, these
f submissions represent a fascinating mixture of the undeniably correct with the obviously false, and I shall have to deal with them in some little detail.

Counsel for the Crown based his first submission largely on *Craddock (Inspector of Taxes) v Zevo Finance Co Ltd* [1944] 1 All ER 566 and *Osborne (Inspector of Taxes) v Steel Barrel Co Ltd* [1942] 1 All ER 634; and in my judgment neither of them supports his contention in the slightest. *Zevo* was a case where the company acquired a parcel of
g shares in exchange for an issue of its own shares. The parcel was a highly speculative parcel, and, although there were Stock Exchange quotations for all the shares comprised therein, it was readily apparent that any attempt to purchase the number of shares comprised in the transaction on the Stock Exchange would have resulted in a very considerable upsurge in prices.

It was in those circumstances that the Crown sought to say that the price at which the
h acquired shares must be included in the accounts of Zevo for tax purposes was their Stock Exchange value, based on the actual quotations. This would have resulted in the shares in Zevo having been issued at a discount. It is not surprising, in those circumstances, that the whole of the argument, and all the speeches in the case, were directed towards rebutting that proposition. Since a company cannot (in general) issue shares for less than their nominal value, the cost of the purchased investments to the company must have
j been at least the nominal value of the shares unless, for some reason, the transaction itself could be impeached as a fraud or a sham, or deliberately framed in a manner intended to obscure the true position.

That case therefore assists in no wise on this proposition of counsel for the Crown. Per contra, what Lord Greene MR said in the Court of Appeal was this ([1944] 1 All ER 566 at 269–270):

'In the everyday case of reconstruction, the shares in the new company allotted to the shareholders of the old company as fully-paid will often, if not in most cases, fetch substantially less than their nominal value if sold in the market. But this does not mean that they are to be treated as having been issued at a discount; or that the price paid by the new company for the assets which it acquires from the old company ought to be treated as something less than the nominal value of the fully-paid shares. The Crown in this case is in fact attempting to depart from the rule (the correctness of which it itself admits) that the figure at which stock-in-trade is to be brought in is its cost to the trader and to substitute the alleged market value of the stock for its cost. Of course, in a case where stock which a company proposes to acquire for shares is deliberately over-valued for the purpose of issuing an inflated amount of share capital, very different considerations apply. But nothing of the kind is present in this case which, as I have already pointed out, is a perfectly proper and normal reconstruction. The propriety of the course adopted is manifest when the uncertainty as to the value of the investments, which is pointed out by the commissioners, is borne in mind. It is, I think, true as a general proposition that, where a company acquires property for fully-paid shares of its own, the price paid by the company is, *prima facie*, the nominal value of the shares. It is for those who assert the contrary to establish it, as could be done, for example, in the suggested case of a deliberately inflated valuation. In the present case the Crown has failed to establish the contrary on the facts as found; and there is no justification for the proposition that, on these facts, the commissioners were bound in law to decide the appeal in favour of the Crown.'

So Lord Greene MR lays down the prima facie rule that the price paid by the company, when it issues shares, is the nominal value of those shares, and it is for those who assert the contrary to establish that fact. So be it. In the present case that fact has been established by the findings of the Special Commissioners that the shares in the two companies acquired by the taxpayer company were valued at considerably more than the nominal amount of the shares issued in exchange by the taxpayer company.

So far as the *Steel Barrel* case is concerned, that is chiefly notable for another remarkable contention on the part of the Crown, namely that since the issue of shares in a company cost that company nothing (beyond, doubtless, the cost of providing the relevant share certificates) stock acquired in exchange for shares should be treated as having been acquired for nothing. In refuting that contention, Lord Greene MR said this when delivering the judgment of the court ([1942] 1 All ER 634 at 638):

'A company cannot issue £1,000 nominal worth of shares for stock of the market value of £500, since shares cannot be issued at a discount. Accordingly, when fully-paid shares are properly issued for a consideration other than cash, the consideration moving from the company must be at the least equal in value to the par value of the shares and must be based on an honest estimate by the directors of the value of the assets acquired.'

When counsel for the Crown first read me that passage I assumed that the words 'consideration moving from the company' must be meant to read 'consideration moving to the company', but on rereading and reflection I now see that this is erroneous. What Lord Greene MR is saying in that passage is that, because shares cannot be issued at a discount, if the company issues shares in exchange for stock, the minimum value which the directors must have placed on that stock, fairly and honestly, is the nominal value of the shares. But this is 'at least'. So long as the value of the assets acquired for the shares is equal to the par value of the shares, there will be no breach of the relevant company code. But it is implicit in his speech that shares may well be issued for more than their nominal value. This is indeed perfectly obvious. If a company whose £1 shares stand in the market at £5 acquires a plot of land worth £5,000 from the vendor in exchange for the issue of shares, it will issue him with 1,000 shares, and not 5,000; and, when taking the plot of land into its accounts, it will obviously do so at the price of £5,000, and not

£1,000. The vendor has received a consideration to the value of £5,000, and correspondingly the company has provided it for him. It is quite idle to think that the Crown can successfully maintain that the cost to the company is only £1,000, being the nominal value of the 1,000 shares, and so they are able to claim some form of tax on a profit of £4,000 if the company finally sells the asset for what it provided for it, namely £5,000.

As regards the second submission of law of counsel for the Crown, I would readily agree that there are many cases where valuations as such are not called for. It is not in respect of every asset that the directors must have a valuation before they purchase it. But thereafter I part company with counsel. In the case I have just indicated, it would clearly be a most glaring breach of the directors' fiduciary duties to the company and its shareholders to issue 4,999 shares to the vendor of the £5,000 property merely because (quite accurately) they honestly estimate that the value of the property is no less than the par value of the shares being issued as consideration therefor. Indeed, it is difficult, if not impossible, to resist the conclusion that, save in special cases, it is the obvious duty of directors, managing the company's affairs to the best of their abilities, to consider very carefully how few shares they can issue to achieve the desired acquisition of any particular asset, and, of course, for that purpose, to have a very firm idea of what are the respective values of the property being acquired and their own company's shares.

Counsel's third submission for the Crown was that it was for the taxpayer company to determine the terms of issue of its shares, and for this purpose he cited *Hilder v Dexter* [1902] AC 474. I do not doubt this as a perfectly general proposition in any way. Who else is there to perform just this very act but the board of directors? But this does not mean that they can do just as they like. The power of raising capital, or acquiring assets, by the issue of shares is, like all the other powers conferred on directors, a fiduciary power to be exercised in the best interests of the company. Accordingly, if what is sought to be implied by this submission is that the company can do what it likes as regards the issue of shares, this is very far indeed from being the case. In *Hilder v Dexter* it was found as a fact that the transaction therein impeached (the issue of shares with an option to take others at a future date at par) was 'a very reasonable and prudent contract to make when it was entered into', and the fact that the value of the shares had increased above par in the interim did not involve that the shares were being issued in contravention of the statutory provisions relating to the payment of commission.

Counsel's next submission for the Crown was that the taxpayer company was entitled to forgo the chance of making a profit on an issue of shares; it was not compellable to issue them at a premium. This, of course, is entirely correct provided, and only provided, there is some good reason, in the interests of the company, for refraining from exacting any premium that might otherwise be exigible. An excellent example of just such an action on the part of a company is to be found in *Lowry (Inspector of Taxes) v Consolidated African Selection Trust Ltd* [1940] 2 All ER 545, [1940] AC 648, where the company, being desirous of showing appreciation of the services rendered by the members of its staff, allotted some shares to them at face value, 5s, when the market value of the shares was £2 3s 9d per share. It then claimed to deduct the difference in value from its profits for income tax purposes, and was quite obviously correctly refused that relief.

But in that case there was a good reason for the action of the company in its own interests. Similarly, if a share is standing in the market at £100 and the company wishes to raise further capital from its shareholders, it may well offer them additional shares at, say, £90 in order to ensure that the whole of the new issue is taken up. Where there is no such reason, the directors will not be justified in issuing shares below the full value. Those who have practised in the field of company law for any length of time will have spent many hours convincing directors that it is wholly wrong for them in such circumstances to issue to themselves and their friends shares at par when they command a premium, however great the company's need for capital may be.

All this was clearly stated by Lord Wright in *Lowry's* case [1940] 2 All ER 545 at 565, [1940] AC 648 at 679 in a classic passage:

> 'It is true that unissued shares are not an asset, in any sense, of the company. What value they have only comes when, and by the fact that, they are issued, just *a* as a deed has no value, and, indeed, no existence, until it is signed, sealed and delivered, or a negotiable instrument until it is issued. Unissued share capital was described by LORD DAVEY in *Hilder* v. *Dexter* ([1902] AC 474 at 480) as potential capital. The power to issue further capital is only a potentiality, but the fact of issue makes it actual capital, and creates the *fasciculus* of rights and liabilities between the company and the shareholder which flow from the share when issued. If the share *b* stands at a premium, the directors *prima facie* owe a duty to the company to obtain for it the full value which they are able to get. It is true that it is within their powers under the Companies Acts to issue it at par, even in such a case, but their duty to the company is not to do so unless for good reason. Normally, they would transfer the difference between the market value and the par value to a premium reserve or similar capital account, but they could justify issuing the share at par on the ground *c* that the difference has been utilised to secure a benefit to the company, as here by paying the extra remuneration to the employees, and, it may be, also by giving them an interest in the company. In my opinion, when the directors did so, the company was incurring an expense on revenue account deductible as such under Sched. D in order to assess the balance of profits and gains. This is none the less so because the premium it acquired would have been, not a trading profit, but a receipt *d* on capital account.'

Now it is true that he dissented, and his conclusion that the company should be allowed to deduct the difference did not find favour with the majority of their Lordships. But the earlier part of that passage has never been queried or dissented from, and is, indeed, obvious good sense. Where the majority of their Lordships in that case parted company with the minority was in refusing to accept that the premiums forgone *e* were equivalent to a payment out. Therefore, it seems to me that counsel's submission for the Crown ought to be turned on its head. It is, in normal circumstances, the duty of the company to issue its shares at the highest premium it can command for them, but for good reason it may issue them for any less amount, obviously not less than par.

Counsel's next submission for the Crown, that the number of shares to be issued was a matter of discretion for the company, not governed by the value of the consideration *f* received, I totally reject. Any director who was a party to the company deliberately paying over the necessary odds for anything would be committing the plainest possible misfeasance towards that company.

I entirely agree with counsel's last submission, namely that the vice in the law at this time was the distribution of a premium obtained on the issue of shares as income. But that one could obtain a premium by an issue of shares in consideration of assets in excess *g* of their nominal value was always recognised. I need do no more than refer to the speech of Lord Romer (another dissenting speech, but again one which on this point has never been criticisable) in *Lowry* [1940] 2 All ER 545 at 574, [1940] AC 648 at 692–693:

> 'Where a company issues its shares at a premium, the premium is a receipt on capital account. It is not a trading profit, and it is not chargeable with income tax. *h* It can, nevertheless, be distributed as dividend among the shareholders, or spent in purchasing stock or machinery, or in any other way that the company thinks fit. However, the company may equally well utilise its power of realising the premium by purchasing, say, stock in trade, or by discharging a liability, without any cash passing through its hands at all. If a company, for example, the £1 shares of which stand at 10 per cent. premium in the market, buys goods of the value of £110 by the *j* issue of 100 fully paid shares to the vendor, the cost price of the goods to the company is £110. If it then sells the goods for £130, its trading profit from the transaction (apart from working charges which can be disregarded) will be £20 and not £30. It will have made a total profit on the transaction of £30, but £10 of this, representing the premium, will be entered as a receipt on capital account. The £20

alone will be taxable. A company, too, in the like circumstances, may discharge an
a existing trading liability of £100 by the issue to its creditor of 1,000 shares for a payment of £1,000. It will not have parted with the £100 but it will have utilised the power of realising the £100 premium by preventing its assets being depleted by that amount. The £100 will, accordingly, be deducted from the trading account, *pro tanto* diminishing the taxable trading profit and a similar amount must be credited in the books as a receipt on capital account.'

b Basing himself on these submissions of the pre-1947 Act law, counsel for the Crown submitted, in effect, that since it was a matter entirely for the taxpayer company how many shares it issued, and that it could issue as many or as few as it liked (subject to not issuing them at a discount), the amount of any non-cash premium (if I may so call a premium derived otherwise than by an issue of shares for cash in excess of their nominal value) was a matter with which the law was wholly unconcerned, and that therefore
c when one came to s 56 one was in fact dealing with a much narrower field than would at first sight appear. He therefore first transposed the opening words of s 56(1) so that they read: 'Where a company issues, whether for cash or otherwise, shares at a premium, a sum equal to the aggregate amount or value of the premiums . . .' Thus, he submitted, the section is really dealing with a case where the shares are being issued at a stated premium, but not being issued for cash. The only example which I was offered of this
d remarkable concept was a case where the assets being acquired were being acquired for £X, to be satisfied by the issue of Y shares of £1 each. In this case, it was submitted, the section would bite, the premium being, of course, £X minus £Y, but that if the transaction had been a simple case of the acquisition of precisely the same assets for Y shares of £1 each, no figure of £X having figured in the terms of issue, then the section would not bite.

e This submission was buttressed by a number of arguments. It was first of all said that it is surprising, if this is not the true construction of the section, that no method of valuation is prescribed: all that is said is 'value of the premiums', which must in that event involve a valuation of some kind; and my attention was drawn to several other sections or paragraphs of schedules in the Companies Act 1948 where the words '"estimated" amounts' and similar words were used. Then it was said that 'premium'
f must have the same meaning in sub-s (3) as it has in sub-s (1); and this is clearly so. So, it was argued, it could only 'form an identifiable part of the company's reserves' if it was in the form of cash, and hence, throughout, the section was dealing with a cash premium. Next it was said that if the contrary construction was correct it was surprising that s 52, dealing with a return of allotments, was unchanged from the provisions of s 42 of the Companies Act 1929; and a similar point was made in relation to the prospectus
g provisions, Sch 4, para 8, and again in Sch 5.

These being the reasons suggested for construing s 56(1) in the manner in which counsel for the Crown would wish the court to construe it, do they in fact assist him so to do? Perhaps at this point I should notice a submission by junior counsel for the Crown to the effect that, although none of the points taken on behalf of the Crown was by itself conclusive, cumulatively they established a good case in law. However, since I do not
h think any of those arguments has any significant validity, I am unable to regard their sum as of any greater validity. Of course the word 'value' must involve a valuation of some kind; but what is a valuation but an estimation, possibly an informed and reasoned estimation, but still an estimation, of what the value is in monetary terms? If the word 'estimated' had been added before the word 'value', would it have improved the subsection, or made it any more certain? I trow not.

j The framers of the section must have realised that, although the Cohen Committee had recommended that the law should jog backwards in this regard, the practical application of such a procedure would be an extremely difficult and hazardous matter, involving, doubtless, if the company had been going for any length of time, even if it were now possible to discover any non-cash premiums or, indeed, even if it were possible to discover any cash premiums, application of the rule in *Clayton's Case* (1902) 18 TLR

731. Accordingly, they took a short and simple course: only those premiums which
were currently identifiable parts of the company's reserves were to be dealt with. But I a
can see no reason why, supposing there had been an issue of shares at a non-cash
premium and that premium had only recently been realised by a sale of the assets
acquired shortly before the 1947 Act came into force, the proceeds of sale (or the
premium part thereof, which, of course, immediately prior to the Act, could have been
distributed as a capital dividend to the shareholders tax free, and hence would be likely
to have been shown separately had it existed) could not have been identified in the b
reserves. In other words, I see no necessary inference to be drawn from sub-s (3) one way
or the other.

Nor can I see (any more than counsel as amicus curiae, with his vast knowledge of
company law, was able to see) any point at all arising from the fact that the provisions of
s 52 and the other prospectus provisions remained unchanged. There was no necessity
to change any of them at all for any purpose, since they one and all simply refer to c
the consideration for the issue of the shares, which does not in any way necessitate
the splitting of that consideration, for those purposes, into nominal and premium
contents.

I can therefore see no rational argument for not construing s 56(1) according to its
obvious meaning and intent, as did Harman J in the *Ropner* case [1951] 2 All ER 994,
[1952] Ch 124. Indeed, the contrary suggestion is in many ways ludicrous; for, in d
substance, according to counsel for the Crown, it is a purely optional section. Its
application will depend on whether or not there is included in the terms of issue the
statement 'The shares are being issued at a premium of £X'. If there is an evil, and there
plainly is an economic evil in allowing assets properly forming part of capital to be
distributed as dividend, that evil is present as much whether the fact that there is a
premium is stated or suppressed. e

Moreover, but here I am sure it is my fault completely, I entirely failed to understand
what counsel for the Crown meant by a premium being 'provided by the terms of
issue'. When he first used that phrase I suggested that it would be a rather odd result if
negotiations had taken place on the basis of certain valuations, but no reference to those
valuations was included in the actual formal contract to take the shares (which is indeed
the position here), and yet there was no premium. Counsel for the Crown hastily stated f
that of course one would have to take all the circumstances of the case into account. This
left me completely baffled as to what he did mean by the terms of offer, and I tried again
in his reply to get him to define them for me rather more closely, but he stated that I was
asking him to define the indefinable. The only thing he was adamant about was that
those terms were not to be confined to the actual contract between the company and the
intending shareholders. I find this point difficult, because it is quite clear that prior to g
the relevant share issue agreements in this case the two capitals of the two companies had
been valued, and all parties must have proceeded on the basis that the shares in the
taxpayer company were being issued at a premium. Counsel for the Crown could give
no explanation which I could comprehend why, if his test was correct and was not
confined to the actual agreements in question, the establishment of a share premium
account was not an inevitable consequence. However, I think the really telling matter h
is that, when asked for an example of the kind of case where a premium would arise in
the case of an issue of shares for a consideration other than cash which would be caught
by s 56(1), the only example that was forthcoming from the Crown was the example to
which I have already referred, namely a purchase for £X to be satisfied by the issue of Y
shares of £1 each. Indeed, I think that, on the Crown's submissions, this is completely
logical and inevitable. But the submission also destroys his whole case. In such an j
example, the premium would obviously be £X minus £Y. One would reach that
conclusion as a pure matter of calculation, and not as a matter of valuation. The
distinction is fundamental: a calculation produces an exact figure, in order to carry it out
one must start from given data and at the end there can be no argument; a valuation
produces a more or less accurate figure, and there is always room for argument. Section

56(1) says clearly 'amount *or value*' of the premiums. The words 'aggregate amount' would in fact have covered both types of premium if counsel's submissions for the Crown had been correct. Certainly there would be nothing to be valued.

So, to summarise this part of the argument, on its face s 56(1) clearly envisages a premium arising on an issue of shares otherwise than for cash. In general, it is the duty of the directors to issue shares in their company for the best equivalent they can obtain, and in a very large number of cases that will mean that they will be able to issue them at a premium, and consequently must do so. The amount of the premium must therefore in all cases be a matter of interest and concern to the directors. That being so, there can be no possible ground for the legislature having made such a ludicrous and totally unworkable distinction between cases where there is a stated and cases where there is no stated premium, and distinct from the factual position whether shares have or have not actually been issued at a premium.

The farcical nature of the Crown's submissions was illustrated by counsel as amicus curiae by considering a case where a company whose shares are standing at a considerable premium purchases an entire business for its shares. It could easily happen that the cash element in the business might be more than the nominal value of the shares so issued. What then? Would it make any difference if the cash content was only just equal to the nominal value of the shares? Would it make any difference if the assets so acquired contained Treasury Stock maturing in a week's time, a fortnight's or a month's? Counsel as amicus curiae also instanced an offer to the shareholders in another company to acquire their shares for cash or shares, one 10p share or £10 cash. Are the shares acquired for shares acquired at 10p each, there being no question of a premium? Or suppose a cash alternative offer by a third party, what then? Or the company buys some shares in the market at the same time as it makes a share for share offer?

All this is simply an extremely graphic and lucid way of illustrating the fact that any attempt to divide cash premiums from non-cash premiums in the light of s 56 is hopeless. Shortly put, whatever is purchased with capital in the shape of shares itself, or an equivalent amount, is itself to be treated as capital. That is the intent of s 56, and, in my judgment, it achieves that end. If the Crown were right, it would only partially achieve that end, and the parts of it dealing with non-cash premiums would be wholly optional.

The matter does not end there, however. Counsel as amicus curiae made a bold submission to me to the effect that, quite apart from s 56, s 149 of the 1948 Act, which provides that a balance sheet must show a true and fair view of the state of the company's affairs, does, in effect, provide to the same effect. He submitted that although accountancy practice is or may be a useful guide, at the end of the day whether accounts showed a true and fair view was a matter of law. Now, as a matter of law, at what price ought one to bring into the balance sheet an asset acquired by an issue of shares? Clearly, at its true value; otherwise, the accounts would not show a true and fair view, and would obviously distort what would be the tax position on a sale.

I agree so far with counsel as amicus curiae, but I think that, in order to make good his submission, one would require to negative the effect of the *Drown* case [1937] 2 All ER 609, [1937] Ch 402, approved as it was by Lord Romer in the *Lowry* case [1940] 2 All ER 545, [1940] AC 648. For, even given that, even without s 56, the taxpayer company would be bound to create a share premium account, I cannot see that, unless somehow one can find some obligation to treat the amount so thrown up as part of the taxpayer company's share capital, it cannot be distributed as it was in the *Drown* case. I think the basic fault here lies not in the presentation of the taxpayer company's accounts but in the ability of the taxpayer company to distribute so-called capital profits or accretions. Be that as it may, I do not intend to rule on that submission one way or the other.

There is, however, yet another provision in the 1948 Act, somewhat like the celebrated (but apocryphal) provision regarding the marriage of the Town Clerk of Leeds, tucked away in para 15 of Sch 8 to the 1948 Act. Schedule 8 is dealing with accounts, and para 15 is in Part II of the schedule, dealing with the position where the company is a holding or subsidiary company. Sub-paragraph (4) deals with the position where group accounts are not submitted, and it runs, so far as material: a

> 'Where group accounts are not submitted, there shall be annexed to the balance sheet a statement showing—(*a*) the reasons why subsidiaries are not dealt with in group accounts; (*b*) the net aggregate amount, so far as it concerns members of the holding company and is not dealt with in the company's accounts, of the subsidiaries' profits after deducting the subsidiaries' losses (or vice versa)—(i) for the respective financial years of the subsidiaries ending with or during the financial year of the b company; and (ii) for their previous financial years since they respectively became the holding company's subsidiary; (*c*) the net aggregate amount of the subsidiaries' profits after deducting the subsidiaries' losses (or vice versa)—(i) for the respective financial years of the subsidiaries ending with or during the financial year of the company; and (ii) for their other financial years since they respectively became the holding company's subsidiary; so far as those profits are dealt with, or provision is c made for those losses, in the company's accounts . . .'

Sub-paragraph (5) then reads as follows:

> 'Paragraphs (*b*) and (*c*) of the last foregoing sub-paragraph shall apply only to profits and losses of a subsidiary which may properly be treated in the holding company's accounts as revenue profits or losses, and the profits or losses attributable d to any shares in a subsidiary for the time being held by the holding company or any other of its subsidiaries shall not (for that or any other purpose) be treated as aforesaid so far as they are profits or losses for the period before the date on or as from which the shares were acquired by the company or any of its subsidiaries, except [and there are some exceptions which do not apply].' e

The question here is simply: are the words 'for . . . any other purpose' completely general, or are they limited in some, and if so what, manner? Counsel for the Crown pointed out that the provisions of Sch 8 are capable of being altered by the Board of Trade under s 454(1) of the 1948 Act, and that it would be somewhat surprising if a provision of this nature were so alterable if it was intended to be given such a general application. He suggested that 'for . . . any other purpose' meant 'for any other purpose in the f accounts of the holding company'. Moreover, he submitted that all that sub-para (5) provided was that the profits in question were not to be treated as *revenue* profits. Be that so: they were still profits, which the company was free to distribute as it thought fit. Finally he submitted that no consistent purpose was to be discerned in those two sub-paragraphs of Sch 8, and that there was no corresponding provision in para 17 of the same schedule. g

To this last point counsel as amicus curiae retorted unanswerably that para 17 was dealing with consolidated accounts, and that the place to which one had to look to discover whether or not sums were distributable by way of dividend was the holding company's own accounts. He also said that whether the Board of Trade had power to amend Sch 8 or not was immaterial; it had to be construed as it stood. Counsel as amicus curiae further submitted that, although this was indeed an odd place to find a general h provision of this nature, there was no doubt at all as to what it did, in terms, provide; and that it cannot possibly have been intended to leave the pre-acquisition profits available for distribution as dividend. What would be the point of a provision which merely robbed them of their character of revenue profits? What conceivable purpose could it serve?

I agree with counsel as amicus curiae. The words 'for . . . any other purpose' are quite j general, and I cannot see how they can be confined in any manner to the purposes of the holding company's accounts. I cannot myself envisage anything in particular to which that could refer.

Accordingly, it appears to me that, at the end of the day, if I felt free to depart from the judgment of Harman J in *Henry Head & Co Ltd v Ropner Holdings Ltd* [1951] 2 All ER 994,

[1952] Ch 124, I should inevitably be driven back to precisely the same conclusions as those to which the learned judge came. The Special Commissioners in the present case conceived it to be their duty to follow the *Ropner* case, which they rightly considered completely covered the facts of the present case, and in so doing they came to an undeniably correct conclusion. The appeal falls to be dismissed.

Appeal dismissed.

Solicitors: *Solicitor of Inland Revenue*; *Treasury Solicitor*.

Rengan Krishnan Esq Barrister.

Dyson v Kerrier District Council

COURT OF APPEAL, CIVIL DIVISION
MEGAW, BRIGHTMAN LJJ AND SIR PATRICK BROWNE
10th, 11th, 27th JUNE 1980

Housing – Homeless person – Person becoming homeless intentionally – Act or omission causing person to cease occupying accommodation available for him – Applicant voluntarily giving up council flat and taking short-term holiday letting – Applicant required to vacate holiday letting – Whether local authority entitled to consider circumstances of accommodation other than that last occupied by applicant – Whether applicant became homeless intentionally – Whether council under duty to house applicant indefinitely or merely temporarily – Housing (Homeless Persons) Act 1977, ss 4(3)(5), 17(1)(2).

In October 1978 the plaintiff, a young woman with a baby, voluntarily surrendered the tenancy of a council flat in Cambridgeshire and went to Cornwall, where she took an unprotected holiday letting of a flat from 10th November 1978 to 31st March 1979. On 22nd February 1979 the plaintiff approached the local housing authority for accommodation. In the case of a person, such as the plaintiff, who was homeless and had a priority need of housing, the authority had a duty by virtue of the Housing (Homeless Persons) Act 1977 either (i) under s 4(5)[a] to provide housing for an indefinite period if the authority were not satisfied that the person had become homeless intentionally or (ii) under s 4(3) merely to provide temporary accommodation to give the person a reasonable opportunity of securing accommodation for herself if they were satisfied that the person had become homeless intentionally. On 19th March the authority decided that, although the plaintiff was then 'threatened with homelessness' because her holiday letting was due to end, her impending homelessness had been caused 'intentionally' by her giving up the flat in Cambridgeshire. The plaintiff was required by court order to vacate the holiday flat on 25th May and on 21st May the authority notified the plaintiff that they considered her homelessness had been 'self-induced' and offered her temporary accommodation at a hotel for one month, which was later extended to six weeks. On 3rd July the authority formally notified the plaintiff that they considered that she had become homeless

---

a Section 4, so far as material, provides:

'... (2) Where—(*a*) [a housing authority] are not satisfied that [a person who has applied to them for accommodation] has a priority need, or (*b*) they are satisfied that he has a priority need but are also satisfied that he became homeless or threatened with homelessness intentionally, their duty is to furnish him with advice and appropriate assistance.

'(3) Where—(*a*) they are satisfied that he is homeless, and (*b*) they are subject to a duty towards him by virtue of subsection (2)(*b*) above, they shall secure that accommodation is made available for his occupation for such period as they consider will give him a reasonable opportunity of himself securing accommodation for his occupation ...

'(5) Where—(*a*) they are satisfied—(i) that he is homeless, and (ii) that he has a priority need, but (*b*) they are not satisfied that he became homeless intentionally, their duty ... is to secure that accommodation becomes available for his occupation ...'

intentionally and that they would not provide any further financial support after 6th July. The plaintiff brought an action against the authority seeking, inter alia, a declaration either that she had not become homeless intentionally and therefore the authority were in breach of their duty under s 4(5) to provide accommodation for an indefinite period, or alternatively that the authority had not provided accommodation for such period as would give her a reasonable opportunity of securing accommodation for herself and were therefore in breach of s 4(3). The plaintiff contended (i) that her voluntary giving up of the flat in Cambridgeshire was irrelevant to the issue of intentional homelessness and that the authority were only entitled to take into consideration the fact that she had been compelled to give up the accommodation she was occupying immediately prior to becoming homeless, and (ii) that the authority had not properly notified her of their decision that they considered that she had become homeless intentionally until 3rd July and had therefore failed in their duty to provide accommodation for a reasonable period to allow her to find her own accommodation. The county court judge dismissed the plaintiff's claim on the ground that the local authority were entitled to find that the plaintiff became homeless intentionally within the meaning of that term in s 17[b] of the 1977 Act because 'intentional homelessness' included an act or omission deliberately contrived in respect of accommodation other than that last occupied by the applicant. The plaintiff appealed.

Held – The appeal would be dismissed for the following reasons—

(1) A person became intentionally homeless within the meaning of s 17(1) of the 1977 Act if he had deliberately done or failed to do anything in consequence of which he ceased to occupy accommodation which was available for his occupation and which it would have been reasonable for him to continue to occupy. The local authority were therefore entitled when deciding that they had no duty under s 4(5) to house the plaintiff permanently to take into account the fact that if she had not surrendered the Cambridgeshire tenancy she would not have become homeless on 25th May. Similarly construed, s 17(2) meant that a person became threatened with homelessness intentionally if he had deliberately done or failed to do anything which was likely to force him to leave accommodation which was available for his occupation and which it would be reasonable for him to continue to occupy. Since the plaintiff would not have found herself threatened with homelessness in March 1979 if she had not surrendered the Cambridgeshire tenancy in October 1978, the local authority were entitled to take the view on 19th March that the plaintiff was threatened with homelessness on 31st March intentionally. It followed therefore that the only duty the local authority owed to the plaintiff on 19th March, when she was threatened with homelessness, was to furnish advice and appropriate assistance under s 4(2) and their only duty on 25th May, when she became homeless, was to secure short-term accommodation for her under s 4(3) (see p 319 *f* to p 320 *c* and *j*, post).

(2) The letter written to the plaintiff on 21st May made it absolutely clear to her that the local authority considered her to be a person who would become homeless intentionally from 25th May. Accordingly, since she was provided with temporary accommodation until 6th July, she had been given at least a month in order to find her own accommodation, and there was no reason for treating the period during which she had had an opportunity to secure accommodation for her occupation as commencing on 3rd July, when she was written a letter which merely confirmed a decision previously made and communicated to her (see p 320 *g* to *j*, post).

Notes

For a housing authority's duties to a homeless person, see 22 Halsbury's Laws (4th Edn) para 513.

---

b Section 17 is set out at p 316 *e* to *g*, post

For the Housing (Homeless Persons) Act 1977, ss 4, 17, see 47 Halsbury's Statutes (3rd Edn) 318, 330.

Cases referred to in judgment

De Falco v Crawley Borough Council, Silvestri v Crawley Borough Council [1980] 1 All ER 913, [1980] 2 WLR 664, CA.

Youngs v Thanet District Council (1980) Times, 20th February, CA.

Appeal

The plaintiff, Fiona Jane Dyson, appealed against the decision of his Honour Judge Chope sitting in the Camborne and Redruth County Court on 16th October 1979 whereby he dismissed the plaintiff's claim in which she sought, inter alia, (i) declarations that she had not become homeless intentionally and that the defendants, Kerrier District Council ('the local authority'), were in breach of their duty under the Housing (Homeless Persons) Act 1977, s 4(3) and (4), or, alternatively, s 4(5), (ii) orders that the local authority secure that accommodation be made available for her, and (iii) damages limited to £2,000. The facts are set out in the judgment of the court.

James Black QC and *David Fletcher* for the plaintiff.
Konrad Schiemann QC and *John Haines* for the local authority.

Cur adv vult

27th June. **BRIGHTMAN LJ** read the following judgment of the court: This is an appeal from a decision of his Honour Judge Chope given on 15th October 1979 in the Camborne and Redruth County Court. It raises questions under the Housing (Homeless Persons) Act 1977, and in particular s 17 of that Act. A dispute arose between the local authority, the Kerrier District Council, and a homeless person, the plaintiff, Miss Fiona Dyson, as a result of which the plaintiff brought an action against the local authority for a declaration that they were bound to secure that accommodation was available for her, and also for damages. The judge dismissed the action. The plaintiff appeals.

We turn first to the Act. The long title of the Act states, as its first purpose, that of making further provision as to the functions of local authorities with respect to persons who are homeless or threatened with homelessness. The material sections are ss 1 to 4, 8 and 17. It is not necessary to read them at length, except s 17, but we will indicate the general scheme of the Act.

Section 1(1) defines a person as 'homeless' if he has no accommodation. He is to be treated as having no accommodation if (among other things) there is no accommodation which he is entitled to occupy by virtue of an interest in it or of an order of the court, or which he has an express or implied licence to occupy. Under sub-s (3) a person is 'threatened with homelessness' if it is likely that he will become homeless within 28 days. Each of such persons is defined by s 2 as having 'a priority need for accommodation' if (among other things) he has a dependent child residing with him.

Section 3 imposes certain preliminary duties on housing authorities in cases of possible homelessness. A housing authority is defined as a local authority for the purposes of the Housing Act 1957. In the present case the Kerrier District Council are the housing authority. Under s 3, if a person applies to a housing authority for accommodation, the authority are required to make inquiries in order to satisfy themselves, first, whether the applicant is homeless or threatened with homelessness, and, if so, whether he had a priority need and whether he became homeless or threatened with homelessness 'intentionally'.

On completion of their inquiries the housing authority have to make certain decisions. If they are satisfied that the applicant is either homeless or threatened with homelessness, duties are imposed on them under the somewhat complex provisions of s 4. The nature of these duties varies according to whether the authority are satisfied that the applicant is homeless or is threatened with homelessness, whether they are satisfied that he has a priority need, and whether they are satisfied that he did not become homeless or threatened with homelessness 'intentionally'. The section, in fact, deals with four categories of applicants who are homeless or threatened with homelessness, although *a* the section is not drafted by reference to categories. Category 1 is the applicant who has no priority need; category 2, the applicant who has a priority need but becomes threatened with homelessness 'intentionally'; in both these cases the duty of the authority is confined to furnishing him with advice and appropriate assistance (as defined); category 3, the applicant who has a priority need and is homeless 'intentionally'; the duty of the authority is not only to furnish advice and appropriate assistance but also to 'secure *b* that accommodation is made available for his occupation for such period as they consider will give him a reasonable opportunity of himself securing accommodation for his 'occupation'; category 4, the applicant who is threatened with homelessness or is homeless 'unintentionally'; the duty of the authority (put shortly) is to secure that accommodation is available for his occupation indefinitely.

The applicant for accommodation will need to know where he stands. So s 8 provides *c* that, on completing their inquiries under s 3, the housing authority are to notify the applicant of their decision whether he is homeless or threatened with homelessness, and, if so, whether he has a priority need, whether he became homeless or threatened with homelessness 'intentionally' and whether they are notifying any other housing authority. In certain circumstances, not arising in this case, the housing authority to whom application has been made may transfer their responsibilities to another housing *d* authority.

Section 17 defines 'intentionally' for the purposes of the Act. The section reads as follows, but only sub-ss (1) and (2) are material for present purposes:

> '(1) Subject to subsection (3) below, for the purposes of this Act a person becomes homeless intentionally if he deliberately does or fails to do anything in consequence of which he ceases to occupy accommodation which is available for his occupation *e* and which it would have been reasonable for him to continue to occupy.
>
> '(2) Subject to subsection (3) below, for the purposes of this Act a person becomes threatened with homelessness intentionally if he deliberately does or fails to do anything the likely result of which is that he will be forced to leave accommodation which is available for his occupation and which it would have been reasonable for him to continue to occupy. *f*
>
> '(3) An act or omission in good faith on the part of a person who was unaware of any relevant fact is not to be treated as deliberate for the purposes of subsection (1) or (2) above.
>
> '(4) Regard may be had, in determining for the purposes of subsections (1) and (2) above whether it would have been reasonable for a person to continue to occupy accommodation, to the general circumstances prevailing in relation to housing in *g* the area of the housing authority to whom he applied for accommodation or for assistance in obtaining accommodation.'

We turn now to the facts. At the beginning of 1978 the plaintiff was expecting a child. At that time she was living with a friend in a rented flat, the details of which are not relevant to this appeal. In July she gave up her flat, and stayed for three weeks in *h* Porthleven with her mother and her sister Janet. She then went to stay with her sister Linda, who had a council flat at Huntingdon. The plaintiff's child Natasha was born in September, when the plaintiff was living with her sister at the Huntingdon address. At the end of September the plaintiff's sister Linda left the Huntingdon flat and moved to other accommodation in Helston, Cornwall. The plaintiff remained for the time being in sole occupation of the Huntingdon flat. On 2nd October or thereabouts the tenancy *j* of the Huntingdon flat was transferred by the local authority into the plaintiff's name. The plaintiff soon made up her mind to leave the Huntingdon flat and to go to Cornwall. On 10th November she signed a tenancy agreement of a flat in Helston, next door to her sister Linda. The tenancy was only for $3\frac{1}{2}$ months, from 10th November 1978 to 31st March 1979. She would have to leave on 31st March 1979 because her tenancy was not protected. It was what is known as a winter letting. It contained a clause under which the tenant acknowledged that she had received notice that the landlord would require possession of the property for holiday letting at the expiry of the term thereby created in accordance with Sch 3, Part II, Case 10B of the Rent Act 1968, as amended. The plaintiff was therefore well aware of her position under that agreement. After she had signed the tenancy agreement, she surrendered the Huntingdon flat to the local authority.

Two months after going to Cornwall, on 19th January 1979, the plaintiff applied to the local housing authority for accommodation. She filled up a printed form and sent it to the Kerrier District Council. She was not quite truthful about the position in her accompanying letter. She represented to the local authority that she was homeless because her sister had left the Huntingdon flat. This was not the case.

On 22nd February the plaintiff called on the welfare officer, Mr Edkins, at Helston. By then the local authority had ascertained the true position in relation to the Huntingdon flat and knew that it had been transferred into her name. Mr Edkins informed the plaintiff that the local authority were going to treat her pending homelessness as 'self-induced'. A letter to this effect was sent to her on the same day signed by the housing officer of the local authority, but the county court judge was not, we think, satisfied that she in fact received it. She called again on 19th March. A letter to the like effect was sent to her on that day. There is no doubt that she received that letter.

The situation on 19th January, when the plaintiff first applied to the local authority, was that the local authority had no duty towards her under the 1977 Act. She was not at that time homeless. Nor was she threatened with homelessness, because more than 28 days would elapse before she was likely to become homeless. Her tenancy of the Helston flat was not due to expire until 31st March. She became 'threatened with homelessness' on or immediately after 3rd March. The duties of the local authority under the Act accordingly then arose, if her previous application for accommodation ought properly to be regarded as brought forward to that date, or at any rate arose when the plaintiff called at the Helston office on 19th March and repeated her application. The judge found as a fact that a decision was taken with relation to the plaintiff on 19th March and that such decision was taken by the housing officer, who signed the letter of 19th March, as the duly authorised agent of the local authority. It is implicit in that letter that the local authority had decided that she was threatened with homelessness and that this was 'intentional' within the meaning of the Act, and it is not in dispute that they recognised that she had a priority need for accommodation within the meaning of the Act.

The plaintiff failed to give up possession of the Helston flat on 31st March. Thereupon she became homeless within the meaning of the Act, because she was not entitled to occupy the premises by virtue of an interest in it or a licence, or an order of the court. She was a mere trespasser. The landlord was compelled to take proceedings. A possession order was made on 18th May, but possession was not ordered to be given up until 25th May. Technically, we think that she may have ceased to be homeless between 18th and 25th May, because she was then in occupation, in a sense, by virtue of a court order. We will treat 25th May as the date on which she finally became homeless.

When the plaintiff became homeless, on the assumption that the local authority were satisfied, and were properly satisfied, that this was 'intentional', they came under a duty under s 4(3) of the Act to secure that accommodation was available for her occupation for such period as they considered would give her a reasonable opportunity of herself securing accommodation for her occupation. Alternatively, if the local authority could not properly have decided that she was threatened with homelessness 'intentionally', they came under a duty to secure that accommodation was available for her occupation indefinitely.

On 21st May the local authority wrote to inform her that they would assist with accommodation for a period of one month at a hotel in Helston as from 25th May, subject to her paying a small weekly amount to the hotel. In fact, the local authority allowed the plaintiff to stay on at the hotel until 6th July. On 3rd July, only three days before she was due to leave, the secretary to the local authority addressed to her a formal letter telling her that, at a meeting of the housing committee held on 2nd July, the following decisions had been reached: (a) that she was homeless, (b) that she had a *a* priority need, (c) that in their opinion she became homeless intentionally, and (d) that they did not propose to notify any other housing authority that her application had been made. The letter also set out the housing committee's reasons for the decision made in para (c).

Two issues arise. First, did the local authority correctly construe and apply s 17 in deciding that she became threatened with homelessness, and became homeless, *b* 'intentionally'? If so, did they secure that accommodation was made available for her occupation for a period which could properly be considered as giving her a reasonable opportunity of herself securing accommodation for her occupation? The first question is the important one. If the plaintiff's homelessness could not properly be treated as 'intentional', then there is no doubt that the local authority became and are liable to secure accommodation for her occupation indefinitely. The second question arises under *c* s 4(3). It depends on whether the local authority had completed their statutory inquiries under s 3 and made their decision at the time when they wrote their letter of 21st May, and whether such letter was a sufficient notification to the plaintiff of their decision, or whether such decision was not made until 2nd July and notified on 3rd July. In the latter case the period of two or three days allowed to her for making her own arrangements to secure accommodation was admittedly inadequate. *d*

The argument on behalf of the plaintiff before the county court judge was that the local authority were not entitled under s 17 to look at what had happened at Huntingdon. The local authority were only entitled to look at what the plaintiff had done or omitted to do in relation to the accommodation she was occupying immediately before she became homeless or threatened with homelessness. By taking into account what happened at Huntingdon, the local authority considered matters which they were *e* not entitled to consider on a proper interpretation of s 17. The judge came to the conclusion that s 17(1) included an act or omission deliberately contrived in respect of accommodation other than that last occupied by the applicant. Section 17(2) was to be construed in parallel manner. The local authority were therefore entitled to find on 19th March that she had become threatened with homelessness intentionally; and that, when she became actually homeless, that also was 'intentional'. He also held that, as she was *f* notified on 19th March that she was being treated as a case of intentional homelessness, she was allowed sufficient time pursuant to s 4(3) for securing her own accommodation.

There are four grounds of appeal specified in the notice of appeal. First, that there was not sufficient evidence to enable the judge to hold that the local authority reached a decision on 19th March. That ground was not pursued. Second, that the judge was wrong in law in his interpretation of s 17 in holding that the local authority were *g* entitled to take the Huntingdon situation into account. Third, that the judge was wrong in holding that the local authority were not obliged to follow a statement in the Code of Guidance issued by the Secretary of State under the provisions of s 12 of the Act, which expresses the view that the most immediate cause of homelessness has greater relevance than past events. That ground was not pursued, having regard to the decision of this court in *De Falco v Crawley Borough Council* [1980] 1 All ER 913, [1980] 2 WLR 664. *h* Fourth, that the judge erred in law in holding that six weeks from the date that the local authority decided that the plaintiff had become homeless or threatened with homelessness intentionally was such period as would give her a reasonable opportunity of securing accommodation for her occupation under s 4(3) of the Act. This ground also was not pursued. The point was, however, taken that the statutory period was not capable of starting before 3rd July, so that the period allowed was only two or three days. *j*

Certain matters are common ground between the parties, which it will be convenient to state. (1) The plaintiff was entitled to occupy the Huntingdon flat and, while she did so, she was not homeless. (2) The plaintiff voluntarily left the Huntingdon flat. (3) The plaintiff knew when she took the Helston flat that her tenancy of it would expire on 31st March. (4) If the plaintiff had not left the Huntingdon flat in October 1978 she would not have found herself threatened with homelessness in March 1979. (5) She applied to the Kerrier District Council for permanent accommodation. (6) This application was refused on the ground that her homelessness was self-induced because she had no need to leave the Huntingdon flat. (7) The court should only interfere if satisfied that the local authority, when dealing with her application for permanent accommodation in Kerrier, was not entitled to take into account the fact that, if she had not left her Huntingdon flat in October 1978, she would not have found herself homeless in March 1979. (8) Subsections (1) and (2) of s 17 of the Act should not be construed in such a way that different results are reached before and after homelessness. There are no policy reasons for drawing any distinction between sub-s (1) and sub-s (2).

As we have already indicated, counsel for the plaintiff submits that, as both sub-s (1) and sub-s (2) are couched in the present tense, they relate only to the existing home, if one exists, or to the last home if none exists. That is to say, sub-s (1) is directed to the case of a homeless person who loses his *last* home because he has done or failed to do something in consequence of which he ceases to occupy that accommodation which is available for his occupation. Subsection (2) is directed to the case of a person who is threatened with the loss of his *existing* home because he does or fails to do something the likely result of which is that he will be forced to leave that accommodation which is available for his occupation.

Neither subsection, it was submitted, can apply to this case. The argument is formidable. On 19th March 1979, when the local authority made their decision, the plaintiff was threatened with homelessness. Therefore, the relevant subsection is sub-s (2). Subsection (2) says that a person becomes threatened with homelessness 'intentionally' if he deliberately does or fails to do anything 'the likely result of which is that he *will be* forced to leave accommodation which *is available* for his occupation'. The Huntingdon flat cannot be treated as that accommodation, because it was not accommodation which, on 19th March, the plaintiff 'will be forced to leave'. She had already left it. Nor could it be said on 19th March that it was accommodation 'which is available' for the plaintiff's occupation, because it was not so available. Nor can the Helston flat be treated as accommodation within the subsection. It was not available for her after 31st March. In the result, it was submitted, neither the Huntingdon flat nor the Helston flat was accommodation within sub-s (2). Nor does sub-s (1) apply. She did not become finally homeless until 25th May. The accommodation which she then ceased to occupy was not accommodation 'which is available' for her occupation.

Although sub-ss (1) and (2) of s 17 are drafted in the present and future tenses, they are in fact also referring to past events. Subsection (1) reads:

> 'A person becomes homeless intentionally if he deliberately does or fails to do anything in consequence of which he ceases to occupy accommodation which is available for his occupation and which it would have been reasonable for him to continue to occupy.'

This subsection is dealing with cause and effect. The subsection states the effect first. The specified effect is the state of being homeless. The subsection specifies that effect and then describes a particular cause which, if it exists, requires the effect to be treated as intentional. The subsection therefore means 'a person becomes homeless intentionally if he deliberately *has* done or failed to do anything in consequence of which he *has* ceased to occupy accommodation which *was* available for his occupation and which it would have been reasonable for him to continue to occupy'. Does that formulation apply to the Huntingdon flat? In our judgment it does. The local authority were entitled to reach the conclusion that the plaintiff became homeless on 25th May intentionally because she deliberately had done something (surrendered the Huntingdon tenancy) in consequence of which she ceased to occupy accommodation (the Huntingdon flat) which was available for her occupation and which it would have been reasonable for her to continue to occupy; and that, therefore, if she had not done that deliberate act she would not have become homeless on 25th May.

In the result, when the plaintiff became homeless on 25th May, the local authority had no duty under s 4(5) to house her permanently.

We must now consider whether a similar result flows from sub-s (2). By parity of reasoning this subsection means that a person becomes threatened with homelessness intentionally if he deliberately *has* done or failed to do anything the likely result of which is that he will be forced to leave accommodation which is available for his occupation and which it would have been reasonable for him to continue to occupy. On 19th March 1979 it could properly be said of the plaintiff that she *had* previously done something (surrendered the Huntingdon tenancy) the likely and indeed the inevitable result of which was that she would be forced to leave accommodation (the Huntingdon flat) which was available for her occupation and which it would have been reasonable for her to continue to occupy; as a result of which she was, on 19th March 1979, threatened with homelessness on 31st March intentionally. Therefore, the local authority could properly take the view, which they did take, on 19th March that sub-s (2) was satisfied.

In the result the only duty of the local authority on 19th March, when the plaintiff was threatened with homelessness, was to furnish advice and appropriate assistance under s 4(2), and their only duty on 25th May, when she became homeless, was to secure short-term accommodation for her under s 4(3).

We must refer briefly once more to the *De Falco* case where it seems possible that a similar point arose, although it was not taken. The facts were these. Mr and Mrs De Falco lived in Italy. They decided to come to England to work. They gave up their home in Italy and arrived in this country in February 1979. They first took a room rent free with Mrs De Falco's brother at Horsham. They left in June because the brother needed the room. They then went to stay with another relative in Crawley. In September this relative gave them what is called in the report 'a notice to quit', as the relative needed the room for others. The De Falcos then applied to the local authority for accommodation under the 1977 Act. The authority decided that they were intentionally homeless within the meaning of s 17. The case came before this court on appeal from the refusal of a motion for interlocutory relief. The appeal proceeded on the basis that the accommodation voluntarily given up was the home in Italy. It was not argued that the only relevant accommodation for the purposes of s 17 was the last accommodation occupied, namely the Crawley house, and that the De Falcos did not give up that accommodation voluntarily. As the point arising in this case was not argued, and in any event it is difficult to tell from the report what (if any) interest in, or licence to occupy, the Horsham and Crawley houses was enjoyed by the De Falcos, the decision is of no assistance to us on this appeal. We also had read to us a report of *Youngs v Thanet District Council* (1980) Times, 20th February. That also was a case of successive places of accommodation, but we do not think that there is any similarity with the case we have to consider.

The only other point is the sufficiency of the period of accommodation which the local authority secured for the plaintiff to enable her to find her own accommodation. The question, put shortly, is whether that period ought to be reckoned from 3rd July 1979, when the formal letter was written by the local authority to the plaintiff, or from an earlier date. The temporary accommodation was provided from 25th May 1979 for a period of one month, subsequently extended. The letter of 21st May, written therefore four days before the plaintiff became homeless, made it absolutely clear to her that she was being considered as a person 'intentionally' homeless who had priority need for accommodation. She was, therefore, being given at least a month in order to find her own accommodation. We can see no reason for treating the statutory period under s 4(3) as commencing on 3rd July when the formal letter was written to her. That letter was merely confirmation of a decision previously made and communicated to her, and is of no particular relevance.

For the reasons indicated we dismiss the appeal.

Appeal dismissed. Leave to appeal to the House of Lords refused.

Solicitors: *Hewitt, Woollacott & Chown*, agents for *Randle, Thomas & Thomas*, Helston (for the plaintiff); *P J Andrews*, Camborne (for the local authority).

Mary Rose Plummer Barrister.

a

Williams and others v Inland Revenue Commissioners

Inland Revenue Commissioners v Williams and others

b

HOUSE OF LORDS

LORD DIPLOCK, VISCOUNT DILHORNE, LORD SALMON, LORD RUSSELL OF KILLOWEN AND LORD KEITH OF KINKEL

23rd, 24th, 25th JUNE, 30th JULY 1980

c *Income tax – Tax advantage – Counteracting – Transaction in securities – Consideration received in connection with distribution of profits of company – Receipt of shares – Property transactions resulting in substantial profit to company wholly owned by taxpayer – Taxpayer exchanging his shares in that company for those in second company, also wholly owned by him, at a premium – First company paying dividend to second company without deduction of tax – Third company unconnected with taxpayer making loans to taxpayer – Second company acquiring all* d *the issued shares in third company – Whether loans by third company transaction in securities – Whether by receiving loans from third company taxpayer obtaining tax advantage – Income and Corporation Taxes Act 1970, ss 460, 461, 466, 467.*

The taxpayers and the wife of one of them held the entire share capital of a property development company, Kithurst. In January 1960 Kithurst acquired at low cost e farmland in Sussex and in 1969 obtained planning permission to develop 31 acres of it. With a view to minimising the substantial liability to tax which would have arisen in respect of the profits arising on a sale of the land, the shareholders entered into a tax avoidance scheme. The scheme was divided into three stages. The first stage consisted of a number of transactions ('the property transactions') by which, between 30th January and 15th February 1970, when Kithurst ceased trading, the freehold title to the land f became vested in Developments, a company owned by the shareholders, leaving Kithurst with a profit of £422,255. The second stage involved the following transactions ('the share transactions'). Shortly before 20th March the shareholders acquired one share each in Gristrim, a specially incorporated company, those shares being the entire issued share capital of that company. The shareholders then exchanged their shares in Kithurst for shares in Gristrim, and a sum of £423,180 was credited by Gristrim in its share premium g account. Kithurst then paid a gross dividend of £422,000 to Gristrim without deduction of tax. The third stage involved the following transactions ('the loan transactions'). A company, Dolerin, in which the shareholders had initially no interest, agreed to lend £84,200 to each of the shareholders personally. The loans were made on terms, inter alia, that no interest should be paid after the first seven days and that although the loans were to be repayable on demand no demand would be made unless repayment was h demanded from all the shareholders. Gristrim then acquired the whole of the issued share capital of Dolerin for £421,250 and the shareholders became the directors of Dolerin. In March 1975 the taxpayers were served with notices under s 460(3)[a] of the Income and Corporation Taxes Act 1970 stating that the Revenue were of the opinion that s 460 applied to them in respect of the transactions. The notices specified the assessments requisite for counteracting the tax advantage alleged to have been obtained j by the taxpayers (a) for the year 1969–70 by transactions involving the exchange of

a Section 460(3), so far as material, provides: 'Where [a person is in a position to obtain or has obtained a tax advantage] in respect of any transaction or transactions, the tax advantage obtained or obtainable by him in consequence thereof shall be counteracted by such . . . adjustments . . . as the Board may specify by notice in writing served on him . . .'

shares in Kithurst for those in Gristrim, and the declaration and payment of a dividend of £422,000 by Kithurst to Gristrim, or, in the alternative, (b) for the year 1970–71 by transactions involving the payment of a sum of cash by way of loan by Dolerin to the shareholders and the subsequent acquisition by Gristrim in February 1971 of the whole of the issued share capital of Dolerin for a consideration of £421,250. It was common ground that the transactions were not carried out for bona fide commercial reasons or in the ordinary course of making or managing investments. The taxpayers contended, however, (a) that the receipt by the shareholders of shares in Gristrim had not conferred on them any tax advantage within s 466[b] of the 1970 Act or (b) (i) that the exchange of shares in Kithurst for those in Gristrim was not a transaction 'whereby' Gristrim received an abnormal amount by way of dividend and that, therefore, the circumstances mentioned in para C of s 461[c] did not exist or (ii) that the shares in Gristrim had not been received by the shareholders 'in connection with' the dividend subsequently paid by Kithurst to Gristrim and, accordingly, the circumstances mentioned in para D of s 461 did not exist, (c) (i) that the money received by the shareholders by way of loan from Dolerin could not confer on the taxpayers any tax advantage within s 466 because it was repayable or, in the alternative, (ii) that the loans were not transactions in securities as defined in s 467(1)[d] and, therefore, any tax advantage obtained from them were not in consequence of transactions in securities within s 460(1)[e] or, in the further alternative, (iii) that as regards the loans neither the circumstances in para C nor those in para D of s 461 existed because 'consideration' in the form of loan moneys did not fall into any of the categories in paras (i), (ii) and (iii) of para C(1) and was not received in connection with the payment of a dividend by Kithurst to Gristrim. The Special Commissioners determined that the transactions involving the exchange of shares were within the circumstances in paras C and D of s 461 and upheld the notices and the consequential assessments for the year 1969–70 and quashed the assessments for the year 1970–71. The taxpayers appealed and the Crown cross-appealed. The judge held that the exchange of shares in Kithurst for those in Gristrim had enabled Kithurst to distribute its profits by way of dividend and consequently the shareholders' receipt of shares in Gristrim was in connection with the payment of a dividend by Kithurst within para D of s 461, and upheld the notices and consequential assessments for the year 1969–70. The taxpayers appealed, contending further that the words 'in connection with the transfer directly or indirectly of assets of a company to which paragraph D ... applies to another such company' in para E(1) of s 461 brought their scheme within the circumstances envisaged by that paragraph and accordingly that they were entitled to the exception or deferment applicable under para E(2) despite the fact that their scheme also came within para D of s 461. Subsequently to the notices and assessments under s 460, assessments to income tax in respect of shortfall in distribution were made on Gristrim under s 289 of the 1970 Act and consequential surtax apportionments were made on the taxpayers under ss 296 and 297 of that Act. The Crown, however, gave an undertaking that if the notices and assessments under s 460 were upheld, assessments and apportionments under ss 289, 296 and 297 would not be proceeded with. The taxpayers referred to those assessments and contended that despite the Crown's undertaking they remained technically liable to assessment in respect of the same receipts under sections of the Act other than s 460, and accordingly it could not be said that in respect of those receipts they had obtained a tax advantage within s 466 by avoiding a possible assessment to tax. The Crown cross-appealed contending that should the taxpayers succeed on their appeals the notices and the consequential assessments on them for the year 1970–71 in respect of transactions involving loans to the shareholders from Dolerin should be upheld. The Court of Appeal allowed the taxpayers' appeal in relation to the notices and consequential assessments for

b Section 466, so far as material, is set out at p 327 *g*, post

c Section 461, so far as material, is set out at p 326 *d e*, post

d Section 467(1), so far as material, is set out at p 328 *a*, post

e Section 460(1), so far as material, is set out at p 326 *b*, post

the year 1969–70, holding that the taxpayers were entitled to the deferment of their
a liability to tax under para E(2) of s 461, and it also allowed the Crown's cross-appeal in
relation to the notices and consequential assessments for the year 1970–71. The taxpayers
appealed and the Crown cross-appealed.

Held – The loans which were received by the shareholders without paying or bearing
any tax thereon and which were repayable to a company under their control (a) were
b 'transactions in securities' within s 467(1) of the 1970 Act and (b) were intended to secure
and did secure a tax advantage to them. Furthermore, the sums received by the
shareholders by way of loans were received by them in connection with the distributions
of profits of Kithurst, a company to which para D of s 461 of the 1970 Act applied, and
represented the value of assets which would have been available for distribution to them
by way of dividends by Kithurst but for the steps taken by Kithurst; accordingly, the
c loan transactions were within the circumstances in para D of s 461. It followed,
therefore, that the Revenue were entitled to counteract the tax advantage obtained by the
taxpayers by the notices they served and the assessments they made for the year 1970–
71. The appeal by the taxpayers and the cross-appeal by the Crown would, therefore, be
dismissed (see p 323 *j*, p 327 *h j* and p 328 *b* to *h*, post).

Notes
d For tax advantage obtained or obtainable in consequence of transactions in securities and
the Inland Revenue Commissioners' power to counteract such tax advantage by making
such adjustments as they may specify by notice served on the person by whom the tax
advantage is obtained or obtainable, see 23 Halsbury's Laws (4th Edn) paras 1461–1464,
and for cases on the subject, see 28(1) Digest (Reissue, 489–494, *1753–1762*.

For the Income and Corporation Taxes Act 1970, ss 289, 296, 297, 460, 461, 466, 467,
e see 33 Halsbury's Statutes (3rd Edn) 394, 403, 405, 591, 595, 600.

Case referred to in opinions
Anysz v Inland Revenue Comrs [1978] STC 296, [1978] TR 323, Digest (Cont Vol E) 311, *1762a*.

f **Consolidated appeals and cross-appeals**
Aubrey Dan Williams, Michael Charles Williams, Peter Alexander Neville Wilson and
John Lewis Bowron ('the taxpayers') appealed pursuant to the leave of the House of Lords
granted on 27th June 1979 and the Crown cross-appealed pursuant to the leave of the
House also granted on 27th June 1979 against the decision of the Court of Appeal (Orr,
Bridge and Cumming-Bruce LJJ) ([1979] STC 598) on 26th February 1979 allowing the
g cross-appeals by the Crown and the appeals by the taxpayers against the decision of
Browne-Wilkinson J ([1978] STC 379) on 21st December 1977 whereby he dismissed
cross-appeals by the Crown and appeals by the taxpayers by way of cases stated by the
Commissioners for the Special Purposes of the Income Tax Acts (the cases are set out at
[1978] STC 381–403) in respect of their dismissal of appeals by the taxpayers against
notices under s 460 of the Income and Corporation Taxes Act 1970 and consequential
h assessments to income tax and surtax. The facts are set out in the opinion of Viscount
Dilhorne.

C N Beattie QC and *George Bretten QC* for the taxpayers.
Donald Rattee QC and *Peter Gibson* for the Crown.

Their Lordships took time for consideration.

j 30th July. The following opinions were delivered.

LORD DIPLOCK. My Lords, I have the advantage of reading in draft the speech
prepared by my noble and learned friend Viscount Dilhorne. I entirely agree with it and
for the reasons he gives I too would dismiss the appeal and the cross-appeal.

VISCOUNT DILHORNE. My Lords, the main question to be determined in this appeal is whether Mr Aubrey Dan Williams and his wife, Mr Michael Williams and two a solicitors, Mr Wilson and Mr Bowron, partners in the firm of Malcolm, Wilson & Cobby ('the taxpayers'), are persons to whom s 460 of the Income and Corporation Taxes Act 1970 applies. If it does, then the Revenue must seek to counteract the tax advantage obtained or obtainable 'on such basis as the Board may specify by notice in writing . . . as being requisite for counteracting the tax advantage so obtained or obtainable' (see s 460(3)). b

The taxpayers were the directors and shareholders of a company called Kithurst Park Estates ('Kithurst') which owned a farm called Hormare Farm at Storrington in Sussex for which it had paid a low price. Some time before 1969 planning permission was obtained for the development for residential purposes of 31 acres of the farm with the result that there was an immediate and very substantial increase in its value.

The taxpayers wanted to realise that value but they were advised that payment of the c betterment levy, corporation tax, shortfall income tax and surtax apportionments would amount to between 98% and 99% of the profit obtained. The Revenue thought that the maximum figure would be 91¼%.

Among the facts found by the commissioners were the following:

> 'In the autumn of 1969 the shareholders in Kithurst were introduced to Mr Bradman and Mr Faber who were directors of a number of companies which Mr d Faber described as property dealing and share dealing companies and were experts in certain tax avoidance devices (on which they had received counsel's advice) and were prepared, in return for a large commission, to make these devices available to clients. The services which Mr Bradman and Mr Faber were willing to provide included the co-operation, as necessary, of companies which they directed and the furnishing of appropriate documentation based on stock drafts which had been e settled by counsel.'

The taxpayers embarked on a scheme supplied by Mr Faber and set out in detail in a letter he wrote on 20th February 1970 in return for a commission of £59,000. They hoped that thereby the payment of tax on the profit which would be realised on the sale of the 31 acres would be avoided and that they would secure the profit for themselves f free of tax.

Section 460 does not apply if a person who is in a position to obtain or has obtained a tax advantage shows that the transaction or transactions were carried out either for bona fide commercial reasons or in the ordinary course of making or managing investments, and that none of them had as their main object, or one of their main objects, to enable tax advantages to be obtained. Not surprisingly the taxpayers did not attempt to show g this in the High Court, the Court of Appeal or this House.

Mr Faber began his letter to Mr Haydon, the accountant for Kithurst, by saying that he understood that Mr Haydon had been advised of certain transactions which had been entered into by Kithurst—

> 'designed to enable that company to dispose of the land at Hormare Farm for approximately £520,000 without any liability to Betterment Levy and without any h material liability to taxation. The proposed transactions were approved by Mr. C. N. Beattie, Q.C. in Conference on the 17th November, 1969 and subsequent in his Written Opinion of the 18th November.'

Mr Faber enclosed a copy of the instructions to taxation counsel and a copy of the written opinion 'which set out in detail the form of the transactions' and said that the j overall scheme was basically divided into three stages of which the first was 'The transactions designed to enable Kithurst to dispose of Hormare Farm without any liability to betterment levy and without any material liability to taxation'.

On 30th January 1970 Kithurst, in accordance with the scheme, leased the farm to one of Mr Faber's companies, Parlev Property Co ('Parlev'), for six years at a rent for the first

three months of £100 and thereafter of £62,550 pa. This was called by Mr Faber 'the
a betterment levy lease'. Its object was, as he said in his letter, to increase the current use value of the farm to its full market value and so to avoid any betterment levy. It was, counsel for the taxpayers said in opening the appeal in this House, not contemplated that that rent would be paid by anyone.

On 31st January 1970 Kithurst granted to Metallic Property Co ('Metallic'), another of Mr Faber's companies, a lease of the farm for 250 years at a rent of £100 pa in return for
b a premium of £521,000 payable by instalments of £100 pa for 249 years with the balance in the 250th year. The lease gave the lessors the right to terminate it at the 49th year and was granted subject to and with the benefit of the betterment levy lease. This Mr Faber called the 'corporation tax lease'.

On 5th February 1970 Parlev surrendered the betterment levy lease to Metallic and the next day Kithurst sold its freehold reversionary interest in the farm to A D Williams
c Developments Ltd ('Developments') for £1,000 subject to the corporation tax lease. The five taxpayers, in addition to being the directors of and shareholders in Kithurst, were directors of and the shareholders in Developments.

In his letter Mr Faber stated that the purpose of the corporation tax lease was to enable Kithurst to dispose of the land in return for a premium 'on what for commercial purposes is a long lease but for taxation purposes, as a result of the lessor's right to
d determine, will be treated as a short lease' with the consequence that Kithurst could elect to pay tax on the instalments of premium, as and when payable, over 250 years. These transactions, Mr Faber said, resulted in a loss.

On 6th February 1970 Developments paid Metallic £521,000 for the surrender of its lease; so, as Developments had bought the freehold for £1,000, it then owned the same freehold interest in the land that Kithurst had had. The same day Kithurst assigned its
e entitlement to the premium to another of Mr Faber's companies, Lekos Investment Co Ltd ('Lekos'), for £521,000. 'In this way,' Mr Faber said, 'Kithurst received virtually the total disposal proceeds which would otherwise have arisen on the sale of the land.'

The same day Metallic lent Lekos £521,000, the amount paid to it by Developments and the amount Lekos agreed to pay Kithurst, and the same day Kithurst lent £522,102·93 to Developments. On 15th February 1970 Kithurst ceased trading. Its
f accounts showed a credit balance on profit and loss account of £422,255.

So far, counsel for the taxpayers said in the course of his opening, no 'real' money was involved and there was 'a mere circulation of money which really scarcely existed' between companies owned by the taxpayers and those of Mr Bradman and Mr Faber in the course of transactions designed to avoid liability to betterment levy, corporation tax, shortfall income tax and surtax apportionments.

g The second stage of the scheme was described by Mr Faber as—

> 'The transactions involving the extraction of the tax free monies from Kithurst by way of a tax free dividend to an interposed holding company controlled by the same shareholders,'

and the third stage as—

h

> 'The final transaction designed to enable the shareholders personally to obtain the benefit of the tax free monies in the form of interest free loans made to them by a company which they ultimately control, so that no liability arises under the provisions of Section 75 of the Finance Act 1965.'

Shortly before 20th March 1970 the taxpayers acquired all the shares in a company
j called Gristrim Investment Co ('Gristrim'), another of Mr Faber's companies, and on that date they agreed to exchange all their shares in Kithurst for shares in Gristrim. On 13th April Developments repaid to Kithurst part of the loan made to it on 6th February 1970 and Kithurst paid a dividend without deduction of tax of £422,000 to Gristrim and Gristrim lent a sum equal or approximately equal thereto to Developments.

Still there was not what counsel for the taxpayers called 'real money' involved.

Nevertheless these transactions involved a very considerable amount of money which had been Kithurst's and which was paid by that company to Gristrim in a tax-free dividend.

The Crown put forward two alternative contentions, the first of which was that the taxpayers had obtained a tax advantage by receiving the shares in Gristrim in exchange for their shares in Kithurst in circumstances to which s 461 of the 1970 Act applied and so were persons to whom s 460 applied. Section 460(1) reads as follows:

> 'Where—(*a*) in any such circumstances as are mentioned in section 461 below, and (*b*) in consequence of a transaction in securities or of the combined effect of two or more such transactions, a person is in a position to obtain, or has obtained, a tax advantage, then . . . this section shall apply to him in respect of that transaction or those transactions . . .'

Section 461 describes five kinds of circumstances. In relation to this case the Crown contended that the circumstances stated in paras C and D of the section were satisfied. They read as follows:

> 'C.—(1) That the person in question receives, in consequence of a transaction whereby any other person—(*a*) subsequently receives, or has received, an abnormal amount by way of dividend; or . . . a consideration which either—(i) is, or represents the value of, assets which are (or apart from anything done by the company in question would have been) available for distribution by way of dividend . . . and the said person so receives the consideration that he does not pay or bear tax on it as income . . .
>
> 'D.—(1) That in connection with the distribution of profits of a company to which this paragraph applies, the person in question so receives as is mentioned in paragraph C(1) above such a consideration as is therein mentioned.
>
> '(2) The companies to which this paragraph applies are—(*a*) any company under the control of not more than five persons . . .'

The Special Commissioners held that the circumstances of this case were covered by paras C and D and that in consequence of transactions in securities the five taxpayers had obtained tax advantages which the Revenue were entitled under s 460(3) to counteract by the notices they had given and the assessments they had made for 1969–70. The commissioners therefore did not find it necessary to consider the Crown's alternative contention.

Browne-Wilkinson J, following his decision in *Anysz v Inland Revenue Comrs* [1978] STC 296, upheld the commissioners' decision that the circumstances came within para D. He therefore also found it unnecessary to consider the Crown's alternative contention.

In the Court of Appeal the taxpayers took and succeeded on a new point. Paragraph E was added to s 461 by s 39 of the Finance Act 1966. It was said that the circumstances set out in this paragraph were a species of those stated in para D and that where para E applied the taxpayer was entitled to the deferment of liability to tax provided by para E(2).

So the Court of Appeal considered the Crown's alternative case and decided that in their favour. From that decision the taxpayers now appeal and the Crown cross-appeals against the Court of Appeal's decision against them on their first contention. The Crown had served notices and made assessments under s 460 for the year 1970–71, the year in which the operation of the scheme was completed and in which each of the taxpayers received interest-free loans of £84,200.

Following on the loan by Gristrim to Developments, in January 1971 Developments sold 30 acres of the land at Hormare Farm for £400,000 to a company not associated with the taxpayers or with Messrs Faber and Bradman. All but £58,000 of that was used to discharge indebtedness of Developments. This was the first occasion on which what counsel for the taxpayers called 'real money' came on the scene.

On 5th February 1971 a £100-company, Dolerin Investment Co ('Dolerin'), was incorporated. Mr Faber and Mr Bradman were its directors and it was a wholly-owned subsidiary of another of their companies, Retsor Trading Co ('Retsor'). It had no assets and no liabilities. On 16th February 1971 Sandelsons, a firm of stockbrokers, agreed to lend Dolerin £410,475 and the next day Retsor agreed to lend that company £10,525, making a total of £421,000. As I have said the amount standing to Kithurst's credit on its profit and loss account when it ceased to trade was £422,255.

The loan made by Sandelsons was repayable on call and in any event, unless otherwise agreed, within seven days. On 16th February, in accordance with instructions given by Mr Faber, the five taxpayers told Sandelsons to buy government stock at a cost of £421,000 and authorised them to hold the stock as security for the loan to Dolerin.

The next day Dolerin entered into agreements with the five taxpayers whereby Dolerin agreed to lend each taxpayer £84,200 interest-free after the first week, making a total of £421,000. The agreements contained a provision that the borrower should not be liable to repay the whole or any part of the loan on demand unless Dolerin at the same time demanded repayment by the other taxpayers. To implement these transactions, 13 cheques were drawn, 12 by Faber companies and the taxpayers and one by Sandelsons for the amount of the loan. All these cheques were cleared simultaneously on 17th February. It is not necessary to refer to them in detail. It suffices to say that five of the cheques, each for £84,200, were drawn by the taxpayers in favour of Sandelsons in payment for the government stock. The loans to Dolerin were repaid and the stock was sold. Sandelsons then divided the proceeds of sale among the taxpayers, Mrs Williams getting £84,216·73 and each of the others £84,216·74.

Gristrim, in which as I have said, the taxpayers held all the shares, called in its loan to Developments and on 24th February paid £421,250 for the whole of the authorised share capital of Dolerin which had been increased to 1,000 shares. On the same day the five taxpayers were appointed the directors of Dolerin.

At the end of these complicated operations the taxpayers received, as the scheme envisaged, interest-free loans almost equivalent to the sum which had stood to the credit of Kithurst when it stopped trading and loans repayable to a company owned by them through Gristrim and of which they were the directors.

The five taxpayers lent the money they had received from Sandelsons to their company, Developments, but this does not in my opinion lead to the conclusion that they did not receive interest-free loans from Dolerin.

As a result of these operations did the taxpayers obtain or were they in a position to obtain a tax advantage, that is to say—

> 'a relief or increased relief from, or repayment or increased repayment of, tax, or the avoidance or reduction of an assessment to tax or the avoidance of a possible assessment thereto, whether the avoidance or reduction is effected by receipts accruing in such a way that the recipient does not pay or bear tax on them, or by a deduction in computing profits or gains' (see s 466(1))?

The taxpayers each received £84,216 without paying or bearing tax thereon. That was the object of the scheme. By the operations in which they engaged they avoided a possible assessment thereon and it is clear beyond all doubt that they obtained or by virtue of these transactions were in a position to obtain a tax advantage.

Did they do so in any of the circumstances mentioned in s 461 and in consequence of a transaction in securities or of the combined effect of two or more such transactions? In my opinion para D of s 461 applies. In connection with the distribution of profits of a company (Kithurst) to which that paragraph applies, they received without paying or bearing tax a consideration which represented the value of assets which would have been available for distribution to them by way of dividend but for the steps taken by that company.

The final question for consideration is: was the tax advantage obtained in consequence of a transaction in securities or of the combined effect of two or more such transactions?

'Securities' is defined in s 467(1) as including shares and stock, and 'transactions in securities' as including— *a*

> 'transactions, of whatever description, relating to securities, and in particular—(i) the purchase, sale or exchange of securities, (ii) the issuing or securing the issue of, or applying or subscribing for, new securities, (iii) the altering, or securing the alteration of, the rights attached to securities.'

The Court of Appeal held that the loans made to the taxpayers came within this *b* definition. I think that they were right to do so. Counsel for the Crown had put forward alternative contentions, one of which was that, it being a condition of the loans that the taxpayers should deposit government stock as security for the loan, the transaction related to securities, the other being that the tax advantage was obtained in consequence of the combined effect of two or more transactions in securities.

I prefer to base my conclusion on the wider ground, though I am far from saying that *c* the Court of Appeal's decision cannot be sustained on the narrower one. It is not, I think, necessary to list the many transactions coming within the definition which were entered into from the inception of the scheme. They were all necessary ingredients of it, intended to secure tax-free gains to the taxpayers and those gains do not cease to be in consequence of those transactions if one or more links in the chain of operations does not come within the definition. *d*

In my opinion, by the receipt of the loans repayable to a company which they now control, they intended to secure and did secure a tax advantage in circumstances which brought them within the scope of s 460.

It is not therefore necessary to consider whether, contrary to the view of the Court of Appeal, they were in a position to obtain or obtained a tax advantage at an earlier stage. If they did, that is no bar to the conclusion that by the receipt of the loans they secured *e* a tax advantage. The Crown's claim has always been in the alternative.

It follows that in my opinion the Revenue were entitled to counteract that tax advantage by the notices they gave and the assessments they made for 1970–71.

In my opinion this appeal should be dismissed for the reasons I have stated. As it is not necessary to decide the Crown's cross-appeal, that too should be dismissed. In my view the taxpayers should pay the costs of the hearing before this House and in the courts *f* below.

LORD SALMON. My Lords, I entirely agree with the speech of my noble and learned friend Viscount Dilhorne and, for the reasons he gives, I would dismiss the appeal and the cross-appeal.

g

LORD RUSSELL OF KILLOWEN. My Lords, I have had the advantage of reading in draft the speech of my noble and learned friend Viscount Dilhorne. I agree with it and with his conclusion that the appeal (and the cross-appeal) be dismissed.

LORD KEITH OF KINKEL. My Lords, I have had the advantage of reading in draft the speech of my noble and learned friend Viscount Dilhorne. I agree with it and would *h* dismiss the appeal for the reasons which he has given.

Taxpayers' appeal and Crown's cross-appeal dismissed.

Solicitors: *Berwin Leighton* (for the taxpayers); *Solicitor of Inland Revenue.*

j

Rengan Krishnan Esq Barrister.

a Kennaway v Thompson and another

COURT OF APPEAL, CIVIL DIVISION
LAWTON, WALLER LJJ AND SIR DAVID CAIRNS
24th, 25th, 26th, 27th MARCH, 30th APRIL 1980

Injunction – Nuisance – Continuing threat of damage – Balance of conflicting interests – Interest b *of public at large conflicting with interest of private individual – Right of private interest to be protected despite interest of public at large – Grant of damages in lieu of injunction – Motor boat club causing noise nuisance to adjoining house owner – Race meetings organised by club attracting large public attendances – Whether private interest of house owner should prevail over public interest in club's race meetings – Whether damages should be awarded in lieu of injunction – Chancery Amendment Act 1858.*

c

The plaintiff owned land near a lake on which a club had organised motor boat races and water skiing since the early 1960s. Although aware of the club's racing activities the plaintiff began building a house on her land in 1969. The plaintiff considered at that time that the club's activities would not interfere with her comfort and enjoyment of the new house. However, by the time the house was completed in 1972 the club was d holding considerably more race meetings and the competing boats had become more powerful and noisy. By 1977 the club had become a centre for motor boat racing at club, national and international level and the number of days on which racing and practising took place on the lake had increased. The plaintiff brought proceedings against the club seeking an injunction restraining the club from causing or permitting excessive noise to come onto her land and restricting motor boat racing on the lake to certain specified e times. At the trial of the action the judge upheld the plaintiff's claim that a nuisance had been caused but refused to grant the injunction sought on the ground that to do so would be oppressive, having regard to the enjoyment of the large numbers of the public who attended the club's races. The judge awarded the plaintiff damages of £1,000 for the nuisance already suffered and £15,000 under the Chancery Amendment Act 1858 for the damage likely to be suffered in the future. The plaintiff appealed against the judge's f refusal to grant the injunction, contending that once she had proved that the club had caused a nuisance which interfered in a substantial and intolerable way with the use and enjoyment of her land she was entitled to an injunction to stop the nuisance. The club conceded that it had caused a nuisance but contended that the judge's exercise of his discretion to award damages in lieu of an injunction should not be disturbed.

g **Held** – Although the plaintiff was not entitled to an injunction restraining all of the club's activities and notwithstanding than an injunction in general terms would be unworkable, the plaintiff was entitled to an injunction restraining the club from carrying on those activities which caused a nuisance to her in the enjoyment and use of her land, despite the public interest in such activities. Accordingly an injunction would be granted restricting the club's racing activities in each year and restricting the noise level of boats h using the lake at other times. The appeal would therefore be allowed and the injunction granted in lieu of the £15,000 damages award (see p 333 *c* to *e* and *h* to p 334 *b*, post).

Shelfer v City of London Electric Lighting Co [1891–4] All ER Rep 838 applied.

Miller v Jackson [1977] 3 All ER 338 considered.

Notes

j For the grant of an injunction to restrain a nuisance, see 28 Halsbury's Laws (3rd Edn) 165–168, paras 239–245, and for cases on the subject, see 36(1) Digest (Reissue) 499–504, 725–772.

For the Chancery Amendment Act 1858, see 25 Halsbury's Statutes (3rd Edn) 203. Section 2 of the 1858 Act was repealed by the Statute Law Revision and Civil Procedure Act 1883, s 3, Sch, but by virtue of the combined effect of s 5 of the 1883 Act, the Statute

Law Revision Act 1898, s 1, and the Supreme Court of Judicature (Consolidation) Act 1925, s 18, the jurisdiction conferred by s 2 of the 1858 Act remains in force. *a*

Cases referred to in judgment

Miller v Jackson [1977] 3 All ER 338, [1977] QB 966, [1977] 3 WLR 20, CA, Digest (Cont Vol E) 466, *752a*.

Shelfer v City of London Electric Lighting Co, Meux's Brewery Co v City of London Electric Lighting Co [1895] 1 Ch 287, [1891–4] All ER Rep 838, 64 LJ Ch 216, 72 LT 34, 12 R *b* 112, CA, 28(2) Digest (Reissue) 1017, *435*.

Appeal

The plaintiff, Mary St Joan Howard Kennaway, appealed against the decision of Mais J on 24th May 1979 whereby he refused to grant the plaintiff an injunction restraining the defendants, Derek Thompson and Audrey Holden sued on their own behalf and on *c* behalf of all other members of the Cotswold Motor Boat Racing Club and all persons who were members from time to time of the Cotswold Motor Boat Racing Club from (i) using or permitting the use of the lake known as Whelford Lake on the west side of Whelford Road, Fairford, Gloucestershire by motorised watercraft, (ii) using or permitting the use of the public address loud speaker system at the lake, or alternatively (iii) carrying on the activities of the club in such a manner as to be, or cause, a nuisance to the plaintiff and *d* unlawfully to interfere with the plaintiff's occupation and enjoyment of her land by causing or permitting excessive noise to come onto it. The judge awarded the plaintiff special damages of £1,000 and damages of £15,000 under the Chancery Amendment Act 1858 for the nuisance caused to her. The facts are set out in the judgment of the court.

e

Michael Kempster QC and *Christopher Mastin-Lee* for the plaintiff.
John Gorman QC and *Richard Wakerley* for the defendants.

Cur adv vult *f*

30th April. **LAWTON LJ** read the following judgment of the court: This appeal, which is from a judgment of Mais J, delivered at Reading on 24th May 1979, is concerned with remedies, not liability. The defendants, who are sued as representatives of the Cotswold Motor Boat Racing Club, have accepted that in this court they have no grounds for challenging the judge's finding that some of the club's activities caused a *g* nuisance to the plaintiff's house, Mallam Waters, near Fairford in Gloucestershire. The judge awarded her £1,000 damages for the damage she had suffered up to the date of the trial and £15,000 damages under the Chancery Amendment Act 1858 (Lord Cairns's Act) for the damage which she is likely to suffer in the future. He refused an injunction. The plaintiff does not want damages. She wants to live in her house without having to put up with a great deal of noise each year from the end of March to the *h* beginning of November, the period during which the club carries on its racing activities on a nearby man-made lake which the judge referred to as the club's water. It was a gravel pit, as was the lake alongside which stands the plaintiff's house.

Both the club's water and Mallam Water are situated about a mile to the east of Fairford. They are separated from one another by a minor public highway. The club's water covers an area of 38·31 acres, and Mallam Water 12·18 acres. The plaintiff's house *j* stands on a spit of land about half-way along Mallam Water. Bordering the road, there is a belt of trees on the west side of Mallam Water. The distance from the plaintiff's house to the starting line for the races organised by the club is 390 yards.

In the early 1960s the club's water began to be used for motor boat racing; but at that time only small boats were used. The plaintiff knew what was going on as she had been brought up in the area and her father owned land to the east of the road, including Mallam Water.

In 1969 the plaintiff, who by this time had become the owner of Mallam Water, her father having died in 1966, applied for planning permission to build a house alongside it. She was granted permission and in May 1972 the house was ready for occupation. When she applied for planning permission the racing activities on the club's water were not such as to make her think that they would interfere with her comfort when she came to live in her house; but between 1969 and 1972 there was a considerable increase in the amount of racing activity on the club's water. This was organised by the club. The boats used for racing were bigger than they had been in the 1960s and were making more noise. This tendency continued after 1972 and by the time proceedings were started in 1977 the club's water had become a well-known centre for motor boat racing at club, national and international levels. In 1977, for example, there were races most weekends between 3rd April and 30th October. There were national meetings on the club's water on five occasions and an international meeting on one. Some of these meetings lasted two days. Before each meeting there would be hours and days of practising. The boats used for the national and international meetings were large. The largest class of boats were supposed to have a noise limit of 85 decibels, with an upward tolerance of a further 10 decibels. Experiments carried out showed that nearly all the large boats took advantage of this tolerance and the noise made by a number exceeded 100 decibels. We do not consider it necessary to go into the details of the evidence about the noise level as there was no issue before us about liability. It suffices to record that we heard tape recordings taken in the plaintiff's house whilst racing, probably with the largest boats, was going on and we saw and heard a sound film taken and recorded during racing at a distance of 25 ft from the club's water's edge. We were all of the opinion that noise caused by the club's activities, which include practising, racing and water skiing, has interfered to a considerable extent with the plaintiff's use and enjoyment of her house. To have to live each year, from about 9 am until dusk each day from the end of March to the beginning of November in the expectation that at any moment, particularly at weekends, she would be subjected to unpleasant noises was a burden which prima facie she ought not to have to bear. The law provides the remedy of injunction for anyone subjected, as the plaintiff has been, and expects to be unless the court intervenes, to such a nuisance.

The judge, however, refused an injunction and made an award of damages under Lord Cairns's Act to compensate her for future nuisance. In his judgment he said that the form of injunction asked for by the plaintiff's counsel was too wide, but he went on as follows:

> 'As I said, the noise at times is quite intolerable and wholly unreasonable and I would be prepared to grant an injunction in terms that the defendants be restrained from using or permitting the use of the waters in such a way as to be a nuisance or cause a nuisance to the plaintiff or to pursue their activities in such a way as to interfere with the plaintiff's reasonable enjoyment and occupation of her premises. But as I indicated . . . if I were to grant such an injunction this would only lead to further litigation almost certainly and it does not appear to me to be the right approach.'

He went on to consider a form of injunction which had been requested at a late stage of the case on behalf of the plaintiff. This would have had the effect of limiting racing to ten days a year, during one bank holiday and two periods of continuous days. He thought this would be unreasonable having regard to the history of the club. He continued as follows:

> 'The question remains as to whether I should grant an injunction. I have considered the question most carefully, and as to whether damages in this case would meet the position—and substantial damages. I have come to the conclusion

> from what I have heard there is considerable public interest in this club, that the public do attend in large numbers and that it would be oppressive in all the circumstances to grant an injunction other than the injunction I have indicated which would merely cause further litigation.'

He then made the awards of damages to which we have referred.

Counsel for the plaintiff has submitted that the judge misdirected himself. What he did, it was said, was to allow the club to buy itself the right to cause a substantial and intolerable nuisance. It was no justification to say that this was for the benefit of that section of the public which was interested in motor boat racing. Once the plaintiff had proved that the club had caused a nuisance which interfered in a substantial and intolerable way with the use and enjoyment of her house she was entitled to have it stopped by injunction.

Counsel for the defendant submitted that this court should not interfere with the exercise of the judge's discretion. He was entitled to take into account the effect which an injunction would have on the club and on those members of the public who enjoyed watching or taking part in motor boat racing.

Counsel for the plaintiff based his submissions primarily on the decision of this court in *Shelfer v City of London Electric Lighting Co* [1895] 1 Ch 287, [1891–4] All ER Rep 838. The opening paragraph of the headnote, which correctly summarises the judgment, is as follows ([1895] 1 Ch 287):

> '*Lord Cairns' Act* (21 and 22 Vict. c. 27), in conferring upon Courts of Equity a jurisdiction to award damages instead of an injunction, has not altered the settled principles upon which those Courts interfered by way of injunction; and in cases of continuing actionable nuisance the jurisdiction so conferred ought only to be exercised under very exceptional circumstances.'

In the judgment, in a much-quoted passage, Lindley LJ said ([1895] 1 Ch 287 at 315–316, [1891–4] All ER Rep 838 at 844):

> '... ever since *Lord Cairns' Act* was passed the Court of Chancery has repudiated the notion that the Legislature intended to turn that Court into a tribunal for legalizing wrongful acts; or in other words, the Court has always protested against the notion that it ought to allow a wrong to continue simply because the wrongdoer is able and willing to pay for the injury he may inflict. Neither has the circumstance that the wrongdoer is in some sense a public benefactor (*e.g.*, a gas or water company or a sewer authority) ever been considered a sufficient reason for refusing to protect by injunction an individual whose rights are being persistently infringed.'

A L Smith LJ, in his judgment, set out what he called a good working rule for the award of damages in substitution for an injunction. His working rule does not apply in this case. The injury to the plaintiff's legal rights is not small; it is not capable of being estimated in terms of money save in the way the judge tried to make an estimate, namely by fixing a figure for the diminution of the value of the plaintiff's house because of the prospect of a continuing nuisance; and the figure he fixed could not be described as small. The principles enunciated in *Shelfer's* case, which is binding on us, have been applied time and time again during the past 85 years. The only case which raises a doubt about the application of the *Shelfer* principles to all cases is *Miller v Jackson* [1977] 3 All ER 338, [1977] QB 966, a decision of this court. The majority, Geoffrey Lane and Cumming-Bruce LJJ, Lord Denning MR dissenting, adjudged that the activities of an old-established cricket club which had been going for over seventy years, had been a nuisance to the plaintiffs by reason of cricket balls landing in their garden. The question then was whether the plaintiffs should be granted an injunction. Geoffrey Lane LJ was of the opinion that one should be granted. Lord Denning MR and Cumming-Bruce LJ thought otherwise. Lord Denning MR said that the public interest should prevail over the private interest. Cumming-Bruce LJ stated that a factor to be taken into account when

exercising the judicial discretion whether to grant an injunction was that the plaintiffs
a had bought their house knowing that it was next to the cricket ground. He thought that
there were special circumstances which should inhibit a court of equity from granting
the injunction claimed. The statement of Lord Denning MR that the public interest
should prevail over the private interest runs counter to the principles enunciated in
Shelfer's case and does not accord with the reason of Cumming-Bruce LJ for refusing an
injunction. We are of the opinion that there is nothing in *Miller v Jackson*, binding on us,
b which qualifies what was decided in *Shelfer*. Any decisions before *Shelfer's* case (and there
were some at first instance as counsel for the defendants pointed out) which give support
for the proposition that the public interest should prevail over the private interest must
be read subject to the decision in *Shelfer's* case.

It follows that the plaintiff was entitled to an injunction and that the judge misdirected
himself in law in adjudging that the appropriate remedy for her was an award of
c damages under Lord Cairns's Act. But she was only entitled to an injunction restraining
the club from activities which caused a nuisance, and not all of their activities did. As the
judge pointed out, and counsel for the plaintiff accepted in this court, an injunction in
general terms would be unworkable.

Our task has been to decide on a form of order which will protect the plaintiff from
the noise which the judge found to be intolerable but which will not stop the club from
d organising activities about which she cannot reasonably complain.

When she decided to build a house alongside Mallam Water she knew that some
motor boat racing and water skiing was done on the club's water and she thought that the
noise which such activities created was tolerable. She cannot now complain about that
kind of noise provided it does not increase in volume by reason of any increase in
activities. The intolerable noise is mostly caused by the large boats; it is these which
e attract the public interest.

Now nearly all of us living in these islands have to put up with a certain amount of
annoyance from our neighbours. Those living in towns may be irritated by their
neighbours' noisy radios or incompetent playing of musical instruments; and they in
turn may be inconvenienced by the noise caused by our guests slamming car doors and
chattering after a late party. Even in the country the lowing of a sick cow or the early
f morning crowing of a farmyard cock may interfere with sleep and comfort. Intervention
by injunction is only justified when the irritating noise causes inconvenience beyond
what other occupiers in the neighbourhood can be expected to bear. The question is
whether the neighbour is using his property reasonably, having regard to the fact that he
has a neighbour. The neighbour who is complaining must remember, too, that the
other man can use his property in a reasonable way and there must be a measure of 'give
g and take, live and let live'.

Understandably the plaintiff finds intolerable the kind of noise which she has had to
suffer for such long periods in the past; but if she knew that she would only have to put
up with such noise on a few occasions between the end of March and the beginning of
November each year, and she also knew when those occasions were likely to occur, she
could make arrangements to be out of her house at the material times. We can see no
h reason, however, why she should have to absent herself from her house for many days so
as to enable the club members and others to make noises which are a nuisance. We
consider it probable that those who are interested in motor boat racing are attracted by
the international and national events, which tend to have the larger and noisier boats.
Justice will be done, we think, if the club is allowed to have, each racing season, one
international event extending over three days, the first day being given over to practice
j and the second and third to racing. In addition there can be two national events, each of
two days but separated from the international event and from each other by at least four
weeks. Finally there can be three club events, each of one day, separated from the
international and national events and each other by three weeks. Any international or
national event not held can be replaced by a club event of one day. No boats creating a
noise of more than 75 decibels are to be used on the club's water at any time other than

when there are events as specified in this judgment. If events are held at weekends, as they probably will be, six weekends, covering a total of ten days, will be available for a
motor boat racing on the club's water. Water skiing, if too many boats are used, can cause a nuisance by noise. The club is not to allow more than six motor boats to be used for water skiing at any one time. An injunction will be granted to restrain motor boat racing, water skiing and the use of boats creating a noise of more than 75 decibels on the club's water save to the extent and in the circumstances indicated.

Appeal allowed. Injunction granted in terms of judgment. Judgment for £1,000 general b
damages for past nuisance to stand. Order for £15,000 special damages discharged.

Solicitors: *Wilmont & Co*, Swindon (for the plaintiff); *John L Davies*, Solihull (for the defendants).

Frances Rustin Barrister. c

Kirby v Manpower Services Commission

EMPLOYMENT APPEAL TRIBUNAL d
SLYNN J, MR A C BLYTON AND MRS M E SUNDERLAND
5th FEBRUARY 1980

Race relations – Discrimination – Discrimination by way of victimisation – Discrimination in circumstances relevant for purposes of race relations legislation – Treatment of person victimised less favourably than other persons – Job centre clerk employed to interview prospective employers e
and employees – Clerk required to treat information received at interviews as confidential – Clerk reporting prospective employers to community relations council alleging racial discrimination – – Clerk's employers moving him to less interesting job – Proceedings later successfully brought against an employer – Clerk bringing complaint against his own employers alleging victimisation – Whether clerk victimised in 'circumstances relevant for the purposes' of legislation – Whether clerk victimised because he gave information 'in connection with proceedings' against an employer f
practising racial discrimination or because his reports to community relations council were something done 'under or by reference to' legislation – Race Relations Act 1976, s 2(1).

The employers, a government agency, ran a job centre. The complainant was employed there as a first tier clerk to interview prospective employees and employers and to collect information from them in the course of his work. He had signed a declaration under the g
Official Secrets Act and was required to treat information received from employees and employers as confidential. The complainant felt strongly about racial discrimination and in three instances, those of a bus company which refused to interview a black man, a nursing home which inquired whether a prospective employee was black, and a club which refused to employ a black girl, he reported the respective employers to the local community relations council alleging that the employers were practising racial h
discrimination. In doing so he breached the employer's confidence in each case. Subsequently the fact that he had reported the bus company and the nursing home was brought to the attention of the complainant's manager, but the manager did not know about the report on the club. The manager interviewed the complainant and decided that he was unsuitable to be a first tier clerk because he had parted with confidential information about the bus company and the nursing home and moved him to the job of j
filing clerk, a less interesting and less responsible job. After the complainant was moved to the job of filing clerk, proceedings were successfully brought against the club for breach of the Race Relations Act 1976. The complainant gave evidence at those proceedings. No proceedings were brought against the bus company or the nursing home. The complainant made a complaint to an industrial tribunal that he had been victimised by his own employers 'in circumstances relevant for the purposes . . . of [the

1976] Act' contrary to s 2(1)[a] of that Act because by removing him to another job they
a had treated him less favourably than they would have treated other persons in those circumstances, and had done so (i) because the complainant had given information 'in connection with proceedings' brought against the club, within s 1(1)(*b*) of the 1976 Act, (ii) because he had done something 'under or by reference to' that Act (ie reported the three employers to the community relations council for them to consider taking proceedings under the Act), within s 2(1)(*c*), and (iii) because he had alleged that the three
b employers had committed acts which would amount to a contravention of the Act, within s 2(1)(*d*). The tribunal found that even though his own employers did not know about the report on the club, and the proceedings against the club were not brought until after the complainant's removal to the job of filing clerk, the report on the club constituted giving information 'in connection with proceedings' against the club within s 2(1)(*b*) and was an act done 'under or by reference to' the 1976 Act within s 2(1)(*c*) and
c also constituted an allegation that an act had been committed which would amount to contravention of the Act within s 2(1)(*c*). However, the tribunal also found that the complainant had not shown that he had been less favourably treated since there was evidence that his employers would have treated anyone else in their employment who gave away confidential information in the same way. The tribunal accordingly dismissed the complaint. The complainant appealed.

d

Held – (1) On the true construction of s 2(1) of the 1976 Act the 'circumstances relevant for the purposes' of the Act in which discrimination could occur were not restricted to the circumstances regarding a person's employment set out in s 4(2)[b] of that Act but extended to any circumstances where one person discriminated against another in the areas with which the Act was concerned, including the field of employment.
e Accordingly, in applying s 2(1) in a case concerning employment the appropriate test was, first, whether the person alleging victimisation had been treated in the employment field less favourably than the employer would have treated other persons in that field (and not whether the complainant had been subjected to a detriment within s 4(2)(*c*)) that being a matter to be judged in the light of the employer's reasons for the complainant's treatment and whether other employees who committed a similar act
f would be treated similarly, and, second, whether the employer had so treated the complainant by reason of any of the matters specified in paras (*a*) to (*d*) of s 2(1) (see p 338 *b* to *g*, p 340 *e f j* and p 341 *d e*, post).

(2) The evidence established that the complainant's employers had moved him to another job because he had given away confidential information and that they would have treated any other employee who did the same in the same way. Accordingly, the
g complainant had not established that his employers had treated him less favourably than they would have treated other employees at the job centre who gave away confidential information, and on that ground the appeal would be dismissed (see p 339 *g h*, p 340 *a* and p 341 *a* to *c* and *h*, post).

(3) In any event, since the complainant's employers did not know about the report on the club, and the proceedings against the club were not commenced until after the
h complainant had been moved, the report and proceedings in regard to the club had to be disregarded in applying s 2(1). Accordingly, the complainant had not shown that he had been moved either (a) because he gave information 'in connection with proceedings', within s 2(1)(*b*), since the alleged victimisation had to occur at a time when the proceedings had been brought, or (b) because he had done something 'under...[the] Act', within s 2(1)(*c*), since that required something to be done under a specific provision of the

j

a Section 2, so far as material, is set out at p 337 *d* to *g*, post

b Section 4(2) provides: 'It is unlawful for a person, in the case of a person employed by him at an establishment in Great Britain, to discriminate against that employee—(*a*) in the terms of employment which he affords him; or (*b*) in the way he affords him access to opportunities for promotion, transfer or training, or to any other benefits, facilities or services, or by refusing or deliberately omitting to afford him access to them; or (*c*) by dismissing him, or subjecting him to any other detriment.'

Act, and the reports to the community relations council on the bus company and the nursing home had not been made under any specific provision of the Act, or (c) because *a*
he had alleged that an act had been committed which would amount to contravention of the Act because, assuming the allegations against the bus company and the nursing home were true, they did not amount to allegations of a contravention of the 1976 Act. However, the complainant had established that he was moved by reason of an act done 'by reference to' the Act, within s 2(1)(*c*), since making a report to a community relations council that there were facts which ought to be investigated and which indicated a *b*
possible breach of the Act was something done 'by reference to' the Act (see p 338 *j* to p 339 *c* and *e* to *g* and p 340 *b c*, post).

Notes

For what constitutes unlawful discrimination generally and in the field of employment, see 4 Halsbury's Laws (4th Edn) paras 1035, 1038.

For the Race Relations Act 1976, ss 1, 2, 4, see 46 Halsbury's Statutes (3rd Edn) 395, *c*
396, 398.

Case referred to in judgment

Ministry of Defence v Jeremiah [1979] 3 All ER 833, [1980] QB 87, [1979] 3 WLR 857, [1980] ICR 13, CA, Digest (Cont Vol E) 408, 72*Ac*(*i*).

d

Appeal

The complainant, Steven John Kirby, appealed against the decision of an industrial tribunal sitting at Bristol made on 20th August 1979 dismissing his complaint against the Manpower Services Commission ('the employers') that they unlawfully discriminated against him, by moving him to another less interesting job, contrary to s 2(1) of the Race Relations Act 1976. The ground of the appeal was that the tribunal erred in law in *e*
interpreting s 2 of the 1976 Act. The facts are set out in the judgment of the appeal tribunal.

Kuttan Menon, legal officer, Commission for Racial Equality, for Mr Kirby.
William Crowther for the employers.

SLYNN J delivered the following judgment of the appeal tribunal: In September 1978, *f*
Mr Kirby, who had been a civil servant for some three years and who apparently had signed a declaration under the Official Secrets Act, was appointed to work at a job centre. Job centres are run by the Manpower Services Commission which is a government agency and is to be treated as a statutory body.

Mr Kirby was given the job of acting as what is called a 'first tier clerk'. That involves interviewing people who came to the job centre who are looking for work and employers *g*
who are looking for employees. If someone comes in who wants a job, the first tier clerk will get in touch with an employer who may have vacancies and will give details of the prospective employee. If necessary, he will arrange an appointment. It is apparently the policy of those responsible for running the job centres that first tier clerks, who are in touch with both employers and employees, should adopt as neutral an attitude as possible. It is their task to collect information and put people in touch with each other, *h*
but they are discouraged from becoming too involved with the affairs of either the employer or the employee. There is a code laid down which gives guidance to civil servants about the implementation of the Race Relations Act 1976, but this case has proceeded on the basis that Mr Kirby may well not have seen a copy of that. It is, however, accepted that when he began to do this work he was told that if he wanted further information or was unsure about any matter he should ask the person in the rank *j*
immediately above him, namely, a second tier officer.

Mr Kirby, who was at the relevant time 23 years of age, felt very strongly about racial discrimination and in the course of his job he apparently came across three incidents which troubled him very much.

He was on one occasion in September 1978 working at his desk when he was overheard by another first tier clerk telephoning to the Council for Community Relations in

Bristol. This caused some concern to the other clerk. Then there was another incident when apparently another employee at the job centre got to know that he had been in touch with the Bristol Council for Community Relations and, as a result, the matter was brought to the attention of Mr Frost, who was the senior manager at the job centre. As a result of the interview which they had, Mr Frost decided that Mr Kirby should no longer work as a first tier clerk. He caused him to be moved to another job in the department. This was a job which someone of his rank would be doing but it was said was of a very less interesting nature. In effect, he was made to do the work of a filing clerk.

As a result of this Mr Kirby brought proceedings before an industrial tribunal alleging that he had been victimised contrary to s 2 of the Race Relations Act 1976. The case was heard by an industrial tribunal which, in the end, dismissed his claim. He now appeals to this tribunal.

The case turns on the proper construction of ss 2 and 4 of the 1976 Act. Section 4 deals with discrimination by employers in the employment field and it provides, amongst other things, that it is unlawful for a person to discriminate against an employee by dismissing him or subjecting him to any other detriment. 'Discrimination' is defined in s 1 of the Act as including the treating on racial grounds of another person less favourably than the employer treats or would treat other people. Section 2 reads as follows, so far as relevant:

> '(1) A person ("the discriminator") discriminates against another person ("the person victimised") in any circumstances relevant for the purposes of any provision of this Act if he treats the person victimised less favourably than in those circumstances he treats or would treat other persons, and does so by reason that the person victimised has—(*a*) brought proceedings . . . or (*b*) given evidence or information in connection with proceedings brought by any person against the discriminator or any other person under this Act; or (*c*) otherwise done anything under or by reference to this Act in relation to the discriminator or any other person; or (*d*) alleged that the discriminator or any other person has committed an act which (whether or not the allegation so states) would amount to a contravention of this Act . . .'

In addition, it is provided that if the discriminator knows that the person victimised intends to do any of those things and he treats him less favourably that too is brought within the ambit of the Act. Section 2 continues:

> '(2) Subsection (1) does not apply to treatment of a person by reason of any allegation made by him if the allegation was false and not made in good faith.'

What is said here is that Mr Kirby gave information 'in connection with proceedings' brought by some person against another person under the statute. Alternatively, he had otherwise done something 'under or by reference to the Act in relation to some other person'. And, thirdly, that he had 'alleged that the discriminator' or some other person 'has committed an act which (whether or not the allegation so states) would amount to a contravention of this Act'.

It all turned on three cases which were referred to the Bristol Council for Community Relations. One of them involved the Bristol Omnibus Co and there Mr Kirby reported to the community relations council that a representative of the bus company had asked if the applicant for the job was black; when told that he was black and that the applicant had been living in Jamaica for the last year, the representative of the bus company refused to give an interview.

The second case involved a nursing home where the person looking for a part-time nurse asked whether the applicant for the job was black; asked why, she said, 'Just like to know what to expect', but, as the applicant for the job was white, the interview was arranged.

The third case involved a coloured girl, a Miss Pasley, who wanted a part-time job as a barmaid at a club. Once the coloured girl came for interview, although the manager was prepared to take her, he told Mr Kirby that the chairman of the club had told him that they must not take on a black girl because it might upset a few of the members. a

Mr Kirby's case, accordingly, was that he had given part of the information 'in connection with proceedings' because in the third case the girl concerned had brought proceedings before an industrial tribunal alleging a breach of the Race Relations Act 1976 and she had succeeded. He said also that he had done things 'by reference to the Act' in relation to other persons because he had given the information to the community relations council in order that they might consider taking proceedings under the 1976 b Act. He also said that he had alleged that the bus company, the nursing home and the club had committed acts which would amount to a contravention of the Act. He was discriminated against in that he was moved for doing these things.

The section, it seems to us, has to be construed as a whole. On the argument we have heard, the first matter to consider is what is meant by the words 'in any circumstances relevant for the purposes of any provision of this Act'. Counsel for the employers was c disposed at first to argue that the relevant circumstances in the present case are those which are set out in s 4 of the 1976 Act and that the relevant one here is subjecting Mr Kirby to a detriment; that one has to ask whether here the employers have treated Mr Kirby less favourably than they would have treated other persons. We do not consider, as we think in the end counsel for the employers himself accepts, that that is the right approach. It seems to us that the words 'any circumstances relevant for the purposes of d any provision of this Act' which appear not only in s 2 but also in s 1 are referring to the areas with which this Act is concerned. 'Any circumstances relevant for the purposes of any provision of this Act' include the field of employment, they include education, they include the provision of goods, facilities, service and premises, and a number of other matters which are specified in the Act. It is only if it is so construed that it is possible to read the phrases 'in any circumstances' and 'in those circumstances' in a way which seems e to us to make sense. So for the present case we have to ask whether there has been discrimination in relation to employment by a person in an establishment in Great Britain of another person. And one then has to ask the question whether the discriminator has treated the person victimised in the circumstances of employment at the establishment in Great Britain less favourably than other persons by reason of one of the matters alleged. So really two questions have to be looked at. The first question is f whether a person (the person victimised) has been treated in the employment field less favourably than the employer would treat other persons in that field. The second question which has to be looked at is whether the employer (the discriminator) has done so by reason of one of the specified matters.

The industrial tribunal were quite satisfied that although Mr Kirby had given evidence in the case brought by Miss Pasley in March 1979 that was long after his removal to the g filing clerk job on 31st October 1978. So they said whether he had been treated less favourably or not did not matter because he had given evidence too late for it to be relied on.

Then, however, they said that he had given evidence or information 'in connection with proceedings' brought by persons against the various bodies to which we have referred. The tribunal there thought it right to read these words 'in connection with h proceedings' in a wide way. They said it was enough that information should be given which led to proceedings. We are sympathetic to that approach, because one should not strive to cut down the language which Parliament has used in this field. But the question remains whether the person alleged to have victimised did so by reason that the person victimised had given information 'in connection with proceedings' brought by any person 'against any other person under the Act'. No proceedings ever were brought j against the bus company or against the nursing home, so they, it seems to us, cannot be said to qualify for this purpose. The industrial tribunal, however, took the view that because on 30th October (that is before Mr Frost moved Mr Kirby to the filing clerk job) Mr Kirby had given information to the community relations council about the club, that was enough. We entirely accept that the giving of information prior to the commencement of proceedings may fall within the section, but it seems to us that before an allegation of victimisation can be made it must be shown that the victimisation has occurred at a time when proceedings have actually been brought. The relevant question is: had the proceedings been brought? If they had, it does not matter whether the information was given before or after the commencement of proceedings so long as it is something which is relied on by the discriminator as a reason for the victimisation. Here the proceedings (which were heard in March) did not, however, begin until 3rd January 1979; that was after Mr Kirby was moved. So, accordingly, we consider that, in finding that the employers had moved Mr Kirby to the new job because he had given information in connection with proceedings brought, the industrial tribunal erred.

They went on to say that the making of a report of alleged discrimination by the club against Miss Pasley was an act done 'by reference to' the Act in relation to another person; alternatively it appears that they are saying that, if it was not done by reference to, it was done 'under' the Act. We are quite satisfied here that the making of a report to the council cannot be said to be something which is done *under* the Act. For it to be done under the Act one must find a specific statutory provision under which the report was made, and there is none. The words 'by reference to' are much more difficult. If it is enough simply to refer to the statute for some act to be done 'by reference to' it, clearly it is possible that a very wide range of activities might be included. If that were so and s 2(1)(*c*) were intended to be a sweeping-up clause, one would have expected it to have followed para (*d*); and the argument is that, because the substance of para (*d*) comes after para (*c*), one should really construe 'by reference to' in very much the same way as one construes the word 'under'. The argument is that one should look for a specific section of the Act and, even though it does not provide for a power to do something, one should ask whether there has been conduct which is only referable to, or explicable by reference to, that particular section.

We have been referred to s 72 as an example. It is said that if reliance is placed on a term of the contract as being void pursuant to that section that is an act which is done by reference to the statute in relation to any other person. We do not find it an easy matter to assess the precise limits of this provision 'by reference to the Act in relation to any other person', but we are prepared to assume, as the industrial tribunal did (and we consider rightly did) that if a report is made to the Race Relations Board, or the Community Relations Commission, that facts are available which ought to be investigated and which indicate a possible breach of the provisions of the 1976 Act, then the making of that report is an act done by reference to the Act in relation to the person against whom it is said discrimination might have occurred. We realise that that is to some extent an overlap with the provisions of para (*d*) of s 2(1), but in our judgment the phrase 'an act done by reference to this Act' is wide enough to include such a report.

So the question is whether there was here a report by reference to the 1976 Act in relation to any other person. It is clear that there was a report about these three incidents. One of them (the third one, the one which led to the proceedings), however, as the tribunal found, was not known to Mr Frost when he moved Mr Kirby to the filing clerk's job. Accordingly, it does not seem to us that it can be said that he moved Mr Kirby by reason that Mr Kirby had reported that third incident to the commission. On the other hand, Mr Kirby did tell Mr Frost of the first two cases, those involving the bus company and the nursing home, and it seems to us that the report of those matters was an act done by reference to the 1976 Act in relation to the persons there involved. So we would on that ground, but not on the ground that something was done under the statute, uphold the decision of the industrial tribunal on that matter.

But the tribunal went further. They found that there had been here an allegation that the discriminator had committed an act which would amount to a contravention of the 1976 Act. They were in some doubt about the first two incidents. No doubt they were not sure whether the refusal of the bus company to hold the interview was due to the fact that the applicant was black or whether it was due to the fact that he had been absent in Jamaica for a period of a year. No doubt they had also some anxiety whether merely asking for information whether or not somebody was black was itself a contravention of the Act. So they merely said that those two incidents may have amounted to a contravention of the Act. We think they were right not to be satisfied that those two incidents would have amounted, had they been assuming them to be true, to a contravention of the Act. It seems to us that what has to be done in these cases is to consider whether the allegation which is made, which must be assumed for present purposes to be true, does amount to an act which would amount to a contravention of the Act. It seems to us here the tribunal was rightly not satisfied that those two first incidents would amount to such a contravention.

The third one, the tribunal were quite satisfied, would amount to a contravention and there really can be no doubt about that. But, as in the case of para (*c*), it appears that when Mr Frost took his decision he did not know about the third incident. He was only told about it some weeks later when Mr Kirby prepared his report. So, it seems to us, on our approach to the construction of this section, that Mr Frost cannot be said to have acted as he did by reason that Mr Kirby had alleged that there had been a contravention of the Act in respect of Miss Pasley. So, accordingly, we think that under para (*d*), as under para (*c*), the tribunal came to a conclusion on their own findings of fact which cannot stand with what we see to be the correct interpretation of the opening words of the section.

But, Mr Kirby succeeds in holding the finding under para (*c*), that what was done had been done by reason of the fact that he had done an act, i e had made a report in relation to the people to whom we have referred. So the next question, taking the sequence adopted by the tribunal, is to go on and ask whether the employers treated Mr Kirby less favourably than they treated, or would treat, other persons by reason of the report which he had made. The proper approach to this part of the section has led to considerable argument before us, as it undoubtedly did before the industrial tribunal. It seems to us that one thing is plain: that it is not right simply to ask whether Mr Kirby was treated in the same way as other people who did one of these acts which are set out in paras (*a*), (*b*), (*c*) and (*d*). If that were law, then the employer could only escape if he could show that he had victimised all the relevant people; he would fail if it were shown that he had only victimised some of them. Nor, on the view which we have taken, is it enough simply to consider whether the detriment which is imposed is the same in all these cases. It seems to us that what has to be looked at is the reason given by the employer for the dismissal or removal and to ask whether other persons who committed an act of a similar kind would be treated in the same way or less favourably.

The tribunal rejected any suggestion here that Mr Kirby's move had nothing to do with the telephone calls to the community relations council. They were quite satisfied that he would not have been moved but for his communicating with the council. But the reason why he was moved was accepted to be that he had given away information which had come to him in confidence as an employee of the job centre. It was felt by those in charge, and indeed by the industrial tribunal, that it was quite wrong for this information which came in confidence to be disclosed to other people. Indeed, the tribunal appear to have been of the view that, however well-intentioned Mr Kirby was, he really might have done quite serious harm to race relations in this particular area by reporting the matter and, more important, it is said he might have discouraged employees, who ought to be encouraged to come to job centres, from so coming. If information about employees and their personal backgrounds (nothing to do with race) is given away, then employees might be deterred from coming. Equally, if employers cannot go to a job centre without information they have given in confidence being used and given for other purposes, then it is said that they will be deterred from coming and in the end harm will be done to the work of the Manpower Services Commission.

The question, it seems to us, which arises in this case for decision is whether it has been shown that these employers treated Mr Kirby less favourably than they would have treated someone in their employment who gave away confidential information whatever its kind. The industrial tribunal looked into this matter. They were quite satisfied that Mr Frost had caused Mr Kirby to be taken away from the job at the desk of a first tier clerk and to be made a filing clerk because he did not consider that he was suitable for this particular work since he had breached the confidence entrusted in him and shown, in the view of his superiors, an error of judgment. Now the question is: would other persons giving confidential information away have been treated any more favourably? The tribunal found that Mr Frost (the manager) would have taken the same view if confidential information had been given to any outside person or body by Mr Kirby or any other civil servant who had not been authorised to give that information. Although they talk only about Mr Frost, we read their decision as meaning here Mr Frost, the manager of the job centre, on behalf of the Manpower Services Commission. Once that evidence is accepted, it seems to us to follow that the tribunal here were not satisfied that Mr Kirby had been treated less favourably than anybody else who gave confidential information away. On the contrary, they were satisfied that he was treated in the same way as they would have been. In those circumstances, even if Mr Kirby was moved because he had made his report to the Bristol Council for Community Relations, he was not 'victimised' within the meaning of this section. It seems to us that the tribunal was entitled on the material before it clearly to come to that conclusion.

We have heard may references to the position of the Official Secrets Act. It has been said that if the motive of the employer, the Crown, is to deal with someone who has committed breaches of the Official Secrets Act, or has violated the special confidence which must obtain in an agency of this kind, that is enough to defeat a claim under the 1976 Act. We do not think that it is enough. It may be that even if someone has committed an act which is a breach of the Official Secrets Act, the employer still may do something which falls foul of the 1976 Act. It seems to us that that is not the right question. The right question in our view is that which we have posed, namely, whether people who give away information of this kind or information which is received in confidence would be treated on broadly the same basis.

It is necessary to add just two short points. We have heard argument about whether there was here any detriment in any event in so far as that is relevant to the decision in the case. It is suggested that the moving of Mr Kirby from the job as a front clerk to a filing clerk was de minimis and cannot amount to a detriment. Counsel for the employers, in our view rightly, has abandoned the argument which was advanced before the tribunal that detriment has to be construed ejusdem generis with dismissal. It seems to us that we should follow what was said in the Court of Appeal in *Ministry of Defence v Jeremiah* [1979] 3 All ER 883 at 837, [1980] QB 87 at 99 where Brandon LJ interpreted 'detriment' as meaning putting under a disadvantage. Lord Denning MR clearly took the view that to require someone to work in less attractive conditions was itself capable of being a detriment (see [1979] 3 All ER 833 at 836, [1980] QB 87 at 97). There is here a finding that this work of filing was less interesting, less responsible and less varied than was the work of a first tier clerk, and we have no doubt here that the tribunal was quite right in its conclusion that there was here a subjecting to a detriment within the meaning of s 4(2)(*c*).

Then, finally, the tribunal make references to the reasons which led Mr Kirby to reveal information to the Bristol Council for Community Relations. Despite those remarks, they have found that the allegations which were made were made by him in good faith. Counsel for the employers has accepted that the complaints which were made, the allegations which were made, were made honestly even if, in the view of the employers, mistakenly and so, accordingly, this claim would not have been barred had it otherwise been entitled to succeed by virtue of the provisions of s 2(2) of the 1976 Act.

In the result, however, despite Mr Menon's admirable arguments on behalf of Mr Kirby, this appeal fails.

Appeal dismissed.

Solicitors: *Osborne, Clarke & Co*, Bristol (for the employers).

K Mydeen Esq Barrister.

Re Davey (deceased)

a

CHANCERY DIVISION
FOX J
12th, 13th MARCH, 2nd APRIL 1980

*Mental health – Patient's property – Execution of will – Order for execution of will – Respondents
to order – Discretion not to make interested person a respondent – Matters to be considered –* b
*Urgency of case – Elderly patient in poor health – Patient married in suspicious circumstances to
man many years younger – Patient executing will shortly before marriage – Will automatically
revoked by marriage – Statutory will executed in same terms as earlier will without notice to
husband – Husband not made respondent to application for statutory will – Whether Court of
Protection having discretion not to make husband a respondent – Whether urgency of case
sufficient reason for not making husband a respondent – Whether Court of Protection may take* c
*into account opportunity for husband to make subsequent application under family provision
legislation – Mental Health Act 1959, s 103(1)(dd) – Court of Protection Rules 1960 (SI 1960
No 1146), rr 12, 21(2).*

*Mental health – Patient's property – Execution of will – Execution pursuant to order of master
of Court of Protection – Execution in accordance with statutory requirements – Whether High* d
*Court having jurisdiction to discharge order and set aside will – Mental Health Act 1959, ss
103(1)(dd), 103A(1)(3).*

In June 1979, when she was 92 years old, O moved into a nursing home. She had never
married and her nearest relatives were two nephews. On 3rd July she granted a power
of attorney for the management of her affairs to two solicitors. On 10th September she e
made a will by which, after bequeathing two small pecuniary legacies, she gave her
residuary estate, worth some £100,000 or so, on trust for division in equal shares
between such of 17 named persons as should survive her, all but one of whom were
related to her by blood or marriage. On 15th October she was examined at the nursing
home by a consultant psychiatrist, who formed the view that she was suffering from
senile mental deterioration to a degree which rendered her incapable of properly f
managing her affairs, although she was able to express definite wishes about the disposal
of her estate. On 15th November and 6th December she was examined by another
consultant psychiatrist who advised that her mentality was sufficiently impaired to
warrant the whole of her estate being placed under the control of the Court of
Protection. On Friday, 14th December another solicitor wrote to the Court of Protection
stating that provided the Official Solicitor was appointed as receiver O herself had no g
objection to the Court of Protection taking control of her affairs. The letter, which
arrived at the Court of Protection on Monday, 17th December, enclosed a copy of a
marriage certificate from which it emerged that on 30th October 1979 at a register office
O had married D, who was 48 years old and who was an employee of and resided at the
nursing home. None of O's relatives were aware of the marriage until it came to their
notice in consequence of the solicitor's letter. On 18th December the Court of Protection h
appointed the Official Solicitor as receiver. On 20th December at the instance of the
Court of Protection the Official Solicitor applied to the Court of Protection for an order
for the execution under s 103(1)(*dd*)[a] of the Mental Health Act 1959 of a will for O in the
same terms as the September will, which, by virtue of s 18 of the Wills Act 1837, would
have been automatically revoked by O's marriage. The application was heard by the
deputy master of the Court of Protection the same day, without notice being given either j
to D or to any of the beneficiaries under the September will. Evidence was given of O's
testamentary capacity, and as a result the deputy master made an order for the execution
in the name and on behalf of O of a will in the same terms as the September will. The

a Section 103(1), so far as material, is set out at p 345 *j* to p 346 *a*, post

deputy master's reasons for ordering the execution of a will without notice to D were (i) that in view of O's age and poor health the matter was urgent and if D were joined as a party there would inevitably be a delay, (ii) that if O died before the court could give orders for the execution of the will it would no longer be possible to challenge the validity of the will and her estate would devolve under an intestacy, the bulk of it going to D, (iii) that the marriage was apparently clandestine, and (iv) that if a statutory will were executed as proposed D could, if he wished, make application for a further statutory will in his favour or if O died beforehand he could make an application under the Inheritance (Provision for Family and Dependants) Act 1975. On 21st December a will was duly executed, the formalities as to signing, attestation and sealing set out in s 103A[b] of the 1959 Act being complied with. D was informed of the will by letter from the Court of Protection dated 21st December. On 27th December O died. D appealed against the order seeking to have it discharged and the will set aside, contending that the deputy master had exercised his discretion wrongly, in that he had reached his decision without notice to D, that he should not have taken into account the possibility of an application under the 1975 Act and that he should have assumed the validity of the marriage.

Held – The appeal would be dismissed for the following reasons—

(1) Under rr 12 and 21(2)[c] of the Court of Protection Rules 1960 the Court of Protection had a discretion as to what persons were to be made respondents to or given notice of an application under s 103(1)(*dd*) of the 1959 Act, and, although in normal circumstances the court would generally insist on the joinder of a person who was adversely affected by the relief sought, in cases of urgency the position might be different; the court had to balance various factors, including, for example, the possibility of an application under the 1975 Act, with a view to reaching a just conclusion. In view of O's age and condition the matter was urgent, and because of the delay that would have been occasioned by joining D as respondent it was, in the circumstances, reasonable for the deputy master to have decided against such a course. If he had refused to make an order at the time and O had died before the matter could have been investigated D would, under the resulting intestacy, have irrevocably taken a very substantial portion of the estate, which might, on investigation of the whole matter and particularly the circumstances of the marriage, have proved very unfair to the beneficiaries under the September will, whereas by making an order the deputy master had in effect preserved the opportunity for all parties to represent their claims fully to the court either by an application by D during O's lifetime for a new statutory will or after her death by an application under the 1975 Act. It followed that the order which the deputy master made was one which offered the widest opportunities for a full investigation of the matter and, therefore, the best prospect of a just result in the end (see p 347 *h*, p 348 *b* to *f* and *j* to p 349 *b*, post).

(2) The circumstances of the marriage were suspicious and it would be quite unreal to say that the Court of Protection should have proceeded on the basis that the marriage was necessarily valid (see p 347 *h*, post).

Per Curiam. Where the formalities as to signing, attestation and sealing set out in s 103A(1) of the 1959 Act have been complied with, the High Court has no jurisdiction to interfere with a will made by a master of the Court of Protection in the exercise of his jurisdiction under s 103(1)(*dd*) of that Act because such a will is, by virtue of s 103A(3), to have the like effect 'for all purposes' as if the patient were capable of making a valid will and the will had been duly executed by the patient (see p 349 *e* to *h* and p 350 *a*, post).

Notes

For the power to order the execution of a statutory will for a person suffering from mental disorder, see 30 Halsbury's Laws (4th Edn) para 1246.

---

b Section 103A, so far as material, is set out at p 349 *c* to *e*, post

c Rules 12 and 21, so far as material, are set out at p 347 *j* to p 348 *a*, post

For the Mental Health Act 1959, ss 103, 103A, see 25 Halsbury's Statutes (3rd Edn) 131, 134. a

For the Court of Protection Rules 1960, rr 12, 21, see 17 Halsbury's Statutory Instruments (Third Reissue) 20, 22.

Cases referred to in judgment

Bennett, Re, Greenwood v Bennett [1913] 2 Ch 318, 82 LJ Ch 506, 109 LT 302, 33 Digest (Repl) 687, *1369*. b

DML, Re [1965] 2 All ER 129, [1965] Ch 1133, [1965] 3 WLR 740, Digest (Cont Vol B) 526, *937a*.

Roberts (deceased), Re, Roberts v Roberts [1978] 3 All ER 225, [1978] 1 WLR 653, CA.

Wheater, Re [1928] Ch 223, 97 LJ Ch 97, 138 LT 433, CA, 33 Digest (Repl) 685, *1343*.

Appeal c

Wallace Lindsay Davey appealed against the order dated 20th December 1979 of the deputy master of the Court of Protection, seeking to have the order discharged and a will executed pursuant thereto by Harold David Spenser Venables, assistant official solicitor, in the name and on behalf of Olive St Barbe Davey on 21st December 1979 set aside. The appeal was heard in chambers and judgment was given in open court. The facts are set out in the judgment. d

Hazel Williamson for Mr Davey.
Peter Rawson for the executors of the will.
Dirik Jackson for the Official Solicitor.

Cur adv vult e

2nd April. **FOX J** read the following judgment: This is an appeal from an order of the deputy master of the Court of Protection directing the execution of a statutory will.

Miss Olive St Barbe (to whom I will refer as 'the patient') was born in the year 1886. For many years she lived in her own house in Highgate. Then, in June 1979, when she was 92 years old, she moved into a private nursing home in London. She had never f married and her nearest relatives were two nephews, Major George St Barbe and Mr Peter St Barbe.

On 3rd July 1979 the patient granted a power of attorney for the management of her affairs to two London solicitors, Mr Riou Benson (to whom I will refer as 'Mr Benson') and Mr Russell. They managed the patient's affairs from then until the appointment of the Official Solicitor as receiver of the patient in December 1979. It seems that on 8th g August 1979 the patient executed another power of attorney in favour of other solicitors, though Mr Benson in his affidavit sworn in support of the application for a receiver states that the patient confirmed that she had no recollection of doing so.

On 10th September 1979 the patient made a will by which, after appointing Mr Benson and Lloyds Bank as executors and bequeathing two small pecuniary legacies, she gave her residuary estate on trust for division in equal shares between such of 17 named h persons as should survive her. Those persons, with the exception of a Mrs Klouda, were related to the patient by blood or marriage. They were Major St Barbe, Mr Peter St Barbe, their children and grandchildren, the wife and former wife of Major St Barbe, and the wives of Major St Barbe's children. Mrs Klouda, I am informed by counsel, ran the nursing home.

On 15th October 1979 the patient was examined at the nursing home by Dr De j Mowbray, a consultant psychiatrist. He found her disorientated in place and time and showing marked impairment of memory, particularly for recent events. For example, she gave her age as 84 and the date as December 25th which she was unable to identify as the date of Christmas. She was unable to state the day of the week; she stated that she was living in St John's Wood though she was in fact living in Kensington. Dr De

Mowbray's view was that the patient was suffering from senile mental deterioration of
a a degree which rendered her incapable of properly managing her affairs, though she was
able to express definite wishes about their broad disposal. Dr De Mowbray was strongly
in favour of the patient's affairs being placed under the control of the Court of Protection.

On 9th November 1979 Mr Benson applied to the Court of Protection for an order
appointing him receiver for the patient. The affidavit of kindred and fortune sworn in
support of the application showed that the patient's main assets consisted of (i) a house
b valued at between £70,000 and £100,000, and (ii) cash amounting to about £30,000.

On 15th November the patient was examined by Dr Donald Blair, also a consultant
psychiatrist, who advised that so far as he could judge the patient's mentality was
sufficiently impaired to warrant the whole of her estate being placed under the control
of the Court of Protection. 'There is no doubt,' he said, 'that her mind is greatly
enfeebled through senility.'

c Major St Barbe was not agreeable to the proposal that Mr Benson be appointed
receiver. Ultimately he agreed to the appointment of the Official Solicitor as receiver.
This was notified to the Court of Protection in a letter from his solicitors dated 10th
December 1979.

On 6th December Dr Blair examined the patient again. His opinion was that 'Her
mentality is definitely permanently and constantly enfeebled and her memory reasoning
d judgment and other intellectual faculties are greatly impaired'. He thought that her
mind and intellect had wilted to such an extent that she was not of testamentary capacity.

On 14th December 1979 (which was a Friday) Mr John Witzenfeld, a solicitor, wrote
to the Court of Protection stating that provided the Official Solicitor was appointed as
receiver the patient herself had no objection to the Court of Protection taking control of
her affairs. The letter enclosed a copy of the patient's marriage certificate. In this
e manner it emerged that the patient had, on 30th October 1979, at the Fulham Register
Office, married the present appellant (to whom I will refer as Mr Davey). He was 48
years of age. He was an employee of, and resided at, the nursing home. None of the
patient's relatives were informed of the marriage until it came to their notice in
consequence of the letter of 14th December.

It is common ground that Mr Witzenfeld's letter of 14th December reached the Court
f of Protection on Monday, 17th December. On 18th December the Court of Protection
made an order appointing the Official Solicitor as receiver. On 20th December the
Official Solicitor, at the instance of the Court of Protection, made an application to the
Court of Protection for an order for the execution of a statutory will for the patient in the
same terms as the will of 10th September 1979. The latter will would, by the operation
of s 18 of the Wills Act 1837, have been automatically revoked by a marriage of the
g patient.

The jurisdiction of the Court of Protection to make a will for a patient is contained in
s 103(1)(*dd*) of the Mental Health Act 1959, as added by s 17(1) of the Administration of
Justice Act 1969. It will be convenient if I first set out the provisions of s 102(1) of the
1959 Act, which are as follows:

h 'The judge may, with respect to the property and affairs of a patient, do or secure
the doing of all such things as appear necessary or expedient—(*a*) for the
maintenance or other benefit of the patient, (*b*) for the maintenance or other benefit
of members of the patient's family, (*c*) for making provision for other persons or
purposes for whom or which the patient might be expected to provide if he were
not mentally disordered, or (*d*) otherwise for administering the patient's affairs.'

j Section 103(1) provides:

'Without prejudice to the generality of the foregoing section, the judge shall have
power to make such orders and give such directions and authorities as he thinks fit
for the purposes of that section, and in particular may for those purposes make
orders or give directions or authorities for . . . (*dd*) the execution for the patient of

> a will making any provision (whether by way of disposing of property or exercising a power or otherwise) which could be made by a will executed by the patient if he were not mentally disordered, so however that in such cases as a nominated judge may direct the power conferred by this paragraph shall not be exercisable except by the Lord Chancellor or a nominated judge . . .'

Section 103(3) provides that the power to order the execution of a will for a patient 'shall not be exercised unless the judge has reason to believe that the patient is incapable of making a valid will . . .'

By Practice Direction [1970] 1 All ER 208, [1970] 1 WLR 259 Ungoed-Thomas J, a nominated judge, directed that the powers conferred by s 103(1)(*dd*) should not be exercisable except by the Lord Chancellor or a nominated judge unless by reason of the amount involved or the general circumstances of the case unreasonable expense or delay would be caused.

By s 100(4) of the 1959 Act the functions expressed to be conferred by the Act on the judge are, in general, exercisable by the Lord Chancellor or by any nominated judge and are also exercisable by the master or deputy master of the Court of Protection.

The Official Solicitor's application for the execution of a statutory will was heard by the deputy master on 20th December 1979 (the same day as the application was issued). That was the penultimate day of the term and I think that unreasonable delay would have been caused by referring the matter to the judge. The contrary indeed is not asserted.

Neither Mr Davey nor any of the beneficiaries under the will of 10th September 1979 was given notice of the application. Mr Benson gave oral evidence on oath to the deputy master. He said that he visited the patient on Thursday, 13th December 1979. She was sitting up but very much slouched. Mr Davey was present but did not mention the marriage. The patient, according to Mr Benson, made no communication either in reply to him or to Mr Davey. Mr Benson formed the view that she did not have any testamentary capacity and would not be capable of appreciating any matter relating to property. On this evidence and that of Dr Blair's examination on 6th December I think that the deputy master would certainly have had reason to believe that the patient was incapable of making a valid will and that accordingly the prohibition contained in s 103(3) was not applicable. Mr Davey does not assert otherwise on this appeal.

At the hearing on 20th December the deputy master made an order directing Mr Venables, the assistant official solicitor, in the name and on behalf of the patient to execute a will in the form of a specified draft (which for practical purposes was the same as the patient's will of 10th September 1979). On 21st December 1979 Mr Venables duly executed the will on behalf of the patient. The various formalities which are required in respect of the execution of such a will by s 103A of the 1959 Act were complied with. The patient died six days later, on 27th December.

The deputy master's reasons for ordering the execution of a will without notice to Mr Davey were, in effect, as follows.

(i) If Mr Davey was joined as a party there would inevitably be delay before the matter could be determined. The patient was 93 years old and in poor health. The matter was, accordingly, one of considerable urgency.

(ii) If the patient died before the court could give directions for the execution of a will, it would no longer be possible to challenge the validity of the marriage and the estate would devolve under an intestacy. The basis of that view is the decision of the Court of Appeal in *Re Roberts (deceased)* [1978] 3 All ER 225, [1978] 1 WLR 653 where it was held that a voidable marriage, whether subsequently annulled or not, is a marriage for the purposes of s 18 of the Wills Act 1837 and therefore automatically revokes an existing will of a party to the marriage. On an intestacy Mr Davey would take, if the estate was sufficient, the statutory legacy of £55,000 plus half the residuary estate.

(iii) The marriage was apparently clandestine, embarked on at short notice and without notification to the patient's relatives.

(iv) If a statutory will was executed as proposed (that is to say in effect restoring the will *a* of September 1979) Mr Davey could, if he wished, make application for a further statutory will in his favour. If the patient died before that could be dealt with, Mr Davey could make an application under the Inheritance (Provision for Family and Dependants) Act 1975.

Mr Davey was informed of the order for the execution of the statutory will by letter from the Court of Protection dated 21st December 1979.

b The present notice of appeal asks that the order for the execution of the statutory will be discharged and that the will be set aside.

In my view it is clear that the deputy master had jurisdiction to direct the execution of the statutory will. The power is expressly conferred by s 103(1) of the 1959 Act. It is true that the power conferred by s 103(1), including the power to direct the execution of a will, are conferred for the purposes of s 102. It is said that the case does not fall within *c* s 102(1)(*b*) since the will is not for the benefit of members of the patient's 'family'; it is said that 'family' does not include collaterals: see *Re DML* [1965] 2 All ER 129, [1965] Ch 1133. But it seems to me that the case falls within s 102(1)(*c*) on the ground that the will makes provision for persons for whom the patient might be expected to provide if she were not mentally disordered. The persons for whom the statutory will makes provision are the same persons as those for whom the patient herself had made provision only three *d* months previously by the September will.

Accordingly, since it is not in dispute that on 20th December the deputy master had reason to believe that the patient was incapable of making a will, I see no reason to doubt the existence of the jurisdiction.

Mr Davey contends, however, that, accepting the existence of jurisdiction, the deputy master exercised his discretion wrongly and that his decision cannot be allowed to *e* stand. It is said that he erred in that (1) he reached his decision without notice to Mr Davey and (2) that he should have assumed the validity of the marriage.

The circumstances with which the deputy master was faced on 20th December were the following. Only three days previously it had come to the notice of the Court of Protection that, on 30th October, the patient had married while she was a patient in the nursing home. She was 93 and Mr Davey was 48. The marriage certificate together with *f* Mr Benson's evidence showed that he was an employee of the nursing home and resided there. Since the patient had only entered the nursing home in June, their acquaintance was presumably comparatively short. From the marriage certificate it appeared that the patient had started to sign her name but only wrote the letter O; she then added her mark. On 15th October, two weeks before the marriage, Dr De Mowbray had found the patient disorientated in place and time and showing marked impairment of memory; *g* she was suffering from senile mental deterioration. The marriage itself was by licence, so there was no previous publication. In fact no relative of the patient had been informed of it. As regards the patient's expectation of life she was a very great age and Mr Benson's evidence before the deputy master was that, at the visit on 13th December, Mr Davey told him that 'She was getting worse quite quickly'. Dr Blair in his report of his visit on 15th November says that the patient was 'obviously suffering from senile *h* physical enfeeblement'.

From these facts, two things emerge. First, the circumstances of the marriage were suspicious, and it is quite unreal to say that the Court of Protection should have proceeded on the basis that the marriage was necessarily valid. Second, the matter was urgent. In view of the patient's age and condition, she might die at any time. In fact she only lived for a few days.

j As to the joinder of parties, by r 12 of the Court of Protection Rules 1960, SI 1960 No 1146, it is provided:

> 'The court may direct that all or any of the relatives of the patient or any other person who appears to the court to be interested in the relief sought by a summons shall be made a respondent to or be given notice of the summons.'

And by r 21(2) it is provided that, on an application under s 103(1)(*dd*) of the 1959 Act—

> 'the receiver shall, unless he is the applicant or one of the applicants, be made a respondent to the application, but except as aforesaid no person shall be made a respondent unless and until the Court so directs.'

The court, therefore, has a discretion as to what persons are to be made respondents to or given notice of the application. No doubt in the normal case the court would generally insist on the joinder of a person who was adversely affected by the relief sought, but in circumstances of urgency the position may be different. The deputy master quite clearly directed his mind to the question whether Mr Davey should be joined as a respondent and decided against it on the ground of delay. In the circumstances I think that that was a reasonable view for the deputy master to take. If Mr Davey had been joined as a respondent it is probable that he would have asked for time to consider putting in evidence and prepare his case; since the application was being heard on 20th December that would, very likely, have delayed matters until well after Christmas. If the deputy master had refused time, it seems most probable that Mr Davey would simply have asserted the validity of the marriage and would have asked that substantial provision be made for him. But that might have affected the interests of the relatives of the patient who would themselves have to be brought before the court to allow them to make representations. All that was bound to cause delay in circumstances where time might be crucial. Looking back, it seems unlikely that it could all have been achieved by 27th December when the patient died.

If the deputy master had decided to do nothing, then if the patient died before the matter could be investigated Mr Davey would, under the intestacy, take irrevocably a very substantial portion of her estate. That might, on an investigation of the whole matter, and particularly the circumstances of the marriage, prove very unfair to the beneficiaries under the September will. On the other hand, by adopting the course which he did, the deputy master preserved, in effect, the opportunity for all parties to represent their claims fully to the court. Either the patient would live long enough for that to be done in her lifetime or she would not. If she lived, it could be done on the application of Mr Davey for a new statutory will. If, as happened, the patient died quickly it seems to me that substantially the same result can be achieved by an application under the Inheritance (Provision for Family and Dependants) Act 1975. Under s 1 of that Act Mr Davey, as the husband of the patient, is entitled to apply to the court for an order under s 2 of the Act on the ground that the patient's will does not make reasonable provision for him. Under s 2 the court could, if it thought proper, make an order, inter alia, for any one or more of the following: (i) periodical payments to Mr Davey out of the estate; (ii) payment to Mr Davey of a lump sum out of the estate; (iii) transfer to Mr Davey of any property comprised in the estate. On such an application Mr Davey and the persons interested under the statutory will could put their respective claims before the court. I should add that it does not appear that any of the beneficiaries under the statutory will would themselves qualify as applicants under s 1 of the 1975 Act.

I do not think that, in substance, there is any material difference in the present case between the factors which the Court of Protection would have been required to consider if the question of what was a proper testamentary disposition for the patient had been fully argued before it and those which the High Court would have to consider on an application under the 1975 Act. I can see that there may be some difference of emphasis; in an application under the 1975 Act, Mr Davey as applicant has to establish that the will does not make reasonable financial provision for him. But in the Court of Protection, the essential question in the end would have been what if anything would be reasonable provision in all the circumstances for the various contestants.

It is said on behalf of Mr Davey that for the deputy master to allow himself to be influenced by the availability of the 1975 Act was an abrogation of his responsibilities. I do not agree with that. The deputy master, in a situation of urgency, had to balance various factors with a view to reaching a just conclusion. It is clear, in my view, that he considered whether the proposed will was a proper will to be made in the circumstances. He concluded that it was. In my judgment, the deputy master in exceptional and difficult circumstances came to a sensible and fair conclusion. If I have any jurisdiction to entertain this appeal I see no reason to interfere with the deputy master's conclusion. I think he was right. It seems to me that the order which he made was one which offered the widest opportunities for a full investigation of the matter and, therefore, the best prospect of a just result in the end.

In fact I do not think that I have any jurisdiction to interfere with the statutory will. It is not necessary for me to decide the matter, but I have heard argument on it and I set out the position broadly as it appears to me.

I should refer first to the provisions of s 103A of the 1959 Act. Subsection (1) provides:

> 'Where under section 103(1) of this Act the judge makes or gives an order, direction or authority requiring or authorising a person . . . to execute a will for a patient, any will executed in pursuance of that order, direction or authority shall be expressed to be signed by the patient acting by the authorised person and shall be . . .'

Then certain formalities as to signing, attestation and sealing are set forth. These formalities were complied with in the present case.

Subsection (3) provides:

> 'Subject to the following provisions of this section, any such will executed in accordance with subsection (1) of this section shall have the like effect for all purposes as if the patient were capable of making a valid will and the will had been executed by him in the manner required by the Wills Act 1837.'

The subsequent provisions of s 103A are not material for present purposes.

In this case the deputy master had jurisdiction to order the execution of the will. Further the will was executed in accordance with subsection (1) of s 103A. The result is that by the operation of s 103A(3) the will is to have the like effect 'for all purposes' as if the patient were capable of making a valid will and the will had been duly executed by her.

The patient is now dead. It seems to me, therefore, that the effect of s 103A(3) is that the statutory will must be treated as if it were a will duly made by her and as if she were of testamentary capacity when she made it. It was her last will. One cannot, I think, in this case get rid of the will simply by attacking the order. The order had no dispositive effect at all. If the patient had died after the order but before the assistant official solicitor executed the will, the patient would have died intestate just as a person of full capacity who gave instructions for a will had died before executing it would die intestate, assuming he left no other will. But the statutory will having been executed, s 103A(3) makes it the patient's will for all purposes. Suppose the deputy master was wrong and that I took the view that the proper order would have been to direct a will under which the estate was divided in some way between Mr Davey and the beneficiaries, or some of them, under the September will. It does not seem to me that the Court of Protection now has any jurisdiction to procure such a distribution. It could not be achieved by order alone. It could only be achieved by revoking the statutory will and making a new will in its place. But that, I think, is impossible. First, it seems to me that the powers of the Court of Protection under s 102 of the 1959 Act came to an end on the patient's death: see, for example, *Re Wheater* [1928] Ch 223 and *Re Bennett* [1913] 2 Ch 318. Second, it is not possible to make a will for, or to revoke the will of, a deceased person, and it cannot, I think, be right to say that in such a case, even though it was not possible to achieve the disposition contemplated by the appellate tribunal, nevertheless the order of that tribunal would, in some way, by itself invalidate the existing will; that seems to me to be wrong in principle and quite likely, in many cases, to produce an unintended, and unfair, intestacy.

In short, the position seems to me to be as follows. The deputy master had jurisdiction to make the order directing the execution of the statutory will. The order, right or wrong, was not a nullity. Accordingly, the will was a will executed in accordance with s 103A(1) of the 1959 Act, and, therefore, by the operation of s 103A(3) has effect, for all purposes, as the patient's will. The patient is dead and the will is irrevocable.

I should add that this is a case where the deputy master had jurisdiction. If he had no jurisdiction (for example because there was no reason to believe that the patient was incapable of making a valid will) different considerations would apply.

The result in my view is that the appeal fails.

Appeal dismissed.

Solicitors: *John A Witzenfeld* (for Mr Davey); *Charles Russell & Co* (for the executors of the will); *Official Solicitor.*

Azza M Abdallah Barrister.

Re Nadler Enterprises Ltd

CHANCERY DIVISION
DILLON J
27th FEBRUARY 1980

Company – Winding up – Preferential payments – Taxes – Value added tax – Group of companies – Representative member – Representative member and another member in liquidation – Unpaid value added tax due from representative member – Whether Crown entitled to claim preferentially in winding up of other member for tax due from representative member – Finance Act 1972, ss 21, 41.

Two companies, X Ltd and Y Ltd, were members of the same group of companies. X Ltd was treated as the representative member of the group for the purposes of s 21[a] of the Finance Act 1972. On 5th March 1976 both companies went into liquidation. On that date a substantial amount of value added tax was due to the Crown from X Ltd in its capacity as the representative member. On the question whether the Crown was entitled by virtue of s 41[b] of the 1972 Act to rank as a preferential creditor in the winding up of Y Ltd in respect of the value added tax due to it from X Ltd as the representative member, for which under s 21, Y Ltd was jointly and severally liable with X Ltd,

Held – Since the liability to tax under s 21(1) of the 1972 Act was joint as well as several, it followed that there was a single obligation and that the tax was automatically due from the various other members of the group as soon as it was due from the representative member. Accordingly, the Crown was entitled to claim preferentially in the liquidation of Y Ltd in respect of the unpaid value added tax due at 5th March 1976 from X Ltd as the representative member of the group (see p 352 *d e* and *h*, post).

Notes

For treatment of groups of companies for purposes of value added tax, see 12 Halsbury's Laws (4th Edn) para 926.

For priority of value added tax in a winding up, see 7 ibid para 1285.

For the Finance Act 1972, ss 21, 41, see 42 Halsbury's Statutes (3rd Edn) 182, 199.

a Section 21, so far as material, is set out at p 351 *e f*, post
b Section 41, so far as material, is set out at p 351 *h*, post

Cases referred to in judgment

a *Baker, Re, ex parte Eastbourne Waterworks Co v Official Receiver* [1954] 2 All ER 790, [1954] 1 WLR 1144, 118 JP 495, 52 LGR 501, 47 R & IT 543, 4 Digest (Reissue) 514, *4463*.
Fastnedge, Re, ex parte Kemp (1874) LR 9 Ch App 383, 43 LJ Bcy 50, 30 LT 109, LJ, 5 Digest (Reissue) 854, *7141*.

Adjourned summons

b By a summons dated 4th September 1979, Leonard Cyril Curtis, the liquidator of Nadler Enterprises Ltd, applied under s 307(1) of the Companies Act 1948 for an order to determine whether the Commissioners of Customs and Excise were entitled to claim preferentially in the liquidation of the company in respect of unpaid value added tax due from Elizabeth Nadler Ltd, the representative member of the group, pursuant to s 21 of the Finance Act 1972. The facts are set out in the judgment.

c

Muir Hunter QC and *Michael Crystal* for the liquidator.
Peter Gibson for the Crown.

DILLON J. I am concerned in this summons with a company called Nadler Enterprises Ltd ('Enterprises'). Enterprises was a subsidiary of a company called Elizabeth Nadler d Ltd ('ENL'). Both Enterprises and ENL went into creditors' voluntary liquidation on 5th May 1976. Before that both Enterprises and ENL and another subsidiary of ENL called Hillingdon Enterprises UK Ltd, with which I am not otherwise concerned, had been the subject of group treatment for value added tax purposes under s 21 of the Finance Act 1972. Section 21(1) reads as follows:

> e 'Where, under the following provisions of this section, any bodies corporate are treated as members of a group any business carried on by a member of the group shall be treated as carried on by the representative member, and—(*a*) any supply of goods or services by a member of the group to another member of the group shall be disregarded; and (*b*) any other supply of goods or services by or to a member of the group shall be treated as a supply by or to the representative member; and (*c*) f any tax paid or payable by a member of the group on the importation of any goods shall be treated as paid or payable by the representative member and the goods shall be treated for the purposes of [certain other sections of the 1972 Act] as imported by the representative member; and all members of the group shall be liable jointly and severally for any tax due from the representative member.'

This group treatment was accorded to the group constituted by ENL, Enterprises and g Hillingdon Enterprises UK Ltd, and ENL was the representative member. It is accepted that Enterprises is jointly and severally liable for any tax due from ENL. What I am concerned with is the extent to which the Commissioners of Customs and Excise are entitled to rank as preferential creditors in the winding up of Enterprises in respect of the value added tax due from ENL as representative member for which Enterprises was jointly and severally liable with ENL. Priority of tax in winding up or bankruptcy is h dealt with by s 41(1) of the Finance Act 1972 which provides:

> 'There shall be included among the debts which ... (*d*) under section 319 of the Companies Act 1948 ... are to be paid in priority to all other debts in the winding up of a company ... the amount of any tax due at the relevant date from the ... company and having become due within the twelve months next before that date.'

j The meaning of the phrase 'tax due at the relevant date ... and having become due within the twelve months next before that date' is the subject of elucidation in s 41(2) of the 1972 Act and s 22 of the Finance Act 1976 which bring in certain apportionment provisions where the relevant date is not at the end of a prescribed accounting period for value added tax purposes, but I do not need to read those provisions. Under s 319 of the Companies Act 1948 the relevant date in the case of a company which has gone into voluntary liquidation is the date of the passing of the winding-up resolution, namely in this case 5th May 1976. The argument for the liquidator is that the priority given by s 41 does not extend to tax due from ENL at the relevant date, but that the scheme, it is said, of group treatment of value added tax is that although all members of the group including Enterprises are jointly and severally liable for the tax, the tax is only due from ENL as the representative member.

Counsel appearing for the liquidator has referred me to observations of Danckwerts J in *Re Baker* [1954] 2 All ER 790 at 793, [1954] 1 WLR 1144 at 1148, where in referring to sections conferring special preference on certain debts he said: '... one must be careful not to extend unduly the privilege or preference in question. The words [of the section], therefore, must be construed with some strictness.'

Bearing that in mind, however, I am nonetheless wholly unable to draw the distinction that counsel for the liquidator would have me draw between tax due at the relevant date from the company and tax for which at the relevant date the company was jointly and severally liable to the Commissioners of Customs and Excise with ENL.

Section 33 of the Finance Act 1972 provides in sub-s (1) that: 'Tax due from any person shall be recoverable as a debt due to the Crown.' I see no reason why that section should not be applied in the context of this group as against Enterprises just as much as against ENL. The 1972 Act is not wholly consistent in its wording throughout. There are references to tax due. There are references to tax payable. There are references to amounts assessed which are to be deemed to be an amount of tax due, and there are references to amounts recoverable as if they were tax due. I do not think the words 'tax due' are a term of art. I think the tax becomes due as soon as it is payable and in the group context, provided for by s 21, there is a liability on all members of the group which is a joint and several liability affecting all members including the representative member. Since it is a joint as well as a several liability there must be a single obligation, and therefore the tax must automatically be due from the various other members of the group as soon as it is due from the representative member, ENL. Moreover some support for the arguments of the Crown is in my judgment provided by the observations of Mellish LJ in *Re Fastnedge, ex parte Kemp* (1874) LR 9 Ch App 383. The actual question the court had to consider in that case was whether certain contingent liabilities due to a firm called Messrs Fastnedge & Co were debts due to that firm which were therefore recoverable by the trustee in the liquidation of the firm.

Mellish LJ said (at 387):

> 'I think that *primâ facie*, and if there be nothing in the context to give them a different construction, [the words "debts due to him"] would include all sums certain which any person is legally liable to pay, whether such sums had become actually payable or not.'

I do not see that there can in principle be much difference between the phrase 'debts due to him' and the converse 'debts due from him'. Therefore, by analogy to what Mellish LJ said, the tax for which Enterprises is liable is due from Enterprises.

In my judgment therefore the Crown is right in contending that it is entitled to preference in respect of the amount of any tax due at the relevant date from ENL as the representative member of the group. That tax is also due at the same date from Enterprises.

The precise form of the declaration then will be that the Crown is entitled to claim preferentially in the liquidation the sum of £55,443·13 in respect of unpaid value added tax, and then no order as to costs except the liquidator's costs to be costs and expenses of liquidation.

Order accordingly.

Solicitors: *Markbys* (for the liquidator); *Solicitor for the Customs and Excise.*

Evelyn M C Budd Barrister.

a

Bankers Trust Co v Shapira and others

COURT OF APPEAL, CIVIL DIVISION
LORD DENNING MR, WALLER AND DUNN LJJ
4th JUNE 1980

b *Equity – Tracing property – Plaintiff seeking to trace money paid under mistake of fact induced by fraud – Power to make interlocutory order for disclosure of bankers' books and correspondence between bank and customer to show amount standing in defendant's account – Defendants outside jurisdiction – Plaintiff unable to effect service on defendants but effecting service on bank – Bank not implicated in fraud – Whether interlocutory order for disclosure should be made against bank.*

c In September 1979 S and F presented for payment to a bank in New York two cheques totalling \$1m which purported to be drawn on a Saudi Arabian bank. The New York bank honoured the cheques and credited \$708,203 to accounts kept by S and F at a discount bank in London. Six months later the Saudi Arabian bank alleged that the cheques were forgeries and took up the matter with the New York bank. The New York bank recredited the Saudi Arabian bank with the \$1m. On 20th May 1980 the New d York bank commenced an action in England against S and F (as first and second defendants) and against the London discount bank (as third defendant) seeking, inter alia, to trace the money they had paid to the discount bank. S and F had gone outside the jurisdiction in circumstances which prevented the New York bank from effecting service on them, but service was effected on the discount bank. On 23rd May the New York bank obtained a Mareva injunction restraining the discount bank from disposing of any e money S and F had paid into that bank, but the judge refused to grant the New York bank's further interlocutory application for an order for discovery against the discount bank requiring it to disclose the sums standing in any accounts of S and F with it and to disclose all the correspondence between it and S and F relating to their accounts and all banking documents, eg cheques drawn on the accounts, debit vouchers and internal memoranda, relating to the accounts. The judge's ground for refusing that application f was that such an order for discovery should not be made so long as the true defendants to the action, S and F, had not been served. The New York bank appealed against the refusal.

Held – The court was entitled, for the purpose of giving effect to a defrauded plaintiff's equitable right to trace his money, to order a bank to disclose the state of, and the g documents and correspondence relating to, the account of a customer who was prima facie guilty of fraud even though the bank had not incurred any personal liability for the fraud, for unless there was the fullest possible disclosure the fund could not be traced. To justify such an order, however, the evidence of fraud against the customer had to be very strong, but, where it was, the customer was disentitled from relying on the confidential relationship between him and his bank to prevent the discovery. Moreover, h such an order for discovery would only be made on terms that the plaintiff gave an undertaking in damages to the bank, paid the bank's expenses of making the discovery and used the documents disclosed solely for the purpose of tracing the money. On that basis, the court would aid the New York bank's claim to trace the money paid to the discount bank by making an order for discovery in the terms sought against that bank. The fact that the true defendants, S and F, had not been served and that a considerable j period of time had elapsed since the fraud had been committed did not, in the circumstance, deprive the court of its power to make the order. The appeal would accordingly be allowed (see p 357 *e f* and *h* to p 358 *h* and p 359 *a b*, post).

Dictum of Lord Denning MR in *Initial Services Ltd v Putterill* [1967] 3 All ER at 148, of Lord Reid in *Norwich Pharmacal Co v Customs and Excise Comrs* [1973] 2 All ER at 948 and *A v C* [1980] 2 All ER 347 applied.

Notes

For the production in evidence of bankers' books, see 3 Halsbury's Laws (4th Edn) paras a 124–126.

For the tracing of property generally, see 16 ibid, para 1460.

Cases referred to in judgments

A v C [1980] 2 All ER 347.

Banque Belge Pour L'Étranger v Hambrouck [1921] 1 KB 321, 90 LJKB 322, 26 Com Cas 72, b CA, 3 Digest (Reissue) 638, *4005*.

Initial Services Ltd v Putterill [1967] 3 All ER 145, [1968] 1 QB 396, [1967] 3 WLR 1032, CA, 28 (2) Digest (Reissue) 1087, *907*.

London and Counties Securities Ltd v Caplan (26th May 1978, unreported).

Mediterranea Reffineria Siciliana Petroli SpA v Mabanaft GmbH [1978] Court of Appeal Transcript 816. c

Norwich Pharmacal Co v Customs and Excise Comrs [1973] 2 All ER 943, [1974] AC 133, [1973] 3 WLR 164, [1974] RPC 101, HL, 18 Digest (Reissue) 8, *23*.

Upmann v Elkan (1871) 7 Ch App 130, 41 LJ Ch 246, 25 LT 813, 36 JP 295, LC; *affg* (1871) LR 12 Eq 140, 28 (2) Digest (Reissue) 1157, *1589*.

Cases also cited d

EMI Ltd v Pandit [1975] 1 All ER 418, [1975] 1 WLR 302.

Third Chandris Shipping Corpn v Unimarine SA [1979] 2 All ER 972, [1979] QB 645, CA.

Tournier v National Provincial and Union Bank of England [1924] 1 KB 461, [1923] All ER 550, CA.

Interlocutory appeal e

In an action commenced by writ dated 20th May 1980 the plaintiffs, Bankers Trust Co, sought (1) against the first and second defendants, Walter Shapira and Max Frei, $US1m as money had and received by them to the plaintiffs' use, or paid to them under a mistake of fact, damages for deceit and/or conspiracy to defraud and a Mareva injunction, (2) against the third defendant, Discount Bank (Overseas) Ltd, $US708,203 as money had and received by it to the plaintiffs' use and, inter alia, the inquiries and accounts necessary f to trace the proceeds of that sum and disclosure of all the bank documents and correspondence relating to the first and second defendants' accounts with the third defendant, and (3) against all three defendants, inter alia, disclosure forthwith of the sums or balances at present standing in any account of the first and second defendants with the third defendant. On the same date the plaintiffs applied by summons for the following interlocutory relief: (1) against the first and second defendants, a Mareva g injunction restraining them from removing from the jurisdiction or otherwise disposing of or dealing with any of their assets within the jurisdiction including any credit balance in any account in their names with the third defendant; (2) against all three defendants, an order that each of them disclose to the plaintiffs forthwith the sums at present standing in any account in the names of the first and second defendants with the third defendant; and (3) as against the third defendant, an order that it disclose to the plaintiffs h forthwith and permit them to take copies of (i) all correspondence passing between the third defendant and the first and second defendants relating to any account with the third defendant in the first or second defendants' names from 15th July 1979 onwards, (ii) all cheques drawn on any account with the third defendant in the names of the first and second defendants from 15th July 1979 onwards, (iii) all debit vouchers, transfer applications and orders and internal memoranda relating to any account with the third j defendant in the first or second defendants' name from 15th July 1979 onwards; (4) an injunction restraining the third defendant from making any payment or transfer out of any account in the name of the first or second defendant at its branch at 63 Hatton Garden, London EC1 or otherwise dealing with such accounts save for payment to the plaintiffs of any sum found due to them. By a judgment given on 23rd May 1980

Mustill J granted the plaintiffs an injunction against the third defendant restraining it *a* from making any payment or transfer out of any account in the name of the first or second defendants at its branch at 63 Hatton Garden or otherwise dealing with such accounts until trial or further order, but made no order under para (2) and (3) of the summons on the ground that an order for discovery against the third defendant ought not to be made at that stage of the proceedings when the first and second defendants who were the true defendants to the action had not been served and were not before the *b* court. The plaintiffs appealed from so much of the judge's order as made no order on paras (2) and (3) of their summons. The facts are set out in the judgment of Lord Denning MR.

Michael Crystal for the plaintiffs.
Nicholas Elliot for the third defendant.
c The first and second defendants were not represented.

LORD DENNING MR. This is a new case. It illustrates something that happens from time to time, frauds made on banks. It appears that on 20th September 1979 two men (Walter Shapira and Max Frei) went into a bank in New York, the Bankers Trust Co. They went into the Middle East section. They presented two apparent cheques, each *d* for $500,000, for payment. The cheques purported to be drawn by the National Commercial Bank in Saudi Arabia on the Bankers Trust Co of 16 Wall Street, New York. One of them was for $500,000 to be paid to Mr Shapira. The other was also for $500,000 to be paid to Mr Shapira.

Bankers Trust honoured the cheques. They let these men have $1m. They acted on the instructions of the two men. I will not go into detail, but I will mention two *e* particular matters. $600,000 was credited to Mr Shapira's account at a London bank in Hatton Garden, the Discount Bank (Overseas) Ltd. They asked that another sum of $108,203 should be credited to Mr Frei's account at a bank in the Cayman Islands. But, as he had no such account there, that sum was also transferred to the Discount Bank in Hatton Garden. So, on the face of it, $708,203 was sent over to the Discount Bank in Hatton Garden. That was in September 1979.

f In some way those cheques got over to the Mecca branch of the Saudi Arabian bank. They apparently honoured them at the time. But six months later, on 10th April 1980, the head office of the National Commercial Bank in Saudi Arabia found that those two cheques were forgeries. They immediately took the matter up with Bankers Trust. I will read part of the letter they wrote:

> *g* 'On looking into these drafts you will find that signatures do not conform in any way to the signatures number 140 and 141 of our officers in our Mecca Branch, that the validating numbers in red do not compare in any way to our validity machine which has the name of our bank on it, that the draft forms are on poor quality paper while our drafts are printed on safety paper with our logo water mark. We therefore consider these drafts are clearly forged and you should have exercised care in encashing them.'

h

When Bankers Trust received that letter, they felt that they were not free from blame themselves. It appears that they did recredit the Saudi Arabian Bank with the money. So Bankers Trust have lost $1m.

They then looked round to see if they could find these rogues. (I call them 'rogues' although it has not been proved yet; but the prima facie evidence against them is *j* strong.) On 20th May 1980 Bankers Trust brought an action. The first defendant was Mr Walter Shapira; the second defendant was Mr Max Frei; and the third defendant was Discount Bank (Overseas) Ltd, with which the moneys were deposited. They did not serve the documents on either Mr Shapira or Mr Frei. We are told, on the evidence, that they investigated the matter. Mr Shapira is now in gaol in Switzerland as a result of a fraud investigation by the Swiss police. Mr Frei is presently believed to be in

Liechtenstein. So they have not served those two. But they have served Discount Bank. The action they have brought is quite clearly to trace and follow these funds which Bankers Trust have been fraudulently deprived of. It operates in common law and in equity as a right to follow and trace the moneys. So they brought this action on 20th May 1980.

Bankers Trust obtained a Mareva injunction in the usual form to stop Discount Bank from disposing of any of the moneys which they had at that time, which Shapira and Frei had paid into Discount Bank. That is common form nowadays in the Commercial Court when it is desired to prevent money being abstracted from the true creditor.

But this case brings out a new point which we have not had before: because Bankers Trust want more information from Discount Bank. They want information as to these accounts. They want to know how much money is now in the accounts. Money has been taken out in the last six months. They want to know what has happened to the money in the accounts. It may have been paid over to third persons; and they may want to follow the money into the hands of those third persons. So they have asked for discovery of the documents relating to the moneys which Discount Bank had, and what has happened to them.

As the question of the form of order has come into question in some of the cases, I would like to read the actual form of order which is sought in this regard by Bankers Trust:

> 'FOR AN ORDER
>
> '(1) Against the first, second and third defendants that each of them do disclose to the plaintiffs forthwith the sums or balances at present standing in any account in either of the names of the first or second defendants at the third defendants.
>
> '(2) Against the third defendants [ie Discount Bank (Overseas) Ltd] that they do disclose to the plaintiffs forthwith and permit the plaintiffs to take copies of the following documents:—(i) all correspondence passing between the third defendants and the first and second defendants relating to any account at the third defendants in the names of either the first and/or second defendants from 20th September 1979 onwards. (ii) all cheques drawn on any account at the third defendants in the names of either the first and/or second defendants from 20th September 1979 onwards. (iii) all debit vouchers, transfer applications and orders and internal memoranda relating to any account at the third defendants in the names of either the first and/or second defendants from 20th September 1979 onwards.'

That is what they applied for in addition to the ordinary Mareva injunction.

The matter came before Mustill J. He refused to make any such order, his reason being that he thought it should not be made whilst the first and second defendants (Mr Shapira and Mr Frei) had not been served.

Counsel has come here today on behalf of Bankers Trust, and asks us to reverse that decision. He has brought to our attention, very usefully, three recent cases (two of them unreported) in which a similar point has arisen. The first one was on 26th May 1978 before Templeman J, *London and Counties Securities Ltd v Caplan*. The plaintiff company had been defrauded by Mr Caplan in the sum of £5m. Mr Caplan was said to have embezzled them. It was desired to obtain information as to the whereabouts of the moneys and what had been done with them. The plaintiffs wanted to trace the moneys to see where they had gone. Templeman J, having considered the matter very carefully, made an order under which the bank was to disclose all the documents and accounts showing where the money had gone.

Then there was a case before this court on 1st December 1978, *Mediterranea Reffineria Siciliana Petroli SpA v Mabanaft GmbH* [1978] Court of Appeal Transcript 816. It was not a fraud on a bank. Nor a fraud at all. Owing to a mistake in a commercial transaction, moneys payable to the plaintiffs were paid to other people. It was desired to trace them. A Mareva injunction was granted and also an order for discovery of documents to discover where the money had gone. Templeman LJ said:

'It is a strong order, but the plaintiffs' case is that there is a trust fund of $3,500,000. This has disappeared; and the gentlemen against whom orders are sought may be able to give information as to where it is and who is in charge of it. A court of equity has never hesitated to use the strongest powers to protect and preserve a trust fund in interlocutory proceedings on the basis that, if the trust fund disappears by the time the action comes to trial, equity will have been invoked in vain.'

The last of the three cases was *A v C* [1980] 2 All ER 347 before Robert Goff J on 18th March 1980. That was a case again of a fraud on a bank. A very large sum of money was involved. It seems to be a case very similar to the present case, but in which the fraudulent rogues (as they may well turn out to be) had been served. It is on that ground distinguishable from the present case. The rogues were served together with the bank. Robert Goff J, after considering the two cases which I have mentioned, said (at 351):

'There is no doubt that this jurisdiction is in a process of development, and that it is still in the course of throwing up problems which have yet to be solved.'

He granted a Mareva injunction; but in addition he made an order for discovery of documents. He did so in order to enable the plaintiffs to trace what had happened to the moneys.

Mustill J had *A v C* before him. He thought it was distinguishable on the ground that in that case the 'rogues' had been served. He refused to order discovery in this case; but he gave leave to appeal in order that the questions of principle could be discussed.

We have had the matter fully argued before us. I would like to express our gratitude to counsel for Bankers Trust for all the submissions he has made in support of the order. Equally to counsel for Discount Bank, who has taken a very proper attitude. He said that the bank are neutral in this matter; but they felt it right to put forward to the court various considerations, such as the confidential relationship between the bank and its customers.

Having heard all that has been said, it seems to me that Mustill J was too hesitant in this matter. In order to enable justice to be done, in order to enable these funds to be traced, it is a very important part of the court's armoury to be able to order discovery. The powers in this regard, and the extent to which they have gone, were exemplified in *Norwich Pharmacal Co v Customs and Excise Comrs* [1973] 2 All ER 943, [1974] AC 133. The customs authorities were perfectly innocent; but they had to disclose the names of infringers of patents whose goods had passed through their hands. Lord Reid said ([1973] 2 All ER 943 at 948, [1974] AC 133 at 175):

'They seem to me to point to a very reasonable principle that if through no fault of his own a person gets mixed up in the tortious acts of others so as to facilitate their wrongdoing he may incur no personal liability but he comes under a duty to assist the person who has been wronged by giving him full information and disclosing the identity of the wrongdoers.'

Lord Reid was referring to the views expressed by Lord Romilly MR and Lord Hatherly LC in *Upmann v Elkan* (1871) LR 12 Eq 140 at 145, 7 Ch App 130 at 133.

So here Discount Bank incur no personal liability: but they got mixed up, through no fault of their own, in the tortious or wrongful acts of these two men; and they come under a duty to assist Bankers Trust by giving them and the court full information and disclosing the identity of the wrongdoers. In this case the particular point is 'full information'.

This new jurisdiction must, of course, be carefully exercised. It is a strong thing to order a bank to disclose the state of its customer's account and the documents and correspondence relating to it. It should only be done when there is a good ground for thinking the money in the bank is the plaintiff's money, as for instance when the customer has got the money by fraud, or other wrongdoing, and paid it into his account

at the bank. The plaintiff, who has been defrauded, has a right in equity to follow the
money. He is entitled, in Atkin LJ's words, to lift the latch of the bankers' door: see a
Banque Belge Pour L'Étranger v Hambrouck [1921] 1 KB 321 at 335. The customer, who has
prima facie been guilty of fraud, cannot bolt the door against him. Owing to his fraud,
he is disentitled from relying on the confidential relationship between him and the
bank: see *Initial Services Ltd v Putterill* [1967] 3 All ER 145 at 148, [1968] 1 QB 396 at
405. If the plaintiff's equity is to be of any avail, he must be given access to the bank's
books and documents, for that is the only way of tracing the money or of knowing what b
has happened to it: see *Mediterranea Reffineria Siciliana Petroli SpA v Mabanaft GmbH*
[1978] Court of Appeal Transcript 816. So the court, in order to give effect to equity, will
be prepared in a proper case to make an order on the bank for their discovery. The
plaintiff must of course give an undertaking in damages to the bank and must pay all and
any expenses to which the bank is put in making the discovery; and the documents, once
seen, must be used solely for the purpose of following and tracing the money, and not for c
any other purpose. With these safeguards, I think the new jurisdiction, already exercised
in the three cases I have referred to, should be affirmed by this court.

Applying this principle, I think the court should go to the aid of Bankers Trust Co. It
should help them follow the money which is clearly theirs, to follow it to the hands in
which it is, and to find out what has become of it since it was put into Discount Bank
(Overseas) Ltd. d

If the courts were to wait until the first and second defendants were served goodness
knows how many weeks might elapse. Meanwhile, if some of it has got into the hands
of third persons, they may dispose of it elsewhere. It seems to me that the fact that the
first and second defendants have not been served does not deprive the court of its power
to make such an order. These two men have gone out of the jurisdiction in circumstances
in which it is clear that the court should do all it can to help the innocent people to find e
out where their money has gone.

In those circumstances, while expressing our indebtedness to both counsel, I would
allow the appeal and make the order as asked in the notice of appeal.

WALLER LJ. I agree. I only add a word or two about three points which were made
by counsel on behalf of Discount Bank (Overseas) Ltd taking, so far as he could, a neutral f
attitude in this matter. He, first of all, emphasised that where the other two parties had
not been served, it was very strong action on the part of the court to order the bank to
break their duty of confidentiality. It was going further, he said, than an Anton Piller
order because, when an Anton Piller order is made, there remains the opportunity of
disobeying it or appealing against it.

Clearly it is undesirable that an order such as this should be lightly made. But the g
answer to this part of counsel's submission, in my judgment, is that here there is very
strong evidence indeed of fraud on the part of the other two defendants, the first and
second defendants. They presented two forged cheques, each for $500,000, and as a
result a total of $1m was transferred to accounts in their names or from which they
would benefit.

Secondly, counsel for Discount Bank submitted that, having regard to the amount of h
time which had gone by, there was no case for making this order now; it could wait until
the normal time for discovery; and indeed Mustill J in his decision adverted to that. But
again, in my opinion, where you have a fraud of this nature, although it may be late, and
although much or perhaps all of the money may be now gone, the sooner that steps are
taken to try and trace where it is the better. If steps are going to be taken, it is important
that they should be taken at the earliest possible moment. j

Thirdly, counsel for Discount Bank expressed concern at the wideness of the order
which it was sought to make, one which required the bank to permit the plaintiffs to
take copies of all correspondence, for example, all debit vouchers, transfer applications
and orders, and internal memoranda. He submitted that the breadth of that order went
far beyond the disclosure which would have to be made under the Bankers' Books

Evidence Act 1879. Again, in my opinion, an order of that breadth is completely
a justified in a case of this sort because, unless there is the fullest possible information, the difficulties of tracing the funds will be well nigh impossible.

On the other side of the coin in relation to that, there must be an implied undertaking on the part of the plaintiffs that the information which they obtain will only be used for the purposes of this action and of course will not be disclosed otherwise.

b **DUNN LJ.** I agree for the reasons given by Lord Denning MR and Waller LJ that this appeal should be allowed.

Appeal allowed. Order in terms sought by the plaintiffs.

Solicitors: *Linklaters & Paines* (for the plaintiffs); *Dawson & Co* (for the third defendant).

c

Sumra Green Barrister.

d Rothmans of Pall Mall (Overseas) Ltd and others v Saudi Arabian Airlines Corporation

QUEEN'S BENCH DIVISION
MUSTILL J
29th OCTOBER, 7th NOVEMBER, 17th DECEMBER 1979

e COURT OF APPEAL, CIVIL DIVISION
ROSKILL AND ORMROD LJJ
13th, 14th MARCH 1980

Carriage by air – Carriage of goods – International carriage – Jurisdiction – Place where carrier ordinarily resident – Ordinarily resident – Goods carried by Saudi Arabian airline with principal
f *place of business outside England but branch office in England – Goods lost – Claim by owners for damages – Writ served at branch office on ground that airline ordinarily resident in England – Whether airline 'ordinarily resident' in England – Whether court should set aside writ and service – Carriage by Air Act 1961, Sch 1, art 28(1).*

The first plaintiffs agreed to sell a consignment of goods to the second plaintiffs in Saudi
g Arabia and arranged in Holland for the defendants, an airline corporation incorporated in Saudi Arabia, to carry the goods from Amsterdam to Jeddah, the carriage being subject to the Warsaw Convention as amended at The Hague in 1955 and as set out in Sch 1 to the Carriage by Air Act 1961. Some of the goods were lost and some damaged on the journey to Jeddah. The plaintiffs issued a writ in England against the defendants claiming damages and served it on the defendants at their branch office in London. In
h so doing, they relied on art 28(1)[a] of the convention which enabled a plaintiff to bring an action for damages against a carrier, in the place, inter alia, where the carrier was 'ordinarily resident'. The defendants, whose principal place of business was outside England, applied to have the writ and service set aside on the ground that the English courts had, in the circumstances, no jurisdiction over the suit by virtue of art 28(1). The plaintiffs contended that, as the defendants had an office in London, they were, within
j the meaning of art 28(1), 'ordinarily resident' within the jurisdiction because the word 'resident' was to be interpreted in the same way as it was in English cases concerning service on foreign corporations under RSC Ord 65, r 3, ie a defendant company was resident within the jurisdiction if it had a place of business there.

a Article 28(1) is set out at p. 361 g, post

Held – The Warsaw Convention, being an international convention, was to be construed without reference to the technical rules of English law or of English legal precedent. On the true construction of art 28(1) of the convention, a foreign corporation was not 'ordinarily resident' within the jurisdiction if it merely had a branch office there. It followed that the defendants' objection to the jurisdiction was well founded and the writ and service would be set aside (see p 370 *e* and *h j*, p 371 *c* to *e* and p 372 *g* to p 373 *d*, post).

Dicta of Lord Wilberforce and of Lord Salmon in *James Buchanan & Co Ltd v Babco Forwarding and Shipping (UK) Ltd* [1977] 3 All ER at 1052 and 1059 applied.

Fothergill v Monarch Airlines Ltd [1979] 3 All ER 445 considered.

Notes

For construction of statutes giving effect to international agreements, see 36 Halsbury's Laws (3rd Edn) 394, para 592, and for cases on the subject, see 44 Digest (Repl) 228, *461–462*.

For the Carriage by Air Act 1961, Sch 1, art 28, see 2 Halsbury's Statutes (3rd Edn) 619.

The decision of the Court of Appeal in *Fothergill v Monarch Airlines Ltd* [1979] 3 All ER 445 was reversed by the House of Lords [1980] 2 All ER 696.

Cases referred to in judgments

Aronowitch v Air France (1978) 383 NE 2d 977.
Buchanan (James) & Co Ltd v Babco Forwarding and Shipping (UK) Ltd [1977] 3 All ER 1048, [1978] AC 141, [1977] 3 WLR 907, [1978] RTR 59, HL, Digest (Cont Vol E) 36, *1435*.
Compagnie Générale Transatlantique v Thomas Law & Co, La Bourgogne [1899] AC 431, 68 LJP 104, 80 LT, 8 Asp MLR 550, HL, 50 Digest (Repl) 319, *515*.
Consorts Tarnay v Varig (28th April 1978) Tribunal de Grande Instance de Paris (First Chamber) 2nd section.
Corocraft Ltd v Pan American Airways Inc [1968] 2 All ER 1059, [1969] 1 QB 616, [1968] 3 WLR 714, [1968] 1 Lloyd's Rep 625; *rvsd* [1969] 1 All ER 82, [1968] 3 WLR 1273, [1968] 2 Lloyd's Rep 459, CA, 8(2) Digest (Reissue) 608, *43*.
Firth v John Mowlem & Co Ltd [1978] 3 All ER 331, [1978] 1 WLR 1184, CA, Digest (Cont Vol E) 663, *2070b*.
Fothergill v Monarch Airlines Ltd [1979] 3 All ER 445, [1980] 1 QB 23, [1979] 3 WLR 491, CA; *affg* [1977] 3 All ER 616, [1978] QB 108, Digest (Cont Vol E) 43, *29a*.
Haggin v Comptoir d'Escompte de Paris (1889) 23 QBD 519, 58 LJQB 508, 61 LT 748, CA, 50 Digest (Repl) 317, *508*.
Hercules (Actiesselkabet Dampskib) v Grand Trunk Pacific Railway Co [1912] 1 KB 222, 81 LJKB 189, 105 LT 695, CA, 13 Digest (Reissue) 378, *3230*.
Karfunkel v Air France (1977) 427 F Supp 971.
Logan v Bank of Scotland [1904] 2 KB 495, 73 LJKB 794, 91 LT 252, CA, 50 Digest (Repl) 315, *500*.
Newby v von Oppen and Colt's Patent Firearms Manufacturing Co (1872) LR 7 QB 293, 41 LJQB 148, 26 LT 164, 13 Digest (Reissue) 374, *3207*.
Nudo and Lovering v Sabena (1962) 207 F Supp 191.
Rotterdamsche Bank NV v British Overseas Airways Corpn [1953] 1 All ER 675, [1953] 1 WLR 493, [1953] 1 Lloyd's Rep 154, 8(2) Digest (Reissue) 602, *27*.
Salah v Saudi Catering and Contracting Co Ltd [1980] Court of Appeal Transcript 315.
Smith v Canadian Pacific Airways Ltd (1971) 452 F 2d 798.
Somportex Ltd v Philadelphia Chewing Gum Corpn [1968] 3 All ER 26, CA, Digest (Cont Vol C) 1081, *1026a*.
Stag Line Ltd v Foscolo, Mango & Co Ltd [1932] AC 328, [1931] All ER Rep 666, 101 LJKB 165, 146 LT 305, 37 Com Cas 54, 18 Asp MLC 266, HL; *affg* [1931] 2 KB 48, 100 LJKB 421, 145 LT 146, 36 Com Cas 213, 18 Asp MLC 210, CA, 41 Digest (Repl) 379, *1698*.
Wilkinson v Barking Corpn [1948] 1 All ER 564, [1948] 1 KB 721, [1948] LJR 1164, 112 JP 215, 46 LGR 169, CA, 50 Digest (Repl) 504, *1803*.

Interlocutory appeal

a The plaintiffs, Rothmans of Pall Mall (Overseas) Ltd and Ahmed & Yousuf Mohammed Abdul Wahab Nagha (a firm) appealed against the order of Master Waldman dated 4th April 1979 allowing the application made by the defendants, Saudi Arabian Airlines Corpn, to have the writ issued on 7th September 1978 by the plaintiffs against the defendants and service thereof set aside. The facts are set out in the judgment of Mustill J.

b

John Roch QC and *Peter Irvin* for the plaintiffs.
Jonathan Mance for the defendants.

Cur adv vult

17th December. **MUSTILL J** read the following judgment: In this case, each party has
c made a procedural mistake. The question is, which is to bear the loss?

The events which gave rise to the dispute are as follows. The first plaintiffs are suppliers of cigarettes. They wished to send a consignment to the second plaintiffs, their purchasers in Saudi Arabia. The carriage was to be performed in two stages: from London to Amsterdam, and thence to Jeddah. For the second stage, they chartered an
d aircraft from the defendants. The flight took place on 3rd October 1976. An air waybill was issued in respect of the carriage, incorporating the terms of the charter. It is common ground that the carriage was subject to the convention known as 'the Warsaw Convention as amended at The Hague, 1955', which I will call 'the convention'.

Statutory effect was given to the convention in the United Kingdom by the Carriage by Air Act 1961. Both parties accept that the present dispute must be judged according to the 1961 Act, even though the contract of carriage was expressed to be subject to the
e law of Saudi Arabia.

Section 1(1) of the 1961 Act provides as follows:

> 'Subject to this section, the provisions of the Convention known as "the Warsaw Convention as amended at The Hague, 1955" as set out in the First Schedule to this Act shall, so far as they relate to the rights and liabilities of carriers, carriers' servants
> f and agents, passengers, consignors, consignees and other persons, and subject to the provisions of this Act, have the force of law in the United Kingdom in relation to any carriage by air to which the Convention applies, irrespective of the nationality of the aircraft performing that carriage . . .'

The English text of the convention is set out in the schedule to the Act and contains the following material provisions:

g

> '*Article* 28 (1) An action for damages must be brought, at the option of the plaintiff, in the territory of one of the High Contracting Parties, either before the court having jurisdiction where the carrier is ordinarily resident, or has his principal place of business, or has an establishment by which the contract has been made or before the court having jurisdiction at the place of destination.
>
> h '(2) Questions of procedure shall be governed by the law of the court seised of the case.
>
> '*Article* 29 (1) The right to damages shall be extinguished if an action is not brought within two years, reckoned from the date of arrival at the destination, or from the date on which the aircraft ought to have arrived, or from the date on which the carriage stopped.
>
> j '(2) The method of calculating the period of limitation shall be determined by the law of the court seised of the case . . .
>
> '*Article* 32 Any clause contained in the contract and all special agreements entered into before the damage occurred by which the parties purport to infringe the rules laid down by this Convention, whether by deciding the law to be applied, or by altering the rules as to jurisdiction, shall be null and void. Nevertheless for the

> carriage of cargo arbitration clauses are allowed, subject to this Convention, if the arbitration is to take place within one of the jurisdictions referred to in the first *a*
> paragraph of Article 28.'

Although the carriage was performed on 3rd October 1976 the second plaintiffs did not take physical delivery of the goods until 14th November 1976. Some time during the first half of November 1976 it was discovered by survey that 188 cartons of cigarettes were missing and that others were damaged by water. According to the survey report, *b*
notice of loss and damage had been given to the defendants on 1st November 1976. It is not clear whether the notification was written. No copy was produced at the hearing. Surveys were carried out on behalf of the plaintiffs. The plaintiffs or their underwriters appointed J S Collyer (Recoveries) Ltd ('Collyers') to act as loss adjusters in respect of the claim.

For months there was silence. Then, on 15th July 1977, Collyers wrote to the *c*
defendants in London stating that they represented goods owners/underwriters, enclosing various documents in support of the claim, and asking for a cheque in settlement. Unfortunately, the letter was wrongly addressed. The plaintiffs do not challenge the defendants' statement that it was never received.

Five months went past, whilst Collyers waited for a reply. Ultimately, having taken up the matter by telephone, they wrote to the defendants' cargo depot at Heathrow *d*
airport, London, enclosing copies of the documents which they had sent with their earlier letter. The defendants acknowledged receipt on 16th December 1977, stating that the files relating to the claim were being forwarded to the system's customer relations department in Jeddah, who would contact Collyers direct. The files referred to consisted solely of the documents which Collyers had sent, since the defendants' offices in England had no connection with the matter, except as recipients of the claim. On *e*
10th January 1978, the Jeddah office wrote to Collyers, acknowledging receipt of the claim and stating that the matter was under investigation.

There was then silence for a further four months, after which Collyers wrote a reminder to the Heathrow office. The latter replied to the effect that they were asking the Jeddah office to advise Collyers as to the present status of the claim, either direct or through the London office. *f*

At some time thereafter, the plaintiffs' underwriters instructed solicitors, who on 10th August 1978 wrote to the Heathrow office, informing the defendants of their appointment, inquiring the current position, and inviting confirmation that liability was accepted in full. Having received no answer, the solicitors wrote a brief reminder on 20th September 1978, to which the defendants replied on 25th September to the effect that they were requesting the Jeddah office to inform the solicitors as to the present status *g*
of the claim, either direct or through the Heathrow office.

By now, the time limit of two years created by art 29 of the convention had less than two weeks to run. The plaintiffs' solicitors evidently had this in mind, for they had already issued a writ on 7th September claiming damages for breach of contract or negligence, or alternatively under the 1961 Act. But they did not say anything about this until 10th November, when they wrote again to the Heathrow office, stating that *h*
'you will of course be aware that the writ has been issued in order to protect the time limit'. (The defendants in fact had no means of knowing this.) The letter went on to say that unless some approach was received within 14 days the writ would be served. By this time, the two year time limit had expired.

The plaintiffs' solicitors received no response to their letter and accordingly served the writ by post, at the defendants' Regent Street office, on the person who had been *j*
nominated to accept service on behalf of the defendants pursuant to s 407 of the Companies Act 1948.

Meanwhile, the defendants had in their turn appointed solicitors, and had telexed to them the wording of the letter of 10th November from the plaintiffs' solicitors. At the time when the writ was served the partner dealing with the matter was away from the office, and it was in the hands of an assistant solicitor, who received the writ when it was forwarded by the defendants after service. The general endorsement on the writ did not a identify the transit on which the goods were being carried at the time of the loss (as it should have done), nor did the only other document available to the assistant solicitor (namely the letter of 10th November 1978) show the termini of the transit, although study of the heading would have disclosed the letters 'AMS/JED', from which someone giving the matter close study could perhaps have deduced that the goods had been sent from Amsterdam to Jeddah. It did not, however, occur to the solicitor that the carriage b might have had nothing to do with England, and that accordingly the English court might have no jursidction. Accordingly, on 7th December 1978 he entered an unconditional appearance on behalf of the defendants. It was not until he had started to look into the facts of the case that he became alive to the possibility that the action should not have been brought in England. Thereupon he reported the matter to his principal. The advice of counsel was sought, and in due course an application was made to the c master for an order that (i) the defendants should have leave to withdraw their unconditional appearance, (ii) the writ and service thereof should be set aside, and in the alternative, (iii) the proceedings should be stayed. On 4th August 1979 the master granted the application. (The formal order gave the plaintiffs leave 'to withdraw their Unconditional Appearance and/or enter a Conditional Appearance herein', as well as ordering that the writ and service thereof should be set aside. The words 'and/or enter d a Conditional Appearance' must be a mistake in the drawing up of the order, and I will treat the matter as if leave had been given to withdraw the unconditional appearance.) The plaintiffs now appeal.

Although in form this appeal is concerned with jurisdiction, it is really a dispute about time limits. If the decision of the master is upheld, the plaintiffs will lose their claim in England, and will be too late to institute proceedings elsewhere. In response to an e inquiry from the court, the defendants' counsel made it plain that the defendants will not waive the time limit, if an action is commenced in another jurisdiction. The defendants' purpose is not to ensure that the action is tried in the correct jurisdiction, but to ensure that it is not tried at all.

In these circumstances, the following issues arise. (1) Does an English court have jurisdiction over the suit by virtue of art 28 of the convention? (2) If not, could the f defendants confer jurisdiction by waiving their right to object to the institution of the suit in England? (3) Did the entry of an unconditional appearance amount to a waiver of their right to object, and, if so, are they now entitled to withdraw their waiver by having the appearance set aside? (4) If the court has a discretion in the matter, should the appearance be set aside in the circumstances of the present case? (5) Should the present action in any event be stayed, on the ground that England is a forum non conveniens?

g Argument on the last of these questions was postponed, since it will only arise if the defendants lose on the remaining issues.

The first question is whether the English court has jurisdiction by virtue of art 28 of the convention. The article lists four places where the action may be brought. Of these two are plainly inapplicable, viz the place where the contract is made, and the place of destination. Counsel for the plaintiffs accepted that although the defendants had a place h of business here (a fact which counsel for the defendants did not dispute) he could not say that it was a principal place of business, within the meaning of the article. But he maintained that the defendants were ordinarily resident in England, by virtue of carrying on business here at two regular offices. In this respect he relied on several reported cases as showing that, quite apart from the mechanism established by ss 407 and 412 of the Companies Act 1948, the defendants could properly have been served with the writ, on j the ground that they were resident here: see *Newby v von Oppen and Colt's Patent Firearms Manufacturing Co* (1872) LR 7 QB 293, *Haggin v Comptoir d'Escompte de Paris* (1889) 23 QBD 519, *Compagnie Générale Transatlantique v Thomas Law & Co, La Bourgogne* [1899] AC 431, *Logan v Bank of Scotland* [1904] 2 KB 495, *Actiesselskabet Dampskib Hercules v Grand Trunk Pacific Railway Co* [1912] 1 KB 222.

I agree that these cases show that the defendants would, in the absence of statutory provisions, have been amenable to direct service in England. But this does not in my view entail that the defendants were properly served under art 28. For both persons and companies, the criterion for service at common law is presence within the jurisdiction. This concept is not easily adapted to the case of a foreign corporation. Not infrequently, the test of presence has been expressed by asking whether the company 'resides' or 'carries on business' within the jurisdiction. But as Buckley LJ pointed out in *Actiesselskabet Dampskib Hercules v Grand Trunk Pacific Railway Co* [1912] 1 KB 222 at 227 these expressions do not appear in the Rules of Court; they are only ways of saying that the company is 'here'. Is that kind of presence sufficient to found judgment under the convention? I think it unlikely that this is what was intended. International conventions of this kind tend to prescribe jurisdiction in narrow terms, on the assumption that the case where the defendant has insufficient assets to satisfy the claims in any of the stipulated countries is catered for by the ready availability of enforcement in other countries which is available via the various conventions on mutual recognition of judgments. In the case of air carriers, who tend to have branch offices, and not merely agencies or local subsidiaries, throughout the world, the possibility of multiple jurisdictions implicit in a wide reading of art 28 is something which the draftsman of the convention is unlikely to have wished to encourage.

Futhermore, on this wider interpretation the concepts of residence and place of business are almost, if not exactly, the same. Yet the possession of a place of business in a country was plainly not intended to found jurisdiction on its own, since art 28 lists a *principal* place of business as one of the four hallmarks of jurisdiction.

In these circumstances, I consider that the words 'where the carrier is ordinarily resident' must be more narrowly construed. The following appear to be the possible readings: (i) the words do not apply to bodies corporate at all; (ii) they mean the place where the body is incorporated; or (iii) they mean the place where the central administration and power of decision of the company is to be found, as in the English tax cases. (See Shawcross and Beaumont on Air Law, 4th Edn, 1977, para 439.)

The choice between these interpretations is difficult. Perhaps some guidance can be obtained from the use of the word 'domicile' in the authoritative French text of the convention. But it is unnecessary to make a choice in the present case: for the defendants do not satisfy any of these tests, so far as England and Wales are concerned. Accordingly, I consider that the objection to the jurisdiction is in principle well founded.

The next issue is whether a party can, by waiver, concede to the court the jurisdiction to entertain actions which by virtue of art 28 ought properly to have been instituted elsewhere. For this purpose, two situations must be distinguished. The first exists where an action is brought in respect of a matter which in the ordinary way the court would have no jurisdiction to entertain, but where it is not precluded from doing so if no objection is taken. Thus, for example, if a plaintiff obtains leave under RSC Ord 11 in a case where it should not have been granted, the action can properly proceed unless an application is made to set aside the writ and service. The objection is one which can be waived, and the entry of an unconditional appearance is an example of such a waiver.

The second situation exists where the objection is not simply that the matter lies outside the jurisdiction of the court, as conferred by the common law or by statute, but is one in respect of which jurisdiction has been actively withdrawn from the court and conferred on another tribunal. The position in such a case was stated by Asquith LJ in *Wilkinson v Barking Corpn* [1948] 1 All ER 564 at 567, [1948] 1 KB 721 at 724 as follows:

> 'It is, undoubtedly, good law that, where a statute creates a right and in plain language gives a specific remedy or appoints a specific tribunal for its enforcement, a party seeking to enforce the right must resort to this remedy or this tribunal and not to others.'

Where the statute is of this kind, it is immaterial whether the parties wish the court to try the action. It must disclaim jurisdiction, since to continue with the action would be contrary to law. Still less can one party by unilateral act confer on the court a jurisdiction which Parliament has said it should not have. Entry of an unconditional appearance does not preclude the defendant from raising the objection at a later stage, since it is the duty of the court not to entertain the dispute.

The defendants maintain that the jurisdictional provisions of the 1961 Act fall into this latter category. If they are right, none of the other questions arise. The defendants need not ask for their appearance to be set aside, but can simply treat the action as a nullity at any stage of the proceedings. At first sight, the defendants' argument receives formidable support from the wording of the Act and convention. Section 1 of the Act says that the convention shall 'have the force of law in the United Kingdom'. Article 28 of the convention prescribes that an action 'must be brought' in one of the specified territories. This is imperative language, enabling the defendants to argue that the legislation creates a self-contained system of rights and liabilities, with its own inbuilt system of remedies independent of any local rules as to choice of law and jurisdiction: see per Donaldson J in *Corocraft v Pan American Airways* [1968] 2 All ER 1059 at 1065–1066 (at first instance), and also *Rotterdamsche Bank v British Overseas Airways Corpn* [1953] 1 All ER 675, [1953] 1 WLR 493. The shape of the legislation is not, so the defendants argue, consistent with the possibility that jurisdiction can be conferred by consent, and still less by unilateral waiver.

Whilst this is a forceful argument, I have been persuaded that it is unsound, for two reasons. First, because the argument ignores the distinction between legislation which changes the jurisdictional rules of the lex fori, and that which takes away the jurisdiction of the local court altogether. The Act undoubtedly has the first of the effects. The court is bound to dissociate itself from a claim brought before it against the will of the defendant, if it is not a tribunal contemplated by art 28: see *Rotterdamsche Bank v British Overseas Airways Corpn*. But it does not to my mind follow that the court must decline jurisdiction even when the defendant does not object. I do not consider that the wording of the convention is strong enough to have this effect. Thus: (1) The fact that art 32 specifically invalidates jurisdictional agreements made before the occurrence of damage suggests that the parties to the convention recognised that a binding agreement on jurisdiction could be made after the event. The plaintiffs did not suggest that an unconditional appearance was a 'special agreement' of the kind referred to in art 28, but the shape of art 32 does at least show that a choice of jurisdiction once a dispute has arisen is not regarded as repugnant to the scheme of the convention. (2) The policy of arts 28 and 32 is in my view twofold: to prevent forum-shopping by the plaintiff, and at the same time to prevent the defendant from imposing, through the medium of his standard conditions of carriage, a choice of jurisdiction likely to be favourable to his interests. Neither of these considerations is hostile to a choice of forum, by agreement or acquiescence, made after the damage has occurred, and at a time when the defendant is in a position freely to decide whether or not to submit.

In a case where the court in which the action is brought has jurisdiction under its own rules, and where the parties are content to have that jurisdiction exercised, I can see nothing in the convention which precludes the court from giving effect to their choice. The English court must of course give full weight to the international obligations assumed by the United Kingdom when becoming a party to the convention; but this is no reason to deny itself a jurisdiction properly exercised under its own procedural law (in the present case via s 412 of the Companies Act 1948) unless the words of the treaty clearly require it to do so. In the present instance, I consider that they do not.

On the next question, which concerns the effect of an unconditional appearance, various questions were developed in argument. For example, what is the relationship between RSC Ord 2, r 1, and RSC Ord 12, r 8? Is it material under the latter rule (as it is under RSC Ord 2, r 1) whether the applicant had knowledge of the irregularity when he performed the act relied on as a waiver? Is it necessary to enter a conditional appearance as a prerequisite to the raising of an objection, in any case other than those listed in RSC Ord 12, r 8? Does a party who enters an unconditional appearance waive the type of objection with which the present appeal is concerned? These are interesting

questions, but it is unnecessary to decide them, for in my view the quality of an
appearance as a waiver must be judged by the law under which the procedure of entering a
an appearance is created: and this quite apart from art 28 (2). To inquire into the status
of an appearance independently of English law is meaningless, since the act is one which
exists only as a reflection of that law. One of the characteristics of an unconditional
appearance under English law is that in appropriate circumstances the court will give the
party leave to withdraw it. This being so, the entry of an appearance cannot be an
outright waiver. It is at best a contingent waiver taking final effect only if the court is not b
asked to, or does not consent to, intervene.

This leads to the fourth issue, namely whether in the particular circumstances of this
case the court should give the defendants leave to withdraw the unconditional
appearance. A question was raised in argument about the extent of the court's discretion
when such an application is made. Does it exist only where the defendant has acted
under a mistake, or is it completely unfettered? To my mind *Firth v John Mowlem & Co* c
Ltd [1978] 3 All ER 331, [1978] 1 WLR 1184 indicates that the latter is the correct view,
although the discretion is one which must be exercised with caution. The point is
however immaterial, for in the present case there was undoubtedly a mistake, rather
than a deliberate if misguided choice, as in *Somportex Ltd v Philadelphia Chewing Gum*
Corpn [1968] 3 All ER 26. The court thus has a discretion. Should it be exercised here?
In one sense, the defendants' stance appears unattractive, for they ask the indulgence of d
the court in order to put right their own mistake, so that they can take advantage of a
mistake by their opponents. Futhermore, much of the lapse of time was due to the
persistent and unexplained failure of the Jeddah office to make any response to the
claim. Indeed, if the writ had been served and an unconditional appearance entered,
before the two-year limit had expired, I would not have granted leave to withdraw the
appearance; for in such a case the plaintiffs could have argued that the entry of an e
unconditional appearance had misled them into believing that there was no problem
over jurisdiction, whereas a conditional appearance would have put them on notice of an
objection, and enabled them at least to consider the institution of proceedings
elsewhere. The case is, however, altogether different, for by the time the plaintiffs'
solicitors wrote their letter of 10th November 1978, and subsequently served the writ,
the claim was already doomed, in the absence of a mistake or indulgence on the part of f
the defendants. Entry of a conditional appearance would not have helped the plaintiffs,
since it was by then too late to commence an action in another jurisdiction. This was the
result of the plaintiffs' own choice, for although they no doubt acted reasonably in
abstaining from proceedings whilst the possibility of a settlement was explored they took
an unnecessary risk in leaving them so late, for there was nothing to prevent them from
taking the usual step of warning the defendants that the proceedings were in the offing g
well within the two-year period, and inviting them to allow an extension of time. If the
Jeddah office had maintained its silence, the plaintiffs could then properly have issued a
writ and served proceedings, whilst continuing to press for a settlement. Instead they
created a situation in which they had conferred on the defendants a vested right under
arts 28 and 29 to be free from all legal proceedings in respect of the claim. The
immunities created by these articles form part of the larger bundle of rights and duties h
created by the convention as between carrier and consignee, and the defendants would
not have been acting unmeritoriously if they had insisted on their enforcement.

The question is, therefore, whether it is just that the defendants should lose their
vested rights simply as a result of their mistake. I do not think that it is. There were
faults on both sides. No doubt the Jeddah and London offices should between them have
given their solicitors better instructions, and the latter should have pressed for more j
information before taking any formal step in the action. Nevertheless, bearing in mind
the short time available for entering an appearance and the fact that the writ did not
identify the transit, it seems to me that the mistake of the person temporarily in charge
of the matter was low on the scale of culpability. I do not consider that a mistake of this
nature should be permitted to deprive the defendants of the valuable right which, as a
result of the plaintiffs' own error of judgment, they had come to possess.

Accordingly, I consider that the master came to the right conclusion, and would dismiss this appeal, save only to the extent that the order should be corrected to eliminate the surplus words which I have already mentioned.

On the view which I have formed, the fifth of the issues listed above does not arise.

Order accordingly.

K Mydeen Esq Barrister.

Appeal

The plaintiffs appealed to the Court of Appeal.

John Roch QC and *Peter Irvin* for the appellants.
Jonathan Mance for the respondents.

ROSKILL LJ. This is an appeal from an interlocutory order made by Mustill J, sitting in chambers, on 17th December 1979. We have had the advantage of a full transcript of the judge's very careful judgment.

The matter came before him on appeal from the master in somewhat unusual circumstances. The dispute arose in form between two plaintiffs, who were respectively the suppliers and purchasers of parcels or cartons of cigarettes sent from London to Amsterdam, and then on from Amsterdam to Jeddah, some of which were lost and other parts of which were damaged in the course of the second part of that transit with Saudi Arabian Airlines, and the airline who, as between themselves and the plaintiffs, were carriers. We were told that there was a sub-charter involved, but that is irrelevant for present purposes.

The dispute is, when viewed realistically, a dispute, as is often the case, between two sets of underwriters, and it gives rise to a somewhat unusual point under art 28 of the Warsaw Convention, which is scheduled to the Carriage by Air Act 1961.

The matter arose in a somewhat unusual way, which adds to the complexities of the case. The plaintiffs issued a writ against the defendants, and as the judge points out, they did so after they had received no response to an earlier letter: they served that writ by post on the defendants' Regent Street office in London on the person who had been nominated to accept service on behalf of the defendants, pursuant to s 407 of the Companies Act 1948. Apparently, it did not immediately occur to the defendants or their advisers that there might be a question under art 28 of the Warsaw Convention whether the defendants were amenable to English jurisdiction in the way in which the plaintiffs alleged by the issue of a writ and by service in that manner, and the defendants' solicitors, it seems, thereupon entered an unconditional appearance. Subsequently it was realised that there was a serious question which ought to be decided: whether or not the defendants were amenable, under art 28, to English jurisdiction, and therefore the defendants sought, properly in those circumstances, to get leave to set aside that unconditional appearance and in place of it to enter a conditional appearance.

The master gave leave so to set aside, and Mustill J dismissed the appeal from the master. A number of points were argued before the judge, but it is conceded that if, on the central point, the judge were right, none of the other points arise. The plaintiffs' case stands or falls on whether they are right and the judge is wrong on what they argue is the true construction of art 28 of the Warsaw Convention.

This precise point does not seem previously to have arisen for decision in this country, although in *Fothergill v Monarch Airlines Ltd* [1979] 3 All ER 445, [1980] QB 23, in this court and before Kerr J at first instance ([1977] 3 All ER 616, [1978] QB 108), this court had to consider, as Kerr J had to consider previously, certain of the problems to which the Warsaw Convention and the Carriage by Air Act 1961 give rise. But although certain problems of construction were there considered by this court, this court did not consider the precise point which we have here, on the true construction of art 28.

Thanks to the industry of solicitors and counsel on both sides, for which we are indebted, a considerable amount of research has been done into the position in other

countries. We have had our attention drawn to a number of decisions in the United States where a similar problem has arisen under art 28 of the Warsaw Convention as *a*
scheduled to the relevant United States legislation. In all of them, so far as I can see, the various courts in different parts of the United States have disclaimed the relevant jurisdiction.

We have also been referred to one interesting French case, and we have been shown, without objection from counsel for the plaintiffs, who has been most co-operative in ensuring that we should see everything which might conceivably be relevant, a number *b*
of telexes which have passed between the defendants' solicitors and various of their agents in other parts of the world, in which they have endeavoured to see what assistance could be derived from decisions in other countries. The search in that direction, however, has not been rewarding.

I venture to question whether much help, as distinct from much interest, can be derived from either the American or the French decisions in question. To my mind, *c*
ultimately I think the question which we have to decide depends on the true construction of art 28 as it is scheduled to the 1961 Act. There is, however, the interesting fact that in the American translation of the French text, as I shall show later, the language used is different from that scheduled to the English Act, a point on which counsel for the plaintiffs very strongly relied. Of course, the French decision was on the French text.

When one looks at the English Act, one finds in s 1 (1) this provision: *d*

> 'Subject to this section, the provisions of the Convention known as "the Warsaw Convention as amended at The Hague, 1955" as set out in the First Schedule to this Act shall, so far as they relate to the rights and liabilities of carriers, carriers' servants and agents, passengers, consignors, consignees and other persons, and subject to the provisions of this Act, have the force of law in the United Kingdom in relation to any carriage by air to which the Convention applies, irrespective of the nationality *e*
> of the aircraft performing that carriage and the Carriage by Air Act, 1932 (which gives effect to the Warsaw Convention in its original form), shall cease to have effect.
>
> '(2) If there is any inconsistency between the text in English in Part I of the First Schedule to this Act and the text in French in Part II of that Schedule, the text in French shall prevail.' [This subsection, so far as my own experience goes, is *f*
> completely new in an English statute.]

Thus we have, and so far as I know this is unique, both the English and French texts being scheduled to the statute, the entirety of the texts in the schedule being given the force of law in the United Kingdom and the provision that in the event of any inconsistency, the French text shall prevail.

Some of the problems to which that provision can give rise were considered by this *g*
court in *Fothergill v Monarch Airlines Ltd* [1979] 3 All ER 445, [1980] QB 23 and both Browne and Geoffrey Lane LJJ appreciated, if I may say so with respect, that that provision could give rise to certain difficulties. For example, Browne LJ said ([1979] 3 All ER 445 at 455, [1980] 1 QB 23 at 42):

> 'It seems to me clear from the dictionaries which are before us . . . that "avarie" is *h*
> a term of art in French law, possibly with different meanings in civil law and maritime law. My knowledge of French is hopelessly inadequate to enable me to decide what "avarie" means in the French language generally, in French law (civil or maritime) or in the context of the French text of this convention. I agree with counsel for the plaintiff that if the defendants wanted to rely on this point they should have called a French lawyer to give expert evidence. Without such evidence, *j*
> I cannot attach any weight to it.'

Geoffrey Lane LJ said ([1979] 3 All ER 445 at 458, [1980] 1 QB 23 at 46–47):

> 'Our atttention was drawn to French definitions of French legal expressions in French dictionaries. Without the assistance of a bilingual expert in French law I found myself unable to understand what if any inconsistency there might be.

Accordingly the problem becomes one of discovering the meaning of the English text as it applies to the facts of this case.'

I do not think it necessary to express any view how a court should approach the problem if and when it has to have recourse to the French text. I begin, as the majority of this court did in *Fothergill's* case, by looking at the English text and I think the right approach to that English text is governed by the views of some, indeed perhaps the majority, of their Lordships in *James Buchanan & Co Ltd v Babco Forwarding and Shipping (UK) Ltd* [1977] 3 All ER 1048, [1978] AC 141. Lord Wilberforce said ([1977] 3 All ER 1048 at 1052, [1978] AC 141 at 152):

> 'The convention of 1956 [ie the Convention on the International Carriage of Goods by Road] is in two languages, English and French, each text being equally authentic. The English text alone appears in the schedule to the 1965 Act [ie the Carriage of Goods by Road Act 1965] and is by that Act (s 1) given the force of law.'

Pausing there, the position is therefore different from the instant case. Lord Wilberforce continued:

> 'Moreover, the contract of carriage seems to have incorporated, contractually, this English text. It might therefore be arguable (though this was not in fact argued), by distinction from a case where the authentic text is, eg, French and the enacted text an English translation, that only the English text ought to be looked at. In my opinion this would be too narrow a view to take, given the expressed objective of the convention to produce uniformity in all contracting states. I think that the correct approach is to interpret the English text which after all is likely to be used by many others than British businessmen, in a normal manner, appropriate for the interpretation of an international convention, unconstrained by technical rules of English law, or by English legal precedent but on broad principles of general acceptation (*Stag Line Ltd v Foscolo, Mango & Co Ltd* [1932] AC 328 at 350, [1931] All ER Rep 666 at 677, per Lord Macmillan). Moreover, it is perfectly legitimate in my opinion to look for assistance, if assistance is needed, to the French text. This is often put in the form that resort may be had to the foreign text if (and only if) the English text is ambiguous, but I think this states the rule too technically.'

Lord Salmon, after reading the relevant words from the English text, said ([1977] 3 All ER 1048 at 1059, [1978] AC 141 at 160):

> 'No doubt these words are flexible and somewhat imprecise; but, especially as they appear in an international convention relating to commercial affairs, they should not be construed pedantically or rigidily but sensibly and broadly.'

I respectfully adopt those two approaches of Lord Wilberforce and Lord Salmon, and I do not find anything in the speeches of the other Law Lords to the contrary effect. Accordingly, I begin by looking at the language of art 28 (1); the judge set this out; it reads thus, and I read the English text:

> 'An action for damages must be brought, at the option of the plaintiff, in the territory of one of the High Contracting Parties, either before the court having jurisdiction where the carrier is ordinarily resident, or has his principal place of business, or has an establishment by which the contract has been made or before the Court having jurisdiction at the place of destination.'

Pausing there for one moment, the English grammar, if one looks at this article pedantically, is far from plain, but it gives a would-be plaintiff at his option four different places where he can sue: first where the carrier is ordinarily resident; second where the carrier has his principal place of business; third where the carrier has an establishment by which the contract has been made; and fourth at the place of destination.

Now the plaintiffs seek to invoke the first of those four places. They do not seek to say that the defendants have their principal place of business in London; they do not seek to say that they have an establishment by which the contract has been made (plainly the contract here was made in Amsterdam and not at the office in Regent Street) and, of course, the destination was in Saudi Arabia, so the fourth option does not apply. The only question here is whether the carrier (that is the defendants) can be said to be 'ordinarily resident' because they have this office in Regent Street in London.

Reliance has been placed before us, as it was placed before the judge, on that well-known group of cases dealing with problems of service on foreign corporations. The judge sets out a number of these cases, and they will be found collected in the notes to RSC Ord 65, r 3. As it happens, Ormrod LJ and I had to consider those cases earlier this week in *Salah v Saudi Catering & Contracting Co Ltd* [1980] Court of Appeal transcript 315 and I do not think it necessary to review them again in this judgment. Their effect is plain: if 'ordinarily resident' in art 28(1) has the meaning for which counsel for the plaintiffs contends, and therefore those cases apply (it is to be noted that those cases speak not of 'ordinarily resident' but of 'resident'), then it is virtually conceded that the defendants were 'resident' or 'ordinarily resident' here. But the central point is this: have those cases or indeed the tax cases to which we have also been referred, any relevance at all, bearing in mind Lord Wilberforce's warning against construing the provisions of a convention by reference to what he called 'the technical rules of English law or English legal precedent'? How much more, if I may say so, does that warning of Lord Wilberforce apply when one is dealing, in those service cases, not so much with technical rules of English substantive law but the technical rules of English procedure regarding service on foreign corporations which carry on business or which can be said to reside within the jurisdiction because they have a place of business or an office of some kind here?

In my judgment, one should look at art 28 (1) without regard to antecedent English decisions in another field. It may be, theoretically I think it is possible, that the four options, as I have called them, given by art 28 might, somewhat exceptionally, coincide, or that any two of them might coincide. Thus, for example, the contract might be made at the carriers' principal place of business, or the place of destination might be a place where the carrier was ordinarily resident, but it is for the plaintiff to select where he wishes to sue, subject to the limitation that he can only sue, as I see it, in one of the four places for which art 28 (1) makes provision.

One is dealing here, not with the question of service as in those English cases, but with the question of jurisdiction. To my mind, and I think the judge took the same view, art 28 creates a self-contained code within the limits of which a plaintiff must found his jurisdiction. He can found that jurisdiction in the courts of the country in any of those four places. As I say, they may be four different places or they may conceivably be the same place.

In the present case it would seem plain that the plaintiffs could have sued in Saudi Arabia; it also seems plain that they could have sued in Holland. But they have sought to sue here on the basis that the existence of the office in Regent Street has the effect that the defendants are 'ordinarily resident' here.

Now that phrase 'ordinarily resident' of course will be found in some of the provisions of RSC Ord 11, but that again brings one back to the technicalities of the English rules of service. More important, after art 28 found its way onto the English statute book under the Carriage by Air Act 1961, RSC Ord 11 was itself amended by adding sub-para (*e*) so as to enable those actions which fell within art 28 to be brought within RSC Ord 11.

For my part, I do not think one finds any guide to the construction of the phrase 'ordinarily resident' in the articles from the English service cases, and I arrive at that conclusion for a number of reasons.

I appreciate the force of the arguments of counsel for the plaintiffs that where one finds the phrase 'ordinarily resident' in other branches of English law, at first sight anyhow, one should give the same meaning to the same phrase in an English statute, but I think that argument loses a great deal of its force when one finds that the context in which this phrase 'ordinarily resident' is used, is the English text of an international convention.

I think there is great force in the point which counsel for the defendants made and
a which I think influenced the judge, that if it were intended that a carrier is 'ordinarily resident' because he has a branch office in a particular place, why are there put, in juxtaposition, the two phrases 'ordinarily resident' and 'principal place of business', because it would have been enough simply to have provided for proceedings to be brought before the court where the carrier is 'ordinarily resident'; instead 'ordinarily resident' is treated as an alternative to the principal place of business. It would be very
b odd, as counsel for the defendants submitted, if 'any place of business' became the 'principal place of business' and I do not see why it would then become necessary to add the provision giving jurisdiction before the court of the place where the contract was made.

I think the true interpretation depends on the fact that this is a self-contained code. The fallacy in the argument of counsel for the plaintiffs seems to me to lie in this: he
c seeks to say that because of the provisions regarding 'ordinarily resident', a would-be plaintiff can sue any foreign corporation in England, irrespective of the provisions of art 28, if that foreign corporation were one against whom he could found jurisdiction under the ordinary English procedural rules illustrated by the provisions of RSC Ord 65, r 3. He is saying that if he can find a foreign corporation which has a branch office here and on which he could serve appropriately because it has that branch office, then that,
d without more ado, makes that foreign corporation 'ordinarily resident' in this country.

So to hold, to my mind, is to apply the technical rules of English procedural law in an alien context where those rules have no logical place at all. Viewing this matter simply as one of the construction of art 28, I find myself in agreement with the judge. I have arrived at that conclusion without reference to the French text of the convention or to the American cases or to the French case to which we have been referred.

e It is of some interest just to look for one moment at the French text. One finds there the French text of the phrase which is translated as 'ordinarily resident', namely 'tribunal du domicile du transporteur aérien'. When one looks at the American cases, one finds that in the relevant American statutory provisions, to which we have been referred, that phrase has been translated differently from the manner in which it has been translated in the English text scheduled to the Carriage by Air Act 1961. I take the text of the
f American statute from the report of *Aronowitch v Air France* in the Supreme Court of Illinois (1978) 383 NE 2d 977. The relevant translation reads:

> 'An action for damages must be brought, at the option of the plaintiff, in the territory of one of the High Contracting Parties, either before the court of the domicile of the carrier or of his principal place of business, or where he has a place of business through which the contract has been made, or before the court at the
> g place of destination.'

Note there that the American translation appears to translate the French word 'domicile' as the same as the technical English word 'domicile'.

So the United States cases to which we have been referred, of which *Aronowitch* is one (and there have been others: *Nudo and Lovering v Sabena* (1962) 207 F Supp 191, *Smith v*
h *Canadian Pacific Airways Ltd* (1971) 452 F 2d 798 and *Karfunkel v Air France* (1977) 427 F Supp 971) all proceed on a text of art 28 which is different from the English text scheduled to the 1961 Act.

Although the conclusions at which the courts in the United States have arrived are in line with the conclusion at which I have arrived, I venture to think that they do not afford a safe guide to the right conclusion in the present case (although they achieve what
j counsel for the defendants claims to be the same desired result), because they are all decisions on a different text.

Similarly, the French case to which we have been referred, *Consorts Tarnay v Varig* (28th April 1978) Tribunal de Grande Instance de Paris (First Chamber, Second Section) turns on the French text and the word 'domicile' to which I have referred. I do not think it necessary to embark in this judgment on the difficult question of the relationship, if that is the right word, between the French word 'domicile' and the English word 'domicile' in its English legal usage, although it is perhaps permissible to say that it is often accepted that those two words in the different languages do not bear the same meaning.

We have been referred to a textbook on Liability on International Air Transport by Madame Georgette Miller, a lady who, we are told, possesses very high professional qualifications, published in New York in August 1977. Page 300, under the rubric 'Ordinary resident and domicile' contains this interesting passage:

> '"Ordinary residence" in the English text and "domicile" in the American text both translate the "domicile" of the French text. There does not appear to have been any case governed by the Warsaw Convention where these notions have been at issue. The reason might be simply that this first ground of jurisdiction seems to be more appropriate for air carriage performed by individuals than for the big corporations which, in fact, perform most of the international carriage by air. This is supported by the drafting history of the provision which reveals that the CITEJA draft did not refer to the carrier's domicile. It was only during the proceedings of the Warsaw Conference, and almost incidentally, that one delegate noted that the principal place of business mentioned in the draft was mainly related to corporations, and that it was necessary to provide a more adequate ground in relation to air carriage performed by individuals. Significant differences exist between the various language versions. According to French law, the domicile of a person is the place where he has his principal residence. The English translation is thus very close to the meaning carried by the French text when it refers to the "ordinary residence" of the carrier. This is not so for the American translation which, by using the word "domicile" refers to a common law concept that is much more rigid than the French concept. Because the domicile of the common law is that place "where a man has his true, fixed and permanent home, and to which, whenever he is absent, he has the intention of returning", a man may change residence many times in the course of his life and retain the same domicile.'

I refer to that interesting passage not because it affords a safe, or indeed any, guide to the solution of the problem with which we are concerned, but because it contains an interesting summary and, I venture to think, a useful warning of the dangers which may arise if one tries to apply the language of the text of other translations to the English text of art 28 which is scheduled alongside the French text in the 1961 Act.

For those reasons, which I have given at some length in deference to the admirable arguments to which we have had the advantage of listening, I would dismiss the appeal.

ORMROD LJ. I have come to the same conclusion. The critical point in this case in my judgment is one of jurisdiction and not a question of the validity of service. If that point is kept firmly in mind some of the difficulties I think disappear.

It is perfectly true that so far as our own jurisdictional rules are concerned, they are much mixed up with our rules as to service, but in this case we are dealing with quite a different problem. In this case the Carriage by Air Act 1961, by incorporating the Warsaw Convention (particularly art 28) has established a code of jurisdiction which is applicable in this country just as much as it is anywhere else. The jurisdictional code is contained in art 28(1) and, as Roskill LJ has already pointed out, it provides four options to the plaintiffs; some of those options in some cases will give a plaintiff a wider opportunity for service than he would have had under our own rules of procedure. So we have to construe the phrase 'ordinarily resident' in that context, a purely jurisdictional context.

In my judgment, counsel for the plaintiffs' argument goes much too far. He says that those words should be construed as they have been construed in a series of cases under RSC Ord 65, r 3, which relate to our own domestic rules as to service; and he says it would be illogical if there were two phrases, or similar phrases, 'ordinarily resident' on the one hand and 'resident' on the other with different meanings. 'Resident' is not actually used in RSC Ord 65, but it has been written into it by a succession of judgments. It would be odd, he says, if this court were to give two different meanings to two such similar phrases. But the circumstances are, in my judgment, quite different.

If he is right in his construction of art 28(1) there is almost no limit to the number of cases which can be started in England by plaintiffs who have nothing whatever to do with this country, concerning accidents or losses which have certainly nothing whatever to do with this country. The airlines would be driven back on the forum conveniens point in order to resist being sued here on claims arising in any part of the world. With great respect to the argument of counsel for the plaintiffs, I cannot think that that is either a sensible or a convenient construction. I think it would indeed be a pedantic one. So I take the view that the plaintiffs in this case cannot show that the defendants are 'ordinarily resident' in this country within the meaning of the section and therefore the action is, as Mustill J held, incompetent.

The only other point that I would make is this: it is worth remembering that the fundamental rule as to jurisdiction in the civil law has always been that the plaintiff sues in the place where the defendant is. The Latin phrase 'forum actus rei' is the old way of expressing it, and in a convention of this kind it would be surprising to find the contracting parties to the convention departing so radically from a concept with which they are familiar and much more so than we are in this country. For those reasons I agree that the appeal must fail.

Appeal dismissed. Leave to appeal to the House of Lords granted.

Solicitors: *Elborne Mitchell & Co* (for the plaintiffs); *Barlow, Lyde & Gilbert* (for the defendants).

Bebe Chua Barrister.

R v Chief Immigration Officer, Gatwick Airport, ex parte Kharrazi

COURT OF APPEAL, CIVIL DIVISION

LORD DENNING MR, WALLER AND DUNN LJJ

30th JUNE, 1st, 9th JULY 1980

Immigration – Leave to enter – Non-patrial – Student – Applicant required to produce to immigration officer proof of acceptance for course of study at school or university – Officer required to refuse entry if not satisfied that applicant would leave United Kingdom on completion of full-time course of study – Full-time course of study – Proof by schoolboy applicant that he was accepted by school for three-year 'O' level course of study – Officer not satisfied that applicant would leave on completion of three-year course because applicant stated that he expected to stay until completion of university study – Refusal by officer to grant applicant leave to enter as a student – Whether officer had interpreted rules correctly – Statement of Changes in Immigration Rules (H C Paper (1979–80) no 394), paras 21, 22.

In 1979 the applicant, a bright 12-year old Iranian boy, was sent by his parents in Iran to school in America, but in 1980, following a change in American policy towards Iranian nationals, he had to leave there. His parents wanted him to continue his education in England and he was accepted by an English public school to do a three-year 'O' level course. On his arrival in the United Kingdom he produced to the immigration officer documents showing that he had been accepted for the 'O' level course at the school and that he had sufficient funds to meet the cost of the course, those being the two

requirements a passenger seeking entry had to meet in order to satisfy para 21[a] of the
immigration rules[b] made under the Immigration Act 1971. He was met at the airport a
by a brother who was studying in England and who planned to remain indefinitely. The
immigration officer interviewed them both and asked them how long the applicant
intended to remain in the United Kingdom. Both told him that the applicant expected
to remain there for up to ten years or as long as it took to complete his secondary
education and go on to university. After considering the applicant's reasons for leaving
America and his family situation, the immigration officer, acting under para 22[c] of the b
rules, refused the applicant leave to enter as a student, on the ground that he was not
satisfied that the applicant intended to leave the country 'on completion' of 'a full-time
course of study'. In so deciding the immigration officer interpreted 'a full-time course
of study' as referring, in relation to the applicant, to the three year 'O' level course for
which he had been accepted and concluded that his answers showed that he did not
intend to leave when that was completed. The applicant applied under RSC Ord 53 for c
judicial review of the immigration officer's decision by way of an order of certiorari to
quash it on the ground that the immigration officer's refusal was unreasonable and
contrary to the immigration rules.

Held – (1) On the true construction of the immigration rules, the 'full-time course of
study' referred to in para 22 was not confined to the 'course of study' mentioned in para
21 for which a prospective entrant had to produce evidence of acceptance, but could d
include (per Lord Denning MR) such full-time course of study as a boy of the applicant's
age might reasonably expect to follow through to its conclusion (ie the attainment of a
degree) even though he had not at that stage been guaranteed a place at a university, or
(per Waller and Dunn LJJ) not only the course of study for which the prospective entrant
had been accepted but a coherent and definite educational proposal of more than one
course of study which was reasonably capable of being carried out by him (see p 378 *g* to e
j, p 382 *a* to *c* and p 383 *g* to *j*, post).

(2) (Waller LJ dissenting) The immigration officer had misinterpreted para 22 by
construing it too narrowly in asking himself whether the applicant intended to leave at
the end of the three-year course rather than whether he intended to leave on the
completion of his expected course of education. In the circumstances the court would
quash the officer's decision and remit the case to him for reconsideration (see p 379 *b*, f
p 380 *b* to *h* and p 383 *j* to p 384 *a* and *d* to *g*, post).

Notes

For the entry of non-patrial students, see 4 Halsbury's Laws (4th Edn) para 984.

For the Immigration Act 1971, ss 1, 3, 4, see 41 Halsbury's Statutes (3rd Edn) 16, 20,
22. g

Cases referred to in judgments

Anisminic Ltd v Foreign Compensation Commission [1969] 1 All ER 208, [1969] 2 AC 147, [1969] 2 WLR 163, HL, Digest (Cont Vol C) 281, *2557b*.

Company, Re a [1980] 1 All ER 284, [1980] 2 WLR 241, CA; *on appeal* sub nom *Re Racal Communications Ltd* [1980] 2 All ER 634, [1980] 3 WLR 181, HL.

Gilmore's Application, Re [1957] 1 All ER 796, sub nom *R v Medical Appeal Tribunal, ex* h
parte Gilmore [1957] 1 QB 574, [1957] 2 WLR 498, CA, 16 Digest (Repl) 482, *3016*.

Pearlman v Keepers and Governors of Harrow School [1979] 1 All ER 365, [1979] QB 56, [1978] 3 WLR 736, 38 P & CR 136, CA, Digest (Cont Vol E) 125, *4476a*.

R v Governor of Pentonville Prison, ex parte Azam [1973] 2 All ER 741, [1974] AC 18, [1973] 2 WLR 949, CA; *affd* [1973] 2 All ER 765, [1974] AC 18, [1973] 2 WLR 1058, 137 JP
626, HL, Digest (Cont Vol D) 24, *101g*. j

R v London Borough of Hillingdon, ex parte Royco Homes Ltd [1974] 2 All ER 643, [1974] 1 QB 720, [1974] 2 WLR 805, 38 JP 505, 72 LGR 516, 28 P & CR 251, DC, Digest (Cont Vol D) 268, *2835d*.

---

a Paragraph 21 is set out at p 375 *j* to p 376 *a*, post

b Statement of Changes in Immigration Rules (HC Paper (1979–80) no 394)

c Paragraph 22 is set out at p 376 *b c*, post

R v Secretary of State for the Home Department, ex parte Hosenball [1977] 3 All ER 452, [1977] 1 WLR 766, 141 JP 626, CA, 2 Digest (Reissue) 214, *1224*.

Cases also cited

Attorney General (on the relation of McWhirter) v Independent Broadcasting Authority [1973] 1 All ER 689, [1973] QB 629, CA.

Liversidge v Anderson [1941] 3 All ER 338, [1942] AC 206, HL.

R v Immigration Appeals Adjudicator, ex parte Perween Khan [1972] 3 All ER 297, [1972] 1 WLR 1058, DC.

R v Lympne Airport Chief Immigration Officer, ex parte Amrik Singh [1968] 3 All ER 163, [1969] 1 QB 333, DC.

R v Secretary of State for the Home Department, ex parte Mughal [1973] 3 All ER 796, [1974] QB 313, CA.

Appeal

The applicant, Khashayar Kharrazi, by his brother and next friend Dariush Kharrazi, applied to the Divisional Court of the Queen's Bench Division for leave to apply for a judicial review by way of (i) an order of certiorari to remove into the court and to quash a decision dated 16th May 1980 by the respondent, the Chief Immigration Officer at Gatwick Airport, to refuse the applicant leave to enter the United Kingdom, and (ii) an order of mandamus directing the respondent to reconsider the case of the applicant in accordance with the law and rules applicable and to direct that the applicant be given leave to enter the United Kingdom. On 6th June 1980 the Divisional Court (Donaldson LJ and Woolf J) refused to give him leave to apply for a judicial review. The applicant applied to the Court of Appeal for leave. On 13th June 1980 the court (Lord Denning MR, Waller and Dunn LJJ) gave him leave and ordered that the hearing be expedited and heard in the Court of Appeal. The facts are set out in the judgment of Lord Denning MR.

Charles Fletcher-Cooke QC and *K S Nathan* for the applicant.
Simon Brown for the respondent.

Cur adv vult

9th July. The following judgments were read.

LORD DENNING MR.

1 Entry for education

To be educated in England is an advantage. It is much sought after. For many years parents in countries overseas have sent their children here to be educated. If they can afford it. They have sent their sons and daughters to our public schools and on to our universities. On finishing here, they have returned to their own countries, often to exercise much influence there, for good. The most distinguished being Jawaharlal Nehru of Harrow and Trinity College, Cambridge. Many have been called to the English Bar and gone back to be prime ministers and judges. Even revolutionaries. Such as Mahatma Gandhi. Some to Sandhurst, and have gone back to become generals and heads of military governments. Like Ayub Khan. Successive Home Secretaries have recognised the value of this beneficent service to the world. Under the immigration rules, we freely admit boys, and girls, of school age whose parents wish them to be educated here and can afford the expense, on the understanding that, when their education is completed, they will return to their home countries. This freedom of education is ensured by the special provisions relating to the entry of students. They are contained in the Statement of Changes in Immigration Rules (HC Paper (1979–80) no 394). We have today to consider their interpretation. Rules 21 and 22 provide:

> '21. A passenger seeking entry to study in the United Kingdom should be admitted (subject to paragraph 13) if he presents a current entry clearance granted for that purpose. An entry clearance will be granted if the applicant produces evidence which satisfies the entry clearance officer that he has been accepted for a

course of study at a university, a college of education or further education, an independent school or any bona fide private educational institution; that the course will occupy the whole or a substantial part of his time; and that he can, without working and without recourse to public funds, meet the cost of the course and of his own maintenance and accommodation and that of any dependants during the course.

'22. An applicant is to be refused an entry clearance as a student if the entry clearance officer is not satisfied that the applicant is able, and intends, to follow a full-time course of study and to leave the country on completion of it. In assessing the case the officer should consider such points as whether the applicant's qualifications are adequate for the course he proposes to follow, and whether there is any evidence of sponsorship by his home government or any other official body. As a general rule an entry clearance is not to be granted unless the applicant proposes to spend not less than 15 hours a week in organised daytime study of a single subject or of related subjects, and is not to be granted for the taking of a correspondence course.'

2 *The young Iranian boy*

Iran is much in the news. So are Iranian nationals. Here is a young boy who seems to have been caught up in the interchanges of nations. He is Khashayar Kharrazi. He was born in Iran on 3rd April 1967. So he is just 13. His father and mother are in Iran where his father is the executive manager of a big agricultural concern. They are very well off. They have three other sons. They have sent all their sons to the United States or England for their education. One of them went to the United States and qualified in computer engineering. He has returned to Iran to work. Another is studying in the United States, doing a course in aerospace programming. Yet another is studying in England and is doing a course for the Higher National Diploma. The fourth and youngest is our present applicant, Khashayar.

When Khashayar was just 12, in June 1979, his mother took him to the United States and enrolled him at a junior high school in Tucson, Arizona. His teacher there gives him a first-class report showing that he has done exceedingly well. His mother had originally entered him as a 'visitor' to the United States, but, after the overthrow of the Shah, the American authorities gave a general permission to Iranian nationals to stay. Later on, when the hostages were imprisoned in Tehran, the American policy changed towards Iranian nationals. Things were so uncomfortable there for this young boy that the family decided to bring him over to England for his education if suitable arrangements could be made. His mother and father had already gone back to Iran. So his brothers did everything. They made inquiries of the British Consul in Los Angeles and of the Home Office in London. They were told that, as long as he had a course and sufficient funds available for his maintenance, he would be granted leave to enter as a student. (That seems to be a convenient summary of paras 21 and 22.) The family arranged for him to be enrolled as a student at one of our smaller public schools, Pierrepont School, Frensham, Farnham, Surrey. The headmaster gave a certificate that—

> 'Khashayar Kharrazi has enrolled and has been accepted to start a three year "O" Level course at Pierrepont School as a boarding student with effect from 1st September 1980.'

Everything being then in order for England, the family arranged for him to be granted voluntary departure from the United States. It was done. His belongings were packed up. His flight booked. All papers got in order so as to show his good faith. His brother Dariush was to meet him at Gatwick, and get him settled in.

3 *Gatwick, 16th May 1980*

On 16th May 1980 the boy arrived at Gatwick airport. An immigration officer, Mr Ladd, interviewed him. The boy was only just 13 but he answered well and produced all his papers. They showed excellent credentials. This is the account given by the immigration officer of the interview:

> 'The Applicant was interviewed throughout in English which he spoke well and
> a there were no language difficulties. I asked the Applicant how long he wished to stay in the United Kingdom. He replied that he wanted leave to enter for 1 year as a student and said that he expected to remain in the United Kingdom for up to 10 years so as to complete his education, taking "O" levels, "A" levels and going on to University.'

The immigration officer then examined his papers. They showed he had ample
b means of support. He had a banker's draft for £1,071·21. He had a letter from Williams & Glyn's Bank showing that his brother here had a credit of £12,000. He had the certificate of enrolment at Pierrepont School for three years. He had a warm letter of support from a well-placed English resident at Camberley saying: '... My wife and I will also be taking more than a passing interest in his well being, both socially and as regards education.'

c After questioning the young boy, the immigration officer then saw his brother Dariush who had come to meet him. He was accompanied by his English young lady whom he expected to marry. The immigration officer asked the brother how long he expected the young boy to remain in England. The brother answered: 'Up to ten years or as long as it takes to complete his education.' The immigration officer consulted his senior. They then told him that the boy was refused entry. They served a notice on the
d boy on 16th May 1980 in these words:

> 'Mr Khashayar KHARRAZI You have asked for leave to enter the United Kingdom as a student but I am not satisfied that you intend to leave the United Kingdom when your studies are completed. I therefore refuse you leave to enter the United Kingdom. I have given directions for your removal to Tehran.'

e Note the word 'studies' in that letter. The brother took that as meaning the completion of his studies at school and university. The brother told the immigration officer that he was prepared to give a bond so as to guarantee that the boy would leave after completion of his studies. But the immigration officer told him that our law in the United Kingdom does not authorise him to accept such bonds.

Having thus refused the boy entry, the immigration officer went off to make
f arrangements for the boy to be sent on the first available flight to Tehran. And he would have gone, but for the intervention of the law. The brother at once went to solicitors. They telephoned to the immigration officer saying that they were applying to the court. On that intimation the immigration officer allowed the boy to be temporarily admitted without prejudice to the position (see the Immigration Act 1971, Sch 2, para 21).

g It so happened that three days later the authorities here put a brake on the entry of Iranian nationals into this country. They could not enter except with a visa. But that did not apply to this boy. Under the immigration rules, as I read them, he ought to have been admitted.

4 *The application for judicial review*

h According to the statute, the boy has a right of appeal to an adjudicator, but *not* 'so long as he is in the United Kingdom'. In order to appeal, the boy would have to go (as ordered) to Iran and to appeal from there (see s 13(1) and (3) of the Immigration Act 1971). This would have been disastrous for the boy's future for several reasons. One is that it would take a long time for the boy's appeal to be heard by an adjudicator. Another is that the appeal would have to be decided on paper. The boy would not be present to speak for
j himself. His appeal might not be heard for months. So that his schooling would be gravely interrupted. And on the latest information, the Iranian law now forbids a student to leave Iran under the age of 18 years. So once back in Iran any hope for his education in England was gone.

In this parlous situation, on 20th May application was made to the Divisional Court for judicial review. The application was made by his brother as his next friend. It was made on the grounds that the refusal of the immigration officer was unreasonable and contrary

to the immigration rules. The Divisional Court refused the application without giving
any reasons. It was renewed before us. We asked for the attendance of the immigration a
authorities. Then for the first time the immigration officer made an affidavit. This
disclosed a new state of affairs. You will remember that the notice refusing entry said:
'I am not satisfied that you intend to leave the United Kingdom when *your studies* are
completed.' The boy, his brother and we ourselves had all assumed that this meant when
he had finished his full-time education, at school and university. But the affidavit of the
immigration officer shows that he interpreted the rule as meaning that he had to intend b
to leave for good as soon as the course at Pierrepont School was completed; and, that as
he intended to go on from school to the university, if he could get in, he was to be refused
entry.

5 The reasoning of the immigration officer

The reasoning of the immigration officer is so important that I will set it out in full: c

> 'I then considered the matter in the light of the Immigration rules then applicable,
> paragraphs 21–24 of the Statement of Changes in Immigration Rules, HC394. It
> appeared that the Applicant had been accepted for a course of study for "O" levels
> and had the financial means to follow the course. *However both the Applicant and his
> brother had indicated that the Applicant's intentions were not limited to the three year course
> and it was evident that he expected to stay in the United Kingdom for up to 10 years or* d
> *more.* He had been required to leave the United States of America and had stated
> that this was because of failure to comply with United States immigration rules. He
> was not without family in the United Kingdom and this situation was likely to
> continue since it appeared that his brother would be seeking to remain
> indefinitely. *Taking all these things together I could not be satisfied that the Applicant
> intended to leave the United Kingdom on completion of his course of study.* I discussed this e
> matter with Chief Immigration Officer S. Woods and with his authority I refused
> the Applicant leave to enter.' (Emphasis mine.)

To my mind that reasoning is only capable of one interpretation: the immigration
officer regards his course of study as being the three-year course. In order to gain entry,
the boy must intend to leave this country for good at the end of his three-year course at
Pierrepont School; and that, as he did not intend to do so, but to go on to the university f
if he could, he had to be refused entry. If this interpretation of the rules be correct, it
means that every boy or girl coming to England, to go to a public school, hoping to go
on to a university, will have to be refused entry. He can only be admitted if he intends
to leave this country for good, not for a holiday, at the end of his public school course,
without going to a university. Such a rule would exclude all the most promising students
who seek to come to England. All of them want to go to the university if they can. g

6 The interpretation of the rules

I can understand the way the immigration officer looked at the rules. He thought that
the words 'a full-time course of study' in para 22 referred back to 'a course of study' in
para 21. That is a possible interpretation but it is a narrow interpretation. So narrow
indeed, and so unjust and unfair that I think it should be rejected. The words 'a full-time h
course of study' in para 22 should be interpreted as meaning 'a full-time course of study'
such as a boy of his age can reasonably expect to follow through to its completion, that
is, to the attainment of a degree, even though he has not yet been guaranteed or accepted
for a place at a university. If he is able and intends to follow such a course, and to leave
for good at the end of it, he comes within para 24. He may be admitted for an
appropriate period depending on the length of the course of study and on his means. j
That fits in well with para 97. The appropriate period might only be for one year. He
should then apply for extensions from time to time under para 98 and they will be
granted to him so long as he is going on with his studies and intends to leave at the end
of them.

There is a sentence in para 24 which enables an immigration officer to admit 'for a
short period' but that is directed to cases where a student comes without sufficient means

to carry him through, or without having been actually enrolled for a course of study at
a a college or school. He can be admitted for a short period so as to enable him to
overcome those difficulties. But that does not apply to this case.

7 The misdirection by the immigration officer

In my opinion, therefore, the immigration officer misdirected himself in point of
law. He did not interpret para 22 correctly. He gave it too narrow an interpretation and
b for that reason refused this boy entry. What then is to be done? Can the immigration
officer's refusal be quashed by the court? Or is the court powerless? Must the boy be
sent to Iran and appeal from there to an adjudicator?

The procedure for judicial review is now governed by RSC Ord 53. The first question
is this: is an immigration officer 'a person or body against whom relief may be granted
by way of an order of mandamus or certiorari?' To my mind he is. He acts under a
c power conferred on him by Parliament to give or refuse leave to enter (see s 4(1) of the
1971 Act). He is bound to apply the rules made by the Secretary of State under the
authority of the statute (see ss 1(4) and 3(2) of the Act). Being a public officer bound to
apply statutory rules, he is amenable to the prerogative writs or, in modern terms,
amenable to judicial review.

The next question is whether this is a case where mandamus or certiorari will lie. If
d the immigration officer had been entrusted with a discretion, and the complaint was
only of the manner of its exercise, then it would not lie: see *R v Secretary of State for the
Home Department, ex parte Hosenball* [1977] 3 All ER 452, [1977] 1 WLR 766. But, if the
immigration officer interprets the rules wrongly, and on that account asks himself the
wrong question, and thus gives the wrong answer to those dependent on it, he does
something which he is not empowered to do. He acts ultra vires. That is made clear by
e the important observations of Lord Diplock in *Re Racal Communications Ltd* [1980] 2 All
ER 634 at 638–639, [1980] 3 WLR 181 at 186–187. These do away with long-standing
distinctions between errors within the jurisdiction and errors without it, by the simple
device which was adumbrated in *Pearlman v Keepers and Governors of Harrow School*
[1979] 1 All ER 365, [1979] QB 56. No administrative tribunal or administrative
authority has jurisdiction to make an error of law on which the decision of the case
f depends. The House said in *Re Racal Communications Ltd* that we were wrong to apply
that concept to the High Court; but left it intact with regard to administrative tribunals
and other administrative authorities. Meaning thereby, as I understand it, all statutory
tribunals and authorities other than the regular courts of law. Even if the statute makes
the decision 'final and conclusive' (*Re Gilmore's Application* [1957] 1 All ER 796, [1957] 1
QB 574) or 'not [to] be called in question in any court' (*Anisminic Ltd v Foreign Compensation
g Commission* [1969] 1 All ER 208, [1969] 2 AC 147) or, what is the same thing, 'not
appealable', nevertheless, so far as administrative tribunals and authorities are concerned,
that exemption is only given on condition that they interpret their rules, and thus their
power, rightly. If it should appear that they make an error of law on which their
decision depends, they do that which they have no jurisdiction to do. 'No jurisdiction'
means 'no power'. They act ultra vires. This approach renders it unnecessary to inquire
h whether there is, or is not, error on the face of the record; nor to inquire what is the
record and what is not. Such bodies have no record as the courts of law have. Suffice it
that it is shown, to the satisfaction of the court, that they have misinterpreted the statute
or the rules under which they are empowered to act. By that very misinterpretation they
go outside their power. Their decision must be quashed.

Incidentally I would make this comment: although we were wrong, according to the
j House of Lords, in *Pearlman v Keepers and Governors of Harrow School* [1979] 1 All ER 365,
[1979] QB 56, and in *Re a Company* [1980] 2 All ER 284, [1980] 2 WLR 241, nevertheless
we did clear up the legal position. We did give guidance to the judges below as to the
way in which the statute in question should be interpreted. Whereas the House of Lords
gave no guidance. They left every judge to do as he liked. Each one could interpret the
statute as he wished, according to the length of his foot, and no one could correct him.
So no one in the profession could advise his client how to act. What a state of affairs!

All that I have just said is, however, subject to this qualification. If there is a convenient remedy by way of appeal to an adjudicator, then certiorari may be refused; and the applicant left to his remedy by way of appeal. But it has been held on countless occasions that the availability of appeal does not debar the court from quashing an order by prerogative writs, either of habeas corpus (see *R v Governor of Pentonville Prison, ex parte Azam* [1973] 2 All ER 741 at 750, [1974] AC 18 at 31) or certiorari (see *R v London Borough of Hillingdon, ex parte Royco Homes Ltd* [1974] 2 All ER 643, [1974] 1 QB 720). It depends on the circumstances of each case. In this present case the remedy by way of appeal is useless. This boy's education, indeed, his whole future, will be ruined if he is sent off by aeroplane to Tehran. Rather than his future be ruined, it is better to quash the refusal; and let the Home Secretary reconsider the case.

8 *Applied to this case*

The immigration officer misdirected himself on the interpretation of the rule. He asked himself the wrong question. As he interpreted the rule, he asked himself: 'Does this boy intend to leave the country for good at the end of his three-year course at Pierrepont School?' The answer was plainly: 'No. He intends to stay on in this country, and go on to the university if he can.' Owing to asking himself that wrong question, the immigration officer refused him leave to enter. But, if the immigration officer had asked himself the right question, he would have asked himself: 'Does this boy intend to leave this country for good as soon as he has completed his expected course of study, at school and university?' If the immigration officer had asked himself that question, he would, I should have thought, on the evidence before him, have answered it in this way: 'The boy says himself that, after he gets his degree, he intends to go back to Iran. His brother (who is here) confirmed it. The brother offers a bond to show their good faith. One of his brothers has gone back there already. We should give them credit for good intentions.' On that evidence, the immigration officer should have been satisfied of the present intention of the boy and should allow him to come in.

There is, moreover, another way in which the immigration officer went wrong. As counsel for the applicant submitted to us, the rules require the immigration officer to look at the *present* intention of the applicant, *subjectively*, not to his *future* intention, *objectively*. Here the immigration officer seems to have asked himself: 'Am I satisfied that this boy *will* leave, or is *likely* to leave, at the end of his course of study?' That is shown by the phrase he used, 'this situation was likely to continue'. That, too, was the wrong question, and resulted in the wrong answer. If he had asked himself the right question: 'What is the boy's present intention?', he might well have been satisfied and allowed him to enter.

Seeing that the immigration officer has asked himself the wrong question, I think his refusal should be quashed. The Home Secretary should consider the case afresh and decide whether he should be given leave to enter or not. I hope he will give him leave for one year anyway; and then extend it if proper. Who knows? If this young boy is admitted here, he may do brilliantly; he may go back to Iran and become a leader in that troubled country. I would give him that chance. I would allow this appeal.

WALLER LJ. Khashayar Kharrazi, whom I will call 'the applicant', is an Iranian citizen and he is aged 13. He went to the United States with his parents in June 1979, and went to school there in Arizona. As a result first of the fall of the Shah and secondly of the taking of the American hostages, the policy of the United States towards Iranians in the United States changed. I do not at this stage go into the details of that save to say that the applicant agreed voluntarily to leave the country before 28th June. His brother who was in the United Kingdom made arrangements for him to go to his school at Farnham to do an 'O' level course of three years commencing in September 1980. Inquiries had been made from the Home Office and his brother understood that provided sufficient funds were available the applicant would be granted leave to enter as a student. On 16th May 1980 the applicant arrived at Gatwick airport, applied for leave to enter as a student and after being interviewed by an immigration officer was refused

leave. The refusal stated: 'You have asked for leave to enter the United Kingdom as a
a student but I am not satisfied that you intend to leave the United Kingdom when your studies are completed.' The applicant now applies for judicial review of that decision with the leave of this court.

The applicant had a letter showing that his brother had considerable funds in this country and the immigration officer then saw his brother. The brother was a final year student doing a National Diploma course at Farnborough Technical College and who had
b been in the country six years and was accompanied by a United Kingdom citizen, Miss Price, his fiancée. The brother was intending to reside in the United Kingdom after marriage. The brother told the immigration officer that the applicant would be likely to remain in the United Kingdom for ten years or as long as it took to complete his education. The immigration officer in his affidavit sets out fully an account of his interview with the applicant and in particular dealing with the applicant's explanation
c of the reasons for leaving the United States. The applicant asserted that the only reason was to continue his education in the United Kingdom, but when asked why he had been ordered to leave the United States he said it was because of immigration regulations. The immigration officer, after considering the matter in the light of the immigration rules, refused the applicant leave to enter in the terms which I have already set out. I will come to the details of his reasoning hereafter.

d The paragraphs of the statement of immigration rules which apply to this case are paras 21 to 24 of HC Paper (1979–80) no 394. Paragraph 21 sets out the conditions under which an entry clearance should be granted. They are: (1) evidence of acceptance for a course of study; (2) that it is whole time; (3) that he has funds for his maintenance and accommodation. Paragraph 22 requires the immigration officer to refuse an entry clearance as a student if he is not satisfied of either of two things, namely: (1) that the
e applicant is able and intends to follow a full-time course of study; and (2) that the applicant intends to leave the country on completion of it. Paragraph 23 has no application to this case. Paragraph 24, in the first part, states that a passenger may be admitted who satisfies the requirements I have already set out, and, in the second part, gives a discretion to the immigration officer to admit somebody who he is satisfied has genuine and realistic intentions of studying for a short period to enable further
f consideration of the case. In my opinion para 24 does not arise if the applicant has been refused an entry clearance because of either of the bars set out in para 22. In other words, if the immigration officer is not satisfied that the applicant intends to follow a full-time course and is able to do so, or is not satisfied that the applicant is able and intends to leave the country on completion of the course, he must refuse an entry clearance.

In order to succeed in this case the applicant must show that the immigration officer's
g conclusion was one to which no reasonable immigration officer could come on the evidence, or that in some other respect the decision was wrong in point of law. It has not been argued that no reasonable officer could come to this conclusion. The point of law depends in part on the construction of paras 21 and 22. In para 21 an entry clearance has to be granted if the applicant produces evidence 'that he has been accepted for a course of study at a university, a college of education etc'. And in para 22 an applicant is to be
h refused if the officer is not satisfied that the applicant 'is able and intends to follow a full-time course of study and to leave the country on completion of it'. Do the words 'a full-time course of study' refer to the course of study at a university etc, mentioned in para 21, or do they have a wider, and if so what, other meaning? Were it not for the consequences of the strict interpretation, I would have come to the conclusion that the words 'course of study' in para 22 mean the same as 'course of study' in para 21.
j However, such a construction would lead to rather surprising results. A boy coming to the United Kingdom planning to go to school and then to university here, even if those plans were fairly clearly fixed, would not be allowed entry because his course at school would terminate and he would have to have an intention to return to his native country. If he intended to go on to university, that would be contrary to the intention and therefore he would have to be refused admission. On the other hand a more liberal construction might involve the admission of applicants as students who had rather vague

plans for courses, one following another, and the intention of the rules would be frustrated. Is the true construction somewhere between these two extremes? Rule 98, which deals with variation of leave to enter or remain, states that 'an extension should be refused if there is reason to believe that the student does not intend to leave at the end of his studies'. That is a wider phrase than is used in para 21 or para 22. In my judgment, the phrase 'full-time course of study' in para 22 is not restricted to precisely the course of study in para 21. On the other hand it does not mean that an intention to do more than one course is necessarily covered by the phrase 'full-time course of study'. A full-time course of study, in my opinion, could include more than one course, provided that they were specific parts of a coherent whole. In other words, arrangements to go to a preparatory school followed by a public school might well be a full-time course of study. They would require separate arrangements but they would be part of a coherent whole. Furthermore, perhaps school followed by university might be a coherent course, but that would depend on the facts, on the ability of the individual and so on. I have come to this conclusion with some hesitation but, on the facts as I now consider them, whether that view is right or whether a restrictive interpretation should be given does not matter in this case.

The immigration officer in his affidavit said this:

> 'It appeared that the Applicant had been accepted for a course of study for "O" levels and had the financial means to follow the course. However, both the Applicant and his brother had indicated that the Applicant's intentions were not limited to the three-year course and it was evident that he expected to stay in the United Kingdom for up to 10 years or more.'

The immigration officer clearly, if it were the strict construction that had to be adopted, was coming to the conclusion that the requirements were not met. But he did not stop there; he went on to consider the reasons for leaving the United States; he went on to consider the fact that there was family in the United Kingdom; he had already set out in detail the circumstances of his brother in the United Kingdom and then he said, at the end of the paragraph: 'Taking all these things together I could not be satisfied that the Applicant intended to leave the United Kingdom on completion of his course of study.' There the immigration officer is following the precise words of para 22. If the immigration officer had been confining himself to the strict construction, he would have not gone further than his first statement, but the fact that he went on and took these other matters into consideration shows, in my view, that he was giving a more liberal construction to the words. Accordingly, in my judgment, the applicant fails to show that there was any error of law in the decision of the immigration officer.

If I had come to the conclusion that the immigration officer had wrongly construed the immigration rules, I would have been in favour of granting the application and of setting the immigration officer's decision aside. Since I am dissenting from Lord Denning MR and Dunn LJ (whose judgment I have seen in advance), I ought to state my view of the effect of granting the application for judicial review. This is not a case of a patrial or of some other person with a qualified right to enter. The applicant is an Iranian citizen and by s 3(1)(*a*) of the Immigration Act 1971, 'he shall not enter the United Kingdom unless given leave to do so in accordance with this Act'. To say that the refusal was made because of an error of law does not give the applicant a right to enter and this court has no power to grant leave to enter. In my opinion the applicant would be in the situation of an alien asking for leave to enter as a student. He has not been granted leave to enter and he would not have been refused if the refusal was wrong in law. It would be for the Secretary of State to ensure that the applicant's case is reconsidered, applying the right principles.

On the view I take these questions do not arise. I have come to the conclusion that this application fails and should be refused. I should add, however, that on this view there are, I think, certain matters which would merit the consideration of the Secretary of State in this particular case. They are these: (1) The applicant came here as a result of

information given to his brother by the Home Office on the one hand and as a result of
a information given by the British Consul in Los Angeles on the other. That information was that he would be admitted as a student to do the studies which had been arranged. (2) Because of that information the applicant arrived here although he had not then obtained entry clearance. (3) In the ordinary way a refusal would mean that an applicant would have to return to his native country and appeal to an adjudicator. In this case however there is information before this court that if the applicant returns to Iran he will
b not be allowed to leave until he is aged 18. In effect, therefore, the applicant is deprived of a right of appeal. This was something which the immigration officer perhaps did not know. (4) It is also possible that there was some misunderstanding in the mind of the immigration officer about the position of the applicant vis-à-vis the American immigration authorities. It may have appeared to the immigration officer that the applicant was not being entirely frank with the American authorities, whereas there is
c before this court an affidavit setting out more fully the situation under American law which could possibly lead to a different conclusion. I emphasise that it is possible; I do not suggest that it necessarily was an important part. These matters are only matters which might be considered by the Secretary of State and do not affect my view that there was no error in law in the immigration officer's decision.

d **DUNN LJ.** If paras 21 and 22 of the immigration rules contained in HC Paper (1979–80) no 394 stood alone in a statute I would feel bound to hold that the words 'full-time course of study' in the first sentence of para 22 referred to the course of study for which the applicant had produced evidence that he had been accepted under para 21, whatever the consequences of that might be. But these rules do not fall to be construed as a statute. They have to be construed by busy immigration officers at all the ports of
e entry. They have to be construed in the light of their intention which clearly is to afford entry to bona fide students who come here for the purpose of their education and studies, and who can support themselves so long as they are here. They also have to be read as a whole. Paragraphs 97 to 99 relate to applications by students to extend their leave for the purpose of continuing their studies, and show that when considering such applications the immigration officer may look beyond the particular course of studies for which the
f applicant was granted leave to stay, and only refuse leave if he has reason to believe that the student does not intend to leave at the end of his extended course of studies.

If a narrow construction is put on the words 'full-time course of study' in the first sentence of para 22, it would mean that a student who came here having been accepted for an initial course of study, but who honestly told the immigration officer that it was his intention to remain if possible for a further course of study, could never obtain
g entry. Whereas if he falsely told the immigration officer he intended to leave on completion of his first course of study, or if he changed his mind, he could be granted leave and then apply for an extension. This seems to me to put a premium on dishonesty and I cannot believe that it was the intention of the rules.

Indeed counsel for the immigration authorities does not seriously suggest that it was. He suggests that the words 'full-time course of study' in the first sentence of para 22
h should not be confined to the course of study for which the applicant has been accepted, but should be given a somewhat wider meaning, so as to include not only that course but also a coherent definite educational proposal reasonably capable in the view of the immigration officer of being carried out by the applicant. The longer the initial course the more difficult it would be for the applicant to satisfy the immigration officer that he has a sufficiently definite educational proposal extending beyond it, so that the
j immigration officer can be satisfied that the applicant intends to leave the country on completion of his total course of studies.

I accept the submission of counsel for the immigration authorities as to the meaning of the words 'full-time course of study' in para 22. The question remains whether in refusing entry the immigration officer in this case adopted that meaning or the narrower meaning to which I have referred above. If he adopted the latter, then he erred in law and his decision cannot stand. His reasoning is set out in his affidavit of 27th June 1980. It is true that he refers to the fact the applicant failed to comply with the immigration rules of the United States of America, and to his family circumstances in this country, as indications that he did not intend to leave the country on completion of his course of studies. But in his affidavit he says:

> 'However both the applicant and his brother had indicated that the Applicant's intentions were not limited to the three year course and it was evident that he expected to stay in the United Kingdom for up to 10 years or more.'

The reference to staying in the United Kingdom for up to ten years or more is referable to an earlier passage in the affidavit when Mr Ladd said:

> 'I asked the Applicant how long he wished to stay in the United Kingdom. He replied he wanted leave to enter for 1 year as a student and said that he expected to remain in the United Kingdom for up to 10 years so as to complete his education, taking "O" levels, "A" levels, and going on to University.'

And in a passage of the affidavit further on the immigration officer said:

> 'When I asked [the applicant's brother] how long he expected the Applicant to remain in the United Kingdom, he said that the period would be up to 10 years or as long as it took to complete his education.'

Although an affidavit of this kind is not to be construed too strictly, those passages indicate to me that the question to which the immigration officer was applying his mind was whether the applicant intended to leave this country on completion of the three-year course of study for which he had been accepted, and as the applicant frankly said he expected to remain here for up to ten years to complete his education the immigration officer refused him entry. He did not apply his mind to the question whether the applicant intended to remain after completion of his full course of education. In that approach I think the immigration officer erred in law.

In reaching that conclusion I attach no blame whatever to the immigration officer. Counsel for the respondent told us that he was instructed to put forward the strict or narrow construction of para 22 as being the correct construction, and it is not unreasonable to assume that it is that narrow construction that has hitherto been generally accepted by the Home Office and immigration officers as being correct. Indeed, as I have already said, it was at first my own reaction, until I realised the full implications of such construction and saw paras 97 to 99. And I can well understand why the immigration officer approached the matter in the way in which he did. However, for the reasons I have given, his decision cannot stand. I too would allow the appeal, but I agree with Waller LJ that this does not mean that the applicant is now entitled as of right to enter as a student, and I would welcome the submissions of counsel as to the appropriate form of order so that his application can be reconsidered in the light of the principles enunciated by this court.

Appeal allowed. Decision of immigration officer quashed. Case remitted to Chief Immigration Officer at Gatwick.

Solicitors: *Donald Nelson & Co* (for the applicant); *Treasury Solicitor*.

Sumra Green Barrister.

a Re Holliday (a bankrupt), ex parte the trustee of the bankrupt v The bankrupt and another

COURT OF APPEAL, CIVIL DIVISION
b BUCKLEY, GOFF LJJ AND SIR DAVID CAIRNS
8th, 9th, 10th, 11th, 12th OCTOBER, 5th DECEMBER 1979
BUCKLEY LJ AND SIR DAVID CAIRNS
8th, 9th MAY 1980

Bankruptcy – Property available for distribution – Matrimonial home – Home held by husband
c *and wife on trust for sale for themselves in equal shares – Exercise of court's discretion to execute trust for sale – Husband and wife divorced – Wife remaining in matrimonial home with three young children of marriage – Husband declared bankrupt on own petition on same day wife applying in divorce proceedings for property transfer order – Wife having no capital and receiving social security allowance – Application by trustee in bankruptcy for order directing sale of house – Whether court should exercise discretion by refusing to order sale – Whether wife's*
d *need to provide home for herself and children should prevail over trustee's need to realise husband's share in house for benefit of creditors – Whether husband's filing of bankruptcy petition to frustrate wife's claim for property transfer order an abuse of process of court – Law of Property Act 1925, s 30 – Matrimonial Causes Act 1973, s 24(1).*

The husband and wife married in 1962 and had three children, all of whom were still
e under the age of 15. In 1970 the husband and wife bought a three-bedroom house for the purpose of providing a matrimonial home. The house was conveyed to them on a trust for sale as joint tenants. The marriage broke down and in 1974 the husband left the wife for another woman, whom he subsequently married. The wife and children remained in the house. The wife petitioned for divorce on the ground of adultery and sought custody of the children and a property adjustment order. She was granted a
f divorce in 1975 and on 3rd March 1976 gave notice of her intention to proceed with her application for a property adjustment order. On the same day the husband filed a bankruptcy petition in the county court and asked for an immediate adjudication order. In accordance with s 6[a] of the Bankruptcy Act 1914 he was at once adjudicated bankrupt. He subsequently filed a statement of affairs disclosing that he was unable to pay his debts. In May 1976 the wife was given custody of the children. The husband's
g trustee in bankruptcy then took steps to realise the husband's interest in the house for the benefit of his creditors and applied in the county court for, inter alia, an order pursuant to s 30[b] of the Law of Property Act 1925 directing that the house be sold and that the wife join in procuring its sale. The wife cross-applied in the county court for annulment of the adjudication order on the grounds that it ought not to have been made because at the date of the bankruptcy petition the husband was able to pay his debts and because his
h petition was a device to prevent her from obtaining a property adjustment order and was therefore an abuse of the process of the court. The bankruptcy proceedings were transferred to the High Court but were not consolidated with the wife's matrimonial proceedings for ancillary relief because there was no jurisdiction to do so. The trustee in bankruptcy formally renewed in the High Court his application for an order directing sale of the house. By an order dated 27th February 1978 the judge dismissed the wife's
j application for annulment of the adjudication order, holding that at 3rd March 1976 the husband was unable to pay his debts and that his petition was not an abuse of the court's process. By a further order dated 6th March the judge granted the trustee's application

a Section 6 is set out at p 388 *j*, post
b Section 30 is set out at p 396 *j* to p 397 *a*, post

and ordered that the matrimonial home be sold with vacant possession and that the wife
join in procuring the sale and deliver up vacant possession by 20th July. However the *a*
judge gave the wife liberty to apply to have the question of sale reconsidered if she filed
further evidence, whereupon the wife filed evidence that she had no capital, was in
receipt of a social security allowance, that the children were attending schools in the near
neighbourhood of the house and that to buy a similar house in that neighbourhood
would cost between £20,000 and £25,000. The wife did not reapply to the judge but
instead appealed against both of his orders, contending, in regard to the order directing *b*
sale of the house, that the court should exercise its discretion by refusing to direct a sale,
on the ground that she and the children ought to be permitted to continue to live in the
house. The only creditors for consideration in the husband's bankruptcy were his
former solicitors to whom he owed approximately £1,260 and a bank to whom he owed
approximately £5,000. At the date of the hearing of the appeal the house was worth
about £34,000, subject to a mortgage of £6,864.

c

Held – (1) Even if the husband's main or sole motive for filing a bankruptcy petition
was to baulk the wife's claim to a transfer of property order that alone did not make the
petition an abuse of the court's process. Furthermore, in all the circumstances the judge
was correct in holding that at 3rd March 1976 the husband was unable to pay his debts.
It followed that the wife's appeal against the order of 27th February 1978 for annulment *d*
of the adjudication would be dismissed (see p 390 *f* to *h*, p 391 *c d* and p 395 *e*, post).

(2) In deciding whether to exercise its discretion under s 30 of the 1925 Act to execute
the trust for sale affecting the matrimonial home on the application of the trustee in
bankruptcy, the court was not required to take into account the power contained in s 24
of the Matrimonial Causes Act 1973 to make a property transfer order transferring the
husband's interest in the house to the wife, because the whole of the husband's beneficial *e*
interest in the house vested in the trustee, and not merely the husband's right to apply
for an order for sale, and the Family Division had no jurisdiction to make an order under
s 24 of the 1973 Act against the trustee. It followed that the exercise of the discretion
under s 30 of the 1925 Act was not required to be referred back to the Family Division
and could be decided by the Chancery Division. However, the court did have a discretion
whether to order execution of the trust for sale and was not bound to exercise that *f*
discretion in the trustee's favour. The guiding principle for the court in exercising the
discretion was that applicable where a marriage had ended by divorce or otherwise, but
without regard to the powers contained in the 1973 Act. Accordingly, the court had to
look at all the circumstances and consider which of the competing claims (ie that of the
trustee seeking to realise the husband's share in the house for the benefit of his creditors
and that of the wife seeking to preserve a home for herself and the children ought to *g*
prevail in equity. However, the need to preserve the house as a home for the children
where they were not beneficiaries under the trust for sale was not a secondary or
collateral object of the trust for sale and did not, therefore, entitle the court to exercise the
discretion by refusing to direct a sale, nor did it prolong beyond the end of the marriage
the secondary or collateral object of the trust of preserving a home for the parties to the
marriage (see p 391 *d* to *g*, p 392 *j* to p 393 *c*, p 394 *b c* and *e* to *h*, p 395 *e* to *j* and p 397 *h*
c d, post); dictum of Buckley LJ in *Burke v Burke* [1974] 2 All ER at 947–948 followed; *Re
Buchanan-Wollaston's Conveyance, Curtis v Buchanan-Wollaston* [1939] 2 All ER 302, *Jones v
Challenger* [1960] 1 All ER 785 and *Re Turner* [1975] 1 All ER 5 applied; *Williams v
Williams* [1977] 1 All ER 28 distinguished.

(3) Balancing the interest of the husband's creditors and the interest of the wife who
was burdened with the obligation to provide a home for the children of the marriage, the *j*
court would order that the house should not be sold without the wife's consent until July
1985 by which time the two eldest children would be over 17 years of age; there would,
however, be liberty to any party to apply in the meantime for a different order. It
followed that the appeal against the order of 6th March 1978 would be allowed (see p 397
h to p 398 *b* and *f j*, post).

Per Buckley LJ. When one of the assets of a bankrupt is an undivided share in land in respect of which the debtor's right to an immediate sale is not an absolute right, that is an asset in the bankruptcy which is liable to be affected by the interest of any other party in that land, and if there are reasons for saying which seem to the court to be good that the trust for sale of the land should not be immediately enforced then the land is an asset which is not immediately available for the benefit of the creditors (see p 397 *g*, post).

Notes

For the property of a bankrupt available for distribution, see 3 Halsbury's Laws (4th Edn) paras 590, 591, and for cases on the subject, see 5 Digest (Reissue) 675–682, *5903–5968*.

For the rights of the trustee in bankruptcy in respect of a matrimonial home, see 22 Halsbury's Laws (4th Edn) para 1052, and for a case on the subject, see 5 Digest (Reissue) 681, *5964*.

For the Law of Property Act 1925, s 30, see 27 Halsbury's Statutes (3rd Edn) 385.

For the Matrimonial Causes Act 1973, s 24, see 43 ibid 566.

Cases referred to in judgments

Bailey (a bankrupt), Re, ex parte the trustee of the bankrupt v Bailey [1977] 2 All ER 26, [1977] 1 WLR 278, DC, Digest (Cont Vol E) 27, *5865a*.

Browne (formerly Pritchard) v Pritchard [1975] 3 All ER 721, [1975] 1 WLR 1366, CA, Digest (Cont Vol D) 427, *6962 Add*.

Buchanan-Wollaston's Conveyance, Re, Curtis v Buchanan-Wollaston [1939] 2 All ER 302, [1939] Ch 738, 108 LJ Ch 281, 160 LT 399, CA, 38 Digest (Repl) 822, *348*.

Burke v Burke [1974] 2 All ER 944, [1974] 1 WLR 1063, CA, Digest (Cont Vol D) 399, *2330c*.

Debtor, Re a, ex parte the trustee v Solomon [1966] 3 All ER 255, sub nom *Re Solomon, a bankrupt, ex parte the trustee of the bankrupt v Solomon* [1967] Ch 573, [1967] 2 WLR 172, 5 Digest (Reissue) 725, *6237*.

Densham (a bankrupt), Re, ex parte the trustee of the bankrupt v Densham [1975] 3 All ER 726, [1975] 1 WLR 1519, 5 Digest (Reissue) 897, *7414*.

Jackson v Jackson [1971] 3 All ER 774, [1971] 1 WLR 1539, CA, 27(1) Digest (Reissue) 99, *704*.

Jones v Challenger [1960] 1 All ER 785, [1961] 1 QB 177, [1960] 2 WLR 695, CA, 47 Digest (Repl) 400, *3595*.

Mayo, Re, Mayo v Mayo [1943] 2 All ER 440, [1943] Ch 302, sub nom *Re Mayo's Will Trusts* 112 LJ Ch 257, 169 LT 205, 47 Digest (Repl) 399, *3593*.

Rawlings v Rawlings [1964] 2 All ER 804, [1964] P 398, [1964] 3 WLR 294, CA, 27(1) Digest (Reissue) 94, *680*.

Turner (a bankrupt), Re, ex parte the trustee of the bankrupt v Turner [1975] 1 All ER 5, [1974] 1 WLR 1556, 5 Digest (Reissue) 681, *5965*.

Williams v Williams [1977] 1 All ER 28, [1976] Ch 278, [1976] 3 WLR 494, CA, Digest (Cont Vol E) 255, *662b*.

Appeal

The wife appealed against the order of Foster J made on 27th February 1978 whereby he dismissed her application for the annulment of an adjudication order made in the Brighton County Court on 3rd March 1976 in respect of her former husband, and against so much of the order of Foster J made on 6th March 1978 whereby, on the motion of the husband's trustee in bankruptcy, he ordered that the former matrimonial home at Thorpe Bay, Essex be sold. The facts are set out in the judgment of Goff LJ.

Muir Hunter QC and *Graham Garner* for the wife.
Robert Pryor for the trustee in bankruptcy.
The husband appeared in person.

Cur adv vult

5th December. The following judgments were read. a

GOFF LJ (delivering the first judgment at the invitation of Buckley LJ). In this case
there are two appeals, both by the bankrupt's wife, who is the second respondent to the
proceedings.

One is against an order made by Foster J on 27th February 1978, whereby he dismissed
an application by the wife to annul an order of the county court at Brighton by which the b
first respondent, whom I shall call the debtor, was adjudicated bankrupt; the other was
made on 6th March 1978, whereby Foster J ordered a sale of the former matrimonial
home in Thorpe Bay, Essex.

The history and relevant facts of the matter are as follows: the debtor and the wife
were married on 15th June 1962 and there were three children of the marriage, one boy
and two girls, born respectively on 6th July 1965, 24th June 1968 and 21st January 1973. c

The Thorpe Bay property was bought in November 1970 for £7,850, of which £6,500
was raised on mortgage. It was conveyed to the debtor and the wife as joint legal and
beneficial owners.

At one stage the trustee in bankruptcy claimed to set this aside, so far as the wife's
interest is concerned, as a voluntary settlement within s 42 of the Bankruptcy Act
1914. For some, no doubt good, reason, probably because of the difficulty of proving d
that the debtor was not able to pay his debts at the date of the purchase without recourse
to the wife's beneficial share, the trustee abandoned that contention, and it is common
ground as between all parties to these proceedings that, although the legal estate is vested
in the debtor and the wife on trust for sale, since his legal estate as trustee did not vest in
his trustee in bankruptcy (see the Bankruptcy Act 1914, s 38), yet as to the net proceeds
of sale and the rents and profits pending sale, they hold it on trust for the trustee in e
bankruptcy and the wife in equal shares absolutely.

The marriage fell apart. The debtor left the wife in May 1974 and went to live with
a Mrs Ball, whom he has since married. The wife petitioned for divorce citing Mrs Ball
as co-respondent. This was at first defended, but later the defence was withdrawn and on
16th April 1975 the court pronounced a decree nisi which was, after some long delay,
ultimately made absolute. In her petition the wife claimed custody of the children and f
ancillary relief including a transfer of property order. These matters were not
conceded. On the contrary the question of custody was bitterly contested.

On 26th November 1975 the wife gave notice that her claims for ancillary relief would
be considered by the court on a date to be fixed.

The debtor first went to live with the co-respondent in a house in Brighton, which he
rented. She has two children, a boy aged 14 and a girl now aged 9, or thereabouts, who
were also living there. They have since all moved into a new home which appears to g
belong to the debtor's present wife.

On or shortly before 3rd March 1976 the wife gave notice of her intention to bring on
her application for ancillary relief, whereupon on that same day the debtor filed his own
petition in the local county court, that is to say Brighton. He asked in it for immediate
adjudication, and accordingly a receiving order was then and there made against him and h
he was at once adjudicated bankrupt. This was in accordance with s 6 of the Bankruptcy
Act 1914, which reads as follows:

> '(1) A debtor's petition shall allege that the debtor is unable to pay his debts, and
> the presentation thereof shall be deemed an act of bankruptcy without the previous
> filing by the debtor of any declaration of inability to pay his debts, and the court
> shall thereupon make a receiving order. j
>
> '(2) A debtor's petition shall not, after presentment, be withdrawn without the
> leave of the court.'

It will be observed that under this section a petitioner is not required to verify his
averment that he is unable to pay his debts, and the debtor did not do so in this case.

On 24th March 1976 the debtor filed a statement of affairs as at 3rd March 1976 which
a disclosed unsecured debts amounting to £1,516, mainly for legal expenses in connection with the divorce proceedings, a partly secured creditor for £5,487 with a security estimated to be worth £800 only, and an overall deficiency of £850.

Next, in May 1976 after bitterly contested proceedings, Faulks J made an order giving the custody of the three children to the wife.

Then the trustee in bankruptcy began to take steps to realise the debtor's interest in the
b property at Thorpe Bay for the benefit of the debtor's creditors. First he issued a notice of application in the county court in which he sought the following relief:

> '1. A Declaration that the joint purchase by and subsequent conveyance into the joint names of the [debtor] and [the wife] of premises [at] Thorpe Bay, Essex on about the 9th November 1970 constituted and was a voluntary settlement or transfer within the meaning of Section 42 of the Bankruptcy Act 1914 by the
> *c* [debtor] to the [wife] and as such is void against the Applicant as Trustee.
>
> '2. A declaration that the Applicant herein is entitled to the whole of the beneficial interest of the said property.
>
> '3. Alternatively a declaration as to the respective interest of the Applicant and the [wife] in the said property.
>
> '4. An order that the said property be sold and that the conduct of such sale be
> *d* given to the Applicant.
>
> '5. An order that the [wife] join with the Applicant in and do such things as are necessary to procure the sale of the said property and that the [debtor] and the [wife] deliver vacant possession of the said property for the purpose of such sale.'

Then he asks for an order as to costs.

e The wife countered this by a motion in the county court to annul the adjudication. The grounds for this application were that the order ought never to have been made because the debtor was not on 3rd March 1976 unable to pay his debts, and because, as she alleges, the petition was an abuse of the process of the court, being a device to prevent her from obtaining a property transfer order. If successful it would follow as of course that the receiving order also must be set aside and the petition dismissed.

f By an order dated 4th July 1977, Browne-Wilkinson J transferred the bankruptcy proceedings to the High Court, but he refused to consolidate them with the matrimonial proceedings on the ground that he had no jurisdiction to do so, and that is not challenged. Accordingly, we could not, even if asked to do so, make any order under the Matrimonial Causes Act 1973. The most we could do would be to transfer the trustee's summons under s 30 to the Family Division or adjourn it until after the hearing of the
g wife's application by that division.

By notice of motion the trustee in bankruptcy formally renewed in the High Court his application to the county court, but both are in identical terms and it is unnecessary to read that notice of motion.

The information as to the means of the wife and the debtor respectively is meagre and to some extent out of date, but according to an affidavit sworn by her on 24th February
h 1977 the debtor is now paying her regularly £20 per week maintenance as ordered, the whole of which is taken by the Department of Health and Social Security which, as appears from her further affidavit sworn on 22nd March 1978, pays her an allowance of £41·56 per week, and she also receives a family allowance of £6·90 per week. Arrears amounting to £300 had accrued under the mortgage, but these were discharged by the department, and she is now paying the current monthly instalments of £67·75 per
j month plus rates, heating and lighting and, of course, she has to provide food and clothing for herself and the children.

She has investments in the Post Office and elsewhere which can only be described as tiny and which bring in only £2 per annum from the Post Office and £2 per annum from dividends, but no other capital or income.

The property at Thorpe Bay is a modern detached house with three bedrooms, sitting room, dining room and kitchen, with a front garden and a large garden at the back. It stands in a secluded close consisting of 11 houses only.

The debtor does not state the amount of his income, but he is apparently employed as an export sales engineer and in an affidavit sworn by the wife on 19th November 1975 she stated her belief that he was then earning £6,500 per annum in that capacity.

He lives with his present wife and her two children in a house which is in her name, and in which I think he does not claim any beneficial interest. There are three to four double bedrooms, one of which he says could be used as a dining room. There is a large kitchen/dining room and lounge, two separate toilets and a bathroom. Although he gives no figures it seems that he has spent considerable sums in or towards extensive alterations and redecoration of those premises.

Foster J heard both motions and made separate orders on them. First, by an order dated 27th February 1978 he dismissed the application for annulment of the adjudication order, and made no order as to costs either before him or in the Brighton County Court, save for a legal aid taxation of the wife's costs. Then on the trustee's motion, by order dated 6th March 1978, he ordered that the Thorpe Bay property be sold with vacant possession but completion not to take place before 31st July 1978, and that the wife join with the trustee in and do all such things as are necessary to procure the sale of the property and do deliver up vacant possession not later than 20th July 1978, with a proviso giving her liberty, if she elected to file evidence on the question of sale on or before 4th April 1978, to apply to have the matter reconsidered. As before, he made no order as to costs save for legal aid taxation.

The wife did elect to file further evidence in an affidavit dated 22nd March 1978, but she did not reapply to Foster J. Instead she appealed from both orders.

The first question which arises on these appeals is whether on 3rd March 1976 the debtor was able to pay his debts, for if so then the receiving order and the adjudication order clearly ought not to have been made.

If, however, he was not so able, then prima facie those orders were rightly made, but counsel for the wife has submitted that even on this hypothesis they are still bad as an abuse of process. Initially he rested this argument solely on the ground that the proper inference from the facts must be that the debtor's motive or purpose was not that of protecting himself from undue pressure by creditors, or to secure a fair distribution of his assets between them, but to baulk the claim the wife was making for a transfer of property order. In my judgment, however, even if this were his main or sole motive (and it may well be that it was) still that cannot alone make the petition an abuse of process. But then counsel for the wife submitted that the petition was an abuse of process if at the time the debtor believed that he was able to pay his debts or filed his petition without directing his mind to that question one way or the other.

There is, however, in my view no evidence to establish either of those postulates, so I turn back to the question whether he was in fact able to pay his debts.

It is clear from the statement of affairs and the revised summary which was put before us that he was insolvent and unable to pay his debts on any showing if the principal sum due under the mortgage had to be taken into account. That was initially an instalment mortgage but owing to default the whole had become due. However, albeit after the receiving order, there was some rearrangement when the debt was reduced by the realisation of an insurance policy held as collateral security, and thereafter the mortgagees have again been content to accept instalments. Counsel for the wife sought to argue that whether by waiver or estoppel the mortgagees had lost the right to claim the outstanding balance of principal.

Even if this were so (and I am not at all satisfied that it would be) the mortgage payments went into arrears as long ago as 1974 and remained so long after 3rd March 1976, so it would seem too late to affect the validity of the receiving order and adjudication. But in my judgment the argument cannot possibly succeed, because the debtor could not meet his other liabilities without recourse to this property and he could not have that without redeeming the mortgage.

Counsel for the wife also challenged the statement of affairs on the ground that it did *a* not give him credit for the wife's liability to contribute to part of the bank overdraft and to a sum of £41 due for rates. In my judgment, however, it would not be right to take that into account, because the debtor was liable for the full amount and could only claim contribution when he had paid more than his fair share; but in any case once one has to take the full amount of the mortgage into account these credits would still leave him on the wrong side.

b There is a note to the revised summary: '(2) assets ignore any beneficial interest in Mrs. Ball's property apparently represented by at least £4,000 of the debt due to the National Westminster Bank.' It may well be that, although the property is in her name alone, if and when it becomes necessary or expedient the debtor or his trustee may be able to establish some beneficial interest in that property, but that is irrelevant for the purpose of considering whether the bankruptcy orders were rightly made, because whatever *c* rights, if any, the trustee in bankruptcy might have, clearly the debtor was not able to have recourse to any beneficial interest in this property at the date when he filed his petition.

For these reasons in my judgment the judge was perfectly correct in holding that at 3rd March 1976 the debtor could not pay his debts and that the petition was not an abuse of the process of the court, and I would dismiss this appeal.

d I turn now to the second appeal. Where property is held on trust for sale and any person interested desires a sale but that is opposed, then the court has in all cases a discretion whether to order a sale or not, but the exercise of that discretion may be very much limited and controlled by the facts and circumstances of the case.

I shall first consider the position as it was before *Williams v Williams* [1977] 1 All ER 28, [1976] Ch 278 and then consider the impact of that case.

e Where the property in question is a matrimonial home, then the provision of a home for both parties is a secondary or collateral object of the trust for sale (see per Devlin LJ in *Jones v Challenger* [1960] 1 All ER 785 at 787, [1961] 1 QB 177 at 181) and the court will not ordinarily order a sale if the marriage be still subsisting and no question of bankruptcy has supervened.

Where, however, the marriage has come to an end by divorce or death of one of the *f* parties, or is dead in fact, though still subsisting at law, then apart from any question how far the secondary or collateral object can be said to be still subsisting if there are young or dependent children, though there remains a discretion it is one in which, as I see it, some very special circumstances need to be shown to induce the court not to order a sale (see *Jones v Challenger* [1960] 1 All ER 785, [1961] 1 QB 177 and *Rawlings v Rawlings* [1964] 2 All ER 804, [1964] P 398).

g In *Jones v Challenger* [1960] 1 All ER 785 at 789, [1961] 1 QB 177 at 183 Devlin J said:

> 'In the case which we have to consider, the house was acquired as the matrimonial home. That was the purpose of the joint tenancy and, for so long as that purpose was still alive, I think that the right test to be applied would be that in *Re Buchanan-Wollaston* ([1939] 2 All ER 302, [1939] Ch 738). But with the end of the marriage, that purpose was dissolved and the primacy of the duty to sell was restored. No *h* doubt there is still a discretion. If the husband wanted time to obtain alternative accommodation, the sale could be postponed for that purpose, but he has not asked for that. If he was prepared to buy out the applicant's interest, it might be proper to allow it, but he has not accepted a suggestion that terms of that sort should be made. In these circumstances, there is no way in which the discretion can properly be exercised except by an order to sell, because, since they cannot now both enjoy *j* occupation of the property, that is the only way whereby the beneficiaries can derive equal benefit from their investment, which is the primary object of the trust.'

Then, after observing, 'If the wife had died and left her share under the trust to a stranger, I think that the house would obviously have had to be sold', he summed up in these words ([1960] 1 All ER 785 at 789, [1961] 1 QB 177 at 184):

> 'I think that the result must be the same whether the test to be applied is derived from the language used in *Re Mayo* ([1943] 2 All ER 440, [1943] Ch 302) or from a
> that used in *Re Buchanan-Wollaston*. Let it be granted that the court must look into all the circumstances; if when the examination is complete, it finds that there is no inequity in selling the property, then it must be sold. The test is not what is reasonable. It is reasonable for the husband to want to go on living in the house and reasonable for the wife to want her share of the trust property in cash. The true question is whether it is inequitable for the wife, once the matrimonial home has b
> gone, to want to realise her investment? Nothing said in the cases which I have cited can be used to suggest that it is, and, in my judgment it clearly is not. The conversion of the property into a form in which both parties can enjoy their rights equally is the prime object of the trust; the preservation of the house as a home for one of them singly is not an object at all. If the true object of the trust is made paramount, as it should be, there is only one order that can be made.' c

Then one must consider on the facts of this case how the matter is affected by the fact that there are young children. In *Rawlings v Rawlings* [1964] 2 All ER 804 at 814, [1964] P 398 at 419 Salmon LJ said:

> 'If there were young children the position would be different. One of the purposes of the trust would no doubt have been to provide a home for them, and d
> whilst that purpose still existed a sale would not generally be ordered. But when those children are grown up and the marriage is dead the purposes of the trust have failed.'

That was no more than a dictum because the only child of the marriage was of full age. If, however, it be accepted, then at all events in the absence of a supervening bankruptcy of one of the parties, if one spouse is living in the home with young children, e
or even probably if they are living there in somebody else's care, the case will be governed by the *Buchanan-Wollaston* principle as applied to a trust for sale with a subsisting secondary or collateral object.

In *Burke v Burke* [1974] 2 All ER 944 at 947–948, [1974] 1 WLR 1063 at 1067, however, Buckley LJ declined to accept this dictum, saying: f

> 'But the interests of the children in the present case, it seems to me, with due respect to Salmon LJ, are interests which are only incidentally to be taken into consideration in that sort of way. They are, as I say, proper to be taken into consideration so far as they affect the equities in the matter as between the two persons entitled to the beneficial interests in the property. But it is not, I think, right to treat this case as though the husband was obliged to make provision for his g
> children by agreeing to retain the property unsold. To do this is, as I think, and as was urged on us by counsel for the husband, to confuse with a problem relating to property, considerations which are relevant to maintenance. Those are two different things. If the property is sold and the means available to the husband in the present case are enhanced by his receiving his share of the proceeds of sale, it may well be that he may find himself exposed to an application for an order for increased h
> maintenance; but that does not seem to me to be a good ground for refusing to give effect to the trust for sale which is the primary provision applicable to this property.'

Davies LJ entirely agreed, but Lawton LJ had reservations, for he thought in general children or prospective children might be considered beneficiaries under the trust for sale, and based his concurring judgment on the fact that the registrar had decided what the beneficial trusts were, namely for the husband and wife in equal shares. j

There may be cases in which the children are beneficiaries, and then, of course, different considerations will apply, but normally in my view that will not be so, nor are they in my judgment in the present case.

So the question is whether to adopt Salmon LJ's view that the existence of young or dependent children prolongs the secondary or collateral purpose, or Buckley LJ's view

that the purpose is ended, but the existence of the children is a factor incidentally to be
a taken into account so far as they affect the equities in the matter as between the persons entitled to the beneficial interests in the property.

With all respect to both the learned Lords Justices concerned, I would prefer the view of Buckley LJ to that of Salmon LJ because as Devlin LJ pointed out in *Jones v Challenger* [1960] 1 All ER 785 at 789, [1961] 1 QB 177 at 184:

> 'The conversion of the property into a form in which both parties can enjoy their
> b rights equally is the prime object of the trust; the preservation of the house as a home for one of them singly is not an object at all. If the true object of the trust is made paramount, as it should be, there is only one order that can be made.'

And in my view the preservation of the house as a home for the children can be no more an object than its preservation as a home for the spouse.

c At this stage, however, I must turn to consider *Williams v Williams* [1977] 1 All ER 28, [1976] Ch 278. There, according to the headnote ([1976] Ch 278 at 279), *Jones v Challenger* and *Burke v Burke* were distinguished. When, however, one looks at the judgments it was said that the approach in those cases was outdated (per Lord Denning MR [1977] 1 All ER 28 at 30, [1976] Ch 278 at 285) or 'a rather narrow, old-fashioned way' per Roskill LJ ([1977] 1 All ER 28 at 31, [1976] Ch 278 at 286).

d This seems to me not so much to be distinguishing cases as saying that having regard to modern thinking and circumstances the court should have regard to different considerations in exercising its discretion.

Whether and how far that makes the authorities conflicting I need not pause to consider for *Jones v Challenger* and *Burke v Burke* on the one hand and *Williams v Williams* and also *Browne v Pritchard* [1975] 3 All ER 721, [1975] 1 WLR 1366 on the other are in
e truth in my judgment distinguishable, since at the time when the first was decided the Matrimonial Proceedings and Property Act 1970 and of course its replacement, the Matrimonial Causes Act 1973, had not been passed, and in the second no argument was based on those statutes.

The distinction clearly appears in this passage in the judgment of Lord Denning MR in *Williams v Williams* [1977] 1 All ER 28 at 31, [1976] Ch 278 at 285–286:

> f 'The truth is that the approach to these cases has been transformed since the Matrimonial Proceedings and Property Act 1970 and the Matrimonial Causes Act 1973, which have given the power to the court, after a divorce, to order the transfer of property. In exercising any discretion under s 30 of the 1925 Act, those Acts must be taken into account. The discretion should be exercised on the principles stated by this court in *Jackson v Jackson* [1971] 3 All ER 774 at 778, [1971] 1 WLR
> g 1539 at 1543. I would add this. An application about a matrimonial home should not be restricted to s 30 of the Law of Property Act 1925. In view of the wide powers of transfer and adjustment which are available under the new matrimonial property legislation, it seems to me that the applications should be made to the Family Division under the relevant provisions. If taken out in another division, they should be transferred to a judge of the Family Division. In this very case it
> h seems to me that the right course (which the wife's advisers ought to have taken before) is that they should now, and at once, take out the appropriate application under s 24 of the 1973 Act for any necessary orders and so on to be made with regard to the house and the property. That application should be brought on together with an application under s 30.'

j Where then the matrimonial jurisdiction is available I would agree that today a spouse wishing to obtain an order for sale should apply to the Family Division and if he or she applies in the Chancery Division the other spouse should apply for an order for transfer to that division and for any ancillary relief he or she may wish to seek under ss 23 and 24 of the Matrimonial Causes Act 1973. That division may then dispose of the problem by a transfer of property order, or may consider the question of sale in combination with an exercise of its powers under ss 23 and 24, and will have regard to the guidelines laid down in s 25.

I need not consider how the matter will stand if a party applies in the Chancery Division for a sale and the other does not seek ancillary relief, since here the wife has done so.

In my judgment, however, *Williams v Williams* itself is clearly distinguishable from the present case which falls within *Jones v Challenger* because of the intervention of the trustee in bankruptcy.

It is argued that makes no difference because the trustee can take no better title than the bankrupt, and that he succeeds to nothing more than the husband's right to apply for an order for sale which, on the *Buchanan-Wollaston* principle, he would be less than likely to obtain. In my judgment, however, that is a fallacy because the whole beneficial share of the debtor has vested in the trustee.

The Family Division has no jurisdiction to make an order against him under s 24, because he is not a party to the marriage, and its power to make an order under s 23 against the debtor is at this stage much circumscribed by the fact that he is bankrupt.

Some reliance was placed by counsel for the wife on s 39 of the Matrimonial Causes Act 1973, which provides as follows:

> 'The fact that a settlement or transfer of property had to be made in order to comply with a property adjustment order shall not prevent that settlement or transfer from being a settlement of property to which section 42(1) of the Bankruptcy Act 1914 (avoidance of certain settlements) applies.'

It has, of course, no direct application because no property adjustment order has been or can now be made, but in so far as it has any relevance it seems to me to tell against counsel for the wife, because it is expressly reserving the trustee's right in bankruptcy to challenge the transfer although, of course, the debtor could not have impeached it in any way.

It seems to me, therefore, that we ought to decide the present case ourselves and not refer it back to the Family Division and that our discretion should be exercised in accordance with the law as established and as I have adumbrated it apart from *Williams v Williams*; so, as it seems to me, we have to decide this case according to the principle of *Jones v Challenger* as applied by me in the bankruptcy cases of *Re Solomon* [1966] 3 All ER 255, [1967] Ch 573; *Re Turner* [1975] 1 All ER 5, [1974] 1 WLR 1556; and *Re Densham* [1975] 3 All ER 726, [1975] 1 WLR 1519. I laid down the relevant principle where there is a bankruptcy in *Re Turner* [1975] 1 All ER 5 at 7, [1974] 1 WLR 1556 at 1558 as follows:

> 'In my judgment, the guiding principle in the exercise of the court's discretion is not whether the trustee or the wife is being reasonable but, in all the circumstances of the case, whose voice in equity ought to prevail.'

I would apply that test to this case.

So we have to decide having regard to all the circumstances, including the fact that there are young children and that the debtor was made bankrupt on his own petition, whose voice, that of the trustee seeking to realise the debtor's share for the benefit of his creditors or that of the wife seeking to preserve a home for herself and the children, ought in equity to prevail. In all those cases I held that the trustee must prevail as did the Divisional Court in *Re Bailey* [1977] 2 All ER 26, [1977] 1 WLR 278.

Nevertheless there is a discretion, and I would hear argument according to these principles on the question whose voice in the circumstances of this case ought to prevail, and in this connection it will be necessary to consider the schooling arrangements at present obtaining, and what could be done if the house were sold, but the evidence at present does not cover this very adequately. The boy is at present attending school in Southend. As to the girls the wife says in her further affidavit of 22nd March 1978:

> 'D is now in her third year at . . . school [in] Thorpe Bay. She previously attended the Infant School which is in the same building. D is now at a very important stage

> of her education as she will be taking the eleven plus examination in January 1979.
> a I am anxious that she should remain at her present school so as her studies will not be disrupted during the crucial period between now and January 1979. In January 1978 S began attending the same Infant School.'

January 1979 is of course now passed and we do not know the result of the eleven plus examination.

In para 12 of this affidavit the wife further says:

b

> 'I have enquired as to local authority housing but there is none available in Thorpe Bay. The nearest is at Shoeburyness, which is quite a different area. I have in any event been informed by the Housing Authority that I am not eligible for council housing. Further, even if such were available I verily believe it would not be possible for the children to keep their pets.'

c In his affidavit, de bene esse the debtor says, as is no doubt true, that Brighton has good educational facilities and plenty more are available in the vicinity, and that the children could keep all their pets in his home.

Having thus decided that we have a discretion and the principles which should govern its exercise, I would now hear further argument whether or not we should confirm Foster J's order that the Thorpe Bay property be sold with vacant possession and if so on
d what terms as to time for completion or otherwise.

Since writing this judgment I have had the advantage of seeing in draft the judgment about to be delivered by Buckley LJ and I would add that I respectfully agree with the procedural steps which he proposes.

Also, I am authorised by Sir David Cairns to say that he agrees with the judgment that I have just read.

e

BUCKLEY LJ. I agree with the judgment delivered by Goff LJ and only wish to add some short observations.

The distinction between *Jones v Challenger* [1960] 1 All ER 785, [1961] 1 QB 177 and *Burke v Burke* [1974] 2 All ER 944, [1974] 1 WLR 1063 on the one hand, and *Williams v Williams* [1977] 1 All ER 28, [1976] Ch 278 on the other is, as Goff LJ has pointed out,
f that in 1961 neither the Matrimonial Proceedings Act 1970 nor the Matrimonial Causes Act 1973 had been enacted and no court had such a power to adjust the property rights of the parties to a dissolved marriage as was conferred by those Acts, and that in *Burke v Burke* no recourse was sought to the power to adjust property rights under the 1973 Act.

I was initially attracted by the proposition that the trustee in bankruptcy could be in no more favourable position than the debtor vis-à-vis the wife. I agree, however, that the
g debtor's whole beneficial interest vested in the trustee in bankruptcy and that the court could not make a transfer of property order against the trustee in bankruptcy under s 24(1)(*a*) of the Matrimonial Causes Act 1973 in the present case, because such an order could only be made against a party to the marriage.

When considering whether in the existing circumstances a sale should be ordered or not, the conflicting legal and moral claims to be taken into account and weighed against
h each other are, as I am at present inclined to think, those of the creditors asserted through the trustee in bankruptcy on the one hand (rather than any claim of the trustee in bankruptcy) and those of the wife on the other, taking all relevant facts, including the existence of the children, into account. Whether the fact that, but for the bankruptcy, no creditor could object to the wife applying for a property adjustment order under the 1973 Act has any relevance in this connection is not a question on which we have heard
j argument and I express no opinion on it.

I agree that in this state of affairs it would be better for us to exercise our discretion in this court rather than send the case to the Family Division. As Goff LJ has pointed out, the evidence which may be relevant as to how we should exercise our discretion is in some respects not very full. If either party wished to supplement it in any way, I would be prepared to entertain an application for leave to file further evidence. In any case I think that the appeal should stand over for a short time to allow counsel to prepare themselves to present such further argument as they may think desirable on the question how the court's discretion should be exercised in the light of our judgments of today.

Appeal stood over to allow for further argument.

8th May. The court heard further argument.

BUCKLEY LJ. This appeal was before this court in October 1979 when the court consisted of Sir David Cairns, Goff LJ and myself. We then held, amongst other things, that it was not open to the wife to obtain a property adjustment order under the Matrimonial Causes Act 1973 against her husband's ('the debtor') trustee in bankruptcy, the trustee not being amenable to that jurisdiction, and so, the matrimonial home being vested in the two parties, the debtor and the wife, as joint tenants on a statutory trust for sale for the benefit of themselves in equal shares, the problem arose whether or not the trustee in bankruptcy was justified in pressing for an immediate sale of the property. At the conclusion of his judgment, Goff LJ said:

> 'So we have to decide having regard to all the circumstances, including the fact that there are young children and that the debtor was made bankrupt on his own petition, whose voice, that of the trustee seeking to realise the debtor's share for the benefit of his creditors or that of the wife seeking to preserve a home for herself and the children, ought in equity to prevail.'

The evidence at that time was not, in the view of the court, very full on the circumstances relevant to the consideration I have just referred to; accordingly the appeal was stood over for the parties to adduce further evidence as they might think fit and for us to deal with that question on a later occasion.

In the interval, most unhappily, Goff LJ has died, but the parties have agreed mutually to the matter now being disposed of by Sir David Cairns and myself.

The former matrimonial home in Thorpe Bay, Essex, is, as I have said, vested in the debtor and the wife as joint tenants on the statutory trust for sale, and in trust for themselves in equal shares beneficially. The debtor has been adjudicated bankrupt on his own petition. We are told that it is necessary for a sum of approximately £7,500 to be found to discharge the obligations and the expenses under that bankruptcy.

The house is said to be worth something of the order of £33,000 to £34,000. There is a mortgage on it, the principal amount of which is now £6,864, so the value of the equity of redemption may be taken to be of the order of £26,500, one half of which would be £13,250. The matrimonial home is a three-bedroomed house, comprising two sitting rooms and a kitchen and, no doubt, what are usually referred to as the usual offices. The family consists of the wife and three children by her marriage to the debtor, a son who is now about 15 years old, a daughter, who will be 12 in June next, and a younger daughter who is now a little over seven years old. With a family of that composition, the wife really needs a three-bedroomed house and that she has at Thorpe Bay. The children are attending schools in the near neighbourhood of that house, and the evidence indicates that to buy another house of comparable capacity in that neighbourhood would cost somewhere between £20,000 and £25,000. The wife is without capital; her present income is I think of the order of £87 a week. The debtor has remarried; he is living with his present wife, the lady for whom he left the wife, in another house; he is employed and is earning quite a reasonably good salary.

In these circumstances we have to consider how we should exercise our discretion under s 30 of the Law of Property Act 1925, which provides:

> 'If the trustees for sale refuse to sell or to exercise any of the powers conferred by either of the last two sections, or any requisite consent cannot be obtained, any person interested may apply to the court for a vesting or other order for giving

> effect to the proposed transaction or for an order directing the trustees for sale to give effect thereto, and the court may make such order as it thinks fit.'

There is no specific transaction in view at the moment, but the trustee in bankruptcy submits that the house should be sold for the benefit of the debtor's creditors and the wife is unwilling, as one of the trustees for sale, to sell, because she contends that she ought to be permitted to continue to live in the house with her three children.

That section confers on the court a broad discretion and as Greene MR observed in *Re Buchanan-Wollaston's Conveyance* [1939] 2 All ER 302 at 308, [1939] Ch 738 at 747:

> '... it seems to me that the court of equity, when asked to enforce the trust for sale, whether one created by a settlement or will or one created by the statute, must look into all the circumstances of the case and consider whether or not, at the particular moment and in the particular circumstances when the application is made to it, it is right and proper that such an order shall be made,'

that is to say, an order for sale of the subject matter of the trust for sale. So we have to consider all the circumstances of the case, and consider whether it is right and proper that the house should be sold now for the benefit of the creditors of the debtor, or whether it is right and proper that it should be retained unsold, the wife being allowed to continue to reside there with her children.

The only creditors, or the only creditors that call for consideration in the bankruptcy, are the debtor's former solicitors, to whom he owes a sum of approximately £1,260 for costs, the debtor's bank, to whom he owes something of the order of £5,000, and the wife's mother, to whom the debtor owes approximately £250 in respect of a loan. The wife's mother is not anxious to press for early repayment of that loan because she does not want to jeopardise the wife's position in regard to the house. So virtually the only creditors whose position has to be considered are the solicitors and the bank.

In these circumstances the wife finds herself saddled with the burden of providing a proper home for her children, which she would be incapable of doing out of her own resources, taking into account the value of her one half share of the equity in the Thorpe Bay property. That situation is attributable to the former conduct of the debtor in leaving the wife and family and going to make a new home for himself with another lady. This seems to me to afford the wife strong and justifiable grounds for saying that it really would be unfair to her, at this juncture and in these circumstances, to enforce the trust for sale. Of course, the creditors are entitled to payment as soon as the debtor is in a position to pay them. They are entitled to payment forthwith; they have an unassailable right to be paid out of the assets of the bankrupt. But in my view, when one of those assets is an undivided share in land in respect of which the debtor's right to an immediate sale is not an absolute right, that is an asset in the bankruptcy which is liable to be affected by the interest of any other party interested in that land, and if there are reasons which seem to the court to be good reasons for saying that the trust for sale of the land should not be immediately enforced, then that is an asset of the bankruptcy which is not immediately available because it cannot be immediately realised for the benefit of the creditors. Balancing the interest of the creditors and the interest of the wife, burdened, as I say, with the obligation to provide a home for the three children of the marriage, in my view the right attitude for the court to adopt is that the house should not be sold at the present juncture. Of course, in fact it cannot be sold without the concurrence of the wife or an order of the court; but in order to make the position clear, for my part I would be disposed to make an order to the effect that the house should not be sold without the consent of the wife or pursuant to an order of the court, before 1st July 1985, by which time the elder daughter will have passed her 17th birthday, and the boy, who is the eldest of the three children, will be older. By that stage the problems confronting the wife will be very different from the problems she has to deal with today.

I would make such an order, although it does not really affect or alter the position as it is today (it has the same effect as if we refused any order) giving any party (that is to say, the wife or the trustee in bankruptcy or the debtor if he has the status to make such an application) liberty to apply in the meantime. When that date, 1st July 1985, is reached, it will of course be open for any party to apply to enforce the trust for sale or to seek to have the trust for sale still not carried into execution. In the meantime, it will be open to any party to apply for some order other than the order which I would favour making.

I would therefore make an order in those terms. I would emphasise that in this case we are only concerned with the exercise of the discretion under s 30 of the Law of Property Act 1925 because, as matters stand at the present time, there is no means of invoking the Matrimonial Causes Act 1973.

I would dispose of the matter in that way.

SIR DAVID CAIRNS. In his judgment delivered on 5th December 1979, with which Buckley LJ and I agreed, Goff LJ said:

> 'So we have to decide having regard to all the circumstances, including the fact that there are young children and that the debtor was made bankrupt on his own petition, whose voice, that of the trustee seeking to realise the debtor's share for the benefit of his creditors or that of the wife seeking to preserve a home for herself and the children, ought in equity to prevail. In all those cases [Goff LJ was there referring to cases which he had mentioned earlier in his judgment] I held that the trustee must prevail as did the Divisional Court in *Re Bailey* [1977] 2 All ER 26, [1977] 1 WLR 278. Nevertheless there is a discretion, and I would hear argument according to these principles on the question whose voice in the circumstances of this case ought to prevail, and in this connection it will be necessary to consider the schooling arrangements at present obtaining, and what could be done if the house were sold . . .'

That passage is part of the decision of this court and it is therefore too late for counsel for the trustee in bankruptcy to argue that the court ought to take no account of the fact that the debtor was made bankrupt on his own petition, or to suggest that the court must always prefer the interests of the creditors to those of the wife and children of the debtor.

I agree with Buckley LJ that in all the circumstances here the voice of the wife, on behalf of herself and the children, should prevail to the extent that the sale of the house should be deferred for a substantial period. I reach that view because I am satisfied that it would at present be very difficult, if not impossible, for the wife to secure another suitable home for the family in or near Thorpe Bay; because it would be upsetting for the children's education if they had to move far away from their present schools, even if it were practicable, having regard to the wife's means, to find an alternative home at some more distant place; because it is highly unlikely that postponement of the payment of the debts would cause any great hardship to any of the creditors; and because none of the creditors thought fit themselves to present a bankruptcy petition and it is quite impossible to know whether any one of them would have done so if the debtor had not himself presented such a petition.

Although there is apparently no previous reported case in which the interests of a debtor's family have been held to prevail over those of creditors in a bankruptcy, there have certainly been earlier cases in which family interests have been considered and set against those of the creditors: see *Re Turner* [1975] 1 All ER 5, [1974] 1 WLR 1556 where it was the wife's interest that was considered, and *Re Bailey* [1977] 2 All ER 26, [1977] 1 WLR 278 where it was the interests of a son of the family.

In the earlier cases the trustee has succeeded, because no sufficiently substantial case of hardship of dependants was established. That is where, in my judgment, this case differs from the earlier ones. It may well be, however, that the hardship for the wife and children would be much less, or would have disappeared altogether, in five years' time or possibly even earlier. I therefore agree that it is appropriate that we should not at this stage defer sale for longer than five years or thereabouts, and that we should leave a

loophole for earlier sale to be applied for if the circumstances change in such a way as to
a warrant it.

Appeal allowed; order of 6th March 1978 discharged to extent indicated in judgment of Buckley LJ; order substituted that house be not sold without the consent of the wife, or pursuant to an order of the court, before 1st July 1985, with liberty to any party to apply meanwhile. Leave to appeal to House of Lords refused.

b

Solicitors: *Jefferies*, Southend on Sea (for the wife); *William Heath & Co* (for the trustee in bankruptcy).

Diana Brahams Barrister.

c

Re Evers's Trust, Papps v Evers

COURT OF APPEAL, CIVIL DIVISION
ORMROD, EVELEIGH AND TEMPLEMAN LJJ
8th, 23rd MAY 1980

d *Trust and trustee – Trust for sale – Refusal of trustees to concur in sale – Unmarried parties living as man and wife – Home purchased jointly out of money provided by both parties – Purpose of trust to provide family home for parties and children – Matters to be considered – How discretion of court to order sale to be exercised – Whether discretion same as that in connection with property adjustment orders under matrimonial causes legislation – Law of Property Act 1925, s 30 – Matrimonial Causes Act 1973, s 24.*

e

In 1974 the parties met and, without marrying, commenced living together as man and wife in the plaintiff's home. Two years later they had a child and at about the same time the defendant's two children from a previous marriage joined them. In 1978 the parties purchased a house for some £14,000 with a joint mortgage of £10,000, a contribution of £2,400 from the defendant and the balance from the plaintiff. The property was
f conveyed to them on trust for sale as joint tenants. In 1979 the parties separated, the defendant and the three children remaining in the house. Because the parties had been unable to agree on a sale of the home, the plaintiff, who was the father of the parties' child, applied to the court, as a person interested, for an order under s 30[a] of the Law of Property Act 1925 for the sale of the house. The trial judge granted the order, but, following the practice in cases under s 24[b] of the Matrimonial Causes Act 1973, directed
g that the sale be postponed until the parties' child attained the age of 16. The plaintiff appealed, contending that he ought to be allowed to take his share out of the house immediately.

Held – In exercising its discretion to execute a trust for sale of property in 'family' cases under s 30 of the 1925 Act the court had to consider both the primary purpose of the
h trust (ie that of a sale) and its underlying purpose (ie that of providing a home not only for the parents but also for the children), but it had no power to adjust the respective property rights of the parties as it had under s 24 of the 1973 Act. Nevertheless, in determining the underlying purpose of a trust in a case under s 30 the interests of children, both legitimate and illegitimate, were a circumstance to be considered. Since,

j a Section 30 is set out at p 401 *e*, post

b Section 24, so far as material, provides: '(1) On granting a decree of divorce, a decree of nullity of marriage or a decree of judicial separation or at any time thereafter ... the court may make ... (*a*) an order that a party to the marriage shall transfer to the other party, to any child of the family or to such person as may be specified in the order for the benefit of such child such property as may be so specified, being property to which the first-mentioned party is entitled ...'

on the evidence, the underlying purpose of the trust was to purchase and provide a
family home for themselves and the three children for the indefinite future and the *a*
plaintiff had no great need to realise his investment, the court would dismiss the
application, leaving it open to the plaintiff to apply again at a later date if circumstances
changed, rather than grant the application but postpone the sale until an arbitrary date
in the future. To that extent the plaintiff's appeal would be dismissed (see p 403 *e f* and
j to p 404 *h*, post).

Re Buchanan-Wollaston's Conveyance [1939] 2 All ER 302, *Jones v Challenger* [1960] 1 All *b*
ER 785, *Burke v Burke* [1974] 2 All ER 944 and *Williams v Williams* [1977] 1 All ER 28
considered.

Notes

For the trustee's powers of sale generally, see 38 Halsbury's Laws (3rd Edn) 1016–1019,
paras 1750–1756, and for cases on the subject, see 47 Digest (Repl) 398–401, *3586–3596*. *c*

For the Law of Property Act 1925, s 30, see 27 Halsbury's Statutes (3rd Edn) 385.

For the Matrimonial Causes Act 1973, s 24, see 43 ibid 566.

Cases referred to in judgment

Browne (formerly Pritchard) v Pritchard [1975] 3 All ER 721, [1975] 1 WLR 1366, CA, Digest (Cont Vol D) 427, *6962Add.*

Buchanan-Wollaston's Conveyance, Re, Curtis v Buchanan-Wollaston [1939] 2 All ER 302, *d*
[1939] Ch 738, 108 LJ Ch 281, 160 LT 399, CA; *affg* [1939] Ch 217, 108 LJ Ch 132, 159 LT 601, 38 Digest (Repl) 822, *348*.

Burke v Burke [1974] 2 All ER 944, [1974] 1 WLR 1063, CA, Digest (Cont Vol D) 399, *2330 c*.

Jones v Challenger [1960] 1 All ER 785, [1961] 1 QB 176, [1960] 2 WLR 695, CA, 47 *e*
Digest (Repl) 400, *3595*.

Martin v Martin [1977] 3 All ER 762, [1978] Fam 12, [1977] 3 WLR 101, CA, Digest (Cont Vol E) 271, *6962Add(i)*.

Mayo Re, Mayo v Mayo [1943] 2 All ER 440, [1943] Ch 302, sub nom *Re Mayo's Will Trusts* 112 LJ Ch 257, 169 LT 205, 47 Digest (Repl) 399, *3593*.

Mesher v Mesher and Hall [1980] 1 All ER 126, CA.

Rawlings v Rawlings [1964] 2 All ER 804, [1964] P 398, [1964] 3 WLR 294, CA, 27(1) *f*
Digest (Reissue) 94, *680*.

Williams v Williams [1977] 1 All ER 28, [1976] Ch 278, [1976] 3 WLR 494, CA, Digest (Cont Vol E) 255, *662 b*.

Appeal

The plaintiff, Raymond Michael Algar Papps ('the father'), appealed against the decision *g*
of his Honour Judge Lipfriend, sitting as a judge of the High Court on 10th December
1979 ordering that the property at Basingstoke, Hampshire, jointly owned by the
plaintiff and the defendant, Carol Jean Evers, and occupied by the defendant, be sold but
that such sale be postponed until the child of the parties attained the age of 16. The facts
are set out in the judgment of the court. *h*

Quentin Edwards QC and *Jane Rodgers* for the father.
Roger Gray QC and *David Bodey* for the mother.

Cur adv vult

2nd May. **ORMROD LJ** read the following judgment of the court: This is an appeal *j*
by Mr Papps, whom we will call 'the father', from part of the judgment of his Honour
Judge Lipfriend, sitting as a judge of the High Court in the Family Division, given on
10th December 1979. The judge had two matters before him, an originating summons
in wardship proceedings by Mrs Evers, whom we will call 'the mother', and an
application by the father under s 30 of the Law of Property Act 1925 for an order for sale
of a cottage near Basingstoke. The judge made an order in the wardship proceedings

giving care and control of the child in question to the mother, and in the s 30 proceedings
a directed that the property be sold but that such sale be postponed until the child attained the age of 16 years or until further order. The father originally appealed against both orders, but at the outset counsel for the father abandoned the appeal in relation to the wardship. The appeal in relation to the s 30 application raises questions of general importance, because it appears to be the first time that this court has had to consider the application of s 30 in relation to a property purchased as a home and held in joint names
b by two persons who are not married to one another. This is a situation which is occurring much more frequently now than in the past and is a social development of considerable importance with which the courts are now likely to have to deal from time to time.

The form of the judge's order bears a close resemblance to, and was obviously derived from, orders made by this court under the Matriomonial Causes Act 1973, s 24, in such
c cases such as *Mesher v Mesher and Hall* [1980] 1 All ER 126, *Browne (formerly Pritchard) v Pritchard* [1975] 3 All ER 721, [1975] 1 WLR 1366 and *Martin v Martin* [1977] 3 All ER 762, [1978] Fam 12; and, in fact, the judge relied expressly on the latter two cases.

At the outset, it must be said that in this respect the judge was in error. The powers of the court under s 30 of the Law of Property Act 1925 are different from the powers which it has under s 24 of the Matrimonial Causes Act 1973; the ambit of the discretion
d is consequently different. Under s 24 the court is empowered to make orders between former husbands and wives, 'adjusting' their respective property rights; under s 30 the court is concerned with the effect to be given to existing property rights, a much more restricted function. Cases arising under s 24, therefore, are not relevant to cases arising under s 30, although some of the considerations to be taken into account are common to both classes.

e Section 30 of the Law of Property Act 1925 is in these terms:

> 'If the trustees for sale refuse to sell or to exercise any of the powers conferred by either of the last two sections, or any requisite consent cannot be obtained, any person interested may apply to the court for a vesting or other order for giving effect to the proposed transaction or for an order directing the trustees for sale to give effect thereto, and the court may make such order as it thinks fit.'

f The section gives the court a discretion to intervene to deal, inter alia, with the situation which arises when the trustees under a trust for sale are unable or unwilling to agree that the property should be sold. In such circumstances, the court can order a sale of the property, and if appropriate impose terms, or it can decline to make an order, leaving the property unsold unless and until the trustees reach agreement or the court makes an order at some future date.

g The usual practice in these cases has been to order a sale and a division of the proceeds of sale, thus giving effect to the express purpose of the trust. But the trust for sale has become a very convenient and much used conveyancing technique. Combined with the statutory power in the trustees to postpone the sale, it can be used to meet a variety of situations, in some of which an actual sale is far from the intentions of the parties at the
h time when the trust for sale comes into existence. So, when asked to exercise its discretionary powers under s 30 to execute the trust, the court must have regard to its underlying purpose. In *Re Buchanan-Wollaston's Conveyance* [1939] 2 All ER 302, [1939] Ch 738 four adjoining landowners purchased a plot of land to prevent it being built on and held it on trust for sale. They also covenanted with one another that the land would not be dealt with except with the unanimous agreement of the trustees. Subsequently one of them wished to sell, but some of the other trustees objected so the plaintiff applied
j to the court under s 30 for an order for sale. At first instance Farwell J refused the order, saying ([1939] Ch 217 at 223):

> 'The question is this: Will the court assist the plaintiff to do an act which would be directly contrary to his contract with the other parties, since it was plainly the intention of the parties to the said contract that the land should not be sold save with the consent of them all?'

His decision was upheld in this court, but on a broader basis. Greene MR said ([1939] 2 All ER 302 at 308, [1939] Ch 738 at 747): a

'... it seems to me that the court of equity, when asked to enforce the trust for sale, whether one created by a settlement or a will or one created by the statute, must look into all the circumstances of the case and consider whether or not, at the particular moment and in the particular circumstances when the application is made to it, it is right and proper that such an order shall be made. In considering a question of that kind, in circumstances such as these, the court is bound to look at b the contract into which the parties have entered and to ask itself the question whether or not the person applying for execution of the trust for sale is a person whose voice should be allowed to prevail.'

Some twenty years later, in *Jones v Challenger* [1960] 1 All ER 785 at 787, [1961] 1 QB at 181, Devlin LJ reviewed the authorities and affirmed this principle: c

'This simple principle [ie that in a trust for sale there is a duty to sell] cannot prevail where the trust itself or the circumstances in which it was made show that there was a secondary or collateral object besides that of sale. Simonds, J. in his judgment in *Re Mayo* ([1943] 2 All ER 440, [1943] Ch 302) said that if there were mala fides, the position would be different. If it be not mala fides, it is at any rate wrong and inequitable for one of the parties to the trust to invoke the letter of the d trust in order to defeat one of its purposes, whether that purpose be written or unwritten, and the court will not permit it.'

In *Jones v Challenger* a house had been purchased by a husband and wife jointly as a home. Subsequently the marriage broke down, the wife left and committed adultery and applied to the court for an order for sale of the property, a leasehold with only a few e years to run. The husband continued to live in the house on his own; there were no children. In these circumstances the court decided that the house should be sold. Devlin LJ said ([1960] 1 All ER 785 at 789, [1961] 1 QB 176 at 183):

'In the case which we have to consider, the house was acquired as the matrimonial home. That was the purpose of the joint tenancy and, for so long as that purpose was still alive, I think that the right test to be applied would be that in *Re Buchanan-* f *Wollaston*. But with the end of the marriage, that purpose was dissolved and the primacy of the duty to sell was restored.'

Had there been children whose home was still in the property, the conclusion in that case might have been different. Later Devlin LJ said ([1960] 1 All ER 785 at 789, [1961] 1 QB 176 at 184): 'The true question is whether it is inequitable for the wife, once the g matrimonial home has gone, to want to realise her investment?'

In *Burke v Burke* [1974] 2 All ER 944, [1974] 1 WLR 1063, however, children were involved. On the husband's application under s 17 the registrar ordered a sale, but postponed it for a year or so to give the wife, who had custody of the children, an opportunity to find an alternative home for them. This court upheld the registrar's order. The application was actually made under s 17 of the Married Women's Property h Act 1882. That section is purely procedural and the principles are the same as under s 30. In giving the leading judgment Buckley LJ took the view that the trust for sale was an immediate binding trust subject to the discretionary power in the court to postpone the execution of the trust for sale, and that the court must have regard to all the relevant circumstances of the case and to the situation of both the beneficial owners. The interests of the children in that case, he thought were ([1974] 2 All ER 944 at 947–948, [1974] 1 j WLR 1063 at 1067)—

'interests which are only incidentally to be taken into consideration in that sort of way. They are, as I say, proper to be taken into consideration so far as they affect the equities in the matter as between the two persons entitled to the beneficial interests in the property. But it is not, I think, right to treat this case as though the husband

> was obliged to make provision for his children by agreeing to retain the property *a* unsold. To do so is, as I think, and as was urged on us by counsel for the husband, to confuse with a problem relating to property, considerations which are relevant to maintenance.'

He expressed disagreement with an obiter dictum of Salmon LJ in the earlier case of *Rawlings v Rawlings* [1964] 2 All ER 804 at 814, [1964] P 398 at 419 where he said:

> *b* 'If there were young children the position would be different. One of the purposes of the trust would no doubt have been to provide a home for them, and whilst that purpose still existed, a sale would not generally be ordered.'

Buckley LJ was plainly anxious to make it clear that the children themselves in such circumstances were not objects of the trust and, therefore, had no beneficial interests in the property, and so were in that sense only 'incidental' to the problem, but we do not *c* think that Salmon LJ thought otherwise. The court in *Burke v Burke* was not referred to the *Buchanan-Wollaston* case, so Buckley LJ does not seem to have considered, in so many words, whether or not the primary purpose of the trust, i e for sale, 'the letter of the trust' in the words of Devlin LJ in *Jones v Challenger* [1960] 1 All ER 785 at 787, [1961] 1 QB 178 at 181, had been affected by the underlying purpose, quoting Devlin LJ again, 'written or unwritten' of providing a home, not only for the parents but also for the *d* children. The dictum of Salmon LJ appears, therefore, to be more in line with the judgments of this court in the *Buchanan-Wollaston* case and in *Jones v Challenger*. Moreover, it is now supported by a dictum of Lord Denning MR in *Williams v Williams* [1977] 1 All ER 28 at 30, [1976] Ch 278 at 285: 'The court, in executing the trust, should regard the primary object as being to provide a home and not a sale.'

This approach to the exercise of the discretion given by s 30 has considerable *e* advantages in these 'family' cases. It enables the court to deal with substance (that is, reality) rather than form (that is, convenience of conveyancing); it brings the exercise of the discretion under this section, so far as possible, into line with the exercise of the discretion given by s 24 of the Matrimonial Causes Act 1973; and it goes some way to eliminating differences between legitimate and illegitimate children in accordance with present legislative policy (see for example the Family Law Reform Act 1969, Part II).

f The relevant facts in the present case must now be examined. There is little or no dispute between the parties about them. Both the mother and the father have been married and divorced. The mother had two children of her marriage, both boys, now aged 10 and 8. She met the father in May 1974. In August 1974 they began to live together at the father's former matrimonial home; the two boys remained in the care of their father, the mother visiting them regularly. Early in 1976 the mother became *g* pregnant by the father and gave birth to the child who is the subject of the wardship proceedings on 22nd December 1976. At about that time the two older boys joined their mother and from then until the separation in August 1979 all five lived together, at first at the father's former matrimonial home, until in April 1978 the parties jointly acquired the cottage which is the subject of these proceedings. This property was purchased for £13,950, of which £10,000 was raised jointly on mortgage. The balance was provided *h* as to £2,400 by the mother and as to £1,050 plus expenses by the father. The mother's contribution was derived from her share of her former matrimonial home. On 28th April 1978 the property was conveyed into their joint names as trustees on a bare trust for sale with power to postpone the sale in trust for themselves as joint tenants.

The irresistible inference from these facts is that, as the judge found, they purchased this property as a family home for themselves and the three children. It is difficult to *j* imagine that the mother, then wholly responsible for two children and partly for the third, would have invested nearly all her capital in the purchase of this property if it was not to be available to her as a home for the children for the indefinite future. It is inconceivable that the father, when he agreed to this joint adventure, could have thought otherwise or contemplated the possibility of an early sale without the consent of the mother. The underlying purpose of the trust was, therefore, to provide a home for all five of them for the indefinite future. Unfortunately, the relationship between the father and the mother broke down very soon, and the parties separated at the beginning of August 1979 in circumstances of great bitterness. This is clearly shown by two dates. On 20th July 1979 the mother issued her originating summons in the wardship proceedings, and on 2nd August 1979 the father issued his application under s 30 for an order for sale of the property.

Counsel for the father argued that the judge had not taken into account that his client's legal liability was limited to providing maintenance for his illegitimate child and did not extend to providing for the mother. That proposition is correct as the law now stands, though it will not be so when s 50 of the Domestic Proceedings and Magistrates' Courts Act 1978 comes into force. That section amends s 4 of the Affiliation Proceedings Act 1957, by empowering magistrates' courts to take account of the needs of the mother. In any event, in the present proceedings the court is not so much concerned with obligations imposed by law on the father as with obligations which he had assumed or must be taken to have assumed.

It was further argued that the father ought to be allowed to 'take his money out' or 'to realise his investment'. In point of fact, his investment amounted to less than one-fifth of the purchase price of the property, and was smaller than the mother's investment. The major part of the purchase price was provided by the mortgagees, and the mother is prepared to accept full responsibility for paying the interest on the mortgage and keeping up the capital repayments. The father has a secure home with his mother. There is no evidence that he has any need to realise his investment. It is an excellent one, combining complete security with considerable capital appreciation in money terms. His share is now said to be worth about £5,000, ie it has more than doubled in value in two years. On the other hand, a sale of the property now would put the mother into a very difficult position because she cannot raise the finance to rehouse herself or meet the cost of borrowing money at present rates. So there is no justification for ordering a sale at the present time.

For these reasons the judge was right not to order an immediate sale, but the form of his actual order is not satisfactory. Under s 30 the primary question is whether the court should come to the aid of the applicant at the 'particular moment, and in the particular circumstances when the application is made to it' (*Re Buchanan-Wollaston's Conveyance* [1939] 2 All ER 302 at 308, [1939] Ch 738 at 747). In the present case, at the present moment and in the existing circumstances, it would be wrong to order a sale. But circumstances may change unpredictably. It may not be appropriate to order a sale when the child reaches 16 years, a purely arbitrary date, or it may become appropriate to do so much sooner, for example on the mother's remarriage or on it becoming financially possible for her to buy the father out. In such circumstances it will probably be wiser simply to dismiss the application while indicating the sort of circumstances which would, prima facie, justify a further application. The ensuing uncertainty is unfortunate, but, under this section, the court has no power to adjust property rights or to redraft the terms of the trust. Ideally, the parties should now negotiate a settlement on the basis that neither of them is in a position to dictate terms. We would, therefore, dismiss the father's appeal, but would vary the order to dismiss the application on the mother's undertaking to discharge the liability under the mortgage, to pay the outgoings and maintain the property, and to indemnify the father so long as she is occupying the property.

Appeal dismissed. Leave to appeal to the House of Lords refused.

24th July. The Appeal Committee of the House of Lords (Lord Salmon, Lord Wilberforce and Lord Russell of Killowen) dismissed a petition by the father for leave to appeal.

Solicitors: *Lamb, Brooks & Bullock*, Basingstoke (for the father); *Snow & Bispham*, Basingstoke (for the mother).

Avtar S Virdi Esq Barrister.

a
Yousif v Salama

COURT OF APPEAL, CIVIL DIVISION
LORD DENNING MR, DONALDSON AND BRIGHTMAN LJJ
7th MAY 1980

b *Practice – Inspection of property – Document not subject matter of action – Interlocutory motion – Ex parte application – Jurisdiction to make order – Discretion to order inspection – Principles on which discretion to be exercised – Plaintiff wishing to support claim by reference to books of account in defendant's custody – Plaintiff fearing that accounts would be destroyed – Whether discretion to order inspection and removal of accounts.*

c The plaintiff purchased goods for the defendants to resell under an agreement whereby the defendants were to pay the plaintiff commission for the goods supplied. For some years transactions took place and commission accrued to the plaintiff but was not paid. The plaintiff visited the defendants' office where he saw the accounts showing the amount of commission due to him. The plaintiff then issued a writ claiming the amount owed and, fearing that the defendants might destroy the two files containing
d the accounts and a diary which contained details of the transactions, applied for an Anton Piller order permitting him to enter the defendants' premises to search and locate the files and diary and remove them to the custody of his solicitor.

Held – The court had a discretion to grant an Anton Piller order to enable the preservation of a document which did not itself form the subject matter of the action,
e where (per Lord Denning MR) the document was the best possible evidence and the plaintiff genuinely feared that the defendant would destroy it prior to the hearing of the action, or (per Donaldson LJ) there was a very clear prima facie case leading the court to fear that the defendant would conceal or destroy essential evidence and that to do so would deprive the plaintiff of any evidence on which to put forward his claim and so
f frustrate the process of justice, or (per Brightman LJ) there was prima facie evidence that essential documents were at risk. On the evidence (Donaldson LJ dissenting), the order would be granted and the appeal allowed (see p 406 *f* to p 407 *a* and *f* to *h* and p 408 *e* to *g*, post).

Anton Piller KG v Manufacturing Processes Ltd [1976] 1 All ER 779 applied.

g **Notes**

For inspection and preservation of property, see 21 Halsbury's Laws (3rd Edn) 419, para 879, and for cases on the subject, see 28(2) Digest (Reissue) 1125, *1234–1242*.

Case referred to in judgments

h *Anton Piller KG v Manufacturing Processes Ltd* [1976] 1 All ER 779, [1976] Ch 55, [1976] 2 WLR 162, [1976] RPC 719, [1976] FSR 129, CA, Digest (Cont Vol E) 338, *1238b*.

Interlocutory appeal

The plaintiff, George Yousif, appealed from the order of Robert Goff J, made in chambers on 6th May 1980, refusing the plaintiff's application for an order permitting him to
j enter the premises of the defendants, Bushra Ibrahim Salama and Selvex Marketing Ltd, for the purpose of searching for and finding files and documents which were contained therein in March 1980 and a 1979 desk diary. The facts are set out in the judgment of Lord Denning MR.

Mary Vitoria for the plaintiff.

Cur adv vult

7th May. The following judgments were read.

LORD DENNING MR. This application raises an interesting new point. The plaintiff says that he made an agreement with the defendant, who was resident in the Middle East. Certain goods were to be purchased in England and dispatched to the Middle East. They were then to be resold there. In respect of those transactions, the plaintiff was to divide the profits between himself and the first defendant: 30% in some cases and 50% in others. That was the agreement.

Several transactions took place for a year or two. A statement of account was rendered by the defendant's limited company (giving the letter of credit references) showing a sum due. Business continued thereafter. Extra commission was accruing. The result was that in March 1980 the plaintiff went with the first defendant to the second defendant company's office to go through the accounts. Two files were produced containing the various accounts. They showed sums due to the plaintiff. Also a desk diary.

The plaintiff, being very anxious about the matter, brought proceedings in the court for the sum due to him. On 16th April 1980 he issued a writ for that purpose. The total sum claimed was £14,000 odd. The writ was served. The solicitors for the defendant wrote to the plaintiff's solicitors saying that they were going to defend the claim strenuously.

The plaintiff then became very anxious about the file and the desk diary he had seen which contained details of the transactions. He became fearful that the defendant would destroy those documents before the actual hearing of the case. On 2nd May 1980 the plaintiff applied for an Anton Piller order. He did not notify the defendant that he was making that application: because he was afraid the defendant would destroy the documents if he were notified. The plaintiff asked that he should be granted an Anton Piller order to enable him to go to the defendant company's offices and inspect the documents before the defendant has an opportunity to destroy them.

In many cases such an order would not be granted. But in this case there is evidence (if it is accepted) which shows the defendant to be untrustworthy. The plaintiff has a legitimate fear that the documents will be destroyed. In the circumstances, it seems to me that it would be proper to make an Anton Piller order to the effect that the plaintiff's solicitor would be able to go and get the documents, take them into his personal custody for a while, make copies of them, and then return the originals to the defendant. He would have to keep them personally himself, and not let them out of his possession. It seems to me that that would be an aid to justice. It would be preserving the evidence in the case. Under RSC Ord 29, r 2, there is a far-reaching power for preserving documents which are the subject matter of the action. These files here are not the subject matter of the action. But they are the best possible evidence to prove the plaintiff's case. There is a genuine fear that, if the plaintiff waits till after the application is heard, the defendant may destroy the documents before the date of the hearing. That is the sort of danger which the Anton Piller order is designed to prevent.

In the particular circumstances of this case, subject to variations in wording which we have discussed with counsel, it seems to me that an Anton Piller order is available. But it should be limited to the documents which were seen to be in the two files at the interview in March, and the desk diary which was also seen at that time. So, with those variations and an undertaking that the documents which are received in pursuance of the Anton Piller order are kept in the solicitor's personal custody, it seems to me that the granting of the order can in no way harm the defendants. It is an aid to justice as far as the plaintiff is concerned. Instead of having to speculate or try and get evidence from elsewhere, it should all be available in the files. It can do no harm to the defendant at all. If he is honest, he will produce the documents in any case. If he is dishonest, that is all the more reason why the order should be made. Meanwhile, once the documents are handed to the plaintiff's solicitor, copies can be made of them and the originals returned to the defendant.

It is an exceptional case. Subject to the variations I have suggested, I would therefore grant an Anton Piller order.

DONALDSON LJ. With great respect to all that has fallen from Lord Denning MR, I have the misfortune to take a rather different view of this case. The relationship between the parties seems to me to be a very common one. The plaintiff is a procuring agent in the Middle East. The terms of his agreement with the first defendant, who is an individual, and the second defendant, which is a company, are both simple and common. They are that he will try to procure business for the two defendants and that he will be paid a commission on any business which he procures and passes to them for execution.

The parties of course have fallen out. Again a common situation. It is true that judges only see the cases that go wrong, so perhaps it is not as universal an ending as the judges might think. Perhaps some agency transactions do reach a successful conclusion. But this is a not uncommon situation again. As a matter of law the defendants are accounting parties if the situation is as set out in the plaintiff's affidavit. Again it is a very common situation that a defendant should be an accounting party, and that much of the information which the plaintiff needs should be in his possession. In those circumstances the ordinary order would be either for an account with all the usual inquiries, which would involve the defendants giving evidence on oath as to what was due and the facts on which that indebtedness was based, or perhaps an order for discovery.

Discovery can be ordered at any stage. It can be ordered even before statement of claim in an appropriate case. But the ordinary basis of litigation in the English courts is that the courts will make orders and that the parties will obey those orders. Thus it is that under an order for discovery one party gives discovery to the other, and I stress the word 'gives'. The party who is entitled to receive discovery has it given to him. He is not empowered to 'take' discovery. What counsel for the plaintiff asks us to do in this case is to make an order that the plaintiff, on an ex parte application, should be entitled, armed with a warrant from this court, to enter the premises of the defendants and *take* discovery.

I regard that as a very serious invasion of the rights of the defendants. Of course there is precedent for doing it. It is in the line of cases descended from *Anton Piller KG v Manufacturing Processes Ltd* [1976] 1 All ER 779, [1976] Ch 55. The essential feature of those cases, as I understand them, is that there is a very clear prima facie case leading the court to fear that the defendant will conceal or destroy essential evidence in the grossest possible contempt of the court, and (this is an important second limb) that should he do so the whole processes of justice will be frustrated because the plaintiff will be left without any evidence to enable him to put forward his claim. In that limited class of case I, for my part, think that the Anton Piller order is absolutely right. No court can stand by and see the processes of justice totally frustrated by a defendant in contempt of its order. But I cannot find anything in this case which brings it within that category. I regard the evidence of an intention to destroy the documentation as flimsy in the extreme. It is based on an allegation of forgery in the indorsement of a cheque. This has nothing whatever to do with the destruction of documents which the plaintiff says that he fears.

The indorsement may not be that of the plaintiff, but if it was authorised there would be no forgery. If it is really said that there has been forgery here, why were the police not informed? It is a criminal offence, not quietly to be put on one side and then trotted out at a convenient moment in support of an application for an Anton Piller order.

Apart from that, it is not irrelevant that the defendant is a relation of the plaintiff's. Family feelings are well-known to be very strong at times, and in a family environment suspicion can grow out of all reason. As I say, I regard the suspicions here as being flimsy in the extreme.

Even if I am wrong about that, it is quite clear, as I see it, that if these documents are destroyed the plaintiff's case will be in no way weakened. In every agency case of this type the starting point of the calculation of commissions is orders placed through the plaintiff and money passing through the hands of the plaintiff or those with whom he could get in touch without any difficulty. The plaintiff can show quite easily how much money has been paid for goods and services which he has procured for the defendants. Starting from that point, it is the defendant who will need the documents in order to prove that the plaintiff is not entitled to a very large commission indeed. And, if the defendant cannot produce the documents, the court will rightly make every presumption in favour of the plaintiff.

Again, it is not a case where there are no documents relating to this type of business so that the plaintiff, so to speak, starts from scratch. The plaintiff has the documents for 1978 and can demonstrate the rate of commission which was payable for that year. There is no suggestion that the basis was altered for 1979. Given the cash flow for 1979, which can be proved without difficulty, I can see no problem for him in proving his prima facie entitlement to commission. The problems will be all for the defendant.

As I say, I think this is a draconian power which should be used in only exceptional cases.

I have considered, of course, whether, as was suggested in argument, it can rightly be said that no harm is done to an honest man by taking discovery from him when eventually he would have been ordered to give it. I think that great harm is done. The people of this country are entitled not to have their privacy and their property invaded by a court order except in very exceptional circumstances. That, in my judgment, is not this case.

I would therefore dismiss the appeal.

BRIGHTMAN LJ. In my view the order sought in this case is justified if, but only if, there is prima facie evidence that essential documents are at risk. If essential documents are at risk, then it seems to me that this court ought to permit the plaintiff to take such steps as are necessary to preserve them.

So there are two questions to be asked. First, are the documents sought to be seized essential to the plaintiff's case? If so, are such documents at serious risk? Might they be dishonestly destroyed?

It is difficult to form any confident view on the merits of the application because inevitably the evidence is one-sided. The defendants have had no opportunity to answer it. But I think on the plaintiff's evidence that there are grounds for saying that the documents in question are essential to the plaintiff's case. I also think that on balance there is sufficient evidence to justify the court in concluding that the documents are at risk. Therefore I would myself favour the grant of an appropriate order.

Appeal allowed.

Solicitors: *Bower, Cotton & Bower* (for the plaintiff).

Frances Rustin Barrister.

Prince Abdul Rahman Bin Turki Al Sudairy v Abu-Taha and another

COURT OF APPEAL, CIVIL DIVISION
LORD DENNING MR, WALLER AND DUNN LJJ
12TH JUNE 1980

Injunction – Interlocutory – Danger that defendant may transfer assets out of jurisdiction – Injunction restraining removal of assets out of the jurisdiction – English defendant – Whether jurisdiction to grant Mareva injunction against defendant resident in England – Whether Mareva jurisdiction restricted to preventing foreigners resident abroad from removing assets out of jurisdiction.

The court has jurisdiction to grant a Mareva injunction against a defendant based in England if the circumstances are such that there is a danger of the defendant absconding or of the assets being removed out of the jurisdiction or disposed of within the jurisdiction or otherwise dealt with so that if the plaintiff obtains judgment he may not be able to have it satisfied (see p 412 *a*, post).

Barclay-Johnson v Yuill p 190, ante, approved.

Notes
For an injunction restraining disposition of property, see 24 Halsbury's Laws (4th Edn) para 1018, and for cases on the subject, see 28(2) Digest (Reissue) 1091–1094, *918–960*.

Cases cited in judgments
Barclay-Johnson v Yuill p 190, ante.
Chartered Bank v Daklouche [1980] 1 All ER 205, [1980] 1 WLR 107, CA.
Gebr Van Weelde Scheepvaart Kantoor BV v Homeric Marine Services Ltd, The Agrabele [1979] 2 Lloyd's Rep 117, Digest (Cont Vol E) 334, *79g*.
Mareva Compania Naviera SA v International Bulkcarriers SA, The Mareva (1975) [1980] 1 All ER 213, [1975] 2 Lloyd's Rep 509, CA, Digest (Cont Vol E) 331, *79b*.
Siskina (Cargo owners) v Distos Compania Naviera SA, The Siskina [1977] 3 All ER 803, [1979] AC 210, [1977] 3 WLR 818, [1978] 1 Lloyd's Rep 1, HL, Digest (Cont Vol E) 660, *782a*.
Third Chandris Shipping Corpn v Unimarine SA, The Pythia, The Angelic Wings, The Genie [1979] 2 All ER 972, [1979] QB 645, [1979] 3 WLR 122, CA, Digest (Cont Vol E) 333, *79e*.

Appeal
By a writ and statement of claim dated 6th February 1980 the plaintiff, His Royal Highness Prince Abdul Rahman Bin Turki Al Sudairy brought an action against the defendants, Awni Othman Abu-Taha and Beda Suleiman Abu-Ghosh, for breach of an oral agreement made in or about March 1977 whereby the defendants agreed to sell to the plaintiffs an Aston Martin Lagonda motor car for the sum of £34,000. On 6th February 1980 Smith J granted an interim injunction restraining the defendants from removing out of the jurisdiction or otherwise disposing of within the jurisdiction any of their assets save in so far as the defendants' assets exceeded £34,000. On 25th February 1980 Robert Goff J discharged the injunction. On 6th June 1980 Peter Pain J reimposed it and on 9th June 1980 Patrick Bennett QC, sitting as a deputy judge of the High Court, discharged it. The plaintiff appealed. The facts are set out in the judgment of Lord Denning MR.

John A Kelly for the plaintiff.
George Lawrence for the defendants.

LORD DENNING MR. This is an unusual case. The plaintiff, Prince Abdul Rahman Al Sudairy, lives in Saudi Arabia. He is a man of great wealth. He entered into negotiations to buy an expensive motor car in England, an Aston Martin Lagonda, for the sum of £34,000. He negotiated with two men, Abu-Ghosh and Abu-Taha. They were two young men. They came originally from Kuwait. According to their own accounts they have been in England for many years and are permanently resident here. They met when they both went to the Bath Technical College and took their 'A' levels there. Abu-Taha went on to Bristol University. Abu-Ghosh went to London University. They afterwards set up business together in office premises on the 6th Floor, 49 Park Lane, London W1. That is a block of offices which houses several Middle East firms. They carried on business under the name of Sarco Enterprises. We know nothing about that firm except that it is said to be registered in Liechtenstein.

In the course of the negotiations for the Aston Martin Lagonda (for £34,000) Prince Abdul Rahman Al Sudairy drew two cheques, one in favour of Abu-Ghosh for £12,000 on 13th March 1978; and the other on 7th February 1979 for £22,000 in favour of Sarco Enterprises. Both those cheques were paid into Barclays Bank (Park Lane branch).

The deal did not go through. The car was not delivered. On 25th November 1979 Abu-Taha purported to return the money. He drew a cheque for £34,000 in favour of Prince Abdul Rahman Al Sudairy. It was drawn on an account at Barclays Bank (Park Lane branch) under the name of Abu-Taha External Account.

The cheque was not honoured. It was returned marked 'Refer to drawer'. Prince Abdul Rahman Al Sudairy sued for his money. He issued a writ on 6th February 1980 against the two young men. He took out a summons under RSC Ord 14. The young men put in affidavits of defence. They denied that they ever agreed to sell the plaintiff an Aston Martin Lagonda motor car. Abu-Taha said that his cheque for £34,000 was not a repayment. It was a loan by him to the plaintiff.

Prince Abdul Rahman Al Sudairy, in support of his claim, seeks a Mareva injunction against these two gentlemen. The summons under RSC Ord 14 is coming on in about a fortnight; and he is fearful that any money they have will have disappeared by the time he gets judgment. It may be transferred to Kuwait, or somewhere else, and it may be difficult to get hold of it. So he asks for a Mareva injunction.

The matter has come before several judges. On 6th February 1980 Smith J granted a Mareva injunction. On 25th February 1980 Robert Goff J discharged it because the defendants swore that they were resident in England. On 6th June 1980 Peter Pain J reimposed it. On 9th June 1980 Mr Patrick Bennett QC, sitting as a deputy judge, discharged it. The plaintiff appeals to this court asking that a Mareva injunction should be granted.

On the hearing before us further affidavits were filed and the case argued inter partes. This further evidence goes far to show that the plaintiff has a strong case for the return of the £34,000. It also shows that, although the defendants are permanently resident within the jurisdiction, they are most secretive about their home addresses. In their affidavits both give their addresses as '6th Floor, 49 Park Lane, London'; but that is a business office. We are told that it is now empty and deserted. Neither of them gives his home address. Abu-Taha says: 'I rent a house in north-west London, where I live with my wife and child. I own two motor cars. Together with the second defendant I own furniture and fittings valued in excess of £25,000.' Abu-Ghosh says: 'I own a house in London, where I live with my wife. I bought it four years ago. I estimate the value to be between £80,000 and £90,000. I own two motor cars valued at approximately £28,000.'

So these two young men, on their own statements, have accumulated great wealth during their short time in business. But neither of them gives his home address, as under the rule each ought to have done. Why not? It leads me to think that they are not at all trustworthy. Their houses may be in the names of nominees so as to prevent creditors getting their hands on them. At any rate, the circumstances suggest to my mind that there is a risk that, if the plaintiff should get judgment, he may find that before he can issue execution, the defendants may have disposed of their assets. They may have taken them out of the jurisdiction or transferred them to someone here.

So the case raises distinctly the question: can a Mareva injunction be granted against
a a defendant who is resident in this country? In *The Agrabele* [1979] 2 Lloyd's Rep 117 Lloyd J held it could not. I can understand his hesitation at first instance in extending the principle of *Mareva Compania Naviera SA v International Bulkcarriers SA, The Mareva* (1975) [1980] 1 All ER 213. But things are moving rapidly. We considered the position in the case of *Chartered Bank v Daklouche* [1980] 1 All ER 205, [1980] 1 WLR 107 and *Third Chandris Shipping Corpn v Unimarine SA* [1979] 2 All ER 972 at 984, [1979] QB 645
b at 667. I intimated there that a Mareva injunction would lie against a person within the jurisdiction. The committee presided over by Payne J considered the problem in their report on the enforcement of judgment debts (Cmnd 3909 (1969), paras 1248–1255). They gave this illustration (para 1252):

> 'Under modern conditions of travel, particularly as the cost of air travel is now within means of many a debtor, the risk of goods and chattels, or substantial sums
> *c* of money being taken out of the country is greatly increased. It is possible to imagine countless circumstances in which a power to restrain a debtor could be justified but one will suffice. A debtor may buy valuable jewellery on credit, ignore demands for payment and ignore a writ or summons. The jeweller may not know where the jewellery is. If he happens to discover that the debtor has booked an air passage and proposes to leave England a few days later and before any progress can
> *d* be made with the action which has been commenced, is there anyone who would argue in these days that the court should not have power to order that the debtor should not remove the jewellery from the jurisdiction or otherwise dispose of it?'

Very recently Sir Robert Megarry V-C has dealt with it fully in *Barclay-Johnson v Yuill* p 190, ante. As a result, I think the time has come for us to grasp the nettle. Lord Hailsham foresaw it when he said in *The Siskina* [1977] 3 All ER 803 at 829, [1979] AC
e 210 at 261:

> 'I believe the truth to be that sooner or later the courts or the legislature will have to choose between the two alternatives. Either the position of a plaintiff making claim against an English based defendant will have to be altered or the principle of the Mareva cases will have to be modified.'

f The courts are now faced with the two alternatives. We have to make the choice. I have no doubt what our choice should be. We must not modify 'the principle of the Mareva cases'. It has proved of such great value to the Commercial Court that it must be retained intact. So we must 'alter the position of a plaintiff making a claim against an English based defendant'. We must do it by putting all defendants on the same footing, no matter whether they be foreign based or English based. The same principle applies
g to both. It was well stated by Sir Robert Megarry V-C in *Barclay-Johnson v Yuill* (see pp 194–195, ante):

> '... the heart and core of the Mareva injunction is the risk of the defendant removing his assets from the jurisdiction and so stultifying any judgment given by the courts in the action ... accordingly, the injunction will restrain the defendant from disposing of [the assets] even within the jurisdiction ... If, then, the essence
> *h* of the jurisdiction is the risk of assets being removed from the jurisdiction, I cannot see why it should be confined to "foreigners", in any sense of that term ... Naturally the risk of removal of assets from the jurisdiction will usually be greater or more obvious in the case of foreign-based defendants, and so the jurisdiction has grown up in relation to them ... Is it really to be said that in relation to Mareva injunctions, there is one law for the foreigner and another for the English ... I do not intend to
> *j* suggest that matters of nationality, domicile, residence and so on are irrelevant in Mareva applications. Any or all of them may be of considerable importance in so far as they bear on the risk of removal ... it must be remembered that since the first Mareva injunction was granted, there has been a significant change, in that within the last year the abolition of exchange control has made it easier for everybody to transfer assets abroad.'

So I would hold that a Mareva injunction can be granted against a man even though he is based in this country if the circumstances are such that there is a danger of his absconding, or a danger of the assets being removed out of the jurisdiction or disposed of within the jurisdiction, or otherwise dealt with so that there is a danger that the plaintiff, if he gets judgment, will not be able to get it satisfied.

That brings me to the particular circumstances of this case. On their own story, these two young men have done extremely well since they left the technical college. They have much money and many assets available to them. But the strange thing is that they have not said a word as to where they live. They have not given us their addresses at all. They had this Liechtenstein concern, but that has wound up. Then, when it comes to their assets, one does not know where they are. They are not British nationals. In the circumstances of this case it seems to me that the court may be apprehensive, and the plaintiff may be apprehensive, that, unless something is done to stop them, they may remove their assets from the jurisdiction or otherwise dispose of them. At all events, pending the time when the summons under RSC Ord 14 has been heard, it seems to me that the plaintiff should be protected; and there should be an injunction in the usual Mareva form restraining the defendants from removing out of the jurisdiction (or otherwise disposing of them within the jurisdiction) any of their assets save in so far as they exceed £34,000.

Of course, £34,000 is the only sum in question here. If they have any more money here, they can remove it. There is nothing to stop them doing that. All this injunction will restrain them from doing is removing the first £34,000. There will be an injunction in the terms asked, that is, to restrain the defendants from disposing of any moneys or assets held to the account of the defendants by Barclays Bank or by the other named firms. I expect the way in which it will be operated will be for the plaintiff to notify Barclays Bank and the named firms of the injunction. On the terms of the injunction being notified to the persons concerned, they will of course recognise the injunction, because, if they were to go against it, they themselves would be guilty of a contempt of court.

I would like to add this. When there is a Mareva injunction of this kind, if the people who are notified of it are put to any expense in regard to it, that expense must be paid by the plaintiff.

This is a proper case for the granting of a Mareva injunction. I would allow the appeal, accordingly.

WALLER LJ. I agree. I would only add this, that the deputy judge in deciding this case refused to grant a Mareva injunction because he was not satisfied that there was a real risk that assets would be removed if an injunction was not granted. But the facts are these: that the two defendants are both foreigners; they are said to be residing here, but in swearing their affidavits they each say 'of 6th Floor, 49 Park Lane, London', which are the premises from which they were trading together which are now said to be closed. In addition to that, a cheque for £34,000, the amount at stake, was not met quite recently. In my judgment, that raises a strong inference that assets may be removed from the jurisdiction, and I agree that this appeal should be allowed.

DUNN LJ. I also agree.

Appeal allowed. Injunction granted until further order. Leave to appeal to the House of Lords refused.

Solicitors: *Peter T James & Co* (for the plaintiff); *Joynson-Hicks & Co* (for the defendants).

Frances Rustin Barrister.

R v Hillingdon Borough Council, ex parte Streeting

QUEEN'S BENCH DIVISION
LORD WIDGERY CJ AND GRIFFITHS J
26th, 27th FEBRUARY 1980

COURT OF APPEAL, CIVIL DIVISION
LORD DENNING MR, WALLER AND DUNN LJJ
1st, 2nd, 3rd, 10th JULY 1980

Housing – Homeless person – Duty of housing authority to provide accommodation – Person coming from abroad and having no local connection with the area of any housing authority in Great Britain – Whether duty extending to person having no local connection with area of any housing authority – Housing (Homeless Persons) Act 1977, s 5(5).

The applicant was born and lived in Ethiopia until 1979, when she arrived in England with her child for the funeral of her English husband. It became impossible for her to return to Ethiopia, and she was granted refugee status by the Home Office which gave her indefinite leave to remain in the United Kingdom. Shortly afterwards she became homeless. Being homeless in Great Britain and homeless abroad, she applied to a housing authority for assistance in obtaining accommodation under the Housing (Homeless Persons) Act 1977. The housing authority provided temporary accommodation and after making inquiries as required by the Act concluded (i) that the applicant had a priority need because of her dependent child and (ii) that the applicant had not become homeless intentionally and was thus entitled under s 4(5)[a] to accommodation provided by the authority. The authority nevertheless decided to refuse to provide permanent accommodation for the applicant and her child on the ground that no duty was owed to her under the 1977 Act because she had no local connection with the area of any housing authority in Great Britain. The applicant applied to the Divisional Court for, and was granted, an order of certiorari to quash the authority's decision. The authority appealed.

Held – Having regard to ss 5(5)[b] and 18(2)[c] of the 1977 Act, which showed that the duty imposed by the Act could exist in circumstances where there was no local connection with the area of any housing authority, and to the fact that immigration controls restricted the number of persons entering the country who were unable to accommodate themselves and their dependants, the duty under the Act imposed on housing authorities to secure accommodation for a homeless person was not limited to persons who had a local connection with the area of a housing authority in Great Britain, but extended to a person from abroad who was unintentionally homeless abroad, who was lawfully in Great Britain and who was otherwise eligible under the 1977 Act for accommodation. In such a case the duty rested on the authority to whom the person from abroad made application. Accordingly, the housing authority owed a duty to the applicant to provide accommodation for her and her child, and the authority's appeal would therefore be dismissed (see p 419 *e* to *g*, p 420 *c* to *j*, p 421 *h* to p 422 *g*, p 424 *e* to *j* and p 425 *b*, post).

R v Bristol City Council, ex parte Browne [1979] 3 All ER 344, *De Falco v Crawley Borough Council* [1980] 1 All ER 913 and *Dyson v Kerrier District Council* p 313, ante, considered.

---

a Section 4(5), so far as material, provides: 'Where—(*a*) [a housing authority] are satisfied—(i) that [a person who has applied to them for accommodation] is homeless, and (ii) that he has a priority need, but (*b*) they are not satisfied that he became homeless intentionally, their duty . . . is to secure that accommodation becomes available for his occupation.'

b Section 5(5) is set out at p 422 *b*, post

c Section 18(2), so far as material, is set out at p 422 *c*, post

Notes

For a housing authority's duties to a homeless person, see 22 Halsbury's Laws (4th Edn) *a* para 513.

For the Housing (Homeless Persons) Act 1977, ss 5, 18, see 47 Halsbury's Statutes (3rd Edn) 319, 330.

Cases referred to in judgments

De Falco v Crawley Borough Council [1980] 1 All ER 913, [1980] QB 460, [1980] 2 WLR *b* 664, CA.

Dyson v Kerrier District Council p 313, ante.

Jefferys v Boosey (1854) 4 HL Cas 815, 3 CLR 625, 24 LJ Ex 81, 23 LTOS 273, 1 Jur NS 615, 10 ER 681, HL, 2 Digest (Reissue) 181, *1066*.

R v Bristol City Council, ex parte Browne [1979] 3 All ER 344, [1979] 1 WLR 1437, DC, Digest (Cont Vol E) 254, *152ab*. *c*

R v Eastbourne (Inhabitants) (1803) 4 East 103, 102 ER 769, 2 Digest (Reissue) 176, *1030*.

Stock v Frank Jones (Tipton) Ltd [1978] 1 All ER 58, [1977] 1 WLR 1288, [1977] ICR 976, CA; *affd* [1978] 1 All ER 948, [1978] 1 WLR 231, [1978] ICR 347, HL, Digest (Cont Vol E) 620, *1560a*.

Thompson v Goold & Co [1910] AC 409, 79 LJKB 905, 103 LT 81, 3 BWCC 392, HL, 34 Digest (Repl) 652, *4494*. *d*

Vickers Sons & Maxim Ltd v Coventry Ordnance Works Ltd [1910] AC 444, 25 RPC 207, 51 Digest (Repl) 570, *2038*.

Cases also cited

Draper (C E B) & Son Ltd v Edward Turner & Son Ltd [1964] 3 All ER 148, [1965] 1 QB 424, CA. *e*

Ealing (London Borough) v Race Relations Board [1972] 1 All ER 105, [1972] AC 342, HL.

R v Bristol Corpn, ex parte Hendy [1974] 1 All ER 1047, [1974] 1 WLR 498, CA.

Tickner v Mole Valley District Council (29th October 1979, unreported).

Application for judicial review

The applicant, Sophia Streeting, applied with the leave of the Divisional Court of the *f* Queen's Bench Division granted on 17th December 1979 for an order of certiorari to quash the decision of Hillingdon Borough Council ('the housing authority') that it owed no duty under the Housing (Homeless Persons) Act 1977 to provide accommodation for her and her child and an order of mandamus directing the housing authority to provide accommodation for them. The facts are set out in the judgment of Griffiths J.

g

Andrew Arden for the applicant.
D Fletcher for the housing authority.

GRIFFITHS J delivered the first judgment at the invitation of Lord Widgery CJ. The applicant, Sophia Streeting, asks for an order of certiorari to quash the decision of Hillingdon Borough Council ('the housing authority') that they owed no duty under the *h* Housing (Homeless Persons) Act 1977 to provide accommodation for her and her child. She also asks for an order of mandamus directing the housing authority to provide accommodation for them.

The 1977 Act imposes a duty on local authorities to provide accommodation for homeless persons. The short point that has to be decided in these proceedings is whether that duty is owed to all homeless persons lawfully in this country or whether it is limited *j* to homeless persons who have or had a local connection with the area of a housing authority in Great Britain. In other words, is any duty owed to a stranger or is it limited to those who live or have lived in this country?

The applicant was born in Ethiopia and lived there until May 1975 when she went through a form of marriage to Alan Streeting, an Englishman. Thereafter she lived with

Alan Streeting as his wife and he cared for her child. In fact she later discovered that Alan
a Streeting was still married at the time he went through the marriage ceremony with her. The couple lived together abroad, visiting this country for periods of leave. During the last two years of his life he provided a flat in Athens for the applicant and her child whilst he was working in Libya. On 27th April 1979 Alan Streeting died of a heart attack in Libya; his body was flown back to England and the applicant and her child flew over to attend his funeral in Yorkshire. On her arrival in this country the applicant was
b at first given a limited permission to stay until 25th November 1979, and she was for the first few weeks accommodated in a hotel at the expense of Alan Streeting's employer.

She was refused permission to live in Greece, and as a result of the political situation she decided that it was impossible for her to return to Ethiopia. She, therefore, applied to the Home Office to be accepted in this country as a refugee. On 28th November the Home Office gave their decision accepting the applicant and her child as refugees in the
c United Kingdom.

In the meantime, on 1st June, the employers had refused to continue to provide hotel accommodation, and the applicant applied to Hillingdon Borough Council for assistance under the 1977 Act. The housing authority provided temporary accommodation for her and her child and proceeded to make inquiries as to her situation pursuant to s 3(1) of the 1977 Act. As a result of these inquiries the authority concluded that she was homeless,
d that because of her dependent child she had a priority need, and that she had not become homeless intentionally. Those findings would normally oblige the housing authority to provide accommodation for the applicant and her child (see s 4(5) of the 1977 Act). But the housing authority refused to provide such permanent accommodation, giving as their reason 'that no duty under the Act was owed to an applicant who has or had no local connection with the area of any housing authority in Great Britain'.

e As a result of interlocutory proceedings between the parties, the applicant is still housed by the housing authority pending the outcome of this hearing.

The phrase 'local connection' appears in various sections of the 1977 Act and is defined in s 18(1) in the following terms:

> 'Any reference in this Act to a person having a local connection with an area is a
> f reference to his having a connection with that area—(*a*) because he is or in the past was normally resident in it and his residence in it is or was of his own choice; or (*b*) because he is employed in it, or (*c*) because of family associations, or (*d*) because of any special circumstances.'

It is admitted that the applicant has no local connection with the area of any housing authority within the meaning of this definition, but it is contended on her behalf that
g this is of no significance because the duty to provide accommodation under ss 3 and 4 of the 1977 Act is expressed to be a duty owed to all homeless persons and is in no way qualified by a requirement that they should have or have had a local connection with any area. The only purpose of introducing the concept of a local connection into the framework of the Act is, it is said, to enable the burden of providing accommodation to be fairly shared between local authorities.

h To this end, s 5 provides an elaborate code under which the housing authority can pass on the burden of housing a person who has no local connection with their area to an authority with which he does have a local connection. A housing authority wishing to pass on this burden, referred to in s 5 as the notifying authority, can only initiate this procedure if they are of opinion that an applicant has no local connection with their area. The authority to which they wish to pass the responsibility, referred to in the
j section as the notified authority, do not have to accept the responsibility unless the applicant does have a local connection with their area.

If the applicant does not have a local connection with either area, it is submitted that the situation is covered specifically by s 5(5), which provides: 'In any other case it shall be the duty of the notifying authority to secure that accommodation becomes available for occupation by the person to whom the notification relates.'

In support of this submission reliance is placed on the Code of Guidance introduced by s 12 of the Act, which provides:

> '(1) In relation to homeless persons and persons threatened with homelessness a relevant authority shall have regard in the exercise of their functions to such guidance as may from time to time be given by the Secretary of State.
> '(2) The Secretary of State may give guidance either generally or to specified descriptions of authorities.'

In pursuance of that section there had been drawn up a Code of Guidance. In the code, in the commentary on s 5(5), one reads: 'If a person has no local connection with the area of any housing authority in Great Britain, the duty to secure accommodation for him rests with the authority to whom he applies.'

The applicant also relies on a passage in the annex to the code which at paragraph A2.2 reads as follows:

> '... Applications for help under the Act from people admitted to the country on a temporary or conditional basis may give rise to special considerations; in dealing with such cases authorities will need to bear in mind that discrimination on grounds of nationality or citizenship is unlawful. There are, however, a variety of circumstances in which people are so admitted; for example, some come to take up approved employment, but for others different requirements are imposed as a condition of entry. In determining how most appropriately to fulfil their obligations under the Act, authorities will need to take account of the particular circumstances of individual cases.'

It is clear from these passages that it never occurred to those responsible for drafting the code that the duty would be limited to those having a local connection. The views expressed in the code are not of course conclusive of the construction of the statute, but in this case they accord with my own view that s 5(5) contemplates and provides for the situation in which neither authority will accept that the homeless person has a local connection with their area, from which it must follow that this duty is owed to such a person, for the subsection provides that accommodation is to be provided in such cases by the notifying authority.

The respondent housing authority concede that there are no express words to be found in the 1977 Act limiting the duty to persons having a local connection. But they submit that it cannot have been the intention of Parliament to impose a duty on local authorities to provide accommodation for all and sundry who choose to pour into this country from abroad and then present themselves as homeless. This, they say, would place an intolerable burden on local authorities, and in particular those like Hillingdon Borough Council whose area is adjacent to a large airport like Heathrow. They therefore submit that the Act must be read as limited to our own homeless and to exclude those coming from abroad in the situation of this applicant, for to read it in any other way would, they say, produce an absurd and unworkable result.

In support of this submission the housing authority rely on the definition of homelessness in s 1(1) of the 1977 Act, which, inter alia, refers to a licence to occupy premises in England and Wales and a right or permission to occupy in Scotland and the lack of reference to any corresponding concept in premises abroad, which they argue indicates that the Act is not concerned with the problem arising from homelessness abroad.

They point to the lack of any machinery under s 5 that would enable an authority to pass this responsibility to an authority in the country from which the applicant had come. They point to the lack of any provisions under which an authority near ports or airports can share the financial burden with other authorities, and finally to the difficulty with which an authority may be faced in trying to determine whether someone coming from abroad has disentitled himself from relief because he has become homeless intentionally.

These submissions might carry more weight if anyone could enter this country and settle here without let or hindrance. But that is not the case. Immigration is strictly controlled, and it is unrealistic to suppose that large numbers of persons would be allowed to enter this country either on a temporary or permanent basis who have nowhere to stay whilst they are here. Of course occasionally it will happen, as in the present case of this applicant whom we have accepted as a refugee, and in such cases no doubt the burden will tend to fall on the authorities near airports and seaports, and I have sympathy for them for it seems hard that the burden should be borne unaided by their ratepayers. But these circumstances were known to Parliament in 1977, and I am wholly unpersuaded by the housing authority's argument that words must be read into this Act to limit the duty to persons with a 'local connection'. Local authorities will be protected from an influx of homeless from abroad by the operation of the immigration rules, and they have the further protection that a person abroad cannot give up his accommodation and then expect to be housed by a local authority under the 1977 Act because by intentionally making himself homeless abroad he will have disentitled himself from relief under the Act (see *De Falco v Crawley Borough Council* [1980] 1 All ER 913, [1980] QB 460). Nor is there anything to prevent an authority from discharging their duty by in fact arranging for accommodation to be provided in the country from which the applicant has come (see *R v Bristol City Council, ex parte Browne* [1979] 3 All ER 344, [1979] 1 WLR 1437).

In my view, a homeless person in this Act includes a person who has no local connections with the area of any authority. The housing authority therefore owe a duty to provide the applicant and her child with accommodation. I reach this conclusion with satisfaction for if ever anyone needed the succour of this Act it is this young woman and her child, homeless refugees in a strange country.

I would therefore grant an order of certiorari to quash the decision of the housing authority dated 13th November 1979 to the effect that they owed no duty under the 1977 Act. In the circumstances I doubt if there is any need for mandamus to go, but I would give liberty to apply if it turned out to be necessary.

LORD WIDGERY CJ. I entirely agree and certiorari will go to quash the decision. We will hear counsel on the question of whether mandamus is necessary because in my experience it rarely is in this kind of situation.

Application for certiorari granted.

Denise Randall Barrister.

Appeal

The housing authority appealed to the Court of Appeal.

Lionel Read QC and *David Fletcher* for the housing authority.
Andrew Arden for the applicant.

Cur adv vult

10th July. The following judgments were read.

LORD DENNING MR. She was born in Ethiopia. Her name was Sophia Abrahim. In 1975 she was 19 years of age. She had a baby son David aged 2. An Englishman then came to Addis Ababa. He was Alan Streeting. He was aged 25. He asked Sophia to marry him. He told her he was divorced, They were united in marriage in Addis Ababa on 17th May 1975. She kept her marriage certificate. He brought her and the baby over to England where they stayed for some weeks. He was employed by an American company and worked in Libya. He took a flat in Athens in Greece. Sophia and her child lived there and he went to and fro to them. He also brought them again to England for a holiday. Then tragedy struck. In Libya he had a heart attack and died. It was on 27th

April 1979. His company flew his body back to England for burial. They arranged for Sophia and her little boy to come here for the funeral. It was at Brighouse in Yorkshire. It then transpired that he had not been divorced at all. His wife was still alive in England. So his marriage to Sophia was a bigamous marriage. It was a nullity. But his company took pity on her. They arranged for her to go back to Greece to sort out her affairs there. They paid her fare. But when she arrived at Athens airport, she was not allowed to enter, on the ground that she had not a valid residency permit. So she returned to England. That was on 25th May 1979. His company then put her and the baby up at an hotel here. But they could not keep her indefinitely. So they went with her to the housing department at Hillingdon. That was on 4th June 1979. They presented her and her child as homeless. The housing department made all sorts of inquiries, from Greece and from Ethiopia, to see if she could be found a home there. But these were all fruitless. The Hillingdon housing department arranged for temporary accommodation for her at a guest house, for bed and breakfast, at £7·75 a night. She also got supplementary benefit (national assistance) from which she could pay for her other meals and clothes etc. But eventually the Hillingdon council decided that they could pay no longer for her accommodation. On 13th November 1979 the Director of Housing at Hillingdon wrote this letter to her:

> '*Housing (Homeless Persons) Act 1977*
>
> 'I have decided that you are not entitled to assistance of this Council pursuant to the Housing (Homeless Persons) Act 1977. The duty under the Act is not owed to an applicant who has or had no local connection with the area of any housing authority within Great Britain. You have admitted that you have no local connection and have never had any local connection with the area of any such housing authority. Further or in the alternative the duty under the Act is not owed to an applicant who is not entitled to remain permanently in Great Britain. You are entitled to remain in Great Britain only until 25th November 1979. Without prejudice to the above contentions, if the statutory duty is owed, then for the purposes of Section 8 of the Act I confirm that I have completed my inquiries under the Act and my findings together with the reasons, where required by law, are as follows: 1. I consider that you are homeless. 2. I am satisfied that you have a priority need. 3. I am not satisfied that you became homeless intentionally. 4. I do not propose to notify any other Housing Authority that your application for assistance in obtaining accommodation has been made.'

Although her leave at first extended only until 25th November 1979 she has since been granted 'refugee status'. That means that she is at liberty to remain here indefinitely. But the question is whether the Hillingdon council are bound to house her and her child.

On receiving that letter Sophia Streeting's advisers applied for judicial review. On an interlocutory application, Kenneth Jones J ordered the council to ensure that accommodation remained available to her. On the final hearing on 27th February 1980 the Divisional Court made an order requiring the Hillingdon council to provide accommodation for her and her child. The council appeal to this court.

The case is regarded by the local authorities as if it were a test case. Mrs Sophia Streeting is undoubtedly homeless in this country. She is also homeless elsewhere. But she has no local connection with England at all. Are the local authority bound to provide accommodation for her indefinitely? At their own expense? So that she takes priority over all the other people on their waiting list. They say that for the seven months from 5th June 1979 to 14th January 1980 they had paid out £1,728·25 for her accommodation, of which she had paid £187·33.

This case raises directly the question: when a man or woman with children come from a foreign country and are homeless here, and are also homeless in their own country, are the local authority here bound under our statute to secure accommodation for them here, and their children?

Counsel for the housing authority put his argument attractively in this way: the
a statute was intended to deal with homelessness in England. It was not intended to deal with homelessness in countries overseas. No person who is homeless overseas should be entitled to come into this country and say: 'I am homeless in my own country. So you must house me here, at your expense.'

He supported this argument by saying that the statute is to be given territorial effect; and not to be construed extra-territorially. I agree with this sentiment. But I think the
b statute can be given territorial effect by reading s 1(1) in this way:

> 'A person is homeless [in this country] for the purposes of this Act if he has no accommodation [in this country], and a person is to be treated as having no accommodation [in this country] for those purposes if there is no accommodation [in this country] . . .'

c

which he is at liberty to occupy and can secure entry to peacefully.

So read, the exceptions in s 1(1)(*a*)(i) and (ii) and s 1(1)(*b*) and (2)(*a*), (*b*) and (*c*) are entirely appropriate. They are dealing with a person who is in this country and not elsewhere; and with accommodation in this country and not elsewhere.

Once you confine the statute in this way to homelessness in this country, you are
d giving it territorial effect. It does not operate extra-territorially. Once this is understood, then I will try to explain (as I sought to do in *De Falco v Crawley Borough Council* [1980] 1 All ER 913, [1980] QB 460) in simple words the position when a person coming from overseas is found to be homeless here. The housing authority comes under an obligation to make inquiries to see whether he has dependent children with him (and thus has a priority need), and whether his homelessness here is intentional or unintentional. If he
e has a priority need and his homelessness overseas was *unintentional*, the housing authority come under a duty to secure that accommodation becomes available for him in this country (see s 4(5)), no matter that he comes here from a country overseas. But, if his homelessness was *intentional*, the housing authority are only bound to house him for a short time: see s 4(2)(*b*). If he has a home outside this country which he can occupy if he wishes, he can be treated as *intentionally* homeless here. If he *has had* a home outside this
f country, which he *could have continued* to occupy if he wished, but he has given it up so as to come here, then again he can be treated as *intentionally* homeless here. That was settled by *De Falco v Crawley Borough Council.* But, if he has not a home elsewhere, and it is not in the least his fault, then he qualifies as being unintentionally homeless: and the housing authority are under a duty to secure that accommodation is available for him indefinitely. But they can perform that duty by finding accommodation for him in the
g country whence he came, and by sending him and the children back there: see *R v Bristol City Council, ex parte Browne* [1979] 3 All ER 344, [1979] 1 WLR 1437.

Counsel for the housing authority put forward two extreme cases, each of which he said would be so absurd that the statute cannot have been intended to apply to them.

The first was when a foreigner has a home overseas which he is at liberty to occupy, but yet he comes over here and is homeless here. Are the housing authority bound to
h secure him with accommodation indefinitely?

The second was when a foreigner, who had no home in his own country, and yet comes over here and is homeless here. Are the housing authority bound to provide accommodation for every foreigner who comes here, pleading that he is homeless in his own country?

The only sensible solution of those absurdities, said counsel for the housing authority,
j was by introducing into s 1 an implication to the effect that a person coming from overseas must have some local connection with this country, before he can claim to have the benefit of the statute. He would read into s 1(1) after 'person' 'being a person having a local connection with this country'. These words 'local connection with this country' are so vague that we pressed counsel to define it more closely. He then said it was to be found in s 18 of the 1977 Act. The person must have *a local connection with an area* in this

country. I cannot accept that suggestion for this simple reason. Many a soldier or sailor in our armed forces has no local connection with any particular area in this country. His parents may be dead. On returning to civilian life he is homeless. He should certainly qualify for the benefits of the statute. And how does he qualify? This is done by the comprehensive words of s 5(5):

> 'In any other case it shall be the duty of the notifying authority to secure that accommodation becomes available for occupation by the person to whom the notification relates.'

Another point on the argument of counsel for the housing authority was this. He acknowledged that, if his submission in this case was correct, it meant that the *De Falco* case was wrongly decided. The De Falcos came from Italy to stay with a brother here in England. They had therefore a local connection with England within s 18. When the brother turned them out, they became homeless in England. Under the guidelines, that was the homelessness which had to be considered. And, as it was unintentional, it was the duty of the local authority to house them. I cannot accept any argument which involves that the *De Falco* case was wrongly decided.

Rejecting counsel's implication, I think the safeguard against his suggested absurdities lies in the control exercised by the immigration authorities. People from foreign countries are not allowed in except under carefully prescribed conditions. For instance, they might have to have a work permit; and that would not be given without arrangements having been made for their accommodation. Or they might be admitted as students; and that would not be given unless proper arrangements had been made. And so forth. It must be comparatively rarely that a foreigner is allowed to enter when he is homeless overseas, and will be homeless here, with no means to support himself or herself.

Of course if he is an illegal entrant, if he enters unlawfully without leave, or if he overstays his leave and remains here unlawfully, the housing authority are under no duty whatever to him. Even though he is homeless here, even though he has no home elsewhere, nevertheless he cannot take any advantage of the 1977 Act. As soon as any such illegality appears, the housing authority can turn him down, and report his case to the immigration authorities. This will exclude many foreigners.

Conclusion

If this Ethiopian lady had been truly married to Alan Streeting, as she believed she was, she would have been entitled to enter England as of right. She ought not to suffer by reason of the unknown invalidity of her marriage. She ought to be treated by this country just as if she had been truly married. If she and her child are homeless, then the statute should apply to them. All the more so seeing that she has no home in any other country. Her homelessness is not due to any fault of hers. It is completely unintentional. In those circumstances, as I read the statute, the housing authority are under a duty to secure that accommodation is available for her. This duty no doubt puts much expense on them. They may have other cases too of homeless people coming into Heathrow, for whom they may have to provide accommodation. But it must be remembered that the airport pays rates and brings money into the area. So the housing authority should shoulder the burden. True this is a meritorious case. There may be others not so meritorious. But, meritorious or not, I hold that, if a foreigner, coming here with a child, is homeless in this country, and is homeless in his own country without his fault, then under the 1977 Act the housing authority are under a duty to provide accommodation for him. I agree with the Divisional Court and would dismiss the appeal.

WALLER LJ. Sophia Streeting is a refugee from Ethiopia with a son aged eight who has been granted refugee status in this country. She claims against the London Borough of Hillingdon ('the housing authority') for accommodation as a homeless person under the Housing (Homeless Persons) Act 1977. The housing authority did not accept that

they were under a duty to provide accommodation for her and she applied to the
a Divisional Court for an order of mandamus directing the authority to provide accommodation for her and her son. On 27th February 1970 the Divisional Court granted an order of certiorari to quash the decision of the authority holding that they were under a duty to Sophia Streeting to provide accommodation. The housing authority now appeal to this court on the ground that the duty is not owed to all homeless persons lawfully in this country but only to those who have, or had, a local
b connection with the area of a housing authority in Great Britain.

The decision in this case depends on a consideration of the 1977 Act. Counsel for the housing authority submits that a careful reading of the statute leads to the conclusion that duties are only owed to homeless persons who have, or have had, a local connection in this country. He relies firstly on the long title to the Act and secondly on the consideration of sections of the Act and in particular ss 5 and 18(1), the former of which
c enables a housing authority to transfer the duty to house to another authority if that other authority is one with which the applicant has a local connection. And s 18(1) defines 'local connection' with an area by present or past residence or employment in it or because of a family association or special circumstances. He submits that there is a presumption that Parliament in passing an Act of Parliament is only dealing with this country and in this particular case was only dealing with England and Wales and
d Scotland which are specified in the Act. It was inherent in his submission that any other interpretation of the Act created anomalies and was unfair to those local authorities which contained within them either ports or airports of arrival from foreign countries.

The Divisional Court had dismissed those considerations and found that the Immigration Acts and rules made thereunder were a safeguard against the entry of persons from abroad who might claim to be considered as homeless. Careful
e consideration of the immigration rules (HC Paper (1979–80) no 394) shows that it is not easy for someone to enter this country who is not able to support himself. Furthermore I do not accept that the anomalies in this case are all on one side; nor is there a substantial injustice. An argument was addressed to the court that it was unfair that one local authority should be responsible for an immigrant who had no connection with this country at all and that if anybody was to be responsible it should be a national
f responsibility. I am satisfied that this argument does not succeed.

As long ago as 1803 in *R v Inhabitants of Eastbourne* (1803) 4 East 103 at 107, 102 ER 769 at 770, Lord Ellenborough CJ in a settlement case said:

> 'As to there being no obligation for maintaining poor foreigners before the statutes ascertaining the different methods of acquiring settlements, the law of humanity, which is anterior to all positive laws, obliges us to afford them relief, to
> g save them from starving . . .'

Those words, with suitable amendment, would cover precisely the relevant argument in the present case. They also show that a statute would not be interpreted so as to exclude benefit to foreigners in this country. The doctrine of extra-territoriality would not apply in such a case.

h There is nothing in the plain meaning of the words of this statute which imposes the limitation proposed on behalf of the applicant and I would follow Viscount Dilhorne in *Stock v Frank Jones (Tipton) Ltd* [1978] 1 All ER 948 at 951, [1978] 1 WLR 231 at 234, in quoting Lord Mersey and Lord Loreburn LC:

> '"It is a strong thing to read into an Act of Parliament words which are not there, and in the absence of clear necessity it is a wrong thing to do" said Lord Mersey in
> j *Thompson v Goold and Co* [1910] AC 409 at 420. "We are not entitled to read words into an Act of Parliament unless clear reason for it is to be found within the four corners of the Act itself" said Lord Loreburn LC in *Vickers, Sons & Maxim Ltd v Evans* [1910] AC 444 at 445.'

If there were any reason to try to read words into the 1977 Act there are two sections which in my view show clearly that this statute should not have the limitation proposed. The first section is s 5(5). Section 5 deals with the responsibility as between housing authorities and by sub-s (1) enables an authority with an applicant who has no local connection with their area to notify another authority where the applicant has an apparent local connection, and sub-ss (2), (3) and (4) deal with problems arising under that notification; but sub-s (5) then reads:

> 'In any other case it shall be the duty of the notifying authority to secure that accommodation becomes available for occupation by the person to whom the notification relates.'

Those words indicate to me that any person without any local connection will be owed the duty by the housing authority who is the notifying authority.

The second section which supports the same view is s 18, and in particular s 18(2). Section 18(1) defines 'local connection', and as I have already mentioned one of the connections may be residence. But sub-s (2) provides that:

> 'Residence in an area is not of a person's own choice for the purposes of subsection (1) above if he became resident in it—(*a*) because he or any person who might reasonably be expected to reside with him—(i) was serving in the regular armed forces of the Crown, or (ii) was detained under the authority of an Act of Parliament ...'

It would follow that if local connection was essential there might well be ex-soldiers who have no local connection in the country at all, even though they are United Kingdom citizens, even though they were born here, because they will have been in the armed services all their working lives. Accordingly I have no doubt that the limitation proposed by the housing authority does not apply and the duty is not limited to those with local connections.

This construction of the 1977 Act does not result in a large number of persons from overseas becoming a burden on local authorities. *R v Bristol City Council, ex parte Browne* [1979] 3 All ER 344, [1979] 1 WLR 1437 and *De Falco v Crawley Borough Council* [1980] 1 All ER 913, [1980] QB 460 indicate that a local authority may fulfil their duty by giving advice to an applicant to return to his or her native land where housing will be available or by considering the circumstances in which the applicant came to this country as perhaps revealing that the applicant was intentionally homeless. These two cases illustrate that a local authority may make full investigation to solve the problem in a way which does not involve the local authority with the obligation of providing housing.

I would dismiss the appeal.

DUNN LJ. The definition of 'homeless person' in s 1(1) of the Housing (Homeless Persons) Act 1977 on the face of it relates to any person who has no accommodation in Great Britain. It is said by counsel on behalf of the housing authority that this construction produces an absurd anomaly because it would mean that a person with accommodation abroad would fall within the definition so that a housing authority would be under a duty to house him. It is said that that cannot have been the intention of Parliament, so that it is necessary to construe this subsection so as to enable the housing authority to look at a person's entitlement to accommodation worldwide; and in order to do that the subsection should be construed so as to limit the definition of 'homeless person' to persons having a 'local connection' with some area of Great Britain, the words 'local connection' being defined as in s 18 of the Act. This, it is said, would be in accordance with the object and purpose of Parliament as set out in the long title, and also in accordance with the principle that statutes should be construed so as to apply territorially and not extra-territorially.

In order to test this submission it is necessary to construe the section in the light of the other provisions of the Act, and to see the nature and extent of the various duties placed on housing authorities at different stages. I start by taking the words of s 1(1) according to their natural and ordinary meaning which leads me to the conclusion that a 'homeless person' as defined by the subsection is any person who has no accommodation in Great

Britain. The only limitation to the word 'person' is that he should be a person who is lawfully here, that is to say, a person who does not require leave to enter, either because he is a citizen of the United Kingdom and Colonies not subject to immigration control, or because he has come from some other part of the Common Travel Area comprising in addition to the United Kingdom the Channel Islands, the Isle of Man and the Irish Republic. Persons lawfully here also include persons who have been granted leave to enter by the immigration control either for a limited period or for settlement. Such persons, including prospective workers from EEC countries, will generally have had to satisfy immigration control that they can maintain and accommodate themselves and their dependants without recourse to public funds.

So illegal immigrants are not persons within the meaning of s 1(1). But if a person lawfully here has no accommodation in Great Britain he may apply to a housing authority, and if the housing authority have reason to believe that in fact he has no accommodation in Great Britain they are at that stage only under a duty to make inquiries to satisfy themselves (1) whether he has a priority need and (2) whether he became homeless intentionally. This duty also exists if the person has accommodation, but cannot secure entry to it, or if occupation of it will probably lead to domestic violence, or if he is likely to become homeless within 28 days. But I will throughout deal with the situation where a person claims to be homeless.

At that initial stage the housing authority may also make inquiries whether the applicant has a local connection with the area of another local authority, and there are provisions in the Act whereby that other local authority may be under a duty to house the applicant. These provisions are not relevant to the circumstances of this case which assumes that the applicant has no local connection with any other area.

Even if the person is homeless, if the housing authority are not satisfied that he has a priority need as defined by s 2(1), they are only under a duty to give the person advice or assistance. If they are so satisfied, they are under a duty to secure that accommodation is made available for him pending their inquiries whether he became homeless intentionally.

Section 17(1) provides:

> 'Subject to subsection (3) below, for the purposes of this Act a person becomes homeless intentionally if he deliberately does or fails to do anything in consequence of which he ceases to occupy accommodation which is available for his occupation and which it would have been reasonable for him to continue to occupy.'

Subsection (3) provides:

> 'An act or omission in good faith on the part of a person who was unaware of any relevant fact is not to be treated as deliberate for the purposes of subsection (1) or (2) above.'

It is at this stage for the first time that any foreign element becomes relevant. Up to this stage the authority will only have been concerned to ascertain whether the person has accommodation in Great Britain and whether he has a priority need. But in considering whether the person has become homeless intentionally the authority are entitled to make inquiries relating to the country whence he came. So in *De Falco v Crawley Borough Council* [1980] 1 All ER 913, [1980] QB 460 Italian families with priority needs who had no accommodation in Great Britain were held to have become homeless intentionally because they voluntarily gave up accommodation in Italy in order to come to England. Whether or not a person becomes homeless intentionally is, like all questions of causation, a matter of fact and degree. It is for the authority to decide having regard to all the circumstances of the particular case. Although the most immediate cause of the homelessness may not have been intentional, the authority are entitled to look at past events, including the circumstances in which foreign applicants left accommodation in their own country (see *De Falco v Crawley Borough Council*, and see *Dyson v Kerrier District Council* p 313, ante, where it was held that although the most immediate cause of the homelessness was that the applicant had been evicted, she was intentionally homeless because she had surrendered a tenancy of a council flat in order to move into the accommodation from which she was evicted).

If the housing authority are satisfied that the person became homeless intentionally, then their only duty is to give him advice and assistance. But, even if they are not satisfied that he became homeless intentionally, they can perform their ultimate duty to secure that accommodation becomes available to him in a number of ways. They can make available accommodation held by them under the Housing Act 1957, in which case he acquires a priority in selection as a tenant, by reason of an amendment to s 113(2) of the 1957 Act; or they can secure that he obtains accommodation from some other person and give him such advice and assistance as will secure that he obtains accommodation from some other person (see s 6). So, if he has come from a foreign country and if as a result of their inquiries the authority are satisfied that some person in the foreign country will provide him with accommodation there, then they can advise him to return to the foreign country and if necessary assist him by paying his fare. This was done in *R v Bristol City Council, ex parte Browne* [1979] 3 All ER 344, [1979] 1 WLR 1437, where Mrs Browne arrived in Bristol from Ireland with her children and applied to the local authority for accommodation. She was homeless in Great Britain and she had a priority need. As a result of their inquiries the local authority ascertained that the housing authorities in Tralee would provide her with accommodation. So they advised her to return to Tralee and offered to pay her fare. This was held by the Divisional Court to be a perfectly proper fulfilment by the local authority of their duty under s 6(1)(*c*) of the 1977 Act. If the contention of counsel for the housing authority in this case is correct, the Bristol corporation would have been under no duty to Mrs Browne at all because she had no local connection with any area of Great Britain, although it is right to say that the Divisional Court decided the case on the narrow ground that the local authority had fulfilled any duty which they had.

The submission that the definition of a homeless person in s 1(1) should be limited to persons with a local connection with an area of Great Britain is also inconsistent with the express provisions of the 1977 Act. Section 5 deals with responsibilities as between housing authorities. Subsections (1) to (4) provide that a local authority to whom application is made by a homeless person, if they are of opinion that the applicant has a local connection with another housing authority's area, may notify that other housing authority accordingly, and it then becomes the duty of the notified authority to secure accommodation for the applicant. Subsection (5) provides:

> 'In any other case it shall be the duty of the notifying authority to secure that accommodation becomes available for occupation by the person to whom the notification relates.'

Those words mean what they say. They expressly negative the limitation of the word 'person' to mean only a person who has a local connection with some area of Great Britain.

But there is another objection to such limitation. Section 18 defines the meaning of 'local connection'. Subsection (2) excludes from that meaning any regular member of the armed forces of the Crown or any person who has been in prison or detained in a mental hospital from having a local connection with an area because of residence or employment in that area. The limitation sought to be placed by counsel for the housing authority on the definition of 'homeless person' would therefore exclude from the protection afforded by this Act many members of the regular forces of the Crown and ex-patients from mental hospitals. I regard this anomaly as more absurd than any suggested by the housing authority in this case.

On the construction that I have so far placed on s 1(1), housing authorities are under the various duties provided by the Act to any person lawfully here, including those who came here from abroad and who have no connection with this country. In a welfare statute of this kind there is nothing wrong in principle with that. In the old settlement cases it was held that a foreigner lawfully here who otherwise qualified was entitled to a

settlement under the poor laws: see *R v Inhabitants of Eastbourne* (1803) 4 East 103, 102 ER
a 769. And foreigners lawfully here have been held to be entitled to the protection of English laws of copyright: see *Jefferys v Boosey* (1854) 4 HL Cas 815 at 955, 10 ER 681 at 736.

I do not share the fears expressed on behalf of the housing authority that this construction would place an intolerable burden on them. Of course it places an additional burden on them, but I see no reason to suppose that it is not a burden intended
b by Parliament. The Act must be read in conjunction with the Immigration Act 1971 and the immigration rules made thereunder. It contains the various safeguards for local authorities to which I have referred and which have been clarified by *De Falco v Crawley Borough Council* and *R v Bristol City Council, ex parte Browne.* I see no reason to limit the words of s 1(1) in the way suggested, and I too would dismiss this appeal.

c *Appeal dismissed.*

Solicitors: *J A Kosky*, Uxbridge (for the housing authority); *Charles Coleman & Co*, Slough (for the applicant).

Sumra Green Barrister.

d

Re Bell's Indenture
Bell and another v Hickley and others

e CHANCERY DIVISION
VINELOTT J
16th, 17th, 18th, 19th, 26th JANUARY 1979

Solicitor – Liability – Trustee – Constructive trustee – Misappropriation of trust money – Liability of solicitor's partner for misappropriation – Money paid into firm's client account in
f *name of express trustees – Money misappropriated by express trustees with solicitor's knowledge – Partner not having actual knowledge of misappropriation and acting throughout honestly and reasonably in regard to firm's affairs but having access to documents inspection of which might have revealed breach of trust – Solicitor liable to replace money as constructive trustee – Whether partner also liable as constructive trustee or under implied terms of partnership.*

g *Trust and trustee – Liability of trustee – Constructive trustee – Sale of trust property in breach of trust and wrongful distribution of proceeds – Solicitor liable as constructive trustee to replace money – Farm sold in breach of trust in 1947 and proceeds wrongfully distributed – Farm resold by purchasers for market value in 1949 – Action by beneficiaries commenced in 1970 – Plaintiffs conceding farm would have been sold in 1949 in course of proper administration of trust – Judgment in action given in 1979 – Estate Duty Office deciding not to charge estate duty on*
h *money replaced – Whether measure of liability the value of farm at date of writ or judgment or price at which farm in fact sold in 1949 – Whether estate duty that would have been payable if trust fund had remained intact should be deducted.*

Between April 1940 and the end of 1947 A and B were the trustees of a compound
j settlement consisting of a marriage settlement made in 1907 and the trusts of the settlor's will, the beneficiaries of the settlement being A, B and others. B was also a trustee of a voluntary settlement of trust funds made in 1930 by A for the benefit of himself and his issue. Another trustee of A's settlement, from 1937 to 1951, was H, who was a partner in the firm of solicitors which acted for A personally and for A and B in their capacity as trustees. From 1940 the firm consisted of H and another partner until the latter died in

October 1947. Between August 1940 and February 1947 approximately £38,000 was
paid into the firm's client account to the credit of A and B in their capacity as trustees, a
that sum being derived from the sale of trust property, including a farm, which belonged
to the compound settlement and which was sold by A and B in breach of trust to facilitate
distribution of the proceeds between them. The farm was sold by A and B to the trustees
of A's settlement for £8,200 and was resold by those trustees in 1949 for £12,400.
Between August 1940 and February 1947 out of the client account standing in the name
of A and B approximately £26,000 was paid to A, B and the trustees of A's settlement. b
Those payments were made in breach of trust and constituted misappropriation of trust
money. H, who knew of the trusts of the compound settlement, assisted in the
misappropriation, but there was no evidence that his partner had actual knowledge of
the misappropriation or that he had exercised other than proper care over the firm's
affairs. A died in 1979. In 1970 the plaintiffs, who were beneficiaries under the
compound settlement, commenced an action against, inter alios, H, the executors of his c
partner, and A's executors, claiming that they were liable to replace the misappropriated
trust money. The claim against H was that he was liable as a constructive trustee of the
money in the client account. The claim against the partner's estate was that the partner
was jointly and severally liable to make good the money misapplied, because, where trust
money was received into a firm's client account and paid out for a purpose which one of
the partners of the firm knew to be a breach of trust, all the partners were liable to make d
good the breach either as constructive trustees or under the principle in ss 10 and 11 of
the Partnership Act 1890 that a firm was liable when one partner acting within the scope
of his authority received a third person's property and misapplied it. The partner's
executors, while admitting that the misapplied money had passed through the firm's
client account and that the partner had had access to documents which if he had
inspected them might have revealed the breaches of trust, denied liability. The plaintiffs e
further contended that the defendants' liability extended to replacing the present value
of the farm, although they admitted that if the farm had not been sold in breach of trust
in 1947 it would have been sold in 1949 in the proper course of administering the
compound settlement for the price of £12,400 at which it was then in fact sold.
Alternatively the plaintiffs contended that the defendants' liability extended to the
proper value of the farm when it was resold in 1949 which was admitted to be £12,400. f
H died in 1972. His executors (against whom the action was carried on) admitted that
H was liable as a constructive trustee to replace the misapplied money but contended that
his liability should be reduced by the amount of the estate duty that would have been
payable on the successive deaths of certain beneficiaries under the compound settlement
if the fund had remained intact, even though the Estate Duty Office accepted that the
misapplied property could not be reconstituted or recovered by tracing and stated that g
estate duty would not be exacted on any money which was replaced. A's executors
sought a similar reduction in liability.

Held – (1) Although a solicitor had the implied authority of his partners to receive trust
money as agent of duly appointed trustees he did not have his partners' implied authority
to constitute himself a constructive trustee of trust money, and where, therefore, a h
solicitor did constitute himself a constructive trustee of trust money then, whether the
money was paid into his private account or into his firm's client account, his partners
were not liable for any misapplication of the money if they had taken no part in, and
were ignorant of, the transactions in question. It followed that the plaintiffs' claim
against the partner was misconceived and failed (see p 437, *d* to *f* and p 442 *e*, post);
dictum of Lord Herschell in *Mara v Browne* [1896] 1 Ch at 208 applied; *Blyth v Fladgate* j
[1891] 1 Ch 337 distinguished.

(2) The defendants' liability in regard to the farm was limited to the value of the farm
at the date when, but for the improper sale in 1947, it would admittedly have been sold,
ie to the sum of £12,400 at which it was sold in 1949, for the court could not enter into
an inquiry into what might have happened to the proceeds of sale of the farm if it had
been retained and later properly sold and the proceeds reinvested (see p 438 *h* to p 439 *b*

and p 442 *e*, post); *Re Massingberd's Settlement, Clark v Trelawney* (1890) 63 LT 296 applied.

(3) No distinction could be drawn between the liability of an express trustee who misappropriated trust money (whether for his own benefit or the benefit of others) and the liability for misappropriation of a person liable as a constructive trustee, the liability in both cases being to replace the money without regard to any fiscal liabilities that might have fallen on the trust fund had it not been misappropriated. Accordingly, estate duty that would have been payable if the trust fund had remained intact was not deductible from the liability of a constructive trustee (such as a solicitor who had constituted himself a constructive trustee) for misappropriation of trust money. It followed that the liability of both H's executors and A's executors to replace the misappropriated money was not subject to any deduction in respect of the estate duty that would have been payable if the fund had remained intact, and thus was not affected by the decision of the Estate Duty Office not to exact duty on any trust money replaced (see p 441 *f* to *j* and p 442 *e f*, post); dictum of Grant MR in *Dornford v Dornford* (1806) 12 Ves at 129 and *British Transport Commission v Gourley* [1955] 3 All ER 796 considered.

Semble. Previous authority to the effect that the date of the writ is the appropriate date for ascertaining the value of property sold in breach of trust which has to be made good would appear to be incorrect as the date of the judgment is the proper date for ascertaining the value of the property (see p 439 *g h*, post); *Re Massingberd's Settlement, Clark v Trelawney* (1890) 63 LT 296 doubted.

Notes

For a solicitor's liability for the acts of his partners, see 36 Halsbury's Laws (3rd Edn) 105, para 140, and for cases on the subject, see 43 Digest (Repl) 407–414, *4334–4386*.

For the measure of liability for breach of trust, see 38 Halsbury's Laws (3rd Edn) 1046–1408, paras 1809, 1810.

Cases referred to in judgment

Blyth v Fladgate [1891] 1 Ch 337, 60 LJ Ch 66, 63 LT 546, 24 Digest (Reissue) 961, *10251*.

Brinsden v Williams [1894] 3 Ch 185, 63 LJ Ch 713, 71 LT 177, 47 Digest (Repl) 192, *1604*.

British Transport Commission v Gourley [1955] 3 All ER 796, [1956] AC 185, [1956] 2 WLR 41, [1955] 2 Lloyd's Rep 475, HL, 17 Digest (Reissue) 88, *34*.

Dornford v Dornford (1806) 12 Ves 127, 33 ER 49, 24 Digest (Reissue) 1034, *11001*.

Fryer, Re, Martindale v Picquot (1857) 3 K & J 317, 26 LJ Ch 398, 29 LTOS 86, 3 Jur NS 485, 69 ER 1129, 47 Digest (Repl) 390, *3504*.

Mara v Browne [1896] 1 Ch 199, 65 LJ Ch 225, 73 LT 638, CA; *rvsg* [1895] 2 Ch 69, 47 Digest (Repl) 191, *1589*.

Massingberd's Settlement, Re, Clark v Trelawney (1890) 63 LT 296, CA; *affg* (1889) 60 LT 620, 47 Digest (Repl) 461, *4117*.

Phillipson v Gatty (1848) 7 Hare 516, 12 LTOS 445, 13 Jur 318, 68 ER 213, 47 Digest (Repl) 522, *4730*.

Vyse v Foster (1872) LR 8 Ch App 309, 42 LJ Ch 245, 27 LT 774, 47 Digest (Repl) 421, *3773*.

Cases also cited

Atkinson v MacKreth (1866) LR 2 Eq 570.

Barker, Re, Ravenshaw v Barker (1898) 77 LT 712.

Barnes v Addy (1874) LR 9 Ch App 244, LJJ.

Belmont Finance Corpn Ltd v Williams Furniture Ltd [1979] 1 All ER 118, [1979] Ch 250, CA.

Dimes v Scott (1827) 4 Russ 195, [1824–34] All ER Rep 653.

Docker v Somes (1834) 2 My & K 655, [1824–34] All ER Rep 402.

Kellaway v Johnson (1842) 5 Beav 319, 49 ER 601.

Lewis, ex parte, Re Leonard (1819) 1 Gl & J 69.

Pauling's Settlement Trusts, Re, Younghusband v Coutts & Co [1963] 3 All ER 1, [1964] Ch 303, CA.

Phipps v Boardman [1966] 3 All ER 721, [1967] 2 AC 46, HL.
Plumer v Gregory (1874) LR 18 Eq 621.
Somerset, Re, Somerset v Earl Poulett [1894] 1 Ch 231, CA.
Wiles v Gresham (1854) 2 Drew 258, 61 ER 718.
Williams-Ashman v Price & Williams [1942] 1 All ER 310, [1942] Ch 219.
Windsor Steam Coal Co (1901) Ltd, Re [1929] 1 Ch 151, CA.

Action

This was an action, commenced by writ dated 6th February 1970, by the plaintiffs, Cecil George Beresford Bell and his brother, Shurland Robin Dumergue Bell, against the following defendants: (1) Anthony North Hickley, a solicitor who at all material times was a partner in the firm of Clowes Hickley & Heaver and who died on 5th September 1972; (2) Alfred John Langton Heaver (who died on 21st January 1973) and (3) Beauchamp Stuart Pell, the executors of Alfred Heaver deceased who at all material times was a partner in the same firm; (4) Marion Babette Bell, the executrix of Mathew Alexander Henry Bell ('Alexander') who died on 6th April 1959; (5) Lady Joan Diana Hall (who died on 23rd July 1975); (6) Matthew Forbes Shurland Bell, (7) Richard John Beresford Bell and (8) Fiona Bell, the second plaintiff's children; (9) Daphne Edith Bridge and (10) Heather Pauline Nutting, the plaintiffs' sisters; and (11) Michael Anthony Petit and (12) Elizabeth North Powell, the executors of Mr Hickley, the first defendant. The plaintiffs claimed against the first four defendants replacement of trust moneys which were the proceeds of sale of property subject to the trusts of a compound settlement consisting of a marriage settlement dated 9th July 1907 and the settlor's will trusts under his will dated 22nd January 1912, misappropriated by the Hon Mary Bell ('Mrs Bell') and Alexander, her son, whilst they were trustees of the compound settlement. At the date of the writ the fifth defendant was the life tenant of the trust fund comprised in the settlement and the plaintiffs and the sixth to tenth defendants were entitled in remainder. Clowes Hickley & Heaver had acted for Mrs Bell and Alexander in their capacity as trustees of the settlement. The facts are set out in the judgment.

D Gidley Scott for the plaintiffs.
Martin Nourse QC and *Nigel Hague* for the first, second, third, eleventh and twelfth defendants.
Roger Horne for the fourth defendant.
The other defendants took no part in the action.

Cur adv vult

26th January. **VINELOTT J** read the following judgment: This action gives rise to a number of issues of importance which relate to certain admitted breaches of trust by the Hon Mary Bell ('Mrs Bell') and her son, Matthew Alexander Henry Bell ('Alexander'), in their capacity as the trustees of, first, a marriage settlement dated 9th July 1907 and, second, the trust of the will of Matthew Gerald Edward Bell, who was the settlor of the property comprised in the marriage settlement and to whom I shall refer as 'the settlor'.

The facts are not in dispute and may be shortly stated as follows. The marriage settlement was an ante-nuptial settlement and was made between the settlor of the first part, Mrs Bell (then a spinster) of the second part, Kathleen Matilda Bell of the third part and Charles John Sackville West and the Hon Alfred Ernest Frederick Yorke (as trustees thereof) of the fourth part. By the settlement, the settlor conveyed certain freehold lands known as the Bourne and Milton Estates to the use of the parties thereto of the fourth part (therein referred to as 'the settlement trustees') for a term of 500 years commencing from the date of the marriage between the settlor and Mrs Bell (which took place on 11th July 1905) on the trusts thereinafter declared and subject thereto to the use that from the date of the said marriage during the remainder of the life of Fanny Cecilia Bell (the settlor's grandmother) the settlor so long as he should live and after his death Mrs Bell so long as she should live should receive a yearly rent-charge of £500 to be charged on and

issuing out of the said settled property and subject and charged as aforesaid to the use of
a the settlor and his assigns during his life with remainder to the use that if Mrs Bell should
survive the settlor she should thenceforth during the remainder of her life receive a
yearly rent-charge of £800 to be charged on and issuing out of all the said settled
property and subject and charged as aforesaid to the use of the settlor in fee simple. By
cl 3 of the marriage settlement it was provided that the said settled property was limited
to the settlement trustees for the said term of 500 years on trust that they should by all
b or any of the means therein set forth or by any other reasonable means raise the said
yearly rent-charge of £500. By cl 6 the settlement trustees were appointed trustees of
the marriage settlement and of every compound settlement consisting of the marriage
settlement and of any subsequent instrument for the purposes of the Settled Land Acts.
By cl 7 the settlor and Mrs Bell during their joint lives and the survivor of them during
his or her life was given power to appoint a new trustee or new trustees of the marriage
c settlement.

The settlor died on 8th May 1926, leaving Mrs Bell surviving him. There was one
child only of the marriage, namely Alexander. By his will dated 22nd January 1912 the
settlor appointed Mrs Bell and Percy Leigh Pemberton to be his executors and trustees.
He devised a dwelling house known as Oswalds, and the premises occupied therewith to
the use of Mrs Bell for life and after her death to the uses declared thereafter of and
d concerning the Bourne and Milton estates. By cl 4 he bequeathed all his chattels in or
about Oswalds in trust to permit Mrs Bell to have the use and enjoyment thereof during
her life and after her death to hold the same on the like trusts as were thereinafter
declared of and concerning the settlor's leasehold, copyhold and customary estates and his
plate and diamonds and furniture in or about his mansion house at Bourne Park. By cl
5, after reciting the marriage settlement and the death of his grandmother, he confirmed
e the marriage settlement and declared that the provisions intended to be made by the will
for Mrs Bell were in addition to the provision made for her by the marriage settlement,
and by cl 6 he devised the Bourne and Milton Estates and his other freehold lands and
hereditaments to the use of Alexander for life, with usual remainders to his sons in tail
male with divers remainders over, which I shall set out in more detail later in this
judgment.

f By cl 7 he declared that if any person to whom an estate in tail male by purchase in the
Bourne and Milton Estates was thereinbefore limited should be born in his lifetime, such
limitation should not take effect and in lieu thereof such person was given a life interest
with usual remainders to his sons in tail male and then daughters in tail male successively
in order of seniority.

Clauses 14 and 15 contain gifts of leasehold, copyhold and customary estates and
g certain specified chattels and the residue of his personal estate on the trusts that would
have been applicable thereto if they had been capital moneys arising on the sale of his real
estate under the Settled Land Acts.

In the events which happened, the effective limitations of the Bourne and Milton
Estates under the joint effect of cll 6 and 7 of the settlor's will were as follows.

First, as I have mentioned, Alexander took a life interest. He died on 6th April
h 1959. On his death, Mrs Bell took a life interest. She died on 7th October 1962. On her
death the settlor's nephew, Edward Charles Sackville West, who later became the fifth
Baron Sackville ('Lord Sackville') took a life interest. He died on 4th July 1965. On his
death, the settlor's niece, who at the date of the will was Diana Sackville West and who
later became Lady Hall, took a life interest. She died on 23rd July 1975 after the
commencement of these proceedings. On her death, the first plaintiff, Cecil George
j Beresford Bell, son of the settlor's cousin, Shurland Bell, took a life interest with
remainder to his sons and then daughters successively according to seniority in tail
male. He has not had any issue. On the death of the first plaintiff, and in the event of
failure of the limitations to his sons and daughters in tail, the first plaintiff's brother,
Shurland Robin Dumergue Bell, if he survives, will take a life interest with remainder to
his sons and then daughters successively according to seniority in tail male. He has two

sons, namely the sixth and seventh defendants, Matthew Forbes Shurland Bell and Richard John Beresford Bell (a minor), and one daughter, namely the eighth defendant, Fiona Bell. On the death of the second plaintiff and in the event of the failure of those limitations in tail, the plaintiffs' elder sister, Daphne Edith Bridge, the ninth defendant, if she survives will similarly take a life interest with remainders to her sons and then daughters successively according to seniority in tail male with remainder to the plaintiffs' younger sister, Heather Pauline Nutting, the tenth defendant, with remainders to her sons and then daughters successively according to seniority in tail male. Neither of the plaintiffs' two sisters has had any children. There is an ultimate remainder to the settlor's own right heir who was in the event Alexander.

The devolution of the trusteeship of the marriage settlement and will is as follows. Probate of the will except settled land was granted on 7th August 1926 to Mrs Bell and Percy Leigh Pemberton, the executors and trustees appointed by the will. Probate of the will limited to land settled by the marriage settlement was granted to the trustees of the marriage settlement on 11th September 1926. By a deed of appointment dated 5th September 1927, Mrs Bell appointed herself and Percy Leigh Pemberton to be the trustees of the marriage settlement in place of the trustees originally appointed. On 24th June 1935 Mrs Bell appointed Charles Leigh Pemberton to be a trustee of the marriage settlement and of the will in place of Percy Leigh Pemberton who died on 25th March 1934. On 17th April 1940 Mrs Bell appointed Alexander to be a trustee of the marriage settlement and of the will in place of Charles Leigh Pemberton who thereby retired. Thus from 17th April 1940 Mrs Bell and Alexander were the trustees of the marriage settlement and the will. No trustees were appointed thereafter until 1st July 1975, when by order of the court in these proceedings the plaintiffs were appointed trustees of the marriage settlement and the will.

As will appear hereafter, by the time of Alexander's death the entirety of the properties subject to the trusts of the marriage settlement and the will had been distributed in breach of trust by Alexander and Mrs Bell.

There is one other settlement that I should mention. On 23rd October 1930 Alexander made a voluntary settlement, the trust fund comprised therein being settled on protective trusts to himself for life with remainder in favour of his issue. On failure of issue, Alexander was given a general testamentary power of appointment. The first trustees were Mrs Bell, Percy Leigh Pemberton and Charles Leigh Pemberton. On 1st February 1937 one Anthony North Hickley was appointed a trustee in place of Charles Leigh Pemberton who, as I have said, died in 1934. By a deed of appointment dated 25th January 1951, one Edythe Frediswide Gallagher, a cousin of Alexander, was appointed a trustee of the voluntary settlement in place of Mr Hickley.

Mr Hickley was at all material times a partner in the firm of Clowes Hickley & Heaver. Between 1937 and 1940 the partners in that firm consisted of Mr Hickley, Sir William Henry Lewthwaite and Alfred Heaver. From 1940 until Mr Heaver's death on 5th October 1947, Mr Hickley and Mr Heaver were the only partners. From Mr Heaver's death until June 1951 Mr Hickley carried on the partnership practice as sole principal. Thereafter the practice was amalgamated with a large London firm.

During a period commencing on or before 15th April 1937 and ending on or after 16th December 1947, the firm of Clowes Hickley & Heaver acted as solicitors for the trustees of the marriage settlement of the will and as solicitor for Alexander personally.

As I have said, the entirety of the property, subject to the trusts of the marriage settlement and the will has now disappeared and so far as can now be ascertained had been distributed in breach of trust during Alexander's lifetime.

Though it is not directly relevant in these proceedings, it is also probable that the funds comprised in the voluntary settlement were also misappropriated and distributed in breach of trust during Alexander's lifetime. Probate of his will was granted to the fourth defendant, Marion Babette Bell, who was the sole beneficiary under his will and the sole executrix thereby appointed on 1st February 1960. The net value of his estate is given in the grant of probate as £2,756 18s 2d, and there is no reference to any settled property.

No grant has ever been taken out to the estate of Mrs Bell. Her estate was of negligible value if indeed it was not insolvent.

No steps were taken by Lord Sackville or Lady Hall to ascertain what had happened to the property comprised in the marriage settlement and the will during their respective lifetimes and indeed they may have been unaware of the life interests given to them by the will. Shortly before 1967, the plaintiffs, who knew by family repute that there had been a settlement of the Bourne and Milton estates, obtained copies of the marriage settlement and the will and instituted inquiries to ascertain what had happened to the trust property. The only sources of information they were able to discover were first the books and records, in particular the client's account, of the firm of Clowes Hickley & Heaver which had passed on amalgamation to their successor firm; and, secondly, evidence filed in proceedings relating to settled chattels which were heard by Farwell J in 1935. The records of Clowes Hickley & Heaver show that between 2nd August 1940 and 28th February 1947, sums amounting in the aggregate to £38,260 3s 11d were paid into the firm's client account to the credit of Mrs Bell and Alexander as trustees of the marriage settlement and will. Those sums were derived from the sale or realisation of trust investments, including a farm known as Churchill Farm and of an item of jewellery.

These records also show that out of those sums payments amounting in the aggregate to £26,237 15s 5d were made to Alexander, to Mrs Bell and to the trustees of the voluntary settlement. By far the larger part was paid to Alexander Bell. Payments amounting to £5,361 6s 6d were made to Mrs Bell and payments amounting to £3,043 17s were made to the trustees of the voluntary settlement.

The largest payment to Mrs Bell was of the sum of £5,293 10s 10d, and it is clear from other documentary evidence that this sum was applied by her in the purchase of two annuities, the purchase having been arranged by Mr Hickley, who received a commission of £52 18s 8d from the insurance company. In addition, the plaintiffs have discovered two payments to Alexander purportedly by way of loan amounting in aggregate to £969 6s 8d, which were never repaid. Those payments were made in 1945. It is not alleged that the payments by way of loan passed through the firm's client account or that Mr Hickley or Mr Heaver knew anything about them.

As regards the settled chattels, I understand that the evidence before Farwell J disclosed that there were settled chattels then in the possession of the trustees. One item of jewellery was included in the proceeds of sale which passed through the firm's account. Again, it is not contended by the plaintiffs that the proceeds of sale of the remaining chattels passed through the firm's account or that Mr Hickley or Mr Heaver knew of any misappropriation of this jewellery. It has been agreed between the plaintiffs and the fourth defendant, representing Alexander's estate, that the value of the jewellery misappropriated is £2,530 13s 4d.

I understand that correspondence and other documents disclosed on discovery show that Mr Hickley knew of the payments out of the client's account to Mrs Bell, Alexander and the trustees of the voluntary settlement (of whom he was one) amounting to £26,237 15s 5d and knew, and indeed could not have failed to have known, that those payments were misappropriations by Mrs Bell and Alexander as trustees of the marriage settlement and will.

Indeed, on 16th December 1947, Mr Hickley was given an indemnity by Alexander and Mrs Bell by which they authorised and requested him, and I cite:

> 'To make available for the use of the said Matthew Alexander Henry Bell all moneys representing capital and income in this settlement which you have had, now have, or in the future will have in your hands and hereby absolutely indemnify you in respect thereof.'

This memorandum is contemporaneous with the last of the misappropriations out of client account that has been discovered, but the memo concludes with the words: 'This request and authority confirms the verbal or written instructions to the above effect given by both of us prior to or since the 25th day of March 1947.' Further, it is clear

from a letter dated 7th February 1947 from Mr Hickley to Mrs Bell that the sale of
Churchill Farm, to which I have referred, was a sale to the trustees of the voluntary *a*
settlement and was made in order to put cash into the hands of Mrs Bell and Alexander
with a view to the distribution of those moneys (amounting to £8,200) between Mrs Bell
and Alexander. In the words of Mr Hickley, Alexander's liabilities were in this way to be
'Contained in the will trust leaving the voluntary settlement on a sound basis'. It is
doubtful whether even the voluntary settlement remained on a sound basis for much
longer. *b*

Mr Hickley died in 1972 after these proceedings had been commenced and on 5th
April 1973 it was ordered that the proceedings be carried on against his executors, the
eleventh and twelfth defendants, Michael Anthony Petit and Elizabeth North Powell.

It is admitted by counsel for Mr Hickley's executors, that in as much as he assisted with
knowledge in the misappropriation of trust moneys held in the trustees' client account
with the firm, he is liable as a constructive trustee to replace at least the amount of those *c*
sums totalling £26,237 15s 5d paid to Alexander and Mrs Bell and the trustees of the
voluntary settlement out of moneys in the client account; subject only to a deduction,
which it is claimed ought to be made, for the estate duty which would have been payable
on the death of Alexander and on subsequent deaths, except that of Mrs Bell, if the trust
fund had remained intact.

The fourth defendant was originally not served with the writ. Her whereabouts at the *d*
time were not known and as it was thought at the time that the assets in Alexander's
estate were very small, no serious efforts were made to trace her. Following Lady Hall's
death, substantial sums fell into Alexander's estate from a settlement in which Lady Hall
had a life interest. Further and successful efforts were made to trace the fourth defendant
who was ultimately found, I understand, in California and a concurrent writ was served
on her. Counsel admits on her behalf that Alexander's estate is liable to make good at *e*
least the sums distributed by him and Mrs Bell in breach of trust. Those sums total
£29,737 15s 5d, being the sum of £26,237 15s 5d paid out of the client account, the
loans amounting to £969 6s 8d and the agreed value of chattels misappropriated of
£2,530 13s 4d. But he also claims that a deduction should be made for the estate duty
that would have been payable on successive deaths, except Mrs Bell's, if the trust fund
had remained intact. *f*

On these facts and admissions three issues fall to be determined. First, it is said by the
plaintiffs that Mr Heaver also became liable, either as a constructive trustee or as a partner
of Mr Hickley to make good the sums wrongly distributed out of his firm's client
account. He died on 5th October 1947. His will was proved on 4th December 1947 by
his widow, Myra Amelia Earnshaw Heaver who died before these proceedings were
commenced, by the second defendant, Alfred John Langton Heaver, who died on 21st *g*
January 1973 and the third defendant, Beauchamp Stuart Pell, who is thus his surviving
executor and represents his estate.

Second, it is said by the plaintiffs that the liability extends to the present value of
Churchill Farm which was sold by the trustees of the marriage settlement and will to the
trustees of the voluntary settlement for £8,200 on 24th February 1947, or alternatively
to the difference between £8,200 and £12,400 which is the price at which Churchill *h*
Farm was sold by the trustees of the voluntary settlement in the open market on 31st
March 1949.

Third, as I have already indicated, the fourth defendant and Mr Hickley's executors
and, so far as liable, Mr Heaver's executors, claim that in ascertaining the moneys which
they are jointly and severally liable to make good to the beneficiaries under the marriage
settlement and the will a deduction should be made in respect of the estate duty which *j*
would have been paid on the deaths of successive life tenants except that of Mrs Bell, if
no defalcations had taken place. Originally, there was a dispute whether Mr Hickley or
his executors were liable to account for the commission of £52 18s 8d received on the
purchase of the annuities by Mrs Bell. At first sight if Mr Hickley is liable to account for
this commission, the beneficiaries under the marriage settlement and will will recover

the same moneys twice over since the commission was paid by the insurance company
a from whom the annuities were purchased by Mrs Bell and Mr Hickley's estate is
admittedly liable to replace the whole of the moneys paid to Mrs Bell and in large
measure used to purchase the annuities. However, the amount at stake is very small and
counsel on behalf of Mr Hickley's estate does not dispute this liability.

I turn therefore to the three main issues.

b *The first issue*

It is admitted on behalf of Mr Heaver's executors that the moneys for the misapplication
of which it is sought to make him and his estate liable passed through his firm's client
account, and that he had in his possession or had access to documents including copies of
the marriage settlement and will and ledger accounts and correspondence between Mrs
Bell, Alexander and Mr Hickley, inspection of which might have led Mr Heaver to
c suspect that breaches of trust were being committed. It is admitted by the plaintiffs that
there is nothing to show that Mr Heaver actually knew of these misappropriations and
it is not contended that Mr Heaver failed to exercise a proper degree of supervision over
the affairs of the firm or failed to make inquiries which a reasonable solicitor in his
position ought to have made and which if he had made might have led to the discovery
of these misapplications. Shortly stated, it is agreed that Mr Heaver acted throughout
d honestly and reasonably.

It is argued by counsel on behalf of the plaintiffs that Mr Heaver is nonetheless jointly
and severally liable to make good the moneys misapplied because, it is said, whenever
trust moneys are received by a firm of solicitors and are paid out for a purpose which any
one of the partners knows to be a breach of trust, all the partners are liable to make good
the breach of trust, either as constructive trustees or alternatively under the general
e principle, embodied in ss 10 and 11 of the Partnership Act 1890, that a firm is liable for
the wrongful act of a partner acting in the ordinary course of business and is liable when
a partner, acting within the scope of his authority, receives the property of a third person
and misapplies it.

For this at first sight somewhat surprising proposition, counsel relies primarily on the
decision of Stirling J in *Blyth v Fladgate* [1891] 1 Ch 337. It is true that there are passages
f in the judgment of Stirling J which taken in isolation appear to lend some support to
counsel's argument. But the passages relied on by counsel, to which I shall refer later in
this judgment, must be read in the light of the very special facts of that case which were
as follows. An antenuptial marriage settlement dated 20th August 1855 was made in
consideration of the marriage that shortly afterwards took place between Mr and Mrs
Blyth. Of the original trustees, one, Arthur Thomas Upton, died on 5th January 1875.
g Another, Philip Patten Blyth died on 30th January 1881 and the third, Henry George
Gordon, who after the death of Philip Patten Blyth was the sole trustee, died on 7th June
1883. Part of the trust fund was invested in a mortgage which was paid off while Henry
George Gordon was the sole trustee, and it was at his direction paid to a firm of solicitors,
Messrs. Fladgate, Smith and Fladgate ('Fladgates'). By the trustee's direction, Fladgates
invested the moneys in Exchequer bills which were deposited with their bankers in their
h name. Henry George Gordon died and, shortly after his death, the husband, Philip
Thomas Blyth interested himself in looking for a suitable mortgage for the investment
of the moneys. On 8th October 1883 he asked one Horace William Smith, a partner in
Fladgates, to look into a possible mortgage security. Mr Smith did so and first reported
unfavourably. Later, some of the difficulties that had troubled him were surmounted
and, prior to 24th February 1884, the Exchequer bills were sold and the proceeds paid to
j the credit of Fladgates with their bankers. Mr Smith drew the attention of the husband
to the fact that there were no trustees of the marriage settlement. There was delay in
getting the consent of one of the trustees proposed by the husband and it was not until
April 1884 that new trustees (including Mr Smith) were appointed.

In the meantime, the moneys held by the firm were advanced on mortgage. A
mortgage deed was executed in favour of the proposed trustees on 13th March 1884.

The advance was imprudent and the securities proved insufficient. An action was brought against the trustees in which they were held to be liable to replace the moneys which had been lost. Subsequently, three other actions were brought and heard together, in the first of which a declaration was sought that Mr Smith's partners in the firm of Fladgates were liable to replace these moneys. In his judgment, Stirling J said (at 351–352):

'The defence of the Messrs. *Fladgate* contained no denial of any part of the allegations made by the statement of claim as to the investment, and regard being had to the admissions in the defence, it must be taken to be admitted by them—first, that the Exchequer bills were in the custody of the firm; secondly, that all the partners knew, or were affected with knowledge that those bills formed part of the funds subject to the trusts of the settlement; and thirdly, that the bills were sold by order of the firm, and that the proceeds were placed to the account of the firm at their bankers. The funds, therefore, came into the custody and under the control of the firm with notice of the trusts upon which they were held; and as against the Plaintiffs in *Blyth* v. *Fladgate*, it lay with the firm to discharge themselves by shewing that the funds were duly applied in accordance with the trusts. That the Messrs. *Fladgate* attempted to do by saying that the funds were paid over to Mr. *Searle* by direction of the trustees of the settlement, on the security of mortgages of real estate, a mode of investment which was within the powers of the trustees, and of the impropriety of which they had no notice. It is to be observed that at the date of the payment to Mr. *Searle*, Messrs. *Smith, Philip William Blyth,* and *Morgan* had not been appointed trustees, and neither the investment of the funds in their names nor the application of them by their direction could, in the first instance, be a discharge to the firm. Messrs. *Smith, Philip William Blyth,* and *Morgan* were however shortly afterwards appointed trustees, and never repudiated the transaction, or disclaimed any interest under the mortgage deed; and under these circumstances it was contended, and I think rightly, that they must be treated as having sanctioned the application of the funds. That sanction, however, would not avail the partners in the firm of Messrs. *Fladgate, Smith, & Fladgate* if they had knowledge or notice that the investment was one which could not properly be made by duly-constituted trustees. It was admitted that neither Mr. *William Mark Fladgate* nor Mr. *William Francis Fladgate* had any actual knowledge of the nature of the security taken for the advance made to Mr. *Searle*; but it was contended that each of them was affected with notice through their partner Mr. *Smith*, to whom the whole of the facts were known. This point requires careful consideration. As I have already said, the matter was brought before Mr. *Smith* by Mr. *Philip Thomas Blyth*, who by his letter of the 8th of October, 1883, asked Mr. *Smith* to "look into this, and see whether this money can be safely lent on it". That letter was addressed to Mr. *Smith* as a member of the firm of Messrs. *Fladgate, Smith, & Fladgate*, and it is clear from the contemporaneous letter of Mr. *Pocock* that the advance was to be made by trustees, and consequently that what Mr. *Smith* was asked to do was to advise whether the security was a safe one for trustees—a matter which falls within the scope of a solicitor's ordinary duties. Mr. *Smith*, as a member of the firm, proceeded to investigate the nature of the security, and ultimately placed himself in communication with Mr. *Searle's* solicitor, received and perused the abstracts of title, made requisitions thereon, and prepared the securities (which were made to himself, Mr. *Philip William Blyth*, and Mr. *Morgan*, the intended new trustees of the settlement), and saw to the due execution of them by the mortgagor. In all that he was acting within the scope of his authority as a partner in the firm of Messrs. *Fladgate, Smith, & Fladgate*, and for the work done by Mr. *Smith*, as such partner, the firm received payment by deducting, in pursuance of an agreement made with Mr. *Searle*, the mortgagor, the sum of £115 14s. 7d. from the money advanced to Mr. *Searle*, which passed through their hands. Mr. *Smith*, therefore, while acting as a member of the firm, became acquainted with the nature of the security on which the money

> under the control of the firm and known by the firm to be a trust fund, was
> a advanced; and the knowledge so acquired by Mr. *Smith* must, as it seems to me, be imputed to the other partners, whose agent he was, for the purpose of dealing with the trust fund under their control. I think, therefore, that the other partners must be taken to have had notice that the security was not of a character suitable for the investment of trust funds, and was one which the trustees of the settlement could not properly sanction as an investment of the funds in the custody of the firm. The
> b partners were consequently implicated in the breach of trust which was committed.'

Counsel for the plaintiffs founds on the statement that 'In all that [he did] he [Mr Smith] was acting within the scope of his authority as a partner in the firm . . .' and on the last two sentences of the passages that I have cited as a sufficient foundation for the proposition on which he relies. But, read in the light of the judgment as a whole, and in
c the light of the very special facts of that case, these passages are capable of a different interpretation. When the Exchequer bills were sold and the proceeds credited to the account of Fladgates with their bankers, the firm (that is, each and every partner) became a constructive trustee of those moneys. It was not open to Fladgates to say that they received the moneys as agents of the trustees. There were no trustees for whom they could be agents. It was therefore the duty of the firm to see that the moneys were
d properly applied in accordance with the powers in the marriage settlement. As Mr Smith, a partner in the firm, negotiated the mortgage and advised as to the adequacy of the security of the advance which was in fact an imprudent one, they could not discharge that duty. The fact that the new trustees, when appointed, did not repudiate the transaction and disclaim any interest under the mortgage deed founded the inference that they had sanctioned the application of the trust fund. But that could not affect the
e pre-existing liability of all the partners in the firm for the breach of trust. That is the explanation of *Blyth v Fladgate* that was advanced in argument by Mr Cozens-Hardy QC in *Brinsden v Williams* [1894] 3 Ch 185 at 187 when he said:

> 'The case of *Blyth* v. *Fladgate* has been misunderstood. In that case one member of a firm, acting as a solicitor in such a way that he had power to bind his partners,
> f took upon himself the management of the trust; he paid money which was entrusted to the firm at a time when there were no actual trustees of the fund on an insufficient security, the sufficiency of which he took upon himself to advise upon. The Court held that he had constituted himself a trustee, and it was the duty of the firm of solicitors to see that the money in their hands was not improperly applied.'

g That that is the correct explanation is, I think, also clear from the subsequent decision of the Court of Appeal in *Mara v Browne* [1896] 1 Ch 199. In that case, the defendants, Hugh Browne and Arthur Browne, practised as solicitors in partnership. One of the plaintiffs, Mrs Mara, was life tenant under a settlement of 30th August 1875 made on her first marriage to a Mr Harold Reeves. Hugh Browne, having been instructed by Mr and
h Mrs Reeves to investigate the affairs of the trust fund, found that there had been gross irregularities on the part of one Bernard Edwin James, a solicitor, and one of the original trustees, his co-trustee being one James Walker. On 7th or 8th January 1884, Arthur Reeves was appointed a trustee in place of Walker but although the deed, which was undated, was executed by Mr and Mrs Harold Reeves, who had the power of appointing new trustees, it was not executed by Walker or Arthur Reeves.

j James remained a trustee on the understanding that he would be replaced when he had made good certain deficiencies in the trust assets and would be replaced by Miss Marian Reeves. The deficiencies were made good and she was appointed a trustee by a deed executed on 9th May 1884 to act jointly with Arthur Reeves, who was her brother.

Between January 1884 and 9th May 1884 moneys were paid by James into a joint account in the name of himself and Arthur Reeves and for the convenience of investment they were paid to Hugh Browne and by him into his private account. He invested the

moneys on various mortgages of building land. The investments were made in every
case with the approval of Mr and Mrs Harold Reeves and Arthur Reeves. James knew a
that the investments were being made out of moneys in the joint account and was
content that this should be done, though he was not consulted about the actual
investments made. Some of the mortgages were imprudent and made in breach of trust,
and it was sought to make Hugh and Arthur Browne liable as constructive trustees. The
argument for the plaintiffs, which was also put by Mr Cozens-Hardy and was accepted by
North J ([1895] 2 Ch 69), was clearly founded on *Blyth v Fladgate*, which was cited. It was b
said that Arthur Reeves was not a trustee at the time when the moneys were invested by
Hugh Browne in the way that I have described, and that Hugh Browne, when he
received the moneys, received them as a constructive trustee. As regards that argument,
Lord Herschell said ([1896] 1 Ch 199 at 206–207):

> 'The moneys sent by Arthur Reeves and James were in every case applied to
> obtaining the investments for the purpose of which they were sent. James, indeed, c
> probably was not made aware, as Arthur Reeves was, of the particulars of the
> proposed investments, and perhaps did not trouble himself about them, but he
> undoubtedly knew that the money was being sent for investment on mortgage
> securities which had been offered, since that very circumstance was employed as a
> means of putting pressure upon him to complete as speedily as possible payment
> into the bank of the full value of the trust estate. It was conceded by Mr. Cozens- d
> Hardy, in his argument for the respondents, that, if the transactions now impeached
> had taken place after the date of the deed of appointment of May, 1884, he could not
> have maintained that the defendant Hugh Browne was to be regarded as a
> constructive trustee. North J. appears to have taken the same view, for he refused
> relief in respect of advances made when the trusteeship was, as he said, full. In my
> opinion, the distinction made is not a sound one. I do not think that it is correct to e
> say that prior to that date there were no trustees. It appears to me that from the
> date, at all events, when the account was opened in the names of Arthur Reeves and
> James, down to the appointment by deed in the May following, those two
> gentlemen were the trustees of the settlement. It may be quite true that, when the
> circumstances of suspicion in relation to James's conduct became known to Arthur
> Reeves after January 11, he was unwilling to be joined with James as trustee, and f
> that, if he had not intermeddled with the trust in any way, the deed of appointment
> executed by Mr. and Mrs. Reeves would have been ineffectual. But, in the
> circumstances which actually occurred, I cannot treat that instrument as a mere
> nullity. Arthur Reeves actually became a joint recipient with James of the whole of
> the trust funds, and jointly with him disposed of them at a time when James,
> though he had expressed his willingness to retire, was still a trustee. It is admitted g
> that Arthur Reeves by so doing subjected himself to the responsibilities of a trustee
> in respect of the trust fund. He became, it is said, a trustee de son tort. But does it
> not seem strange thus to designate him when he had, immediately before this, been
> appointed a trustee with his assent by those who were competent to make the
> appointment? It is surely more reasonable to refer his acts as trustee to this
> appointment than to treat them as tortious. In my opinion, therefore, the h
> trusteeship was full during the period covered by the transactions in question as
> truly as it was after the subsequent 9th of May, and the learned counsel for the
> respondents made, in my opinion, no greater concession than he was compelled to
> make when he conceded that, if the money had come into Hugh Browne's hands
> from duly appointed trustees for application upon specific investments, his
> responsibility would have been that of a solicitor, and not of a trustee.' j

Any liability of Hugh Browne (or his brother) as a solicitor would of course have been founded on negligence, and it was accepted that it was too late to found an action on that ground. This passage is wholly inconsistent with the proposition also advanced by counsel for the plaintiffs that whenever a solicitor receives trust moneys, knowing them to be trust moneys, he, and if the moneys are paid into the firm's client account, his partners, become liable as constructive trustees and can only escape liability by showing that the moneys were applied in accordance with the terms of the trust.

Counsel for the plaintiffs sought to distinguish *Mara v Browne* on the ground that the moneys were paid into Hugh Browne's private account. But I do not think that is a valid ground of distinction. If counsel's proposition were well-founded, Hugh Browne, at least, would have been a constructive trustee. But the decision is of importance for another reason. At the end of his judgment Lord Herschell said ([1896] 1 Ch 199 at 208):

> 'What I have already said is sufficient to dispose of the action. But I desire to add that, even if in the circumstances of this case Hugh Browne had been held liable as a trustee, I should still have come to the conclusion that the defendant Arthur Browne was not so liable. The only case against him is that, during the period covered by these transactions, he was in partnership as a solicitor with the other defendant. He took no part in them, and was ignorant of their nature. In my opinion, it is not within the scope of the implied authority of a partner in such a business that he should so act as to make himself a constructive trustee, and thereby subject his partner to the same liability.'

A L Smith and Rigby LJJ made observations to the same effect (at 208, 214). Although elliptically expressed, as I understand the judgment, what Lord Herschell is saying is that a solicitor has the implied authority of his partners to receive trust moneys as agent of the trustees but does not have any implied authority to constitute himself a constructive trustee. Nor, I would add, does a solicitor in the ordinary course of his practice have the implied authority of his co-partners to accept office as a trustee and so make his co-partners liable for a misapplication of the trust property; as to this last point, see *Re Fryer, Martindale v Picquot* (1857) 3 K & J 317, 69 ER 1129, where it was held that the partners of a solicitor who received money as a trustee which was lost were not liable for his default, the moneys having been received by him as trustee and not as a solicitor.

If that is the correct principle, it can make no difference to the liability of the partners of a solicitor who does constitute himself a constructive trustee whether the moneys are paid into his private account or into his firm's client account. In *Blyth v Fladgate* the firm became trustees because there were no trustees at the time when trust moneys were received by them and they could not therefore be considered agents of the trustees.

In my judgment therefore the claim against Mr Heaver's executors is misconceived.

The second issue

Churchill Farm was an asset of the compound settlement constituted by the marriage settlement and the will. It was sold on 24th February 1947 to the trustees of the voluntary settlement for the sum of £8,200. It is clear from the letter of 7th February 1947 from Mr Hickley to Mrs Bell to which I have referred, that it was sold in order to facilitate the distribution of the proceeds in breach of trust between Mrs Bell and Alexander. Churchill Farm was sold by the trustees of the voluntary settlement on 31st March 1949 for the sum of £12,400.

Counsel contends on behalf of the plaintiffs that the liability of Mrs Bell, Alexander and Mr Hickley or their respective estates is to replace the present value of Churchill Farm or alternatively the value of Churchill Farm when it was resold by the trustees of the voluntary settlement.

As originally formulated, this claim was founded primarily on the fact that Mr Hickley was a trustee of the marriage settlement and the will on the one hand and of the voluntary settlement on the other hand. It was said, I think rightly, that the sale was voidable, without proof of undervalue, by any beneficiary interested under the marriage settlement and will because a trustee cannot sell to himself or to one of a number which includes himself. As against Mr Hickley's estate, counsel for the plaintiffs also relied on the fact that Mr Hickley was solicitor to the trustees of the marriage settlement and will and one of the purchasing trustees. However, in opening his case, counsel for the plaintiffs sought leave to amend to put his case on the alternative and simpler ground, that as the sale by the trustees of the marriage settlement and the will was made to *a* facilitate a breach of trust, the sale was itself a breach of trust and that the liability of the trustees of Mr Hickley as constructive trustee is to restore the assets disposed of in breach of trust.

Counsel on behalf of Mr Hickley's and Mr Heaver's executors and counsel on behalf of Alexander's executrix agreed not to oppose this application on terms that the plaintiffs admitted as a fact that if Churchill Farm had not been sold in breach of trust it would *b* have been sold in the ordinary course of administration of the trusts of the marriage settlement and will at the date and the price at which it was in fact sold by the trustees of the voluntary settlement. In the absence of an admission, evidence would, I understand, have been called to establish these facts. However, counsel on behalf of the plaintiffs, was prepared to make this admission.

Counsel for the plaintiffs relied on the well-known decision of the Court of Appeal in *c* *Re Massingberd's Settlement, Clark v Trelawney* (1890) 63 LT 296. In that case, trustees of a settlement sold a sum of consols in 1875 in order that the proceeds might be invested in a mortgage. The mortgage was a contributory mortgage on family estates and the investment on a contributory mortgage was not permitted by the powers of investment in the settlement. In 1879 under a rearrangement of the mortgages on the family estates, a mortgage in the names of the trustees was substituted for the contributory *d* mortgage but the consent of the tenant for life (which was required under the settlement to any change of investment) was not obtained. The mortgage was paid off in full in 1887. The question was whether the trustees were liable to replace the consols sold in 1875. It was also argued that the tenant for life had by his conduct acquiesced in the rearrangement in 1879, that the mortgage was therefore thereafter a proper investment and the trustee's liability could not extend beyond the sum which would have been *e* necessary to replace the consols sold in 1875 at the price of consols ruling in 1879. It was held by a very strong Court of Appeal (Cotton, Bowen and Fry LJJ) that the tenant for life had not consented to the substituted mortgage in 1879 and (following the earlier decision in *Phillipson v Gatty* (1848) 7 Hare 516, 68 ER 213) that the trustees were liable to replace the consols sold in 1875 at the higher prices ruling in 1887.

Counsel for the executors of Mr Hickley and Mr Heaver, while reserving the right to *f* challenge the correctness of this decision in a higher court, accepted that it is an authority binding on me for the proposition that if a trust investment is sold with a view to the application of the proceeds in breach of trust, prima facie the liability of the trustees is to replace the investment sold and not merely to make good the proceeds misapplied. He also submitted that it is implicit in the judgment of the Court of Appeal that if the consent of the tenant for life had been obtained in 1879 to the substituted mortgage, the *g* liability of the trustees would have been limited to the cost of replacing the consols sold in 1875 at the prices ruling in 1879 on the footing that the consols would in any event have been sold in 1879 in order to make an investment which, ex hypothesi, would have been a proper one. I accept that submission. The question whether the substituted investment was made in breach of trust is dealt with at length in the judgment and this question was only relevant on the basis submitted by counsel for the executors. *h*

Counsel contends that similarly the liability of Mrs Bell, Alexander and Mr Hickley is limited to the value of Churchill Farm at the date when, but for the improper sale, it would admittedly have been sold and properly sold, that is in 1949, and at the price at which it was sold, which again is admitted to have been a proper price. Counsel for the plaintiffs points out, rightly, that if the farm had been retained and sold with a view to reinvestment in 1949, the proceeds might have been invested in another farm, the value *j* of which, like Churchill Farm, probably would have kept pace with the rise in value of agricultural land generally, though he accepts that apart from land, other investments permitted by the marriage settlement and the will would, at least until 1961, have been more likely to have depreciated than to have appreciated in value. He says with considerable force that an order compelling the trustees and Mr Hickley to make good

the present value of Churchill Farm does a kind of rough justice or at least a less rough
a justice than restoring mere monetary value in 1949.

This is one of the many problems to which inflation gives rise. No wholly fair solution can, it seems to me, be devised. But I have come to the conclusion, after some hesitation, that the submission of counsel for the executors of Mr Hickley and Mr Heaver must be accepted. It is difficult to see how the court could enter into an inquiry into what might have happened to the proceeds of sale of the farm if it had been retained and
b properly sold with a view to the reinvestment of the proceeds.

I can see that the court might well be slow to accept evidence that an investment sold with a view to the application of the proceeds of sale in breach of trust would have been sold at a later date if it had not been sold in breach of trust, but in view of the admissions made by counsel for the plaintiffs, this difficulty does not arise in the present case.

As regards the alternative claims of counsel for the plaintiffs, first that the sale by the
c trustees of the marriage settlement and will to the trustees of the voluntary settlement was voidable by the beneficiaries under the marriage settlement and will without proof of under-value and second that Mr Hickley's estate is liable on the further ground that he was solicitor to the trustees of the marriage settlement and will and one of the trustees of the voluntary settlement, it was accepted by counsel for the plaintiffs, in my judgment rightly, that the measure of compensation could be no greater than that appropriate to
d the claim founded on *Re Massingberd*. I do not propose to say more about these claims except that, without in any way deciding the point, I have some difficulty in seeing how either claim, if otherwise well-founded, could extend beyond an account of the actual profit made by the trustees of the voluntary settlement.

There is however, one other point which I should deal with. In *Re Massingberd* the trustees were ordered to make good the difference between the proceeds of the consols
e sold in 1875 and the cost of replacing the consols at the date of the writ. Counsel for the plaintiffs argued that the correct date should have been the date of the judgment of Kay J (ie 7th February 1889). In *Re Massingberd* the real issue was whether, if the trustees were liable at all, they were liable for more than the difference between the proceeds of sale of the consols sold in 1875 and the cost of replacing the consols at the date of the substituted mortgage in 1879. No argument was directed to the question whether the
f appropriate date was the date of the writ or the date of the judgment. It seems likely that, having regard to the stability of the price of consols over short periods in the 19th century, the difference in price between the date of the writ and the date of the judgment of Kay J was insignificant.

In the case of an action in common law founded in detinue, damages for non-return of the chattel are assessed according to the value at the date of the judgment. I have been
g unable to find any other comparable type of claim where damages are assessed according to value at the issue of a writ. Accordingly, if I had been able to accept counsel for the plaintiffs' main submission, it would, in my judgment, have been open to me to treat the decision of Kay J and of the Court of Appeal in *Re Massingberd*, so far as specifying the date of the writ as the date for ascertaining the value of the property sold in breach of trust to be made good, as an observation made per incuriam and to have substituted the
h date of judgment.

The third issue

I turn to the third and last issue. If the fund subject to the trusts of the marriage settlement and will had not been distributed in breach of trust, estate duty for which the trustees would have been accountable would have been payable on the successive deaths
j of Alexander (but not Mrs Bell having regard to the surviving spouse exemption), Lord Sackville and Lady Hall. The estate duty on the death of Alexander would have been small, having regard to his modest estate; but estate duty would have been payable on the death of Lord Sackville at a rate I understand of some 50% or 60%, and on the death of Lady Hall at a lower but still not inconsiderable rate.

Since these proceedings were commenced, there has been considerable correspondence

between on the one hand the several firms of solicitors acting for the plaintiffs, for the
estates of Mr Hickley and Mr Heaver, and for the estate of Alexander, and, on the other a
hand, the Estate Duty Office. It is only necessary to refer to two of these letters.

In a letter dated 10th May 1974 the Estate Duty Office, in reply to a letter from the
solicitors acting for Mr Hickley's solicitors, confirmed that no claim for estate duty would
be made 'In respect of properties settled by' the settlor's will on the death of any of the
persons who were given life interests by the will, and that—

> 'Without restricting the generality of this assurance . . . it proceeds on the view, b
> which I am content to accept, that it is presently and practicably impossible to
> recover or reconstitute the properties so settled (which was, it is gathered, dissipated
> in breach of trust during the lifetime of the first life tenant, Matthew A H Bell).'

This assurance was in effect repeated in a letter to the plaintiffs' solicitors dated 10th
September 1974, which is in response to a question whether estate duty would be payable c
in respect of moneys recovered from the estate of Mr Hickley. The Estate Duty Office
said:

> 'I confirm that this Office would not seek to raise claims for Estate Duty against
> the estate of the above named deceased in connection with the deaths of Matthew
> A H Bell . . . and the Fifth Baron Sackville . . . a. if Mr Hickley's estate is ordered by d
> the Court to replace the missing Trust Funds; b. if the Action is settled by way of
> damages payable to, or apportioned between, the persons contingently entitled to
> the remainder; or c. if the action is settled on any other terms under which the
> Executors of Mr. A N Hickley and/or Mr A Heaver should agree to make any
> payment or payments. I may say that claims would in fact have been raised only if
> it had been possible to recover or reconstitute to any extent the property which was e
> dissipated if such recovery or reconstitution could have taken place by way of the
> process known as "tracing". From the information supplied to this Office, it does
> not seem that there is any possibility of the funds or any part of them being
> "traced".'

It is accepted by all the parties that it is not possible, and I quote, 'to recover or
reconstitute to any extent the property which was dissipated by any process of "tracing"'. f

In these circumstances it is argued by counsel for Mr Hickley's executors that at least
as regards the claim against Mr Hickley's estate, the compensation recoverable for the
breach of trust for which he is liable (that is, in effect, the payments made out of the
client's account to Alexander and Mrs Bell and the trustees of the voluntary settlement)
should be limited to the sums wrongly distributed (in the case of Churchill Farm its
value in 1949) less the estate duty that would have been payable on the successive deaths g
if those moneys or Churchill Farm had been retained (and in the case of Churchill Farm
sold at a proper price in 1949). The principle, says counsel, is compensation and not
punishment. In the case of a trustee, actual or constructive, who has not himself taken
the trust property his liability is to make good the fund of which the beneficiaries have
been deprived as nearly as possible in the state in which it would have been if no breach
of trust had been committed. He found some support, though he did not pretend to find h
very strong support, in the statement of general principle in Lewin on Trusts (16th Edn,
1964, p 664) where the liability for breach of trust is put in this way:

> 'If a trustee commits a breach of trust, the beneficiary is entitled to commence
> civil proceedings against the trustee to recover compensation from him personally
> for the loss which the trust estate has sustained; and if he has a vested interest and j
> has reason to apprehend that the trustee is going abroad, he may obtain a writ of *ne
> exeat regno*.'

He relied also on the decision of Grant MR in *Dornford v Dornford* (1806) 12 Ves 127,
33 ER 49, a case where an executor holding a legacy in trust for an infant with a direction

to accumulate became bankrupt and a claim was made against the estate for interest at
a the rate of 5%, with rests. Grant MR said (12 Ves 127 at 129, 33 ER 49):

> '... the question is, what is the obligation, which this Court attaches upon the
> breach of such a duty. That obligation is equivalent to the contract of the party.
> This Court says "if you neglect your duty, and keep the money yourself, your
> obligation is to put the infant in the same situation, as if you had not done so." The
> b Court does not inquire into the particular benefit, that has been made; but fastens
> upon the party an obligation to make good the situation of the *Cestuis que Trust*.'

The obligation, says counsel, adopting these words, is not simply to restore the fund
without regard to intermediate fiscal charges but to make good the situation of the
cestuis que trust by restoring something equivalent to the fund in which, apart from a
breach of trust, they would have enjoyed their interest.

c Counsel for Alexander started by submitting that the same principle should apply to
all those breaches of trust to which Alexander was a party including those where he put
the trust moneys into his own pocket. He pointed to the fact that if the Estate Duty
Office had claimed duty on Lady Hall's death on moneys recovered by the plaintiffs from
Alexander's estate, they would, in effect, be claiming duty twice on the same death in
respect of the same property inasmuch as Alexander's estate is substantially derived from
d a reversionary interest under a settlement in which Lady Hall had a life interest. That
may be so, but I do not myself see how it advances the argument of counsel for
Alexander's executors. In the course of his argument counsel was at least disposed to
accept that Alexander's estate was liable to replace all moneys paid to Alexander directly
or indirectly through the voluntary settlement without any deduction for the estate duty
which would have been payable but for his defalcations, though he adopted the
e arguments of counsel for Mr Hickley's executors as regards moneys paid to Mrs Bell and
the difference between the actual proceeds of Churchill Farm received by the trustees of
the marriage settlement and will and the proceeds received by the trustees of the
voluntary settlement on its subsequent sale.

I find myself unable to accept these submissions. There can to my mind be no doubt
that a trustee who has himself defrauded his beneficiaries by taking trust moneys for his
f own purposes is liable to restore the moneys he has taken without regard to any fiscal
liabilities that might have fallen on the trust fund if he had not misappropriated the
funds. If, as a result of, for instance, a decision of the Estate Duty Office not to charge
estate duty on the restored fund there is a windfall, the windfall cannot be allowed to
benefit the defaulting trustee. Equally, if he has sold an investment in order to
misappropriate the proceeds, he must restore the investment or if it is shown or admitted
g that the investment would have been sold at a later date (as in the case of Churchill Farm)
restore its value at that later date.

In my judgment no valid distinction can be drawn between the position of a trustee
who has misappropriated for his own benefit and a trustee who has deliberately
misappropriated trust moneys for the benefit of someone else. It would to my mind be
absurd to impose a lesser liability to a trustee who has deliberately misappropriated trust
h moneys by paying them to, for instance, his wife or children. And in my judgment a
third party who has made himself liable as a constructive trustee by assisting with
knowledge of the trust in a misappropriation of trust moneys by the trustee, whether for
his own benefit or for the benefit of someone else, can be in no better position than an
express trustee. The suggested distinction between a solicitor who is also a trustee and
who joins in a misappropriation by his co-trustee on the one hand, and a solicitor acting
j for trustees who assists with knowledge in a misappropriation by the trustees on the
other hand, is to my mind an arbitrary and irrational one.

Counsel for the plaintiffs suggested that a distinction can be drawn between a
deliberate misappropriation of trust moneys by a trustee, whether for his own benefit or
for the benefit of a stranger to the trust, and a breach of trust consciously committed but
committed for the benefit of the trust estate, as for instance in *Vyse v Foster* (1872) LR 8

Ch App 309, and that in this latter case the court might limit the liability of the trustee to such amount as was necessary to reconstitute the fund in the state in which it would *a* have been if no breach of trust had been committed. I can see force in this suggested distinction but it does not arise for decision in this case and I express no opinion on it.

I was, not surprisingly, referred by counsel for Mr Hickley's and Mr Heaver's executors to the decision of the House of Lords in *British Transport Commission v Gourley* [1955] 3 All ER 796, [1956] AC 185. He urged that the principle established in that case should logically apply to an action by a beneficiary to recover the loss suffered by him personally, *b* for instance, an action by a life tenant or the estate of a deceased life tenant to recover income of which he was deprived by reason of the misappropriation of trust moneys by a trustee. But such an action in my judgment has nothing in common with an action against a defendant who has misappropriated money or property to restore that which he has wrongfully taken or its value. If an analogy is to be found to an action to reconstitute a trust fund a closer analogy would seem to me to be an action to recover the moneys of *c* a firm which had been misappropriated by an employee if, for example, at a time when the employee was thought to be untraceable or the moneys otherwise irrecoverable the employer reached an agreement with the Revenue under which the moneys were written off thus reducing the employer's taxable profits for that year. The decision in *Gourley's* case does not as I see it entail the conclusion that the employer could only recover a net sum equal to the moneys misappropriated less the tax which the employer *d* would have had to pay but for this misappropriation and the subsequent agreement with the Revenue, leaving the fraudulent employee free to enjoy the balance.

Summary

In my judgment, therefore, the action so far as brought against Mr Heaver's executors is not well-founded. The joint and several liability of Mr Hickley's executors and *e* Alexander's executrix as regards Churchill Farm is limited to the replacement of the value of that farm at the time when it was sold by the voluntary settlement trustees. But the joint and several liabilities of Mr Hickley's executors and Alexander's executrix to replace trust moneys misappropriated by Alexander and Mrs Bell is not affected by the decision of the Estate Duty Office that the moneys replaced will not attract estate duty on the death of Alexander, Lord Sackville and Lady Hall. *f*

Order accordingly.

Solicitors: *Macdonald, Stacey & Co* (for the plaintiffs); *Radcliffes & Co* (for the first, second, third, eleventh and twelfth defendants); *Rooks Rider & Co* (for the fourth defendant).

Jacqueline Metcalfe Barrister.

a

Cresswell (Valuation Officer) v BOC Ltd

COURT OF APPEAL, CIVIL DIVISION
MEGAW, EVELEIGH AND WATKINS LJJ
24th JUNE 1980

b *Rates – Exemption – Agricultural premises – Agricultural buildings – Buildings used for keeping or breeding of livestock – Livestock – Fish bred and kept in tanks for sale as food – Whether fish raised for food constituting livestock – General Rate Act 1967, s 26 – Rating Act 1971, ss 1(3), 2(1)(a).*

The respondents were the owners of premises used to breed and keep fish, mainly rainbow trout, for sale as food. The premises were included in the valuation list for
c rating purposes. The respondents appealed to a local valuation court, which deleted the premises from the valuation list on the ground that the buildings were 'agricultural buildings' within the meaning of s 26[a] of the General Rate Act 1967, as extended by ss 1 and 2 of the Rating Act 1971, and therefore exempt from rates. The valuation officer appealed to the Lands Tribunal which held that 'livestock' in s 1(3)[b] of the 1971 Act
d included fish and that therefore the buildings were 'agricultural buildings' and exempt from rates because they were 'used for the keeping and breeding of livestock' within s 2(1)(a)[c] of that Act. The valuation officer appealed to the Court of Appeal.

Held – On the true construction of s 2(1)(a) of the 1971 Act 'livestock' used in its ordinary meaning but in an agricultural context referred to domestic animals or birds which would ordinarily be regarded as livestock, and that was reinforced by the fact that
e s 1(3) which extended the meaning of 'livestock' nevertheless referred to mammals or birds. On that basis fish were not 'livestock', and buildings in which they were bred and kept were not agricultural buildings and were not exempt from rates. The valuation officer's appeal would therefore be allowed (see p 445 *f* to p 446 *a*, p 447 *c* and *f* to *j* and p 448 *f g*, post).
f *Wallace v Assessor for Perth and Kinross* 1975 SLT 118 followed.

Notes

For exemptions of agricultural land and buildings from rating, see 32 Halsbury's Laws (3rd Edn) 47, para 64, and for extension of definition of agricultural buildings for the purposes of derating, see Supplement thereto, para 64A.
For the General Rate Act 1967, s 26, see 27 Halsbury's Statutes (3rd Edn) 106.
g For the Rating Act 1971, ss 1, 2, see 41 ibid 1169, 1170.

Cases referred to in judgments

Belmont Farm Ltd v Minister of Housing and Local Government (1962) 60 LGR 319, 13 P & CR 417, DC, 45 Digest (Repl) 327, *13*.
h *Brutus v Cozens* [1972] 2 All ER 1297, [1973] AC 854, [1972] 3 WLR 521, 136 JP 636, 56 Cr App R 799, HL, 15 Digest (Reissue) 910, *7807*.
Wallace v Assessor for Perth and Kinross 1975 SLT 118.

Cases also cited

Dilworth v Stamps Comrs, Dilworth v Land and Income Tax Comrs [1899] AC 99, PC.
j *Minister of Agriculture, Fisheries and Food v Appleton* [1969] 3 All ER 1051, [1970] 1 QB 221, DC.

---

a Section 26, so far as material, is set out at p 444 *f*, post
b Section 1(3) is set out at p 444 *j*, post
c Section 2(1), so far as material, is set out at p 444 *h*, post

Normanton (Earl) v Giles [1980] 1 All ER 106, [1980] 1 WLR 28, HL.
Strathclyde Region (Assessor) v Isle of Jura Fish Farm (9th October 1979, unreported), Lands Valuation Appeal Court.

Appeal
G D Cresswell ('the valuation officer') appealed against the decision of the Lands Tribunal (president Sir Douglas Frank QC) dated 26th February 1979 dismissing the valuation officer's appeal from a decision of a local valuation court for Cumbria given on 2nd November 1976 whereby the local valuation court determined that the description and assessment of the hereditament described as 'Weighbridge and premises, Low Plains, Castlerigg, Cumbria', entered in the valuation list with an assessment of rateable value of £100, be deleted from the list on the ground that the premises were an agricultural hereditament and exempt from rates. The premises were owned by the respondents, BOC Ltd, and occupied by Shearwater Fish Farming Ltd, a subsidiary of BOC Ltd. It was agreed that if the premises were held to be rateable they should be entered in the valuation list with an assessment of gross value of £2,850 and rateable value of £2,347. The facts are set out in the judgment of Eveleigh LJ.

Alan Fletcher for the valuation officer.
Guy Seward for the respondents.

EVELEIGH LJ delivered the first judgment at the invitation of Megaw LJ. This is an appeal from the decision of the Lands Tribunal, dated 26th February 1979, dismissing an appeal by this appellant from a decision of the local valuation court for Cumbria given on 2nd November 1976, which ordered the deletion of the description and assessment of a hereditament described as 'Weighbridge and premises, Low Plains, Castlerigg, Cumbria' from the valuation list. The point in dispute in the case is whether fish bred and kept in tanks for sale as food are 'livestock' within the meaning of s 2 of the Rating Act 1971.

Section 26(1) of the General Rate Act 1967 provides: 'No agricultural land or agricultural buildings shall be liable to be rated or be included in any valuation list or in any rate'. 'Agricultural land' is defined in s 26(3) and 'agricultural buildings' in s 26(4).

The Rating Act 1971 extended the definitions. The marginal note to s 1 of the 1971 Act reads: 'Extension of definition of "agricultural buildings" and "agricultural land" for purposes of derating in England and Wales'; and s 1(1) reads:

> 'In section 26 of the General Rate Act 1967 (in this Part of this Act referred to as "the principal section")—(*a*) the expression "agricultural buildings" shall include any building which is an agricultural building by virtue of section 2, 3 or 4 of this Act . . .'

We are not concerned in this appeal with the expression 'agricultural land', which is referred to in s 1(1)(*b*). So one then turns to s 2(1) of the 1971 Act which, reads:

> 'Subject to subsections (2) to (4) of this section, each of the following is an agricultural building by virtue of this section—(*a*) any building used for the keeping or breeding of livestock . . .'

The word 'livestock' is referred to again in s 1(3), which reads:

> 'In this Part of this Act "livestock" includes any mammal or bird kept for the production of food or wool or for the purpose of its use in the farming of land.'

The premises in question are situated in Low Plains, Castlerigg, Cumbria. At that site operations were carried on for the production of edible fish, mainly rainbow trout. Eggs were imported from California and other parts of the world. They were placed in small tanks on racks. Later, young fish were transferred to other circular tanks, where they developed into fry, and the fish were fed in those tanks. They were finally removed for sale as food.

Now, the president of the Lands Tribunal, who came to the conclusion that the premises were exempt from rating, arrived at the conclusion that the fish in question were 'livestock'. He said: 'In my judgment the ordinary meaning of the word in an agricultural context is something which is alive and is stocked for the purposes of providing food.'

Counsel for the appellant, the valuation officer, has submitted that s 1(3) is restrictive of any possibly wide meaning that might be given to 'livestock' standing on its own in s 2. It is to be noted that there is no specific definition of the word 'livestock' in the Act. Therefore, he says, the livestock with which one is concerned is mammal or bird for the purposes set out in s 1(3). Counsel for the respondents, however, has said that in the first instance one should look at s 2 and ask the question: is the fish 'livestock' or not? and that question should be approached in a general way, regarding the word 'livestock' as having a meaning of creatures that are not deadstock. He says that s 1(3) is extensive and not restrictive, but is for the purpose of this case irrelevant, because, applying the natural meaning of the word 'livestock', the fish in question already come within the meaning of that word in s 2.

He also has submitted to this court that the decision of the Lands Tribunal was in effect a decision of fact, applying a possible and reasonable meaning of the word 'livestock', and has submitted that this court cannot go behind that decision. For that submission he has relied on *Brutus v Cozens* [1972] 2 All ER 1297, [1973] AC 854, and in particular on the words of Lord Reid (see [1972] 2 All ER 1297 at 1299, [1973] AC 854 at 861). It is not necessary to recite that well-known passage, but counsel has summarised the case by saying that where a statute uses an ordinary word and a judicial authority has the task of deciding whether or not something comes within the meaning of that word, then, unless the decision is so unreasonable that the court can say that no reasonable tribunal could arrive at that conclusion, we must not interfere. To my mind, there is a short answer to that point, namely, that the learned president in fact gave his definition of the word 'livestock' in the passage which I have already quoted; this court is in a position, therefore, of seeing the meaning that he ascribed to that word, and if this court itself ascribes a different meaning, then of course the court can interfere, for it would then be a question of law whether or not the Lands Tribunal applied the correct definition to the word in question. For myself, I have come to the conclusion that the learned president did not apply the correct definition, but employed a definition that was wider than that justified by the wording in the 1971 Act.

For myself, I would be inclined, at a first look at s 2, to say that 'livestock' there contemplates domestic animals or birds which are found on agricultural premises and which are supported by the land. In my judgment, s 2 is the basic section granting relief, and the word 'livestock' is there used in its ordinary meaning, but in an agricultural context. The agricultural context is, of course, made clear by the fact that what is being extended by the 1971 Act is the definition of 'agricultural buildings' and 'agricultural land'. Indeed, the heading of Part I of the 1971 Act reads 'Agricultural derating in England and Wales'. So, consequently, it is livestock which one, in the ordinary sense of the word, associates with agriculture; and, to my mind, that does refer to domestic animals.

Taking that view, as I do, of s 2 of the Act, I regard s 1(3) as extensive. It will allow to be brought within the exemption provided by the statute animals of an uncommon kind which may be kept for the production of food or wool or for the purposes of use in the farming of land, and could therefore include animals that are not usually regarded as domestic. For the present case, I would first look at s 2 and having decided, as I say, that the fish in this case do not come within the ordinary meaning of the word 'livestock' in an agricultural context, I would go no further. However, as an aid to construction of 'livestock' in s 2, I think it is permissible to have regard to s 1(3), and it seems to me that Parliament is there revealing the kind of creature that it has in mind in the use of the word 'livestock' in s 2. By s 1(3) it is in effect saying that of the mammals and birds which one ordinarily regards as being livestock, there may be some in addition to those and they shall be given special protection if kept for the purposes set out in that subsection. But the use of the words 'mammal' and 'bird' to my mind provides a clue to the kind of creature contemplated in the broad use of the word 'livestock' in s 2.

In *Wallace v Assessor for Perth and Kinross* 1975 SLT 118 the court, in deciding a case the facts of which were very similar to those of the present case (but, of course, there applying ss 5(2)(*a*) and 6 of the 1971 Act, which applied to Scotland), came to the conclusion that the fish were not livestock. Lord Fraser said (at 120):

> 'As I have already said, the solution of the problem is, in my opinion, not to be found by reference to the Agricultural Holdings (Scotland) Act 1949 but only by reference to the definition in s. 5(6) of the Rating Act 1971. In that subsection the word "livestock" is said to "include any mammal or bird kept for the production of food . . ." The fact that Parliament thought it necessary to make express provision for including such mammals and birds shows, in my opinion, that the word "livestock" cannot by itself have been intended to include all kinds of living creatures; if that had been intended, there would have been no need to make the special provision for mammals and birds. That view is powerfully reinforced by consideration of s. 6 of the 1971 Act which provides that a building occupied and used solely in connection with the keeping of bees shall be treated as agricultural lands and heritages. Again, if the word "livestock" in s. 5(6) was enough by itself to cover all kinds of living creatures, there would have been no need to make special provision for bees. It follows, in my opinion, that the word "livestock" in s. 5(6) must have some more limited meaning. That meaning may perhaps be found in earlier cases under the Valuation Acts, dealing with the word "livestock", or, if that limitation be too strict, it must at least be found by reference to the context, which is that of agricultural buildings and agriculture.'

The sections there quoted are, of course, the sections which apply to Scotland, but the wording used is the same as that to be found in Part I of the 1971 Act applying to England and Wales. Furthermore, s 3 of the Act makes similar provision as is found in the legislation relating to Scotland in connection with beekeeping. The reasoning, therefore, of Lord Fraser is equally applicable, in my view, in construing the sections relating to England and Wales.

We have, in the course of argument, been referred to a number of other Acts of Parliament in which the word 'livestock' appears. For myself, I do not find them very helpful. They appear in different settings; in the Town and Country Planning Act 1947, for example, in relation to planning law. In each case, when construing a word which is in general use, it is important to have regard to the context in which it is used. For those reasons, I do not find references to decisions under those other Acts helpful in coming to a decision on this Act.

I therefore would allow this appeal.

WATKINS LJ. The learned president of the Lands Tribunal, whose decision is appealed against to this court, found that the word 'livestock' as used in Part I of the Rating Act 1971 could, reasonably and properly construed, include fish. The ordinary meaning of the word in an agricultural context, he said, is something which is alive and is stocked for the purposes of providing food. He appears to have thought that this decision did not arise out of a question of law. Construction of a word or phrase contained in a section of an Act of Parliament, whether or not it is used in conjunction with the provisions contained in other sections of the same Act, involves inevitably in my opinion a question of law. So this appeal arises out of a question of law: what is the proper construction to be put on the word 'livestock' as it is used in the 1971 Act?

In *Belmont Farm Ltd v Minister of Housing and Local Government* (1962) 13 P & CR 417 at 421 Lord Parker CJ, in dealing with the construction of the identical word, said:

> 'It may be that this is rather a matter of first impression, but I confess that I
> a approach it in this way: Of course, on one view "livestock" can be said to be used in
> contradiction to dead stock, and to include any animal whatsoever. In some contexts
> that might be so, but it seems to me that in the context of agriculture, as here, it has
> some less extensive meaning. What exact meaning should be given to it if it stood
> alone in this agricultural context, I do not propose to determine. I think that it is
> sufficient to say that there must be a limitation in that context on what I may call
> b the wide dictionary meaning. I find it unnecessary to decide what it would mean
> if it stood alone because it does not stand alone, and the words in brackets that follow
> assist in determining what is meant by "livestock".'

If it is permissible to have regard only to first impressions in deciding what
construction should be put on the word 'livestock' in the present case, I should be driven
to the view that by no stretch of the imagination could fish be said to be 'livestock' in the
c agricultural context and more especially when the word is regarded within the contexts
in which it is used in the Act. If it is impermissible to determine such a matter on that
basis, it becomes necessary to examine how this word has been interpreted or construed
in other Acts of Parliament. I begin with the Agriculture Act 1947, where in s 109(3)
'livestock' is interpreted as: '"livestock" includes any creature kept for the production of
d food, wool, skins or fur, or for the purpose of its use in the farming of land.'

The Town and Country Planning Act 1947, by s 119(1), applied a similar
interpretation. Under the heading of the word 'agriculture' and, in brackets, following
the word 'livestock', it is provided: 'including any creature kept for the production of
food, wool, skins or fur, or for the purpose of its use in the farming of land.'

In the Agricultural Holdings Act 1948 the provisions of s 94 gave the word a somewhat
e wider interpretation. The provisions reads:

> '"livestock" includes any creature kept for the production of food, wool, skins or
> fur or for the purpose of its use in the farming of land or the carrying on in relation
> to land of any agricultural activity.'

More recently, the Selective Employment Payments Act 1966, by s 10 thereof,
f provided: '"agriculture" includes ... livestock breeding and keeping', and '"livestock"
includes any creature kept for the production of food, wool, skins or fur, or for the
purposes of its use in the farming of land', and so on.

It is noteworthy that in the Rating Act 1971 there is no reference whatsoever to
'creatures', to 'furs' or to 'skins'. All that appears in association with the word 'livestock'
are 'mammal' and 'bird', which seems to indicate an intention to give a more restricted
meaning to the word than has been given in previous legislation. It can in my opinion
g properly be said that, so far as the 1971 Act is concerned, 'livestock' is restricted in its
meaning so as to include only something which is either a mammal or a bird.

Accordingly, I see no reason for including fish within the category of the 'livestock'
referred to in the Act, whether they be bred or farmed in tanks, ponds, lakes or
reservoirs.

h I too would allow this appeal.

MEGAW LJ. I also agree that this appeal should succeed. Whether or not the contents
of s 1(3) of the Rating Act 1971 are strictly to be called a definition, having regard to the
fact that the word used is 'includes', I have no doubt that that section must have, at least,
j an important bearing on the construction of s 2(1)(*a*) of the same Act, where that
subsection refers to 'any building used for the keeping or breeding of livestock'. I am
comforted to note that Lord Fraser, in his judgment in *Wallace v Assessor for Perth and
Kinross* 1975 SLT 118 at 120, refers to the provisions of the 1971 Act applicable to
Scotland, which correspond identically with the provisions of s 1(3), in relation to
England, as 'a definition'. Lord Fraser says:

> 'As I have already said, the solution of the problem is, in my opinion, not to be found by reference to the Agricultural Holdings (Scotland) Act 1949 but only by reference to the definition in s. 5(6) of the Rating Act 1971.'

Section 5(6) is the subsection corresponding to s 1(3) in relation to England.

I agree respectfully and entirely with the way in which the issue was expressed and decided by Lord Robertson in his judgment in the same case (at 121–122). There Lord Robertson set out the terms of s 5(6) of the 1971 Act, which he says 'defines "livestock" in the following terms'. He then went on:

> 'If "livestock" *includes* any mammal or bird, it was argued, it must embrace other species, such as fish. This was the first time that "livestock" had been defined in a Rating Act. The important question was the purpose for which the living creature was kept, and if, as in the present case, fish were kept for the production of food in the same way as cattle or sheep, then the definition was wide enought to embrace fish. This argument is attractive, but, in my opinion, it must fail. The phrase "includes any mammal or bird kept for the production of food", in my view, covers some mammals or birds which otherwise might be excluded from the word "livestock" for valuation and rating purposes. It cannot be read as covering species of living creatures other than mammals or birds. If Parliament had intended the word "livestock" to include fish it would have been simple to say so. This view is underlined by s. 6 of the 1971 Act [I pause to say that corresponds to s 3 of the Act in relation to England], which deals specially with bees; if it had been intended that the definition of "livestock" in s. 5(6) should cover all species of living creatures, s. 6 would have been unnecessary. [I pause there to say that I find that an unanswerable argument on the question of construction.] In my opinion fish are excluded from the definition of "livestock" in s. 5(6) of the 1971 Act, and the argument that the subjects of appeal are entitled to be treated as "livestock buildings" in terms of s. 5 therefore fails.'

Lord Keith concurred in the judgments of Lord Fraser and Lord Robertson. As I understand it, therefore, Lord Keith was concurring in the ratio decidendi of Lord Robertson's judgment which is in the passage which I have just read.

If, contrary to my view, the provisions of s 1(3) of the 1971 Act were not to be treated as relevant for the question of the construction of the meaning of 'livestock' in s 2(1)(*a*), I would nevertheless arrive at the same result, agreeing, as I do, with the views which Eveleigh LJ has expressed as to the meaning to be given to 'livestock' in the absence of any assistance from the context of the Act or other provisions of the Act.

I agree, therefore, that the question of law stated by the learned president of the Lands Tribunal falls to be answered No, and the appeal should be allowed.

Appeal allowed; hereditament to be entered in valuation list at the gross value of £2,850, rateable value £2,347.

Solicitors: *Solicitor of Inland Revenue; G W Beck* (for the respondents).

Mary Rose Plummer Barrister.

a
Newman v Bennett

QUEEN'S BENCH DIVISION
WALLER LJ AND PARK J
19th, 20th, 21st MAY 1980

b *Commons – Right of common – Common of pasture by reason of vicinage – Whether common of vicinage a right of common or merely providing a defence to a claim for trespass.*

A byelaw made by the verderers of the New Forest provided that no commoner or 'other person in exercise of any right of common of pasture' should suffer a bovine animal to which the byelaw applied to be depastured in the forest unless certain requirements were
c complied with. The appellant enjoyed a right of common of pasture over the wastes of a manor contiguous to, but not forming part of, the New Forest. In consequence of that right he also had a common of pasture pur vicinage over the neighbouring New Forest land and cattle depastured on the manor could and did freely roam across the borders of the manor onto New Forest land. The appellant's cows were found grazing in the New Forest contrary to the requirements of the byelaw. The appellant was charged with
d contravening the byelaw and was found guilty by the verderers and fined. He appealed contending that the privilege of vicinage did not confer a right but merely provided a defence to a claim for trespass by straying cattle and that, accordingly, no offence against the byelaw had been committed because he was not a person who had depastured his cattle on New Forest land in exercise of any 'right' of common.

e **Held** – Common of pasture pur vicinage was a right of common, and not merely an excuse for trespass, but the right was limited in character, being determinable by fencing off the neighbouring land. It followed that the appellant in allowing his cattle to depasture on New Forest land was exercising a right of common of pasture, within the meaning of the byelaw, and was subject to the byelaw. The appeal would therefore be dismissed (see p 454 *c* to *e* and *j* and p 455 *a* and *d e*, post).

f Dictum of Archibald J in *Cape v Scott* (1874) LR 9 QB at 277 followed.

Dicta of Parke B in *Jones v Robin* (1847) 10 QB at 632 and of Jessel MR in *Sewers Comrs v Glasse* (1874) LR 19 Eq at 161 considered.

Notes

For classification of rights of common and for common of pasture by reason of vicinage,
g see 6 Halsbury's Laws (4th Edn) paras 507, 566–569, and for cases on common by vicinage, see 11 Digest (Reissue) 12–13, *110–137*.

Cases referred to in judgments

Cape v Scott (1874) LR 9 QB 269, 43 LJQB 65, 30 LT 87, 38 JP 263, 11 Digest (Reissue) 50, *744*.

h *Corbet's Case* (1585) 7 Co Rep 5a, 77 ER 417, 11 Digest (Reissue) 24, *305*.

Hall v Harding (1769) 4 Burr 2426, 1 Wm Bl 673, 98 ER 271, 11 Digest (Reissue) 50, *742*.

Jones v Robin (1847) 10 QB 620, 17 LJQB 121, 12 Jur 308, 116 ER 235, Ex Ch; *affg* (1845) 10 QB 581, 15 LJQB 15, 11 Digest (Reissue) 12, *113*.

Sewers Comrs v Glasse (1874) LR 19 Eq 134, 44 LJ Ch 129, 31 LT 495, 11 Digest (Reissue) 12, *116*.

j
Cases also cited

Arlett v Ellis (1827) 7 B & C 346, [1824–34] All ER Rep 294.

Clarke v Tinker (1847) 10 QB 604, 116 ER 230.

Combe v Combe [1951] 1 All ER 767, [1951] 2 KB 215, CA.

Heath v Elliott (1838) 4 Bing NC 388, 132 ER 836.

Low v Bouverie [1891] 3 Ch 82, [1891–4] All ER Rep 348, CA.
Prichard v Powell (1845) 10 QB 589, 116 ER 224. a
Tool Metal Manufacturing Co v Tungsten Electric Co [1955] 2 All ER 657, [1955] 1 WLR 761, HL.
Tyrringham's Case (1584) 4 Co Rep 36b, [1558–1774] All ER Rep 646.
Wells v Pearcy (1835) 1 Bing NC 556, 131 ER 1232.

Case stated b

This was a case stated by the verderers of the New Forest in respect of their adjudication as a court of swainmote sitting at Lyndhurst, Hampshire on 24th April 1978. On 8th November 1977 three informations were preferred by the respondent, Raymond Harold Bennett, against the appellant, Alfred Walter Newman, alleging that on 16th August 1977 at Pundle Green, Bartley, in the New Forest in the county of Hampshire, acting in the due exercise of his right or rights of common in the New Forest, he suffered a Friesian c horned cow, a black Hereford cow and a Jersey horned cow belonging to him to depasture in the forest when they were not duly marked by one of the agisters and the appropriate payment was not made for such marking contrary to byelaw 4A(1) of the New Forest. The verderers found the following facts. (i) On 16th August 1977 the respondent and Raymond George Stickland, both duly appointed agisters in the New Forest, went to Pundle Green, Bartley, and there found three animals, namely, a Jersey d horned cow, a Friesian horned cow and a black Hereford cow, grazing on the forest. The animals were all born before 1st January 1977. (ii) The animals belonged to the appellant and had not been inspected and marked by the agisters of the New Forest nor had any fee been paid pursuant to the byelaw in respect of the animals. (iii) Pundle Green was in the perambulation of the New Forest and was part of forest land as described in s 3 of the New Forest Act 1877. (iv) The appellant enjoyed right of common of pasture over the e wastes of the manor of Minstead and a right of common of pasture pur vicinage over forest land by reason of his right of common of pasture over the manor of Minstead. (v) The land comprised in the manor of Minstead was contiguous to but not part of the New Forest and cattle depastured on the manor of Minstead freely roamed in the absence of any restraint, across the borders of the manor onto forest land, and similarly cattle depastured on the New Forest freely roamed over the lands forming the wastes of the f manor of Minstead. (vi) The appellant had not turned out the animals on the forest during the winter months of 1976–77 but had turned the animals out to pasture on the land at the manor of Minstead on an unspecified date early in 1977. (vii) The appellant made no attempt or arrangement to restrain the animals from wandering across the borders of the manor of Minstead onto forest land and was content that they should so do. The appellant had seen the animals on the forest earlier in the year and had made no g attempt to drive them back so that they were within the curtilage of the manor of Minstead.

After hearing the contentions of the parties, the verderers were of the opinion: (i) that there was no right of vicinage as a separate right attaching to animals depastured on common land and that vicinage was a means by which a commoner of one common, in this case the common of Minstead, obtained rights of common of pasture over the land h of another common, in this case the New Forest, and vice versa; (ii) that if the appellant took no steps to prevent his cattle from lawfully straying from the manor of Minstead onto forest land then he suffered his animals to be depastured on the forest within the meaning of byelaw 4A(1) and that byelaw applied whether the animals were continuously, temporarily or intermittently on the forest; (iii) that the rights of common over the manor of Minstead were not affected by the byelaws and there was no derogation from j the common rights over the manorial wastes of the manor of Minstead, but there was an interference with the right of common of pasture pur vicinage enjoyed over forest land by the commoners of Minstead in that that right was now modified by the requirement that persons exercising the right should comply with the byelaws made by the verderers of the New Forest and in so far as that amounted to a derogation from the common rights enjoyed by the commoners of Minstead it was a derogation authorised by statute, the byelaws having been properly made under the terms of the New Forest Acts 1877 and 1949; (iv) that the appellant had committed the three offences with which he was charged.

The appellant was fined £2 on each offence and ordered to pay £10 costs in respect of each offence, the payments of the fines and costs being stayed for 28 days and, in the event of notice requiring a case to be stated being given, further stayed pending the decision of the Divisional Court on the case stated. The appellant appealed.

The question for the opinion of the court was whether the verderers had come to a correct determination and decision in point of law, and if not the verderers requested the court to make a reversal or amendment of the decision or to remit the matter to them with the opinion of the court thereon.

Ian McCulloch and *Caroline Abele* for the appellant.
Christopher Clark for the respondent.

WALLER LJ. This is an appeal by way of case stated from a decision of the verderers of the New Forest sitting as a court of swainmote at Lyndhurst. That court is a court originally established by s 25 of the New Forest Act 1877 and now by s 8 of the New Forest Act 1949. By s 9 of the 1949 Act the verderers are empowered to make byelaws. Section 9(1) reads:

> 'The matters as to which under section twenty-five of the Act of 1877 the verderers may make, alter, add to or repeal byelaws shall include—(*a*) general measures for maintaining the health of animals at large in the Forest . . . (*c*) the application to animals entitled to be in the Forest otherwise than by virtue of a right of common of the same provisions for marking and control as applied to animals entitled to be there by virtue of such a right . . .'

Then by sub-s (3):

> 'The power of the verderers under paragraph (3) of section twenty-three of the Act of 1877 to levy sums from the commoners by means of marking fees shall extend to all persons owning animals entitled to be in the Forest . . .'

The byelaws now in force are the New Forest (Confirmation of Byelaws) Order 1962, SI 1962 No 596, to which there is a schedule setting out the byelaws, and this case is concerned with byelaw 4A. That reads as follows:

> '(1) No commoner or other person in exercise of any right of common of pasture, and no person pursuant to any permission given under section 2 of the said Act of 1879, shall in any year cause or suffer a bovine animal to which this byelaw applies to be depastured in the Forest unless [certain requirements have been complied with] . . .'

Three identical informations were heard by the verderers, identical save that each one related to a different animal. I will read one of them. The appellant on 16th August 1977—

> 'at Pundle Green Bartley in the New Forest in the County of Hants acting in the due exercise of his right or rights of common in the said New Forest did suffer a certain animal to wit a Friesian horned cow belonging to the [appellant] to depasture in the Forest when the same was not duly marked by one of the Agisters and the appropriate payment made for such marking contrary to byelaw number 4A(1) of the said New Forest made in that behalf and to the form that the statute in such case made and provided.'

The facts were that on 16th August the respondent and another named Stickland, both duly appointed agisters in the New Forest, went to Pundle Green, Bartley, and there found three animals, namely, a Jersey horned cow, a Friesian horned cow and a black Hereford cow, grazing on the forest. They were all born before 1st January 1977, so that put them in one of the categories which I have not actually read.

The animals belonged to the appellant and had not been inspected by the agisters of the New Forest, nor had any fee been paid pursuant to the said byelaws in respect of the said animals.

Pundle Green is in the perambulation of the New Forest and is part of forest land as described in s 3 of the New Forest Act 1877.

The appellant enjoys right of common of pasture over the wastes of the manor of Minstead and a right of common of pasture pur vicinage over forest land by reason of his right of common of pasture over the manor of Minstead. I need not read the other facts found by the verderers.

The verderers were referred to 6 Halsbury's Laws (4th Edn) para 566 and no other authority. They found the appellant guilty of three charges and imposed fines which are irrelevant for the purposes of these proceedings. They asked the question in their case whether they were right in coming to that conclusion or not.

Paragraph 507 of 6 Halsbury's Laws (4th Edn) sets out the classification of rights of common and says: 'Rights of common are either (1) appendant, (2) appurtenant, (3) in gross, or (4) by reason of vicinage.'

Paragraph 566 says:

> 'Common of pasture by reason of vicinage exists where the commonable beasts belonging to the inhabitants of one town or manor have been accustomed time out of mind to stray into the fields or wastes of an adjoining town or manor without molestation. The right must have existed from time immemorial, or for a period which the law accepts as proof that it has so existed.'

The beginning of the next sub-paragraph reads: 'It has been said not to be a right, but only an excuse for trespass.'

Counsel for the appellant in this case has relied in particular on that passage that the privilege or whatever of vicinage is not a right but only an excuse for trespass; in other words that it does not confer any right on any individual but merely a possibility of defence. If anybody sought to seize beasts, having strayed from the manor of Minstead for example into the New Forest, as distress for trespassing, there is a good defence that they were there by rights of vicinage.

This court has had to consider whether or not the verderers were right and were correct in coming to the conclusion that this was a right or whether counsel's argument that it was not is correct. If he is correct, no offence was committed. If he is wrong, then the words 'no other person in exercise of any right of common of pasture' would clearly apply to the appellant.

The earliest authority on vicinage is contained in Blackstone's Commentaries (23rd Edn, 1854, bk 2, ch 3, pp 34–35):

> 'Common *because of vicinage*, or neighbourhood, is where the inhabitants of two townships which lie contiguous to each other, have usually intercommoned with one another; the beasts of the one straying mutually into the other's fields, without any molestation from either. This is indeed only a permissive right, intended to excuse what in strictness is a trespass in both, and to prevent a multiplicity of suits . . .'

There it was being described as a right, albeit a permissive right.

Counsel for the appellant cited to the court a number of cases at first instance in the early part of the nineteenth century which I do not here repeat because he also cited *Jones v Robin* (1847) 10 QB 620, 116 ER 235, in the Exchequer Chamber. That was a case where the plaintiff was suing for trespass because her sheep had been distrained and impounded by the defendant. The defendant's defence, among other things, was that the sheep were there by right of vicinage.

The judgment of the court was given by Parke B, and at the beginning of his
a judgment he said (10 QB 620 at 632, 116 ER 235 at 240):

> 'It must be considered to be established that a common, or as it is sometimes called feeding, *Corbet's case* ((1585) 7 Co Rep 5a, 77 ER 417) pur cause de vicinage, is not properly a right of common or profit à prendre, but rather an excuse for a trespass . . . Lord Coke says that the person entitled cannot put in his cattle into the adjoining waste, but they must escape into it . . .'

b So counsel for the appellant submitted that there it was being said it was not a right but merely a defence.

But further in the same judgment Parke B goes on (10 QB 620 at 634–635, 116 ER 235 at 241):

> 'In one precedent of the late Mr. Serjeant Williams it is pleaded as a right by
> *c* custom for cattle depasturing and feeding, not stating in what right; in another, an ancient usage for common pur cause &c. for all having either right of pasturage or common of pasture.'

So that does not clearly support or destroy the argument of counsel for the appellant.

In 1874, however, there were two decisions, one *Cape v Scott* (1874) LR 9 QB 269
d where the headnote reads:

> 'The principle laid down in *Hall v Harding* ((1769) 4 Burr 2426, 98 ER 271) that one commoner cannot distrain the cattle of another commoner because they come upon the commonable land by colour of right, applies to common pur cause de vicinage as well as to common appurtenant.'

e Blackburn J picks up the phrase 'colour of right' which had been used in *Hall v Harding*. For instance, he said (at 275):

> 'It was urged, therefore, that common pur cause de vicinage was not a matter of strict right, inasmuch as it can be put an end to by inclosure so that the commonable lands will not lie open to each other, and that, as the plaintiff relies on a right of this kind, the defendants are entitled to distrain in case of a surcharge.'

f He was using the word 'right', although in another passage (at 274) he refers to it as 'a colour of right', picking up the phrase which had been used in *Hall v Harding*. Quain J also picked up the same phrase (at 277), namely, 'colour of right'. But Archibald J said (at 277):

> 'Now common pur cause de vicinage was in its origin a mere excuse for a trespass;
> *g* but although this circumstance may explain the way in which the right came originally into existence, yet unquestionably it has grown into a right resting on a sort of prescriptive licence, subject to this limitation, that by an act lawful in itself either party may inclose so as to prevent the cattle from straying, and by that means may put an end to the right.'

h Counsel for the appellant submitted that there Archibald J was going beyond that which was said by either of the other two judges, but in my opinion, there is nothing inconsistent in what he said. Blackburn J was simply picking up a phrase that had been used in *Hall v Harding*; so indeed was Quain J, and they were not saying anything that was in any way different from Archibald J.

There was another case in the same year, *Sewers Comrs v Glasse* (1874) LR 19 Eq 134,
j where again there was as one of the issues the question whether or not there was a right of common or of vicinage. The nature of the right was being both discussed in the course of argument and being considered in the course of the judgment of Jessell MR. Both in the arguments for the plaintiff by Mr Manisty (at 142–144) and Mr Williams (at 144–146) it was described as a right. Mr Williams used the phrase 'the rights must be reciprocal', and in the argument of Mr Southgate for the defendant (at 146–147) the

phrase was described as 'a right'; in other words, the argument was based on both sides as if vicinage was a right and not a mere shield, as counsel for the appellant in this case *a*
was arguing.

Jessel MR uses this phrase (at 161):

> 'In common of vicinage there is a limitation of the right of this sort. Neither party can put on the commons more beasts than his own common will maintain ...' *b*

In other words, Jessel MR is there saying it is a right, but it is a right limited to the number of beasts, for example, in this case the number of beasts which could be properly put on the manor of Minstead, and it would not be permissible to put more in the New Forest by reason of vicinage.

In my opinion, the authors of Halsbury in the paragraph which I read at the beginning (6 Halsbury's Laws (4th Edn) para 507) correctly divide the rights of common in the way *c*
in which they did, that is to say as appendant, appurtenant, in gross or by reason of vicinage. While it may be useful as a shield against trespass (and in the cases to which counsel for the appellant referred the argument was always a defence to the distress, the animals being seized), it is still a right of common, though limited in character because it is determinable. It can be determined by fencing off, and however impracticable that might be in the present case, it is a theoretical possibility. *d*

Accordingly, in my judgment, I have come to the conclusion that the appellant with a right of pasture over the wastes of the manor of Minstead had a right of common of pasture pur vicinage over the forest land and that he was another person in exercise of any right of common of pasture within the meaning of byelaw 4A. Accordingly, I would answer the question posed by the verderers in the affirmative, that they came to a correct determination and decision in point of law. *e*

PARK J. I agree. The main question, and indeed the only question, argued in this appeal is whether the appellant was a person to whom byelaw 4A applied. That means whether at the relevant time he was a 'commoner or other person in exercise of any right of common'.

The appellant enjoys the right of common of pasture over the wastes of the manor of *f*
Minstead and in consequence has a common of pasture pur vicinage over forest land by reason of his right of common of pasture over the manor of Minstead. The land comprised in the manor of Minstead is contiguous but not part of the New Forest, and cattle depastured on the manor of Minstead can and do freely roam in the absence of any restraint across the borders of the manor on to forest land, and similarly cattle depastured on the New Forest can and do freely roam over the lands forming the wastes of the *g*
manor of Minstead.

The question is whether common of pasture pur vicinage is part and parcel of the right of common of pasture. That is whether there is a *right* of common pasture pur vicinage, or whether, as counsel for the appellant contends, common pasture pur vicinage is merely an excuse for trespass.

The words in byelaw 4A(1) were first used in byelaws of the New Forest passed in *h*
1954. At that time the verderers knew very well of the problem posed by cattle straying into the New Forest. In order to be able properly to control all cattle in the New Forest, it was essential for owners of straying cattle to be subject to the byelaws.

The question is therefore, whether the draftsman of the byelaw achieved that aim by the words used. I agree with Waller LJ that the law relating to common of pasture by reason of vicinage is accurately stated in 6 Halsbury's Laws (4th Edn) paras 566–588. In *j*
those paragraphs common of pasture by reason of vicinage is referred to over and over again as a right.

The verderers' opinion expressed in the case is:

> 'That there is no right of vicinage as a separate right attaching to animals depastured on common land and that vicinage was a means by which a commoner

> of one common, in this case the common of Minstead, obtained rights of common
> a of pasture over the lands of another common, in this case the New Forest, and vice versa.'

I think that the verderers' opinion is right. In my judgment, therefore, the appellant was a commoner or other person exercising at the relevant time a right of common of pasture and the byelaw applied to him.

The next question is whether in breach of the byelaw the appellant suffered the three
b cows to be depastured in the forest. The case states its findings in these words:

> 'The Appellant made no attempt or arrangement to restrain the animals from wandering across the borders of the manor of Minstead on to Forest land and was content that they should so do. The Appellant had seen the animals on the Forest earlier in the year and had made no attempt to drive them back so that they were
> c within the curtilage of the manor of Minstead . . . That if the Appellant took no steps to prevent his cattle from lawfully straying from the manor of Minstead on to Forest land then he suffered his animals to be depastured on the Forest within the meaning of bye-law 4A (1) and this bye-law applied whether the animals were continuously, temporarily or intermittently on the Forest.'

Once again I think the verderers came to the right opinion. It seems to me that, if the
d appellant as the owner of a cow knows that unless he takes steps to prevent it from straying onto New Forest land the cow will inevitably roam onto that land for the purpose of grazing there, then the appellant can rightly be held to have suffered the cow to be depastured there, especially if he has persistently failed to restrain it. If the appellant in those circumstances is unwilling to take steps to prevent such depasturing, then he can avoid the consequences either by arranging for an agister to mark the cow
e and by making the appropriate payment or by seeking the verderers' permission to allow his cows to depasture in the forest pursuant to s 2 of the 1879 Act. If he does either he will not contravene these byelaws.

For these reasons I too would answer the question in the way that Waller LJ has said.

Appeal dismissed.

f

Solicitors: *Woodford & Ackroyd*, Southampton (for the appellant); *Ewing, Hickman & Clark*, Southampton (for the respondent).

N P Metcalfe Esq Barrister.

Parsons v F W Woolworth & Co Ltd a

QUEEN'S BENCH DIVISION
DONALDSON LJ AND BRISTOW J
24th APRIL 1980

Case stated – Limitation of time – Need to comply with statutory requirements – Draft case stated issued to parties out of time b *– Applicant for case stated requesting that issue of draft case be delayed – Whether delay fatal to hearing of case – Whether court should exercise discretion to refuse to hear case stated – Magistrates' Courts Rules 1968 (SI 1968 No 1920), r 65A.*

The applicant, acting on behalf of a local authority, preferred informations against the respondent. The informations were dismissed by the justices, and the applicant then applied within the time required by the Magistrates' Courts Rules 1968 for the justices c to state a case for the opinion of the Divisional Court of the Queen's Bench Division. Under r 65A of the 1968 rules the justices' clerk was required to issue the draft case to the parties within 21 days after receipt of the application. The clerk was ready to issue the draft case within that time but, as he was entitled to do, he asked the applicant to enter into a recognisance before the case was issued. The applicant, who was not prepared to enter into a recognisance until he had received authority to do so from the local authority, d requested the clerk to delay the issue of the draft case. Because of the ensuing delay the case was not issued to the parties until 47 days after the prescribed time. When the case stated came on for hearing the respondent contended that the court should not proceed to hear it because it had not been issued within the time laid down by r 65A.

Held – Rule 65A of the 1968 rules was directory and not mandatory and did not go to the e jurisdiction of the High Court to hear and adjudicate on a case stated. Accordingly, the court had a discretion whether it would hear the case and, since the party seeking to have the case heard and determined by the court had himself been responsible for the delay and in view of the necessity for a prompt trial of criminal matters, in the exercise of that discretion the court would decline to adjudicate on the case stated (see p 458 *g* to f p 459 *b*, post).

Moore v Hewitt [1947] 2 All ER 270, *Rippington v Hicks & Son (Oxford) Ltd* [1949] 1 All ER 239 and *Whittingham v Nattrass (note)* [1958] 3 All ER 145 followed.

Notes

For an application to the justices to state a case, see 29 Halsbury's Laws (4th Edn) 266, para 478, and for cases on the subject, see 33 Digest (Repl) 315, *1394–1401*. g

For time limits for stating a case, see 29 Halsbury's Laws (4th Edn) para 478, and for cases on the subject, see 33 Digest (Repl) 319, *1426–1430*.

For the Magistrates' Courts Rules 1968, r 65A, see 13 Halsbury's Statutory Instruments (Third Reissue) 64.

Cases referred to in judgment h

Moore v Hewitt [1947] 2 All ER 270, [1947] 1 KB 831, [1947] LJR 1276, 177 LT 576, 111 JP 483, 45 LGR 558, DC, 33 Digest (Repl) 319, *1427*.

Rippington v Hicks & Son (Oxford) Ltd [1949] 1 All ER 239, 113 JP 121, 49 LGR 265, DC, 33 Digest (Repl) 319, *1429*.

Whittingham v Nattrass [1958] 3 All ER 145n, 102 Sol Jo 637, 33 Digest (Repl) 319, *1430*. i

Case stated

This was an appeal by case stated by the justices for the county of Worcestershire acting in and for the petty sessional division of Kidderminster in respect of their adjudication as a magistrates' court sitting at Kidderminster. On 30th June 1977 seven informations were preferred by the applicant, Phillip Geoffrey Parsons, a trading standards officer

employed by the Worcestershire County Council, against the respondent, F W
a Woolworth & Co Ltd, that on 24th November 1976 the respondent offered to supply
certain specified items of food by means of an advertisement in an issue of a specified
magazine which indicated that the items were being offered at a price less than that at
which they were in fact being offered, contrary to s 11(2) of the Trade Descriptions Act
1968. Having found the relevant facts and considered the submissions of the parties the
justices dismissed the informations. The applicant appealed. When the case came on for
b hearing in the High Court the respondent contended that the court should not proceed
to hear it on the ground that the application to the justices to state a case for the opinion
of the court had been made out of time. The facts are set out in the judgment of
Donaldson LJ.

Anthony Scrivener QC and *Stephen Martin* for the applicant.
c *Susan Jackson* for the respondent.

DONALDSON LJ. This matter comes before the court in the form of a preliminary
application that the court do not proceed to hear a case stated by the Kidderminster
justices at the request of the prosecutor, they having dismissed seven informations which
had been preferred against F W Woolworth & Co Ltd alleging offences under the Trade
d Descriptions Act 1968.

Unless it be thought from that rather bald description of the matter that some fearful
crime was being alleged against Woolworth, I ought in fairness to say that the complaint
in essence was this. Woolworth had said that certain goods would be offered for sale at
a reduced price. They advertised this information in Woman's Own magazine which
comes out weekly, and this particular issue was dated 27th November 1976. The essence
e of the matter was whether Woolworth had in fact placed the goods on sale at the reduced
price on the date when they should have done in accordance with the Act. But we are
not concerned with that aspect of the matter.

We are concerned at this stage with the preliminary point that the timetable required
under the Magistrates' Courts Rules 1968, SI 1968 No 1920, was not complied with and
what was the effect of that non-compliance. The timetable is provided by rr 65, 65A and
f 66. Each of those rules has as an adjunct a separate paragraph in r 67 dealing with
extensions of time. It is a three-stage operation. Rule 65 is concerned with the
application to the justices by the aggrieved party to state a case. Rule 65A is concerned
with the issue of a draft case and its study by the parties making representations as to
what amendments should be made. Rule 66 consists of the final settlement of the case
and its submission to the parties.

g Let me go back to r 65. That requires that an application for the case stated under
s 87(1) of the Magistrates' Courts Act 1952 shall be made in writing and signed by or on
behalf of the applicant and shall identify the question or questions of law or jurisdiction
on which the opinion of the High Court is sought. The 1952 Act itself provides that the
application should be made within 14 days after the day of the magistrates' court
decision.

h This decision was reached on 12th September. The latest date for making the
application to the justices to state a case was 26th September. The application was made
in due time by the applicant prosecutor on 21st September. Under r 65A, within 21 days
after receipt of an application made in accordance with r 65 the clerk of the magistrates
whose decision is questioned shall, unless the justices refuse to state a case (which was not
the position here), send a draft case in which are stated the matters required under r 68
j to the applicant or his solicitor and send a copy thereof to the respondent or his
solicitor. Then the parties have 21 days in which to make representations. The
magistrates' clerk was obliged within 21 days after receipt of the application on 21st
September to issue a draft case to the parties. That step should have been taken by 12th
October.

In fact the draft case was prepared by the justices' clerk and was ready for issue to the parties on 11th October within due time, so no criticism can be made of the justices' clerk. However, he was asked by the applicant, who was of course a servant of the local *a* authority, to delay the issue of this draft because authority to pursue these proceedings was required from a committee of the council and the chairman was not apparently prepared to take responsibility in the usual way for dealing with it as a matter of urgency subject to subsequent ratification.

It was not a case of a single delay. There were several delays. There was a great deal of correspondence. As I say, the applicant could not get backing from his local authority *b* and the magistrates' clerk sat on the draft case meanwhile.

It would, I think, have been a matter of some criticism of the magistrates' clerk if he had been prepared not to issue a draft case merely because an applicant, and in particular a local authority applicant, chose to ask him not to do so. It is of the highest importance that justices' clerks realise that, closely though they may in many cases have to work with the local authorities concerned, they are an independent judicial authority, and local *c* authorities are not entitled to any greater consideration than any other litigant or party to a criminal proceeding. But that is not this case because the justices' clerk was entitled to require, and did require, the applicant to enter into a recognisance before the draft case was sent forward to the parties. The applicant who could not get backing from his local authority, was naturally not prepared to enter into the recognisance, so there was a perfectly good constitutional reason for this draft case not being forwarded to the *d* parties. It was ready to be sent on 11th October, but was in fact sent on 28th November, well out of time.

Rule 67(1) deals with the position where there is a failure to comply with the time limits in r 65A, and it does so in these terms:

> 'If the clerk of a magistrates' court is unable to send to the applicant a draft case *e* under paragraph (1) of rule 65A of these Rules within the time required by that paragraph, he shall do so as soon as practicable thereafter and the provisions of that rule shall apply accordingly; but in that event the clerk shall attach to the draft case, and to the final case when it is sent to the applicant or his solicitor under rule 66(3), a statement of the delay and the reasons therefor.'

As I read rr 65A and 67(1), between them they provide a '21 days plus' time limit, that *f* is to say 21 days if the justices' clerk can send the draft case out within that time, and '21 days plus' whatever may be necessary in order to enable him to send it out if he cannot. But of course on the facts of this case he could have sent the draft case out on 11th October, so there is no room for any extension of time under r 67(1). It is not, I may say, an extension of time that he grants or the court grants. It is an automatic extension of time arising by operation of the rule as applied to the facts. There is a plain breach of the *g* rule.

What is the consequence of that? As I understand the authorities under the old rules (and I refer to *Moore v Hewitt* [1947] 2 All ER 270, [1947] KB 831, *Rippington v Hicks & Son (Oxford) Ltd* [1949] 1 All ER 239 and *Whittingham v Nattrass* [1958] 3 All ER 145n) these rules or their predecessors (and the same applies to these rules) do not go to the jurisdiction in this court to hear and adjudicate on a case stated; they are directory, as *h* Lord Goddard CJ put it in those cases, and not mandatory. Those cases do show an approach under the old rules (and I see no reason why the court should adopt a different approach under these rules) that they will decline to hear a case where the party seeking to have the case heard and determined by the Divisional Court has himself been the author of the delay or responsible for the delay in some way. That seems to me to be this case. *j*

I agree with the remarks of Lord Goddard CJ about the necessity for a prompt trial of criminal matters. Of course it is unfortunately true that the delay here is negligible as compared with the delay which has arisen in the Divisional Court list itself. No individual judge can accept responsibility for that, but collectively we must of course appear, as Bristow J was putting it to counsel for the applicant, in white gown, if not in

sackcloth and ashes. But the fact remains that the principle that there shall be no delay
a by the parties in bringing these matters forward and complying with the rules is one of vast importance.

For my part, for that reason I would decline to adjudicate on the case stated. We can discuss the exact form of the order and whether we dismiss it or not, but I would decline to proceed further with the matter.

b **BRISTOW J.** I agree.

Application dismissed.

Solicitors: *Sharpe, Pritchard & Co*, agents for *J W Renney*, Worcester (for the applicant); *Lovell, White & King* (for the respondent).

c Dilys Tausz Barrister.

Robinson v Whittle

d

QUEEN'S BENCH DIVISION
DONALDSON LJ AND BRISTOW J
2nd MAY 1980

Case stated – Limitation of time – Need to comply with statutory requirements – Application
e *made to magistrates within time prescribed by statute – Application not identifying question for opinion of High Court and consequently not complying with rules – Supplementary application complying with rules made after expiration of time prescribed by statute – Whether delay fatal to hearing of case – Magistrates' Courts Act 1952, s 87(2) – Magistrates' Courts Rules 1968 (SI 1968 No 1920), r 65(1).*

f *Animal – Protection – Bird – Offence – Defence – Action necessary to prevent serious damage to crops and property – Farmer putting down poison for birds – Farmer not able to shoot birds and bird scarers found to be ineffective – Whether defence available to charge of using poison for killing birds – Protection of Birds Act 1954, ss 4(2)(a), 5(1)(b).*

The respondent was a farmer who produced arable crops and kept pigs. Rooks and other
g birds from trees on land adjacent to the respondent's farm caused considerable damage to his crops and ate his pigs' food, causing an annual loss of about £2,500. Because the trees were amongst houses on land which was not his the respondent was not able to shoot out the rookeries, and experiments with bird scarers had proved ineffective. The respondent put down a poisonous substance with a view to killing the birds, and was charged on an information alleging offences against s 5(1)(*b*)[a] of the Protection of Birds
h Act 1954. The respondent contended that his action was necessary for the purpose of preventing serious damage to his crops, and that he was therefore entitled to rely on the defence provided by s 4(2)(*a*)[b] of the 1954 Act. The magistrates accepted that contention and dismissed the information. The prosecutor made an application to the magistrates to state a case for the opinion of the High Court. Although the application was made within the 21 days specified in s 87(2)[c] of the Magistrates' Courts Act 1952, it did not
j comply with the requirement of r 65(1)[d] of the Magistrates' Courts Rules 1968 that it

a Section 5(1), so far as material, is set out at p 463 *d*, post
b Section 4(2), so far as material, is set out at p 463 *a*, post
c Section 87(2), is set out at p 461 *d*, post
d Rule 65(1) is set out at p 461 *h*, post

should identify the question of law or jurisdiction on which the opinion of the High Court was sought. Accordingly a supplementary notice was filed by the prosecutor, but a outside the 21-day period provided by s 87(2). At the hearing of the appeal the respondent raised the additional point that, since the application complying with the requirement of r 65(1) was not made until after the expiration of the 21-day period provided by s 87(2), the High Court had no jurisdiction to adjudicate on the case.

Held – (1) Rule 65(1) of the 1968 rules was directory and not mandatory, and did not go b to the jurisdiction of the High Court to hear and adjudicate on a case stated. Provided that the application to the magistrates to state a case was made within the 21 days specified in s 87(2) of the 1952 Act, any irregularity arising because of a failure to comply with the provisions of r 65 could be corrected at any time before the case came before the High Court (see p 462 *e* and p 463 *g*, post); *Moore v Hewitt* [1947] 2 All ER 270 followed; *Lockhart v St Albans Corpn* (1888) 21 QBD 188 distinguished. c

(2) On its true construction s 4(2)(*a*) of the 1954 Act only provided a defence to the offence of killing a bird, and that was not the offence, namely the placing of poison, with which the respondent had been charged. It followed that the magistrates were wrong to dismiss the information, but in view of the delay involved before the case reached the court it was inappropriate in the circumstances to send it back to the magistrates with a direction to convict (see p 463 *c* and *e* to *h*, post). d

Semble. The general exceptions contained in s 4 of the 1954 Act apply only to ss 1 and 3 and orders made under s 3 of that Act (see p 463 *c* and *g*, post).

Notes

For applications to magistrates to state a case and for the time limits, see 29 Halsbury's Laws (4th Edn) para 478, and for cases on the subject, see 33 Digest (Repl) 315–316, e *1426–1430*.

For the protection of wild birds, see 2 Halsbury's Laws (4th Edn) paras 326–337, and for cases on the subject, see 2 Digest (Reissue) 430, *2387–2396*.

For the Magistrates' Court Act 1952, s 87, see 21 Halsbury's Statutes (3rd Edn) 258.

For the Protection of Birds Act 1954, ss 4, 5, see 2 ibid 196, 198.

For the Magistrates' Courts Rules 1968, r 65, see 13 Halsbury's Statutory Instruments f (Third Reissue) 63.

As from a day to be appointed s 87 of the 1952 Act is to be replaced by s 111 of the Magistrates' Courts Act 1980.

Cases referred to in judgments

Lockhart v St Albans Corpn (1888) 21 QBD 188, 57 LJMC 118, sub nom *Rutter v St Albans* g *Corpn, Lockhart v St Albans Corpn* 52 JP 420, CA, 33 Digest (Repl) 315, *1392*

Michael v Gowland [1977] 2 All ER 328, [1977] 1 WLR 296, 141 JP 343, DC, Digest (Cont Vol E) 400, *1399a*.

Moore v Hewitt [1947] 2 All ER 270, [1947] 1 KB 831, [1947] LJR 1276, 177 LT 576, 111 JP 483, 45 LGR 558, DC, 33 Digest (Repl) 319, *1427*

h

Case also cited

Goldmen v Eade [1945] 1 All ER 154, [1945] 1 KB 57, DC.

Case stated

This was an appeal by way of case stated by the justices for the county of Oxfordshire acting in and for the petty sessional division of Bullingdon in respect of their adjudication j as a magistrates' court sitting at Harcourt House, Marston Road, Oxford on 26th January 1978 whereby they dismissed an information dated 16th December 1977 preferred by Peter John Robinson ('the applicant') against the respondent, Richard A B Whittle, alleging that between 22nd and 26th June 1977 at Northfield Farm, Burcot in the county of Oxfordshire the respondent did use a poisonous substance for the purpose of killing wild birds contrary to s 5(1)(*b*) of the Protection of Birds Act 1954 as amended. The facts are set out in the judgment of Donaldson LJ.

Robert Turner for the applicant.
Stewart Jones for the respondent.

DONALDSON LJ. In this case we are concerned with a preliminary objection going to our jurisdiction to hear an appeal by way of case stated by the Bullingdon magistates sitting in Oxford. The basis of the objection is this. Section 87 of the Magistrates' Courts Act 1952 provides:

> '(1) Any person who was a party to any proceeding before a magistrates' court or is aggrieved by the conviction, order, determination or other proceeding of the court may question the proceeding on the ground that it is wrong in law or is in excess of jurisdiction by applying to the justices composing the court to state a case for the opinion of the High Court on the question of law or jurisdiction involved: Provided that a person shall not make an application under this section in respect of a decision against which he has a right of appeal to the High Court or which by virtue of any enactment passed after the thirty-first day of December, eighteen hundred and seventy-nine, is final.
>
> '(2) An application under the preceding subsection shall be made within twenty-one days after the day on which the decision of the magistrates' court was given ...'

Within that period the applicant in this case made an application to the magistrates in these terms:

> '[the respondent] being dissatisfied and aggrieved with your determination upon the hearing of the said information alleging that [the respondent] did use a poisonous substance for the purpose of killing wild birds contrary to section 5(1)(*b*) of the Protection of Birds Act 1954 as amended by the Protection of Birds Act 1967 and the Protection of Birds (Amendment) Act 1976, as being wrong in law, hereby, pursuant to the provisions of the Magistrates' Courts Act 1952 Section 87, applies to you to state and sign a case setting forth the facts and grounds of your such determination for the opinion thereof of the Queen's Bench Division of the High Court of Justice.'

I have quoted the application fully because it complies precisely with the requirements of s 87(1) of the 1952 Act, and it was served on the magistrates within the time limit provided by sub-s (2).

But it is said for the respondent that it was a bad notice, because it failed to comply with the Magistrates' Courts Rules 1968, SI 1968 No 1920, and in particular with r 65(1), which reads:

> 'An application under section 87(1) of the Act shall be made in writing and signed by or on behalf of the applicant and shall identify the question or questions of law or jurisdiction on which the opinion of the High Court is sought.'

That point was taken by the clerk to the magistrates or somebody below, and in consequence a supplementary notice was filed outside the 21-day period, specifying precisely the point of law. Accordingly there was compliance with the rules, but outside the 21-day period provided by the statute. There was compliance with the statute within the 21-day period.

It has been held by the Divisional Court of the Family Division in *Michael v Gowland* [1977] 2 All ER 328, [1977] 1 WLR 296 that there is no power in the Divisional Court to extend the time for giving notice under the statute. Thus it is not open to us to regularise the situation by any extension of time. It follows that we are faced with having to decide whether the original notice was a nullity, in which case the second notice would be out of time and we would have no jurisdiction, or whether it was only irregular and, if so, whether the irregularity could be corrected by amending the original *a* notice outside the 21-day period, provided always that the irregularity was corrected before the matter came before this court.

We have been referred to a number of cases under the Summary Jurisdiction Act 1879, beginning with *Lockhart v St Albans Corpn* (1888) 21 QBD 188. These cases are all distinguishable, because in s 33 of the 1879 Act, which is the equivalent of s 87 of the 1952 Act, there was a subsection which provided that 'The application [i e the application *b* referred to in sub-s (1)] shall be made and the case stated within such time and in such manner as may be from time to time directed by rules under this Act . . .' There is no such provision in the 1952 Act.

It follows that we have to consider whether the rule-making body which made the Magistrates' Courts Rules had power to deprive an applicant of a plain right conferred on him by statute, or whether, when it purported to do this, it was acting ultra vires. The *c* alternative view is that the rules are directory, and while directions must be complied with, they do not go to jurisdiction.

There is authority, apart from principle, which suggests that the rules are directory. It is to be found in *Moore v Hewitt* [1947] 2 All ER 270, [1947] 1 KB 831. In that case Lord Goddard CJ was dealing with a different rule which required the magistrates to state a case within the period of three months, but he said in terms that the court had *d* power in its discretion to allow the case to be heard and that the rule was directory and not mandatory.

In my judgment r 65 (1) is to be treated as directory and not mandatory. An application must be made within three weeks to comply with the terms of s 87. If it complies with that section, but does not comply with the rules, that irregularity can be corrected, even if it is corrected outside the 21-day period specified by the statute, *e* provided always that it is corrected before the case comes before this court. In other words the original application in this case was not a nullity. As it was not a nullity, it can be, and has been, corrected.

We now come to the substance of the case stated by the Oxfordshire magistrates sitting in Oxford, against which the applicant has appealed.

An information was preferred by the applicant charging the respondent with using a *f* poisonous substance for the purpose of killing wild birds contrary to s 5(1)(*b*) of the Protection of Birds Act 1954, as amended by the 1967 and 1976 Acts.

The facts found by the magistrates were these. The respondent was a farmer farming between Burcot-on-Thames and Dorchester. His farm was bounded on the east and north by the River Thames. The produce of his farm was partly arable and partly livestock. The arable crops were winter barley, spring barley, maize and potatoes. In *g* addition he had a breeding herd of about 280 sows housed in small ark huts on an outdoor system. There were considerable rookeries in the trees which stood on the opposite side of the river. The rooks and birds from these trees descended in large numbers (by large numbers it appears we are talking of the order of 2,000).

Not surprisingly they caused considerable damage to the respondent's crops and ate his pigs' food, causing an estimated loss of £2,000 to £3,000 a year. He had a problem *h* because the trees in which the rookeries stood were amongst houses on land which was not his, and it was not possible for him to shoot out these rookeries. Furthermore, because of the nearness of the houses, it was not reasonable for him to use any of the scarers which produce large explosions. Apparently he had experimented with a rotating scarer. That was quite ineffective. So, as the magistrates found, either he had to put up with his loss and the rooks or he had to get rid of them by poisoning, and on 24th June *j* 1977 he did just that. He put down a poisonous substance, alpha-chlorelose, with a view to killing the rooks.

He was prosecuted, and he raised a defence under s 4(2) of the 1954 Act. Section 4(2) provides:

> 'Notwithstanding any of the provisions of section one or of any order made under section three of this Act, a person shall not be found guilty of an offence against this Act—(*a*) by reason of the killing or injuring of, or an attempt to kill, a wild bird other than a bird included in the First Schedule to this Act if he satisfies the court before whom he is charged that his action was necessary for the purpose of preventing serious damage to crops, vegetables, fruit, growing timber or any other form of property or to fisheries . . .'

The magistrates found as a fact that the respondent's action was necessary for this purpose. They found that he had killed the rooks. Accordingly they held that this section applied and that the respondent had a complete defence.

I have some sympathy with the magistrates in reaching that conclusion. At first blush the Act might be thought to say that. But it does not in fact say anything of the sort. It is not as clearly drafted as it might be. In fact the general exceptions in s 4 probably apply only to s 1, orders made under s 3 and s 3 itself. But whether that is right or not, they produce a defence only to the offence of killing. The offence with which the respondent was charged was not killing. He is equally guilty under s 5 if not one single rook had taken the poison or if they had only been made ill by it, because the provisions of s 5 are these:

> '(1) If, save as may be authorised by a licence granted under section ten of this Act, any person . . . (*b*) uses for the purpose of killing or taking any wild bird any such article as aforesaid [including poison], whether or not of such a nature and so placed as aforesaid, or any net, baited board, bird-lime or substance of a like nature to bird-lime . . . he shall be guilty of an offence . . .'

It is the placing of the poison which is the offence, not the killing. It follows that s 4 provides no defence.

The respondent should have applied for a licence. We have been told that licences are rarely granted. That may very well be the case for obvious reasons. But this may equally have been a case where the situation is very unusual and the Secretary of State might perhaps have considered it appropriate to allow the respondent to use an appropriate poison. I say nothing about that. My decision would only be that the magistrates were wrong.

For reasons which are no fault of either party to the proceedings, this is a very stale case. The decision was reached in January 1978. In those circumstances, I think, and the prosecutor does not dissent, that it would be inappropriate to send it back to the magistrates with a direction to convict. In fact the prosecutor's only interest is to secure an authoritative construction of the 1954 Act. That he has done. Therefore I would make no order save to answer the question of law in terms of the judgment which I have given.

BRISTOW J. I agree.

No order. Question of law answered in terms of judgment of Donaldson LJ.

Solicitors: *Baileys, Shaw & Gillett* (for the applicant); *A H Franklin & Son*, Oxford (for the respondent).

Dilys Tausz Barrister.

R v Bromley Magistrates' Court, ex parte Waitrose Ltd a

QUEEN'S BENCH DIVISION
WALLER LJ AND PARK J
22nd MAY 1980

b

Case stated – Limitation of time – Need to comply with statutory requirements – Application made to magistrates within time prescribed by statute – Application not identifying question for opinion of High Court and consequently not complying with rules – Whether applicant may correct original application outside time limit for making application – Magistrates' Courts Act 1952, s 87(2) – Magistrates' Courts Rules 1968 (SI 1968 No 1920), r 65(1).

c

Where an applicant applies to magistrates to state a case and does so within the 21 days specified in s 87(2)[a] of the Magistrates' Courts Act 1952 but fails to comply with the requirement of r 65(1)[b] of the Magistrates' Court Rules 1968 that the application 'shall identify the question ... of law ... or jurisdiction on which the opinion of the High Court is sought', the applicant may correct the original application outside the 21-day time limit laid down by s 87(2) provided the amendment is made within a reasonable d
time thereafter (see p 466 *a* to *c*, post).

Notes
For applications to magistrates to state a case and for the time limits, see 29 Halsbury's Laws (4th Edn) para 478, and for cases on the subject, see 33 Digest (Repl) 315–316, 1426–1430. e

For the Magistrates' Courts Act 1952, s 87, see 21 Halsbury's Statutes (3rd Edn) 258.

For the Magistrates' Courts Rules 1968, r 65, see 13 Halsbury's Statutory Instruments (Third Reissue) 63.

As from a day to be appointed s 87 of the 1952 Act is to be replaced by s 111 of the Magistrates' Courts Act 1980.

f

Application for judicial review
Waitrose Ltd applied pursuant to the leave of the Divisional Court of the Queen's Bench Division given on 22nd May 1980 for an order of mandamus requiring the justices for the petty sessional division of Bromley in the County of Kent to state a case for the opinion of the High Court on the determination by them in respect of a charge of theft heard by them sitting as a magistrates' court on 29th February 1980 whereby they found g
that there was no case to answer against the accused. The facts are set out in the judgment of Waller LJ.

Peter Digney for the applicants.
John Tonna for the magistrates.

h

WALLER LJ. This is an application by Waitrose Ltd for leave to apply for judicial review of a decision of the Bromley Magistrates' Court on 29th February 1980. On that day evidence was given concerning an alleged case of shoplifting. As a result of a submission the case was dismissed.

---

a Section 87(2) provides: 'An application [to magistrates to state a case for the opinion of the High Court] under the preceding subsection shall be made within twenty-one days after the day on which the decision of the magistrates' court was given.' j

b Rule 65(1), so far as material, provides: 'An application under section 87(1) of the [1952] Act ... shall identify the question or questions of law or jurisdiction on which the opinion of the High Court is sought.'

The question arises whether or not the magistrates, having been requested to state a case and having refused to state a case on the grounds that the notice was out of time, should now be directed to state a case. The application is for an order of mandamus addressed to the magistrates.

The case for the applicants is that on the evidence given, assuming it was accepted by the magistrates (and it does not seem that there are facts set out in their draft case which could reasonably be in dispute), the submission which was made should have been rejected if the submission is correctly set out in the draft case, the submission being one which certainly, in our view, is of no substance whatever.

The magistrates refused to state a case because they said that the notice had not been served in time, and it is true that the notice did not arrive at the magistrates' clerk's office until well out of time. It had apparently been, among other places, to the county court, but there is evidence before us (which I do not think is challenged by counsel for the magistrates) by a clerk in the employ of the solicitors for the applicants that the notice was delivered by hand within time.

Before us today a different point is taken by counsel on behalf of the magistrates, namely that, although a notice was served in time, it was not a good notice, and it was not a good notice because it did not comply with r 65 of the Magistrates' Courts Rules 1968, SI 1968 No 1920.

The form of the notice was taken from a precedent which dated from before the 1968 rules, and it was this:

> 'WHEREAS a complaint wherein Police (Waitrose Bromley) was complainant and Prosecutor and Alfred Bullock was Defendant was heard before and determined by the Magistrates Court sitting at Bromley on the 29th February, 1980. NOW WE Police (Waitrose Bromley), being aggrieved and dissatisfied with your determination upon the Hearing of the above Complaint as being erroneous in point of law and/or in excess of jurisdiction hereby apply, pursuant to section 87 of the Magistrates' Courts Act 1952, to you to state and sign a Case setting forth the facts and the grounds of such your determination, in order that we may take the opinion thereof to the High Court of Justice.'

The magistrates submit that, since the point of law is not there clearly stated, this notice was bad and it is not permissible to extend the time to correct it once the 21 days has passed.

The law before the 1968 rules did not require the point of law to be stated, and the short time now of 21 days, since the Criminal Law Act 1977 (originally it was 14 days), imposed is obviously so that the magistrates may be given notice when the matter is still fresh in their minds so that they can recollect the facts.

The question which has been argued before us is whether the rule, which requires a question or questions of law or jurisdiction on which the opinion of the High Court is sought to be contained in the application, is mandatory, in which case it would not be possible for time to be extended, or whether it is directory, in which case it would be possible for time to be extended.

In support of the submission that it is mandatory, counsel for the magistrates has referred us to an article in the Justice of the Peace journal in which it is said that Lord Widgery CJ in two cases in 1977 added an observation that magistrates would be entitled to refuse to state a case if the case failed to identify the point of law on which the case was to be stated. Whether that observation is accurately and fully reported or not I do not know, but it is clear from the form of it that it was not something that had been argued in the course of the case and was an observation made in the course of dismissing what was an absolutely hopeless case.

Before the 1968 rules were corrected, it was clear that the statute imposed a mandatory period. The question is: did the 1968 rules increase the onus in a mandatory fashion. The word in the rule is 'shall', but, in my judgment, one must look realistically at a problem of this sort and consider the situation with which the rules are intended to deal. Obviously it is of the greatest importance that at the earliest possible time the magistrates should have their attention drawn to the fact that they are being required to state a case. Obviously it is important that, if possible, they should be fully apprised of the grounds on which they are required to state that case, setting out the point of law and so on. But, in my judgment, it is not inevitably fatal to an applicant if he fails properly to state the point of law within the time if he corrects the notice within a reasonable time.

In this particular case, the sole question being whether or not the magistrates were entitled to dismiss the case on the evidence before them, it is, I think arguable, as Park J has said, that very little more in the way of words would be required in this notice. However that may be, it is in my judgment, permissible for the notice to be amplified within such time as the magistrates would think it proper. In this case I would be in favour of ordering the magistrates to state a case on facts which, on the face of them, do seem to produce a strong case.

PARK J. I agree.

Order of mandamus granted.

9th June. The court refused to certify, under s 1(2) of the Administration of Justice Act 1960, that a point of law of general public importance was involved in the decision.

Solicitors: *Underwood & Co* (for the applicant); *R L Preece*, Bromley (for the magistrates).

Dilys Tausz Barrister.

O'May and others v City of London Real Property Co Ltd

COURT OF APPEAL, CIVIL DIVISION
BUCKLEY, SHAW AND BRIGHTMAN LJJ
13th, 14th, 17th, 18th, 19th MARCH, 19th JUNE 1980

Landlord and tenant – Business premises – Terms of new tenancy – Inclusion of service charge over and above reserved rent – Landlord offering tenant new three-year lease containing new provisions as to service charge – Landlord claiming proportion of amount expended by him on services and repairs to building as service charge from tenant – Reserved rent to be consequentially reduced – Landlord thus obtaining clear lease free of burden of services and repairs – Whether service charge merely part of rent payable or variation of terms of tenancy – Whether transfer of risk and burden of services and repairs from landlord and tenant fair and reasonable – Landlord and Tenant Act 1954, ss 34, 35.

The tenants leased office premises comprising one floor and basement car parking in an office building owned by the landlord. The tenants' lease was for a term of five years from 25th March 1972 at an annual rent equivalent to £9·39 per square foot. The landlord was responsible for maintenance, repairs and services in respect of the building and any structural damage, without recourse to the tenants. On the expiry of the lease the landlord agreed to offer the tenants a new lease until 24th March 1982 but wished to change the nature of the lease to a 'clear lease' by which responsibility for all outgoings on maintenance, repairs and services to the building would be transferred to the tenants. The landlord would thus receive a clear rent unaffected by fluctuations in the cost of outgoings, which in turn would make the building more attractive to prospective purchasers and enhance its capital value. Accordingly, the landlord offered the tenants a new lease under which the landlord was still obliged to provide all services for the

building and to repair, maintain and decorate it both externally and internally (except
a for that part demised to the tenants) but the tenants were to pay an additional rent, or service charge, over and above the reserved rent, being a proportion of the amount expended by the landlord on services and repairs each year and an estimated amount to cover internal and external decoration and the depreciation of plant and equipment such as lifts and boilers. It was agreed that if the new lease was on the same terms as before the appropriate rent would be £10·50 per square foot. In return for the tenant paying the
b service charge under the new lease the landlord offered to reduce the reserved rent by 50p per square foot, that being an agreed assessment of the additional liability to be borne by the tenants in so far as that liability could be valued. The tenants refused to accept the terms of the new lease and applied to the court under Part II of the Landlord and Tenant Act 1954 for the grant of a new tenancy. The judge held that the imposition of the service charge amounted to a variation of the 'terms of the tenancy . . . other than
c . . . as to duration . . . and rent' and therefore that in default of agreement between the parties the terms of the new tenancy were to be determined by the court under s 35[a] of the 1954 Act having regard 'to the terms of the current tenancy and to all relevant circumstances'. The judge then held that in making that determination the court had to apply three tests, which he then applied, finding (i) that the party demanding the variation (ie the landlord) had shown a valid reason for doing so, namely the increase in
d the capital value of the building that would result, (ii) that the party resisting the change (ie the tenants) would in principle be adequately compensated by the consequential adjustment of the rent by the proposed reduction of 50p per square foot, and (iii) that the proposed variation would not materially impair the security of the tenants in carrying on their business or profession. Having applied those three tests the judge went on to hold that the clear lease proposed by the landlords was fair and reasonable in all the
e circumstances. The tenants appealed. At the hearing of the appeal the landlord contended that the service charge was merely part of 'the rent payable under [the] tenancy' and therefore under s 34[b] of the 1954 Act it was to be determined by the court merely on the basis of whether the premises 'might reasonably be expected to be let in the open market' at the proposed rent having regard to the other terms of the tenancy. The landlord was able to show that, because of a shortage of superior office
f accommodation of the type occupied by the tenants, it would have no difficulty in arranging a new letting on a clear lease on the terms proposed.

Held – (1) Because the imposition of the service charge amounted to a collateral variation of the tenants' obligations it was a variation of 'the terms of the tenancy' other than as to duration and rent, and therefore fell to be considered under s 35 of the 1954 Act and not
g under s 34 thereof as merely part of the rent payable under the lease (see p 470 *c*, p 473 *g* and p 474 *a* to *c* and *f*, post).

(2) In deciding the case under s 35 the judge had applied the correct three tests. However, although the landlord had shown a valid reason for demanding a variation of the terms of the lease, applying the second test the tenants would not be adequately compensated for the increased burden thrust on them by the proposed reduction in
h rent. The proposal for a service charge transferred the long term risks of the landlord to a short term tenant who would in effect become the landlord's insurer against unknown contingencies of undefined cost in return for the limited compensation of a reduced rental over the short period of the lease. The risk thus transferred to the tenants could prove to be wholly out of proportion to the very limited interest held by them. Because the proposed variation altered the terms of the lease so drastically and so adversely to the
j tenants the court would not impose them on them. The appeal would accordingly be allowed (see p 470 *e h*, p 471 *b* to *g*, p 472 *c d*, p 473 *g* to *j* and p 474 *a* and *d* to *g*, post).

---

a Section 35 is set out at p 470 *d*, post

b Section 34, so far as material, is set out at p 470 *b*, post

Notes

For the terms of a new tenancy of business premises, see 23 Halsbury's Laws (3rd Edn) a
898–899, paras 1723–1726.

For the Landlord and Tenant Act 1954, s 35, see 18 Halsbury's Statutes (3rd Edn) 574.

Case referred to in judgments

Cardshops Ltd v Davies [1971] 2 All ER 721, [1971] 1 WLR 591, 22 P & CR 499, [1971] RVR 151, CA, 31(2) Digest (Reissue) 960, *7777*. b

Cases also cited

Attorney General v HRH Prince Ernest Augustus of Hanover [1957] 1 All ER 49, [1957] AC 436, HL.
Bailey (C H) Ltd v Memorial Enterprises Ltd [1974] 1 All ER 1003, [1974] 1 WLR 728, CA.
Bandar Property Holdings Ltd v J S Darwen (Successors) Ltd [1968] 2 All ER 305. c
Clements (Charles) (London) Ltd v Rank City Wall Ltd (1978) 246 Estates Gazette 739.
Fawke v Viscount Chelsea [1979] 3 All ER 568, [1980] QB 441, CA.
Finchbourne Ltd v Rodrigues [1976] 3 All ER 581, CA.
Gold v Brighton Corpn [1956] 3 All ER 442, [1956] 1 WLR 1291, CA.

Appeal d

The plaintiffs, Donald Robert O'May and 13 other named partners practising as Ince & Co, a firm of solicitors ('the tenants'), appealed against the decision of Goulding J dated 18th December 1978 ordering the grant of a new tenancy to the tenants by the defendants, City of London Real Property Co Ltd ('the landlord'), in terms proposed by the landlord in respect of premises leased by the tenants from the landlord at Knollys House, Byward Street in the City of London. The tenants had applied by originating e
summons dated 20th January 1977 for the grant of a new tenancy pursuant to Part II of the Landlord and Tenant Act 1954. The facts are set out in the judgments of Shaw LJ.

Derek Wood QC and *Jonathan Gaunt* for the tenants
Ronald Bernstein QC and *Benjamin Levy* for the landlord.

f

Cur adv vult

19th June. The following judgments were read.

SHAW LJ (delivering the first judgment at the invitation of Buckley LJ). This is an appeal by the plaintiff tenants from a decision of Goulding J given on 18th December g
1978 in determining their application for the grant of a new tenancy of business premises on terms proposed by the landlord but not agreed to by the tenants. They contend that those terms imposed on them burdens and risks which had hitherto been borne by the landlord, and that, although the new rent made allowance for this shift of burden and risk, the judge was wrong in approving those terms in that he failed, in so doing, to give due effect to the requirements of s 35 of the Landlord and Tenant Act h
1954.

The premises in question comprise the fifth floor of an office building of modern construction, Knollys House, having been completed in 1962. The owner landlord is a property company of good standing. The plaintiff tenants are a firm of solicitors of high repute. They were granted a lease of the relevant premises for a term of five years from 25th March 1972. The rent reserved was £65,421 per annum, and there were in j
addition certain charges for services such as the heating of the demised premises and the lighting of the general parts of the building. The effective rent for office floor space was £9·39 per square foot.

The new lease sought is one which it is agreed shall expire on 24th March 1982; it is also agreed that if the terms of that lease were made to correspond substantially to those of the lease which was current when the tenants' application came to be determined, the rent per square foot should be £10·50. The landlord is not, however, willing to reproduce those terms in the new lease. Hitherto the landlord has borne the burden of keeping the general building in repair and servicing it, and has been responsible for any damage to the structure. The incidence of these liabilities, practical and financial, has of course been reflected in the rents reserved in the lettings of different parts of Knollys House; but the respective tenants have had to bear a determinate finite liability while the landlord has carried a contingent liability without any finite limit save perhaps the cost of restoration in the event of total destruction of the building. The landlord now wishes to transfer this contingent and immeasurable liability to tenants in appropriate proportions. To offset this shift of burden the landlord proposes a rent of £10 per square foot instead of £10·50 per square foot. It is agreed by valuation experts on both sides that so far as the liability in question can be translated into monetary terms, 50p per square foot appears to be the right figure to measure the additional liability cast on the tenants. Whether over any given period in which tenants are called on to pay for repairs and services affecting the general building they will have to provide a sum less than or more than the saving in rent must however remain a matter of conjecture and speculation. In the long term the concession of 50p per square foot may provide a true approximation. In the short term the odds must be uncertain either way.

The landlord's attitude in this regard derives from business reasons manifested in the contemporary property market. The disposal of office buildings in which the landlords receive 'clear rents' from the various lettings under what are called 'clear leases' is not only facilitated but is made more profitable than in situations where the landlord carries the primary liability for the maintenance, repair and servicing of the general structure and can look to the tenants for contribution only in regard to part of the expenditure thereby incurred.

The reason is obvious enough. If all outgoings in respect of an office building are covered by the tenants' obligations, the income which accrues to the landlord from the property is subject to no fluctuation in the costs of outgoings. The 'clear lease' removes any speculative element. Investment in a building let under clear leases is thus rendered more secure and attractive. Its capital value is correspondingly enhanced and it is rendered more saleable, especially to pension funds and other investment institutions.

Owners of office blocks are turning more and more to the type of letting envisaged in the expression 'clear lease'. So long as there is a scarcity of superior office accommodation in the City of London and its environs, tenants will continue to accept the form of letting which imposes on them a share of the burden which has in the past normally fallen on the landlord or reversioner.

Counsel who has argued this appeal on behalf of the respondent landlord produced impressive statistics in support of the proposition that recent new lettings have been on a 'clear lease' basis; and he has submitted that inasmuch as the rents reserved are less than they would have been if the old system had been pursued, and less by a figure which, it is common ground, represents as far as can be ascertained the financial burden of the shift of liability, there can be no reason for the tenants to complain of, let alone to resist, the landlord's proposals.

This may well be true in the case of a new letting. In general an owner of property is entitled to dispose of it on such terms as he chooses, if a tenant can be found. Where, however, a prospective letting lies in the penumbra of some statutory provision, the position is not so plain; a careful examination of that provision may reveal that the landlord's liberty of disposition can and should be qualified even where it may appear superficially that a new burden on an existing tenant is compensated for by a relaxation in regard to the rent reserved. Is there a true offset of burden and benefit, or may it be that there is not a real equivalence between the one and the other?

In the present case counsel for the landlord has contended that as it is universally accepted that the tenants' projected new burden is represented in money terms by 50p per square foot of the tenants' office space, and as it is agreed also that the rent has been reduced correspondingly, the tenants suffer no detriment by reason of this departure from the terms of their original lease. He further submitted that the court has no greater *a* responsibility in such circumstances than to apply the provisions of s 34 of the 1954 Act to the situation thus simply depicted. Section 34 provides:

> '(1) The rent payable under a tenancy granted by order of the court under this Part of this Act shall be such as may be agreed between the landlord and the tenant or as, in default of such agreement, may be determined by the court to be that at which, having regard to the terms of the tenancy (other than those relating to rent), *b* the holding might reasonably be expected to be let in the open market by a willing lessor . . .'

This argument would suffice to identify and to delimit the court's function if the amount of the rent was the only factor in issue between the parties; but what is proposed, and what Goulding J approved, was a collateral variation of the obligations of the tenants *c* in regard to general maintenance, repairs and servicing.

This, in my opinion, necessarily attracts the application of s 35 which reads:

> 'The terms of a tenancy granted by order of the court under this Part of this Act (other than terms as to the duration thereof and as to the rent payable thereunder) shall be such as may be agreed between the landlord and the tenant or as, in default *d* of such agreement, may be determined by the court; and in determining those terms the court shall have regard to the terms of the current tenancy and to all relevant circumstances.'

The judge considered this in applying the first of the three tests he enunciated. He posed the question: 'Has the party demanding a variation of the terms of his current *e* tenancy shown a reason for doing so?' He went on to cite a passage from the judgment of Widgery LJ in *Cardshops Ltd v Davies* [1971] 2 All ER 721 at 726, [1971] 1 WLR 591 at 596 where it is stated:

> 'Section 35 . . . shows that the terms of the new tenancy must be fixed having regard (inter alia) to the terms of the current tenancy; and a departure from the terms of the current tenancy is something which . . . requires to have a reason *f* attributed to it.'

One need hardly add that the reason put forward must have validity in the circumstances to which it relates. In the present case the landlord avers that the value of Knollys House as an investment would be greatly augmented (by £1m or £2m) if it was entirely let on clear leases, and that, with the court's approval where necessary, such a *g* situation could be achieved within a relatively short period. From the landlord's standpoint this is a powerful reason. In the world of property and commerce there could hardly be a stronger one.

One may therefore pass to the second test propounded by Goulding J which I would respectfully adopt, namely: 'Will the party resisting the change be in principle adequately compensated by the consequential adjustment of open market rent under s 34?' I read *h* the passages in his judgment dealing with what I consider to be the crucial question in this appeal. He said:

> 'Secondly, the tenants can in principle be adequately compensated for the proposed change of terms by a diminution of the open market rent to be fixed under s 34 of the 1954 Act. The tenants' own expert witness, Mr Baker, found no difficulty in agreeing a figure for that purpose. He was very conscious of the *j* tenants' objection to the uncertainties of the comprehensive service charge and to their lack of control of the landlord's future expenditure. Nevertheless he was satisfied that the agreed rent reduction of 50p per square foot, or £4,950 in all, was a fair compensation in all the circumstances. If I have understood correctly the figures produced by Mr Treagus, the landlord's chief surveyor and one of its

> directors, the acceptance of the landlord's terms would increase the service charge by
> a about £2,700 per annum on the basis of figures relating to a year which ended in March 1978. The remaining £2,250 (approximately) per annum can be regarded as compensation, and it is agreed to be a fair compensation, for the transfer of uncertainties from the landlord to the tenants in respect of the three years to end in March 1982.'

It is here that, regretfully, I find myself parting company with the judge. The
b advantage conferred on the landlord by a clear lease is the freedom from factors which are of uncertain outcome and which elude absolute quantification and lend themselves to what at best is a conjectural assessment, however informed the source. That freedom removes an element of risk from the landlord's financial situation; but the element of risk is not obliterated. It is transferred to the tenant. In the outcome, the diminution in the rent, though 'fair compensation' when in prospect, may prove in actuality to be
c wholly inadequate as the years go by. If the risk is disadvantageous and therefore unacceptable to the landlord at a commensurable rent why should it be more acceptable and less disadvantageous to the tenants albeit at a reduced rent? This is the more so since they are not in the business of property management and property dealing. The status of an individual landlord is, in these days, generally of longer duration than that of a particular tenant. This is especially the case with office lettings, which are often for
d successive relatively short terms. A landlord can spread the risk of deterioration, dilapidation and depreciation over a longer period and possibly over several properties; tenants have neither the opportunity nor the interest to do so. A risk which is normally acceptable to a landlord as an incident of his ownership of property may be oppressive and intolerable to a tenant whose interest in the premises he occupies is coextensive with his tenure and will not survive it. As for the general building of which those premises
e form part, he has only a very limited interest which does not extend to responsibility for its overall maintenance.

It is, I think, unnecessary to discuss the detail of the terms by which the landlord seeks to achieve a clear lease. In general terms the plan is that subject to certain safeguards against abuse the landlord retains the practical responsibility for deciding what is required in the nature of repair, restoration, renewal and services. While the cost is to be
f defrayed by the sitting tenants throughout Knollys House, the figures involved are those certified by the landlord's accountant subject in the case of dispute to a final determination by a surveyor or engineer nominated as provided in the lease.

The third test in Goulding J's analysis was whether the proposed change would materially impair the security of the tenant in carrying on their business or profession. In the circumstances of this case I do not think that the proposed change has any impact
g on that aspect of the tenants' situation. I respectfully agree with the judge in this regard.

Having enunciated the tests and applied them, he then considered, following the language of s 33 of the 1954 Act, whether the clear lease propounded by the landlord was 'reasonable in all the circumstances'. He sums the matter up thus:

> 'So I come to the final and comprehensive question, whether the proposed
> h variation of terms is fair and reasonable as between the parties. One is here in the realm of pure discretion, where it is hardest to condense in words the dialogue of the intracranial jury room. On the main question of introducing a clear lease I can only say that, weighing the landlord's reasons against the tenants' objections, taking into account the terms of the current tenancy, and remembering the compensating diminution of fixed rent, I think it fair and reasonable to adopt the landlord's terms,
> j and I cannot see that any other elements of the case point to an opposite conclusion.'

If the landlord's proposals survive the three individual tests prescribed in the course of the judgment below, it is true that the outcome is then, to use the words of the judge, 'in the realm of pure discretion'. Perhaps it is rather a matter of impression. Whichever it may be, this court would not, and should not on a matter of discretion, interfere in any other than an extreme case where the court of first instance had palpably misdirected

itself. This is not remotely the position in the present case. The judge, in the course of a pellucid judgment, has arrayed the arguments, devised the proper tests and considered a
their individual effect. None the less, I do not think that in the present case the ultimate stage which calls for the exercise of discretion considering the overall reasonableness of the landlord's proposals is reached, for they fail to pass the second test.

In my judgment the landlord's terms introduce a radical change in the balance of rights and responsibilities, of advantage and detriment, of security and risk. The tenants are justified in rejecting those terms in so far as they seek to achieve a clear lease. The b
objections are not to be dismissed as captious and they should be met. I would accordingly allow the appeal.

In the course of the hearing of the appeal, counsel for the tenants submitted a modified version of the landlord's proposals which his clients were prepared to agree. I would set aside the order of the court below and substitute an order incorporating the form devised on behalf of the tenants. c

BRIGHTMAN LJ (read by Shaw LJ). I agree that this appeal should be allowed. In so doing I differ with considerable hesitation from the carefully reasoned judgment of Goulding J.

The form taken by the draft lease annexed to the order under appeal is as follows, so d
far as relevant. The term of the lease is three years from March 1979. There are expressed to be three rents: first, a fixed rent of £100,700 a year; second, by way of further or additional rent, a proportionate part of certain insurance premiums paid from time to time by the landlord in respect of the building of which the demised premises form part (this is called an insurance rent); third, by way of further or additional rent, a service charge calculated and payable in the manner set out in the first schedule. Clause e
2 contains a covenant by the lessees to keep the interior of the demised premises in repair and decorated. Clause 3 contains a number of covenants on the part of the landlord which can be summarised as follows: (1) to provide heating; (2) to clean the common parts; (3) to keep the exterior and interior of the building in repair, other than the demised premises; and (4) to provide the services mentioned in paras 1 to 11 of Part I of the second schedule; this is sub-cl (1)(iv), and I shall have to refer to it later. f

The function of the first schedule is exclusively to calculate the service charge, as indeed the opening words of the schedule proclaim. Put shortly, the schedule provides that the service charge is to consist of the fair and reasonable proportion, to be certified by the landlord's surveyor, of the total of five items: item (a), the actual or estimated cost in any year of the term of providing the services mentioned in paras 1 to 11 of Part I of the second schedule; (these are the services which the landlord covenanted to provide in g
cl 3(1)(iv) of the body of the lease); item (b), a management fee, on which nothing turns; item (c), certain VAT, on which nothing turns; item (d)(i), an amount to be revised annually by the landlord at its discretion, towards the estimated cost of replacing lifts, boilers and other equipment on the basis of certain life expectancies; and item (d)(ii), a similar annual amount towards the estimated cost of the decoration of the exterior and common parts of the interior of the building calculated on the footing that such work h
will be carried out at the end of specified periods. Paragraphs 1 to 11 of Part I of the second schedule, which represent item (a) above, comprise various items of routine expenditure but most importantly include also '*repairing, maintaining*, cleaning, painting and decorating *the structure exterior* and common parts of the building . . . plant and equipment . . . and all drains pipes wires' etc.

The scheme of the draft, therefore, is to impose on the landlord the obligation to j
provide all the services to the building and to repair, maintain and decorate the building, both externally and internally (except the demised premises), but to entitle the landlord to recover, as additional rent, a proportion of the money which is spent on services and on external and internal repairs, plus a yearly sum which can best be described as estimated provision for depreciation of lifts, boilers and other equipment and for external

and internal decorations. The service rent so collected from the tenants, though gauged
a by reference to actual or estimated expenditure, becomes in the hands of the landlord its
absolute property to deal with as it pleases. If all leases are on the same basis, which is not
yet the case, the effect will be to extract from the tenants in each year sums which are
calculated to recover or recoup the whole financial burden of the landlord's compliance
with the covenants of the lease, in order to leave the fixed rent in the hands of the
landlord as clear profit exonerated from the burden of all outgoings.

b The scheme of the Landlord and Tenant Act 1954, in the case of the renewal of
tenancies within the Act, is to give the court jurisdiction to determine, in default of
agreement between landlord and tenant, the duration of the new tenancy, the rent
payable under the new tenancy, and the other terms of the new tenancy. This is
achieved by ss 33, 34 and 35 respectively. The test to be applied under each section is
different. As it is impossible to determine the proper rent payable under a tenancy until
c the other terms of the tenancy have been determined, it follows that the parties must
agree, or the court must determine, the duration of the tenancy and the terms other than
duration and rent, before determining rent. In other words, the court must perform its
function under ss 33 and 35 before it approaches its task under s 34. The case was argued
below as if the provisions governing the payment of the service rent were terms which
fell to be determined pursuant to s 35 of the Act on the basis that they were 'terms of a
d tenancy other than terms as to the duration thereof and as to the rent payable
thereunder'. If such provisions fall within s 35, the court is required in reaching its
determination to 'have regard to the terms of the current tenancy and to all relevant
circumstances'. This approach lets in arguments based on a comparison between the old
lease and the proposed new lease and allows the tenant to challenge the justification for
transferring the financial responsibility for the building as a whole from the shoulders of
e the lessors to the shoulders of the lessees. If, however, the service rent is part of 'the rent
payable under the tenancy', then the matter has to be determined under s 34. Under this
section the court would have to decide whether the fixed rent, the insurance rent and the
service rent constitute rents 'at which, having regard to the terms of the tenancy (other
than those relating to rent) the holding might reasonably be expected to be let in the
open market by a willing lessor', disregarding certain features which are not relevant to
f the instant case.

The judge appreciated the existence of what I may term the s 34 argument, but as the point had not been taken he expressed no conclusion on its validity. The point has, however, been taken before us, and this appeal cannot properly be dealt with under the 1954 Act unless this court first comes to the conclusion whether the proper section to apply to the service charge, which is the main bone of contention, is s 34 or s 35.

g I agree entirely with Shaw LJ that this case has to be considered under s 35 and not
under s 34, because the substantial issue is not the amount or calculation of the rent but
the incidence of certain unusual financial burdens which will have the effect of
controlling the rent. Approaching the case on this basis, and applying the three tests
enunciated by Goulding J, I entirely agree with Shaw LJ that a short term tenant, such as
the plaintiffs, is not adequately compensated by a small reduction in rent for the
h assumption of the financial risks implicit in the maintenance of the structure of an office
block. Those risks are proper to be borne by the owner of the inheritance or of a long
term of years but are not appropriate to be borne by one who is in possession for three
years and has no further interest save a limited statutory security of tenure. Such risks
are indeterminate in amount and could prove to be wholly out of proportion to the very
limited interest held by a short term tenant. No doubt they can be quantified annually
j when averaged over a number of years, and better still when averaged over a number of
properties. But they are not capable of being fairly allowed for, by way of a reduction of
rent, when the tenancy has only a few years to run. The tenant in such a case would be
made the insurer of the landlord against unknown contingencies of undefined cost. I
wholly agree with the approach of Shaw LJ, and I respectfully adopt the entirety of his
reasoning. I would accordingly allow the appeal.

BUCKLEY LJ. I fully agree with both of the judgments which have been delivered. I concur in the view that this case falls to be considered under s 35 of the Landlord and Tenant Act 1954 rather than under s 34. Section 35 requires the court, in determining what the terms of a new tenancy granted by order of the court shall be, to have regard to the terms of the current tenancy. If the intention of the legislature had been merely that the sitting tenant should have a pre-emptive right to a tenancy on such terms as could be negotiated on the open market between a willing lessor and a willing lessee at the relevant time for a lease of the holding with vacant possession, that intention would have been easily and clearly expressed, but not in the language of s 35; the terms of the current tenancy would be irrelevant.

The section does not require the new tenancy to be on the same terms as the current tenancy. All relevant circumstances must be considered, but the section makes clear that the terms of the current tenancy are relevant. This must be, in my opinion, because the legislature intended that, in the absence of relevant circumstances leading to some other conclusion, the new tenancy should, mutatis mutandis, be on similar terms to the existing tenancy. Any departure from those terms requires explanation, that is to say justification: see *Cardshops Ltd v Davies* [1971] 2 All ER 721 at 726, [1971] 1 WLR 591 at 596.

The effect of the proposed modification of the terms of the existing tenancy in the present case is to make the tenants insurers of the landlord against risks connected with the structure of the building which under the terms of the existing lease have to be borne by the landlord. They are risks which are inherent in the ownership of the building. The reduction in the rental which is said to compensate the tenants for assuming these risks is far from being an indemnity against them. The tenants might find themselves at any time unexpectedly and unforeseeably saddled with heavy capital expenditure for which the reduction in rent would by no means compensate them, except possibly in the very long run; but, as has already been pointed out, a particular tenant may fill that role only for a relatively short period and compensation which is only compensation on a very long term basis would be no comfort to him.

The proposed alterations in the terms of the lease, in my judgment, alter the mutual relations of the landlord and the tenants so drastically, and so adversely to the tenants, that the court could not in the exercise of its discretion properly impose them on the tenants under the 1954 Act in the absence of some more cogent reason than can be discovered in this case.

For these reasons, and for those already given by Shaw and Brightman LJJ, I agree that this appeal should be allowed.

Appeal allowed. Leave to appeal to the House of Lords.

Solicitors: *Ince & Co* (for the tenants); *Nabarro Nathanson & Co* (for the landlord).

Diana Brahams Barrister.

Buttes Gas and Oil Co v Hammer and others (No 3)

Occidental Petroleum Corporation v Buttes Gas and Oil Co and another (No 2)

COURT OF APPEAL, CIVIL DIVISION
LORD DENNING MR, DONALDSON AND BRIGHTMAN LJJ
8th, 9th, 12th, 13th, 14th, 15th, 16th, 19th, 20th MAY, 25th JUNE 1980

Discovery – Privilege – Production contrary to public interest – Public interest of United Kingdom – Confidential documents of foreign sovereign state concerning international territorial dispute – United Kingdom involved in dispute under treaty with foreign state – Dispute between two oil companies over area of concessions granted by adjoining foreign states – Action for slander brought by one company against other – Second company counterclaiming for libel and for conspiracy between first company and sovereign ruler – Territorial dispute between foreign states the underlying issue in action – Whether public interest immunity extending to confidential documents of foreign ruler relating to territorial dispute acquired by first company from ruler granting concession – Whether documents privileged from production.

Discovery – Privilege – Production contrary to public interest – Foreign state privilege – Whether documents protected from production if disclosure would injure interests of foreign state – Whether foreign state privilege recognised in English law.

Discovery – Legal professional privilege – Document coming into existence after litigation anticipated – Privilege in aid of anticipated litigation where several persons having common interest in litigation – Confidential documents originating from person not a party to the litigation but having interest in it and same solicitor as party to litigation – Whether common interest conferring legal professional privilege on documents in hands of party to the litigation – Whether privilege waived by reference to documents in party's pleadings – Whether allegation of fraud disentitling claim to privilege.

Sharjah and Umm al Qaiwain ('UAQ') were adjacent sovereign states in the Persian Gulf whose foreign relations were conducted by the United Kingdom government under treaty. In 1969 and 1970 the two states were in dispute over an island in the gulf, Abu Musa, and in particular whether Sharjah's territorial waters extended 12 miles around Abu Musa or were restricted to a 3-mile limit. In November 1969 the ruler of UAQ granted an oil concession to Occidental, an American corporation, giving them the right to exploit oil in UAQ's territory including the area underneath its territorial waters. A map attached to the concession agreement showed UAQ's territorial waters as extending up to the 3-mile limit of Abu Musa's waters. The concession was executed in the presence of a representative of the United Kingdom government. In December the ruler of Sharjah granted an oil concession to Buttes, another American corporation, over the island, its territorial waters and the sea bed beneath those waters. That agreement was approved by the United Kingdom government in the belief that Sharjah had sovereignty over Abu Musa and that its territorial waters were limited to three miles. In February 1970 Occidental discovered oil nine miles from Abu Musa. Both companies claimed exclusive rights to the site by virtue of their respective concession agreements. Occidental relied on the map attached to their agreement. Buttes claimed that Sharjah's territorial waters, and their concession area, extended to 12 miles from the island. The exact deliniation of the territorial rights of Sharjah and UAQ was therefore at the centre of the dispute between Buttes and Occidental. Furthermore, it was clear that the interests of Buttes and the ruler of Sharjah in the right to drill for oil on the site were identical, while on the other side there was a similar identity of interest between Occidental and the ruler of UAQ. By 2nd April 1970 all parties anticipated that there would be litigation over the dispute. To support Buttes's claim the ruler of Sharjah, by a decree which he said he had made in September 1969 but which was not published until 5th April 1970, claimed that Sharjah's territorial waters extended to 12 miles around Abu Musa. The decree if made in September 1969 thus ante-dated Occidental's concession. The ruler of Sharjah, lacking modern communications of his own, used Buttes's telex system to obtain legal advice on his territorial rights from lawyers in the United Kingdom and the United States, and in consequence Buttes acquired copies of confidential documents belonging to the ruler, such as state documents relating to his sovereignty and correspondence with his legal advisers, the United Kingdom government and other sovereign rulers in the area. In 1970 the United Kingdom government appointed a mediator to try to resolve the territorial conflict between Sharjah and UAQ, and Buttes were given copies of correspondence between the ruler of Sharjah and the mediator.

In July 1970 Buttes issued a circular to shareholders commenting on Occidental's activities. In October Occidental's chairman stated at a press conference in London that the ruler of Sharjah had conspired with Buttes to increase Buttes's concession area to 12 miles around Abu Musa by fraudulently back dating the decree of 10th September 1969. Buttes issued a writ against Occidental and their chairman claiming damages for slander. Occidental served a defence in which they pleaded justification and counterclaimed for damages for fraudulent conspiracy by Buttes with the ruler of Sharjah and libel by Buttes in their shareholders' circular. In May 1978 Buttes, in compliance with RSC Ord 26, r 2, served a list of documents on Occidental but claimed that particular documents were protected from production because of either legal professional privilege or 'foreign state privilege', i e that production was contrary to the public interest because it would be injurious to the interests of foreign sovereign states. The claim to legal professional privilege arose out of the fact that both Buttes and the ruler of Sharjah had instructed the same firm of London solicitors, the ruler in June 1970 and Buttes in October 1970, and the ruler had consented to documents held by the firm on his behalf being used by the firm in their capacity as legal advisers to Buttes. The claim of foreign state privilege arose out of the fact that the documents in question were communications by or to the ruler of Sharjah for the purpose of the territorial dispute over Abu Musa, copies of advice to the ruler in connection with the dispute, communications between the ruler and the United Kingdom government (which was involved by virtue of its treaties with the states concerned in the dispute) and communications with the ruler's legal advisers and other foreign rulers. These documents had been made available to Buttes by the ruler in confidence, and the ruler, although not a party to the action, indicated that he wished to maintain their confidentiality and did not want them produced for inspection. Occidental's claim for discovery of the disputed documents was upheld by the master, but on appeal by Buttes the judge held that, although 'foreign state privilege' was unknown in English law, all the documents, apart from some which were ordered to be produced for inspection, were protected by legal professional privilege because Buttes and the ruler had a common solicitor and a common interest in the pending litigation. The judge further held that Buttes had not lost their entitlement to legal professional privilege because of the allegation of fraud by Occidental or because they had waived the privilege in regard to some of the documents by referring to them in their pleadings. Occidental appealed, while Buttes cross-appealed in respect of those documents which had been ordered to be produced (other than some which they had already produced). On the hearing of the appeal Buttes maintained their claim to legal professional privilege but relied on public interest immunity, i e the public interest of the United Kingdom, instead of foreign state privilege.

Held – The appeal would be dismissed and the cross-appeal allowed, because all the disputed documents were protected from production, for the following reasons—

(1) (Per Lord Denning MR) English courts should not act as arbiters in a dispute between private litigants where the underlying issue was a dispute between sovereign

rulers as to their territorial jurisdiction, and therefore as a matter of its general discretion
a under RSC Ord 24, r 11[a] (rather than because of any public interest immunity) the court
should not order production of any of the disputed documents. Although on its face the
action was a claim for libel, slander and conspiracy between Buttes and Occidental, the
underlying issue was the territorial dispute between the rulers of Sharjah and UAQ, and,
since the object of the discovery was to condemn the ruler of Sharjah as a conspirator who
had conspired with Buttes to extend his territorial waters, to order discovery would be
b contrary to the comity of nations. Moreover, since ten years had elapsed between the
commencement of the action and the stage at which discovery was being sought, it was
inappropriate for the court, in the exercise of its discretion, to allow further delay by
ordering discovery (see p 482 *j*, p 483 *d* to *g* and p 487 *d* to *f*, post); *Hesperides Hotels Ltd
v Muftizade* [1978] 2 All ER 1168 applied.

(2) (Per Donaldson and Brightman LJJ) It was in the public interest of the United
c Kingdom that the contents of confidential documents addressed to or emanating from
a sovereign state, or concerning the interests of a foreign state in connection with an
international territorial dispute, should be immune from production in private litigation
unless the sovereign concerned consented to production, because (per Donaldson LJ)
there was a public interest in the maintenance of international comity which the English
courts, as an emanation of the Crown and acting in the name of the Crown, should give
d effect to, and (per Brightman LJ) the resolution of a territorial dispute between sovereign
states being a political question, it was undesirable that an English court should force
disclosure of confidential documents for the ostensible purpose of pronouncing,
indirectly in private litigation, on the merits of the territorial dispute. In the
circumstances (per Donaldson and Brightman LJJ) the public interest in refraining from
ordering discovery outweighed the public interest in the achievement of justice by full
e disclosure of documents, and accordingly the documents in question were protected
from production on the ground of public interest immunity (see p 493 *e* to *j*, p 500 *a* to
d and p 501 *c*, post); *Hesperides Hotels Ltd v Muftizade* [1978] 2 All ER 1168 applied.

(3) Alternatively, legal professional privilege applied where two persons had a
common interest in anticipated litigation and a common solicitor and exchanged
information for the dominant purpose of informing each other of the facts or issues or
f of advice received in respect of the litigation, and documents exchanged in such
circumstances were privileged from production in the hands of either person even
though only one of them was a party to the litigation. Accordingly, since Buttes and the
ruler of Sharjah had a common interest in the litigation between Buttes and Occidental
and had a common solicitor, the documents obtained by Buttes from the ruler were
protected by legal professional privilege (see p 483 *h j*, p 484 *a* to *c*, p 485 *b* to *j*, p 486 *a*
g to *d*, p 490 *c* to *e* and p 502 *b* to *d*, post); *Jenkyns v Bushby* (1866) LR 2 Eq 547 applied.

(4) The bare reference by Buttes to some of the documents in their pleadings did not
waive the legal professional privilege from production nor, in the circumstances, did the
allegation of fraud against Buttes disentitle them from relying on that privilege from
production (see p 486 *d* to *g*, p 490 *f* to *j*, p 501 *b* and p 502 *e f*, post).

Per Curiam. Foreign state privilege is unknown to English law (see p 487 *c*, p 489 *e f*
h *h j* and p 497 *j*, post).

Per Lord Denning MR. If an original document is not entitled to legal professional
privilege then neither is a copy of the document made by a solicitor for the purpose of
litigation, because, if the original is not privileged and can be given in evidence under a
subpoena duces tecum, to make the copy discoverable would merely accelerate
production of the document itself (see p 484 *g h*, post); *The Palermo* (1883) 9 PD 6 and
j *Watson v Cammell Laird & Co (Shipbuilders & Engineers)* Ltd [1959] 2 All ER 757
disapproved.

Notes

For public interest and Crown privilege, see 13 Halsbury's Laws (4th Edn) paras 86–91,
and for cases on the subject, see 18 Digest (Reissue) 154–160, *1265–1301*.

---

a Rule 11, so far as material, is set out at p 495 *h*, post

For legal professional privilege, see 13 Halsbury's Laws (4th Edn) paras 71–84, and for cases on the privilege for communications between legal adviser and third party where litigation contemplated or pending and for waiver of privilege, see 18 Digest (Reissue) 116–122, 163, *883–942*, *1303–1308*.

Cases referred to in judgments

Anderson v Bank of British Columbia (1876) 2 Ch D 644, [1874–80] All ER Rep 396, 45 LJ Ch 449, 35 LT 76, 3 Char Pr Cas 212, CA, 18 Digest (Reissue) 114, *867*.

British South Africa Co v Companhia de Moçambique [1893] AC 602, [1891–4] All ER Rep 640, 63 LJQB 70, 69 LT 604, 6 R 1, HL, 11 Digest (Reissue) 398, *388*.

Bustros v White (1876) 1 QBD 423, 45 LJQB 642, 34 LT 835, 3 Char Pr Cas 229, CA, 18 Digest (Reissue) 71, *499*.

Buttes Gas and Oil Co v Hammer (No 2), Occidental Petroleum Corpn v Buttes Gas and Oil Co [1975] 2 All ER 51, [1975] QB 557, [1975] 2 WLR 425, Digest (Cont Vol D) 111, *491a*.

Chadwick v Bowman (1886) 16 QBD 561, 54 LT 16, DC, 18 Digest (Reissue) 117, *898*.

D v National Society for the Prevention of Cruelty to Children [1977] 1 All ER 589, [1978] AC 171, [1977] 2 WLR 201, HL, Digest (Cont Vol E) 185, *1301b*.

Hesperides Hotels Ltd v Muftizade [1978] 2 All ER 1168, [1979] AC 508, [1978] 3 WLR 378, 142 JP 541, HL, Digest (Cont Vol E) 90, *398a*.

Jenkyns v Bushby (1866) LR 2 Eq 547, 35 LJ Ch 820, 15 LT 310, 12 Jur NS 558, 18 Digest (Reissue) 105, *773*.

Palermo, The (1883) 9 PD 6, 53 LJP 6, 49 LT 551, 5 Asp MLC 165, CA, 18 Digest (Reissue) 116, *896*.

Rahimtoola v Nizam of Hyderabad [1957] 3 All ER 441, [1958] AC 379, [1957] 3 WLR 884, HL, 1(1) Digest (Reissue) 60, *389*.

Rogers v Secretary of State for the Home Department, Gaming Board for Great Britain v Rogers [1972] 2 All ER 1057, [1973] AC 388, [1972] 3 WLR 279, 136 JP 574, HL; *affg in part* sub nom *R v Lewes Justices, ex parte Secretary of State for the Home Department* [1971] 2 All ER 1126, [1972] 1 QB 232, [1971] 2 WLR 1466, 135 JP 442, DC, Digest (Cont Vol D) 267, *2835c*.

Taylor v Batten (1878) 4 QBD 85, 48 LJQB 72, 39 LT 408, CA, 18 Digest (Reissue) 53, *378*.

Watson v Cammell Laird & Co (Shipbuilders & Engineers) Ltd [1959] 2 All ER 757, [1959] 1 WLR 702, [1959] 2 Lloyd's Rep 175, CA, 18 Digest (Reissue) 117, *899*.

Waugh v British Railways Board [1979] 2 All ER 1169, [1980] AC 521, [1979] 3 WLR 150, HL, Digest (Cont Vol E) 183, *943(1)*.

Cases also cited

Bassford v Blakesley (1842) 6 Beav 131, 49 ER 775.

Brunswick (Duke) v King of Hanover (1842) 6 Beav 1, 49 ER 724.

Busch v Stevens [1962] 1 All ER 412, [1963] 1 QB 1.

Calcraft v Guest [1898] 1 QB 759, CA.

Crescent Farm (Sidcup) Sports Ltd v Sterling Offices Ltd [1971] 3 All ER 1192, [1972] Ch 553.

Crompton (Alfred) Amusement Machines Ltd v Customs and Excise Comrs [1971] 2 All ER 843, [1972] 2 QB 102.

Crompton (Alfred) Amusement Machines Ltd v Customs and Excise Comrs (No 2) [1973] 2 All ER 1169, [1974] AC 405, HL.

Gamlen Chemical Co Ltd v Rochem [1980] 1 All ER 1049, [1980] 1 WLR 614, CA.

Gartside v Outram (1856) 26 LJ Ch 113.

Graham v Bogle [1924] 1 IR 68.

Juan Ysmael & Co Inc v Government of Republic of Indonesia [1954] 3 All ER 236, [1955] AC 72, PC.

Kearsley v Philips (1883) 10 QBD 465, CA.

Land Corpn of Canada v Puleston (1884) Bitt Rep in Ch 176.

Learoyd v Halifax Joint Stock Banking Co [1893] 1 Ch 686.

Lyell v Kennedy (No 3) (1884) 27 Ch D 1, [1881–5] All ER Rep 814, CA.

Mexborough (Earl) v Whitwood Urban District Council [1897] 2 QB 111, CA.

Munet v Morgan (1873) LR 8 Ch App 361, LC and LJJ.
Newton v Chaplin (1850) 10 CB 356, 138 ER 114.
Pearce v Foster (1885) 15 QBD 114, CA.
Rattenberry v Munro (1910) 103 LT 560.
Roberts v Oppenheim (1884) 26 Ch D 724, CA.
Rochefoucauld v Boustead (1896) 65 LJ Ch 794.
Schneider v Leigh [1955] 2 All ER 173, [1955] 2 QB 195, CA.
United States of America v Dollfus Mieg et Compagnie SA [1952] 1 All ER 572, [1952] AC 582, HL.
Whitworth, Re, O'Rourke v Darbishire [1919] 1 Ch 320, CA; *affd* [1920] AC 581, [1920] All ER Rep 1, HL.
Williams v Quebrada Railway, Land and Copper Co [1895] 2 Ch 751.

Interlocutory appeal and cross-appeal

By an order of Master Warren dated 8th January 1979 in an action between the plaintiffs, Buttes Gas and Oil Co ('Buttes') and the defendants, Dr Armand Hammer and Occidental Petroleum Corpn ('Occidental'), and a counterclaim between Occidental as plaintiffs and Buttes and John Boreta as defendants Buttes were ordered to produce for inspection by the Dr Hammer and Occidental, the documents listed in para (2) of Part 2 of the first schedule to Buttes's preliminary list of documents. Buttes appealed and by an order dated 31st July 1979 McNeill J ordered that the documents listed in para (2) were privileged from production, save for those listed in sub-paras (c), (d)(ii), (d)(iii) and (g) of para (2) and four documents referred to in Buttes's reply and defence to counterclaim served on 2nd May 1975 which the judge ordered Buttes to produce for inspection. Dr Hammer and Occidental appealed. Their grounds of appeal were that the judge erred in deciding (1) that the documents held to be privileged from production were protected from production by legal professional privilege as documents brought into existence for the dominant purpose of obtaining legal advice in pending or anticipated litigation because they had been obtained by Buttes from a third party with a common interest and a common legal adviser for the purpose of exchanging information and/or receiving advice from the legal adviser in connection with the litigation, (2) that Dr Hammer and Occidental had not sufficiently made out a charge of fraud to which the documents held to be privileged were relevant so as to prevent them from being privileged from production, (3) that Buttes had not waived any privilege in regard to the documents by setting out parts of them, or summarising their contents, in their pleadings, and (4) that Dr Hammer and Occidental were not entitled to production because the documents belonged to a third party. Buttes cross-appealed against that part of the judge's order as ordered them to produce for inspection the documents listed in sub-paras (c), (d)(ii), (d)(iii) and (g) of para (2). Their grounds of appeal were (1) that the judge misdirected himself in holding that the English courts did not recognise claims to privilege from production for inspection on the ground that production was claimed to be injurious to the interest of a foreign state and (2) that he had misdirected himself in holding that Buttes's claim that the documents listed in para (2) of their list of documents were privileged from production as being confidential correspondence with and/or documents obtained in confidence from Her Majesty's government and/or from an independent foreign sovereign, and/or were communications passing between Her Majesty's government and/or the foreign sovereign and/or another state was not a sufficient claim either on behalf of the foreign sovereign or on behalf of the Buttes. The facts are set out in the judgment of Lord Denning MR.

Colin Ross-Munro QC and *Murray Rosen* for Dr Hammer.
Mark Littman QC, Elihu Lauterpacht QC, Murray Rosen and *Andrzej J Kolodziej* for Occidental.
Maurice Bathurst QC, Anthony Evans QC and *John Previté* for Buttes and Mr Boreta.

Cur adv vult

20th June. The following judgments were read.

LORD DENNING MR. Abu Musa is a small island in the Arabian Gulf. Early in 1970 oil was discovered nine miles off its shore. Each of two American oil companies claimed the right to exploit it. They started litigating about it in October 1970. Now ten years later the action is nowhere near trial. It has only reached the stage of discovery of documents. On this interlocutory point the argument before us took nine days, with five leading counsel and as many juniors. We have had excursions into the law of the sea, of territorial waters and the continental shelf, into sovereign immunity and diplomatic immunity, into the rules of court and goodness knows what else. No expense has been spared. No stone left unturned. McNeill J in the court below exploded. Even at that stage, when the application was before him, he said that the length of the proceedings was 'outrageous and comes perilously near to an abuse of the process of the court'. Even more when it reaches us nearly a year later. Still we must go on with it. It looks like outdoing *Jarndyce v Jarndyce* (see Dickens, Bleak House) except that these litigants are not likely to run out of money.

Discovery of documents is an important step in the course of an action. Each side has to disclose to the other the documents which he has in his possession, custody or power relating to the issues in the action. These issues are defined by the pleadings. To these I will turn. But to make them intelligible, I have included a map. I would also ask the reader to go back to the previous time when this case was before us. It is reported in *Buttes Gas and Oil Co v Hammer (No 2)* [1975] 2 All ER 51, [1975] 1 QB 557. [For earlier proceedings see *Buttes Gas and Oil Co v Hammer* [1971] 3 All ER 1025.]

The two companies are Occidental and Buttes. Each of them claimed under a local ruler. In November 1969 Occidental was granted an oil concession by the ruler of Umm al Qaiwain ('UAQ'). In December 1969 Buttes was granted an oil concession by the ruler

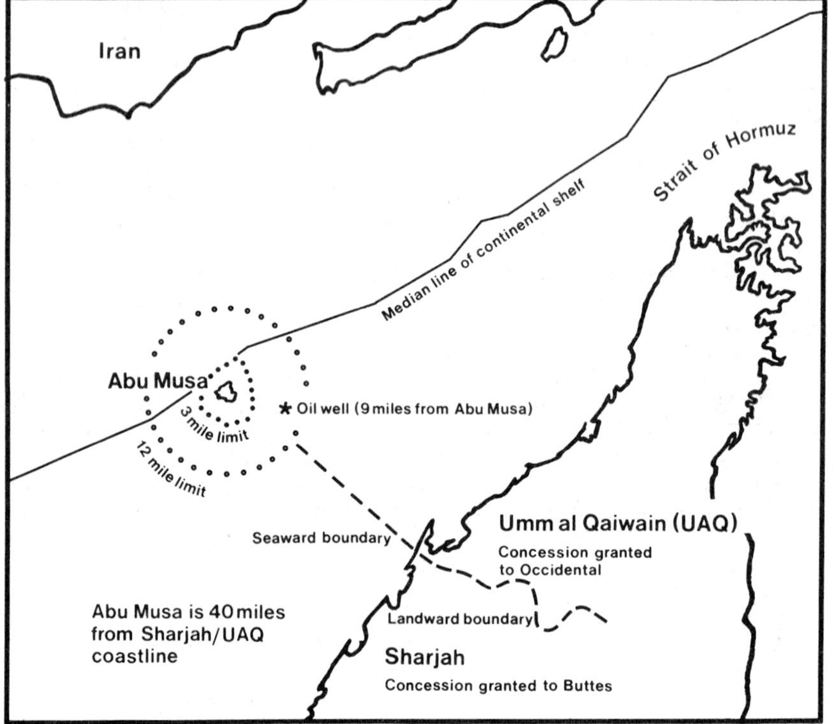

of Sharjah. Each of these oil concessions was made with the approval of Her Majesty's government which at that time controlled the external affairs of these rulers.

The concession to Occidental

I would not like to attribute any blame to Her Majesty's government, but in some ways they contributed to the misunderstandings that arose. The source of the trouble was a map which was annexed to the oil concession which the ruler of UAQ granted to Occidental on 18th November 1969. The 'concession area' was defined by reference to a map attached to the concession. It appeared to show the 'concession area' as extending from the coast of the mainland outwards for 37 miles up to the 3-mile limit of the island of Abu Musa. This concession agreement was executed by the ruler of UAQ 'in the presence of D. J. McCarthy, Head of the Arabian Department, Foreign and Commonwealth Office'. It was executed by Dr Armand Hammer on behalf of Occidental.

The concession to Buttes

By contrast the concession granted by the ruler of Sharjah to Buttes on 29th December 1969 had no map attached to it. The 'concession area' was defined by words only. It was—

> 'all the territorial waters of the main land of Sharjah, all islands within the jurisdiction of the Ruler and the territorial waters of the said islands and all the area of the seabed and subsoil lying beneath the waters of the Arabian Gulf continues to the said territorial waters.'

That agreement was approved by Her Majesty's government *in the belief* that the territorial waters of Sharjah were 3 nautical miles, that the island of Abu Musa was within the jurisdiction of the ruler of Sharjah, and consequently that the concession area to Buttes only extended as far as the 3-mile limit round Abu Musa. That was, however, only the *belief* of Her Majesty's government. There was nothing in the concession to support it. The 'concession area' was defined as extending to the 'territorial waters' without saying whether they were 3 miles or 12 miles.

The discovery of oil

In February 1970 oil was discovered at a point nine miles out from Abu Musa. Each of the oil companies claimed it. Occidental claimed that it fell within their concession area as shown on the map attached to their concession. Buttes claimed it on the footing that their concession area extended not merely to the 3-mile limit but to the 12-mile limit round Abu Musa. In support of their claim Buttes sent a delegation to London. It included their legal adviser, Mr Northcutt Ely. They saw Mr Holding of the Foreign and Commonwealth Office. In a letter to him of 20th March 1970 they said that they wished to know 'the breadth of the territorial sea' which the ruler of Sharjah 'can properly claim around the Island of Abu Musa'. They said that—

> 'a twelve-mile territorial sea belt has been proclaimed by Iran, Iraq, Kuwait and Saudi Arabia. This width of the territorial sea would, therefore, appear to be the prevailing rule of international law in the Arabian Gulf.'

As a result of these discussions, Buttes decided that their concession area extended to the 12-mile limit; that the oil found nine miles out fell within their concession area. So they decided to drill a well there. By a letter dated 23rd March 1970 Buttes asked the ruler of Sharjah for his approval of their drilling there. He gave his approval.

Occidental hotly disputed this claim by Buttes. They claimed that they had a right to drill for oil at this point. They relied on the map attached to their concession.

Both sides notified the political agent of Her Majesty's government stationed at Dubai of their intention to drill at this 9-mile point. Then followed much diplomatic activity, and sea activity, by both sides. In the end Buttes succeeded and Occidental failed. Buttes drilled for oil at the 9-mile point and transported the oil to the United States. Occidental started hundreds of actions in the United States against Buttes, claiming that the oil was theirs. But these actions were all stayed because the United States' courts would not allow them to go on.

The decrees

When the dispute became acute early in April 1970, the ruler of Sharjah produced a homemade decree which he said that he had made six months earlier on 10th September 1969 (before he granted the concession to Buttes). In that decree he had declared that the extent of the territorial waters of Sharjah and the islands was 12 nautical miles. Occidental say that that homemade decree was a fraud. It was not made, they say, until early April 1970, and then back dated to September 1969 so as to ante-date the concession of December 1969.

On 5th April 1970 the ruler of Sharjah issued a formal decree in which he declared that—

> 'The Territorial Sea of the Emirate of Sharjah and its Dependencies extends into the open sea to a distance of twelve nautical miles from the base lines on the coasts of the mainland and of the islands of the Emirate.'

The pleadings

Buttes in their statement of claim complain that on 5th October 1970, at a press conference in London, Dr Hammer of Occidental slandered them. He said (1) that the ruler of Sharjah conspired with Buttes to increase the concession area from 3 miles to 12 miles and (2) that the ruler of Sharjah fraudulently back dated the decree of 10th September 1969 so as to give him 12 miles from September 1969, whereas it was in truth not made till late March 1970.

Occidental and Dr Hammer in their defence plead that the words were true in substance and in fact. They counterclaim for damages for conspiracy. Also for libel in an earlier letter of Buttes to their shareholders.

The issues

The issues that arise are, first, what was the area of the concession granted by the ruler of UAQ to Occidental in November 1969? Second, what was the area of the concession granted by the ruler of Sharjah to Buttes in December 1969? Third, if Occidental was validly granted an area which included the 9-mile point, did the ruler of Sharjah, in collaboration with Buttes, fraudulently conspire to deprive Occidental of it?

International implications

Seeing that each ruler granted a concession over *all the territorial waters that he had*, these issues inevitably involve an inquiry into the territorial jurisdiction of two sovereign rulers. Furthermore, the charge of conspiracy inevitably involves an inquiry into the conduct of a sovereign ruler in his legislative capacity, ie in making his legislative decrees.

If the ruler of Sharjah had been an ordinary citizen and not a sovereign he would have been a necessary and proper party to the action. He would have been joined as a plaintiff, or at any rate as a defendant to the counterclaim. But he has not been joined. No doubt because he is entitled to sovereign immunity. The reason why he could claim sovereign immunity is because the action calls into question his conduct in his international relations and his conduct in his legislative capacity: see the principle which I sought to enunciate in *Rahimtoola v Nizam of Hyderabad* [1957] 3 All ER 441, [1958] AC 379 and the State Immunity Act 1978.

Judicial restraint

Now this is clear: it would be most unfortunate if these courts were to act as judicial arbiters over an international dispute about territorial waters or if the ruler of Sharjah were to be condemned for his conduct as a sovereign in his absence. It would be contrary to the comity on which sovereign immunity is founded. So much so that I am beginning to think now that we were in error in 1975 when we allowed this action to continue. The argument then turned altogether on the act of state doctrine. Since that time we have the benefit of some wise advice given by the legal adviser to the Department of State in Washington. It arose in the hundreds of actions between Occidental and Buttes, raising this very dispute, to which the ruler of Sharjah was not a party. The legal adviser gave his advice on 12th May 1978. He discarded any reliance on the act of state doctrine. He advised the courts of the United States to abstain from any consideration of the dispute even though it arose in the context of actions by Occidental against Buttes. He said:

> 'We do not believe that this judicial self-restraint should turn on such analytical questions as whether the so-called Act of State doctrine which is traditionally limited to governmental actions within the territory of the respective state can apply to an exercise of disputed territorial jurisdiction. It rather follows from the general notion that national courts should not assume the function of arbiters of territorial conflicts between third powers even in the context of a dispute between private parties.'

This doctrine is parallel to that stated in the recent case of *Hesperides Hotels Ltd v Muftizade* [1978] 2 All ER 1168, [1979] AC 508 where the House of Lords declined to enter into a dispute about land in Cyprus even though it arose in the context of a claim for trespass and conspiracy.

To my mind, therefore, our courts in England should not act as arbiters in this dispute between Buttes and Occidental. Although the action is framed in slander, conspiracy and libel, nevertheless it is at bottom a dispute between two sovereign rulers as to their territorial waters carried on through their powerful oil concessionaires, Buttes and Occidental. As such it is, or was, so politically sensitive that these courts should be very wary before taking any part in it.

There is no application before us to stay further proceedings in this action but we can still show our judicial restraint by not ordering discovery of documents.

After all, the power to order discovery is discretionary. There have grown up rules about legal professional privilege, public interest and the like; these we have to apply: see *Bustros v White* (1876) 1 QBD 423; but whenever a new case arises, it comes back to discretion. This is to my mind a new case. The object of the discovery here is to condemn the ruler of Sharjah and Buttes as conspirators, conspiring together to extend the territorial waters of the ruler of Sharjah so as to defraud Occidental. In the exercise of their discretion the courts should not give their aid to discovery made with that object, so contrary to the comity of nations, not at any rate when the ruler of Sharjah objects. Nor in a case which has dragged on so long that it is high time it was brought to an end.

On this simple ground, I would dismiss the appeal and allow the cross-appeal.

Legal professional privilege

In case this be wrong, however, I must go on to consider the claim for legal professional privilege. The arguments became complicated beyond belief. Largely because a distinction was drawn between Buttes (who are the party to the litigation) and the ruler of Sharjah (who is no party to it). Such as questions as to who held the originals and who held the copies and so forth. Countless cases were cited. Few were of any help.

I would sweep away all those distinctions. Although this litigation is between Buttes and Occidental, we must remember that standing alongside them in the selfsame interest are the rulers of Sharjah and UAQ respectively. McNeill J thought that this gave rise to special considerations, and I agree with him. There is a privilege which may be called a 'common interest' privilege. That is a privilege in aid of anticipated litigation in which several persons have a common interest. It often happens in litigation that a plaintiff or defendant has other persons standing alongside him who have the selfsame interest as he and who have consulted lawyers on the selfsame points as he but who have not been made parties to the action. Maybe for economy or for simplicity or what you will. All exchange counsels' opinions. All collect information for the purpose of litigation. All make copies. All await the outcome with the same anxious anticipation because it affects each as much as it does the others. Instances come readily to mind. Owners of adjoining houses complain of a nuisance which affects them both equally. Both take legal advice.

Both exchange relevant documents. But only one is a plaintiff. An author writes a book and gets it published. It is said to contain a libel or to be an infringement of copyright. Both author and publisher take legal advice. Both exchange documents. But only one is made a defendant.

In all such cases I think the courts should, for the purposes of discovery, treat all the persons interested as if they were partners in a single firm or departments in a single company. Each can avail himself of the privilege in aid of litigation. Each can collect information for the use of his or the other's legal adviser. Each can hold originals and each make copies. And so forth. All are the subject of the privilege in aid of anticipated litigation, even though it should transpire that, when the litigation is afterwards commenced, only one of them is made a party to it. No matter that one has the originals and the other has the copies. All are privileged.

Having swept away the distinctions, it is possible to state the principles simply. Privilege in aid of litigation can be divided into two distinct classes.

The first is legal professional privilege properly so called. It extends to all communications between the client and his legal adviser for the purpose of obtaining advice. It exists whether litigation is anticipated or not.

The second only attaches to communications which at their inception come into existence with the dominant purpose of being used in aid of pending or contemplated litigation. That was settled by the House of Lords in *Waugh v British Railways Board* [1979] 2 All ER 1169, [1980] AC 521. It is not necessary that they should have come into existence at the instance of the lawyer. It is sufficient if they have come into existence at the instance of the party himself with the dominant purpose of being used in the anticipated litigation. The House approved of the short statement by James LJ in *Anderson v Bank of British Columbia* (1876) 2 Ch D 644 at 656, [1874–80] All ER Rep 396 at 399: '... as you have no right to see your adversary's brief, you have no right to see that which comes into existence merely as the materials for that brief.' Lord Simon emphasised the word 'merely' [see [1979] 2 All ER 1169 at 1177, [1980] AC 521 at 537).

In applying this principle, a word is necessary about copies. If the original document is privileged (as having come originally into existence with the dominant purpose aforesaid), so also is any copy made by the solicitor. But, if the original is not privileged, a copy of it also is not privileged, even though it was made by a solicitor for the purpose of the litigation: see *Chadwick v Boorman* (1886) 16 QBD 561. There are some cases which appear to give a privilege to copies on their own account, even when the originals are not privileged. They range from *The Palermo* (1883) 9 PD 6 down to *Watson v Cammell Laird & Co (Shipbuilders & Engineers) Ltd* [1959] 2 All ER 757, [1959] 1 WLR 702. But those cases are suspect. They were adversely commented on by the 16th report of the Law Reform Commission on Privilege in Civil Proceedings (Cmnd 3472 (1967)). Since *Waugh's* case it is open to us to reconsider them. In my opinion, if the original is not privileged, neither is a copy made by the solicitor privileged. For this simple reason: the original (not being privileged) can be brought into court under a subpoena duces tecum and put in evidence at the trial. By making the copy discoverable, we only give accelerated production to the document itself. That was pointed out by Winn LJ's committee in the report of the Committee on Personal Injuries Litigation (Cmnd 3691 (1968), para 304).

Applied to the present case, the material date for all concerned is 2nd April 1970. That is the agreed date when litigation was anticipated. It does not matter that the ruler of Sharjah did not instruct Coward Chance until 2nd June 1970; nor that Buttes did not instruct them until 5th October 1970; nor that the ruler changed over in 1979 to Lovell, White & King. Nor does it matter that some documents originated with the ruler and he sent copies to Buttes; or that other documents originated with Buttes and they sent copies to the ruler and Coward Chance. We have simply to take the date 2nd April 1970 as the date when litigation was contemplated by all concerned.

Having thus cleared the air, I turn to consider the various classes of documents for which privilege is claimed. They were put up in bundles with a general description. So general that the description conveyed little of their contents. Nor was the claim verified by an affidavit in the accustomed formula. All was done very informally. So much so that we asked to see the documents ourselves, as we often do nowadays, so as to judge whether they were the subject of privilege or not. I will now take samples and give my opinion about them.

The report of Judge Dweik

In the summer of 1969 the ruler of Sharjah wanted to know the legal position about the sea bed and continental shelf. He asked Judge Dweik, a Jordanian judge, to investigate and report to him on it. The judge made his report in Arabic and submitted it to the ruler. It is clearly privileged on the first basis of privilege, namely communications between client and lawyer for the purpose of obtaining advice. The report is privileged even though made before any concession was granted or any litigation anticipated. (This is category (d)(i) of para (2) of Part 2 of the first schedule to Buttes's list of documents.)

The report of Coward Chance and associates

At some time after litigation was anticipated, Mr M E Bathurst QC, Mr Northcutt Ely and Messrs Coward Chance made a report to the ruler of Sharjah setting out their opinion as to the legal position of Abu Musa and its territorial waters. That report has been given a limited circulation. Excerpts from it will be found in the textbooks by Professor Al-Baharna, and reference to it by Dr El-Hakim. It is clearly privileged on the first basis being legal advice given by lawyers to the client. (This is category (a)(iii) of para 2 of Part 2 of the first schedule to Buttes's list. The same applies to categories (m) and (n) of para (2) in so far as they apply to advice given to the ruler of Sharjah by his legal advisers (regarding Sharjah's sea-bed rights in the area offshore Abu Musa); and to advice given to Buttes by their legal advisers on those rights.)

Communications with Her Majesty's government before 2nd April 1970

In February and March 1970, before litigation was anticipated, representatives from Buttes visited the Foreign and Commonwealth Office in London to seek information about the offshore boundaries of Sharjah. Mr Holding gave them a note about it in February 1970, and Buttes wrote a long letter on 20th March 1970 to Mr Holding referring to their meeting and requesting further information. In addition letters passed between Buttes and Mr Bullard, the political agent of Her Majesty's government in Dubai, dated 25th March and 1st April 1970. Seeing that these all took place before litigation was anticipated, i e before 2nd April 1970, I do not think they are protected by the privilege in aid of litigation. This applies to those of the documents in para (2) categories (b) and (c) which passed before 2nd April 1970.

Communications with Her Majesty's government after 2nd April 1970

After 2nd April 1970 the representatives of Buttes and the ruler of Sharjah had correspondence with Mr Bullard, the political agent of Her Majesty's government in Dubai and with Mr Acland of the Foreign and Commonwealth Office in London relating to the extent of the territorial waters and of the concession area. This correspondence is privileged only if it came into existence with the dominant purpose of being used in the dispute then raging between Occidental and Buttes. I doubt whether that was the dominant purpose. The real purpose was to sort out the tangle about the concessions. At any rate, that is the test to be applied to categories (a)(i)(ii) and (b) and (c) of para (2) in so far as the correspondence passed after 2nd April 1970 and to the documents in categories (k)(i) and (l) which all took place after 2nd April 1970.

The mediation documents

In August 1970 Her Majesty's government appointed a mediator, Sir Gawain Bell, to seek to resolve the difference between the rulers, and consequently the rights of the oil companies. The mediation was unsuccessful. But in the course of it the ruler of Sharjah submitted a comprehensive dossier which contained a complete record of all that had taken place. It was prepared for him by his advisers. They attached to it copies of all the documents relating to the dispute, including those by or to Buttes or Her Majesty's government. The dossier and the accompanying documents have been given a considerable circulation already. They have been handed to commentators. The textbooks contain references to them and extracts from them.

In so far as the dossier contained submissions by way of argument to the mediator they would be privileged. Like a brief. The dominant purpose was for use in the mediation. In so far as the dossier contained an appendix with copies of original documents, those are privileged according to whether or not the originals were privileged. If the originals came into existence before litigation was anticipated, ie, before 2nd April 1970, the copies are not privileged. If they came into existence after 2nd April 1970 the copies will be privileged if the originals came into existence for the dominant purpose of the anticipated litigation. This test must be applied to categories (e), (f) and (g) of para (2).

Correspondence with other states

After litigation was anticipated, the ruler of Sharjah had correspondence with the rulers of other emirates of the Trucial States and Iran, all relating to rights in regard to the sea-bed area. I doubt whether this came into existence for the dominant purpose of the anticipated litigation. If so, it is not privileged. This covers categories (h) and (j) of para (2).

Documents referred to in the pleadings

In general, it is clear that if a party refers in his pleading to a document the other side are entitled to require it to be produced: see RSC Ord 24, r 10(1) and (2); but it is open to the pleader to object to its production: see Ord 24, r 11(1)(*a*).

Buttes in their amended reply and defence to counterclaim referred to a number of documents. By pleading them, Buttes show that they intend to rely on them. They should make them available for production. If and in so far as they contend that those documents are the subject of a privilege, they should amend their pleading by striking out all reference to them.

Fraud

No privilege can be invoked so as to cover up fraud or iniquity. But this principle must not be carried too far. No person faced with an allegation of fraud could safely ask for legal advice. To do away with the privilege at the discovery stage there must be strong evidence of fraud such that the court can say: 'This is such an obvious fraud that he should not be allowed to shelter behind the cloak of privilege.' The judge was not prepared so to hold in this case. Nor am I.

Conclusion on privilege

The documents should be reconsidered by the parties in the light of the principles I have tried to state. It seems to me that many of them would not be privileged.

Sir Michael Palliser's letters

A question arose whether the Crown would claim 'Crown privilege' or, as it is now called, public interest privilege. The question was referred to the Foreign and Commonwealth Office. On 11th May 1978 the Permanent Under-Secretary of State, Sir Michael Palliser, said: 'The Foreign and Commonwealth Office know of no overriding considerations of the national interest which would warrant intervention by the Crown in these proceedings.' On 2nd May 1980 on further information, Sir Michael confirmed that view, saying: 'The Foreign and Commonwealth Office does not consider that there should be an intervention by the Crown in these proceedings.'

So far so good. No public interest privilege asserted on behalf of the Crown. But Sir Michael followed it with this cryptic sentence:

> 'It appears to be open to you to submit to the Court that as matter of general

> principle confidential communications between States should, in the public interest, not be adduced in evidence without the consent of the States concerned, a principle to which the Foreign and Commonwealth Office would certainly presubscribe.'

I am afraid that I would not myself presubscribe to that principle or post-subscribe to it. It is so widely stated that it would cover not only communications about territorial boundaries but also commercial communications. It would give a power of veto to either of the states superior to that given to the Crown itself. In any case it would only cover a minor part of the documents in this case. Most of them are not 'confidential communications between States', but confidential communications between a state and oil companies, or between a state and legal advisers and others.

Foreign state privilege

A point much canvassed before the master and the judge was whether a foreign state could intervene and claim a privilege for itself by which the foreign state could prevent the disclosure of any documents, if it considered that such disclosure was inimical to its own public interest. Both the master and the judge rejected this submission. I entirely agree with them. If such a principle were admitted into our law, it would give a foreign state a power of veto which we do not afford to Her Majesty's government itself.

Conclusion

I return to where I started. This is merely an application for discovery of documents. Yet it has taken the master, the judge and the Court of Appeal many days of argument and many pages of judgments. All the territorial matters under discussion have passed into history. They were settled by international agreement eight years ago. The continental shelf of the Arabian Gulf has been apportioned out. The oil revenues have been divided by agreement. All that is left is this interminable action arising out of a speech by Dr Armand Hammer on 5th October 1970 at the Great Eastern Hotel in London. It is high time to let bygones be bygones. I would not allow any further discovery by either side. Let these two oil companies fight it out as best they can with such materials as they have available or can get hold of. By subpoena or otherwise. There is quite enough of it in all conscience. Take out a summons for directions. Either side can demand that it be tried by a jury. I pity the jury. Set the action down for trial at once. Let it hang about no longer. For goodness sake get rid of it one way or the other.

DONALDSON LJ (read by Brightman LJ). This is not the first occasion on which cries of 'I have been libelled' have been used as a means of inducing the court to embark on an inquiry which it would otherwise have declined. Nor will it be the last. But it certainly has very unusual features.

To start with, neither the parties nor the subject of the inquiry have anything to do with England. The parties are United States corporations and citizens. The underlying dispute is between Arabian Gulf subsidiaries of these corporations. Others concerned are the rulers of two of the Trucial States, now the United Arab Emirates, and Her Majesty's government. The bone of contention is, of course, oil.

The parties have attempted to litigate the underlying dispute in several hundred actions in the United States, which is a much more appropriate forum, but have been stopped by the act of state doctrine of United States law. They no doubt regarded it as a happy accident when each made statements which the other felt could ground actions in the English courts for defamation and thus allow the resumption of hostilities in a forum in which this doctrine is not yet applied with the same rigour.

These hostilities have much of the character of trench warfare. The events in issue occurred in 1969 and 1970. The action was begun with reasonable promptitude by a writ dated 15th October 1970. Thereafter the parties dug in. In 1974 there was foray which involved this court in consideration of the width of the act of state doctrine in English law (see *Buttes Gas and Oil Co v Hammer* (*No* 2) [1975] 2 All ER 51, [1975] QB 557) and the parties are now back again in connection with Occidental's claims to be entitled to inspect certain documents, the existence of which has been disclosed in Buttes's list of documents.

As I have said, jurisdiction is based on allegations that each party defamed the other within this country. However, Occidental has taken the opportunity to add a counterclaim for damages for fraudulent conspiracy. The conspirators are described as being Buttes, the ruler of Sharjah and unidentified 'others'. But in its essentials the alleged conspiracy, like the pleas of justification in the defence to the claim for slander and to the counterclaim for libel, involve investigating and determining the underlying dispute.

That dispute can be simply stated. In 1969 and 1970 Sharjah and Umm al Qaiwain ('UAQ') were adjacent territories in the Trucial States. The foreign relations of both were conducted by Her Majesty's government pursuant to treaty, but the state of Sharjah and its ruler were respectively recognised by Her Majesty's government as a sovereign state and a sovereign ruler. I do not doubt, although there is no certificate from the Secretary of State to this effect, that the same is true of UAQ and of its ruler. On 18th November 1969 the ruler of UAQ granted a concession to the local subsidiary of Occidental entitling them, in substance, to search for and exploit any oil which they could find in that territory, including land subjacent to its territorial waters and its continental shelf. On 29th December 1969 the Sharjah subsidiary of Buttes were granted a similar concession in relation to the territory of Sharjah including the island of Abu Musa, which is some 37 miles from the mainland.

In theory there could be no conflict between these concessions, but in fact it was otherwise and both parties set out to drill for oil at a point about nine miles south-east of the island of Abu Musa. This was not a coincidence. They had been exchanging seismic and similar information and this was a highly promising spot. As each claimed exclusive rights by virtue of its own concession, it will be clear that the exact deliniation of the boundaries of the continental shelf of the two states and of the territory subjacent to the territorial waters of Abu Musa lies at the heart of the dispute. Such problems are the staple diet of distinguished international jurists acting as arbitrators, but have rarely if ever before been visited on an unsuspecting, and probably unappreciative, English common jury. Yet that is what is contemplated in this case.

If the nature of the conflict is refined still further, it comes down to this, that Sharjah has claimed a 12-mile territorial sea by virtue of a decree of the ruler dated September 1969, but not published until April 1970, and that UAQ has claimed that Sharjah's territorial sea in way of Abu Musa is limited to 3 miles. The drilling location was outside the 3-mile and within the 12-mile limit. It seems that Sharjah's case may be stronger in international law if this decree was in fact made when it was dated, but Occidental allege that it was actually made in April 1970 and fraudulently back dated. Buttes are said to have been parties to this fraud. For good measure there is an argument on the extent of the respective continental shelves, irrespective of the decree or of its effect, to make confusion finally confounded. Iran has claimed sovereignty of Abu Musa which, if correct, might affect the seaward end of the respective continental shelves and the validity of both concessions.

Against that background I turn to the dispute on the right to inspect the documents disclosed in Part 2 of the first schedule to Buttes's list of documents. Nothing has ever turned on para (1). All those documents are admittedly protected by the legal professional privilege which obtains whether or not litigation is contemplated or pending. This was referred to in the argument as 'limb 1' privilege. This claim to refuse inspection is conceded. Battle has, however, been joined on para (2) which describes 14 groups of documents which, in Buttes's submission, should not be inspected by Occidental. It is therefore necessary to say a word about the nature of these documents and how they came into Buttes's possession.

From the time when, or perhaps even before, it was apparent that Occidental and Buttes were both claiming the right to drill for oil in the same area, it was clear that the interest of Buttes and that of the ruler of Sharjah were identical. Both wanted to make sure that the oilfields of Sharjah were as extensive as possible. There was a similar, and conflicting, identity of interest between Occidental and UAQ. The ruler of Sharjah needed to obtain the best possible legal advice and, in the light of that advice, to make forceful diplomatic representations to the other rulers of the Trucial States, to Iran and to Her Majesty's government. Access to this essential advice could be obtained via the United States and the United Kingdom, but the ruler had no modern communications. Buttes's local office, however, had all the latest forms of communication. And so it came about that Buttes and the ruler of Sharjah co-operated. Buttes discussed his position with him and sent and received messages and advice on his behalf. They were given copies of unpublished state documents relating to the sovereignty of Sharjah over Abu Musa, of the correspondence between the ruler and his legal advisers with Her Majesty's government, and of the correspondence between the ruler and the rulers of other emirates of the Trucial States. When, in due course, a mediator was appointed, they were given copies of correspondence between the ruler and the mediator. This correspondence was expressly agreed by the mediator to be confidential, it being of a 'without prejudice' nature. In addition, they supported the ruler by themselves corresponding with Her Majesty's government and attending and taking notes at meetings between the ruler's advisers and that government. In June 1970 the ruler retained Messrs Coward Chance as his English solicitors and in October 1970, when this action began, Buttes followed suit. The ruler thereupon authorised Coward Chance to make available to Buttes all or most of the relevant documents which theretofore they had held solely on behalf of the ruler. All these documents came into the hands of Buttes directly or indirectly from the ruler and were held by them under seal of confidentiality. At all stages in this action the ruler has instructed Buttes to maintain this confidentiality, but he has not himself intervened in the action.

Now confidentiality is an essential pre-condition for resistance to an application under RSC Ord 24, r 11(2) for an order requiring production of documents for inspection. But it is not itself a ground of resistance. Something more is required. And so it came about that before Master Warren Buttes relied on what they called 'foreign state privilege'. This was defined by McNeill J as 'a principle . . . whereby documents are privileged from production on the ground that production would be injurious to the interests of a foreign state'. This claim failed before the master and it is, indeed, a head of privilege unknown to the law.

On appeal to McNeill J Buttes took the same point, but in addition sought to assert legal professional privilege. This was an unusual plea because, with the exception of the documents referred to in para (2)(m), or some of them, none of the documents could be described as communications passing between Buttes or their legal advisers (limb (1), legal professional privilege) or documents obtained or coming into existence for the purpose of Buttes's obtaining legal advice or the prosecution of their claim or their defence to the counterclaim (limb 2). They had all been obtained or came into existence for the ruler's purposes. What Buttes were really asserting was legal professional privilege at one stage removed, a derivative claim, based on the community of interest and activity between themselves and the ruler. Occidental joined issue. They also alleged that in any event any privilege had been waived in so far as the documents were referred to in Buttes's pleadings. Finally, Occidental denied that privilege could be claimed in the light of the fact that fraud was in issue.

McNeill J held that foreign state privilege, as he had defined it, was unknown to English law. He said that he found it impossible to see how an English court could determine whether or not the public interest of a foreign sovereign was adversely affected by the production of documents. I am not sure how difficult that would really have been in the present case, bearing in mind the political volatility of the region and the sensitivity of the documents relating to territorial claims. However, in other cases there could be great difficulties and I agree with the judge that this is a head of privilege from production for inspection which is wholly unknown to English law. Furthermore, as defined, it does not seem to me to be a natural development of any known form of privilege or immunity.

The judge then turned to the claim for legal professional privilege. He rejected the claim in relation to certain of the documents, on the ground that they had already been *a*
published or for other reasons were not confidential or that the claim was as yet insufficiently made out. However, he refused an order for production of most of the documents. The primary basis of his decision was that the documents were the ruler's own documents and not those of Buttes. He reached this conclusion on the basis that the ruler could demand their return at any time and that Buttes's interest was one of 'defeasible possession'. I do not think that this can be a correct basis for refusing an order *b*
for production. The documents were rightly included in Buttes's list as being in their possession, custody or power, because 'possession' is not limited to an indefeasible possession and, even if it were, all these documents were without doubt in the 'custody' of Buttes even if they were the ruler's own documents. In fact, it was admitted that many of the copy documents were the property of Buttes.

But McNeill J held in the alternative that these documents were protected by legal *c*
professional privilege. The proposition which he accepted was this:

> 'If two parties with a common interest and a common solicitor exchange information for the dominant purpose of informing each of them of the facts, issue and advice and of both, or either, obtaining legal advice or further legal advice in respect of contemplated or pending litigation, the documents or copy documents containing that information are privileged from production in the hands of either.' *d*

There is, I think, a difficulty in applying this proposition literally to the facts of this case, since it was only after October 1970 that Buttes and the ruler had a common solicitor. But I think that some such proposition must be correct. Take the case of a block of flats. The landlord takes proceedings against a particular tenant and the dispute concerns a term of the lease which is common to all the tenancies. The tenant might *e*
well circulate all other tenants in confidence with a copy of counsel's opinion which he had obtained. If the landlord were then to join another tenant as an additional defendant, could he obtain production of the copy of the opinion? I think not. But I prefer to reserve this point for further consideration in another case in which the facts are less unusual and the point essential to the decision.

Since legal professional privilege could be defeated by waiver or, subject to certain *f*
qualifications, by fraud, the judge considered both these issues.

So far as fraud was concerned, McNeill J said:

> 'I should be surprised if a jury, bearing in mind that fraudulent conspiracy is also a criminal offence, found the plaintiff company guilty on the evidence which is presently available. Indeed, I regard the allegation of fraud as no more than the key to an intended fishing operation, to be carried out in the hope that discovery of *g*
> otherwise privileged documents will produce some peg on which the defendants could seek to justify and to sustain the counterclaim.'

I respectfully agree and find it unnecessary to express any view on how strong a prima facie case of fraud is necessary to defeat a claim for disclosure based on legal professional privilege, but something exceptional is called for. *h*

On waiver McNeill J held that reference in the pleadings to a document or to its contents does not of itself waive any privilege which attaches to it. It must be right that a bare reference to a document in a pleading does not waive any privilege attaching to it as otherwise there would be no scope for taking objection under RSC Ord 24, r 11(1), when a notice was served under r 10(1). If, on the other hand, a document is reproduced in full in the pleading, its confidentiality is gone and no question of privilege could *j*
arise. Where the line is drawn between these two extremes may be a matter of some nicety, but I do not think that it is necessary to reach a conclusion in the present case, which does not, in my judgment, turn on so narrow an issue as waiver in relation to the few documents which are referred to in the pleadings.

I now turn to what I regard as the decisive issue in the case, namely public interest immunity from disclosure. Let me make it clear that this is quite different from 'foreign

sovereign immunity' which was debated below. That turned on the public interest of
a the foreign sovereign or state. This turns on the public interest of this country. It is an
issue which has only arisen in this court and counsel for Occidental were a little aggrieved
that it did not feature in the notice of appeal. However, it is a point which the court is
bound to take of its own motion if it thinks that it arises (see *Rogers v Secretary of State for
the Home Department* [1972] 2 All ER 1057, [1973] AC 388 (the *Lewes Justices* case) and it
has been fully argued.

b Any question of public interest immunity from disclosure must involve a balancing
of competing interests. In one scale is always the very heavy weight of the public interest
that in legal proceedings the truth shall come out. Full disclosure of all relevant
documents in the hands of the parties is a most powerful aid to the achievement of this
result. In this case we have to consider the weight in the other scale and to decide how
the balance is to be struck.

c As was said by Lord Morris in the *Lewes Justices* case [1972] 2 All ER 1057 at 1064,
[1973] AC 388 at 405, 'a Minister of the Crown often has very special knowledge
concerning the public interest and a court can be greatly helped if it is informed of the
views of the Minister'. No doubt with this in view, Buttes's solicitors at a fairly early
stage in the proceedings, inquired of the Treasury Solicitor whether the Crown wished
to intervene. The answer given by Sir Michael Palliser, the Permanent Under-Secretary
d of State to the Foreign and Commonwealth Office, is contained in a letter dated 11th May
1978. It is in these terms:

> 'We have given careful consideration to all aspects of the matter which you have
> drawn to my attention. While I understand the desire of His Highness the Ruler of
> Sharjah that certain documents should not be disclosed in the current legal
> proceedings, the Foreign and Commonwealth Office know of no overriding
> e considerations of the national interest which would warrant intervention by the
> Crown in those proceedings.'

On 22nd April 1980, just before the hearing in this court, Buttes's solicitors wrote
again to Sir Michael inquiring whether, in the light of recent events in the Gulf area, the
views of Her Majesty's government were the same as in 1978. The reply dated 2nd May
f 1980 was as follows:

> 'I confirm that the Foreign and Commonwealth Office view remains as set out in
> my letter of 11 May 1978 to you. The Foreign and Commonwealth Office does not
> consider that there should be an intervention by the Crown in these proceedings.
> I call your attention to the statement by Lord Simon of Glaisdale in *R v Lewes JJ*
> ([1972] 2 All ER 1057 at 1066, [1973] AC 388 at 407), where he made it plain that
> g immunity was a rule of law and that there was no necessity for the Crown to
> intervene, adding that any litigant or witness may draw attention to the nature of
> the evidence with a view to its being excluded. It appears to be open to you to
> submit to the Court that as a matter of general principle confidential communications
> between States should, in the public interest, not be adduced in evidence without
> the consent of the States concerned, a principle to which the Foreign and
> h Commonwealth Office would certainly presubscribe.'

It must be remembered that the Crown was a principal actor in the dispute at an
international diplomatic level. Accordingly there can be many and diverse considerations
which had to be weighed in deciding whether it wished to intervene in circumstances in
which such intervention might be construed as support for Sharjah as against UAQ.
j Whilst a commercial compromise has been reached between these two emirates and Iran,
all concerned have maintained their claims to an exclusive right to oil exploration and
recovery in the disputed area. I understand this letter as affirming the view that it was
thought inappropriate for the Crown to intervene in these proceedings, but as putting
forward, for the consideration of the court, the much wider issue of whether, and to what
extent, English public interest is served by the courts ordering a litigant to break the
confidentiality of communications between foreign sovereign states and that of the

mediation proceedings without the consent of all the states concerned. This question
arises irrespective of whether the United Kingdom is one of those states. a

This was, in effect, the position which was considered by the United States government
when the present dispute came before the United States courts. As a result, the legal
adviser to the State Department wrote to the assistant attorney general of the Land and
Natural Resources Division of the Department of Justice in the following terms on 12th
May 1978:

> 'It is our understanding that the disposition of this case would require a b
> determination of the disputed boundary between Umm Al Qaiwain on the one
> hand and Sharjah and Iran on the other at the time Umm Al Qaiwain granted the
> concession in issue to Occidental. It is our view that it would be contrary to the
> foreign relations interests of the United States if our domestic courts were to
> adjudicate boundary controversies between third countries and in particular that
> controversy involved here. The extent of territorial sovereignty is a highly sensitive c
> issue to foreign governments. Territorial disputes are generally considered of
> national significance and politically delicate. Even arrangements for the peaceful
> settlement of territorial differences are often a matter of continued sensitivity.
> These considerations are applicable to the question of Umm Al Qaiwain's sovereignty
> over the continental shelf surrounding Abu Musa at the time of the concession to
> Occidental and to the subsequent arrangements worked out among the affected d
> states. For these reasons, the Department of State considers that it would be
> potentially harmful to the conduct of our foreign relations were a United States
> court to rule on the territorial issue involved in this case. We believe that the
> political sensitivity of territorial issues, the need for unquestionable U.S. neutrality
> and the harm to our foreign relations which may otherwise ensue, as well as the
> evidentiary and jurisprudential difficulties for a U.S. court to determine such issues, e
> are compelling grounds for judicial abstention. We do not believe that this judicial
> self-restraint should turn on such analytical questions as whether the so-called Act
> of State doctrine which is traditionally limited to governmental actions within the
> territory of the respective state can apply to an exercise of disputed territorial
> jurisdiction. It rather follows from the general notion that national courts should
> not assume the function of arbiters of territorial conflicts between third powers f
> even in the context of a dispute between private parties. As a result, we are of the
> view that the court should be encouraged to refrain from setting the extent of Umm
> Al Qaiwain's sovereign rights in the continental shelf between its coast and Abu
> Musa at the time of its grant of the concession to Occidental.'

For my part I find the views expressed compellingly persuasive regardless of what may g
be the act of state doctrine of the law of the United States.

However, there are other considerations which point in the same direction. The
newly enacted States Immunity Act 1978, provides by s 1:

> '(1) A State is immune from the jurisdiction of the courts of the United Kingdom
> except as provided in the following provisions of this Part of this Act.
>
> '(2) A court shall give effect to the immunity conferred by this section even h
> though the State does not appear in the proceedings in question.'

Subsection (2) of s 1 is mandatory and nothing in the subsequent sections derogates
from this requirement in the context of the facts of this case. The non-appearance of the
ruler of Sharjah is not voluntary in that he probably cannot take advantage of s 2(4)(*b*) of
the 1978 Act in order to intervene and assert his claim to confidentiality of state j
documents obtained by Buttes from him because he has no property in many of them.
Section 2(4)(*b*) would not apply and, were he to intervene, he would be deemed to have
submitted to the jurisdiction. In the context of a dispute of this nature, such a result
would be unacceptable to any sovereign. Whilst the 1978 Act is not applicable since the
ruler of Sharjah is not directly being subjected to the jurisdiction of the court in these
proceedings, he would no doubt regard this as a somewhat technical point if the court

intended ultimately to determine whether in 1969–70 he did or did not exercise a sovereign rights over the disputed area. This consideration also points in the direction of the court refusing to order Buttes to break the ruler's confidence.

We were also referred to the Diplomatic Privileges Act 1964, and to Sch 1 which reproduces certain articles from the Vienna Convention on Diplomatic Relations of 1961. By art 24 'The archives and documents of the mission shall be inviolable at any time and wherever they may be.' As counsel for Buttes pointed out, it would be more b than a little odd if these documents, which are, or are copies of, documents of the head of state himself, should enjoy less protection than documents of his diplomatic agents.

Last, but by no means least, it is necessary to bear in mind the court's attitude to determining the title to foreign land. Whether the cause of action is conspiracy or defamation, the rights of the parties can only be determined if the court is prepared to adjudicate on the sovereign rights of the ruler of Sharjah, a right more fundamental and c involving political questions of far greater delicacy than is involved in an adjudication on the title to foreign land. Yet the courts have refused to adjudicate on the title to foreign land, whatever the form of the cause of action, for precisely this reason: see the reconsideration of the rule in *British South Africa Co v Companhia de Moçambique* [1893] AC 602, [1891–4] All ER Rep 640, in *Hesperides Hotels Ltd v Muftizade* [1978] 2 All ER 1168, [1979] AC 508, a case in which, as here, the cause of action was conspiracy.

d Some of these considerations point to the wisdom of the court declining to try the action at all, but that option may no longer be open in the light of the decision of this court in 1974 ([1975] 2 All ER 51, [1975] QB 557) and the refusal of the House of Lords to give leave to appeal. It may be doubted whether that decision would have been the same if that court had had the benefit, as we have had, of full argument on the international law involved in Sharjah's claims to sovereignty and had been aware how e complex and evenly balanced is the issue. But that decision, like those arguments, is I think irrelevant for present purposes. It cannot bind us to order disclosure of these documents.

The public interest in the maintenance of international comity, a standard of international behaviour which can be epitomised as 'do as you would be done by', is very great. The courts are wholly independent of the executive, but they are an emanation of f the Crown and they act in the name of the Crown. Giving the fullest weight to the public interest in the achievement of justice between litigants, I have no doubt that this is more than counterbalanced in this case by the public interest in refraining, in the name of the Crown, from ordering the disclosure for inspection of the documents the subject matter of this application. All of them are impressed by a seal of confidentiality from which Buttes have not been released by the ruler of Sharjah. Indeed, he has continually g reaffirmed his insistence on that confidentiality being maintained. In many cases the nature of the documents is such that other heads of state would be entitled equally to demand that their confidentiality be maintained. In so far as any of the documents were received otherwise than from the ruler, they were communications or records which came into existence or were acquired by Buttes only because Buttes were invited by the ruler to take part in and be privy to confidential negotiations with other states and with h the mediator.

Six documents have been disclosed by Buttes pursuant to the judge's order. None of them were confidential. With the exception of those documents, I would dismiss the appeal and allow the cross-appeal substituting an order refusing to require disclosure of the documents for inspection.

j **BRIGHTMAN LJ.** This is an appeal and cross-appeal from an order of McNeill J made on 31st July 1979. It relates to the right of the defendants to the production of certain confidential documents disclosed on discovery by the plaintiffs. There is both an action and a counterclaim. The action is by Buttes Gas and Oil Co ('Buttes') and their president against Occidental Petroleum Corpn ('Occidental') and their chairman for slander. The counterclaim is by Occidental against Buttes and their president alleging libel and conspiracy.

The background to the action and counterclaim is the stretch of water in the Persian (Arabian) Gulf which lies between Iran to the north and the emirates of Sharjah and Umm al Qaiwain ('UAQ') to the south. Between the emirates and Iran is an island called Abu Musa. This island lies about forty miles off the southern shore of the Gulf. Sovereignty over Abu Musa is a matter of dispute, still unresolved, between Iran and the ruler of Sharjah. The dispute dates back to Victorian days. The waters off Abu Musa were also the subject matter of dispute, that is to say, whether the right to explore and exploit the seabed could be exercised by the ruler of UAQ on continental shelf principles up to the 3-mile limit round the island of Abu Musa, or only to the 12-mile limit.

The bone of contention between Buttes and Occidental is an oil well which lies about eight miles off the east coast of Abu Musa, thus outside the 3-mile limit but within the 12-mile limit. The claim of Occidental to exploit the oil well depended on a concession granted by the ruler of UAQ to Occidental's wholly-owned subsidiary, Occidental of Umm al Qaiwain Inc, under an agreement dated 18th November 1969. The area of the concession was defined by reference to a map. The area purported to extend from the coastline of UAQ seawards to a median line between UAQ and Iran, but excluding a 3-mile belt round the island of Abu Musa. The concession therefore purported to include the site of the oil well which was later discovered off the island. The signatories to the agreement acted on the basis that three miles represented the limit of the seabed over which the ruler of Sharjah had rights. The signature of the ruler of UAQ to the agreement was witnessed by the head of the Arabian Department of the Foreign and Commonwealth Office of Her Majesty's government, and the agreement must be regarded as having had the approval of the United Kingdom.

The claim of Buttes to exploit the well depended on a concession granted to them on 9th December 1969 by the ruler of Sharjah. The concession area was expressed to include the territorial waters of the islands within the jurisdiction of the ruler, and all the area of the sea bed and subsoil lying beneath the waters of the Gulf contiguous to such territorial waters.

In February 1970 Occidental, as a result of prospecting in their supposed concession area, located oil. Buttes, as a result of an exchange of seismic information, deduced the existence of oil in the same location. In March Buttes applied to the British political agent at Dubai for the necessary approval to drill on the site. This was refused by the political agent on the ground that the site was in Occidental's concession area. However, the ruler of Sharjah, in order to support Buttes's claim, made known the fact that a decree already existed over his signature declaring that the territorial waters of Sharjah and its dependencies and islands extended to 12 miles. This decree bore the date 10th September 1969 and therefore antedated Occidental's concession agreement. A supplemental decree, on which nothing turns, was made by the ruler on 5th April 1970. Occidental assert that the 1969 decree was in fact made in 1970, but was backdated for fraudulent purposes and is a forgery.

On 1st June 1970 Occidental started to move a drilling rig into position, but the rig was turned back by a gunboat of the Royal Navy. These happenings gave rise to a great deal of diplomatic activity and to a great deal of litigation. I will deal with the litigation first, and then turn to the diplomatic activity.

The earliest action was one by Occidental against the Ministry of Defence, the Attorney General and the commanding officer of the gunboat. It was started in June 1970 but was discontinued in the following year and no more need be said about it.

In June 1970 Occidental brought proceedings against Buttes in California to make good their claim to the concession; but in 1971 the District Court, whose decision was affirmed by the Federal Court of Appeals, ruled that the court was without jurisdiction because the case involved the competing territorial claims of foreign states, and such claims were not competent to be adjudicated on by an American court. An attempted appeal to the Supreme Court was denied.

In July 1970 Buttes complained in a circular to their shareholders about the activities of Occidental and in October of the same year Occidental responded more forcibly at a press conference held in London. The consequence of this was that on 15th October

Buttes began the present action by a writ against Occidental and their chairman, Dr Hammer, claiming damages for slander. Occidental served a defence in April 1972, 18 months later. They pleaded justification. They added a counterclaim against Buttes and Mr Boreta, their president, alleging a conspiracy between Buttes and the ruler of Sharjah to defraud Occidental of their concession. They also claimed damages for an alleged libel contained in the circular. Buttes served a reply in May 1975 in which they pleaded justification to the charge of libel.

This was not the only litigation. Between 1974 and 1978 a great number of actions were instituted by Occidental in the United States to intercept oil cargoes shipped out of the Persian Gulf by Buttes, but finally the United States Court of Appeals injuncted Occidental against pursuing further claims, and the United States Supreme Court in 1979 denied an appeal.

I turn to the diplomatic activity. Since 1968 it had been known that the United Kingdom was intending to bring to an end its agreements with the Trucial States and to end its political presence in the area. In May 1970 Iran once more pressed its claim to sovereign rights over Abu Musa and the territorial waters round the island to a width of 12 miles. It became highly desirable to defuse the situation. Her Majesty's government, through the Foreign and Commonwealth Office, provided the services of Sir Gawain Bell as mediator, but mediation did not prove to be fruitful. However, a settlement was ultimately reached in November 1971 between Iran and the ruler of Sharjah under which the competing claims of both states were maintained, the island was occupied (in part only) by Iran, and the exploitation of the petroleum resources of Abu Musa and its sea bed was committed to Buttes on the basis that the oil royalties would be equally divided between Iran and Sharjah. The ruler of Sharjah was assassinated two months later. Agreement was also reached between Sharjah and UAQ under which a proportion of the former's oil royalties in respect of Abu Musa and its waters was to be paid to UAQ. In 1973 UAQ formally terminated Occidental's oil concession, thus leaving Buttes triumphant in the field.

I will turn now to the legal representation of some of the parties to these disputes. The former ruler of Sharjah had retained as his legal adviser a judge of a neighbouring Arab state, Judge Yusri Dweik. In 1969 Judge Dweik produced for the ruler a report on the sea bed and continental shelf. At a later date, on 2nd April 1970, the ruler retained the services of an American attorney, Mr Northcott Ely, of Washington DC. In June the ruler retained Messrs Coward Chance as his London solicitors. In October Buttes, then about to embark on the present action in the Queen's Bench Division, sought and obtained the consent of the ruler to Messrs Coward Chance acting for themselves as well. The interests of the ruler and of Buttes were, in this context, identical.

The action between Buttes and Occidental now comes before us on a procedural point. It arises under RSC Ord 24, which deals with discovery and inspection of documents. Under Ord 24, r 2, a party to an action is required to make discovery of the documents which are or have been in his possession, custody or power relating to any matter in question in the action. Under r 9 a party who has served a list of documents, and under r 10 a party in whose pleadings a document is referred to, is prima facie obliged on request to produce that document for inspection by the other side. Under r 11, if a party objects to produce any document for inspection, 'the Court *may* . . . make an order for production' (emphasis mine). Some documents are privileged from production. This privilege is recognised but not defined by r 5(2). Legal professional privilege is the common class of privileged document. Rule 15 reflects another quite different head of protection:

> 'The foregoing provisions of this Order shall be without prejudice to any rule of law which authorises or requires the withholding of any document on the ground that the disclosure of it would be injurious to the public interest.'

In May 1978 Buttes and Mr Boreta served a list of documents in compliance with Ord 24, r 2. They objected to the production of the documents specified in Part 2 of the first schedule to that list. Part 2 is divided into two paragraphs. Legal professional privilege was claimed and is not challenged in respect of the documents in para (1), these consisting of the ordinary communications in the action between legal adviser and client and suchlike. Paragraph (2) describes in general terms 14 categories of documents, lettered (a) to (n), in respect of which two claims were made. First, it was said that they were privileged from production—

> 'by reason of the said classes of documents being confidential correspondence with and/or documents obtained in confidence from Her Majesty's Government and/or the Ruler of Sharjah, being an independent foreign sovereign, and/or are communications passing between Her Majesty's Government and/or the said Ruler of Sharjah and/or the Imperial Government of Iran.'

Alternatively 'the said documents are in many cases privileged from production by reason of legal professional privilege'. Second, it was said that—

> 'production of the classes of documents described in para (2) would be contrary to the public interest and/or to the legitimate interests of the said foreign sovereign states.'

These claims of privilege and immunity from production are challenged by the Occidental. The challenge was upheld by the master in toto, and Buttes appealed.

The appeal came before McNeill J in the summer of 1979. At an early stage in his judgment he said this:

> 'In my view, that an action for slander, with a counterclaim for damages for fraudulent conspiracy and libel, has not, nearly nine years after the issue of the writ, even reached the stage of an application for directions is outrageous and comes perilously near to an abuse of the process of the court.'

I indorse that observation.

Three issues were argued before the judge. First, whether the English courts recognise a principle called in argument 'foreign state privilege' whereby documents are privileged from production on the ground that production would be injurious to the public interest of a foreign sovereign state. Second, whether the documents listed, or any of them, were privileged from production in the hands of Buttes on the ground of legal professional privilege notwithstanding that the legal professional privilege originated with the ruler of Sharjah. Third, if either claim of privilege was well-founded, whether it was lost by fraud or waiver.

On the first issue the judge held that there was no separate head of privilege described as foreign state privilege. He then examined and analysed each of the different categories of document and decided that all the categories were entitled to legal professional privilege in the hands of Buttes except category (c), part of category (d) and category (g), and four of the documents referred to in the reply and defence to counterclaim. He decided the issue of fraud and waiver in favour of Buttes.

Buttes cross-appeal in respect of categories (c), (d) and (g), but not in respect of the four pleaded documents, which have in fact now been disclosed.

During the course of the argument in this court, Buttes have maintained the claim of legal professional privilege, but have not argued for the existence of a head of privilege described as foreign state privilege. Instead, as often happens on appeal, the argument has taken a different turn. What is now relied on is 'public interest immunity', the public interest being that of the United Kingdom.

I propose to consider first the question of public interest immunity, because if this objection is properly taken it will affect the extent to which it is necessary to go into the question of legal professional privilege.

The documents for which protection is claimed are, as I have said, divided by Buttes into 14 categories. But I have found more descriptive the seven groups into which counsel for Occidental has been able to distill them: (1) advice to the ruler of Sharjah; (2) communications between the ruler of Sharjah and Her Majesty's government; (3) communications between the ruler of Sharjah and other sovereign states;

(4) communications between the ruler of Sharjah or his legal advisers and Her Majesty's government and Sir Gawain Bell relating to the mediation attempted by Her Majesty's government; (5) a confidential note prepared by the Foreign and Commonwealth Office at the request of Coward Chance as the legal advisers of the ruler of Sharjah, relating to Iranian claims to sovereignty over the island of Abu Musa; (6) communications between Buttes and representatives of Her Majesty's government relating to drilling rights off the shores of Abu Musa; and (7) correspondence and documents passing between the ruler of Sharjah or Buttes and the rulers of the other emirates relating to the claims of Sharjah and Iran.

Buttes profess themselves as willing from their own point of view to produce all or most of these documents, but they claim that all are regarded by the present ruler of Sharjah as confidential and have always been treated by him and his predecessor as confidential. This view was first adumbrated in a letter dated 10th February 1977 from Mr Northcutt Ely to Coward Chance, and has been vigorously maintained at all times since.

By a letter dated 6th May 1978 sent by telex from the ruler of Sharjah to Coward Chance, the ruler said this:

> 'We are told that [Occidental] has applied to the English Court for an order that [Buttes] disclose in the proceedings a number of documents in their possession, including documents passing between our government, the British government, the government of the Iran and our brother rulers in the United Arab Emirates. These documents relate to confidential matters of state between our government and the other governments involved—matters which were resolved directly between us many years ago. We would inform you that the government of Sharjah does not wish that these confidential documents be published in the proceedings in London, or elsewhere, and we ask that your clients should inform the Foreign and Commonwealth Office that the confidentiality of these documents is maintained.'

The views of Her Majesty's government were sought by Coward Chance acting as solicitors for Buttes. In a letter dated 11th May 1978 Sir Michael Palliser, the Permanent Under-Secretary of State in the Foreign and Commonwealth Office, replied as follows:

> 'While I understand the desire of His Highness the Ruler of Sharjah that certain documents should not be disclosed in the current legal proceedings, the Foreign and Commonwealth Office know of no overriding considerations of the national interest which would warrant intervention by the Crown in those proceedings.'

In view of recent events in this part of the world, the matter was raised a second time shortly before the start of this appeal. The Under-Secretary of State confirmed his previous reply but added:

> 'I call your attention to the statement of Lord Simon of Glaisdale in *R v Lewes JJ* ([1972] 2 All ER 1057 at 1066, [1973] AC 388 at 407), where he made it plain that immunity was a rule of law and that there was no necessity for the Crown to intervene, adding that any litigant or witness may draw attention to the nature of the evidence with a view to its being excluded. It appears to be open to you to submit to the Court that as a matter of general principle confidential communications between States should, in the public interest, not be adduced in evidence without the consent of the States concerned . . .'

As I have said earlier, there is no principle of 'foreign state privilege' which is sought to be maintained in this court, nor in my view could it be successfully argued for. Nor, on the authorities, can it be claimed that a document is protected from inspection merely because it has reached the hands of a party to litigation in strictest confidence. The importance of ascertaining and protecting the rights of litigants outweighs the importance of maintaining a confidence.

It is an axiom of the law of discovery that documents may be protected from production by reasons of state. This was formerly known as Crown privilege but that name is now out of fashion because it is not a matter of privilege and it is not confined to the Crown. It is now usually called 'public interest immunity'. The rule is that certain evidence is inadmissible on the ground that its adduction would be contrary to the public interest of the United Kingdom. The public interest which demands that the evidence be withheld has to be weighed against the public interest that in the administration of justice the courts should have the fullest possible access to all relevant material. Once the former public interest is held to outweigh the latter, the immunity arises: see the speech of Lord Simon in *Rogers v Secretary of State for the Home Department* [1972] 2 All ER 1057 at 1066, [1973] AC 388 at 407 (the *Lewes Justices* case).

RSC Ord 25, r 11 is in terms discretionary, and it is tempting to suppose that the categories of public interest can be infinitely extended to meet the circumstances of each individual case so that in the end the court would have the widest discretion. This is not a permissible approach, as was made clear by the speech of Lord Hailsham in *D v National Society for the Prevention of Cruelty to Children* [1977] 1 All ER 589 at 600–601, [1978] AC 171 at 224–226, from which I will read these extracts:

> 'The appellants argued, in effect, for a general extension in range of the nature of the exceptions to the rule in favour of disclosure. This, it was suggested, could be summarised in a number of broad propositions, all in support of the view that, where an identifiable public interest in non-disclosure can be established, either there is a firm rule against disclosure (e g legal professional privilege or state secrets) or the court has a discretion whether or not to order disclosure, and that this discretion must be exercised against disclosure in all cases where, after balancing the relevant considerations, the court decides that the public interest in non-disclosure outweighs the ordinary public interest in disclosure. The appellants contended that new cases will arise from time to time calling for a protection from disclosure in classes of case to which it was not previously extended, and that the courts had in practice shown great flexibility in adapting these principles to new situations as and when these arise... The contentions have at least the merit of propounding a lucid and coherent system. Nevertheless, I am compelled to say that, in the breadth and generality with which they were put forward, I do not find them acceptable. They seem to me to give far too little weight to the general importance of the principle that, in all cases before them, the courts should insist on parties and witnesses disclosing the truth, the whole truth, and nothing but the truth, where this would assist the decision of the matters in dispute. In the second place, I consider that the acceptance of these principles would lead both to uncertainty and inconsistency in the administration of justice. If they were to be accepted, we should remember that we should be laying down a large innovation not merely in the law of discovery, but equally in the law of evidence, which has to be administered not merely in the High Court, but in the Crown Court, the county courts, and the magistrates' courts throughout the land. What is the public interest to be identified? On what principles can it be defined? On what principles is the weighing-up process to proceed? To what extent, if at all, can the right to non-disclosure be waived? Can secondary or extraneous evidence of the fact not disclosed be permitted? To what extent should the Crown be notified of the fact that the issue has been raised? These questions are all manageable if the categories of privilege from disclosure and public interest are considered to be limited. Indeed, reported authority, which is voluminous, shows that largely they have been solved. But to yield to the appellants' argument on this part of the case would be to set the whole question once more at large, not merely over the admitted categories and the existing field but over a much wider, indeed over an undefined, field. Thirdly, and perhaps more important, the invitation of the appellants seems to me to run counter to the general tradition of the development of doctrine preferred by the English courts. This proceeds through evolution by extension or analogy of recognised principles and reported precedents. Bold statements of general principle based on a review of the total field are more appropriate to legislation by Parliament which has at its command techniques of enquiry, sources of information and a width of worldly-wise

> experience, far less restricted than those available to the courts in the course of contested litigation between adversaries. On the other hand, I find equally unattractive the more restricted and even, occasionally, pedantic view of the authorities advanced on behalf of the respondent. This was based on a rigid distinction, for some purposes valuable, between privilege and public interest, and an insistence on a narrow view of the nature of the interest of the public, reflected in the reasoning of the majority in the Court of Appeal, which would virtually have restricted the public interest cases to the narrower interests of the central organs of the state, or what might be strictly called the public service. The effect of the argument would not merely limit the ambit of possible categories of exception to the general rule. In my view, it would virtually ensure that the categories would now have to be regarded as effectively closed . . . The result of this is that I approach the problem with a caution greater than that contended for by the appellants, but with a willingness to extend established principles by analogy and legitimate extrapolation more flexible than that contended for by the respondent.'

The objection of 'public interest immunity' may be raised not only by the Crown but also by a private litigant or the court itself: see the speech of Lord Pearson in the *Lewes Justices* case [1972] 2 All ER 1057 at 1065, [1973] AC 388 at 406. It is clearly the duty of the court to take the point if it arises. It is therefore immaterial in the present case that the point was not argued before McNeill J and is not raised by Buttes's cross-notice. The documents to the production of which objection is made were confidential when they came into existence and the copies which came into the hands of Buttes reached their hands in confidence. They emanated from, or came to, or were concerned with the affairs of, sovereign states. They all arose in connection with an international dispute between sovereign states, a dispute in which the United Kingdom was involved as having a special treaty relationship with three of such states. Does a 'public interest' of the United Kingdom exist which ought to be placed in the scales against disclosure? What is the extent of that interest? Is it analogous to any recognised head of public interest? Does it outweigh the 'public interest' that all relevant documents in the hands of a party shall be produced if not protected by privilege?

Where the public interest is involved it is invaluable to have the view of the appropriate minister of Her Majesty's government, although the final responsibility for weighing the matter rests with the court and not with any officer of the executive: see Lord Pearson in the *Lewes Justices* case [1972] 2 All ER 1057 at 1065, [1973] AC 388 at 406. In the instant case, the executive do not seek to intervene.

It is easier to consider the problem by reference to specific documents. For this purpose I propose to select one document and one class of document for particular consideration.

Category (d) includes a confidential report on the sea bed and continental shelf prepared by Judge Dweik on the instructions of, and for, the ruler of Sharjah in 1969. Categories (e) and (f) consist of correspondence and documents passing between (1) the ruler of Sharjah and Her Majesty's government, and (2) the ruler and Sir Gawain Bell, relating to the mediation arranged in 1970 by Her Majesty's government. The parties to that mediation were the emirates of Sharjah, Ajman and UAQ. On 11th August 1970, at a meeting in London between the mediator and the representatives of the ruler of Sharjah, Sir Gawain Bell assured the ruler's advisers that all documents submitted for the purposes of the mediation would be treated on a private and confidential basis.

The ruler of Sharjah made the above report, correspondence and documents available to Buttes in strict confidence. He did so because Buttes had a mutual interest with him in the issues raised by the territorial dispute. So we have a situation in which the ruler of a foreign state has passed to a private person in strict confidence a report which he commissioned from his own legal adviser as to the extent of his territorial rights as sovereign; and documents submitted to a mediator under the express seal of confidence for the purpose of settling a dispute as to such sovereign rights. Is an order now to issue from the court, without the consent of the ruler, causing these documents to be revealed and thus breaching the confidence which clearly attaches to them?

In my view it is in the public interest of the United Kingdom that the contents of confidential documents addressed to or emanating from sovereign states, or concerning the interests of sovereign states arising in connection with an international territorial dispute between sovereign states, shall not be ordered by the courts of this country to be disclosed by a private litigant without the consent of the sovereign states concerned. I think that such an immunity is a public interest of the United Kingdom and I think that it outweighs the public interest that justice shall be administered on the basis of full disclosure of all relevant unprivileged documents. It is analogous to but is clearly distinguishable from the public interest immunity which may attach to confidential documents of Her Majesty's government. The resolution of a territorial dispute between sovereign states is a political question, and it is undesirable that an English court should be seen to be forcing the disclosure of documents, prima facie of a confidential nature, for the ostensible purpose of pronouncing, albeit indirectly, on the merits of such a dispute. Furthermore, I think that such a rule is consistent with the fact that the courts of this country have no jurisdiction to determine the title to foreign land, even if the action is dressed up as a claim of conspiracy: see *Hesperides Hotels Ltd v Muftizade* [1978] 2 All ER 1168, [1979] AC 508.

The 'public interest' which I have endeavoured to define should, in my view, carry decisive weight in the present case. But I think that there is room for doubt whether public interest immunity would necessarily protect from disclosure all the documents which are broadly described in Buttes's list of documents, notably category (c), 'Communications between [Buttes] and representatives of Her Majesty's Government in 1970 and 1971 relating to drilling rights offshore Abu Musa'. Rule 5(1) of RSC Ord 24 states that a list of documents must—

> 'enumerate the documents in a convenient order and as shortly as possible but describing each of them or, in the case of bundles of documents of the same nature, each bundle, sufficiently to enable it to be identified.'

Rule 5(2) reads:

> 'If it is desired to claim that any documents are privileged from production, the claim must be made in the list of documents with a sufficient statement of the grounds of the privilege.'

As stated in the notes to r 5 in the Supreme Court Practice 1979 (vol 1, p 409, para 24/5/2), the provisions for enumeration and description are to enable the court to see whether the rule or order for discovery has been complied with, and to enable it to make an order for production which is clear and can be enforced, but not of course so as to enable the other party to discover the contents of the document from the description. The accepted principle is that laid down by this court in *Taylor v Batten* (1878) 4 QBD 85 at 88. By analogy I am disposed to think that the documents for which public interest immunity is claimed should be properly enumerated and described and duly sworn to. The compilation of a proper list of documents would also have the advantage of enabling Lovell, White & King, the present solicitors to the ruler of Sharjah, to give effect to para 9 of their letter dated 13th July 1979 to Occidental's solicitors, when (in connection with a possible adjournment of the hearing before the master) they said this:

> 'We believe that, given sufficient time, we might be able to make some recommendations to His Highness which would enable all interests to be appropriately covered, including the interests of Sharjah and other Sovereign States, and also the specific interests of [Buttes] and [Occidental] in the disclosure of documents relevant to the issues between them in this litigation.'

It might well be that the requisite consents would be forthcoming to the disclosure of further documents. However, I gather that neither Lord Denning MR nor Donaldson LJ favours this course. My preference for it is subsidiary to my main conclusion. Having indicated that viewpoint, I leave the matter there.

Once the court comes to the conclusion that on balance the public interest of the
a United Kingdom requires that an order for production should not be made, the question whether immunity from disclosure has been lost by waiver on the part of the party possessing the document does not arise. It is not open to a party to litigation to waive the public interest. If, for example, a litigant is in possession of a relevant document containing a vital defence secret, the litigant cannot consent to its disclosure against the public interest. That goes without saying. Likewise if it is against the public interest
b that the court should order the disclosure of a confidential document concerning the territorial rights of a sovereign state, a litigant cannot waive that immunity. So no more needs to be said about waiver in the context of public interest.

I agree with the conclusion of McNeill J that there is no prima facie case of fraud, and I intend to add nothing of my own in relation to this topic.

I accordingly reach the conclusion that the appeal should be dismissed and the cross-
c appeal allowed, on the basis of the requirements of public interest immunity. In case, however, this approach is wrong, I propose to express my opinion on the question of legal professional privilege. Documents so privileged from production are commonly said to fall into two classes: (1) confidential communications between legal adviser and client for the purpose of the provision of legal advice, and (2) communications between legal adviser and a third party which come into existence after the dispute has begun or been
d foreseen for the dominant purpose of assisting the client in such dispute. It will be recalled that Judge Dweik was retained by the ruler as his legal adviser in 1969, that Mr Northcutt Ely was so retained from 2nd April 1970, that Messrs Coward Chance were so retained from 2nd June 1970 and that Messrs Coward Chance were advising both the ruler and Buttes from 5th October 1970. None of the documents sought to be withheld by Buttes come within limb (1) protection so far as Buttes are concerned, although a
e number would fall within limb (1) so far as the ruler is concerned if he were involved in the litigation.

McNeill J found that the documents came from three sources: (1) some were copies of messages transmitted to and from the ruler by means of telex facilities available to Buttes; (2) some were copies of documents held by Coward Chance as the ruler's solicitors which the ruler allowed Coward Chance to hold as Buttes's solicitors as well as his own;
f (3) some were copies of documents passed by the ruler direct to Buttes for transmission to Coward Chance for the purpose of obtaining advice.

I agree with the judge that no claim to limb (1) privilege can be made by Buttes on behalf of or in the right of the ruler.

The judge found as a fact that the copy telex messages (source (1) above) are held by Buttes only in a derivative or secretarial capacity in the right of the ruler and that the
g ruler can demand their return at any time and that Buttes could not resist that demand. I see no reason for rejecting that finding of fact. Therefore I think that the court should refuse to order production for the simple reason that, on such finding of fact, the ruler could frustrate the order at will. Indeed I have no doubt that he would so demand if advised of the position in time. In such circumstances it would be wrong for the court to make an order for production which might turn out to be futile.

h As regards the remaining documents the judge said this:

> '[Buttes] and the ruler had a common interest in resisting the claim of UAQ and [Occidental] to the disputed location, because any diminution of their rights to grant and enjoy a drilling concession there would deprive the ruler of sovereign rights and revenues actual or potential and [Buttes] of their drilling rights and of
> j any profits which might have accrued to them therefrom. If, as I find to be the fact on the material before me, the ruler supplied [Buttes] with documents for transmission to Coward Chance so that they might both be advised, or if, as I find to be the fact, Coward Chance after 5th October 1970 held for [Buttes] as well as for the ruler documents or copy documents (which previously they had held for the ruler alone) for the purpose of advising both the ruler and [Buttes] about that

> litigation (or the word "dispute" would do, because I do not think it matters that the contemplated litigation was not then, as it has turned out to be, an action for a
> slander) the real issue, and the dominant issue, on which advice was required and on which litigation was contemplated or pending was about the right to explore and drill for oil in the disputed location. I think it follows, from the material before me and the inferences properly to be drawn from that material, that the dominant purpose in providing those documents to the common solicitor was for the common advice of [Buttes] and the ruler.' b

The judge then spelt out his proposition of law, with which I agree, that if two parties with a common interest and a common solicitor exchange information for the dominant purpose of informing each other of the facts, or the issues, or advice received, or of obtaining legal advice in respect of contemplated or pending litigation, the documents or copies containing that information are privileged from production in the hands of each. I think that this proposition follows from *Jenkyns v Bushby* (1866) LR 2 Eq 547 and c
other cases in the same line and is a legitimate extension of the principle that protects confidential communications between co-plaintiffs or co-defendants for the purposes of an action.

I differ from the judge only on minor points. (1) The judge found against privilege in respect of categories (c) and (g) (communications between Buttes and Her Majesty's government and communications between Buttes and the mediator). I would allow the d
claim to privilege to the extent indicated in the judgment of Lord Denning MR for the reasons which he gives. (2) The judge allowed the claim to privilege in respect of category (h) (correspondence and documents passing between the ruler of Sharjah or Buttes and the rulers of other Trucial States in 1970 and 1971 relating to Sharjah's sovereignty over Abu Musa and its rights in the sea bed offshore Abu Musa). As I understand the papers, no claim to legal professional privilege is made in respect of that e
category.

So far as waiver by pleading is concerned, I agree with the judge that reference to a document or to its contents in a pleading does not waive any legal professional privilege attached to it. It is to my mind equally clear that a party cannot rely on a privileged document so pleaded without thereby waiving the privilege. Therefore sooner or later Buttes will have to decide whether to forgo privilege in respect of a privileged document f
which is pleaded or to abandon reliance on it. If they sit on the fence until the trial (if any) begins or is in actual progress, they will do so at their own risk. Circumstances might arise in which the other side could properly claim to be entitled to an adjournment at Buttes's expense. Whether Occidental could force Buttes to step down from the fence prior to the trial by an application to strike out a pleaded document in respect of which privilege is maintained does not arise for decision on this appeal, but I would think that g
Occidental might be able to do this.

For the reasons given at the beginning of this judgment, I would dismiss the appeal and allow the cross-appeal; in other words, for my part I would make no order for production against Buttes.

Appeal dismissed. Cross-appeal allowed. Leave to appeal to the House of Lords refused. h

Solicitors: *Coward Chance* (for Buttes and Mr Boreta); *Herbert Smith & Co* (for Occidental and Dr Hammer).

Frances Rustin Barrister.

a Attorney General of the Duchy of Lancaster v G E Overton (Farms) Ltd

CHANCERY DIVISION
DILLON J
b 23rd, 24th, 25th, 26th JUNE 1980

Treasure trove – Crown's right to treasure trove – Coins – Silver coins – Whether Crown's right to treasure trove limited to articles of gold and silver.

Some 7,811 third century Roman coins were found on land owned and occupied by the
c defendants within the liberties of the Duchy of Lancaster. The coins, known as antoniniani, were made of alloys of silver and base metal. When originally introduced in AD 215 antoniniani had a silver content of about 50% but the discovered coins dated for the most part from the period AD 260 to 280 by which time the silver content had fallen to between 1·4% and 18%. Analysis of 15 of the discovered coins showed the silver content to range from 0·2% to 18%. The Attorney General of the Duchy of Lancaster
d claimed that the coins were treasure trove and as such were the property of the duchy. The defendants denied that the coins were treasure trove and claimed them as their property.

Held – The prerogative right of the Crown to treasure trove was limited to articles of gold and silver, and in the case of coins did not extend to coins made of other metals. Whether a particular coin or object was made of silver was a question for the judge of fact
e to decide, and on the evidence none of the coins was a silver coin and they could not therefore be claimed as treasure trove by the duchy (see p 506 *c d* and *f g* and p 507 *j* to p 508 *a* and *c d*, post).

Case of Mines (1568) 1 Plowd 310 and dictum of Viscount Simon in *Palser v Grinling* [1948] 1 All ER at 11 applied.

f **Notes**

For meaning of treasure trove, see 8 Halsbury's Laws (4th Edn) para 1513, and for cases on the subject, see 11 Digest (Reissue) 784, 943–944.

Cases referred to in judgment

Case of Mines, R v Earl of Northumberland (1568) 1 Plowd 310, 75 ER 472, 11 Digest
g (Reissue) 780, 917.
Elwes v Brigg Gas Co (1886) 33 Ch D 562, [1886–90] All ER Rep 559, 55 LJ Ch 734, 55 LT 831, 33 Digest (Repl) 727, 40.
Palser v Grinling, Property Holding Co Ltd v Mischeff [1948] 1 All ER 1, [1948] AC 291, [1948] LJR 600, HL, 31(2) Digest (Reissue) 1017, 8072.

h **Cases also cited**

Attorney-General v Moore [1893] 1 Ch 676, [1891–4] All ER Rep 880.
Attorney-General v Trustees of the British Museum [1903] 2 Ch 598.
R v Thomas and Willett (1863) Le & Ca 313, 169 ER 1409, CCR.
R v Toole (1867) 11 Cox CC 75, CCA(Ir).
Westwood v Cann [1952] 2 All ER 349, [1952] 2 QB 887, CA.

j **Action**

By a statement of claim dated 17th May 1977 the Attorney General of the Duchy of Lancaster brought an action against the defendants, G E Overton (Farms) Ltd, alleging that 7,811 Roman coins made of silver alloy found in Quarry Field, Coleby, Lincolnshire, in March 1975, had been concealed in the earth in an earthenware urn, and, the owner of the coins at the time they were concealed being unknown, the coins were treasure trove belonging to the Crown. By order dated 29th November 1978 the action was transferred from the Lincoln District Registry of the Queen's Bench Division to the Chancery Division of the High Court in London. The facts are set out in the judgment of Dillon J.

John L Knox QC and *Hubert Picarda* for the Attorney General.
Igor Judge QC and *Collingwood Thompson* for the defendants.

DILLON J. I am asked to decide in these proceedings whether some 7,811 third century coins, which were found in March 1975 in a field at Coleby in Lincolnshire, are treasure trove or not.

It so happens that this particular land at Coleby is within the liberties of the Duchy of Lancaster, although, of course, not within the duchy itself, and so the contest is between the Attorney General for the duchy, claiming in reliance on the Crown's prerogative right to treasure trove, and the defendants, G E Overton (Farms) Ltd, the fee simple owners and occupiers of the field in question. If the coins are not treasure trove they are the property of the owner of the soil and not of the finder.

As is usual in cases of treasure trove a coroner's inquest was held, and it was found at the inquest that the coins were treasure trove. It is however common ground that the decision at the inquest is not conclusive. Indeed the main argument of the defendants is that these coins are such as in law are not capable of being treasure trove.

I shall have to refer to the coins in question in more detail later in this judgment. For the present it is sufficient to say that they are antoniniani, minted, for the most part, over the period from AD 260 to 280. They are made of alloys of silver and a base metal and are properly to be described as of argentiferous bronze or argentiferous copper. The percentage of silver varies but is, in the greater part of the sample which has been sorted and cleaned, low.

Counsel for the Attorney General has therefore formulated two questions for consideration. (1) Is the right of the Crown to treasure trove limited, even where coins are concerned, to articles of gold and silver, or does it extend to coins of other metals? (2) What is the criterion to be applied in deciding whether a coin is a silver coin, if the Crown's right is limited to coins of gold and silver?

The coin that is 100% pure silver is virtually unknown, because silver is a soft metal. English and, later, British silver coins from the Conquest until 1920 were of sterling silver, 92·5% silver, except for a short period in mid-Tudor times from 1544 to 1553 when the coinage was very considerably debased.

As to what is treasure trove, Sir Edward Coke says categorically (3 Co Inst 132):

> 'Treasure trove is when any gold or silver, in coin, plate, or bullyon hath been of ancient time hidden, wheresoever it be found, whereof no person can prove any property, it doth belong to the king, or to some lord or other by the king's grant, or prescription.'

He adds: '*Gold or silver* For if it be of any other metall, it is no treasure; and if it be no treasure, it belongs not to the king, for it must be treasure trove.' Again he says (2 Co Inst 576): '. . . nothing is said to be treasure trove but gold and silver.'

In Chitty's Prerogatives of the Crown of 1820 it is stated (p 152):

> '*Treasure trove*, is where any gold or silver in coin or plate or bullion is found concealed in a house, or in the earth, or other private place, the owner thereof being unknown, in which case the treasure belongs to the King or his grantee, having the franchise of treasure trove.'

The substance of these definitions, and specifically the limitation of treasure trove to articles of gold and silver is repeated in leading modern text books. See, for example, 8

Halsbury's Laws (4th Edn) para 1513; Russell on Crime (12th Edn, 1964, p 1497);
a Megarry and Wade on the Law of Real Property (4th Edn, 1975, p 71).

Similarly in *Elwes v Brigg Gas Co* (1886) 33 Ch D 562 at 567, [1886–90] All ER Rep 559 at 562 Chitty J, in an obiter statement which in my judgment reflects the accepted view, after referring to a jar which had been found containing Roman coins added: '. . . not gold or silver coins, and therefore not falling within the royal prerogative of treasure trove . . .'

b The prerogative right of the Crown to treasure trove was established in English law many centuries before Sir Edward Coke's time. It had no counterpart in Roman law and seems to have come into English law from some Scandinavian or Germanic source. Some very slight inferential indication that treasure trove was regarded, even in early medieval times, as applying only to articles of gold and silver is afforded by the so-called Leges Edwardii Confessoris. This work was issued between AD 1130 and 1135 and is not
c regarded as very reliable or of high authority. The assertion however that (and I quote a translation)—

> 'Treasures from the earth belong to the king, unless they be found in a church or in a cemetery, and even if they be found there the gold belongs to the king and half the silver and the other half to the church . . .'

d even if inaccurate as a statement of the King's rights is a slight indication that only articles of gold and silver were then regarded as being treasure trove.

Until recently the Crown accepted that only articles of gold and silver could be treasure trove. In statements promulgated by the Home Office in 1930 and 1955 it is categorically stated that coins and other ancient objects of copper, bronze or any other base metal are not treasure trove.

e Despite, however, the main current of opinion as to what is treasure trove, the Attorney General now contends that the true view is wider and that hoards of coins of any metal may be treasure trove. The argument is supported by reference to jurists of the highest eminence, and it is said that if the Crown prerogative was initially not limited to articles of gold and silver the wider prerogative cannot have been lost by disuse over recent centuries.

f It is convenient to refer first to Bracton (2 De Legibus et Consuetudinibus Angliæ 338). He refers to treasure trove as being treasure (and I quote a translation), 'to wit silver or gold or other kind of metal', found in any place whatever. A little further on in the same passage he refers to treasure as being (and again I quote from the translation) 'a certain old deposit of money or other metal of which there is no memory so that now it has no owner'. This was around 1250. Some sixty years earlier Glanville (Tractatus de
g Legibus et Consuetudinibus Regni Angliæ) in referring to the offence of the fraudulent concealment of treasure trove describes the object found as '*aliquod genus metalli*', some kind of metal, and does not state that it must be gold or silver.

Five centuries after Bracton, Sir William Blackstone in his Commentaries (bk 1, ch 8, para 13) refers to treasure trove as being—

> 'where any money or coin, gold, silver, plate, or bullion, is found hidden *in* the
> h earth, or other private place, the owner thereof being unknown; in which case the treasure belongs to the King.'

This definition does not limit the money or coin to gold or silver coin, and it is this definition which counsel for the Attorney General asks me to accept.

What Blackstone says, however, seems to be no more than a synthesis of Bracton and
j Coke, with both of whose works he was of course familiar, without independent support. Unless therefore Bracton (and Glanville) are broadly right, there is no reason for preferring Blackstone to Sir Edward Coke. Indeed, there is some reason against, since it would not have been natural, even in Blackstone's time when copper coinage had been in circulation in England for nearly a hundred years, to regard a hoard of bronze or copper, as opposed to gold or silver coins, as treasure. Moreover Blackstone appears to

refer the King's right to treasure trove to the same original as the King's right to mines, which was limited to mines of gold and silver.

So far as Bracton is concerned, his reference to other kinds of metal is plainly deliberate since he has taken, and extended by that reference, the definition of treasure by the Roman jurist Paulus, which had in fact nothing to do with any Crown prerogative. It may be that Bracton considered it logical that the prerogative of treasure trove should extend to coins and other articles of value not made of gold or silver. But I can see no evidence, beyond these two passages in Bracton and Glanville, that the prerogative ever did so extend.

If I were satisfied that the prerogative had originally extended to coins not of gold or silver, I would attach great weight to counsel for the Attorney General's argument that the Crown prerogative cannot be lost by mere disuse. But that argument has no weight in the absence of proof that the prerogative did extend to coins of non-precious metals.

In *Case of Mines* (1568) 1 Plowd 310, 75 ER 472 the court decided the extent of the Crown's prerogative right to mines of gold and silver on the basis of consuetudo, what the Crown had always had. By a parallel approach I conclude that Coke and Chitty are right and that it is not shown that the Crown has ever had as treasure trove coins that are not of gold or silver.

Counsel for the Attorney General pointed out that whereas in early times articles taken by the Crown as treasure trove went into the King's Exchequer to help to defray the cost of government the position is now very different in that the Crown's right to treasure trove has, for the past 100 years, been used not as a source of revenue but as a means of preserving interesting antiquities for the benefit of the nation as a whole. However the Crown cannot unilaterally extend its prerogative rights. That is a matter for Parliament. The fact that the object achieved by the law of treasure trove is now different cannot warrant the courts, without parliamentary sanction, either in extending the prerogative to articles not of gold or silver, or in adopting a wider or more relaxed definition of what are articles of silver.

The position however in which the preservation for the nation of recently discovered antiquities depends on a prerogative which originated for quite different purposes is not satisfactory and the topic is one which could well merit the attention of Parliament so as to adopt criteria in keeping with modern thinking and the ways of modern life.

Taking the view therefore that the prerogative is limited to articles of gold or silver, I turn to consider whether these coins fall within that description.

It is convenient to say a little about the coinage of the Roman empire.

Initially the emperors issued a gold coin, the aureus, a silver coin, the denarius, and various lesser coins of base metal. Under Augustus the silver content of the denarius was 95% to 98%. In the year of the four emperors it was 92% or 93% and under Vespasian it dropped to under 90%. Despite a recovery under Domitian the decline continued under Hadrian and Antoninus, and under Marcus Aurelius the percentage dropped to below 80%. Under Septimius Severus the silver content fell to 50%.

The coins with which I am concerned are antoniniani, and the antoninianus was first introduced by Septimius Severus's son, Caracalla, in 215. It was intended to have double the purchasing power of the denarius, but was not double the weight. Antoniniani were issued from 215 to 219 and denarii were also issued during this period. The percentage purity of the two was roughly the same. From 219 to 238 no antoniniani were issued, but in 238 the antoninianus was reintroduced and the denarius went out of circulation. Antoniniani continued to be issued (but not denarii) from 238 until 294 when the emperor Diocletian carried out a reform of the currency and introduced fresh coins. When the antoninianus was reintroduced in 238 its silver content was only 30%, and thereafter the content declined. From 260 to 274 there were separate emperors of the Gallic Empire who issued their own coins, but the silver content of the coins of the Gallic Empire was roughly the same as the percentage content of the contemporary coins of the Central Empire.

Of the 7,811 coins found at Coleby, a sample of 923 have been cleaned and examined in the British Museum. Of this sample it has been possible to identify 869 according to the emperor by whom they were issued.

According to details shown in the exhibit, 120 were minted in the sole reign of the emperor Gallienus, whose dates are from AD 260 to 268. One bears the image of Salonina, the wife of Gallienus. A further 118 are from the reign of Claudius II (268 to 270), 12 from the reign of Quintillus (AD 270) and one each from the reigns of Tacitus (275 to 276) and Probus (276 to 281). Eleven are coins of the Gallic emperor Postumus (260 to 268), 157 of the Gallic emperor Victorinus (268 to 270), and 334 and 114, respectively, of the Gallic emperors Tetricus I and Tetricus II, who reigned over the period 270 to 275. In addition it is known that one at least of the coins in the find not included in the sample is an antoninianus of the emperor Philip I, who reigned from 244 to 249.

Accepted metallurgical research shows that under the sole reign of Gallienus the silver content of antoniniani varied between 18% and 1·5%, probably declining as the reign progressed. Under Claudius II, Quintillus, Tacitus and Probus, the content did not exceed 5%. Under the Gallic emperor Postumus the percentage varied from 21% to 4% and under Victorinus it varied from 6·8% to 1·4%. Under Tetricus I and II it barely exceeded 1·5% at best. It appears that in 274 the emperor Aurelian endeavoured to reform the currency of the Central Empire by raising the silver content of the antoninianus to a modest 4·5% but the attempt does not seem to have been very successful.

There has been little analysis of the coins in the find with which I am concerned. At an early stage 15 of the coins were analysed. These showed percentages of silver ranging from 5·85% to 0·2% but no record survives to show from which reigns these coins came. Eleven of the 15 coins analysed showed percentages of less than 3%.

More recently one coin of the reign of Tacitus has been analysed by X-ray fluorescence and shown to have a silver content of 5% and one from the reign of the Gallic emperor Postumus has been similarly analysed and shown to have a silver content of 18%. These two coins, and the one from the reign of Probus, are the only ones in the sheets put before me to show any trace of silvering to the naked eye.

The pattern shown by the metallurgical research indicates that the silver in the antoniniani issued in these various reigns, whatever its percentage, was included deliberately in the alloy and was not there by chance.

Counsel for the Attorney General argues that when the antoninianus was first introduced by Caracalla in 215 it had the same 50% silver content as the denarius, which was a silver coin, and it was intended to be a double denarius. Therefore, as he submits, the antoninianus of Caracalla was, and was intended to be, a silver coin. He goes on to submit that the same reasoning is to be applied when the antoninianus was reintroduced in 238 and replaced the denarius, and that thereafter, however debased, the antoninianus remained a silver coin. He distinguished the follis, introduced by Diocletian in 294, on the basis that the follis was never intended to be other than a bronze coin, albeit with a silver element.

It does not seem to me to follow, however, that the coins in this find with which I am concerned are silver coins, even if the coins issued by Caracalla in 215 were silver. I am not concerned with Caracalla's coins and the argument based on them seems to get near to saying that a cupro-nickel shilling issued in 1955 is silver because a shilling issued in 1915 or 1895 was silver and there was a continuous issue of shillings, albeit with different monarchs' heads, in the meantime.

I prefer counsel for the defendants' submission, which he supports by analogy by reference to the observations of Viscount Simon in *Palser v Grinling* [1948] 1 All ER 1 at 11, [1948] AC 291 at 317, that the question whether a particular coin or object is of silver is for the judge of fact to decide as best he can on all the evidence, without being bound by any hard and fast rule or fixed percentage of silver content.

By this test, and even giving particular attention to the three coins of Tacitus, Probus and Postumus which show visible traces of silver, I conclude that none of the coins in this

find (of which I take the sample of 923 to be a fair sample) is a silver coin. On the detailed
evidence now before me it would be perverse for any jury to hold them to be silver a
coins. They cannot therefore be treasure trove.

A further question that was canvassed in argument is whether these coins can be said
to have been hidden. It is one of the requirements of the definition of treasure trove that
the coin concerned must have been, as Sir Edward Coke put it, 'of ancient time hidden',
or as Chitty put it, 'concealed in a house, or in the earth, or other private place'. The
evidence is that these coins were found by the use of a metal detector, in or around a b
broken urn, buried in the earth in a field at a level lower than would ordinarily be
reached by a ploughshare. There is, as always in these cases, no satisfactory evidence of
what the topography was in the third century or whether there were or were not
buildings around. But it is difficult to suppose that anyone would have placed such a
large number of coins in an urn in what seems to have been a rural locality rather than
a town if he were not hiding them. There is therefore slight evidence that they were c
hidden and this, in the absence of any more satisfactory explanation, would be sufficient
to establish a claim of treasure trove if, contrary to my view, the coins were silver coins
or coins that are not silver coins were capable of being treasure trove. As it is, however,
on the view of the law that I take and on my view that these are not silver coins I reject
the Attorney General's claim that these coins are treasure trove.

Order accordingly. d

Solicitors: *Frere, Cholmeley & Co* (for the Attorney General); *Bolton & Lowe*, agents for *Epton & Co*, Lincoln (for the defendants).

Evelyn M C Budd Barrister.

a R v Hatfield Justices, ex parte Castle

QUEEN'S BENCH DIVISION
WALLER LJ AND PARK J
22nd MAY 1980

b *Magistrates – Summary trial – Offence triable summarily or on indictment – Minor offence of criminal damage – Offence triable only summarily unless forming part of series of offences of same or similar character – Factors constituting offences of similar character – Accused charged with damaging police uniform valued at £23, using threatening words and behaviour likely to occasion breach of peace, assaulting a constable and wilfully obstructing constable – Last three offences triable summarily only – Whether offence of criminal damage to uniform triable summarily only* *c* *– Whether one of several offences of 'similar character' – Criminal Law Act 1977, s 23(7)(a).*

The defendant was charged with committing four offences on the same day. The first three offences, namely using threatening words and behaviour likely to occasion a breach of the peace, assaulting a police constable in the execution of his duty and wilfully obstructing a police constable, were offences triable summarily only. The fourth offence, *d* that of damaging a police uniform contrary to s 1(1) of the Criminal Damage Act 1971, was triable either summarily or on indictment. The magistrates, in considering the most suitable mode of trial having regard to the value involved, as they were required to do under s 23(1)[a] of the Criminal Law Act 1977, determined that the value involved in the criminal damage offence was £23 and thus below the £200 limit prescribed by s 23 for offences triable either way. However the magistrates then decided to proceed with *e* the criminal damage offence under s 23(7) as if it was an offence triable summarily or on indictment, and not under s 23(2) as if it was triable summarily only, on the ground that the criminal damage offence was one of several offences 'with which [the defendant was] charged on the same occasion' and which appeared 'to constitute or form part of a series of . . . offences of the same or a similar character', within s 23(7)(*a*). The defendant elected for trial by jury on the criminal damage charge and the magistrates therefore *f* adjourned that charge for committal proceedings to take place. The prosecution applied for an order prohibiting the magistrates from hearing the committal proceedings and for an order of mandamus directing them to hear the charge of criminal damage summarily, on the ground that the four offences charged were not offences of a similar character within s 23(7)(*a*), and therefore under s 23(1) and (2) the criminal damage charge was required to be tried summarily.

g

Held – For s 23(7)(*a*) of the 1977 Act to apply the offence charged and the other offences with which the accused was charged on the same occasion had to be part of a series and similar in fact and law and had further to be similar in being offences which were triable either way, that is summarily or on indictment. Since the offence of criminal damage and the other offences charged did not have those similar characteristics, it followed that *h* s 23(7)(*a*) was not applicable and under s 23(1) and (2) the criminal damage offence was required to be tried summarily. The orders sought would accordingly issue (see p 511 *j* to p 512 *c* and *e* to *h*, post).

Ludlow v Metropolitan Police Comr [1970] 1 All ER 567 applied.

Notes

j For the procedure for determining the mode of trial of minor offences of criminal damage, see 29 Halsbury's Laws (4th Edn) para 304.

For the Criminal Law Act 1977, s 23, see 47 Halsbury's Statutes (3rd Edn) 703.

---

a Section 23, so far as is material, is set out at p 511 *a* to *e*, post

Cases referred to in judgment

Ludlow v Metropolitan Police Comr [1970] 1 All ER 567, [1971] AC 29, [1970] 2 WLR 521, a
134 JP 277, 54 Cr App R 233, HL, 14 (1) Digest (Reissue) 301, *2304*.

R v Camberwell Green Magistrates, ex parte Prescott [1979] Court of Appeal Transcript 356.

Case also cited

R v Considine [1980] Crim LR 179.

b

Application for judicial review

Pursuant to leave given by Booth J on 11th April 1980 Inspector Douglas Castle of the Hertfordshire Constabulary ('the applicant') applied for (1) an order prohibiting justices for the petty sessional division of Hatfield in the County of Hertford sitting as a magistrates' court at Hatfield from further proceeding as examining magistrates under s 21 of the Criminal Law Act 1977 in regard to a charge brought against the defendant, c
Stephen James Mark Healy, that on 24th December 1979 he without lawful excuse damaged a police uniform tunic belonging to the Hertfordshire Constabulary intending to damage it or being reckless whether it would be damaged, contrary to s 1(1) of the Criminal Damage Act 1971 and (2) an order of mandamus directed to the magistrates requiring them to hear that charge by way of summary trial, pursuant to s 23(2) of the 1977 Act. The grounds of the application were that when the magistrates asked the d
defendant whether he consented to be tried summarily or wished to be tried by jury under s 21(3) of the 1977 Act and when he elected for trial by jury in determining to hear the charge as examining magistrates, the magistrates were acting in excess of their jurisdiction because by virtue of s 23 of and Sch 4 to the 1977 Act the charge, which related to damage to the value of only £23·67, was triable only by way of summary trial. The facts are set out in the judgment of Waller LJ. e

Jonathan Haworth for the applicant.
James P Wadsworth for the defendant.

WALLER LJ. This is an application by Inspector Castle ('the applicant') for leave to apply for judicial review of a determination made on 10th March 1980 by the Hatfield f
justices sitting at Hatfield magistrates' court. The application is for an order prohibiting the magistrates from committing the defendant for trial on a charge of criminal damage and involves the consideration of s 23(7) of the Criminal Law Act 1977.

The defendant was charged before the Hatfield magistrates with four offences that he did, on 24th December 1979, use threatening words and behaviour whereby a breach of the peace was likely to be occasioned, contrary to s 5 of the Public Order Act 1936, as g
amended. On the same day he assaulted a constable in the execution of his duty, contrary to s 51(1) of the Police Act 1964 and on the same day, without lawful excuse, he damaged a police uniform, contrary to s 1(1) of the Criminal Damage Act 1971. On the same day he wilfully obstructed the constable, acting in the execution of his duty, contrary to s51(3) of the 1964 Act.

The value of the damage to the police uniform tunic amounted to £23.67. The h
magistrates in their affidavit go on to say, not surprisingly, that they were of opinion that the damage to the police uniform tunic did not exceed £200 and that the provision of s 23(7)(*a*) applied to the offence of damaging a police uniform and that the offence of criminal damage was suitable for summary trial. It is to be noted that the other three offences were triable summarily only. When the court proceeded in accordance with the provisions of s 21 of the 1977 Act, the defendant elected to be tried by jury. j

The magistrates, having had their attention drawn to an article in the Justice of the Peace (Criminal Damage—Which Way Now, 2nd December 1978, p 684), came to the conclusion that the defendant was entitled to elect trial by jury, and it is that issue which comes before us.

Sections 19 to 23 of the 1977 Act deal with procedure for determining the mode of

trial of offences which are triable either way. Section 23(1) deals particularly with certain
a offences which are triable either way but are made triable summarily if the value
involved is small.

Section 23(1) provides:

> 'If the offence charged ... is one of those mentioned in the first column of
> Schedule 4 to this Act [which include offences under s 1 of the Criminal Damage
> Act 1971] ... then, subject to subsection (7) below, the court shall, before proceeding
> b in accordance with section 20 above [ie considering which mode of trial appears
> more suitable], consider whether, having regard to any representations made by the
> prosecutor or the accused, the value involved (as defined in subsection (10) below)
> appears to the court to exceed the relevant sum ...'

It was in relation to that that the magistrates came to the opinion that the relevant sum
c was £23·67. As the section goes on to say, 'For the purposes of this section the relevant
sum is £200', it was below that sum.

Then s 23(2) provides:

> 'If ... the value involved does not exceed the relevant sum, the court shall
> proceed as if the offence were triable only summarily, and sections 20 to 22 above
> shall not apply.'

d

But s 23(7) reads as follows:

> 'Subsection (1) above shall not apply where the offence charged—(*a*) is one of two
> or more offences with which the accused is charged on the same occasion and which
> appear to the court to constitute or form part of a series of two or more offences of
> the same or a similar character ...'

e

Counsel for the applicant submits to this court that the offences here were neither of
a similar character nor did they constitute what formed part of a series. They all
occurred, submits counsel, at virtually the same time. They all occurred in relation to
the same officer and therefore they were not part of a series. The time probably was not
more than a minute or two. Secondly, they were not offences of a similar character.

f Threatening words and behaviour whereby a breach of the peace is likely to be
occasioned, contrary to s 5 of the 1971 Act, has nothing in common with criminal
damage. Assaulting a constable has nothing in common with criminal damage except
that the damage was to a constable's uniform, but criminal damage may be done to
anything. Criminal damage has nothing in common with wilful obstruction of a
constable in the execution of his duty.

g Counsel for the applicant submits that the authority of the Court of Appeal decided
after the article in the Justice of the Peace makes that clear. He referred firstly to the case
of *R v Camberwell Green Magistrates, ex parte Prescott* [1979] Court of Appeal Transcript
356 which was a case where the magistrate had refused to give the defendant the right
to elect trial by jury. The episode was one where the defendant obstructed a police officer
while he was looking for somebody and, in obstructing him, damaged a pair of his
h trousers to the value of £12. There was an offence of obstructing a police officer in the
course of his duty and of criminal damage to trousers so that it was similar to at any rate
part of the offences charged in this case. Ormrod LJ said:

> 'When one turns to the nature of the offences charged in this case, one is an
> offence of obstructing a police officer in the course of his duty and the other is the
> offence of criminal damage to the officer's trousers. It seems to be plain beyond any
> j question that the two offences are not of the same or similar character, nor can I see
> on the facts of this case how these two offences could possibly be described as a
> "series". There is no series.'

He went on to dismiss the appeal.

If one applies that decision to the present case, clearly the obstruction is not similar to criminal damage. In my judgment, equally clearly, insulting behaviour is not similar to criminal damage. Nor is the offence of assault similar to criminal damage. There may be occasions when they are similar in what happens but they are not similar offences.

Counsel for the applicant has drawn attention to a passage in the speech of Lord Pearson in *Ludlow v Metropolitan Police Comr* [1970] 1 All ER 567, [1971] AC 29 where Lord Pearson was considering the elements of similarity for the purpose of the Indictments Act 1915, Sch 1, r 3. The argument apparently having been on the one side that it was factual similarity and on the other side legal similarity, Lord Pearson expressed the following view ([1970] 1 All ER 567 at 573, [1971] AC 29 at 39):

> 'I think the proper conclusion to be drawn from the judgments as a whole [ie the judgments of the Court of Appeal] is that both the law and the facts have been and should be taken into account in deciding whether offences are similar or dissimilar in character.'

Both of those requirements have to be present.

What had happened in the present case produced a very extraordinary state of affairs. The offence of criminal damage of an amount of £23 was in many ways rather less serious than the other offences with which the defendant was charged. Assault on a police constable is more serious in the ordinary way than criminal damage of a small amount. The public order offence may well be more serious. Obstructing a police constable in the course of his duty may well be more serious than criminal damage itself.

The result of the magistrates feeling compelled to send this case for trial (compelled by the article in the Justice of the Peace) was that he was being sent for trial certainly for no more serious offence than the others with which he was charged, and almost certainly for a rather less serious offence, which is a rather extraordinary result. None of those others were triable other than summarily.

In my judgment, one of the essentials to comply with s 23(7)(*a*) is that the offences which are said to be of the same or similar character should have the characteristic, among others, of being triable either way. The words of this subsection follow closely the words of r 9 of the Indictment Rules 1971, SI 1971 No 1253, which are concerned with offences which can be tried on indictment, and one can understand those words being used to enable offences to be tried together on indictment when they are all triable either way. In my opinion, that is one of the characteristics that should apply.

In my judgment, in this case the magistrates were wrong in the conclusion to which they came, albeit they were misled by the article in the Justice of the Peace and that, in order for s 23(7)(*a*) to apply, there has to be similarity of fact; there has to be similarity in law; there has to be the characteristic of similarity in that they are all triable either way and they must form part of a series. In this particular case it is not necessary to decide whether these offences formed part of a series. It is sufficient to say that none of the other characteristics were present and therefore the court was not obliged to consider s 23(7), and the offence of criminal damage remained an offence that was triable only summarily.

PARK J. I agree.

Order prohibiting the justices from committing the defendant for trial and an order of mandamus directing them to hear the charge under s 1(1) of the Criminal Damage Act 1971 summarily.

Solicitors: *Pellys*, Bishop's Stortford (for the applicant); *Bretherton & Co*, St Albans (for the defendant).

Dilys Tausz Barrister.

Re Berkeley Securities (Property) Ltd

CHANCERY DIVISION
VINELOTT J
31st MARCH, 1st APRIL, 16th MAY 1980

Company – Winding up – Application of bankruptcy rules – Proof and ranking of claims – Unliquidated claim for damages in tort – Company in compulsory liquidation – Secretary of State instituting action on behalf of company to recover money from another company – Third company agreeing to purchase assets of other company and seeking to bring proceedings against company being wound up for damages for negligent misstatement regarding other company's assets – Whether leave to bring proceedings should be granted – Whether claim for unliquidated damages in tort capable of proof in compulsory winding up of company – Whether if leave given leave should extend to allowing proceedings to proceed to trial to enable application for proceedings to be heard with action – Companies Act 1948, ss 231, 317.

A company (Berkeley) was in compulsory liquidation. Pursuant to s 37(1)[a] of the Companies Act 1967 the Secretary of State for Trade and Industry, acting in the public interest, commenced an action ('the main action') on behalf of Berkeley against another company (Atlantic) seeking to recover, inter alia, money in respect of a purported loan of £400,000 by Atlantic to Berkeley which it was alleged was not paid to Berkeley but was used by Atlantic for other purposes. Even if the action succeeded Berkeley would remain insolvent. A further company (PGA), which had entered into an agreement with Atlantic to purchase its assets on the footing that they included a debt from Berkeley of £400,000, thereby stood to be adversely affected if the action succeeded. Further, at the time of the agreement Berkeley had confirmed to Atlantic's accountants that it was a debtor of Atlantic's in the sum of £400,000, and PGA, to the extent that any sum was recovered from Atlantic in the main action in respect of the purported loan, wished to bring proceedings against Berkeley for damages for the negligent misstatement that it was Atlantic's debtor. PGA accordingly sought leave under s 231[b] of the Companies Act 1948 to bring its action and to have it heard together with the related main action. Unless PGA issued a writ against Berkeley within nine months its claim would be time-barred. The registrar refused PGA's application for leave to bring its action. PGA appealed. On the appeal Berkeley's liquidators objected to leave being granted on the ground that s 317[c] of the 1948 Act required that the bankruptcy rules should prevail in a winding up of an insolvent company, and since under those rules a claim for damages in tort which was unliquidated at the date of the receiving order was excluded from proof in a bankruptcy, therefore, so the liquidators contended, an unliquidated claim for damages in tort was incapable of proof in the winding up of an insolvent company so long as the company remain insolvent; alternatively, the liquidators contended, if leave were granted to PGA it should be restricted to the commencement of proceedings and should not extend to allowing the proceedings to proceed to trial (which would enable an application to be made for PGA's claim and the main action to be tried together), because the Secretary of State had no power under s 37 of the 1967 Act to defend PGA's claim.

---

a Section 37(1) provides: 'If, from any report made under section 168 of the principal Act or from any information or document obtained under Part III of this Act or section 18 or 19 of the Protection of Depositors Act 1963 it appears to the Board of Trade that any civil proceedings ought in the public interest to be brought by any body corporate, they may themselves bring such proceedings in the name and on behalf of the body corporate.'

b Section 231, so far as material, provides: 'When a winding-up order has been made . . . no action or proceeding shall be proceeded with or commenced against the company except by leave of the court and subject to such terms as the court may impose.'

c Section 317 is set out at p 523 *j* to p 524 *j*, post

Held – (1) A literal application of the bankruptcy rules in the winding up of an insolvent company would lead to absurdity because, although a company being wound up by the *a* court was initially treated as an insolvent company to which s 317 of the 1948 Act would apply, later in the winding up it might be found to be solvent in which case s 316[d] of that Act would apply and then an unliquidated claim for damages in tort could be proved in the winding up. It was therefore necessary to modify the bankruptcy rules to fit into the scheme of a winding up. Accordingly, s 317, properly construed, did not operate to exclude from the winding up of an insolvent company a claim for damages in tort which *b* was unliquidated at the commencement of the winding up, but only excluded such a claim from proof in the winding up if, at the time the claimant came in to prove, the claim had not become a liquidated claim by judgment. Where the claim, if made good, would result in the company being insolvent, then, until the claim became liquidated, the initial presumption that the company was insolvent could not be rebutted and there could be no return to contributories of the company. However, when the claim became *c* liquidated the claimant was entitled to a dividend out of the undistributed assets of the company, although he could not disturb prior distribution to creditors (see p 523 *b* and p 528 *j* to p 529 *a* and *d* to *h*, post); dictum of Vaughan Williams LJ in *Re Whitaker* [1901] 1 Ch at 12–13 and *Re McMurdo* [1902] 2 Ch 684 applied.

(2) Such a construction of s 317 of the 1948 Act was heavily in favour of leave being given under s 231 of the Act to bring proceedings for damages in tort against a company *d* being wound up by the court which was or might be insolvent, and, unless there were special circumstances, fairness required that leave should be given to prosecute such a claim to judgment. However, because the Secretary of State had no interest in defending PGA's claim, since his statutory charge for the costs and expenses of the main action would have priority over any damages or costs recoverable by PGA in its claim, and because he had no power under s 37 of the 1967 Act to finance a defence by Berkeley to *e* PGA's claim, and Berkeley itself had no means to finance a defence, the main action should be heard first without PGA's claim being heard with it. Accordingly, PGA would be granted leave but limited to issuing a writ and serving a statement of claim so that its claim would not become statute-barred, and the court would direct that no further steps in its claim should be taken until the main action had been heard (see p 530 *b c* and *j* to p 531 *a* and *e* to p 532 *a*, post); dictum of Brightman LJ in *Re Aro Co Ltd* [1980] 1 All ER *f* at 1076 applied.

Per Curiam. It is not easy to see why, in bankruptcy, an unliquidated claim for damages in tort alone should be excluded from proof (see p 530 *c d*, post).

Notes

For the application of bankruptcy rules in the winding up of an insolvent company, see *g* 7 Halsbury's Laws (4th Edn) para 1276, and for cases on the subject, see 10 Digest (Reissue) 1063–1066, *6524–6544*.

For the effect of a winding up order on an action or proceeding against a company, see 7 Halsbury's Laws (4th Edn) para 1044, and for cases on the subject, see 10 Digest (Reissue) 1097–1098, *6740–6743*.

For the Companies Act 1948, ss 231, 317, see 5 Halsbury's Statutes (3rd Edn) 299, 344. *h*

Cases referred to in judgment

Aro Co Ltd, Re [1980] 1 All ER 1067, [1980] Ch 196, [1980] 2 WLR 453, CA.

Barned's Banking Co, Re, Kellock's Case, Re Xeres Wine Shipping Co, ex parte Alliance Bank (1868) LR 3 Ch App 769, 39 LJ Ch 112, 18 LT 671, LJJ, 10 Digest (Reissue) 1081, *6627*.

Baum, Ex parte, re Edwards (1874) LR 9 Ch App 673, 44 LJ Bcy 25, 31 LT 12, LJJ, 5 Digest *j* (Reissue) 1082, *8663*.

Brownsea Haven Properties Ltd v Poole Corpn [1958] 1 All ER 205, [1958] Ch 574, [1958] 2 WLR 137, 122 JP 97, 56 LGR 91, CA, 11 Digest (Reissue) 261, *158a*.

d Section 316 is set out at p 523 *a*, post

Fine Industrial Commodities Ltd, Re [1955] 3 All ER 707, [1956] Ch 256, [1955] 3 WLR 940, 10 Digest (Reissue) 1062, *6519*.
a
Fryer v Ewart [1902] AC 187, 71 LJ Ch 433, 9 Mans 281, sub nom *Watney, Combe, Reid & Co v Ewart* 86 LT 242, HL, 31(2) Digest (Reissue) 837, *6926*.
Great Orme Tramways Co, Re (1934) 50 TLR 450, 10 Digest (Reissue) 1052, *6465*.
Grosvenor Metal Co Ltd, Re [1949] 2 All ER 948, [1950] Ch 63, 10 Digest (Reissue) 1103, *6782*.
b *Hopkins, Re, ex parte De Stedingk* (1902) 86 LT 676, CA, 4 Digest (Reissue) 343, *3057*.
Leng, Re, Tarn v Emmerson [1895] 1 Ch 652, [1895–9] All ER Rep 1210, 64 LJ Ch 468, 72 LT 407, CA, 24 Digest (Reissue) 803, *8610*.
Mason v Bogg (1837) 2 My & Cr 443, 40 ER 709, 24 Digest (Reissue) 811, *8676*.
McMurdo, Re, Penfield v McMurdo [1902] 2 Ch 684, 71 LJ Ch 691, 86 LT 814, CA, 4 Digest (Reissue) 410, *3602*.
c *Milan Tramways Co, Re, ex parte Theys* (1884) 25 Ch D 587, 53 LJ Ch 1008, 50 LT 545, CA, 10 Digest (Reissue) 1070, *6570*.
Newman, Re, ex parte Brooke (1876) 3 Ch D 494, CA, 4 Digest (Reissue) 352, *3132*.
Whitaker, Re, Whitaker v Palmer [1901] 1 Ch 9, 70 LJ Ch 6, 83 LT 449, CA, 24 Digest (Reissue) 807, *8639*.
Withernsea Brickworks, Re (1880) 16 Ch D 337, 50 LJ Ch 185, 43 LT 713, CA, 10 Digest (Reissue) 1102, *6780*.
d
Wyley v Exhall Coal Mining Co (1864) 33 Beav 538, 55 ER 478, 10 Digest (Reissue) 1099, *6751*.

Case also cited

Post Office v Norwich Union Fire Insurance Society Ltd [1967] 1 All ER 577, [1967] 2 QB 363.

e

Motion

By an order dated 1st February 1980 Mr Registrar Bradburn refused an application by Property Growth Assurance Co Ltd ('PGA') under s 231 of the Companies Act 1948 for leave to commence proceedings in the Chancery Division of the High Court against
f Berkeley Securities (Property) Ltd ('Berkeley') for damages, or alternatively for an inquiry as to damages and an order for payment of the sum found due on taking the inquiry, notwithstanding an order dated 19th May 1975 to wind up Berkeley. By notice of motion dated 12th February 1980 PGA applied for an order discharging the registrar's order and for an order giving PGA leave to commence the proceedings or such other order as seemed just to the court. The respondents to the motion were David Llewellyn
g Morgan and Malcolm Gee, the joint liquidators of Berkeley. The facts are set out in the judgment.

Conrad Dehn QC and *Michael Brindle* for PGA.
Andrew Morritt QC and *Philip Heslop* for the liquidators.

h

Cur adv vult

16th May. **VINELOTT J** read the following judgment: This is an appeal by Property Growth Assurance Co Ltd (which I will call 'PGA') against an order of Mr Registrar Bradburn whereby he refused an application by PGA made pursuant to s 231 of the
j Companies Act 1948 for leave to bring an action against Berkeley Securities (Property) Ltd (which I will call 'Berkeley'). Berkeley is in compulsory liquidation, a winding-up order having been made on 19th May 1975 on a creditors' petition which was presented on 8th April 1975. The proposed action is an action for damages for negligent misrepresentation, and the loss which it is sought to recover will be suffered if, and only if, Berkeley succeeds in another action which has been commenced by the Secretary of

State for Trade in the name and on behalf of Berkeley pursuant to the powers conferred on him by s 37 of the Companies Act 1967.

An explanation of the issues raised in that action (which I will call 'the main action') is a necessary prologue to an analysis of the questions raised by PGA's application for leave to bring proceedings against Berkeley.

The main action

At all material times Berkeley carried on business as a property investment company, the acquisition of its portfolio being financed by moneys deposited with Berkeley by members of the public on interest-bearing deposit accounts. The accounts of Berkeley for the last accounting period before the making of the winding-up order, that is, the year ended 31st December 1974, showed that at 31st December 1974 there were 337 depositors and that the aggregate amount owed to them at that date was approximately £410,000. Berkeley's records also reveal that at 27th June 1974 its portfolio of investment in property and ground rents was professionally valued at £631,130, and that that portfolio (which I will call 'the property portfolio') was then unincumbered. At the commencement of the winding up the property portfolio appeared to be incumbered by, amongst other things, a debenture (which I will call 'the Atlantic debenture') dated 31st December 1974 and purportedly securing the repayment of a sum of £400,000 to a company then known as Atlantic Assurance Co Ltd, which has since changed its name to Property Growth Pensions and Annuities Ltd (which I will call 'Atlantic'). The repayment of the sum secured by the Atlantic debenture was guaranteed by a company, Celoware Builders (which I will call 'Celoware'), one Timothy John Angus, one Robin Christopher Scott-Brown, a company then known as Seven Oaks Financial Holdings Ltd, which is now known as the Currency Index Deposit Co Ltd (which I will call 'Cidco'), and by one Anna Christina Scott-Brown.

The property portfolio also appeared to be incumbered by a debenture dated 1st January 1975 and granted by Berkeley to Cidco, which purported to create a floating charge to secure payment to Cidco of £57,215, and a legal mortgage of that date also granted to Cidco by way of collateral security. Apart from the property portfolio, the assets of Berkeley available to its creditors amounted in value to a little over £8,000, a sum which will be absorbed by the costs and expenses of the winding up. The realisable value of the property portfolio was substantially less than £400,000 and, if the Atlantic debenture is valid, there will be nothing for Berkeley's other creditors, whatever may be the fate of the debenture and mortgage in favour of Cidco.

In those circumstances the joint liquidators of Berkeley caused a full investigation to be carried out to ascertain whether the Atlantic debenture and the debenture and mortgage in favour of Cidco were valid and binding on Berkeley. Following that investigation, the Secretary of State for Trade decided that it was in the public interest that proceedings be brought in the name and on behalf of Berkeley to set aside the Atlantic debenture and to recover from Atlantic any moneys received by it by dealings with the Atlantic debenture or the Berkeley property portfolio. I will return to the powers conferred by s 37 and the position of the Secretary of State in relation to costs later in this judgment. The main action is, of course, brought by the Secretary of State for Trade through the offices of the Treasury Solicitor.

The issues in the main action are very complex. A brief summary will suffice for the purposes of this judgment. The main action relates primarily to two transactions which are as follows.

(1) It is alleged that on 28th June 1974 the entire issued share capital of Berkeley, amounting to 10 million shares of 1p each, was sold by its then shareholders to Cidco at the price of £450,000; that the sum of £450,000 was lent by Atlantic to Cidco, a company controlled by the Scott-Browns, and secured by a legal charge on the property portfolio; and that the legal charge (i) was not made for the purposes or benefit of Berkeley, which received no consideration, (ii) was a misapplication of Berkeley's property and ultra vires, and (iii) was made to provide security for a loan made to enable

Cidco to purchase the Berkeley shares in contravention of s 54 of the Companies Act 1948. It is further alleged that Atlantic knew or ought to have known the purposes for which the legal charge was made, and that the legal charge was either ineffective to create any interest in or security over the property portfolio, or, if it was effective for that purpose, that Atlantic held any benefit it obtained as a constructive trustee for Berkeley. The professional valuation of the property portfolio, to which I have referred, was made for the purposes of that transaction.

It is also alleged in the main action that in September 1974 Berkeley raised the sum of £184,750 by sale of part of the property portfolio, out of which the sum of £112,000 was paid to Atlantic as to £100,000 in part repayment of the loan to Cidco secured on the property portfolio by the mortgage of 28th June 1974 and as to £12,000 by way of penalty for early redemption. It is claimed against Atlantic that it is liable to account to Berkeley for that sum with interest.

(2) It is alleged that in or about October 1974 negotiations commenced for the acquisition of the issued share capital of Berkeley by Celoware, which was controlled by Mr Angus, the negotiations being conducted by Mr Robin Scott-Brown on behalf of Cidco and Mr Angus on behalf of Celoware; that as a result of those negotiations Celoware agreed to buy the Berkeley shares for £513,000, the purchase being conditional upon the repayment of the loan, then £350,000 plus interest, to Cidco from Atlantic, secured by the mortgage of 28th June 1974; that by a series of complex transactions, which it is unnecessary to describe in detail, the sum of £513,000 was paid out of Berkeley's moneys to Celoware; and that a sum of £400,000 purportedly paid to Berkeley and secured by the Atlantic debenture of 31st December 1974 was not paid to Berkeley but was used in part to discharge the debt due from Cidco and secured by the charge of 28th June 1974 (which with interest amounted to £388,342) and in part to meet a commitment fee of £8,000 and interest payable in advance of January 1975 of £7,134·24, the balance of £3,476·24 being retained by Atlantic's solicitors to meet their charges.

It is accordingly alleged that the Atlantic debenture was not made for the purposes or for the benefit of Berkeley; that the creation of the charge was a misapplication of Berkeley's assets and ultra vires; and that it was made to give financial assistance to Celoware to assist in the purchase of Berkeley's shares in contravention of s 54.

It is claimed as against Atlantic that it knew or ought to have known the purposes for which the Atlantic debenture was created; that the Atlantic debenture constituted an application of Berkeley's property otherwise than for its benefit; and that accordingly (i) the Atlantic debenture was not effective to create any interest in or charge over Berkeley's assets in favour of Atlantic; or alternatively (ii) that if it was effective to create any such interest or charge, Atlantic held any such interest or charge as a constructive trustee for Berkeley.

I should mention for completeness that it is also alleged that in January 1975 Berkeley raised approximately £19,000 by sale of part of the property portfolio and that part of the proceeds of sale was paid to Atlantic in partial discharge of the sums secured by the Atlantic debenture. Berkeley again claims repayment of any sums so paid with interest.

Those are the main claims against Atlantic. They are, of course, coupled with claims against the Scott-Browns and Mr Angus, and other directors and shareholders of Cidco and Celoware, and against Cidco and Celoware themselves. Other parties, in particular the solicitors acting for Atlantic, have been joined as third parties. If the action succeeds, there will be difficult and complex questions of contribution to be resolved. But a further claim is made against Atlantic which is coupled with a claim against Williams & Glyn's Bank Ltd (which I will call 'Williams & Glyn's'). That further claim is founded on events which took place between 31st December 1974 and the presentation of the petition for the winding up of Berkeley. To those events I now turn.

For many years before 1974 Atlantic carried on the business of life assurance. It was a wholly-owned subsidiary of Atlantic Assurance Holdings Company Ltd (which I will call 'Holdings') which in turn was owned as to 52% by, or by companies controlled by, a Mr Pollard, and as to 48% by, or by companies controlled by, a company called

Cornwallis Estates Ltd (which I will call 'Cornwallis'). Cornwallis was owned as to 75%
by Kayrealm Ltd and as to 25% by, or by a company controlled by, Williams & Glyn's. a
In 1974 Cornwallis and Kayrealm were in financial difficulties. An informal committee
of creditors of Cornwallis had been appointed. Later, on 11th February 1975 Cornwallis
went into a creditors' voluntary winding up. Williams & Glyn's had also appointed a
receiver of Kayrealm Ltd. Atlantic in turn was in financial difficulties. Between 6th
December 1973 and 10th May 1974 the Secretary of State for Trade issued notices
pursuant to the Insurance Companies Amendment Act 1973 requiring Atlantic to b
maintain in the United Kingdom assets equivalent to a specified porportion of its net
domestic liabilities and to vest them in a trustee approved by the Secretary of State.
Williams & Glyn's, on appointing a receiver of Kayrealm, gave the Secretary of State an
assurance, which was published, that it would take steps to safeguard the interests of
Atlantic's policyholders. Following that assurance, Williams & Glyn's looked for a
reputable assurance company which would take over Atlantic or its life assurance business c
and which could be relied on to meet Atlantic's liabilities to policyholders. PGA was
approached. The assets of Atlantic available to meet claims of policyholders included a
portfolio of loans secured on land (which I will call 'the loan portfolio') of an aggregate
face value of some £6·1 million. PGA was unwilling to take over Atlantic, and so
indirectly assume responsibility for ensuring that claims of its policyholders were met,
unless a purchaser could be found who would take over the loan portfolio, which d
comprised approximately half the assets available to meet the claims of policyholders, at
par. In these circumstances the following arrangement was entered into.

By an agreement dated 20th February 1975 (which I will call 'the Atlantic share
agreement') to which, amongst others, PGA, Mr Pollard, Williams & Glyn's, Holdings
and Atlantic were parties, it was agreed, amongst other things, that PGA would purchase
from Holdings the entire issued share capital of Atlantic. Under the Atlantic share e
agreement Holdings and Mr Pollard entered into a series of warranties which included
first, a warranty that information given to accountants and actuaries instructed by PGA
to make a full investigation into the affairs of Atlantic was, when given, true and was
given after making all proper inquiries, and remained true at the date of the agreement;
and secondly, a warranty that all information known or which should have been known,
or which pending completion should become or have become known to them, and f
which was material to a purchaser of the shares of Atlantic, had been supplied to PGA or
its investigating accountants and actuaries acting in connection with the investigation to
which I have referred.

It was also a term of the Atlantic share agreement that Atlantic and Williams & Glyn's
would enter into a contemporaneous agreement in the form of a draft annexed thereto.
By that agreement, which was duly executed (and which I will call 'the Atlantic loan g
portfolio agreement'), it was agreed that Atlantic would sell and Williams & Glyn's
would purchase the loan portfolio, Williams & Glyn's paying therefor a sum equal to the
face value of the loans as at 31st December 1974, subject to a provision for adjustment in
respect of repayments or further advances since 31st December 1974. Under the Atlantic
loan portfolio agreement the consideration, £6,125,735 payable (subject to adjustment)
by Williams & Glyn's, was to be paid into a deposit account in the name of Atlantic and h
withdrawn by instalments on 1st March and 1st September 1976 with interest. The loan
portfolio, of course, included the loan purportedly made to Berkeley. Assignments were
duly executed by Atlantic vesting the benefit of the loan portfolio and the securities
therefor in Williams & Glyn's. One of the assignments, which is dated 25th March 1975,
and which was made in a form annexed to the agreement, was an assignment of the
benefit of the debt apparently due from Berkeley and of the benefit of the Atlantic j
debenture. The debt is stated to be £400,000, although, as I have mentioned, some
repayments may have been made in January 1975. By the assignment Atlantic gave
Williams & Glyn's the same covenants of title as would have been implied under s 76 (1)
of the Law of Property Act 1925 if Atlantic had transferred and had been expressed to
transfer both as settlor and as mortgagor.

In the statement of claim in the main action Berkeley claim delivery up and
a cancellation of the Atlantic debenture and an account of all moneys received by or on behalf of Williams & Glyn's in respect of assets purportedly charged by the Atlantic debenture. Berkeley claim in the alternative that if the Atlantic debenture was effective to create any interest in or security over the property portfolio, Atlantic was a constructive trustee thereof and is liable to account for the sum of £400,000, the part of the total consideration paid by Williams & Glyn's for the Atlantic loan portfolio which is
b attributable to the Atlantic debenture. That sum has been retained on deposit with Williams & Glyn's in the name of Atlantic, and with accrued interest amounted on 31st December last to £702,857·29, since when further interest has accrued. Williams & Glyn's has, of course, refused to pay this sum to Atlantic pending the hearing of the main action, and indeed at an earlier stage Williams & Glyn's interpleaded, though the interpleader proceedings have been stayed since the commencement of the main action.

c In third party proceedings Williams & Glyn's claims an indemnity from Atlantic against any moneys for which Williams & Glyn's is liable to account to Berkeley in respect of its dealings with the properties charged by the Atlantic debenture under the first of the two heads of claim I have mentioned. Atlantic claim an indemnity from Williams & Glyn's in the event that Berkeley succeed in recovering the sum of £400,000 with accrued interest held by Williams & Glyn's on deposit in the name of Atlantic.
d There are other cross-claims and claims for indemnity or contribution against others concerned with the creation of the legal charge of 28th June 1974 and the Atlantic debenture. Further, Williams & Glyn's has commenced an action against the guarantors of the Atlantic debenture and Atlantic has commenced an action against Holdings and Mr Pollard under the warranties in the Atlantic share agreement to which I have referred. This latter action has, I understand, been ordered to be tried immediately after the trial of the main action.

e There is, as counsel for PGA accepts, and indeed asserts, a possibility that the final outcome of this welter of claims and cross-claims will be that Atlantic will either be held liable to indemnify Williams & Glyn's against money recovered by Berkeley under the first head of claim, or alternatively will be held liable as a constructive trustee under the second head of claim, and in either event will either fail to make good a claim for
f indemnity or contribution, or in the case of persons other than Williams & Glyn's will make good a claim for indemnity or contribution but fail to recover. If that happens, PGA will suffer in that it bought the shares of Atlantic on the footing that the assets of Atlantic included the loan portfolio which would be taken over by Williams & Glyn's at the face value of the loans. To the extent of any loss which falls on Atlantic, and indirectly on PGA, as a result of recovery from Atlantic of the sum of £112,000 paid to
g Atlantic in September 1974 in reduction of the debt due from Cidco and by way of penalty for early redemption, PGA would appear to have no remedy against Berkeley or Williams & Glyn's. But to the extent of any sums recovered from Atlantic in respect of the loan of £400,000 and of any dealings with the Berkeley property portfolio since 31st December 1974, PGA asserts that it has a claim for damages against Berkeley. That claim is the subject matter of the proposed action.

h

The proposed action

The claim which PGA wishes to bring against Berkeley is by comparison with the complex and interlocking claims in the main action a straightforward one. The Atlantic share agreement was expressed to be made subject to certain conditions being satisfied before the close of business on 20th February 1975, that is, the date of the Atlantic share
j agreement. One of the conditions was that before completion of the agreement a balance sheet and a profit and loss account of Atlantic for the year ended 31st December 1974 would be prepared on an agreed basis and approved by the directors of Atlantic and certified by Atlantic's auditors, who were Price Waterhouse & Co, before completion of the agreement. PGA also instructed Price Waterhouse & Co to carry out the investigation into the financial affairs of Atlantic which I have already mentioned. I have already

referred to the warranty in the Atlantic share agreement by Holdings and Mr Pollard as to the accuracy and completeness of the information to be supplied to PGA and its investigating accountants.

Price Waterhouse & Co's report was, in fact, furnished to PGA before the date of the Atlantic share agreement, namely on 29th January 1975. A draft balance sheet and profit and loss account were appended to the report. While Price Waterhouse & Co were preparing the accounts of Atlantic for the year ended 31st December 1974, a letter dated 3rd January 1975 was sent by the accounts department of Atlantic to Berkeley enclosing a statement of account as at close of business on 31st December 1974. The letter stated that 'as part of their normal audit procedure, our Auditors, Price Waterhouse & Co, request direct confirmation of the amount outstanding at 31st December, 1974'. Berkeley were asked to complete an enclosed letter of confirmation and to return it in an enclosed stamped-addressed envelope to Price Waterhouse & Co. It is alleged in the draft statement of claim in the proposed action that Berkeley signed and sent this letter of confirmation to Price Waterhouse & Co, that it was received by Price Waterhouse & Co on or shortly before 16th January 1975, that is, before the date of Price Waterhouse & Co's report to PGA, and that—

> 'In reliance upon that letter of confirmation Price Waterhouse & Company (as Berkeley knew or ought reasonably to have foreseen they would) included Berkeley as a debtor of Atlantic in the sum of £400,000 (as at 31st December 1974) in the accounts of Atlantic which they were preparing and auditing.'

It is further alleged that Berkeley owed a duty to exercise reasonable care in and about dealings with the letter and inquiry of 3rd January 1975 and in sending that letter of confirmation to any person whom it knew or ought reasonably to have foreseen would or might rely on accounts prepared in reliance on the letter of confirmation, including any intending purchaser of shares of Atlantic; that in reliance on Atlantic's accounts PGA entered into the Atlantic share agreement and that letter of confirmation was a breach of Berkeley's duty of care. It is said that if that letter of confirmation had not been sent PGA would not have entered into the Atlantic share agreement without further safeguards, or alternatively would not have paid as large a sum as it in fact paid for the Atlantic shares.

Those are the issues which it is sought to raise. It is said by counsel for PGA, with I think considerable force, that although the claim is a contingent claim, in that it will only arise if the claims by Berkeley in relation to the Atlantic debenture ultimately fall to be borne by Atlantic (in addition to any liability in respect of properties sold in September 1976), nonetheless the main action and the proposed action by PGA should, if possible, be consolidated and heard concurrently, or alternatively should be heard consecutively but by the same judge and in such a way that all parties to both actions are bound by findings of fact in the main action. Counsel points out that the letter of confirmation sent by Berkeley in reply to Atlantic's letter of 3rd January 1975 is relied on by Williams & Glyn's in their defence (where the letter is said to have been signed by Mr Angus) as founding an estoppel. Williams & Glyn's claim that they relied on the accounts drawn up by Price Waterhouse & Co, which in turn were drawn up in reliance on that letter, when they agreed to pay £6,125,735 for the Atlantic loan portfolio. It is said by counsel for PGA that the circumstances in which the letter of confirmation was sent, and the extent to which Price Waterhouse & Co relied, and were intended to rely on it, are relied on in Williams & Glyn's defence and are equally relevant to the proposed action, and that justice and convenience require that the main action and the proposed action be heard either concurrently or consecutively by the same judge, so as to avoid the expense of having the same issues tried twice and the risk that there will be inconsistent findings of fact in the two actions. Counsel for PGA also points out that there is a danger that unless a writ is issued by PGA before 20th February 1981, PGA's claim will be barred by limitation.

The situation in the main action, as I understand it, is that as between Berkeley and the defendants pleadings are closed, subject to compliance with certain outstanding requests for particulars, but that the defences to certain third party statements of claim have yet to be delivered. Discovery is not yet complete. It is unlikely that an action of this complexity, and with matters of pleading and discovery as yet incomplete, will be ready for trial by 20th February 1981.

The objections to leave

In an affidavit sworn by Mr David Francis Campbell Evans, a partner in Wilde Sapte, the solicitors instructed by the liquidators to act for Berkeley, a number of objections are raised to the grant of leave to bring the proposed action. With one exception they appear to me to be without substance, and I can deal with them very briefly.

First, it is said that s 54 is designed to protect a company and its creditors from the misuse of a company's assets in financing transactions involving its own share capital, and that as Mr Angus, who signed the letter relied on in the proposed action, participated in the alleged breaches of s 54, it would be inequitable to allow an action to proceed founded on that letter, which will result, if successful, in a sum equal to any moneys recovered by Berkeley from Atlantic being in return recovered from Berkeley by PGA. That objection is, I think, wholly misconceived. There is no suggestion that PGA or anyone connected with PGA was in any way involved in the breaches of s 54 or had any knowledge or failed to make any reasonable inquiry that would have revealed those breaches. I can see nothing inequitable in allowing PGA to rely on a representation that Berkeley was indebted to Atlantic as founding a claim for damages if PGA can show further that because the loan infringed s 54, the statement was false, and secondly, that PGA was entitled to rely, and did rely, on it in entering into the Atlantic share agreement.

Second, it is said that Berkeley has no assets available to defend the proposed action, and that if PGA obtains judgment in default of appearance or defence and as a result PGA is entitled to rank as an unsecured creditor, then the depositors on whose behalf the Secretary of State for Trade has intervened by bringing the main action will receive a much reduced dividend instead of the whole, or substantially the whole, of their deposits. It is said that in these circumstances the proposed action 'if allowed to proceed at this stage will effectively frustrate the entire purpose of the main proceedings'. In so far as this objection is founded on Berkeley's inability to finance its defence to the proposed action, I will return to it later in this judgment. In so far as the objection is founded on the more general proposition that no proceedings should be allowed which might diminish the fund available to meet the claims of Berkeley's depositors, it is in my judgment also misconceived. The fact that the transactions attacked in the main action have had the practical result of stripping Berkeley of assets derived originally from depositors, leaving nothing to answer their claims, or even to finance litigation to remedy the wrong to Berkeley, and indirectly the depositors, no doubt founded the decision of the Secretary of State for Trade that it was in the public interest that the main action should be brought. But the main action is brought on behalf of Berkeley and not on behalf of the depositors, and any moneys recovered in the main action will, after payment of costs not recovered from the defendants, form part of the assets of Berkeley to be administered in the winding up. It would, I think, be quite wrong to refuse leave under s 231 in order to prefer one class of creditor to a claimant innocent of participation in or of knowledge, actual or constructive, of any misuse of the company's moneys. Nor, if it were relevant, do I see how the moral claims of depositors, many of whom were no doubt attacted by the lure of very high rates of interest, are to be weighed against the claims of PGA which, on the evidence before me, appears to have taken part in a rescue operation designed to protect holders of policies issued by Atlantic.

Third, it is said that in the absence of any allegation that Berkeley knew or ought to have known that PGA was contemplating the purchase of Atlantic or its assets (and there is no such specific allegation in the draft statement of claim in the proposed action) the proposed action is bound to fail. I do not think it would be right to refuse leave on that ground. The claim in the proposed action is that Berkeley owed a duty of care to anyone who might rely on accounts of Berkeley which had been drawn on the basis that Berkeley owed Atlantic the sum of £400,000, and that that duty extended to anyone who might purchase the shares of Atlantic. The question whether Berkeley's duty of care extended so far is not one which can be answered in the abstract. It can only be answered in the full context of the circumstances as they existed at the time and of the facts known to Mr Angus and others concerned with Berkeley's affairs who were aware of the inquiry and the answer to it.

Fourth, it is said that there would be no advantage to the parties in having the two actions tried together, in particular no substantial saving of costs, and that, by contrast, if Atlantic were to succeed in its defence or to recover against other defendants or third parties, costs incurred in prosecuting the proposed action will have been thrown away. On the material before me the advantage of having the two actions tried together appear to me to be overwhelming. The factual background of the two actions is the same and many of the issues overlap, in particular the defence of estoppel raised in Williams & Glyn's defence. It appears to me unlikely that there will be any further documentary evidence relevant to the proposed action which is not relevant to the main action, and the attendance of most, if not all, the witnesses whose oral evidence will be needed at the trial of the proposed action will also be required at the trial of the main action. Of course, if Atlantic successfully defend the main action or recover any moneys they are ordered to pay Berkeley from other defendants or third parties, PGA will fail to establish damage and the proposed action will fail. That is a feature which the proposed action shares with many of the third party proceedings and with PGA's action against Holdings and Mr Pollard. To that extent PGA will be at risk as to costs. It is not in my judgment a reason for refusing leave. I cannot on this application decide whether the main action and the proposed action should be tried concurrently or consecutively before the same judge. That question will have to be decided in applications for directions in the main action and the proposed action. But in my opinion it would be wrong to preclude that course by refusing leave to PGA to commence and prosecute the proposed action.

In my judgment, therefore, there is no substance in these objections. However, in the course of argument two other objections were raised. The first objection made is that the claim in the proposed action being a claim for unliquidated damages in tort would not be capable, even if liquidated by judgment, of being proved in the winding up so long as Berkeley is insolvent. It is said, with some force, that there is no real prospect that even if Berkeley succeeds in all the claims in the main action and recovers the £112,000 realised and paid to Atlantic in September 1974, the £513,000 paid to Celoware in December 1974 and the £19,000 realised and paid to Atlantic in January 1975 (and that, apart from interest, appears to be the maximum that Berkeley could recover) Berkeley will still be unable to meet in full the costs and expenses of the winding up and the claims of depositors (including interest, so far as permissible under the bankruptcy rules). Therefore, it is said it would be futile and a waste of money to allow the proposed action to proceed. That objection was raised for the first time in argument. It is inconsistent with the first of the two objections I have already considered, which are founded on the assumption that, in the words of Mr Evans's affidavit, if PGA recovers judgment in the proposed action it 'would be entitled to rank as an unsecured creditor in Berkeley's liquidation and prove into the fund recovered by the liquidators'.

The second objection is that Berkeley has no moneys with which to defend the proposed action. It is said that the Secretary of State for Trade has power to bring the main action in the name of, and on behalf of, Berkeley but no power to spend public money in defending proceedings against Berkeley. In those circumstances it is said that it would be impractical for the main action and the proposed action to be heard together or consecutively, and that if leave is granted, it should be limited to the commencement of the proposed action. I will deal with these two objections in turn.

The first objection

Section 316 of the Companies Act 1948 reads as follows:

> 'In every winding up (subject, in the case of insolvent companies, to the application in accordance with the provisions of this Act of the law of bankruptcy) all debts payable on a contingency, and all claims against the company, present or future, certain or contingent, ascertained or sounding only in damages, shall be admissible to proof against the company, a just estimate being made, so far as possible, of the value of such debts or claims as may be subject to any contingency or sound only in damages, or for some other reason do not bear a certain value.'

Save for the words in brackets at the beginning of that section, s 316 reproduces in substantially the same words s 158 of the Companies Act 1862. A similar section has appeared in every intermediate Companies Act. It is clearly wide enough to admit to proof an unliquidated claim for damages for tort: see *Wyley v Exhall Coal Mining Co* (1864) 33 Beav 538, 55 ER 478, a case decided under the 1862 Act. Under the 1862 Act proof and adjudication of claims and liabilities were governed by a general order made by the Lord Chancellor, the Master of the Rolls and the Vice-Chancellor pursuant to powers conferred by the 1862 Act. In the administration of the affairs of an insolvent company the court followed the practice of the Court of Chancery in administering an insolvent estate. The practice of the Court of Chancery in administering an insolvent estate was altered by s 10 of the Supreme Court of Judicature (1873) Amendment Act 1875 which amended and re-enacted s 25(1) of the Supreme Court of Judicature Act 1873 which had never come into operation. Section 10, so far as material, reads as follows:

> 'Sub-section one of clause twenty-five of the principal Act is hereby repealed, and instead thereof the following enactment shall take effect; (that is to say), in the administration by the Court of the assets of any person who may die after the commencement of this Act, and whose estate may prove to be insufficient for the payment in full of his debts and liabilities, and in the winding up of any company under the Companies Acts, 1862 and 1867, whose assets may prove to be insufficient for the payment of its debts and liabilities and the costs of winding up, the same rules shall prevail and be observed as to the respective rights of secured and unsecured creditors, and as to debts and liabilities provable, and as to the valuation of annuities and future and contingent liabilities respectively, as may be in force for the time being under the Law of Bankruptcy with respect to the estates of persons adjudged bankrupt; and all persons who in any such case would be entitled to prove for and receive dividends out of the estate of any such deceased person, or out of the assets of any such company, may come in under the decree or order for the administration of such estate, or under the winding up of such company, and make such claims against the same as they may respectively be entitled to by virtue of this Act.'

Section 10, so far as it related to companies, was repealed by the Companies (Consolidation) Act 1908 and reproduced in s 207 of that Act. Section 10 was finally repealed by the Administration of Estates Act 1925,. so far as it related to the administration of insolvent estates, and was replaced by s 34(1) of that Act. Section 207 of the 1908 Act was replaced by s 262 of the 1929 Act and in turn by s 317 of the 1948 Act.

Section 206 of the 1908 Act reproduced s 158 of the Companies Act 1862, except for the addition of the words '(subject in the case of insolvent companies to the application in accordance with the provisions of this Act of the law of bankruptcy)'. Section 206 was in turn replaced by s 261 of the 1929 Act, and is now s 316 of the 1948 Act which I have already read, and which is in the same terms as s 206 of the 1908 Act.

Section 317 which, as I have said, replaced or re-enacted sections of the Companies Act which replaced s 10, is not in precisely the same terms as s 10. It reads as follows:

> 'In the winding up of an insolvent company registered in England the same rules

> shall prevail and be observed with regard to the respective rights of secured and
> unsecured creditors and to debts provable and to the valuation of annuities and a
> future and contingent liabilities as are in force for the time being under the law of
> bankruptcy in England with respect to the estates of persons adjudged bankrupt,
> and all persons who in any such case would be entitled to prove for and receive
> dividends out of the assets of the company may come in under the winding up and
> make such claims against the company as they respectively are entitled to by virtue
> of this section.' b

Section 10 of the 1875 Act gave rise to many conflicting decisions. The problem was
whether s 10 merely swept away the well-known rule in Chancery known as the rule in
Mason v Bogg (1837) 2 My & Cr 443, 40 ER 709 that a secured creditor could realise his
security and prove against the estate for the whole of his debt, subject only to the
limitation that he could not recover more than 20 shillings in the pound; he was not
bound (as is a secured creditor under the bankruptcy rules) to elect to abandon his c
security and prove for the whole debt or to realise his security and prove for the
balance. The rule in *Mason v Bogg* was applied to the liquidation of an insolvent company
under the 1862 Act: see the decision of the Court of Appeal in *Kellock's Case* (1868) LR 3
Ch App 769. Initially the court gave a narrow interpretation to s 10 and held in a
number of cases that s 10 reversed *Mason v Bogg* and *Kellock's Case*, but did not introduce
into the administration of insolvent estates or into the winding up of insolvent companies d
the other rules applicable to the administration of the property of a bankrupt. Thus in
Re Withernsea Brickworks (1880) 16 Ch D 337 at 341 James LJ said:

> 'The Legislature, finding a well-known difference in the law as to proof by a
> secured creditor in administration by the Court of Chancery and in bankruptcy,
> intended to introduce the bankruptcy rule that a secured creditor could only prove e
> for the balance of his debt after deducting the value of his security.'

Lush LJ said (at 343):

> 'The whole object of sect. 10 as it appears to me, was to make this rule in
> bankruptcy applicable to administration of the assets of deceased persons, and to
> winding-up.' f

But in later decisions the court gave a wider construction to s 10. In *Re Whitaker*
[1901] 1 Ch 9, which is the watershed between the old and the modern construction of
s 10 and its successors, the question was whether s 10 introduced into the administration
of an insolvent estate the old bankruptcy rule that voluntary creditors are to be paid pari
passu with creditors for value and not, as under the Chancery practice, postponed to
them. In explaining the effect of s 10 Rigby LJ said (at 12): g

> 'Sect. 10 provides (among other things) that the rules for the time being in force
> in bankruptcy as to debts provable shall apply in the administration by the High
> Court of the estate of a deceased insolvent. Upon the true construction of the words,
> I think they do not simply deal with the proof of debts. The same rules are to
> prevail "as to debts and liabilities provable". I cannot read those words as meaning h
> simply "as to the proof of debts and liabilities". I think they mean that whatever
> general rules are in force in the Court of Bankruptcy for the time being with regard
> to debts and liabilities provable shall apply in the administration of insolvent estates
> in Chancery. Now undoubtedly in bankruptcy (it does not matter how it came
> about) the rule as to debts and liabilities provable is that all those debts and liabilities,
> whether contracted for value or not, shall rank pari passu. I think we should be j
> cutting down unduly the plain words of s. 10 if we were to allow the old rule of the
> Court of Chancery to override in the present case the existing rule in regard to
> bankruptcy.'

Similarly, Vaughan Williams LJ said (at 12–13):

> 'One thing is quite clear, namely, that the section does not mean that in all respects the results of a bankruptcy, and the consequent administration of the estate, and the results of the death of an insolvent and the consequent administration of his estate, are to be absolutely identical. It was long ago decided that, notwithstanding s. 10, you must still apply only in bankruptcy those bankruptcy rules, whether statutory or otherwise, which go to augment the bankrupt's assets as against third persons. So far it is plain that there is intended to be a distinction between bankruptcy and the consequent administration and death followed by administration of the insolvent estate of the deceased. The section itself seems to me to point to an intention that the uniformity (if I may use the expression) shall be limited to some particular subjects, because it says "the same rules shall prevail and be observed as to the respective rights of secured and unsecured creditors, and as to debts and liabilities provable, and as to the valuation of annuities and future and contingent liabilities respectively". The section specifies four heads as to which uniformity is for the future to prevail. And, in my view, we have in construing it to determine what are the limits of the four heads specified, and then to see whether this rule of administration in Chancery, whereby voluntary creditors were postponed to creditors for value, is still to prevail.'

That, of course, is not in any way a binding authority on the proposition before me, but applying the principle there stated, and indeed construing the language of s 10, unfettered by any presumption that it was intended only to reverse the rule in *Mason v Bogg*, it is to my mind plain that s 10 and its successor section, now s 317, restricts debts provable in the winding up of an insolvent company to those which are provable under the bankruptcy law, and that only those persons who would be entitled to prove for and be entitled to dividends out of the assets of a bankrupt are entitled to prove in the winding up.

I turn, therefore, to consider what debts and liabilities are capable of proof in bankruptcy.

Section 30 of the Bankruptcy Act 1914 reads as follows:

> '(1) Demands in the nature of unliquidated damages arising otherwise than by reason of a contract, promise, or breach of trust shall not be provable in bankruptcy.
>
> '(2) A person having notice of any act of bankruptcy available against the debtor shall not prove under the order for any debt or liability contracted by the debtor subsequently to the date of his so having notice.
>
> '(3) Save as aforesaid, all debts and liabilities, present or future, certain or contingent, to which the debtor is subject at the date of the receiving order, or to which he may become subject before his discharge by reason of any obligation incurred before the date of the receiving order, shall be deemed to be debts provable in bankruptcy . . .'

Subsection (5) gives to any person aggrieved by any estimate by the trustee in bankruptcy a right to appeal to the court, and sub-ss (6) and (7) read:

> '(6) If, in the opinion of the court, the value of the debt or liability is incapable of being fairly estimated, the court may make an order to that effect, and thereupon the debt or liability shall, for the purposes of this Act, be deemed to be a debt not provable in bankruptcy.
>
> '(7) If, in the opinion of the court, the value of the debt or liability is capable of being fairly estimated, the court may direct the value to be assessed before the court itself without the intervention of a jury . . .'

This section is in substantially the same terms as s 31 of the Bankruptcy Act 1869 which it replaced. The only material difference is that the exception of claims for damages for breach of trust from the general exclusion of demands in the nature of unliquidated damages does not appear in the 1869 Act. As amended, sub-s (1) appears to exclude from proof only unliquidated claims for damages in tort. The rule as to tort before the 1869 Act was that damages in an action for tort were not a provable debt *a* unless judgment had actually been signed before adjudication. Section 31 preserved that rule. It was a rule which frequently operated to the benefit of a plaintiff who had not obtained judgment and who wished to preserve his claim against the defendant and to enforce it after discharge. Thus in *Ex parte Baum* (1874) LR 9 Ch App 673 an action was started by a firm of bankers against two defendants who carried on business as commission agents. The action was started on 3rd September 1873. The plaintiffs *b* claimed first, damages for breach of contract in refusing to accept certain bills, and secondly, damages for fraudulent misrepresentation. The defendants put in a defence, but before trial the defendants filed a petition for liquidation by arrangement of the affairs of the firm under the procedure in s 125 of the 1869 Act, which had the same effect for present purposes as a petition for adjudication. The defendants then applied to the registrar to restrain the plaintiffs from proceeding with the action. The registrar had *c* power to make such an order if, and only if, the claim in the action was one in respect of a liability provable in the liquidation. It was held by the Court of Appeal that the claim, so far as it was founded on a fraudulent misrepresentation, was not so provable, and that accordingly the court had no power to restrain the plaintiffs from bringing the action, though the plaintiffs were put to their election between proceeding on the claim for damages in tort and proving for damages in breach of contract. *d*

Similarly, in *Re Newman* (1876) 3 Ch D 494 the plaintiff, a Miss Brooke, commenced proceedings against an omnibus proprietor, Newman, for damages for a tort committed by one of his servants. The action was tried on 14th January 1876, when the plaintiff obtained a verdict for £50. The defendant moved to have the verdict entered for him. That motion was heard and refused on 26th April. The court ordered judgment to be entered for the plaintiff for £50 and costs. On 6th May, before judgment was signed, the *e* defendant filed a liquidation petition. An order was made by the bankruptcy registrar restraining further proceedings by the plaintiff until after the first meeting of the defendant's creditors. On 3rd June the creditors resolved to accept a composition, and a second meeting was called for 13th June to confirm the resolution. On 9th June the injunction against further proceedings by the plaintiff was continued until after 17th June, but with liberty for the plaintiff to sign judgment in the action. On 13th June the *f* resolution for a composition was confirmed. On 17th June the plaintiff signed judgment for £50 damages and £83 10s 4d for costs. Later the registrar made an order perpetually restraining the plaintiff from proceeding on the judgment. The effect of the order was to leave her without remedy. She could neither prove nor enforce her judgment. An appeal by the plaintiff was allowed. James LJ said (at 496):

> 'The first clause of sect. 31 contains clear negative words, and was, I think, meant *g* to preserve the old law with regard to the proof in bankruptcy of damages for a tort. Certainly, under the old law damages in an action of tort were not a provable debt in bankruptcy until judgment had been signed. The old law as to that remains, in my opinion, now exactly as it was. Unless judgment has been signed damages for a tort are not included in the second clause of the section commencing with the words "save as aforesaid"; and when judgment for such damages is signed *h* after the adjudication the amount of the judgment is not a debt or liability to which the bankrupt is subject at the date of the adjudication, or to which he has become subject afterwards by reason of any obligation incurred previously to the adjudication'

Mellish LJ added (at 497): *j*

> '... the costs, being a mere addition or appurtenance to the damages, must follow the same rule as that to which they are attached.'

That is still the law, though today judgment is entered and not signed.

Counsel for the liquidators founded his argument on this principle of bankruptcy law. The argument, shortly stated, is that a debt or liability is provable in the winding

up of an insolvent company only if it would have been provable if the company had been
a an individual and if a receiving order had been made. A claim for damages for tort is not
so provable unless liquidated by judgment entered before the date of the receiving
order. Similarly, it is said, the provisions of s 317 'must be treated as applicable to every
company in liquidation unless and until it is shewn that its assets are in fact sufficient for
the payment of its liabilities and the costs of winding up': see per Lord Macnaghten in
Fryer v Ewart [1902] AC 187 at 192, a decision on s 10 of the 1875 Act approving *Re*
b *Milan Tramways Co* (1884) 25 Ch D 587. Therefore, it is said, until it is shown that the
assets of a company which is being wound up by the court are sufficient for the payment
of its debts and liabilities and the costs of winding up, no claim for unliquidated damages
for tort can be proved. By contrast, once it is shown that the company is solvent, the
claim for unliquidated damages for tort becomes provable under s 316 of the 1948 Act
though, unlike bankruptcy, the leave of the court is required under s 231 before the
c claim can be liquidated by judgment in proceedings whether commenced before or after
the winding up.

In support of this argument counsel for the liquidators relied on a statement in Gower
on Modern Company Law (4th Edn, 1979, p 730) which reads as follows:

> 'Prima facie, therefore, every sort of claim, whether in contract, tort or otherwise,
> can be proved. This is, however, subject to an important limitation in the case of
> d insolvent companies, for there "the same rules shall prevail . . . with regard to the
> respective rights of secured and unsecured creditors, and to debts provable, and to
> valuation of . . . future and contingent liabilities" as are in force under the law of
> bankruptcy. This does not have the effect of incorporating all the rules of
> bankruptcy law, but only those applying to the three matters specifically
> mentioned. But it does mean that a debt not provable in bankruptcy cannot be
> e proved, and this excludes claims for unliquidated damages arising otherwise than
> by reason of contract or breach of trust, for example, unliquidated damages in tort.
> It is therefore vital that a creditor whose sole claim is in tort, should not delay in
> enforcing his rights against a company if its financial stability is in doubt. Should
> it go into liquidation before his claim has become liquidated by a judgment or
> agreement he will be barred unless it proves to be solvent. His position is even
> f worse than in the case of bankruptcy, where his claim, not being provable, will not
> be ended by the bankrupt's discharge so that he could sue him thereafter. This,
> however, will not be open to him in the case of a company's winding up, for the
> company will cease to exist.'

The only other textbook which deals specifically with this point is Pennington's
g Company Law (4th Edn, 1979), where the opposite view is taken. The author says
(p 763):

> 'The debts and liabilities which may be proved under the Bankruptcy Act 1914,
> are as widely defined as those which may be proved in the winding up of a solvent
> company, save that in bankruptcy claims for unliquidated damages arising otherwise
> than by reason of a contract, promise or breach of trust, are not provable.
> h Consequently, claims for torts committed by an insolvent company cannot be
> proved in its winding up, but, with leave of the court when necessary, the claimant
> may sue the company, and then prove in the winding up for the amount of his
> judgment debt.'

No authority was cited by counsel for the liquidators or is cited by Professor Gower or
j Professor Pennington. However, the most recent edition of Williams on Bankruptcy
(19th Edn, 1979, p 161) refers in the notes on s 30 of the 1914 Act to a decision of Eve J
in *Re Great Orme Tramways Co* (1934) 50 TLR 450 where the appellant, a confectioner's
assistant, on holiday in Llandudno bought a return ticket on a tramway to the top of the
Great Orme. On the return journey the tram got out of control and she was seriously
injured. An order for the compulsory winding up of the company was made and a proof
of debt was lodged claiming damages for tortious negligence on the part of the

defendants' servants. Later a proof was lodged claiming damages for breach of a contract to carry her safely and securely. The liquidator rejected both claims in reliance on s 262 a
of the Companies Act 1929, the immediate precursor of s 317, and on s 30 of the Bankruptcy Act 1914. Eve J said (at 450):

> '... he must allow the appellant to substitute the proof based on contract lodged in November for the proof of August in tort. It seemed rather an extraordinary thing to have an inquiry in winding-up Chambers as to the damages which Miss Beesley had sustained, but there must be such an inquiry. All the claims arising out b
> of the accident and provable in the liquidation must be proved in order to ascertain what was the total amount of them. There must be an affidavit by the liquidator showing the total assets and the amount of the claims, what was the possible dividend, and, therefore, for what amounts the claims should be admitted.'

Eve J thus assumed that in the winding up of an insolvent company an unliquidated c
claim for damages in tort could not be proved, but he did not decide the point. There was no argument to the contrary. The only point decided was that the appellant, if she abandoned the claim in tort, could prove the coextensive claim for breach of contract, a proposition which is, of course, well established in bankruptcy law: see *Re Hopkins* (1902) 86 LT 676, a case which was cited to Eve J. The decision is, therefore, not even of persuasive authority. d

The argument elaborated by counsel for the liquidators is at first sight a formidable one, but it leads, as it seems to me, to absurd consequences. The following example will suffice as an illustration. Suppose that a three-quarters majority of the members of a company, with assets of £100,000, and liquidated debts of £50,000, and no other liabilities except an unliquidated claim for damages in tort in respect of which proceedings have been commenced against the company, resolves by special resolution e
that the company be wound up by the court. The majority might, if counsel's argument is right, pass such a resolution with a view to stultifying the plaintiff's claim. The claim, let it be supposed, is one which the company has been advised is almost certain to succeed and is for damages which are likely with costs to exceed £75,000. If the value of that claim is taken into account, the company is insolvent. If counsel's argument is well founded, the consequence must be that the claim in tort, being unliquidated at the f
commencement of the winding up, cannot be proved. But it is still a liability of the company within s 316 and, as it seems to me, a liability the existence of which would prevent a distribution of surplus assets to the contributories pursuant to s 302. Is the company then solvent or insolvent? The question appears to present a paradox worthy of Epimenides. Both an affirmative and a negative answer lead to a contradiction. If the company is treated as an insolvent company to which s 317 applies the claim is excluded, g
and if the claim is excluded the company is solvent. If the company is treated as a solvent company to which s 316 applies, the admission of the claim makes the company insolvent. Counsel's preferred answer, as I understand his argument, is that the claim in tort must be disregarded altogether and the surplus assets distributed amongst the contributories. If that is right then the effect of s 317 is not so much paradoxical as mischievous. It may be that, faced with such a situation, the plaintiff in the action for h
unliquidated damages in tort could limit his claim to such a sum as with the costs and expenses of the winding up would not exceed the surplus assets of the company, and then prove under s 316. But if counsel's argument is well founded, there is no way in which he can prove and receive a dividend pari passu with other creditors.

The consequences which flow from a literal application of the bankruptcy rules in the winding up of an insolvent company are so absurd as to compel the conclusion that the j
bankruptcy rules must be modified in some way if they are to fit into the scheme of the winding up of an insolvent company. As Vaughan Williams LJ said in *Re Whitaker* [1901] 1 Ch 9 at 12, in the passage I have already cited:

> '... the section does not mean that in all respects the results of a bankruptcy, and the consequent administration of the estate, and the results of the death of an

> insolvent and the consequent administration of his estate, are to be absolutely *a* identical.'

The fallacy in the construction of counsel for the liquidators lies, I think, in equating a winding up order and receiving order, and treating s 317 as excluding a claim in tort which has not been liquidated by judgment before the commencement of the winding up. A receiving order operates both to protect the debtor from claims in respect of debts *b* provable in bankruptcy and to preserve his assets for distribution amongst creditors whose debts are so provable. Once a receiving order has been made then, unless the receiving order is stayed or rescinded, the bankrupt's assets must be administered in accordance with the statutory scheme. If an order is made for a company to be wound up by the court, it will be treated as an insolvent company until it is shown that its assets are in fact sufficient for the payment of its liabilities and the costs and expenses of the winding up: see *Fryer v Ewart* [1902] AC 187 and *Re Milan Tramways Co* (1884) 25 Ch D *c* 587 (those were decisions on s 10 of the 1875 Act, which applied to a case when the company's assets 'may prove to be insufficient for the payment of its debts and liabilities and the costs of winding up', and that language is more susceptible of the construction adopted in those cases than s 317 and the predecessor sections in the 1908 and 1929 Acts which refer simply to 'the winding up of an insolvent company'. However, those cases have always been treated as equally applicable to the sections of the Companies Act *d* which replaced s 10). On the other hand, although a company which is being wound up by the court is to be treated initially as insolvent, the company may later be shown to be solvent; then 'the court must be deemed to be no longer winding up an insolvent company but to be winding up a company which is solvent': see *Re Fine Industrial Commodities Ltd* [1956] Ch 256 at 262 per Vaisey J. Similarly, a company which is shown in the course of the winding up to be solvent may become again insolvent because the *e* surplus of assets over liabilities is insufficient to meet the costs and expenses of the winding up: see *Re Leng* [1895] 1 Ch D 652 at 658, [1895–9] All ER Rep 1210 at 1213 per Lindley LJ (that was a case concerning the administration of an insolvent estate, but this principle would be equally applicable to the winding up of an insolvent company). A proof in respect of a claim for damages for tort which is unliquidated at the commencement of the winding up cannot be first admissible and then excluded and, *f* perhaps, become again admissible according to the vicissitudes of the company's apparent financial health.

The answer to counsel for the liquidators' argument in my judgment is that s 317 does not operate to exclude a claim for damages for tort which has not been liquidated at the commencement of the winding up but only to exclude from proof a claim for damages for tort which has not been liquidated by judgment at the time when the claimant comes *g* in to prove. In the meantime, although the claim has not been liquidated by judgment, then, if the amount of the claim is such that if made good it will have the result that the company will be insolvent, the presumption that the company is insolvent cannot be rebutted and no return can be made to contributories. That produces a sensible and workable scheme. The claimant will not be entitled to disturb prior distributions to *h* other creditors although, as regards any undistributed assets, he will be entitled to a dividend out of the undistributed assets equal to dividends distributed to those whose proof has already been accepted. That has always been the rule in bankruptcy. Vaughan Williams LJ said in *Re McMurdo* [1902] 2 Ch 684 at 699:

> 'Now, according to my experience of bankruptcy practice, there never has been any doubt as to the right of a creditor, whether he is a secured creditor or whether *j* he is an unsecured creditor, to come in and prove at any time during the administration, provided only that he does not by his proof interfere with the prior distribution of the estate amongst the creditors, and subject always, in cases in which he has to come in and ask for leave to prove, to any terms which the Court may think it just to impose; and, of course, in every case in which there has been a time limited for coming in to prove, although the lapse of that time without proof

> does not prevent the creditor from proving afterwards, subject to the conditions which I have mentioned, in every such case he can only come in and prove with the leave of the Court. If that is so, leave must be granted upon such terms as the Court may think just.'

The rule is now embodied in s 65 of and para 14 of Sch 2 to the 1914 Act. In *Re McMurdo* the bankruptcy rule was applied pursuant to s 10 of the Supreme Court of Judicature (1873) Amendment Act 1875, the administration of an insolvent estate. It must apply equally to the winding up of an insolvent company.

If that is the true effect of s 317, then consideration of s 317 must weigh heavily in favour of leave being given. PGA will be unable to prove until its claim has been liquidated by a judgment. The claim having been clearly formulated, though not yet made in any action, it would be wrong if any distribution were to be made until it has been determined, and it must be in the interests of the other creditors of Berkeley that it be determined at the earliest possible date.

There is one other matter which I should mention. It is not easy to see why an unliquidated claim for damages in tort should alone be excluded from proof in bankruptcy. It seems that historically the rule was that whenever damages were—

> 'contingent and uncertain, as in some cases of demands founded in contract, and in all cases of torts, where both the right to any damages at all, and also the amount of them, depend upon circumstances of which a jury alone can properly judge, and which, therefore, it requires the intervention of a jury to ascertain, such damages are not capable of proof under a commission.'

(See the passage in Eden's Bankruptcy Law (1st Edn, 1860, p 129), cited in Williams on Bankruptcy (16th Edn, 1949, p 155).) The rule was gradually relaxed by the courts in cases where the damages could be easily ascertained. The rule was further relaxed by s 153 of the Bankruptcy Act 1861; then, as regards all claims for damages for breach of contract, by s 30(1) of the Bankruptcy Act 1869; and then, as regards claims for damages for breach of trust, by s 30(1) of the Bankruptcy Act 1914. The continued exclusion of unliquidated claims in tort appears to me to be difficult to justify. As the editor of Williams on Bankruptcy observed (16th Edn, 1949, p 156): 'In practice creditors seem to have found no difficulty in swearing to the amount of their claims. A creditor may swear to a certain amount "and upwards".' Claims in contract may be no less difficult of ascertainment and evaluation than claims in tort and, indeed, there are cases where the claim can equally well be formulated for damages for tort or for breach of contract (compare *Re Great Orme Tramways Co* (1934) 50 TLR 450). It is to the modern lawyer anomalous that the question whether a claim is provable in bankruptcy should turn on the technical classification of the form of action. I draw attention to this point because the reform of bankruptcy law is currently being considered by the Cork Committee (the Insolvency Law Review Committee). It is a point which the Cork Committee might wish to consider before it reports.

The second objection

The effect of s 37(3) of the Companies Act 1967, read together with s 170(1) and (3) of the Companies Act 1948, is to give the Secretary of State for Trade a charge on any moneys or property recovered in an action instituted by him under s 37(1) for the costs and expenses of the action; subject to that charge the Secretary of State is liable under s 37(2) of the 1967 Act to indemnify the company in whose name or on whose behalf the claim is brought against any costs or expenses incurred by the Secretary of State and not recovered from other parties. In the present case the Treasury Solicitor acts for the Secretary of State in the main action. The second objection raised is that the Secretary of State has no power under s 37 or otherwise to defend the proposed action. The Secretary of State will have no interest in any moneys recovered which remain after meeting the charge for the costs and expenses of the main action; and the Secretary of State can have no interest in defending the proposed action in order to protect his charge for the costs and expenses of the main action against any damages or costs which may be recovered by

PGA in the proposed action, since the statutory charge will have priority over them. In a these circumstances, it is said, the Crown has no such interest in the subject matter in dispute in the proposed action as would justify the Treasury Solicitor in acting on behalf of Berkeley in its role as defendant to the proposed action: see *Brownsea Haven Properties Ltd v Poole Corpn* [1958] 1 All ER 205 at 208–211, [1958] Ch 574 at 591–594, per Lord Evershed MR. Berkeley has no money with which it can instruct other solicitors to act on its behalf and instruct counsel in relation to the proposed action. Although the b opposition to PGA's present application has, I understand, been financed by the Secretary of State for Trade, counsel for the liquidators made it clear that the Secretary of State, despite his concern to protect depositors from what is represented in Mr Evans's affidavit as an inequitable claim by PGA, takes the view that he has no power to make public money available for that purpose. It is common ground that I would have no jurisdiction to order that Berkeley's costs of defending the proposed action be made a charge on the c sum held by Williams & Glyn's to the account of Atlantic. Further, even if moneys could be made available to finance Berkeley's defence, the fact that the Treasury Solicitor would be unable to act for Berkeley in relation to the proposed action, and that other solicitors and counsel would have to be employed, would largely, if not wholly, destroy any practical benefit that might otherwise have been obtained by allowing the proposed action to proceed to trial in order that an application might be made for the two actions d to be tried together.

The situation is not a very satisfactory one. If the main action had been brought by Berkeley on its own behalf, it would be no answer for Berkeley to say in opposing PGA's application for leave to bring the proposed action that it could not afford to defend it. But the main action is brought on behalf of Berkeley by someone who has no interest in and claims to have no power to finance a defence to an action which, if successful, will e deprive Berkeley of the benefit of its success. This situation may, again, merit further consideration by the legislature. But as the law stands, it produces in my judgment an insuperable objection to permitting the proposed action to proceed to trial before the main action has been heard.

Conclusion

f I was referred by counsel for the liquidators to the judgment of Brightman LJ in *Re Aro Co Ltd* [1980] 1 All ER 1067 at 1076, [1980] Ch 196 at 209 where, giving the judgment of the Court of Appeal, he approved the statement of Vaisey J in *Re Grosvenor Metal Co Ltd* [1950] Ch 63 at 65 that s 325(1)(*c*) of the Companies Act 1948 'seems to give the court a free hand to do what is right and fair according to the circumstances of each case', and held that statement of principle to be equally applicable to the exercise of the g court's discretion under s 231.

In my judgment, unless there are very special circumstances, fairness requires that leave should be given to a litigant who seeks to bring or to continue an action for damages for tort against a company which is being wound up by the court, and which is or may be insolvent. For the liability he seeks to enforce will be admissible for proof if, and only if, liquidated by a judgment before the assets of the company are distributed h in the winding up. That principle must apply a fortiori where, as here, the action may be barred by limitation unless brought promptly and where, as here, it can conveniently be tried together with another related action brought by the company. If matters rested there, I would have no hesitation in granting PGA leave to bring and prosecute the proposed action to judgment leaving PGA to apply in the main action for an order that the two actions be heard together. But I am satisfied that, having regard to the very j special circumstances I have outlined, there is no way in which the main action and the proposed action can be heard together, and that it would be unfair to allow any considerable expense to be incurred in relation to the proposed action until after the main action has been heard. In these circumstances, the only course I can take is to give leave to PGA to issue the writ and serve its statement of claim in the proposed action, and to give leave to Berkeley to serve its defence and to serve any third party proceedings it may be advised to bring. It may be that arrangements can be made without specific

directions for lists of documents to be exchanged, if there are any documents which have
not been already disclosed in the main action. But I must direct that no further step be a
taken in the proposed action without the further leave of the court.

Order accordingly. Leave to appeal to both parties.

Solicitors: *Linklaters & Paines* (for PGA); *Wilde Sapte* (for the liquidators).

b

Jacqueline Metcalfe Barrister.

Re Salmon (deceased), Coard v National Westminster Bank Ltd and others c

CHANCERY DIVISION
SIR ROBERT MEGARRY V-C
12th, 27th JUNE 1980

*Family provision – Time for application – Extension – Refusal of application to extend time –
Originating summons issued 5½ months out of time – Delay caused wholly by plaintiff – No* d
*warning to defendants that claim might be made – Estate already distributed – Whether court
should exercise discretion to extend time – Guidelines on exercise of discretion – Inheritance
(Provision for Family and Dependants) Act 1975, s 4.*

The plaintiff ('the widow') married her husband in 1932 but left him in 1944 after the
marriage proved to be unhappy. The parties never saw each other again although they e
were never divorced. In 1978 the husband died leaving an estate of £75,000. Letters of
administration were granted to a bank on 15th December 1978, and by virtue of s 4[a] of
the Inheritance (Provision for Family and Dependants) Act 1975 the six-month time
limit for making application under the Act for financial provision out of the estate ran
from that date and expired on 15th June 1979. In February 1979 a friend of the widow's
wrote to the bank asking on her behalf for an ex gratia payment in lieu of taking f
proceedings under the 1975 Act, but the bank refused and stated that the widow should
take such action as she was advised. On 2nd April solicitors were instructed on the
widow's behalf, and in the belief that the widow would require legal aid they applied to
a legal aid committee on 24th April. The application was not for an emergency
certificate, and no attempt was made either to warn the bank of pending proceedings or
to institute proceedings before the time limit expired. On 30th July the legal aid g
committee issued a certificate limited to obtaining counsel's opinion. Counsel requested
a conference with the widow which was held on 18th September, and on 4th October the
legal aid committee authorised proceedings under the 1975 Act to be commenced.
Counsel settled the papers on 12th October, but an originating summons was not issued
until 27th November. On 31st October the solicitors wrote to the bank for the first time
to inform it of the proposed proceedings and to ask that if the estate had not been h
distributed the bank should take no action to do so. In fact most of the estate had by then
been distributed. In her summons the widow requested 'the permission of the court'
under s 4 to make her application out of time.

Held – Permission to the widow under s 4 of the 1975 Act to apply out of time for
financial provision out of the estate of her deceased husband would be refused because j
(i) the delay was substantial and the fault was wholly on the widow's side, (ii) there had
been no negotiations while time was running and no warning was given to the bank that
an extension of time was to be sought, (iii) almost all of the estate had been distributed

a Section 4 is set out at p 536 *a*, post.

and no warning had been given to the bank that a claim might be made, (iv) the widow probably had a remedy in negligence against her solicitors, and (v) it would be unjust to the beneficiaries to extend what was a substantive statutory time limit when the widow had such a remedy against her solicitors (see p 538 *e* to *j*, post).

Re Ruttie [1969] 3 All ER 1633 and *Re Gonin* [1977] 2 All ER 720 considered.

Guidelines on the exercise of the court's discretion under s 4 to extend the time limit for making application under the 1975 Act (see p 537 *a* to p 538 *f*, post).

Notes

For the time applying for an order for financial provision out of a deceased person's estate, see 17 Halsbury's Laws (4th Edn) para 1326, and for cases on the subject, see 24 Digest (Reissue) 714–718, *7699–7712*.

For the Inheritance (Provision for Family and Dependants) Act 1975, s 4, see 45 Halsbury's Statutes (3rd Edn) 503.

Cases referred to in judgment

Allen v Sir Alfred McAlpine & Sons Ltd, Bostic v Bermondsey and Southwark Group Hospital Management Committee, Sternberg v Hammond [1968] 1 All ER 543, [1968] 2 QB 229, [1968] 2 WLR 366, CA, Digest (Cont Vol C) 1091, *2262b*.

Cohen v Snelling, Lubovsky v Snelling [1943] 2 All ER 577, [1944] KB 44, 113 LJKB 14, 170 LT 2, CA, 32 Digest (Reissue) 470, *3619*.

Gonin (deceased), Re, Gonin v Garmeson [1977] 2 All ER 720, [1979] Ch 16, [1977] 3 WLR 379, Digest (Cont Vol E) 237, *291a*.

Ruttie (deceased), Re, Ruttie v Saul [1969] 3 All ER 1633, [1970] 1 WLR 89, 24 Digest (Reissue) 718, *7711*.

Simson (deceased), Re, Simson v National Provincial Bank Ltd [1949] 2 All ER 826, [1950] Ch 38, 24 Digest (Reissue) 722, *7741*.

Wright v John Bagnall & Sons Ltd [1900] 2 QB 240, 69 LJQB 551, 82 LT 346, 64 JP 420, CA, 34 Digest (Repl) 657, *4535*.

Originating summons

The plaintiff, Linda Ellen Coard the widow of Alfred Edward Salmon deceased, issued a summons dated 27th November 1979 against the defendants, National Westminster Bank Ltd ('the bank'), the administrator of the deceased's estate Elsie Jameson, Gladys Jameson and Olive Salmon, the beneficiaries named in his will, seeking (i) the permission of the court to make application under the Inheritance (Provision for Family and Dependants) Act 1975 notwithstanding that a period of six months from the date on which the bank had been granted letters of administration had expired, and (ii) an order that such reasonable financial provision as the court thought fit be made for the widow out of the deceased's estate. The facts are set out in the judgment.

P R Simpson for the widow.
J D Martineau for the defendants.

Cur adv vult

27th June. **SIR ROBERT MEGARRY V-C** read the following judgment: This case discloses a sorry story. The plaintiff is a widow who wishes to obtain an order under the Inheritance (Provision for Family and Dependants) Act 1975 that reasonable financial provision be made for her out of the estate of her deceased husband. As a necessary preliminary, she seeks the permission of the court under s 4 of that Act to make her application for an order notwithstanding that six months have elapsed since representation to her husband's estate was first taken out.

The marriage lasted long de jure, but was relatively brief de facto. The parties married on 12th April 1932; he was 37 and she was 24. The marriage was unhappy, and after

1934 sexual intercourse was rare. There were no children of the marriage. The couple
lived over the shop in which the husband, assisted by the wife, sold confectionery, a
newspapers and tobacco, seven days a week. He allowed her only £1 a week for their
food, and her requests for more money led to arguments; he was, she said, very mean.
In 1941 she took the opportunity of working as a Post Office telephonist, despite the
husband's objections; but she still helped in the shop in her spare time, as well as doing
the housework. After a quarrel about money in 1944, she left him and returned to her
parents. She never saw him again. b

In 1945, the wife left her Post Office job, and eventually, in 1953, went to work as a
telephonist on a liner. There she met a Mr Coard, who was employed as a printer on
board, and soon they decided to leave the liner and live together in England. They lived
together as man and wife until he died in October 1974. In 1955 and again in 1962 her
husband had made some moves towards getting a divorce; but nothing came of it, and
not until after Mr Coard died did she discover that she might have been able to take c
divorce proceedings herself.

The husband died on 11th October 1978: he was over 83 years old. He left a will dated
16th June 1961. This appointed two ladies, the second and third defendants, as executors,
made various gifts to them, gave £1,000 to the fourth defendant, who was his sister, and
left the residue equally between the second, third and fourth defendants. One provision
in the will expressed the husband's appreciation of the very great kindness of the second d
and third defendants to him in his loneliness while residing in Portishead. They are
elderly ladies, in their late seventies or early eighties. They renounced probate, and
letters of administration cum testamento annexo were granted to the first defendant ('the
bank'), on 15th December 1978. The net estate, I may say, is of the order of £75,000.

Thus far, there is nothing very striking about the case. Although the marriage existed
in law for over 46 years, it had become unhappy within some two years, and ceased to e
exist with any reality after twelve years; and this was emphasised when the wife formed
her stable relationship with Mr Coard in 1953. The husband never paid the wife
anything after she left him in 1944, and there was nothing which provided any link
between them. The marriage was as dead as a marriage well could be.

When the widow (as I shall now call her) heard of her husband's death, she consulted
a friend of hers, a Mr Chambers, who was a Fellow of the Institute of Legal Executives. f
On 14th February 1979 he wrote to the solicitors for the bank, seeking an ex gratia
payment for the widow 'rather than consider proceedings under the Family Inheritance
Provisions Act'. The bank's solicitors acknowledged this, and then on 23rd March they
wrote to say that the bank was unable to make any payment from the estate, and that the
widow 'must therefore take such action as she is advised'. That letter was not answered;
but on 2nd April the solicitors who are now acting for the widow were instructed by Mr g
Chambers on her behalf with a view to instituting proceedings under the 1975 Act. At
this time, some 2½ months of the six months time limit for commencing proceedings
under the Act remained unexpired: under s 4, the period ran from the grant of letters of
administration on 15th December 1978, and so would expire on 15th June 1979. The
solicitor consulted, a Mr Whyte, says that Mr Chambers told him that the widow did not
have sufficient means to institute proceedings and that she would need legal aid. Mr h
Whyte got the necessary forms signed, and sent them to the local secretary of the legal aid
committee on 24th April. He says that he did not feel it necessary to apply for an
emergency certificate as about four months had passed since the grant of letters of
administration, 'and the urgency of the matter was implicit in the application itself.
Furthermore a claim had already been notified to the Administrators by the said Mr
Albert Chambers'. j

In that state of affairs, 15th June came and went without anything further
happening. Due to pressure of work, Mr Whyte says, the last day for instituting
proceedings passed by unnoticed by him since he had convinced himself that he would
hear from the legal aid committee well within the two months. Far from dealing with
the application within two months, the legal aid committee took over three months. On

30th July, when it was already six weeks too late to commence proceedings without leave of the court, a legal aid certificate limited to obtaining counsel's opinion on the merits was issued, with no authority to institute proceedings. On 8th August the solicitors instructed counsel to advise on the merits, and, not surprisingly, he felt unable to do this without holding a conference at which the widow would be present. This conference took place on 18th September, and the result was that on 4th October the limitation on the widow's legal aid certificate was removed, 'whereafter', says Mr Whyte, 'the writ was issued as quickly as possible'. In fact, counsel informed me that he settled the originating summons and supporting affidavits on 12th October; and not until 27th November, some six weeks later, was the originating summons issued, some 5½ months late.

Perhaps the most striking feature of this sorry tale is what was not done. For nearly seven months after they were first consulted, the solicitors did absolutely nothing to inform the bank that proceedings under the Act were contemplated and, later, in preparation. Not until 31st October 1979, almost seven months after they were instructed, did the solicitors write to the bank's solicitors to tell them of the contemplated proceedings, and ask that, if the estate had not been distributed, they should take no action for the time being. Mr Whyte's statement that a claim had already been notified to the bank by Mr Chambers will stand no examination. No claim under the Act had been made. What had been sought was a mere ex gratia payment, and this had been rejected in language which in terms left it to the widow to take such action as she might be advised. To this there had been no answer, and so the bank was left with no inkling that there might be proceedings under the Act. Once the six months had expired, the bank had consulted their own solicitors in order to discover whether anything more had been heard from the widow; and as nothing had been heard, the bank proceeded to distribute the estate. The bulk of the distribution was carried out between 27th June, shortly after the six months had expired, and 11th November, shortly after the widow's solicitors wrote their first letter to the bank's solicitors.

There are obviously many questions to be asked. One is why the widow's solicitors did not at least write a warning letter to the bank soon after they were instructed. Another is why the legal aid committee took over three months to deal with the application: the six months time limit for applications under the Act must surely be notorious in all legal aid offices. Another is why the widow's solicitors were not stirred into activity when the arrival of the limited legal aid certificate of 30th July must have reminded Mr Whyte of the time limit within which he had so confidently expected the legal aid committee to act. A letter to the bank's solicitors at this stage would at least have put the bank and the beneficiaries on notice of the claim, and perhaps would have suspended the distribution. The evidence before me, however, left these and other questions unanswered; and counsel for the widow was unable to answer them, even on instructions. Mr Whyte, I was told, was believed to be in Scotland, and could not be reached. It therefore seemed to me that the plaintiff ought to be given the opportunity of supplementing the evidence, in case there was some factor affecting her claim which had not been disclosed, and so I allowed just under a week for this purpose. In the event, however, I was told that it was not desired to supplement the evidence, so that it was necessary to deal with the case as it stands. This morning, counsel for the widow informed me that he could make a statement on instructions as to what the solicitor would have said had he sworn an affidavit; but in the circumstances it did not seem to me to be proper to allow to be stated on instructions at the last minute what the solicitor had declined to put in an affidavit which he had been given the opportunity of swearing.

The only question before me is whether the widow should be given permission to apply under the 1975 Act notwithstanding the expiration of the time limit. The statutory time limit has gone through three stages. Under the Inheritance (Family Provision) Act 1938 there was no power to extend the time. The Intestates' Estates Act 1952, Sch 3, gave the court power to extend the six months if satisfied that it would 'operate unfairly' in consequence of certain specified matters, such as the discovery of a will or codicil involving a substantial change in the disposition of the estate. The Family

Provision Act 1966 removed the limitation to specified matters, and substituted a provision which, in essence, is the same as that now contained in s 4 of the 1975 Act. *a* That reads as follows:

> 'An application for an order under section 2 of this Act shall not, except with the permission of the court, be made after the end of the period of six months from the date on which representation with respect to the estate of the deceased is first taken out.' *b*

This gives no guidance whatever to the court as to any principles on which the jurisdiction to extend the time is to be exercised: the words 'except with the permission of the court' could hardly be more neutral. There is, however, some assistance to be obtained from the two authorities which counsel for the widow cited, *Re Ruttie* [1969] 3 All ER 1633, [1970] 1 WLR 89 and *Re Gonin* [1977] 2 All ER 720; the report of the latter case at [1979] Ch 16, I may say, omits what the judge said about the extension of time. *c*

In *Re Ruttie* the plaintiff was six weeks out of time. Substantial negotiations between solicitors had begun well within time, and these included not only possible terms of compromise, but also discussions of a complex issue whether the plaintiff and her deceased husband were Polish so that there was community of property. The plaintiff had also been ill for some weeks during these negotiations, and in the negotiations her solicitors had overlooked the expiry of the time limit. In those circumstances, Ungoed-Thomas *d* J held that time should be extended. If it was not, there would be serious hardship to the plaintiff, who was poor; and the extension would cause no prejudice to the defendant save the loss of the advantage of the time limit, a loss which the statute contemplated by giving the court power to extend the time. The judge pointed out that it was dangerous to establish prematurely any guiding principles without wide experience of cases which could not be envisaged beforehand, and that he was in the early *e* days of the history of the unfettered discretion. (See [1969] 3 All ER 1633 at 1637, [1970] 1 WLR 89 at 93–94.)

The unfettered discretion has now existed for some 14 years; but in that time there has been little reported authority to add to our knowledge on the subject. There is, however, one point in *Re Ruttie* that I think should be emphasised, and that is the existence of the negotiations in that case before the time expired. This, of course, necessarily meant that *f* the defendant was fully aware of the claim within time; but it also had a further possible significance. I will take the Fatal Accidents Act 1846. Section 3 required that any action under the Act 'be commenced' within 12 months of the death. If in negotiations within that time the defendant admitted liability, but the action was not brought until after time had run, the defendant might be precluded from relying on the lapse of time: *Cohen v Snelling, Lubovsky v Snelling* [1943] 2 All ER 577, [1944] KB 44, applying *Wright v John* *g* *Bagnall & Sons Ltd* [1900] 2 QB 240. This point was not discussed in argument, and I shall not pursue it at length. Yet it does seem to me that the existence of negotiations within the time limit is a factor which may point towards extending time under the 1975 Act. If while time is running out you negotiate with a claimant on a basis which accepts liability but disputes quantum, you must not be surprised if the court refuses to allow you to rely on the expiry of time, or if, having power to extend the time, the court *h* exercises it.

Re Gonin was very different from *Re Ruttie*. In *Re Gonin* the application was made nearly 2½ years late, and Walton J said that the only real suggestion why time should be extended was that the plaintiff alleged that her solicitors had given her wrong advice. It was contended that there would be no prejudice to the defendants if time were to be extended; but, said the judge, it is always prejudicial to anybody not to receive money *j* that they are due to receive at the earliest possible moment. Accordingly, an extension of time was refused.

I am anxious not to go further than is proper in attempting to discover guidelines in exercising the court's discretion under s 4. I bear in mind what Ungoed-Thomas J said on this; and in saying what I do, I disclaim any intention to lay down principles, though

I am not sure that it makes it much better to use the term 'guidelines' in place of 'principles'. However, after 14 years I think that some progress can be made towards identifying some guidelines. A number of points seem reasonably plain. The first two are sufficiently supported by *Re Ruttie* [1969] 3 All ER 1633 at 1636, [1970] 1 WLR 89 at 93. First, the discretion is unfettered. No restrictions or requirements of any kind are laid down in the Act. The discretion is thus plainly one that is to be exercised judicially, and in accordance with what is just and proper. Second, I think that the onus lies on the plaintiff to establish sufficient grounds for taking the case out of the general rule, and depriving those who are protected by it of its benefits. Further, the time limit is a substantive provision laid down in the Act itself, and is not a mere procedural time limit imposed by rules of court which will be treated with the indulgence appropriate to procedural rules. The burden on the applicant is thus, I think, no triviality: the applicant must make out a substantial case for it being just and proper for the court to exercise its statutory discretion to extend the time.

In addition to the two points which emerge from *Re Ruttie*, there are others which I think can properly be considered in deciding whether or not to extend time. In my view, a third point is that it must be material to consider how promptly and in what circumstances the applicant has sought the permission of the court after the time limit has expired. This is not, of course, a crude matter of simply looking at the length of time that has been allowed to elapse: it is not a mere matter of comparing, for instance, the six weeks of *Re Ruttie* with the 2½ years of *Re Gonin*. The whole of the circumstances must be looked at, and not least the reasons for the delay, and also the promptitude with which, by letter before action or otherwise, the claimant gave warning to the defendants of the proposed application. Thus if the warning was given within time, but for some good reason the proceedings were not commenced until a short while after time had run, I would expect the applicant's task to be relatively simple. Where there has been some error or oversight, an obvious question is whether the applicant has done all that was reasonably possible to put matters right promptly, and keep the defendants informed. As I have said more than once, it is not only Heaven that helps those who help themselves.

This leads to a fourth point. For the reasons that I have already given, I think that it is obviously material whether or not negotiations have been commenced within the time limit; for if they have, and time has run out while they are proceeding, this is likely to encourage the court to extend the time. Negotiations commenced after the time limit might also aid the applicant, at any rate if the defendants have not taken the point that time has expired.

Fifth, I think that it is also relevant to consider whether or not the estate has been distributed before a claim under the Act has been made or notified. Section 20(1) provides that the Act is not to make a personal representative liable for distributing the estate after the six months has ended on the ground that he ought to have taken account of the possibility that the court might permit an application to be made after the six months; but this provision does not prejudice any power to recover, by reason of the making of an order under the Act, any part of the estate so distributed. The end of the six months thus marks a change from a period when any distribution by the personal representatives is made at their own risk (see *Re Simson (deceased)* [1949] 2 All ER 826, [1950] Ch 38) to a period where there is some statutory protection for a distribution.

So far as the beneficiaries are concerned, there will usually be a real psychological change when the estate is distributed. Before the distribution, they would have only the expectation of payment; and if they are entitled to a share of residue, they will often have a considerable degree of uncertainty as to the amount. After the distribution, they have the money itself, and know the exact amount. If an order is made under the Act, the difference will be the difference between the prospect of receiving in due course less than they had hoped, and on the other hand having something that they had already received and regarded as their own taken away from them. For most people, there is a real difference between the bird in the hand and the bird in the bush. In addition, of course, the beneficiaries are more likely to have changed their position in reliance on the

benefaction if they have actually received it than if it lies merely in prospect. If it is always prejudicial to claimants not to receive money that they are entitled to receive at *a*
the earliest possible moment, it is likely to be even more prejudicial to have taken away from them money that they have actually received and have begun to enjoy. The point is strengthened if they have changed their position in reliance on what they have received, as by making purchases or gifts that they otherwise would not have made. However, I shall not pursue this, as there is no evidence of any change of position in the case before me. *b*

Sixth, I think that it is relevant to consider whether a refusal to extend the time would leave the claimant without redress against anybody. In *Re Gonin* [1977] 2 All ER 720 at 736 Walton J considered the possibility that the plaintiff might sue her solicitors in negligence if in fact it was due to their faulty advice that her claim was not made in time. Although the subject matter is different, there seems to me to be considerable force in the approach to be found in the line of cases associated with the name of *Allen v* *c*
Sir Alfred McAlpine & Sons Ltd [1968] 1 All ER 543, [1968] 2 QB 229, on dismissing actions for want of prosecution. Even if the plaintiff personally is completely blameless, the delays of his or her solicitors must be treated as the delays of the plaintiff, though injustice to the plaintiff will often be avoided by the existence of the plaintiff's right to sue the solicitors for negligence: see particularly per Diplock LJ ([1968] 1 All ER 543 at 553–554, [1968] 2 QB 229 at 256–257). There may appear to be some logical difficulty *d*
in making the decision whether the defendants should escape liability under the 1975 Act depend in any degree on whether the responsibility for the delay was that of the plaintiff personally or was that of the plaintiff's solicitors: the liability of the defendants, it may be said, ought not to depend on the distribution of fault between the plaintiff and his or her solicitors. Nevertheless, however logic may affect the defendants' position, there is a real and plain difference to a plaintiff between having a claim against his or her *e*
solicitors instead of against the defendants, and having no claim against anybody.

I am far from saying that the six considerations that I have stated are exhaustive: plainly they are not. I think, however, that they suffice for the present case. Here, the delay is substantial. It was some 4½ months before the bank was even warned of the proposed proceedings, and a further unexplained month before proceedings were actually commenced. The fault for the delay is wholly on the widow's side: none of the *f*
delay can be laid to the charge of the defendants or of extraneous factors over which the widow had no control. Such explanations of the delay as have been given are inadequate and insubstantial. Even when the widow's solicitors realised that they would have to seek an extension of time, they did nothing prompt either to seek the extension or to warn the bank that they intended to do so. There were, of course, no negotiations either within time or out of time. Further, while the solicitors were delaying, nearly all the *g*
estate was being distributed to the beneficiaries without, of course, any warning that a claim had been made that might result in the beneficiaries having to give back some of the money that they were receiving.

In those circumstances, can the widow be said to have made out a sufficient case for extending a substantive statutory time limit, and not one that is merely procedural, when there lies to hand, if no extension is granted, possible, and indeed probable, *h*
proceedings for negligence against the solicitors who were responsible for the delay and have put forward such unsatisfactory explanations? Would it be just to extend the time so that the beneficiaries must pay (if the claim succeeds) and the solicitors will escape? It seems to me that the answer must be No. Even if the burden on an applicant for an extension of time is less than I have stated it to be, and time should readily be extended, I would give the same answer. *j*

In saying this, it is right that I should make it clear that Mr Whyte's affidavit contains very proper expressions of regret, and an express acceptance of the fact that the widow herself has been guilty of no delay. He has made no attempt to shuffle off responsibility onto others. He referred to the daily pressure of work in an extremely busy office, and there is no reason to doubt this or to underestimate the problems in such an office. Mr

Whyte also stated that it was not until the widow had sworn her affidavit that he realised that she had sufficient means to issue a writ to protect her position pending her application for legal aid: the affidavit shows that she has a maisonette which she bought in 1978 for £7,250, an income of a little over £1,600 a year net of tax and savings of some £220. Mr Whyte said that Mr Chambers had impressed on him that the widow had no means at all. Even if that be accepted to the full, there is much that it does not explain. Thus it does not explain why no letter was written to the bank until the claim was 4½ months out of time: the case would have been so different if only in April the solicitors had sent the bank a simple letter of the type so often seen, stating that the widow was applying for legal aid in order to claim under the Act. Again, if there were thought to be sufficient reasons for not seeking an emergency legal aid certificate initially, there is not a word of explanation why such a certificate was not sought when the legal aid committee at last issued their limited certificate, six weeks after time had expired, and so reminded the solicitors of the widow's claim, and of the self-evident urgency of the matter that Mr Whyte had seen in the application for legal aid.

That brings me to one matter that was relied on both by counsel for the defendants and by counsel for the widow. This is the assertion of counsel for the widow that, despite the net estate having the substantial value of some £75,000, the widow's claim was likely to be small, in view of the history of the marriage. The rival contentions come down to saying on the one hand that as the claim would be small there would be no great hardship to the defendants if it was allowed to proceed, and on the other hand that elderly ladies ought not to be exposed to the worries and uncertainties of litigation when nothing much is being claimed. I can see a certain amount of force in each submission, but nothing that affects the conclusion that I have reached, namely that permission for the widow to make an application under the 1975 Act notwithstanding the expiration of the six months must be refused. I so hold.

There is one matter that I must add. During the hearing I attempted to discover how it was that the legal aid authorities took so long to deal with the widow's application for legal aid, and how it was that they initially issued a certificate which excluded the main thing that was needed promptly, namely legal aid for the commencement of proceedings. Counsel for the widow could give me no information whatever, and Mr Whyte, whose affidavit says nothing about it, has not taken the opportunity that I afforded him of dealing with this, and other matters about which I inquired, in a further affidavit. There is nothing to suggest that the widow's solicitors even asked about it. I do not think it right to leave matters in that state: the widow has been ill-served by the legal profession, and others may suffer in a similar way. Accordingly, I direct that this judgment be transcribed at the public expense, and that the registrar send a copy of the transcript to the secretary of the appropriate legal aid committee, seeking an explanation. When the registrar has received a reply, which I hope will be prompt, I shall consider whether to take any further action, either in court or out. In addition, I have no doubt that counsel for the widow will give her proper advice as to the apparent conflict of interest between her and her solicitors.

Summons dismissed.

Solicitors: *Thomas Boyd Whyte*, Bexleyheath (for the widow); *Hextall, Erskine & Co*, agents for *Cartwrights*, Bristol (for the defendants).

Azza M Abdallah Barrister.

McQuaid v Anderton a

QUEEN'S BENCH DIVISION AT MANCHESTER
LORD WIDGERY CJ, ROSKILL LJ AND HEILBRON J
20th FEBRUARY 1980

Road traffic – Driving – Using driver's controls for purpose of directing movement of car – Accused sitting in driver's seat of car and controlling it while it was being towed – Whether accused 'driving' towed car – Road Traffic Act 1972, s 99(b). b

The appellant, who was disqualified for holding or obtaining a driving licence, sat in the driver's seat of a car while it was being towed by means of a tow rope connected to another vehicle. c The appellant steered the towed car and was able to use its brakes as and when required. He was charged with driving a motor vehicle while disqualified contrary to s 99(*b*)[a] of the Road Traffic Act 1972. At his trial he contended that sitting in the driver's seat of a towed vehicle did not constitute 'driving' for the purposes of s 99. On appeal against conviction,

Held – On the true construction of s 99 of the 1972 Act the essence of 'driving' in the d context of driving while disqualified was the use of the driver's controls in order to direct the movement of the car, the method of propulsion being irrelevant. The appellant had therefore been rightly convicted and his appeal would be dismissed (see p 542 *c* to *e* and p 543 *b* and *e* to *g*, post).

R v MacDonagh [1974] 2 All ER 257 applied.

Dictum of Lord Goddard CJ in *Wallace v Major* [1946] 2 All ER at 88–89 disapproved. e

Notes

For the meaning of 'driving' in the road traffic legislation, see 33 Halsbury's Laws (3rd Edn) 450, para 768, and for cases on the subject, see 45 Digest (Repl) 103, *331–337*.

For the Road Traffic Act 1972, s 99, see 42 Halsbury's Statutes (3rd Edn) 1751.

f

Cases referred to in judgments

Anderson v Transport Department [1964] NZLR 881.

R v MacDonagh [1974] 2 All ER 257, [1974] QB 448, [1974] 2 WLR 529, 138 JP 488, 59 Cr App R 55, CA, Digest (Cont Vol D) 896, *425*.

R v Pearson (8th May 1978, unreported) Crown Court at Bodmin.

R v Roberts [1964] 2 All ER 541, [1965] 1 QB 85, [1964] 3 WLR 180, 128 JP 395, 48 Cr g App R 296, CCA, 45 Digest (Repl) 103, *337*.

Wallace v Major [1946] 2 All ER 87, [1946] KB 473, 115 LJKB 402, 175 LT 84, 110 JP 231, 44 LGR 237, DC, 45 Digest (Repl) 87, *289*.

Case stated

On 29th August 1977 an information was laid by the respondent before the justices for the county of Greater Manchester sitting in Manchester against the appellant, Eugene h Francis McQuaid, that he, being a person disqualified for holding or obtaining a licence to drive, did drive a motor vehicle contrary to s 99 of the Road Traffic Act 1972. At the hearing on 1st November 1972 the magistrates found the appellant to have been 'driving' within the meaning of the 1972 Act and convicted and fined him £3 and endorsed his driving licence. He appealed against his conviction by way of case stated. The facts are j set out in the judgment of Heilbron J.

F E Coles for the appellant.
P J Brennan for the respondent.

---

a Section 99, so far as material, is set out at p 541 *c*, post

HEILBRON J delivered the first judgment at the invitation of Lord Widgery CJ. This is an appeal by way of case stated by the justices for the county of Greater Manchester sitting in Manchester who, on 1st November 1977, convicted the appellant of driving a motor vehicle whilst disqualified within the meaning of s 99 of the Road Traffic Act 1972. He was fined £3 and his driving licence was endorsed.

The justices found the following facts which were not disputed. On 29th August 1977 the appellant was a disqualified driver by order of the court; a motor vehicle was being towed along Matthews Lane, Manchester by another vehicle by means of a tow rope; and the appellant was sitting in the driver's seat of the motor vehicle being towed. Counsel for the appellant conceded that he was steering by means of the vehicle's steering wheel and that the braking system of the towed vehicle was operative.

By s 99 of the Road Traffic Act 1972 it is provided:

> 'If a person disqualified for holding or obtaining a licence ... (*b*) while he is so disqualified drives on a road a motor vehicle ... he shall be guilty of an offence.'

There is no definition in the Act of the word 'drive' or 'drives' and that word clearly encompasses a variety of ways in which a person may be described as 'driving a motor vehicle'.

This activity primarily envisages a person sitting in the driving seat directing and controlling the movement of the vehicle by means of a steering wheel, using the brakes as and when required, the engine being used for propulsion. But that apart, many of the other ways in which persons may be said and have been held to drive, have been considered in authorities covering such widely diverse types of driving as, for example, a man sitting in the driving seat controlling the vehicle by means of the steering wheel and brakes, whilst another person or persons or another car pushes the relevant vehicle. The vehicle in question may be allowed to coast downhill in neutral with the engine switched off, but still with the person sitting in the car at the steering wheel with his foot at the ready, so as to be able to apply the brakes. There are instances of a person being held to be a driver though not sitting in the driving seat but exercising sufficient, though not necessarily full, control from the passenger seat so as to cast himself in the role of a driver.

The matter is not devoid of authority and reliance has been placed by counsel for the appellant in his most helpful submission on the case of *Wallace v Major* [1946] 2 All ER 87, [1946] KB 473, where, in a case concerned with a charge of dangerous driving, the respondent, who was at the steering wheel of a broken-down car on tow by another car, was acquitted by the justices. Lord Goddard CJ held, when the matter came before him by way of case stated, that, first of all, and this was the prime matter with which he was concerned, s 121 of the Road Traffic Act 1930 did not apply because the provision in that section contemplated two persons being in charge of the same vehicle and the appellant was not a driver, in any event within the meaning of that Act. Counsel has referred us to the judgment of Lord Goddard CJ in which he stated that in his view the person in the driving seat of a towed vehicle could not be described as a driver. One reason was that, although he was controlling it to some extent, he did not have full control, and, another, that he could not retain a full view of the road and traffic ahead. Lord Goddard CJ also referred to the latter difficulty arising under the Motor Vehicles (Construction and Use) Regulations 1941, SR & O 1941 No 398.

Counsel submitted that in reliance on the decision in *Wallace v Major* the appellant should have been acquitted.

The matter was, however, recently and authoritatively considered by the full Court of Appeal, Lord Widgery CJ, Scarman LJ, Thesiger, Bristow and May JJ, in *R v MacDonagh* [1974] 2 All ER 257, [1974] QB 448. When Lord Widgery CJ gave the judgment of the court *Wallace v Major* was considered but its authority doubted. Although the facts in *R v MacDonagh* were not the same as the facts in the instant case, save that the appellant was also disqualified for driving, it was there held that 'driving' could not extend to the activity of a person who was not in the car, had both feet on the road and was making no use of the controls apart from an occasional adjustment of the steering wheel. The appeal was allowed, but the facts of that case were far removed from these here, for the appellant in *R v MacDonagh* was not in the car at all.

Lord Widgery CJ referred to the infinite number of ways in which a person may control the movement of a motor vehicle, apart from the orthodox one of sitting in the driving seat and using the engine for propulsion, including some of the manifold ways to which I have referred in which a car can be driven, and he pointed out that, although the word 'drive' must be given a wide meaning, the courts must be alert to see that the net is not thrown so widely that it includes activities which cannot be said to be driving a motor vehicle in any ordinary use of that word in the English language (see [1974] 2 All ER 257 at 259, [1974] QB 448 at 451). Unless this is done absurdity may result. Although counsel did not restrict himself to that particular aspect he would no doubt want to rely on it. What he would say, I assume from the rest of his submission, is that the net cannot be thrown wide enough to encompass a man at the seat of a towed vehicle.

Lord Widgery CJ added ([1974] 2 All ER 257 at 258, [1974] QB 448 at 451):

> 'The Act does not define the word "drive" and in its simplest meaning we think that it refers to a person using the driver's controls for the purpose of directing the movement of the vehicle. [Pausing there, certainly the appellant in this case was directing the movement of the vehicle.] It matters not that the vehicle is not moving under its own power, or is being driven by the force of gravity, or even that it is being pushed by other well-wishers. The essence of driving is the use of the driver's controls in order to direct the movement, however that movement is produced.'

As to the argument put forward by counsel that propulsion is at the basis of these cases, it was made clear in that case that it is not. Lord Widgery CJ referring to the decision of Lord Goddard CJ said ([1974] 2 All ER 257 at 259–260, [1974] QB 448 at 452):

> 'Whilst we adopt Lord Goddard CJ's approach to penal legislation, we respectfully doubt whether the correct conclusion was reached on the facts of that case. The court seems to have regarded the defendant as merely a steersman, and to have ignored his responsibility for the use of the brakes . . . [He added, with reference to *R v Roberts* [1964] 2 All ER 541, [1965] 1 QB 85:] We would draw attention to the two factors to which Lord Parker CJ refers: first, that the alleged driver must be in the driving seat, or in control of the steering wheel, and, secondly, that his activities are nevertheless not to be held to amount to driving unless they come within the ordinary meaning of that word.'

Here the appellant was certainly in the driving seat and in control of the steering wheel. Counsel submitted that the word 'driver' in this case was not used in the ordinary way. The justices, no doubt exercising their common sense as magistrates usually do, apparently had no hesitation in coming to the conclusion that the appellant was a driver.

One can, I think, test this matter in a number of different ways by asking oneself certain questions. Suppose, for instance, there was no one at the wheel of the towed vehicle: would not an ordinary bystander, in common sense, say, perhaps with some alarm, 'There is no driver in that car'; and although the facts were somewhat different in *Anderson v Transport Department* [1964] NZLR 881 when a towed vehicle snaked dangerously about the road due to the careless control of the man who was at the wheel of the other car, he was held to be guilty of dangerous driving. What would happen therefore if there was no one to brake the towed vehicle when an emergency arose ahead of the leading vehicle?

One might also ask oneself the question not answered by the newspaper report of a case in the Crown Court at Bodmin (*R v Pearson* (8th May 1978, unreported)) produced by counsel: could a drunken man safely purport to steer and control the brakes of a

towed vehicle? One has only to ask that question to see how naturally the word 'driver'
a covers the position of a person steering, controlling and having the ability, as he should
have, to brake when necessary. As to the criticism that the word 'driver' is not used in
its natural and ordinary meaning when a person is in the driving seat of a towed vehicle,
the only alternative word that could be suggested was that of 'towee'.

Therefore, without straining its connotation, giving the word its ordinary meaning,
and adopting the test proposed in *R v MacDonagh*, in my judgment 'the extent and
b degree' to which the appellant must have been controlling this vehicle comprises an
activity which the justices correctly described as driving, and he was rightly convicted.

ROSKILL LJ. I entirely agree that this appeal fails and should be dismissed. The case
stated by the justices of this city is, if I may be allowed to say so, a model of its kind. It
occupies no more than 2½ pages of typescript. The facts are set out with admirable
c succinctness and we are asked to say whether their decision that this man was guilty of
the offence charged is right in point of law.

Counsel for the appellant in this court (and whoever represented the appellant in the
court below made the same submission) rested largely on the decision of the Divisional
Court in *Wallace v Major* [1946] 2 All ER 87, [1946] KB 473. I confess with the utmost
respect for Lord Goddard CJ that when counsel read the relevant passages ([1946] 2 All
d ER 87 at 88–89, [1946] KB 473 at 477–478) I wondered if that case had been correctly
decided, though of course sitting in the Divisional Court we would have been bound by
the decision if there had been no subsequent authority. I was not then aware of the
decision to which attention has been drawn of a five judge Court of Appeal, Criminal
Division, in *MacDonagh's* case [1974] 2 All ER 257, [1974] QB 448. Heilbron J has read
the relevant passages in the judgment of this court delivered by Lord Widgery CJ, and I
e will not repeat what was there said. It seems to me plain that what Lord Goddard CJ and
the other members of the court said in *Wallace v Major* cannot stand alongside with the
judgment of the full court in *MacDonagh's* case. This appeal will have served a useful
purpose if the ghost of *Wallace v Major* is now finally exorcised.

It is worth drawing attention to the fact that in Stone's Justices' Manual (1979, vol 2,
p 3607) *Wallace v Major* is referred to but (correctly) is doubted, with a reference to *R v*
f *MacDonagh*. That passage will, no doubt, be revised in the next edition much to the
relief of justices hereafter concerned with these problems.

I agree the appeal should be dismissed and the question we are asked, whether the
determination was right in point of law, be answered Yes, it was.

LORD WIDGERY CJ. I agree with both judgments. The law hereafter on these
g points is that laid down in *R v MacDonagh* and justices will be well advised to apply that
authority and no other. The appeal will be dismissed.

Appeal dismissed.

Solicitors: *Pariser & Co* Manchester (for the appellant); *D S Gandy*, Manchester (for the
respondent).

M Denise Chorlton Barrister.

Poland and another v Earl Cadogan and another a

COURT OF APPEAL, CIVIL DIVISION
MEGAW, WALLER AND EVELEIGH LJJ
15th, 17th, 25th JULY 1980

b

Landlord and tenant – Leasehold enfranchisement – Tenant occupying house as his residence – Occupation in right of the tenancy – Tenant not physically in occupation for three of past five years – Tenant making arrangements to sublet property – Mortgagees taking possession of property for part of five year period – Whether tenant 'occupying the house as his residence' – Whether tenant qualified to acquire freehold – Leasehold Reform Act 1967, s 1(1)(b).

c

On 17th December 1973 the lease of a house and premises created on 21st June 1960 for
a term of 21½ years from 25th March 1960 to 29th September 1981 at a ground rent of
£150 per annum was assigned to the applicants. The lease was a long lease at a low rent
and fell within the provisions of the Leasehold Reform Act 1967. On the same date as
the deed of assignment the applicants created a legal charge over the property. The
applicants went into occupation, but in August 1974 went abroad for two months. On d
their return they lived in the house until October 1975 when they went on a long ocean
voyage. They instructed estate agents to sublet the property while they were away, but
in the event the house was never sublet. A handyman and cook were left in the house
and for a few months the mother of one of the applicants lived there. The ground rent
due on 25th December 1975 was not paid and the mortgage instalments fell into
arrear. The daughter of the applicants, who had been left in charge of the property, e
could not trace the applicants. In 1976 severe storm damage was caused to the house
rendering it uninhabitable and in December 1976 the mortgagees took possession and
changed the locks. If the applicants had moved back in without discharging their
outstanding debt the mortgagees would have ejected them. In January 1977 the
applicants returned to the United Kingdom. In March they were handed the keys of the
house by the mortgagees but they acknowledged that they held them to the order of the f
mortgagees, that the mortgagees were in lawful possession and that they, the applicants,
had no right to possession. In September the mortgagees handed back the legal possession
of the house to the applicants but the applicants could not reoccupy the house until 30th
May 1979 because, until then, it was unfit. On 18th December 1978 the applicants
notified the landlords of their desire to acquire the freehold of the house but the
landlords disputed their right. The applicants therefore applied to the county court for g
an order that they were entitled by virtue of s 1[a] of the 1967 Act to acquire the freehold
on the ground that they were occupying the house as their residence and had been doing
so for the past five years. The judge granted the order sought. The landlords appealed,
contending that the applicants were not occupying the house from August 1975 (when
they went abroad) up to and including the date of the notice, and that, in any event, they
were not occupying the house between December 1976 and September 1977 when the h
mortgagees were in possession, and, accordingly, had not been occupying the house as
their residence for the past five years and were therefore not entitled to acquire the
freehold.

Held – Whether a tenant was occupying a house as his residence for the purposes of s 1
of the 1967 Act when he was not physically in it was a question of fact and degree. The j
tenant might occupy premises as his residence even though he was absent for a long
period, provided he was keeping it ready for habitation whenever he was pleased to go

a Section 1, so far as material, is set out at p 547 *c* to *f*, post

into it, but the onus was on him to show that the steps which he had taken to maintain
a occupation were clear. However, a tenant could not be said to be occupying a house as his residence during a period of time in respect of which he had no intention of occupying or residing in it because of his belief, albeit erroneous, that he had given up his legal right to occupy or reside in the house, since he had, in respect of that period of time, no intention of asserting or exercising an immediate right of possession, which was an essential element of occupation. The arrangements made by the applicants for
b subletting while they were abroad were such as to make them cease to occupy the house as their residence during that period since they had no animus possidendi. Likewise the applicants could not be regarded as occupying the house as their residence during the period when the mortgagees had lawfully taken possession and would have lawfully prevented the applicants from residing in the house had they sought to do so. It followed therefore that the applicants had not been 'occupying the house as [their] residence, for
c the past five years' within s 1(1)(*b*) of the 1967 Act, and, accordingly, were not qualified to acquire the freehold of the house under that Act. The appeal would therefore be allowed (see p 548 *a* to *c*, p 549 *a* and *e* to *g* and p 550 *j* to p 551 *a* and *g*, post).

Observations on the meaning of 'occupation' for the purposes of s 1 of the 1967 Act (see p 548 *h* to p 549 *e*, p 550 *e* to *j* and p 551 *c* to *g*, post).

d **Notes**

For circumstances in which a tenant is to be regarded as occupying a house as his residence, see Supplement to 23 Halsbury's Laws (3rd Edn) para 1752.

For the Leasehold Reform Act 1967, s 1, see 18 Halsbury's Statutes (3rd Edn) 634.

Cases referred to in judgments

e *Brown v Brash* [1948] 1 All ER 922, [1948] 2 KB 247, [1948] LJR 1544, CA, 31(2) Digest (Reissue) 984, 7905.

Gibbons, Re, Gibbons v Gibbons [1920] 1 Ch 372, 89 LJ Ch 148, 122 LT 710, 40 Digest (Repl) 800, 2807.

Martin Estates Co Ltd v Watt and Hunter [1925] NI 79, 31(2) Digest (Reissue) 1007, *2762.

Poowong Shire v Gillen [1907] VLR 37.

f *R v St Pancras Assessment Committee* (1877) 2 QBD 581, 46 LJMC 243, sub nom *Willing v St Pancras Assessment Committee* 37 LT 126, 41 JP 662, Ryde Rat App (1871–85) 188, 38 Digest (Repl) 469, 5.

Cases also cited

Bushford v Falco [1954] 1 All ER 957, [1954] 1 WLR 672, CA.

g *Gofor Investments Ltd v Roberts* (1975) 29 P & CR 366, CA.

Haskins v Lewis [1931] 2 KB 1, [1930] All ER Rep 297, CA.

Methuen-Campbell v Walters [1979] 1 All ER 606, [1979] QB 525, CA.

Morris Holdings Ltd v Manders Property (Wolverhampton) Ltd [1976] 2 All ER 205, [1976] 1 WLR 533, CA.

Skinner v Geary [1931] 2 KB 546, [1931] All ER Rep 302, CA.

h

Appeal

The Rt Hon William Gerald Charles, Earl Cadogan, and Cadogan Holdings Ltd ('the landlords') appealed against the judgment of his Honour Judge Parker QC dated 22nd January 1980 by which he declared that the applicants, Trevor Peter Gordon Poland and his wife Lorette Elizabeth Poland, were entitled by virtue of the provisions of the
j Leasehold Reform Act 1967 to acquire the freehold of a house and premises situate at and known as 3 Cheyne Gardens, London SW3. The facts are set out in the judgment of Waller LJ.

William Poulton for the landlords.
Alan Steinfeld for the applicants.

Cur adv vult

25th July. The following judgments were read.

WALLER LJ (delivering the first judgment at the invitation of Megaw LJ). This is an appeal from the decision of his Honour Judge Parker QC sitting at West London County Court when he declared that the applicants, Commander and Mrs Poland, were entitled to acquire the freehold of a house and premises known as 3 Cheyne Gardens, London SW3. By a lease dated 1st June 1960, 3 Cheyne Gardens was demised to a Mr and Mrs Haire for 21½ years from 25th March 1960 to 29th September 1981 at a rent of £150 per annum. This was a long lease at a low rent. The lease was assigned to Commander and Mrs Poland on 13th December 1973 who, on the same date, charged the property to First National Securities Ltd for £17,500. The notice of claim under the Leasehold Reform Act 1967 is dated 18th December 1978, that is to say, the first possible date. By virtue of s 1 of the 1967 Act the tenant had to show residence for the last five years (or he could have shown five out of the last ten years). During the greater part of the five years Commander Poland did not physically occupy the property, and the question is whether the judge was right to hold that, notwithstanding that fact, the details of which I shall set out shortly, he can be said to have occupied the house as his residence for those five years.

Commander Poland went into occupation of the house but in August 1974 he went abroad, returning in November. He wrote to the landlords before leaving, saying: 'For your information I am going away for about two months on 4th August. I may be letting the house whilst I am away.' In 1975 he again went abroad. The judge found that the applicants 'left England for the purpose of sailing "Matchless" (their yacht) to South Africa thence to Brazil, from there to the United States where they intended to take part in the Newport–Bermuda race, and eventually bring "Matchless" back to England'. Before going, Commander Poland wrote asking for a licence to sublet. Whilst he was away, he left behind Mr and Mrs Rentjel as handyman and cook, and, for a period, Mrs Poland's mother, who lived in South Africa, stayed in the house for some months. The property was left with Harrods to let if they could. The judge found that the ground rent due on 25th December 1975 was not paid and the mortgage instalments fell into arrear. The applicants' daughter, Mrs Fisher, was left in charge, but neither she nor her brother could trace the applicants.

I do not set out the details of what happened during the remainder of 1976, save to say that, on or about 17th December 1976, Mr Wordley, on behalf of the mortgagees, took possession of the house and changed the locks. The judge found that, by 21st December, they had taken possession and this fact had been made clear to the Poland family. Mr Wordley was threatening to sell the furniture from the house, but held his hand when Mrs Fisher said that her father would be returning shortly.

The house suffered considerable storm damage. 1976 was the long, hot summer, and the gutters had become blocked. When there was very heavy rainfall in the autumn rainwater poured into the house and ceilings were damaged. Mr and Mrs Rentjel left. Mr Wordley had been faced with the security of his mortgage deteriorating as a result of flood damage.

The applicants returned to the United Kingdom in January 1977. On 15th February 1977 a letter was written on behalf of Mr Wordley to the landlords, saying: 'Will you please note that our clients are now mortgagees in possession of 3 Cheyne Gardens, S.W.3 and in future all demands for ground rent should be made to them care of ourselves.' When asked about the relationship between Commander Poland and himself, Mr Wordley said, concerning this period: 'Commander Poland would have been ejected if he had moved back in without making some payment to us', and, in another answer: 'If he had discharged the outstanding debt we would have let him back in, but not until then.'

On 18th March Commander Poland was handed the keys but, by letter of the same date, he acknowledged that he held the keys of the property to the order of Mr Wordley and agreed to return them on demand, and he acknowledged to Mr Wordley: 'That you peaceably obtained lawful possession with the consent of my family and continue to remain lawful mortgagee in lawful possession. (2) That I have no right to possession at the present time.' On 5th September 1977 Commander Poland signed a letter to Mr Wordley in the following terms: 'I acknowledge that I no longer hold the keys of 3 Cheyne Gardens, S.W.3 to your order and that I am lawful mortgagor in possession subject to the terms and conditions of the original ... mortgage.' The applicants reoccupied the house on 30th May 1979. This was the earliest date on which it was possible to reoccupy the house because, until then, it was unfit.

The learned judge held that, on 18th December 1978, Commander Poland was occupying the house as his residence and he had been doing so for the last five years. Accordingly, he had the right to acquire the freehold. The landlords now appeal.

Section 1 of the Leasehold Reform Act 1967 (in so far as it affects tenancies created on or before 18th February 1966) reads as follows:

> '*Tenants entitled to enfranchisement or extension.*—(1) This Part of this Act shall have effect to confer on a tenant of a leasehold house, occupying the house as his residence, a right to acquire on fair terms the freehold or an extended lease of the house and premises where—(*a*) his tenancy is a long tenancy at a low rent and ... the rateable value of the house and premises on the appropriate days is not (or was not) more than [£750] or, if it is in Greater London, than [£1,500]; and (*b*) at the relevant time (that is to say, at the time when he gives notice in accordance with this Act of his desire to have the freehold or to have an extended lease, as the case may be) he has been tenant of the house under a long tenancy at a low rent, and occupying it as his residence, for the last five years or for periods amounting to five years in the last ten years; and to confer the like right in the other cases for which provision is made in this Part of this Act.
>
> '(2) In this Part of this Act references, in relation to any tenancy, to the tenant occupying a house as his residence shall be construed as applying where, but only where, the tenant is, in right of the tenancy, occupying it as his only or main residence (whether or not he uses it also for other purposes); but—(*a*) references to a person occupying a house shall apply where he occupies it in part only ...'

It is submitted on behalf of the landlords, firstly, that the applicants were not occupying the house from the time in 1975 when they went abroad up to and including the date of the notice; secondly, that, in any event, they were not occupying the house from the time that the mortgagees took possession in December 1976. The county court judge found in favour of the applicants on both points.

I will deal first with the second of the above submissions, namely, the effect of the mortgage.

The judge found facts as follows. On a date in December 1976—

> 'in a series of telephone calls or at a meeting he [Mr Wordley] told Mr and Mrs Fisher [the daughter of the applicants] and Mr P K Poland that he was advised that First National could enter into possession as mortgagees by changing the locks and that is what they intended to do. No member of the Poland family made any protest. Mr Wordley obtained keys from the builder and changed the locks.'

Then the judge went on in dealing with this particular point and said:

> 'There must be many circumstances in which the actions of a mortgagee in seeking to enforce his charge might well prevent the mortgagor from occupying premises as his residence. The mortgagee might arrange for supplies of water and electricity to be cut off, he might (as First National threatened to do) sell the furniture and household effects. There may well be circumstances in which the changing of the locks would be sufficient. It is important, however, to look at the changing of the locks in this case in its context. At the time the house was uninhabitable. Commander and Mrs Poland could not have lived there even if they

> had wanted to. Certainly Mr Wordley did not expect them to. I bear in mind that Mr Wordley said: "Commander Poland would have been ejected if he had moved a back in without making some payment to us".'

The judge then said that, because the threat to sell the furniture was not carried out, because Commander Poland was allowed to go to the premises and was given keys, and because the premises were uninhabitable, he came to the conclusion that the actions of the First National did not interrupt the applicants' occupancy.

I cannot agree. The question is: was Commander Poland 'occupying the house as his b residence'? The fact that he went to the house by permission of Mr Wordley cannot make him occupy it as his residence. It was certainly not in right of a tenancy, as sub-s (2) requires, when he went there. Furthermore, in the letter of 18th March 1977, Commander Poland made it absolutely clear that he was going with the permission of Mr Wordley and not otherwise. In my judgment, it cannot possibly be said that Commander Poland was occupying the house as his residence between December 1976 c and 5th September 1977.

I now consider the argument which the landlords regard as more important, namely, whether the applicants were or were not occupying the house as their residence from October 1975 until the time of the notice.

In argument before the county court judge it was submitted that, having regard to the terms of s 3(2) of the Rent Act 1968, cases decided under the Rent Act did not assist in d deciding what was required to comply with s 1 of the Leasehold Reform Act 1967. Reference has also been made to *Brown v Brash* [1948] 1 All ER 922, [1948] 2 KB 247. I have found the analysis of occupation in the judgment of Asquith LJ extremely helpful. But, in my opinion, it is also helpful to look at both sections, i e s 3(2) of the Rent Act 1968 as well as s 1 of the Leasehold Reform Act 1967, in order to ascertain the way in which s 1 of the Leasehold Reform Act should be interpreted. Section 1 requires the e tenant to have been 'occupying the house as his residence for the last five years' and, by sub-s (2), that is to be construed as 'applying where, but *only where*, the tenant is in right of the tenancy occupying it as his only or main residence'. I emphasise the words 'only where' because it shows that the section should be applied strictly. Section 3(2) of the Rent Act 1968 reads as follows:

f

> 'In paragraph (*a*) of subsection (1) above and in Schedule 1 to this Act, the phrase "if and so long as he occupies the dwelling-house as his residence" shall be construed as requiring the fulfilment of the same, and only the same, qualifications (whether as to residence or otherwise) as had to be fulfilled before the commencement of this Act to entitle a tenant, within the meaning of the Increase of Rent and Mortgage Interest (Restrictions) Act 1920, to retain possession, by virtue of that Act and not by g virtue of a tenancy, of a dwellinghouse to which that Act applied.'

It is important to notice the words 'the same, and only the same, qualifications'.

It seems to me that, comparing those two sections, they are each confining the definition strictly but strictly with different emphases. In the Rent Act the meaning of 'occupation' is to be construed for the purposes of the Rent Act as it had been up to that time. Were it not for s 3 there might be other qualifications to be included. The object h of the Rent Act was to provide accommodation for persons, and, in cases under the Rent Acts, occupation had been very much discussed and the law made clear. In the Leasehold Reform Act, which is concerned with conferring the right to acquire on fair terms a freehold or extended lease of the house, occupation is restricted to those cases where, and only where, 'the tenant is, in right of the tenancy, occupying [the house] as his only or main residence'. j

There is a further provision in the Leasehold Reform Act which enables a tenant to qualify if he has occupied the house as his residence 'for the last five years or for periods amounting to five years in the last ten years'. This clearly contemplates periods when the residential occupation is interrupted. But, if the interruptions were to be confined to sublettings, I would have expected the subsection to say so.

How should the test be applied in relation to the Leasehold Reform Act? Going away
a for a short holiday clearly does not involve a break, but, when asking whether the tenant is occupying it as his residence when he is not physically living in it, the court must look more critically than under the Rent Act. As in the case of the Rent Act it is a question of fact and degree; but to adopt precisely the same criteria does not give effect to the differences, eg 'and only the same' in the Rent Act and the five years out of ten which qualifies under the Leasehold Reform Act. The difference lies in the purposes of the two
b Acts. The Rent Acts are to provide accommodation and the court need only look at the qualifications established prior to 1968. The Leasehold Reform Act is to enable a tenant to acquire compulsorily a greater interest in his house. It confers a right on a tenant who can fulfil certain conditions to acquire compulsorily the freehold belonging to his landlord on terms prescribed in the Act. The terms are laid down in the Act to be fair terms but, nevertheless, the landlord has no choice. It is compulsory.

c In my opinion, the words 'where, but only where' themselves imply a strict approach and, therefore, 'occupying it as his only or main residence' must be approached to see whether the occupation has been of a nature to entitle the tenants to the benefit of a compulsory freehold or extended lease. Furthermore, the phrase 'occupying as' implies an existing state of affairs. It is not 'for the purpose of' his only residence. It is 'as his only residence'. Once it becomes clear that the tenant is not physically in occupation the onus
d is firmly on him to show that the steps which he has taken to maintain occupation are clear. Going away for a short holiday is simple but the longer the period the more difficult it becomes to infer continued occupation. If the family (wife or children) are still in physical occupation, then the position is clear, but to infer occupation because furniture is left in the house or because there is a caretaker requires closer examination. If the period is short the inference of continued occupation may be easy, but where many
e months are concerned very much more doubtful. The tenant does not lose the benefit of his periods of genuine occupation because of the provisions allowing aggregation.

I should be reluctant to upset the judgment of the county court judge on a question of primary fact, but there is no dispute about the primary facts. Here the question is one of mixed fact and law. It is the approach to these primary facts and the inferences to be drawn.

f In my judgment, bearing in mind the considerations that I have mentioned above as to the different emphasis and approach under the Leasehold Reform Act and accepting, as I do, the findings of primary fact by the learned judge, I am satisfied that Commander Poland's arrangements about subletting were such as to make him cease to occupy the house as his residence. He was physically abroad and had left it to his daughter and Harrods to sublet. It was not a mere intention. In my judgment, from the time he left
g the house having that intention he was no longer 'occupying it as his only or main residence'.

I would, therefore, allow the appeal.

EVELEIGH LJ (read by Waller LJ). In 14 Halsbury's Laws (3rd Edn) 15, para 21, it is stated:

h 'An occupier is one who actually exercises the rights of an owner in possession. The primary element of occupation is possession, but it includes something more, for mere legal possession cannot constitute an occupation. The owner of a vacant house is in possession, though not in occupation; but, if he furnishes the house and keeps it ready for habitation, he is an occupier, though he may not have resided in it for a considerable time ... So a trader occupies premises by merely keeping his stock, tools, vehicles or other goods upon those premises. A merchant or business man occupies an office or counting-house by using it during ordinary hours by himself or his clerks for the purpose of his business.'

In *R v St Pancras Assessment Committee* (1877) 2 QBD 581 at 588, Lush J said:

'Occupation includes possession as its primary element, but it also includes

> something more. Legal possession does not, of itself, constitute an occupation. The owner of a vacant house is in possesion, and may maintain trespass against anyone *a* who invades it, but as long as he leaves it vacant he is not rateable for it as an occupier. If, however, he furnishes it, and keeps it ready for habitation whenever he pleases to go into it, he is an occupier, though he may not reside in it one day in a year.'

That passage was adopted by Hood J in *Poowong Shire v Gillen* [1907] VLR 37 at 40.

In *Martin Estates Co Ltd v Watt and Hunter* [1925] NI 79 at 85, Moore LJ said: *b*

> '"Occupation" means that the owner is in actual physical enjoyment of the house, property or estate by himself, his agents or servants. Strictly speaking, "occupation" by the owner cannot include the case of sub-tenants for the actual occupation is in them. A limited form of occupation is "residence" . . . [which] must involve the dwelling for some period of the year on the premises personally of the owner or his *c* family, or alternatively, at least, of his domestic servants.'

I find assistance in the present case from the above quotations but must, of course, bear in mind that we have to construe the precise words 'occupying it as his residence' in s 1 of the Leasehold Reform Act 1967. I do not regard these words as the equivalent of 'lives and resides'. In *Re Gibbons, Gibbons v Gibbons* [1920] 1 Ch 372 at 379 Lord Sterndale MR said: *d*

> 'The difference between the words "reside" and "occupy" and "enjoy the use of" is perfectly well known. If he meant to restrict it to residence I do not see the reason for his not using the appropriate word "reside".'

I am of the opinion that a person may occupy premises as his residence, even though he is absent for a very long period. It may well be, however, that a long absence will *e* necessitate the acquisition of another residence which will prevent the tenant from claiming that the premises were his 'only or main residence', which is the requirement of s 1(2) of the Act. It seems to me that, if a person takes the tenancy of a house and furnishes it and keeps it ready for his own habitation 'whenever he pleases to go into it', he is, as Lush J said, an occupier though he may not reside in it one day in a year, and I would further say that he occupies it as a residence. Moreover, I would say that he *f* *occupies* it as his residence provided that it is understood that the expression 'his residence' is not used in a context which implies his main residence. It means he keeps it for himself to live in. If, however, he sublets the property, he ceases to occupy it as his residence because, as Moore LJ explained, the occupation is in the subtenant. It may not be inaccurate, however, still to refer to the premises as his residence. That in isolation would be a permissible description of the property, but it does not mean that he is in *g* occupation.

However, in considering the present case, one must concentrate on the actual words 'occupying it as his residence, for the last five years or for periods amounting to five years in the last ten years' in the Act. The words 'occupying it as his residence' taken in conjunction with the recognition of periods amounting to five years in the last ten years indicate to me that the period or periods contemplated by the subsection are those *h* periods when he is using and enjoying the property as a residence for himself. He may do this although he is absent from the premises. In such a case, as I have said, the premises may then be unlikely to be his main residence.

The facts referred to in the judgment of Waller LJ and those specifically emphasised by Megaw LJ lead to the conclusion, in my judgment, that Commander Poland was not during the disputed period occupying the premises as his residence. He was not keeping *j* it ready for habitation by himself whenever he was pleased to go into it. He did not intend to exercise his right as a tenant to occupy the house as his residence at any time during that period.

During the period when the mortgagees were in possession the case permits of a short answer. Commander Poland could not exercise the rights of an owner in possession and could not be regarded as the occupier.

MEGAW LJ. I agree that this appeal should be allowed.

When the applicants left England in early October 1975 they intended that the house should be sublet. They left instructions that the necessary steps should be taken to that end. An estate agent had, in fact, been instructed. It appears from the evidence that Commander Poland, during his absence abroad, believed, or at least hoped, that the house had in fact been let, in accordance with his intention. That was at least one reason why, according to Commander Poland, the rent which became due from him to his landlords remained unpaid during his absence abroad. He believed that those whom he had left in charge of his affairs (in so far as he did leave anyone in charge) would be in funds to pay, and would be duly paying, the rent out of the money which they as his agents were receiving, so he thought, from the subletting.

Whatever may be the relationship between the criteria applicable, respectively, in assessing 'occupying as his residence' in s 1 of the Leasehold Reform Act 1967 and in s 3(2) of the Rent Act 1968, it seems to me that, as regards the former statutory provision, a tenant cannot be said to be occupying a house as his residence during a period of time in respect of which he has no intention of occupying it or residing in it because of his belief, or expectation, whether it is accurate or not, that he has given up his legal right to occupy or reside in the house. He has, in respect of that period of time, to use the expression used in the judgment of the court in *Brown v Brash* [1948] 1 All ER 922 at 926, [1948] 2 KB 247 at 255, no 'animus possidendi': no intention of asserting or exercising an immediate right of possession. That is an essential element.

The tenant may have the intention of resuming occupation as his residence in the future. For the purposes of s 1 of the 1967 Act, progress toward the achievement of the five-year qualification period may resume after intermission. But the period of intermission cannot itself count towards the five-year period. 'Occupying as his residence' necessarily involves as one essential element, at any rate where the tenant is not, in the ordinary sense of the words, actually living in the house, the tenant's own state of mind as to his relationship with, his legal rights as to occupation of, the house. If his own state of mind is the belief or expectation that he has by his own act put it outside his lawful right to occupy the house as his residence, as and when he wills, during a period of time, then he cannot be regarded as occupying it as his residence during that period. He has no animus possidendi.

With great respect to the learned judge and to his very careful judgment, I disagree also with his conclusion that the applicants could, on any permissible interpretation of s 1 of the 1967 Act, be regarded as occupying the house as their residence between December 1976 and September 1977, when the mortgagees had lawfully taken possession and would have lawfully prevented the tenants from residing in the house if they had sought to do so.

Appeal allowed. Leave to appeal to the House of Lords refused.

Solicitors: *Reynolds, Porter, Chamberlain* (for the landlords); *Lee & Pembertons* (for the applicants).

Mary Rose Plummer Barrister.

Maidstone Borough Council v Mortimer a

QUEEN'S BENCH DIVISION
WALLER LJ AND PARK J
22nd MAY, 9th JUNE 1980

Town and country planning – Trees – Preservation order – Prohibition of wilful destruction of trees – Offence – Mens rea – Whether knowledge of preservation order a necessary ingredient of offence – Town and Country Planning Act 1971, s 102(1). b

The respondent cut down an oak tree which unknown to him was the subject of a tree preservation order made by the local council under s 60(1)[a] of the Town and Country Planning Act 1971. The council laid an information against the respondent charging c
him with contravention of the order contrary to s 102(1)[b] of the 1971 Act. The justices dismissed the information on the ground that knowledge of the existence of the order was a necessary ingredient of an offence under s 102(1). The council appealed.

Held – Having regard to the mischief which ss 59, 60 and 62 of the 1971 Act were intended to prevent, namely that no tree which was the subject of a preservation order should be cut down or destroyed without consent, and to the fact that s 102(1) of that Act d
was not capable of two interpretations one of which was more favourable to the respondent, s 102 on its true construction applied to tree felling carried out in contravention of a preservation order either with or without knowledge of the order. Accordingly, knowledge of the existence of an order was not a necessary ingredient of the offence created by s 102(1) and did not have to be proved by the prosecutor. The council's appeal would therefore be allowed (see p 554 *e* and p 555 *d* to *f* and *j* to p 556 e
a, post).

Dicta of Wright J in *Sherras v De Rutzen* [1895–9] All ER Rep at 1169 and of Lord Reid in *Sweet v Parsley* [1969] 1 All ER at 350 applied.

Notes

For prohibition of cutting trees which are subject to a preservation order, see 37 f
Halsbury's Laws (3rd Edn) 460–462, paras 581–583.

For the Town and Country Planning Act 1971, ss 59, 60, 62, 102, see 41 Halsbury's Statutes (3rd Edn) 1659, 1660, 1663, 1711.

Cases referred to in judgments

Barnet London Borough Council v Eastern Electricity Board [1973] 2 All ER 319, [1973] 1 g
WLR 430, 137 JP 486, 71 LGR 254, 25 P & CR 261, DC, Digest (Cont Vol D) 935, *156d*.

Lim Chin Aik v R [1963] 1 All ER 223, [1963] AC 160, [1963] 2 WLR 42, PC, 2 Digest (Reissue) 194, **839*.

Sherras v De Rutzen [1895] 1 QB 918, [1895–9] All ER Rep 1167, 64 LJMC 218, 72 LT 839, 59 JP 440, 18 Cox CC 157, 15 R 388, DC, 30 Digest (Reissue) 110, *731*. h

Sweet v Parsley [1969] 1 All ER 347, [1970] AC 132, [1969] 2 WLR 470, 133 JP 188, 53 Cr App R 221, HL, 15 Digest (Reissue) 1084, *9179*.

Case stated

Maidstone Borough Council ('the local authority') appealed by way of case stated by the justices for the County of Kent in respect of their adjudication as a magistrates' court sitting at Maidstone on 22nd August 1978 whereby they dismissed an information j
preferred by the local authority against the respondent, John Mortimer, that on 13th January 1978 at Headcorn he contravened the provisions of the County of Kent

a Section 60(1), so far as material, is set out at p 554 *b c*, post
b Section 102(1) is set out at p 553 *d*, post

(Hollingbourne Rural District) Tree Preservation (No 2) Order 1964 in that he wilfully
a destroyed an oak tree to which the order applied. The facts are set out in the judgment of Park J.

Harry B Sales for the local authority.
David Davies for the respondent.

b

Cur adv vult

9th June. The following judgments were read.

PARK J (delivering the first judgment at the invitation of Waller LJ). This is an appeal by case stated by the Maidstone Borough Council against the dismissal by the Maidstone
c justices on 22nd August 1978 of an information against the respondent charging him that he did on Friday, 13th January 1978, at 11 Rushford Close, Headcorn, contravene the provisions of the County of Kent (Hollingbourne Rural District) Tree Preservation (No 2) Order 1964, and that without the consent of the Maidstone Borough Council he did wilfully destroy an oak tree specified as T2 in Sch 1 to the order and on the plan annexed thereto, contrary to s 102(1) of the Town and Country Planning Act 1971.
d Section 102(1) provides:

> 'If any person, in contravention of a tree preservation order, cuts down or wilfully destroys a tree, or tops or lops a tree in such a manner as to be likely to destroy it, he shall be guilty of an offence and liable on summary conviction to a fine not exceeding £250 or twice the sum which appears to the court to be the value of the tree, whichever is the greater.'

e

On this appeal, the question for determination is whether on a charge under s 102(1) knowledge of the wrongfulness of the accused's act has to be proved by establishing that he knew of the existence of the tree preservation order in respect of the tree the subject matter of the charge.

The respondent is by occupation a tree feller. He was employed by a Mrs Twydell to
f cut down a fully mature oak tree which was subject to the tree preservation order referred to in the information. Mrs Twydell told the respondent, as she honestly believed to be the case, that she had received permission from the parks department of the local authority to cause the tree to be felled. No such consent had in fact been given. After the respondent had made one cut in the tree he was told by a Mr Woodcock, the vice-chairman of the parish council, that he believed that the tree was the subject of
g a tree preservation order. Mr Woodcock requested the respondent to stop the tree felling operation until the arrival of a Mr Musker who would be able to confirm, or otherwise, the existence of such an order. The respondent, in reliance on the accuracy of Mrs Twydell's information, made a further cut in the tree.

The combined effect of the two cuts made the tree dangerous so that a council official, who eventually arrived at the scene, ordered the felling of the tree to be completed.
h The justices held that, by his deliberate act in making cuts in the tree, the respondent had wilfully destroyed the tree. In arriving at that conclusion the justices followed the decision of this court in *Barnet London Borough Council v Eastern Electricity Board* [1973] 2 All ER 319, [1973] 1 WLR 430, where it was held that if a person inflicted on a tree so radical an injury that in all the circumstances a competent forester, taking into account its situation, e g its proximity to a highway, would decide that it ought to be felled, that
j person would have 'wilfully destroyed' the tree within s 29(1)(*a*) of the Town and Country Planning Act 1962.

No serious challenge is made or could be made on the respondent's behalf to this finding. The justices nevertheless acquitted the respondent because, in their opinion, knowledge of the existence of the tree preservation order was an essential ingredient of an offence under s 102(1) and the respondent did not have that knowledge.

I think it is necessary to consider first those sections of the Town and Country Planning Act 1971 which deal with tree preservation in order to determine the mischief with which this part of the statute is intended to deal.

Section 59 imposes on the local planning authority the duty of ensuring, whenever it is appropriate, that, when granting planning permission for any development, adequate provision is made, by the imposition of conditions, for the preservation or planting of trees and to make such tree preservation orders under s 60 as may be necessary in connection with the grant of such permission to give effect to the conditions imposed.

Section 60(1) says:

> 'If it appears to a local planning authority that it is expedient in the interests of amenity to make provision for the preservation of trees or woodlands in their area, they may for that purpose make [a tree preservation order] with respect to such trees . . . as may be specified in the order; and, in particular, provisions may be made by any such order—(*a*) for prohibiting . . . the cutting down, topping, lopping or wilful destruction of trees except with the consent of the local planning authority . . .'

I need not refer to the remainder of s 60.

Section 62 deals with the replacement of any tree in respect of which a tree preservation order is in force. If such a tree is removed or destroyed in contravention of the order, it is the duty of the owner of the land, unless he obtains dispensation from the local authority, to plant another tree of an appropriate size and species at the same place as soon as he reasonably can.

Thus s 102 is the section whereby the provisions of s 60 are enforced and s 103 relates to the enforcement of s 62.

In my judgment, therefore, these sections demonstrate that Parliament intended that no tree the subject of a tree preservation order should be cut down or wilfully destroyed or topped or lopped in such a manner as to be likely to destroy it without the consent of the local authority. Plainly it is of the utmost public importance that such trees should be preserved. The risk to their continued existence in these days of extensive building operations, which encroach further and further into rural areas, is very great. It is not a difficult task for any member of the public wishing to interfere with the shape, size or continued existence of a tree to obtain from the local authority reliable information on the question whether the tree is the subject of a preservation order and, if so, to seek the authority's consent to the operation proposed. (Mrs Twydell appears to have made a most perfunctory inquiry of the wrong department of the local authority and to have misunderstood or misinterpreted whatever it was she claims to have been told.) Thus, there can be no hardship to a member of the public in having on or near land which he owns or occupies any protected tree.

For these reasons, in my judgment, s 102(1) is a section to which the words of Wright J in *Sherras v De Rutzen* [1895] 1 QB 918 at 921–922, [1895–9] All ER Rep 1167 at 1169 can be applied:

> 'There is a presumption that mens rea, an evil intention, or a knowledge of the wrongfulness of the act, is an essential ingredient in every offence; but that presumption is liable to be displaced either by the words of the statute creating the offence or by the subject-matter with which it deals, and both must be considered . . . [The] principal classes of exceptions may perhaps be reduced to three. One is a class of acts which . . . are not criminal in any real sense, but are acts which in the public interest are prohibited under a penalty.'

I need not refer to the two other classes of exceptions he mentions.

In *Sweet v Parsley* [1969] 1 All ER 347 at 350, [1970] AC 132 at 149 Lord Reid referred to Wright J's words in *Sherras v De Rutzen*. He said:

> 'In the absence of a clear indication in the Act that an offence is intended to be an absolute offence, it is necessary to go outside the Act and examine all relevant

> circumstances in order to establish that this must have been the intention of Parliament. I say "must have been", because it is a universal principle that if a penal provision is reasonably capable of two interpretations, that interpretation which is most favourable to the accused must be adopted. What, then, are the circumstances which it is proper to take into account? In the well-known case of *Sherras* v. *De Rutzen*, WRIGHT, J., only mentioned the subject-matter with which the Act deals. But he was there dealing with something which was one of a class of acts which "are not criminal in any real sense, but are acts which in the public interest are prohibited under a penalty". It does not in the least follow that, when one is dealing with a truly criminal act, it is sufficient merely to have regard to the subject-matter of the enactment. One must put oneself in the position of a legislator. It has long been the practice to recognise absolute offences in this class of quasi-criminal acts, and one can safely assume that, when Parliament is passing new legislation dealing with this class of offences, its silence as to mens rea means that the old practice is to apply.'

In deciding whether this section of the 1971 Act is one to which 'the old practice' is to be applied, I think it is right to bear in mind that if it were the law that no conviction could be obtained under s 102(1) unless the prosecution could discharge the often impossible burden of proving that the accused knew of the existence of the relevant tree preservation order that subsection would have little, if any, deterrent effect, so that protected trees could be felled or otherwise destroyed without any appreciable risk of a penalty being incurred by the wrongdoer.

The question is: is the language of s 102(1) reasonably capable of two interpretations, so that the interpretation most favourable to the accused must be adopted? In my judgment, having regard to the nature of the tree preservation sections of the 1971 Act, to the mischief with which those sections was intended to deal and to the fact that the section relates to 'acts which in the public interest are prohibited under a penalty', s 102(1) is not capable of two interpretations. I do not think that the section was intended to be interpreted or should be interpreted as making the cutting down or wilful destruction of a tree or the topping or lopping of a tree in such a manner as to be likely to destroy it an offence only if the accused had knowledge of the existence of the preservation order. In my judgment, no such proof is necessary.

For these reasons, I would allow the appeal and, on the facts found, direct the justices to convict the respondent on the information. It is, I think, right to add, first, that as the respondent was evidently misled by the information he had received from Mrs Twydell that fact can be reflected in the penalty imposed on him and, second, that no criticism of the justices' decision can be or is made, since the point on which the appeal in my view is allowed was either not taken or not fully argued before them.

WALLER LJ. I agree with the judgment which has just been delivered. I only add a few words to deal with an argument advanced on behalf of the respondent. It was argued that the words 'in contravention of a tree preservation order' which occur in s 102(1) of the Town and Country Planning Act 1971 indicated that it was necessary to prove conscious contravention, and reliance was placed on some observations of Lord Evershed in *Lim Chin Aik v R* [1963] 1 All ER 223 at 229–230, [1963] AC 160 at 176. Section 62(1) of the 1971 Act, which deals with replacement, reads:

> 'If any tree in respect of which a tree preservation order is for the time being in force, other than a tree to which the order applies as part of a woodland, is removed or destroyed in contravention of the order [and then follow some provisions about cutting down which is authorised; the subsection concludes:] it shall be the duty of the owner of the land, unless on his application the local planning authority dispense with this requirement, to plant another tree of an appropriate size and species at the same place as soon as he reasonably can.'

It is clear, from both that subsection and s 103, that the phrase 'in contravention of' applies to any felling other than felling authorised by the appropriate authority. The phrase therefore covers not only felling which is done with knowledge of a tree preservation order but also felling which was done in ignorance of a tree preservation order. The same meaning would, in my opinion, clearly be given to the same phrase in s 102(1).

Appeal allowed.

Solicitors: *Sharpe, Pritchard & Co*, agents for *K B Rogers*, Maidstone (for the local authority); *Hallett & Co*, Ashford (for the respondent).

Dilys Tausz Barrister.

China-Pacific SA v Food Corporation of India

The Winson

COURT OF APPEAL, CIVIL DIVISION

MEGAW, BRIDGE AND CUMMING-BRUCE LJJ

23rd, 24th, 25th, 28th, 29th, 30th APRIL 1980

Shipping – Salvage – Cargo – Storage expenses – Agreement – Vessel stranding – Master signing Lloyd's standard salvage agreement on behalf of shipowner and cargo owner – Arrangements made by salvors for storage of cargo ashore – Voyage abandoned by shipowner – No necessity or emergency requiring salvors to store cargo in order to preserve it – Whether shipowner or cargo owner liable for storage expenses ashore.

Estoppel – Promissory estoppel – Reliance on representation – Nature of representation relied on – Representation required to be unequivocal promise – Plaintiff relying on advice of defendant's solicitor that defendant liable in law to plaintiff and on discussion between plaintiff's and defendant's counsel prior to arbitration – Whether matters relied on by plaintiff constituting representations giving rise to promissory estoppel.

In October 1974 the cargo owners chartered a vessel from the shipowners to carry a cargo of wheat from the United States of America to India. The charterparty provided, inter alia, that freight should be 'deemed earned upon safe arrival' of the cargo, that the vessel was to have a lien on the cargo for all freight, demurrage and average, and that the entire freight was to be at all times at the risk of the shipowners. On 21st January 1975, during the course of the voyage, the vessel stranded on a reef in the South China Sea, some 420 miles from Manila. The following day the ship's managing agents in Hong Kong signed a Lloyd's standard form of salvage agreement with the salvors expressed to be made by the master 'as agent for the vessel, her cargo and freight and the respective owners thereof'. Under the agreement the salvors agreed to use their best endeavours to salve the vessel and/or cargo and deliver them to a safe port. The services were to be rendered and accepted on the principle of 'no cure—no pay'. Between 10th February and 20th April the salvors performed salvage services which resulted in the saving of 15,429 tonnes of wheat, in six parcels. The parcels were taken by the salvors from the vessel, put into craft which they provided and taken to Manila where they were off-loaded and put into store so that they might be preserved in good condition. All the arrangements for stevedoring and the storage in Manila were made by the salvors. On 24th April the shipowners abandoned the voyage and notified the cargo owners accordingly. On 5th August the cargo owners, who had given a guarantee in respect of their proportion of the salvage award, took possession of the salved cargo at Manila. The cargo owners refused to pay the salvors the expenses they incurred in off-loading and storing the salved cargo after its arrival in Manila and before 24th April, when the voyage was abandoned. The salvors brought an action against the cargo owners in respect of those expenses. The cargo owners denied liability, contending, inter alia, that the shipowners were liable to pay those expenses because the cargo was deliverable to the shipowners and not to the cargo owners on its arrival in Manila. The trial judge ([1979] 2 All ER 35) held that the cargo owners were liable for those expenses. On appeal by the cargo owners, the salvors, by cross-notice, contended that even if the cargo was deliverable to the shipowners nevertheless the cargo owners were estopped from denying liability because they had, by their agents, represented to the salvors by their agents that they, the cargo owners, were liable for the post-salvage expenses. The representation was said to have been made as the result of the combined effect of what was set out in a letter from the cargo owners' solicitors to the salvors' solicitors and what was said in a discussion between counsel for the salvors and for the cargo owners prior to arbitration.

Held – The appeal would be allowed for the following reasons—

(1) Since a shipowner was under a contractual obligation and was entitled, under the charterparty, to carry the cargo to its destination in order to earn his freight, he was entitled to remain in possession of the cargo by himself or through a sub-bailee unless or until the voyage was abandoned or frustrated. Accordingly, where a salvor took possession of a cargo under a salvage agreement, his obligation when the cargo or part of it had been brought to a place of safety and his services under the agreement terminated was (in the absence of special circumstances, such as where the shipowner could not be found or refused to take delivery of the cargo or declared a disinterest in it and the salvor had notified the cargo owner of the position) to deliver the cargo back to the shipowner and not to the cargo owner. On the evidence it could not be said that the shipowners had either been invited by the salvors to take delivery of the cargo at Manila or indicated a refusal to do so, or that the cargo owners had been so informed. The primary obligation for the preservation of the cargo therefore remained on the shipowners (see p 561 *a* to p 562 *a*, p 567 *j* and p 568 *b e f*, post).

(2) Although the salvors were bailees of the salved cargo from the cargo owners by virtue of the salvage agreement, and as bailees were obliged to take all reasonable steps to ensure that the cargo was properly cared for and were therefore entitled to reimbursement from the cargo owners of the expenses incurred in carrying out their duty, once their contractual duty had ended with the cargo being brought to a place of safety they were not entitled to recover from the cargo owners their expenses incurred in keeping the cargo from damage or destruction in the absence of necessity or an emergency that they should so act to preserve it. The relevant time for considering whether there was such a necessity or an emergency was the time when the existence of the supposed emergency became apparent, eg by the arrival or expected arrival of the salved cargo at a port of safety with no arrangements having been made for its off-loading or for its preservation in proper storage. Since it could not be said that the conduct of the salvors in arranging for the off-loading and storing of the salved cargo was founded on, or related to, any relevant emergency or relevant necessity, the salvors could not look to the cargo owners for reimbursement of the expenses claimed (see p 562 *f* to p 563 *j*, p 567 *j* and p 568 *b* to *f*, post).

(3) The salvors could only succeed on the issue of estoppel if the representation could be treated as the foundation of a promissory estoppel, one of the essential attributes of which was the unequivocality of the promise or assurance relied on, but since the matters relied on by the salvors as constituting the promise were not unequivocal and at best were an indication that the cargo owners had been advised by their solicitors that they were liable in law to the salvors for the expenses claimed, the cargo owners were not estopped from denying liability (see p 566 *j*, p 567 *g* to *j* and p 568 *e f*, post).

Decision of Lloyd J [1979] 2 All ER 35 reversed.

Notes

For the salvor's right to a reward, see 35 Halsbury's Laws (3rd Edn) 733, para 1112, and for cases on the subject, see 42 Digest (Repl) 1040–1041, *8565–8577*. a

Cases referred to in judgments

Central London Property Trust Ltd v High Trees House Ltd [1956] 1 All ER 256, [1947] KB 130, [1947] LJR 77, 175 LT 332, 21 Digest (Repl) 376, *1133*.

Delantera Amadora SA v Bristol Channel Shiprepairers Ltd and Swansea Dry Docks Co, The Katingaki [1976] 2 Lloyd's Rep 372, Digest (Cont Vol E) 563, *9153a*. b

Gaudet v Brown, Brown v Gaudet, Geipel v Cornforth, Cargo ex Argos, The Hewsons (1873) LR 5 PC 134, 42 LJ Adm 1, 28 LT 77, 1 Asp MLC 519, PC, 41 Digest (Repl) 391, *1782*.

Gokal Chand-Jagan Nath v Nand Ram Das-Atma Ram [1938] 4 All ER 407, [1939] AC 106, 108 LJPC 9, PC, 1(1) Digest (Reissue) 525, *3659*.

Great Northern Railway Co v Swaffield (1874) LR 9 Exch 132, [1874–80] All ER Rep 1065, 43 LJ Ex 89, 30 LT 562, 8(1) Digest (Reissue) 41, *225*. c

Notara v Henderson (1872) LR 7 QB 225, 41 LJQB 158, 26 LT 442, 1 Asp MLC 278, Ex Ch, 41 Digest (Repl) 391, *1783*.

Somes v British Empire Shipping Co (1860) 8 HL Cas 338, 30 LJQB 229, 2 LT 547, 6 Jur NS 761, 11 ER 459, 42 Digest (Repl) 1101, *9153*.

Woodhouse AC Israel Cocoa Ltd SA v Nigerian Produce Marketing Co Ltd [1972] 2 All ER 271, [1972] AC 741, [1972] 2 WLR 1090, [1972] 1 Lloyd's Rep 439, HL; *affg* [1971] 1 All ER 665, [1971] 2 QB 23, [1971] 2 WLR 272, CA, Digest (Cont Vol D) 313, *1291a*. d

Cases also cited

Alan (W J) & Co Ltd v El Nasr Export & Import Co [1972] 2 All ER 127, [1972] 2 QB 189, CA. e

Craven-Ellis v Canons Ltd [1936] 2 All ER 1066, [1936] 2 KB 403, CA.

Falcke v Scottish Imperial Insurance Co (1886) 34 Ch D 234, CA.

Gilchrist, Watt and Sanderson Pty Ltd v York Products Pty Ltd [1970] 3 All ER 825, [1970] 1 WLR 1262, PC.

Greenwood v Bennett [1972] 3 All ER 586, [1973] QB 195, CA. f

Hingston v Wendt (1876) 1 QBD 367, DC.

Morris v C W Martin & Sons Ltd [1965] 2 All ER 725, [1966] 1 QB 716, CA.

Nippon Menkwa Kabushiki Kaisha (Japan Cotton Trading Co Ltd) v Dawsons Bank Ltd (1935) 51 Ll L Rep 147, PC.

Peace, The (1856) Swa 115, 166 ER 1048.

Petrinovic & Co Ltd v Mission Francaise des Transports Maritimes (1941) 71 Ll L Rep 208.

Raisby, The (1885) 10 PD 114. g

Rose v Bank of Australasia [1894] AC 687, HL.

Société Franco-Tunisienne D'Armement v Sidermar SPA [1960] 2 All ER 529, [1961] 2 QB 278.

United Overseas Bank v Jiwani [1977] 1 All ER 734, [1976] 1 WLR 964.

h

Appeal

The defendants, the Food Corpn of India ('the cargo owners'), appealed against the judgment and order of Lloyd J on 28th July 1978 ([1979] 2 All ER 35) whereby the defendants were ordered to pay to the plaintiffs, China-Pacific SA ('the salvors'), a quantum meruit payment of $US 110,982·25 plus interest of $US 29,177·68 at 8% per annum to date of judgment for services rendered by the salvors to a cargo of wheat j belonging to the cargo owners from the wreck of the steam tanker Winson. The facts are set out in the judgment of Megaw LJ.

Gordon Pollock QC and *Simon Crookenden* for the cargo owners.
Anthony Clarke QC and *Jeremy Russell* for the salvors.

MEGAW LJ. This is an appeal from the judgment of Lloyd J ([1979] 2 All ER 35), delivered on 28th July 1978. The appellants, who were the defendants in the action, are the Food Corpn of India; they were the charterers of a vessel, the Winson, under a charterparty dated 9th October 1974. That charterparty was for the carriage of a cargo of wheat from the United States of America to India. The charterers duly loaded a cargo of some 37,000 tons of wheat. They were, at all material times, the owners of the wheat; I shall call them 'the cargo owners'. The owners of the Winson were Winson Tankers SA of Panama, which I understand to have been a one-ship company. I shall call them 'the shipowners'.

The charterparty, which was a Baltimore Berth Grain Charterparty, Steamer, Form C, with many pages of additional clauses added to it, provided that freight should be 'deemed earned upon safe arrival', in effect, of the cargo at the port of discharge. But by another clause in the charterparty 50% of the freight was to be paid within seven days of bills of lading being signed, 40% on the arrival of the cargo and the remaining 10% after settlement of what is described as 'despatch/demurrage'. The vessel was to have a lien on the cargo for all freight, demurrage or average. The entire freight was to be at all times at the risk of the vessel's owners. It is not necessary to refer to any of the other provisions of the charterparty.

In the course of the voyage, on 21st January 1975, the Winson stranded on the North Danger Reef in the South China Sea, some 420 miles from Manila in the Philippines. On 22nd January the ship's managing agents in Hong Kong signed a Lloyd's standard form of salvage agreement, 'no cure—no pay'. The salvors, the plaintiffs in the action, who are the respondents in this appeal, were referred to in the Lloyd's form as 'the contractor'; they are China-Pacific SA. I shall refer to them as 'the salvors'. There is no dispute but that the agreement in the Lloyd's form was an agreement which was duly and properly made on behalf of three parties, and that it was binding on each of them. The three parties are the salvors, the shipowners and the cargo owners. The first sentence of cl 1 of the salvage agreement reads:

> '(1) The contractor agrees to use his best endeavours to salve the S.S. Winson and/or her cargo and take them into [and then the blank space for the port of safety was not filled in] or other place to be hereafter agreed.'

It then provided that the services should be rendered and accepted as salvage services on the principle of 'no cure—no pay', and provisions for arbitration were incorporated.

Clause 16 of the form was as follows:

> 'The Master or other person signing this Agreement on behalf of the property to be salved enters into this Agreement as Agent for the vessel, her cargo and freight and the respective owners thereof and binds each (but not the one for the other or himself personally) to the due performance thereof.'

The salvors performed salvage services which resulted in the saving of 15,429 metric tons of the wheat, in six separate parcels, between 10th February and 20th April 1975. These parcels were taken by the salvors out of the wrecked Winson; they were put into craft provided by the salvors, and were taken in those craft to Manila, where they were off-loaded and put into store, partly in a vessel and partly in a bonded warehouse. The claim in this action is in respect of the expenses incurred in the off-loading and storage of salved cargo up to 24th April 1975.

On 24th April the shipowners abandoned the voyage and notified the cargo owners accordingly. It is not suggested in this action that, as between the shipowners and the cargo owners, the shipowners were not lawfully entitled in the circumstances to abandon the voyage when they did so, and thus put an end to the obligations of the parties as to any further performance under the contract of carriage.

On 23rd April a guarantee had been given on behalf of the cargo owners in respect of the cargo owners' proportion of any salvage award. That did not cover, or certainly did not necessarily cover, the expenses which are here in question, which relate to things done after completion of the salvage services. In June a compromise agreement was made without prejudice to the contentions of either side as to liability for the matters which have come into dispute in this action. For the cargo owners a total sum of $223,542·78 was paid to the salvors, representing expenses incurred by the salvors in connection with the salved cargo at Manila from 15th April to 15th June 1975, with an undertaking by the cargo owners to pay any further, post-15th June, expenses thereafter. The date, 15th April, would seem to have been a mistake for 24th April, the date on which notice of abandonment of the voyage was given by the shipowners; but neither side now raises any point on that mistake.

On 5th August the cargo owners took possession of the salved cargo in Manila, on the basis of that compromise agreement, which left open the issue as to liability for the expenses with which this case is concerned.

Thereafter a Lloyd's salvage arbitration was held, on 30th January 1976. The arbitrator was Mr Barry Sheen QC. He made an award in favour of the salvors. The salvors appealed under the procedure for appeal in such salvage arbitrations, on the question of the amount of the award. On that appeal the appeal arbitrator, Mr Roland Adams QC, increased the amount of the award. The detail of those proceedings, and of the awards, is not material to the issues in this case, except in respect of an issue as to estoppel.

As I have indicated, expenses were incurred in Manila as the various parcels of cargo arrived in the salvors' craft, salved from the Winson and carried the 420 miles to Manila. The expenses included the expense of removing and stevedoring the wheat out of the salvors' craft in which it had been carried to Manila, and thereafter the expenses of the storage of the salved wheat in order that it might be preserved in good condition. The total cost of the stevedoring and storage of the salved cargo was $383,392·90. It is agreed between the parties that this is a reasonable amount. The cargo owners accepted, at any rate at one time, that they were responsible for the reimbursement to the salvors of that part of the expenses in connection with the salved cargo which was referable to the period from 24th April to 5th August 1975. I should say, however, to avoid any possibility of misunderstanding, that I understood counsel for the cargo owners in his submissions to us not to concede that the cargo owners were liable, even for those expenses incurred by reference to the period after the abandonment of the voyage. But as I see it, there is no need to pursue that question on this appeal, which relates to the expenses referable to the period ending on 24th April.

The cargo owners deny that they are liable to pay that part of those expenses which is referable to the period between the arrival in Manila of the respective parcels of salved cargo and 24th April, when the voyage from the United States to India was abandoned. The amount in question in relation to that period, or rather, those periods, because they start at the various dates when the six respective parcels arrived at Manila, has been agreed to be $110,982·25. The cargo owners say that they are not liable to the salvors to reimburse them for those expenses, which the salvors have paid. If the salvors have any remedy in law, say the cargo owners, it is against the shipowners and not against the cargo owners. Lloyd J held that the cargo owners were liable. The cargo owners appeal. The salvors, by cross-notice, raise a question of estoppel, which was, indeed, in their pleadings when the action was heard before Lloyd J, but which was not dealt with in that action because in the circumstance of Lloyd J's decision on other matters it became unnecessary to decide it.

The cargo owners' primary submission is that the essential issue is: to whom was the cargo deliverable when each consignment of it, unloaded from the stranded Winson and loaded into the craft supplied by the salvors, arrived at Manila? The cargo owners contend that possession of the salved cargo was deliverable by the salvors to the shipowners, not to the cargo owners. If it be right that, on the correct principle of law as applied to the facts of this case, the salvors were required to deliver the cargo to the shipowners, not to the cargo owners, on its arrival piece by piece at Manila, then, say the cargo owners, they, the cargo owners, cannot be made liable for the expenses incurred in the stevedoring of the salved cargo out of the salvors' craft at Manila, or in its storage at Manila at any rate up to the date of the abandonment of the voyage. I think that the question as stated by counsel for the cargo owners is indeed the vital question, and that the answer to it in effect decides the appeal, subject only to the further question of estoppel raised on behalf of the salvors. I leave the question of estoppel for the time being, and consider the primary question as stated.

In my judgment, with great respect to the contrary view held by Lloyd J, counsel for the cargo owners has established his proposition that, where a salvor takes possession of the whole or part of a cargo of a vessel, after a casualty, under a salvage agreement such as that with which we are here concerned, then, when the cargo, or part of it, has been brought by the salvors to a place of safety, the salvors' obligation, in the absence of special circumstances, is to deliver that cargo back to the shipowners, not to deliver it to the cargo owners. I am not here considering the question of the security that might properly be required by the salvor as a condition for delivering cargo, whether to the shipowners or to the cargo owners. The salvage services to cargo, covered by the agreement, terminate in respect of that part of the cargo when the cargo is brought to a place of safety. It is the duty of the shipowner, vis-à-vis the cargo owner, under his contract of carriage, the charterparty, to carry the goods on to the contractual destination, unless the adventure has been frustrated or is abandoned by consent of the parties to it. The adventure is not necessarily frustrated even though the vessel in which the goods were being carried may itself be unable to continue the contract voyage. The shipowner, even so, has a right, though not a duty, to complete the adventure by carrying the cargo, or the surviving cargo, in another vessel. These propositions of law are covered by authority which I understand is not in dispute; therefore I shall not cite the authority. Of course, the adventure may be frustrated. The salvor may not know that this has happened, or that the shipowner has given notice to the cargo owner of the abandonment of the voyage. There may, therefore, be at any rate theoretical difficulties for the salvor, since, if the voyage has been abandoned, the cargo owner would be entitled, at any rate vis-à-vis the shipowner, to have the salved cargo delivered to him.

But, as a general proposition, both principle and convenience appear to me to lead to the conclusion contended for by counsel for the cargo owners. The shipowner, unless and until the voyage is abandoned or frustrated, is the person who is entitled to the possession of the goods which he is under a contractual obligation, and is contractually entitled, to carry to the destination, which, in some cases, he has to carry to their destination in order to earn his freight. It is right, however, to say that in modern times that last consideration is of much less importance in general than it once was.

I accept the propositions of counsel for the cargo owners on this point. They were summarised in his argument as follows. (1) The shipowners are entitled to remain in possession of the cargo by themselves or through sub-bailees until the contractual voyage is terminated. (2) Unless the shipowners abandon the voyage they are entitled to continue the voyage in order to earn their freight. (3) Shipowners have a possessory lien and it is not to be implied that they would lightly give it up. (4) The cargo owners are entitled to look to the shipowners to do all that is necessary and reasonable to safeguard the cargo wherever the ultimate cost of the steps taken may fall. (5) As the converse to (4), cargo owners have no right to seek to take possession of the cargo in order to take any steps which they may consider necessary. (6) It is more practicable that cargo should be delivered to the shipowner than to the cargo owner.

This general principle is no doubt subject to exceptions. One state of facts which might very probably constitute a valid exception is a case in which the shipowner cannot be found when the salvor has brought the cargo to the port of safety; or, a less improbable example, if the shipowner, knowing that the cargo has arrived, or is likely to arrive, at the place of safety, nevertheless indicates to the salvor that he does not wish or intend to take delivery of the salved cargo. If that were the position in the present case the cargo owners would, in my opinion, be in, at least, a very difficult position if they sought to contend that they were not liable for the expenses here in question, at any rate, if the salvors had told the cargo owners that the shipowners had declared a disinterest in, or a refusal to take delivery of, the cargo.

But on the evidential material in this case, obscure and unsatisfactory as much of it is,

I am persuaded by counsel's analysis that it would be wrong to hold that the shipowners had either been invited by the salvors to take delivery of the cargo at Manila, or had *a* indicated a refusal to do so, or that the cargo owners had been so informed. The most that can be said on the obscure evidence is that the salvors had at an early stage discussed the matter of the storage of the salved cargo with the shipowners' representatives, by telex, I think, rather than by any oral discussions. But it appears that it was the salvors, not the shipowners, who arranged for the stevedoring and the storage in Manila of the salved cargo. The cargo owners knew that the salvors were intending so to do and had *b* done so. But there was never any demand, or even a request to the cargo owners that they should take delivery in Manila before, at any rate, the first two loads of the salved cargo had arrived, had been stevedored out of the salvors' craft and had been put in storage; and that had been done on the salvors' instructions and, in the first instance at any rate, at their expense. The arrangements had all been made by the salvors, or by agents acting for them, without any indication, so far as one can see from the telexes and *c* the correspondence, that the salvors were requiring the cargo owners to make arrangements on their own account to take care of the cargo when the salvage services ended by the arrival of the cargo at Manila. The letter from the salvors' solicitors, dated 25th February 1975 (see [1979] 2 All ER 35 at 40) does not, in my view, operate to affect the cargo owners' liability in relation to arrangements made and expenses incurred, whether before or after the date of that letter. The primary obligation was still on the *d* shipowners; nothing appears to have been said to the cargo owners to tell them that the shipowners were declining to accept what was their obligation as to the preservation of the cargo on the conclusion of the salvage services.

The primary answer of the salvors, in their submissions before us, was that it does not matter whether the obligation to take delivery of the salved cargo at Manila was an obligation of the cargo owners or of the shipowners. They did, indeed, submit that, if it *e* mattered, the court should hold that it was the cargo owners who were obliged to take delivery. As I have said, I do not think that that is right. But, say the salvors, even if the primary obligation to take delivery of the salved cargo rested on the shipowners, none the less the salvors were bailees of the salved cargo. They were bailees directly from the cargo owners by reason of the provisions of the Lloyd's salvage agreement, and in particular cl 16 of that agreement. Even if the salvors were to be treated, not as bailees *f* but as sub-bailees (the shipowners being the bailees) it would make no difference. From this latter proposition, as I understand it, counsel for the cargo owners did not in the end dissent; he did not rely on the argument that the position would be different in law if the salvors were sub-bailees rather than direct bailees by virtue of the Lloyd's salvage agreement. As bailees, the salvors were obliged to take all reasonable steps to ensure that the salved cargo was properly cared for; that it was duly discharged from the salvors' *g* vessels and duly stored, pending on-carriage or other disposal of it. If the salvors carried out that duty, and incurred expenses, they were, as a matter of law, entitled to reimbursement of those expenses from the owner of the goods. That is the submission on behalf of the salvors.

This argument is set out, in a note of 'plaintiffs' propositions' which counsel for the salvors helpfully put before us, in these words: 'Where a bailee incurs reasonable expenses *h* as a bailee he is entitled to recover those expenses and reasonable remuneration in relation thereto from the bailor. The same is true as between a bailor and a sub-bailee.'

I need not lengthen this judgment by seeking to summarise or expound the cases relied on by the salvors for this proposition, cases such as *Gaudet v Brown* (1873) LR 5 PC 134, *Great Northern Railway Co v Swaffield* (1874) LR 9 Exch 132, [1874–80] All ER Rep 1065, *Notara v Henderson* (1882) LR 7 QB 225, and others. For the cargo owners the *j* general principle was accepted, subject to a qualification which, it was submitted, is vital in this case. That qualification is that where, as here, the bailee's contractual duty has ended, the existence of a duty on his part to incur expenses, recoverable from the goods' owner, in keeping the goods bailed from damage or destruction, depends on there being something which can properly be called an element of necessity that the bailee should so

act in order to preserve the goods. If, on the facts of this case, it were properly to be
a accepted that the salvors, when they brought these craftloads of salved cargo into port in Manila, had made their arrangements, at their own initial expense, to off-load the salved cargo and to store it, simply, or primarily, for the benefit of the cargo owners, because an emergency had arisen, then the salvors might well be entitled (subject to the lien point which I shall mention hereafter) to recover the expenses which they had reasonably incurred for the benefit of the cargo owners. But that is simply not this case. There is
b no basis in the material before us for any finding that the conduct of the salvors in arranging for the stevedoring of the cargo out of the salvors' carrying craft, and the storage of that salved cargo, was founded on, or related to, any relevant emergency or any relevant necessity. If there had been any such basis, the salvors would certainly have taken steps to convey to the cargo owners, of whose identity they were well aware, the unequivocal demand that the cargo owners should make arrangements, or authorise the
c salvors on their behalf and at their expense to make arrangements, to receive the cargo or to take over the responsibility for it, on the basis that the cargo would otherwise be left to perish. There was no suggestion, other than the letter of 25th February 1975 to which I have already referred, that the cargo owners should send, or appoint, representatives in Manila who would be responsible for taking delivery of, and arranging for the storage of, the cargo. The letter of 25th February seems to have been, at most, a demand or request
d that the cargo owners should take delivery from the salvors of cargo stored by them, the salvors, in Manila.

With great respect, I am unable to accept the view expressed by Lloyd J in his judgment that 'the only point of time at which necessity could be relevant was when Lloyd's Open Form was signed' (see [1979] 2 All ER 35 at 44). The relevant time, for the purpose of considering whether there was a necessity, or an emergency, which brought
e into operation the right of the bailee to incur expenses on behalf of the bailor is, as submitted by counsel for the cargo owners, the time when the existence of the supposed emergency became apparent. The emergency would be the arrival, or expected arrival, of salved cargo at Manila, with no arrangements for its off-loading or for its preservation in proper storage having been made or put in hand. There never was, so far as one can ascertain from the evidential matter here, such an emergency.

f I am also, with great respect, unable to accept on the facts of this case that there can be said to have been here a 'necessity' because of 'inability to obtain proper instructions'. It may well be that the cargo owners can fairly be criticised for maintaining a remarkable and prolonged silence; but it was not until at least two instalments of the salved cargo had arrived in Manila that the salvors, through their London solicitors, for the first time even suggested to the cargo owners that they should 'accept delivery of the cargo'. I need
g not repeat what I have said about that letter of 25th February.

In the circumstances, having regard to all that had already happened, and the complete absence of any suggestion by the salvors to the cargo owners that the shipowners were refusing, or falling down on their duty, to be responsible for the salved cargo, I am unable to regard that belated request as evidencing, or giving rise to the existence of, a case of emergency or necessity such as would warrant the recognition of an obligation on
h the cargo owners of responsibility for reimbursement of the salvors for either past or future expenditure. If the salvors were to look to anyone for the charges which they had incurred for the arrangements that they had themselves, as volunteers, made for the off-loading and storing of the salved cargo, it would be to the shipowners that they should look, as being the persons primarily responsible for accepting delivery of the cargo when it was brought to the place of safety. The salvors, perfectly properly, were concerned to
j maintain a lien on the salved cargo. It was, I have no doubt on the material before us, with that in mind that they did what they did.

The submissions which the salvors made on the basis of agency of necessity do not, in my opinion, avail them, essentially for the same reasons. I would merely say in passing, with very great respect to the learned editors of the highly-regarded and authoritative textbook, Goff and Jones on The Law of Restitution, that the proposition stated in the second edition (1978, p 266, para (1)) does not appear to me to be supported by the authority cited for it in the footnote. That passage reads: 'It is apparently enough if the agent asked his principal for instructions but the principal ignored his request.' The authority cited is *Gokal Chand-Jagan Nath v Nand Ram Das-Atma Ram* [1938] 4 All ER 407, [1939] AC 106. As I say, perusal of that case does not appear to me to provide support for the proposition. There may well be cases in which a failure to give instructions, when the owner of the goods is asked by the bailee to give instructions, may be relevant and may give rise to an obligation on the bailee to reimburse; but in the present case, on the view that I have already stated, that question does not here arise.

I referred a short time ago to a further point, which has been described as being the lien point. I do not propose in the circumstances to express any views on that further point, which was raised on behalf of the cargo owners, which they submit would enable them to defeat the salvors' claim even if they were held to be wrong on the issues which I have already discussed. I would merely mention that this further point is based on the authority of *Somes v British Empire Shipping Co* (1860) 8 HL Cas 338, 11 ER 459. The first paragraph of the headnote of the report reads: 'A person who has a lien upon a chattel for a debt cannot, if he keeps it to enforce payment, add, to the amount for which the lien exists, a charge for keeping the chattel till the debt is paid.' That authority was cited recently by Brandon J in *Delantera Amadora SA v Bristol Channel Shiprepairers Ltd and Swansea Dry Docks Co, The Katingaki* [1976] 2 Lloyd's Rep 372. It is clear that, although *The Katingaki* was mentioned in the course of counsel's speech before Lloyd J, the point now raised for the cargo owners was not developed as it has been developed before us by counsel for the cargo owners. If it had been so developed, I have no doubt that Lloyd J would have referred to it and discussed it in his judgment. I do not find it necessary or desirable to express any views on that issue.

I turn finally to the estoppel point. I do not find it necessary to go into the rather unfortunate manner in which this point has been dealt with in these proceedings. The result at one time appeared likely to be that this court was being placed in a position of serious embarrassment, which it would be extremely difficult to resolve in a way which would be procedurally sensible and would be fair to the parties. In the end, however, having heard submissions on the issue, I am satisfied that we are in a position properly to decide the point, and I do not propose to go further into the matters to which I have referred; no useful purpose would be served by so doing.

The estoppel point is raised in the pleadings in the action, in the points of reply. The salvors say that the cargo owners are estopped from denying liability to the plaintiffs for the sum claimed in this action. The representation which is said to have been made is 'that the defendants [the cargo owners] by their said agents represented to the plaintiffs [the salvors] by their said agents that the defendants were liable for the post-salvage charges herein sued upon'. That representation is said to have been made as the result of the combined effect of what was set out in a letter dated 29th January 1976 from the cargo owners' solicitors to the salvors' solicitors, and what was said in a discussion between counsel for the salvors and for the cargo owners on 30th January 1976.

The Lloyd's salvage arbitration was due to be held, before Mr Barry Sheen, on 30th January 1976. The parties were seeking to arrive at an agreed value of the salved property, which in this case was the cargo alone. The amount of the salvage award might (it is sufficient for this purpose to say 'might') be affected in some degree by the value of the salved property. The cargo owners were thus concerned to keep any agreed value as low as possible, and the salvors were concerned to keep it as high as possible.

At that time the amount of the expenses which are in dispute in this action was thought by both parties to be \$174,173·91, instead of the \$110,982·25 which is now known to be the correct figure. I mention that merely by way of explanation of the point as it arose; the fact that there was that error is immaterial.

The letter to which I have referred, of 29th January 1976 from the cargo owners' solicitors to the salvors' solicitors, in the first paragraph, states: '. . . we [that is, the cargo owners' solicitors] are prepared to recommend to our clients [that is, the cargo owners] to agree the sound value of the cargo at U.S.$2,266,223·61.' Then the cargo owners' solicitors were concerned to seek to obtain agreement to deductions being made from that figure in order to arrive at the relevant agreed value for the purposes of the salvage arbitration. The third paragraph of the letter starts with these sentences:

> 'As regards deductions, apart from the deduction of U.S.$272,410·65, we consider that the sum of U.S.$174,173·91 [I pause to say that that is the figure with which we are concerned] should also be deducted from the sound value of the cargo although this sum is to be claimed by your clients from our clients in the arbitration. We have advised our clients that they are liable for the sum of $174,173·91. In this respect, we write without prejudice.'

Then, later in the letter, this is said:

> 'Therefore, agreeing your figure (although subject to instructions) of U.S.$2,226,223·61 as the sound value of the cargo, we shall contend that there should be a total deduction of U.S.$823,084·67, the resultant salved value of the cargo being [and then the subtraction sum is done].'

So that is the cargo owners' solicitors saying that the amount of the charges with which we are concerned in these present proceedings, which are now agreed to be approximately $110,000, should not be included as a part of the salved value. The basis on which the suggestion was being made, that the salvors' representatives should agree to that deduction, was presumably contained in the sentence 'We have advised our clients that they are liable' for that sum, though it is right to add that they said that in this respect they wrote without prejudice.

Then, on the morning of 30th January 1976, before the salvage arbitration began, counsel who then represented the respective parties (not being counsel who appeared before us on the appeal) met to try to arrive at an agreed figure of salved value. We have before us an agreed note, prepared and signed by the two counsel concerned, of their recollection of what took place at that discussion. It is agreed for the purposes of this appeal, in order to avoid the necessity that would otherwise have arisen of evidence being taken, possibly from counsel concerned, that it should be assumed that the note is inaccurate in one respect, namely that a representative of the cargo owners' solicitors was present. That is what the agreed note of counsel says, but for the cargo owners it is said that counsel's recollection on that was inaccurate and, so far as the salvors are concerned, they are prepared for the purposes of this appeal to accept that that assumption should be made. It is fair to say that counsel's note appears to have been agreed, as a result, I think, of something that was said by a judge who dealt with an earlier stage of these proceedings, on 4th July 1978. That was a very long time after the discussions in question. Counsel have obviously done their best. I think it is remarkable and very helpful that they should have remembered what they have remembered. In any case, so far as the presence or absence of the solicitors for the cargo owners at the discussion that morning is concerned, I do not think that it makes any difference, and therefore the concession that has been made on behalf of the salvors is one that does not harm them in any way. If I had thought that it made a difference, I should have hesitated as to the propriety of accepting the concession. For myself, although we were invited to do so, I would not be prepared, in the circumstances here, and I would not regard it as proper, to go outside that note agreed by counsel, otherwise than on the basis of the whole matter being sent back for further consideration by counsel concerned, who have sought to assist the court in this way.

The agreed note sets out that counsel then representing the salvors put forward a sound value of the cargo on the basis, fob Manila, of $2,266,223, which we have already seen in the letter of the previous day. It is recorded that counsel for the cargo owners accepted both that basis of sound valuation and that figure.

Then the note goes on to refer to deductions. It records that counsel for the cargo owners 'for the purpose of the discussion then put forward the following deductions', and there are then set out seven suggested deductions, lettered from (a) to (g). Presumably those deductions were put forward by counsel on instructions, though some suggestion *a* has been made in submissions on behalf of the cargo owners that it should be assumed that counsel was not instructed on those matters. The one with which we are concerned is (g): 'Unpaid post-salvage expenses: $174,173.' The agreed note of counsel contains the parenthesis under that item: '(at that stage both parties bona fide but mistakenly believed the unpaid expenses to amount to $174,173 and not $110,982 as was and is in fact the correct figure).' *b*

Then the note goes on to record: 'These deductions were dealt with as follows'. I need not bother with (a), (b), (c), (d), (e) or (f), in respect of all of which, in one way or another, agreement was reached between counsel. I read the note relating to (g), simply substituting for the initials which appear in the note the words 'counsel for the salvors' or 'counsel for the cargo owners' as the case may be:

c

> '[Counsel for the salvors] disputed this deduction on the ground that the sum of $174,173, although due, had not been paid. [Counsel for the cargo owners] then pointed out that, if the Defendants were liable to pay the sum, it ought properly to constitute a deduction irrespective of whether or not it had actually been paid. [Counsel for the salvors] accepted the correctness of [counsel for the cargo owners'] argument in principle but continued to resist the allowance of the deduction *d* because of the Defendants' prolonged and (in the Plaintiffs' view) unwarrantable failure to pay the relevant charges. [Counsel for the cargo owners] then suggested the resolution of the problem by the compromise of the deduction at about one half of the figure claimed, ie $87,086. [Counsel for the salvors] agreed to that.'

So those suggested deductions were made, including that deduction. The result was that *e* when the salvage arbitration took place, the arbitrator was told that the salved value was agreed and that it was agreed at a figure which was arrived at by including, amongst other deductions, a deduction of one-half of the supposed expenses which are in question in this action.

It is said for the salvors that the cargo owners, through their authorised representatives, by virtue of the letter and what happened between counsel on that occasion, made a *f* representation to the authorised representatives of the salvors that the cargo owners were liable for the post-salvage charges claimed in this action. In his submission to this court, junior counsel for the salvors submitted that the representation consisted of the cargo owners' representatives saying that they, the cargo owners, would pay these charges. The salvors, it is said, relied on that representation to their detriment by agreeing, as a result of it, that the agreed salved value of the cargo was of a lower value than they would have *g* agreed if it had not been for the representation.

I would wish to pay tribute to the admirably clear and careful advocacy of junior counsel for the salvors on this issue. If I may say so, he has said everything that could be said, and he has said it as well as it could be said. It is no fault of his that, as I think, the salvors' case on estoppel cannot succeed.

It has been attacked by counsel for the cargo owners on a substantial number of *h* different grounds; I do not find it necessary to discuss them all.

The supposed representation is not, and cannot be dressed up as being, a representation of fact. If it were a representation by the cargo owners, 'we are liable', it would, in the dichotomy which has been drawn for this purpose, be a representation of law. If what was said is to be construed as 'we will pay', it would be a promise. The salvors could, indeed, succeed on this issue only if this were properly to be treated as a promissory *j* estoppel. But, for a promissory estoppel, apart from other conditions, it has to be shown that there is something which is a quite unequivocal statement.

I would refer to a passage in the textbook Estoppel by Representation by Spencer, Bower and Turner (3rd Edn, 1977, p 375, para 347), where, in the chapter dealing with promissory estoppel, this is said:

> 'While a *representation of existing fact* is necessary for the foundation of a true estoppel, the words or conduct necessary to support a promissory estoppel are essentially different in quality. They consist of a *promise or assurance as to the future conduct of a promisor*, on which the promisee relies to act to his detriment. Not only does this follow *ex vi termini* from the very term "promissory estoppel", but it is clearly stated as a principal attribute of the estoppel in the cases from which the doctrine takes its origin.' (Author's emphasis.)

Then there are citations from *Central London Property Trust Ltd v High Trees House Ltd* [1956] 1 All ER 256, [1947] KB 130 and other cases.

The learned editor goes on (at p 376):

> 'When promissory estoppel is invoked, the promise or assurance necessary to support it is inevitably less than a promise binding upon the parties *in contract*—it would not be necessary to invoke the doctrine of promissory estoppel at all if the promise had contractual force. But nevertheless the promise supporting a promissory estoppel is closely analogous in many respects to a promise having contractual effect. One of its essential attributes is the same degree of *unequivocality* which, if the same assurance had been given full consideration, would have clothed it with contractual effect. This was the rock upon which the plea of promissory estoppel foundered, both in the Court of Appeal and in the House of Lords, in *Woodhouse A. C. Israel Cocoa S.A. v. Nigerian Produce Marketing Limited* ([1972] 2 All ER 271, [1972] AC 741). In his judgment in the Court of Appeal ([1971] 1 All ER 665 at 672, [1971] 2 QB 23 at 59–60) LORD DENNING M.R. referred to the "extraordinary consequences" of holding that an assurance ineffectual (by reason of its indefiniteness) to *vary* a contract was yet definite enough to support a promissory estoppel bringing about the same result.' (Author's emphasis.)

In the circumstances with which we are concerned here, promissory estoppel would not have been necessary for the purpose for which it so often is necessary, namely, because of the absence of anything which can technically be called consideration moving from the person to whom the promise is offered or the representation is made.

In the present case it could not be suggested that there was absence of consideration. If here there were an offer which could have amounted to a contractual offer if accepted, there would have been consideration flowing from the salvors, namely their agreement, in consideration of the cargo owners' promise to accept liability for the expenses, themselves to accept in the salvage arbitration a lower figure for the salved value of the cargo than they would otherwise have agreed. Therefore, if there were here a case on behalf of the salvors, I should have thought that it would have been a case that would have founded itself in contract. It does not found itself in contract. The reason is that what is said to be the promise is not unequivocal. At the best it was an indication by solicitors instructed on behalf of the cargo owners that they, the solicitors, had advised their clients that their clients were liable in law to the salvors in this claim for expenses. But that would not be enough, as I see it, to constitute either an offer which would give rise by acceptance to a contract to pay those sums or a representation which could be treated as giving rise to a promissory estoppel. The matters put forward as constituting representation are not unequivocal.

For that reason, without going into the other reasons (and I think there are other serious difficulties in the way of the salvors in relation to their claim for estoppel) I would hold that they cannot succeed on that issue.

It follows, therefore, that on this appeal, as a whole, I would hold that the appeal must be allowed.

BRIDGE LJ. I entirely agree with the judgment that has been delivered by Megaw LJ; I add only a very short word of my own in deference to the learned judge, from whose decision we are differing, on what seems to be the central issue in the appeal.

Under Lloyd's standard form of salvage agreement, on the termination of salvage services, who has the primary right and duty to retake possession of the salved cargo? Is it the shipowner, or is it the cargo owner? This is, as it seems to me, the critical question on which this appeal turns.

Many considerations have been urged on us by counsel on both sides in argument, as bearing on the answer to this question. But in my judgment, the decisive consideration is simply this: that at all events, as long as the shipowner is, or may be, able to continue the voyage in the original vessel he has, as against the cargo owner, both the right and the duty to do so. He is entitled to earn his freight; he is entitled to a lien on the cargo, both for freight and for average. It follows in my view that the shipowner is both bound and entitled to take possession of the salved cargo, and if he incurs expenses in taking care of the cargo following successful salvage operations these are his primary liability, subject to his right to recover a contribution from the cargo owner as general average.

In this situation therefore, it seems to me clear that the salvor, if he incurs expenses in the care of the cargo after determination of the salvage services, must look to the shipowner to recoup them. So long as he has a right of recourse to the shipowner, he cannot claim that a situation of emergency, or necessity, has arisen which entitles him to recover direct from the cargo owner the expenses which he has incurred.

Quite a different situation will no doubt arise once the voyage is abandoned. Again if, apart from abandonment, the shipowner repudiates his obligations (as, for example, by refusing to accept the cargo from the salvor) it may well be that the salvor can then claim that such an emergency or necessity has arisen as to entitle him to take appropriate steps for the preservation of the cargo in discharge of a duty owed directly to the cargo owner such as to give rise to a correlative right to recover his expenses from the cargo owner. But I cannot discover anything in the somewhat exiguous evidence before the court that indicates that any such situation arose in the present case.

For these reasons, in addition to those given by Megaw LJ, I too would allow this appeal.

CUMMING-BRUCE LJ. I agree with both judgments.

Appeal allowed. Leave to appeal to the House of Lords refused.

23rd July. The Appeal Committee of the House of Lords (Lord Wilberforce, Lord Salmon and Lord Russell of Killowen) granted leave to appeal.

Solicitors: *Stocken & Co* (for the cargo owners); *Constant & Constant* (for the salvors).

Mary Rose Plummer Barrister.

a Booth v Ellard (Inspector of Taxes)

COURT OF APPEAL, CIVIL DIVISION
BUCKLEY, ACKNER AND OLIVER LJJ
20th MAY 1980

b *Capital gains tax – Settlement – Beneficiary becoming absolutely entitled to settled property –*
Beneficiary entitled as against trustee – Plurality of beneficial owners – Family controlled
company – Taxpayer and other family shareholders transferring shares to trustees – Trustees to
hold shares for 15 years – Taxpayer and shareholders restricted in their right to dispose of shares
– Taxpayer's interest in his shares the same as interest of other family shareholders – Whether
taxpayer absolutely entitled to his shares as against the trustees – Finance Act 1965, s 22(5).

c Pursuant to an agreement dated 29th August 1972 the taxpayer and 11 other
shareholders, all members of the same family ('the family shareholders'), transferred
their shares in B Ltd to trustees to be held by them on the terms set out in the
agreement. Under the agreement the trust was to continue until 31st December 1987
subject to termination by notice given by a majority, in terms of settled shares, of the
d persons entitled under the trust. The income from the trust fund, subject to
administrative expenses, was distributable among the shareholders in proportion to the
number of shares to which they were entitled. If a family shareholder failed to give
written instructions how the voting rights in respect of his shares were to be exercised at
a general meeting of the company, the trustees were entitled to exercise those voting
rights as they thought fit. If an offer was made or a scheme proposed for the acquisition
e of the family shareholdings and if the trustees were notified by family shareholders who
between them were entitled to not less than three-quarters of the shares that they wished
their shares to be so acquired, the trustees were to take such action as in their opinion was
likely to result in the disposal of all the family shareholdings to the best advantage of the
family shareholders. In the event of a rights issue by the company each family
shareholder was to be given the opportunity to notify the trustees within a specified
f period whether he intended to take up the rights. If a family shareholder failed to notify
the trustees within the specified period the trustees were entitled to dispose of the rights
as they thought fit and were required to pay the proceeds of sale to the shareholder
entitled to the shares in respect of which the rights had arisen. The taxpayer was assessed
to capital gains tax for the year 1972–73 on the basis that the transfer of his shares to the
trustees constituted a chargeable disposal. The taxpayer appealed contending, inter alia,
g that he was absolutely entitled to the shares as against the trustees within s 22(5)[a] of the
Finance Act 1965 since all the family shareholders had the same interest in the trust and
could, by acting together, direct how the trustees should deal with the fund, and that
accordingly, for the purposes of capital gains tax, there was no chargeable disposal. The
Special Commissioners upheld the assessment on the grounds that although the taxpayer
and the other family shareholders, by combining, could put an end to the trust,
h nevertheless, in so doing they could not properly be regarded as acting 'jointly' or as
'tenants in common' or concurrently and that the terms of the agreement were
inconsistent with absolute ownership. The judge allowed the taxpayer's appeal ([1978]
3 All ER 298), on the ground that the taxpayer was absolutely entitled to the shares as
against the trustees and, accordingly, in transferring his shares to the trustees the taxpayer
had not made a chargeable disposal. The Crown appealed.

j **Held** – Although the effect of the trust was to subject all the trust shares to the powers
and discretions conferred on the trustees for the collective benefit of the settlors, the
measure of the beneficial interest of each of the settlors remained unaffected by the trust

a Section 22(5) is set out at p 571 *h j*, post

(subject to the trustees' powers and discretions, which the settlors could collectively override), and there was no transfer of any beneficial interest from any one of them to *a*
any other. Thus, on a true view of the facts, by participating in the pooling arrangement the taxpayer never lost his interest in the shares and was absolutely entitled to them as against the trustees within s 22(5) of the 1965 Act. It followed, therefore, that the transfer of shares to the trustees under the agreement did not constitute a chargeable disposal. The appeal would, accordingly be dismissed (see p 574 *c* to *e* and *j* to p 575 *a* and *c* to *g* and p 576 *b* to *d*, post). *b*

Kidson (Inspector of Taxes) v Macdonald [1974] 1 All ER 849 and *Stephenson (Inspector of Taxes) v Barclays Bank Trust Co Ltd* [1975] 1 All ER 625 followed.

Decision of Goulding J [1978] 3 All ER 298 affirmed.

Notes

For capital gains tax in relation to settled property, see 5 Halsbury's Laws (4th Edn) paras *c*
45–48.

For the Finance Act 1965, s 22, see 34 Halsbury's Statutes (3rd Edn) 877.

With effect from 6th April 1979, s 22(5) of the 1965 Act was replaced by the Capital Gains Tax Act 1979, s 46(1).

Cases referred to in judgments *d*

Kidson (Inspector of Taxes) v Macdonald [1974] 1 All ER 849, [1974] Ch 339, [1974] 2 WLR 566, [1974] STC 54, 49 Tax Cas 503, 52 ATC 318, [1973] TR 259, Digest (Cont Vol D) 471, *1448a*.

Stephenson (Inspector of Taxes) v Barclays Bank Trust Co Ltd [1975] 1 All ER 625, [1975] 1 WLR 882, [1975] STC 151, 53 ATC 351, [1974] TR 343, Digest (Cont Vol D) 473, *1448d*. *e*

Cases also cited

Aberdeen Construction Group Ltd v Inland Revenue Comrs [1978] 1 All ER 962, [1978] AC 885, [1978] STC 127, HL.

Hoare Trustees v Gardner (Inspector of Taxes) [1978] 1 All ER 791, [1979] Ch 10, [1978] STC 89. *f*

Kipping, Re, Kipping v Kipping [1914] 1 Ch 62, CA.

Weiner's Will Trusts, Re, Wyner v Braithwaite [1956] 2 All ER 482, [1956] 1 WLR 579.

Appeal

The Crown appealed against an order of Goulding J ([1978] 3 All ER 298, [1978] 1 WLR 927) reversing, on an appeal by way of case stated by John Sebastian Macaulay Booth ('the *g*
taxpayer'), the determination of the Special Commissioners upholding the assessment to capital gains tax made on him for the year 1972–73 in respect of the transfer of his shares in Booth (International Holdings) Ltd to trustees to be held by them on the terms of an agreement dated 29th August 1972. The facts are set out in the judgment of Buckley LJ.

Andrew Morritt QC and *C H McCall* for the Crown. *h*

D J Nicholls QC, J E Holroyd Pearce QC and *A G Wilson* for the taxpayer.

BUCKLEY LJ. This is an appeal from a judgment of Goulding J ([1978] 3 All ER 298, [1978] 1 WLR 927) delivered on 28th February 1978 on an appeal by the taxpayer from a decision of the Special Commissioners, who upheld in principle an assessment of the taxpayer to capital gains tax for the year 1972–73. The learned judge allowed the *j*
taxpayer's appeal. The Crown now appeals to this court from that decision.

The detailed facts are set out in para 4 of the case stated (the case stated is set out at [1978] 3 All ER 299–307). They arise out of the circumstances that in August 1972 the taxpayer and members of his family held, either beneficially or as trustees, 432,299 of the 600,000 issued shares of a company called Booth (International Holdings) Ltd, and that

it was then in contemplation that in the near future application would be made for
a permission to deal in, and a quotation for, the company's shares on the London Stock Exchange. This would necessitate sales on the market of a substantial part of the family's holdings. The family was anxious to retain effective control of the company as far as possible. With that object 270,091 shares of the company held by members of the family (approximately 45% of the issued share capital) were transferred to trustees to be held on the terms of an agreement set out in full in the case. They included 55,000
b shares transferred by the taxpayer. Some of these he owned beneficially and some he held as trustee, but that is, I think, irrelevant to what we have to decide.

Stating it as shortly as I can (for the document can be read in the case) the substance of the agreement is as follows. The trust is to continue until 31st December 1987 unless determined earlier under cl 3 by a majority, in terms of settled shares, of the persons entitled under the trust. The income (subject to administrative expenses) is distributable
c amongst the participants in the arrangement in proportion to the number of shares to which they are respectively entitled. Subject to receiving a prescribed notice, the trustees are to exercise voting rights on the shares as the several participants direct in respect of the shares to which they are respectively entitled, subject to which the trustees may vote as they think fit. In the event of any offer being made to acquire all or any part of the shares, if a specified majority of the participants wish to dispose of their shares, the
d trustees are to take such action as in their opinion is likely to result in all the trust shares being disposed of to the best advantage. In the event of any duty becoming payable in respect of any of the trust shares by reason of a death, the trustees are, if so requested, to sell sufficient shares to pay the duty, and the person entitled to those shares may charge the shares to raise any such duty. A participant is entitled to dispose of his beneficial interest in any shares to which he is beneficially entitled under the trust, subject to
e restrictions of a kind which are familiar in the regulations of private companies, involving the giving of a disposal notice and a right of pre-emption for other participants at a fair value, and provision is made for the personal representatives of a deceased participant to be deemed to have given a disposal notice in certain circumstances which might result in the deceased's shares going outside the family circle. Possible rights issues and bonus issues are also dealt with. On the determination of the trust the shares
f then held by the trustees are to be transferred to the participants then respectively entitled to them.

The question for decision is whether, by reason of his transferring 55,000 shares of the company to the trustees, the taxpayer became liable to capital gains tax. That tax was brought into existence by the Finance Act 1965, Part III. The relevant sections for present purposes are ss 19(1) and (3), 20(1), 22(1), (4) and (5) and 45(1). Reference should
g also be made to Sch 13, para 9, to the Finance Act 1969, which explains the meaning in this context of the expression 'absolutely entitled as against the trustee'. Section 45(1) defines 'settled property' as meaning (subject to an irrelevant qualification) 'any property held in trust other than property to which section 22(5) of this Act applies'. The question in the present case is whether the case falls within s 22(5) or not. If it does so, the taxpayer is not liable for tax on his disposal of the 55,000 shares; if it does not, he is.

h Section 22(5) is in the following terms:

> 'In relation to assets held by a person as nominee for another person, or as trustee for another person absolutely entitled as against the trustee, or for any person who would be so entitled but for being an infant or other person under disability (or for two or more persons who are or would be jointly so entitled), this Part of this Act
> j shall apply as if the property were vested in, and the acts of the nominee or trustee in relation to the assets were the acts of, the person or persons for whom he is the nominee or trustee (acquisitions from or disposals to him by that person or persons being disregarded accordingly).'

Breaking this down, selecting only the words appropriate to a case such as the present and reading it first as applicable to a single person absolutely entitled, the subsection reads thus:

> 'In relation to assets held by a person as trustee for another person . . . absolutely entitled as against the trustee . . . this Part of this Act shall apply as if the property were vested in, and the acts of the . . . trustee in relation to the assets were the acts of, the person . . . for whom he is . . . trustee . . .'

Let me now read it as it must be read in relation to two or more persons absolutely entitled; that would read as follows:

> 'In relation to assets held by a person . . . as trustee . . . for two or more [other] persons jointly [absolutely entitled as against the trustee] . . . this Part of this Act shall apply as if the property were vested in, and the acts of the . . . trustee in relation to the assets were the acts of, the . . . persons for whom he is . . . trustee . . .'

The words in brackets which close the subsection enunciate a consequence of what precedes them. They are '(acquisitions from or disposals to him by that person or persons being disregarded accordingly)'. Here 'him' refers to the trustee and 'that person or persons' refers to the person or persons beneficially entitled.

So if A transfers shares into the name of B as his nominee, or as trustee of a trust under which B holds the shares for A absolutely, the shares are to be treated for capital gains tax purposes as though they remained vested in A, and the disposal by A to B is to be disregarded, as also is any reacquisition of the shares by A from B.

The present case is not so simple as that, because there were 12 distinct settlors, treating joint settlors as single entities. They brought various numbers of shares into the trust. They did not retain any beneficial interest in the specific shares which they brought in. Each settlor became entitled, subject to the provisions of the trust, to the number of shares which he brought in, but the shares to which each settlor was entitled were unspecified shares in the pool.

The meaning of the word 'jointly' in s 22(5) has been considered in two cases, the correctness of the decisions in which has not been questioned before us. In *Kidson (Inspector of Taxes) v Macdonald* [1974] 1 All ER 849, [1974] Ch 339 Foster J was concerned with a case in which two gentlemen had bought land in 1960 and 1961 in their joint names as joint tenants on trust for sale and to hold the net proceeds of sale in trust for themselves as tenants in common. In 1966 one of them died and his legal personal representatives sold his share in the land at a profit. The question was whether the vendors were liable to capital gains tax. That they were so was clear, unless they were exempt under Sch 7, para 13, to the 1965 Act which, so far as relevant, reads as follows:

> 'No chargeable gain shall accrue on the disposal of an interest created by or arising under a settlement . . . by the person for whose benefit the interest was created by the terms of the settlement . . .'

So, if the interest disposed of by the vendors was one created by or arising under a settlement for the purposes of Part III of the 1965 Act, the vendors were exempt from tax. Having regard to the definition of 'settled property' in s 45(1), the judge held that the deceased's interest arose under a settlement unless s 22(5) was applicable. So it was in the taxpayer's interest in that case to contend that s 22(5) did not apply. Foster J held that in s 22(5) 'jointly' was not used in a technical sense, but meant concurrently or in common. So the tenants in common were jointly entitled within the meaning of the subsection and as against the trustee they were together absolutely entitled. On that basis Foster J held that the taxpayers were not exempt from tax.

In *Stephenson (Inspector of Taxes) v Barclays Bank Trust Co* [1975] 1 All ER 625, [1975] 1 WLR 882 Walton J was concerned with a fund in which two beneficiaries under a will became absolutely entitled in possession to a fund as tenants in common on the execution in 1969 of a deed of family arrangement. In the course of his judgment Walton J drew a distinction between successive beneficial interests and the interests of persons 'jointly

entitled' within the meaning of s 22(5). Walton J said ([1975] 1 All ER 625 at 638, [1975]
a 1 WLR 882 at 890):

> 'The definition says "jointly"; it does not say "together". I think this is because it is intended to comprise persons who are, as it were, in the same interest. This is a point which was alluded to by Foster J in *Kidson v Macdonald* [1974] 1 All ER 849 at 858, [1974] Ch 339 at 350. If property is settled on A for life with remainder to B,
> b A and B are "together" entitled absolutely as against the trustees, but they are not so entitled "jointly", "concurrently", or as "tenants in common".'

In the present case counsel for the Crown has submitted that s 22(5) is not applicable because the taxpayer did not transfer his shares to the trustees on trust for himself alone but to be held as part of a pool in which all the participants had interests. Alternatively, he says that if the taxpayer's shares were held specifically in trust for him he was not
c entitled to direct the trustees how to deal with them. On the first point counsel for the Crown says that the relevant consideration is whether the trustees held the shares transferred by the taxpayer in trust for him and him alone as a person absolutely entitled as against the trustees.

Counsel for the taxpayer submits that one should not look at the taxpayer in isolation. On the creation of the trust the several settlors who contributed shares to the
d pool were, counsel says, concurrently and absolutely entitled to the settled property as against the trustees; they could, by a unanimous act, have put an end to the settlement at any time and without recourse to any provision for termination contained in the agreement. No beneficial interest passed from anyone to anyone in consequence of the trust. What had previously been owned by several owners in several ownerships coalesced in a trust fund which was held in trust for the same persons and in proportions
e corresponding to the proportions of their previous several ownerships. In such a state of affairs counsel for the taxpayer submits that s 22(5) applies. He does not suggest that this would necessarily be so in any case except one in which (a) the beneficial interests of the several persons beneficially interested under the trust amounted in the aggregate to the whole beneficial interest in the property subject to the trust and (b) those interests were all concurrent. In the light of the two cases which I have cited, I understand 'concurrent'
f in this context to mean coexistent and of the same quality. Taking (a) with (b), it seems to me that this must mean that the interest of every person having a beneficial interest must be an absolute interest in some part of, or share in, the property. Given that such interests amount in the aggregate to the entire beneficial interest in the fund, then, assuming that the persons beneficially interested are all sui juris (and there is no suggestion to the contrary here) it must follow that they have it in their power to put an
g end to the trust summarily at any moment, notwithstanding any powers or discretions conferred on the trustees by the terms of the trust or by operation of law.

In the circumstances of the present case, counsel for the taxpayer submits, all the 12 settlors who contributed shares to the pool comprised in the trust were together collectively and concurrently entitled absolutely to the whole trust fund as against the trustees, within the meaning of s 22(5). Collectively they could put a summary end to
h the trust and so destroy or override any discretion or power vested in the trustees. They were consequently jointly entitled to the trust property absolutely as against the trustees within the meaning of s 22(5). So one must treat the shares as vested in the settlors and treat the acts of the trustees as the acts of the settlors, with the consequence, as counsel for the taxpayer contends, that the position must be viewed as though none of the settlors had disposed of his or her or their shares.

j The logic of this argument seems to me to be unassailable unless it can be said that by participating in the pooling arrangement the several settlors lost their existing beneficial interest in their own particular shares and become entitled merely to an undivided or unappropriated share in the pool formed by their several contributions and that, because the latter interest was different from the former, there were dispositions not merely of the shares themselves but of the anterior beneficial ownerships of specified shares.

Counsel for the taxpayer concedes that if A transferred shares to B in trust as to nine-tenths for himself absolutely and as to one-tenth for C absolutely there would, for the purposes of the 1965 Act, be a chargeable disposal of one-tenth of the shares though not of the nine-tenths. This, he submits, is because, although A and C would be jointly absolutely entitled to the trust shares as against B, s 22(5) would require the one-tenth to be treated as vested not in A (which would negative any disposal by A to B) but in C (which could only be the case if A had made a disposal of the shares comprised in the one-tenth). To the extent of that one-tenth, A would have parted with the shares.

Can it, then, be argued successfully that in the present case all the several settlors did in fact make a chargeable disposal of their shares because under s 22(5) all the shares which are subject to the trust are to be treated as vested in the settlors collectively, whereas before the inception of the trust they were vested in them severally? I think not. The effect of the trust was to subject all the trust shares to powers and discretions conferred on the trustees for what was conceived to be the collective benefit of the settlors, but, subject to those powers and discretions which the settlors collectively could override, the measure of the beneficial interests of the settlors remained unaffected by the trust. There was no transfer of any beneficial interest from any one of them to any other. This is, in my judgment, the answer to counsel's first contention for the Crown to the effect that the taxpayer did not transfer his shares to the trustees in trust for himself alone.

On the true view of the facts the taxpayer, in my view, never lost his interest in 55,000 shares of the company. He subjected that interest to certain restraints, as did the other settlors in respect of their shares, but it was at all times within their collective power to abolish those restraints, whereupon each settlor would become absolutely entitled to the same number of shares as he had brought into the trust.

Counsel's second submission for the Crown does not, in my opinion, require consideration. It depends on the premise that the taxpayer's original 55,000 shares were specifically held on trust for him. This was not, in my opinion, the effect of the agreement. Goulding J expressed his conclusion and his reasons for it in this way ([1978] 3 All ER 298 at 312–313, [1978] 1 WLR 927 at 935):

> 'Looking at the judgments by which I have to be guided, of Foster and Walton JJ, I find that they appear to lay down at most two requirements for the application of s 22(5) where there is a plurality of beneficial owners. The first requirement is that the interests of the beneficial owners must be concurrent and not successive, like the interests of a life tenant on the one hand, and a remainderman or reversioner on the other. That is distinctly stated in *Kidson (Inspector of Taxes) v Macdonald* [1974] 1 All ER 849 at 857–858, [1974] Ch 339 at 349, where Foster J said: "If, however, one has a trust for A for life with remainder to B absolutely, A and B together are able to direct the trustees how to deal with the settled property, but such a limitation is clearly settled property and is not excluded by s 22(5)." That was also stated in *Stephenson (Inspector of Taxes) v Barclays Bank Trust Co Ltd* [1975] 1 All ER 625 at 638, [1975] 1 WLR 882 at 890 in the passage I have already read. The second requirement for the application of s 22(5) which may be found in the reported cases is that the interests of the co-owners should be, as Walton J put it, the same. Again the passage is that to which I have already referred, where Walton J said: "The definition says 'jointly'; it does not say 'together'. I think this is because it is intended to comprise persons who are, as it were, in the same interest." The reference, I think, is certainly to a similarity of interests in quality, not equality in quantity, because I do not think there is any hint in the decision that tenants in common in unequal shares could be treated differently from tenants in common in equal shares. Those two tests appear to me to be satisfied in the present case. The interests of the different shareholders within the agreement are concurrent. That is to say, they all coexist in time during the same period of the agreement, and they are the same in Walton J's sense; that is, each shareholder has, pro rata with regard

> to the size of his original holding, the same sort of rights as every other. Each is a subject to a right of pre-emption for the benefit of the others, but each has the benefit of the right of pre-emption against all the others. I can find no warrant in the two reported cases for adding a third requirement, which, as appears from the summary of the argument that I have given, is elusive to conceive and hard to define in words. [That is, I think, a reference to an argument presented to Goulding J by counsel for the Crown. Goulding J went on:] Does the language of the statute b itself clearly require this third attribute of nominee property? [I pause here to interject that 'nominee property' was a term that the learned judge adopted to describe property falling within s 22(5). He went on:] I think not. We know that the word "jointly" must be taken in a popular sense, not the technical sense of joint tenancy in English law; and then we have to see what is the relevant character of property falling under s 22(5). [He went on to give his reasons for rejecting c counsel's argument for the Crown, and said:] Accordingly, while accepting that the word "jointly" is not to be technically construed and embraces all concurrent interests, and while accepting also that the concurrent interests must have a qualitative similarity one to another (though it will be for future cases, no doubt, to define how far that requirement goes), I see no reason to introduce any further refinement in the test. It follows that in my judgment, on the true construction of d the agreement and the facts found in the present case, the shares comprised in the agreement are nominee property and not settled property for the purposes of capital gains tax.'

With those observations of Goulding J I fully agree.

For these reasons, in my judgment this appeal fails and should be dismissed.

e **ACKNER LJ.** I agree; there is nothing that I can usefully add.

OLIVER LJ. I also agree. Where several separate owners of property pool their property through the medium of a trust in such a way that their respective beneficial proprietary interests under the trust reflect precisely the individual property interests which they separately had before the creation of the trust, nobody would say, I think, f using language in its ordinary sense, that they had disposed of their property except in the purely technical sense that the legal ownership has been transferred to the trustees. To tax such a technical disposition as one producing a capital gain would be capricious and it seems to me that counsel for the taxpayer is right in saying that s 22(5) of the Finance Act 1965 was introduced precisely to avoid so unreasonable a result. When, of course, a trust is created as a result of which the beneficial owner disposes of the whole g or part of his beneficial interest, there is pro tanto a disposition attracting capital gains tax on the interest disposed of. Thus, if A declares himself a trustee of a one-tenth share of particular property for B, he has clearly disposed of the one-tenth and the tax becomes payable on any gain notionally found to be made on the disposition. If A does the same thing in a different way, namely by transferring the property to C and D as trustees on trust for himself and B in the proportions of nine-tenths and one-tenth, it would be h entirely unreasonable to treat the disposition to the trustees as a disposition attracting tax on a notional gain made on the whole interest. Hence 22(5), which in effect directs that where assets are held by trustees either for a single person absolutely entitled as against the trustee, or for two or more persons who are jointly absolutely entitled as against the trustees, the position is to be looked at as if the assets were vested in the beneficiaries, disposals *by those beneficiaries* to the trustees being disregarded. In other words, you are j to look through the trustees to the beneficiaries in this situation to determine whether there has been any disposition attracting capital gains tax.

This does not, of course, mean that the creation of a trust for the same persons who previously owned the trust property, but in proportions different from those in which they previously owned it, will escape tax. The disposal to the trustees may have to be

disregarded under s 22(5), but there will still have been pro tanto a disposal of the
beneficial interest. a

The Crown does not seek to challenge the construction put by the courts on the words
'absolutely entitled as against the trustee' and 'jointly so entitled' in the subsection, in
Kidson (Inspector of Taxes) v Macdonald [1974] 1 All ER 849, [1974] Ch 339 and *Stephenson*
(Inspector of Taxes) v Barclays Bank Trust Co Ltd [1975] 1 All ER 625, [1975] 1 WLR 882.
It seems to me inevitably to follow in the instant case that the trust here under
consideration was one where the beneficiaries are, and were at all material times, jointly b
and absolutely entitled as against the trustees to the assets vested in the trustees, since
their interests are both concurrent and qualitatively identical, and they can collectively,
at any time, terminate the trust and direct the actions of the trustees. The transfers to the
trustees, therefore, fall to be ignored, and the question of whether there was a taxable
disposition has to be determined as between the beneficiaries themselves. On this
analysis there was, for the reasons given by Buckley LJ, no such disposal. Their interests c
in the mass precisely reflect the individual interests which they had before the deed was
entered into.

In my judgment, therefore, the learned judge reached the correct conclusion, and I
would dismiss the appeal. I do so with the more satisfaction since the result seems to me
to be in accordance with the common sense and commercial reality of the matter. This
was no more than a shareholders' voting agreement carried out through the medium of d
a trust, and it would seem capricious and unreasonable to tax these shareholders on a
wholly illusory gain simply because of the technical machinery which they chose to
adopt to effect an end which involved no quantitative alteration in their separate and
individual beneficial entitlements.

Appeal dismissed. e

Solicitors: *Solicitor of Inland Revenue*; *Herbert Smith & Co* (for the taxpayer).

Edwina Epstein Barrister.

Gunton v London Borough of Richmond upon Thames

COURT OF APPEAL, CIVIL DIVISION
BUCKLEY, SHAW AND BRIGHTMAN LJJ
26th, 27th, 28th, 31st MARCH, 2nd APRIL, 3rd JULY 1980

Master and servant – Contract of service – Unilateral repudiation of contract by employer – Wrongful dismissal – Effect – Employer wrongfully dismissing employee by not following correct dismissal procedure – Whether wrongful dismissal automatically terminating contract – Whether wrongful dismissal merely a repudiation which does not bring contract to an end until accepted by employee.

In 1968 the plaintiff was employed by a borough council on terms of employment which stated that the appointment was terminable on one month's notice. His contract of employment subsequently incorporated regulations made by the council prescribing the procedure to be followed regarding the suspension and dismissal of officers for breaches of discipline. That procedure incorporated a series of stages, including a hearing by an appeals committee, which would normally take considerably longer than a month to implement. In 1975 the council decided that the plaintiff's conduct was inconsistent with the terms of his contract and that he should be dismissed. On 6th November 1975 the council wrote to the plaintiff informing him of its intention to dismiss him and giving him notice of his right of appeal. The council thus decided to treat the dismissal as a disciplinary matter, but in proceeding directly to the appeal stage it disregarded certain preliminary steps of the procedure for dismissal on disciplinary grounds. The plaintiff replied the same day giving notice of appeal, and an appeal committee was convened on 9th December. The committee, after hearing submissions by the plaintiff on the merits, recommended on 12th January 1976 that the dismissal be confirmed. On 13th January the council wrote to the plaintiff informing him that his contract was terminated as from 14th February and that he was forthwith no longer required to attend his place of work. The plaintiff issued a writ, seeking a declaration that the termination of his employment was illegal, ultra vires and void and that he remained an employee of the council, or alternatively damages. The judge held that the council's letter of 13th January had not effectively terminated the plaintiff's employment in law and made a declaration that the plaintiff was entitled to an inquiry as to damages on the basis that he was entitled to remain in the council's employment until the normal retiring age unless he became redundant or liable to dismissal under the disciplinary procedure. The council accepted that the letter of 13th January was not a valid dismissal of the plaintiff but appealed against the order as to damages and the basis on which the inquiry had been ordered. The council contended that the notice of 13th January was a repudiation of the contract which automatically terminated the contract and that it followed that the plaintiff was entitled by way of damages to one month's salary (being the length of notice to which he was entitled under his contract) from the date the contract was terminated (ie 14th January) and that was in fact what he had been paid.

Held – (1) (Shaw LJ dissenting) Although the council had power, by virtue of the express term in the plaintiff's letter of appointment, to dismiss the plaintiff simply on a month's notice on grounds other than disciplinary grounds, once the council had decided to dismiss the plaintiff on disciplinary grounds it was required to carry out all the steps of the appeal procedure that applied, and as it had admittedly failed to do so the council had wrongfully dismissed the plaintiff on 13th January 1976 (see p 584 *d* to *f*, p 590 *e* to *g* and p 593 *b* to *h*, post).

(2) (Shaw LJ dissenting) The wrongful dismissal of an employee did not put an immediate end to the contract of service because, applying the ordinary principles of the doctrine of repudiation, it was merely a repudiation of the contract by the employer

which only resulted in termination of the contract when it was accepted by the employee. It followed that the council's wrongful dismissal of the plaintiff on 13th *a* January did not immediately terminate the plaintiff's contract of service and in particular did not destroy his right under his contract not to be dismissed on disciplinary grounds until the prescribed disciplinary procedures had been carried out, and to be compensated accordingly if they were not (see p 588 *j* to p 589 *b* and p 594 *a*, post); dictum of Jenkins LJ in *Vine v National Dock Labour Board* [1956] 1 All ER at 8, *Francis v Municipal Councillors of Kuala Lumpur* [1962] 3 All ER 633, *Denmark Productions Ltd v Boscobel Productions Ltd* *b* [1968] 3 All ER 513, *Decro-Wall International SA v Practitioners in Marketing Ltd* [1971] 2 All ER 216, *Hill v C A Parsons & Co Ltd* [1971] 3 All ER 1345, *Sanders v Ernest A Neale Ltd* [1974] 3 All ER 327, *Ivory v Palmer* [1975] ICR 340 and *Thomas Marshall (Exports) Ltd v Guinle* [1978] 3 All ER 193 considered.

(3) (Per Shaw LJ) Having regard to the fact that specific performance would not be ordered to enforce a contract of service, the wrongful dismissal of an employee was to be *c* regarded as a total repudiation of the contract which automatically destroyed the contractual relationship, leaving the employee to be compensated in damages according to ordinary principles. Accordingly, although the council's dismissal of the plaintiff on 13th January may have been wrongful it nevertheless brought his contract to an end and he was entitled to damages as a result (see p 582 *e* to p 583 *e*, post); *Sanders v Ernest A Neale Ltd* [1974] 3 All ER 327 followed. *d*

(4) The plaintiff was accordingly entitled to damages assessed on the basis of his salary for the period from 14th January until the date when the proper disciplinary procedure if carried out expeditiously might reasonably have been concluded, plus one month's notice; the one month's salary received by the plaintiff for the month ending 14th February and salary in any other employment during the period of assessment were to be deducted from the damages so assessed. An order for an inquiry as to damages on that *e* basis would be substituted for the order made by the judge (see p 583 *h j*, p 590 *h*, p 591 *d* to *h* and p 594 *c d*, post).

Per Buckley LJ. Because a wrongfully dismissed servant has, in the absence of special circumstances, no option but to accept the employer's repudiation of the contract and because the employee is almost invariably bound, under his duty to mitigate the damage, to seek other employment which will almost invariably prevent him from being in a *f* position to perform his obligations of service under the original contract, the court should readily infer that a wrongfully dismissed employee has accepted the employer's repudiation (see p 589 *d* to *g*, post).

Notes

For wrongful dismissal and remedies therefor, see 16 Halsbury's Laws (4th Edn) paras 649–654, and for cases on the subject, see 34 Digest (Repl) 124–125, *842–844*. *g*

For an innocent party's rights on repudiation of a contract, see 9 Halsbury's Laws (4th Edn) paras 551–553, and for cases on the subject, see 12 Digest (Repl) 411–416, *3032–3049*.

For what amounts to repudiation, see 9 Halsbury's Laws (4th Edn), para 546, and for cases on the subject, see 12 Digest (Repl) 151–153, *961–975*. *h*

Cases referred to in judgments

Decro-Wall International SA v Practitioners in Marketing Ltd [1971] 2 All ER 216, [1971] 1 WLR 361, CA, 12 Digest (Reissue) 415, *3049*.

Denmark Productions Ltd v Boscobel Productions Ltd [1968] 3 All ER 513, [1969] 1 QB 699, [1968] 3 WLR 841, 28(2) Digest (Reissue) 677, *147*.

Francis v Municipal Councillors of Kuala Lumpur [1962] 3 All ER 633, [1962] 1 WLR 1411, *j* PC, 30 Digest (Reissue) 210, *317*.

Heyman v Darwins Ltd [1942] 1 All ER 337, [1942] AC 356, 111 LJKB 241, 166 LT 306, HL, 3 Digest (Reissue) 88, *453*.

Hill v C A Parsons & Co Ltd [1971] 3 All ER 1345, [1972] Ch 305, [1971] 3 WLR 995, CA, Digest (Cont Vol D) 539, *702a*.

Hochster v De la Tour (1853) 2 E & B 678, 1 CLR 846, 22 LJQB 455, 22 LTOS 171, 17 Jur 972, 118 ER 922, 34 Digest (Repl) 127, *861*.

Howard v Pickford Tool Co Ltd [1951] 1 KB 417, CA, 30 Digest (Reissue) 206, *293*.

Ivory v Palmer [1975] ICR 340, CA, Digest (Cont Vol E) 361, *1736a*.

Johnstone v Milling (1886) 16 QBD 460, 55 LJQB 162, 54 LT 629, 50 JP 694, 12 Digest (Reissue) 412, *3033*.

Marshall (Thomas) (Exports) Ltd v Guinle [1978] 3 All ER 193, [1979] Ch 227, [1978] 3 WLR 116, [1978] ICR 905, Digest (Cont Vol E) 420, *1056d*.

Sanders v Ernest A Neale Ltd [1974] 3 All ER 327, [1974] ICR 565, [1974] ITR 395, [1975] KILR 77, [1974] IRLR 236, NIRC, Digest (Cont Vol D) 673, *816Ao*.

Vine v National Dock Labour Board [1956] 3 All ER 939, [1957] AC 488, [1957] 2 WLR 106, [1956] 2 Lloyd's Rep 567, HL; *rvsg in part* [1956] 1 All ER 1, [1956] 1 QB 658, [1956] 2 WLR 311, [1955] 2 Lloyd's Rep 531, CA, 30 Digest (Reissue) 208, *311*.

Cases also cited

Atlantic Underwriting Agencies Ltd v Compagnia di Assicurazione di Milano SpA [1979] 2 Lloyd's Rep 240.

Barber v Manchester Regional Hospital Board [1958] 1 All ER 322, [1958] 1 WLR 181.

Cooper v Wilson [1937] 2 All ER 726, [1937] 2 KB 309, CA.

Fisher v Jackson [1891] 2 Ch 84.

Fisher v York Trailer Co Ltd [1979] ICR 834.

Greater London Council v Connolly [1970] 1 All ER 870, [1970] 1 QB 100, CA.

Hanson v Radcliffe Urban District Council [1922] 2 Ch 490, CA.

Jones v Lee [1980] ICR 310, CA.

Malloch v Aberdeen Corpn [1971] 2 All ER 1278, [1971] 1 WLR 1578, HL.

Marriot v Oxford and District Co-operative Society Ltd [1969] 3 All ER 1126, [1970] 1 QB 186, CA.

McClelland v Northern Ireland General Health Services Board [1957] 2 All ER 129, [1957] 1 WLR 594, HL.

Palmer v Inverness Hospitals Board 1963 SC 311.

Photo Production Ltd v Securicor Transport Ltd [1980] 1 All ER 556, [1980] 2 WLR 283, HL.

Price v Sunderland Corpn [1956] 3 All ER 153, [1956] 1 WLR 1253.

Rasool v Hepworth Pipe Co Ltd [1980] ICR 494.

Ridge v Baldwin [1963] 2 All ER 66, [1964] AC 40, HL.

Short v Poole Corpn [1926] Ch 66, CA.

Smith v Macnally [1912] 1 Ch 816.

Stevenson v United Road Transport Union [1977] 2 All ER 941, [1977] ICR 389, CA.

Taylor v National Union of Seamen [1967] 1 All ER 766, [1967] 1 WLR 532.

Vidyodaya University of Ceylon v Silva [1964] 3 All ER 865, [1965] 1 WLR 77, PC.

Western Excavating (ECC) Ltd v Sharp [1978] 1 All ER 713, [1978] QB 761, CA.

White & Carter (Councils) Ltd v McGregor [1961] 3 All ER 1178, [1962] AC 413, HL.

Appeal

The defendant, the London Borough of Richmond upon Thames ('the council'), appealed against the order of his Honour Judge Rubin QC sitting as a judge of the High Court on 26th October 1978 that the plaintiff, Norman George Gunton, was entitled to (i) a declaration that a notice dated 13th January 1976 purporting to dismiss the plaintiff from the council's employment was ineffective lawfully to terminate his contract of service, and (ii) an inquiry as to damages on the basis that the plaintiff was entitled to remain in the council's employment until his normal retiring age for an employee of his standing unless in the meantime he became redundant or liable to be dismissed under the disciplinary procedure incorporated into his contract of service. By a respondent's notice under RSC Ord 59, r 6 the plaintiff sought, inter alia, a declaration that he at all material times had been and remained a registrar in the council's education department and clerk to the governors of Twickenham College of Technology, or that he so remained until 26th October 1978 or until 31st August 1977. The facts are set out in the judgment of Shaw LJ. a

James Goudie for the plaintiff.
James Mitchell and *Edward Bailey* for the council.

Cur adv vult b

3rd July. The following judgments were read.

SHAW LJ (delivering the first judgment at the invitation of Buckley LJ). This is an appeal by the defendant in the action (whom I shall call 'the council') against a judgment of his Honour Judge Rubin QC sitting as a judge of the High Court in the Chancery Division, which he gave on 26th October 1978. By that judgment he granted declaratory c
relief to the plaintiff in relation to his contract of service with the council. By his cross-notice the plaintiff asks this court to enlarge the scope of the declaratory order made by the judge.

The history of the matter goes back for some years. The council, through its education department, was responsible at material times for the administration of the Twickenham College of Technology (to which I shall refer as 'the college'). In 1968 it was seeking a d
registrar for that institution. The plaintiff applied for the position and was successful. On 3rd May 1968 the town clerk for the council wrote to the plaintiff in these terms:

> 'Dear Sir,
>
> 'I confirm your appointment as a Registrar in the Education Department initially at Twickenham College of Technology with effect from 1st July 1968. Your annual commencing salary will be [and that is set out, with the addition of London e
> weighting]. Your appointment will be terminable by one month's notice in writing on either side and will be subject to the National Scheme of Conditions of Service for Local Authorities A.P.T. and Clerical Services which will govern your period of probationary service and any entitlements during holidays and sickness, and to any regulations which may be made by this Council and in force from time to time f
> ... It is a condition of employment that you may be subject to transfer to any other establishment within the Borough should the need arise.'

The plaintiff responded promptly. On 4th May 1968 he wrote to the town clerk thanking him for confirming the appointment, and thereafter duly commenced in the employment of the council at the college in the capacity of registrar. As appears from the town clerk's letter the contract of service thus brought about was to be subject to the g
National Conditions of Service for Local Authorities and to any regulations made from time to time by the council, which was the nominal employer. There was explicit provision for the termination of the appointment by one month's notice on either side. It is common ground that there was incorporated a disciplinary code entitled 'Regulations as to Staff Discipline' which prescribed the procedure to be followed in regard to the suspension and dismissal of officers for breaches of discipline. That procedure involved h
a series of stages including, in cases of suspension or dismissal, a hearing by an appeals committee of which the employee concerned must be given not less than a week's notice in writing. It is manifest that the course of the steps or stages to be taken will generally be prolonged beyond a month from the time when they are initiated. How is this code as to dismissal for breaches of discipline to be reconciled with the express provision for the termination of the plaintiff's contract of service by one month's notice on either j
side? A possible solution is that the code extends or varies that express provision where the council purports to dismiss on disciplinary grounds, but that in any other circumstances the contract of service may be determined by reference to the express provision. This, however, would produce a grotesque result, for it would mean that the council could, without assigning any reason, terminate the plaintiff's employment by a

month's notice, but could not, if it complained of misconduct on his part, determine that employment save by what might prove a long and protracted process. As this apparent contractual anomaly lies at the root of the matters to be resolved in examining the judgment which is appealed, I think it as well to indicate at the outset the view which I have formed as to the interaction of the stated contractual term of notice, and the procedure in relation to dismissal for breaches of discipline which it is accepted forms part of the plaintiff's contract of employment. For myself, I do not consider that the regulations as to staff discipline were designed to deprive the council of its contractual power to determine the contract of service by one month's notice; nor in my view did they have that result. If, however, the council exercised that right and was called on before an industrial tribunal to justify a dismissal on some disciplinary ground as being fair, it might be very difficult for the council to establish that the dismissal was not unfair if the code had not been followed. The plaintiff would then be accorded appropriate redress by the industrial tribunal pursuant to the statutory provisions in that regard. On the other hand, if the code had been fully observed, the onus on the council to demonstrate that the dismissal was fair would be relatively easy to discharge.

With this digression I return to the history. The plaintiff duly took up his appointment as registrar. At some stage he was required by 'articles of government relating to the college to act also as clerk to the governors'. This could hardly have added greatly to the burdens of his office. It did not in my view constitute a distinct and separate employment, and was no more than an extended definition of his function as registrar.

Unhappily as time went on, the plaintiff's conduct in the discharge of his duties did not commend itself to his superiors in the department of education of the council. By November 1975 the director of education felt constrained to recommend the plaintiff's dismissal 'on the ground of his conduct being wholly inconsistent with the terms of his contract'. On 6th November the town clerk wrote to the plaintiff, saying:

> 'As you will be aware, the appointment of Registrar is subject to such conditions of service as the Council may determine and, in this connection, the Council's "Regulations as to staff discipline including dismissal and suspension of officers and workmen" apply. Accordingly, I enclose a copy of these Regulations and draw your attention to Regulation 13 as the result of the operation of which Regulation 7 and those following, as appropriate, are brought into effect. Further, in accordance with Regulation 7, I hereby convey to you the decision to recommend your dismissal from the Council's service and give you notice of your right to appeal against this decision. If you wish so to appeal please give me notice thereof within the period specified in Regulation 7.'

In taking this action, the introductory steps prescribed by the regulations as to staff discipline had been short-circuited. It may be that they were considered to be inappropriate in the case of a senior executive like the registrar, although he clearly came within their scope.

However, the reaction of the plaintiff was not to refute the validity or effectiveness of the dismissal foreshadowed by the recommendation referred to in the town clerk's letter. Instead he wrote on the same day saying: 'In reply to your letter dated 6th November 1975 I give notice of appeal in accordance with Section 7 of the Regulations referred to.' An appeal committee was duly convened and it conducted a hearing of an appeal by the plaintiff. He was represented and the matter was argued, not on any technical point of compliance with the regulations but on the general merits. In adopting this course I would myself have been prepared to hold that the plaintiff had waived and forgone any objection to the validity of his prospective dismissal founded on a failure to follow the code precisely. The process of appeal was the ultimate step in determining the propriety of the dismissal. It was a step which he sought and in which he participated.

The appeal was opened on 9th December 1975, when the plaintiff attended and had the advantage of being represented by a district officer of his union, the National

Association of Local Government Officers. After being heard in part the appeal was adjourned to 12th January 1976, when the plaintiff again attended and was represented this time by counsel who appeared on his behalf in this appeal. The appeal committee's decision was adverse to the plaintiff. Accordingly, the town clerk, in his capacity as chief executive of the council, wrote on the following day giving the plaintiff notice that his contract was terminated on 14th February 1976. The concluding sentence of the letter read: 'As from the receipt of this letter you will not be required for the performance of any of your duties to attend at your place of work.'

In the face of this plain intimation that he would not be permitted to perform his erstwhile functions, the plaintiff understandably and sensibly kept away from the college. He regarded himself as dismissed de facto; but not, as thereafter became apparent, de jure. On 11th February 1976 he issued a writ, by which he claimed a declaration—

> 'that the purported termination of his appointment as Registrar and Clerk to the Governors of the College is illegal, ultra vires and void and that [he] at all material times has been and remains Registrar and Clerk to the Governors of the College.'

In seeking this form of relief, the plaintiff ventured into a vexed area of the common law. It is trite enough that the wrongful repudiation of a contract does not, in general, determine the contract. It is for the innocent party to decide whether he will treat the contract as at an end and seek redress by way of damages, or whether he will regard the contract as still subsisting and call for performance in accordance with the contractual terms. In the sphere of employment this basic exposition of the law is not easy or possible to reconcile with the realities of life. While damages as a universal remedy for breach of contract may generally serve to redress the injury done to the injured party, it may not always in itself be an adequate remedy. Specific performance in lieu of, or as an adjunct to, damages may be both necessary and appropriate to give that party his due. It is therefore practical and legitimate to give the party not in default the option of treating the contract as still subsisting notwithstanding the repudiation by the other party; if he elects to treat the contract as still subsisting he may seek and obtain those supplemental or auxiliary remedies which serve more effectively to compensate him or to provide him with a fulfilment of his expectations under the contract. This practical basis for according an election to the injured party has no reality in relation to a contract of service where the repudiation takes the form of an express and direct termination of the contract in contravention of its terms. I would describe this as a *total* repudiation which is at once destructive of the contractual relationship. There may conceivably be a different legal result where the repudiation is oblique and arises indirectly as, for example, where the employer seeks to change the nature of the work required to be done or the times of employment; but I cannot see how the undertaking to employ on the one hand, and the undertaking to serve on the other, can survive an out-and-out dismissal by the employer or a complete and intended withdrawal of his service by the employee. It has long been recognised that an order for specific performance will not be made in relation to a contract of service. Therefore, as it seems to me, there can be no logical justification for the proposition that a contract of service survives a total repudiation by one side or the other. If the only real redress is damages, how can its measure or scope be affected according to whether the contract is regarded as still subsisting or as at an end? To preserve the bare contractual relationship is an empty formality. The servant who is wrongfully dismissed cannot claim his wage for services he is not given the opportunity of rendering; and the master whose servant refuses to serve him cannot compel that servant to perform his contracted duties. In this context remedies and rights are inextricably bound together. It is meaningless to say that the contract of service differs from other contracts only in relation to the availability of remedies in the event of breach. The difference is fundamental, for there is no legal substitute for voluntary performance.

I have had the advantage of reading in draft the judgment of Buckley LJ. He has, if

I may respectfully say so, collected and collated in logical and historical development the
a principal authorities in this dubious field. I gratefully accept his analysis of the cases and his survey of the ebb and flow of the tide of judicial opinion. In the end one is left in the slack water of first principles. While it is true that arbitrary repudiation by one contracting party cannot of itself terminate a contract so as to relieve that party of the obligation to perform his contractual obligation, the application of this principle cannot, in real terms, go beyond those situations in which the law can compel performance. The
b preservation of the contractual relationship is necessarily coterminous with the ability of the law to compel performance. Where it cannot, it is the scope of damages that must afford appropriate redress to the injured party. I would therefore follow those decisions cited in this sense in Buckley LJ's judgment and in particular that of Donaldson J in *Sanders v Ernest A Neale Ltd* [1974] 3 All ER 327.

To return to the facts of the present case, how could it profit the plaintiff to get the
c declaration he claimed? It might be a salve to his amour propre, but it is not the function of the courts to provide this. He cannot remain idle and demand his salary for he has not earned it. If he claims damages he must, by implication, treat his contract of service as at an end for the court will not also reinstate him by an order for specific performance; and if he is reduced to claiming damages he must show that he has taken reasonable steps to mitigate his loss. Indeed he has since his dismissal had other employments for short
d terms. If it were necessary to look that far, I would regard his so doing as an acceptance of the council's repudiation of his contract of service. I do not, however, think it is necessary. The dismissal in January 1976 may have been wrongful, but in my judgment it brought the contract to employ the plaintiff to a summary end. The measure of his damage is to be determined on ordinary and elementary principles. He is not assisted in that regard by, and does not need, any declaration. It is a form of relief not normally
e appropriate in relation to contracts of service. Counsel for the plaintiff contended that a peculiar and special status attached to the plaintiff's position as clerk to the governors because it was a public office. Counsel submitted also that public authorities stood in a special and more responsible situation in law in regard to contracts with employees than did ordinary employers. With all respect to the products of his research and his persuasive presentation of them, I find no warrant for either proposition. There are
f situations in which the impact of some statutory provision on the status of an employee gives rise to special considerations and consequences. The relationship between the council and the plaintiff was free from such trammels. The only peculiarities it presents arise from his conduct in the performance of his duties while he was at the college and the excursions in law which he has pursued since he left that institution.

The views I have expressed in the course of this judgment differ in two respects from
g those which commend themselves to Buckley and Brightman LJJ. They relate to the possible determination of a contract of service by unilateral repudiation and to the impact of the disciplinary code on the right to determine the contract between the plaintiff and the college by one month's notice. As I, though diffidently, maintain the view I have stated, it may be as well to point out that the practical outcome, in the circumstances of this case, is virtually the same. Whether the plaintiff is entitled to
h damages because on the one hand his contract was not determined by a valid notice, or because on the other hand, although it was so determined, he suffered damage as a result of the code not having been observed, the measure of damages would be much the same. This is plainly demonstrated by the time scale set out in the judgment of Brightman LJ which I have had the advantage of reading in draft.

I would accordingly respectfully agree that the declaration which will be proposed by
j Buckley LJ in the course of his judgment meets the justice of this case, and I would substitute it for the declaration made by the judge.

BUCKLEY LJ. This case involves an interesting question on the law of master and servant, on which there has been much judicial difference of opinion. That question is whether the wrongful dismissal of a servant puts an immediate end to the contract of service, or whether it operates as a repudiation of the contract by the master which results in termination of the contract only when that repudiation is accepted by the servant.

Before I come to that question I should first say something about the terms of the plaintiff's contract of service as to its termination by notice.

The letter of appointment dated 3rd May 1968 expressly stated that the appointment would be terminable by one month's notice in writing on either side. It also stated that the appointment would be subject to any regulations which might be made by the council and in force from time to time. At a later date in, I think, July 1972, the council adopted 'Regulations as to Staff Discipline including Dismissal and Suspension of Officers and Workmen'. It is common ground that these regulations thereupon became part of the terms of the plaintiff's employment. The effect of this, in the learned judge's view, was to fetter the council's power to dismiss the plaintiff on a month's notice to the extent necessary to give effect to the regulations. It seems that the judge thought that the consequence of this was to abrogate the power of the council to dismiss the plaintiff on a month's notice, for he directed that the inquiry as to damages for wrongful dismissal which he ordered should be conducted on the basis that the plaintiff was entitled to remain in the council's employment until the normal retirement age for a servant of his standing, unless in the meantime he became redundant or became liable to be dismissed under the disciplinary procedure incorporated into his contract of service. That direction seems to be consistent only with the view that the council no longer had power to terminate the contract on a month's notice otherwise than at normal retirement age, on grounds of redundancy, or on disciplinary grounds. I feel unable to accept this view, for its seems to me that the express term about notice in the letter of appointment should only be treated as modified, if at all, by regulations subsequently adopted by the council to the extent that such regulations are irreconcilable with the continued operation of the express term. The adoption of the disciplinary regulations does not appear to me to be in any respect inconsistent with the continued power of the council to dismiss the plaintiff on a month's notice on grounds other than disciplinary grounds. I am, however, myself of the opinion that the adoption of the disciplinary regulations and their consequent incorporation in the plaintiff's contract of service did disenable the council from dismissing the plaintiff on disciplinary grounds until the procedure prescribed by those regulations had been carried out. The council accepts that in the present case that procedure was not fully carried out, although it is fair to say that the extent of the failure does not seem to me to have been such as to prejudice the plaintiff in any important respect, for he was afforded an opportunity to appeal against his dismissal and was given what appears to be accepted as having been a fair hearing. The judge reached the conclusion that, since the council had not fully complied with the regulations, the letter of 13th January 1976 was not effective lawfully to determine the plaintiff's contract of service. There is no appeal against that part of his decision. Consequently I proceed on the basis that the council's dismissal of the plaintiff was wrongful. It was nevertheless a dismissal and de facto it brought the plaintiff's employment by the council to an end.

It is at this stage that the question to which I referred at the outset of this judgment arises. In *Vine v National Dock Labour Board* [1956] 1 All ER 1 at 8, [1956] 1 QB 658 at 674 Jenkins LJ said:

> 'In the ordinary case of master and servant, however, the repudiation or the wrongful dismissal puts an end to the contract, and a claim for damages arises. It is necessarily a claim for damages and nothing more. The nature of the bargain is such that it can be nothing more.'

That was not an ordinary master and servant case: the plaintiff was a dock labourer employed in a pool of available dock labour under a statutory scheme. The defendant board was the employer of all the men in the pool, but they worked for shipowners or charterers to whom they were allocated by the board. Unless a man was employed in the pool he could not earn his living as a stevedore in the port at all. The observation which I have quoted from Jenkins LJ's judgment was consequently no more than an obiter

dictum. It was, however, approved by Viscount Kilmuir LC in the House of Lords on
a appeal ([1956] 3 All ER 939 at 944, [1957] AC 488 at 500):

> 'This is an entirely different situation from the ordinary master and servant case. There, if the master wrongfully dismisses the servant, either summarily or by giving insufficient notice, the employment is effectively terminated, albeit in breach of contract.'

b This also was an obiter dictum. I do not think that Viscount Kilmuir LC should be understood as saying anything different from what Jenkins LJ, with whom he expressed entire agreement, had said, although it might, I suppose, be suggested that Viscount Kilmuir LC was speaking only of the end of the de facto employment, whereas Jenkins LJ was speaking of the end of the contract of service.

The next case in chronological sequence which I should mention is *Francis v Municipal*
c *Councillors of Kuala Lumpur* [1962] 3 All ER 633, [1962] 1 WLR 1411, a case before the Judicial Committee of the Privy Council. The plaintiff was employed by the defendant municipal council as a clerk. The council purported to dismiss him. This dismissal was held to be ultra vires because by the terms of the ordinance establishing the council the only power to dismiss the plaintiff was vested not in the council but in its president. The plaintiff claimed a declaration that he was still employed by the municipality, his
d dismissal having been a nullity. The Judicial Committee said ([1962] 3 All ER 633 at 637, [1962] 1 WLR 1411 at 1417):

> 'Their Lordships consider that it is beyond doubt that on Oct. 1, 1957, there was de facto a dismissal of the appellant by his employers, the respondents. On that date he was excluded from the council's premises. Since then he has not done any work for the council. In these circumstances it seems to their Lordships that the appellant
> *e* must be treated as having been wrongly dismissed on Oct. 1, 1957, and that his remedy lies in a claim for damages. It would be wholly unreal to accede to the contention that since Oct. 1, 1957, he had continued to be, and that he still continues to be, in the employment of the respondents.'

So far the reasoning of the Judicial Committee appears to me to be consistent, or at least
f reconcilable, with Jenkins LJ's dictum. The Judicial Committee, however, went on to say ([1962] 3 All ER 633 at 637, [1962] 1 WLR 1411 at 1417):

> 'In their Lordships' view, when there has been a purported termination of a contract of service a declaration to the effect that the contract of service still subsists will rarely be made. This is a consequence of the general principle of law that the courts will not grant specific performance of contracts of service. Special
> *g* circumstances will be required before such a declaration is made and its making will normally be in the discretion of the court. In their Lordships' view there are no circumstances in the present case which would make it either just or proper to make such a declaration.'

This clearly implies that there may be circumstances in which a purported termination
h of a contract of service may not in law determine the contract. The Judicial Committee could hardly have held otherwise in the face of the decision of the House of Lords in *Vine's* case, but they emphasised that in their view such a declaration should only be made in special circumstances. In *Vine's* case the special circumstance was the statutory nature of the National Dock Labour Scheme, which gave the plaintiff a statutory status over and above his rights under his contract of service, so that as the judgments in that
j case make plain, *Vine's* case was not just an ordinary master and servant case. In the *Francis* case on the other hand the Judicial Committee declined to advise the grant of a declaration notwithstanding that no notice of dismissal had been given by the only person competent to dismiss the plaintiff, so that the relation of master and servant had been ended only by the de facto exclusion of the plaintiff from his employment.

Denmark Productions Ltd v Boscobel Productions Ltd [1968] 3 All ER 513, [1969] 1 QB 699 was not a case of a contract of personal service but of a contract for services. Nevertheless both Harman and Salmon LJJ referred to the consequences of wrongful dismissal of an *a* employee under an ordinary contract of personal service. Harman LJ said ([1968] 3 All ER 513 at 533, [1969] 1 QB 699 at 737):

> 'An employee dismissed in breach of his contract of employment cannot choose to treat the contract as subsisting and sue for an account of profits which he would have earned to the end of the contractual period: he must sue for damages for the wrongful dismissal and must of course mitigate those damages so far as he *b* reasonably can.'

This appears to me to be entirely consistent with Jenkins LJ's dictum. Salmon LJ employed language which is perhaps not quite so explicit but still appears to me to concur with Jenkins LJ's view. He said ([1968] 3 All ER 513 at 524, [1969] 1 QB 699 at 726): *c*

> 'It has long been well settled that if a man employed under a contract of personal service is wrongfully dismissed he has no claim for remuneration due under the contract after the repudiation. His only money claim is for damages for having been prevented from earning his remuneration ... His sole money claim is for damages and he must do everything he reasonably can to mitigate them.' *d*

So far the tide of opinion, as it seems to me, runs strongly in the direction set by Jenkins LJ.

In 1971, however, it turned. In *Decro-Wall International SA v Practitioners in Marketing Ltd* [1971] 2 All ER 216 at 223, [1971] 1 WLR 361 at 369 Salmon LJ said:

> 'I doubt whether a wrongful dismissal brings a contract of service to an end in law, although no doubt in practice it does. Under such a contract a servant has a *e* right to remuneration, including what are sometimes called fringe benefits, in return for services. If the master, in breach of contract, refuses to employ the servant, it is trite law that the contract will not be specifically enforced. As I hope I made plain in the *Denmark Productions* case, the only result is that the servant, albeit he has been prevented from rendering services by the master's breach, cannot recover remuneration under the contract because he has not earned it. He has not *f* rendered the services for which remuneration is payable. His only money claim is for damages for being wrongfully prevented from earning his remuneration. And like anyone else claiming damages for breach of contract he is under a duty to take reasonable steps to minimise the loss he has suffered through the breach. He must do his best to find suitable alternative employment. If he does not do so, he prejudices his claim for damages. I doubt whether, in law, a contract of service can *g* be unilaterally determined by the master's breach.'

Sachs LJ expressed a similar view (see [1971] 2 All ER 216 at 228–229, [1971] 1 WLR 361 at 375–376). Both Salmon and Sachs LJJ, however, recognised that the dismissed servant's remedy must lie only in damages and that he could not sue in debt for remuneration under the contract in respect of any period after his employment had actually ceased. *h* Once again the case was not concerned with a contract of personal service and the observations to which I have referred were obiter.

The next case to be mentioned, *Hill v C A Parsons Ltd* [1971] 3 All ER 1345, [1972] Ch 305, was a decision on a contract of personal service, but an unusual one. The defendants dismissed the plaintiff from their service. They gave only one month's notice, which was held to be too short, so that the dismissal was wrongful. The defendants had been *j* unwilling to dismiss the plaintiff and were only induced to do so by organised industrial pressure. They were quite willing to re-employ him if they could legitimately and practically do so. The plaintiff sought an interlocutory injunction to restrain the defendants until trial or further order from implementing the notice of dismissal. The defendants' primary submission was that a wrongful repudiation of a contract of service terminates that contract irrespective of whether or not the other party elects to accept it. Sachs LJ swam strongly with the anti-Jenkins LJ tide. He said ([1971] 3 All ER 1345 at 1354, [1972] Ch 305 at 319):

> 'In [the *Decro-Wall* case] it was not necessary to determine the point which is now once more under discussion: nor, this being an interlocutory appeal, is it strictly necessary here. But having now heard the matter so well argued again it is only right to say that I feel reinforced in the view, of which I am now convinced, that the defendants' primary contention is wrong.'

Lord Denning MR, on the other hand, may be described as having been content to remain in the slack water between ebb and flow. He said ([1971] 3 All ER 1345 at 1349–1350, [1972] Ch 305 at 314):

> 'Suppose, however, that the master insists on the employment terminating on the named day? What is the consequence in law? *In the ordinary course of things*, the relationship of master and servant thereupon comes to an end; for it is inconsistent with the confidential nature of the relationship that it should continue contrary to the will of one of the parties thereto. [He then referred to what Viscount Kilmuir LC said in *Vine's* case and continued:] Accordingly, the servant cannot claim specific performance of the contract of employment. Nor can he claim wages as such after the relationship has been determined. He is left to his remedy in damages against the master for breach of the contract to continue the relationship for the contractual period. He gets damages for the time he would have served if he had been given proper notice less, of course, anything he has, or ought to have, earned in alternative employment.' (Emphasis Lord Denning MR's.)

He went on, however, to make plain that in his view de facto dismissal did not always put an end to the relationship, which can be consistent only with the view that de facto dismissal does not in all circumstances automatically terminate the contract of master and servant. Stamp LJ assumed for the purpose of his judgment, without expressing an opinion on the point, that the plaintiff's contract of service was still subsisting, the plaintiff not having accepted the defendant's repudiation. In the event the court granted an interlocutory injunction restraining the defendant from relying on the abortive notice.

In *Sanders v Ernest A Neale Ltd* [1974] 3 All ER 327 Donaldson J, delivering the judgment of the National Industrial Relations Court, distinguished *Hill v C A Parsons Ltd* as a case where, notwithstanding the wrongful dismissal, the mutual confidence of the parties continued. The court held that wrongful dismissal terminates a contract of personal service without the necessity for acceptance by the injured party (see [1974] 3 All ER 327 at 333). This is, I think, the only decision in which the Jenkins LJ doctrine, if I can call it such, features as part of the ratio decidendi in what can be described as an ordinary master and servant case.

In *Ivory v Palmer* [1975] ICR 340 Cairns and Roskill LJJ were able to avoid committing themselves to either view on the disputed question because they found themselves able to hold that the defendant, who had been summarily dismissed by the plaintiff and was claiming damages for wrongful dismissal, had in fact accepted the dismissal (see per Cairns LJ at 346 and per Roskill LJ at 352). Browne LJ, on the other hand, held (at 354) that the ordinary doctrine of repudiation and acceptance was not applicable to contracts of personal service.

Finally in *Thomas Marshall (Exports) Ltd v Guinle* [1978] 3 All ER 193 at 202, 205, [1979] Ch 227 at 239, 243 Sir Robert Megarry V-C, in a judgment in which he usefully reviewed the authorities, held that a contract of personal service was no exception to the general rule that repudiation did not automatically discharge the contract.

So there are two decisions at what I may perhaps (somewhat inaccurately) call first instance level, namely *Sanders v Ernest A Neale Ltd* and *Thomas Marshall (Exports) Ltd v Guinle*, one of which goes one way on the question under discussion and one the other way; a decision in this court in *Hill v C A Parsons Ltd* (which I think Roskill LJ in *Ivory v Palmer* [1975] ICR 340 at 351 rightly described as a very special case) in which one member of this court, Sachs LJ, came down firmly against wrongful dismissal automatically putting an end to a contract of personal service, but the other two members of the court left the matter somewhat at large; a decision of this court in *Ivory v Palmer* in which it was not found necessary to reach a decision one way or the other on the question under discussion, but in which Browne LJ clearly favoured the automatic termination view; and a decision of the Judicial Committee of the Privy council in *Francis v Municipal Council of Kuala Lumpur*, in which a de facto, but ultra vires, dismissal was held to give rise only to a liability in damages for wrongful dismissal. It is worthy of note that in the *Francis* case no reference is made to the plaintiff having accepted a repudiation by the defendant municipality of his contract of service. If, however, a dismissed servant sues for damages for wrongful dismissal, he must by so doing accept the master's repudiation of the contract. I am inclined to think that this may in truth be the explanation of Jenkins LJ's dictum.

Counsel for the council has based his argument on a submission that an unequivocal dismissal of an employee, whether by express words or by necessary implication, of itself terminates the contract of employment.

In *Howard v Pickford Tool Co* [1951] 1 KB 417 at 421 Asquith LJ employed a colourful phrase: 'An unaccepted repudiation is a thing writ in water and of no value to anybody: it confers no legal rights of any sort or kind.' It is common ground that in respect of the generality of contracts that is good law. As Viscount Simon LC said in *Heyman v Darwins Ltd* [1942] 1 All ER 337 at 341, [1942] AC 356 at 361:

> 'However, repudiation by one party standing alone does not terminate the contract. It takes two to end it, by repudiation, on the one side, and acceptance of the repudiation, on the other.'

The principle was recognised a hundred years ago in such cases as *Hochster v De la Tour* (1853) 2 E & B 678, 118 ER 922 and *Johnstone v Milling* (1886) 16 QBD 460. The basis of the doctrine is that, where a party to a contract before the date for performance has arrived evinces an intention not to perform his part of the contract, he has committed no breach until the date for performance arrives. Nevertheless the innocent party will be relieved of his obligations under the contract, if he so chooses, so as to render him free to arrange his affairs unhampered by the continued existence of those obligations. It is for the innocent party to elect whether he wishes to be so relieved, which he does by accepting the repudiatory act of the guilty party as a repudiation of his, the guilty party's, obligations under the contract. In those circumstances the innocent party may treat the guilty party as having committed an entire breach of the contract notwithstanding that the time for performance has not yet arrived. Where the time for performance of part of the guilty party's obligations has arrived but some of those obligations remain executory, the position is the same as regards those obligations which remain executory as it is in respect of all the guilty party's obligations where none of them has yet become due for performance. If the guilty party has evinced an intention not to perform those obligations of his which remain executory, the innocent party may elect to treat himself as discharged from all obligations on his part to perform the contract any further. He does so by accepting the guilty party's repudiation of his outstanding obligations under the contract, in which case the innocent party may treat the guilty party as having committed an entire breach of all his outstanding obligations under the contract notwithstanding that the time for performance of those obligations, or some of them, may not yet have arrived.

Why should the doctrine operate differently in the case of contracts of personal service from the way in which it operates in respect of other contracts? I for my part can discover no reason why it should do so in principle. It cannot be because the court will not decree specific performance of a contract of personal service, for there are innumerable kinds of contract which the court would not order to be specifically enforced to which the doctrine would undoubtedly apply. For similar reasons it cannot, in my opinion, be because a contract of personal service involves a relationship of mutual confidence, or because the obligations of a master and a servant are mutually dependent on co-operation between the parties. If one party to a contract of personal service were to repudiate it before the time for performance had arrived, there would be no breach of contract until the time for performance and no cause of action until then, unless the innocent party chose to create one by accepting the repudiation. I can only conclude that the doctrine does apply to contracts of personal service as it applies to the generality of contracts.

However, cases of wrongful dismissal in breach of a contract of personal service have certain special features. In the first place, as the term 'wrongful dismissal' implies, they always occur after the employment has begun and so involve an immediate breach by the master of his obligation to continue to employ the servant. Secondly, a wrongful dismissal is almost invariably repudiatory in character; it is very rarely that there can be any expectation that the master will relent and take the servant back into his service under the contract. Thirdly, the servant cannot sue in debt under the contract for remuneration in respect of any period after the wrongful dismissal, because the right to receive remuneration and the obligation to render services are mutually interdependent. Fourthly, the servant must come under an immediate duty to mitigate his damages and so must almost invariably be bound to seek other employment in fulfilment of that obligation; it would be very rarely that he could expect to find other employment, or could mitigate his damages in any other way, which would leave him free to return to his original employer's service at any moment, should the original employer relent. It follows, in my view, that at least as soon as the servant finds, and enters into, other employment he must put it out of his power to perform any continuing obligations on his part to serve his original employer. At this stage, if not earlier, the servant must, I think, be taken to have accepted his wrongful dismissal as a repudiatory breach leading to a determination of the contract of service.

Finally, in a case of wrongful dismissal, in the absence of special circumstances the damages recoverable on the footing of an accepted repudiation must, I think, be as great as, and most probably greater than, any damages which could be recovered on the footing of an affirmation of the contract by the innocent party and of the contract consequently remaining in operation.

So, as was recognised in the *Decro-Wall* case and in *Ivory v Palmer*, a wrongfully dismissed servant really has, in the absence of special circumstances, no option but to accept the master's repudiation of the contract.

It consequently seems to me that, in the absence of special circumstances, in a case of wrongful dismissal the court should easily infer that the innocent party has accepted the guilty party's repudiation of the contract. I do not think, however, that it is impossible that in some cases incidental or collateral terms might cause the injured party to want to keep the contract on foot.

In the present case the plaintiff has accepted the repudiation. He did so at the trial, if not earlier.

Where a servant is wrongfully dismissed, he is entitled, subject to mitigation, to damages equivalent to the wages he would have earned under the contract from the date of dismissal to the end of the contract. The date when the contract would have come to an end, however, must be ascertained on the assumption that the employer would have exercised any power he may have had to bring the contract to an end in the way most beneficial to himself, that is to say, that he would have determined the contract at the earliest date at which he could properly do so: see McGregor on Damages (13th Edn, 1972) paras 884, 886, 888.

If a master, who is entitled to dismiss a servant on not less than three months' notice, wrongfully purports to dismiss the servant summarily, the dismissal, being wrongful, is a nullity and the servant can recover as damages for breach of contract three months' remuneration and no more, subject to mitigation, that is to say, remuneration for the three months following the summary dismissal. If the master wrongfully purports to dismiss the servant on a month's notice and continues to employ him and pay him during that month, no breach occurs until the servant is excluded from his employment at the end of the month, in which case he would be entitled, subject to mitigation, to damages equivalent to three months' remuneration from the date of exclusion. If the master were to pay the servant one month's remuneration in lieu of notice and were to exclude him from his employment forthwith, there would be an immediate breach of the contract by the master; the servant would be entitled to three months' remuneration by way of damages, but would have to give credit for the one month's remuneration paid in lieu of notice.

Suppose, however, that the master were to dismiss the servant summarily or on a month's notice, and the facts were such as to justify the view that the servant did not accept the master's repudiation of the contract until the end of ten weeks from the servant's exclusion from his employment. In such a case, if I am right in supposing acceptance of a repudiation to be requisite in master and servant cases, the master would be guilty of a breach of contract continuing de die in diem for refusing to offer the servant employment from the date of exclusion down to the date of acceptance, and thereafter for damages on the basis of a wrongful repudiation of the contract. Could the servant properly claim damages under the second head in relation to a period of three months from the date of acceptance as well as damages under the first head in relation to the 10 week period? In my judgment, he clearly could not. His cause of action would have arisen when he was wrongfully excluded from his employment. The subsequent acceptance of the repudiation would not create a new cause of action, although it might affect the remedy available for that cause of action. The question must, I think, be for how long the servant could have insisted at the date of the commencement of his cause of action on being continued by the master in his employment.

In the present case, in my view, the council could, on 13th January 1976, have determined the plaintiff's contract of service on 14th February 1976 without assigning any reason or for any given reason other than a disciplinary reason. They did not, however, do so. It is common ground that the letter of 13th January 1976 purported to relate the plaintiff's dismissal to disciplinary matters. Counsel for the council, as I understood his argument, submitted that that circumstance was not significant; the plaintiff received one month's notice, which was all that he was entitled to insist on. As I have already indicated, I feel unable to accept that view because, in my opinion, the effect of the incorporation in the contract of the disciplinary regulations was to entitle the plaintiff not to be dismissed on disciplinary grounds until the disciplinary procedures prescribed by the regulations had been carried out. Some of the preliminary stages of those procedures never were carried out. Accordingly, in my judgment, the plaintiff was entitled at 14th January 1976, when he was excluded from his employment, to insist on a right not to be dismissed on disciplinary grounds until the disciplinary procedures were recommenced and carried out in due order but with reasonable expedition. Consequently in my view the period by reference to which the amount of damages recovered by the plaintiff in this case should be assessed is a reasonable period from 14th January 1976 for carrying out those procedures, plus one month, the plaintiff giving credit for one month's salary which he received in respect of the month ended 14th February 1976 and for anything earned in other employment during the period.

Counsel for the plaintiff referred us to a number of cases in which employers of persons in the public service, such as school teachers, were held to be disentitled to dismiss employees otherwise than in accordance with particular procedures or on limited grounds. I do not find those authorities helpful in the present case, in which, as it seems to me, the plaintiff's rights were purely contractual. They were not entrenched by any statutory or other extra-contractual provisions. Nor, in my opinion, was the discretionary power of the council to dismiss the plaintiff on a month's notice limited in any way apart from the terms of the contract of employment itself, relating to disciplinary matters. It was suggested that the plaintiff's position as clerk to the governors was an office in respect of which he had some particular status. I feel unable to take this view. The plaintiff's employment was as a registrar in the education department of the council. He was initially assigned to the position of registrar at the Twickenham College of Technology. The articles of government of the Twickenham College, which came into operation on 1st April 1972, provided in para 2(e): 'The registrar of the College shall act as clerk to the Governors.' The effect of this article, in my view, was not to invest the plaintiff with an office as clerk to the governors, but merely to provide that the registrar from time to time of the college should perform the functions of clerk to the governors. The council could, in my view, quite properly have transferred the plaintiff at any time from his post as registrar to the Twickenham College of Technology to any other registrarship within their educational department. The plaintiff would thereupon have ceased to have been clothed with the duty of discharging the functions of clerk to the governors. The duty to act as clerk to the governors was, I think, no more than part of the plaintiff's duties as registrar of the college.

In my judgment, this is not a case in which any declaratory relief is really necessary; but the declaration contained in the judge's order that the letter of 13th January 1976 was ineffective lawfully to determine the contract of service of the plaintiff with the council as a registrar in the education department of the council and clerk to the governors of the Twickenham College of Technology is, in my view, correct in law and inoffensive in its effect. I see no particular reason for interfering with that part of the order.

The next declaration contained in the order that the plaintiff is entitled if he so wishes to treat his exclusion from the service of the council on 14th February 1976 as a repudiation of the contract is, in my opinion, inaccurate in the respect that the plaintiff was in fact excluded from the service of the council on 14th January 1976. I would accordingly substitute that date for 14th February 1976 in the declaration and in that part of the order directing an inquiry as to damages. I would discharge that part of the order which directs on what basis the inquiry should be conducted and I would substitute a direction that the inquiry should be conducted on the basis indicated in this judgment.

I would accordingly vary the order of the judge to the extent which I have indicated.

BRIGHTMAN LJ. I have reached the same conclusion as Buckley LJ. That is to say, the plaintiff is entitled to an order for an inquiry as to the damages sustained by him by reason of his wrongful exclusion from the service of the council from 14th January 1976 until the expiration of a notional one month's notice served on the day when the proper disciplinary procedures, if followed, could have been concluded. This day should be determined by estimating a reasonable period from 14th January 1976 for the purpose of expeditiously commencing, carrying out and concluding the disciplinary procedures contained in the 'Regulations as to Staff Discipline'. Not all those procedures are relevant to the estimation of this period. The relevant procedures are, in my opinion, those defined in paras 3, 4(b) and (c), 5, 6, 7, 9, 10, 11 and 12 of the regulations. Without having heard argument, and therefore without expressing a concluded view, I have in mind that a period of two months should be sufficient for the purpose indicated, making three months in all from 14th January.

By a letter dated 13th January 1976 the council purported to terminate the plaintiff's contract of employment as from 14th February, on the basis that the plaintiff would be paid his salary down to that date but would forthwith be excluded from (the letter says 'not required . . . to attend at') his place of work. That letter was admittedly wrongful because the council was not entitled by the contract to dismiss the plaintiff on a disciplinary ground without observing the agreed disciplinary procedures, which by an oversight and without any practical injustice to the plaintiff were in this case disregarded. The council's letter in my view involved an immediate breach of contract by them because the plaintiff, although to be paid for a month, was immediately excluded from his place of work. I should however add that, like Shaw LJ, I would have been prepared to hold that the plaintiff had waived any objection to the validity of the process which he sought and in which he participated.

By his writ issued on 11th February 1976 the plaintiff sought a declaration that the purported termination of his contract of employment was unlawful. In my opinion there is no objection to that declaration for what it may be worth. He also sought a declaration that he 'at all material times has been and remains Registrar and Clerk to the Governors of the College'. In the alternative the plaintiff claims, by amendment, an inquiry as to damages on the basis that he was entitled to remain in the council's employment until normal retirement age unless (i) he became redundant or (ii) he became liable to dismissal under the disciplinary procedure, due allowance being made for the plaintiff's duty to mitigate his loss by seeking alternative employment.

By his order the judge declared that the letter of 13th January 1976 was ineffective lawfully to determine the plaintiff's contract. His order then recorded that the plaintiff by his counsel elected to treat his exclusion from the council's service on 14th February 1976 as a repudiation of his contract of service and elected to claim damages at common law. However, I would myself have thought that the contract was repudiated from 14th January when the plaintiff was excluded from his place of work, but the point is in practice of no materiality because the plaintiff was paid his entire salary until 14th February.

The order then directed that the inquiry should be conducted—

> 'on the basis that [the plaintiff] was entitled to remain in the Council's employment until the normal retirement age for a servant of his standing unless in the meantime he became redundant or became liable to be dismissed under the disciplinary procedure incorporated into his contract of service. Due allowance ought to be made for [the plaintiff's] duty to mitigate his loss by seeking suitable alternative employment.'

I cannot see any justification for that entitlement.

The notice of appeal raises one challenge only to that order. It asserts that the inquiry—

> 'should be conducted upon the basis that, pursuant to the aforesaid contract of service, [the council was] entitled at any time to give the plaintiff one month's notice in writing of termination thereof.'

So the council's claim amounts to this, that the admitted invalidity of the notice served on 13th January 1976 can be disregarded because the plaintiff could on that day have been dismissed on one month's notice on non-disciplinary grounds.

An employee's remedy, if he is unlawfully dismissed by his employer, is damages. He cannot obtain an order for specific performance because it is not available to compel performance of a contract of service against an unwilling employer. He cannot sue for his salary or wages as such. By necessity his remedy is confined to damages. An unlawful dismissal is ex hypothesi a premature dismissal. The damages recoverable, having regard to the plaintiff's duty to mitigate his damages, are the moneys needed to compensate the plaintiff for his net loss of salary or wages during the period for which the defendant was bound by his contract to employ the plaintiff. In the case of a fixed term contract, the assessment will extend over that fixed term. In the case of a contract terminable by notice, the assessment will extend over the period which would have had to elapse before the defendant could lawfully have dismissed the plaintiff (see McGregor on Damages (13th Edn, 1972) paras 884–888).

So the first inquiry which has to be made in this case is whether the plaintiff was serving under a fixed term contract or a contract determinable by notice or some other type of contract.

The plaintiff's counsel sought to argue that there was some special law which applied to contracts of service entered into by a statutory authority with its employees. He called it an aspect of administrative law. A statutory authority, he submitted, could not give an employee notice of dismissal without some good reason. Such a notice would be ultra vires, because a statutory authority had a statutory duty to act with propriety.

I accept that a statutory authority has to act reasonably and that it should exercise
a reasonably its statutory powers to hire and fire its servants. But I do not know of any
principle of law which confers on a public employee a greater security of tenure than is
enjoyed under a comparable contract of employment with a non-statutory authority.

The only problem on this aspect of the case which arises is that the plaintiff's letter of
appointment from the council stated that 'your appointment will be terminable by one
month's notice on either side', while at the same time the contract of employment
b incorporated 'Regulations as to Staff Discipline' applicable to allegations of inefficiency,
misconduct or indiscipline. These regulations have the effect of defining the steps
required to be taken in the interests of the employer and the employee before the head
of department can recommend dismissal to the appropriate committee of the council.
The result was that the council had under the contract a right to dismiss the plaintiff on
one month's notice, but that it could not lawfully act on a recommendation for dismissal
c on a disciplinary ground unless the disciplinary procedure had been followed; the
completion of this procedure was a condition precedent to a valid recommendation for
dismissal on a disciplinary ground.

What then is the legal position if a notice of requisite contractual length is given to
determine an employee's contract of service, but such notice is the result of a
recommendation improperly made and on which the defendant could not lawfully
d act? The plaintiff has suffered a wrong, and so far as damages can do so, he must be put
in the same position as if the wrong had not been done. To assess the damages, the
invalid notice should be disregarded. It was a nullity. It should be assumed that the
council gave, as it could have done, a valid one month's notice at the earliest permissible
date. It was argued that a valid one month's notice could have been given on the same
day as the void one month's notice, but this proposition would make a complete nonsense
e of the protection which purports to be afforded by the disciplinary code, and I reject the
submission. The council was intending to dismiss on a disciplinary ground. It would be
inconsistent with the terms of the contract for the council to be treated as entitled to give
a month's notice until the day when the disciplinary procedures could have been
completed.

Much argument in this case has been devoted to the vexed question of the legal result
f of an unlawful repudiation of a contract of service which is not accepted by the other
side. The council has argued, and there are many dicta in the cases which it can turn to
its advantage, that a wrongful repudiation of a contract of service results in an 'automatic'
termination of the contract although the innocent party has not accepted, and indeed has
expressly rejected, the attempted repudiation. If, as I think, the council wrongfully
repudiated the contract on 13th January 1976, the acceptance of this proposition would
g presumably mean that the contract would cease to exist on 14th January and that the
plaintiff became on that day entitled to damages to be assessed by reference to the
month's notice to which he was entitled under the contract, which would be offset by the
month's salary in fact paid. But I have to confess that it has never been completely clear
to me where the council's argument logically leads if accepted in this case. What I am
clear about in my own mind is that this contract cannot be read so as to entitle the council
h to disregard the disciplinary procedures with impunity. But I would add, in parentheses,
as I have indicated, that I think it is unlikely that the plaintiff suffered any injustice by
the council's oversight.

It is clear beyond argument that a wrongfully dismissed employee cannot sue for his
salary or wages as such, but only for damages. It is also, in my view, equally clear that
such an employee cannot assert that he still retains his employment under the contract.
j If a servant is dismissed and excluded from his employment, it is absurd to suppose that
he still occupies the status of a servant. Quite plainly he does not. The relationship of
master and servant has been broken, albeit wrongfully by one side alone. The same
would apply to a contract for services, such as an agency. If a two-year agency contract
is made between principal and agent, and the principal wrongfully repudiates the
contract of agency after only one year, quite plainly the agent cannot hold himself out as

still being the agent of the principal. He is not. The relationship of principal and agent has been broken. I do not think it follows, however, from the rupture of the status of *a* master and servant or principal and agent, that the contract of service or the contract of agency has been terminated by the wrongful act of the master or the principal. What has been determined is only the status or relationship. So in the result the servant cannot sue in debt for his wages, which he is wrongfully deprived of the opportunity to earn, or for his fringe benefits, such as the house which the carpenter in *Ivory v Palmer* [1975] ICR 340 had the right to occupy as part of his emoluments. As the relationship of master and *b* servant is gone, the servant cannot claim the reward for services no longer rendered. But it does not follow that every right and obligation under the contract is extinguished. An obligation which is not of necessity dependent on the existence of the relationship of master and servant may well survive, such as the right of the master in *Thomas Marshall (Exports) Ltd v Guinle* [1975] 3 All ER 193, [1979] Ch 227 that the servant should not during the term of the contract deal on his own account with customers of the plaintiff *c* company.

As indicated, I am of the view that the relationship of master and servant was broken on 13th January 1976 but that this did not deprive the plaintiff of his contractual right to be protected from a notice of dismissal for an alleged disciplinary offence before the contractual disciplinary procedures had been duly completed. The plaintiff is therefore in my view entitled to an inquiry as to damages on the basis which I indicated at the *d* beginning of this judgment. I would vary the order accordingly.

Order accordingly.

Solicitors: *Bartlett & Gluckstein, Crawley & de Reya* (for the plaintiff); *Sharpe, Prichard & Co*, agents for *A W B Goode*, Twickenham (for the council). *e*

Frances Rustin Barrister.

Heywood v Hull Prison Board of Visitors and another *f*

CHANCERY DIVISION
GOULDING J
16th APRIL 1980

g

Judicial review – Declaration – Circumvention of procedure for application for judicial review – Action for declaration circumventing procedure for judicial review – Plaintiff found guilty of disciplinary offences by board of prison visitors – Plaintiff issuing writ in Chancery Division for declaration that adjudication of board null and void – Application by board for order to stop plaintiff proceeding except by way of application for judicial review in Queen's Bench Division – Whether proceedings in Chancery Division should be allowed to continue – RSC Ord 53. *h*

The defendant board of prison visitors found the plaintiff guilty of certain disciplinary offences and imposed various penalties on him. The plaintiff considered that the board had failed to observe the rules of natural justice but instead of applying under RSC Ord 53[a] to the Divisional Court of the Queen's Bench Division for leave to bring proceedings *j* against the board by way of judicial review, he issued a writ and statement of claim in the Chancery Division seeking a declaration that the board's adjudication was null and void. The board contended that the plaintiff's proper remedy was to apply for judicial

a Order 53, so far as material, is set out at p 597 *f g*, post

review under RSC Ord 53 and sought an order that all further proceedings in the
a Chancery action be stayed.

Held – Although technically a plaintiff could apply under the Rules of the Supreme Court for a declaration either by bringing an action in the Chancery Division or by applying for judicial review in the Queen's Bench Division, in practice a plaintiff should not be permitted to seek relief by way of an action for a declaration if he was challenging
b the decision of a body, such as a board of prison visitors, which was exercising a judicial function, and was in fact indirectly seeking a judicial review. Instead, the plaintiff should be required to use the procedure provided by RSC Ord 53, because (i) a plaintiff should not be able to obviate the need for obtaining leave under RSC Ord 53 by bringing an action in the Chancery Division, and (ii) the Queen's Bench Division was, by reason of its long experience of such cases, better equipped than the Chancery Division to deal
c expeditiously with them. It followed that the board's application would be granted and the plaintiff's action in the Chancery Division stayed (see p 597 *h j*, p 598 *a* to *h*, p 600 *c* and p 601 *b* to *g* and *j* to p 602 *b*, post).

De Falco v Crawley Borough Council [1980] 1 All ER 913 distinguished.

Notes

d For application for leave under RSC Ord 53, r 1, see 11 Halsbury's Laws (4th Edn) para 1545.

Cases referred to in judgment

Barnard v National Dock Labour Board [1953] 1 All ER 1113, [1953] 2 QB 18, [1953] 2 WLR 995, [1953] 1 Lloyd's Rep 371, CA, 30 Digest (Reissue) 208, *310*.

e *De Falco v Crawley Borough Council* [1980] 1 All ER 913, [1980] QB 460, [1980] 2 WLR 664, 78 LGR 180, CA.

Meade v London Borough of Haringey [1979] 2 All ER 1016, [1979] 1 WLR 637, [1979] ICR 494, 77 LGR 577, CA.

Pyx Granite Co Ltd v Ministry of Housing and Local Government [1959] 3 All ER 1, [1960] AC 260, [1959] 3 WLR 346, 123 JP 429, 58 LGR 1, 10 P & CR 319, HL, 30 Digest (Reissue)
f 202, *277*.

R v Hull Prison Board of Visitors, ex parte St Germain, R v Wandsworth Prison Board of Visitors, ex parte Rosa [1979] 1 All ER 701, [1979] QB 425, [1979] 2 WLR 42, 68 Cr App R 212, CA.

Taylor v National Assistance Board [1956] 2 All ER 445, [1956] P 470; *rvsd* [1957] 1 All ER 183, [1957] P 101, [1957] 2 WLR 189, CA; *affd* [1957] 3 All ER 703, [1958] AC 532,
g [1958] 2 WLR 11, HL, 50 Digest (Repl) 488, *1710*.

Thornton v Kirklees Metropolitan Borough Council [1979] 2 All ER 349, [1979] QB 626, [1979] 3 WLR 1, 77 LGR 417, CA.

Uppal v Home Office [1978] Court of Appeal Transcript 719, (1978) Times, 11th November, 123 Sol Jo 17, CA; *rvsg* (1978) Times, 21st October.

h **Case also cited**

Sirros v Moore [1974] 3 All ER 776, [1975] QB 118, CA.

Motion

By a writ dated 28th February 1980 the plaintiff, Joseph Bernard Paul Michael Heywood, brought an action against the defendants, the Hull Prison Board of Visitors and the
j Home Office, in which he claimed a declaration that an adjudication of the board of visitors, dated 12th October 1976, was null and void on the ground that the board had failed to observe the rules of natural justice. By a notice of motion, dated 31st March 1980, the defendants applied for an order, under the inherent jurisdiction of the court or under RSC Ord 18, r 19, that all further proceedings in the action be stayed or that the indorsement of the writ and statement of claim be struck out and the action dismissed

on the ground that the action was an abuse of the process of the court and that before the commencement of proceedings against the defendants in respect of the matters of complaint alleged in the writ and statement of claim the leave of the Divisional Court of the Queen's Bench Division should have been, and should be, sought under RSC Ord 53. The facts are set out in the judgment.

Peter Gibson for the defendants.
Lord Gifford for the plaintiff.

GOULDING J. I have before me a motion on the part of the defendants in an action brought by Joseph Bernard Paul Michael Heywood as plaintiff against two defendants, namely, the Board of Visitors of Hull Prison and the Home Office. The plaintiff was a prisoner at Hull in the summer of 1976 at the time of the well-known disturbances that then took place there. In consequence of those disturbances, a large number of prisoners were charged with various breaches of discipline before the Board of Visitors of Hull Prison, the present first-named defendants. The plaintiff was charged with two specific offences alleged to have taken place on 31st August 1976, the charges being laid, as I understand, on 12th October in that year. On the next day, 13th October, the board of visitors found the charges proved and sentenced the plaintiff to various penalties, including a loss of remission of sentence amounting to 250 days.

Some of the prisoners who were the subject of disciplinary proceedings after the Hull disturbances sought relief from the decisions of the board of visitors by way of application for certiorari. The Divisional Court of the Queen's Bench Division took the view that that remedy was not available in such a case. However, some of those concerned appealed to the Court of Appeal, that is to the Civil Division of the Court of Appeal, and there the decision of the Divisional Court was reversed and it was held that the determinations of the board of visitors could be called in question by way of certiorari. That case is reported as *R v Hull Prison Board of Visitors, ex parte St Germain* [1979] 1 All ER 701, [1979] QB 425.

After the decision of the Court of Appeal, the plaintiff quickly came to know of it and took steps to seek legal aid and to endeavour to bring proceedings for his own benefit. There were, it is conceded, delays on the plaintiff's side and it is said (though I have no evidence on the point, but it is said by counsel on his behalf) that he personally was not to blame in the matter. I will so assume for the purposes of my judgment. However, in the event, the plaintiff did not seek relief by certiorari proceedings in the Queen's Bench Division, which would now have to be brought under RSC Ord 53 by way of an application for judicial review. Instead, he issued a writ in the Chancery Division. That writ was issued on 28th February 1980. It is indorsed generally for one item of relief only, namely 'a declaration that the adjudication of the Board of Visitors on the 12th October 1976 is null and void'.

On 26th March the plaintiff gave notice of a motion seeking an order for a speedy trial of the action. That is plainly a necessary move on his part, because he is now, so I am informed, only detained in prison in consequence of the loss of remission of 250 days by the sentence of the board of visitors. Accordingly, unless he can obtain relief reasonably quickly, it will be of no benefit to him in that regard.

The notice of motion given on behalf of the plaintiff has been overtaken by a cross-notice of motion on the part of both defendants, the board of visitors and the Home Office. That seeks—

> 'an Order under the inherent jurisdiction of the Court or under Order 18, Rule 19, of the Rules of the Supreme Court, that all further proceedings in the action be stayed or that the indorsement of the Writ and the Statement of Claim herein be struck out and this action dismissed, on the ground that the action is an abuse of the process of the Court and that before the commencement of any proceedings against the Defendants in respect of the matters of complaint alleged in the said Writ and

> said Statement of Claim the leave of the Divisional Court of the Queen's Bench a Division should have been and should be sought under Order 53 of the said Rules.'

Very properly and logically, it has been agreed that I should hear the defendants' motion first.

Several matters are, in my judgment, quite clear when one comes to consider the contentions put forward on behalf of the defendants. First of all, all relief by way of judicial declaration, whether or not accompanied by relief of a more practical character, b is equitable or statutory in origin. The common law of England itself knew of no such remedy. Secondly, there is ample and indisputable authority that all declaratory relief is in the discretion of the court, and there is authority of long standing that where the declaration sought is (as it were) independent (I mean where it is not introductory or ancillary to some other specific relief) the discretion is to be exercised with caution. Thirdly, under the Rules of the Supreme Court, which have the force of statute, in the c form in which they stand at present and in the circumstances of the present case, there are at least two methods indicated of seeking a declaration from the court. One is in RSC Ord 15, r 16 which says:

> 'No action or other proceedings shall be open to objection on the ground that a merely declaratory judgment or order is sought thereby, and the Court may make binding declarations of right whether or not any consequential relief is or could be d claimed.'

While that applies to all proceedings in the High Court, it looks primarily at actions, that is actions in the ordinary sense, begun by writ or originating summons, and it makes it clear that a writ or originating summons cannot be objected to merely because it asks for nothing but a declaration. So there is one way indicated of seeking such relief from e the court. But in the present case there is an alternative and more special mode of approach indicated by RSC Ord 53, which has been extensively revised quite recently, in 1977. I will read Ord 53, r 1, which is divided into two paragraphs:

> '(1) An application for (*a*) an order of mandamus, prohibition or certiorari, or (*b*) an injunction under section 9 of the Administration of Justice (Miscellaneous Provisions) Act 1938 restraining a person from acting in any office in which he is f not entitled to act, shall be made by way of an application for judicial review in accordance with the provisions of this Order.
>
> '(2) An application for a declaration or an injunction (not being an injunction mentioned in paragraph (1)(*b*)) may be made by way of an application for judicial review, and on such an application the Court may grant the declaration or injunction claimed if it considers that, having regard to (*a*) the nature of the matters in respect g of which relief may be granted by way of an order of mandamus, prohibition or certiorari, (*b*) the nature of the persons and bodies against whom relief may be granted by way of such order, and (*c*) all the circumstances of the case, it would be just and convenient for the declaration or injunction to be granted on an application for judicial review.'

h The order goes on to provide for a preliminary ex parte application for leave to bring proceedings by way of judicial review and then for the substantive application to be made by originating notice of motion. Clearly, that procedure is appropriate to the present case. Reference to the facts and the judgment of the Court of Appeal in *St Germain's* case shows plainly that relief sought against a decision of a board of prison visitors would fall within the scope of Ord 53, r 1 and a declaration might suitably be j claimed by an application for judicial review. Fourthly (and I am still dealing with matters that I consider clear), although the present case in its subject matter is clearly and properly within the scope of Ord 53, the court has jurisdiction to give a declaration in an action commenced by writ or originating summons. The existence of that concurrent jurisdiction seems to me to be sufficiently established by reported cases, of which it will be enough to refer to *Barnard v National Dock Labour Board* [1953] 1 All ER 1113, [1953]

2 QB 18, *Taylor v National Assistance Board* [1956] 2 All ER 445, [1956] P 470, and *De Falco v Crawley Borough Council* [1980] 1 All ER 913, [1980] QB 460. The fifth and last of the points which in my judgment are clear is that, looking at the matter from the point of view of a court seeking to apply the existing Rules of the Supreme Court in the interests of justice, it is obviously undesirable that the plaintiff should seek relief by action rather than by application for judicial review.

There are a number of considerations which to my mind justify that opinion. First of all, the Rules of the Supreme Court as they stand must be construed as a whole. Where, in a code of procedural rules, carefully designed machinery is provided for determining a special class of issues or questions, it is in general inconvenient to use some broader form of process designed to cover not only that, but much larger categories of question. Secondly, Ord 53, r 3(1) requires a would-be applicant for judicial review to obtain preliminary leave ex parte from a Divisional Court of the Queen's Bench Division or in vacation from a judge in chambers. There are very good reasons (among them an economy of public time and the avoidance of injustice to persons whom it is desired to make respondents) for that requirement of preliminary leave. If an action commenced by writ or originating summons is used instead of the machinery of Ord 53, that requirement of leave is circumvented. Thirdly, by Ord 53, r 4, certain requirements of expedition are laid down to be observed by an applicant for judicial review, though they are not inflexible and within limits the court has a discretion as to their application. Once again, there are very good reasons for such a requirement. Once again, the provisions of the rule are obviated if the relief is sought by action instead of by application for judicial review. In the present case the plaintiff or his advisers (for whom he is responsible) have, it may be, been guilty of some delay. It is no recommendation of the plaintiff's application that that has happened, though of course he may on investigation be able to excuse himself. Fourthly, Ord 53, r 9(4) provides that where an order of certiorari is sought and obtained, the court may, in addition to quashing the decision to which the application relates, remit the matter to the court, tribunal or authority concerned, with a direction to reconsider it and reach a decision in accordance with the findings of the court. No such convenient machinery for remission of the cause is available in an action for a declaration. Fifthly, in proceedings seeking a review of a judicial or quasi-judicial determination, the machinery of an action as to discovery and giving of evidence may result in placing members of the tribunal concerned in a position not really compatible with the free and proper discharge of their public functions, or at least result in attempts to put them in that position. In the present case counsel for the plaintiff has contemplated the possibility (though he by no means says it will be a necessity) of cross-examining members of the board of visitors. In principle, that seems to me an undesirable way of dealing with such questions. Sixthly, proceedings under Ord 53 have to be brought in the Queen's Bench Division, and that division has had and daily obtains a larger experience in these questions about administrative or quasi-judicial proceedings by bodies that are not courts in the full sense than the Chancery Division has. That last point is of little weight, because it could be met, if necessary, by an order for transfer to the Queen's Bench Division.

Those matters seem to me, as I have said, tolerably plain. But now I leave what is clear for the question that I have to decide. I think I have to ask myself in the end this question: is the impropriety of using the procedure of an action in the present case so gross that the court, in exercising its undoubted power to regulate its own business and avoid abuse of its process, can stop an action that is within the court's jurisdiction to determine and that might conceivably succeed, stop it at the earliest stage, when the issues have not yet been defined by pleadings, nor elucidated by particulars or discovery, simply in order to force the plaintiff to use the proper machinery in the light of the rules considered as a whole?

Now, this question is not free from previous observations by judges and learned writers. On behalf of the plaintiff, I have been directed, among other things, to the report of the Law Commission on remedies in administrative law (Cmnd 6407 (1976)), which I am told led to the revision of RSC Ord 53. The report says this (at para 34):

> 'In the light of our consultation, we are clearly of the opinion that the new procedure we envisage in respect of applications to the Divisional Court should not be exclusive in the sense that it would become the only way by which issues relating to the acts or omissions of public authorities could come before the courts.'

Consistently with that recommendation Ord 53, as appears from the passages that I have read, while providing that in a suitable case an application for a declaration or an injunction may be made by way of judicial review, leaves it open, so far as any express words are concerned, to the applicant to proceed by action. There is, in other words, no rule of exclusion contained in Ord 53.

Then I was referred also to what Professor de Smith says in his book, Judicial Review of Administrative Action (3rd Edn, 1973, p 459). Discussing the remedy of a declaratory judgment in cases of administrative law, the learned author asks: 'Is jurisdiction to award a declaration excluded if another non-statutory remedy is available in the High Court and is equally or more appropriate?' He answers this question with a citation from an earlier writer (Borchard, Declaratory Judgments (2nd Edn, 1933, p 318)):

> 'There is great force in the view that "it ought not to make any difference to judges through which door the petitioner enters the judicial forum, provided he is lawfully there and the court is in a position to grant him relief".'

Somewhat similar language was employed by Lord Denning MR in *De Falco v Crawley Borough Council* [1980] 1 All ER 913 at 920, [1980] QB 460 at 476, a case relating to the duties of a housing authority under the Housing (Homeless Persons) Act 1977. He said:

> 'During the hearing, a point was raised about the procedure adopted by the plaintiffs. They issued writs in the High Court claiming declarations and an injunction. It was suggested that they should have applied for judicial review, because that was the more appropriate machinery. Now the interesting thing is that this new Act, the Housing (Homeless Persons) Act 1977, contained nothing about remedies. It does not say what is to be done if the local authority fails to perform any of the duties imposed by the statute. It has been held by this court that, if the council fails to provide accommodation as required by s 3(4), the applicant can claim damages in the county court: see *Thornton v Kirklees Metropolitan Borough Council* [1979] 2 All ER 349, [1979] QB 626. I am very ready to follow that decision and indeed to carry it further, because this is a statute which is passed for the protection of private persons, in their capacity as private persons. It is not passed for the benefit of the public at large. In such a case it is well settled that, if a public authority fails to perform its statutory duty, the person or persons concerned can bring a civil action for damages or an injunction: see *Meade v London Borough of Haringey* [1979] 2 All ER 1016 at 1023, [1979] 1 WLR 637 at 646, Wade on Administrative Law (4th Edn, 1977, p 633–634) and the Law Commission's Report on Remedies in Administrative Law (1976) (Cmnd 6407, para 22). No doubt such a person could, at his option, bring proceedings for judicial review under the new RSC Ord 53. In those proceedings he could get a declaration and an injunction equally well. He could get interim relief also. So the applicant has an option. He can either go by action in the High Court or county court, or by an application for judicial review.'

That conclusion, that the plaintiffs in the *De Falco* case had rightly proceeded by way of action for declarations and an injunction, was shared by the other two members of the Court of Appeal who decided the case, Bridge LJ and Sir David Cairns. It is only, I think, of limited assistance to the plaintiff in the present case, because Lord Denning MR founded his observations on the hypothesis that the proceedings with which he was concerned were for the enforcement of a statute passed for the protection of private persons, and not passed for the benefit of the public at large. Also I think the Court of Appeal, in considering that the applicant had an option, were not concerned how far in the preliminary stages of the proceedings the court can interfere with initial freedom of choice. So far as they go, the observations in *De Falco's* case reinforce the suggestion in

Professor de Smith's book that it ought not to make any difference to judges through which door the petitioner enters the forum.

However, there has been much said that points in the other direction. As long ago as 1960, in *Pyx Granite Co Ltd v Ministry of Housing and Local Government* [1959] 3 All ER 1 at 8, [1960] AC 260 at 290, Lord Goddard said:

> 'It was also argued that, if there was a remedy obtainable in the High Court, it must be by way of certiorari. I know of no authority for saying that, if an order or decision can be attacked by certiorari, the court is debarred from granting a declaration in an appropriate case. The remedies are not mutually exclusive though, no doubt, there are some orders, notably convictions before justices, where the only appropriate remedy is certiorari.'

Thus Lord Goddard recognised the existence of a class of case in which a High Court declaration would not be an appropriate way of attacking a tribunal's decision, and there is at least a sufficient resemblance between the functions of justices of the peace and those of a board of prison visitors, operating in either case in the exercise of their judicial functions, for one to be on one's guard after reading what he said.

Now I come to what has been mainly relied on by the defendants in the present case, that is, a pronouncement by the Court of Appeal in an immigration case of *Uppal v Home Office* [1978] Court of Appeal Transcript 719, (1978) Times, 11th November. It has not been fully reported, but I have been furnished with a transcript of the proceedings. The case was one in which an application for a declaration in a matter of the immigration laws had been made to Sir Robert Megarry V-C in the Chancery Division (1978) Times, 21st October. It failed. One of the grounds argued on behalf of the Home Office against the plaintiffs was that they ought to have proceeded in the Queen's Bench Division. That argument was rejected. Sir Robert Megarry V-C, as will be seen in a moment, thought the proceedings in the Chancery Division were properly brought and should be decided on the merits. When the plaintiffs brought on their appeal in the Court of Appeal they decided, at what appears to have been an early stage, to abandon it and were content to submit to an order dismissing the appeal. The Court of Appeal were much concerned at certain observations of the judge below and, after some brief discussion with counsel, proceeded to express their views for the guidance, as it would appear, of the profession and the courts. The observations in question were made by Roskill LJ, but can be taken to be those of the court, as Geoffrey Lane LJ and Sir David Cairns expressed their agreement without qualification. As the case is not fully reported I will read the greater part of what Roskill LJ said. After mentioning the abandonment of the appeal, Roskill LJ continued:

> 'There is, however, one difficulty which this court feels it should refer to, and that relates to the procedure which was adopted in this case. The relief sought against the Secretary of State was in form indistinguishable from an application for judicial review under RSC Ord 53. But the proceedings were not taken before the Divisional Court: nor was leave sought from the Divisional Court under Ord 53. On the contrary, an originating summons was issued in the Chancery Division, the applicants being the plaintiffs to that summons and the Secretary of State the defendant ... [Roskill LJ then cited part of the judgment of Sir Robert Megarry V-C below:] "First, [counsel for the Home Office] said that these were the wrong proceedings in the wrong division; the plaintiffs ought to have sought some prerogative order by way of judicial review in the Queen's Bench, and so no declaration should be granted. I do not accept this; nor do I accept counsel's watered-down version, seeking that I should make some obiter pronouncement that such cases ought to be brought in the Queen's Bench. Where two or more different types of proceedings are possible in the same court (and of course the Chancery Division and the Queen's Bench Division are both parts of the High Court) then I do not see why the plaintiffs should not be free to bring whatever type of proceeding they choose. I readily accept that the Queen's Bench Division has had a far greater

> experience of immigration cases than the Chancery Division has had; but that cannot require a plaintiff to proceed for judicial review in the Queen's Bench if he wishes to proceed for a declaration in the Chancery Division. I do not think the Chancery Division can be regarded as being avid for this jurisdiction: but it would be wrong to turn away or discourage a plaintiff who elects to bring one form of proceedings instead of the other." [Roskill LJ then continued:] With the greatest respect to Sir Robert Megarry V-C I find myself unable to agree with the latter part of that passage. There is no doubt, and [counsel for the Home Office] before us had not sought to say otherwise, that in theory the Chancery Division has jurisdiction to entertain an application of this kind. But, as I said a moment ago, this application is in principle indistinguishable from an application for judicial review; and, where an application for judicial review is sought, then as Ord 53, r 3(1) provides, that application must be made to the Divisional Court. I feel bound to say that I find it not a little surprising that this form of procedure has been chosen rather than an application to the Divisional Court for judicial review. It is the Divisional Court which is equipped by reason of its experience, expertise and long practice to deal with these matters and to deal with them expeditiously; and I express the hope that in future it is the Divisional Court to which this type of problem will be submitted and that the temptation to deal with immigration problems by way of an originating summons in proceedings for a declaration in the Chancery Division will be avoided. [After summarising Ord 53, r 1 Roskill LJ concluded:] There is, as I said a moment ago, and [counsel] has not argued otherwise, jurisdiction in the Chancery Division to hear an application of this kind, but it would be wrong that this procedure should be adopted in order to bypass the need for getting leave from the Divisional Court to move for the relevant order where what in truth is sought is judicial review. As this is a matter of some general importance, I venture to make that criticism of what Sir Robert Megarry V-C said with the greatest respect to him.'

Now, it is not possible, in my judgment, to confine the force of the observations in *Uppal v Home Office* to immigration cases. The reasons given by Roskill LJ in the passage that I have read apply equally to the present case. The observance by applicants of the requirements of Ord 53 with regard to preliminary leave and as to prompt timing are equally necessary or desirable in attempts to question the decisions of prison visitors as in attempts to question decisions of the immigration authorities. The superior experience and practice of the Queen's Bench Division are equally obvious in the present class of case. The judges of that division, who are accustomed to sit in the Criminal Division of the Court of Appeal and in the Crown Court and in the Queen's Bench Divisional Court itself, have in general quite plainly more acquaintance than the judges of the Chancery Division with this sort of subject matter.

Secondly, it was suggested on behalf of the plaintiff that there is no persuasive authority in the pronouncement in *Uppal v Home Office*, because it is inconsistent with the actual decision of the Court of Appeal in *De Falco v Crawley Borough Council* [1980] 1 All ER 913, [1980] QB 460. I think that is not so. As I have just shown in referring to the remarks of Lord Denning MR in *De Falco v Crawley Borough Council*, the legislation there under consideration was of a special character directed to the protection of individual homeless persons. Whether or not the language used in the Court of Appeal fits comfortably together in the two cases, there is nothing in the decision in *De Falco's* case that is inconsistent with what was said in *Uppal's* case. The status of what was said in *Uppal's* case is, of course, unusual. The appeal was dismissed by consent, but the court felt constrained to express its view that part of the judgment below was erroneous. That being so, whether or not the views of the court are technically binding on me, they are clearly deserving of the greatest respect, because they were made for the guidance of both the profession and the lower courts. It seems to me that if the formulation of the matter in *Uppal's* case is correct, if indeed it is wrong that the procedure of an action should be adopted in order to bypass the need for getting leave from the Divisional Court, then in the present case it is my duty to put a stop at an early stage to the action. Although I have

some sympathy for the opinion expressed by Professor de Smith in his book and by Sir Robert Megarry V-C in *Uppal v Home Office* that, if the rules appear to leave the plaintiff a
with a choice of procedure, he should be allowed to have it, judicial discipline requires me to follow the view of the whole court in *Uppal's* case, whether technically binding or not. The observance of judicial discipline in the hierarchy of courts in this country seems to me much more important than any particular considerations affecting the plaintiff in this individual case.

For those reasons, the defendants' motion succeeds and, subject to any observations of b
counsel, the proper order will be that I stay all further proceedings in the action.

Order accordingly.

Solicitors: *Treasury Solicitor; Sidney Torrance & Co* agents for *Barrington, Black, Austin & Co*, Leeds (for the plaintiff). c

Evelyn M C Budd Barrister.

Megarity v D J Ryan & Sons Ltd (No 2) d

COURT OF APPEAL, CIVIL DIVISION
LORD ROSKILL AND ORMROD LJ
27th JUNE 1980

Legal aid – Unassisted person's costs out of legal aid fund – Costs incurred by successful unassisted party – Costs incurred in proceedings between him and party receiving legal aid – e
Proceedings – Interlocutory appeal – Interlocutory appeal in action in Queen's Bench Division for damages for personal injuries – Interlocutory appeal by legally aided plaintiff dismissed – Whether power to order payment of unassisted defendant's costs of appeal out of legal aid fund – Whether interlocutory appeal 'proceedings' in connection with which plaintiff receiving legal aid – Legal Aid Act 1974, s 13(1).

f

The plaintiff was granted a legal aid certificate in respect of the entirety of his proceedings against the defendants in the Queen's Bench Division for damages for personal injuries. The defendants, who denied liability, were not legally aided. The defendants obtained from the judge in chambers an interlocutory order requiring the plaintiff to submit unconditionally to examination by the defendants' medical adviser. The legal aid committee authorised the plaintiff to appeal against the order but did not issue a separate g
legal aid certificate in respect of the appeal. The Court of Appeal dismissed the interlocutory appeal and ordered that the defendants' costs of the appeal be paid out of the legal aid fund, since in the court's opinion, it was just and equitable that they should be so paid. The Law Society objected to the order contending that the Court of Appeal had no power under s 13(1)[a] of the Legal Aid Act 1974 to make it because the 'proceedings' in connection with which the plaintiff was receiving legal aid, within h
s 13(1), were the whole action, and since the whole action had not yet been decided, it could not be said on determination of the interlocutory appeal that the 'proceedings [were] finally decided' in favour of the unassisted party (the defendants) within s 13(1), so as to empower the court to make an order for payment of the defendants' costs out of the legal aid fund.

j

Held – An interlocutory appeal to the Court of Appeal in an action in the Queen's Bench Division amounted to 'proceedings' between the assisted party and the unassisted party within s 13(1) of the 1974 Act and accordingly, on the determination of such an appeal,

a Section 13 (1) is set out at p 604 j, post

the court had power under s 13(1) to order payment out of the legal aid fund of the
a successful unassisted party's costs of the appeal since, on the determination of the interlocutory appeal, the 'proceedings' in point had been 'finally determined' in favour of the unassisted party within s 13(1). It followed that the Court of Appeal had power to order the defendants' costs of the interlocutory appeal to be paid out of the legal aid fund (see p 607 *j* and p 608 *c d* and *g*, post).

Dicta of Diplock LJ in *Mills v Mills* [1963] 2 All ER at 240 and of Lord Parker CJ in *R*
b *v Area Committee No 1 (London) Legal Aid Area* [1967] 2 All ER at 422 considered.

Notes

For the Legal Aid Act 1974, s 13, see 44 Halsbury's Statutes (3rd Edn) 1053.

Cases referred to in judgments

c *General Accident Fire and Life Assurance Corpn v Foster* [1972] 3 All ER 877, [1973] QB 50, [1972] 3 WLR 657, [1972] 2 Lloyd's Rep 288, CA, Digest (Cont Vol D) 1053, *1733d*.

Mills v Mills [1963] 2 All ER 237, [1963] P 329, [1963] 2 WLR 831, CA, 50 Digest (Repl) 494, *1752*.

R v Area Committee No 1 (London) Legal Aid Area, ex parte Rondel [1967] 2 All ER 419, [1967] 2 QB 482, [1967] 2 WLR 1358, DC, Digest (Cont Vol C) 1087, *1713a*.

d *Wozniak v Wozniak* [1953] 1 All ER 1192, [1953] P 179, [1953] 2 WLR 1075, CA, 50 Digest (Repl) 493, *1746*.

Cases also cited

Maynard v Osmond (No 2) [1979] 1 All ER 483, [1979] 1 WLR 31, CA.

Shiloh Spinners Ltd v Harding (No 2) [1973] 1 All ER 966, [1973] 1 WLR 518, HL.

e

Application for costs

In an action for personal injuries by the plaintiff, Brian Megarity, against the defendants, D J Ryan & Sons Ltd, the Court of Appeal (Roskill and Ormrod LJJ) ([1980] 2 All ER 832, [1980] 1 WLR 1237) on 13th March 1980 gave judgment for the defendants in an interlocutory appeal by the plaintiff against an order of Hollings J made on 4th February
f 1980 that all further proceedings in the action be stayed until the plaintiff submitted unconditionally to examination by the defendants' medical adviser. The plaintiff was legally aided but the defendants, being a body corporate, were not. At the conclusion of the interlocutory appeal the court ordered that, subject to any objection by the Law Society, the defendants' costs of the interlocutory appeal be paid by the legal aid fund. The Law Society objected to that order on the ground that the proceedings were not, for the purposes of s 13(1) of the Legal Aid Act 1974, finally decided in favour of the
g unassisted party, i e the defendants, when the interlocutory appeal was decided and at the conclusion of that appeal the Court of Appeal had no power to make an order under s 13(1) in favour of the defendants against the legal aid fund.

Duncan Matheson for the Law Society.
G W Wingate-Saul for the defendants.
h The plaintiff did not appear.

LORD ROSKILL. On 13th March 1980 there came before this court, consisting of Ormrod LJ and myself, an interlocutory appeal from an order made by Hollings J sitting in Manchester on 4th February 1980. The judge had given leave for that appeal. It was an appeal by the plaintiff in a personal injuries case, who objected to submitting to a
j medical examination at the instance of the defendants unless the defendants first agreed that he (the plaintiff) or his advisers should be given a copy of any resulting medical report. The district registrar upheld the plaintiff's objection, but the judge reversed the district registrar and we in this court (in a judgment which I gave and with which Ormrod LJ agreed) agreed with Hollings J (see [1980] 2 All ER 832, [1980] 1 WLR 1237). In that respect we followed an earlier judgment of Cusack J.

The plaintiff was legally aided; the defendants were not. We dismissed the appeal without calling on counsel who was appearing for the defendants in this court. He has a reminded us that either in the judgment which I gave or in the course of the argument afterwards I described the appeal as without merit, as indeed from my present recollection of the case I thought it was. As a result, counsel for the defendants applied for an order that the defendants' costs of the appeal (an interlocutory appeal brought by leave of the judge in chambers) should be paid by the legal aid fund. After some discussion, which is not (quite rightly) recorded in the transcript, we made that order, subject, of course, to b the Law Society's usual right to object.

In many of these cases the Law Society do not object; they accept the burden. Then the unassisted person's costs in the Court of Appeal come out of the legal aid fund and thus are borne by the taxpayer. But in the instant case the Law Society have objected. We have had the advantage of a very full and careful argument, for which we are greatly indebted, by counsel for the Law Society and by counsel for the defendants whether or c not the order which Ormrod LJ and I tentatively made was an order within the powers of the Court of Appeal. Counsel for the Law Society has grasped the nettle and has said (and it is, so far as I am aware, the first time that this argument has been advanced in this court, but that certainly does not mean that it is wrong) that the Court of Appeal when it dismisses an interlocutory appeal in favour of an unassisted person and against an assisted person who has brought the appeal, has no power at that juncture to make an d order under s 13(1) of the Legal Aid Act 1974, in favour of the unassisted person and against the legal aid fund. I ought, perhaps, also to say that, to the best of my recollection, the order which this court made in the instant case is one which has been made on interlocutory appeals on a number of previous occasions. We have, therefore, looked at the matter very carefully indeed.

We have been referred to a number of authorities, which I will mention in more detail e in a moment, but I want to make this point at this juncture: many were decided under statutes that were on the statute book before the Legal Aid Act 1974 was passed. Before that Act (which was a consolidating Act) the powers of the court in relation to these matters came from at least three different statutes, and most of the cases which came before the court arose either under the Legal Aid and Advice Act 1949, such as *Mills v Mills* [1963] 2 All ER 237, [1963] P 329, or under the Legal Aid Act 1964, such as *General* f *Accident Life and Fire Assurance Corpn v Foster* [1972] 3 All ER 877, [1973] 1 QB 50. When one looks at the judgments in those cases one sees that the Court of Appeal, on both occasions, referred to, and only to, the language of the statute concerned, which did not cover as wide a field as the 1974 Act. They therefore construed what are the crucial words here, namely 'any proceedings' and 'those proceedings' in s 13(1) of the 1974 Act in the context in which the corresponding words appeared in the earlier statutes, the g 1949 Act and the 1964 Act. Now, of course, when you have a consolidating Act covering a wider field, it is natural to look at all the places in that statute where those words or the word 'proceedings' appear; but it is difficult to think that when Parliament consolidated this legislation it intended the words 'proceeding' or 'proceedings' in the 1974 Act to bear any different meaning from that which it had previously been held to bear under the earlier legislation. h

With that introduction, let me turn to the relevant statutory provisions. I do not propose to read all that have been referred to. Section 13 of the 1974 Act reads thus:

> '(1) Where a party receives legal aid in connection with any proceedings between him and a party not receiving legal aid (in this and section 14 below referred to as 'the unassisted party') and those proceedings are finally decided in favour of the j unassisted party, the court by which the proceedings are so decided may, subject to the provisions to this section, make an order for the payment to the unassisted party out of the legal aid fund of the whole of any part of the costs incurred by him in those proceedings.
>
> '(2) An order may be made under this section in respect of any costs if (and only if) the court is satisfied that it is just and equitable in all the circumstances that

provision for those costs should be made out of public funds; and before making
a such an order the court shall in every case (whether or not application is made in that behalf) consider what orders should be made for costs against the party receiving legal aid and for determining his liability in respect of such costs.'

Pausing there, with reference to sub-s (2) I would interpose this: first, neither Ormrod LJ nor I had any doubt but that it was just and equitable in all the circumstances that the defendants' costs should come out of the legal aid fund; secondly, we performed our duty
b of considering what order should be made against the plaintiff as 'the party receiving legal aid', and our answer was that, in the light of the information we then had, he should not make any contribution.

I continue with s 13:

'(3) Without prejudice to subsection (2) above, no order shall be made under this
c section in respect of costs incurred in a court of first instance, whether by that court or by any appellate court, unless [I leave out para (*a*) because that deals with courts of first instance] (*b*) the court is satisfied that the unassisted party will suffer severe financial hardship unless the order is made.

'(4) An order under this section shall not be made by any court in respect of costs incurred by the unassisted party in any proceedings in which, apart from this
d section, no order would be made for the payment of his costs . . .'

Section 14 was relied on. I will read sub-s (1):

'Regulations may make provision—(*a*) for determining the proceedings which are or are not to be treated as separate proceedings for the purposes of section 13 above . . .'

e and I need not read the rest of that. I go to s 14(3) and (4), to which Ormrod LJ referred during argument. I will not read sub-s (3), but sub-s (4) reads thus:

'Where a court decides any proceedings in favour of the unassisted party and an appeal lies (with or without leave) against that decision, the court may, if it thinks fit, make or refuse to make an order under section 13 above forthwith, but any
f order so made shall not take effect—(*a*) where leave to appeal is required, unless the time limited for applications for leave to appeal expires without leave being granted; (*b*) where leave to appeal is granted or is not required, unless the time limited for appeal expires without an appeal being brought.'

I will not read sub-s (5), though counsel for the Law Society referred us to it, or Sch 1.

I can go to the Legal Aid (General) Regulations 1971, SI 1971 No 62, which were made
g under the earlier legislation. Regulation 6 provides:

'(1) A certificate may be issued in respect of—(*a*) one or more steps to assert or dispute a claim; or (*b*) the whole or part of—(i) proceedings in a court of first instance, or (ii) proceedings in an appellate court; but no certificate shall relate to proceedings (other than interlocutory appeals) both in a court of first instance and
h in an appellate court or to proceedings in more than one appellate court.

'(2) Unless a certificate otherwise provides it shall not without the authority of the appropriate committee given under regulation 15(1) extend to . . . (*c*) lodging an interlocutory appeal . . .'

and I think that is all we need.

We were referred to reg 20 but I need not read it. I will go to the Legal Aid (Costs of
j Successful Unassisted Parties) Regulations 1964, SI 1964 No 1276. I need only refer to reg 2 of those regulations:

'Any proceedings in respect of which a separate civil aid certificate *could* [and I emphasise the word 'could'] properly be issued under the General Regulations to a person receiving legal aid shall be treated as separate proceedings for the purposes of the Act.'

In the present case the plaintiff was the beneficiary of a legal aid certificate for the entirety of his proceedings. He was not issued with a separate certificate for the instant *a* interlocutory appeal, but authority was given for that interlocutory appeal to be brought. But I cannot think that the answer to the problem we have to resolve can depend on the administrative consideration whether or not he was issued with a single legal aid certificate but one which requires special authority to bring an interlocutory appeal or with two or more different legal aid certificates. The essential point, when one looks at s 13(1) is whether or not he has received legal aid in connection with 'any *b* proceedings' and those proceedings are 'finally' decided in favour of the unassisted party.

Counsel for the Law Society's argument was to this effect: that the plaintiff did receive legal aid in connection with the action; it is the action which is 'any proceedings' and those proceedings have not been, and will not be, finally decided in favour of the unassisted party unless and until (if ever) there is judgment for the defendants in the action. I should say that liability in this action is still in issue. *c*

Counsel for the defendants' argument is that the plaintiff has received legal aid in connection with this interlocutory appeal; the 'any proceedings' are the interlocutory appeal, and 'those proceedings' (being the interlocutory appeal) have been finally decided in favour of the unassisted party, namely the defendants/respondents in this appeal.

Both sides have referred us to a number of cases. For my own part, without any disrespect, I doubt if one gets much help from the cases in resolving what is basically a *d* question of construction, but as we have been referred to them I mention some of them if only to dispose of some of the arguments.

In chronological order, the first was *Wozniak v Wozniak* [1953] 1 All ER 1192, [1953] P 179. The relevant provision in that case was wholly different from the current statutory provisions. Further, what Denning LJ said had reference only to an order wrongly made by a trial judge; Denning LJ had not in mind the position of the Court of *e* Appeal.

Next chronologically is *Mills v Mills* [1963] 2 All ER 237, [1963] P 329, again a decision of this court. In proceedings in what was then the Probate, Divorce and Admiralty Division, the husband got a limited legal aid certificate enabling him to defend the wife's claim for alimony and maintenance. He was not given legal aid to defend her claim for dissolution of marriage. In due course the judge granted her a decree nisi and ordered *f* the husband to pay the costs of the petition. The husband appealed to this court on the ground that he ought to have had the benefit of his legal aid certificate in respect of all the costs, including the costs of the petition, and not merely the costs of contesting the claim for alimony and maintenance. His Honour Judge Herbert (sitting as a Special Commissioner) rejected that argument and this court had no difficulty in affirming that judge without calling on counsel for the wife. The judgment of the court was given by *g* Diplock LJ. After reading the relevant regulations, Diplock LJ said ([1963] 2 All ER 237 at 240, [1963] P 329 at 337):

> 'I have a good deal of sympathy with that argument where it applies to petitions for dissolution of marriage in which a petitioner, even in an undefended petition, has to prove his or her case and costs are incurred, and if I could find some way of treating "proceedings" in para. (e) in a different sense from the word "proceedings" *h* in other parts of the same subsection, I would gladly do so; but, as a matter of construction, that seems to me to be quite impossible. Consequently, the result of the construction contended for by counsel for the husband would be this: not merely that where an assisted person has a limited certificate limited to disputing part, and part only, of the claim, would he be entitled not to have an order for costs made against him except under the conditions laid down in para. (e), but he would *j* also be entitled under para. (b) and para. (d) to have paid out of the legal aid fund the costs of the very matter in respect of which he was not given a certificate. The result of that construction would mean, so far as I can see, that there would be no power on the part of a legal aid committee to give a certificate limited to part of the proceedings in a court, for such attempted limitation would be a brutum fulmen.'

That passage, of course, was not directed to the point currently at issue, but its
a underlying philosophy seems to me to be a pointer in the direction of what I regard as the true construction of s 13(1).

In *R v Area Committee No 1 (London) Legal Aid Area, ex parte Rondel* [1967] 2 All ER 419 at 422, [1967] 2 QB 482 at 491, a decision of the Divisional Court, Lord Parker CJ said:

> 'Counsel for the applicant, in his able argument before this court, begins by submitting, and for my part I think he is undoubtedly right, that where proceedings
> *b* are referred to in the Act and in the regulations, those proceedings are not confined to actions but involve all proceedings of an interlocutory nature. I find it unnecessary to refer to all the matters to support that view.'

Lord Parker CJ went on to refer to *Mills v Mills.* Plainly Lord Parker CJ had no difficulty in taking the view that 'proceedings' in the relevant legislation included
c interlocutory proceedings.

In *General Accident, Fire and Life Assurance Corpn v Foster* [1972] 3 All ER 877 at 880, [1973] QB 50 at 55, there is this passage in the judgment of Lord Denning MR:

> 'The matter is governed by s 1(1) and (2) of the Legal Aid Act 1964. [Pausing there, those are the corresponding subsections to s 13(1) and (2) of the 1974 Act.] The first point is: what are the "proceedings"? Are they the proceedings from the
> *d* beginning to the end—from the very first time when legal aid was granted? I think not. The only "proceedings" with which we are concerned is the interlocutory appeal to this court, which we heard on 19th January 1971; and for which, no doubt, a separate legal aid certificate was granted. [Whether Lord Denning MR was right in making that last observation is, if I may say so with respect, doubtful, but it does not matter.] The second point is whether "those proceedings", ie the
> *e* interlocutory appeal, were "finally decided in favour of the assisted party"? When are proceedings "finally decided in favour" of a party, especially in a case like this where the result was not wholly in his favour?'

It has been pointed out by counsel for the Law Society that it was conceded by Mr Hames QC for the Law Society in the *General Accident* case that 'proceedings' included
f interlocutory proceedings. That that concession was made clearly emerges from the opening sentence of Sachs LJ's judgment where he said ([1972] 3 All ER 877 at 881, [1973] QB 50 at 56):

> 'On three preliminary points there was no dispute in this court. The first was that the interlocutory appeal to this court was clearly a separate proceeding for the
> *g* purpose of considering the effect of s 1 of the Legal Aid Act 1964.'

The fact that that concession was made on that occasion does not mean that it was rightly made, and we have looked at the whole matter de novo. But it seems to me that if one looks at the relevant words in s 1(1) and (2) of the 1964 Act it was inevitable that Mr Hames should have made that concession, and when I look at the corresponding and identical words in s 13(1) and (2) of the 1974 Act, I am unable to give them a different
h meaning from that which they bore when that provision appeared in isolation in the 1964 Act. It is true that if one goes through, as counsel for the Law Society has carefully taken us through, other sections not in the 1964 Act but in other Acts now consolidated in the 1974 Act, one can find, as one often does find in statutes, the word 'proceedings' used in different senses in different places, but I think the concession was rightly made. I would have no hesitation in construing the words 'any proceedings' as including an
j interlocutory appeal to this court in an ordinary Queen's Bench action. If one asks while the interlocutory appeal is going on, 'In what proceedings are the plaintiff and the defendant engaging?', I think the man in the street would say, 'An interlocutory appeal in the Court of Appeal'. They would not at that stage say they are engaging in a personal injury action in the High Court. On that point I therefore reject counsel for the Law Society's argument.

It is, perhaps, worth considering what the practical consequences would be if that argument were allowed to succeed. Ormrod LJ drew attention to those consequences. *a* What is the Court of Appeal to do in a case in which it dismisses an appeal by an assisted person in favour of an unassisted person? It is suggested that the matter would then have to await a decision until after the trial judge finally decides the case. That would involve the trial judge usurping, if I may be forgiven the word, the powers of the Court of Appeal over costs in matters before this court. It would involve endless delay. The trial judge would not know what the Court of Appeal would have done if it had had power to do *b* that which ex hypothesi it could not. It was further said that this court could not finally determine the amount of the assisted person's contribution unless and until the result of the action was known, because his means would vary according to the result. It is true his means may so vary, but the Court of Appeal has to take its decision on the best information available to it at the time the appeal is dismissed. After all, if the matter were left to the trial judge it may be that on the day of judgment the plaintiff, if *c* successful, might be worth a certain amount, but the next day he might be worth a great deal more if he had won a football pool or had a successful day at the races. It seems to me that it is within the powers of the Court of Appeal to determine this matter once and for all (subject, of course, to due compliance with the other provisions of s 13) at the end of the interlocutory appeal. I have no hesitation in holding that this court does have power, at the conclusion of an interlocutory appeal, to decide this matter because *d* interlocutory appeals are 'any proceedings' between the assisted person and a party not receiving legal aid, and those 'proceedings' will have been 'finally determined', as they were in the present case, in favour of the unassisted party.

Though grateful for counsel for the Law Society's excellent argument, I would, therefore, decide this issue in favour of the defendants.

I would just add this to my judgment. Counsel for the Law Society mentioned that *e* the Law Society had not been informed of our tentative order until a considerable number of weeks had elapsed after our judgment on 13th March 1980. I confess that I thought, and I understand Ormrod LJ shares my view, that when this court made such an order, the court would have informed the Law Society of the order that had been made, but we have been told by the associate that that is not now the practice. We are told that it was the assisted person's solicitors who notified the Law Society. That cannot *f* be the right way for the Law Society to be notified. But I do not think it is a matter on which we ought to express any final view. Perhaps the Law Society, if they wish to raise it, would be good enough to take it up direct with the Master of the Rolls. It is a matter on which there should be some uniform practice.

g

ORMROD LJ. I agree and would only add very few words of my own.

If counsel for the Law Society's argument is right, s 13(1) of the Legal Aid Act 1974 has to be read thus:

> 'Where a party receives legal aid in connection with any proceedings [that is in the sense of an action or claim or some similar proceeding] between him and a party *h* not receiving legal aid . . . and those proceedings [that means the whole action] are finally decided in favour of the unassisted party, the court by which the proceedings [that is the whole action] are so decided may, subject to the provisions of this section, make an order for the payment to the unassisted party out of the legal aid fund of the whole or any part of the costs incurred by him in *those* proceedings [that is the whole action].'

j

It therefore follows, if counsel for the Law Society is right, that at the end of the case the trial judge will be asked to make an order for costs in favour of the unassisted party, as against the fund in a case such as this, in respect of part of those costs, namely the costs of an unsuccessful appeal to this court. Then the judge would have to deal with the awkward problem of sub-s (3), because the 'proceedings' will be proceedings in the court of first instance, in which case the court has to be satisfied on the severe financial hardship point.

The truth is I think, with respect to counsel for the Law Society, that ss 13 and 14, as Lord Roskill has said, come from an entirely separate piece of legislation, the Legal Aid Act 1964, which was passed expressly to deal with the problem which had been omitted from the 1949 Act of the unassisted party's costs, about which there had been a certain amount of feeling and which eventually was dealt with by the 1964 Act to protect unassisted parties who were successful. It seems to me that logically we should construe ss 13 and 14 in exactly the same way as the court would have construed them when they were in a separate statute.

That was done in *General Accident Fire and Life Assurance Corpn v Foster* [1972] 3 All ER 877, [1973] QB 50, and I, for my part, attach some significance to the fact that Mr Hames QC who was appearing for the Law Society in that case conceded that the interlocutory appeal was a separate proceeding for the purposes of the 1964 Act. He is a man who has enormous experience of handling legal aid points and he would be the last person, I venture to think with respect, to make a concession unless it was well founded. I also obtain a little assistance and a little comfort from what Sachs LJ said. He, too, had a long association with the legal aid scheme, long before 1949, and we find him saying ([1972] 3 All ER 877 at 881, [1973] QB 50 at 56):

> 'On three preliminary points there was no dispute in this court. The first was that the interlocutory appeal to this court was *clearly a separate proceeding for the purpose of considering the effect of s 1 of the Legal Aid Act 1964*.' (Emphasis mine.)

That, I must confess, impressed me a good deal. It would be very odd if that concession by Mr Hames and that view expressed by Sachs LJ proved to be wrong. For my part, I would require a lot of convincing before I came to a different view on the construction of these two subsections. When one adds to that counsel for the Law Society's admission in this court that the effect of his construction would, if accepted, effectively make it impossible for this court to make an order for costs in favour of an assisted party against the legal aid fund in an interlocutory appeal, then I can only say that before being forced to that conclusion I should require to see very, very clear statutory provisions leading to that conclusion.

I take the same view as Lord Roskill, and, indeed, the view of this court in the *General Accident* case, that if we look at these two sections in isolation the answer is obvious. Looked at in the body of the legal aid legislation as a whole it is easy to get tied in many ways, and counsel for the Law Society is an admirable spinner of webs in that connection. I agree that the existing order should stand.

Order that defendants recover their costs of the interlocutory appeal against the legal aid fund, such costs to include today's costs. Leave to appeal to the House of Lords refused.

Solicitors: *David Edwards*, Secretary, Legal Aid (for the Law Society); *James Chapman & Co* (for the defendants).

Dilys Tausz Barrister.

Rahman v Kirklees Area Health Authority a

COURT OF APPEAL, CIVIL DIVISION
ORMROD AND CUMMING-BRUCE LJJ
22nd NOVEMBER 1979

Practice – Evidence – Expert evidence – Disclosure to other parties – Action for medical b
negligence – Disclosure of reports – Number of medical witnesses – Whether action for medical negligence an exception to general rule requiring disclosure of medical reports in personal injuries actions – Whether sufficient reason for non-disclosure – Whether number of medical witnesses should be limited in action for medical negligence – RSC Ord 38, r 37.

The plaintiff brought an action against a hospital authority alleging negligence by the c
hospital staff in respect of her medical treatment while she was in hospital. The authority denied liability. On the hearing of an appeal in respect of the plaintiff's summons for directions the judge ordered that there should not be mutual disclosure of medical reports or any limitation on the number of medical witnesses called on either side. The plaintiff appealed seeking an order that (i) medical reports be mutually disclosed and (ii)
the number of medical witnesses be limited to three on each side. On the issue of d
mutual disclosure of medical reports, the plaintiff contended that RSC Ord 38, r 37(1)[a] obliged the court to order mutual disclosure of medical reports in all personal injury actions unless it considered that 'there was sufficient reason for not doing so' and that this applied to actions alleging medical negligence notwithstanding that by r 37(2) the court might if it thought fit treat the fact that the pleadings contained an allegation of medical
negligence 'as sufficient reason' for not directing mutual disclosure. The plaintiff further e
contended that there was not sufficient reason for refusing disclosure because the facts were not in dispute. On the issue of the number of medical witnesses to be allowed, the plaintiff contended that not to limit the number would be onerous to her because, having regard to the nature of her allegations, the authority would be likely to call a large number of medical witnesses.

Held – The appeal would be dismissed and the judge's order upheld, for the following f
reasons—

(1) On the issue of mutual disclosure of medical reports, RSC Ord 38, r 37(2) expressly distinguished actions for medical negligence from other actions for personal injuries in order to indicate that in an action for medical negligence the court ought not to order disclosure of medical reports unless there was some unusual feature in the case. The
reason for that distinction was that it was common for the defendant's expert in a g
medical negligence case to be given proofs of the evidence of those whose acts and omissions were under scrutiny in order to found his expert opinion, and therefore disclosure of his report would in fact disclose to the other side a summary of the defendant's proofs of evidence, and (per Ormrod LJ) the character of the expert evidence in a medical negligence case differed from expert evidence in an action for personal
injuries properly so called. Since there was no material before the judge to justify h
disclosure of the authority's medical reports, it followed that the judge's order was right (see p 612 *f* to *h*, p 613 *f* and p 614 *a b e* to *g* and *j* to p 615 *b*, post).

(2) Having regard to the nature of the plaintiff's allegations of medical negligence, it was not appropriate to restrict the number of medical witnesses either side should be allowed to call (see p 613 *j* to p 614 *b* and *j* to p 615 *b*, post).

j

Notes

RSC Ord 38, r 37, has been substituted by RSC (Amendment No 2) 1980, SI 1980 No 1010, r 10(2), with effect from 1st October 1980.

---

a Rule 37, so far as material, is set out at p 612 *b c*, post

Interlocutory appeal

a By a writ dated 4th December 1978 the plaintiff, Joan Rahman, claimed against the defendants, Kirklees Area Health Authority, the occupier of Staincliffe General Hospital and Staincliffe Maternity Unit, Dewsbury, West Yorkshire and the employer of the persons engaged in the care and treatment of patients at the hospital and unit, damages for negligence in the plaintiff's treatment in 1976 for delivery of a child. The defendants denied negligence. By an order dated 24th May 1979 made on the plaintiff's summons *b* for directions Mr District Registrar Lamb, inter alia, ordered (by Direction 23) that medical reports be exchanged, and if not agreed the medical evidence be limited to one witness for each party. The defendants appealed and on 27th June 1979 Mais J in chambers allowed the appeal and ordered that Direction 23 be deleted from the summons for directions and that no limit be imposed on the number of medical witnesses to be called by either side. The plaintiff appealed seeking mutual disclosure of medical reports *c* and limitation of the medical witnesses to three for each party. The facts are set out in the judgment of Cumming-Bruce LJ.

John M Collins for the plaintiff.
Ian Kennedy QC and *Robert Taylor* for the defendants.

d **CUMMING-BRUCE LJ** delivered the first judgment at the invitation of Ormrod LJ. This is an action for medical negligence. The negligence alleged is that by reason of the failure of the defendants, by their doctors, surgeons or other servants, to exercise proper skill and care, the plaintiff was subjected to delivery by Caesarian section which, if it could not have been avoided altogether by proper diagnostic skill, was at any rate not carried out at the right time or at all, before the death of the baby. There is an allegation *e* that during the period immediately preceding the birth there was a want of proper supervision of the plaintiff by the appropriate specialist eyes or hands; and there is a further allegation that the defendants re-established a cyntocinon drip without proper consultation and without proper consideration of harmful effects.

The defence admitted some facts that could not be controverted and accepted that the plaintiff had had a stillbirth and was found to have suffered a uterine rupture, which led *f* to drastic surgical interference. The defendants content themselves with a denial of negligence, putting the plaintiff to proof of matters of fact alleged.

The summons for directions came before the registrar and, after ordering discovery of documents, he made the following order:

> 'Medical Reports be exchanged and that if not agreed medical evidence be limited *g* to one witness for each party whose reports have been exchanged . . . Trial Place Leeds. Mode Judge alone.'

There was an appeal against that order and, on the appeal, the judge allowed the appeal and ordered that—

> 'direction number 23 be deleted from the Summons for Directions herein and no *h* limit be imposed on the number of Medical expert witnesses to be called on either side.'

Item 23 on the summons for directions is the item dealing with the agreement of medical reports and the restriction of medical witnesses. The plaintiff appeals.

Counsel for the plaintiff appeals two parts of the judge's order. He seeks an order that—

j

> '(1) The Plaintiffs and Defendants do mutually disclose medical reports within forty two days (2) Such reports be agreed if possible (3) Unless such reports are agreed the parties be at liberty to call experts on medical matters limited to those witnesses whose reports have been disclosed and limited to three witnesses for each party.'

I come first to the appeal in relation to the judge's decision that there should be no mutual disclosure of medical reports. The relevant rule is RSC Ord 38, r 37, which appears in the Rules of the Supreme Court in relation to actions for personal injuries and bears that heading. The rule reads:

> '(1) Where in an action for personal injuries an application is made under rule 36(1) in respect of oral expert evidence relating to medical matters, then, unless the Court considers that there is sufficient reason for not doing so, it shall direct that the substance of the evidence be disclosed in the form of a written report or reports to such other parties and within such period as the Court may specify.
>
> '(2) The Court may, if it thinks fit, treat any of the following circumstances as a sufficient reason for not giving a direction under paragraph (1):—(*a*) that the pleadings contain an allegation of a negligent act or omission in the course of medical treatment; or (*b*) that the expert evidence may contain an expression of opinion—(i) as to the manner in which the personal injuries were sustained . . .'

Counsel for the plaintiff submitted that on a scrutiny of para (1) it is clear that the starting point is that the court shall direct disclosure of the reports of expert witnesses, subject only to the proviso that such a direction shall not be given 'unless the Court considers that there is sufficient reason for not doing so.' He also submitted that para (2) does no more than give some illustrations of certain kinds of case which are not intended to be exhaustive, and are selected by the Rules Committee only as illustrations of certain kinds of situation in which the court may find there is sufficient reason for refusing disclosure. So construing or explaining Ord 38, r 37, counsel for the plaintiff submits that, on the issues in this case (although it is, of course, a medical negligence case because that is what the pleadings allege), when the issue raised by the pleadings are considered, there is nothing so special about them as to make it right in the exercise of the judge's duty to find that a sufficient reason for refusing disclosure has been shown.

For myself, I do not accept the explanation and effect of Ord 38, r 37, propounded by counsel for the plaintiff. Paragraph (2) of that rule goes further than merely indicating as illustrations the kinds of situation which might appropriately be regarded as sufficient reasons for refusing to direct exchange of reports. In my view, the Rules Committee has clearly thought it appropriate expressly to distinguish the situation where expert evidence is being called in other kinds of actions for damages for personal injuries, from the forensic situation that obtains where an allegation of medical negligence is made as a cause of action. For myself, I can see at once the common sense of that distinction, because one of the features of an expert report for the defendants in a medical negligence case is that, in order to found an opinion, it is commonly necessary for the expert to be given all, or most, of the proofs of fact, of all those persons whose acts and omissions are under scrutiny in the proceedings. It would be strange indeed if, by means of a direction under Ord 38, r 37, the court, on a sidewind, made an order in which it was implicit that the defendants' proofs of evidence would be shown to the other side in summary form. The plaintiff has the right, by reference to orders for discovery of documents and interrogatories, to obtain from the defendants such evidence of fact as lies in their possession, subject to the practice of the courts in relation to discovery of documents and interrogatories.

Although, as counsel for the plaintiff has rightly stated, the history of procedure in civil actions has been developing over the last generation in that parties are encouraged to hold their cards less closely to their chests, that development has certainly not reached the stage of imposing on a defendant a duty to disclose his proof of evidence, save in so far as discovery is obtainable through discovery of documents and interrogatories. For the purposes of construing or appreciating the intent of Ord 38, r 37, it is helpful, in my view, also to look at the next rule, r 38, which has the heading 'Other expert evidence'. It is, I think, helpful to observe that in Ord 38, r 38, para (2) reads:

> 'In deciding whether to give a direction under paragraph (1) the Court shall have regard to all the circumstances and may, to such extent as it thinks fit, treat any of

the following circumstances as affording a sufficient reason for not giving such a a direction [for exchange of reports]:—(*a*) that the expert evidence is or will be based to any material extent upon a version of the facts in dispute between the parties; or (*b*) that the expert evidence is or will be based to any material extent upon facts which are neither—(i) ascertainable by the expert by the exercise of his own powers of observation, nor (ii) within his general professional knowledge and experience.'

I focus on RSC Ord 38, r 38(2)(*a*), and observe that the Rules Committee, in relation b to other expert evidence (ie other than medical evidence in actions for personal injuries), contemplated that it would not be appropriate to exchange reports if the expert evidence will be based to any material extent on a version of the facts in dispute between the parties. Counsel for the plaintiff submitted that the facts are not really in dispute, because there cannot be a dispute about the sad history of the plaintiff over the period in June and July 1976 which culminated in the death of the baby and an ensuing c hysterectomy.

That is, in my view, a gross over-simplification of the realities. Matters in dispute, having regard to the allegations in the statement of claim, are likely to be the detail of the history of supervision, diagnosis and treatment from day to day and at certain stages, from hour to hour; and there may very well be the most substantial dispute about what the facts were in relation to such supervision, diagnosis and treatment. The experts, d whom the defendants would seek to call, are likely to be persons with appropriate professional qualifications who will state what the proper standards of skill and care are in relation to the different kinds of problem posed by the plaintiff during the relevant period; and, in order to form such an opinion, it will be necessary for such experts to be given by the defendants' solicitors what may well amount to a summary of the proofs of all the professional persons who were responsible for the supervision, diagnosis, medical, e surgical and nursing care of the plaintiff over the relevant period of a month or six weeks. It is by reflecting on such considerations that the decision of the Rules Committee to draft Ord 37, r 38(2)(*a*), in the form in which it was is to be explained. For my part I do not accept counsel for the plaintiff's interpretation of Ord 38, r 37(2), and I can find no reason in the material before the judge which would justify this court in varying the order that the judge made in deciding not to give a direction for the disclosure of expert f medical reports in this case. I would go further and say that, if I were to consider the subject matter afresh, I would think that the judge's order was plainly right.

The second matter that arises is on the limitation of medical witnesses. In the summons for directions issued by the plaintiff the application was, I understand, for a limitation of expert evidence to two witnesses to each party. For some reason which remains obscure to me the registrar made a rather startling order that the medical reports g be 'exchanged and that if not agreed medical evidence be limited to one witness for each party whose reports have been exchanged'. A mere superficial scrutiny of the issues raised by the particulars of negligence in the statement of claim is sufficient to show that that figure is quite certainly wrong. It may well be, first, that a number of different kinds of medical speciality may be involved and, second, that both plaintiff and defendants may reasonably wish to call more than one witness dealing with any relevant h specialist experience connected with the issues in the case.

The judge decided not to limit the number of witnesses. Counsel for the plaintiff submits that that is onerous and subjects the plaintiff, a mere patient, to the prospect of litigation in which a whole string of men of medical learning may be marshalled to follow each other into the witness box to obscure the truth out of a misguided sense of loyalty to a member or members of their profession charged with negligence. The j history of medical negligence actions, I think, can be said to show that counsel's apprehensions are not wholly fanciful but, as against that, this court should not approach a case on the basis that the defendants, a public authority, will consciously try to abuse their position.

Secondly, having looked at the allegations in the statement of claim, it does appear to me, innocent though I am of professional medical knowledge, to be the kind of case in which the defendants ought to be at liberty to decide what kinds of medical specialists to call, and ought also not to be restricted in deciding whether it is necessary and sensible to call more than one medical witness on any particular kind of speciality.

For those reasons I would uphold the judge's order and dismiss the appeal.

ORMROD LJ. I agree and I have only a few words to add of my own.

If counsel for the plaintiff is right in his contention in this case, it produces the most extraordinary result. Under RSC 38, r 37, the court is obliged to order the exchange of medical reports unless it considers there is sufficient reason for not doing so. Under RSC 38, r 38, on the other hand, the court is simply left with a general discretion whether to order or not to order the disclosure of other expert reports. If counsel for the plaintiff's construction of r 37 is right, it would mean that medical negligence cases are singled out from all other kinds of negligence by experts for quite separate and different treatment. The court would be prima facie under a duty in medical negligence cases to order an exchange of reports, whereas in other kinds of professional negligence cases, such as solicitors or engineers or architects, there would be no such onus on the court or onus on the persons objecting to the disclosure to make it good.

I am bound to say I do not think that Ord 38, r 37, is particularly well drafted. It appears to me, from the use of the phrase 'action for personal injuries' in the first line of the rule, that the draftsman contemplated what everybody calls an action for personal injuries, which is a running-down case or a factory accident or something similar. I do not think I have ever heard of a medical negligence case spoken about as an action for personal injuries, although of course in a sense it is. There is no doubt that the burden of r 37 is directed to the case with which we are all so familiar, where the question is the extent of the injuries suffered by the person as a result of somebody else's negligence and the prognosis of those injuries, a standard form of medical report in a personal injury action. Expert evidence in an action for medical negligence or for professional negligence takes on an entirely different character, because the evidence is directed not to what the patient's condition is now or was as a result of the accident or what it is going to be in the course of time in order that damages can be assessed. The expert evidence in this case is directed to the crucial question: was the treatment correct or reasonable in the circumstances? That is an enormous difference. No doubt that is why in para (2) of r 37 the draftsman specifically mentioned negligent acts in the course of medical treatment, intending apparently not to take actions for medical negligence out of the rule altogether, but to give the court the broadest of hints that the court should not order disclosure of reports in such cases unless there is some unusual feature. I cannot help feeling that it would have been better, if the draftsman intended there to be an exception, to have made it a clear exception.

The same comment, with less force, to my mind applies to the provision in para (2)(*b*)(i) of r 37, which indicates that the court may if it thinks fit treat as a sufficient reason for not giving a direction the fact that the expert evidence may contain an expression of opinion as to the manner in which the personal injuries were sustained. That is another example of the medical expert evidence going to liability and not to quantum of damages. The same applies to para (2)(*b*)(ii), 'as to the genuineness of the symptoms of which complaint is made': that goes to liability. It looks as though the draftsman of the rule shrank from putting on the court the duty to order disclosure of the reports when those reports were directed to the issue of liability as opposed to damages.

In my judgment, the rule is not at all happily phrased and, when one looks at r 38, which is permissive in contrast to r 37, one sees then, as Cumming-Bruce LJ has already pointed out, a series of circumstances which will take the expert evidence out of the rule of disclosure.

For all those reasons it seems to me plain that the judge was right in his view that this was not a case for making any direction at all under r 37, and I agree with what Cumming-Bruce LJ has said as to the number of witnesses. In a case like this I do not, for my part, see any useful purpose whatever in limiting the number of witnesses. If the defendants or plaintiff choose to try to abuse the position by calling an innumerable number of witnesses they may well end up by damaging their own case in nine out of ten cases, and the trial judge can deal with it himself.

I would dismiss this appeal.

Appeal dismissed.

Solicitors: *Kingsley, Napley & Co*, agents for *Stapleton Gardner & Co*, Dewsbury (for the plaintiff); *Hempsons*, agents for *R H D Chapman*, Harrogate (for the defendants).

Sumra Green Barrister.

Swain and another v Law Society

CHANCERY DIVISION

SLADE J

18th, 19th, 20th, 21st FEBRUARY, 17th MARCH 1980

Insurance – Liability insurance – Professional indemnity insurance – Solicitors – Law Society's group scheme – Law Society authorised to 'take out and maintain insurance with authorised insurers' – Law Society arranging master policy with specified insurers – Law Society requiring all solicitors to participate in group scheme and pay premiums set under master policy – Whether scheme within Law Society's authority to take out and maintain insurance with authorised insurers – Solicitors Act 1974, s 37(2)(b).

Insurance – Commission – Professional indemnity insurance – Solicitors – Law Society's group scheme – Law Society arranging master policy with specified insurers through brokers – Law Society and brokers agreeing to share commission – Whether Law Society accountable to individual solicitors for commission received – Whether Law Society in a fiduciary relationship with solicitors when making commission agreement with brokers.

By virtue of s 37 of the Solicitors Act 1974 the Law Society was empowered to make rules for compulsory professional indemnity insurance against claims made against solicitors in respect of civil liability for professional negligence or breach of duty. Under s 37(1)[a] the society had a general rule-making power to make rules concerning indemnity against loss arising from claims in respect of civil liability incurred by solicitors, while s 37(2)[b] specified that 'for the purpose of providing such indemnity' such rules could (a) authorise the society to establish and maintain its own indemnity fund, or (b) authorise the society to 'take out and maintain insurance with authorised insurers', or (c) require solicitors to take out and maintain insurance individually with authorised insurers. The society opted for a group scheme whereby it arranged indemnity insurance through a particular firm of brokers and then required solicitors to participate in the scheme or else risk being refused a practising certificate. Accordingly, the society entered into a contract with specified insurers in November 1975 and later made the Solicitors' Indemnity Rules 1975 which provided for the society to take out and maintain with authorised insurers a 'master policy' and required solicitors to pay the premiums prescribed under that policy and to produce a certificate of insurance issued under the master policy when applying each year for a practising certificate. By s 37(3)(*c*)[c] of the 1974 Act the society was authorised to require solicitors to 'make payments by way of premium on any insurance policy maintained by the Society [under s 37(2)(*b*)]'. The master policy, which was

a Section 37 (1) is set out at p 619 *j* to p 620 *a*, post

b Section 37 (2) is set out at p 620 *c*, post

c Section 37 (3) is set out at p 620 *e* to *h*, post

deemed to form part of the indemnity rules, was arranged by the society with specified insurers. The policy recited that the insurers agreed 'with the Law Society on behalf of a all solicitors . . . required to be insured' by the indemnity rules to provide such insurance and provided for fixed premiums according to whether a solicitor was a partner or sole practitioner and later according to whether a solicitor practised in Inner London or elsewhere. A specified firm were to act as sole brokers under the scheme and all claims were required to be submitted to them. The brokers agreed that in return for being appointed sole brokers they would share with the society commission received by them b from the insurers, and in fact the society received substantial amounts of revenue from this source. This agreement ('the commission arrangement') was made in May 1976 following renegotiation by the society and the brokers of an earlier commission agreement made in February 1975 in respect of the voluntary insurance scheme which the society ran in conjunction with the brokers prior to the compulsory scheme set up in November 1975. The February 1975 agreement provided for such renegotiation at the c request of either party in the event of the introduction of a compulsory indemnity insurance scheme. As a result of the renegotiation the society received a much greater share of the commission than before.

The plaintiffs were two practising solicitors who considered that given freedom of choice they could obtain better insurance cover at a lower premium than that available under the society's scheme. They took out an originating summons seeking declarations d (i) that the society had no power under s 37 to make the indemnity rules, which were therefore null and void, and (ii) that the society was not entitled to retain for its own purposes commission received by it from the brokers in respect of premiums paid by individual solicitors but was instead accountable to them for the commission. On the question of the legality or otherwise of the rules the plaintiffs contended (i) that s 37(2)(*b*) under which the rules were admittedly made only authorised the society to take out and e maintain insurance for itself and on its own behalf and not as agent or trustee for other persons which, the plaintiffs contended, was the effect of the group scheme embodied in the rules and the master policy, (ii) that the master policy did not amount to the 'taking out' of insurance because the master policy was not a policy of insurance but merely an undertaking to provide insurance, which the society was unable to enforce since it had not given any consideration in return, and (iii) that the effect of the rules was to require f solicitors to take out and maintain insurance with specified insurers of the society's choice whereas s 37(2)(*b*) merely required solicitors to effect insurance with any insurers who were 'authorised insurers'. On the question of the society's accountability for the share of the commission received by it the plaintiffs contended that the general principle of equity that a person such as an agent or a trustee who by the use of his fiduciary position derived a profit from a third party was required to account to his principal or g beneficiary for the profit so obtained was applicable to the commission received by the society. The society contended, inter alia, that the methods of providing indemnity insurance set out in s 37(2) were not exhaustive and that the general rule-making power conferred by s 37(1) was wide enough to authorise the making of the rules. The society conceded that if that was not the case the rules had to fall within the authority conferred by s 37(2)(*b*) if they were to be intra vires since neither s 37(2)(*a*) nor s 37(2)(*c*) was h appropriate to confer authority for the making of the group scheme.

Held – (1) Applying the principle expressio unius est exclusio alterius the three methods specified in s 37(2) of the 1974 Act were exhaustive of the permitted methods by which the society might provide indemnity insurance for solicitors, since the rule-making power conferred on the society was to be construed restrictively, having regard to the j drastic nature of the sanction for non-compliance, and also because the powers conferred on the society by s 37(2) were not expressed to be without prejudice to the society's general rule-making power contained in s 37(1). The society could not therefore claim that the rules were intra vires by virtue of having been made under s 37(1) (see p 619 *h j*, p 621 *b d* to *f* and *j* to p 622 *a* and p 626 *j*, post); dicta of Hargrave J in *Drinkwater v*

Arthur (1871) 10 SCR (NSW) at 222 and of Lord Macmillan in *Canadian National Railways v Canada Steamship Lines Ltd* [1945] AC at 211 applied.

(2) On the true construction of the master policy, the society had entered into the insurance agreement with the insurers not on its own account nor as agent for solicitors but as trustee for solicitors whether ascertained or not, so as to entitle solicitors as beneficiaries under the trust to require the insurers to provide insurance in accordance with the terms of the certificate and on payment of the specified premium. However, the power contained in s 37(2)(*b*) authorising or requiring the society 'to take out and maintain insurance with authorised insurers' was wide enough to permit the society to take out insurance on behalf of solicitors because (a) the 'loss' in respect of which the insurance was to be effected was loss suffered by solicitors, (b) the premium payments by solicitors referred to in s 37(3)(*c*) were unlikely to be in respect of a policy taken out by the society on its own behalf, (c) it was not necessarily to be presumed that Parliament did not intend the society to have power to create a monopoly of professional indemnity insurance, and (d) it was logical for Parliament to have made provisions for the society to make group arrangements for and on behalf of solicitors (see p 620 *b*, p 624 *e f* and p 628 *d* to p 629 *c* and *e*, post).

(3) The society properly fulfilled its obligations under s 37(2)(*b*) to 'take out and maintain insurance with authorised insurers' if (a) it entered into contractual arrangements under which the authorised insurers agreed to provide insurance cover for solicitors on specified terms and on payment of specified premiums by solicitors and (b) the society subsequently procured that such premiums were paid. Although the master policy did not in terms impose any obligations on the society but imposed obligations solely on the insurers, it was an inevitable inference that the insurers only agreed to provide the insurance specified on the premiums quoted if the society for its part procured that all solicitors required by the 1974 Act to be insured effected their insurance with the insurers and that the society impliedly undertook to enforce the indemnity rules to ensure that that happened. That amounted to consideration on the society's part and the master policy thus involved mutually enforceable contractual arrangements, and that being so the master policy was not ultra vires s 37(2)(*b*) on the ground that it did not constitute a proper 'taking out' of insurance (see p 630 *a* to *h* and p 635 *j* to p 636 *a* and *d e*, post).

(4) Unlike a scheme under s 37(2)(*c*) under which it would have been ultra vires for the rules to have compelled solicitors to have taken out insurance with specified insurers, a group scheme arranged by the society under s 37(2)(*b*) was not required to give individual solicitors freedom to choose their own insurers since to do so would be incompatible with the very existence of a group scheme (see p 630 *h* to p 631 *d*, post).

(5) On the question of the society's accountability for its share of the commission, although the society contracted with the insurers as trustees for solicitors the consequent fiduciary relationship was not created until the contract had been concluded, and since the society had received the profit in question as the result of its right to renegotiate the commission arrangement, which right had accrued to it in February 1975 before the contract was concluded in November 1975, it could not be said that the profit was received as the result of its fiduciary relationship with solicitors. Nor could it be said that the society was acting in a fiduciary relationship when renegotiating the commission arrangement, since the mere fact that the society was to hold the benefit of each of the master policy contracts as trustee for the individual solicitors concerned did not show that it was acting in a fiduciary capacity when negotiating the commission arrangement and it was not to be presumed, having regard to the fact that the society was a professional body, that Parliament intended that the society would negotiate the insurance scheme in a fiduciary capacity (see p 637 *e* to *j* and p 638 *c* to p 639 *d*, post); *Boardman v Phipps* [1966] 3 All ER 721 distinguished.

(6) It followed that the plaintiffs were not entitled to the declarations sought, but neither, since the plaintiffs had not brought the proceedings in a representative capacity, was it appropriate to make declarations that the rules were invalid, though that was not

to be taken as indicating any doubt as to their validity (see p 631 *c d* and p 640 *a b* and *e f*, post). a

Notes

For professional indemnity insurance, see 25 Halsbury's Laws (4th Edn) paras 719–724, and for cases on professional negligence, see 29 Digest (Repl) 516, *3624–3627*.

For the Solicitors Act 1974, s 37, see 44 Halsbury's Statutes (3rd Edn) 1508.

Cases referred to in judgment b

Blackburn v Flavelle (1881) 6 App Cas 628, 50 LJPC 58, 45 LT 52, PC, 17 Digest (Reissue) 345, *1128*.

Boardman v Phipps [1966] 3 All ER 721, [1967] 2 AC 46, [1966] 3 WLR 1009, HL, Digest (Cont Vol B) 732, *3295*.

Bray v Ford [1896] AC 44, [1895–9] All ER Rep 1009, 65 LJQB 213, 73 LT 609, HL, 51 Digest (Repl) 856, *4070*. c

Canadian National Railways v Canada Steamship Lines Ltd [1945] AC 204, 114 LJPC 60, PC, 38 Digest (Repl) 435, **1286*.

Drinkwater v Arthur (1871) 10 SCR (NSW) 193.

Hooper v Exeter Corpn (1887) 56 LJQB 457, 12 Digest (Reissue) 689, *4970*.

Morgan v Palmer (1824) 2 B & C 729, 4 Dow & Ry KB 283, 2 Dow & Ry MC 232, 2 LJOSKB 145, 107 ER 554, 12 Digest (Reissue) 688, *4965*. d

Regal (Hastings) Ltd v Gulliver [1942] 1 All ER 378, [1967] AC 134, HL, 9 Digest (Reissue) 532, *3181*.

Shaw v Applegate [1978] 1 All ER 123, [1977] 1 WLR 970, 35 P & CR 181, CA, Digest (Cont Vol E) 336, *235a*.

Thompson v Adams (1889) 23 QBD 361, 29 Digest (Repl) 94, *413*. e

Cases also cited

Barclay v Cousins (1802) 2 East 544, 102 ER 478.

Fair v McIver (1812) 16 East 130, 104 ER 1038.

Jaglom v Excess Insurance Co Ltd [1972] 1 All ER 267, [1972] 2 QB 250.

Adjourned summons f

The plaintiffs, James Midwood Swain and Alan Stephen McLaren, who were practising solicitors, applied by an originating summons dated 25th October 1979 issued against the defendant, the Law Society, seeking (1) a declaration that on the true construction of s 37 of the Solicitors Act 1974 and the Solicitors' Indemnity Rules 1975, the Solicitors' Indemnity Rules 1978 and the Solicitors' Indemnity Rules 1979 the Council of the Law Society had no power to make all or any such rules, which were accordingly null and void, and (2) the determination of the question whether, on the true construction of the g
1974 Act and the indemnity rules and in the events which had happened, the Law Society was entitled to retain for its own purposes the commission received by it from London Assurance Brokers Ltd in respect of premiums paid by individual solicitors pursuant to the society's Solicitors' Indemnity Insurance Scheme, or whether it was accountable for such commission to individual solicitors or otherwise. On 30th January h
1980 the plaintiffs issued a summons seeking an order for inspection of documents constituting the master policy in accordance with which the Law Society provided insurance to solicitors in accordance with the indemnity rules. The facts are set out in the judgment.

Leonard Lewis QC and *Martin Roth* for the plaintiffs.
Robert Alexander QC and *Patrick Phillips* for the Law Society. j

Cur adv vult

17th March. **SLADE J** read the following judgment: In this originating summons the plaintiffs are two practising solicitors and the defendant is the Law Society. The summons raises two questions relating to the Law Society's Solicitors' Indemnity

Insurance Scheme. These must be of importance to all practising solicitors. The first challenges the validity of the rules made by the Council of the Law Society pursuant to which the scheme has been introduced. It is suggested that the council had no power to make these rules, from which it would follow that the scheme itself is not binding on solicitors. The second question asks the court to decide whether, in the events which have happened, the Law Society is entitled to retain for its own purposes the commission received by it in respect of premiums paid by individual solicitors pursuant to the scheme or whether it is accountable to them for this commission.

The rules

Until 1975 there existed no general scheme of insurance for solicitors who wished to obtain indemnity insurance against claims in respect of civil liability for professional negligence or breach of duty. Solicitors who wished to obtain such insurance sought it on the insurance market, either with or without the intervention of insurance agents or brokers. They were free to negotiate terms suiting their individual requirements with such insurance companies as were prepared to engage in this class of business. Lloyd's of London and various insurance companies of repute offered competitive terms.

For some years, however, many persons had been of the opinion that some form of scheme making professional indemnity insurance for solicitors compulsory was desirable, having regard to the increasing incidence of claims against solicitors. In 1972 a special committee of the Law Society wrote a report for its council recommending (inter alia) that the introduction of a single compulsory professional indemnity insurance scheme for all solicitor-principals in private practice should be approved in principle, subject to satisfactory terms being negotiated and administrative arrangements being made. It further recommended that any statutory powers required to implement this recommendation should be sought as soon as possible, after certain consultation.

Statutory provision for the introduction of such a scheme was first made by s 10 of the Solicitors (Amendment) Act 1974. That Act, however, was almost immediately superseded by a consolidating enactment, the Solicitors Act 1974, which received the royal assent on 31st July 1974 and came into force on 1st May 1975. I will refer to this as 'the Act'.

The method adopted by the legislature in the Act, so as to enable the introduction of a compulsory professional indemnity insurance scheme, essentially embodied two features. The first was to empower the council with the concurrence of the Master of the Rolls to make rules concerning such indemnity, in such manner as to apply to solicitors or any class of solicitors. These rules are referred to in the Act as 'indemnity rules'. The second was to empower the Law Society to withhold a practising certificate from any person who does not satisfy it that he is complying with any indemnity rules or is exempt from them.

Section 1 of the Act disqualifies from acting as a solicitor any person who does not have a current practising certificate. Section 10(1) sets out the conditions as to which a person must satisfy the Law Society if he is to be entitled to a practising certificate. One of these conditions, set out in para (*e*), is 'that he is complying with any indemnity rules or is exempt from them'.

There can thus be no doubt that the legislature contemplated that compliance with any relevant indemnity rules, which the Council of the Law Society might see fit to make in the proper exercise of its statutory powers, with the concurrence of the Master of the Rolls, should be an inescapable condition precedent to practise as a solicitor. However, I accept the general submission made on behalf of the plaintiffs that the drastic nature of the sanction which the legislature introduced for non-compliance afford grounds for concluding that the wording of the power to make indemnity rules, conferred on the council by s 37 of the Act, should be construed more narrowly than broadly.

Section 37(1) reads as follows:

> 'The Council, with the concurrence of the Master of the Rolls, may make rules (in this Act referred to as "indemnity rules") concerning indemnity against loss

> arising from claims in respect of any description of civil liability incurred—(*a*) by a solicitor or former solicitor in connection with his practice or with any trust of a
> which he is or formerly was a trustee; (*b*) by an employee or former employee of a solicitor or former solicitor in connection with that solicitor's practice or with any trust of which that solicitor or the employee is or formerly was a trustee.'

'The Council' is defined by s 87 of the Act as meaning the Council of the Law Society. I pause to observe that the expression 'loss arising from claims', in the context of s 37(1), plainly refers to loss suffered by *solicitors* as a result of claims made against them, in b
respect of liability incurred by them. It is not apt to refer to any loss which may be suffered either by their clients or by the Law Society itself.

Section 37(2) of the Act then proceeds to list three methods which indemnity rules may specify for the purpose of providing for the indemnity. It reads:

> 'For the purpose of providing such indemnity, indemnity rules—(*a*) may c
> authorise or require the Society to establish and maintain a fund or funds; (*b*) may authorise or require the Society to take out and maintain insurance with authorised insurers; (*c*) may require solicitors or any specified class of solicitors to take out and maintain insurance with authorised insurers.'

With reference to s 37(2)(*b*) and (*c*), the expression 'authorised insurers' is defined by s 87 of the Act as meaning 'a person [sic] permitted under the Insurance Companies Act d
1974 to carry on liability insurance business or pecuniary loss insurance business'. Thus the council has no control over the list of 'authorised insurers' falling within this definition.

Section 37(3) of the Act contains certain ancillary provisions designed further to define or to extend the rule-making powers of the council. It provides:

e

> 'Without prejudice to the generality of subsections (1) and (2), indemnity rules—(*a*) may specify the terms and conditions on which indemnity is to be available, and any circumstances in which the right to it is to be excluded or modified; (*b*) may provide for the management, administration and protection of any fund maintained by virtue of subsection (2)(*a*) and require solicitors or any class of solicitors to make payments to any such fund; (*c*) may require solicitors or any class of solicitors to f
> make payments by way of premium on any insurance policy maintained by the Society by virtue of subsection (2)(*b*); (*d*) may prescribe the conditions which an insurance policy must satisfy for the purposes of subsection (2)(*c*); (*e*) may authorise the Society to determine the amount of any payments required by the rules, subject to such limits, or in accordance with such provisions, as may be prescribed by the rules; (*f*) may specify circumstances in which, where a solicitor for whom g
> indemnity is provided has failed to comply with the rules, the Society or insurers may take proceedings against him in respect of sums paid by way of indemnity in connection with a matter in relation to which he has failed to comply; (*g*) may specify circumstances in which solicitors are exempt from the rules; (*h*) may empower the Council to take such steps as they consider necessary or expedient to ascertain whether or not the rules are being complied with; and (*i*) may contain h
> incidental, procedural or supplementary provisions.'

Section 37(4) of the Act provides:

> 'If any solicitor fails to comply with indemnity rules, any person may make a complaint in respect of that failure to the Tribunal.'

'The Tribunal' is defined by s 87 of the Act as meaning the Solicitors Disciplinary j
Tribunal.

Section 37(5) reads:

> 'The Society shall have power, without prejudice to any of its other powers, to carry into effect any arrangements which it considers necessary or expedient for the purpose of indemnity under this section.'

It is common ground that s 37(5) of the Act does not itself give the council power to make rules, but that its rule-making powers are to be found in sub-ss (1), (2) and (3). A subsidiary argument has been advanced in the alternative by counsel for the Law Society to the effect that the three permissible methods of providing the indemnity specified by s 37(2) do not constitute an exhaustive list of the methods which may be adopted for this purpose when rules come to be made. It is submitted that s 37(2) takes effect without prejudice to the generality of the rule-making power conferred by s 37(1). I think it may be convenient to deal at once with this argument, which I feel unable to accept. In my judgment this is a case where the maxim expressio unius est exclusio alterius applies.

In *Blackburn v Flavelle* (1881) 6 App Cas 628 at 634 the Privy Council approved the following exposition of the principle contained in the judgment of Hargrave J in *Drinkwater v Arthur* (1871) 10 SCR (NSW) 193 at 222:

> 'Now, if there be any one rule of law clearer than another, as to the construction of all statutes and all written instruments (as for example, sales under powers in deeds and wills), it is this—that where the Legislature or the parties to any instrument have *expressly* prescribed one or more particular modes of sale or other dealing with property, such *expressions* always exclude any *other* mode, except as specifically authorised.' (Hargrave J's emphasis.)

As illustrated by the decision of the Privy Council in *Canadian National Railways v Canada Steamship Lines Ltd* [1945] AC 204 at 211, the maxim is not one to be applied invariably and regardless of the context. Nevertheless in the particular context of s 37(2) of the Act, I think it reasonably clear that it should be applied, particularly for the following reasons. First, as I have already said, the general approach of the court should in my judgment be to construe the rule-making power conferred on the council restrictively rather than otherwise. It seems inherently improbable that the legislature should have intended to give the council carte blanche in selecting methods of providing for the indemnity, subject only to obtaining the approval of the Master of the Rolls. Second, the wording of s 37(2) of the Act, following the same pattern as s 37(3), could easily have provided that sub-s (2) should operate 'without prejudice to the generality of subsection (1)'. Significantly, sub-s (2) is prefaced with no such provision. I can see no sufficient ground for concluding that the list contained in sub-s (2) is anything but exhaustive in relation to the permitted methods of providing the indemnity.

There are, however, certain points of construction which are, I think, common ground in relation to s 37(2) of the Act.

First, under sub-s (2)(*a*), rules could be made authorising the Law Society to establish and maintain its own indemnity insurance fund. Furthermore, by virtue of sub-s (3)(*b*), rules could require solicitors or any class of solicitors to make payments to any such fund.

Second, under sub-s (2)(*c*), rules could be made requiring solicitors or any specified class of solicitors to take out and maintain their own insurance with 'authorised insurers', as defined by the Act. Furthermore, by virtue of sub-s (3)(*d*), rules could prescribe the conditions which an insurance policy must satisfy for this purpose.

Third, however, as counsel on its behalf expressly conceded, it would not be open to the Law Society, in reliance on sub-ss (2)(*c*) and (3)(*d*), to make rules requiring solicitors to take out and maintain insurance with *specified* insurers nominated in the rules. In other words, if rules follow the route envisaged by sub-ss (2)(*c*) and (3)(*d*), the solicitors affected are to be left at liberty to effect insurance with insurers of their own choice, provided only that they are 'authorised insurers' as defined by the Act and any conditions prescribed by the rules as being conditions which a policy must satisfy are duly complied with.

The present dispute as to the construction of the Act substantially concerns the meaning and effect of sub-ss (2)(*b*) and (3)(*c*) of s 37. What has happened is that the Law Society has made or purported to make rules providing for an indemnity scheme, but these rules, as is common ground, do not on any footing fall within the authority conferred on it by sub-s (2)(*a*) or (2)(*c*). It has been submitted as a subsidiary argument on behalf of the Law Society that, quite apart from sub-s (2), the general rule-making

power conferred by sub-s (1) was wide enough to authorise the making of these rules. I reject this argument, however, because, for reasons already stated, I think that the a
alternative methods of providing for the indemnity, which are specified in sub-s (2), are exhaustive. It follows that, if the rules are to be valid, they must be shown to fall within the authority conferred by sub-s (2)(*b*), read in conjunction with sub-s (3)(*c*). After this introduction I now turn to the rules themselves.

On 12th December 1975, the Council of the Law Society, in purported exercise of the authority conferred on it by s 37 of the Act and with the previous concurrence of the b
Master of the Rolls, made what were named, by r 1, 'the Solicitors' Indemnity Rules 1975'. Rule 1 provided that the rules should come into operation immediately, except r 3, which should come into operation on 1st September 1976. Rules 2 and 3 provided as follows:

> '2. The Society is hereby authorised to take out and maintain with authorised insurers a Master Policy in the form set out in the Schedule hereto and to arrange for c
> the issue to solicitors to whom these Rules apply Certificates of Insurance in the form there set out. The provisions of the said Master Policy and Certificate of Insurance shall be deemed to form part of these Rules.
>
> '3. Every solicitor to whom these Rules apply shall pay the premiums payable by him under the said Master Policy and Certificate of Insurance as soon as they fall due and shall comply with such of the provisions of the said Master Policy and Certificate d
> of Insurance as apply to him.'

Rule 4(1) provided that the rules applied to every solicitor 'who is, or is held out to the public as, a principal in private practice in England and Wales'. Rule 5 conferred on the council 'power in any case or class of case to waive in writing any of the provisions of these Rules and revoke any such waiver'. I need not read the other provisions of the rules e
themselves.

They were, however, accompanied by explanatory notes. Two of these explanatory notes, though not forming part of the rules, are worth reading as helping to explain the mechanics of the scheme as envisaged by the council. The note to rr 1 and 2 explained:

> 'The Master Policy referred to in Rule 2 is to be taken out immediately to enable solicitors to whom the Rules apply to become insured under it on a voluntary basis f
> as soon as their current insurance expires. It will not, however, be compulsory for them to be insured under the Master Policy until 1st September, 1976, and accordingly Rule 3 does not come into operation until that date. Thereafter every solicitor to whom the Rules apply will be required to produce evidence of compliance with them on applying for a practising certificate.'

g

The note to r 3 explained:

> 'The amount of indemnity provided under the Master Policy is the *minimum* which must be held by every solicitor to whom the Rules apply. That amount will not necessarily reflect what each individual solicitor and firm as a matter of prudence should consider to be the amount of indemnity appropriate to their case, in the light
> of their commitment.' h

In the event, since 1st September 1976 the Law Society has regarded the scheme as having become compulsory and has required every solicitor to whom the rules apply to produce a certificate of insurance on applying annually for a practising certificate.

On a very first reading, the authority given by r 2 to the Law Society to take out and maintain with authorised insurers a master policy would appear to fall fairly and squarely j
within the wording of s 37(2)(*b*) of the Act. The provision in r 3 requiring solicitors to make payments by way of premium under the master policy would similarly at first sight appear to fall fairly and squarely within the wording of s 37(3)(*c*). The position, however, is not as simple as that, if only because the provisions of the proposed master policy and certificate of insurance set out in the schedule to the rules are, as is expressly stated, deemed to form part of them.

I therefore turn to examine first the terms of the proposed master policy scheduled to the 1975 rules. Clause 1 provided as follows:

> 'The Insurers agree with The Law Society on behalf of all solicitors from time to time required to be insured by Indemnity Rules made under s. 37 of the Solicitors' Act 1974, and on behalf of former solicitors, to provide such insurance in accordance with the terms of the Certificate attached hereto. Subject as hereinafter appears in respect of former solicitors, such Certificate will be issued annually on request on receipt of the premium payable in accordance with Clauses 2 and 3 hereof.'

Clause 2 provided:

> 'This Policy commences on the 12th day of December, 1975, and shall be extended on the 1st day of September, 1976, and the 1st day of September 1977, for a further 12 months' period in each case. At each extension date the rates of premium payable in respect of the year next following shall be the annual rates of premium applicable in respect of the immediately preceding period as increased by 12½%, or by 75% of the percentage increase in the official retail price index during the previous year to 31st May, whichever percentage shall be the greater. This Policy can be extended subsequently for successive periods of one year on each 1st day of September subject to the rates of premium for each renewal being agreed by the Insurers and The Law Society at least 12 months before such renewal. In the event of any failure so to agree such rates of renewal premium all cover under this Policy shall cease on the expiry of the period for which the Policy was last extended.'

Clause 3(*a*) provided:

> 'In respect of the period of insurance prior to the 1st day of September, 1976, the premium payable hereunder shall be pro rata to the annual premium of £387·50 per sole practitioner and £310·00 per partner. For the period of insurance commencing on the 1st September, 1976 and subsequent periods of insurance the premiums for solicitors who are first required to be insured hereunder during the period of insurance shall be calculated pro rata to the premiums which applied at the beginning of the relevant period of insurance.'

By way of parenthesis, I mention that the equivalent rates of premium agreed between the insurers and the Law Society since the scheme became compulsory on 1st September 1976 were for the year ending 31st August 1977 £435 and £348, and for the year ending 31st August 1978 £490 and £392.

Clause 3(*b*) set out a scale in accordance with which the premiums for part-time sole practitioners would be calculated. Clause 4 provided that all claims and notices required to be given to the assured under the terms of the attached certificate should be notified to London Insurance Brokers Ltd on behalf of the insurers. The last-mentioned company were defined by cl 4 as 'the Brokers'. For brevity I shall from time to time refer to them as 'LIB'. Clause 4 also contained a number of provisions in accordance with which LIB were to handle claims. I need only read cl 4(*e*):

> 'In handling claims and potential claims against the Assured, the Brokers shall act as agents for the Assured and, subject to such disclosure as may be necessary to the Insurers or as required by them in accordance with the terms of this Policy and the attached Certificate, shall be under a duty of confidence to the Assured; and in particular neither the Brokers nor the Insurers shall disclose information about any individual or firm to The Law Society without his or their consent.'

LIB were thus to act as sole brokers under the scheme, a point which will have some significance in the context of commission.

Of the remaining four clauses of the proposed master policy scheduled to the 1975 rules, I need only read cll 6 and 7:

> '6. Authority is hereby given by the Insurers to the Brokers to issue on behalf of

the Insurers to solicitors seeking insurance in accordance with Clause 1 hereof certificates in the form attached hereto.

'7. Expressions used in this Policy have the meanings given to them by the Certificate attached hereto.'

I pause to make a few observations in relation to this form of proposed master policy, and in particular cl 1 thereof, which is of crucial importance in the present case. The phrase 'on behalf of all solicitors from time to time required to be insured by Indemnity Rules made under s. 37 of the Solicitors' Act 1974, and on behalf of former solicitors' appearing in that clause makes it clear that the Law Society would not be entering into the agreement on its behalf and for its own benefit. There have been suggestions on both sides in the present case that the Law Society would be entering into it as *agent* on behalf of the persons from time to time falling into the two categories. A large number of such persons, however, would not be ascertained or capable of ascertainment at the date when the master policy would be effected. As I understand the law, if a contract is to be effectively concluded by a principal as agent for another party, that party must be both in existence and ascertainable (even if not actually ascertained) at the date of the contract. If he is not in existence and ascertainable at that date the supposed principal cannot even subsequently ratify it (see 1 Halsbury's Laws (4th Edn) paras 760–761).

A similar restriction, however, does not apply where a person enters into a contract with another on the footing that he is to hold the benefit of the contract as *trustee* for third parties. The third parties are then beneficiaries under the trust created by the contract and may be entitled to enforce this trust, even though they were unascertained at the date of the contract (see 16 Halsbury's Laws (4th Edn) para 1341, and the cases there cited). In my judgment it is reasonably clear that the effect of the phrase which I have quoted from cl 1 of the draft master policy is this: on its true construction it indicates the intention of the makers of the rules that the Law Society should enter into the agreement of insurance as *trustee* for the persons, ascertained and unascertained, referred to in that clause, the purpose of the provision being to entitle such persons, as beneficiaries under the trust, to require the insurers to provide them with insurance in accordance with the terms of the proposed certificate, on paying the specified premium.

The form of proposed certificate of insurance scheduled to the 1975 rules began with the following words:

> 'This is to certify that in accordance with the authorisation granted to the undersigned under the Master Policy referred to in the Schedule by the Insurers subscribing such Master Policy (hereinafter called "The Insurers") insurance is granted by the Insurers in accordance with the terms and conditions following, and in consideration of the payment of the premium stated in the Schedule.'

There then followed a series of definitions. They included definitions of 'the Solicitor' as meaning the person named as such in the schedule, and 'the Period of Insurance' as the period specified in the schedule. 'The Assured' was defined as meaning—

> 'the Solicitor, any person employed in connection with the Practice (including any articled clerk, and any solicitor who is a Consultant or Associate in the Firm), and the estate and/or the legal representatives of any of the foregoing, to the intent that each of the foregoing shall be severally insured hereunder.'

The expressions 'the Practice', 'the Firm' and 'Partner' were also defined.

Clause 2(*a*) of the proposed certificate provided that, on the terms and conditions therein contained, the insurers should indemnify the assured against all loss to the assured wheresoever occurring arising from any claim or claims first made against the assured or the firm during the period of insurance, in respect of any description of civil liability whatsoever incurred in connection with the practice. This general provision was followed by a restriction on liability set out in cl 2(*b*), which provided that the liability of the insurers under the certificate and any other certificate issued under the master policy should not exceed in respect of each such claim and claimant's costs the sum insured specified in the schedule, and in addition certain costs and expenses.

Clause 3 contained a number of special conditions. Sub-clause (*c*) provided (inter alia) that, if on the 'relevant date' the solicitor was practising in partnership with one or more solicitors, the schedule should be deemed to specify as the sum insured in respect of that claim an amount of £30,000 multiplied by the number in partnership on the relevant date or on 1st September preceding that date, whichever number was greatest. For this purpose the number by which the amount of £30,000 fell to be multiplied was called 'the multiplier'. 'The relevant date' was defined substantially as meaning the date when the claim was first made against the assured or the date, if earlier, when circumstances which might give rise thereto first came to the notice of the solicitor or of any partners of his.

Clause 4 of the proposed certificate contained a number of general conditions. Sub-clause (*d*) provided that notices to the insurers to be given thereunder should be deemed to be properly made if given to LIB.

Clause 5 of the certificate contained a number of general exclusions, of which sub-cl (*a*) read as follows:

> 'This insurance shall not indemnify the Assured in respect of the first £250 of any one claim or (in the case of any claim to which Special Condition (c) applies) the first £250 multiplied by the Multiplier.'

Finally the form of certificate contained a schedule in the following form, with a number of blanks left to be completed:

'SCHEDULE

'Certificate No.: Master Policy No.:

'1. The solicitor:

'2. Address(es) at which the Solicitor practises:

'3. Period of Insurance:

'4. Sum insured: £50,000 each claim (Sole practitioner)
£30,000 each claim (Partner)—see Special Condition 3(c)

'5. Premium:

The schedule thus contemplated that, with the exception of item 4, each item would be completed as appropriate in the individual case.

Thus the pattern of the form of master policy and certificate of insurance scheduled to the 1975 rules was, in my judgment, this. The Law Society was to enter into a contract with the insurers on the terms of the master policy, on the footing that it would hold the benefit of the contract as trustee for the persons referred to in cl 1 of the master policy, and that the contract would entitle such persons, as beneficiaries under the trust, on paying the designated premium, to require the insurers to issue them a policy on the terms specified in the certificate of insurance. By virtue of cl 6 of the master policy, LIB would possess authority from the insurers to issue, on their behalf, such a certificate to any solicitor seeking insurance in accordance with cl 1 of the master policy. Whenever an individual solicitor should pay to the insurers through LIB the appropriate premium and receive his certificate of insurance, a further contract would come into being between him and the insurers, quite separate from that between them and the Law Society.

In due course, in or about early 1978, the terms of the master policy and certificate of insurance were renegotiated, in respect of the ensuing year beginning on 1st September 1978.

On 7th July 1978 the Council of the Law Society, with the concurrence of the Master of the Rolls, made the Solicitors' Indemnity Rules 1978, which were expressed, by r 1, to come into operation on 1st September 1978, and were designed to incorporate these renegotiated terms.

Rules 2 and 3 provided as follows:

> '2. The Solicitors' Indemnity Rules 1975 shall remain in full force and effect save

that the forms of Master Policy and Certificate of Insurance set out in the Schedule
hereto shall be substituted for those set out in the Schedule to those Rules and shall *a*
be deemed to be the forms of Master Policy and Certificate of Insurance referred to
in Rule 2 of those Rules.

'3. In all other respects the Solicitors' Indemnity Rules 1975 are confirmed.'

The form of master policy scheduled to the 1978 rules was similar, though not
identical, to the form scheduled to the 1975 rules. I need only refer to two differences. *b*
The policy was expressed to commence on 1st September 1978. The premiums payable
under it were substantially increased, to £658 per solicitor per annum, but for any
solicitor practising within the Inner London area the annual premium was to be £888.
The form of certificate scheduled to the 1978 rules was similar, though not identical, to
the form scheduled to the 1975 rules. One variation included the substitution of the
figure of £400 for the figure £250 in condition 5(*a*). *c*

On 27th July 1979 the Council of the Law Society, with the concurrence of the Master
of the Rolls, made the Solicitors' Indemnity Rules 1979, which were expressed by r 1 to
come into operation on 1st September 1979. Their purpose was simply to incorporate
the renegotiated terms of the master policy and certificate of insurance coming into
effect on 1st September 1979. They followed mutatis mutandis the form of the 1978
rules. The annual premiums were increased to £926 for those practising in Inner *d*
London and to £712 for other solicitors.

It is common ground that there are no differences between the respective provisions
of the 1975 rules, the 1978 rules and the 1979 rules, or the forms respectively scheduled
thereto, which are material for the purpose of the question of construction which the
court has to decide in relation to the Act and those rules. Accordingly any references
hereafter to 'the rules', 'the master policy' or 'the certificate' are, save where the context *e*
otherwise requires, equally applicable to any one of the three sets of rules, master policy
and certificate.

A large volume of evidence has been filed on both sides, dealing with alleged merits
or demerits of the present indemnity scheme. These are clearly matters on which
opinions inside the solicitors' branch of the legal profession can and do greatly vary. This
is indicated by the fact that a poll conducted by the Law Society in November 1975 *f*
among solicitors holding current practising certificates resulted in 10,531 votes being
cast in favour of the scheme and 7,455 against it. It is understandable that the plaintiffs
should have wished to point out what they consider to be a number of disadvantages or
anomalies involved in it. I have no doubt that they genuinely consider that, given
freedom of choice, they could obtain for themselves better cover from insurance
companies of good reputation at a smaller premium than is being charged by the *g*
insurers with whom the Law Society has made its arrangements. It is equally
understandable that the Law Society should have wished to answer such evidence by
pointing out anticipated benefits from a group scheme of this kind.

However, I think it neither necessary nor appropriate to enter into the debate or to
attempt any evaluation of the merits of the scheme in this judgment, which relates to
bare questions of law. The court, in construing the Act and the rules, must have regard *h*
to any admissible evidence as to surrounding circumstances. In carrying out the process
of construction, it is, I think, also entitled to have regard to any self-evident consequences
of any particular interpretation. In my judgment, however, for present purposes, it is
wholly irrelevant that another kind of scheme might have been either better or worse
than that provided for by the rules and schedules which form part of them.

Though a number of supporting submissions have been put forward on behalf of the *j*
plaintiffs, their challenge to the validity of the rules, as advanced by counsel rests, I think,
principally on the following propositions, though I do not reproduce them verbatim
from his argument.

(1) Section 37(2) of the Act contains an exhaustive list of the methods by which
indemnity rules may provide for the indemnity required to support an indemnity
scheme. I have already indicated that I accept this proposition.

(2) Section 37(2)(*a*) is irrelevant for present purposes. So is s 37(2)(*c*), because, while this subsection, read in conjunction with s 37(3)(*d*), empowers the Law Society to make rules requiring solicitors or any class of solicitors to take out and maintain insurance with any 'authorised insurers', as defined by s 87 of the Act, on conditions prescribed in the rules, s 37(2)(*c*) does not authorise the making of rules which require insurance to be effected with a *specified* insurer. As I have already indicated, this proposition, unlike the first, is common ground and I accept it.

(3) The Law Society can therefore support the rules as having been made intra vires if, but only if, it can show that they fall within the authority given to the council by s 37(2)(*b*) and (3)(*c*) of the Act. I accept this proposition.

(4) However, it is submitted, the only authority conferred on the Council of the Law Society by s 37(2)(*b*) is an authority to make rules authorising or requiring the Law Society to take out and maintain insurance *for itself and on its own behalf.* The subsection does not empower the council to make rules enabling the Law Society to take out and maintain insurance *as agent or trustee for other persons.* If the existing rules and schedules or any part thereof purport to provide for the 'taking out and maintenance' of insurance by the Law Society at all, within the meaning of s 37(2)(*b*) (which is not admitted), such insurance is not to be effected by the Law Society on its own behalf but as purported agent or trustee for the individual solicitors concerned. On this ground alone, it is submitted, the rules are ultra vires.

(5) Further or alternatively, it is submitted, the rules are ultra vires because they cannot on any footing be said to authorise or require the Law Society to 'take out and maintain' insurance. The so-called master policy referred to in the rules, so it is said, would not in truth be a policy of insurance at all. It would at most represent an undertaking by the insurers to provide insurance on certain terms to those solicitors who paid the premiums. Since the Law Society would have given no consideration for this undertaking, so it is submitted, it would not be in a position to enforce it.

(6) The general effect of the rules, it is submitted, is to do the very thing which s 37(2)(*c*) contemplates shall not be done, namely, to require solicitors to take out and maintain insurance on prescribed terms with *specified* insurers of the Law Society's choice, as opposed to any authorised insurers of their own choice.

I hope and believe that these six propositions fairly embody the substance (though not the form) of counsel's principal arguments for the plaintiffs on question 1 raised by this summons.

Having already dealt with the first three propositions, I shall now proceed to consider the fourth. It is common ground that the rules and schedules do not provide for the taking out and maintenance by the Law Society of insurance *on its own behalf.* The argument on this proposition has therefore centred round the question: is the wording of s 37(2)(*b*) wide enough to permit the making by the council of rules which authorise the Law Society to make contractual arrangements for insurance indemnity against loss of the nature referred to in the section, not on its own behalf, but on behalf of those solicitors from time to time required to be insured by rules under the Act and on behalf of former solicitors?

Counsel for the plaintiffs submitted that the answer to this question must be No. As he pointed out, s 37(2)(*b*) does not in specific terms provide that indemnity rules may empower the Law Society to effect and maintain insurance on behalf of other persons. Such a power of insurance, he observed, would enable it to create a monopoly of insurance in restraint of trade in regard to the solicitors affected. In these circumstances, he submitted, only the plainest words or inevitable implication would justify the interpretation of the subsection as authorising the conferring of such power. No such inevitable implication, he suggested, arises here. On the contrary, it was said, s 37(2)(*c*) gives a strong indication that Parliament never contemplated that, through the introduction of rules, solicitors should ever find themselves bound to a particular insurer or insurers selected by the Law Society.

If it be right that s 37(2)(*b*) only contemplates the effecting and maintenance of insurance by the Law Society on its own behalf, it is relevant to consider what are the circumstances that Parliament may be deemed to have had in mind, in which the Law Society might wish to take out insurance on its own behalf for the purpose of implementing an indemnity insurance scheme. Counsel for the plaintiffs suggested two such circumstances. First, the Law Society might establish its own fund for the purpose of meeting claims, as envisaged by s 37(2)(*a*). In this event, it would or might wish to effect insurance on its own behalf, to protect the fund against the risk of exhaustion by large or numerous claims and to make sure that it could at all times meet its commitments. Second, the Law Society, without establishing a fund, might decide that the appropriate course was to give an undertaking to solicitors to indemnify them against loss. In this event, again it would or might wish to take out insurance to protect itself against its own potential liability. These, the plaintiffs submitted, were the two contingencies which Parliament must be deemed to have contemplated in enacting s 37(2)(*b*) of the Act; I do not think that any other contingencies were suggested.

A subsidiary argument advanced by counsel for the Law Society, in opposition to these contentions, was to the effect that, even in the two contingencies mentioned, the Law Society would have no insurable interest, within the meaning of the Life Assurance Act 1774, entitling it to take out insurance on its own behalf. I do not, however, need to consider this argument or the submissions advanced by counsel in opposition to it, because I am satisfied that there are other more powerful reasons which compel a much broader construction of s 37(2)(*b*) than the plaintiffs attribute to this subsection.

First, the rules which s 37 authorises the council to make are described by s 37(1) as rules 'concerning indemnity against loss arising from claims' of the nature referred to in the section. As I have already said, the 'loss' referred to in this context is loss suffered by solicitors. Prima facie, therefore, I would expect that the insurance envisaged by s 37(2)(*b*) would be insurance against loss of the nature referred to in the preceding subsection, that is to say, insurance against loss suffered *by solicitors*, not loss suffered by the Law Society.

Second, the plaintiffs' argument on the construction of s 37(2)(*b*) appears to me to attach inadequate weight to the wording of s 37(3)(*c*), which provides that rules may require solicitors to make payments by way of premium on any insurance policy maintained by the society by virtue of sub-s (2)(*b*). I accept that, as counsel for the plaintiffs pointed out, it is a perfectly possible arrangement for X to make payments by way of premium on an insurance policy which is being maintained by Y on Y's own behalf. Nevertheless it seems to me quite unrealistic to suppose that Parliament, in including s 37(3)(*c*), was directing its mind to a policy maintained by the Law Society on its own behalf. Let it be supposed that the Law Society had either established its own fund or had agreed to indemnify solicitors in the manner suggested by counsel for the plaintiffs. Let it further be supposed that it then wished to insure itself against the commitments which it had thus assumed. It is to my mind inconceivable that it would think it convenient or appropriate to leave the premiums required to maintain a policy of this nature, taken out for its own protection, to be actually paid not by itself, but pro rata by the thousands or tens of thousands of individual solicitors concerned. The situation, however, would be quite different, if the insurance were to be arranged by the Law Society simply on behalf of such individual solicitors. In this case there would be nothing in the least inconvenient or inappropriate in leaving each solicitor to pay the premiums applicable to himself. Thus in my judgment the wording of s 37(3)(*c*) strongly suggests that the type of policy at least primarily (if not solely) envisaged by that subsection is a policy taken out on behalf of solicitors, not on behalf of the Law Society. Correspondingly this wording lends support to the conclusion that a similar type of policy is at least primarily (if not solely) envisaged by s 37(2)(*b*).

Third, the argument based on the alleged presumption that Parliament would not have intended to confer on the Law Society the power to create a monopoly of professional indemnity insurance is in my judgment fallacious. According to the plaintiffs' own submissions, rules could be made empowering the Law Society, first, to establish its own indemnity fund, second to insure that fund for its own benefit with one set of insurers of its own choice, and, third, to require solicitors to pay the premiums on such insurance. In this event individual solicitors, when being called on to pay such premiums, would have had no opportunity whatever to choose their own insurers, so that in this sense a monopoly of insurance would once again have been arranged by the Law Society. Accordingly the monopoly argument affords no good reason for construing s 37(2)(*b*) as not referring to the taking out and maintenance by the Law Society of insurance on behalf of solicitors.

Fourth, I think that common sense suggests that this is the method of providing the indemnity which Parliament must have had primarily in mind in enacting s 37(2)(*b*). It seems to me that three obvious possible alternative routes would have been likely to spring to the mind of anyone considering methods of providing for a compulsory insurance scheme for solicitors. The first route would have involved the establishment and maintenance by the Law Society of its own fund, to be financed by contributions to the fund from solicitors. This route was duly provided for by s 37(2)(*a*) and (3)(*b*) of the Act. The second route would have involved a direction to solicitors to take out and maintain insurance on prescribed conditions with authorised insurers. This route was duly provided for by s 37(2)(*c*) and (3)(*d*) of the Act. The third route would have involved the Law Society first itself making group arrangements with insurers under which the insurers bound themselves to grant insurance on agreed terms and in an agreed form to individual solicitors who paid a specified premium and subsequently requiring solicitors to take up the insurance rights thus arranged for them. If Parliament had omitted to provide for the third route, it would indeed have been a strange omission. I do not think it did. The route was in my judgment provided for by s 37(2)(*c*) and (3)(*c*).

For all these reasons, I conclude that s 37(2)(*b*) on its true construction does empower the council to make rules authorising or requiring the Law Society to take out and maintain insurance with authorised insurers on behalf of solicitors, on the footing that it is to be a trustee of the benefit of the contract for the solicitors affected. I do not think it necessary to decide the further question whether the subsection would also permit the making of rules enabling the Law Society to effect insurance on its own behalf. I am inclined to think that the subsection is not directed to this kind of insurance at all. The Law Society in any event, I understand, has power under its own charter to insure itself. Furthermore, if it contemplated establishing its own fund and wished to be given specific power to insure itself in relation to that fund, such power could no doubt be conferred under s 37(3)(*i*) of the Act, under which indemnity rules may contain 'incidental, procedural or supplementary provisions'. Further or alternatively it would appear to me that s 37(5) would be wide enough, even in the absence of any specific rule to this effect, to empower the Law Society to insure itself in relation to any such fund. However, I leave open this further point arising on s 37(2)(*b*), which requires no decision.

I now turn to what I have described as the fifth of the principal propositions put forward on behalf of the plaintiffs. It is clear that, if a rule is to be justified as falling within the authority given to the council by s 37(2)(*b*), it must at very least authorise or require the Law Society to 'take out and maintain insurance'. The points taken against the Law Society in this context substantially resolve themselves to these. Though the rules in terms authorise the Law Society to take out and maintain with authorised insurers a master policy, the proposed master policy, even if issued by the insurers in the form contemplated, would not, it is suggested, in truth involve the 'taking out' of any insurance by the Law Society within the meaning of s 37(2)(*b*). The taking out of insurance, it is said, necessarily presupposes the existence of enforceable contractual arrangements between the grantor and grantee of the policy in question. Here, it is suggested, the documentation scheduled to the rules envisages no enforceable contractual arrangements between the insurers and the Law Society. The form of master policy even if issued, it is submitted, would constitute at most an undertaking given by the insurers to the Law Society to provide insurance on specified terms to solicitors who paid the appropriate premium. It is submitted that such undertaking could not be enforced by the Law Society, because it would have given no consideration for it.

It is the fact that the form of master policy, like most other insurance policies, in terms imposes obligations solely on the insurers; in terms it imposes none on the Law Society. Nevertheless it seems to me an inevitable inference from the forms of the documents scheduled to the rules that the insurers will have agreed to provide the specified insurance, and will have quoted the rates of premiums payable, on the basis that, during the currency of the master policy, the Law Society will for its part require all solicitors from time to time required to be insured by rules made under s 37 of the Act to effect their insurance with those insurers. The following features to be found in the documentation lead me to this conclusion.

(i) By cl 1 of the master policy, the agreement on the part of the insurers is expressed to be made with the Law Society 'on behalf of all solicitors from time to time required to be insured by Indemnity Rules made under s. 37 of the Solicitors' Act 1974, and on behalf of former solicitors . . .'

(ii) The master policy makes express reference to the rules and the rules themselves provide that they apply to every solicitor who is or is held out to the public as a principal in private practice in England and Wales. True it is that the rules empower the council in any case or class of case to waive in writing any of the provisions of the rules; but, if the rules are waived in such manner as to exempt a particular solicitor from the requirement to be insured which is imposed by the rules, such solicitor no longer falls within the ambit of cl 1 of the master policy, so that the insurers have no legitimate ground of complaint. In this respect, as in other respects, the rules themselves and the form of master policy tally with one another.

(iii) The rules themselves further provide that every solicitor to whom the rules apply shall pay the premiums payable by him under the master policy and certificate of insurance, as soon as they fall due.

(iv) The rules, as the insurers must be well aware, are made in exercise of an authority conferred by the Act, s 10 of which obliges the Law Society to grant to a solicitor a practising certificate only if it is satisfed that he is complying with the rules or is exempt from them.

Against this background, it seems to me that, from the form of documentation annexed to the rules, when read with the rules, the inevitable inference is that the Law Society for its part is implicitly undertaking with the insurers to enforce the rules during the currency of the master policy, so as to procure that all solicitors who are from time to time required by the rules to be insured will be insured with those insurers. It follows that in my judgment the rules and the documentation scheduled to them envisage that the Law Society will have given consideration for the agreement on the part of the insurers set out in cl 1 of the master policy and that the proposed master policy will thus involve mutually enforceable contractual arrangements.

In my judgment the Law Society can properly be said to 'take out and maintain insurance with authorised insurers', within the meaning of s 37(2)(*b*) of the Act, if it enters into contractual arrangements under which 'authorised insurers' agree to provide insurance cover for solicitors, on specified terms and on the payment by the solicitors of specified premiums, and if the Law Society subsequently procures that such premiums are paid. It follows that I must reject what I have described as the fifth proposition put forward on behalf of the plaintiffs.

Finally in this context I must deal shortly with their sixth proposition. I have already accepted that s 37(2)(*c*) does not contemplate insurance on prescribed terms to be taken out with specified insurers. However, to conclude from this that s 37(2)(*b*) likewise does not so contemplate seems to me to involve a non sequitur. For practical purposes, quite different considerations will apply to a group insurance scheme from those which apply to a system such as is envisaged by s 37(2)(*c*). In the case of a system of the latter nature, requiring solicitors to effect their own insurance on prescribed conditions but without the protection of any group scheme arranged and maintained by the Law Society, it would perhaps seem only reasonable that solicitors should be left free to select their own insurers, provided only that such insurers fall within the definition of 'authorised insurers' and are prepared to offer insurance on the prescribed conditions.

If, however, a group scheme has been arranged by the Law Society, the commercial need to preserve such individual freedom of choice is far less compelling and indeed is likely to be incompatible with the very existence of a group scheme. The kind of indemnity scheme envisaged by s 37(2)(*a*) manifestly would not confer the freedom of choice to which the plaintiffs attach such importance. Likewise, even if the construction which the plaintiffs themselves place on s 37(2)(*b*) be the correct one, a scheme constituted thereunder would not be likely to confer such freedom. In these circumstances I think there is no substance in the plaintiffs' sixth proposition.

For all these reasons I conclude that this challenge to the validity of the rules must fail. Paragraph 1 of the amended originating summons seeks a declaration that—

> 'upon the true construction of Section 37 of the above-mentioned Act and of the Rules hereinafter mentioned the Council of the Law Society had no power to make all or any of The Solicitors Indemnity Rules 1975, The Solicitors Indemnity Rules 1978 and The Solicitors Indemnity Rules 1979 and the said Rules are accordingly null and void.'

I must decline to make any such declaration. Since the plaintiffs do not purport to bring these proceedings in any representative capacity, I do not propose to make a declaration in the contrary sense, though I will in due course hear counsel on this point.

Commission

Paragraph 2 of the originating summons asks the question—

> 'Whether upon the true construction of the said Act and Rules and in the events which have happened the Law Society is entitled to retain for its own purposes the commission received by it from London Insurance Brokers Limited in respect of premiums paid by individual Solicitors pursuant to the said scheme or whether it is accountable for the same to such individual Solicitors or otherwise.'

For the purpose of dealing with this question, unlike the first question, it is necessary to consider the manner in which the rules were actually implemented and the arrangements which were made in regard to commission. Though the originating summons refers to the commission in question as having been received by the Law Society, the evidence shows that it has in fact been received by the Law Society's wholly-owned company, Law Society Services Ltd, which I will call 'LSS'. This company was established several years ago. Through it the Law Society conducts its various trading activities, the receipt of commissions being one such activity.

By an agreement dated 6th February 1975 the Law Society and LSS had appointed LIB as insurance brokers to LSS and to operate the Law Society's then existing insurance advisory service on terms (inter alia) that, in the event of the introduction of a compulsory professional indemnity insurance scheme for solicitors, the provisions of this agreement could be renegotiated at the request of any party.

After the Council of the Law Society had decided to adopt proposals for the introduction of a compulsory scheme by way of a single master policy, taken out by the society, debate in the profession was encouraged. Two circulars were issued by the council in May 1975. One of them summarised in question and answer form the main features of the proposed scheme. It included the question: 'What arrangements are proposed under the Scheme for commission on premiums?' The answer given was as follows:

> 'The brokers to the Scheme (L.I.B.) will be remunerated on the usual commission basis from which they will meet the major cost of operating the Scheme and handling claims. Hitherto the Society, through the Insurance Advisory Service, has received a share of the brokers' commission and as regards solicitors' professional indemnity business this amounted to approximately £46,000 gross in 1974 (the equivalent of nearly £2 on a practising certificate fee). The existing arrangements with L.I.B. require the Society to provide premises and defray certain quite

> substantial costs in relation to staff. Under the Scheme it is likely that if the existing arrangements are continued the commission income to the Society will be of the order of £250,000 per annum gross. The benefit of the net excess receipts will inure for the profession as a whole, but, subject to taxation and other important considerations, the Council will consider whether the surplus can be appropriately earmarked for possible future improvements in the Scheme. The surplus, however it is generally applied, will correspondingly reduce future calls upon the practising members of the profession.'

In October 1975, the president of the Law Society sent to all solicitors with practising certificates a letter setting out the council's arguments in favour of the master policy scheme as recommended by it and enclosing a voting card asking for a Yes or No answer to the question whether the recipient was in favour of the scheme. This letter contained the following paragraph:

> 'Although individual solicitors will no longer receive the benefit of commission, it will be payable by the Insurers, and The Law Society will receive a share after operating expenses have been deducted. This will enure for the benefit of the profession, thus mitigating future increases in the Practising Certificate Fee.'

The result of the vote was published in the Law Society's Gazette in November 1975 and as I have said showed a majority in favour of the scheme. The Law Society, according to the affidavit evidence of Mr D A Marshall, its present vice-president designate, treated this vote as an indorsement of the proposal that the Law Society should take the benefit of payments by way of commission as an incident of the master policy scheme. This proposal had certainly been clearly announced to the profession in the preceding documentation to which I have referred.

Normally, as Mr Marshall states in his first affidavit, professional indemnity insurance is effected by professional firms, whether solicitors or otherwise, through an insurance broker, who receives payment by receipt of brokerage from the insurer with whom the policy is effected. It made obvious commercial sense that the Law Society, as the price of permitting LIB to act as sole brokers under the scheme, should demand a share of the commission which would otherwise be received and wholly retained by LIB in respect of premiums paid on policies effected by solicitors pursuant to the master policy scheme.

On 11th May 1976 a written agreement was entered into between the Law Society and LSS of the first part, LIB of the second part and others of the third and fourth parts ('the 1976 agreement'). The 1976 agreement recited (inter alia) the wish of the Law Society and LSS to terminate the appointment of LIB as insurance broker to LSS under the agreement of 6th February 1975 and to enter into a new agreement on the terms thereinafter appearing. The Law Society and LSS thereby appointed LIB with effect 'on and from 1st October 1975' as (inter alia) insurance broker to the Law Society for the purposes of the master policy and insurance broker to LSS in respect of all 'solicitors business', as defined in the agreement, and as managing insurance broker of the 'service', as therein defined. The 1976 agreement further provided that LSS should be entitled to a commission in respect of each year equal to 40% of the 'net brokerage earned by the service' (as defined therein), up to and including £700,000, and 30% of the net brokerage earned by the service in excess of £700,000. This was the broad pattern of the 1976 agreement. I do not think that its detailed provisions are material for present purposes.

Mr Marshall states in an affidavit that, from the outset, it was appreciated by the Law Society that, as all solicitors would be required to pay premiums for the master policy, benefits received under the agreement with LIB should demonstrably be applied for the benefit of the profession as a whole, and not merely of those solicitors who were members of the Law Society.

The consolidated accounts of the Law Society and LSS for the year ended 31st December 1976 show a sum of £412,864 as having been received by LSS under the heading 'Insurance Advisory Service—Commission receivable'. The equivalent figure similarly shown in such accounts for the year ended 31st December 1977 is £365,000. The equivalent figure shown in such accounts for the year ended 31st December 1978 is £670,185, such large increase presumably being principally due to increased rates of premium. The greater part of these sums represented commission in respect of the master policy scheme. The accounts for this most recent year show a sum of £150,000 as set aside for a specific reserve under the heading 'Professional indemnity insurance'. Mr Marshall explains that this sum has been set aside to be available towards the initial capital of an insurance company, if the profession should wish to adopt an element of self-insurance. His unchallenged evidence is that no part of the commission income received by LSS and attributable to the scheme has been allocated for the sole benefit of members of the Law Society, but that the whole of such income has been allocated for the benefit of the profession as a whole.

Mr Marshall in his evidence, at least implicitly, suggests that for these reasons, if for no others, the plaintiffs can have no legitimate grounds of complaint in regard to the receipt of these sums by way of commission by the Law Society or by LSS. He points out that, but for them, the Law Society would either have been unable to discharge its functions properly or would in fact have raised the income by other means, probably by increasing the cost of a practising certificate. Similar considerations (among others) were urged by the Law Society's counsel.

I see the practical force of submissions along these lines and think they would have been highly relevant if any attack was being made on the integrity of those persons who have been responsible for introducing or administering the Law Society's insurance scheme. No such attack, however, has been made by the plaintiffs. They have not sought in any way to impugn the good faith of these persons or to suggest that full disclosure has not been made to the profession, either of the Law Society's intentions with regard to commission or of its actual receipts and dealings with commission. Their attack on the rights of the Law Society or LSS to retain the share of commission received by it is based not at all on the manner in which the moneys have been dealt with when received but on quite different grounds, to which I now turn.

The plaintiffs' submissions under this head have been presented on three alternative footings, namely: (1) that the rules are valid and that the Law Society has operated in accordance with them; (2) that the rules are valid, but the Law Society has *not* operated in accordance with them; (3) that the rules are invalid.

Since I have already decided that the rules have been validly made, the arguments presented on the last of these three footings do not need to be further considered. I think it will be convenient to dispose of the argument presented on the second footing, before reverting to the first, which is in my view by far the more significant.

During the course of counsel's opening speech on behalf of the plaintiffs, it became clear (if it had not been made clear before) that one of the reasons why the plaintiffs would be submitting that the Law Society had not operated in accordance with the rules was this. The evidence adduced by the Law Society, it was suggested, did not establish that the insurers had either actually issued to the Law Society any document constituting a master policy or had even contractually bound themselves to provide insurance on the terms of such a policy.

The submission that no contract existed on the particular facts was in this context based not so much on alleged lack of consideration moving from the Law Society (I have already dealt with this point) as on the alleged absence of any finally agreed arrangements between the parties. The force of this submission, if a good one, would have been that it could hardly be said that the Law Society had 'taken out' a master policy in accordance with the rules if it had neither received a document issued by the insurers, which could be said to constitute the master policy, nor had the contractual right to require the insurers to provide insurance on the terms of such a policy.

To meet these points, during the course of the hearing, the Law Society put in two further affidavits, both sworn on 20th February 1980, one by Mr Marshall and the other by Mr M J Herniman, the managing director of LIB. Mr Marshall and Mr Herniman were both cross-examined on these affidavits on behalf of the plaintiffs. As a result, there has in the end been a large volume of detailed evidence before the court describing not *a* only the general practice of Lloyd's with regard to the issue of policies, but also the manner in which the particular arrangements relating to the master policies in the present case were negotiated and implemented. On the basis of this further evidence, I am satisfied that the suggestion that these arrangements never got beyond the stage of mere negotiation is insupportable in regard to any of the three periods covered by the respective sets of rules. Indeed, as I understood him, counsel for the plaintiffs in his final *b* speech did not seek to persist with this suggestion, his attack then being on a somewhat narrower front.

In these circumstances, I do not think it necessary to particularise in any detail the evidence as to the manner in which the three sets of contractual arrangements were concluded between the Law Society and the insurers. It will, I think, suffice merely to summarise my conclusions as to these arrangements and to explain the points still taken *c* by the plaintiffs in this context.

I shall begin with the 1975 rules. The cover required for the period 1975 to 31st August 1978 was provided as to 62·5% by certain underwriting members of Lloyd's, as to 22·5% by Guardian Royal Exchange Assurance Ltd ('Guardian'), as to 7·5% by Royal Insurance Group, as to 3·5% by Legal and General Assurance Society Ltd and as to 4% by General Accident Fire and Life Assurance Corporation Ltd ('General Accident'). The list *d* of syndicates of Lloyd's underwriters thus participating, together with the percentages of the risk respectively assumed by them, are to be found set out in a file, containing a binding authority given by the underwriters to LIB, a form of master policy and a form of certificate of insurance, which was submitted to the Lloyd's policy signing office ('the LPSO'), stamped and sealed by it and dated 23rd March 1976. A policy (numbered 892/76/NSPI/P) was in fact issued to the Law Society by the LPSO on 23rd March 1976, *e* at the same time as it stamped, sealed and dated the file. A companies' collective policy (numbered 76/NSPI/P) was subsequently issued by the four insurance companies on 5th October 1976. Each of these two policies had attached to it a copy of the form of master policy scheduled to the 1975 rules. However, the schedule to each policy expressed insurance to be afforded thereunder merely in respect of 'former partners in accordance with the attached master policy'. The schedules stated that insurance in respect of *f* solicitors required to be insured under s 37 of the Act was afforded by individual certificates of insurance. In other words, as I read them, neither policy purported itself to afford insurance in respect of such solicitors. In these circumstances, while the purpose of the issue of these two policies in this particular form is not entirely clear to me, I cannot accept the submission of the Law Society that the policies themselves constituted master policies of the nature contemplated by the 1975 rules. They may *g* have been master policies in ordinary parlance, but were not master policies of this particular nature. Nor, so far as the evidence shows, was any other document issued by the insurers of that nature. I am, however, satisfied on the evidence that on 18th November 1975 a final draft of the 1975 rules was in existence and on that date a contract was concluded between the Law Society and the insurers concerned covering the period from that date until 31st August 1978 and conditional on the 1975 rules being actually *h* made, which gave the Law Society the same contractual rights against the insurers as it would have had if a policy in the form of the master policy scheduled to the 1975 rules had actually been issued to it.

The cover required for the period 1st September 1978 to 31st August 1979 was provided as to 73·5% by certain underwriting members of Lloyd's, as to 22·5% by Guardian and as to 4% by General Accident. The list of syndicates of Lloyd's underwriters *j* thus participating, together with the percentages of the risk respectively assumed by them, are to be found set out in a file, containing a binding authority given by the underwriters to LIB, a form of master policy and a form of certificate of insurance, which was submitted to the LPSO, stamped and sealed by it and dated 17th January 1979. In respect of this period, no actual Lloyd's policy was issued and no actual companies' collective policy was issued. I am, however, satisfied on the evidence that, before 1st September 1978, a contract had been concluded between the Law Society and the insurers concerned, covering the year in question, which gave the Law Society the same contractual rights against the insurers as it would have had if a policy in the form of the master policy scheduled to the 1978 rules had been actually issued to it.

The cover required for the period 1st September 1979 to 31st August 1980 was provided as to 63·5% by certain underwriting members of Lloyd's, as to 32·5% by Guardian and as to 4% by General Accident. The list of syndicates of Lloyd's underwriters thus participating, together with the percentages of the risk respectively assumed by them, are to be found set out in a file, containing a binding authority given by the underwriters to LIB, a form of master policy and a form of certificate of insurance, which was submitted to the LPSO, stamped and sealed by it and dated 28th January 1980. In respect of this period, no actual Lloyd's policy has been issued by the LPSO and no actual companies' collective policy has been issued. I am, however, satisfied on the evidence that, before 1st September 1979, a contract had been concluded between the Law Society and the insurers concerned, covering the period in question, which gives the Law Society the same contractual rights against the insurers as it would have had if a policy in the form of the master policy scheduled to the 1979 rules had been actually issued to it.

As I have indicated, counsel for the plaintiffs, as I understood him, having heard all the evidence, implicitly accepted that (subject to his point as to lack of consideration, which I have rejected) the Law Society had acquired contractual rights against the insurers of the nature which I have indicated before each set of rules came into force. In the end, his submissions that the Law Society has been in breach of the rules rested on much narrower grounds.

First he submitted in effect that, on the true construction of each set of rules, the authority thereby conferred on the Law Society to implement the scheme was conditional on its actually obtaining a document issued by the insurers, which could be identified as itself constituting the proposed master policy referred to in the rules. It would not suffice, he submitted, for the Law Society to have entered into a contract with the insurers, under which the insurers undertook to offer insurance to solicitors on the terms of the master policy; the society would not have complied with the rules unless it could point to a specific document which itself constituted the master policy. This was no mere technicality, counsel for the plaintiffs suggested; the Law Society should be in a position on demand to produce to any careful solicitor, who was called on to pay a premium on any policy pursuant to the rules, formal documentation evidencing the rights which the Law Society had purported to secure on his behalf.

The validity of this line of argument depends on the meaning to be attributed to the phrase 'take out and maintain' in each set of rules. Special considerations may apply to marine insurance because of the provisions of the Marine Insurance Act 1906, with which this case is not concerned. A contract of non-marine insurance, however, may be concluded, and the insurers correspondingly put on risk, as soon as the parties have reached final agreement to this effect. A complete and binding contract may for example be concluded simply by the initialling by underwriters of a slip containing particulars of the proposed insurance and showing the risks covered (see for example *Thompson v Adams* (1889) 23 QBD 361). Mr Herniman's evidence confirms what I think is a point of common knowledge, namely that in practice formal policies are frequently not issued for some weeks after payment of the premium and inception of the risk and that in many cases formal master policies are never issued.

In these circumstances, a person may, in my judgment, properly be said to 'take out' a policy of insurance in a specified form within ordinary legal parlance as soon as he obtains contractual rights against the insurers of the same nature as those which he would have if such a formal policy had actually been issued. I can see no special context in the three sets of rules to justify attributing to the phrase 'take out' a more restricted meaning than this. It follows that in my judgment the Law Society 'took out' a master policy in the forms set out in the schedule to each of the respective sets of rules, within

the meaning of such rules, as soon as it acquired contractual rights against the insurers of
the same nature as it would have had if a master policy in the relevant form had been a
actually issued. Likewise in my judgment it thereafter 'maintained' such master policies
within such meaning by requiring solicitors to pay premiums on individual policies in
accordance with its provisions. Despite their counsel's reference to 'careful solicitors',
there is no evidence that the plaintiffs themselves ever made any inquiry of the Law
Society as to the taking out of the three master policies before these proceedings were
issued. If, however, they had done so, the nature of the evidence which the Law Society b
would have been entitled to adduce in answer to this inquiry would not in my judgment
have been restricted to formal master policies actually issued by the insurers. It could,
for example, have included reference to the files dated 23rd March 1976, 17th January
1979 and 28th January 1980 to which I have already referred.

The second alternative ground on which counsel for the plaintiffs submitted that the
Law Society was in breach of the rules was a short one, relating solely to the 1975 rules. c
Mr Herniman's evidence shows that, in relation to the Law Society, the insurers finally
accepted the risk on 18th November 1975, while the 1975 rules were not made until
12th December 1975. It was submitted that the authority conferred on the Law Society
by those rules only covered the taking out of a policy *after* the rules had been made. To
use a colloquialism, it was suggested that the Law Society 'jumped the gun'. I think there
is no substance in this point. It was necessarily implicit in all the contractual d
arrangements between the Law Society and the insurers that the operation of these
arrangements was to be conditional on the 1975 rules being finally made in the form
envisaged. These arrangements thus became finally operative on 12th December 1975
and not before. This, in my judgment, was the date when the Law Society 'took out'
insurance within the meaning of the 1975 rules.

For these reasons the plaintiffs have not satisfied me that the Law Society has been e
acting in breach of the rules. I must therefore reject such of their arguments relating to
commission as are based on the footing that the Law Society has been in such breach, just
as I reject their arguments based on the footing that the rules are invalid. This makes it
unnecessary to deal with two authorities cited by counsel for the plaintiffs relating to the
position where money is improperly obtained under colour of an office, namely *Hooper
v Exeter Corpn* (1887) 56 LJQB 457 and *Morgan v Palmer* (1824) 2 B & C 729, 107 ER 554. f

I now turn to consider the plaintiffs' submissions based on the footing that the rules are
valid and that the Law Society has acted in accordance with them in taking out and
maintaining master policies. The springboard of their arguments in this context is the
general principle of equity that a person (such as an agent or trustee) who, by the use of
a fiduciary position, derives a profit from a third party must account to his principal or
beneficiary for the profit so obtained. Even where a fiduciary relationship is established,
a defendant required to account for the profit may successfully resist the claim on the g
ground that it was received with the knowledge and assent of the principal or beneficiary
concerned (see, for example, *Boardman v Phipps* [1966] 3 All ER 721 at 744, [1967] 2 AC
46 at 105 per Lord Hodson). Furthermore, the right may be lost by a sufficient degree
of acquiescence even without express consent. With these exceptions, however, the
principle, if applicable at all, is a strict one. As Lord Russell said in *Regal (Hastings) Ltd v* h
Gulliver [1942] 1 All ER 378 at 386, [1967] 2 AC 134 at 144:

> 'The rule of equity which insists on those, who by use of a fiduciary position make
> a profit, being liable to account for that profit, in no way depends on fraud, or
> absence of *bona fides*; or upon such questions or considerations as whether the profit
> would or should otherwise have gone to the plaintiff, or whether the profiteer was j
> under a duty to obtain the source of the profit for the plaintiff, or whether he took
> a risk or acted as he did for the benefit of the plaintiff, or whether the plaintiff has
> in fact been damaged or benefited by his action. The liability arises from the mere
> fact of a profit having, in the stated circumstances, been made. The profiteer,
> however honest and well-intentioned, cannot escape the risk of being called upon to
> account.'

The principle that a person in a fiduciary capacity must not make a profit out of his
a trust is 'part of the wider rule that a trustee must not place himself in a position where his duty and his interest may conflict' (see *Boardman v Phipps* [1966] 3 All ER 721 at 746, [1967] 2 AC 46 at 123 per Lord Upjohn.

Lord Herschell in *Bray v Ford* [1896] AC 44 at 51, [1895–99] All ER Rep 1009 at 1011, explained the reason for the rule as follows:

> b 'It does not appear to me that this rule is, as has been said, founded upon principles of morality. I regard it rather as based on the consideration that, human nature being what it is, there is danger, in such circumstances, of the person holding a fiduciary position being swayed by interest rather than by duty, and thus prejudicing those whom he was bound to protect.'

Counsel for the plaintiffs pointed out that, according to the terms of the master policy set
c out in the schedule to each set of rules, the Law Society was contracting 'on behalf of all solicitors from time to time required to be insured by Indemnity Rules made under s. 37 of the Solicitors' Act 1974, and on behalf of former solicitors'. These very words showed, he submitted, that the Law Society was not contracting with the insurers on its own behalf, but simply as agent or trustee for the solicitors concerned. From this it was suggested that, in contracting, the Law Society must inevitably have been acting in a
d fiduciary capacity in relation to such solicitors.

Furthermore, it was suggested, there was an inevitable conflict between the interests of such solicitors, who would be concerned to see the premiums on all insurance arranged under the master policy kept as low as possible, and the interests of the Law Society, which would take increased benefits from higher premiums in the form of an increased share of the commission. In these circumstances, while it was not suggested
e that the Law Society had in fact been influenced by such unworthy motives in making the various arrangements with the insurers, it was submitted that the inflexible rule of equity already mentioned must be applicable to all its rigour, save to the extent that defences, such as acquiescence or waiver, may be available to the Law Society.

If I am right in my conclusion that the Law Society entered into the contract with the insurers on the footing that it was to hold it as trustee for the solicitors concerned, then
f it does seem to me inevitably to follow that *as soon as the contract had been concluded* there existed a fiduciary relationship between the Law Society and such solicitors. Thereafter, I think, any such solicitor would have been entitled to call for the Law Society's co-operation, so far as necessary, in enforcing his rights (as beneficiary under the trust created by the contract) to obtain insurance cover from the insurers.

However, proof of a post-contract fiduciary relationship would not itself suffice to
g entitle the plaintiffs to invoke the equitable principles exemplified in *Boardman v Phipps* unless it were shown that the profit in question had been received by the Law Society as a result of the use of this post-contract fiduciary position. I do not think that this has been shown. True it is that the 1976 agreement was in point of time actually entered into long after the contract between the Law Society and the insurers had been concluded in 1975. The Law Society, however, found itself in a position in 1976 to conclude the
h advantageous arrangement relating to commission, not by virtue of its then subsisting fiduciary relationship to the solicitors affected by the scheme, but because of the negotiation of the original contract with the insurers. Under this contract LIB had derived the certain prospect of receiving large sums of commission on insurance effected by individual solicitors during the currency of that contract and the hope of receiving further similar large sums if the contract was renewed. It was the negotiation of this
j contract which placed the Law Society in a position to demand rights to participate in the commission; its subsequent fiduciary position had nothing to do with the matter.

In the circumstances, the relevant question seems to me to be whether the Law Society must be treated as having acted in a fiduciary relationship to the solicitors affected, *in negotiating the original contract with the insurers*. If, but only if, the answer to this question be Yes, the claim of the plaintiffs based on the principle of *Boardman v Phipps* begins to have substantial force in law.

It might at first sight be assumed that, in any case where A enters into a contract with
B on the footing that A is to be trustee for C of any rights acquired under the contract, a
then A must necessarily be in a fiduciary relationship to C in negotiating the contract.
In my judgment, however, any such general assumption would be fallacious. Merely
because A is to hold the benefit of the contract, when concluded, as trustee for C, it by no
means necessarily follows that A was acting in a fiduciary capacity during the stage of
negotiation. Everything must depend on the particular circumstances. To take one
example, albeit far removed from the present facts: if a grandfather, out of natural love b
and affection for his grandchild were to enter into a contract with insurers, whereunder
he was to hold certain benefits as trustee for his infant grandchild, it could not, I conceive,
be suggested that he was acting in a fiduciary relationship to the grandchild in negotiating
the contract. Correspondingly, even if, as a consequence of negotiating such contract,
the grandfather were to obtain commission, or a share of the commission, paid by the
insurers in respect of the issue of the relevant policy, it could not be suggested that he was c
accountable to the grandchild for such commission.

Thus the mere fact that the Law Society was to hold the benefit of each of the master
policy contracts when concluded as trustee for the individual solicitors concerned does
not show that it was acting in a fiduciary capacity in relation to such solicitors in
negotiating those arrangements. Are there then any other factors which establish the
existence of such a fiduciary relationship during the pre-contract stage? d

Counsel for the plaintiffs emphasised that, as a result of the introduction of the master
policy scheme, the Law Society has become the possessor of a very substantial new source
of income. It would be remarkable, he suggested, if Parliament, in passing the Act and
thereby enabling the Law Society to introduce a compulsory scheme, contemplated that
the Law Society would thereby be enabled to increase its spendable income by several
hundred thousand pounds. This, he suggested, is one reason in itself for concluding that e
the suggested fiduciary relationship exists.

I do not think there is any substance in this point based on the supposed intentions of
Parliament. First, the express power conferred on the Law Society by s 37(5) of the Act,
which empowered it to carry into effect any arrangements which it considered expedient
for the purpose of indemnity under the section, was indubitably wide enough to enable
it to enter into a prudent, commercial arrangement such as the 1976 agreement. Second, f
Parliament is hardly likely to have assumed, as does the plaintiffs' argument, that there
is an inherent conflict of interest between the Law Society and the members of the
solicitors' profession, which the Law Society exists to serve. The suggestion of conflict of
interest on these present facts seems to me an unrealistic one. The position might be
quite different if the person receiving the commission were an individual and not the
professional body which is itself responsible for the affairs of the solicitors' profession. g
Third, if Parliament had directed its mind to the question of commission, it would no
doubt have appreciated that the Law Society already has a large number of powers and
duties, which are usually exercised through its council and are designed to enable it to
advance or protect the interests, usefulness and efficiency of the profession. Nevertheless,
it could not, I conceive, be argued (and has not been argued in the present case) that the
Law Society or the council, in the ordinary exercise of its general powers, acts in a h
fiduciary capacity in relation to individual solicitors, even in those frequent instances
where such exercise is likely to affect their pockets. If solicitors are dissatisfied with the
manner in which the council is exercising its powers and discretions, their normal
remedy is by way of exercise of their rights under the Law Society's byelaws, and not by
reliance on the principles of equity.

For all these reasons, I see no a priori reason for presuming that Parliament, in j
conferring on the council the power to make rules authorising the Law Society to take
out and maintain insurance with authorised insurers for the purpose of providing
indemnity, contemplated that the society would be negotiating such insurance in a
fiduciary capacity. A similar observation applies to the rules themselves which actually
authorised the taking out of such insurance; at least if read without reference to the

scheduled form of master policy, they do not suggest that the society will be negotiating
a any policy otherwise than pursuant to its normal functions as the governing body of the solicitors' branch of the legal profession.

In the end, in my judgment, the argument that the Law Society, in discharging the particular function of negotiating contracts of insurance with the insurers in 1975, 1978 and 1979, was acting in a fiduciary capacity in relation to the solicitors concerned must depend wholly and exclusively on the phrase 'on behalf of all solicitors [etc]' to be found
b in cl 1 of each form of master policy. But for these words, the argument, I conceive, would not get off the ground. In my judgment, however, for reasons already appearing, such dependence is ill founded. This phrase by itself by no means necessarily imports that the Law Society was acting in a fiduciary capacity vis-à-vis the individual solicitors concerned in negotiating contracts; in this respect its import is quite neutral.

I can see no other sufficient grounds for holding that the performance of this particular
c function imposed on the Law Society equitable obligations to individual solicitors of a nature which it would not ordinarily assume in negotiating commercial contracts which it considered to be in the interests of the solicitors' profession. Accordingly, in my judgment, the existence of the relevant fiduciary relationship at the relevant time, which the plaintiffs must establish if they are to succeed under this head, has not been established.

d In these circumstances it is unnecessary to make any decision on the alternative submissions made by the Law Society to the effect that, on any footing, acquiescence now debars these two particular plaintiffs from seeking to enforce any equitable rights, which they might otherwise possess, to compel the Law Society to account for commission. It is common ground that a legal or equitable right may be lost if the situation is such that 'it would be dishonest, or unconscionable, for the plaintiff, or for the person having the
e right sought to be enforced, to continue to seek to enforce it' (see *Shaw v Applegate* [1978] All ER 123 at 131, [1977] 1 WLR 970 at 978 per Buckley LJ). Furthermore it appears from the judgment of Goff LJ in that case that it is easier to establish a case of acquiescence where, as in the present case, the right is equitable only (see [1978] 1 All ER 123 at 132, [1977] 1 WLR 970 at 979).

No attack has been made on the honesty of these two plaintiffs. It has, however, been
f forcefully submitted on behalf of the Law Society that, as matters stand, it would be unconscionable for the plaintiffs to seek to enforce the rights to participate in commission which they now claim. As I have illustrated, in May and October 1975 the Law Society made full disclosure to solicitors that, if and when the master policy scheme was introduced, it would be receiving a share of the brokers' commission on the relevant policies and that it intended to apply this for the benefit of the profession as a whole
g (thereby implicitly informing solicitors that it did not intend to account to them individually for it). It is not suggested that the plaintiffs were unaware of these announcements. Subsequently every set of annual accounts of the Law Society has disclosed the existence of the commission and its receipt by LSS. The evidence shows that all sums thus received have been applied or allocated for the benefit of the whole profession. The plaintiffs have not suggested that they were not, at all material times,
h aware of the contents of the Law Society's successive sets of accounts and of the manner in which these sums were actually dealt with. And yet, until the actual issue of the present originating summons, so far as the evidence shows, they did not by any communication to the Law Society dispute or question in any way its right to participate in the commission and to apply it in the manner indicated. It would appear that, so far as the Law Society was concerned, their complaints were directed simply against the
j existence of a compulsory insurance scheme, which deprived them of the freedom to select their own insurers.

In these circumstances, the defence based on acquiescence would in my judgment at least have considerable force in relation to these plaintiffs' claims, if it were necessary to consider it. As things are, however, I express no conclusion on this point.

Subject to the submissions of counsel as to the precise form of relief to be granted, I propose to declare in answer to para 2 of the originating summons that, on the true construction of the Act and the rules, and in the events which have happened, the Law *a* Society is not bound to account to either of the plaintiffs for any part of any commission received by it or by LSS from LIB in respect of premiums paid by individual solicitors pursuant to the Solicitors' Indemnity Insurance Scheme. This not being a representative action, I propose not to make any wider declaration than this, but again I will hear counsel on this point.

[His Lordship heard argument on the point and on the question of costs. His Lordship *b* continued:] In these circumstances it seems to me that the plaintiffs' summons of 30th January was amply justified, though I entirely accept that the Law Society's solicitors were acting throughout with the best of intentions, and no one has attempted to suggest otherwise. I further think that in all the circumstances, because of the way that the matter was conducted on the Law Society's side in relation to the adduction of the evidence to which I have been referring, there has been a certain amount of unnecessary *c* expenditure of time in the hearing itself. I think that both sides are to some extent to blame for the misunderstandings that have occurred, but on the whole I think the fault must be laid more at the Law Society's door in this context.

In these circumstances therefore, I propose to direct that the Law Society should pay the costs of the summons of 30th January, and to direct in effect that they make a modest contribution to the plaintiffs' costs of the main summons. Taking all factors into *d* consideration, I think that the proper order will be that the plaintiffs, who have been unsuccessful on the main summons, should be directed to pay four-fifths only of the Law Society's costs of this summons, instead of the whole lot, which I would otherwise have directed them to pay.

In relation to the relief to be granted on the main summons, I think both parties are content that I should make a declaration in answer to para 2 in the form that I have *e* already indicated.

I have considered counsel's invitation on behalf of the Law Society that I should make an affirmative declaration in answer to para 1, but on the whole, in this non-representative action, I remain of the view that I should not do that, though, by declining to make a positive declaration that I regard the rules as valid, I do not wish to be taken in any way as suggesting that I think there is any doubt on the matter. As will have appeared from *f* my judgment, my own view is that these rules are valid and intra vires; but I think it is right to leave it formally open to other persons to take such other points on them as they may see fit to take in the future.

Order accordingly.

g

Solicitors: *Lovell Son & Pitfield*, agents for *Pethybridges*, Bodmin (for the plaintiffs), *Slaughter & May* (for the Law Society).

Jacqueline Metcalfe Barrister.

a Re a debtor (No 2A of 1980, Colchester)

CHANCERY DIVISION
GOULDING J
18th MARCH 1980

Bankruptcy – Receiving order – Rescission – Jurisdiction of court – Transfer of proceedings from
b *High Court to county court after receiving order made in High Court – Whether county court having jurisdiction to rescind receiving order – Whether proceedings required to be transferred back to High Court for rescission of receiving order – Bankruptcy Act 1914, s 100(2).*

A receiving order was made in the High Court against the debtor on the petition of the Inland Revenue. Pursuant to s 100(2)[a] of the Bankruptcy Act 1914 and r 21[b] of the
c Bankruptcy Rules 1952 the High Court ordered the proceedings to be transferred to the county court. The debtor made provision for payment of his debts in full before a preliminary examination was held in the county court and applied in the county court for rescission of the receiving order, pursuant to s 108(1)[c] of the 1914 Act. The official receiver of the county court applied to the High Court to have the proceedings transferred back to the High Court on the ground that the receiving order having been made in the
d High Court only the High Court could rescind it. The debtor resisted the application and requested that the county court should rescind the receiving order. It was the prevailing practice in the county court for that court itself to rescind a receiving order made in the High Court where the proceedings had thereafter been transferred to the county court, but there was doubt about the lawfulness of the practice.

e **Held** – Where proceedings were 'transferred' under s 100(2) of the 1914 Act from one court to another court having parallel jurisdiction in bankruptcy, that effected a replacement of the first court by the second court for all the purposes of the 1914 Act so that what could have been done in the first court could be done in the second court without the first court being brought into the matter. It followed that the prevailing practice was lawful and that it was unnecessary to order the proceedings against the
f debtor to be transferred back to the High Court. Accordingly, the receiving order could be rescinded in the county court (see p 645 *j* to p 646 *g*, post).

Re Hughes (1887) 4 Morr 73 and *Re Maugham* (1888) 21 QBD 21 distinguished.

Notes

For transfer of bankruptcy proceedings, see 3 Halsbury's Laws (4th Edn) para 966, and for
g cases on the subject, see 4 Digest (Reissue) 169–172, *1497–1536*.

For the Bankruptcy Act 1914, s 100, see 3 Halsbury's Statutes (3rd Edn) 129.

Cases referred to in judgment

Hughes, Re, ex parte Hughes (1887) 4 Morr 73, DC, 4 Digest (Reissue) 186, *1651*.
h *Maugham, Re, ex parte Maugham* (1888) 21 QBD 21, 57 LJQB 487, 59 LT 253, DC, 4 Digest (Reissue) 186, *1648*.

Application

By an application dated 11th March 1980 the official receiver of the Colchester and Clacton County Court applied to the High Court for an order that bankruptcy proceedings against the debtor to be transferred from the county court to the High Court
j for the purpose of rescinding the receiving order made against the debtor in the High

---

a Section 100(2) is set out at p 643 *b*, post
b Rule 21 is set out at p 643 *d*, post
c Section 108(1) is set out at p 643 *h*, post

Court prior to the transfer of the proceedings to the county court. The application was heard in chambers but judgment was given by Goulding J in open court. The facts are a set out in the judgment.

Mr A H S Robertshaw, Senior Legal Assistant, Department of Trade and Industry, for the official receiver.
Martin Mann for the debtor.

GOULDING J. This is an application which I have heard during the forenoon at b chambers. I propose to give my judgment in open court as I think it may be of some procedural interest to those engaged in bankruptcy business.

The application concerns a debtor and is made by an official receiver in Essex. I will read the official receiver's affidavit rather than his formal application, as it states concisely the material facts and shows the relief sought:

> c
> 'A receiving order was made against the above-named debtor in the High Court of Justice on 4th March, 1980, on the petition of the Commissioners of Inland Revenue dated 28th November, 1979. By order of the High Court of Justice dated 5th March, 1980, the proceedings were transferred to the county court. The debtor has not yet attended on the official receiver for preliminary examination but he has stated that he estimates his liabilities do not exceed £20,000 and that he has assets d estimated to be worth £500,000. The debtor has further stated that he has instructed his solicitor [and the name and the address of the solicitor are then given] to make immediate application to the court for a stay of advertisement of the proceedings and the rescission of the receiving order. I have been informed by the said solicitor that such application and an accompanying affidavit is in the course of preparation. The official receiver accordingly makes application for the transfer of e the proceedings back to the High Court of Justice.'

The debtor was represented at chambers by counsel who resisted the application, saying that a transfer was unnecessary and that the county court should be requested, and should accede to a request, to rescind the receiving order. The official receiver supported the view of the debtor on grounds of past practice and convenience. I found the question not altogether an easy one and I have seriously considered whether I ought not to adjourn f it for the assistance of a properly instructed amicus curiae. However, any delay may be of some hardship to the debtor, who has a business near Harwich, and I have also had the advantage of a great deal of help at chambers from Mr Robertshaw, who is an assistant solicitor with the Department of Trade and has directed my mind to a number of matters that I might otherwise have overlooked. Accordingly, I think it is my duty to give judgment forthwith. g

To explain how the difficulty arises I should refer to some sections in the Bankruptcy Act 1914. Section 96(1) provides that the court having jurisdiction in bankruptcy shall be the High Court and the county court, and later subsections of the same section provide that only certain county courts selected by the Lord Chancellor shall exercise bankruptcy jurisdiction. Section 98 was no doubt designed to meet the convenience of debtors. It provides: h

> '(1) If the debtor by or against whom a bankruptcy petition is presented has resided or carried on business within the London bankruptcy district as defined by this Act for the greater part of the six months immediately preceding the presentation of the petition, or for a longer period during those six months than in the district of any county court, or is not resident in England, or if the petitioning j creditor is unable to ascertain the residence of the debtor, the petition shall be presented to the High Court.
>
> '(2) In any other case the petition shall be presented to the county court for the district in which the debtor has resided or carried on business for the longest period during the six months immediately preceding the presentation of the petition.

> '(3) Nothing in this section shall invalidate a proceeding by reason of its being taken in a wrong court.'

Section 99 defines the London bankruptcy district and I need not pause over that.

Section 100 provides:

> '(1) Subject to the provisions of this Act, every court having original jurisdiction in bankruptcy shall have jurisdiction throughout England.
>
> '(2) Any proceedings in bankruptcy may at any time, and at any stage thereof, and either with or without application from any of the parties thereto, be transferred by any prescribed authority and in the prescribed manner from one court to another court, or may, by the like authority, be retained in the court in which the proceedings were commenced, although it may not be the court in which the proceedings ought to have been commenced . . .'

There is a third subsection to which I will refer at a later stage in my judgment.

To complete the picture as regards transfer I will read rr 21 and 22 from the Bankruptcy Rules 1952 (SI 1952 No 2113 and SI 1972 No 529):

> '21. The Judge of the High Court may order the proceedings in any matter under the Act to be transferred from a county court to the High Court; the Judge of the High Court or, where an application for transfer is made by the Official Receiver, a Registrar of the High Court may order the proceedings in any matter under the Act to be transferred from the High Court to a county court.
>
> '22. The Judge of a county court having jurisdiction in bankruptcy may order the proceedings in any matter under the Act which have been commenced or are pending in his court to be transferred to any other county court having jurisdiction in bankruptcy.'

It will be remembered that s 98 of the 1914 Act directed presentation of a bankruptcy petition in a court to be determined primarily by the location of the debtor's residence or business. The Crown, or at any rate a number of the emanations of the Crown, claim that the Crown is not bound by the provisions of s 98 and may present a bankruptcy petition in any of the statutory jurisdictions of its choice. I express no opinion on that claim, I have not looked into it and it is not necessary to do so for the purposes of the present application. I believe it has been unsuccessfully challenged before a registrar of the High Court in bankruptcy. So far as I know there is no reported authority on it. I mention that to indicate how the present case arose and its general bearing. The departments that are perhaps the most active in presenting bankruptcy petitions, namely the Board of Inland Revenue, the Board of Customs and Excise and I think also the Department of Health and Social Security, are in the habit of presenting petitions in the High Court in a great number of cases. Once a receiving order has been obtained application is made under s 100 for transfer to a convenient county court.

Now I turn to s 108(1):

> 'Every court having jurisdiction in bankruptcy under this Act may review, rescind or vary any order made by it under its bankruptcy jurisdiction.'

That subsection is in everyday use, debtors having a strong propensity to desire that orders made in the bankruptcy courts may be rescinded or varied. One of the common types of application under s 108(1) is for the rescission of a receiving order. Among the most usual applications, or perhaps I should say among the most usual successful applications, for rescission of a receiving order are two kinds: one where there is a fatal defect in the bankruptcy notice or the petition on which the receiving order was founded, and the other, like the present case, where the debtor makes provision for paying all his debts in full. As I have said a great number of Crown petitions in bankruptcy are constantly being presented to the High Court and after a receiving order has been made the proceedings are transferred to a county court; and of that great

number there is continually a substantial proportion wherein reason is shown on one ground or another for the rescission of the receiving order. And I am told by those who a
are in a position to know the practice that county courts with bankruptcy jurisdiction have long been in the habit in such cases of themselves rescinding the receiving order where a proper application has been made and not successfully opposed. Doubts, as again I am informed, have recently arisen among official receivers whether the county court can properly rescind receiving orders where the proceedings have been transferred from the High Court after such an order has been made. Those doubts appear to have b
arisen from an order made by consent some months ago in the Divisional Court in bankruptcy. To the best of my recollection there was no argument addressed to the court; the court simply on the request of the parties made an order by consent. However that may be, doubts have now arisen and hence the present application by the official receiver of the Colchester and Clacton County Court for transfer of the proceedings back to the High Court so that the receiving order may be rescinded. c

There are two authorities which seem to be of some persuasive weight against the practice that has hitherto prevailed. One is *Re Hughes* (1887) 4 Morr 73. That was a case before a Divisional Court consisting of Mathew and Cave JJ. Application had been made by a creditor under the Debtors Act 1869 in the Brighton County Court for the committal of the debtor to prison, and under s 103(5) of the Bankruptcy Act 1883, the county court declined to commit and in lieu thereof, with the consent of the creditor, made a d
receiving order against the debtor. At the same time the county court transferred the proceedings to the London court in bankruptcy, that being the proper court in which a bankruptcy petition should have been presented against that particular debtor. The debtor, as soon as he heard of the receiving order, paid the debt and sought the rescission of the receiving order. He came to the Divisional Court by way of appeal from the receiving order itself in the county court. The debtor's counsel is reported (at 74) to have e
said to the Divisional Court:

> '... difficulty arose as to the rehearing. The County Court judge could not do so because of the transfer. The Registrar in London could not, because the order had been made in the County Court in Brighton.'

Cave J said (at 75): f

> 'This court is not the Court of Appeal from the London Bankruptcy Court. I think you ought to go to the County Court Judge to rehear. If he refuses, you can then come here. I think the case should stand over for you to ask the County Court Judge to rehear. You may say that, in our opinion, the County Court Judge has authority to rehear you under the circumstances.'

Mathew J concurred. g

I may say that the provisions regarding transfer and review and rescission in the 1883 Act were for present purposes the same as those in the 1914 Act.

The other authority to which I should refer is *Re Maugham* (1888) 21 QBD 21, again a decision of a Divisional Court. This case raised no question of transfer, but it did raise a question as to the interpretation of what is now s 108 of the Bankruptcy Act 1914, then s 104 of the 1883 Act. In *Maugham's* case the petition had been dismissed by the registrar h
of the county court. Then a creditor's solicitor gave notice of intention to apply for an order rescinding or varying the registrar's order and substituting the applicant's name for the original petitioning creditor. That application was not heard by the county court registrar, but by the county court judge himself, and he gave judgment as prayed, rescinding the registrar's order of dismissal and substituting a new petitioning creditor. The debtor and some other creditors appealed. The Divisional Court allowed their j
appeal on two alternative grounds, whereof only one is of interest for present purposes. Cave J said (at 22–23):

> '... the order dismissing the petition was made by the registrar and the application to rescind it was made to the judge. In my opinion the order which the

> learned judge then made was clearly illegal. There is not a vestige of a pretence for
> a saying that a county court judge can be asked to review the order of the registrar any more than for saying that a registrar can be asked to review the order of a judge. Each of these authorities has his own work, and under s. 104 [that corresponds with the present s 108] can review, vary, or rescind his own order; their jurisdiction is distinct, and to hold that the one can vary or rescind the order of the other would be to give an appeal not given by the statute, and which does not exist.'

b The other member of the court was A L Smith J, who said (at 23):

> 'I am entirely of the same opinion. I will only add that I think the proper construction of s. 104, sub-s. 1, is that the same Court that makes the order can review, rescind, or vary it. If the registrar makes the order, he is the Court that
> c makes it, and he alone is the Court which can review or rescind it, and the same power is given to the judge, the Divisional Court and the Court of Appeal. But no one of these Courts can review, rescind, or vary the order of any other unless a right of appeal is clearly given by the statute.'

Having heard these authorities discussed and having reflected on them I am of opinion
d that they both ought to be distinguished from the present case. As I have occasion to say almost every day the authority of any decision must always be considered secundum subjectam materiam: you find what the judge meant by considering what he was thinking of and within what limits argument was addressed to him. In *Re Hughes* there appears to have been no one before the Divisional Court except the debtor. That is not surprising. If the debt had been paid neither the petitioning creditor nor, unless he
e knew of some other material circumstance, the official receiver would be very interested in the appeal designed to get the receiving order removed. So far as the report shows the debtor's counsel simply told the court of the difficulty that had arisen, the county court judge could not rescind the order because of the transfer and the registrar in London could not do it because it had been made in the county court. The court seems to have accepted that without any investigation of the law and provided an immediate way out
f by saying, 'Go back to the county court and say that it is our opinion it can be done there.' I do not expect it took very long because there is reported a more substantial case, with leading counsel on both sides, heard and disposed of on the same day. I do not think, therefore, that *Re Hughes* can be considered as expressing an opinion of the Divisional Court that the transferee court was unable to review an order of the transferor court.

g *Re Maugham* does of course contain considered observations which if taken quite literally would be fatal to the debtor's contention in the present case, because A L Smith J said that he thought the proper construction of the section was that the same court which makes the order can review, rescind or vary. But he was thinking, as was the other member of the court, Cave J, of competition between the concurrent jurisdictions in the county court of the registrar and the judge. He was not thinking at all of the
h possible effect of transfer, and I do not expect that the transfer section was ever in the mind of the Divisional Court at all. Accordingly, one has to consider the meaning of the word 'transferred' in the section authorising transfer. The decision in *Re Maugham* does not of course mean that an application to review or rescind must be disposed of by the very same individual who made the original order. If there is a change in the personality of the county court judge or the county court registrar the successor is
j perfectly able to review or rescind the order his predecessor has made, the jurisdiction being that of the court and not of the individual. One has to ask whether a transferee court, where transfer has been ordered, is really in a different position from an individual successor to the maker of the order. There is nothing in the scheme of the 1914 Act, so far as I have been able to see, that makes it inherently improbable that a county court should sometimes be in a position to review or rescind an order of the High Court. The

county court is not an inferior or secondary court for the purpose of exercising bankruptcy jurisdiction. Section 103 of the 1914 Act says: a

> 'A county court shall, for the purposes of its bankruptcy jurisdiction, in addition to the ordinary powers of the court, have all the powers and jurisdiction of the High Court, and the orders of the court may be enforced accordingly in manner prescribed.'

Any practical difficulty about the determination of difficult questions of law in a b county court is met by s 100(3), which enables the county court judge, if he so wishes, and compels him if all the parties to the proceedings desire, to state a case for the opinion of the High Court on a question of law. Accordingly, I do not start with any notion that it is improbable that a county court could rescind a High Court order. I go back to s 100, where, without further explanation of the term 'transfer', it is simply said that 'Any proceedings in bankruptcy may at any time etc' be transferred from one court to another c court. The natural meaning of that in my opinion is to effect a universal replacement of the first court by the second court for all the purposes of the Act, so that what could have been done in the first court can now be done in the second court without having to bring the first court into the matter any more. It is pointed out that there is a possible difficulty in the proviso to s 105(1) of the 1914 Act. That is the subsection which authorises every court with jurisdiction in bankruptcy to decide all questions, whether d of law or fact, which arise in any case of bankruptcy coming within the cognisance of the court. There is a proviso in these terms:

> 'Provided that the jurisdiction hereby given shall not be exercised by the county court for the purpose of adjudicating upon any claim, not arising out of the bankruptcy, which might heretofore have been enforced by action in the High Court, unless all parties to the proceeding consent thereto, or the money, money's e worth, or right in dispute does not, in the opinion of the Judge, exceed in value two hundred pounds.'

It is true that that proviso might make it necessary where bankruptcy proceedings have been transferred from the High Court to the county court either to transfer them back or to permit the commencement of an independent action in order to decide some f collateral matter arising in the bankruptcy. But that one point does not seem to me to limit the natural meaning of the transfer provision in s 100. Accordingly, I am of the view that the prevailing practice is not unlawful and that the receiving order made in the High Court may after transfer be rescinded by the transferee county court.

It has been said in discussion at chambers that there is difficulty created by the words 'by it' in s 108. It will be remembered that the provision is: 'Every court having g jurisdiction in bankruptcy under this Act may review, rescind or vary any order made by it.' I can only say, trying to give the words their natural meaning, that where provision is made for transfer of legal proceedings from one court to another court having a parallel jurisdiction, then when a valid order of transfer has been made, as in a children's game, the transferor ceases to be 'it' and the transferee becomes 'it'. Accordingly, I make no order on the application. The county court may, of course, be informed of my reasons h for doing so.

Order accordingly.

Solicitors: *Official Receiver*; *Ellison & Co*, Dovercourt (for the debtor).

Evelyn M C Budd Barrister.

a # Watson v Lucas

COURT OF APPEAL, CIVIL DIVISION
STEPHENSON, OLIVER LJJ AND SIR DAVID CAIRNS
19th, 20th JUNE, 4th JULY 1980

b *Rent restriction – Death of tenant – Claim by friend to remain in possession – Defendant cohabiting with widow in widow's flat for 19 years – Both defendant and widow retaining own names – Defendant remaining married to wife but refusing reconciliation – Defendant remaining in flat after widow's death – Whether defendant entitled to succeed widow as statutory tenant – Whether defendant 'a member of the original tenant's family' – Rent Act 1977, Sch 1, para 3.*

c The defendant married in 1953 but after a year his wife left him. They were never reconciled but there was no divorce. In 1958 the defendant went to live with a widow some 15 years his senior in her flat. The widow was a protected tenant of the flat. The defendant and the widow lived in all respects as a married couple although they both continued to use their own surnames except when visiting a club that the defendant belonged to. There were no children of the union. In 1969 the defendant's wife sought d a reconciliation but the defendant refused to leave the widow and remained with her until her death in 1977. After the death of the widow the defendant continued to reside in the flat and when the plaintiff, the owner of the flat, brought an action against him to recover possession he contended that he was entitled to remain in possession because he had become, by virtue of s 2(5)[a] of and para 3[b] of Sch 1 to the Rent Act 1977, the statutory tenant by succession on the widow's death because he was 'a member of the original e tenant's [i e the widow's] family' within the meaning of para 3. The county court judge, having taken into consideration (i) that the defendant had remained married to another woman throughout the period of cohabitation with the widow and (ii) that with one minor exception the defendant and the widow had continued to use their own names, held that the defendant was not a member of the widow's family and ordered that possession be given up to the plaintiff. The defendant appealed.

f

Held (Oliver LJ dissenting) – The appeal would be allowed for the following reasons—

(1) A man who remained married to another woman throughout the time he lived with a protected tenant was not thereby barred from becoming a member of the tenant's 'family' for the purposes of para 3 of Sch 1 to the 1977 Act, since (Oliver LJ concurring) it was quite possible for a man to have two families. Furthermore, the assumption by g one party of the other's name and a public assumption by both parties of the status of marriage by their holding out that they were married were merely indicators in favour of the relationship being a 'family' one but the reverse was not true, i e the retention by the parties of their own names and the absence of a public holding out that they were married did not necessarily indicate that the relationship was not a family one (see p 651 *j* to p 652 *c* and p 658 *a b* and *g h*, post).

h (2) Applying the test that the relationship had to have sufficient stability and permanence for an ordinary man at the time of the tenant's death to say that the parties were members of one another's family, the defendant's marriage to another woman, the retention by the defendant and the widow of their own names and the absence of any pretence that a marriage existed were not sufficient to outweigh the evidence of a long-lasting and stable relationship as illustrated by the defendant's refusal of a reconciliation j with his wife. The defendant was therefore a member of the widow's family for the purposes of para 3 of Sch 1 to the 1977 Act and was entitled to retain possession of the flat (see p 650 *b* to *d*, p 652 *c* to *h*, p 653 *b* to *j* and p 658 *e* to *h*, post); *Dyson Holdings Ltd v Fox* [1975] 3 All ER 1030 applied.

---

a Section 2(5) is set out at p 649 *c*, post
b Paragraph 3 is set out at p 649 *d*, post

Notes

For succession to a statutory tenancy on the death of an original tenant, see 23 Halsbury's Laws (3rd Edn) 811, para 1590, and for cases on the subject, see 31(2) Digest (Reissue) 987–997, *7919–7964*.

For the Rent Act 1977, s 2, Sch 1, para 3, see 47 Halsbury's Statutes (3rd Edn) 396, 556.

Cases referred to in judgments

Brock v Wollams [1949] 1 All ER 715, [1949] 2 KB 388, CA, 31(2) Digest (Reissue) 991, *7942*.

Carega Properties SA v Sharratt [1979] 2 All ER 1084, [1979] 1 WLR 928, HL, Digest (Cont Vol E) 380, *7956a*.

Dyson Holdings Ltd v Fox [1975] 3 All ER 1030, [1976] QB 503, [1975] 3 WLR 744, CA, Digest (Cont Vol D) 592, *7946a*.

Gammons v Ekins [1950] 2 All ER 140, [1950] 2 KB 328, CA, 31(2) Digest (Reissue) 992, *7944*.

Hawes v Evenden [1953] 2 All ER 737, [1953] 1 WLR 1169, CA, 31(2) Digest (Reissue) 992, *7946*.

Helby v Rafferty [1978] 3 All ER 1016, [1979] 1 WLR 13, CA, Digest (Cont Vol E) 379, *7947a*.

Ross v Collins [1964] 1 All ER 861, [1964] 1 WLR 425, 31(2) Digest (Reissue) 995, *7956*.

Salter v Lask, Lask v Cohen [1925] 1 KB 584, 94 LJKB 522, 132 LT 830, 23 LGR 327, DC, 31(2) Digest (Reissue) 989, *7928*.

Trowchurch Ltd v Pammer (28th March 1980, unreported).

Appeal

The defendant, Dennis Lucas, appealed against the judgment of his Honour Judge Granville Slack given at the Willesden County Court on 4th January 1980 ordering the defendant to deliver up possession of premises at 21 St Julian's Road, London NW6 to the plaintiff, Edith Watson, the owner of the premises. The facts are set out in the judgment of Stephenson LJ.

Mark George for Mr Lucas.
Christopher Semken for Mrs Watson.

4th July. The following judgments were read.

Cur adv vult

STEPHENSON LJ. On 29th February 1980 his Honour Judge Granville Slack declared in the Willesden County Court that Mr Lucas, the defendant to proceedings brought against him by the plaintiff, Mrs Watson, was not a member of the family of a Mrs Sullivan. Mrs Sullivan had been the protected tenant of a basement flat in 21 St Julian's Road, London NW6 when she died on 21st June 1977. Mr Lucas had been residing with her there at the time of her death and, as the judge held, contrary to Mrs Watson's evidence, for many years before her death. Mrs Watson bought the freehold of the whole house, no 21, in 1962, subject to Mrs Sullivan's tenancy of the basement flat, and lived there on and off from 1962 to 1979. When she gave Mr Lucas notice to quit, as she did in 1977 and again in 1979, he was therefore entitled to remain in occupation of the flat as a statutory tenant by succession pursuant to s 2(1)(*b*) of the Rent Act 1977 and para 3 of Sch 1 thereto, provided he was a member of her family. In his defence he raised that plea. The judge rejected it. He appeals against the judge's decision.

A good deal turns on this question and the outcome of this appeal because Mr Lucas's continued occupation of the flat has prevented Mrs Watson from completing work on the house which was required by the local authority; and that led Mrs Watson to couple with her claim for possession a claim for damages limited to £2,000 and Mr Lucas to counterclaim an injunction and damages limited to £1,000. Those proceedings the judge adjourned pending the hearing of this appeal.

The statutory provisions on which Mr Lucas relies are these. Section 2(1) of the Rent Act 1977 provides:

> 'Subject to this Part of this Act—(*a*) after the termination of a protected tenancy of a dwelling-house the person who, immediately before that termination, was the protected tenant of the dwelling-house shall, if and so long as he occupies the dwelling-house as his residence, be the statutory tenant of it; and (*b*) Part I of Schedule 1 to this Act shall have effect for determining what person (if any) is the statutory tenant of a dwelling-house at any time after the death of a person who, immediately before his death, was either a protected tenant of the dwelling-house or the statutory tenant of it by virtue of paragraph (*a*) above.'

Section 2(5) provides:

> 'A person who becomes a statutory tenant as mentioned in subsection 1(*b*) above is, in this Act, referred to as a statutory tenant by succession.'

Schedule 1 to the Act contains these three paragraphs:

> '2. If the original tenant was a man who died leaving a widow who was residing with him at his death then, after his death, the widow shall be the statutory tenant if and so long as she occupies the dwelling-house as her residence.
>
> '3. Where paragraph 2 above does not apply, but a person who was a member of the original tenant's family was residing with him at the time of and for the period of 6 months immediately before his death then, after his death, that person or if there is more than one such person such one of them as may be decided by agreement, or in default of agreement by the county court, shall be the statutory tenant if and so long as he occupies the dwelling-house as his residence.
>
> '4. A person who becomes the statutory tenant of a dwelling-house by virtue of paragraph 2 or 3 above is in this Part of this Schedule referred to as "the first successor".'

This protection was first conferred by s 12(1)(*g*) of the Increase of Rent and Mortgage Interest (Restrictions) Act 1920 by defining the expression tenant to include a member of his (or her) family residing with him at the time of his death. Section 13 of the 1933 amending Act introduced the qualification of residence for not less than six months.

The facts are these. Mr Lucas was born in 1933. He married at 20 and had one child, but after about a year his wife left him to go to Ireland and later had two more children. A few years later he got to know Mrs Sullivan. She was a widow with two children, who had been living in this flat with her husband since 1943 and with his children since his death in 1956. After about a year's acquaintance he moved into the flat with her. That was in 1958 when he was 24 or 25 and she was 40, having been born in 1918. Her daughter had already married and left home. Her son, who gave evidence for Mr Lucas, was then a schoolboy and continued to live in the flat with his mother and Mr Lucas until he married in 1964.

From 1958 until her death in 1977 Mr Lucas and Mrs Sullivan lived together in the flat as husband and wife, and he lives there still with another woman. The flat consists of two rooms used as bedrooms when the son was there, a kitchen and a hall, with its own front door and an outside water-closet. They slept in the same bed and had sexual intercourse, but no children. They both worked and he contributed out of his earnings to the housekeeping expenses. She paid the rent and the bills, which were all in her name. They never married. He could have divorced his wife but he never did. Indeed about 1969 she came over from Ireland and asked for a reconciliation, but he refused; he would not leave Mrs Sullivan, and his wife went back to Ireland.

The county court judge described the relationship between Mr Lucas and Mrs Sullivan in his note:

> 'For the most part they retained their own names, with one exception, regarding

> the ex-serviceman's club, of which Mr Lucas was a member before he met Mrs
> Sullivan. He could take her there as his wife, and she was regarded as his missis. a
> When they went on excursions, it was as Mr and Mrs Lucas. There is no evidence
> that he ever used her name until after her death. He used his own name, and
> usually she continued to use her own name.'

This is the only respect in which they did not live as a married couple. There was no
evidence from other relations or friends as to how they were regarded. Her son said: 'It
was as if they were married.' Both the Sullivan children called Mr Lucas 'Dennis' and his b
mother referred to him as 'Dennis' when speaking to her son. So their relationship was
no different from that of stepfather and stepson.

Was Mr Lucas a member of Mrs Sullivan's family? On the authority of *Brock v
Wollams* [1949] 1 All ER 715 at 718, [1949] 2 KB 388 at 395 per Cohen LJ the question
the county court judge should and did ask himself is: 'Would an ordinary man,
addressing his mind to the question whether [Mr Lucas] was a member of her family or c
not, have answered "Yes" or "No"?'

We are bound by the decision of this court in *Dyson Holdings Ltd v Fox* [1975] 3 All ER
1030 at 1035, [1976] QB 503 at 511 per James LJ to place the ordinary man not in 1920,
when Parliament first used the phrase in this context, but in 1977, when Mrs Sullivan
died. And we have also to place him in possession of the evidence which the judge had
before he gives his answer. d

Gammans v Ekins [1950] 2 All ER 140, [1950] 2 KB 328 would seem to have answered
the question for us, for in that case this court decided that an unmarried man, who had
lived with a tenant as man and wife for some twenty years before her death (see [1950]
2 All ER 140 at 141) and taken her name, and had no children, was not a member of her
family because (as I read the judgments) to hold that he was would be an abuse of
language and presuppose an intention of Parliament to reward immorality with e
irremovability: the party to a union out of wedlock is out of the statutory protection.
But the decision was held by *Dyson Holdings Ltd v Fox* to be no longer valid, either (per
Lord Denning MR) because it was wrongly decided or (per James and Bridge LJJ) because
it was outdated and no longer applied the popular meaning which would guide the
ordinary man's answer.

These are only three of the reported cases in which the question who is a member of f
a deceased's tenant's family has been extensively canvassed since the 1920 Act first made
an answer necessary. The hope expressed in the most recent case in this court, *Helby v
Rafferty* [1978] 3 All ER 1016, [1979] 1 WLR 13, that all these cases, including *Dyson
Holdings Ltd v Fox*, might be reviewed by the House of Lords was disappointed by the
House in *Carega Properties SA v Sharratt* [1979] 2 All ER 1084, [1979] 1 WLR 928. It
would, in my judgment and in Hamlet's words (1. ii. 133), be 'weary, stale, flat and g
unprofitable' to go through them all again. The judge went carefully through them and
counsel for the defendant has taken us through them. I am satisfied that the decisive
question for us is whether this case is distinguishable from *Dyson Holdings Ltd v Fox*. It
is submitted for the defendant that it is not and that the county court judge was only able
to distinguish it on a ground which is erroneous in law or does not distinguish it in
fact. In that case this court decided that an unmarried woman, who had lived with an h
unmarried man as man and wife for 21 years before his death, but without children, and
had taken his name, was a member of his family residing with him at the time of his
death because, in the view of the majority, the union was permanent and stable enough
to make her a member of his family in the eyes of the ordinary man and in the popular
meaning of that phrase in 1975, or in 1961 when the man died.

That decision and its ratio have been doubted and distinguished by this court in *Helby* j
v Rafferty. It was doubted because it did not follow the earlier decision of this court in
Gammans v Ekins on a ground which seemed inconsistent with recognised principles of
statutory construction. It was distinguished on the facts there found by the county court
judge, not because the deceased tenant was (as in this case) a woman and the defendant,
who claimed to be a member of her family residing with her at the time of and for the

period of six months immediately before her death, was (as here) a man but because during their five years' cohabitation the parties never pretended to be married and the tenant wished to remain independent, so that their relationship lacked the permanence and stability necessary to create a family unit. All three members of this court in *Helby v Rafferty* regarded *Dyson Holdings Ltd v Fox* as binding on them, and we must do the same. To go back to *Gammans v Ekins* would be to introduce impermanence and instability into our own decisions in this case. Only the House of Lords can reinstate *Gammans v Ekins* and that they have so far declined to do.

In *Carega Properties SA v Sharratt* [1979] 2 All ER 1084 at 1085, [1979] 1 WLR 928 at 930 Lord Diplock said:

> 'The facts of the instant case, if they are not unique, are certainly most unusual, and for that reason they do not, in my opinion, provide a suitable occasion for this House to undertake a general consideration of what persons may be included in the expression "a member of the original tenant's family" where at the time of the tenant's death there did exist between him and the claimant to a statutory tenancy by succession a relationship of one or other of the various kinds to which I have referred above. In particular, the difficult question posed by *Dyson Holdings Ltd v Fox* as to the extent, if any, to which changed social attitudes towards cohabitation between unmarried couples and the offspring of such liaisons may have enlarged the meaning of the expression "family" in the Rent Act 1968 does not arise in the instant case and is best left for consideration in the light of the actual facts of a case in which it does arise.'

But can *Dyson Holdings Ltd v Fox* be distinguished? The county court judge thought it could. In the note of his judgment he said:

> 'One feature not present in any of those cases was that Mr Lucas was a married man, and so long as he was a married man he could not become her husband in law, and I think that is a very important factor. He deliberately chose to remain a married man. Each remained independent of the other; each usually used his or her own name, Lucas or Sullivan. The Lucases and Sullivans were Catholics, and deliberately chose not to get a divorce after 1969. This is not an easy case in which to apply the test, but I come to the conclusion that the defendant was not a member of Mrs Sullivan's family, indeed could not become a member of her family so long as he remained a married man. If the ordinary man was aware of all the circumstances, he would say they were not members of the same family. Mr Lucas never got himself in a position to marry Mrs Sullivan. The facts have to be weighed. Mr Lucas remained a married man, he was never a member of Mrs Sullivan's family. The conclusion I reach is that Mr Lucas was not a member of Mrs Sullivan's family.'

As I read his judgment he denied Mr Lucas the protection of the statute because (1) usually he and Mrs Sullivan kept their own names and so remained independent of each other and (2) Mr Lucas deliberately chose not to get a divorce from his legal wife and so get into a position to marry Mrs Sullivan. The county court judge seems to have regarded his married status as an absolute bar to his being in fact a member of her family. He was there accepting the argument of counsel for the plaintiff, plainly recorded in the judge's note of the evidence and argument and repeated in this court, that a man cannot have two families; Mr Lucas had a family in Ireland and not having legally rid himself of his wife and children in Ireland he could not be a member of another family here.

That is, in my view, a plain error of law. The ordinary man often has two families, one by his first wife and another by his second, and often has, or at any rate knows, a man who has one by his wife and another by his mistress. I can see no legal impossibility in a man being a member of both families, though he will have difficulty in fact in residing with more than one and it will be impossible in fact for him to reside with more than

one, as required by the statute, if he is to succeed to a protected tenancy. And the question whether he is a member of his mistress's family cannot any longer be decided a
by any moral preference for the family to which his lawful wife belongs. There is no authority on the point, although it could have been taken in *Trowchurch Ltd v Pammer* (28th March 1980, unreported) in the Bloomsbury and Marylebone County Court, and may yet be taken on the appeal to this court which we were told is pending. But I agree with the submission of counsel for Mr Lucas that there is no rule of law that a man who remains married throughout the time he has been living with an original tenant other b
than his wife may not become a member of the original tenant's family.

This error of law entitles us to reverse the judge's decision if he was wrong in treating Mr Lucas's married status, and the retention of their own names by himself and Mrs Sullivan with that one exception, as features of their relationship inconsistent with a family relationship between them in the eyes of an ordinary 1977 man.

I agree with the judge that Mr Lucas's remaining married is an important factor, as c
may be the retention of the couple's own names. But not in this case. For both factors are of importance, in my judgment, only as indications of independence and instability. The retention of the woman's name may indicate both, as I think it did in *Helby v Rafferty*, but, if it does not indicate either, it has little relevance to the right answer to the ordinary man's question. Without the guidance given in *Dyson v Fox*, I might have thought that both factors might influence his answer, but I understand the d
ratio of the majority decision as holding that a union between a man and a woman, which in all the circumstances, known and unknown to the ordinary man, looks permanent and stable to him, creates a family unit and both parties are members of it, whether or not it consists of more than those two. It was held long ago by the Divisional Court that a husband could be a member of his wife's family (in fact there was a young child, but the decision does not seem to have turned on that fact): see *Salter v Lask* [1925] e
1 KB 584. And we are prevented by *Dyson Holdings Ltd v Fox* from regarding children as necessary to constitute a family, although I think we are still permitted to regard their absence as a possible indication of impermanence. The question 'Is there a family?' or 'Has he a family?' is the wrong question, because there 'a family' means or may mean children. If this approach is right, and Mr Lucas's decision to remain married is not an absolute impediment to membership of another woman's family but a factor to be f
weighed with all others including their decision to keep their own names in every part of their life together but one, I am of opinion that it was plainly outweighed by his refusal to give Mrs Sullivan up and return to his wife and by his continuing to live with Mrs Sullivan till she died some eight years later. The judge must have given these two factors of names and marriage far too much weight or this refusal to be reconciled far too little, or he could not have answered the relevant question as he did. These two factors, g
in my judgment, are of far too little weight to contradict the evidence that this was a lasting, indeed a lifelong, association, more permanent and stable than many marriages including Mr Lucas's own; and I doubt if the judge could have given them enough weight to justify his decision had he not fallen into the error of regarding Mr Lucas's membership of Mrs Sullivan's family as incompatible with his married status.

Holding this man to be a member of this woman's family will not promote the h
support of marriage or the reduction of illicit unions, which were among the avowed objects of divorce reform stated in the preamble to Sir Alan Herbert's Matrimonial Causes Act 1937. But, though these objects might have influenced the judges who decided *Gammans v Ekins*, they had lost their relevance to the interpretation of this provision of the Rent Acts a quarter of a century later. Their irrelevance in other fields has been recognised by Parliament, as demonstrated by the Domestic Violence and j
Matrimonial Proceedings Act 1976, s 2(2), the Supplementary Benefits Act 1976, Sch 1, para 3(1)(*b*) and, I would add, more directly by the concept of a family in the Family Income Supplements Act 1970, s 1(1), which provides:

> 'For the purposes of this Act a family shall consist of the following members of a household—(*a*) one man or single woman engaged, and normally engaged, in

remunerative full-time work; and (*b*) if the person mentioned in paragraph (*a*) *a* above is a man and the household includes a woman to whom he is married or who lives with him as his wife, that woman; and (*c*) the child or children whose requirements are provided for, in whole or in part, by the person or either of the persons mentioned in the preceding paragraphs.'

The emphasis which in 1976 this court in *Dyson Holdings Ltd v Fox* put on the permanence and stability of an extra-marital relationship in constituting a family for the *b* purpose of this provision led the court to regard the county court judge's answer that Miss Fox was not a member of Mr Wright's family as plainly wrong. I cannot find enough difference between her position and that of Mr Lucas to allow of Judge Granville Slack's answer that he was not a member of Mrs Sullivan's family being right.

I do not find it helpful to consider a couple's adoption of a common name to conceal the fact that the parties are not married to be a 'masquerading' (Asquith LJ's term in *c* *Gamman v Ekins* [1950] 2 All ER 140 at 142, [1950] 2 KB 328 at 331) or a 'charade' (Stamp LJ's term in *Helby v Rafferty* [1978] 3 All ER 1016 at 1020, [1979] 1 WLR 13 at 191). Counsel for Mrs Watson argued that it was essential to a family relationship that there should be a public assumption of the status of marriage by passing off or holding out; but though that may indicate an intention that the association shall last its absence does not negative that intention and would be less likely to be thought to do so with every year *d* that goes by.

It was held in *Brock v Wollams* [1949] 1 All ER 715, [1949] 2 KB 388 that, where the parties could not have been granted a legal adoption, a de facto adoption might constitute a family for the purpose of succession to a statutory tenancy. So a married couple who keep their own names may constitute a family de facto when there was not and could not be a marriage de jure. If the de facto cohabitation is strong enough to repel an attempt *e* by the other party to the legal marriage to put an end to the cohabitation, as in this case, I do not see why it should be prevented from being, as well as being treated as, a family relationship in its ordinary popular meaning because the couple did not pose as married persons. In spite of their separate names they could, by the time Mrs Sullivan came to die, have come to be regarded as husband and wife, 'as if they were married'. That is how Mrs Sullivan's son told the judge that he regarded them when Mr Lucas moved in; and *f* that I suspect was Mrs Watson's view of them which led her to pretend in the witness box that, though she had been living in the house since 1962, she knew nothing of his living in her basement flat until a few months before Mrs Sullivan's death.

The ordinary man has to consider whether a man or a woman is a member of a family in the light of the facts, and whatever may have been held before *Dyson Holdings Ltd v Fox* I do not think a judge, putting himself in the place of the ordinary man, can consider an *g* association which has every outward appearance of marriage, except the false pretence of being married, as not constituting a family. If it looks like a marriage in the old and perhaps obsolete sense of a lifelong union, with nothing casual or temporary about it, it is a family until the House of Lords declares (as counsel for Mrs Watson reserves his right to ask them to declare) that the case of *Dyson Holdings Ltd v Fox* was wrongly decided because the reasoning of the majority was wrong. The time has gone by when the courts *h* can hold such a union not to be 'familial' simply because the parties to it do not pretend to be married in due form of law.

I have no wish to extend *Dyson Holdings Ltd v Fox*, but we are bound to follow it; nor do I wish to differ from an experienced county court judge on the meaning and application of what ought to be plain English words, but we are bound to move with the times.

j I would accordingly hold, not without reluctance, that the judge's decision was wrong. I would allow the appeal and declare that Mr Lucas was a member of Mrs Sullivan's family.

OLIVER LJ. The question raised on this appeal is a short and at first sight a simple one. It is whether, in the circumstances which have already been stated in the judgment of Stephenson LJ, the defendant who had lived on terms of intimacy for some twenty years with the tenant of the basement flat at the plaintiff's premises at 21 St Julian's Road, *a* London NW6 until the tenant's death in 1977 was a member of the tenant's family. If he was, then, under the provisions of the Rent Act 1977, Sch 1, para 3, he is entitled to continue to occupy the flat as a statutory tenant in succession to her. If he was not, as the judge held, then the plaintiff is entitled to possession of the flat and the appeal must be dismissed.

The particular provision under which Mr Lucas claims to remain in the premises as *b* the successor to the original tenant is one which has formed part of the Rent Act legislation in substantially, although not exactly, the same form since 1920 and it has been the subject of judicial construction in a number of cases. One of the curiosities of the statutory provisions is that, while they cater expressly for the position of the widow of the tenant residing with him at his death, there is no corresponding reference to a widower, so that if he is given any protection at all it is solely as a member of his late *c* wife's 'family'. It was, however, held as long ago as 1925 that the expression 'family' was apt to include the surviving husband of the tenant (see *Salter v Lask* [1925] 1 KB 584).

The matter was taken a step further in 1949 in *Brock v Wollams* [1949] 1 All ER 715, [1949] 2 KB 388 in which the expression 'family' was held to include an informally adopted child and in 1953 in *Hawes v Evenden* [1953] 2 All ER 737, [1953] 1 WLR 1169, a unanimous Court of Appeal held that an unmarried lady who had lived with the tenant *d* for 12 years prior to his death and had had two children by him was entitled, in the circumstances that she and the children were living together with him as one family unit, to be considered a member of his family. It is clear, however, that in that case the conclusive features were the birth of the children and the establishment and continuance of what the ordinary man would regard as a single family unit.

The court there applied the test propounded by Cohen LJ in *Brock v Wollams*, namely, *e* would the ordinary man answer Yes or No to the question whether the person claiming the protection of the Act was a member of the tenant's 'family'. *Hawes v Evenden* answered a question which had been left unanswered in the earlier decision of *Gammans v Ekins* [1950] 2 All ER 140, [1950] 2 KB 328. In that case, in which the position was uncomplicated by the birth of any children, the Court of Appeal firmly and unanimously rejected a claim by a man who, although unmarried, had lived with the tenant for some *f* years prior to her death as her husband to be a member of her family.

Had the matter rested there, the instant case would have presented no difficulty and, speaking for myself, I should, even unassisted by authority, have required little argument to persuade me to the same conclusion as that reached in *Gammans v Ekins*. In 1976 however a very similar case came before the Court of Appeal again in *Dyson Holdings Ltd v Fox* [1975] 3 All ER 1030, [1976] QB 503. That was a very hard case of an elderly lady *g* of 74 who, although unmarried in fact, had lived with the tenant to all outward appearances as his wife for 40 years until his death in 1961. The 21 years immediately preceding his death were spent in the premises of which possession was sought and she had continued to reside there after his death up to the date of the hearing. She had taken the tenant's name and, as Lord Denning MR expressed it, 'In every respect they were man and wife save that they had not gone through a ceremony of marriage'. The court *h* held unanimously that she was a member of the tenant's family and the majority decision (that of James and Bridge LJJ) was based on two propositions, that is to say, first that the word 'family' fell to be construed, not according to its accepted meaning at the time when the legislation was enacted, but, at any rate as I read the majority judgments, according to its accepted meaning at the time of the hearing, and second that there had, since *Gammans v Ekins*, taken place such a change in social attitudes as to justify the *j* conclusion that the ordinary man would, given a sufficient degree of apparent stability and permanence in an extra-marital relationship, say that the parties to it were members of one another's 'family'. In this way the court, whilst accepting that *Gammans v Ekins* was binding on it, felt able to distinguish that case from the case before it. One of the curious facts of the case is that, although the tenant in that case had died in 1961 (which would have appeared, prima facie, to be the appropriate time for deciding whether the defendant was a member of his family), the court seems to have disregarded the fact that between 1961 and the hearing the Court of Appeal had, in 1964, considered the case of *Gammans v Ekins* in *Ross v Collins* [1964] 1 All ER 861, [1964] 1 WLR 425 and had unanimously followed and applied it. *Ross v Collins* was cited in *Dyson* but does not appear to have been referred to in any of the judgments. So what the court actually did in 1975 was to apply to the word 'family' in the context of the tenant's death in 1961 a meaning contrary to that which had subsequently been applied to it as the correct meaning by the Court of Appeal in 1964.

It is, I think, true to say that the ratio of the *Dyson* case has not met with universal approbation. In particular in *Helby v Rafferty* [1978] 3 All ER 1016, [1979] 1 WLR 13 the Court of Appeal expressed certain reservations about the approach to construction adopted by the court in *Dyson*. However, it recognised that *Dyson* was binding on it (although it distinguished the case before it on the facts).

Although I think that in the light of *Ross v Collins* it is arguable (I put it no higher) that there are in fact two conflicting decisions of the Court of Appeal as to the meaning to be applied to the word 'family', this was not argued before us and I am content to adopt as the starting position in the instant case that the *Dyson* case is binding on this court. The only question is whether the county court judge was right in distinguishing it. What he had to do was to ask himself the question: 'In the circumstances of the instant case would the ordinary man, cognisant of the relevant facts, say that the defendant in *this* case was a member of the tenant's family?'; and in asking himself that question he had to bear in mind the way in which the matter was put by Bridge LJ in the *Dyson* case when he said ([1975] 3 All ER 1030 at 1036, [1976] QB 503 at 513):

> 'The ordinary man in 1975 would, in my opinion, certainly say that the parties to such a union, provided it had the appropriate degree of apparent permanence and stability, were members of a single family whether they had children or not.'

The instant case is markedly similar in many respects to the *Dyson* case. The parties had shared the same dwelling for many years, each contributing to the household expenses, and there was every outward indication that, had it not been for the tenant's death, they would have gone on living together indefinitely. It differs from the *Dyson* case, however, in three respects. First, it was the female partner who was the tenant and the male who survived. Second, neither party sought, save on occasions when they went together to, or on outings organised by, a club of which the defendant was a member, to convey the impression that their relationship was anything other than an extra-marital one. The tenant was a widow and continued to be known by her married name of 'Mrs Sullivan'. The defendant continued to be known as 'Mr Lucas'. Third, whereas the parties in the *Dyson* case were a bachelor and a spinster respectively and thus able to marry if they wished, the defendant in the instant case was, at all material times, a married man with a wife and child living in Ireland. His evidence was that his wife had left him about a year after his marriage (which had taken place some five years before he went to live with Mrs Sullivan) taking the child of the marriage with her. She had two further children by another man in Ireland but in about 1969 she came back to him seeking a reconciliation which he declined. He continued to live with Mrs Sullivan and his wife returned to Ireland. She, apparently, was a Roman Catholic and did not want a divorce, and he took no steps to obtain one although he was aware that he could petition on the ground of 5 years' separation.

It was this last matter to which the judge attached particular importance. I do not think that it was argued that the first ground of distinction which I have mentioned carried any weight and the judge does not mention it. That clearly, I think, must be right because the test enunciated in the *Dyson* case clearly cannot depend for its application on whether the survivor is male or female. He does appear to have taken some account of the fact that they normally and habitually used their own names. But the matter to which he attached very great importance was the fact that the defendant remained, at his own election, a married man. He said: a

> 'So long as he was a married man he could not become her husband in law, and I think that is a very important factor. He deliberately chose to remain a married man. Each remained independent of the other, each usually used his or her own name, Lucas or Sullivan. The Lucases and Sullivans were Catholics, and deliberately chose not to get a divorce after 1969.' b

The judge then continued (and this is the passage in his judgment which is particularly criticised by counsel for the defendant):

> 'This is not an easy case in which to apply the test [that is the test of what the ordinary man would conclude] but I come to the conclusion that the defendant was not a member of Mrs Sullivan's family, indeed could not become a member of her c family so long as he remained a married man.'

What is said about this is that this shows that the judge misdirected himself because, instead of looking, as the *Dyson* case directs him to do, at the question of whether as a matter of *fact* the relationship was one of such stability and permanence as to justify the inference that the parties were members of each other's 'family', he considered only the d legal impediment to their actually marrying and treated that, as a matter of *law*, as an insurmountable impediment. It is, I think, dangerous to seek to construe a judgment, and, particularly, an extempore judgment, as if it were a statute and I do not, for my part, put on it the interpretation for which the defendant contends. The reference to the inability of the defendant to become a member of the tenant's family appears to have been something of an afterthought and I do not read it as more than a consideration e which the judge treated as reinforcing the conclusion of fact at which he had arrived. One has to bear in mind that this passage came at the conclusion of two pages of notes of judgment in which the judge exhaustively reviewed the facts which had been proved, a review which would have been wholly unnecessary if the judge had really taken the view that a decision in the defendant's favour was precluded by what would, on this view, have been the only relevant fact, namely that he remained married to someone else. f That it formed a very important factor in his decision, however, is beyond doubt, and the real question on this appeal is, as it seems to me, whether he was right to attribute any weight to it and, if so, whether he attached undue weight to it. Now the essential question was one of fact: was the relationship one which displayed the requisite qualities of *apparent* permanence and stability not simply to constitute what the ordinary man might categorise as a permanent relationship but to constitute what he would categorise g as a *de facto family* relationship? In reaching the answer to that question I do not think that the judge was wrong to take into account both the manner in which the parties to the relationship treated themselves and their actual status. In the instant case the defendant and Mrs Sullivan never appear (except for the purely temporary purpose of satisfying the social susceptibilities of the other members of the defendant's club) to have sought to convey to the world at large any impression that they were other than what h they were in fact, that is to say, two people who were not husband and wife but had chosen to live together. As I read the learned judge's judgment he did attach some significance to this and I do not, for my part, think that he was wrong to do so. Whilst it may seem startling at first to attribute to persons who engage in a masquerade a higher status than that attributable to persons who do not seek to pose as other than what in fact they are, such a step is, to some extent, inherent in the very process of attributing the j status of 'family' to those who do not in fact possess it. Normally one expects members of a family to be related by blood or marriage, and the application of the term to what are loosely called 'de facto' relationships involves the artificial attribution to the persons concerned of a blood or de jure relationship which they do not in fact possess. In reaching a decision, therefore, whether the case is a proper one to make such an attribution, having regard to what the ordinary man would conclude, it cannot I think be irrelevant to consider how the parties treated themselves and whether they themselves manifested any desire to be so treated vis-à-vis their friends and neighbours by publicly assuming the appearance and incidents of a family unit. If they themselves openly treated themselves as engaged only in a concubinage which each was free to continue or not and from which each was free to withdraw at will and without obligation, then this does appear to me to be at least a factor to be taken into account in considering whether (to apply the test propounded by Bridge LJ in the *Dyson* case) the relationship had a sufficient degree of apparent permanence. That is not to say that pretence is a virtue but merely that one should not be too ready to accord to persons in the position of the defendant and Mrs Sullivan in the instant case the incidents of a status which they never sought to claim for themselves. Equally, they did not seek to put themselves in a position in which they could commit themselves de jure to a permanent relationship involving mutual obligations although they knew that they could do so and the judge inferred from this that they had elected to preserve their independence. Of course, the same could be said of the parties in the *Dyson* case, and thus it is argued that there is no valid distinction between the two cases. In the ultimate analysis, however, the question is: what would the ordinary man conclude in the circumstances of the particular case? Here the defendant had, at all material times, a de jure wife who was alive and who, as a matter of law, constituted, with the child of his marriage, his family, so that the case raises directly for decision the question which was postulated by counsel in the *Dyson* case [1976] QB 503 at 505 and not specifically answered by the Court of Appeal. That position he elected to continue, and the ordinary man could, I think, be pardoned if he concluded that the defendant was intending, for whatever reason, social, religious, economic or merely idiosyncratic, to preserve the familial status which the law and his church had imposed on him by his marriage rather than to substitute a different and de facto familial relationship to which he was not prepared to commit himself de jure or even as a matter of outward semblance. Counsel for the defendant has drawn our attention to the provisions of the Supplementary Benefits Act 1976 and the Domestic Violence and Matrimonial Proceedings Act 1976 to support the submission that Parliament, in concurrence with current social mores, now recognises extra-marital relationships such as that with which the instant case is concerned as deserving of the law's protection. But I am not, speaking for myself, much impressed by that argument, because the question is not whether the law will now countenance relationships which might previously have been disapproved, but whether the ordinary man would regard the relationship between a man and his concubine of many years as being a 'family' relationship. Indeed the argument is a double-edged one, for if we are to have reference to other statutes, it can with equal force be pointed out that when Parliament in 1975 came to extend the ambit of the Inheritance (Family Provision) Act 1938 to persons in the position of, for instance, Mrs Sullivan in the instant case, it felt it necessary to alter the title to the Inheritance (Provision for Family *and Dependants*) Act. I cannot help feeling that if the defendant had, for instance, gone to a solicitor in 1976 in order to have a will prepared and had been asked 'Have you any family?' his answer would have been, 'Yes, I have a wife and child in Ireland, but I have not seen them for years and I want to leave my property to a lady with whom I am living.'

Essentially every case of this kind turns on its own facts and the impression that these facts make on the mind of the judge assuming for the purpose the mantle of the ordinary man. Speaking for myself I would regard the decision in the *Dyson* case as one which rested on its own peculiar facts and as standing at the very limit of any ordinarily accepted or acceptable definition of a family relationship. I would certainly not regard it as establishing a principle which is susceptible of further extension or which ought to be extended. The judge in the instant case had the difficult task of applying to the facts before him a test which, though neither an easy one nor a certain one, is certainly one which required him to consider all the available factors. The decision was essentially one which depended on the inferences to be drawn from all of the facts before him, which included the fact that the defendant was and remained by choice married to a lady who was living at the material time and who was the mother of his only child. a

If and so far as the judge was of opinion that the continued existence of the defendant's marriage was, in itself, and by itself, an absolute answer in law to his claim, I respectfully disagree. I think, however, that it was one factor, and a not unimportant factor, to be taken into account, although I accept that a man may sometimes have two families. One possible inference to be drawn from it was that, however agreeable and convenient his relationship with Mrs Sullivan may have been, he was not prepared to make himself b
responsible for her maintenance and support indefinitely or to put himself in a position in which he might have become susceptible to pressure to convert the relationship into a permanent one by marrying her. I have to confess to more than one change of mind during the course of the very full arguments presented to us, but I have concluded, not without hesitation, that I am not prepared to say that the judge, who saw and heard the witnesses, in making his assessment as a whole and in reaching the conclusion which he c
did reach on all the facts, was wrong to attribute weight to the factors which I have mentioned. They are, in my judgment, factors which do distinguish the instant case from the *Dyson* case, and I would dismiss the appeal.

SIR DAVID CAIRNS. I do not find the test of Cohen LJ as helpful in this case as it was in *Brock v Wollams* [1949] 1 All ER 715, [1949] 2 KB 388. To the question 'Was Mr Lucas d
a member of Mrs Sullivan's family?', I have no idea what 'an ordinary man' would answer. Stephenson LJ would answer Yes and Oliver LJ would answer No.

I agree with both my brethren that we should proceed on the basis that *Dyson Holdings Ltd v Fox* [1975] 3 All ER 1030, [1976] QB 503 was rightly decided, though I respectfully share the doubts that have been expressed about that decision and I recognise the force of the reasoning of Oliver LJ based on *Ross v Collins* [1964] 1 All ER 1016, [1964] 1 WLR e
425.

I have reached the conclusion that this case cannot sensibly be differentiated from *Dyson Holdings Ltd v Fox.* I attach little or no importance to the continued use by Mr Lucas and Mrs Sullivan of different surnames. It is the relations between the man and the woman that are relevant rather than the appearance that they present to the public. In this case the permanence of the relationship is not in doubt. f

That Mr Lucas had a wife in Ireland is to my mind, having regard to the brevity of cohabitation, the long separation and the refusal by Mr Lucas of reconciliation, neither an absolute bar to his being considered a member of Mrs Sullivan's family nor a weighty reason for finding as a fact that he should not be so considered. Even if he could be regarded as a member of his wife's family (which I doubt) I agree with Stephenson LJ that it is perfectly possible for a man to be a member of more than one family. g

In my opinion the judge was wrong in law in holding that the very fact of Mr Lucas's continuing state of marriage prevented him being a member of Mrs Sullivan's family. If this part of his judgment cannot strictly be considered to be one of the rationes decidendi I think it coloured his approach to the question of fact and led him to attach excessive weight to that matter.

For these reasons I agree with Stephenson LJ that the appeal should be allowed. h

Appeal allowed. Leave to appeal to the House of Lords granted.

Solicitors: *Powell Magrath & Co* (for Mr Lucas); *Sylvester, Amiel & Co* (for Mrs Watson).

Patricia Hargrove Barrister.

a Wynne v Wynne and Jeffers

COURT OF APPEAL, CIVIL DIVISION
BRIDGE, CUMMING-BRUCE AND EVELEIGH LJJ
16th MAY 1980

b *Divorce – Financial provision – Application – Investigation by registrar – Extent of registrar's jurisdiction – Petitioner suspecting that respondent receiving financial support from person named as co-respondent in divorce suit – Petitioner applying for order that co-respondent file affidavit of means in ancillary proceedings – Whether registrar having jurisdiction to make order – Matrimonial Causes Rules 1977 (SI 1977 No 344), r 77 (5).*

c Shortly after separating from his wife the husband, who was in lucrative employment, went to live with Miss J in a luxurious house in Knightsbridge. The wife petitioned for a divorce, naming Miss J as co-respondent, and, in addition, applied for ancillary relief. She was granted a decree of divorce, but before the hearing of her application for ancillary relief the husband lost his job. He did not however stop living in the house in Knightsbridge. The wife thought that he was being supported financially by Miss J and
d that it would be relevant for the court to know the extent of the support when considering the matters which it had to take into account under s 25(1)(*a*) and (*b*) of the Matrimonial Causes Act 1973. The wife therefore applied for an order under r 77(5)[a] of the Matrimonial Causes Rules 1977 requiring Miss J to file an affidavit of her means for the purposes of the ancillary proceedings.

e **Held** – On the true construction of r 77(5) of the 1977 rules, the court had no jurisdiction to order a stranger to the lis to file an affidavit of means. It followed that as Miss J was not a party to the ancillary proceedings she could not be required to file such an affidavit, the fact that she had been a party to the divorce proceedings being irrelevant. Accordingly the wife's application would be dismissed (see p 662 *b c f*, p 663 *f j* and p 664 *d* to *j*, post).

f

Notes

For affidavits of property and income in ancillary relief proceedings after divorce, see 13 Halsbury's Laws (4th Edn) paras 1070–1071.

For the Matrimonial Causes Act 1973, s 25, see 43 Halsbury's Statutes (3rd Edn) 567.

For the Matrimonial Causes Rules 1977, r 77, see 10 Halsbury's Statutory Instruments
g (4th Reissue) 266.

Cases referred to in judgments

West v West (1972) Times, 16th December.

Wilkinson v Wilkinson (1979) 10 Fam Law 48, 123 Sol Jo 752.

h **Appeal**

The wife, the petitioner in divorce proceedings against the respondent husband, appealed against an order of Bush J, dated 22nd February 1980, dismissing her appeal against an order of Mr Registrar Kenworthy, dated 27th December 1979, whereby he dismissed an application which she made, in the course of ancillary proceedings for financial relief against the husband, for an order that the person named as co-respondent in the divorce
j proceedings should file an affidavit of means. The facts are set out in the judgment of Bridge LJ.

---

a Rule 77(5) is set out at p 661 *d*, post

Joseph Jackson QC and *J J Davies* for the wife.
John E A Samuels for the husband.
J P Harris QC and *Christopher Sumner* for the co-respondent.

BRIDGE LJ. This is an appeal from an order of Bush J made on 22nd February 1980 dismissing an appeal from Mr Registrar Kenworthy on 27th December 1979 whereby he refused an application by the petitioner wife, in the course of ancillary proceedings for financial relief against the respondent husband, for an order that the lady co-respondent should file an affidavit of her means. As the sole point in the appeal is whether the court has jurisdiction to make such an order as that which the petitioner wife was seeking, it will be possible to deal with the matter quite shortly. Both the registrar and the judge held that there was no such jurisdiction. It is against the judge's decision to that effect that the present appeal is brought.

The parties are American. They were married in June 1960 in the United States. There are two children, sons born in 1966 and 1968. The parties have lived in England since 1967 and since 1972 in Maida Vale. In February 1978 the husband left the wife and set up house with the co-respondent in Knightsbridge. On 25th May 1978 the wife petitioned initially for judicial separation on the ground of her husband's adultery. In due course the petition was amended to seek dissolution of the marriage and on 24th May 1979 a decree nisi was pronounced on the husband's admitted adultery, albeit with no finding of adultery proved against the co-respondent. The decree was made absolute on 14th September 1979.

At the time when the parties separated, the husband was in lucrative employment and, when that state of affairs still subsisted on 16th March 1979, Mr Registrar Kenworthy made an order for maintenance pending suit in favour of the wife in the sum of £6,000 a year and in favour of each child in the sum of £3,000 a year. Very shortly after that order was made, the husband's employment was terminated in circumstances which have aroused considerable suspicion on the part of the wife and her advisers. The husband continued to comply with the order for maintenance for a time but ceased, I think, in about August 1979. On 8th November 1979 an order was made suspending payment as from 1st October 1979. Meanwhile the husband continued to live in Knightsbridge with the co-respondent in an extremely luxurious house or apartment. He says that these premises belong to his former employers and that he is under threat of eviction from them, but so far that threat has not materialised. The wife's case is that he is being supported to a substantial extent by the co-respondent who herself has a business which she carries on.

The basis of the application for an order that the co-respondent should make an affidavit of her means is that her means would be relevant to two questions which, in the wife's application for ancillary relief, the court will have to consider under s 25(1)(*a*) and (*b*) of the Matrimonial Causes Act 1973, namely the income and earning capacity, property and other financial resources which each of the parties to the marriage has or is likely to have in the foreseeable future and the financial needs, obligations and responsibilities which each of the parties to the marriage has or is likely to have in the foreseeable future.

When the wife's application for the order in dispute was originally made, it was made on the basis that she was entitled to know what the co-respondent's means were in order to minimise any suggestion that might be made by the husband that she was a burden to him. Now the position is reversed, and it is now contended that the relevance of the co-respondent's means is to show the extent to which she is able to support, and is in fact supporting or contributing to the support of, the respondent husband.

In the end, the issue of jurisdiction raises a short point on the construction of the Matrimonial Causes Rules 1977, SI 1977 No 344. It is to those rules that I now turn. By r 73(2) and (3) it is provided as follows:

> '(2) Where a respondent or a petitioner is served with a notice in Form 11 or 13 in respect of an application for ancillary relief, not being an application to which

> rule 74 or 75 applies [I interpose in parenthesis that this is not such an application], then, unless the parties are agreed upon the terms of the proposed order, he shall, within 14 days after service of the notice, file an affidavit in answer to the application containing full particulars of his property and income . . .
>
> '(3) Within 14 days after service of any affidavit under paragraph (2) or within such other time as the court may fix, the applicant shall file an affidavit in reply containing full particulars of his property and income.'

So the effect of that rule is that, as soon as proceedings are instituted for ancillary financial relief, both spouses are under an obligation within the stated limits of time under the rule to file affidavits containing 'full particulars' of their property and income.

I do not think I need refer to anything in r 74 or r 75, which, as I have said, are not applicable to the present case and I can go straight on to r 77 and read paras (4) and (5):

> '(4) Any party to an application for ancillary relief may by letter require any other party to give further information concerning any matter contained in any affidavit filed by or on behalf of that other party or any other relevant matter, or to furnish a list of relevant documents or to allow inspection of any such document, and may, in default of compliance by such other party, apply to the registrar for directions.'

Then we come to what is in the end the crucial paragraph:

> '(5) At the hearing of an application for ancillary relief the registrar shall, subject to rules 78, 79, 80 and 81, investigate the allegations made in support of and in answer to the application, and may take evidence orally and may order the attendance of any person for the purpose of being examined or cross-examined, and may at any stage of the proceedings order the discovery and production of any document or require further affidavits.'

Before approaching the construction of that paragraph on which in the end this appeal turns, it is right that I should refer to two decided cases which have been drawn to our attention by counsel for the wife. *West v West* (1972) Times, 16th December is reported very shortly. It was a case where a dissolution was sought on the ground of five years' separation and was opposed by the wife on the ground of grave financial hardship. The Times report records that the judge in the course of the proceedings made an order that an affidavit should be made by the lady with whom the husband was then living, disclosing her income and financial resources. There is nothing to indicate that the court was presented with any argument on the rule which then applied, which was in similar terms, so far as material, to the rule with which we are concerned, to the effect that under the rule there was no jurisdiction in the judge to make such an order as he did make.

A much more recent decision was by Booth J, *Wilkinson v Wilkinson* (1979) 10 Fam Law 48, where she was asked to make, and did make, an order at the instance of the respondent wife that the petitioner husband's second wife, whom he had married since the divorce proceedings, should make an affidavit of her means. In that case the petitioner husband was not represented by counsel. Although the judge pays tribute to the skill with which the husband had presented his own case, it again does not appear from her judgment, of which we have a transcript, that the point of jurisdiction now raised before us was canvassed there. What was canvassed there was the question whether the affidavit of means which the original wife was seeking from the new wife was one which would properly be relevant. The judge resolved that question affirmatively and therefore made the order requiring it.

I do not regard either of those cases, which would not in any event, of course, be binding on this court, as having much, if any, significance in throwing light on the point which we are called on to decide, since, as I have indicated, it does not appear that in either of them the point was argued. It is, of course, perfectly clear from the language of r 77(5) that when it comes to the effective hearing of this wife's claim for ancillary financial relief the co-respondent can be ordered to attend and to give evidence, to be examined or cross-examined, but the critical question is whether the concluding words of the rule on their true construction permit an order to be made now that she should make an affidavit of her means. I will read those concluding words again: 'and may at any stage of the proceedings order the discovery and production of any document or require further affidavits.' They follow the comma after the word 'cross-examined'. It is to be observed that this paragraph falls into two parts because the whole of the rule down to the word 'cross-examined' is concerned with the proceedings at the hearing of the application, whereas the concluding words, which I have reread, are, as they expressly state, concerned with the power of the court exercisable at any stage of the proceedings.

Having been much assisted by the argument of counsel on both sides, in the end I have reached a clear conclusion in this matter that the registrar and the judge were right in the view that they reached that they had no jurisdiction to order an affidavit to be made by the co-respondent in this case. Counsel for the wife has put his argument boldly on the footing that the rule gives power to the court to order an affidavit to be made by any third party; any person, that is to say, who is not a party to the proceedings. In a subsidiary argument he did rely on the circumstance that this co-respondent was a party to the suit. In my judgment that really is quite irrelevant. Apart from the fact that there was no finding against her in the suit, on any view she cannot properly be regarded as a party to the lis which is involved in ancillary proceedings for financial relief. So, in my judgment, counsel is right to put his argument on the broad proposition that the rule empowers an order to be made against any stranger requiring that stranger to make an affidavit, because only if it is so widely construed is it available for the purpose for which it is invoked in this case.

I think the reasons which have brought me to the conclusion that the registrar and the judge were right in giving the words of the rule the restrictive construction they did give them may fairly be put under five headings. First, it seems to me that the whole phrase 'may at any stage of the proceedings order the discovery and production of any document or require further affidavits' must be read in the same sense. To put it conveniently in the form in which the question was posed by counsel for the husband, the question is whether one should read that entire phrase as if it concluded with the words 'from the parties' or with the words 'from any person'. I have no doubt whatsoever that the power which the rule confers of ordering discovery of any document must be understood as a power which is limited to exercise against one of the parties to the lis.

Second, in my judgment, one is entitled to draw a significant conclusion from the contrast between the concluding phrase of the paragraph and the phrase which immediately precedes it, because the phrase immediately preceding it includes the words in terms 'may order the attendance of any person for the purpose of being examined or cross-examined'. If the draftsman of the rule thought it necessary to include that phrase 'of any person' in order to make clear the breadth and scope of the power which he was conferring, then, had he intended the same breadth and scope to attach to the power to order discovery and production of documents or further affidavits, I should have expected him to say so in terms.

The third, and perhaps most significant, pointer, in my judgment, to the proper construction of this rule lies in this consideration, that it will only be in the rarest cases that it will be possible to say that a person who is a stranger to the lis involved in a party's claim to ancillary financial relief ought, in the words which are used in r 73, as the spouses are required to do, to make an affidavit containing full particulars of his or her property and income. It will only be in the rarest cases where it will be possible to say that full information about property and income of the third party, whether the third party is a new spouse, a new mistress, a new lover, a rich uncle or a mother or any other friend or relation from whom one of the spouses has expectations, will be relevant to the issue which the court has to consider under s 25 of the 1973 Act. Indeed, at the end of the day, I do not think counsel for the wife in this case was contending that, if the court had jurisdiction, the order which it would be appropriate to make against this co-respondent would be an order that she gave full particulars of her property and income.

In his reply he formulated the order which he was suggesting would define the scope of
a the affidavit which she should be required to make, namely that she should be required
to state from February 1978, the date when she and the husband began cohabiting, what
contributions she had made, in what form and from what source, to the support of the
respondent. But once it is recognised that, if this power is a power to order strangers to
the lis to make affidavits, it will in ninety-nine cases out of a hundred be necessary
carefully to define the scope of the affidavits they are required to make, one is really
b driven to recognise that, so construed, this is an order which empowers the court to
interrogate, in advance of the hearing, a witness who is not a party to the lis. That is such
an exceptional proceeding that I would need the clearest possible statutory language to
drive me to the conclusion that that was what the legislature had intended.

Fourth, it has been pointed out that, whereas only minimal expense, for which a
witness can in any event expect to be recompensed, is involved in attending a hearing as
c a witness, if a witness is a stranger to the lis and is required by such an order as is
suggested should be made here to make an affidavit, that will almost inevitably involve
that witness in incurring a good deal of expense. It is a little difficult to see that such an
order can properly be made and how the witness can be recompensed for that expense.
It may indeed be, if a witness who is required to make a full affidavit of means has
complicated financial affairs on which his or her means depend, that he or she will be
d involved in a very large investigation in order to make full disclosure. Moreover,
however carefully the terms of the order requiring the witness to make an affidavit were
to be formulated, the witness would never under such an order enjoy the same degree of
protection against being required to disclose matters which are not really relevant as he
or she would enjoy giving evidence orally at the hearing. If a witness is simply ordered
to attend a hearing to be examined or cross-examined, each question which is put can be
e the subject of objection if it is not a proper question and does not seek to elicit relevant
information. A blanket order, however carefully formulated, requiring a witness to
make an affidavit covering defined subject matter will always be in danger of requiring
that witness to put in evidence in his or her affidavit more than is strictly relevant and
more than is strictly necessary.

Fifth and finally, it does seem to me that, if one looks simply at the language of these
f concluding words of r 77(5), they bear very much more naturally the restricted
construction for which counsel for the husband and counsel for the co-respondent have
contended, and which the registrar and the judge adopted, than the very wide
construction urged on us by counsel for the wife. I rely particularly on the last two
words of the rule, 'further affidavits'. What are the affidavits further to? Counsel for the
wife submits that 'further affidavits' simply means affidavits in addition to those which
g are already in evidence in the proceedings, affidavits which may come from anybody.
If that was so, I find it very difficult to see what the purpose was of introducing the word
'further'. It would have been perfectly simple to say 'may require affidavits'. To my
mind, in carefully drafted rules such as these, one expects each word to have its own
particular significance. If I ask myself what the significance is of the word 'further' in the
phrase 'require further affidavits' at the end of r 77(5), I find the answer by harking back
h to r 73. Under r 73 both the spouses have been required to make affidavits containing
full particulars of their property and income. If those particulars were not as full as they
ought to be, then further particulars of their property and income would be required,
and, in order that those further particulars should be forthcoming, it is the most natural
phrase in the world to use to say those parties should be required to make 'further
affidavits'.

j For those reasons I have come to the conclusion that the registrar and the judge were
right in the view they took here that they had no jurisdiction. I would dismiss this
appeal.

CUMMING-BRUCE LJ. I agree with the order proposed by Bridge LJ. The power that the court exercises in relation to financial provision is to be collected from s 23 of the Matrimonial Causes Act 1973, and the matters to which the court is to have regard under ss 23 and 24 are to be collected from s 25 of that Act. It is perfectly clear from the words of s 25 that all the circumstances of the case are to be regarded, and matters specifically regarded as possibly being relevant will include the financial resources which each of the parties have or are likely to have in the foreseeable future and their financial needs at present and in the foreseeable future. So where one of the parties, whether the applicant or the respondent to an application for financial provision or property adjustment, is in fact receiving support from a third party which increases his or her resources or reduces his or her needs or, alternatively, if the party is likely to be in that position in the foreseeable future, the facts relevant to such present or foreseeable support or reduction of needs are relevant to the inquiry that is imposed on the court under ss 23, 24, and 25.

In my view, the machinery for the conduct of the investigation is to be collected from the Matrimonial Causes Rules 1977, rr 73 and 74 and for this purpose particularly r 77. Rule 73, as Bridge LJ has explained, empowers the court at the inception of the application to require of the parties the filing of affidavits to give full particulars of property and income. When one comes to r 77, paras (4) and (5) are the relevant paragraphs. Paragraph (4) provides for the eliciting of information from another party, and, like Bridge LJ, I take the term 'other party' to mean parties to the lis with which the application for ancillary relief is concerned. It does not include a third party, even though such third party may be indirectly interested in the result. By para (5) the wide power given, in the last two lines, to the court that it 'may at any stage of the proceedings order the discovery and production of any document or require further affidavits', in my view should not be construed to give the court a power to exercise what I regard as a drastic power against strangers to the suit.

Counsel for the wife made a forceful submission that in many cases it was not practicable to do justice to an applicant or a respondent without the powers now sought. I disagree. I take the view that the first four lines of r 77(5) award the court all the necessary powers to elicit relevant evidence and to see relevant documents. Where I differ from counsel is about the stage at which the court has the power to obtain the information and the method by which the information may be obtained. I cannot find in para (5), as I interpret it, any power to require an affidavit from a stranger to the lis. There is a power on the hearing of the application to take evidence orally, to order the attendance of any person for the purpose of being examined or cross-examined, and, in my view, after the exercise of such powers on the hearing of the application, the court then has the power to take such steps as are necessary with a view to ordering the production of any document.

I fully agree with the reasons given by Bridge LJ with this qualification. My experience in relation to applications for financial provision is limited, but such experience as I have has led me to the view that it is not an infrequent situation for the court to need, in order to do justice, to have full information about the financial resources of third parties who are either spouses or cohabitees to a party to the suit. Where I depart from the submission of counsel is as to the stage and the machinery for obtaining such information when it is necessary. In my view there is no jurisdiction either to order an affidavit of means from a stranger to the suit or to order the more limited affidavit that counsel submitted might be more appropriate, namely an affidavit setting out the factual quantum of support. I too would dismiss this appeal.

EVELEIGH LJ. I agree that the appeal should be dismissed for the five reasons stated by Bridge LJ.

Appeal dismissed.

Solicitors: *Bernard Sheridan & Co* (for the wife); *Jaques & Co* (for the husband); *Plant, Gold & Co* (for the co-respondent).

Avtar S Virdi Esq Barrister.

Re a debtor, ex parte Viscount of the Royal Court of Jersey

CHANCERY DIVISION
GOULDING J
10th, 11th, 12th, 14th, 17th, 18th, 19th, 20th, 21st, 24th, 25th, 26th MARCH, 28th, 29th, 30th APRIL, 1st, 15th MAY 1980

Bankruptcy – Order in aid of British court – Scope of orders in aid – British court having jurisdiction in matters of bankruptcy – Désastre proceedings in Royal Court of Jersey against insolvent debtor – Order initiating proceedings authorising Viscount of Jersey Court to sequestrate all debtor's movable property – Debtor leaving Jersey for England before order made – Jersey court requesting English court to make order in aid and to appoint Viscount as receiver of debtor's movable property in England – Whether jurisdiction to make order in aid – Whether courts of Channel Islands 'British courts' – Whether Jersey court having jurisdiction in 'bankruptcy' in désastre proceedings – Whether English court entitled to scrutinise validity of requesting court's anterior proceedings – Whether désastre proceedings extending to debtor's assets wherever situated and to property acquired after order initiating désastre proceedings – Bankruptcy Act 1914, s 122.

The debtor, an English solicitor, practised as such in Jersey. In 1976 he got into financial difficulties there and on 19th November 1976 an order was made in the Royal Court of Jersey, on the application of a petitioning creditor, declaring the debtor's goods 'en désastre'. The désastre procedure was that most frequently used in Jersey to dispose of an insolvent debtor's affairs. It had points both of resemblance to and of difference from an English bankruptcy. The points of difference included the exclusion in désastre proceedings of the debtor's immovable property from the assets realisable, the absence of provision for discharging a debtor and, possibly, the absence of vesting of the debtor's property in the Viscount of the Royal Court (its principal executive officer) in the same manner as an English bankrupt's property vested in the trustee in bankruptcy. Moreover, the law and practice regarding désastre proceedings were not defined in any written code but merely by judicial practice which was not precisely recorded in writing; there were, however, written rules of the Royal Court defining procedure. The order of 19th November 1976 authorised the Viscount to sequestrate all the debtor's movable property for the benefit of those who might be entitled. The debtor had finally left Jersey some days before the order was made and had come to England where he set up successfully in practice as a solicitor. The Royal Court, pursuant to s 122[a] of the Bankruptcy Act 1914, requested the English bankruptcy court to grant the Viscount an order in aid under s 122, and to appoint him receiver of the debtor's movable property in England, to enable him to discharge his duties under the désastre proceedings in Jersey. A formal application to the English court was made by the Viscount in the terms of the request. The debtor contended that the court was not entitled to make an order in aid because (1) the request for aid did not fall within the terms of s 122 since (i) the Royal Court was not a 'British Court elsewhere', ie outside the United Kingdom, and (ii) in relation to désastre proceedings the Royal Court was not a court having jurisdiction in 'bankruptcy' because désastre proceedings were not 'matters of bankruptcy', (2) the Viscount's rights and duties under the désastre proceedings were limited to the debtor's assets in Jersey, and (3) the désastre proceedings were from the beginning invalid either because the debtor had finally left Jersey before the order of 19th November 1976 was made or because the petitioning creditor was not in all the circumstances qualified as such. The debtor contended alternatively that the Viscount's conduct of the désastre proceedings in Jersey

a Section 122 is set out at p 668, *j* to p 669 *a*, post

disentitled him from assistance from the English court. Finally the debtor contended that if the English court appointed the Viscount receiver of the debtor's assets in England his receivership should be restricted to the debtor's assets in England at the date of the order of 19th November 1976 initiating the désastre proceedings. The Viscount called an expert witness on the law of Jersey, namely the Solicitor General for Jersey, who testified that under Jersey law all the movable assets of a debtor including those situated outside Jersey were caught by désastre proceedings, and that an order en désastre extended to assets acquired by the debtor after that order was made and before the termination of the désastre proceedings. The debtor did not call any expert evidence.

Held – The application for an order in aid would be granted for the following reasons—

(1) The application fell within the terms of s 122 of the 1914 Act because—

(a) the courts of the Channel Islands were 'British courts' within s 122, for the legislative authority of the United Kingdom Parliament over the Channel Islands and the appellate jurisdiction over the islands of the Judicial Committee of the Privy Council were testimony that the Crown had sovereignty over the Channel Islands in right of England (see p 671 *f j* and p 676 *d*, post); dictum of Lord Maugham in *Renouf v Attorney General for Jersey* [1936] 1 All ER at 937–938 and *Minquiers and Ecréhos Case* [1953] ICJ 1 considered;

(b) on the basis that the word 'bankruptcy' in s 122 referred to a class of judicial or administrative process dealing with insolvent persons and not merely to the personal condition of insolvency, the word was to be construed in a wide sense since the section was designed to produce co-operation between courts acting under different systems of law. Accordingly, a form of procedure could be described as 'bankruptcy' within s 122 even though it did not reproduce all the main features of the English procedure of bankruptcy so long as it provided by established legal rules for the administration of the debtor's assets, whether with or without exceptions, with a view to satisfying his debts, whether with or without exceptions. It followed that désastre proceedings were 'matters of bankruptcy' and the Royal Court was therefore a court having jurisdiction in 'bankruptcy' for neither the exclusion in désastre proceedings of the debtor's immovable property, the absence of provision for final discharge of the debtor nor the possibility that the Viscount did not have the proprietary title to the debtor's assets of an English trustee in bankruptcy prevented the désastre proceedings from being a matter of 'bankruptcy'; furthermore, viewed in the round, désastre proceedings had been developed for the very purposes which were essential to bankruptcy in a broad sense and contained nothing repugnant to that conception (see p 675 *e* to *j* and p 676 *a* to *e*, post); dictum of Dodd J in *Re Bolton* [1920] 2 IR at 327 applied.

(2) On the uncontroverted expert evidence to that effect désastre proceedings extended to the debtor's movable assets wherever they were situated. But in any event, as the request to the English court was plainly on its face a request that the Viscount be put in possession of the debtor's assets in England, that was, in the absence of strong evidence to the contrary, sufficient to show that the Royal Court had jurisdiction over those assets and entitled the English court to grant an order in aid of the exercise of that jurisdiction (see p 676 *g* to *j*, post).

(3) Once the English court was satisfied that a request for aid fell within s 122 it did not have any general duty to scrutinise the requesting court's anterior proceedings, although if it were proved that those proceedings were bad under the proper law of the requesting court, or offended against an overriding principle of public policy, the English court might refuse aid. In all the circumstances, neither the allegations that the désastre proceedings were invalid nor those regarding the Viscount's conduct of the proceedings were well founded (see p 676 *j* and p 677 *b* to *d* and *h j*, post); dicta of Farwell J in *Re Osborn* [1931–32] B & CR at 194 and of Lord Lowry LCJ in *Re Jackson* [1973] NI at 71–72 applied.

(4) The court should accept the Solicitor General's evidence, and would find that the Viscount was entitled to possession of property of the debtor acquired after the order of

19th November 1976, even though the court considered the Solicitor General's authorities to be less persuasive than he did (see p 678 *f* to *h*, post); *A/S Tallinna Laevauhisus v Estonian State Steamship Line* (1946) 80 Ll L Rep 99 applied.

Notes

For orders in aid, see 3 Halsbury's Laws (4th Edn) para 985, and for cases on the subject, see 4 Digest (Reissue) 43, 51, *362*, *418–422*.

For the Bankruptcy Act 1914, s 122, see 3 Halsbury's Statutes (3rd Edn) 139.

Cases referred to in judgment

A/S Tallinna Laevauhisus v Estonian State Steamship Line (1946) 80 Ll L Rep 99, CA; *affg* 175 LT 285, 29 Digest (Repl) 114, *587*.

Bolton, Re [1920] 2 IR 324, 5 Digest (Reissue) 745, **3044*.

Debtor (No 452 of 1948), Re a, ex parte the debtor v Le Mee-Power [1949] 1 All ER 652, [1949] LJR 1112, CA, 4 Digest (Reissue) 176, *1580*.

Désastre Overseas Insurance Brokers Ltd, Re [1966] JJ 547.

Gibbons, Re [1960] I Jur Rep 60.

Gosset, Re (1886) 210 Ex 457, 211 Ex 71.

Government of India, Ministry of Finance (Revenue Division) v Taylor [1955] 1 All ER 292, [1955] AC 491, [1955] 2 WLR 303, [1955] TR 9, 48 R & IT 98, sub nom *Re Delhi Electric Supply and Traction Co Ltd* 34 ATC 10, HL, 11 Digest (Reissue) 341, *8*.

Jackson (a bankrupt in the Republic of Ireland), Re [1973] NI 67.

James (an insolvent) (Attorney General intervening), Re [1977] 1 All ER 364, [1977] Ch 41, [1977] 2 WLR 1, CA.

Le Brun v Lemprière (1893) 76 Exs 455.

Minquiers and Ecréhos Case [1953] ICJ 1.

Osborn, Re, ex parte the trustee [1931–1932] B & CR 189, 5 Digest (Reissue) 743, *6379*.

Renouf v Attorney General for Jersey [1936] 1 All ER 936, [1936] AC 445, 105 LJPC 84, 155 LT 1, 30 Cox CC 397, PC, 8(2) Digest (Reissue) 853, *990*.

Viscount v Jersey Services Co (1954) Ltd [1966] JJ 651.

Cases also cited

Anantapadmanabhaswami v Official Receiver of Secunderabad [1933] AC 394, PC.

Attorney General v Times Newspapers Ltd [1972] 3 All ER 1136, [1974] AC 273, HL.

Attorney General for the Isle of Man v Mylchreest (1879) 4 App Cas 294, PC.

Bergerem v Marsh [1921] B & CR 195.

Bullen (a bankrupt in England), Re [1930] IR 82.

Callender, Sykes & Co v Colonial Secretary of Lagos [1891] AC 460, PC.

Cohen (a bankrupt), Re, ex parte the bankrupt v Inland Revenue Comrs [1950] 2 All ER 36, CA.

Cohen v Mitchell [1890] 25 QBD 262, CA.

Concha v Murrietta, De Mora v Concha (1889) 40 Ch D 543, CA.

De Beéche v South American Stores (Gath and Chaves) Ltd [1935] AC 148, [1934] All ER Rep 284, HL.

Gregory (No 396 of 1933), Re, Trustee v Patriarch of Jerusalem (No 2) (1934) 103 LJ Ch 267, [1934–5] B & CR 62.

Jerusalem-Jaffa District Governor v Suleiman Murra [1926] AC 321, PC.

Kooperman, Re [1928] B & CR 49.

Rickett, Re, ex parte Insecticide Activated Products v Official Receiver [1949] 1 All ER 737.

Wellington (Duke), Re, Glentanar v Wellington [1947] 2 All ER 854, [1948] Ch 118, CA.

Whitehouse v Jordan [1980] 1 All ER 650, CA.

Adjourned application

By an application dated 16th January 1979 the Viscount of the Royal Court of Jersey applied to a registrar in bankruptcy for an order in aid pursuant to s 122 of the

Bankruptcy Act 1914 and for the appointment of the Viscount as receiver (without
security) of all the movable property of the debtor situate in England, with liberty to a
realise and sell the property, to give effect to the order in aid. In support of the
application a notice of motion dated 15th January 1979 was served on the debtor. By an
order dated 15th June 1979 Mr Registrar Wheaton adjourned the appplication into open
court for hearing before the judge sitting in bankruptcy. The facts are set out in the
judgment.

b

Muir Hunter QC and *John Briggs* for the debtor.
Michael Crystal for the Viscount.

Cur adv vult

15th May. **GOULDING J** read the following judgment: This application is concerned
with the affairs of M, to whom I will refer as 'the debtor'. The debtor is a solicitor of the c
Supreme Court and formerly carried on practice in Leicester and in Nottingham. In
1974 or thereabouts he began to practise, again as an English solicitor, in the island of
Jersey also, and early in 1975 he disposed of his Leicester and Nottingham practice, save
for continuing employment therein as a consultant. Thenceforward he lived and carried
on his profession in Jersey. In the latter part of 1976 the debtor found himself in
financial difficulties and on 19th November 1976 an order of the Royal Court of the d
island initiated a process of sequestration of his movable property, known under the local
law as procedure 'en désastre'. The order was made on the application of a company
called J de Ackary & Co Ltd, which claimed to be a creditor of the debtor. I shall read the
English version of the court's order:

> 'IN THE ROYAL COURT OF THE ISLAND OF JERSEY e
>
> 'IN THE YEAR ONE THOUSAND NINE HUNDRED AND SEVENTY-SIX, THE NINETEENTH DAY OF NOVEMBER.
>
> 'The limited liability Company known as "J. de Ackary and Company Limited", a creditor of [the debtor], was given leave to declare the goods of the [the debtor] en désastre.
>
> 'THEREFORE the Court has authorised the Viscount to sequestrate by inventory all f
> the personal property, account books, documents of title, papers and proofs of debt of the [debtor] and to receive the accounts and other debts which may be due to him, the whole for the benefit of those who may be entitled; and it is ordered that the present Act be published by the Officer of the Court at the customary place and posted in the lobby of the Royal Court, so that all persons may have knowledge thereof. g
>
> 'And the said Officer is charged with the execution of all that is ordered by the present Act; the whole at the cost of the said limited liability Company, "J. de Ackary and Company Limited", which may be recovered from the property of the [debtor].'

I shall have to consider hereafter the legal effect of an order en désastre. Suffice it for
the moment to say that the Viscount, or Vicomte as he is called in French, is the principal h
executive officer of the Royal Court. Some days before the date of the order the debtor
had come to England, and he has not returned to Jersey. He has established a practice as
a solicitor in the West End of London and appears to be making a very good living. In
those circumstances the Royal Court of Jersey decided to set in motion the procedure of
s 122 of the Bankruptcy Act 1914. The section provides as follows: j

> 'The High Court, the county courts, the courts having jurisdiction in bankruptcy in Scotland and Ireland, and every British court elsewhere having jurisdiction in bankruptcy or insolvency, and the officers of those courts respectively, shall severally act in aid of and be auxiliary to each other in all matters of bankruptcy and an order of the court seeking aid, with a request to another of the said courts, shall be deemed

sufficient to enable the latter court to exercise, in regard to the matters directed by the order, such jurisdiction as either the court which made the request, or the court to which the request is made, could exercise in regard to similar matters within their respective jurisdictions.'

A request pursuant to the section was made to this court on behalf of the Jersey court on 2nd January 1979; the document issues from the Bailiff's Chambers, Jersey, it is addressed to the High Court of Justice, In Bankruptcy, Royal Courts of Justice, Strand, London WC2, and is in these words:

> 'WHEREAS Philip Francis Misson, Viscount and Chief Executive Officer of the Royal Court of Jersey ("the Viscount") was charged by Act of the said Court dated the 19th November, 1976, to sequestrate by inventory all the personal property, account books, documents of title, papers and proofs of debt of [the debtor], and to receive the accounts and other debts which may be due to [the debtor], the whole for the benefit of those who may be entitled, a true copy and translation of which Act is annexed, I, the undersigned, Herbert Frank Cobbold Ereaut, Knight, Bailiff and Chief Justice in and for the Island of Jersey do hereby request the High Court of Justice, In Bankruptcy, to grant to the Viscount an Order in Aid under the provisions of Section 122 of the Bankruptcy Act, 1914, to enable the Viscount to discharge the duties conferred upon him by the said Act of the Royal Court of Jersey and without prejudice to the generality of the foregoing to appoint the Viscount as Receiver (without security) of all the moveable property of [the debtor] situate in England with liberty to realise and to sell the same and with authority to take such steps and do such acts and things as may be necessary for these purposes.
>
> 'This 2nd day of January 1979.'

The instrument bears the signature of the Bailiff of Jersey and the seal of the court there.

On 16th January 1979 formal application was made to this court, by solicitors in London acting for the Viscount, to make an order in aid in response to the Jersey court's request, and a notice of motion dated 15th January 1979 was served on the debtor in support thereof. The application, and the notice of motion, follow the letter of request in proposing the appointment of the Viscount as receiver (without security) of all the debtor's movable property situate in England with liberty to realise and to sell the same, and with authority to take such steps and do such acts and things as may be necessary for those purposes. An order in substantially that form was made by Farwell J in *Re Osborn* [1931–2] B & CR 189 in favour of a trustee in bankruptcy appointed under Manx law.

The application in the present case came before Mr Registrar Wheaton. After an adjournment, and after reading affidavit evidence and hearing counsel for both sides, he formed the opinion that the matter involved a question of difficulty, and at the request of the debtor adjourned it for hearing in open court before the judge, pursuant to the practice orders of this court, commonly known as the Cave orders. The order of the learned registrar thus adjourning the application is dated 15th June 1979 and, as required by the Cave orders, it contains a statement of the apprehended questions of difficulty. It is in that condition that the Viscount's application now comes before me. I may say at once that, having regard to the course of argument, it will not be necessary for me to attempt an answer to all the specified questions in the form in which they are set out.

A number of witnesses have sworn affidavits in this motion, and have been cross-examined before me. The debtor himself, although careful not to give any answer that was demonstrably incorrect, seemed to me evasive in some parts of his cross-examination. With that exception I find all the evidence to have been given with frankness and to the best of the witnesses' ability.

The law of Jersey, as is well known, is derived from the ancient customary law of Normandy, as modified by subsequent legislation, both insular and imperial. Like the common law of England, the original customary law of Jersey has been developed not only by statutory enactments, but also by a long process of exposition, and of adaptation to the changing needs of society. However, whereas the present state of English law, so far as not codified by statute, is abundantly explained by a wealth of reported and fully reasoned decisions of appellate courts and in a great number of authoritative textbooks, the written materials for the ascertainment of modern Jersey law are comparatively meagre, and textbooks are very few. The reasons for decisions in the Royal Court are often expressed concisely and without lengthy discussion of principle. Accordingly, important parts of the law still reside in the breasts of the judges and legal practitioners of the island, and it is not always possible to find a persuasive answer to a legal problem by mere study of published material.

I have had only one witness of Jersey law, namely Mr Philip Martin Bailhache. Mr Bailhache is Her Majesty's Solicitor General for Jersey. He has held that office for over five years. He swore two affidavits in support of the Viscount's case and was exhaustively cross-examined on them by counsel for the debtor.

Counsel for the debtor subsequently submitted in argument that Mr Bailhache's evidence ought to be rejected altogether as that of a person not suitably qualified by knowledge or experience to be competent to give expert evidence on the law of Jersey. Alternatively, he argued that on the like grounds, and on the additional ground of his alleged partiality, Mr Bailhache's testimony was of little weight. Counsel objected to the witness's youth: he is 34. He said that when in private practice in Jersey Mr Bailhache was in no way a specialist in désastre proceedings, and that as a law officer he is largely occupied by matters of the criminal law. He also dwelt on the assistance Mr Bailhache obtained from members of his staff in the preparation of his evidence and in his researches for this purpose into the law of désastre. I was not impressed by those criticisms, which pay no attention to the conditions of a small jurisdiction, where the entire legal profession comprises only a few dozen persons and there is little professional specialisation. I doubt whether any more expert witness than Mr Bailhache could have been found among the present members of the insular Bar.

Mr Bailhache was then said to lack the independence required of a proper expert witness. Both he and the Viscount are officers of the Crown in Jersey, and it was suggested that the government of the island is concerned to see its constitutional position established in relation to applications of this kind. As a law officer Mr Bailhache is from time to time consulted by the Viscount (who, however, largely employs private practitioners) and there has of course been discussion between them in the preparation of this application to the English court. Counsel for the debtor also invoked an occurrence in the spring of 1975, when an advocate acting for the debtor made an informal approach to Mr Bailhache to see whether the debtor could safely carry on business in certain offices in St Helier without obtaining a licence under a particular Jersey law. This last occurrence seems to me wholly innocent and quite irrelevant. As to the supposed influence on Mr Bailhache of his official interests, I observed him at length in the witness box, and perceived no trace of bias or partiality, only the natural and proper care of every expert witness to bring out matters helpful to the party calling him. I regard his testimony as highly valuable and persuasive.

The debtor claims in the first place that the present application does not fall within s 122 of the Bankruptcy Act 1914, and that for more than one reason. He says that the Royal Court of Jersey is not a 'British court elsewhere', ie, outside the United Kingdom, within the meaning of the section. Further or alternatively, it is not, so far as the procedure here in question is concerned, a court 'having jurisdiction in bankruptcy or insolvency', and thirdly, the proceedings against the debtor are not 'matters of bankruptcy' within the section.

I can deal quite shortly with the first question argued. A great deal of evidence has been presented to me regarding the history and constitutional position of the Channel Islands. Their political relationship with the British Crown and the United Kingdom is, however, very well known and I believe I can take judicial notice of it. Whether that is so or not, the evidence leaves the essential facts in no doubt, and I do not find it necessary to seek the opinion of the Home Office. I respectfully differ from the learned editors of

Williams and Muir Hunter on Bankruptcy (19th Edn, 1979, p 475) in not finding the status of the island courts as British courts at all obscure.

A brief summary of the constitutional history of the island of Jersey will be found in the opinion of the Judicial Committee delivered by Lord Maugham in *Renouf v Attorney General for Jersey* [1936] 1 All ER 936 at 937–938, [1936] AC 445 at 460 in these terms:

> 'It may be added the Island of Jersey is not a colony, or, to use the old phrase, "a plantation". It is part or parcel of the ancient Duchy of Normandy, which came into the possession of William, Duke of Normandy, in A.D. 933, and remained attached to the English Crown when Philip II of France conquered the rest of Normandy from King John. It has its own constitution, and is governed by its own laws . . .'

Counsel for the debtor relied particularly on the memorial or pleading on behalf of the government of the United Kingdom submitted to the International Court of Justice in the case concerning the islets known as the Minquiers and the Ecréhos, decided by the court in 1953 (*Minquiers and Ecréhos case* [1953] ICJ 1). It contains the following passage (at 46):

> 'The Channel Islands are included among the British Isles, but do not form part of the United Kingdom. The laws of the Channel Islands are based on the ancient customs of the Duchy of Normandy, of which they formed part until 1205. The sovereignty of the King of England is, to the present day, only admitted in his right as Duke of Normandy. The Channel Islands are subject to the legislative supremacy of the United Kingdom Parliament, which is exercised for them in relation to such subjects as nationality and defence. The legislative assemblies of Jersey and Guernsey, known as the States, have power to pass Acts which require the approval of the King in Council. The Channel Islands possess their own courts from which an appeal lies to the Judicial Committee of the Privy Council in London.'

Counsel for the debtor emphasised the reference to the Crown's sovereignty in right of Normandy, and said that therefore the Channel Islands are not possessions of the *British* Crown at all. It is, however, far too late today, whatever may have been the position during the lives of the Conqueror's sons, to think of England and Jersey as connected by a mere personal union of Crowns, like Great Britain and Hanover before the accession of Queen Victoria. The legislative authority of the Parliament at Westminster and the appellate jurisdiction of the Privy Council, mentioned in the very passage I have just read, are testimony to the contrary. As long ago as the middle of the seventeenth century, Sir Matthew Hale concluded a discussion of the royal prerogative as to the Channel Islands with this sentence:

> 'And now by long usage these islands are annexed unto the crown of England, and though not *infra regnum*, yet they are *infra dominium regni sui Angliae*.'

(see The Prerogatives of the King, ch 3 (Selden Society (1976) vol 92, p 42)).

The significance of the words quoted, for present purposes, will be appreciated by observing that the chapter is divided into two sections, dealing respectively with territories held in right of the Crown of England as parcel thereof or annexed thereto, and those enjoyed by the King of England in a distinct capacity. The Channel Islands are found in the middle of the former section, lodged between the Kingdom of Man and the town of Berwick. I should perhaps add that I was not referred by counsel to the judgment of the International Court of Justice in the *Minquiers* case. It clearly recognises, or assumes, that sovereignty over the Channel Islands belongs to the United Kingdom.

I have no doubt at all (with or without the assistance of *Re James* [1977] 1 All ER 364, [1977] Ch 41) that at the date of the Bankruptcy Act 1914 the Royal Court of Jersey was a British court within the meaning of s 122. The evidence makes it abundantly clear that, disregarding the temporary episode of enemy occupation during the war of 1939–45, there has been no relevant constitutional change since that date, and it is, in my judgment, equally clear that the court is within the words of the section today.

I do not find it necessary to distinguish between the other two points taken on the language of s 122 of the 1914 Act. If proceedings en désastre before the Royal Court of Jersey are matters of bankruptcy within the section, the court is necessarily a court having jurisdiction in bankruptcy or insolvency within the section. The expression 'bankruptcy or insolvency' may possibly have been used to avoid doubt in jurisdictions which may retain the distinction, long since superseded in England, between the bankruptcy of traders and the insolvency of other persons. That, however, is mere conjecture on my part.

I ask then, whether désastre is a matter of bankruptcy.

The procedure of declaration 'en désastre' is one of several alternative methods available to dispose of the affairs of an insolvent debtor under the law of Jersey. It appears to be the procedure most frequently used in practice at the present day. It was no part of the original Norman law of the island, nor was it introduced by legislative enactment, although a number of enactments refer to and recognise it: see La Loi (1867) au sujet des débiteurs et créanciers; La Loi (1904) (amendment no 2) sur la propriété foncière; and the Interpretation (Jersey) Law 1954, art 13, on the meaning of bankruptcy. The law and practice of désastre have been elaborated by the evolving practice of the Royal Court over the last 200 years or thereabouts. The procedure is now defined by the rules set out in Part 12 of the Royal Court Rules 1968, as amended, but that is by no means a complete code comparable with the 1914 English Act. An authoritative examination of the modern law of désastre is to be found in the judgment of the Royal Court in *Re Désastre Overseas Insurance Brokers Ltd* [1966] JJ 547. After reviewing the history of the procedure from its origins at the end of the eighteenth century, the court summarised the present state of the law as follows (at 551–552):

> 'We conclude that whereas it may well have been the case that in its original form the "désastre" was invented to consolidate the claims of numerous creditors and to preserve a status of equality between them, its scope has been enlarged over the years and may now be defined as follows. A désastre is a declaration of bankruptcy, the effect of which is to deprive an insolvent debtor of the possession of his moveable estate and to vest that possession in Her Majesty's Viscount whose duty it is to get in and liquidate that estate for the benefit of the creditors who prove their claims.'

Another case before the Royal Court in the same year was *Viscount v Jersey Services Co (1954) Ltd* [1966] JJ 651. It raised a question in dispute between the Viscount acting in a désastre and a third party alleged by him to have assets of the debtor. The court said this (at 652):

> 'As C.S. Le Gros says in his "Droit Coutumier de Jersey", at p. 75, "Le désastre est un procédure qui a pour but d'établir l'égalité entre les créanciers d'un débiteur insolvable dans la distribution de ses biens-mobiliers après paiement des préférences accordées". In effect, the authority given to the Viscount is to make a general arrest on all the assets of the debtor for the benefit of all the creditors and is in no way different from an authority given to him to arrest assets for the benefit of a single creditor. If, therefore, the ownership of any assets is disputed, the question can only be settled by this Court and the nature of the action to be taken in this connexion will depend on the circumstances of the case.'

To show clearly how the désastre procedure operates in practice it will, I think, be worth while to read in extenso Part 12 of the Royal Court Rules of 1968 I have referred to. Omitting cross-headings, it is as follows:

> '12/1.—(1) When the goods of a debtor are declared "en désastre", the procedure prescribed by this Part of these Rules shall apply.
>
> '(2) In this Part of these Rules, unless the context otherwise requires—"claim"

includes a claim for repossession of goods and a claim for rent, but does not include a claim for an unliquidated sum; "creditor" includes a person claiming repossession of goods.

'12/2.—(1) The Viscount shall, with the least possible delay after the declaration "en désastre" of the goods of a debtor, cause a notice to be published in the Jersey Gazette, and in such newspapers as he may deem appropriate, requiring every creditor to file with him a statement of claim.

'(2) The Viscount shall specify in such notice the date by which statements of claim are to be filed, which date shall be not less than forty and not more than sixty days from the date of the Act of the Court declaring the goods of the debtor "en désastre".

'12/3.—(1) The Court may refuse to receive the declaration "en désastre" of the goods of a debtor—(*a*) where the declaration is made by the creditor, unless it states that he has a claim against the debtor and that to the best of his knowledge and belief the debtor is insolvent but has realisable assets, and contains a statement of the claim and of the grounds on which he believes the debtor to be insolvent; (*b*) where the declaration is made by the debtor, unless it states that he is insolvent but has realisable assets; and, in either case, the declaration is verified by affidavit.

'(2) The Court shall refuse to receive a declaration "en désastre" made by a creditor where the claim of the creditor is one for repossession of goods.

'12/4.—(1) Every creditor shall, if required by notice in writing given to him by the Viscount, produce to the Viscount within such time as may be specified in the notice—(*a*) such documents as may be necessary to substantiate his claim; (*b*) an affidavit of proof of debt.

'(2) Where a creditor claims that any amount due to him is a privileged debt ranking for payment in priority to ordinary debts he shall so state in his statement of claim.

'(3) A creditor who has a surety ("caution") shall so state in his statement of claim.

'(4) A creditor who has obtained a final judgment the effect of which has been suspended by the declaration "en désastre" shall, in lieu of filing a statement of claim, file a copy of the Act recording the judgment, together with a bill of the costs incurred in obtaining the judgment which he is entitled to recover from the debtor.

'12/5.—(1) On the expiration of the time fixed in pursuance of Rule 12/2(2) the Viscount shall fix a time during which the statements of claim, together with the documents in support thereof, that have been filed may be inspected by the debtor and by any creditor or other person interested.

'(2) Notice of such time shall be published in the Jersey Gazette and in any newspaper in which a notice has been published in pursuance of Rule 12/2(1) and, if the whereabouts of the debtor are known to the Viscount, shall be given in writing to the debtor.

'12/6. A creditor who does not send full particulars of his claim within the time fixed by the Viscount or who does not comply with Rule 12/4(1) shall be deemed to have forfeited his right to participate in the distribution of the assets of the debtor under Rule 12/13.

'12/7. Where the debtor or any creditor or person interested wishes to oppose the admission of any claim, including a claim that any amount should rank as a privileged debt, he shall, within one month from the expiration of the time fixed in pursuance of Rule 12/5(1), lodge with the Viscount a statement in writing setting forth the grounds on which he opposes the admission of such claim.

'12/8. On the expiration of the time fixed for the lodging of statements opposing the admission of claims, the Viscount shall examine the claims and any statements that have been lodged in pursuance of Rule 12/7 and shall ascertain, so far as he is able, to which of such claims the debtor is liable, and whether any amounts claimed as privileged debts may properly rank as such, and shall give notice of his decisions in accordance with Rule 12/9.

'12/9.—(1) The notice required by Rule 12/8 shall be given—(*a*) to every person claiming to be a creditor whose claim or any part thereof has not been allowed by the Viscount, or having been allowed by him has not been allowed to rank as a privileged debt; and (*b*) to every person whose opposition to the admission of a claim has been set aside by the Viscount.

'(2) Where any person to whom notice has been given as aforesaid is dissatisfied with the decision of the Viscount he shall within fourteen days of the date of such notice notify the Viscount that he wishes application to be made to the Court for the reversal or variation of the decision, and the Viscount shall apply to the Court for a date to be fixed for the hearing of all such applications.

'12/10. Where there have been mutual credits, mutual debts or other mutual dealings between the debtor and a creditor, an account shall be taken of what is due from the one party to the other in respect of such mutual dealings, and the sum due from one party shall be set off against any sum due from the other party, and the balance of the account, and no more, shall be claimed or paid on either side respectively.

'12/11. Where the debtor is in possession of goods in virtue of a hire-purchase agreement, the Viscount may settle the debtor's indebtedness under such agreement if he considers that it would be in the interest of the creditors to do so.

'12/12. Where a creditor has a right of action against the debtor for the recovery of an unliquidated sum or for the cancellation of a lease, he shall not file a claim for such relief in the manner provided by these Rules but may institute proceedings against the debtor in the Royal Court.

'12/13. On the expiration of the period of fourteen days prescribed by Rule 12/9(2) or, if any applications have been made to the Court in pursuance of the said Rule, on the determination of all such applications, the Viscount shall distribute the assets among the persons entitled to receive the same in accordance with their respective claims as allowed.

'12/14. After the goods of a debtor have been declared "en désastre", the Viscount may—(*a*) at any time, sell perishable goods belonging to the debtor; (*b*) after the date specified by him in pursuance of Rule 12/2(2), sell any other goods belonging to the debtor.

'12/15. Where a receiving order in bankruptcy has been made under the law for the time being in force in any part of the United Kingdom in respect of the estate of a person whose goods have been declared "en désastre", it shall not be obligatory for creditors whose claims have been admitted in accordance with such law to file individual statements of claim, but instead the person charged with the administration in bankruptcy of such person's estate may file with the Viscount a bulk statement of claim on their behalf.'

It will be obvious that the désastre procedure has points both of resemblance to, and of difference from, an English statutory bankruptcy. Among the most important similarities are (1) the seizure and realisation of an insolvent debtor's assets for the benefit of his creditors, (2) the rateable distribution, subject to preferences, of the proceeds of realisation of the assets among those creditors who prove their claims in the proceedings, and (3) the protection of the debtor, and also of the creditors inter se, from the enforcement of individual debts during the pendency of the process.

Among striking differences between the English and Jersey procedures are to be noticed: (1) the exclusion of immovable property from the assets realisable en désastre, (2) the absence of any discharge of the debtor from debts proved in désastre proceedings, so far as not recovered therein, (3) possibly (and of this I shall say more later) the absence of an actual vesting of property in the Viscount, similar to that effected by s 53 of the 1914 Act and (4) the absence of any express provision for the alimentary maintenance of the debtor, such as that contained in ss 38 and 51 of the 1914 Act.

Counsel for the debtor relied on all these points in his submission that désastre proceedings are not matters of bankruptcy within s 122, and also (perhaps most strongly of all) on the circumstance that they are not defined and regulated by statutory law, but a by judicial practice, nowhere to be found (except as to matters within the 1968 Rules) precisely set out in writing. He said in effect that Parliament can never have intended to burden the courts with an obligation of mutual aid unless the court which is asked for aid can examine without doubt or difficulty the system it is requested to support. This argument wholly fails to convince me. Suppose two British courts were to conduct their insolvency business according to practically similar rules, in the one jurisdiction reduced b to a statutory code, and in the other established as unwritten customary law. It could not be right, in my judgment, to treat one court as entitled to invoke s 122, and the other not.

The 1914 Act does not define 'bankruptcy' for the purposes of s 122, and I shall not attempt to supply a definition that Parliament has not thought fit to provide. I confine myself to such interpretation of the section as is necessary to determine whether this court can act in aid of the Jersey court in the present case. The word 'bankruptcy' may c mean on the one hand the condition of a person who cannot or will not pay his creditors, or, on the other hand, a judicial or administrative process for dealing with persons in that state. The first use of the word is familiar in the Scottish expression 'notour bankruptcy', which I take to be a state of demonstrable insolvency evidenced in one of the ways, now defined by statute, which supply the necessary foundation for the judicial process of sequestration. In England we are more inclined to use the word in the second sense, not d designating a debtor as bankrupt until he has been the subject of adjudication under the 1914 Act. If in s 122 the word 'bankruptcy', occurring as it does in the expression 'jurisdiction in bankruptcy or insolvency' and 'all matters of bankruptcy', is given the first meaning, then clearly, in my opinion, the present case is within the section, for both the High Court and the Jersey court have jurisdiction in relation to insolvent debtors and the désastre is one method by which the latter deals with them. If, however, as is well e arguable, 'bankruptcy' in s 122 refers not to a personal condition but to a class of judicial or administrative process, then one has to ask what are the essential characteristics of such process and does the désastre procedure fall within that class.

To my mind, if any form of procedure is to be described as 'bankruptcy' it must at least provide for the administration of the debtor's assets, with or without the exception of particular classes of assets, with a view to satisfying his debts, again with or without f exceptions, according to established legal rules. Such procedure may have one or more of at least three purposes, first to protect the creditors from one another, so that an overactive or unscrupulous creditor does not get an unfair advantage over his fellows; secondly, the protection of creditors from a dishonest debtor who secretes his property, or absconds, or gives fraudulent preferences; and thirdly, the protection of the debtor from the extreme enforcement of the legal rights of his respective creditors. The objects g are not, in practice, separate and independent. In particular the pursuit of the first tends to attain in some measure the third, for the restraint imposed on creditors to secure justice or equality between them necessarily gives some relief to the insolvent debtor. The word 'bankruptcy' in s 122, if indeed it refers at all to the *process* of bankruptcy, must, in my judgment, be construed in a wide sense, for the section is designed to produce co-operation between courts acting under different systems of law, and it would h be much restricted if extended only to jurisdictions that reproduce all the main features of English procedure. Dodd J took much the same view of a similar provision in the Bankruptcy Amendment (Ireland) Act 1872: see *Re Bolton* [1920] 2 IR 324 at 327.

Approaching the matter in that spirit, I do not think that the exclusion of immovable property from the distributable estate can of itself prevent an insolvency process from being a matter of bankruptcy, nor, in my view, is a final discharge of the debtor an j essential feature of bankruptcy sensu lato. Dodd J pointed out in the case I have just mentioned that no such discharge was provided by the old laws for the relief of non-mercantile debtors.

I turn then to the third point. A good deal of evidence and argument has been applied to the question whether under the désastre procedure the assets of a debtor subject to such procedure vest as property in the Viscount, as the property of an English bankrupt passes to his trustee under s 53 of the 1914 Act. Mr Bailhache takes the view that they do so vest, but this was hotly contested by counsel for the debtor. The point does not seem to have been the subject of express decision in the Jersey court, nor of exposition by any authoritative textbook writer. Notwithstanding the learned argument to which I have listened, I cannot see that I need make any finding about it on this motion. Whether the Viscount in a Jersey désastre has the proprietary title of an English trustee in bankruptcy, or whether as an alternative he is clothed only with full powers to realise the assets of the debtor and liquidate his affairs, somewhat like the liquidator of an English company, it is in my judgment equally appropriate (if the circumstances otherwise require it) for this court to make an order in aid of the Jersey Court under the 1914 Act.

The fourth point of difference between English bankruptcy and the désastre procedure, among those that I enumerated just now, is in my opinion of little importance, for although there is no express rule on the subject, Mr Bailhache proved that by well understood practice the Viscount has, and exercises, a discretion to allow a sufficient maintenance to debtors en désastre.

But even if no one particular defect takes the Jersey procedure outside the intendment of s 122, is it, when regarded in the round, so different from the general idea of bankruptcy that it must be excluded from the scope of the section? I think not, for the désastre scheme seems to me to have been developed for the very purposes that I find essential to bankruptcy in a broad sense and to contain nothing repugnant to that conception.

Thus the debtor's defence founded on the construction of s 122 of the 1914 Act must, in my judgment, fail. He makes, however, a number of other objections to the Viscount's application. He asserts among other things, that the rights and duties of the Viscount in a désastre are limited to movable assets within the Bailiwick of Jersey. The Viscount says they are in principle exercisable over the debtor's movables wherever they may be located. It is well settled that bankruptcy proceedings outside the United Kingdom will be recognised as affecting the debtor's movables in England if the jurisdiction of the foreign court is recognised by English law and the foreign law itself extends to such assets. I have been referred to no judicial decision in Jersey which expounds the territorial limits, or freedom from limits, of an order en désastre. Mr Bailhache in his evidence expressed the opinion that under the law of Jersey all the debtor's movable assets are caught by the order, wherever in the world they may be found. He also mentioned cases in which the Viscount has enforced his claim outside the island. In one case, in 1958, he said, the Viscount went to the South of France and obtained the assistance of the French court to collect and sell a motor cruiser for the benefit of creditors who had proved in a désastre. And in another, very recent, case the Viscount by virtue of a request from the Jersey court, obtained an order in aid from the county court at Southampton. On this question Mr Bailhache's opinion remained unshaken and I have no hesitation in accepting it as correct. There is, however, in my judgment, another weighty matter to be considered in this regard. The request of the Royal Court, which I have already read in full, given under the hand and seal of the Bailiff and Chief Justice of the island, requests this court to put the Viscount in possession of all the debtor's movable property situate in England. By s 122 of the 1914 Act such a request is deemed sufficient to enable this court to exercise in the relevant matter, the jurisdiction either of the requesting court or of itself. Counsel for the debtor says the request was obtained ex parte at chambers, without any public hearing. That is no doubt so, but the terms of the request, which I read out at the beginning of this judgment, are perfectly plain on the face of the document, and it would require strong evidence to convince me in these circumstances that a British court overseas had fundamentally mistaken the territorial extent of its own process under its own law.

Now I turn to several objections made by the debtor to the institution and conduct of these particular proceedings against him in Jersey. I do not think that this court, when requested for aid under s 122 of the 1914 Act, has any general duty to scrutinise the requesting court's transactions once it is satisfied that the case falls within the scope of the section. Farwell J said in *Re Osborn* [1931–32] B & CR 189 at 194:

> 'There not being any such conflict [ie, conflict with a concurrent English *a* bankruptcy] I think this Court is bound to give all the assistance that it can.'

Lord Lowry LCJ took the same view of the section in *Re Jackson* [1973] NI 67, preferring it to that expressed by Walsh J in the Irish case of *Re Gibbons* [1960] I Jur Rep 60 where Walsh J thought such provisions to be merely enabling and discretionary. I respectfully agree with Farwell J and Lord Lowry CJ, while recognising that the court might have to *b* refuse aid if it were proved that the anterior proceedings were hopelessly bad under their own proper law, or that they offended against some overriding principle of English public policy.

The debtor here has suggested that the désastre was invalid from the start, either because he had finally left the island a few days before the declaration was made, or because the petitioning creditor, J de Ackary & Co Ltd, was not duly qualified as such, in *c* consequence of arrangements made by the debtor to secure his release after that company had procured his imprisonment under a process known as ordre provisoire. I am not satisfied that either of those averments is well founded in Jersey law. The second was, and the first could have been, raised by the debtor in an application which he made at an early stage to the Royal Court to (as the phrase goes) 'lift the désastre'. The application was dismissed by order dated 30th December 1976, from which the debtor did not *d* appeal.

Alternatively, counsel for the debtor contends that the character of the Viscount's conduct of the debtor's affairs must disentitle him to an English court's assistance. The Viscount is criticised for not having given evidence personally, and for having left that duty to his subordinate, Michael Wilkins. Mr Wilkins is senior administrative assistant in the Viscount's department and head of the désastre section. As such he has control of *e* the debtor's désastre, subject to the Viscount's directions and supervision. It is also said that the Viscount is not as active as he should be in questioning and repelling the claims of doubtful creditors in the désastre. But, most of all, the Viscount is attacked for consistently declining to give any indication, in advance of his appointment as receiver, of the course he is likely to adopt concerning three items which, according to counsel for the debtor, may be of great value and which are said to constitute the debtor's principal *f* assets in England. The first is the debtor's interest under an agreement with one Graham John Burton, to whom he sold his former practice in the Midlands in 1975. It is the subject of a pending action in the Commercial Court here. There are a number of defendants in addition to Mr Burton himself, including the Viscount, against whom the debtor seeks a declaration that he is not interested in, and an injunction restraining him from claiming, the subject matter of the action. The validity and effect of the désastre *g* proceedings appear to be in issue on the pleadings in that action. The second of the alleged major assets is a claim against several defendants for damages for professional negligence, for conversion of certain shares, and for conspiracy to defraud, arising out of transactions of the debtor in Jersey. That claim is the subject of another pending action in the Queen's Bench Division. The third asset consists of the goodwill and other constituents of the debtor's present practice as a solicitor in London.

h Those various complaints do not persuade me to deny relief to the Viscount. I see nothing improper in deputing Mr Wilkins to give evidence, for he has direct personal knowledge of the désastre; and I entirely decline, on an application under s 122 of the 1914 Act, to investigate the reception or rejection of proofs of debt in Jersey. The Viscount seems to me to act prudently in waiting till he has control of the English assets and can fully investigate them, before saying, or indeed deciding, how they are to be *j* dealt with. As to the pending actions I will assume, but without professing to decide, that they give me the same discretion to postpone making an order in aid as to defer a receiving order in an English bankruptcy: see *Re a Debtor (No 452 of 1948)* [1949] 1 All ER 652. On that footing I am decidedly of opinion that I ought not to adjourn the Viscount's application to await the result of either of the actions.

One other matter was mentioned from time to time in argument, but never really came to a head. It is said that the Viscount has on occasion allowed the revenue authorities of the United Kingdom to prove in a Jersey désastre, contrary to the established principle of international law exemplified by *Government of India v Taylor* [1955] 1 All ER 292, [1955] AC 491. If this is indeed the fact, it is certainly not, in my judgment, a reason for the refusal of aid by a court of the United Kingdom itself.

I have still to deal with one point, which has troubled me more than any other in this interesting case. Counsel for the debtor submits that even if I accede to the Viscount's application to be appointed receiver of the debtor's movable property in England, his receivership should be restricted to property which is or represents assets belonging to the debtor at the date of the order giving leave to declare his goods en désastre, to which assets alone, he says, the Viscount's rights and duties extend. But counsel for the Viscount maintains that they also catch the debtor's after-acquired movable assets during the period between the initial order and the termination of the désastre proceedings. Until 1964 that termination was marked by a formal order of the Royal Court, known as an 'acte généralle', made on the adjudication of the proving creditors' claims (itself called the 'passation des causes'). Mr Bailhache's evidence indicates, and I accept it, that under the present practice the equivalent date is the final determination of the creditors' claims by the Viscount or on appeal by the court. Mr Bailhache expressed a clear opinion that such after-acquired property does constitute assets distributable in the désastre. In support of his opinion he referred in particular to *Re Gosset* (1886) 210 Ex 457 and to the action of *Le Brun v Lemprière* (1893) 76 Exs 455. The earlier case does not seem to me to carry the matter far, as it merely authorised the Viscount to carry on the debtor's business during the désastre proceedings at the cost of the estate. *Le Brun v Lemprière* is not only consistent with Mr Bailhache's proposition but also suggestive that it may be correct but (as I read the case) the judgment did not, and did not need to, expressly affirm it. He could not produce any more cogent precedent or any textbook authority, nor could he testify to any prevalent professional opinion in the island. On this point, unlike that of the territorial extent of a désastre, I get no help (in one direction or the other) from the terms of the Jersey court's request. I could have wished the question to be referred to the Royal Court under the British Law Ascertainment Act 1859. However, one party having called expert evidence and the other not, and neither party having asked me to remit a case under that Act, I am in the end dependent as to this important matter on the evidence before me, which, in substance, is simply Mr Bailhache's expert opinion. He swore that in his view from the authorities which he cited, the Royal Court, if the question arose, would come to the decision that after-acquired property does fall within the jurisdiction of the Viscount. Mr Bailhache expressed himself as having no doubt on the point, and even though I find his authorities less persuasive than he does, he after all is, in my judgment, an expert of the highest quality on the law of Jersey. Accordingly, obeying the admonitions of the Court of Appeal in *A/S Tallinna Laevauhisus v Estonian State Steamship Line* (1946) 80 Ll L Rep 99, I accept Mr Bailhache's opinion and find that the Viscount is entitled to the possession of after-acquired property accordingly.

The Viscount's motion accordingly succeeds. Precedents of orders in aid are to be found in Farwell J's case of *Re Osborn*, which I have cited and in two Irish cases that I have already referred to, namely *Re Bolton* and *Re Jackson*. In my view the *Osborn* order contains undertakings and directions that, with slight adaptation, will be suitable in the present case, omitting, of course, the paragraph touching immovable property. If junior counsel can agree minutes of order on those lines I am content that the order should go accordingly. If any difficulty arises, it can be mentioned to me at short notice.

Order accordingly.

Solicitors: *Geoffrey Myerson & Co* (for the debtor); *Durrant Piesse* (for the Viscount).

Evelyn M C Budd Barrister.

a

R v London Borough of Barnet, ex parte Shah and another

QUEEN'S BENCH DIVISION
ORMROD LJ, KILNER BROWN AND MCNEILL JJ
23rd, 24th JUNE, 18th JULY 1980

b

Education – University – Grant for study – Local authority grant – Eligibility – Student entitled to grant from local authority for university study if ordinarily resident in United Kingdom for three years – Ordinarily resident – Education Act 1962, s 1 – Local Education Authority Awards Regulations 1979 (SI 1979 No 889), reg 13(a).

c The applicants, N and J, were both foreign-born students who applied for, and were refused, local authority grants for their university education. Both applicants were born in Kenya and came to England in 1976 when aged 17. N came with his parents and was admitted for an indefinite period for the purpose of settling in England. His parents returned to Kenya shortly after, while he stayed with relations in England, attended school in England and returned to Kenya during the summer holidays. J arrived in d England on his own and was admitted for two months under a student's entry certificate which was extended from time to time. He had no right of entry into the United Kingdom. He stayed with his brother and attended secondary school. In 1979 each applicant made an application to his local education authority for a grant in respect of his university education, pursuant to s 1[a] of the Education Act 1962. The authority refused both applications on the ground that neither applicant had been 'ordinarily resident' in e the United Kingdom for the preceding three years as required by reg 13 (a)[b] of the Local Education Authority Awards Regulations 1979. Each applicant applied for orders of certiorari to quash the authority's decision and mandamus to compel the authority to make a grant. Since it was not disputed that each applicant had been present in England for three years the question arose whether they had been 'ordinarily resident' during that f time. The authority contended that the correct test was whether the applicants had made their 'real home' in England, while the applicants contended that the words were to be given their natural and ordinary meaning.

Held – The concept of 'ordinary residence' embodied a number of different factors, such as time, intention and continuity, each of which might carry different weight according to the context in which, and purpose for which, it was used in a particular statute. On g the true construction of reg 13(*a*) of the 1979 regulations the phrase 'ordinarily resident' was used to distinguish between persons who were resident for general (or 'ordinary') purposes and those who were resident for a specific, special or limited purpose. An important, but not the only, test in ascertaining the person's purpose or reason for being in the United Kingdom and his intention in coming and remaining there was to ask why h that person was in the country. Applying that test, N had come to England for the purpose of settling, i e for all ordinary purposes of living, and not for the specific purpose of being educated, and was therefore 'ordinarily resident' and entitled to a grant. J on the other hand had arrived with the specific purpose of studying, qualifying and then leaving and was thus not 'ordinarily resident' and not entitled to a grant (see p 683 *j*, p 684 *b*, p 685 *h j*, p 687 *d* and p 688 *b* to *h*, post).

j *Clarke v Insurance Office of Australia Ltd* [1965] 1 Lloyd's Rep 308 approved.

Inland Revenue Comrs v Lysaght [1928] All ER Rep 575, *Levene v Inland Revenue Comrs* [1928] All ER Rep 746, *Stransky v Stransky* [1954] 2 All ER 536, *Miesegaes v Inland Revenue Comrs* (1957) 37 Tax Cas 493 considered

a Section 1, so far as material, is set out at p 682 *a b*, post
b Regulation 13, so far as material, is set out at p 681 *b*, post

Notes

For eligibility for mandatory awards by local education authorities for university study, see 15 Halsbury's Laws (4th Edn) paras 240–258.

For the Education Act 1962, s 1, see 11 Halsbury's Statutes (3rd Edn) 315.

Cases referred to in judgment

Clarke v Insurance Office of Australia Ltd [1965] 1 Lloyd's Rep 308, Digest (Cont Vol B) 458, *3653b*.

Fox v Stirk [1970] 3 All ER 7, [1970] 2 QB 463, [1970] 3 WLR 147, 134 JP 576, [1970] RA 330, CA, Digest (Cont Vol C) 320, *75a*.

Judd v Judd (1957) 75 WN (NSW) 147.

Hopkins v Hopkins [1950] 2 All ER 1035, [1951] P 116, 11 Digest (Reissue) 526, *1116*.

Inland Revenue Comrs v Lysaght [1928] AC 234, [1928] All ER Rep 575, 97 LJKB 385, 139 LT 6, 13 Tax Cas 511, HL, 28(1) Digest (Reissue) 359, *1310*.

Levene v Inland Revenue Comrs [1928] AC 217, [1928] All ER Rep 746, 97 LJKB 377, 139 LT 1, 13 Tax Cas 486, HL, 28(1) Digest (Reissue) 359, *1309*.

Lewis v Lewis [1956] 1 All ER 375, [1956] 1 WLR 200, 11 Digest (Reissue) 526, *1118*.

Macrae v Macrae [1949] 2 All ER 34, [1949] P 397, [1949] LJR 1671, 113 JP 342, 47 LGR 537, CA, 27(2) Digest (Reissue) 952, *7689*.

Miesegaes v Inland Revenue Comrs (1957) 37 Tax Cas 493, [1957] TR 231, 36 ATC 201, 50 R & IT 643, CA.

Stransky v Stransky [1954] 2 All ER 536, [1954] P 428, [1954] 3 WLR 123, 11 Digest (Reissue) 355, *69*.

Thomson v Minister of National Revenue [1946] SCR 209, 28(1) Digest (Reissue) 376, **1019*.

Young, Re (1875) 1 Tax Cas 57, 28(1) Digest (Reissue) 360, **996*.

Cases also cited

Abdul Manan, Re [1971] 2 All ER 1016, [1971] 1 WLR 859, CA.

Bicknell v Brosnan [1953] 1 All ER 1126, [1953] 2 QB 77.

Gout v Cimitian [1922] 1 AC 105, PC.

Applications for judicial review

The applicants, Nilish Ramniklal Lalji Shah and Jitendra Umedchand Harakchand Shah, applied by separate applications and with the leave of the Divisional Court of the Queen's Bench Division granted on 23rd January 1980 for orders of certiorari to quash the decision of the London Borough of Barnet ('the local education authority') refusing to bestow a major award on the applicants and orders of mandamus directing the local education authority to reconsider the applicants' claims for a major award. The applicant Jitendra Shah further sought a declaration (i) that the local education authority's refusal to bestow an award on him in respect of his attendance at a university course constituted an unlawful failure by the authority to perform their statutory duty, (ii) that the applicant was entitled to an award, (iii) that the applicant was at the material time ordinarily resident in the authority's area and had been ordinarily resident there for a period of three years immediately preceding his course, and (iv) that the authority had misdirected itself in holding that the applicant had not been ordinarily resident as required by the Education Act 1962 and the Local Education Authority Awards Regulations 1979, SI 1979 No 889. The facts are set out in the judgment of the court.

Anthony Lester QC and *K S Nathan* for the applicants.
Anthony Scrivener QC and *R A Barratt* for the local education authority.
Simon D Brown as amicus curiae.

Cur adv vult

18th July. **ORMROD LJ** read the following judgment of the court: In these two cases, which raise the same point of law and have been heard together, Mr Nilish Shah and Mr Jitendra Shah apply by way of judicial review for orders of certiorari and mandamus in respect of decisions by the London Borough of Barnet, in its capacity as local education authority, that neither of the applicants is eligible for an award (or grant) under s 1 of the Education Act 1962. Regulation 13(*a*) of the Local Education Authority Awards Regulations 1979, SI 1979 No 889, made under this Act provides:

> 'An authority shall not be under a duty to bestow an award in respect of a person's attendance at a course—(*a*) upon a person who has not been ordinarily resident, throughout the three years preceding the first year of the course in question, in the United Kingdom or, in the case of such a person as is mentioned in Regulation 9(1)(*b*), has not been so resident in the European Economic Community . . .'

In each case the ground for refusing to make an award was that the applicant had not been ordinarily resident throughout the preceding three years in the United Kingdom. The present applications, therefore, turn on the construction of that familiar phrase 'ordinarily resident' which seems so convenient to the draftsman but proves difficult and troublesome to everyone who has to consider and apply it. The question is of great importance to all local education authorities and to many students. Both applicants, by leave of the court, have amended their applications to ask in the alternative for various declarations.

The two Shahs are in no way related or connected with each other and their cases differ significantly on their facts. For convenience we shall refer to them as 'Nilish' and 'Jitendra' respectively, and the London Borough of Barnet as the 'local education authority'.

Counsel who has appeared for both applicants has put their respective cases succinctly, and with force and clarity, for which we are grateful. He submitted that we should follow, though with due caution, the three well-known tax cases, *Levene v Inland Revenue Comrs* [1928] AC 217, [1928] All ER Rep 746, *Inland Revenue Comrs v Lysaght* [1928] AC 234, [1928] All ER Rep 575 and *Miesegaes v Inland Revenue Comrs* (1957) 37 Tax Cas 493, reject the 'real home' test suggested by Karminski J in *Stransky v Stransky* [1954] 2 All ER 536, [1954] P 428, and give the words their natural and ordinary meaning. Counsel for the local education authority, on the other hand, submitted with equal force and brevity that we should adopt the 'real home' test and not follow the tax cases. Alternatively, we should construe the words in their legislative context. Counsel who appeared as amicus curiae, mainly on questions of immigration law, has also helped us on the main issue. He supported counsel for the local education authority on the tax cases and submitted that they should not be regarded as of general application because tax law accepts the concept that a person may be 'ordinarily resident' in more than one place at the same time, a concept which is not applicable in the present context or in other contexts in which this phrase is used. We are grateful to him for his assistance.

We have not found the tax cases very helpful in the solution of out present problem because they were concerned with a different situation. Each decides only that there was evidence on which the Special Commissioners could find 'ordinary residence' as a matter of fact. Much of the speeches and judgments, though of the highest authority, are, therefore, essentially obiter dicta. Nor do we derive much assistance from *Stransky v Stransky* which was again concerned with a different situation. We do not think that Karminski J intended his use of the phrase 'real home' to be of general application. We have also experienced considerable difficulty in ascertaining the 'natural and ordinary' meaning of the words in question. To determine the 'ordinary' meaning of 'ordinarily' is something of a linguistic feat in itself. Nor is the word 'resident' at all easy. It is not much used in ordinary speech, and then without precision.

In these circumstances we think that the problem is best approached from first principles. Any tentative conclusion as to construction can then be examined in the light of the reported cases.

Our task is to construe the phrase 'ordinarily resident' in its legislative context, giving
the words, so far as possible, their natural and ordinary meaning in that context. Section a
1 of the 1962 Act, so far as material, reads:

> '(1) It shall be the duty of every education authority, subject to and in accordance
> with regulations made under this Act, to bestow awards on persons who—(*a*) are
> ordinarily resident in the area of the authority, and (*b*) possess the requisite
> educational qualifications, in respect of their attendance at courses to which this b
> section applies . . .'

Regulation 13(*a*) limits the scope of this duty to persons who have been ordinarily
resident throughout the preceding three years in the United Kingdom.

There are, therefore, two classes of person, differentiated by the phrase 'ordinarily
resident'. To be eligible for an award a person must not only be 'resident' in the United
Kingdom, he must also be 'ordinarily resident', and in a position to show that he has had c
this quality of residence for the three years immediately preceding the beginning of his
course of study.

The 1962 Act, in s 1, provides for bestowing awards on certain persons. 'Bestow' is an
unusual word to find in an Act of Parliament and carries a special connotation. It is
commonly used in connection with words such as 'bounty' or 'favours' or some similar
charitable or quasi-charitable act. d

It is, therefore, to be expected that Parliament intended to distinguish between persons
whose connection with the United Kingdom was sufficiently close to justify their being
helped or supported by awards from public funds to pursue their studies in the United
Kingdom and those whose connection lacked this quality. Mere residence, even for a
period of three years, would not be enough; the residence must have a certain quality;
that quality is identified by the use of the word 'ordinarily'. e

The phrase 'ordinarily resident' is used in a variety of legislative contexts. It has
become, in fact, a point on a scale which ranges from mere presence in this country
through 'resident', 'ordinarily resident', 'habitually resident' to 'domicle' which is widely
used to specify the nature and quality of the association between person and place which
brings the person within the scope of the particular enactment. Mere presence within f
the jurisdiction is enough to permit good service of a writ or other forms of process in
most cases; in some, eg the Carriage by Air Act 1961, more is required. Article 28 of the
Warsaw Convention specifies the defendant's ordinary residence or principal place of
business as the prerequisite for jurisdiction. Residence alone is enough for the
Representation of the People Act 1949. Habitual residence for one year or domicile is
required to give jurisdiction in matrimonial proceedings (see the Domicile and
Matrimonial Proceedings Act 1973, s 5). Habitual residence or nationality is required for g
the recognition of foreign divorces (see Recognition of Divorces and Legal Separations
Act 1971, s 3).

What then are the characteristics of ordinary residence which distinguish it from
residence without this qualification? In answering this question we have derived great
assistance from the judgment of Smith J in *Clarke v Insurance Office of Australia* [1965] h
1 Lloyd's Rep 308 at 310–311, a case in the Supreme Court of Victoria. We cannot do
better than to read in full what he said:

> 'The words "ordinarily residing with" are common English words and here there
> is no context requiring that they should be given other than their natural meaning
> in accordance with the accepted usage of English. Even in such circumstances,
> however, there can be difficulty and doubt as to their applicability to particular sets j
> of facts, because the conception to which the words have reference does not have a
> clearly definable content or fixed boundaries. It is a conception as to the extent of
> the association and the strength of the connection between two persons as members
> of one household or domestic establishment; and whether the extent and strength
> of the connection are such, in any given case, as to make the words fairly applicable,

> is a question of degree. Moreover that question depends upon an assessment of a
> a combination of factors; and combinations may be found to be adequate though
> they differ widely, both in the weighting of factors and in the identity of the factors
> present. The situation is similar to that discussed by Mr. Justice Rand in the
> following passage from his judgment in *Thomson v. Minister of National Revenue*
> ([1946] SCR 209 at 224), where the expression under consideration was "ordinarily
> resident": ". . . The enquiry lies between the certainty of fixed and sole residence and
> b the uncertain line that separates it from occasional or casual presence, the line of
> contrast with what is understood by the words 'stay' or 'visit' into which residence
> can become attenuated; and the difference may frequently be a matter of sensing
> than (*sic*) of a clear differentiation of factors. The gradation of degree of time,
> object, intention, continuity and other relevant circumstances, shows, I think, that
> in common parlance 'residing' is not a term of invariable elements, all of which
> c must be satisfied in each instance. It is quite impossible to give it a precise and
> inclusive definition. It is highly flexible, and its many shades of meaning vary not
> only in the contexts of different matters, but also in different aspects of the same
> matter. In one case it is satisfied by certain elements, in another by others, some
> common, some new." The duration of residence and the comparative times spent
> in different places or households, will, of course, commonly be a great importance,
> d but they are not factors which are necessarily decisive. They may be outweighed by
> other factors: compare *Levene v. Commissioners of Inland Revenue* ([1928] AC 217,
> [1928] All ER Rep 746); *Commissioners of Inland Revenue v. Lysaght* ([1928] AC 234,
> [1928] All ER Rep 575); *Thomson v. Minister of National Revenue* ([1946] SCR 209 at
> 228, 232); *Hopkins v. Hopkins* ([1950] 2 All ER 1035, [1951] P 116); *Judd v. Judd*
> ((1957) 75 WN (NSW) 147). In some circumstances, for example, a man may
> e properly be said to be "ordinarily residing" at a place immediately after he begins to
> reside there. For it may be his intention to reside there permanently and he may
> have severed his connections with all previous places of residence: cf. *Macrae v.
> Macrae* ([1949] 2 All ER 34 at 36, [1949] P 397 at 403); *Lewis v. Lewis* ([1956] 1 All
> ER 375 at 377, [1956] 1 WLR 200 at 203). To take another illustration, if a ship's
> officer spends all but a few weeks of the year at sea, and spends those weeks with his
> f wife and children in the home in which they live, it would be an appropriate use of
> language to say that he ordinarily resided with his wife; compare *In re Young* ((1875)
> 1 Tax Cas 57). And the same would be true of, say, a wool buyer whose occupation
> prevented him from being at home with his wife and family for more than a few
> weeks in the year, and who followed a regular round of sales and spent longer
> periods lodging at particular hotels than at the home. In such cases the strength of
> g the bond that ties the man to his family and their household makes up for the short
> duration of his stays in the home. Again if a person has once become so connected
> with a particular household that it would be regarded as his permanent home, and
> absence from it, even if of long duration and spent in only one other household, will
> not, in general, be regarded as changing the place where he ordinarily resides, so
> long as the move is for a special limited purpose and is not intended to be permanent
> h or to continue indefinitely: compare, as regards the relative unimportance of a
> "residing" which is for a special purpose and not for general purposes of living with
> "its accessories in social relations, interests, and conveniences": *Thomson v. Minister of
> National Revenue* ([1946] SCR 209 at 224–225), and *In re Young* ((1875) 1 Tax Cas 57);
> and in relation to the continuing importance of the connection with a permanent
> home until there is clear severance [then there is a reference to several other cases].'

j We think that the most significant point which emerges from this analysis is that the
concept of 'ordinary residence' embodies a number of different factors such as time,
intention and continuity, each of which may carry a different weight according to the
context in which, and the purpose for which, the phrase 'ordinarily resident' is used in
a particular statute. An illustration of this is to be found in the National Service Act
1948, s 34(4) which, exceptionally, defines 'ordinarily resident' as excluding residence

'only for the purposes of attending a course of education', and residence for 'a temporary purpose only'.

Some help may be obtained from the relevant entries in the dictionaries. For example, the Shorter Oxford Dictionary shows that the words 'ordinary' or 'ordinarily' may be used as the antonym of 'exceptional' or 'special' or 'extraordinary' or as a synonym for 'regular'. In each case the shade of meaning is different and, as Smith J pointed out, one shade may be appropriate in one legislative context and another in another. We think that in reg 13(*a*) 'ordinarily resident' is used to distinguish between those who are resident for general (ie ordinary) purposes, and others who are resident for a specific or limited purpose.

There is nothing in the tax cases, *Levene v Inland Revenue Comrs* [1928] AC 217, [1928] All ER Rep 746 and *Lysaght v Inland Revenue Comrs* [1928] AC 234, All ER Rep 575, when carefully examined, which is inconsistent with this provisional conclusion although there are obiter dicta which at first sight might appear to be. The House of Lords was not really concerned in either case with the distinction between 'resident' and 'ordinarily resident'. Both cases were primarily concerned with the meaning of 'resident'; 'ordinarily resident' was a subsidiary issue to which little attention was paid. The main issue was whether the individuals concerned were entitled to exemption from income tax on interest on securities of British possessions under r 2(*d*) of the General Rules applicable to Sch C, as persons 'not resident' in the United Kingdom; the subsidiary question arose under the Income Tax Act 1918, s 46, which exempted persons not 'ordinarily resident' in the United Kingdom from income tax on interest on war loan. It might have seemed a little anomalous if Mr Levene and Mr Lysaght had been subject to tax on their income from securities of British possessions yet not subject to tax on the interest from their holdings of war loan.

These cases have been cited very frequently as authority for the meaning of 'ordinarily resident', almost always for the dicta which are to be found in the speeches. Insufficient attention has been paid, in our view, to the reasons given by the Special Commissioners for finding that these two men were resident and ordinarily resident in this country. In the case of *Levene* the Special Commissioners' reasons are given and they read as follows ([1928] AC 217 at 222, [1928] All ER Rep 746 at 749):

> 'These are in our opinion questions of degree, and taking into consideration all the facts put before us in regard to the appellant's past and present life, the regularity and length of his visits here, his ties with this country, and his freedom from attachments abroad, we have come to the conclusion that at least until January, 1925, when the appellant took a lease of a flat in Monte Carlo, he continued to be resident in the United Kingdom. The claims for the years in question therefore fail.'

In *Lysaght's* case [1928] AC 234 at 238, [1928] All ER Rep 575 at 557 the reasons refer specially to his former ties with this country, to the length of time spent by him in this country during the year in question and to the regularity of his visits.

We were also referred to the case of *Miesegaes v Inland Revenue Comrs* (1957) 37 Tax Cas 493, another case under s 46 of the 1918 Act, in which a schoolboy at Harrow was held to be 'ordinarily resident' in this country. The facts are altogether unusual. The boy came to this country with his father as a refugee from Holland in 1939. As an extra-statutory concession, the father was not regarded as ordinarily resident. In 1946 he went to live in Switzerland but died there in July 1948. The questions was whether the boy was ordinarily resident in this country during the years 1947–48 to 1951–52. After his father's death the boy had no home anywhere but spent by far the greater part of his time in England either at school or with an aunt or with his former governess. It was submitted that his presence here during the relevant period was for the special purpose of schooling, but the Special Commissioners rejected that submission because 'in our opinion that consideration did not in the circumstances of the case point very strongly to the conclusion that he was not resident here' (at 495). In our opinion the judgments in the Court of Appeal must be read in the light of these very unusual circumstances of a schoolboy with no alternative residence but his boarding school. Plainly he was not here for the special purpose of education; after his father's death he had nowhere else to go. On the special facts of the case the observations of both Pearce and Morris LJJ as to the meaning of 'ordinarily resident' were entirely appropriate. As statements of general application they were, in our view, too widely expressed, and being in the context obiter dicta are not binding on us.

In *Stransky v Stransky* [1954] 2 All ER 536, [1954] P 428 Karminski J had to construe the meaning of 'ordinarily resident' in the context of the Matrimonial Causes Act 1950, s 18(1)(*b*) which gave the court jurisdiction to grant a decree of divorce to a wife not domiciled here, who had been ordinarily resident in England for three years immediately preceding the filing of her petition.

During the three-year period she was away from this country for 15 months living with her husband in temporary accommodation in Munich due to the exigencies of her husband's employment but returning from time to time to the flat which was never let and kept ready for her occupation. She was held to have been ordinarily resident here during the whole period. The learned judge said ([1954] 2 All ER 536 at 541, [1954] P 428 at 437): 'I can find no intention on the wife's part to make Munich her home for an indefinite period.' The case is constantly cited as authority for the 'real home' test, but it is clear from the judgment that this was just one of the tests and the one which seemed most appropriate on the facts of that case (see [1954] 2 All ER 536 at 541, [1954] P 428 at 437).

Macrae v Macrae [1949] 2 All ER 34, [1949] P 397 is an illustration of the weight which, in a proper case, may be given to intention. Mr Macrae established ordinary residence in Scotland immediately on his return there from England following the breakdown of his marriage because, from that moment, he intended to make his home in Scotland for an indefinite period.

Hopkins v Hopkins [1950] 2 All ER 1035 at 1039, [1951] P 116 at 122 is sometimes cited for the proposition that the addition of the adverb 'ordinarily' lends no added meaning to the word 'resident'. Pilcher J actually said: '... on the facts of this particular case at least—the qualifying adverb "ordinarily" adds nothing to the adjective "resident".'

Fox v Stirk [1970] 3 All ER 7, [1970] 2 QB 463 does not throw any light on the present problem. It merely established that a student at a university is 'resident' in the area of the university for the purposes of the Representation of the People Act 1949.

It is convenient, at this stage, to deal with a subsidiary argument put forward by counsel for the applicants based on s 34(4) of the National Service Act 1948. He submitted that this section demonstrates that when Parliament intends to restrict the meaning of the words 'ordinarily resident' it does so by express enactment. Apart from the principle that one Act is not to be construed by reference to other and unconnected legislation, it seems probable that in the National Service Act Parliament was anxious to make doubly sure that persons not intended to be subject to national service were not caught by the ambiguity of the words themselves. It is a pity that this precedent is not followed more often when draftsmen use, as they so often do, this deceptively simple phrase.

In our judgment, therefore, an important, though not the only, element to be considered in ascertaining whether an individual is 'ordinarily resident' in the United Kingdom for the purposes of reg 13(*a*) is the purpose of, or the reason for, his presence in the United Kingdom and his intention in coming and remaining here. 'Why is he in this country?' is a relevant question. If the answer is for a specific or limited purpose, rather than the general purposes of living here, he will not be 'ordinarily resident' within the meaning of this regulation.

The facts of each case must now be considered separately.

Nilish

Nilish Shah was born in Kenya on 15th July 1959. He is a citizen of Kenya and holds a Kenyan passport issued to him on 14th July 1976. His parents were then living in Kenya and are citizens of the United Kingdom and Colonies. On 1st August 1976 his father obtained from the British High Commission in Nairobi, a 'special voucher' entitling him to enter the United Kingdom for 'settlement' within the meaning of the Immigration Act 1971. On the same day his mother obtained an entry certificate marked 'Accompany Husband–Settlement'. Nilish himself was given an entry certificate on the same day marked 'Accompany Parents–Settlement'. The family arrived at Heathrow on 7th August 1976. All three were given leave to enter for an indefinite period.

Nilish has been living at New Southgate in London since that date. The house belongs to his father, grandfather and an uncle. He attended the Hendon College of Further Education from September 1976 to June 1977 and Southgate Technical College from September 1977 to June 1979, and has passed his O and A levels in various subjects. He has been accepted by the University of Manchester Institute for Science and Technology to read for a BSc degree in Management Science. He started this course on 2nd October 1979. His name now appears on the electoral roll for the area in which he lives. He states in his affidavit that he is 'settled' in the United Kingdom, and that there are no conditions limiting his stay in this country. In August 1979 he applied to the local education authority for a major award under the Education Act 1962. The evidence, therefore, appears to indicate that he has been resident in the United Kingdom since 7th August 1976 for all purposes, including 'settlement' as that word is used in immigration law. However, he has not been living with his parents. They returned to Kenya 5 weeks after their arrival in this country. Their passports show that they left on 10th September 1976 since when they have been living in Kenya. Both are entitled to 'readmission' to the United Kingdom if they wish. Nilish has returned to Kenya during the summer holidays each year.

The local education authority's decision on his eligibility for an award was conveyed in a letter dated 28th August 1979. The letter reads:

> 'I refer to your application for a major award to assist you with your proposed course of study. To qualify for a major award a student must have been ordinarily resident in the United Kingdom for three years prior to 1st September in the year the course commences. In accordance with guidance from the Department of Education and Science and from information available it appears that your real home is not in the United Kingdom and, thus, you fail to fulfil the requirements of this regulation. I, therefore, write to advise you that your application cannot be approved.'

The reasons for this decision are given in an affidavit, sworn by Mr Jack Dawkins, the director of educational services, on 26th February 1980. They read as follows:

> '13. The matters taken into consideration by the Authority in determining as a matter of fact whether the Applicant was ordinarily resident in its area in September 1979 were that:—(a) The Applicant had permission to enter the United Kingdom as a dependent of his parents who, on the occasion of his entry he accompanied and were admitted for settlement. (b) His parents however left the United Kingdom only 5 weeks later on the 10th September 1976 and have not returned since that date. (c) The Applicant is now over 18 years of age and his parents have not been resident in the United Kingdom for a period of more than two years nor had they lived in this country for most of their lives, when they left. (d) The Applicant is a citizen of the Republic of Kenya and a passport holder of that country. (e) He has regularly returned to the home of his parents in Nairobi during each of the summer holiday periods during his full time course of studies in this country. (f) Since August 1976 the Applicant has been continuously engaged in studies at colleges of further education in the Authority's area for which purpose he has remained in this country.

> '14. At the time of his application to the Authority, the Applicant's parents were no longer settled in the United Kingdom and his circumstances have therefore changed from those that obtained upon his original entry into this country. It appeared to the Authority that the Applicant's real home was in Nairobi in Kenya to which he returned in the summer holidays.'

The local education authority are not to be criticised for applying the 'real home' test, because they were following the advice of the Department of Education and Science in a circular dated 27th January 1978. Nor is the department, because the authorities are not in a satisfactory state. However, for reasons given above, we do not think that the 'real home' test by itself is particularly helpful; it is certainly not conclusive.

The return of the parents to Kenya after such a brief stay makes this case quite exceptional. We think that the only ground for saying that Nilish's real home is in Kenya would be the assumption that the 'real home' of young people aged 17 or 18 (Nilish was 17 on arrival) is with their parents. Even assuming that the local education authority applied the right test, we do not think there is any evidence to support their decision.

Applying what we hold to be the correct test, and in the absence of any suggestion that the father and mother did not intend to settle in the United Kingdom, the only proper inference appears to be that Nilish came to this country for the purpose of settling here, ie for all ordinary purposes of living and not for the specific purpose of being educated here, and has been so residing here since August 1976. We would hold that, on the material before us, there is no evidence on which the local education authority could decide that he was ineligible for an award under reg 13(*a*).

Jitendra

Jitendra's case has significant differences on its facts. He, too, was born in Kenya, and at almost the same time, 19th July 1959. He is a citizen of the United Kingdom and Colonies, but has no right of entry to this country. On 20th June 1976 he was granted a student's entry certificate by the British High Commission in Kenya. He arrived at Heathrow on 26th August 1976 and was given leave to enter the United Kingdom for two months on condition that he did not enter employment or engage in any business or profession. This leave has been extended on the same basis from time to time. His parents still live in Kenya. Since his arrival he has been living in London N12 at the home of his brother, Mr D U Shah. From September 1976 to July 1979 he was a student at Southgate Technical College. He has A levels in four subjects. He has obtained a place at Newcastle University to read for a degree in dental science. He applied to the local education authority for an award under s 1 of the 1962 Act but his application was rejected. The local education authority's decision was conveyed to him in a letter dated 1st August 1979. It is in precisely the same terms as the letter to Nilish, quoted above. In his affidavit in this case, Mr Jack Dawkins summarised the reasons for the local education authority's decision as follows:

> '12. The matters taken into consideration by the Authority in determining as a matter of fact whether the Applicant was ordinarily resident in its area in September 1979 were that:—(a) The Applicant had permission to remain in this country only as a student for a limited period. (b) The Applicant had been permitted to enter this country only upon the basis that he had been accepted for and intended to follow a full time course of study at a College within the Authority's area. (c) The Applicant was able to meet the cost of his course and his own maintenance. (d) The Applicant will be required to leave the country on the completion of his studies and expiry of extensions to his original entry clearance. (e) The Applicant's parents have remained resident at their home in Nairobi in Kenya. (f) Throughout the period in which the Applicant has remained in the Authority's area he has pursued the course of studies for which he was given his original entry clearance.
>
> '13. Upon consideration of each and all these matters the Authority concluded

> that the real home of the Applicant was in Nairobi in Kenya and determined to refuse his application for a Major Award, which refusal was notified to the Applicant by letter dated the 1st August 1979.'

It is clear that para 12(a), (b) and (d), contain the substantive ground for deciding that Jitendra was not ordinarily resident in the United Kingdom over the period of three years, although in para 13 Mr Dawkins refers to the 'real home' test. We need not repeat our comments on this.

In our judgment the evidence clearly establishes that Jitendra came to this country as a student, for a limited period only, and for a specific or limited purpose, namely to study and, if possible, obtain a professional qualification. For this purpose the terms on which he was permitted by the immigration authorities to enter the United Kingdom are evidence, and strong evidence, of his purpose in coming here and the reasons why he has remained here since 1976. His immigration status is not in itself conclusive but it justifies this inference.

It is only necessary to refer briefly to the immigration rules. The Statement of Immigration Rules for Control on Entry: Commonwealth Citizens (HC Paper (1972–73) no 79) treats students as 'passengers coming for temporary purposes'. Rule 18 requires the applicant for entry clearance to satisfy the officer that he has been accepted for a course of full-time study, and that he can meet the cost of the course and of his own maintenance. Under r 19 he must satisfy the officer that he intends to leave the country on completion of the course. The Statement of Immigration Rules for Control after Entry: Commonwealth Citizens (HC Paper 1972–73 no 80) provides in r 13 that on an extension of leave the student 'may be reminded that he will be expected to leave at the end of his studies'.

The contrast between these two cases brings out very clearly the difference between 'resident' and 'ordinarily resident' in the legislative context of reg 13(*a*). Nilish's answer to the question 'Why are you here?' would be 'To live, to study and to remain'; Jitendra's answer could only be 'To study, to qualify if possible and then to leave'.

We are fortified in our construction of this regulation by the reflection that it is almost inconceivable that Parliament could have intended to bestow major awards for higher education, out of public funds, on persons permitted to enter this country on a temporary basis, solely for the purpose of engaging in courses of study at their own expense. Such an improbable result is not to be accepted if it can properly be avoided.

The conclusion, therefore, is that in the case of Nilish there was no evidence before the local education authority on which they could properly decide that he had not been ordinarily resident in the United Kingdom for the relevant period, and that he was ineligible for an award under the Act. In the case of Jitendra, on the other hand, there was evidence which entitled the local education authority to decide that he was ineligible for such an award on the ground that he had not been ordinarily resident in this country for the relevant period or at all.

If necessary we will hear counsel on the form of order in Nilish's case but he appears to be entitled to an order quashing the local education authority's decision of 28th August 1979 and an order directing them to reconsider his application for an award. In the case of Jitendra we dismiss the application for judicial review and for any of the declarations claimed.

Orders of certiorari and mandamus granted in the case of Nilish Shah. Application of Jitendra Shah dismissed.

Solicitors: *Jaques & Co* (for the applicants); *E M Bennett*, Hendon (for the local authority); *Treasury Solicitor.*

Dilys Tausz Barrister.

a

Cicutti v Suffolk County Council

CHANCERY DIVISION
SIR ROBERT MEGARRY V-C
22nd, 25th JULY 1980

b *Education – University – Grant for study – Local authority grant – Eligibility – Student entitled to grant from local authority for university study if ordinarily resident in United Kingdom for three years – Ordinarily resident – Education Act 1962, s 1 – Local Education Authority Awards Regulations 1979 (SI 1979 No 889), reg 13(a).*

The plaintiff was born in Italy of Italian parents in 1961. His parents wished him to have
c an English education, and from 1971 when he was aged 10½ until June 1979 the plaintiff attended boarding school in England. In October 1979 he commenced studying at university in England. After the death of his mother in 1969 his father remained in Italy, and between 1976 and 1979 the plaintiff spent four holidays in Rome with his father and five holidays in England staying with friends or working. The plaintiff was an Italian citizen although he had applied in England to be naturalised. Although he had
d been given permission by the immigration authorities to remain in the United Kingdom for periods of six months, which were extended from time to time, as a citizen of an EEC member state he was entitled to remain and work in the United Kingdom. He applied to a local education authority for a grant in respect of his university education, pursuant to s 1[a] of the Education Act 1962. The authority refused his application on the ground that he had not been 'ordinarily resident' in the United Kingdom for the preceding three
e years as required by reg 13(*a*)[b] of the Local Education Authority Awards Regulations 1979. The plaintiff brought an action against the authority seeking a declaration that he was entitled to a grant. The authority conceded that whether the plaintiff was ordinarily resident in England turned on his intention but contended that, although he may have had a genuine intention of remaining in England to live and work, a mere state of mind was not sufficient and the intention to remain had to be manifested by physical facts
f which demonstrated a change in the character of the residence.

Held – In assessing whether an applicant for a local authority grant for his university education had the requisite intention to remain in the United Kingdom in order to be 'ordinarily resident' there for the purpose of reg 13(*a*) of the 1979 regulations, physical manifestations of that intention, although they could assist in determining whether the applicant had a genuine intention, were not essential for that purpose. Although the
g plaintiff had originally arrived in the United Kingdom for the specific purpose of being educated there, he had by the time the authority considered his application formed a genuine intention of remaining there, and that was sufficient to make him 'ordinarily resident' for the purpose of reg 13(*a*). The plaintiff was accordingly entitled to the declaration sought (see p 693 *e f* and p 694 *j* to p 695 *a* and *e* to *j*, post).

h *R v London Borough of Barnet, ex parte Shah* p 679, ante, applied.

Notes

For eligibility for mandatory awards by local education authorities for university study, see 15 Halsbury's Laws (4th Edn) paras 240–258.

For the Education Act 1962, s 1, see 11 Halsbury's Statutes (3rd Edn) 315.

j

Cases referred to in judgment

Clarke v Insurance Office of Australia Ltd [1965] 1 Lloyd's Rep 308, Digest (Cont Vol B) 458, *3653b*.

---

a Section 1, so far as material, is set out at p 690 *h*, post

b Regulation 13, so far as material, is set out at p 690 *h j*, post

Cunliffe v Goodman [1950] 1 All ER 720, [1950] 2 KB 237, CA, 31(2) Digest (Reissue) 641, *5217*. a
Inland Revenue Comrs v Lysaght [1928] AC 234, [1928] All ER Rep 575, 97 LJKB 385, 139 LT 6, 13 Tax Cas 511, HL, 28(1) Digest (Reissue) 359, *1310*.
Levene v Inland Revenue Comrs [1928] AC 217, [1928] All ER Rep 746, 97 LJKB 377, 139 LT 1, 13 Tax Cas 486, HL, 28(1) Digest (Reissue) 359, *1309*.
R v London Borough of Barnet, ex parte Shah p 679, ante.
Stransky v Stransky [1954] 2 All ER 536, [1954] P 428, [1954] 3 WLR 123, 11 Digest b
(Reissue) 355, *69*.

Originating summons

By an originating summons dated 12th December 1979, the plaintiff, Ambrose Cicutti, sought a declaration (i) that the refusal of the defendants, Suffolk County Council, by a letter dated 18th June 1979, to bestow an award on the plaintiff in respect of his c
attendance at a course at Warwick University pursuant to s 1 of the Education Act 1962 and reg 13 of the Local Education Authority Awards Regulations 1978 constituted an unlawful failure to perform their statutory duty, (ii) that the plaintiff was entitled to an award in respect of the course pursuant to the 1962 Act and the 1978 regulations, (iii) that the plaintiff was at the material time ordinarily resident in the area of the defendants for a period of three years immediately preceding the course and (iv) that the defendants d
had misdirected themselves in holding that the plaintiff had not been ordinarily resident as required by the 1962 Act and the 1978 regulations. The plaintiff further sought an order requiring the defendants to bestow an award on him in respect of his course or alternatively to consider whether he was ordinarily resident according to the proper legal test. The facts are set out in the judgment.

e

Michael Beloff for the plaintiff.
Anthony Dinkin for the defendants.

Cur adv vult

25th July. **SIR ROBERT MEGARRY V-C** read the following judgment: This case f
turns on the complex meaning of the simple term 'ordinarily resident' in relation to awards by local education authorities for courses leading to a first degree at a university. The plaintiff applied to the defendants, a county council, for such an award on 15th May 1979; and on 1st June 1979 the defendants refused the award on the ground that the plaintiff did not meet the statutory requirements of residence. The plaintiff accordingly seeks a declaration which will establish his right to an award. There is no g
dispute about any other requirements for an award; the only question is on the expression 'ordinarily resident'.

That term comes into the matter in two ways. First, there are the words of qualification in the Education Act 1962, s 1(1)(*a*). Subsection (1) enacts that it is the duty of every local education authority, subject to and in accordance with regulations made under the Act, 'to bestow awards on persons who—(*a*) are ordinarily resident in the area h
of the authority ...' Second, there are the words of disqualification in regulations made under the Act, the Local Education Authority Awards Regulations 1979, SI 1979 No 889. By reg 13(*a*) an authority is under no duty to bestow an award in respect of a person's attendance at a course 'upon a person who has not been ordinarily resident, throughout the three years preceding the first year of the course in question, in the United Kingdom ...' There is then a reference to the European Economic Community j
in the alternative which it is agreed has no application in the present case. At the time of the refusal of the award, the regulations in force were the 1978 regulations (SI 1978 No 1097); but so far as is relevant to this case, the corresponding provisions in those regulations, though worded a little differently, are the same in substance. The questions before me are thus (1) whether at the time of the decision on or about 1st June 1979 (for

that, I think, must be the relevant time) the plaintiff was 'ordinarily resident' in the defendants' area, and so was entitled to an award, and (2) if he was, whether during the three years prior to the beginning of the plaintiff's university course in October 1979 the plaintiff had not throughout been 'ordinarily resident' in the United Kingdom, and so was disqualified from requiring the award to be made.

The facts are relatively simple, and are not in dispute. The plaintiff has sworn two affidavits, the second being in answer to certain questions put to him by the defendants; and the defendants have been content to argue the case on the contents of these two affidavits and their exhibits, without putting in evidence of their own. The plaintiff was born in Rome on 10th March 1961, so that he is between 19 and $19\frac{1}{2}$ years old. His father is an Italian citizen and lives in Rome. His mother died in 1969. He himself is still an Italian citizen, though he has applied for naturalisation here; I do not know when. His parents wished him to have an English education, and so in September 1971, when he was $10\frac{1}{2}$, he was sent as a boarder to the preparatory section of a college in Ipswich; and shortly afterwards he was moved to the college itself. He continued there until the end of the summer term in June 1979. In October 1979 he began reading for a history degree at Warwick University. During the three years from October 1976 to October 1979, he spent one summer and three Christmas holidays in Rome, and three Easter and two summer holidays in England, working during the last of these, but otherwise staying with friends. Save for the holidays in Rome, he has remained throughout in this country.

Apart from the question of intention, about which there was much argument, those are the basic facts. It was accepted that there was no difference as regards being 'ordinarily resident' between the plaintiff's position on 1st June 1979 and his position throughout the three-year period which began in October 1976, or, for that matter, his position today. Nor was it contended that the plaintiff was resident in the area of any local education authority other than that of the defendants. The whole question is whether the plaintiff's presence in the defendants' area and in the United Kingdom had the quality required to make him 'ordinarily resident' within the meaning of the two statutory provisions.

The argument between counsel for the plaintiff and counsel for the defendants naturally centred on the recent decision of a Queen's Bench Divisional Court in *R v London Borough of Barnet, ex parte Shah* p 679, ante. In that case, there was an extended consideration of the meaning and effect of the term 'ordinarily resident' in the statutory provisions which are now before me. The court consisted of Ormrod LJ, Kilner Brown and McNeill JJ, and it was Ormrod LJ who delivered the only judgment; it was the judgment of the court. The facts were materially different from those in the case before me. There were two applications for judicial review of the refusal of the local education authority in question to make awards. Each applicant had been born in Kenya and came to England in August 1976, aged some 17 years. One of them, a citizen of Kenya, came with his parents, and was admitted for an indefinite period to settle here. After five weeks, his parents returned to Kenya; he remained here, living with relations but returning to Kenya for the summer holidays each year. In his case, the court quashed the local education authority's decision to refuse an award, and directed that authority to reconsider the award. The court held that there was no evidence to support the local education authority's refusal of the award. In the other case, the applicant, a citizen of the United Kingdom and Colonies who had no right of entry here, came here alone with a student's entry certificate, and was given leave to enter for two months, a leave which was extended from time to time. He became a student at a technical college and lived with his brother; nothing is said about visits to Kenya or anywhere else. In his case the application for judicial review was dismissed.

Counsel for both sides argued the case on the footing that the *Barnet* case, as I shall call it, was binding on me, though counsel for the plaintiff delicately indicated an alternative line of argument that he would otherwise have pursued. I do not propose to analyse the case in detail, though I must consider the ratio. After quoting from the judgment of

Smith J in the Australian case of *Clarke v Insurance Office of Australia Ltd* [1965] 1 Lloyd's Rep 308 at 310–311, Ormrod LJ said (at p 683, ante): a

> 'We think that the most significant point which emerges from this analysis is that the concept of "ordinary residence" embodies a number of different factors, such as time, intention and continuity, each of which may carry a different weight according to the context in which, and the purpose for which, the phrase "ordinarily resident" is used in a particular statute.' b

He then said (at p 684, ante) that in reg 13(*a*) 'ordinarily resident' was—

> 'used to distinguish between those who are resident for general (ie ordinary) purposes, and others who are resident for a specific or special or limited purpose.'

After considering a variety of decisions, many on income tax, and concluding that there was nothing in them, when carefully examined, which was inconsistent with this c conclusion, Ormrod LJ concluded (at p 685, ante) that—

> '... an important, though not the only, element to be considered in ascertaining whether an individual is "ordinarily resident" in the United Kingdom for the purposes of reg 13(*a*) is the purpose of, or the reason for, his presence in the United Kingdom and his intention in coming and remaining here. "Why is he in this country?" is a relevant question. If the answer is for a specific or limited purpose, d rather than the general purposes of living here, he will not be "ordinarily resident" within the meaning of this regulation.'

The court, I should say, rejected the 'real home' test based on *Stransky v Stransky* [1954] 2 All ER 536, [1954] P 428.

These principles were then applied to the two individual cases, with the result that in e the first of them it was held that the applicant, who was referred to as 'Nilish', had come to the country 'for the purpose of settling here, that is for all ordinary purposes of living and not for the specific purpose of being educated here, and has been so residing here since August 1976'. The other applicant, who was referred to as 'Jitendra', had come 'as a student, for a limited period only, and for a specific or limited purpose, namely to study and if possible, obtain a professional qualification'; and the terms on which he was f permitted to enter were strong evidence of his purpose in coming here and his reasons for remaining here. Ormrod LJ said (at p 688, ante):

> 'The contrast between these two cases brings out very clearly the difference between "resident" and "ordinarily resident" in the legislative context of reg 13(*a*). Nilish's answer to the question "Why are you here?" would be "To live, to study and to remain"; Jitendra's answer could only be "To study, to qualify if possible and then g to leave".'

On this, it might perhaps be questioned whether Jitendra's answer might not have added to it the additional phrase 'To live', since he had resided in England for over three years, and if asked where he was living it is not easy to see why he should not say that he was living in England. However special and limited the purpose in going to another country, h a man may still say that he lives there if he has gone there for any substantial period. He who goes as a visiting professor to Harvard for a year surely lives in Cambridge, Massachusetts, for that year. The real difference between the two hypothetical answers seems to me to lie in the contrast between the concluding phrases, between 'to remain' and 'then to leave'.

With that, I can turn to the question of intention in the case now before me. This was j at the centre of the argument. On the evidence, it is clear that the plaintiff initially came to England for the purpose of being educated here. It is not disputed that subsequently he formed the intention of remaining here, and living and working here. It does not appear precisely when or how or why he formed that intention, but the defendants accept that it occurred at some time before October 1976 when the three-year period

began to run. They also accept that it is a perfectly genuine intention and not a spurious
a intention asserted for the purpose of obtaining an award. As a student of Italian
nationality the plaintiff is subject to immigration control, and his passport shows that
when on 7th January 1979 he returned to England from his last Christmas holiday in
Rome, he was given leave to remain for six months; and doubtless this leave has been
duly renewed from time to time. In any case, counsel for the defendants accepted that
no significance could be attached to the restriction of the leave to remain to six months.
b He also accepted that when the plaintiff left Warwick University he would, as a citizen
of a Common Market country, be entitled under the right of establishment to remain
here to work even if he had not by then become naturalised here. His intention is to
pursue a career in the Civil Service, though counsel were not able to tell me whether for
this British nationality is requisite.

The case accordingly raises questions not only of the effect of a person's intentions on
c the quality of his residence here, but also of the result of a change of intention after the
initial entry into the country. Counsel for the defendants said that the *Barnet* case made
it plain that the plaintiff would have failed if his intention on first entering the country
had remained unchanged, since that intention was to come here merely for the specific
limited purpose of being educated here. Everything therefore depended on the effect of
the plaintiff's change of intention. A mere intention to remain here was not enough,
d counsel said, even though it was a perfectly genuine intention to remain here
permanently. There must be more than a mere state of mind: there must be some
translation of that state of mind into physical facts which demonstrated a change in the
character of the residence. Pressed for examples of such facts, counsel suggested the
acquisition of a home here, even if it was merely a single room in a boarding house or the
home of a friend. Another indication would be the existence of a place in which to keep
e personal belongings, or some arrangements for this purpose; and yet another would be
the making of financial arrangements here, as by opening a bank account. A further
example would be the severance of connections with all previous places of residence.

I found these contentions unconvincing. I can well see that in deciding whether or not
an asserted intention is genuine, the presence or absence of indicia such as these may well
be a matter of some importance. But once it is accepted, as it has been in this case, that
f the intention is perfectly genuine, I do not see why the presence or absence of such
indicia should affect the matter. Furthermore, in the case of somebody who at all
material times has been a schoolboy, I can see little reality in suggesting that he ought to
have acquired a home here. There would be no sense in paying rent or some equivalent
for even a single room when for three-quarters of the year he was boarding at school.
Indeed, if somebody did that, it might suggest that he was attempting to manufacture
g evidence to bolster up an intention of dubious genuineness. As for personal belongings,
those of most schoolboys are usually of modest bulk, and those which are not left at
school for the holidays may readily be taken to wherever the boy spends his holidays.
Nor is there anything in the question of bank accounts and other financial arrangements,
for, on instructions, counsel for the plaintiff told me, without demur by counsel for the
defendants, that the plaintiff had long had an account with both a bank and a building
h society here. Lastly, I cannot see why the severance of connections with all previous
places of residence should be a requisite of holding the plaintiff to be ordinarily resident
here, especially when his only previous place of residence is his father's home. Many an
adult retains close connections with his parents' home without thereby doing anything
to suggest that he is not ordinarily resident elsewhere. The idea of such a severance
comes, I think, from the judgment of Smith J in *Clarke's* case (at 311); and there it was
j used for the quite different purpose of indicating a way in which a man may be said to
be 'ordinarily resident' at a new place as soon as he begins to reside there.

For his part, counsel for the plaintiff at first accepted that a mere intention to remain
here was not enough, as there must in addition be the ability to carry out that
intention. However, in view of the celebrated passage in the judgment of Asquith LJ in
Cunliffe v Goodman [1950] 1 All ER 720 at 724, [1950] 2 KB 237 at 253, I suggested that

such an ability was implicit in the word 'intention' itself, and distinguished it from mere matters of hope or desire. A man cannot truly be said to 'intend' something unless he has *a* at least a reasonable prospect of bringing it about by his own act. On that footing, counsel for the plaintiff ultimately contended that a genuine intention sufficed per se, and alternatively that such an intention must be supplemented by the taking of such steps as the person concerned could reasonably be expected to take. Here, the person was a schoolboy, and the change in where he spent his holidays sufficed for the purpose.

I propose to consider the matter by stages. *b*

(1) From the *Barnet* case it seems clear that 'ordinarily resident' is a concept which requires the examination of a variety of factors, including time, intention and continuity, and that the weight to be given to those factors depends on the context in which the phrase appears, and the purpose for which the statute uses the phrase.

(2) The purpose for which the phrase is used in s 1 of the 1962 Act and reg 13(*a*) of the 1979 regulations is, I think, to define the local education authority which is required to *c* make the award, to define the applicants who are entitled to such awards, and to exclude those who lack a sufficient connection with the particular local education authority, or with the United Kingdom, thereby preventing abuses of the system of awards. Quoad the applicant, the statutory provisions are enacted in relation to the conferring of a benefit, as contrasted with provisions imposing a burden, such as legislation for taxation or national service. *d*

(3) The *Barnet* case establishes that the test is not one of what is the 'real home' of the applicant. Instead, the dividing line is between those who are in this country for some specific or limited purpose, and those who on the other hand are present for the general purposes of living here. What must be ascertained is the purpose or reason for that presence, and the intention of the person in coming here, and also in remaining here. These are matters which cannot be determined without ascertaining the intention of the *e* person concerned.

(4) The *Barnet* case indicates that in the term 'ordinarily resident', the word 'ordinarily' is primarily directed not to duration but to purpose. The question is not so much where the person is to be found 'ordinarily', in the sense of 'usually' or 'habitually', and with some degree of continuity (as opposed to 'unusually' or 'extraordinarily'), but whether the quality of the residence is 'ordinary' and general, rather than merely for some special *f* or limited purpose. No doubt there must be residence for a sufficient length of time and with a sufficient degree of continuity to be capable of supporting the contention that the residence is ordinary in its quality; but it is that quality of ordinariness which is of the essence, and not the duration or continuity. The Divisional Court rejected indications to the contrary which may be found in Revenue cases such as *Levene v Inland Revenue Comrs* [1928] AC 217 at 225, [1928] All ER Rep 746 at 750 and *Inland Revenue Comrs v Lysaght* *g* [1928] AC 234 at 243, [1928] All ER Rep 575 at 580; and on the footing that I was bound by the *Barnet* case, no submissions were put before me on these cases.

(5) It seems to me that the intention to be considered is the intention that exists at the time in question. Under s 1(1)(*a*) of the 1962 Act, that time is, I think, the time of the decision by the local education authority, both for general reasons and by reason of the use of the present tense; the verb is 'are'. Under reg 13(*a*) of the 1978 regulations, the *h* time is the whole of the three-year period. I say nothing about fluctuations of intention during that period, for no such point arises in this case. Intentions which existed previously, or came into being subsequently, do not seem to me to be relevant except so far as they throw some light on the intention at the relevant time. A person who comes to this country with one intention and then asserts that at the relevant time a different intention had come into being may well find it harder to convince the local education *j* authority or the court than a person whose case is based on his original intention having remained unchanged throughout.

(6) I do not think that there is any requirement that for this purpose an intention must be supported by any particular physical or other manifestation. Provided an intention is genuine, and is a true intention in the sense that the person concerned has at least a reasonable prospect of carrying out what he says that he intends, I think that it can

suffice for this purpose. As I have suggested, physical or other manifestations of the intention may play their part in supporting or detracting from the existence of a genuine intention; but I do not regard their presence or absence as being of the essence.

If those are the correct principles, then it is plain that some applicants for awards will have a strong motive for asserting that they have an intention which will entitle them to an award, and so, it may be said, the door to an abuse of the system will stand ajar. As this contention was not advanced in argument I shall not say much about it; but it may assist those concerned if I say something. First, it is clear that motive and intention are distinct; an intention is not vitiated merely because the person forming it has a self-interest in doing so. Indeed, the stronger the motive for forming the intention, the more likely it is that it will truly be formed. The question is whether the intention does exist, and not why it was formed. Second, nobody can form a genuine intention to live in this country for general purposes if he has no right to be here save for a limited time and purpose, and no real expectations of having these limitations removed. Third, I would regard it as an important part of the functions of a local education authority to scrutinise with care any such asserted intention, and to investigate any that appear to be doubtful or suspicious. Fourth, in any case I am bound by the statutory language and, it seems, by the construction put on it by the Divisional Court. If that language, so construed, is considered to be too relaxed, no doubt it will be amended or qualified by a further statutory instrument.

I return to the facts of the case before me. Counsel for the defendants understandably stressed the plaintiff's Italian origin and connections. His father and his father's home are in Italy; he has no home over here, apart from what has been provided by his school and then his university; he is an Italian citizen with an Italian passport which states his residence to be Rome; he is being maintained from Italy by his father; and until in 1977 he began to spend most of his school holidays here, he spent all of them in Italy. Further, he had no connection with the United Kingdom until he came here, and then he came only for the special and limited purpose of being educated here. I agree that if you look to the past, Italy plainly predominates. But look, as one must, at the three-year period, and look at his intentions and his daily life then, and Italy retreats into the background. It is obviously probable that he will be able to remain here to finish his degree course, and after that the right of establishment will enable him to work here, as he intends. Not only is his intention of remaining here admittedly genuine, and capable of being put into effect, but also, in spending most of his school holidays here and in applying for naturalisation, the plaintiff has been acting in accordance with that intention. The old pattern of his life has been superseded by the new; and in my judgment that new pattern was and is a pattern of being here for the general purpose of living here. The mere existence of foreign connections seems to me to be per se of small importance in considering where a person is 'ordinarily resident'; what matters far more is where he moves and dwells and has his being, and for what purposes he does so. His centre of gravity, once in Rome and Italy, came to be in Ipswich and the United Kingdom.

It therefore seems to me that counsel for the plaintiff's contentions are right in their essentials. As the action is for a declaration and not merely for certiorari, the question is not whether there was or was not sufficient evidence to support the decision of the defendants, but what the relevant rights of the plaintiff are. I shall therefore make a suitable declaration in his favour: the precise terms are for consideration. I will add that if, contrary to the *Barnet* case, 'ordinarily' had to be construed in the sense of 'usually' or 'habitually', my present impression is that I would have reached the same conclusion on the facts of this case, unless, indeed, counsel for the defendants had been able to put before me some authority or contention that at the moment I cannot envisage.

Declaration accordingly.

Solicitors: *Iliffe & Edwards*, agents for *Prettys*, Ipswich (for the plaintiff); *Sharpe, Pritchard & Co*, agents for *K O Hall*, Ipswich (for the defendants).

Azza M Abdallah Barrister.

Daly v General Steam Navigation Co Ltd a

COURT OF APPEAL, CIVIL DIVISION
ORMROD, BRIDGE AND TEMPLEMAN LJJ
20th MAY 1980

Damages – Measure of damages – Plaintiff's partial loss of ability to perform housekeeping duties b
– Plaintiff not employing domestic help in period between accident and trial – Whether loss separate head of damage – Whether estimated cost of employing help proper measure of both pre-trial and future loss.

The plaintiff, a housewife aged 34 with young children, was seriously injured due to the
defendants' negligence and suffered permanent disability in her right arm. Her claim
for damages against the defendant included a claim on her own behalf for partial loss of c
her ability to do her housework in respect of both the period between the accident and
the trial (the pre-trial period) and the future years. The plaintiff did not in fact employ
domestic help in the pre-trial period since her husband and his sister helped her in the
house. The trial judge treated the whole of the plaintiff's claim for loss of housekeeping
ability as a separate head of damage, and not as an element of the general damages for
pain, suffering and loss of amenity, and measured that head of damage according to the d
estimated cost of employing the necessary domestic help. He awarded the plaintiff (i)
£2,691 for the loss of housekeeping ability in the pre-trial period (a period of 299 weeks)
on the basis that during that period the plaintiff needed domestic help for 10 hours a
week at a cost of 90p per hour, and (ii) £8,736 for loss of housekeeping ability in respect
of future years on the basis that she would need domestic help for eight hours a week for
the rest of her life at a cost of £1·40 per hour to which he applied a multiplier of 15. e
Taking into account other heads of damage the judge awarded a global sum of
£21,116. The defendants appealed against the awards for loss of housekeeping ability.

Held – The appeal would be dismissed for the following reasons:

(1) In regard to the future loss of housekeeping ability, the proper measure of damages
was the estimated cost of employing domestic help for eight hours a week during the f
plaintiff's life expectancy, even though she might not use the award to employ domestic
help and might struggle to do the housekeeping herself and use the award for another
purpose, for the award so assessed represented the court's view of reasonable compensation
for the future loss of housekeeping ability. Accordingly, the judge's award of £8,736 for
the future loss was a proper sum to award (see p 701 *b* to *f*, p 702 *h j* and p 703 *d* and *h j*,
post). g

(2) In regard to the pre-trial period, however, the court had to look at the actual loss
sustained by the plaintiff, and therefore, in regard to that period, it was not correct to
evaluate the loss of housekeeping ability by reference to the amount it would have cost
to employ the necessary domestic help when the plaintiff had not in fact employed such
help. The pre-trial loss properly fell to be assessed as part of the plaintiff's general
damages for pain, suffering and loss of amenity by considering to what extent her h
difficulties in performing her housekeeping duties due to her disability had increased
those damages. However, the application of the proper measure to the pre-trial loss of
housekeeping ability resulted in the same global figure of damages as that arrived at by
the judge (see p 701 *j*, p 702 *a* to *c f* and *h j* and p 703 *d* to *f*, post).

Notes

For the general principles of damages for personal injuries, see 12 Halsbury's Laws (4th j
Edn) paras 1146–1147.

Cases referred to in judgments

Cookson v Knowles [1978] 2 All ER 604, [1979] AC 556, [1978] 2 WLR 978, [1978] 2 Lloyd's Rep 315, HL, Digest (Cont Vol E) 462, *1437a*.

Donnelly v Joyce [1973] 3 All ER 475, [1974] QB 454, [1973] 3 WLR 514, [1973] 2 Lloyd's Rep 130, CA, 17 Digest (Reissue) 117, *193*.
Hay v Hughes [1975] 1 All ER 257, [1975] QB 790, [1975] 2 WLR 34, [1975] 1 Lloyd's Rep 12, CA, 36(1) Digest (Reissue) 370, *1491*.
Pickett v British Rail Engineering Ltd [1979] 1 All ER 774, [1980] AC 136, [1979] 1 Lloyd's Rep 519, HL, Digest (Cont Vol E) 459, *1314b*.

Appeal

This was an appeal by the defendants, General Steam Navigation Co Ltd, against the judgment of Brandon J delivered on 10th July 1978 giving judgment for the plaintiff, Mrs Veronica Daly, on her claim for damages for personal injuries, in the total sum of £21,116 and awarding interest from the date of the accident to the date of his judgment at half the short term investment rate on £4,380 of that sum comprising £1,689 special damages and £2,691 awarded for the plaintiff's partial loss of housekeeping ability up to the date of trial. The judge awarded no interest on the balance of the damages. The plaintiff cross-appealed seeking payment of interest at the short term investment rate on the sum of £8,000 awarded as damages for pain, suffering and loss of amenity. The facts are set out in the judgment of Bridge LJ.

Patrick Bennett QC and *M N Howard* for the defendants.
Adrian Hamilton QC and *Alan Pardoe* for the plaintiff.

BRIDGE LJ delivered the first judgment at the invitation of Ormrod LJ. On 7th July 1971 the plaintiff was a passenger on a vessel belonging to the defendants. She was going to travel from Rosslare in Ireland to somewhere on the Continent of Europe, when she met with a most grievous accident which caused her extremely serious injuries to her right shoulder and arm.

In due course she claimed damages against the defendants, and the matter came for trial before Brandon J who, on 10th July 1978, gave judgment for the plaintiff in a sum of damages which was made up of a number of different items.

He awarded £1,689 special damages, £2,691 for what he described as the 'plaintiff's partial loss of housekeeping capacity up to the date of trial', and £8,736 in respect of the plaintiff's future partial loss of housekeeping capacity. Finally, for pain and suffering and loss of amenity, he awarded a sum of £8,000. He aggregated the special damage with the partial loss of housekeeping figure up to the date of trial, making a total of £4,380, and on that figure he awarded interest from the date of the accident to the date of judgment at half the short term investment rate, and on the balance of the judgment he awarded no interest.

The essence of the appeal before the court against the judgment is directed at the awards which the judge made for what he described as 'partial loss of housekeeping capacity', and at a late stage a cross-appeal has been entered on behalf of the plaintiff, complaining of the judge's failure to award interest on the damages in respect of pain and suffering and loss of amenity.

I have said that the plaintiff suffered extremely severe injuries to her right shoulder and arm. The nature of those injuries, the history of the long series of visits to hospital which the plaintiff had to undergo, and the consequences of the injuries are all accurately and succinctly summarised in the judgment of Brandon J. I could not equal, let alone improve, on that summary if I tried. I therefore propose to adopt what the judge said in his judgment:

> '*The damages issue.* After the accident the plaintiff was taken by ambulance to Wexford County Hospital and detained there. She was found to have a comminuted fracture of the right shoulder and paralysis of the right arm. An operation was carried out on her during the night, consisting of open reduction and fixation with a four hole plate with four screws. This involved a surgical incision on the

anterolateral surface of the right shoulder. On 9th June 1971, the plaintiff was
transferred to St Mary's Orthopaedic Hospital, Cappagh. She was found to have a
extensive bruising of the right side of the neck, the right shoulder and the right
arm, and laceration of the medial side of the arm. There was no muscle reaction at
all in the right arm. She was treated with physiotherapy and discharged home on
6th August 1971. On 22nd August 1971, a plaster was applied, and on 8th
September she was examined again at Cappagh Hospital where fresh X-rays were
taken. It was found that the bruising had gone and that a 4 inch surgical incision b
on the anterolateral side of her arm and a 3 inch laceration on the posterolateral side
had both healed. The fracture, however, had not united and there was very little
movement of the shoulder joint. There was some flexion movement in the fingers
and thumb of her right hand, but no dorsiflexion movement in either the fingers
or the wrist joint. The conclusion was reached that there had been damage to the
nerve supply of her right arm. Arrangements were made to have her return to the c
hospital for a further bonegraft operation consisting of the removal of bone from
the iliac crest and the placing of it round the fracture in the right shoulder. On 13th
September 1971, the plaintiff was readmitted to Cappagh Hospital, and on 15th
September the bonegraft operation was carried out. On 22nd September a plaster
was applied, and on 4th November she was discharged home again. On 29th
November she went into Cappagh Hospital again and the plaster was removed. On d
22nd December she was allowed home again. On 31st December 1971 and during
the first two weeks of January 1972 the plaintiff attended as an out-patient at St
Vincent's Hospital for treatment by physiotherapy. She was in Cappagh Hospital
again from 12th to 21st January, presumably for observation, and from 26th to 28th
January, when a pin which had been put in her shoulder was removed. She had
further spells in Cappagh Hospital; from 31st January to 4th February, and from 7th e
February to 11th February. She then continued to receive physiotherapy as an out-
patient at St Anthony's rehabilitation centre until 19th May 1972. The plaintiff's
shoulder was still very stiff and it was recommended in May that she should have
manipulative treatment in hospital. She went into Cappagh Hospital again from
26th to 28th September 1972, to receive such treatment, and there was a slight
increase in the movement of her shoulder as a result. In May 1973, a further f
examination showed that there had been some improvement in the function of the
plaintiff's right hand. The main problems were stiffness in the shoulder and the
absence of any extension movement of the wrist. The fracture itself had now
united. In August and September 1973, the doctors decided that the plaintiff
should have a further operation, consisting of tendon transplant, but, due to
industrial action, there was a delay of several months in making the necessary g
arrangements. On 4th February 1974, she went into Cappagh Hospital again for
this further operation, in which flexor muscles were transferred to the back of her
wrist. On 14th February she returned home again in plaster, which remained on
until 19th March. From then until the end of April she received further treatment
by physiotherapy at St Vincent's Rehabilitation Centre. On the 2nd May 1974, she
was examined again. Her shoulder was painful. She had one quarter of the normal h
range of movement at the shoulder joint. The transplanted tendons were working
and there was some extension movement at the wrist. On 15th July 1974, there was
another examination. The transplant was working and the grip of her hand was
fair, but there was no extension movement of the wrist against resistance. Exercises
at home were recommended. The last examination of the plaintiff took place on
28th July 1975. There was abduction movement at the right shoulder of 90°, but j
this was only possible when the arm was held forward. She was unable to lift her
arm above shoulder level. All the movement was between the shoulder blade and
the underlying chest wall. There was no active or passive abduction movement at
the shoulder joint. There was only a very small amount of rotation at the
shoulder. As regards the elbow joint, there was full extension movement, flexion
of 10° from a right angle position, full pronation movement, and one quarter of

> normal supination movement. As regards the fingers, there was full extension
> a movement except for a slight terminal restriction of the little finger which was
> slightly clawed; full flexion at all finger joints and half normal flexion at all knuckle
> joints. The hand grip was fair. As regards the wrist, there was good power of wrist
> flexion but dorsiflexion, though present, was not active against resistance. As
> regards the muscles, charting showed that there was good power in the small
> muscles of the right shoulder; the deltoid muscle had more than half normal
> b strength; there was some slight weakness of the elbow flexor muscles; there was
> considerable weakness of all muscles which extend the wrist and fingers; the flexor
> muscles were strong; there was some weakness in the small muscles of the hand;
> and there was some diminution of sensation in the hand and forearm. There was
> no evidence that the plaintiff's condition had improved significantly since that last
> examination of July 1975, which can therefore be regarded as showing her final
> c condition after all medical treatment to improve it had been given. The plaintiff's
> accident, besides producing the physical injuries and consequences of them which
> I have described, also had a serious psychological effect on her. She suffered from
> severe depression, and there was an adverse effect on her relationship with Mr Daly
> which put her marriage under strain. She has also suffered from dizzy spells from
> time to time and from insomnia.'

d The consequences of the extremely grave injuries which she sustained were
summarised by the plaintiff in particulars which were also adopted by the judge as part
of his judgment and held by him to have been fully substantiated. I will read them:

> '(i) As a result of the injuries caused to her in the accident the plaintiff, who was
> before the accident right-handed, has been rendered unable to carry out activities
> e requiring full use of her right arm including (a) ordinary housework such as ironing
> and vacuum-cleaning and making of beds, (b) gardening, (c) driving, bicycling; this
> has entailed giving up singing with a choral society since a car is essential to get to
> rehearsals, (d) washing her own hair, (e) playing tennis. (ii) In addition because she
> is more prone to falling because she cannot hold on with her right hand and because
> the consequences of falling on her right arm would be serious she cannot use easily
> f public transport or go out on ice or snow or stand on chairs or ladders. (iii) She is in
> continual pain which increases in winter. (iv) The scars have affected her appearance
> and attractiveness. She and her husband have had consequential problems in their
> marriage. There has been considerable stress and depression. (v) She is no longer
> able to enjoy the beach which she did before. (vi) She has found it difficult to
> exercise a proper supervision of her children and the consequent family difficulties
> g have distressed her. Her son is now at a boarding school. She has been precluded
> from increasing her family. (vii) The opportunities of paid work have diminished
> because she used her right hand to write.'

The plaintiff was a lady of 34 years of age at the time of the accident, so presumably she
is now 42 or 43. At the time of the accident she had two children, a boy aged 10 and a
h daughter aged 11. The judge accepted that the intention of the plaintiff and her husband
was to increase their family by up to another two children, but that the consequences of
the accident have been such as to render that impracticable, so that one of the matters to
be weighed in the scale in assessing general damages was her loss of a chance of an
enlarged family.

The special damages of £1,689 included an amount of £633 which had been paid or
j which was due to be paid to the plaintiff's sister-in-law, who had come into the family
household and who had undertaken the housekeeping work for the husband and the
children during the very considerable period when the plaintiff had been in hospital. In
addition, as originally pleaded, there had been a claim for loss of earnings suffered by the
husband in giving up part-time employment which he would otherwise have been in a
position to undertake and would have undertaken, but which he had been unable to do
because of the necessity to assist his wife in running the home.

At the trial, the claim for that loss of part-time earnings by the husband was abandoned, and there was substituted a claim on behalf of the wife to recover damages in respect of *a* the impairment of her ability to undertake housekeeping duties, both in respect of the years between the accident and the trial, and in respect of future years, based on the estimated cost of employing the domestic help which would be necessary to make good the plaintiff's own inability to undertake all the work needed to be done in and about the household. It is essentially this claim which forms the subject matter of the dispute in this appeal. *b*

The judge said this about the argument which had been addressed to him:

> 'I have considered first whether it is right to treat the plaintiff's partial loss of housekeeping capacity as a separate head of damage, or whether it should be regarded only as one element in the loss of the amenities of life for which general damages have to be awarded.' *c*

That single sentence really summarises the issue which has been canvassed before us in this court. The judge went on:

> 'Having considered the matter, I have reached the conclusion that this disability should be treated as a separate head of damage. When a person in paid employment suffers a total or partial loss of earnings by reason of disability, such loss is invariably *d* treated as a separate head of damage, with separate assessments of past and future loss. Where the person concerned is a housewife, who is disabled wholly or partly from doing housekeeping in her own home, she does not suffer an actual loss of earnings, and unless a substitute is employed, she may not suffer any pecuniary loss at all. Nevertheless, she is just as much disabled from doing her unpaid job as an employed person is disabled from doing his paid one, and I think that she is, in *e* principle, entitled to be compensated separately for her loss in a similar way.'

Basically, that is the proposition which counsel for the defendants challenges. The judge went on:

> 'As to the method of assessing the amount of the loss, I think that one way of doing it, though not necessarily the only way, is to take the cost of employing *f* someone else to do the work which the plaintiff has been in the past, and will be in the future, incapacitated from doing. It was contended for the defendants that this method was only permissible if another person had in fact been so employed in the past, and would in fact be so employed in the future. I do not, however, accept this contention as correct. The Dalys did not have the resources to employ such assistance in the past, but I do not think that the plaintiff's loss should be assessed at *g* a lower figure on this account. The loss occurred and the cost of employing someone else is no more than a way of measuring it.'

The judge then proceeded to adopt that measure of quantifying this head of damage, and he came to the conclusion that excluding the periods of time when Miss Daly, the sister-in-law, had been engaged in housekeeping duties in the absence of the plaintiff's wife, the total period when the wife was coping as best she could, with the aid of her *h* husband and daughter, amounted to 299 weeks, and that the reasonable figure to take as an average figure for the cost per hour of employing a daily help during those weeks would be 90p, and that the assistance which the plaintiff had needed but had not had in the shape of paid daily help would have been 10 hours per week. That is how he arrived at the figure which I have mentioned earlier in this judgment for partial loss of housekeeping capacity up to the date of trial of £2,691 which was 299 weeks at £9 a *j* week.

He then went on to deal with future loss, and said:

> 'I think that it would be reasonable to regard the average number of hours for which assistance will be needed in the future as eight hours per week. As to cost, on

> the footing that the present rate is £1·40 per hour, the weekly cost comes to £11·20, and the annual cost to £582·40.'

He then pointed out that the necessity to continue housekeeping was one which would remain with the plaintiff for the rest of her life and was likely to be 30 years or more, and so the judge took a multiplier of 15, and that is how he arrived at his estimate of the future partial loss of housekeeping capacity in the figure of £8,736.

I approach first the judge's assessment of the future loss in this respect. It has been energetically argued by counsel for the defendants that before future loss of capacity to undertake housekeeping duties can properly be assessed at the estimated cost of employing some third person to come in and do that which the plaintiff is unable to do for herself, the plaintiff has to satisfy the court that she has a firm intention in any event that such a person shall be employed. For my part, I am quite unable to see why that should be so. Once the judge had concluded that to put the plaintiff, so far as money could do so, in the position in which she would have been if she had never been injured, she was going to need, in the future, domestic assistance for eight hours a week, it seems to me that it was entirely reasonable and entirely in accordance with principle in assessing damages, to say that the estimated cost of employing labour for that time, for an appropriate number of years having regard to the plaintiff's expectation of life, was the proper measure of her damages under this heading. It is really quite immaterial, in my judgment, whether having received those damages the plaintiff chooses to alleviate her own housekeeping burden which is an excessively heavy one, having regard to her considerable disability to undertake housekeeping tasks, by employing the labour which has been taken as the basis of the estimate on which damages have been awarded, or whether she chooses to continue to struggle with the housekeeping on her own and to spend the damages which have been awarded to her on other luxuries which she would otherwise be unable to afford.

The essence of the matter is that the eight hours domestic assistance, which is the basis of the estimate on which the damages are awarded, represents the court's view of what she reasonably needs to compensate her for her own disabilities.

Accordingly, so far as the appeal challenges the inclusion in the overall estimate of damages of the judge's figure of £8,736 as an estimate of the wife's future partial loss of housekeeping capacity, I think it fails.

As a matter of strict logic it might seem to follow from that, that the same reasoning ought to apply to the period elapsing before trial, but if that is the strictly logical conclusion, then I think there is a fallacy in the logic somewhere. Looking at the matter as one not so much of logic as of practical reality, the fact is that the plaintiff is unable to say that she has incurred the cost of employing the labour which no doubt she needed in the years which intervened between the accident and the trial (ignoring the time when she was in hospital). What she has done and what she has had to do for lack of means to do otherwise, has been to manage as best she could with all the disabilities from which she was suffering and with the assistance of such help as her husband and daughter were able to give her.

Counsel for the plaintiff has argued strenuously that the judge's award under this head, the figure of £2,691 based on 299 weeks domestic help at £9 a week, can be understood as his evaluation of the domestic help which was rendered to the wife by her husband and daughter, but although this may have been pleaded and argued, I can find no trace of any such finding in the reasoning of the judge's judgment. With the utmost respect to the judge, I cannot think, that as a matter of principle, it is a correct method of evaluating what is essentially an element in the plaintiff's pain and suffering and loss of amenity caused by the additional difficulties she has had in doing her housekeeping work, to take the figure which it would have cost her to employ someone whom she has not in fact employed in the past, to take that burden off her shoulders.

What the judge certainly could have done, and I think should have done if the claim had been maintained, would have been to have added to the special damages the amount of the loss of part-time earnings which the husband had sustained, which was a figure either proved or agreed as I have mentioned earlier in the sum of £930, which was necessitated by his obligation to spend his time assisting his wife in the home.

But apart from that element of strictly special damage, I think the proper approach to this aspect of the case would have been for the judge to ask himself to what extent the difficulties which the plaintiff had had to contend with in performing her housekeeping duties in the face of the disabilities from which she suffered, ought to have increased the sum awarded to her for pain and suffering and loss of amenity.

Having said that, when I come to look at the figures awarded by the judge for damages here, and in particular at what I must say seems to me to be the rather parsimonious figure of £8,000 for pain and suffering and loss of amenity (even accepting that the judge was going to add to that £8,736 for future loss of housekeeping capacity) although I am satisfied that the judge arrived at his global figure by the wrong route, applying strictly accurate principles of assessment of damages, I am by no means satisfied that in the event the global figure at which he arrived was the wrong figure.

I test the matter in this way: if the judge had accepted that he was going to add £8,736 for future loss of housekeeping capacity (which as I have already explained I think he was entitled to do) and if the judge had said, 'Damages for pain and suffering and loss of amenity, £10,000 and an additional £930 special damages for the husband's loss of partial earnings which had resulted from his necessity to assist his wife in the house', then I do not think he could have been faulted at all. In fact, if I took those figures, that would be increasing the total award, and that is something which, subject to the question of interest, we are not invited to do on the plaintiff's behalf.

So the way in which I would adjust the figure is this: I would add to the £8,000 as the judge's award for pain and suffering and loss of amenity first £2,691 (which is the judge's assessment of partial loss of housekeeping capacity up to the date of trial) making £10,691, but I would deduct from that £930, the husband's partial loss of earning capacity which ought to be treated as special damages. That results in the general damage figure coming to £9,761 and the special damage figure becoming £2,619, that is £1,689 plus £930. Subject to the adjustment of the method by which the global award is arrived at, and subject to the question of interest which is the subject of a cross-appeal, I would dismiss the defendants' appeal.

So far as interest is concerned, it is true that the cross-notice of appeal claiming interest on the award of damages for pain and suffering and loss of amenity in accordance with the decision of the House of Lords in *Pickett v British Rail Engineering Ltd* [1979] 1 All ER 774, [1980] AC 136, was made at a late stage. The reason why the judge did not award interest on that element in the damages was because he was guided at the date of this trial by the observations of the Court of Appeal in *Cookson v Knowles* [1978] 2 All ER 604, [1979] AC 556 which have been subsequently disapproved in *Pickett's* case. Once the cross-notice is allowed to be entered, as clearly it should be, counsel for the defendants concedes he has no answer to the claim for interest on that part of the award of general damages which represents pain and suffering and loss of amenity at the short term interest rate from the date of the trial.

I would, accordingly, allow the cross-appeal to the extent that it is necessary to give effect to that adjustment.

TEMPLEMAN LJ. I agree. Taking the figure of special damages, the judge calculated that the figure for special damages was £1,689 including the cost of employing Miss Daly as a full time housekeeper during the period when the plaintiff was in hospital. That figure of £1,689 is the actual loss suffered prior to the trial.

In addition, there was an actual loss suffered prior to the trial of £930·48 being the sum lost by Mr Daly by having to give up his part-time employment, and the justification for including that as a loss by the plaintiff is to be found in the case of *Donnelly v Joyce* [1973] 3 All ER 475, [1974] QB 454. That gives a total special damage figure of £2,619. That leaves general damages, and those general damages had to take into account past and future. There were past damages in so far as Mrs Daly's inability to perform her housekeeping duties exceeded the actual loss for which account has already been taken, namely the amount paid to Miss Daly and the sums paid for Mr Daly. Then of course, there must be general damages for loss and damage in the future.

The future loss is estimated at £8,736, that being the cost of providing housekeeping services which Mrs Daly in future will be unable to perform. Then there are past and future damages in respect of pain, suffering and loss of amenities but excluding housekeeping loss for which credit has already been given. £1,760 damages for the past added to £8,000 for the future produces the figure of £9,760.

Adding all those three together, namely damages for the past and loss and damage for the future, the global figure which the judge gave, as Bridge LJ has said, is well within bounds.

In the result, it seems to me the special damages amount to £2,619 and the general damages amount to £18,496; and the addition of general damages and special damages brings up the figure to the global figure reached by the judge, namely £21,116.

ORMROD LJ. I agree with both judgments which have been given. The basic principle in all these cases is to arrive at a figure of compensation for the plaintiff which is fair to both parties. So far as the special damage is concerned, that, as I have always understood, represents actual loss, 'actual' as opposed to 'estimated' loss. So far as the general damage is concerned, that loss necessarily has to be estimated.

By reason of the rules relating to interest, it is necessary now to subdivide these awards in order to distinguish between that part of the award which the plaintiff was entitled to have paid to her, in theory, at the time of the issue of the writ, from sums the loss of which she will only experience in the future.

So far as the approach to the loss of housekeeping ability is concerned, I would deprecate talking about 'capacities' in this connection. The words 'incapacity' and 'capacity' are extraordinarily vague words on which much can be built on rather insecure foundations. What we have to do is to look, so far as the pre-trial loss is concerned, at the actual loss that has been sustained.

It is perfectly true that the plaintiff is entitled to some compensation for the loss of her ability to do her housekeeping during that period, but I agree that this is properly to be included in the estimated general damage.

I would venture to repeat what I said in my judgment in *Hay v Hughes* [1975] 1 All ER 257 at 275, [1975] QB 790 at 818, namely that in trying to assess what is a fair compensation in an internal family situation, it is not necessarily at all reliable to have regard to market values of housekeepers or other comparable people. It introduces a wildly artificial concept if one resorts to that and talks about compensating the husband in this case at a rate of a daily woman at so many hours a week. It simply does not represent reality at all. The nearest one can get to reality in a case like this is to see what the husband has actually lost, and thanks to *Donnelly v Joyce* [1973] 3 All ER 475, [1974] QB 454 we are no longer in any difficulty about replacing such loss for members of the family.

So far as the future loss is concerned, I entirely agree with what Bridge LJ has said. The judge's method of assessing that part of general damage represented by the future cost, at least in theory, of supplementing the plaintiff's capacity to do her housework, seems to me to be perfectly reasonable. It has to be quantified in some way, not on an £sd basis, but one has to be able to get the order of magnitude of the sum to be awarded, and the way the judge did it, by calculating the number of days a week, and hours per day and cost per hour of the housekeeping assistance seems to me to be a reasonable approach to it. The figure may be too high, in which case it can be scaled down, but it is as good a guide as one could think of.

In the result, I agree with the order proposed by Bridge LJ, unless counsel has anything to say on the question of interest.

Appeal dismissed. Cross-appeal allowed to extent necessary to give effect to adjustment. Special damages of £2,619 to carry interest at half short term investment rate from date of accident. a
General damages of £9,761 to carry interest at short term investment rate from date of writ.

Solicitors: *Stocken & Co* (for the plaintiff); *Ingledew, Brown, Bennison & Garrett* (for the defendants).

Bebe Chua Barrister. b

Practice Directions

QUEEN'S BENCH DIVISION c

Land registration – Production of register of title – Order for production – Procedure – Ex parte application.

The requirement that an application under the Land Registration Rules 1967, SI 1967 No
761, should be made by summons is hereby revoked and such application may be made d
ex parte on affidavit.

Accordingly, the Practice Direction of 23rd June 1970 ([1970] 3 All ER 70, [1970] 1 WLR 1158) should be amended by deleting the words 'should be made by summons pursuant to RSC Ord 32, r 1' and substituting therefor the words 'may be made by an ex parte application'.

This direction is made with the concurrence of the Chief Chancery Master. e

SIR JACK I H JACOB QC
10th October 1980 Senior Master of the Supreme Court.

f

CHANCERY DIVISION

Costs – Assessment in chambers – Chancery Division – Assessment by master – Monetary limit.

1. Since 1975 the limit of costs which may be assessed or settled in chambers by a master has been £500, with defined exceptions. This limit is now raised to £1,500.

2. The Practice Direction of 25th July 1975 ([1975] 3 All ER 224, [1975] 1 WLR 1202) g
is amended accordingly.

By direction of the Vice-Chancellor.

EDMUND HEWARD
22nd October 1980 Chief Master.

Barrass v Reeve

a

QUEEN'S BENCH DIVISION
WALLER LJ AND PARK J
20th MAY 1980

National insurance – Offence – Knowingly making false statement or representation for purpose
b *of obtaining benefit – Ingredients of offence – Claimant knowingly making false statement in claim form – Claimant's purpose in making false statement merely to deceive his employer – Claimant unaware that his statement would affect amount of benefit payable – Whether offence committed – Whether necessary to prove that false statement made with intention of obtaining benefit – Social Security Act 1975, s 146(3)(c)(i).*

c On 4th March 1977 the defendant declared in a form claiming benefit under the Social Security Act 1975 that he had become unfit to work on Monday, 28th February 1977, and had last worked on Friday, 25th February 1977. However he had in fact worked from 28th February to 2nd March and been paid for his services. An information was preferred against him alleging that for the purpose of obtaining benefit for himself under the 1975 Act he had knowingly made a false representation, contrary to s
d 146(3)(c)(i)[a] of the Act. The defendant admitted that he had made a false statement but said that he had only done so in order to deceive his employer. The justices found that on completing the form he had believed that his claim for benefit was only from 4th March 1977 and that he had not known that benefit would in fact be paid from the date on which he had declared in the form that he was unfit to work. They dismissed the information on the ground that the false representation had not been made 'for the
e purpose of obtaining any benefit . . . under [the] Act' for himself. On appeal by the prosecutor,

Held – In order to prove an offence under s 146(3)(c)(i) of the 1975 Act it was not necessary to show that the false representation was made with the intention of obtaining benefit under the Act. It was sufficient to establish that the person claiming the benefit
f made a representation which he knew to be false. It followed that the appeal would be allowed and the case remitted to the justices with a direction to convict the defendant (see p 707 *j* to p 708 *b* and p 709 *f g*, post).

Stevens & Steeds Ltd and Evans v King [1943] 1 All ER 314 applied.
Moore v Branton (1974) 118 Sol Jo 405 not followed.

g **Notes**

For social security benefits, see 27 Halsbury's Laws (3rd Edn) 702, para 1278.
For the Social Security Act 1975, s 146, see 45 Halsbury's Statutes (3rd Edn) 1244.

Cases referred to in judgments

Clear v Smith [1980] Crim LR 246, DC.
h *Moore v Branton* (1974) 118 Sol Jo 405, DC.
Stevens & Steeds Ltd and Evans v King [1943] 1 All ER 314, 41 LGR 108, DC, 25 Digest (Repl) 152, 635.

Case stated

This was a case stated by justices for the county of Humberside, acting in and for the
j petty sessional division of Grimsby borough, in respect of their adjudication as a magistrates' court sitting at Grimsby.

On 2nd March 1978 an information was preferred by the appellant, Maureen Barrass, against the respondent, George William Reeve, that he on 7th March 1977 at Grimsby,

a Section 146(3), so far as material, is set out at p 707 *d*, post

for the purpose of obtaining for himself benefit under the Social Security Act 1975, knowingly made a false representation, namely that he had last worked on 25th February *a* 1977, whereas he had worked on subsequent days assisting in the boarding of the vessel Globtik Venus, contrary to s 146(3) of the Social Security Act 1975.

The justices heard the information on 24th May 1978 and found the following facts: (a) The respondent signed and completed a benefit claim form on 4th March 1977 declaring that he had become unfit for work on Monday, 28th February 1977, and that he had last worked on Friday, 25th February 1977. (b) The respondent was engaged by *b* Globtik Management Ltd between 28th February 1977 and 2nd March 1977 and was paid for his services. (c) The respondent knew the statement as to the last date on which he had worked on the claim form was false. (d) The respondent completed the claim form on 4th March 1977, on which date the doctor examined him and advised that he should refrain from work for ten days.

It was contended by the appellant that having completed the declaration on the claim *c* form, which was admitted to contain a false statement which was made knowingly albeit to deceive his employer, and not having shown any way in which he intended to prevent benefit paid to him wrongly, the justices should have concluded that the respondent had knowingly made the false representation for the purpose of obtaining benefit for himself.

It was conceded by the respondent that he had made a false statement, but that it was only to deceive his employer, and it was contended that mens rea had to be shown to exist *d* for the purpose alleged in the information.

The justices were referred to *Moore v Branton* (1974) 118 Sol Jo 405.

They were of the opinion (a) that the respondent, on completing the form, believed his claim for benefit was from 4th March 1977 and was ignorant of the fact that waiting days would count from 28th February 1977, (b) that the respondent had completed the form in the way he did to deceive his employer so that he would not lose his job, (c) that that *e* deception, whilst reprehensible, did not amount to mens rea so far as the offence was concerned, i e it was not made for the purpose of obtaining benefit for the respondent under the 1975 Act, (d) that, being satisfied that the respondent had believed what he had put could not affect the date from which he would be paid benefit, the justices should follow the ruling in *Moore v Branton*. Accordingly the justices dismissed the information.

The question for the opinion of the High Court was whether the justices were entitled *f* to conclude that the respondent had not been guilty of the offence.

Simon D Brown for the appellant.
Peter Morrell for the respondent.

WALLER LJ. This is an appeal by way of case stated from the justices for the county *g* of Humberside sitting at Grimsby.

On 24th May 1978 they heard an information which had been preferred on 2nd March 1978 alleging that for the purpose of obtaining for himself benefit under the Social Security Act 1975 the respondent knowingly made a false representation, namely that he had last worked on 25th February 1977, whereas he worked on subsequent days assisting in the boarding of the vessel Globtik Venus, contrary to s 146(3) of the 1975 Act. *h*

The situation was that the respondent was regularly employed by one employer and had worked for him up to and including Friday, 25th February 1977. On 28th February the respondent did some other work assisting in the boarding of the vessel Globtik Venus and he took part in assisting in the boarding on 2nd March. Then two days later, on 4th March, he filled in a form claiming benefit. The form said this:

> 'Q. When did you become unfit to work? *A*. On Monday 28th Feb. Q. On what *j* day did you last work? *A*. On Friday 25th Feb.'

and then finished stating the time he had finished. That form was signed by the respondent on Friday, 4th March 1977.

The justices, having heard the case (and I do not think it is necessary to refer to any other of the facts), found that the respondent conceded that he had made a false statement but that he had only made it to deceive his employer. As it was submitted that mens rea had to be shown to exist for the purpose alleged in the information, that is to say for the purpose of obtaining benefit, they were of opinion that he, completing the form, believed his claim for benefit was from 4th March and was ignorant of the fact that waiting days would count from 28th February. In other words, he did in fact obtain slightly more benefit than he would otherwise have done, but he was ignorant of that. As they found that he believed that what he had put could not affect the date from which he would be paid benefit, they followed the ruling in *Moore v Branton* (1974) 118 Sol Jo 405 and accordingly dismissed the information. The question they ask is whether or not they came to a correct conclusion.

The issue which has been argued before this court is whether or not there is a third ingredient in the offence or whether it consists only of two. The first ingredient is: was there a false representation? The second is: was the false representation known to be false? The third, and this is the one in issue, is: was it falsely made for the purpose of obtaining benefit?

Section 146(3) of the Social Security Act 1975 provides:

> 'If a person . . . (*c*) for the purpose of obtaining any benefit or other payment under this Act, whether for himself or some other person, or for any other purpose connected with this Act—(i) knowingly makes any false statement or false representation . . . he shall be liable on summary conviction to a fine not more than £400, or to imprisonment for a term not more than 3 months, or to both.'

The justices in their finding, having come to the conclusion that the falsity of the declaration by the respondent was not made for the purpose of obtaining extra benefit, acquitted him.

It is submitted by counsel for the appellant that in doing so the justices were in error. He relied first on *Stevens & Steeds Ltd and Evans v King* [1943] 1 All ER 314, a decision of this court, where a case under reg 42 of the Rationing Order 1939 (SR & O 1939 No 1856) was considered by this court. That regulation provided:

> 'A person shall not: for the purpose of obtaining any rationed food make any statement which he knows to be false in a material particular or recklessly make any statement which he knows to be false in a material particular . . .'

The only difference between the form of that regulation and the subsection with which we are concerned is the part which deals with a reckless statement.

The court came to the conclusion there that, where statements were made which were false, the fact that the falsity did not in itself achieve any benefit from the regulations was not something which made any difference to the offence.

Viscount Caldecote CJ in giving judgment said (at 315):

> 'Therefore, in the ordinary sense of the words, it seems to me that these documents were made for the purpose of obtaining rationed food, although it is possible that the evidence would not have justified a finding that they attempted to obtain any rationed food by means of such reckless statement. It is of obvious importance to the food department to have accurate returns for the purpose of distributing available supplies and of estimating the supplies which will be required in the future. I have come to the conclusion, therefore, that in respect of those three articles of food, as well as in the case of the cheese, there was evidence upon which the magistrates could come to the conclusion that an offence had been committed under art. 42.'

The effect of that decision was that the court came to the conclusion that it was not an ingredient of the offence that the representation should be falsely made in order to achieve a greater benefit from the rationing restrictions.

That authority would appear to show that when similar words are used in s 146(3)(*c*)

of the 1975 Act the same consequences would follow; in other words, 'for the purpose of obtaining any benefit or other payment under this Act . . . knowingly makes any false a
statement or false representation'. In other words, the form is 'for the purpose of obtaining benefit' and if in that form a false representation is knowingly made the offence would have been committed. The appellant submits that one does not have to go further and show that it was actually falsely made with the object of obtaining extra benefit.

The difficulty in the way of that construction, which I am bound to say strikes me as b
the correct construction, is the decision of *Moore v Branton* which was referred to by the justices in this case. That was a case where the appellant was claiming benefit under the Ministry of Social Security Act 1966 (the Supplementary Benefit Act 1966) and she had to make a regular declaration as to the state in which she was living. She was obtaining benefit because she was separated from her husband and was living alone. There was a weekend when, in an effort to obtain a reconciliation, the husband spent either one or c
two nights in the house. The form warned the appellant that if any part of the declaration was not true it would be a criminal offence. One of the things that she was required to state was whether there was a change of circumstance, including the question of whether somebody had come to live in the house or whether anybody now living in the house had gone away. She did not disclose that. The allegation was that she failed to disclose something which under the provisions of the book she was required to d
disclose and represented (and this was her representation) that she was entitled to the sum of £18·10 whereas this was not true because she had become reconciled with her husband.

The justices came to the conclusion that there was a trial reconciliation, but this court came to the conclusion that in reality there was no reconciliation. What they found in terms is that her failure to make a disclosure about the trial reconciliation was not a e
dishonest failure with the object of swindling the Department of Social Security, and there is no doubt whatever that that was true.

The difficulty arises in this way, that this court came to the conclusion that there was no misstatement that there had been no change of circumstances. Bristow J came to the conclusion that it was very doubtful whether as a matter of law her husband coming at the weekend was within the paragraph at all. f

But in the course of his judgment he said that, in his view, s 29 created a criminal offence which involved mens rea in the true sense. In explaining what the true sense was, he said:

> 'In my judgment the evil aimed at by s 29 is getting money out of the Department of Social Security by dishonesty. In this case the justices find specifically that Mrs Moore was not dishonest in what she did; she did not think, and they found that her g
> evidence to that effect was true, that what happened in her case would have affected the amount of her benefit.'

If that were the end of what Bristow J said, that would be inconsistent with the view that I have just expressed, but he went on:

> 'Indeed, when one looks at the terms of para 6 of the coloured pages of the h
> allowance book, it is doubtful whether as a matter of law her husband's coming for weekends falls within para 6(5)(*c*) at all. Whether it does or not, the justices' findings are that she genuinely did not believe that her failure to disclose that partial reconciliation was something which could affect the amount of the social security she was receiving.'

j

The note of that, we are told, in Stone's Justices' Manual (112th Edn, 1980, vol 2, p 4188) does not fully represent the decision of the court. This court in *Clear v Smith* [1980] Crim LR 246 had to consider again similar words in relation to s 29 of the Supplementary Benefit Act 1966. There the false statement was that the appellant had done no work on any day in a week when in fact he had been doing work for which he had not been paid.

Lord Widgery CJ, in the course of his judgment, said:

> 'But the matter does not necessarily stop there, because we have been given a transcript of *Moore v Branton*. It is a decision of this court of 7th May 1974, and it is concerned with a matter very close to the present case because it is concerned with a declaration made by a person in receipt of supplementary benefit which was said later on to be false and to have produced the same criminal responsibility which is produced in the instant case before us.'

Then Lord Widgery CJ set out briefly the facts and said:

> 'That does not mean of course that the question of mens rea is wholly outside this case. It seems to me, I must say, to have a very limited application. But [counsel for the respondent] submits, and I would not be disposed to quarrel with him, that, if the objective test is satisfied in this case, as it is, all that is further necessary is to prove that the appellant knew when he signed the declaration that it was false.'

Wien J said:

> 'It was submitted on behalf of the appellant that the mens rea in this case was an intention to defraud. I venture to disagree. All that had to be proved was that for the purpose of obtaining for himself benefit under the Supplementary Benefit Act 1966, this appellant made a representation which he knew to be false, namely, that he had done no work on some particular days. What that means is that he knowingly made a declaration that was false. It would also follow of course that he could not know that it was false unless he was dishonest. That finding has in fact been made.'

As it seems to me, that decision of the court, which was given on 4th February 1980 and of which we have a transcript, is wholly in line with the earlier decision on the defence regulation in *Stevens & Steeds Ltd and Evans v King*. If it is inconsistent with *Moore v Branton*, I would think it was right to follow the later case of *Clear v Smith*. But, as counsel for the appellant has indicated, there is a difference in the facts of *Moore v Branton* in that the representation which was the basis of the case was that she was entitled to the sum of £18·10 which was rather different to the factual representations with which we are concerned.

In my judgment, the plain words of s 146(3) are covered if a person, for the purpose of obtaining any benefit or other payments under the 1975 Act, knowingly makes any false statement or false representation. There are no words to say 'with intent to obtain money' or anything of that sort. In my judgment, the offence is committed when there is a false representation made which the person claiming benefit knows to be false. I would, therefore, allow this appeal.

PARK J. I agree.

Appeal allowed. Case remitted to justices with a direction to convict.

Solicitors: *Solicitor, Department of Health and Social Security* (for the appellant); *John Barkers*, Grimsby (for the respondent).

N P Metcalfe Esq Barrister.

Greasley and others v Cooke

COURT OF APPEAL, CIVIL DIVISION
LORD DENNING MR, WALLER AND DUNN LJJ
17th, 18th JUNE 1980

Estoppel – Conduct – Conduct leading representee to act to his detriment – Representation – Detriment – Burden of proof – Representee led to believe she could remain in house for remainder of her life – Belief induced by assurances and conduct – Whether representee required to prove that she had acted to her detriment in relying on assurances – Whether assurances raising equity in representee's favour – Whether representee presumed to have acted on faith of assurances – Whether representor required to prove that representee had not acted to her detriment or prejudice by remaining in house.

In 1938 the defendant, then aged 16, was employed as a maid in the house of a widower and his four children. In 1946 one of the sons, Kenneth, became attached to the defendant and they lived in the house as man and wife. Two years later the widower died and the defendant remained in the house with Kenneth and acted as an unpaid housekeeper for his brothers Hedley and Howard for a short time until they left the house, and then looked after his mentally ill sister until she died in 1975. By his will the widower left the house equally to Kenneth and Howard, and on their respective deaths Kenneth left his share to Hedley, and Howard's share passed on intestacy to his two daughters. In possession proceedings brought against her by Hedley and Howard's daughters, the defendant counterclaimed for a declaration entitling her to remain in the house rent free for the rest of her life. The trial judge found that the defendant's belief that she could remain in the house for as long as she wished had been induced by assurances and the conduct of Kenneth and Hedley, but that she had failed to prove that she had acted to her detriment in relying on those assurances. Accordingly he refused to grant the declaration. The defendant appealed.

Held – The assurances given by the representors, Kenneth and Hedley, that the defendant could remain in the house for as long as she wished raised an equity in the defendant's favour and it was to be presumed that the defendant had acted on the faith of those assurances. The burden of proof was therefore on the plaintiffs to establish that the defendant had not acted to her detriment or her prejudice by remaining there. Since on the facts the plaintiffs had not established that, the appeal would be allowed (see p 713 *c* to p 714 *a* and *f g* and p 715 *c* to *f*, post).

Dicta of Lord Cranworth LJ in *Reynell v Sprye* (1852) 1 De GM & G at 708, of Jessel MR in *Smith v Chadwick* (1882) 20 Ch D at 44 and of Lord Denning MR in *Brikom Investments Ltd v Carr* [1979] 2 All ER at 759 applied.

Notes

For estoppel by conduct, see 16 Halsbury's Laws (4th Edn) paras 1609–1619, and for cases on the subject, see 21 Digest (Repl) 411–461, *1310–1601*.

Cases referred to in judgments

Brikom Investments Ltd v Carr [1979] 2 All ER 753, [1979] QB 467, [1979] 2 WLR 737, 38 P & CR 326, CA, Digest (Cont Vol E) 366, *4870b*.

Crabb v Arun District Council [1975] 3 All ER 865, [1976] Ch 179, [1975] 3 WLR 847, CA, Digest (Cont Vol D) 312, *1250a*.

Inwards v Baker [1965] 1 All ER 446, [1965] 2 QB 29, [1965] 2 WLR 212, CA, Digest (Cont Vol B) 242, *2579a*.

Moorgate Mercantile Co Ltd v Twitchings [1976] 2 All ER 641, [1977] AC 890, [1976] 3 WLR 66, [1976] RTR 437, HL; *rvsg* [1975] 3 All ER 314, [1976] QB 225, [1975] 3 WLR 286, CA, Digest (Cont Vol E) 211, *1109a*.

Pascoe v Turner [1979] 2 All ER 945, [1979] 1 WLR 431, CA, Digest (Cont Vol E) 214, *1222b*.
Reynell v Sprye (1852) 1 De GM & G 660, 21 LJ Ch 633, 42 ER 710, LJJ, 35 Digest (Repl) 120, *189*.
Smith v Chadwick (1882) 20 Ch D 27, 51 LJ Ch 597, 46 LT 702, CA; *affd* (1884) 9 App Cas 187, 53 LJ Ch 872, 50 LT 697, HL, 35 Digest (Repl) 51, *456*.

Cases also cited
Bull v Bull [1965] 1 All ER 1057, [1968] P 618.
Sharpe (a bankrupt) Re, ex parte the trustee of the bankrupt v Sharpe [1980] 1 All ER 198, [1980] 1 WLR 219.

Appeal
By a writ dated 6th February 1978 the plaintiffs, Hedley Marsden Greasley, Margaret Mary Greasley and Audrey Jessie Baker, brought an action against the defendant, Doris Cooke, for possession of premises at 32 George Street, Riddings, Derbyshire. The defendant counterclaimed for a declaration that she was entitled to occupy the premises rent free for the remainder of her life. At the trial in the Alfreton County Court the plaintiffs withdrew their claim for possession. On 12th July 1979 his Honour Judge Brooke Willis ordered that the defendant's counterclaim be dismissed. The defendant appealed. The facts are set out in the judgment of Lord Denning MR.

James Leckie for the plaintiffs.
John H Weeks for the defendant.

LORD DENNING MR. This is a family case. The lady most concerned is Miss Doris Cooke. In 1938, when she was 16, she went as a maidservant to help in the house of a widower, Mr Arthur Greasley. He was a butcher. He had his house and shop at 32 George Street, Riddings, Derbyshire. He had three sons and a daughter. They were teenagers. Doris Cooke, at the age of 16, went into that house as a maidservant. She was paid 10s a week.

Ten years later in 1948 the widower died. Doris Cooke stayed on. She looked after the family for nearly 30 years until 1975. During that time some members of the family had left; others had died; and she was left alone in the house. The house has become vested in some surviving members of the family. They wish to turn Doris Cooke out. She is 62 years old now. This is her home. The judge has ordered her out. She appeals.

I must tell more of the story. When Doris Cooke was in her twenties, living in the house, one of the sons, Kenneth, formed an attachment for her. She and Kenneth lived as husband and wife from 1946 onwards. Kenneth ran the butcher's shop and Doris Cooke, living as his wife, ran the household. Two other sons left. Hedley left and got married. He had no children. Howard, another son, left and got married. He had three children. The daughter Clarice remained. She was very ill mentally. The position was that, for many years, Kenneth was living there with Doris Cooke as his wife. Clarice, the invalid daughter, was looked after by them both, but particularly by Doris Cooke. Doris Cooke was entirely one of the family.

The title of the house descended in this way: old Arthur Greasley, before any of the sons were married or had left, made a will by which he left the house to two of his sons, Howard and Kenneth, in equal shares. Howard died. He did not make a will. His half-share, on his intestacy, went to his children. Kenneth and Clarice died in 1975. Kenneth left his half-share to Hedley. So the title was in Hedley and the children of Howard. After Kenneth's death in 1975 they gave Doris Cooke notice to quit. They brought proceedings to turn her out of the house. They said she had no title: she was not a tenant, she paid no rent, and had no status in the house at all.

The matter was taken to the county court. Pleadings passed between the parties. I will read a paragraph from the defence:

> 'The defendant received no payment from any person for her services after the death of Arthur Greasley in 1948. The defendant reasonably believed and was *a*
> encouraged by members of the family to believe that she could regard the property as her home for the rest of her life and accordingly did not ask for any payment.'

On that ground she asked to be allowed to stay in the house for the rest of her days and she counterclaimed for a declaration that she was entitled to occupy it rent free for the rest of her life. Then the case came on before the county court judge. It took a most unusual course. The plaintiffs, Hedley and Howard's daughters, had instructed a *b*
solicitor. Their solicitor simply got up and said that he withdrew the claim for possession against the defendant, Doris Cooke. Counsel for the defendant rose and said, 'But there is my counterclaim to be dealt with.' The judge said, 'Yes, you must prove your counterclaim. You must prove that she is entitled to be there for the rest of her life.' So counsel called the defendant and asked her a few questions. She said, according to the judge's note: *c*

> 'Lived there 42 years. I went there in service to Mr Arthur Greasley. I was 16 years . . . [she went through the story as I have told it] Kenneth died he had no children. Clarice died 20/8/75 mental trouble from 1947. Paid 10/- week by Arthur Greasley. Not pd wages after that. I looked after house Clarice, Kenneth & I looked after . . . Kenneth sd he would do the right thing by me. Hedley sd no *d*
> need to worry I'd be looked after. . .'

The plaintiffs' solicitor did not cross-examine. He asked no questions. He said nothing. Counsel for the defendant submitted that the counterclaim succeeded and he should have the declaration sought. The judge was troubled. He pointed out that the defendant had spent no money on the house. Counsel referred to *Pascoe v Turner* [1978] 2 All ER 945, [1979] 1 WLR 431 and to Snell's Principles of Equity (27th Edn, 1973 p *e*
565). The judge reserved his decision.

On giving judgment the judge rejected the defendant's counterclaim. She appeals, and for a very good reason. If her counterclaim fails it means that she has no right to stay in the house at all. The plaintiffs can bring an action tomorrow and evict her. Their counsel told us that was indeed their intention. She will have no answer because the issue will be res judicata. *f*

The judge made this important finding:

> 'On the facts that I have found I am prepared to accept, although the evidence is not very strong, that the defendant believed, because of what was said to her by Kenneth and Hedley, that she would be allowed to live at and remain in the house as long as she wished, though if Kenneth "intended to do the right thing by her" one *g*
> might have expected him to do so by his will.'

Having made that finding, the judge propounded this proposition of law:

> 'If the defendant is to succeed she has to prove that she acted to her detriment *as a result of her belief* and that the owners of the house encouraged her in her actions or stood by knowing that her actions were because of her belief. In both *Inwards v* *h*
> *Baker* [1965] 1 All ER 446, [1965] 2 QB 29 and *Pascoe v Turner* [1979] 2 All ER 945, [1979] 1 WLR 431 it was the expenditure of money on the property which raised the equity which provided the estoppel. There is no question of any expenditure of money in this case . . . I have not the slightest doubt that the defendant did that [ie looked after Kenneth and the mentally ill Clarice] and that looking after the mentally ill Clarice was an unpleasant and hard task, but the vital question is: has *j*
> she proved that she did that work without payment because of her belief that she would be entitled to live in the house as long as she wished? . . . I have accepted that they led her to believe she would be able to remain in the house . . . That means that long after any question as to the defendant's future arose she was doing all those acts which she has to prove were done relying on her belief that she would be able to

> remain in the house as long as she wished . . . There is no evidence which satisfies me that the defendant acted in any way to her detriment as a result of the belief induced in her mind by the words or conduct of Kenneth or Hedley. That means then she is not entitled to call on equity to protect her from what would otherwise be inequitable.'

The judge decided the case on that point. Before us counsel sought to raise many other points on behalf of the plaintiffs. But we cannot go into them. We must insist that the only points which can be raised on appeal are those which were considered by the judge in the county court.

The first point is on the burden of proof, Counsel for the defendant referred us to many cases, such as *Reynell v Sprye* (1852) 1 De GM & G 660 at 708, 42 ER 710 at 728, *Smith v Chadwick* (1882) 20 Ch D 27 at 44 and *Brikom Investments Ltd v Carr* [1979] 2 All ER 753 at 759, [1979] QB 467 at 482–483 where I said that, when a person makes a representation intending that another should act on it—

> 'It is no answer for the maker to say: "You would have gone on with the transaction anyway." That must be mere speculation. No one can be sure what he would, or would not, have done in a hypothetical state of affairs which never took place . . . Once it is shown that a representation was calculated to influence the judgment of a reasonable man, the presumption is that he was so influenced.'

So here. These statements to the defendant were calculated to influence her, so as to put her mind at rest, so that she should not worry about being turned out. No one can say what she would have done if Kenneth and Hedley had not made those statements. It is quite possible that she would have said to herself: 'I am not married to Kenneth. I am on my own. What will happen to me if anything happens to him? I had better look out for another job now rather than stay here where I have no security.' So, instead of looking for another job, she stayed on in the house looking after Kenneth and Clarice. There is a presumption that she did so relying on the assurances given to her by Kenneth and Hedley. The burden is not on her but on them to prove that she did not rely on their assurances. They did not prove it, nor did their representatives. So she is presumed to have relied on them. So on the burden of proof it seems to me that the judge was in error.

The second point is about the need for some expenditure of money, some detriment, before a person can acquire any interest in a house or any right to stay in it as long as he wishes. It so happens that in many of these cases of proprietary estoppel there has been expenditure of money. But that is not a necessary element. I see that in Snell on Equity (27th Edn, 1973, p 565) it is said that A must have incurred expenditure or otherwise have prejudiced himself'. But I do not think that that is necessary. It is sufficient if the party, to whom the assurance is given, acts on the faith of it, in such circumstances that it would be unjust and inequitable for the party making the assurance to go back on it (see *Moorgate v Twitchings* [1975] 3 All ER 314, [1976] 1 QB 225 and *Crabb v Arun District Council* [1975] 3 All ER 865 at 871, [1976] 1 Ch 179 at 188). Applying those principles here it can be seen that the assurances given by Kenneth and Hedley to the defendant, leading her to believe that she would be allowed to stay in the house as long as she wished, raised an equity in her favour. There was no need for her to prove that she acted on the faith of those assurances. It is to be presumed that she did so. There is no need for her to prove that she acted to her detriment or to her prejudice. Suffice it that she stayed on in the house, looking after Kenneth and Clarice, when otherwise she might have left and got a job elsewhere. The equity having thus been raised in her favour, it is for the courts of equity to decide in what way that equity should be satisfied. In this case it should be by allowing her to stay on in the house as long as she wishes.

I would therefore allow the appeal and grant a declaration on the counterclaim that the defendant is entitled to occupy 32 George Street, Riddings, rent free so long as she wishes to stay there.

WALLER LJ. I agree. I agree that it was unfortunate that the plaintiffs took no part in the hearing before the learned county court judge, but the judge heard the defendant give evidence on her counterclaim. He was addressed by counsel on her behalf, and he reserved judgment. He clearly found that it was not an easy question to decide, although it appears that at the time when he reserved judgment he was rather more concerned with the possibility of detriment and the absence of any specific financial detriment which the defendant could show. But, when he considered the matter, he delivered his judgment and he made certain clear findings. He found:

> 'At some time and probably more than once after the death of Arthur Greasley Kenneth told the defendant he would do the right thing by her [Kenneth was the member of the family with whom the defendant was living. Then another finding:] At some time Hedley told the defendant that she had no need to worry; she would be looked after.'

The judge did, in considering his reserved judgment, put the onus fairly and squarely on the defendant. He said:

> 'If the defendant is to succeed she has to prove that she acted to her detriment *as a result of her belief* . . . Has she proved that she did that work without payment because of her belief that she would be entitled to live in the house as long as she wished? . . . long before any question as to the defendant's future arose she was doing all those acts which she has to prove were done relying on her belief.'

Then he made the findings which counsel for the plaintiffs has submitted to this court were findings of fact which this court should not interfere with, namely:

> 'I am satisfied that the defendant looked after Kenneth and the house in which they lived with Clarice because she was living with Kenneth as his wife . . . There is no evidence which satisfies me that the defendant acted in any way to her detriment as a result of the belief induced in her mind by the words or conduct of Kenneth or Hedley.'

It was a difficult question, not a simple question, which the judge had to consider; and one cannot help being sympathetic in that he had to consider it in the absence of argument from the plaintiffs, and, as an explanation for his getting the onus of proof wrong in this particular case, that is probably the main reason. However, I am satisfied that he did, unfortunately, and that he was in error in the way in which he put the onus of proof. I would just quote the words of Lord Cranworth LJ in the case mentioned by Lord Denning MR, namely *Reynell v Sprye* 1 De GM & G 660 at 707–708, 42 ER 710 at 728, where, having set out some statements made by one of the parties, he said this:

> 'Every one of these considerations would be material ingredients towards enabling Sir T. Reynell to form his judgment as to whether he should or should not accede to the proposal of Capt. Sprye. If he had not received what was equivalent to an assurance that Mr. Yonge considered the proposed division of the property as the usual course of conducting business on such occasions, and if he had not been led to suppose that his interest was contingent, depending on the chance of his surviving Mrs. Williams Reynall, and then only to be recovered by expensive and doubtful litigation, it may well be that he would not have acted as he did;—perhaps he might, perhaps he might not. But this is a matter on which I do not feel called upon or indeed at liberty to speculate.'

A similar statement was made by Jessel MR, also in a case cited by Lord Denning MR, *Smith v Chadwick* (1882) 20 Ch D 27 at 44 where he said this:

> 'Again, on the question of the materiality of the statement, if the Court sees on the face of it that it is of such a nature as would induce a person to enter into the contract, or would tend to induce him to do so, or that it would be a part of the

> inducement, to enter into the contract, the inference is, if he entered into the contract, that he acted on the inducement so held out, and you want no evidence that he did so act . . . But unless it is shewn in one way or the other that he did not rely on the statement the inference follows.'

In my judgment, if the judge had been referred to those cases, he would have started from a quite different position in considering the facts. He would have had before him the finding of fact which I have just quoted, namely that Hedley said that she had no need to worry; she would be looked after; which indicates that there was in that conversation the possibility of worry in the defendant's mind. Whether it was said after she said, 'I am worried about what is going to happen to me', or whether it was just volunteered, it is certainly something which would tend to induce a course of conduct on her part.

Counsel admitted in the course of argument that a finding the other way could not have been attacked. If the judge had had in mind those cases, he would have come in my judgment to a different conclusion, namely, because of the fact that the defendant continued over all those years not only to live with Kenneth but to look after Clarice who was mentally ill, and as Lord Denning MR has said was a difficult person to look after, he would have come to the conclusion that the evidence showed that there was something which tended to induce a course of conduct, and it would be wrong to speculate what the defendant would have done if those inducements had not existed.

Accordingly I agree with Lord Denning MR that this appeal should be allowed and that the declaration should be made in the form asked.

DUNN LJ. I also agree, and would only add this. The circumstances of this case were very exceptional. The plaintiffs withdrew their claim for possession in the county court and, although they were represented by a solicitor, took no part in defending the counterclaim and indeed did not resist it.

The judge considered his judgment and found for the defendant on every point except one, and that is the only point that we can consider on this appeal. It is a narrow point. There is no doubt that for proprietary estoppel to arise the person claiming must have incurred expenditure or otherwise have prejudiced himself or acted to his detriment. The only question before us is as to the burden of proof of the detriment. The judge thought that the onus lay on the claimant to prove it. I agree that in that he fell into error for the reasons given by Waller LJ, and I also would allow this appeal.

Appeal allowed. Declaration in terms sought in counterclaim.

Solicitors: *Wrinch & Fisher*, agents for *Rickards & Cleaver*, Alfreton (for the plaintiffs); *Waterhouse & Co*, agents for *Robinsons*, Ilkeston (for the defendant).

Frances Rustin Barrister.

Jaggard v Dickinson a

QUEEN'S BENCH DIVISION
DONALDSON LJ AND MUSTILL J
15th, 25th JULY 1980

Criminal law – Damage to property – Property belonging to another – Belief of accused – Belief that owner would have consented to damage to property – Belief honestly held but induced by b *drunkenness – Whether belief induced by drunkenness a defence to charge of damage to property – Criminal Damage Act 1971, s 5(2)(3).*

The appellant, late at night and while drunk, broke two windows and damaged a curtain in another person's house while attempting to break into the house believing it to be the house of a friend in the same street. The two houses were identical and the appellant's c relationship with the friend was such that she had his consent to treat his house as if it was her own. The appellant was charged with damaging property belonging to another without lawful excuse, contrary to s 1(1)[a] of the Criminal Damage Act 1971. At the hearing in the magistrates' court she relied on the defence afforded by s 5(2) and (3)[b] of the 1971 Act, namely that she honestly believed that she had a lawful excuse for damaging the property in question because, as a result of her drunkenness, she believed d that she was breaking into her friend's house and that he would have consented to her breaking in and causing the damage. The magistrates held that she was not entitled to rely on the defence in s 5(2) because her belief that she had a lawful excuse was induced by her drunkenness. Accordingly they convicted her. She appealed. On the appeal the prosecutor contended that since drunkenness did not negative the mens rea required for an offence under s 1(1), because it was an offence of basic intent, and absence of lawful e excuse was an element of that offence, drunkenness could not be relied on to support a defence under s 5(2).

Held – Section 5(2) and (3) of the 1971 Act specifically required the court, when deciding whether there was an honest belief that there was lawful excuse to damage property, to consider a defendant's actual state of belief, and that belief could be honestly held within f s 5(3) even though it was induced by intoxication. The magistrates were therefore in error in deciding that the appellant could not rely on the defence under s 5(2) because she was drunk. The appeal would therefore be allowed and the conviction quashed (see p 719 *a b e j* and p 720 *a* and *d* to *f*, post).

Director of Public Prosecutions v Majewski [1976] 2 All ER 142 distinguished.

g

Notes

For lawful excuse as a defence to a charge of damaging property, see 11 Halsbury's Laws (4th Edn) para 1310, and for cases on destroying or damaging property, see 15 Digest (Reissue) 1439–1440, *12,690–12,693*.

For the effect of drink as a defence for crime, see 11 Halsbury's Laws (4th Edn) para 28, and for cases on the subject, see 14(1) Digest (Reissue) 49–54, *232–259*. h

For the Criminal Damage Act 1971, ss 1, 5, see 41 Halsbury's Statutes (3rd Edn) 409, 412.

Cases referred to in judgments

Director of Public Prosecutions v Majewski [1976] 2 All ER 142, [1977] AC 443, [1976] 2 WLR 623, 140 JP 315, 62 Cr App R 262, HL, 14(1) Digest (Reissue) 54, *258*. j

Director of Public Prosecutions v Morgan [1975] 2 All ER 922, [1976] AC 182, [1975] 2 WLR 913, 139 JP 476, 61 Cr App R 136, HL, 15 Digest (Reissue) 1212, *10,398*.

---

a Section 1(1) is set out at p 718 *c d*, post

b Section 5, so far as material, is set out at p 718 *e f*, post

R v O'Driscoll (1977) 65 Cr App R 50, CA, Digest (Cont Vol E) 126, *251a*.

R v Smith (David Raymond) [1974] 1 All ER 632, [1974] QB 354, [1974] 2 WLR 20, 138 JP 236, 58 Crim App R 320, CA, 15 Digest (Reissue) 1439, *12,690*.

R v Stephenson [1979] 2 All ER 1198, [1979] QB 695, [1979] 3 WLR 193, 143 JP 592, CA, Digest (Cont Vol E) 161, *12,692a*.

Case stated

This was a case stated by justices for the County of Essex acting in and for the petty sessional division of Thurrock in respect of their adjudication as a magistrates' court sitting at Grays, Essex.

On 12th October 1978 an information was preferred by the respondent, Detective Chief Inspector James Alexander Dickinson, against the appellant, Beverley Anne Jaggard, that on 11th October 1978 at South Ockendon, Essex, she, without lawful excuse, damaged two window panes and a length of net curtain belonging to Patricia Ann Raven intending to damage them or being reckless whether they would be damaged, contrary to s 1(1) of the Criminal Damage Act 1971.

The magistrates found the following facts. 35 Carnach Green, South Ockendon, which was occupied by Mrs Raven, and 67 Carnach Green, South Ockendon, which was occupied by Ronald Frederick Heyfron, were externally identical properties. The appellant did not know Mrs Raven and had no contact with her prior to the events giving rise to the charge against the appellant. The appellant did know Mr Heyfron and their relationship was such that she had his consent at any time to treat his property as if it was her own. At 10.45 pm on the day of the offence the appellant was in state of self-induced intoxication and ordered a taxi to take her to 67 Carnach Green, Mr Heyfron's property, but the taxi delivered her to 35 Carnach Green, Mrs Raven's property. She entered the garden of 35 Carnach Green and was ordered by Mrs Raven to remove herself. The appellant then broke the window in the hallway of 35 Carnach Green and then broke the window in the back door of the premises, damaging a net curtain, and gained entry to 35 Carnach Green.

The appellant contended that at the time she broke into 35 Carnach Green she had a genuine belief she was breaking into 67 Carnach Green and that her relationship with Mr Heyfron was such that she had his consent to break into 67 Carnach Green, and she relied on s 5(2) of the 1971 Act as affording her a defence to the charge. The prosecutor contended that she could not rely on the defence in s 5(2) because the damaged property belonged to someone other than Mr Heyfron and because the appellant was in a state of self-induced intoxication.

The magistrates were of the opinion that the appellant believed she was breaking into 67 Carnach Green but that this belief was not a genuine and honest mistake because it was induced by a state of intoxication. Accordingly, they convicted the appellant, fined her £20 and ordered her to pay costs of £10·55 to the prosecutor.

The question for the opinion of the High Court was whether the magistrates were right in deciding that a defendant charged with an offence under s 1 of the 1971 Act could not rely on the defence afforded by s 5 of that Act if the belief relied on was brought about by a state of self-induced intoxication.

Nigel Lithman for the appellant.
Andrew Collins for the respondent.

Cur adv vult

25th July. The following judgments were read.

MUSTILL J (delivering the first judgment at the invitation of Donaldson LJ). On 21st March 1979 the appellant was convicted by the justices for the County of Essex on a charge of damaging property contrary to s 1(1) of the Criminal Damage Act 1971. She now appeals to this court by way of case stated.

The facts set out in the case are short but striking. On the evening of 12th October 1978 the appellant had been drinking. At 10.45 pm she engaged a taxi to take her to 67 Carnach Green, South Ockendon, a house occupied by Mr R F Heyfron, a gentleman with whom she had a relationship such that, in the words of the magistrates, she had his consent at any time to treat his property as if it was her own. Alighting from the taxi, she entered the garden but was asked to leave by a Mrs Raven who was a stranger to her. Persisting, she broke the glass in the hallway of the house. She then went to the back door where she broke another window and gained entry to the house, damaging a net curtain in the process. At some time thereafter, in circumstances not described by the magistrates, it became clear that the house was not 67 Carnach Green but 35 Carnach Green, a house of identical outward appearance, occupied by Mrs Raven. The magistrates have found that the appellant did believe that she was breaking into the property of Mr Heyfron but that this mistake was induced by a state of self-induced intoxication.

In these circumstances, the respondent prosecuted the appellant for an offence under s 1(1) of the 1971 Act which reads as follows:

> 'A person who without lawful excuse destroys or damages any property belonging to another intending to destroy or damage any such property or being reckless as to whether any such property would be destroyed or damaged shall be guilty of an offence.'

At the hearing before the magistrates the appellant relied on the following provisions of s 5 of the 1971 Act:

> '(2) A person charged with an offence to which this section applies shall, whether or not he would be treated for the purposes of this Act as having a lawful excuse apart from this subsection, be treated for those purposes as having a lawful excuse— (*a*) if at the time of the act or acts alleged to constitute the offence he believed that the person or persons whom he believed to be entitled to consent to the destruction of or damage to the property in question had so consented, or would have so consented to it if he or they had known of the destruction or damage and its circumstances . . .
>
> '(3) For the purposes of this section it is immaterial whether a belief is justified or not if it is honestly held . . .'

It is convenient to refer to the exculpatory provisions of s 5(2) as if they created a defence whilst recognising that the burden of disproving the facts referred to by the subsection remains on the prosecution. The magistrates held that the appellant was not entitled to rely on s 5(2) since the belief relied on was brought about by a state of self-induced intoxication.

In support of the conviction counsel for the respondent advanced an argument which may be summarised as follows. (i) Where an offence is one of 'basic intent', in contrast to one of 'specific intent', the fact that the accused was in a state of self-induced intoxication at the time when he did the acts constituting the actus reus does not prevent him from possessing the mens rea necessary to constitute the offence: see *Director of Public Prosecutions v Morgan* [1975] 2 All ER 922, [1976] AC 182, *Director of Public Prosecutions v Majewski* [1976] 2 All ER 142, [1977] AC 443. (ii) Section 1(1) of the 1971 Act creates an offence of basic intent: see *R v Stephenson* [1979] 2 All ER 1198, [1979] QB 695. (iii) Section 5(3) has no bearing on the present issue. It does not create a separate defence, but is no more than a partial definition of the expression 'without lawful excuse' in s 1(1). The absence of lawful excuse forms an element in the mens rea: see *R v Smith* [1974] 1 All ER 632 at 636, [1974] QB 354 at 360. Accordingly, since drunkenness does not negative mens rea in crimes of basic intent, it cannot be relied on as part of a defence based on s 5(2).

Whilst this is an attractive submission, we consider it to be unsound, for the following reasons. In the first place, the argument transfers the distinction between offences of specific and of basic intent to a context in which it has no place. The distinction is material where the defendant relies on his own drunkenness as a ground for denying that he had the degree of intention or recklessness required in order to constitute the offence. Here, by contrast, the appellant does not rely on her drunkenness to displace an inference of intent or recklessness; indeed she does not rely on it at all. Her defence is founded on the state of belief called for by s 5(2). True, the fact of the appellant's intoxication was relevant to the defence under s 5(2) for it helped to explain what would otherwise have been inexplicable, and hence lent colour to her evidence about the state of her belief. This is not the same as using drunkenness to rebut an inference of intention or recklessness. Belief, like intention or recklessness, is a state of mind; but they are not the same states of mind.

Can it nevertheless be said that, even if the context is different, the principles established by *Majewski* ought to be applied to this new situation? If the basis of the decision in *Majewski* had been that drunkenness does not prevent a person from having an intent or being reckless, then there would be grounds for saying that it should equally be left out of account when deciding on his state of belief. But this is not in our view what *Majewski* decided. The House of Lords did not conclude that intoxication was irrelevant to the fact of the defendant's state of mind, but rather that, whatever might have been his actual state of mind, he should for reasons of policy be precluded from relying on any alteration in that state brought about by self-induced intoxication. The same considerations of policy apply to the intent or recklessness which is the mens rea of the offence created by s 1(1) and that offence is accordingly regarded as one of basic intent (see *R v Stephenson*). It is indeed essential that this should be so, for drink so often plays a part in offences of criminal damage, and to admit drunkenness as a potential means of escaping liability would provide much too ready a means of avoiding conviction. But these considerations do not apply to a case where Parliament has specifically required the court to consider the defendant's actual state of belief, not the state of belief which ought to have existed. This seems to us to show that the court is required by s 5(3) to focus on the existence of the belief, not its intellectual soundness; and a belief can be just as much honestly held if it is induced by intoxication as if it stems from stupidity, forgetfulness or inattention.

It was, however, urged that we could not properly read s 5(2) in isolation from s 1(1), which forms the context of the words 'without lawful excuse' partially defined by s 5(2). Once the words are put in context, so it is maintained, it can be seen that the law must treat drunkenness in the same way in relation to lawful excuse (and hence belief) as it does to intention and recklessness, for they are all part of the mens rea of the offence. To fragment the mens rea, so as to treat one part of it as affected by drunkenness in one way and the remainder as affected in a different way, would make the law impossibly complicated to enforce.

If it had been necessary to decide whether, for all purposes, the mens rea of an offence under s 1(1) extends as far as an intent (or recklessness) as to the existence of a lawful excuse, I should have wished to consider the observations of James LJ, delivering the judgment of the Court of Appeal in *R v Smith* [1974] 1 All ER 632 at 636, [1974] QB 354 at 360. I do not however find it necessary to reach a conclusion on this matter and will only say that I am not at present convinced that, when these observations are read in the context of the judgment as a whole, they have the meaning which the respondent has sought to put on them. In my view, however, the answer to the argument lies in the fact that any distinctions which have to be drawn as to the relevance of drunkenness to the two subsections arises from the scheme of the 1971 Act itself. No doubt the mens rea is in general indivisible, with no distinction being possible as regards the effect of drunkenness. But Parliament has specifically isolated one subjective element, in the shape of honest belief, and has given it separate treatment and its own special gloss in s 5(3). This being so, there is nothing objectionable in giving it special treatment as regards drunkenness, in accordance with the natural meaning of its words.

In these circumstances, I would hold that the magistrates were in error when they decided that the defence furnished to the appellant by s 5(2) was lost because she was drunk at the time. I would therefore allow the appeal.

DONALDSON LJ. I agree, but in deference to the very careful arguments with which we have been assisted in this case, I would like to express my own view, albeit briefly. a

As I understand the law as expounded in *R v Majewski* [1976] 2 All ER 142, [1977] AC 443, where self-induced intoxication in fact deprives an accused person of the mental ability to form a relevant intent but otherwise the essential ingredients of the offence are proved, his liability to conviction will depend on whether the relevant intent was a general, or basic, intent or a specific intent. If only a general or basic intent is required, the effects of the intoxication cannot be relied on. Aliter, if a specific intent is required. b The distinction between a general, or basic, intent and a specific intent is that, whereas the former extends only to the actus reus, a specific intent extends beyond it.

The actus reus in s 1(1) of the Criminal Damage Act 1971 consists of destroying or damaging the property of another and the mens rea, consisting of an intent or recklessness and absence of lawful excuse, is co-extensive (see *R v Smith* [1974] 1 All ER 632 at 636, [1974] QB 354 at 360 per James LJ). Accordingly this is a crime of basic c intent and was so held in *R v O'Driscoll* (1977) 65 Cr App R 50 at 55, where Waller LJ also pointed to the contrast between s 1(1) and s 1(2), where a further and specific intent was required, namely an intent by the criminal damage to endanger the life of another.

If, therefore, the 1971 Act had not contained s 5 there would be no problem. The appellant would have been rightly convicted. The question for us, and so far as I know it is a completely novel question, is whether s 5 makes any difference. d

The law in relation to self-induced intoxication and crimes of basic intent is without doubt an exception to the general rule that the prosecution must prove the actual existence of the relevant intent, be it basic or specific (see *R v Stephenson* [1979] 2 All ER 1198 at 1204, [1979] QB 695 at 704 per Geoffrey Lane LJ). And in s 5 Parliament has very specifically extended what would otherwise be regarded as 'lawful excuse' by providing that it is immaterial whether the relevant belief is justified or not provided e that it is honestly held. The justification for what I may call the *Majewski* exception, although it is much older than that decision, is said to be that the course of conduct inducing the intoxication supplies the evidence of mens rea (see [1976] 2 All ER 142 at 150–151, [1977] AC 443 at 474–475) per Lord Elwyn-Jones LC. It seems to me that to hold that this substituted mens rea overrides so specific a statutory provision involves reading s 5(2) as if it provided that 'for the purposes of this section it is immaterial f whether a belief is justified or not if it is honestly held provided that the honesty of the belief is not attributable only to self-induced intoxication'. I cannot so construe the section and I too would therefore allow the appeal.

Appeal allowed. Conviction quashed.

g

The court refused leave to appeal to the House of Lords but certified under s 1(2) of the Administration of Justice Act 1960 that the following point of law of general public importance was involved in the decision: whether it is a defence to a charge under s 1(1) of the Criminal Damage Act 1971 that a defendant, as a result of self-induced intoxication, has an honest belief that a state of affairs exists that in all other respects constitutes a lawful excuse within s 5(2)(a) and (3) of that Act. h

Solicitors: *Roberts-Morgan, Shaen, Roscoe & Co*, Stanford-le-Hope (for the appellant); *T Hambrey Jones*, Chelmsford (for the respondent).

Denise Randall Barrister.

Trendtex Trading Corporation and another v Crédit Suisse

QUEEN'S BENCH DIVISION
ROBERT GOFF J
30th MARCH 1979

COURT OF APPEAL, CIVIL DIVISION
LORD DENNING MR, BRIDGE AND OLIVER LJJ
25th, 26th, 27th, 28th, 31st MARCH, 1st APRIL, 2nd MAY 1980

Maintenance of action – Common interest – Commercial and financial interest – Cause of action – Assignment – Bank financing corporation in commercial transaction – Corporation bringing action against third party in respect of that transaction – Bank guaranteeing corporation's legal costs – Corporation assigning to bank its rights of action against third party – Whether assignment valid – Whether bank having sufficient interest in subject matter of action.

Practice – Stay of proceedings – Foreign jurisdiction clause – Agreement made in Switzerland containing purported assignment by Swiss corporation to Swiss bank of its rights of action in England against another – Agreement providing that all disputes regarding it to be determined by Swiss court – Bank selling rights of action to third party for large sum – Corporation bringing action in England against bank claiming assignment void – Application for stay of proceedings – Whether Switzerland appropriate forum for dispute – Whether application should be granted.

In 1975 the first plaintiff, a Swiss corporation ('Trendtex'), contracted to sell to an English company 240,000 tonnes of cement c i f Lagos. Under a letter of credit to be issued by the Central Bank of Nigeria ('CBN') the English company agreed to pay the purchase price and demurrage. CBN issued the letter of credit but subsequently failed to honour it, with the result that Trendtex was left heavily indebted to the defendants, a Swiss bank ('Crédit Suisse'), which had from the outset provided finance to Trendtex to enable it to fulfil its contractual obligations to the English company. Thus, Crédit Suisse had issued and honoured letters of credit in respect of cement purchased by Trendtex from its suppliers, and had issued and honoured guarantees to shipowners from whom Trendtex had chartered ships to carry the cement to Lagos, and had then debited Trendtex accordingly. Trendtex issued a writ in England against CBN claiming $US14,000,000 by way of damages. Crédit Suisse, whose only substantial prospect of payment lay in the success of the litigation, agreed to guarantee all the legal fees and costs incurred by Trendtex in the proceedings. CBN successfully pleaded sovereign immunity and the writ was set aside by the High Court. Trendtex appealed to the Court of Appeal which allowed the appeal but gave CBN leave to appeal to the House of Lords, so that the matter was still unsettled. From the autumn of 1976 Crédit Suisse, who were not Trendtex's only creditors, had been anxious to secure their advances to Trendtex. By a series of agreements made between September and November 1976 Trendtex purported to assign to Crédit Suisse by way of security its cause of action against CBN. Crédit Suisse however wanted an outright assignment of Trendtex's claim against CBN. At a meeting in Geneva on 4th January 1978 their Swiss lawyer, P, told Trendtex that he had received an offer from a third party to buy Trendtex's right of action against CBN for $US800,000 and that Crédit Suisse would make Trendtex bankrupt unless Trendtex assigned the right of action outright to Crédit Suisse and allowed them to make their own terms with the third party. Later the same day an agreement was signed in Geneva whereby Trendtex released to Crédit Suisse its residual rights of action against CBN, acknowledged that it had no further interest in the action, gave P a power of attorney to enable him to settle its action against CBN, and deposited 90% of its shares, which were owned by the second plaintiff, a Liechtenstein corporation ('Temo'), with P, in return for which Crédit Suisse agreed to pay off all Trendtex's other creditors. The agreement expressly stated *a* that it was to be governed by Swiss law and that 'Any dispute regarding its conclusion, interpretation or fulfilment [was to] be judged by the Court of Geneva, exclusive of any other jurisdiction'. On 9th January P, on behalf of Crédit Suisse, assigned to a third party (whose identity P never disclosed) all the rights of action against CBN for $US1,100,000. On 12th February P negotiated a settlement in Nigeria of the action against CBN for $US8,000,000. In March Trendtex and and Temo brought an action in England against *b* Crédit Suisse claiming (i) that the agreements of the autumn of 1976 and of 4th January 1978 were void as constituting an assignment of a bare cause of action and therefore the cause of action against CBN should be declared to remain vested in Trendtex, (ii) that Trendtex was induced to enter into the agreement of 4th January 1978 by illegal pressure, (iii) that P was in breach of a fiduciary duty to Trendtex for which Crédit Suisse were vicariously liable and accordingly liable to account to Trendtex for moneys received, *c* and (iv) the return of the shares to Temo. Crédit Suisse applied for a stay of the proceedings under the inherent jurisdiction of the court and/or on the ground that Trendtex's claim constituted a dispute within the exclusive jurisdiction clause in the agreement of 4th January 1978. The plaintiffs argued (i) that by English law the assignment was illegal and unenforceable because, as an assignment of a bare cause of action, it savoured of maintenance and champerty and that accordingly, whatever the *d* proper law of the agreement of 4th January 1978 was, English law would not enforce the agreement by giving effect to the exclusive jurisdiction clause, (ii) that even if the assignment was valid the proceedings should continue in England because discovery of documents could be had there but not in Switzerland. The judge granted the stay on the grounds that the plaintiffs had failed to show sufficient cause why effect should not be given to the exclusive jurisdiction clause, that everything pointed to Switzerland as the *e* more appropriate forum and that the advantages of a trial in England were not such as to outweigh the Swiss connection. The plaintiffs appealed.

Held – (1) Although a personal right to litigate (ie one which was by its nature personal to oneself, such as a claim in tort or under a personal and non-assignable contract) could not be assigned, an impersonal right to litigate (ie one which was by its nature a *f* proprietary right) could be assigned provided that the circumstances reasonably warranted it. On the evidence Crédit Suisse had a sufficiently genuine and legitimate interest in the subject matter of Trendtex's action against CBN to justify them in maintaining a suit and in taking a charge on the proceeds of it and there was in the circumstances no reason why that interest should not justify the assignment to Crédit Suisse of the whole cause of action. It followed that the purported assignment was valid *g* (see p 741 *d e*, p 742 *d e g*, p 743 *b h j*, p 744 *d* to *g*, p 745 *e*, p 752 *j* to p 753 *d g* and p 757 *d* to *f* and *h j*, post); *Martell v Consett Iron Co Ltd* [1955] 1 All ER 481 approved; *British Cash and Parcel Conveyors Ltd v Lamson Store Service Co Ltd* [1908] 1 KB 1006, *Martell v Consett Iron Co Ltd* [1955] 1 All ER 481, *Hill v Archbold* [1967] 3 All ER 110 and *Mackender v Feldia AG* [1966] 3 All ER 847 applied; *Glegg v Bromley* [1912] 3 KB 474, *County Hotel and Wine Co Ltd v London and North Western Railway Co* [1921] 1 AC 85, *Re Trepca Mines Ltd* *h* [1962] 3 All ER 351 and *Compania Colombiana de Seguros v Pacific Steam Navigation Co* [1964] 1 All ER 216 considered.

(2) The proper law of the agreement was Swiss law and (per Bridge and Oliver LJJ) even if the agreement of 4th January 1978 did not itself effect an assignment but was made in contemplation of procuring an assignment in the future of Trendtex's cause of action to a third party who did not have a legitimate and genuine interest in the subject *j* matter of the action, it did not follow that because an English court would not enforce such an agreement the agreement as a whole was void by Swiss law. The question whether the agreement gave rise to enforceable rights and duties was 'a dispute regarding [the] conclusion, interpretation or fulfilment' of the agreement within the exclusive jurisdiction clause and fell to be determined by Swiss law (see p 744 *g h*, p 745 *d e*, and p 758 *d* to *f*, post).

(3) The judge had not erred in principle in exercising his discretion in favour of giving effect to the exclusive jurisdiction clause. Nor were there any grounds for interfering with the exercise of his discretion in favour of staying the proceedings in relation to that part of the plaintiffs' claim which did not depend on the assignment. In all the circumstances Switzerland was the more appropriate forum, and there was no reason to suppose that justice would not be done there merely because Switzerland had no process for compelling discovery of documents (see p 744 *h* to p 745 *e* and p 758 *e* to p 759 *a*, post); *MacShannon v Rockware Glass Ltd* [1978] 1 All ER 625 applied.

Per Curiam. Although the abolition of criminal and civil liability for maintenance and champerty did not affect any rule of law by which a contract was to be treated as contrary to public policy or otherwise illegal, the trend of recent authority was against striking down agreements merely because they savoured of maintenance (see p 741 *c* to *f*, p 742 *d e g*, p 743 *b h j*, p 745 *e* and p 748 *g h*, post).

Notes

For assignment of rights of action, see 6 Halsbury's Laws (4th Edn) paras 15, 86, 87, and for cases on the subject, see 8(2) Digest (Reissue) 504–507, *100–122*.

For maintenance and champerty in relation to assignment of fruits of litigation, see 9 Halsbury's Laws (4th Edn) paras 400–401, 404.

Cases referred to in judgments

Alabaster v Harness [1895] 1 QB 339, [1891–4] All ER Rep 817, 64 LJQB 76, 71 LT 740, 14 R 54, CA.

Atlantic Star, The, Atlantic Star (owners) v Bona Spes (owners) [1973] 2 All ER 175, [1974] AC 436, [1973] 2 WLR 795, HL, 11 Digest (Reissue) 645, *1777*.

British Cash and Parcel Conveyors Ltd v Lamson Store Service Co Ltd [1908] 1 KB 1006, 77 LJKB 649, 98 LT 875, CA, 26 Digest (Repl) 230, *1780*.

Compania Colombiana de Seguros v Pacific Steam Navigation Co, Empressa de Telefona de Bogota v Pacific Steam Navigation Co [1964] 1 All ER 216, [1965] 1 QB 101, [1964] 2 WLR 484, [1963] 2 Lloyd's Rep 479, 8(2) Digest (Reissue) 506, *110*.

County Hotel and Wine Co Ltd v London and North Western Railway Co [1918] 2 KB 251, 87 LJKB 849, 119 LT 38, 17 LGR 274; *on appeal* [1921] 1 AC 85, 89 LJKB 918, 124 LT 99, 17 LGR 598, HL, 38 Digest (Repl) 349, *351*.

Dawson v Great Northern and City Railway Co [1904] 1 KB 277, 73 LJKB 174, 90 LT 20, 68 JP 214; *rvsd on other grounds* [1905] 1 KB 260, [1904–7] All ER Rep 913, 74 LJKB 190, 92 LT 137, 69 JP 29, CA, 8(2) Digest (Reissue) 507, *116*, *120*.

Defries v Milne [1913] 1 Ch 98, 82 LJ Ch 1, 107 LT 593, CA, 8(2) Digest (Reissue) 507, *117*.

Dickinson v Burrell, Stourton v Burrell (1866) LR 1 Eq 337, 35 Beav 257, 35 LJ Ch 371, 13 LT 660, 12 Jur NS 199.

Eleftheria, The, (The Eleftheria cargo owners) v The Eleftheria (owners) [1969] 2 All ER 641, [1970] P 94, [1969] 2 WLR 1073, [1969] 1 Lloyd's Rep 237, 11 Digest (Reissue) 633, *1691*.

Ellis v Torrington [1920] 1 KB 399, 89 LJKB 369, 122 LT 361, CA, 8(2) Digest (Reissue) 506, *108*.

Fitzroy v Cave [1905] 2 KB 364, 74 LJKB 829, CA.

Glegg v Bromley [1912] 3 KB 474, 81 LJKB 1081, 106 LT 825, CA, 8(2) Digest (Reissue) 507, *118*.

Grell v Levy (1864) 16 CBNS 73, 9 LT 721, 10 Jur NS 210, 143 ER 1052.

Guy v Churchill (1888) 40 Ch D 481, 58 LJ Ch 345, 60 LT 473.

Heyman v Darwins Ltd [1942] 1 All ER 337, [1942] AC 356, 111 LJKB 241, 166 LT 306, HL, 3 Digest (Reissue) 88, *453*.

Hill v Archbold [1967] 3 All ER 110, [1968] 1 QB 686, [1967] 3 WLR 1218, CA, Digest (Cont Vol C) 3, *634a*.

Holden v Thompson [1907] 2 KB 489, 76 LJKB 889, 97 LT 138.

Hughes v Pump House Hotel Co [1902] 2 KB 190, [1900–3] All ER Rep 480, 71 LJKB 630, 86 LT 794, CA, 8(2) Digest (Reissue) 521, *226*.

Interseas Shipping Co SA v Banco di Bilbao [1978] Court of Appeal Transcript 329.

Kemp v Baerselman [1906] 2 KB 604, 75 LJKB 873, CA, 12 Digest (Reissue) 724, *5243*.
Laurent v Sale & Co (a firm) [1963] 2 All ER 63, [1963] 1 WLR 829, [1963] 1 Lloyd's Rep 157, Digest (Cont Vol A) 3, *823a*.
Mackender v Feldia AG [1966] 3 All ER 847, [1967] 2 QB 590, [1967] 2 WLR 119, CA, 50 Digest (Repl) 341, *689*.
MacShannon v Rockware Glass Ltd [1978] 1 All ER 625, [1978] AC 795, [1978] 2 WLR 362, HL, Digest (Cont Vol E) 99, *1691a*.
Martell v Consett Iron Co Ltd [1955] 1 All ER 481, [1955] Ch 363, [1955] 2 WLR 463, CA; *affg* [1954] 3 All ER 339, [1955] Ch 363, [1954] 3 WLR 648, 8(2) Digest (Reissue) 632, *115*.
May v Lane (1894) 64 LJQB 236, 71 LT 869, 14 R 149, CA, 8(2) Digest (Reissue) 504, *101*.
Neville v London Express Newspapers Ltd [1919] AC 368, [1918–19] All ER Rep 61, 88 LJKB 282, 120 LT 299, HL, 51 Digest (Repl) 861, 862, *4115*, *4131*.
Ogdens Ltd v Weinberg (1906) 95 LT 567, HL, 8(2) Digest (Reissue) 539, *346*.
Plating Co v Farquharson (1881) 17 Ch D 49, 50 LJ Ch 406, 44 LT 389, 45 JP 568, CA, 16 Digest (Repl) 34, *284*.
Prosser v Edmonds (1835) 1 Y & C Ex 481, 160 ER 196, 8(2) Digest (Reissue) 500, *75*.
St Pierre v South American Stores (Gath & Chaves) Ltd [1936] 1 KB 382, [1935] All ER Rep 408, 105 LJKB 436, 154 LT 546, CA, 11 Digest (Reissue) 399, *392*.
Seear v Lawson (1880) 15 Ch D 426, 49 LT Bcy 69, 42 LT 893, CA.
Torkington v Magee [1902] 2 KB 427, 71 LJKB 712, 87 LT 304, DC; *rvsd on other grounds* [1903] 1 KB 644, 72 LJKB 336, 88 LT 443, CA, 8(2) Digest (Reissue) 505, *103*.
Trendtex Trading Corpn v Central Bank of Nigeria [1977] 1 All ER 881, [1977] QB 529, [1977] 2 WLR 356, [1977] 1 Lloyd's Rep 581, [1977] 2 CMLR 465, CA: *rvsg* [1976] 3 All ER 437, [1976] 1 WLR 868, [1976] 2 CMLR 668, 1(1) Digest (Reissue) 59, *382*.
Trepca Mines Ltd, Re [1960] 3 All ER 304, [1960] 1 WLR 1273, CA, Digest (Cont Vol A) 195, 251, *7180b*, *1203a*.
Trepca Mines Ltd, Re (Application of Radomir Nicola Pachitch (Pasic)) [1962] 3 All ER 351, [1963] Ch 199, [1962] 3 WLR 955, CA, Digest (Cont Vol A) 3, *777a*.
Wallersteiner v Moir (No 2), Moir v Wallersteiner (No 2) [1975] 1 All ER 849, [1975] QB 373, 508n, [1975] 2 WLR 389, CA, Digest (Cont Vol D) 570, *518a*.
Williams v Protheroe (1829) 5 Bing 309, 2 Y & J 129, 2 Moo & P 779, 130 ER 1080, Ex Ch.
Zapata Off-Shore Co v The Bremen and Unterweser Reederei GmbH, The Chaparrall [1972] 2 Lloyd's Rep 315.

Cases also cited

Adolf Warski, The, and the Sniadecki [1976] 2 Lloyd's Rep 241, CA.
Anziani, Re, Herbert v Christopherson [1930] 1 Ch 407.
Bank Voor Handel en Scheepvaart NV v Administrator of Hungarian Property [1954] 1 All ER 969, [1954] AC 584, HL; *rvsg* [1952] 2 All ER 956, [1953] 1 QB 248, CA.
British Anzani (Felixstowe) Ltd v International Marine Management (UK) Ltd [1979] 2 All ER 1063, [1980] QB 137.
Carvalho v Hull Blyth (Angola) Ltd [1979] 3 All ER 280, [1979] 1 WLR 1228, CA.
Cast Shipping Ltd v Tradax Export SA, The Hellas in Eternity [1979] 2 Lloyd's Rep 280, CA.
Castanho v Brown & Root (UK) Ltd [1980] 1 All ER 689; *rvsd* p 72, ante, [1980] 1 WLR 833, CA.
Castellain v Preston (1883) 11 QBD 380.
Danish Mercantile Co Ltd v Beaumont [1951] 1 All ER 925, [1951] Ch 680, CA.
Earle's Shipping and Engineering Co v Atlantic Transport Co (1899) 43 Sol Jo 691.
Farrell v Secretary of State for Defence [1980] 1 All ER 166, HL.
Fehmarn, The [1958] 1 All ER 333, [1958] 1 WLR 159, CA.
Joachimson (N) v Swiss Bank Corpn [1921] 3 KB 110, CA.
Haseldine v Hosken [1933] 1 KB 822.
Hispano Americana Mercantil SA v Central Bank of Nigeria [1979] 2 Lloyd's Rep 277, CA.

Hutley v Hutley (1873) LR 8 QB 112, 42 LJQB 52.
a *Kislovodsk, The* [1980] 1 Lloyd's Rep 183.
Makefjell, The [1975] 1 Lloyd's Rep 528; *affd* [1976] 2 Lloyd's Rep 29, CA.
Republica de Guatemala v Nunez [1927] 1 QB 669.
Trans Trust SPRL v Danubian Trading Co Ltd [1952] 1 All ER 970, [1952] 2 QB 297, CA.
Unterweser Reederei GmbH v Zapata Off-Shore Co, The Chaparrall [1968] 2 Lloyd's Rep 158, CA.
b *Whitworth Street Estates (Manchester) Ltd v James Miller and Partners Ltd* [1970] 1 All ER 796, [1970] AC 583, HL.

Summons

By a writ issued on 29th March 1978, and subsequently amended, the first plaintiffs, Trendtex Trading Corpn ('Trendtex'), a company incorporated in accordance with the c laws of Switzerland, and the second plaintiffs, Temo Anstalt ('Temo'), a corporation established in accordance with the laws of the principality of Liechtenstein, brought an action against the defendant, Crédit Suisse, a company incorporated in accordance with the laws of Switzerland, seeking (1) declarations that (a) Trendtex's cause of action for damages in an action in the High Court of Justice, Queen's Bench Division, Commercial Court, entitled *Trendtex Trading Corpn v Central Bank of Nigeria* was and at all material d times remained the sole property of Trendtex, and (b) that Trendtex's cause of action in that case was at all material times incapable of lawful assignment under English law, (2) a declaration that the assignment or purported assignment of the cause of action to Crédit Suisse by a declaration of assignment dated 6th September 1976 and/or by a declaration of surrender dated 26th November 1976 and/or by a written agreement made between Trendtex and Crédit Suisse dated 4th January 1978 was void and of no effect, (3) a e declaration that a written agreement dated 4th January 1978 and made between Trendtex, Dr Vital Hauser (the director of Trendtex) and Crédit Suisse was void and of no effect, (4) alternatively, an order that that agreement be set aside, (5) a declaration that all moneys held or received by Crédit Suisse in the name of Trendtex, or alternatively all moneys held or received by them which were proceeds of any settlement of the action in the High Court entitled *Trendtex Trading Corpn v Central Bank of Nigeria* was the property f of Trendtex, (6) an injunction to restrain Crédit Suisse by themselves, their servants or agents or otherwise howsoever from disposing of or otherwise dealing with any moneys received by them or of any of them within the jurisdiction of the court for the benefit of Trendtex without the consent of Trendtex and Temo or alternatively without an order of the court (other than the sum of $US1,500,000 together with interest thereon currently owed by Trendtex to Crédit Suisse), (7) an account of what had become of the g sum of $US8,000,000 or such other sum as Crédit Suisse received on the settlement of the proceedings on behalf of and for the benefit of Trendtex, (8) an order that Crédit Suisse pay Trendtex and Temo such sum as might be found due to Trendtex on the taking of such account, (9) damages for breach of duty owed to Trendtex by Crédit Suisse as bankers and/or agents of Trendtex and interest thereon pursuant to the Law Reform (Miscellaneous Provisions) Act 1934, (10) delivery up to Temo of all the shares in h Trendtex, the property of Temo, held by Maître Patry on behalf of Crédit Suisse, (11) further or other relief. By a summons dated 20th October 1978 Crédit Suisse applied for orders (i) that under RSC Ord 15, r 6 and/or under the inherent jurisdiction of the court the name of Trendtex be struck out as a plaintiff and that the action so far as brought by Trendtex be dismissed or all further proceedings by Trendtex be stayed on the ground that neither Trendtex nor the persons authorised to act on behalf of Trendtex authorised j the action to be brought by Trendtex, (ii) that the solicitors who commenced and carried on the proceedings in the name of Trendtex pay the costs occasioned thereby, (iii) that claims (1) to (8) in the amended writ be stayed on the ground that they constituted disputes regarding the conclusion, interpretation or fulfilment of an agreement dated 4th January 1978 by art 8 whereof the parties agreed that any such dispute should be judged by the Court of Geneva, Switzerland, exclusive of any other jurisdiction, (iv) that the amended writ be struck out under RSC Ord 18, r 19 and/or under the inherent jurisdiction of the court on the ground that the claims therein were frivolous and/or vexatious and/or an abuse of the process of the court. The facts are set out in the judgment of Robert Goff J.

Christopher French QC and *David Hunt* for Crédit Suisse.
Stanley Brodie QC and *Stephen Nathan* for Trendtex and Temo.

ROBERT GOFF J. There is before the court a summons issued by the defendants in the action, Crédit Suisse, in which they claim relief on various grounds against the plaintiffs, Trendtex Trading Corpn and Temo Anstalt, and their solicitors, Messrs Herbert Oppenheimer Nathan & Vandyk. Before I set out the nature of the relief claimed in the summons, I propose to summarise the background to the matter as it appears from the affidavit evidence before me, which will, I think, make it more easy to appreciate the nature of the relief claimed.

The first plaintiff, which I shall refer to as 'Trendtex', is a Swiss corporation. Its capital consists of 100,000 Swiss francs in respect of which there have been issued 100 bearer shares of 1,000 Swiss francs each. The second plaintiff, which I shall refer to as 'Temo', is a Liechtenstein anstalt, which claims to be the owner of all the shares in Trendtex. The defendants are a Swiss bank. I should mention also at this stage the names of four persons who figure largely in this case. First, Mr Alan London and Dr John Kennedy, both of whom claim to have been appointed general managers of Trendtex; Mr London also claims to own or control Temo. The third person is Dr Hauser, a lawyer practising in Zurich, who was at all material times the sole director and administrator of Trendtex, no doubt in accordance with provisions of Swiss law requiring a Swiss resident to hold this post. The fourth person who figures very largely in the story is another Swiss lawyer, Dr Patry, who acted on behalf of Crédit Suisse.

The story begins on 24th July 1975, when Trendtex entered into a contract for the sale to Pan-African Export and Import Co of 240,000 metric tons of cement, cif Lagos/Apapa. Under the contract, Pan-African was responsible for demurrage incurred at the discharging port. Payment of the purchase price and demurrage was to be made under a letter of credit to be issued by the Central Bank of Nigeria (which I shall refer to as 'CBN'), the terms of which were incorporated into the sale contract. The letter of credit was duly issued, Trendtex being notified by the Midland Bank in London, CBN's London corresponding bank, where the documents were to be presented. The Midland Bank did not however confirm the letter of credit. Both the sale contract and the letter of credit were governed by English law. The first four shipments of cement, which were shipped in August and September 1975, were duly paid for. However this was the period of great congestion in the port of Lagos; and all those four ships came on demurrage on various dates in September and October. Two more shipments were made by Trendtex; and then Trendtex began to run into trouble with the letter of credit. CBN refused to accept documents presented in October in respect of the fifth shipment, and refused to pay for substantial demurrage due on two of the earlier shipments. As a result Trendtex treated CBN as in repudiation of its obligations under the letter of credit, and on 4th November 1975 commenced proceedings against CBN in the English courts, claiming a substantial sum by way of damages, their total claim amounting to some $US14,000,000. Trendtex also obtained a Mareva injunction restraining CBN from disposing of certain assets in the jurisdiction. However, on 16th December 1975 CBN issued a summons asking for an order that the proceedings be set aside on the ground of sovereign immunity; and on 26th March 1976 Donaldson J set aside the writ and discharged the injunction (see *Trendtex Trading Corpn v Central Bank of Nigeria* [1976] 3 All ER 437, [1976] 1 WLR 868).

Now Trendtex was a customer of Crédit Suisse. Crédit Suisse acted for Trendtex in and about the cement transaction, opening letters of credit in favour of the German suppliers from whom Trendtex purchased the cement; they also issued guarantees to certain shipowners, and in particular to a company called Intermare Transport GmbH, *a* which appears to have acted in some capacity in relation to the ships chartered to carry the cement.

As a result of CBN's failure to honour the letter of credit, Trendtex ran into severe financial difficulties. Its account with Crédit Suisse ran into debt, largely because of demurrage paid by Crédit Suisse which CBN failed to pay for under the letter of credit. In order to assist Trendtex to recover damages from CBN, and no doubt in the hope that *b* thereby Trendtex would be able to discharge its indebtedness to them, Crédit Suisse agreed in November 1975 to guarantee all the legal fees and costs incurred by Trendtex's English solicitors, Messrs Theodore Goddard, in the proceedings against CBN. This arrangement was made through a Mr Köstner, the then manager of Crédit Suisse's Lausanne branch. In November 1975 Crédit Suisse acting on behalf of Trendtex sold the fifth and sixth cargoes of cement, which had not been paid for under the letter of credit, *c* to a Swiss company called Utex SA; Trendtex was however later to claim that, under this transaction, Crédit Suisse unwisely obtained no bank guarantee against Utex's obligation to pay discharging port demurrage.

Trendtex appealed to the Court of Appeal against the decision of Donaldson J; but, before the appeal came on for hearing, certain documents were executed by Trendtex in favour of Crédit Suisse, apparently intended to secure Crédit Suisse's advance to *d* Trendtex. First, on 6th September 1976, Trendtex through Dr Hauser issued a declaration of assignment, assigning to Crédit Suisse all its claims arising out of the contract as between it and Pan-African; but no reference was made in that document to claims against CBN. Subsequently, however, on 26th November 1976, Dr Hauser on behalf of Trendtex executed in favour of Crédit Suisse a document entitled 'Declaration of Surrender', whereby Trendtex surrendered to Crédit Suisse all its claims arising from *e* its contract with Pan-African and from the letter of credit issued by CBN, to the full extent of its indebtedness to Crédit Suisse. By the same document Crédit Suisse were empowered either in the name of Trendtex or their own name to enforce all claims arising out of the contract against CBN.

The appeal from the decision of Donaldson J was successful, the Court of Appeal on 13th January 1977 allowing the appeal (see [1977] 1 All ER 881, [1977] QB 529), but *f* granting CBN leave to appeal to the House of Lords. On 20th April 1977 CBN presented their petition to the House of Lords. However, in March 1977 Messrs Theodore Goddard received an indication from CBN's solicitors that CBN were prepared to enter into negotiations for settlement of the claim. Crédit Suisse then appointed a Swiss lawyer, Dr Patry, to investigate the possibility of settlement; this gentleman figures very large in the story from this time on. In June, Dr Patry began to take a strong line on behalf of Crédit *g* Suisse vis-à-vis Trendtex. On a visit to Messrs Theodore Goddard on 8th June Dr Patry revealed his main concern to be to recover the sum outstanding from Trendtex to Crédit Suisse; he also asserted that, under a previous document (presumably the surrender of 26th November 1976), Trendtex had assigned *all* its rights to Crédit Suisse. On 16th June, at a meeting with Dr Hauser in Switzerland, Dr Patry proposed that Trendtex should renounce every claim against CBN to Crédit Suisse, in return for Crédit Suisse *h* giving up their claims against Trendtex and settling all relative claims, including in particular a very substantial claim by Intermare for demurrage; if Trendtex did not agree to this proposal, Dr Patry threatened that Crédit Suisse would call in their loan and so render Trendtex bankrupt. The manner of Dr Patry's approach to Dr Hauser provoked a strong protest by Dr Hauser to Crédit Suisse. He proposed a meeting in London, to be attended by both Dr Kennedy and Mr London, and by Mr Carrington of Theodore *j* Goddard. In answer, Dr Patry wrote to Dr Hauser a long and strong letter dated 14th July, asserting that by the surrender of 26th November Trendtex had surrendered all its rights under the letter of credit with CBN, and taking a very strong line as to the nature of Crédit Suisse's rights vis-à-vis Trendtex. Trendtex was later to maintain that, by virtue of the meetings of 8th and 16th June, and the letter of 14th July, Dr Patry exerted or attempted to exert pressure on Trendtex. Meanwhile, by letter dated 18th July, Dr Patry asserted to Theodore Goddard that Crédit Suisse alone were entitled to give Theodore Goddard instructions as to proceedings against CBN, and as to any negotiations with CBN. Trendtex, on the other hand, was disputing liability to pay sums which Crédit Suisse had paid to Intermare, claiming that Crédit Suisse had entered into their guarantee with Intermare without Trendtex's authority; and it was also denying liability to reimburse Crédit Suisse in respect of demurrage payments which Utex had failed to pay, claiming that lack of satisfaction of Utex's demurrage liability was due to Crédit Suisse's failure to cover this liability with a bank guarantee.

As a result of these various disputes a meeting was held on 21st September 1977 at Dr Patry's office in Geneva. Mr London, Dr Kennedy and Dr Hauser attended on behalf of Trendtex. There is considerable dispute as to what was agreed at that meeting; rival versions were subsequently advanced by Mr London, Dr Hauser and Dr Patry. However, Trendtex and Temo, plaintiffs in the present action, now claim, relying on Mr London's version, that agreement was reached in the following terms: (i) Crédit Suisse would be responsible for paying or settling the claims of Intermare and the shipowners; (ii) Crédit Suisse would remove from Trendtex's overdraft the demurrage payments debited to its account arising from Utex's failure to pay them and would seek to negotiate a settlement of a claim against Utex; (iii) the overdraft of Trendtex was agreed at a maximum sum of $1,500,000 to be paid from the proceeds of any settlement negotiated with CBN; (iv) Dr Patry on behalf of Crédit Suisse undertook to attempt to settle the litigation with CBN for the sum of $3,000,000, by direct negotiation with CBN through political channels, subject to any proposed settlement at a lesser sum being submitted to Trendtex for its approval; (v) Trendtex would endeavour to find its own channels through which to achieve the same settlement with CBN; (vi) a settlement of the litigation in the sum of $3,000,000 was to be divided as to $1,500,000 each to Trendtex and Crédit Suisse save that (a) Crédit Suisse would receive $1,500,000 whether the settlement agreed was more or less than $3,000,000 and (b) any settlement in excess of $3,000,000 would accrue for the account of Trendtex; (vii) pending settlement, Theodore Goddard were to continue with the litigation.

However, shortly after the meeting Dr Patry set out in a letter to Dr Hauser dated 30th September 1977 his version of what was agreed at the meeting, which differed in some material respects from Mr London's version. I do not think it is necessary for me in this judgment to go into the details of this difference of opinion. Some time later, on 3rd November 1977, Dr Hauser sent a letter to Dr Patry, challenging certain points in the letter: it is difficult to reconcile Dr Hauser's view of the agreement with either Mr London's or Dr Patry's. On the following day, 4th November, Dr Patry responded with a telex containing his comments on Dr Hauser's comments and ending with the words:

> 'Kindly confirm with me this morning because we need to finish with this matter. Should full and final agreement not be possible today, Crédit Suisse will again take up all its rights against [Trendtex].'

On the same day, 4th November, Dr Hauser responded with further comments by telex. This appears to have been followed by a telephone conversation; and on 7th November Dr Patry sent a new letter confirming the agreement between the parties. The letter ended with the words: 'Kindly return a copy of this letter signed by you by way of agreement.' This Dr Hauser did on 14th November; and Crédit Suisse and Dr Patry maintain that the letter of 7th November, countersigned by Dr Hauser, contains the definitive version of the agreement between the parties following the meeting of 21st September. The agreement recorded in the letter may be summarised as follows. (1) It was recorded that the total sum owed by Trendtex to Crédit Suisse was about $3,400,000, and that Utex owed Crédit Suisse about $2,200,000. (2) Trendtex transferred, in partial payment of its obligations to Crédit Suisse, all its rights against Intermare and Utex or other companies in the Utex group. Crédit Suisse were free to negotiate settlements with those companies, for the benefit of Crédit Suisse, and would, without obligation, try to obtain a release from Intermare of its claims against Trendtex. (3) In consideration of the transfer in (2) above, the total debt of Trendtex to Crédit Suisse was reduced to $1,500,000, on which interest would accrue. (4) Crédit Suisse were authorised to settle, if possible, the proceedings in London against CBN, provided the settlement was at least in the sum of $3,000,000. If a settlement could only be obtained for a lesser sum, Crédit Suisse were bound to inform Trendtex; but Trendtex could only oppose such a settlement if it paid within 30 days the capital sum due to Crédit Suisse, or if it showed that the settlement was for too low a figure. (5) 'The rights of TTC [Trendtex] with regard to the Central Bank of Nigeria are wholly and irrevocably ceded to Crédit Suisse to guarantee TTC's debt such as it is laid out in paragraph (3) above.'

In their statement of claim, the plaintiffs object to a number of the passages in this letter, on the ground that they do not accurately record the agreement reached on 21st September. The passages are set out in the statement of claim: I do not think it is necessary for me to record them in this judgment.

On 10th December a meeting took place in London attended by Dr Kennedy, Dr Hauser, Mr Carrington and an accountant. At the meeting it was reported (apparently by Dr Hauser) that Dr Patry had tried to settle with CBN through diplomatic channels, without success. It was also reported that Intermare had presented a claim to Trendtex in a sum of about 4,000,000 Swiss francs. There was a clear danger that Intermare might drive Trendtex into bankruptcy. There was a discussion of a proposal by Dr Patry that Crédit Suisse might rescue Trendtex from its difficulties by taking over all Trendtex's obligations, at least to Intermare, apparently on the basis of buying outright all Trendtex's rights, including its rights against CBN, for a nominal sum, and also discharging Trendtex's obligation to Crédit Suisse. Dr Kennedy was opposed to this proposal; but Dr Hauser appears to have favoured it. No mention appears to have been made at this meeting of any proposal or negotiation by Crédit Suisse to dispose of Trendtex's rights against CBN to a third party.

There followed correspondence in which Dr Hauser urged on Mr London acceptance of such a deal. On 21st December Dr Patry in a telex to Dr Hauser reminded him that, in a telephone call on 22nd November, and subsequently, he had informed Dr Hauser that Crédit Suisse had the possibility of 'realising' (presumably selling) Trendtex's rights against CBN for a substantial sum; a figure of $800,000 was mentioned. Dr Patry claimed that, under the terms of the letter of 7th November, Crédit Suisse were free to dispose of Trendtex's rights against CBN for that sum. He however made himself available for a meeting in the first week of January. The next day Dr Hauser informed Mr London that Trendtex had no more money, and proposed that the company should be put into liquidation.

A meeting took place in Switzerland on 4th January, at which a formal agreement was concluded, the parties to the agreement being Trendtex, Dr Hauser and Crédit Suisse. In general terms, the agreement provided for an out and out assignment by Trendtex to Crédit Suisse of all its rights against CBN. Crédit Suisse were to pay $388,000 to Trendtex on (i) a statement by Dr Hauser to Crédit Suisse that, by collecting that sum, he had been able to obtain a release from Trendtex's creditors and (ii) releases from Trendtex's creditors. In addition, Crédit Suisse committed themselves to pay a further $72,000 to a certain Nigerian company (Banu Plateau Enterprises) if it established a valid claim against Trendtex. To give Crédit Suisse 'proper control of the good fulfilment by TTC [Trendtex] of its obligations and undertakings hereunder', Dr Hauser undertook three things: (i) to deposit 90% of the shares of Trendtex with Dr Patry, to be kept by Dr Patry 'in escrow until such time that Dr. Patry thinks he can return the shares to Dr Hauser'; (ii) to complete the formalities necessary to enable Dr Patry, as long as he held the shares in escrow, to exercise the voting rights appertaining to them, as he deemed fit; (iii) to hand over to Dr Patry his resignation as director of Trendtex to be used by Dr Patry at the time of Dr Patry's sole choice. Apparently the remaining 10% of the shares in Trendtex had already been pledged to Temo as security for a loan.

The final article (art 6) of the agreement read as follows:

> 'This Agreement is governed by Swiss law. Any dispute regarding its conclusion, interpretation or fulfilment shall be judged by the Court of Geneva, exclusive of any other jurisdiction.'

Dr Hauser duly handed over to Dr Patry the bearer shares representing 90% of the shares in Trendtex, and his resignation; and he provided Dr Patry with a power of attorney to act on behalf of Trendtex. Mr London and Dr Kennedy provided Dr Patry with a letter in which they undertook not to interfere with the proceedings against CBN in London, or in any negotiations for settlement of those proceedings.

The hearing of CBN's appeal to the House of Lords was expected to commence in April 1978. However in March 1978 Mr London heard that Dr Patry, acting on behalf of Trendtex, had agreed to a settlement with CBN in a sum of $8,000,000. This appears to have provoked considerable suspicions in the minds of Mr London and Dr Kennedy that Crédit Suisse, having persuaded them to enter into the agreement of 4th January on the basis that there was available a possibility of disposing of Trendtex's rights against CBN for a sum of $800,000, had in fact known at the time of the possibility of settling the claim for a very much larger sum. On 22nd March Mr London inquired of Dr Patry by telex whether the news was correct. On 28th March, no doubt at the instigation of Mr London, Dr Hauser, on behalf of Trendtex, informed Dr Patry by letter that the power of attorney given to him was withdrawn, and Dr Hauser also demanded return of the 90% shares in Trendtex. On the following day, 29th March, Messrs Herbert Oppenheimer, Nathan & Vandyk commenced the present proceedings against Crédit Suisse in this country, in the name of Trendtex and Temo, apparently on the instructions of Mr London and Dr Kennedy, with a view to setting aside the agreement of 4th January 1978 and recovering the proceeds of the settlement with CBN.

These events provoked a strong reaction by Dr Patry who, in a long telex to Dr Hauser dated 30th March, repudiated any suggestion that Crédit Suisse or he himself had any knowledge at the date of signing the agreement of 4th January of any intention on the part of the Nigerians to negotiate, and stated that in fact Crédit Suisse had disposed of Trendtex's rights to an unnamed third party on 9th January for $1,000,000, out of which $388,000 had been paid over to Dr Hauser, who had provided Dr Patry with the statement and releases required under the agreement. Dr Patry required Dr Hauser to withdraw the terms of his telex of 28th March, and immediately to instruct Messrs Herbert Oppenheimer, Nathan & Vandyk that they had no authority to act on behalf of Trendtex and that they must withdraw the present action. He warned Dr Hauser that, if his instructions were not complied with, an action would be started the next day in Geneva against Dr Hauser and Trendtex. Dr Hauser on the same day withdrew his telex of 28th March; but he explained to Dr Patry that on the basis of the information available to him on 28th March he had to take the action which he then took, and that since he had given no instructions to Messrs Oppenheimers he could not countermand them. However, Dr Hauser subsequently informed Messrs Oppenheimers that they had no authority to act on behalf of Trendtex. Meanwhile on 5th April Messrs Theodore Goddard, who are acting for Crédit Suisse in these proceedings, queried with Messrs Oppenheimers whether they had authority to issue proceedings on behalf of Trendtex. Despite this, and despite further protests by Dr Patry, the proceedings have not been withdrawn; and it is in these proceedings that the summons now before me has been issued.

There is documentary evidence before the court, confirmed by Dr Patry, that the negotiations leading to the settlement with the Nigerians were in fact conducted by Dr Patry, who visited Lagos for this purpose and attended a meeting there on 13th February 1978, and that the final settlement in the sum of $8,000,000 was signed by Dr Patry on behalf of Trendtex on 24th February. The identity of the party for whose benefit Dr Patry acted has not been disclosed by Crédit Suisse or by Dr Patry. In an affidavit sworn in these proceedings, Dr Patry stated: 'I have not "refused" to disclose the identity of the purchaser nor do I consider the identity or its omission significant. It is irrelevant.' There followed an attempt by the plaintiffs in the present action to freeze in this country the $8,000,000 paid under the settlement negotiations, by means of a Mareva injunction. That attempt was unsuccessful, the money having already been remitted to Switzerland.

On 30th August 1978, presumably at the instance of Dr Patry, a meeting was held in Switzerland, attended by Dr Patry and Dr Hauser, at which they purported to put Trendtex into liquidation, and to confirm the terms of the agreement of 4th January. Mr London and Dr Kennedy did not however learn of this meeting until November 1978. They claim that the meeting was of no effect, on the ground that Temo should have been represented at the meeting as owner of the shares in Trendtex.

The writ in the present action, as subsequently amended, claims the following relief: (1) a declaration that Trendtex's cause of action against CBN was and at all times remained the sole property of Trendtex; (2) a declaration that the assignment or purported assignment of the said cause of action to Crédit Suisse on 6th September 1976 and/or 26th November 1976 and/or 4th January 1978 was void and of no effect; (3) a declaration that the agreement of 4th January 1976 was void and of no effect; or alternatively (4) an order that the agreement be set aside; (5) a declaration that all moneys received by Crédit Suisse which are the proceeds of the settlement of Trendtex's action against CBN are the property of Trendtex; (6) an injunction to restrain Crédit Suisse from disposing of any such moneys received by Crédit Suisse within the jurisdiction (except for $1,500,000 owed by Trendtex to Crédit Suisse); (7) an account of such moneys; (8) an order that Crédit Suisse pay Trendtex such sum as is found due to it on the taking of such account; (9) damages for breach of duty by Crédit Suisse to Trendtex as banker and/or agent; (10) delivery up to Temo of all the shares in Trendtex held by Dr Patry on behalf of Crédit Suisse.

On 1st October 1978 the statement of claim was served in the action. From that document, it appears that the ground on which the plaintiffs claim that the assignment of Trendtex's rights against CBN is void is that it offends against the law relating to champerty and maintenance; and that they seek to have the agreement of 4th January 1978 set aside on the ground that Trendtex was induced to enter into it 'by the exercise of undue influence, economic duress and commercial pressure arising out of the unequal bargaining position of the parties', as alleged in the statement of claim.

Having set out the background of the matter, as it appears from the documents before me, I come to the summons, which was issued by the defendants, Crédit Suisse, on 20th October 1978. In the summons, Crédit Suisse ask for relief under four heads: (1) that under RSC Ord 15, r 6 and/or under the inherent jurisdiction of the court the name of Trendtex be struck out and that the action so far as brought by Trendtex be dismissed or all further proceedings by Trendtex be stayed on the ground that neither Trendtex nor the persons authorised to act on behalf of Trendtex authorised the action to be brought by Trendtex; (2) that Messrs Oppenheimers pay the costs occasioned by the proceedings; (3) that the claims in the writ and the statement of claim be stayed under the inherent jurisdiction of the court and/or on the ground that they constitute disputes regarding the conclusion, interpretation or fulfilment of the agreement of 4th January 1978, by art 6 whereof the parties agreed that any such dispute should be judged by the Court of Geneva, exclusive of any other jurisdiction; (4) that the amended writ and/or statement of claim be struck out under RSC Ord 18, r 19, and/or under the inherent jurisdiction of the court on the ground that the claims therein were frivolous and/or vexatious and/or an abuse of the process of the court.

The fourth head of relief has not been pursued. So far as concerns the relief claimed under paras (1) and (2), which relate to the authority of Trendtex's solicitors to commence these proceedings, there is a clear dispute on the facts which cannot be decided on the affidavit evidence before me. It has therefore been agreed that I should deal with the relief claimed under para (3) in the first instance.

Under para (3) of the summons, Crédit Suisse asked for a stay on two grounds, first on the ground that the court should, in its discretion, give effect to the exclusive jurisdiction clause in the agreement of 4th January 1978 and second, under the inherent jurisdiction of the court on the principles stated by the House of Lords in *MacShannon v Rockware Glass Ltd* [1978] 1 All ER 625, [1978] AC 795. I shall consider first the application based on the exclusive jurisdiction clause. The clause (art 6) provides as follows:

> 'This Agreement is governed by Swiss Law. Any dispute regarding its conclusion, interpretation or fulfilment shall be judged by the Court of Geneva, exclusive of any a other jurisdiction.'

Now there are three points to note about this clause. First, it contains an express agreement that the contract is governed by Swiss law; in consequence, it is not in dispute that the proper law of the contract is Swiss. Second, the agreement conferring exclusive jurisdiction on the Court of Geneva covers disputes regarding the conclusion of the b contract, which I understand to be disputes regarding its formation. Third, wide though the clause is, it is not wide enough to embrace all the disputed claims in the present case. It clearly does not apply to Temo's claim to the return of the shares in Trendtex, and to damages for their wrongful detention; nor in my judgment does it apply to the claim by Trendtex for damages for breach of fiduciary duty. It is however in wide enough terms to apply to the claim that the contract is contrary to public policy, void and of no c effect, on the ground that the assignment by Trendtex of its claim to damages against CBN offended against the law relating to champerty and maintenance, or that Trendtex was induced to enter into the contract by the exercise of undue influence, economic duress and commercial pressure.

For Trendtex, counsel launched a frontal attack on Crédit Suisse's application founded on the clause. He submitted that, by English law, the assignment was plainly illegal and d unenforceable because, as an assignment of a bare cause of action, it savoured of maintenance or champerty, and on well-established principles a purported assignment of such a cause of action was unenforceable in English law. It followed that, whatever the proper law of the contract, English law would not enforce the contract by giving effect to the exclusive jurisdiction clause. In support of this submission, he relied on dicta of Diplock LJ in *Mackender v Feldia AG* [1966] 3 All ER 847 at 851, [1967] 2 QB 590 at 601, e and in particular the statement that 'English courts will not enforce an agreement, whatever be its proper law, if it is contrary to English law, whether statute law or common law . . .'

Counsel for Trendtex took me through the authorities on champerty and maintenance; and it appears that, on the evidence before me, there is much substance in his submission that the agreement of 4th January 1978, if sued on in the English courts, would on the f present state of the authorities be held to be unenforceable. On the authorities, the English courts do not enforce an assignment of a bare right of action, because it savours of or is likely to lead to maintenance: see *Glegg v Bromley* [1912] 3 KB 474 at 490 per Parker J. It follows that the court does not inquire whether the particular assignment will lead to maintenance; it strikes down the whole class of assignments on the grounds that such assignments are likely to lead to maintenance. The only way in which an g assignment can be upheld is by showing that it does not fall within the class, i e that it is not an assignment of a bare right of action; this can be done by showing, for example, that the right assigned is a simple debt (which equity always treated as property), or that what is being assigned is not the cause of action but the proceeds of its enforcement (which is an assignment of property), or, which is most relevant for present purposes, that the assignee already had, independently of the assignment, an interest in the right h assigned. Counsel for Crédit Suisse argued that they had a sufficient interest in Trendtex's cause of action against CBN; true, Crédit Suisse had no proprietary interest, but this was no case of officious intermeddling, Crédit Suisse having a legitimate commercial interest in the cause of action arising out of the complex financial arrangements between Crédit Suisse and Trendtex which went beyond the mere relationship of banker and customer. There was no logic, he submitted, in restricting the interest, which in this j context prevents the cause of action from being a bare cause of action, to a proprietary interest. I have considerable sympathy for this point of view. I must confess to being unhappy that a transaction which businessmen in Switzerland may well regard as so unobjectionable that they would enter into it without appreciating that there was any possibility of it being ineffective should be held to be contrary to public policy in this country. But on the authorities as they stand it appears that the interest must be a proprietary interest, either an interest in other property to which the cause of action is ancillary, or an interest in the cause of action itself in the sense that the assignor was under a pre-existing duty to enforce it for the benefit of the assignee (as does a trustee for his beneficiary, a trustee in bankruptcy for a creditor of the bankrupt, or an assured for an insurer who is subrogated to the benefit of the cause of action). A mere creditor of the assignee has as such no interest in a cause of action of the assignor, even one which, if enforced, might lead to the creditor being paid; this is implicit in *Glegg v Bromley* itself. I do not think that it is open to a judge of first instance to widen the class as counsel for Crédit Suisse suggests; if that step is to be taken judicially, it can only be taken by a higher court. For these reasons I am satisfied (though I do not propose finally to decide the point, since it is an issue to be decided in the action on the evidence then called), that there is much force in counsel for Trendtex's submission that the assignment to Crédit Suisse by Trendtex of its cause of action against CBN was unenforceable by English law.

Even so, I do not consider that this provides a short answer to Crédit Suisse's application based on the exclusive jurisdiction clause. In his judgment in *Mackender v Feldia AG*, Diplock LJ drew a distinction between an agreement and a contract, the latter being an agreement which gives rise to legally enforceable rights and duties; he considered that the question whether an agreement did give rise to such rights and duties was to be decided by reference to the proper law of the agreement. That case was concerned with a policy of insurance containing a provision that the policy should be governed exclusively by Belgian law and that any disputes arising under the policy should be exclusively subject to the Belgian jurisdiction; and Diplock LJ held that a question whether their undoubted agreement embodied in the policy, which included the parties' choice of Belgian law as its proper law, gave rise to any legally enforceable rights and duties under Belgian law, was a dispute arising under the agreement, ie the policy, and therefore fell to be decided according to Belgian law in the Belgian courts to which both parties had agreed to submit. Likewise in the present case the question whether the agreement of 4th January 1978 gave rise to any legally enforceable rights and duties under Swiss law is a dispute regarding the conclusion, interpretation and/or fulfilment of the agreement, and as such is within the clause.

On the evidence of Swiss law before me, since the agreement of 4th January 1978 concerns the assignability of rights which arise from another contract to which the law of a foreign jurisdiction applies, by Swiss law the assignability of the rights has to be examined by the Swiss court in the light of the law of the foreign jurisdiction; and if the right cannot be lawfully assigned under the law of the foreign jurisdiction, the *assignment* is 'invalid' under Swiss law. But it does not follow from this that the *contract* is void by Swiss law. Furthermore, if the exclusive jurisdiction clause is given effect to, it is for the Court of Geneva to decide first, by English law, whether or not Trendtex's cause of action is 'assignable' in accordance with the meaning of that expression as understood in Swiss law, and second, if the court concludes that it is not, to decide in accordance with Swiss law what effect is to be given to the agreement itself.

It follows that counsel for Trendtex's short cut is not open to him. I have therefore to consider on ordinary principles whether I should or should not, in the exercise of my jurisdiction, grant a stay of proceedings on this ground. It is well established that I should grant a stay in respect of any disputes within the exclusive jurisdiction clause unless strong cause for not doing so is shown, and that the burden of proving such strong cause is on the plaintiff, in the present case, Trendtex: see *The Eleftheria* [1969] 2 All ER 641 at 648, [1970] P 94 at 99 per Brandon J. Brandon J went on to state that, in exercising its discretion, the court should take into account all the circumstances of the particular case, and he listed certain matters which might properly be regarded, though it is clear that he did not intend that list to be exhaustive. Brandon J did not state the principle on which the court should exercise its discretion; in my judgment, the principle is that the court should exercise its discretion to grant a stay unless the plaintiff proves that, in all the circumstances, it would be unjust to do so.

I think it right at this stage to refer to the second ground on which Crédit Suisse are seeking a stay, viz. that the court should grant a stay under the inherent jurisdiction of the court. The law has developed very considerably over the past few years. The accepted principle for many years was the principle stated by Scott LJ in *St Pierre v South American Stores (Gath & Chaves) Ltd* [1936] 1 KB 382 at 398, [1935] All ER Rep 408 at 414 under which the defendant had to show that the plaintiff's conduct in commencing proceedings in this country was 'oppressive' or 'vexatious' or otherwise would be an abuse of the process of the court. *The Atlantic Star* [1973] 2 All ER 175, [1974] AC 436 saw a considerable loosening of that principle, by giving a more liberal interpretation to the words 'oppressive' and 'vexatious'; in *MacShannon v Rockware Glass Ltd* [1978] 1 All ER 625, [1978] AC 795 the development has been taken a stage further, and it is now no longer appropriate to have regard to those words as providing a suitable test. The decision in *MacShannon's* case was unanimous; but, in stating the principles to be applied, there are some differences between the approaches adopted by their Lordships. It is my duty to distil from their speeches the principles which I should apply in the present case. As I understand it those principles are as follows:

(1) '... the real test of stay depends on what the court in its discretion considers that justice demands' (see [1978] 1 All ER 625 at 636, [1978] AC 795 at 819 per Lord Salmon).

(2) The court must first consider whether there is another jurisdiction which is clearly more appropriate than England for the trial of the action. (a) Such a jurisdiction has been called the 'natural or appropriate forum' (see [1978] 1 All ER 625 at 631, [1978] AC 795 at 812 per Lord Diplock) or the 'natural forum' (see [1978] 1 All ER 625 at 636, [1978] AC 795 at 818 per Lord Salmon). The court looks for another forum which is clearly more appropriate, because the court will not lightly stay an action properly commenced in this country (see [1978] 1 All ER 625 at 629, 636, [1978] AC 795 at 810, 818 per Lord Diplock and Lord Salmon), the reason being that, since the jurisdiction of the English court has been competently invoked, a stay should not be granted without good reason (see [1978] 1 All ER 625 at 642, [1978] AC 795 at 826 per Lord Keith). (b) The burden rests on the defendant to prove the existence of such other jurisdiction. (c) In considering whether there is another jurisdiction which is clearly more appropriate the court will consider all the circumstances of the particular case, including, for example, where the cause of action arose, the connection of the parties with any particular jurisdiction, the applicable law, the availability of witnesses and the saving of costs.

(3) If the court concludes that there is another clearly more appropriate jurisdiction, then two slightly different tests have been adumbrated. (a) A stay will be granted unless the plaintiff shows that a stay would deprive him of a legitimate personal or juridical advantage available to him in England (see [1978] 1 All ER 625 at 630, 639, [1978] AC 795 at 812, 822, per Lord Diplock, approved generally by Lord Fraser). (b) The burden of proof remains on the defendant. If he can show that trial in England would afford the plaintiff no real advantage, it would be unjust to refuse a stay. But, if trial in England would offer the plaintiff a real advantage, then a balance must be struck and the court must decide in its discretion whether justice demands a stay (see [1978] 1 All ER 625 at 636, 645, [1978] AC 795 at 819, 829 per Lord Salmon and Lord Keith).

On either test the court will only consider advantages to the plaintiff which are real, ie objectively demonstrated. (It is not clear which of these two approaches enjoyed the support of Lord Russell; but from the general tenor of his speech I infer that he preferred the latter.)

(4) If the court concludes that there is no other clearly more appropriate jurisdiction, then only Lord Keith appears to have considered that a stay might be granted. Such a case must surely be very rare.

I propose to apply the principles set out in (1), (2) and (3) (b) above.

It will at once be apparent that the principles now applicable are not far different from those applicable in the case of an exclusive jurisdiction clause. But there are important differences. First, in the case of an exclusive jurisdiction clause, the burden of proving that there is strong cause for not granting a stay rests on the plaintiff, because the parties have chosen the foreign jurisdiction. But in other cases, where no such choice has been made, the burden of proof (including the burden of proving that there is another clearly more appropriate forum) rests on the defendant. There is another important point of a difference. If the parties have chosen to submit their disputes to the exclusive jurisdiction of a foreign court it is difficult to see how either can in ordinary circumstances complain of the procedure of that court; whereas the mere fact that there exists another more appropriate forum should not of itself preclude the plaintiff from seeking to obtain the benefit of a procedural advantage in the English jurisdiction.

I shall, as I have already indicated, first consider whether I should exercise my discretion b to stay the proceedings or any part of them by reason of the exclusive jurisdiction clause. I shall consider the various matters in the same order as Brandon J chose to list them in *The Eleftheria* [1969] 2 All ER 641, [1970] P 94. First of all, evidence. The greater part of the evidence is situated in Switzerland. Dr Patry and Dr Hauser, who will both be very important witnesses, are in Switzerland; other possible witnesses in Switzerland, though less important, are Dr Patry's brother and a Maître Bovet. All witnesses from the c bank (and in particular Mr Köstner) are in Switzerland. Witnesses from outside Switzerland are Dr Kennedy (and, less important, Mr Carrington) from England, and Mr London from New York. Mr Carrington has given an undertaking to go to Switzerland to give evidence. The documentary evidence is in Switzerland; some is in English, some in French and some in German; if instructions are to be taken about these documents much will have come from Switzerland. In so far as language is important, Swiss d professional men are bilingual in French and German, and generally have a good working knowledge of English; the converse is not true of English professional men. Under this head, the case is strongly orientated towards Switzerland.

Second, the applicable law. The law on one crucial issue, viz whether Trendtex's cause of action is assignable, will fall to be decided by English law. But that apart, everything else falls to be decided by Swiss law. The whole framework of the action is Swiss. e Although 'assignability' of the cause of action is to be decided by English law, the meaning of that term, which was a matter of some dispute before me, is a question of Swiss law. If it should be held that the cause of action is not assignable, the assignments will be held 'invalid'; it must be decided with reference to Swiss law what that means, and what effect that has on the contract of 4th January 1978. In particular the legal effect of the ratification of 30th August 1978, and of the consequences of putting Trendtex into f liquidation, are matters to be decided by Swiss law. Furthermore, in so far as the contract itself is affected by the invalidity of the assignment, the questions how far, and on what principles, the transaction can be undone, will have to be decided with reference to Swiss law, bearing in mind that the transaction has been executed, that the principal subject matter (Trendtex's cause of action against CBN) has apparently ceased to exist, and that third party rights may have intervened. It is for Swiss law to decide the effect of any g undue influence, economic duress or commercial pressure on the validity of the contract. Again, the claim in respect of the alleged breach of fiduciary duty by Dr Patry, and the responsibility (if any) of Crédit Suisse for his actions, fall to be decided by Swiss law. Finally, the whole of Temo's claim to the shares in Trendtex is a matter to be decided under Swiss law; in particular, the construction of the agreement of 4th January 1978, on which that claim may depend, is a matter to be decided under Swiss law. Under h this head, despite the importance of the champerty issue which is to be decided with reference to English law, the connection with Swiss law is overwhelming.

Third, the parties. Two of the parties to the action are Swiss; the third is a Liechtenstein anstalt, and Liechtenstein has a closer connection with Switzerland than with any other country.

Fourth, I am satisfied that the defendants, Crédit Suisse, do genuinely desire trial in j Switzerland. This is not a case where they are seeking to invoke the jurisdiction of some strange and distant forum, but are rather seeking to have the matter tried in the country with which all three parties are most closely connected. Counsel for Trendtex attempted to persuade me otherwise; but his submissions, which consisted largely of a catalogue of points which might be construed as prejudicial to Crédit Suisse on the merits of the case, fell far short of persuading me that Crédit Suisse did not wish the case to be tried in

Switzerland. It may well be that Crédit Suisse are hoping to take advantage of the procedure of the Swiss courts, in so far as it assists them to do so; but I do not regard that as inconsistent in this case with a genuine desire to have the matter tried in Switzerland.

Fifth, the plaintiffs would not be prejudiced by having to sue in Switzerland because they would be deprived of security for their claim, or because they could not enforce a judgment, or because they would be unlikely to obtain a fair trial. Counsel did however submit that there were other disadvantages which Trendtex would suffer if the action was brought in Switzerland. First, he said that if the action was stayed, it would suffer delay; I cannot see that that is of any relevance, since the delay would arise from the choice of Trendtex in commencing proceedings here. Second, he said that the Swiss courts would have to grapple with the English law of champerty and maintenance; but in my judgment Swiss law is far more relevant to the action as a whole than English law. Third, he said that his client would lose the benefit of procedure under RSC Ord 14 which Temo desired to invoke in respect of its claim for the delivery up of the shares in Trendtex; I have however no evidence that no procedure for summary judgment is available in Switzerland, and anyway I do not regard this point as of fundamental importance. Fourth, he said that there was no procedure in Switzerland under which proceedings could be brought by minority shareholders; however, since he submits that Temo is plainly entitled to all the shares in Trendtex, this submission is (on his own argument) of minor importance, and on the evidence Swiss law provides for alternative remedies. Fifth, he said that under Swiss law (art 31 of the Swiss Contract Law), if a party influenced by (inter alia) threat fails, within one year, to declare to the other party that he is not bound by the contract, or fails to demand restitution, then the contract is deemed to be ratified. Such period runs, in the case of a threat, from the time of its removal. Ratification of the contract does not however of itself bar a claim for damages; and in any event Trendtex has an alternative claim for damages for breach of fiduciary duty. Furthermore, the English proceedings were commenced within the year, and the statement of claim was delivered on 1st October 1978, also within the year; if (as counsel for Trendtex contends) Temo is entitled to recover its shares as of right, it can cure by ratification any want of authority of Messrs Oppenheimers in starting the proceedings, and so defeat the time bar. Finally, the English court would (on the present authorities) give effect to the time bar if it bars the right, and not just the remedy; on the evidence before me, I have no sufficient guidance to conclude whether under Swiss law the right or the remedy is barred, but it is certainly at least possible that it is the right. For all these reasons, I doubt whether there would be any disadvantage to Trendtex from the time bar, if the matter proceeded in Switzerland. But even if there was, the fact remains that Trendtex has agreed to the Swiss jurisdiction; and, having done so, I would not be inclined to assist Trendtex to escape from the procedural consequences of that choice.

This last comment is of particular relevance to the last and by far the most substantial of the disadvantages on which counsel for Trendtex relied. This was that the process of discovery is much more restricted in Switzerland than it is in this country. On the evidence before me, it appears that in a commercial case such as the present there is no procedure for the discovery of documents or for interrogatories. If it appears to the judge that a party is withholding facts or documents which might involve a fraud, he may refer that part of the case to a criminal judge who can investigate and seize all the documents of the party concerned; this procedure can also be instituted by a private party. But such a procedure is very different from the English procedure, under which discovery and inspection of all relevant documents is required as a matter of course, subject to well-known exceptions, and under which interrogatories may be ordered in an appropriate case. It was submitted by counsel for Trendtex, with much force, that the present case is one in which discovery will be of great importance; with that I agree. But if the parties have agreed to submit their dispute to the jurisdiction of a court in which no such right exists, I find it difficult to see why this should be a ground for refusing to give effect to their agreement; by choosing the court, they have chosen the procedure, and I do not consider that the fact that a procedure which is generally applicable in the chosen jurisdiction is not helpful to a plaintiff in a particular case is a good reason for refusing to give effect to the contractual choice of forum.

Subject to one matter, I do not consider that the plaintiffs have shown sufficient cause to persuade me not to give effect to the exclusive jurisdiction clause. That one matter is that certain heads of claim are outside the scope of the clause, although related to the heads of claim within the clause. Without deciding whether this one matter should of itself impel me to decline to give effect to the clause, I propose next to consider, in the light of the foregoing, the question whether a stay should be granted under the inherent jurisdiction of the court, on the principles stated in *MacShannon's* case.

I have already set out these principles as I understand them. I have also set out, in considering the application for a stay under the exclusive jurisdiction clause, the relevant matters to be taken into account. I have first to consider whether there is another forum clearly more appropriate than England for the trial of this action. Plainly, Switzerland is such a forum, for the reasons I have already given. Next, would trial in England offer the plaintiffs a real advantage? This question must also be answered in the affirmative. First, they have the advantage that the champerty issue would be decided in this country; but, more important, the plaintiffs have the advantage of the English procedure for the purpose of obtaining discovery of documents and, if necessary and appropriate, interrogatories. This is moreover, as I have already indicated, a particularly valuable advantage to the plaintiffs in the present case; and this is so especially in relation to Trendtex's claim for damages for breach of fiduciary duty, which falls outside the ambit of the exclusive jurisdiction clause. In these circumstances, I have to strike a balance and consider whether justice demands a stay of proceedings.

In considering this question, I have to take into account all relevant circumstances. Now I have no doubt that, in some cases, the advantage to a plaintiff of discovery in this country may be such that the court may, in its discretion, consider it right to refuse to grant a stay; indeed, an example of such a case is *Interseas Shipping Co SA v Banco di Bilbao* [1978] Court of Appeal Transcript 329. However, no two cases are the same; and the present case has the additional feature of the exclusive jurisdiction clause, under which the parties have agreed that disputes within the clause, which include a substantial part of the subject matter of the present action, should be tried in the Court of Geneva. Furthermore, I have already held that (subject to the fact that there are two related heads of claim in the present proceedings which fall outside the clause) the plaintiffs have not satisfied me that the clause should not be given effect. This is, in my judgment, an important factor to be taken into account when deciding whether the court should exercise its inherent jurisdiction to stay the proceedings. I consider that this factor in particular outweighs the advantage to the plaintiffs. The plaintiffs have already agreed to submit themselves to the jurisdiction of a Swiss court, and therefore to accept their procedure, in respect of a substantial part of the matter in dispute. Further, Temo's claim to the shares in Trendtex, although outside the ambit of the clause, appears to depend very largely on questions of Swiss law, including the construction of the agreement of 4th January 1978 and the validity of that agreement. In my judgment, while giving full weight to the advantage to be derived by the plaintiffs if they have the benefit of discovery and possibly interrogatories in this country, and to the advantage of having the champerty issue decided here, these matters are outweighed by the overwhelmingly strong Swiss connection in all aspects of the case (including the availability of evidence, the applicability of Swiss law, the connection of the parties with Switzerland and the consequent saving of costs), coupled with the choice by the parties of the Swiss forum for the resolution of a substantial part of the dispute.

I therefore decide, in the exercise of my discretion, to accede to the defendant's application that the proceedings should be stayed.

Application granted. Action stayed. Leave to appeal granted.

K Mydeen Esq Barrister.

Appeal

Trendtex and Temo appealed against so much of the order of Robert Goff J, dated 24th April 1979, as ordered that all further proceedings in the action be stayed.

Stanley Brodie QC and *Stephen Nathan* for Trendtex and Temo.
Richard Yorke QC and *David Hunt* for Crédit Suisse.

Cur adv vult

2nd May. The following judgments were read.

LORD DENNING MR. The Trendtex Trading Corpn (I will call it 'Trendtex') is elusive. It is a Swiss corporation with 100 bearer shares all held by a Liechtenstein corporation. It has emerged from obscurity. It has provided us with much food for thought, and much material for the law reports. Last time it was the international law on sovereign immunity. This time it is the common law of champerty and maintenance. The first part of the story is told in *Trendtex Trading Corpn v Central Bank of Nigeria* [1977] 1 All ER 881, [1977] 1 QB 529. You should read it there so as to be able to follow the second part which I will recount now. It concerns the way in which Trendtex financed its dealings. It did it through the well-known bankers, Crédit Suisse.

Trendtex as creditors of the Central Bank of Nigeria

At the end of the first part, Trendtex was in a strong position. It was the beneficiary under a letter of credit which had been issued by the Central Bank of Nigeria. That bank had defaulted. Trendtex had a good cause of action against the bank for damages. Trendtex put it as $14,000,000. The bank had raised a plea of sovereign immunity, but that had been rejected by the Court of Appeal. There was an appeal pending to the House of Lords. So Trendtex was not home and dry. It might lose all if the House of Lords upheld the bank's plea of sovereign immunity. Even if the appeal to the House of Lords failed, Trendtex had still a long way to go. It had to prove the amount of damage it had suffered. It might fall far short of the $14,000,000 it had claimed. The legal position was simply that Trendtex had a cause of action for damages which it had reduced into possession by bringing proceedings in the English courts.

Crédit Suisse as creditors of Trendtex

Now in all its transactions Trendtex had been financed by Crédit Suisse. When Trendtex bought the 240,000 tonnes of cement, it asked Crédit Suisse to issue a letter of credit for the price. Crédit Suisse honoured their letter of credit and debited Trendtex with the amount. When the ships were delayed off Lagos, and demurrage accrued, Crédit Suisse paid the amounts and debited Trendtex accordingly. When Trendtex brought proceedings in the English courts against the Central Bank of Nigeria, and instructed Theodore Goddard & Co, English solicitors, to act for it, Crédit Suisse guaranteed the payment of the costs. There was some controversy as to the amount which Trendtex owed Crédit Suisse; but it seems to have been somewhere between $3,000,000 and $5,000,000.

Crédit Suisse seek an assignment of Trendtex's cause of action

Trendtex had some other creditors too. These had to be reckoned with some time or other. But Crédit Suisse were by far the largest creditors. They had their eyes on the one asset of Trendtex, on its chose in action against the Central Bank of Nigeria. Crédit Suisse wanted to get it assigned to them for their own benefit. They appointed a lawyer, Maître Patry of Geneva, to act for it in relation to all Trendtex matters. He brought pressure to bear on Trendtex by threatening to make it bankrupt unless it assigned to Crédit Suisse the benefit of its chose in action against the Central Bank of Nigeria. He also opened up negotiations with the Central Bank of Nigeria to see what they would pay to settle Trendtex's claim against them.

The negotiations were long and complex. But they came to a climax on 4th January

1978 at a meeting in Geneva. Maître Patry of Geneva represented Crédit Suisse. Dr
a Hauser of Zürich represented Trendtex. There was an important representation made by Maître Patry to Dr Hauser which can be interpreted as follows: 'I have got an offer from a third party. He will buy the right of action [of Trendtex against the Central Bank of Nigeria] for $800,000. I cannot get more. But I must ask Trendtex to assign the right of action outright to Crédit Suisse, and allow Crédit Suisse to make their own terms with the third party. Unless you agree to this, I will force Trendtex into liquidation.'

b

The assignment is made to Crédit Suisse

On the faith of that representation, an agreement was drawn up in writing and signed in Geneva on that very day, 4th January 1978. It was long and detailed. But its principal terms were: (1) Trendtex assigned to Crédit Suisse all its rights of action against the Central Bank of Nigeria, not as security but out and out for the sole and exclusive benefit
c of Crédit Suisse (or the third party purchaser); and Trendtex acknowledged that it had no further interest in the legal action conducted in London; (2) Crédit Suisse paid off all the other creditors of Trendtex or put money at its disposal to pay them; (3) Trendtex gave Maître Patry a power of attorney to enable him to settle its claim against the Central Bank of Nigeria; (4) Dr Hauser deposited 90% of Trendtex's shares with Maître Patry so as to give him full control over Trendtex. (Note: Trendtex is a Swiss corporation. It has a
d capital of 100 bearer shares of 1,000 Swiss francs each. Those 100 bearer shares were owned by Temo Anstalt, a Liechtenstein corporation. Temo Anstalt had bearer shares which were owned by Mr London of New York. Under the assignment 90 of Trendtex's shares were deposited with Maître Patry); (5) Finally, there was this important clause (art 6):

e 'This Agreement is governed by Swiss law. Any dispute regarding its conclusion, interpretation or fulfilment shall be judged by the Court of Geneva, exclusive of any other jurisdiction.'

The first surprise

That agreement was signed on Friday, 4th January 1978. Then, on Wednesday, 9th
f January, Maître Patry on behalf of Crédit Suisse assigned to a third party all the rights of action (of Trendtex against the Central Bank of Nigeria) for $1,100,000. So over the weekend Crédit Suisse (or Maître Patry) had got an increase of $300,000, over and above the $800,000 which they had said was the uttermost offer. An increase of 37½%.

The second surprise

g A bigger surprise was yet to come. Five weeks later, on 12th or 13th February, Maître Patry went out to Nigeria. He took with him the power of attorney authorising him to act on behalf of Trendtex. He also took his 90 bearer shares to support it. He negotiated with the Nigerians a settlement of the action of Trendtex against the Central Bank of Nigeria. They paid $8,000,000 to settle the case. Presumably Maître Patry handed it over to the third party. So the third party made a profit of $6,900,000. He only paid
h $1,100,000 on 9th January 1978 for the rights of action; and here he was in February 1978 getting $8,000,000 for them.

The mysterious third party

Who was this mysterious third party who made this huge profit? Maître Patry refuses to disclose his identity. In an affidavit he says:

j

'... it was agreed and stipulated with the purchaser that the identity of the purchaser should not be disclosed. That stipulation was and continues to be binding upon me as the person who acted on behalf of [Crédit Suisse] in relation to the transfer and I am not, therefore, at liberty to disclose the purchaser's identity without permission of the purchaser which is not forthcoming.'

Mr London is furious

Now, apart from Dr Hauser in Switzerland, Trendtex had other representatives, Mr London and Dr Kennedy. They had participated in all the negotiations. When they discovered that the Nigerians had paid $8,000,000 to settle the claim, they were furious. They felt that Maître Patry had played a dirty trick on Trendtex. They thought that he must all along have had, hidden up his sleeve, this settlement of $8,000,000. And yet he had put forward the offer by a third party of $800,000 as all that could be obtained.

The English proceedings

So Mr London and Dr Kennedy went to Herbert Oppenheimer, Nathan & Vandyk, solicitors, in London and issued a writ in the High Court of Justice in England. They named as plaintiffs Trendtex and its holding company Temo Anstalt. They named Crédit Suisse as defendants. They claimed that the assignment of 4th January 1978 was invalid and should be set aside. They claimed that the $8,000,000 belonged to them and asked for an account of what had become of it. Temo Anstalt asked for the return of the 90% of the shares which Maître Patry had kept.

Crédit Suisse retaliated by an application to strike out the name of Trendtex on the ground that Mr London and Dr Kennedy had no right to use it, and also to stay the proceedings on the ground that the parties had agreed to the exclusive jurisdiction of the Swiss courts.

On 30th March 1979 Robert Goff J stayed the proceedings. He was influenced considerably by the exclusive jurisdiction clause. On the appeal before us, two points of law were argued. First, was the assignment of 4th January 1978 valid or invalid? If it was invalid, that was decisive of the whole case. The exclusive jurisdiction clause fell with it. There was no bar to the proceedings continuing in England. Second, even if the assignment of 4th January 1978 was valid, it was submitted that the proceedings should continue in England, because discovery of documents could be had here, but not in Switzerland.

The validity of the assignment

The right of action of Trendtex against the Central Bank of Nigeria was a chose in action. It was reduced into the possession of Trendtex by the issue of the writ in the High Court in England. It was situate in England. The question whether it was assignable at all is governed by the law of England. That is clear from the private international law as enunciated in our textbooks in England: see Dicey and Morris on the Conflict of Laws (9th Edn, 1973, pp 506, 547, rr 78 and 83); and it is acknowledged by the Swiss lawyers. Dr Baechi of the University of Zürich says:

> 'The assignability of the rights has to be examined by the Swiss Court in the light of the law of the foreign jurisdiction (see Schnitzler "Handbuch des Intern. Privatrechtes" (3rd Edn, p 580)). If the right cannot be lawfully assigned under the law of that foreign jurisdiction the assignment is invalid under Swiss law.'

Dr Perret of the Bar of Geneva agreed, saying that—

> 'The Swiss Court would look to English law to decide whether [Trendtex's] claim against the Central Bank of Nigeria could be assigned at all. It would not look to English law to decide whether the agreement actually had assigned those rights.'

We must therefore turn to English law to decide whether the chose in action (the right of action by Trendtex against the Central Bank of Nigeria) was capable of being assigned at all. It was submitted by counsel for Trendtex that it was incapable of being assigned at all. It was, he said, the assignment of a bare right to litigate, which has for centuries been held to be bad as offending against the law of maintenance and champerty. He admitted that there were many exceptions to that rule, but he submitted that this case did not come within any of the exceptions hitherto recognised.

The effect of the Criminal Law Act 1967

a Now this is the first case, I believe, in which we have been called on to consider the effect on assignments of the Criminal Law Act 1967. It abolished the crime of maintenance, including champerty, so that no one can be punished for it. It did away with the tort of maintenance, including champerty, so that no one can be made liable for it. By striking down both the crime and the tort, it seems to me that the statute struck down our old cases as to what constitutes maintenance, including champerty, in so far as
b they were based on an outdated public policy. But it did not strike down our modern cases in so far as they carry out the public policy to today. These are preserved by s 14(2), which says:

> 'The abolition of criminal and civil liability under the law of England and Wales for maintenance and champerty shall not affect any rule of that law [that is the law of England and Wales] as to the cases in which a contract is to be treated as contrary
> c to public policy or otherwise illegal.'

Maintenance today

So far as maintenance itself is concerned (without champerty), the modern public policy is to be found in *British Cash and Parcel Conveyors Ltd v Lamson Store Service Co Ltd* [1908] 1 KB 1006, *Martell v Consett Iron Co Ltd* [1955] 1 All ER 481, [1955] Ch 363 and
d *Hill v Archbold* [1967] 3 All ER 110, [1968] 1 QB 686 (decided just before the passing of the 1967 Act). It is perfectly legitimate today for one person to support another in bringing or resisting an action (as by paying the costs of it), provided that he has a legitimate and genuine interest in the result of it and the circumstances are such as reasonably to warrant his giving his support. As I said in *Hill v Archbold* [1967] 3 All ER 110 at 112, [1968] 1 QB 686 at 694:

> e 'Much maintenance is considered justifiable today which would in 1914 have been considered obnoxious. Most of the actions in our courts are supported by some association or other, or by the State itself. Very few litigants bring suits, or defend them, at their own expense. Most claims by workmen against their employers are paid for by a trade union. Most defences of motorists are paid for by
> f insurance companies. This is perfectly justifiable and is accepted by everyone as lawful, provided always that the one who supports the litigation, if it fails, pays the costs of the other side.'

Champerty today as affecting lawyers

So far as champerty is concerned, there is need for some updating. Champerty is a species of maintenance; but it is a particularly obnoxious form of it. It exists when the
g maintainer seeks to make a profit out of another man's action, by taking the proceeds of it, or part of them, for himself. Modern public policy condemns champerty in a lawyer whenever he seeks to recover not only his proper costs but also a portion of the damages for himself, or when he conducts a case on the basis that he is to be paid if he wins but not if he loses. As I said in *Re Trepca Mines Ltd* [1962] 3 All ER 351 at 355, [1963] Ch 199 at 219:

> h 'The reason why the common law condemns champerty is because of the abuses to which it may give rise. The common law fears that the champertous maintainer might be tempted, for his own personal gain, to inflame the damages, to suppress evidence or even to suborn witnesses.'

This reason is still valid after the 1967 Act. In *Wallersteiner v Moir (No 2)* [1975] 1 All
j ER 849 at 860, [1975] QB 373, at 394, I said:

> 'It was suggested to us that the only reason why "contingency fees" were not allowed in England was because they offended against the criminal law as to champerty; and that, now that criminal liability is abolished, the courts were free to hold that contingency fees were lawful. I cannot accept this contention. The

reason why contingency fees are in general unlawful is that they are contrary to public policy as we understand it in England.' *a*

They *are* contrary to modern public policy.

Champerty in former times as affecting assignments

Now I come to another aspect of champerty. It is when a man has a 'bare right to litigate'. Can it be lawfully assigned to a purchaser? Under the old notions of public *b* policy, such an assignment was always unlawful. It was said by all that 'a chose in action is not assignable ... No case can be found which decides that such a right can be the subject of assignment, either at law or in equity': see *Prosser v Edmonds* (1835) 1 Y & C Ex 481 at 499, 160 ER 196 at 203. The only exception was where property of some kind or other was assigned, and there was attached, as incidental to it, a right to bring an action (see *Dawson v Great Northern and City Railway Co* [1905] 1 KB 260 at 270–271, [1904–7] All ER Rep 913 at 916–917; *Ellis v Torrington* [1920] 1 KB 399); or an undisputed debt *c* was assigned, because this was regarded as a piece of property (see *Fitzroy v Cava* [1905] 2 KB 364 at 373). Apart from these exceptions it was unlawful to assign a right of action for a disputed debt or for damages for breach of contract or for tort.

Champerty today as affecting assignments *d*

That old rule has not been able to survive into modern times. Just as the old law about maintenance (without champerty) was brought up to date by *Martell v Consett Iron Co Ltd* [1955] 1 All ER 481, [1955] Ch 363, so the time has come when we should bring the law about assignments up to date. Just as in maintenance, it is sufficient if the maintainer has a legitimate and genuine interest in the subject matter, and the circumstances are such as reasonably to warrant his support of the action or defence; so in an assignment of a *e* chose in action, it is valid if the assignee has a legitimate and genuine interest in the subject matter and the circumstances are such as reasonably to warrant the assignment of it to him. I realise that, like in maintenance and in champerty, this new policy will give rise to questions such as: what is a legitimate and genuine interest? What circumstances are such as reasonably to warrant the assignment? These questions are only to be solved in our English way, by case to case as the judges come to decide them. *f* Thus there will be built up a body of case law to guide practitioners for the future. But meanwhile I will take from the books some instances when the assignment of a chose in action should be held to be valid.

(i) Incidental to property

Just as in former times, so in modern times, an assignment of a chose in action is assignable when it is incidental to an assignment of other property; or when an *g* undisputed debt is assigned. In such cases the assignee has a legitimate and genuine interest, in the shape of the property which he is acquiring, and the circumstances do reasonably warrant the assignment of that which is incidental to it.

(ii) Assignment to a creditor

Take now a man who brings an action for damages for breach of contract, and becomes *h* bankrupt whilst the action is still going on. His trustee can sell the chose in action to one of the creditors of the bankrupt, on the terms that the creditor can take the fruits of the action for himself. The creditor is not limited to the amount of the debt owing to him, but can take the whole proceeds: see *Guy v Churchill* (1888) 40 Ch D 481. Now suppose that the man who brings the action does not become bankrupt, but is in financial difficulty, and to save his business assigns the chose in action to one of his creditors. Is *j* there any ground of public policy why he should not do so? If his trustee in bankruptcy could do so, why should not he? Cannot the creditor likewise take the fruits of the action, not limited to the amount of his debt? And does not the same apply even when the man is not in financial difficulty? At any rate when the creditor does not take undue advantage of the debtor, and is able and willing to pay the costs of the action, if he loses.

(*iii*) *Assignment to an insurer*

a Take next a man who has insured his goods against loss or damage and he suffers the loss of or damage to them by the fault of a wrongdoer. He has a right of action in tort. The insurance company can, of course, pay him compensation and be subrogated to his claim against the wrongdoer to recoup themselves, but no more. But as an alternative the man can assign his right of action to the insurance company out and out; and the insurance company can take the fruits of the action for themselves. They are not limited
b to the amount which they have paid to their customer: see *Compania Colombiana de Seguros v Pacific Steam Navigation Co* [1964] 1 All ER 216, [1965] 1 QB 101. They have a legitimate and genuine interest and the circumstances are such as reasonably to warrant the assignment.

(*iv*) *Assignment of the proceeds*

Take next a case where one lady, Mrs Glegg, brought an action against another lady for
c damages for slander. The plaintiff owed a large sum to her husband, and wanting to borrow more from him, so as to pay her solicitor's costs in the action, she assigned to him 'all that the interest sum of money or premises to which she is or may become entitled' in the action or by settlement of it. That assignment was held to be good and not against public policy: see *Glegg v Bromley* [1912] 3 KB 474. But, suppose she had used different words and assigned 'all the right of action for damages', would that have made any
d difference? On principle, I should think not. There is no reason in public policy why the law should permit the assignment of the *proceeds* of a right of action and refuse to allow the assignment of the right of action itself. In either case the assignee is the one concerned to bring the action to trial or settlement. He promotes the litigation, and not the assignor.

But *Glegg v Bromley* was an exceptional case. The cause of action was for slander, a
e personal tort. Such a cause of action is not in general assignable. Hence the need to say that it was only the proceeds which could be assigned.

(*v*) *Assignments in the case of personal torts*

Torts can be divided into two broad classes: those relating to persons and those relating to property. So far as personal torts are concerned, like damages for libel or slander, or for assault, or for personal injury, the judges have often said that they cannot be
f assigned. This, I think, still holds good. There are good reasons of public policy for not allowing an assignment, because of the danger that the assignee may buy up the claim at a small figure and use it to get a big profit for himself. In short, all the evils which our forefathers saw in champerty. In such cases the assignee has no legitimate and genuine interest in the chose in action, and the circumstances are not such as reasonably to warrant the assignment.

g

(*vi*) *Assignment of damages for breach of contract*

Take next a case where a man sells goods on an instalment basis, and after a time the buyer repudiates the contract and the repudiation is accepted. The seller is left with a claim for the price of the unpaid instalment and damages for repudiation. The seller can certainly assign the debt to a purchaser. Can he not also assign the chose in action for
h damages? The point was discussed by McCardie J in *County Hotel and Wine Co Ltd v London and North Western Railway Co* [1918] 2 KB 251. He saw nothing in public policy to prevent the assignment. Nor do I. Just as a party to a contract can assign the benefit of it (*before* there is a breach) (see *Hughes v Pump House Hotel Co* [1902] 2 KB 190, [1900–3] All ER Rep 480) so also he should be able to assign the benefit of the right to sue for damages (*after* there is a breach); provided always that he is able and willing to pay the
j costs of the action if he loses; and that it is not a contract of a personal nature which is not assignable at all (see *Kemp v Baerselman* [1906] 2 KB 604). And provided also that it is made for good and sufficient consideration such as reasonably to warrant the assignment. If the assignee takes three-quarters of the damages, the circumstances may not be such as to warrant the assignment: see *Laurent v Sale & Co* [1963] 2 All ER 63, [1963] 1 WLR 829.

(vii) Assignments in the case of torts to property

In many cases of loss of or damage to property, the cause of action can be framed either as damages for breach of contract or as damages for tort. If I am right in thinking that damages for breach of contract are capable of assignment, for good and sufficient consideration, so also it would seem that damages in tort, for loss of or damage to property, can be assigned, provided the assignment is for good and sufficient consideration. The two cases of *Dawson v Great Northern and City Railway Co* [1905] 1 KB 260, [1904–7] All ER Rep 913, and *Defries v Milne* [1913] 1 Ch 98 are often cited to show that damages for tort are not assignable. But they were decided on the footing that the damages were not for tort but in respect of claims for compensation and breach of contract respectively. But nowadays they would be valid if they were regarded as an assignment of damages for tort. There is no reason in public policy for making any difference. We must do away with all that hair-splitting.

(viii) Assignee's name

There has been much discussion as to the scope of the words 'debt or other legal thing in action' in s 25 of the Supreme Court of Judicature Act 1873, now s 136 of the Law of Property Act 1925. It seems to me that in modern times the words 'legal thing in action' should be given their proper legal significance. They include a right to sue for a disputed debt or for damages for breach of contract or in tort for loss of or damage to property. At one time they were given a restricted interpretation because of the old law of champerty and maintenance: see *May v Lane* (1894) 64 LJQB 236 at 238 per Rigby LJ, as explained in *Torkington v Magee* [1902] 2 KB 427 at 433–434. But now that the old law of champerty and maintenance has gone, it seems to me that, whenever a legal thing in action can lawfully be assigned, the assignee can sue in his own name provided he gives proper notice, and is able and willing to pay the costs of the action if he loses.

The old saying that you cannot assign a 'bare right to litigate' is gone. The correct proposition is that you cannot assign a personal right to litigate, that is, which is in its nature personal to you yourself. But you can assign an impersonal right to litigate, that is, which is in its nature, a proprietory right, provided that the circumstances are such as reasonably to warrant it.

The present case

Returning now to the present case, it is clear to my mind that Crédit Suisse had a legitimate and genuine interest in the right of action by Trendtex against the Central Bank of Nigeria. They had financed the transaction which had given rise to the right of action. They were creditors of Trendtex for large amounts arising out of those transactions. This interest was such as reasonably to warrant the assignment to them. So the right of action was capable of assignment in English law. The assignment was valid.

The effect of the assignment

The assignment being valid, the effect of it depends on the proper law of the contract of assignment: see Dicey and Morris on the Conflict of Laws (9th Edn, 1973, p 551, r 84). That was Swiss law. At once we come on to the clause which gives exclusive jurisdiction to the Court of Geneva. That clause must be given full effect unless its enforcement would be unreasonable and unjust or that the clause was invoked for such reasons as fraud or overreaching: see *The Chaparrall*, [1972] 2 Lloyd's Rep 315 at 321.

The claims of Trendtex do not rest on the contract of assignment. They are based on the suggested invalidity of the assignment itself or on breach of fiduciary duty; the claim of Trendtex for the return of the 90 shares does not depend on the assignment. So I do not think the clause about choice of jurisdiction really applies here. We have to see what is the forum conveniens for the decision of this dispute: see *MacShannon v Rockware Glass Ltd* [1978] 1 All ER 625, [1978] AC 795. In this case everything points to Switzerland. All the impugned transactions took place in Switzerland; Trendtex and Crédit Suisse are Swiss corporations, Swiss lawyers took a leading part, coupled with an excursion by a Swiss lawyer to Nigeria. The forum conveniens is Switzerland.

Discovery

The dispute should clearly be tried in Switzerland except for one matter which does *a* give rise to concern. There is no process for compelling discovery of documents in the civil courts of Switzerland. But I cannot believe that this means that justice cannot be had in Switzerland. I should expect that, if a defendant in a commercial case does not produce the documents in his possession, or, for instance, does not disclose the name of the third party here, the Swiss court would draw inferences against him. Maître Patry *b* says in his affidavit:

> '... under the Swiss civil litigation system the judge not only questions the witnesses first (having already seen the detailed statements of facts and law prepared by both parties) but also takes an independent interest in establishing the truth of a situation.'

c In other words, not an adversarial system, but an investigative system. Moreover, Maître Patry says in his affidavit:

> 'The most important witnesses (Dr Hauser and myself) are resident in Switzerland and available to the Swiss Courts ... we are both professional persons acting in such capacity and it is proper that our actions should be judged in the light of our professional as well as our general responsibilities before the Courts of our own *d* country.'

Those reasons are quite sufficient to my mind to show that the claims of Trendtex and of Temo should be tried in Switzerland, and not in England.

I would dismiss the appeal, accordingly.

e **BRIDGE LJ.** I have had the advantage of reading in draft the judgment to be delivered by Oliver LJ. I agree with it and for the reasons expressed in that judgment I too would dismiss this appeal.

OLIVER LJ. This appeal arises out of an extremely complicated background, the facts of which have been set out in detail in the judgment of Robert Goff J. The salient facts *f* have already been summarised in the judgment of Lord Denning MR, and I will not take up time by repeating them. In considering, however, the validity and effect of the agreement of 4th January 1978 on which the defendants' application for a stay was based there are, I think, two particular aspects of the matter which are of some importance. The first is the very close commercial involvement which the defendants had, right from the inception, with the contract entered into by the plaintiff, to which, if I may, I will *g* refer by the shorthand title 'Trendtex', and with the letter of credit issued by the Central Bank of Nigeria ('CBN'). Trendtex had, in 1974, bound itself by contract to supply to Pan-African Export and Import Co Ltd ('Pan-African'), a quantity of 240,000 metric tons of cement c i f Lagos/Apapa and the letter of credit was issued to Trendtex by CBN under the terms of that contract to cover the price payable by Pan-African and demurrage. Trendtex could never have undertaken those contractual obligations without the *h* financial assistance of the defendants, Crédit Suisse, for it was not itself a manufacturer or supplier of cement. It relied, for fulfilment of its contract with Pan-African, on procuring supplies to be shipped from German suppliers, Alsen-Breitenburg of Hamburg, at a rather lower price than that which was payable under the contract with Pan-African. To enable that to be done it was necessary for a letter of credit to be issued in favour of the German suppliers to cover each shipment, and this was done by Crédit *j* Suisse at Trendtex's request. Crédit Suisse also issued guarantees to certain shipowners, among them a German company called Intermare Transport GmbH ('Intermare'), through whom Trendtex chartered the ships. So far the transaction represented a perfectly normal international commercial dealing with Crédit Suisse providing back-to-back financing. On each consignment of cement being shipped by the German suppliers, the latter presented the shipping documents and invoices to Crédit Suisse's corresponding

bank and received payment under a letter of credit issued by Crédit Suisse to cover the shipment, and Crédit Suisse debited Trendtex's account accordingly. The documents a
received by Crédit Suisse would then be presented by them to the Midland Bank (CBN's corresponding bank in London) and the payments received by Crédit Suisse under the letter of credit issued by CBN would then be credited to Trendtex's account with Crédit Suisse.

When CBN suspended payment under the letter of credit issued by them, Crédit Suisse had, of course, already paid to the German suppliers at Trendtex's request the price b
of the cargoes shipped, on presentation of the shipping documents, under their letter of credit and this, together with demurrage payable under their guarantees to the shipowners, was duly and properly debited to Trendtex's account. This left Trendtex in a serious financial position.

It had treated CBN as being in repudiation of their contract constituted by the letter of credit and had, on 4th November 1975, commenced proceedings against CBN in this c
country claiming a sum of some $US14,000,000 by way of damages. It had also succeeded in obtaining an injunction freezing a sufficiency of CBN's assets in this country to meet that claim. But it had not the resources for prolonged litigation. Thus when, on 26th March 1976, an order was made setting aside the writ and dissolving the injunction on the ground of CBN's sovereign immunity (see *Trendtex Trading Corpn v Central Bank of Nigeria* [1976] 3 All ER 437, [1976] 1 WLR 868), Trendtex found itself d
with a heavy indebtedness to Crédit Suisse and the prospect of some prolonged and expensive litigation in an appellate court, with no certainty of a successful outcome, before it could raise the money to meet its obligations. Crédit Suisse's own position, however, was not much more enviable. They had financed Trendtex's purchase in the comfortable knowledge that their possession of the shipping documents would enable them to recoup themselves under the letter of credit issued by CBN and they now found e
themselves in a position where their only substantial prospect of payment lay in the success of the litigation which Trendtex was conducting in England. It would be difficult to find more closely interwoven commercial interests and it is not, therefore, surprising to find Crédit Suisse agreeing to support Trendtex in pursuing the matter to the Court of Appeal (see [1977] 1 All ER 881, [1977] 1 QB 529) and beyond if necessary. Not to have done so would have been disastrous for them. In November 1975 f
a Mr Köstner, the manager of Crédit Suisse's Lausanne branch, committed Crédit Suisse to guaranteeing all the legal fees and costs incurred by Trendtex's English solicitors, Messrs Theodore Goddard, in the proceedings against CBN.

But Crédit Suisse were not Trendtex's only creditors and they became desirous of obtaining some security not only for their debt but also for the not insubstantial investment which they were being called on to make in the litigation, and it was the g
effecting of and the progressive improvement in the Crédit Suisse's security which ultimately gave rise to the present proceedings.

That brings me to the other matter which seems to me to be of some importance, and that is that the agreement of 4th January 1978 was merely the culmination of a series of agreements between Crédit Suisse and Trendtex under which Trendtex had already purported to assign to Crédit Suisse its cause of action against CBN. On 6th September h
1976 Dr Hauser, Trendtex's sole administrator and director, had sent to Mr Köstner what was described as a 'General Declaration of Assignment' by Trendtex of the six specified contracts for the shipment of cement which had taken place before CBN's repudiation of their obligations. There were, so far as appears at any rate, no pending proceedings against Pan-African, but this document authorised Crédit Suisse to pursue in Trendtex's name all claims arising out of the contracts and bound Trendtex to supplement the j
agreement with individual documents. This agreement did not mention the claim against CBN, but on 26th November 1976 Dr Hauser sent a further 'Declaration of Surrender' expressed to be in fulfilment of the 6th September agreement and surrendering to Crédit Suisse all claims arising from the Pan-African contract and the letter of credit 'to the full extent of the indebtedness to the transferee', and empowering

Crédit Suisse to enforce all claims arising from CBN's letter of credit either in their own name or in that of Trendtex. It was on the basis of this document that the defendants financed Trendtex's appeal to the Court of Appeal, which was successful.

Yet a further document was prepared on 7th November 1977 and signed by Dr Hauser on 14th November, purporting to record an agreement reached at a meeting held on 21st September 1977 at which Trendtex's indebtedness to Crédit Suisse was reduced from $3,400,000 to $1,500,000 on agreed terms which included an authority to Crédit Suisse to settle the proceedings against CBN for not less than $3,000,000 and a further total irrevocable cession of Trendtex's rights against CBN by way of guarantee of Trendtex's debt.

Thus the position at 4th January 1978 was that Trendtex's claim, if assignable at all, had already been effectively assigned to Crédit Suisse but only by way of security for the amount owing to them. The agreement of 4th January in fact recited the previous assignment of 26th November 1976; that an offer to buy Trendtex's rights for $800,000 had been received from a third party, and that a sale had been opposed by Trendtex because of its position vis-à-vis its other creditors. It went on to recite that Crédit Suisse were ready to advance a part of the anticipated proceeds of sale in satisfaction of the claims of such other creditors in order to treat them substantially in the same way as Crédit Suisse themselves were being treated.

The operative provisions of this agreement have already been summarised by Lord Denning MR and I need not further refer to them save to notice that there was no express assignment of Trendtex's right of action against CBN as such (it being assumed that that had already taken place) but, in effect, a release of any residual interest which Trendtex had. Trendtex agreed not to oppose a sale of its rights for such consideration as Crédit Suisse might determine and irrevocably recognised that it had no further interest in the proceedings.

Having regard to the wide discrepancy of the sum received in settlement and the sum for which Trendtex had been told that the claim was about to be sold and also to the relatively short time which elapsed between the agreement of 4th January and the ultimate settlement, it is not altogether surprising that, when Mr London heard about it in March, a query was raised in his mind whether at the date of the agreement, Crédit Suisse or their representative might not have been aware that there existed a possibility of settling for a very much larger sum than the $800,000 referred to in the agreement. Thus the present action was commenced on 29th March 1978 by Trendtex and Temo Anstalt ('Temo'), the Liechtenstein anstalt which claims to be beneficially entitled to the shares in Trendtex, claiming, first, that the agreements of 4th January 1978 and of 26th November 1976 were void as constituting assignments of a bare cause of action and a declaration that the cause of action against CBN remained vested in Trendtex; second, that Trendtex was induced to enter into the agreement of 4th January by illegal pressure; third, that Maître Patry was in breach of a fiduciary duty to Trendtex for which Crédit Suisse were vicariously liable and liable to account accordingly to Trendtex for moneys received; and, fourth, the return of the shares to Temo. On Crédit Suisse's summons to stay the proceedings, it was strenuously argued before Robert Goff J that the assignment of Trendtex's cause of action against CBN was champertous and incapable of enforcement in England. The judge did not in terms decide that question, although he expressed the view that there were very strong arguments in favour of the plaintiffs' (Trendtex and Temo) contention. He held, however, that, even if the argument were correct, that did not conclude the matter, since the question whether the agreement itself (assuming it to be inoperative as an assignment) gave rise to legally enforceable duties under Swiss law was a dispute which fell within the exclusive jurisdiction clause. He then considered, on the evidence before him and in accordance with the principles set out in the judgment of Brandon J in *The Eleftheria* [1969] 2 All ER 641, [1970] P 94, whether Trendtex had discharged the onus of showing that it would be unjust to give effect to that clause by granting a stay. He concluded that it had not. He also considered, in relation to Temo's claim and the claims based on breach of fiduciary duty, whether, in accordance with the principles laid down by the House of Lords in *MacShannon v Rockware Glass Ltd* [1978] 1 All ER 625, [1978] AC 795, there was a more appropriate forum for the trial of issues between the parties, and whether trial in England would offer to Trendtex and Temo some real advantage of which they would be deprived if the dispute were tried in the appropriate forum. He concluded that everything pointed to Switzerland as a more appropriate forum, and that the advantages of trial in England were not such as to outweigh what he described as 'the overwhelmingly Swiss connection'; and he granted the stay accordingly.

In this court the main thrust of counsel for Trendtex has been a challenge to the view which the judge expressed that the issue of maintenance and champerty, which he expressly avoided deciding, did not constitute a short cut which effectively concluded the matter, and indeed the court has been pressed by both sides to decide in terms whether the relevant agreements were void for maintenance or champerty since, whether the dispute is tried in England or in Switzerland, that is a matter which will in any event have to be determined. Counsel for Trendtex puts it higher, as he did before the judge. He contends that, if the point is decided in his favour, it is conclusive of the matter, at any rate so far as concerns Crédit Suisse's reliance on art 6 of the agreement of 4th January (the exclusive jurisdiction clause).

The judge was, he contends, wrong to treat the assignment as something separable from the agreement. The agreement was, he submits, an assignment and nothing but an assignment. As such, its validity falls to be determined by the lex situs of the chose in action, that is to say, England, where the action against CBN was being litigated. By English law it was illegal and void as a whole and the invalidity extends to the exclusive jurisdiction clause itself (see *Heyman v Darwins Ltd* [1942] 1 All ER 337, [1942] AC 356).

Whether counsel for Trendtex is right or wrong about this, the question of the champertous nature of the agreement is one which lies at the threshold of his argument and it does, as it seems to me, require to be resolved conclusively before one ever gets to the ulterior question of the effect, supposing the assignments to be champertous, which that has on the agreement as a whole. Nor, indeed, is it inappropriate that concepts having their origins in the ancient fear entertained by English lawyers of the abuse of legal process, which was endemic in medieval times, should once again be reappraised in the light of current notions of public policy and of international trading practices. Robert Goff J in the instant case said (at p 732, ante):

> 'I must confess to being unhappy that a transaction which businessmen in Switzerland may well regard as *so* unobjectionable that they would enter into it without appreciating that there was any possibility of it being ineffective should be held to be contrary to public policy in this country.' (My emphasis.)

I share that unhappiness. Maintenance and champerty, which once attracted criminal penalties and founded claims for tortious damages, have, since 1967, ceased to do so (see the Criminal Law Act 1967, ss 13(1) and 14(1)). Only in the field of contractual rights and duties do they still cast their shadow (see s 14(2)) and even in this field the trend of all the recent authorities has been to foreshorten the shadow. Danckwerts J in *Martell v Consett Iron Co Ltd* [1954] 3 All ER 339 at 347, [1955] Ch 363 at 382, observed that 'unless the law of maintenance is capable of keeping up with modern thought it must die in a lingering and discredited old age'; and in *Hill v Archbold* [1967] 3 All ER 110 at 114, [1968] 1 QB 686 at 697, the same judge said:

> 'the law of maintenance depends on the question of public policy, and public policy . . . is not a fixed and immutable matter. It is a conception which, if it has any sense at all, must be alterable by the passage of time.'

There is, I think, a clear requirement of public policy that officers of the court should be inhibited from putting themselves in a position where their own interests may conflict with their duties to the court by the agreement, for instance, of so-called 'contingency fees'; and there may well be valid reasons why personal rights of action for tortious damage should not, in general, be the subject matter of assignment or partition.

a But outside these categories, and speaking only for myself, I question whether, in the year 1980, our jurisprudence ought still to have room for distinctions, which owe more to sophistry than to logic, between choses in action and what are described as 'bare' rights of action or between strictly proprietary and purely commercial or financial interests. Maintenance is a very ancient concept and its history is one of a progressive alleviation of a strictness which at one time even forbade the giving of evidence except under
b subpoena. It may be defined as the rendering by one person, improperly, of assistance to another in prosecuting or defending proceedings in which the person so rendering assistance has no legitimate interest. Champerty was merely an aggravated form of maintenance and was constituted by an agreement between the maintainer and the maintained for the division of the proceeds of the suit. Apart from the additional element of partition it was, in its essentials, no different from maintenance, although it
c does seem clear that at least some of the exceptional circumstances (for instance, kinship between maintainer and maintained) which came to be recognised as justifying maintenance would not necessarily be recognised as justifying champertous agreements.

As regards these the law was particularly strict, the reason being said to be that the champertous interest of a maintainer might lead him to abuse the process of the court by suborning witnesses, suppressing evidence and so on. What endowed champerty with
d particular importance in the development of the law was the extension of the suspicion entertained in cases of maintenance in consideration of the division of the spoils (campus partitio) to cases of outright transfer of the whole benefit of a cause of action not necessarily involving maintenance, an extension which had a profound effect on the law relating to the assignability of choses in action. Equity, it was said, refused to lend its assistance to certain assignments, not because they were in fact champertous but because
e they 'savoured of maintenance and champerty'.

It would not, I think, be helpful to seek to trace the historical development of the doctrines through a maze of contradictory cases and sometimes oversubtle distinctions which merely illustrate changing views of public policy. The line of recent authorities starts with the judgment of Danckwerts J in *Martell v Consett Iron Co Ltd* [1954] 3 All ER 339, [1955] Ch 363 (subsequently affirmed on appeal [1955] 1 All ER 481, [1955] Ch
f 363) which is the locus classicus of the modern law on the subject, and it is really unnecessary to go behind this save to the extent of illustrating the two streams of development which are visible, that is to say, first, the extension of the type of interest which the law regards as justifying the maintenance by one man of another's action and, second, the broadening of the category of interests which are treated by the law as capable of assignment, both matters of critical importance in the instant case in the light of the
g submissions of counsel for Trendtex.

I hope that I do not do injustice to these submissions if I summarise them as follows. First, it is said that, however far the law may have progressed, it has not yet gone so far as to permit the maintenance of an action by a person who has anything less than a proprietary interest in the subject matter of the proceedings unless he can bring himself within one or other of the established exceptions, such as close relationship, charity or
h membership of a group or association of persons having a common interest in the outcome. Second, it is submitted that, even if, contrary to counsel's first submission, a purely financial or commercial interest is sufficient to entitle a person to maintain proceedings (in the sense that, at the time when maintenance was an actionable wrong, such interest would have afforded a defence to an action in tort), nothing short of a proprietary interest in the subject matter can justify an agreement which involves the
j receipt by the maintainer of any part of the proceeds of the action. Third, it is said that, even were it permissible for a person having only a financial interest in the solvency of a party to the action to maintain the action and to take a charge on the future proceeds for what is due to him, it is never permissible for such a person to take an assignment, either outright or by way of charge, of the cause of action, and any agreement under which he purports to do so will be illegal and void.

As regards counsel's first submission, the judge expressed the view that, on the authorities as they stand, the interest which justifies a third party in maintaining an action must be either a proprietary interest, that is to say either an interest in property to which the cause of action is ancillary, or an interest in the cause of action itself in the sense that the assignor was under some pre-existing duty to enforce it for the benefit of the assignee. It is not, however, clear how far, in reaching that conclusion, the judge had had the benefit of the numerous authorities cited in this court. Even in the nineteenth century the courts seem to have been aware of and anxious to avoid the inconvenience of a doctrine which hampered normal and legitimate commercial transactions, and, although originally the tendency was to avoid the inconvenience by attaching the cause of action to some often quite illusory proprietary interest, the tendency of the later cases was towards a franker recognition of commercial realities. In *Williams v Protheroe* (1829) 5 Bing 309, 130 ER 1080 it was held that there was no objection, on the sale of certain customary hereditaments, to an assignment of the benefit of a pending action between the vendor and one of the tenants of the estate for arrears of rent due and dilapidations accrued prior to the date of the sale. In 1866 a similar principle was applied in quite different circumstances in *Dickinson v Burrell* (1866) LR 1 Eq 337. Here the plaintiffs were the trustees of a voluntary settlement executed in 1864, the only property in which was in fact the settlor's claim in equity to have set aside two conveyances of his share in a certain estate. The deed recited those conveyances and that the settlor disputed their validity but proceeded to convey the settlor's share of the estate to the plaintiffs 'upon trust to recover the same'. In fact, therefore, the 'property' in the settlement existed only if and so far as the claim to set aside the earlier conveyance could be pursued and succeeded. Nevertheless Lord Romilly MR held that the deed was not champertous saying (at 342):

> 'The distinction is this: if *James Dickinson* had sold or conveyed the right to sue to set aside the indenture ... without conveying the property, or his interest in the property, which is the subject of that indenture, that would not have enabled the grantee, *A.B.*, to maintain this bill; but if *A.B.* had bought the whole of the interest of *James Dickinson* in the property, then it would. The right of suit is a right incidental to the property conveyed ...'

Since the property could not be obtained without proceeding with the suit and had, therefore, no practical existence unless the suit succeeded, this seems to me, I am bound to say, to be a distinction without a difference, and the case is an illustration of the somewhat shadowy nature of the interest which, even in those days, the court would entertain as justifying the maintenance of an action.

In *Plating Co v Farquharson* (1881) 17 Ch D 49 the common interest which manufacturers in a particular industry had in resisting an action by a patentee against one of them was recognised as a sufficient interest to justify the maintenance of his defence, and this was carried one stage further by the Court of Appeal in *British Cash and Parcel Conveyors Ltd v Lamson Store Service Co Ltd* [1908] 1 KB 1006. This is an important case in the present context and it is surprising that, apart from a brief reference in *Neville v London Express Newspapers Ltd* [1919] AC 368, [1918–19] All ER Rep 61, it does not seem to have been referred to in any of the subsequent decisions in this branch of the law prior to *Martell v Consett Iron Co Ltd* [1955] 1 All ER 481, [1955] Ch 363. It was an action for the tort of maintenance in which the plaintiffs' complaint was that the defendants, who were rival manufacturers, had installed their equipment in premises of certain customers of the plaintiffs indemnifying those customers against any claims which the plaintiffs might make against them for breach of contract. Pursuant to those indemnities the defendants had in fact maintained the defences of certain actions by the plaintiffs. The Court of Appeal unanimously reversed the trial judge and held that the defendants were not liable for maintenance since they were acting in the legitimate defence of their own commercial interests.

Cozens-Hardy MR was content to say (at 1012):

> '... the defendants had a business interest, a commercial interest, which fully justified the indemnities or guarantees which they gave. And on this short ground I think the appeal must be allowed ...'

Fletcher Moulton LJ in his judgment observed that the old common law of maintenance was, even then, to a large extent obsolete. He said (at 1013–1014):

> 'Speaking for myself, I doubt whether any of the attempts at giving definitions of what constitutes maintenance in the present day are either successful or useful. They suffer from the vice of being based upon definitions of ancient date which were framed to express the law at a time when it was radically different from what it is at the present day, and these old definitions are sought to be made serviceable by strings of exceptions which are neither based on any logical principle nor in their nature afford any warrant that they are exhaustive. These exceptions only indicate such cases as have suggested themselves to the mind of the Court, and it is impossible to be certain that there are not many other exceptions which have equal validity ...'

and he referred to *Holden v Thompson* [1907] 2 KB 489 as an example, a case in which community of religion was accepted as a justification for assisting a co-religionist in a dispute relating to religious matters. That maintenance as a civil wrong still existed he did not doubt, but it was directed at what he described (at 1014) as—

> 'wanton and officious meddling with disputes of others in which the defendant has no interest whatever, and where the assistance he renders to the one or the other party is without justification or excuse.'

The 'legitimate defence of their own business interests' was, he held (at 1016), a sufficient ground for the indemnity which gave rise to the action.

Buckley LJ's judgment was to the same effect. He said (at 1020–1021):

> 'The cases ... divide themselves into two classes—the one where the person accused of maintenance has a common interest with the party to the litigation (an instance of which is *Plating Co.* v. *Farquharson* ((1881) 17 Ch D 49)), and the other where the party charged with maintenance has no such interest, in which case he is guilty of maintenance unless his case falls within certain exceptions which have from early times been specifically allowed. The respondents pressed us with an argument which I think was fallacious, that the party accused of maintenance is guilty of an offence unless he falls within some one of these exceptions, relying for that purpose upon the judgment of Lord Esher in *Alabaster* v. *Harness* ([1895] 1 QB 339, [1891–4] All ER Rep 817). The point in *Alabaster* v. *Harness* was that the action as to which the question arose was an action for libel, and Lord Esher commenced his judgment by pointing out that that was a personal action which in point of law concerns only the person who brings it. In other words it was one of the class of cases in which there was no common interest and in which maintenance was established if the case did not fall within one of the specific exceptions. That does not in any way affect the proposition, which I think is true, that it is not maintenance to uphold a party in litigation in whose result the party accused of maintenance has a real and bona fide interest.'

I have already referred to the classic judgment of Danckwerts J in *Martell v Consett Iron Co Ltd* [1954] 3 All ER 339, [1955] 1 Ch 363. Before coming to his conclusion in that case it is worth noting, on the way, the citation (which he adopted) from the speech of Lord Shaw in *Neville v London Express Newspapers Ltd* [1919] AC 368 at 414, [1918–19] All ER Rep 61 at 84, where he said:

> 'What remains of the doctrine deserves, in these circumstances, a scrupulous examination; and I am of opinion that the test of maintenance is the test of the quality of the act itself as it bears upon the attainment of justice in the particular

> case, and that the test either of tort or of offence is primarily whether it contains that
> quality which is essential both by the statute and the common law of England.' a

Danckwerts J stated what I take to be the correct principle when he said ([1954] 3 All
ER 339 at 350, [1955] Ch 363 at 387):

> 'Support of legal proceedings, based on a bona fide community of *pecuniary*
> interest or religion or principles or problems, is quite different and, in my view, the
> law would be wrong and oppressive if such support were to be treated as a crime or b
> a civil wrong. But I do not believe that the law is in that condition.' (My emphasis.)

Danckwerts J's judgment was affirmed by the Court of Appeal, and, although his
judgment is itself treated as the classical exposition of the law on the subject, it is worth
referring in the context of the submissions in the instant case to the following passage
from the judgment of Jenkins LJ ([1955] 1 All ER 481 at 498–499, [1955] Ch 363 at 414–
415). He pointed out that the cases which had been cited by counsel for the appellants, c
indicating that the interest required to rebut an allegation of maintenance must be one
of a proprietary nature, had all been cases where the actions concerned had been of an
essentially personal nature, and that the observations as to the common interest required
had to be considered in that context. He continued ([1955] 1 All ER 481 at 498–499,
[1955] Ch 363 at 415–416):

d

> 'Be that as it may . . . It seems to me that *British Cash & Parcel Conveyors, Ltd.* v.
> *Lamson Store Service Co., Ltd.* ([1908] 1 KB 1006) at all events shows that it is not
> illegal maintenance for a person to support the defence of an action in respect of a
> claim against which he has, as part of a legitimate business transaction, agreed to
> indemnify the defendant, and I cannot reconcile this with a strict application of the
> principle that maintenance can only be justified on the ground of common interest e
> where the maintainer has some interest recognised by the law in the subject-matter
> of, or some issue in, the action. In such a case, the maintainer no doubt has a
> financial interest in the result of the action, but only because he has chosen to give
> the indemnity. The mere fact that he has given the indemnity surely cannot suffice
> to give him a common interest within the meaning of the principle. Otherwise,
> every maintainer who effected the maintenance of an action by giving an indemnity f
> against damages and costs to the defendant, or against costs to the plaintiff, could
> plead by way of justification the common interest thus acquired, which is clearly
> not so. In my view, therefore, the true justification in cases such as *British Cash &*
> *Parcel Conveyors, Ltd.* v. *Lamson Store Service Co., Ltd*, must be that the maintainer,
> having given the indemnity in the course of a legitimate and genuine business
> transaction, has a legitimate and genuine business interest in the result of the action g
> which suffices to justify him in maintaining the defendant (as in *British Cash &*
> *Parcel Conveyors, Ltd.* v. *Lamson Store Service Co., Ltd* itself) or, as it might equally well
> be, the plaintiff. This leads me to conclude that a person who has a legitimate and
> genuine business interest in the result of an action must be taken for the purposes
> of the rule against maintenance to have an interest recognised by the law in the
> subject-matter of the action.' h

Finally there is *Hill v Archbold* [1967] 3 All ER 110, [1968] 1 QB 686, decided in 1967,
which again stresses the need to look at the doctrine in the light of modern conditions
and the altered considerations of public policy which those conditions require. As Lord
Denning MR said ([1967] 3 All ER 110 at 112, [1968] 1 QB 686 at 694):

> 'A person is still guilty of maintenance if he supports litigation in which he has j
> no legitimate concern without just cause or excuse. But the bounds of "legitimate
> concern" have been widened: and "just cause or excuse" has been readily found.'

Now it is not necessary for present purposes to seek any exhaustive definition of what
now constitutes a 'just cause or excuse', although for my part I would be disposed to hold

that such just cause at least exists wherever the maintainer has a genuine pre-existing
a financial interest in maintaining the solvency of the person whose action he maintains. In *Guy v Churchill* (1888) 40 Ch D 481, Chitty J treated it as beyond question that creditors under a bankruptcy or in a liquidation had a sufficient interest to enable them to maintain an action or defence by the trustee or liquidator. Granted that this is explicable on the ground that a bankruptcy or liquidation produces in the creditors a proprietary interest in the assets of the estate, it is difficult to see why, commercially, a creditor does
b not have at least as great an interest in preserving the solvency of his debtor and preventing him from becoming bankrupt. It is not, however, necessary, in my judgment, to go so far because it seems to me that, however defined, a sufficient interest existed in the instant case where, from the inception, Crédit Suisse had been intimately concerned with the transactions in respect of which CBN's letter of credit was issued and where, as is perfectly plain, they had relied and been led to rely on that letter of credit in
c making their own considerable outlay on behalf of Trendtex. I entertain no doubt whatever that this gave them a sufficient interest in maintaining Trendtex's action, and it follows that I would reject the first submission of counsel for Trendtex.

Turning then to the second submission of counsel for Trendtex, I am unable to follow why, once it is established that there is a sufficient interest in a third party to justify his supporting another's action, that interest should not equally justify his participating in
d the proceeds of the action, for instance, by taking a charge on such proceeds for what is due to him and for expenses incurred in supporting the litigation. It is perfectly true that in *Re Trepca Mines Ltd* [1962] 3 All ER 351 at 355, [1963] Ch 199 at 219 Lord Denning MR observed that champerty was a species of maintenance for which the common law rarely admits of any just cause or excuse, but that was in the context of an agreement under which the third party who supported the litigation had no conceivable
e interest in it beyond that which he had acquired by purchasing a share in it. All the authorities concur in pronouncing that champerty is merely a species of maintenance, and it is clear from *Glegg v Bromley* [1912] 3 KB 474 that the mere agreement to participate in the proceeds of an action without maintaining it does not constitute champerty. If, therefore, the supporting of the action is itself justified by a sufficient interest in the person lending support, so that he does not (or did not prior to 1967)
f commit the offence of maintenance, the fact that he participates in the proceeds cannot logically render him guilty of an offence which, by definition, depends on his also being guilty of maintenance.

In any event, the law, as it seems to me, must again take account of the changes in public policy which have occurred during the past half-century, for the whole of our system of legal aid is founded on the principle that the Law Society's legal aid fund has
g a first charge on any property preserved or recovered as a result of the litigation which it has been called on to support. In my judgment, the quality of interest required to justify an agreement which is otherwise champertous is no different from that required to justify an agreement which is otherwise void for maintenance. This seems, if authority be needed for the proposition, to have been the view of Scrutton LJ in *Ellis v Torrington* [1920] 1 KB 399 at 412:

h

> 'Champerty is only a particular form of maintenance, namely, where the person who maintains takes as a reward a share in the property recovered. When the person who assists is himself interested in the subject matter of the suit before its commencement there is neither champerty nor maintenance.'

Furthermore, *Guy v Churchill* (1888) 40 Ch D 481 is an authority directly contrary to
j the proposition of counsel for Trendtex.

But, if it is permissible for a person who has a legitimate interest in the proceedings to maintain them and to take a charge on the proceeds to the extent of his interest, is it also permissible for him to take an assignment of the cause of action itself, whether by way of charge or outright? Counsel for Trendtex submits that it is not, and cites *Glegg v Bromley* [1912] 3 KB 474 for the proposition that such an assignment is illegal and void.

I do not, for my part, think that *Glegg v Bromley* is authority for any such proposition, and the very fact that it has been cited as such is indicative of the confusion of thought which *a* surrounds the subject. What *Glegg v Bromley* decided was that whilst a cause of action in *tort* was incapable of assignment (as it always has been in English law) there was no legal objection to the granting, without any question of the grantee maintaining the action, of a charge on the future proceeds even of an action in tort. It did not decide, and did not purport to decide, that causes of action other than strictly personal claims in tort were not assignable, much less that a purported assignment was void on the ground of illegality. *b* One cannot read the cases without a growing sense of bewilderment at the apparent contradictions, and I cannot help feeling that there is some confusion at the base of the submission of counsel for Trendtex. To say, as he was constrained to say, that even though an action might legitimately be supported and even though a charge might be taken in the proceeds yet nevertheless the law will strike down as illegal an assignment of the cause of action itself seems to me to confuse the form with the substance. As *c* Collins MR observed in *Fitzroy v Cave* [1905] 2 KB 364 at 369: 'So long as the real transaction is the same, the form in which it is carried out ought not to alter the legal effect.'

The argument of counsel for Trendtex is based essentially on two propositions: (1) the law does not permit the assignment of a right to litigate, and (2) any agreement purporting to include or constitute such an assignment is not only ineffective as an *d* assignment but is illegal and void ab initio as being champertous. Implicit in the first of these propositions is the further proposition that once it has become clear that a particular chose can be recovered only by a resort to litigation it ceases to be assignable. None of these propositions is universally true. No doubt the ancient notions of maintenance and champerty lie at the root of the non-assignability of certain causes of action, but the immediate reason why an assignment of what was described as a 'bare' right of action was *e* ineffective was that equity refused to lend its aid to enforcing the assignment. Such an assignment was therefore inoperative, and the reason why it was inoperative was that it 'savoured of or was likely to lead to maintenance' (see the judgment of Parker J in *Glegg v Bromley* [1912] 3 KB 474 at 490). But it does not follow from the fact that a court of equity would not, on this ground, lend its assistance to an assignment that any transaction of which the assignment formed part was itself illegal and void. Thus in *Glegg v Bromley* *f* itself Fletcher Moulton LJ observed (at 488):

> 'We are all agreed that you cannot assign a cause of action for a personal wrong, and I am not sure that some of the words here might not bear a meaning which would cover such an assignment. But if this be so the only effect would be that those particular words would be inoperative. Their presence would not invalidate the whole deed, because there is nothing in the way of maintenance or champerty *g* in this assignment.'

The reluctance of equity to lend assistance to the assignment of a right which was essentially no more than a right to carry on litigation survived the general statutory assignability of choses in action in s 25 of the Supreme Court of Judicature Act 1873, which was construed as excluding from the ambit of the expression 'chose in action' *h* rights the assignment of which would not, prior to the Act, have been enforced in equity (see *Torkington v Magee* [1902] 2 KB 427 at 430 per Channell J); but it is impossible to read the cases without discerning a measure of inconsistency and illogicality. On one point all the authorities agree, namely that a personal cause of action in tort never was and still is not generally assignable, although even here exception has, commercially, had to be made in the case of insurance contracts, where the insurer is subrogated to the rights of *j* the insured (see *Compagnia Colombiana de Seguros v Pacific Steam Navigation Co* [1964] 1 All ER 216 at 231, [1965] 1 QB 101 at 110 per Roskill J). But where, as here, what is in issue is the assignability of the right to recover damages for breach of contract the position is far less clear. What is it (if anything) that distinguishes the assignment of the benefit of a subsisting contract from the assignment of a right to enforce a contract the performance of which has been withheld? What logical dividing line is there between the innocent assignee of a contract and the champertous assignee of the right to sue for damages for its breach? Why is it to be assumed that the former will behave with total rectitude whilst the latter may suppress evidence, suborn witnesses and advance inflated and unsustainable claims? Authority gives no certain answer. Originally, claims for damages for breach of contract appear to have been treated as no different, as regards assignability, from personal claims for damages in tort. An exception was, however, made at an early stage in the case of an assignment by a trustee in bankruptcy. *Seer v Lawson* (1880) 15 Ch D 426 was a case of an assignment after action commenced, by a trustee in bankruptcy. The argument, which prevailed both before Bacon V-C and the Court of Appeal, was that the right of action, a claim to set aside a conveyance on the ground that it was, in fact, a mortgage, was 'property' of the bankrupt which it was the trustee's duty to realise under the Bankruptcy Act 1869, and the dichotomy between 'personal' claims and 'property' claims appears most clearly in the argument. Looked at in terms of the danger of maintenance and champerty it is difficult to see why, logically, a purchaser from the trustee in bankruptcy of the original claimant should be less prone to misconduct than a purchaser from the claimant himself before the bankruptcy; and it is not without interest that both Jessel MR and James LJ, although content to assume that the right of action would not have been assignable but for the bankruptcy, were by no means convinced that this was so.

Passages, however, in the judgments of Lord Esher MR and Rigby LJ in *May v Lane* (1894) 64 LJQB 236 show nevertheless that the view remained that a right, for instance, to recover damages for breach of contract (which might have been thought to be truly, on analysis, a right of property) was equated with a truly personal right such as a right to sue for damages for defamation or for assault. Lord Esher MR said (at 237): 'But even assuming he could have been sued, an action could only have been brought to recover damages for breach of contract, and such a right of action is not assignable.' It is difficult, if I may say so respectfully, to see why not. It is a right not in essence personal, except in a case of a purely personal contract; it is a right having a value of its own which depends not at all even on the continued existence of the owner of the right. It passes to his personal representatives. It passes to his trustee in bankruptcy and can be sold by him. On what basis, one may ask, does it fall to be equated with a personal right to sue for personal injury? The subsequent cases appear to me to demonstrate a movement away from this concept, a movement sometimes achieved by the perhaps somewhat artificial device of attaching the right of action, as had been done over half a century earlier in *Dickinson v Burrell* (1866) LR 1 Eq 337, to a more or less notional property right. The same distinction between the assignment of the benefit of a contract prior to breach and the assignment of the right to sue on a breach which predated the assignment was drawn by Channell J in *Torkington v Magee* [1902] 2 KB 427. Shortly afterwards, however, in *Dawson v Great Britain and City Railway Co* [1905] 1 KB 260, [1904–7] All ER Rep 913 the Court of Appeal upheld an assignment of a right to claim compensation for injury under s 68 of the Lands Clauses Consolidation Act 1845 on the ground that, contrary to counsel's argument, it was not a claim for 'damages for a wrongful act' (and therefore not assignable) but was the price payable for the exercise of statutory powers and thus itself a property right. It is, I think, important to note that, although the court attached great weight to the circumstances that the assignment was incidental and subsidiary to a conveyance of the land, they were prepared to hold that it was good even if regarded apart from that conveyance (see [1905] 1 KB 260 at 271, [1904–7] All ER Rep 913 at 917). Again, in *Ogdens Ltd v Weinberg* (1906) 95 LT 567 the House of Lords upheld an assignment by a trustee in bankruptcy as part of the assets of the bankrupt's business of a claim for damages for a breach of contract which had occurred prior to the bankruptcy. Lord Loreburn LC said that the contract 'although unperformed, was nevertheless not annulled, so as to prevent any person entitled to sue on it from bringing his action for damages for breach of it'. In *Compania Colombiana de Seguros v Pacific Steam Navigation Co* [1964] 1 All ER 216 at 230, [1965] 1 QB 101 at 119, Roskill J distinguished this case from the assignment of a 'bare' cause of action on the ground that the House of Lords were there dealing with 'an executory contract unperformed by breach, the a contractual rights whereunder survived sufficiently to be susceptible to assignment'. This, as it seems to me, is another way of saying that the right to enforce the contract, in the only way which the law provided, that is, by an action for damages for breach, was itself a property right and not a 'bare' right.

That interpretation seems to me to be reinforced by the decision of the Court of Appeal in *Fitzroy v Cave* [1905] 2 KB 364, where the plaintiff had taken from the b defendant's trade creditors an absolute assignment of the amounts due to them, undertaking to pay to the creditors whatever might be realised after payment of the necessary costs of recovery. The plaintiff frankly avowed that he had no interest in the matter beyond that of making the defendant bankrupt and so removing him as a director of a company in which he was interested. On the face of it, this seems about as plain a case of maintenance as there could well be. It is interesting to note the argument c of the plaintiff's counsel which is reported thus (at 366):

> 'There are authorities no doubt which shew that an assignment of a mere right of action, such as a right of action for damages for defamation, is invalid as amounting to maintenance ... But an assignment of anything in the nature of property is valid.'

d

Collins MR observed that, unless actions to recover debts were incapable of being the subject of maintenance, this was a clear case of the assignment of a bare right of litigation. The court held, however, that the effect of s 25(6) of the Supreme Court of Judicature Act 1873 was to make any debt assignable and that to use the words of Cozens-Hardy LJ (at 373): 'Henceforth in all Courts a debt must be regarded as a piece of property e capable of legal assignment in the same sense as a bale of goods.' But what, it may be asked, is it that segregates a 'debt' from any other contractual right, save that the sum due is liquidated? What in fact was assigned in *Fitzroy v Cave* was the right to sue for the price of goods sold and delivered for which the defendant had failed to pay, that is to say the right to enforce a contract of sale which had already been broken at the time of the assignment. f

Again, in *Defries v Milne* [1913] 1 Ch 98 the Court of Appeal held that an assignment of a claim for damages for waste was a claim in tort and was not assignable, but both Farwell and Hamilton LJJ seem to have considered that the assignment of the right to sue on the contract (the pre-existing breach of which was recited in the asisignment) was valid.

In this state of the authorities, McCardie J in *County Hotel and Wine Co Ltd v London and* g *North Western Railway Co* [1918] 2 KB 251 was prepared to hold that in a case where a contract creates a property right capable of assignment the mere fact that the other contracting party has repudiated his obligation cannot affect assignability. Having referred to the recognition of the assignability of debts by s 25(6) of the Supreme Court of Judicature Act 1873, he observed (at 258–260):

h

> 'Such being the state of things, it would seem strange indeed to hold that a debt could not be assigned after the debtor had repudiated the debt by refusing to pay. Can a debtor destroy the assignability of a debt by repudiating his obligation of payment? ... I can well understand that causes of action strictly founded on tort, for example, libel or assault, should not on grounds of public policy be assignable. So, too, there are contractual causes, breach of promise of marriage, which may not, for j obvious reasons, be assignable. But much of the law of champerty is coloured by the mediæval notion that choses in action were not assignable because they amounted to sales of a right to litigate ... I can see no reason why damages for breach of contract should not in some cases be capable of assignment without infringement of the public interests. Take, for example, a case where the contract

> admittedly fixes the damages for breach at a liquidated sum and provides that it may be sued for as a debt. What reason of public policy should prevent the assignment of such sum if public policy permits the assignment of a disputed debt?'

McCardie J concluded (at 261) by holding in terms that—

> 'a defendant cannot destroy the assignability of a right of property, whether it be a contract or other form of property, by committing a breach of contract by repudiation prior to the assignment.'

His decision was affirmed by the Court of Appeal, but on quite different grounds, and I cannot trace that it has been referred to in any of the subsequent cases bearing on assignment of choses in action. If correct, however, McCardie J's view was in line with what had been said by the House of Lords in *Ogdens Ltd v Weinberg* (1906) 95 LT 567, and it suggests that the true dichotomy is not between contractual rights and 'bare' rights to litigate, but between strictly personal claims, such as claims in tort or under personal and non-assignable contracts, and claims to enforce what may properly be described as proprietary rights.

This, I am bound to say, appears to me to be a much more logical and practical distinction, and it has the additional merit in the year 1980 of absolving the court from striking down, on the basis of archaic doctrine which, if not entirely obsolete, is at least obsolescent, transactions which are perfectly familiar and accepted by lawyers in continental countries where much of the modern business of this nation is conducted. For my part, I would be prepared to hold that where a cause of action arises out of a right which was itself assignable the cause of action equally remains assignable or, if one must use the language of the older cases, that it is not a 'bare' right to litigate but itself a right of property. So to hold does not, I think, violate current notions of public policy. It does not, for instance, follow that because a particular right may be generally assignable there may not still be circumstances in which on grounds of public policy the law would refuse to enforce an assignment. Such a case as *Grell v Levy* (1864) 16 CBNS 73, 143 ER 1052, for instance, which turned to some extent on the special position of an English solicitor, would equally, I think, be decided in the same way today, not on the ground that the cause of action to which it related is not assignable (it plainly would be in the light of *Fitzroy v Cave* [1905] 2 KB 364) but because an English court will not permit one of its own officers to put himself in a position in which his interest and duty may conflict. It may be questioned whether such a dichotomy is not irreconcilable with the decision of this court in *Re Trepca Mines Ltd* [1962] 3 All ER 351, [1963] Ch 199. I do not think that it is. That case was concerned with the effect of a solicitor's participation in an agreement held to be champertous, but the argument as to champerty was addressed to the question of whether a proof in a liquidation could be the subject matter of a champertous agreement. No argument was addressed to, nor did the court consider, the nature or assignability of the claim on which the proof in the liquidation was based, which, in any event, was of a most shadowy nature and seems, in so far as it could be pursued at all, to have been a claim for damages for tort and not for breach of contract (see the judgment of Harman LJ in [1960] 1 WLR 1273 at 1282).

It is not, however, necessary to go to this extent for the purposes of the present case. So far as the agreement of the 4th January falls to be treated as an assignment to Crédit Suisse, the short answer to the contention of counsel for Trendtex is, in my judgment, this: that, just as in *Guy v Churchill* (1888) 40 Ch D 481 Chitty J found it inconceivable that an interest which would have supported an out and out assignment would not also support an agreement for the division of the proceeds, so it is to me equally inconceivable that an interest which would justify Crédit Suisse in maintaining the suit and in taking a charge on the proceeds does not equally justify the assignment to them of the whole cause of action.

But there is an alternative submission which must be noted, for it is said that,

whatever interest Crédit Suisse themselves might have had, the agreement of 4th January 1978 was one which, if it did not itself effect an assignment, was at least made in a
contemplation of, and indeed for the express purpose of, procuring an assignment in the future of Trendtex's cause of action against CBN to a third party who might not have and in the event (at least so it may be assumed) did not have, on any analysis, any interest in the matter at all beyond that which was generated by paying the price of the assignment. Thus it is said the agreement was one which, however it was expressed, was in fact for a purpose illegal under English law and was therefore one which an English b
court will not enforce. There seem to me to be a number of answers to this. In the first place, if I am right in the views which I have expressed regarding assignability, the submission does not start. But second, and assuming that I am wrong, it is necessary to look at the agreement to see what in fact it does. As counsel for Crédit Suisse has pointed out in his analysis, it does not in fact assign anything. It starts from the postulate that Trendtex's cause of action had already been effectively assigned in November 1976 by c
way of security and provides that Trendtex will not object to an assignment by Crédit Suisse to a third party. It contains a number of other provisions which are designed to clear accounts between Trendtex and Crédit Suisse and to enable Trendtex to deal with its other creditors. I agree with Robert Goff J that, assuming that the contemplated transaction with the third party was in fact one to which English law does not give effect and which therefore would be treated equally as ineffective by the Swiss court, it does not d
follow that the agreement as a whole is void by Swiss law. There was nothing ex facie necessarily illegal in the agreement. Whether any assignment under it fell foul of the English rules with regard to maintenance or champerty would depend on the identity and interest of the unidentified third party, and in my judgment the judge was right in applying to the exclusive jurisdiction clause the reasoning of Diplock LJ in *Mackender v Feldia AG* [1966] 3 All ER 847, [1967] 2 QB 590 and in holding that the question whether e
the agreement gave rise to enforceable rights and duties was a dispute regarding the conclusion, interpretation or fulfilment of the agreement, was within the clause, and fell to be determined according to the proper law of the agreement. Once that was determined, it was a matter for the judge's discretion whether or not to give effect to the exclusive jurisdiction clause by granting the stay sought by Crédit Suisse, and I can see no ground on which it could be said that the judge erred in principle in exercising his f
discretion. Much has been made of the superiority of the English process of discovery, and particular emphasis has been given to the desirability of this by obliquely tendentious references to the conduct and state of knowledge of Maître Patry who, be it noted, has not been made a party to the action and against whom fraud has not been alleged. Counsel for Trendtex has told us that this was considered but that it was thought improper on the evidence to plead fraud. I wish to say no more about that than to repeat what was once g
said by Scrutton LJ (quoted by Lord Denning MR in *Re Trepca Mines Ltd* [1962] 3 All ER 351 at 356, [1963] Ch 199 at 221): 'I object to dealing with charges of fraud or dishonesty unless they are distinctly alleged and as distinctly proved.' The judge dealt fully with the question of discovery in his judgment and I would not differ from his reasoning or from his conclusion.

In relation to that part of the claim which lies outside the agreement of 4th January h
1978, Robert Goff J analysed and applied the principles laid down in the House of Lords in *MacShannon v Rockware Glass Ltd* [1978] 1 All ER 625, [1978] AC 795. Criticism has been directed at this part of the judgment because, it is said, the judge took into account an impermissible factor, namely that the parties had already agreed, in the agreement of 4th January, on the Swiss court as an appropriate forum. This, of course, was not a factor present in the *MacShannon* case, but speaking for myself I would not consider it j
inappropriate, when weighing in the balance what is an appropriate forum for the hearing of a given dispute, to take account of the fact that two of the parties to that dispute have already, in relation to another matter which is not merely closely allied with it but is inextricably involved with it, themselves agreed on a suitable forum.

None of the arguments so strenuously advanced on behalf of Trendtex have persuaded me that this court ought to interfere with the exercise of the judge's discretion and accordingly I too would dismiss the appeal.

Appeal dismissed. Leave to appeal to the House of Lords granted on terms that the plaintiffs give proper security for costs.

Solicitors: *Herbert Oppenheimer, Nathan & Vandyk* (for the plaintiffs); *Theodore Goddard & Co* (for the defendants).

Sumra Green Barrister.

Stafford Winfield Cook & Partners Ltd v Winfield

CHANCERY DIVISION
SIR ROBERT MEGARRY V-C
10th, 21st, 31st MARCH 1980

Practice – Transfer of proceedings between divisions of High Court – Jury trial available as of right in action begun in Queen's Bench Division where fraud in issue – Action begun in Chancery Division including allegation of fraud – Plaintiff's claim not depending on establishing fraud against defendant – Whether right to have action transferred to Queen's Bench Division to obtain jury trial – Whether fraud 'in issue' – Whether court should exercise discretion to transfer action – Administration of Justice (*Miscellaneous Provisions*) *Act 1933, s 6*(*1*) *– RSC Ord 4, r 3*(*1*).

The defendant's husband was a director of the plaintiff company from 1962 until 1976. She herself was also a director of the company from February 1975 until 1976. Between 1971 and December 1975 the company made payments to the defendant, totalling over £10,000, against invoices rendered by her to the company for consultancy fees. Subsequently the company suspected that the invoices had been shams designed to conceal payments improperly procured by the husband out of the company's assets in order to maintain the defendant (from whom he was separated), so it commenced an action by writ in the Chancery Division seeking, inter alia, (i) a declaration that the defendant and her husband had wrongfully misapplied the company's money, (ii) an order requiring the defendant to pay to the company a sum representing the money which she had received as constructive trustee from the company, and (iii) damages, inter alia, for fraud. In its statement of claim the company made no mention of fraud but alleged that the defendant had not performed, and had never intended to perform, any services in respect of the invoices, that the payments were made for no consideration and were ultra vires the company and were effected by the defendant and her husband in breach of their fiduciary duties to the company, and that they had conspired together to have the money paid to her in breach of their duties to the company and had converted the sums to her use. The defendant applied by summons for the action to be transferred to the Queen's Bench Division on the ground that she was entitled under s 6(1)(*a*)[a] of the

[a] Section 6(1), so far as material, provides: 'Subject as hereinafter provided, if, on the application of any party to an action to be tried in the King's Bench Division of the High Court made not later than such time before the trial as may be limited by rules of court, the Court or a judge is satisfied that—(*a*) a charge of fraud against that party . . . is in issue, the action shall be ordered to be tried with a jury unless the Court or judge is of opinion that the trial thereof requires any prolonged examination of documents or accounts or any scientific or local investigation which cannot conveniently be made with a jury; but, save as aforesaid, any action to be tried in that Division may, in the discretion of the Court or a judge, be ordered to be tried either with or without a jury . . .'

Administration of Justice (Miscellaneous Provisions) Act 1933 to have the action tried by jury in that division because 'a charge of fraud' was 'in issue' against her. a

Held – (1) Although a litigant who was charged with fraud was given the right by s 6 of the 1933 Act to demand trial by jury if the action was brought in the Queen's Bench Division, he was given no such right if the action was brought in the Chancery Division and could not, as of right, require the action to be transferred from the Chancery Division to the Queen's Bench Division merely on the ground that he wanted a trial by b jury. The court could, however, in the exercise of its discretion under RSC Ord 4, r 3(1)[b], order such an action to be transferred to the Queen's Bench Division if it thought that it was appropriate to do so (ie if it considered that the case was one which was suitable for trial by jury and was of such a nature that the interests of justice required the transfer to be made) (see p 765 *f* to p 766 *b*, post); *Ruston v Tobin* (1879) 10 Ch D 558 and *International Producers Ltd v Forbes* [1922] WN 76 considered. c

(2) In s 6 of the 1933 Act the word 'fraud' was not used in a general sense of dishonesty. It meant an intentional misrepresentation (or in some cases concealment) of fact made by one party with the intention of inducing another party to act on it, and thereby inducing the other party to act on it to his detriment. Furthermore, although a charge of 'fraud' within s 6 might be made without specifically using the word 'fraud', for a case to come within s 6(1) fraud had to be in issue between the parties in the sense d of being a question which had to be decided in order to determine the rights of the parties (see p 766 *b* to *e*, post); *Davy v Garrett* (1878) 7 Ch D 473, *Everett v Islington Guardians* [1923] 1 KB 44 and *Barclays Bank Ltd v Cole* [1966] 3 All ER 948 applied.

(3) The defendant's summons would be dismissed because (a) the case was not one in which a charge of fraud against her was in issue within s 6, since the company was not required to prove fraud in respect of any of the claims which it had made against her in e its statement of claim, and (b) in any event, even if a charge of fraud against her was in issue, she had not established that the case was an appropriate one for the court to exercise its discretionary power under RSC Ord 4, r 3(1), to order the action to be transferred to the Queen's Bench Division (see p 766 *g* to *j* and p 767 *h* to p 768 *d*, post); *Jenkins v Bushby* [1891] 1 Ch 484 and *Williams v Beesley* [1973] 3 All ER 144 applied.

f

Notes

For the right to trial by jury, see 30 Halsbury's Laws (3rd Edn) 376, para 700, and for cases on the subject, see 51 Digest (Repl) 648–651, *2564–2582*.

For the Administration of Justice (Miscellaneous Provisions) Act 1933, s 6, see 25 Halsbury's Statutes (3rd Edn) 749.

g

Cases referred to in judgment

Back v Hay (1877) 5 Ch D 235, 36 LT 295, 9 Digest (Reissue) 135, *750*.

Barclays Bank Ltd v Cole [1966] 3 All ER 948, [1967] 2 QB 738, [1967] 2 WLR 166, CA, 51 Digest (Repl) 650, *2577*.

Clarke v Cookson (1875) 2 Ch D 746, 45 LJ Ch 752.

Davy v Garrett (1878) 7 Ch D 473, 47 LJ Ch 218, 38 LT 77, CA, 50 Digest (Repl) 16, *115*. h

Derry v Peek (1889) 14 App Cas 337, [1886–90] All ER Rep 1, 58 LJ Ch 864, 61 LT 265, 54 JP 148, 1 Meg 292, HL, 9 Digest (Reissue) 123, *650*.

Duport Steels Ltd v Sirs [1980] 1 All ER 529, [1980] 1 WLR 142, HL.

Everett v Islington Guardians [1923] 1 KB 44, 92 LJKB 250, 128 LT 447, 87 JP 61, DC, 13 Digest (Reissue) 469, *3881*.

Hope v Great Western Railway Co [1937] 1 All ER 625, [1937] 2 KB 130, 106 LJKB 563, j 156 LT 331, CA, 51 Digest (Repl) 649, *2573*.

---

b Rule 3(1) provides: 'A cause or matter may, at any stage of the proceedings therein, be transferred from one Division to another by order of the Court made in the Division in which the cause or matter is proceeding.'

International Producers Ltd v Forbes [1922] WN 76, 66 Sol Jo 333, 51 Digest (Repl) 649,
a 2571.

Jenkins v Bushby [1891] 1 Ch 484, 60 LJ Ch 254, 64 LT 213, CA; *subsequent proceedings* (1893) Lords Journals 177, HL, 51 Digest (Repl) 651, 2591.

Pacaya Rubber and Produce Co Ltd, Re [1913] 1 Ch 218, 82 LJ Ch 134, 108 LT 21, 20 Mans 37, CA, 10 Digest (Reissue) 1114, 6885.

Reese River Silver Mining Co v Smith (1869) LR 4 HL 64, 39 LJ Ch 849, HL; *affg* sub nom
b *Re Reese River Silver Mining Co, Smith's Case* (1867) 2 Ch App 604, LJJ, 9 Digest (Reissue) 132, 726.

Ruston v Tobin (1879) 10 Ch D 558, 40 LT 111, CA, 51 Digest (Repl) 651, 2585.

Warner v Murdoch (1877) 4 Ch D 750, 46 LJ Ch 121, 35 LT 748, CA, 51 Digest (Repl) 653, 2603.

Williams v Beesley [1973] 3 All ER 144, [1973] 1 WLR 1295, HL, Digest (Cont Vol D)
c 1059, 2572a.

Summons

This was an application by the defendant, Wendy Madeleine Helen Styles Winfield, for an order (i) transferring to the Queen's Bench Division the action which had been brought against her in the Chancery Division by the plaintiff, Stafford Winfield Cook
d & Partners Ltd ('the company'), and (ii) directing that the trial of the action should be with a jury. The facts are set out in the judgment.

R G B McCombe for the company.
Christopher Allen for the defendant

e 31st March. **SIR ROBERT MEGARRY V-C** read the following judgment: This is a summons by the defendant to have the action transferred to the Queen's Bench Division, there to have a trial by jury. The action is brought by a company called Stafford Winfield Cook & Partners Ltd which went into liquidation in April 1976. I shall call it 'the company'. The defendant is a widow. Her late husband was a director of the company from 1962 until it went into liquidation, and the defendant, too, was a director
f from February 1975. The dispute is in respect of sums amounting to rather over £12,500 paid by the company to the defendant during the period from July 1971 to December 1975. The sums originally claimed were a little over £10,000, and the receipt of these has been admitted. The larger figure was subsequently inserted in the statement of claim by way of amendment, and I have not seen any amended defence. There is also an alternative claim for rather over £3,000 (which originally was for a little over £1,100)
g for mistaken overpayments; but nothing at this stage turns on this or on the precise figures.

What is in issue is the company's allegation that whereas the payments purported to have been made against invoices rendered to the company by the defendant for consultancy fees or services rendered by her to the company, in fact the defendant did not perform, and never intended to perform, any services in respect of the invoices. The
h payments were made for no consideration, says the company, were made ultra vires and in breach of the fiduciary duties of the defendant and her husband, and were made, and were intended by the defendant and her husband to be made, as a provision by him for her maintenance; they had admittedly ceased to live together in about March 1972. The defendant, says the company, knew or ought to have known that the money belonged to the company and was improperly paid from the company's assets, and that the
j husband paid it dishonestly in breach of his duties to the company. There is an allegation of conspiracy between the defendant and her husband, and of conversion by the defendant, and that the defendant is liable to account as a constructive trustee. The relief sought is a declaration that the defendant and her husband wrongfully misapplied the company's moneys, an order for the defendant to pay the company the larger sum as representing money received by her as a constructive trustee for the company, damages,

an alternative claim for an order to pay the smaller sum of a little over £3,000 as money had and received to the company's use, interest, and various consequential relief. From *a* first to last the word 'fraud' is not used, though in the writ there was a claim for 'damages for fraud'.

The defence is basically a denial of most of the allegations in the statement of claim, and an assertion that the invoices were rendered in respect of design consultancy work carried out by the defendant at the company's request from time to time. In essence, the central issue is whether or not the invoices were genuine invoices for work genuinely *b* done by the defendant for the company, or whether they are shams, designed to conceal payments improperly procured by the husband out of the company's assets in order to maintain the defendant. On that, two main questions have been admirably argued by counsel for the company and counsel for the defendant. The first is whether this case is a case in which 'a charge of fraud' against the defendant 'is in issue' within the meaning of the Administration of Justice (Miscellaneous Provisions) Act 1933, s 6(1), and the *c* second is whether, if it is, the discretion of the court under RSC Ord 4, r 3(1), to transfer the case to the Queen's Bench Division, where the defendant may claim trial by jury as of right, ought to be exercised. Counsel for the defendant accepted that if he did not succeed on the first point, his claim to a transfer must fail.

It was common ground that if there was to be a trial by jury, the action must be transferred to the Queen's Bench Division, since there is no machinery for jury trial in *d* the Chancery Division. Indeed, *Clarke v Cookson* (1876) 2 Ch D 746 at 748 shows that Jessel MR and all three Vice-Chancellors (Malins, Bacon and Hall V-CC) considered that the terms of the Supreme Court of Judicature Act 1873 precluded trial by jury in the Chancery Division; and in *Warner v Murdoch* (1877) 4 Ch D 750 this was approved by the Court of Appeal. On one view, the first point to decide is whether there is in fact a charge of fraud; but before I do that I think that it is desirable to consider what provision has *e* been made by statute for trial by jury where fraud is charged. This has changed considerably over the years, as counsel for the company demonstrated in his careful survey.

Under RSC Ord 36 set out in the Supreme Court of Judicature Act 1875, Sch 1, the mode of trial was to be specified in the notice of trial by the party giving the notice, with the right for the other party, if trial by jury had not been specified, then to give notice *f* requiring trial by jury; and the court had a discretion to direct trial without a jury in certain respects: see rr 2, 3, 4 and 26. Fraud was not specially mentioned, and no special rule was laid down for the Chancery Division.

This provision was varied by the Rules of the Supreme Court 1883. Order 36, r 2 allowed either party, by notice, to require a jury in cases of slander, libel, false imprisonment, malicious prosecution, seduction or breach of promise of marriage. This *g* rule, too, made no mention of fraud. Causes or matters assigned to the Chancery Division by the Supreme Court of Judicature Act 1873 (see s 34, and also s 35, and s 11 of the 1875 Act) were directed, by the new provisions of r 3, to be tried by a judge without a jury unless the court or a judge otherwise ordered; and r 4 repeated the previous discretion of the court to direct trial without a jury in certain respects. Rule 5 introduced a new power for the court or a judge to direct trial without a jury of any *h* cause, matter or issue requiring any prolonged examination of documents or accounts, or any scientific or local investigation, which could not conveniently be made with a jury. Rule 6 then, a little surprisingly, provided that in any other cause or matter any party could on application insist on trial by jury. That, of course, left untouched the Chancery Division (r 3: see *Jenkins v Bushby* [1891] 1 Ch 484), and the matters under r 5; but I say that it seems a little surprising because r 2 provided for the right to a jury in the *j* six specified cases of libel, slander and so on, and this hardly presaged the general right to trial by jury which r 6 gave. The only difference seems to be that under r 2 the litigant exercised his right to a jury by giving notice, and under r 6 he did it by making application. In the absence of any exercise of the right to a jury, or an order for jury trial, r 7 provided for a trial without a jury.

It seems to have been the Juries Act 1918 which introduced fraud for the first time into this subject; at any rate, no earlier provision has been cited to me. This was professedly an Act 'to limit the right to a jury in certain civil cases'; and s 1 provided that all trials 'in the High Court' should be by a judge alone. There were then certain provisos, one of which, proviso (*b*), enabled any party to claim trial by jury as of right if 'fraud is alleged', or there was a claim for libel, and so on. On this, counsel for the company commented that it would be a little strange if in limiting the right to a jury the Act had in fact extended it by enabling the litigant in the Chancery Division in a case in which fraud was alleged to claim a jury as of right, whereas previously the trial would have been by a judge alone unless it had been otherwise ordered. The Act, indeed, made no separate mention of the Chancery Division, but spoke generally of the High Court. Proviso (*c*) to s 1, however, empowered the court to direct trial by jury if a party applied for it, and the matter was 'more fit' to be tried with a jury.

This enactment came before Peterson J in *International Producers Ltd v Forbes* [1922] WN 76. The action had been commenced in the Chancery Division, and there were allegations of fraudulent misrepresentation and corrupt bargain. The defendant claimed the right to a jury under proviso (*b*), and also under the court's discretion under proviso (*c*) and generally. The case is somewhat shortly reported (I was told that the only other report was in the Solicitors' Journal (66 Sol Jo 333) and was equally brief), but it is plain that the judge did not accept the contention that proviso (*b*) applied to the Chancery Division. He rejected the idea that matters assigned to the Chancery Division such as dissolution of partnerships, setting aside deeds, and specific performance, in which allegations of fraud were common, would entitle the defendant to demand a jury and have the action which statute had assigned to the Chancery Division transferred to the King's Bench Division. The Act showed an intention to limit the right to a jury, and not to extend it to the Chancery Division where the right to a jury had never existed before. What proviso (*b*) contemplated was an application for a jury, and not an application for transfer to another division in which a jury could be obtained; it was restricted to cases where, apart from the Act, the court had power to direct trial by jury. Further, the judge saw no reason for exercising his power to transfer the case to the King's Bench Division, or for thinking that it would be tried more satisfactorily there; and so he refused the application.

At the time of that decision, the Administration of Justice Act 1920 had been enacted, but s 2 of it had not been brought into force. Section 2 dealt with trial by jury in civil cases. Subsection (1) gave the court power to direct trial without a jury 'in the High Court' if either party applied for it and the court was satisfied that the matter 'cannot as conveniently be tried with a jury as without a jury'. Proviso (*a*), however, prohibited trial without a jury if fraud was alleged, or there was a claim for libel and so on, unless both parties consented. These provisions were superseded by the Administration of Justice Act 1925, s 3. This provided that s 2 of the 1920 Act should cease to have effect, and that rules of court could prescribe which trials in the High Court were to be with a jury and which without. Until then, the rules of court which were in force immediately before the 1918 Act was passed were to have effect.

Fraud thus lost the position which the 1918 Act had conferred on it. This was, however, restored by the Administration of Justice (Miscellaneous Provisions) Act 1933, s 6. This is in force today, save that as a result of the Law Reform (Miscellaneous Provisions) Act 1970, breach of promise of marriage has disappeared from the familiar list of six causes of action, beginning with libel. Seduction, abolished by the same Act, still remains; I know not why, but it does not matter. Section 6 of the 1933 Act provides that on the application of any party to an action 'to be tried in the King's Bench Division of the High Court', if the court or a judge is satisfied that a charge of fraud against that party, or a claim for libel and so on, is in issue, the action must be tried with a jury, unless the court or judge is of opinion that the trial 'requires any prolonged examination of documents or accounts or any scientific or local investigation which cannot conveniently be made with a jury'. Subject to this, any 'action to be tried in that Division' may, in the discretion of the court or a judge, be ordered to be tried either with or without a jury. For some while after the 1933 Act was passed, the ancestors of the rule which now stands as RSC Ord 33, r 5, repeated the substance of much of s 6 of the Act; the present rule avoids this, though like the section it is specifically confined to actions 'to be tried in the Queen's Bench Division'.

I pause there. Section 1 of the 1918 Act had conferred the right to a trial by jury in a case 'in the High Court' if fraud was alleged. *International Producers Ltd v Forbes* [1922] WN 76 had shown that this gave no right to demand a jury in actions in the Chancery Division; and then, in 1933, the section in the Act which gave a litigant charged with fraud the right to demand a jury was in terms confined to an action 'to be tried in the King's Bench Division of the High Court'. In those circumstances, there is plainly much force in the contention that Parliament meant what it said, and did not intend to confer any right to a jury on a litigant charged with fraud in the Chancery Division by the indirect method of making it obligatory for the Chancery Division to transfer any such case to the Queen's Bench Division in order to give him a statutory right to a jury. I should certainly be surprised if a charge of fraud in a matrimonial cause were held to give a right to trial by jury despite r 43(1) of the Matrimonial Causes Rules 1977, SI 1977 No 344. The power to transfer a case from one division to another given by RSC Ord 4, r 3, appears to be purely a matter for the discretion of the court (to be exercised, of course, on proper principles), for the verb is 'may', without more. Is it right to say that a party charged with fraud who has been given no right to a jury is entitled to require the power to transfer the case to be exercised in order to confer on him the right to a jury which Parliament has refrained from giving him? Alternatively, can it be said that because the right to a jury has been given to a party charged with fraud in the Queen's Bench Division, that is a strong or compelling reason for the court to exercise its discretion to transfer to the Queen's Bench Division a case in the Chancery Division in which that party has no right to a jury?

Questions such as these plainly lead to others. In particular, what is the reason for not giving the right to litigants in the Chancery Division? May not a party charged with fraud legitimately ask why the right to the jury that he seeks should depend on whether the division in which the plaintiff has issued the writ is the Queen's Bench Division or the Chancery Division? Does anything turn on whether the assignment to the Chancery Division is obligatory or optional? In other words, does anything turn on whether the proceedings have been assigned to the Chancery Division by force of the Supreme Court of Judicature (Consolidation) Act 1925, s 56, which specifically assigns certain types of action to that division, or whether the action is one which, although it could have been commenced in either the Chancery Division or the Queen's Bench Division, has in fact been assigned to the Chancery Division by the plaintiff exercising his right under s 58 to assign it to that division simply by marking the writ with the name of that division? Section 56, I may say, replaced s 54 of the 1873 Act, and s 58 replaced s 35 of the 1873 Act and s 11 of the 1875 Act, the old and the new provisions being substantially to the same effect in what is material.

In considering these questions, it seems plain that many of the matters specifically assigned to the Chancery Division by s 56 of the 1925 Act are inherently unlikely to be suitable for trial by jury. Further, nobody can practise or sit in this division for long without being well aware that many allegations of fraud are made and tried by a judge sitting alone. I have already referred to what Peterson J said in *International Producers Ltd v Forbes*; and there are a number of older authorities to the same effect, even if one does not go the whole way with Malins V-C in saying that 'questions of fraud have always been considered to be peculiarly within the jurisdiction of the Court of Chancery': see *Back v Hay* (1877) 5 Ch D 235 at 240; and see 241. In *Rushton v Tobin* (1879) 10 Ch D 558 the action was brought in the Chancery Division to have an agreement induced by the fraudulent misrepresentations of the defendant set aside and cancelled, for repayment of the money paid under the agreement, and damages. The plaintiff required trial by jury, and the defendant thereupon moved for trial by a judge alone. One obvious point against the plaintiff was that if he had wanted a jury, he should have issued his writ in one of the common law divisions of the High Court, instead of coming into Chancery. The plaintiff sought to meet this by saying that he had been forced to come into Chancery because actions for cancellation of written instruments were assigned to the Chancery Division by s 34 of the 1873 Act; but Malins V-C held that as cancellation was not essential to the relief claimed, there was no need for the plaintiff to have sued in the Chancery Division.

That aspect of the case is not, of course, directly in point in the present case; but (at 562) Malins V-C went on to rest his decision on a further ground. '... independently of these considerations', he said, the case was one of setting aside a transaction on the ground that it was brought about by fraud. As he had pointed out in many cases:

> '... that is peculiarly, and always has been considered peculiarly the jurisdiction of the Court of Chancery when that Court existed, and is the jurisdiction and business of this Court now that it is simply called the Chancery Division. There are no cases of that nature, however complicated, however difficult, however lengthy, which this Court has not been in the habit of dealing with, and which it does not deal with almost constantly. It is therefore, and always has been, considered the peculiar tribunal for trying these questions, and being so, I could not send such a case to be tried by a jury unless I was absolutely satisfied that justice could not be obtained here, or that there is an absolute right on the part of the Plaintiffs to take the Defendant to a jury.'

In the Court of Appeal (at 565) Jessel MR observed that there must be a 'very strong case' before the Court of Appeal would interfere with the discretion of a judge as to the way in which a case before him should be tried. He then said that Malins V-C:

> 'went on the ground that this was a kind of case which had always been tried in Chancery, and never at Common Law; not a case turning on a single misstatement, but on a series of representations, so that there was no single question of fact which could be conveniently submitted to a jury. It is no part of my duty to say what I should have done if this case had come before me in the first instance, but I do unhesitatingly say that I should have done what the Vice-Chancellor has done.'

With this, James and Bramwell LJJ concurred.

Both on the authorities and on principle it seems to me that the position may be summarised as follows:

(1) A litigant who is charged with fraud has been given by statute the right to demand a jury if the action is brought in the Queen's Bench Division, but not if the action is brought in Chancery.

(2) Such a litigant has been given no right to require the action to be transferred from the Chancery Division to the Queen's Bench Division simply in order to obtain the jury to which, ex hypothesi, he has no right.

(3) These consequences flow from the language of the statute and the rules; but if reasons for them are sought, one reason may well be that many of the matters proceeding in the Chancery Division are of a nature which makes them inherently unsuitable for trial by jury, irrespective of fraud; and the inclusion of a charge of fraud does not make suitable for jury trial proceedings which are unsuitable. Another reason may lie in the long experience that the Chancery Division has had in hearing cases of fraud which arise in the types of case usually to be found in that division.

(4) The power to transfer proceedings from (inter alia) the Chancery Division to the Queen's Bench Division which is given by Ord 4, r 3(1), provides something of a safety-valve. It would be open to the court to exercise the power in a case in which fraud is charged which (a) is suitable for trial by jury, and (b) is of a nature such that the interests of justice sufficiently require that the transfer should be made.

(5) Any contention that the plaintiff has deliberately issued his writ in the Chancery Division in order to deprive the defendant of the right to a jury which he would have had

if the writ had been issued in the Queen's Bench Division can be dealt with adequately under the court's power to transfer the action. This may occur when the assignment of the case to the Chancery Division was made by the plaintiff exercising his option under the Supreme Court of Judicature (Consolidation) Act 1925, s 58, in a case where there is no obligatory assignment to the Chancery Division under s 56, especially where the subject matter of the action has no particular Chancery element.

With these considerations in mind, I turn to the other main head, ie whether in fact in this case 'a charge of fraud against that party [namely, the defendant] . . . is in issue' within the meaning of those words in the Administration of Justice (Miscellaneous Provisions) Act 1933, s 6(1)(*a*). Certain matters are clear. First, the word 'fraud' is used not in any general sense of dishonesty, but as meaning an intentional misrepresentation (or in some cases concealment) of fact made by one party with the intention of inducing another party to act on it, and thereby inducing the other party to act on it to his detriment. In other words, 'fraud' means 'fraud' in the sense of *Derry v Peek* (1889) 14 App Cas 337, [1886–90] All ER Rep 1: see *Barclays Bank Ltd v Cole* [1966] 3 All ER 948 at 950, [1967] 2 QB 738 at 744–745, where robbery was held not to be fraud for this purpose. Second, it is plain that a charge of fraud may be made without using the word 'fraud'. This is so where a defendant is said to have made representations to the plaintiff on which he intended the plaintiff to act, and the representations were untrue, and were known to the defendant to be untrue: see *Davy v Garrett* (1878) 7 Ch D 473 at 489. Third, it is settled that a mere superadded allegation of fraud will not suffice: there must be a charge of fraud which will have to be decided in order to determine the rights of the parties. Thus if the only issue is whether or not goods have been paid for, an allegation that the defendant was fraudulent does not give him the right to a jury: see *Everett v Islington Guardians* [1923] 1 KB 44 at 46. That case depended on the action being one 'in which fraud is alleged' so that the present requirement that fraud should be 'in issue' strongly reinforces the decision.

Counsel's contentions for the company on the point really fell under two main headings. First, he said that the essence of the company's case was to recover money from the defendant which she had received as a constructive trustee, and that success in such a claim in no way depended on proving fraud against the defendant. However fraudulent the defendant's husband may have been, fraud on the defendant's part was not a necessary ingredient for success by the company. Second, he said that there was plainly no question of the defendant having deceived the representative of the company with whom she dealt (namely, her husband), since the company's case was that the two of them were acting in concert, with the husband probably the prime mover.

Now the claim in respect of the alleged constructive trust obviously does not depend on the company establishing fraud against the defendant, and the same applies to the claim for money had and received to the company's use. There is, indeed, a claim for damages; since the Misrepresentation Act 1967, s 2, such a claim may succeed without proving that the misrepresentation was fraudulent; and the charge of conspiracy to pay the money in breach of duty to the company is not a charge of fraud. It seems to me that the company could succeed in all that is claimed without establishing that the defendant is guilty of *Derry v Peek* fraud. Obviously the company's claims against the defendant involve grave imputations against her; but that is not enough to bring the case within the statute. Counsel for the defendant took me on an interesting tour of a number of criminal and other authorities on aiding and abetting, on accessories before the fact, on imputing an agent's knowledge to his principal, and on lifting the corporate veil; but I do not think that I need discuss them. For the reasons that I have given I do not consider that this is a case in which a charge of fraud against the defendant is in issue. Accordingly, even if the case were to be transferred to the Queen's Bench Division, the defendant would have no right to a jury.

If I am wrong in that, and a charge of fraud against the defendant is in issue, then there is the question whether I ought to transfer the case to the Queen's Bench Division. First, as I have mentioned, RSC Ord 4, r 3(1), simply provides that the proceedings 'may' be transferred, without more; and this, I think, gives the court a discretion, to be exercised a on proper principles. Second, I think that, on ordinary principles, it is for the litigant who seeks the transfer to make out a sufficient case for the power to be exercised. Certainly the onus rests on an applicant who asks for a discretionary power to order trial by jury to be exercised: see *Jenkins v Bushby* [1891] 1 Ch 484. Third, the fact that the transfer will give the defendant the right to claim a jury, and that that is what she wants, is only one of the factors to be borne in mind. Others include the nature of the case, the b suitability or otherwise of the Chancery Division for deciding the case as compared with the suitability of a trial by jury (and this includes the probability of a trial by judge alone being shorter and cheaper), as well as the wishes of the other party to the litigation. In deciding whether there should be trial by jury, the court must act fairly to all parties: see *Williams v Beesley* [1973] 3 All ER 144, [1973] 1 WLR 1295.

Counsel for the defendant advanced a contention that the cases in which the suitability c of the Chancery Division for trying cases of fraud had been asserted were cases where the fraud was mere equitable fraud, and not those where there was *Derry v Peek* fraud. I do not think that he made good this proposition. Thus *Ruston v Tobin*, which I have already discussed, seems to me to be a plain case in which *Derry v Peek* fraud was charged. However, in the course of his submissions counsel cited *Re Pacaya Rubber and Produce Co Ltd* [1913] 1 Ch 218; and it was a dictum of Kennedy LJ in that case which perhaps d helped him most. The case was one in which an order for transfer to the Chancery Division had been made in respect of an action in the King's Bench Division for fraudulent misrepresentations in the prospectus of a company which was being wound up by the Companies Court. Both Neville J and the Court of Appeal held that the transfer had been rightly made; and Neville J reiterated (at 223) the view that the Chancery Division was not unfitted to deal with allegations of fraud, because both that e division and the old Court of Chancery were largely concerned with cases of that kind. That, of course, was a case in which the transfer would take away the right to a jury, and not a transfer which, like the transfer sought in the present case, would confer the right to a jury. Kennedy LJ said (at 225) that if the directors of the company had taken up the position that the charge of fraud 'was a serious charge', which they wished to have tried by a jury, he would have come to a different conclusion, since it would be right to have f a trial by jury in such a case. Counsel for the defendant, of course, strongly relied on this dictum. He linked it with a reference to some words of Lord Cairns in *Reese River Silver Mining Co v Smith* (1869) LR 4 HL 64 at 79, another case of an allegedly fraudulent company prospectus. There, Lord Cairns refrained from entering into any question regarding 'fraud in the more invidious sense', and said that it was quite possible that the directors were ignorant of the untruth of the statements in their prospectus, though they g would still be civilly liable for them.

Now I would accept that one of the factors to be borne in mind in considering a transfer is the degree of gravity of the charges made against the defendant, and especially that of any charges of fraud. But that is only one of the factors. It has to be weighed against all the other factors in the case. Here, the claim is based on a whole series of invoices, and whether the work alleged in them to have been done by the defendant had h in fact been done or not. This comes close to the words in the judgment of Jessel MR in *Ruston v Tobin* (1879) 10 Ch D 558 at 565 that I have already quoted, that of a case not 'turning on a single misstatement, but on a series of representations, so that there was no single question of fact which could be conveniently submitted to a jury'. Furthermore, I cannot see any circumstances of especial gravity in the charge of fraud made against the defendant in this case, nor anything which makes it unsuitable for trial in the Chancery j Division. Indeed, there is force in counsel's contention for the company that a case about the doctrine of constructive trusts in relation to a company, and the fiduciary duties of directors, with an allegation of ultra vires to boot, is not very suitable fare for a jury, even though there are also allegations of fraud and dishonesty. The natural home for such a case may well be said to be the Chancery Division, where such matters are almost a commonplace, so that the case ought to stay where it is. I should add that there is indeed

a sizeable bundle of invoices to be examined; but although I do not accept counsel's
contention for the company that the trial requires a 'prolonged examination of *a*
documents or accounts which cannot conveniently be made with a jury' so as to satisfy
the statutory requirement for excluding trial by jury even in cases of fraud, I think that
the invoices make a small contribution towards preferring trial by a judge alone.

Looking at the case as a whole, it seems to me that not only is there no strong case for
a transfer, but there is, on balance, no case at all: the factors in favour of a transfer are
outweighed by those in favour of the case remaining where it is. The matter is an *b*
anxious one because as I understand it, both on the older authorities (to which may be
added *Hope v Great Western Railway Co* [1937] 1 All ER 625, [1937] 2 KB 130) and also
on the recent statement of the House of Lords in *Duport Steels Ltd v Sirs* [1980] 1 All ER
529, [1980] 1 WLR 142 (a case on a quite different point), in discretionary matters the
discretion is that of the judge at first instance, and it will not readily be interfered with
on appeal. I have tried to express the major considerations in this judgment in accordance *c*
with the submissions put before me, but of course it is not practicable to set forth every
single matter that is of any possible relevance. I can only say that, looked at as a whole,
the case appears to be entirely appropriate to the Chancery Division; and even on the
assumption that a charge of fraud against the defendant is in issue, no case has been made
out which would justify the case being transferred to the Queen's Bench Division.
Accordingly, the application fails, and the summons will be dismissed. *d*

Summons dismissed.

Solicitors: *William F Prior & Co* (for the company); *Gregsons* (for the defendant).

Azza M Abdallah Barrister.

a

Jobling v Associated Dairies Ltd

COURT OF APPEAL, CIVIL DIVISION
STEPHENSON, ACKNER LJJ AND DAME ELIZABETH LANE
1st, 2nd, 3rd, 11th JULY 1980

b *Damages – Personal injury – Amount of damages – Subsequent further injury to plaintiff – Supervening disease – Plaintiff's back injured in accident resulting from defendant's breach of statutory duty – Back injury impairing plaintiff's capacity to work – Plaintiff subsequently rendered totally unfit for work because of spinal disease unconnected with accident – Claim for loss of earnings – Whether damages for injury originally caused by defendant should be reduced by reason of supervening disease.*

c In 1973 the plaintiff slipped and fell on the defendants' premises, the accident being caused by the defendants' breach of statutory duty. The plaintiff sustained a back injury and was thereafter able to do only light work, which was frequently interrupted because of the injury. In 1976 he was found to be suffering from a disease of the spine which was not connected with the accident but which rendered him wholly unfit to work. The plaintiff brought an action against the defendants in respect of the 1973 accident and at d the trial in 1979 damages were assessed as if the disease had not supervened. Accordingly the plaintiff was awarded, inter alia, a sum for loss of earnings based on 50% capacity from 1976 until the date of the trial and for seven years thereafter. The defendants appealed on the grounds that from 1976 the plaintiff's incapacity to work was due to circumstances wholly unconnected with their tortious act and that they should not be required to compensate him for it.

e

Held – Although it was settled law that where a plaintiff was injured by two successive and independent tortfeasors the liability of the first did not fall to be reduced by reason of the injury done by the second unless that second injury either diminished the disability of the plaintiff or shortened his expectation of life, nevertheless, when an injury caused to a plaintiff by a tort was obliterated by, and submerged in, a greater f injury caused by a supervening illness or other non-tortious event, the liability of the tortfeasor ceased. Accordingly, the defendants were liable for the incapacity directly resulting from the plaintiff's fall, but that liability fell to be reduced appropriately in consequence of his supervening illness; they were not, however, liable for loss of earnings from the time when the illness had rendered him wholly unable to work. The appeal would therefore be allowed (see p 772 *j* to p 773 *a* and p 776 *e* and *j* to p 777 *a*, post).

g Dictum of Latey J in *Hodgson v General Electricity Co Ltd* [1978] 2 Lloyd's Rep at 211 adopted.

Baker v Willoughby [1969] 3 All ER 1528 distinguished.

Notes

For the measure of damages in personal injuries cases, see 12 Halsbury's Laws (4th Edn) h paras 1138–1158, and for cases on the subject, see 17 Digest (Reissue) 112–118, *168–200*.

Cases referred to in judgment

Baker v Willoughby [1969] 3 All ER 1528, [1970] AC 467, [1970] 2 WLR 50, HL; *rvsg* [1969] 2 All ER 549, [1970] AC 467, [1969] 2 WLR 489, CA, 17 Digest (Reissue) 115, *186*.

j *Curwen v James* [1963] 2 All ER 619, [1963] 1 WLR 748, CA, 36(1) Digest (Reissue) 378, *1522*.

Harwood v Wyken Colliery Co [1913] 2 KB 158, 82 LJKB 414, 108 LT 283, 6 BWCC 225, CA, 34 Digest (Repl) 562, *3848*.

Hodgson v General Electricity Co Ltd [1978] 2 Lloyd's Rep 210.

Jones v National Coal Board (13th December 1976, unreported).

Phillips v London and South Western Railway Co (1879) 5 CPD 280, [1874–80] All ER Rep
1176, 49 LJQB 223, 42 LT 6, 44 JP 217, CA, 17 Digest (Reissue) 221, 932. a

Appeal

The defendants, Associated Dairies Ltd, appealed against the judgment of Reeve J at
Newcastle upon Tyne on 26th March 1979 awarding the plaintiff, Alexander Jobling, the
sum of £17,950 and interest, in the plaintiff's action against the defendants for
negligence and/or breach of statutory duty. The facts are set out in the judgment of the b
court.

L D Lawton QC and *Simon Hawkesworth* for the defendants.
Robin Stewart QC and *Keith Walmsley* for Mr Jobling.

Cur adv vult c

11th July. **ACKNER LJ** read the following judgment of the court: On 1st June 1972
the respondent, Mr Alexander Jobling, was engaged by the defendents to act as manager
of a butcher's shop, Farm Stores Ltd, at Shield Road, Byker, Newcastle upon Tyne. This
was a relatively small shop at which there were employed, apart from Mr Jobling, six
female staff of whom two worked full time and four part time. The only other employee d
of the defendants with whom we are concerned in these proceedings was a Mr Dunk
who was the area supervisor of this and 12 other shops.

Some six months after his employment began, that is on 15th January 1973, Mr
Jobling slipped and fell in the shop premises thereby injuring his back. The accident
happened in these circumstances. At about 11.00 am he went into the refrigerator room
whose approximate dimensions were 8 ft by 4 ft to collect a forequarter of beef, weighing e
about 140 lb, which was hanging on a hook. He placed the forequarter on his shoulder,
disengaged it from the hook, turned towards the door to go out of the refrigerator and
in taking his first step forward, his foot slipped under him and he fell backwards. He
slipped because the floor was wet.

The source of this wetness was the refrigerator. It was an old one and constantly gave
trouble, with the result that Mr Jobling regularly had to call on the services of a firm of f
refrigeration engineers. This was the result of condensation within the refrigerator
which should have been collected into a tray within the refrigerator and drained off by
a pipe into a bucket. The trouble was that the tray leaked with the result that all the
moisture was not collected into the bucket.

The floor of the shop was scrubbed daily to remove grease, fat and blood from it. At
the beginning of the day and thereafter attempts were made to keep it dry by mopping g
it up two or three times daily. However these mopping-up operations were only
partially successful. Within a very short time of it being completed the floor became
slippery again. To mitigate the effect of the water on the floor, sawdust was used when
Mr Jobling took over in June 1972 and it continued to be used until about the beginning
of December 1972, that is some six weeks before his accident, when Mr Dunk in
compliance with company policy in regard to regulations concerning hygiene, ordered h
the practice to be stopped. Thereupon Mr Jobling, realising the danger of the slippery
conditions of the floor, asked Mr Dunk to supply duckboards for the purpose of reducing
or removing that danger. Mr Dunk, however, did not take kindly to the request, gave
an evasive or temporising answer and fobbed Mr Jobling off with promises when on
several occasions he repeated the request over the telephone. No duckboards or other
means of counteracting the slipperiness of the floor were ever provided. j

It is common ground that the Offices, Shops and Railway Premises Act 1963 applied
to the premises. It was accordingly alleged in Mr Jobling's statement of claim that the
defendants were in breach of s 16 of the Act in that they failed, in so far as was reasonably
practicable, to maintain the floor of the meat refrigerator properly or at all or to keep it
free from substances (namely water), likely to cause persons to slip. On the facts set out

above Reeve J, on 26th March 1979, held that the defendants were in breach of their obligations under that section of the Act.

Although when opened this appeal was not only against the decision of the judge as to the quantum of damages, but also as to his finding of liability, counsel for the defendants subsequently confined his submissions to the sums awarded by the judge both by way of general and special damages. We therefore now turn to consider the injuries which Mr Jobling suffered.

As a result of his fall Mr Jobling sustained a prolapsed intervertebral disc which produced low back pain and sciatica. He was given physiotherapy treatment which produced some improvements so that on 30th September 1973 he was able to take up employment in a butcher's shop in a supervisory capacity involving no lifting. He was able, although in considerable pain, to continue in that employment until April 1974, though during that period he was off work because of the state of his back during January and February. In June 1974 he took further employment, which was periodically interrupted by reason of his condition until January 1975, when he fell down some stairs and aggravated that condition. He has not worked since then. The judge held that the 1975 fall was directly referable to the 1973 accident. The judge further held that he was not fit to return to work before October 1975.

However, unknown to Mr Jobling, an injury to his neck which he sustained in 1956 and from which he had thought he had made a full recovery was proving disabling. He was found in 1976 to be suffering from spondylotic myelopathy, that is to say, he had damage to the cervical spinal cord at the C4, 6 and 7 level particularly on the left side. This is a condition which normally occurs naturally and is due to ischaemia, that is poor blood supply to the cord consequent on degenerative spondylosis. An agreed medical report by the consultant surgeon, Mr Todd, acting for the plaintiff, and the consultant neurologist, Dr Foster, acting for the defendants, stated that this myelopathy became disabling about the middle or end of 1976 and that the effect of this myelopathy has of itself been such as to render the plaintiff wholly unfit to work. This they agreed was the main disability and that it was unrelated to the 1973 accident. They further agreed that due to the accident of 1973 there was continuing back pain which they described as being 'somewhat disabling'.

General damages

When considering the damages which he should award for pain, suffering and loss of amenities, the judge in substance set out five items in the last report of Mr Todd (28th February 1979) under the heading 'Present complaints', but he omitted to have regard to a later part of that report where the surgeon set out his opinion and in particular stated that the condition of Mr Jobling's left arm, the cramping pains in his legs, his difficulty with walking and the tendency for his urine to dribble away were due to cervical myelopathy. The learned judge only omitted item 6 in the list of complaints, which related specifically to the pain in the neck and the deterioration in the strength of the left arm and numbness in the fingers of the left hand. It was accordingly common ground that the items which he should have taken into account were limited to the continuing back pain, some sciatic radiation to the left leg and the consequences that any bending, lifting or stooping makes Mr Jobling's back worse.

Mr Jobling was born in July 1925 and was therefore nearly 54 when the action was tried. Up until the time of his accident he led an active life, enjoyed walking and swimming and was particularly fond of gardening. He has been unable since the accident to enjoy these activities.

The judge awarded £6,000 general damages. We see nothing wrong with this figure, on the assumption that the judge was entitled on the agreed medical evidence to take into account all the matters he enumerated. It follows that if he had eliminated those items which he should not have included and to which reference has been made above, he himself would have awarded a lesser figure. In our judgment the lesser figure should have been £4,000 and we accordingly allow the appeal in relation to general damages by substituting this figure. a

Loss of earnings

It is however in relation to the loss of earnings from the middle or end of 1976, when Mr Jobling's myelopathy rendered him wholly unfit to work, that a question of some difficulty arises. Although the judge treated the myelopathy as lying dormant for many years, only manifesting itself in 1976, it is common ground that neither of the two b doctors was able to say whether on the balance of probabilities the myelopathy was present at the time of the accident. Counsel for Mr Jobling conceded before us that, if proper interpretation of the agreed joint report by the doctors had been that the myelopathy was a pre-existing condition, then he would have accepted that the defendants had injured a person with a very limited working life, and accordingly he would have only been able to recover loss of earnings up to the time when the c myelopathy rendered his client wholly unfit for work, that is up to the middle or end of 1976. It was the whole basis of his contention that the myelopathy was a disease or disability which supervened for the first time after the accident. It was not a quiescent condition which had pre-existed for some years before the accident and had only manifested itself after the accident. It was for this reason he relied on the two authorities referred to in the judgment, namely *Harwood v Wyken Colliery Co* [1913] 2 KB 158 and d *Baker v Willoughby* [1969] 3 All ER 1528, [1970] AC 467. He contended before the learned judge that the plaintiff's disabilities could be regarded as having two causes, the accident and the myelopathy, and the latter could not diminish the amount of damages payable in respect of the accident.

Counsel who appeared at the trial for the employers argued that a distinction is to be drawn between a supervening disease and a disability caused by a supervening tort, e which was the position in *Baker's* case. The judge did not accept the validity of such a distinction and considered himself, on the authority of *Baker's* case, obliged to leave out of account the disability caused to Mr Jobling by the myelopathy in assessing the damages resulting from the 1973 accident. He considered that what he had to decide was the extent to which Mr Jobling's earning capacity had been reduced by the injury to his back alone. He put to himself the question: had the myelopathy not supervened, to f what extent and from what date would he have been able to undertake sedentary work, albeit periodically interrupted by occasions when he would have probably been off work? He decided that the proper approach was to assess the damages on the basis of a 50% loss of earnings capacity. He thus arrived at a figure for special damages for the period starting at the beginning of 1976 and continuing up to the date of trial ($3\frac{1}{4}$ years) and then by applying a multiplier of seven he calculated the loss of future earnings at g £13,650.

Counsel for Mr Jobling is correct in contending that there are observations in *Baker v Willoughby* which, although obiter, lend support to the proposition that there is no distinction to be drawn between a supervening event which is tortious and one which is not. But this particular problem was not before the House of Lords and accordingly it did not have the benefit of the argument which we have had nor that which was so h commended by Latey J in *Hodgson v General Electricity Co Ltd* [1978] 2 Lloyd's Rep 210. In that case a grinder and milling machine operator, while doing his work in September 1971, suffered a severe injury to his left hand. After a very long period of medical treatment, involving the amputation of three fingers, he was left with a deformed and very defective hand. In mid-1976 a serious heart condition developed, wholly unconnected with the injury. He became unfit for all work from that date. He j contended, relying on *Baker v Willoughby*, that he was entitled to his full notional pre-accident earnings for the balance of his expectation of life, which was $7\frac{1}{2}$ years from the date of the trial. Latey J decided that, as the incapacity of the plaintiff to earn anything from mid-1976 was not due to any wrong which the defendant did to him in 1971 but was due to his heart disease which came on him unconnected with anything the defendants did, he could see no reason in logic or justice why they should be required to compensate him for loss of earnings from that date, 1976. He followed a decision of Forbes J in *Jones v National Coal Board* (13th December 1976, unreported) where the learned judge, obiter, took the same view of the law.

It is helpful in a dispute of this kind to go back to first principles. (1) Damages are intended to compensate the plaintiff for his loss arising out of the tortious act and no more. (2) A tortfeasor takes his victim as he finds him, in the sense that a defendant who injures an already disabled man need only compensate him as such. (3) The court must never speculate when it knows the true facts. Thus, when assessing damages the court must have regard to events which have happened since the date of the accident and must be guided by those events so far as they have made certain that which would otherwise be uncertain. This principle is well illustrated by *Curwen v James* [1963] 2 All ER 619, [1963] 1 WLR 748 where this court held (as the law then stood) that the remarriage of a widow had to be taken into account in assessing damages under the Fatal Accidents Act 1846, even though the remarriage took place after the trial and before the appeal. (4) In order to give a plaintiff fair and reasonable compensation for his loss of earnings capacity it has to be borne in mind in relation to the future that—

> 'if no accident had happened, nevertheless many circumstances might have happened to prevent the plaintiff from earning his previous income; he may be disabled by illness, he is subject to the ordinary accidents and vicissitudes of life; and if all these circumstances of which no evidence can be given are looked at, it will be impossible to exactly estimate them; yet if the jury wholly passed them over they will go wrong, because these accidents and vicissitudes ought to be taken into account.'

(See *Phillips v London and South Western Railway Co* (1879) 5 CPD 280 at 291 per Brett LJ; cf [1874–80] All ER Rep 1176 at 1181.)

It is because of these well-accepted principles that counsel for Mr Jobling unhesitantly made the following concessions. (a) If a plaintiff suffers from a pre-existing disability, albeit in another part of the body, which was likely to manifest itself with totally disabling symptoms, then he would receive no compensation for loss of earnings caused by a tortious act, once that disablement commenced or was considered likely to commence. (b) Accordingly he accepted that if the plaintiff's myelopathy had been dormant and had manifested itself in 1976, without any connection with the 1973 trauma, then there could be no claim for loss of wages after that date. (c) Morever if the 1973 trauma had accelerated the inevitable onset of the symptoms from the assumed dormant myelopathy by, say, three years, then there would be no claim for loss of wages as from 1979. (d) If after the accident, but by the date of trial, an event had taken place which reduces the plaintiff's life expectancy then this is a factor that must be taken into account in assessing damages.

Counsel however contends that a valid distinction in principle is to be drawn between a plaintiff whose inability to work, post the accident, is due to symptoms that emanate from a quiescent disease but which manifest themselves for the first time after the accident, and a plaintiff who has the selfsame disability as a result of a disease whose inception occurs after the accident. He thus draws a distinction between a condition which has its inception immediately before the plaintiff suffers the tortious injury and immediately after. He further draws a distinction between an event which supervenes after the tortious injury which reduces the life expectation and one which reduces only working life expectation.

To translate counsel's contentions into two simple examples, assume the case of a plaintiff who, on 2nd January, was knocked down by a motor cycle, with the result that his capacity for gainful employment was reduced by 20%. On 3rd January he was rendered permanently incapable of work by reason of a paralysis. If the condition which gave rise to the paralysis was already in existence on 1st January, albeit dormant, the plaintiff has no claim for loss of wages save for one day. If, however, the inception of the paralysis truly occurred on the day after the accident, he would be entitled to claim compensation for a 20% reduction in working capacity for the rest of what would have been assumed, without the paralysis, to be his working life.

However, the event which supervenes after the accident does not have to be a disease. It would equally follow, on counsel's submission, that if the plaintiff on 3rd January, as a result solely of his own negligence, was knocked down by a motor coach and thereby rendered totally incapable of further work, this incapacity would have to be wholly ignored and the plaintiff awarded his future loss of earnings, as if that event had never occurred. On the other hand if this later accident, for which the plaintiff was wholly to blame, had affected not his capacity to work, but only his expectation of life, then his claim for future loss of earnings would have to be reduced to reflect that reduction.

The results which flow from the submissions of counsel for Mr Jobling seems to run so counter to the majority of the basic principles to which reference has been made above and to be so devoid of logic and fairness as to be quite unacceptable, unless clear authority makes this obligatory.

The first of the two authorities relied on by counsel and referred to above, *Harwood v Wyken Colliery Co* [1913] 2 KB 158, involved a claim by a workman for compensation under the Workmen's Compensation Act 1906. Mr Harwood was a miner aged 59 who on 20th October 1911, whilst working in the respondents' mine, injured his right knee. They paid him compensation until May 1912 but thereafter ceased doing so, because it was discovered in the previous month that he was suffering from a heart disease which also incapacitated him from work. It is not apparent from the report whether this was a pre-existing disease which first manifested itself some six months after the accident or whether its inception occurred after the accident. Hamilton LJ, with whom Cozens-Hardy MR agreed, based his decision to allow the workman's appeal on his construction of the statute which he described as a 'compensation' Act, compensating the workman in a new and statutory manner in respect of a wholly statutory right. He stated that it could not be said of the plaintiff that partial incapacity for work had not resulted and was not still resulting from the injury. All that could be said was that such partial incapacity was not still resulting 'solely' from the injury. To read the word 'solely' into the Act after the word 'injury' was not interpretation but legislation, unless the context or the scheme of the Act demonstrated that the legislature so intended. He contrasted the plaintiff's statutory right to compensation with his right to claim damages at common law, where a jury would have to be directed, inter alia, to consider the possibility of 'future diminution or loss of earnings arising independently of the cause of action, from increasing age, from accident or illness in futuro, and so forth' (see [1913] 2 KB 158 at 170). We do not read the judgment of Buckley LJ as necessarily taking a contrary view. He concluded that while the compensation was only for the continuing consequences of the injury measured by diminished capacity to earn wages, still a subsequent supervening cause left the consequences of that diminished capacity still existent and only added a further diminished capacity.

The essential foundation of the submissions of counsel for Mr Jobling is the decision in the House of Lords in *Baker v Willoughby* [1969] 3 All ER 1528, [1970] AC 467, referred to earlier in this judgment. In that case the plaintiff was crossing a main highway when he was knocked down by the defendant's car and his left leg was injured. However, before his claim in respect of this injury was heard, he was shot in the left leg during an armed robbery and his leg had to be amputated. It was accordingly argued that since the second incident had removed the very limb from which the earlier disability had stemmed, no loss suffered by the plaintiff after his leg was amputated could be attributed to the defendant's negligence. The second accident had obliterated the effect of the first and accordingly all loss suffered thereafter was attributable to the second incident. The trial judge awarded him damages for pain, discomfort, loss of amenities and loss of earning power. He declined to take into account, in his assessment of the damages, the effect of the amputation of the left leg. The plaintiff was compensated on the basis that there was stiffness, weakness and pain in the left ankle and that he might sustain arthritis in his left leg, the amputated leg, in later years.

In the Court of Appeal counsel conceded on behalf of the plaintiff that if a workman claims against his employer for personal injuries causing permanent partial loss of earning capacity, but by the date of trial he has been reduced to permanent complete incapacity for work by disease or some pure accident wholly unconnected with the original injury, his damages for future incapacity would properly be reduced and might in some cases have to be reduced to nil (see [1969] 2 All ER 549 at 555, [1970] AC 467 at 481 per Fenton Atkinson LJ). Again it is apparent from the judgments that the plaintiff did not seek to attack the logic of the argument that, since damages are intended to compensate the plaintiff for his loss arising out of the tortious act and no more, where the consequences of a tortious act come to an end before trial, whether by recovery or supervening disease or further injury, the defendant's liability should cease. It was however contended that the argument should be rejected in the case of a subsequent pretrial disability *caused by a second tort* because of its unjust consequences. By way of illustration the example was given of a foreman steel erector earning £40 per week who had a serious fall owing to his employer's neglect and injured a leg to such an extent that he could not climb again and was reduced to desk work at £15 per week. Such a man's claim for loss of future earnings might be £10,000. Suppose that before trial he had a motor accident which resulted in the paralysis of both legs. On the principle that a tortfeasor takes his victim as he finds him, the driver responsible for the second accident would compensate the plaintiff as a £15 per week man and if the employer escaped responsibility for loss of wages subsequent to the second accident, the plaintiff would never recover the £10,000 to which he was clearly entitled. Thus the plaintiff would fall between two stools and be deprived of the damages which he would have recovered had there been only one incident. It was understandably urged that if that was the law it would be in a ridiculous and unjust state.

The Court of Appeal considered that there was a fallacy in that argument, because, if the second tortfeasor has to take the victim as he finds him, there was no good reason why the damages payable by the second tortfeasor should not include a figure to cover the compensation for loss of future earnings which the victim would have received for the original injuries but for the second tortious injury.

The House of Lords did not accept the view taken by the Court of Appeal. Applying the general rule that a wrongdoer must take the plaintiff as he finds him, the robber was not responsible or liable for the damage caused by the first tortfeasor. He would only have to pay for the additional loss to the plaintiff by reason of his having an artificial limb instead of a stiff leg. The House of Lords rejected the contention that the plaintiff's damages should be decreased by the fact of the second injury. Lord Reid, with whose opinion Lord Guest, Viscount Dilhorne and Lord Donovan agreed, stated that, if the second injuries merely became a concurrent cause of the disabilities caused by the injury inflicted by the first tortfeasor, then they cannot diminish the damages. Thus the unacceptable result of putting a plaintiff, who had been injured by two successive and independent torts, in a worse position than if he had suffered the selfsame injuries at the hands of a single tortfeasor was avoided.

Counsel for Mr Jobling recognised, however, on the facts of *Baker's* case, the difficulty in maintaining that the injuries sustained to the leg in the first accident was still a cause of the diminished mobility, the loss of earning capacity and a potential source of severe arthritis, when the consequences of the second accident were totally to remove the injured leg. True enough Lord Reid accepted that if the result of the amputation was that the plaintiff suffered no more pain from his first injury, then he could not recover for the pain he would never suffer. But then he would never have arthritis, nor would there be any loss of mobility through stiffness or weakness of the left ankle because it no longer existed. How could it be said that the injury to the left leg, resulting from the original accident, was still operating as one of two concurrent causes both producing disability? Counsel for Mr Jobling felt obliged in these circumstances to submit that the first accident had to be *deemed* to be a concurrent cause.

Lord Pearson in his speech recognised that the argument that the consequences of the original accident had been submerged and obliterated by the greater consequences of the supervening event was 'formidable'. He added, however: 'But it must not be allowed to succeed, because it produces manifest injustice' (see [1969] 3 All ER 1528 at 1535, [1970] AC 467 at 495). He dealt in detail with the nature of the injustice, illustrating the gap in damages which would result from applying the principle, which he accepted had to be applied, that the second tortfeasor was entitled to take his victim as he found him. He referred to what he described as 'the ingenious attempt' made in the Court of Appeal to fill the gap by holding that the damages recoverable from the second tortfeasor would include a novel head of damages, viz the diminution of the plaintiff's damages recoverable from the first tortfeasor. However he did not consider that that would be an admissible head of damage. He held that the original accident caused 'a devaluation' of the plaintiff in the sense that it produced a general reduction of his capacity to do things, to earn money and to enjoy life. For that devaluation the original tortfeasor should be and remain responsible for the full extent, unless something happened which either reduced the devaluation or shortened the expectation of life, thus reducing the period over which the plaintiff would suffer from the devaluation. Where the supervening event was a tort, he considered the second tortfeasor should be responsible for the additional devaluation caused by him.

The repeated references made both in the Court of Appeal and in the House of Lords to the need to avoid the clear injustice which would result if the plaintiff fell between the two tortfeasors, the first one saying that the loss ceased on the occurrence of the second accident and the second one saying that he was only obliged to pay damages on the basis that he took his victim as he found him, appear to have involved an element of policy entering into the decision. An exception appears to have been made in order to do justice. Thus it is settled law that where a plaintiff is injured by two tortfeasors, his damages do not fall to be reduced as a result of the injuries sustained in the second accident, unless before the assessment of the damages something has happened which either diminishes the devaluation or shortens his expectation of life. Although counsel for Mr Jobling is fully entitled to urge that the speeches in the House of Lords may tend to support the proposition that damages should equally be awarded against the tortfeasor inflicting the initial injury where the further injury is *non-tortious*, this was, as previously stated, not the case in point before the House of Lords. Accordingly there is no binding authority obliging this court to reach that conclusion.

If we were thus to extend the decision in *Baker v Willoughby*, we would not be curing, but creating, manifest injustices. We would be obliging, as the examples given earlier demonstrate, a defendant to pay damages far in excess of the loss which his tortious act created. We would be requiring judges to close their eyes to events which happened since the accident, as indeed counsel for Mr Jobling accepted. He was obliged to concede that, although a judge must take into account the vicissitudes of life, he must exclude the possibility of all future accidents and diseases except fatal ones. Thus, when considering the expectation of working life of, say, a steel erector plaintiff, no defendant would be entitled to seek to establish that the steel erector had shortly before trial been obliged to give up that occupation, because of a non-tortious accident, sustained either at his work or elsewhere, which rendered him incapable of further following that occupation. No evidence would be admissible to establish that an injured plaintiff, seeking damages for loss of future earnings, was working or proposing to work in circumstances where he might well contract a disabling disease. If the seeds of the post-accident illness could be established prior to the accident, then the damages which he could claim would fall to be reduced. If they were implanted immediately after, the situation was reversed. This artificiality can in our judgment be supported by neither principle nor sound sense and we accordingly reject the argument.

We refer once more to the final agreed medical fact: 'The effect of the myelopathy has of itself been such as to render the plaintiff wholly unfit to work.' We accordingly adopt, mutatis mutandis, the words of Latey J in *Hodgson's* case [1978] 2 Lloyd's Rep 210 at 211. The incapacity of the plaintiff to earn anything from mid or late 1976 was not due to any wrong which the defendants did to him in 1973, but was due to the myelopathy which came on him unconnected with anything the defendants did.

For the reasons given we reduce the award of general damages from £6,000 to £4,000,
a and make the appropriate reduction to the special damages for loss of earnings up to the hearing of the action in March 1979 and quash the award for future loss of earnings.

Appeal allowed. Judgment of Reeve J varied. Leave to appeal to the House of Lords granted.

Solicitors: *Berrymans*, agents for *Crutes*, Newcastle upon Tyne (for the defendant); *Carney*
b *Joyce & Co*, Newcastle upon Tyne (for Mr Jobling).

Patricia Hargrove Barrister.

R v Mason

c

COURT OF APPEAL, CRIMINAL DIVISION
LAWTON LJ, MICHAEL DAVIES AND BALCOMBE JJ
22nd, 23rd MAY, 3rd JUNE 1980

Jury – Jury vetting – Antecedents of member of panel – Legality of jury vetting.

d

Jury – Juror – Challenge – Right to stand by jurors – Crown's right to stand by jurors – Right exercisable without provable valid objection until panel exhausted – Thereafter Crown required to show valid objection.

The practice of supplying prosecuting counsel in a criminal trial with information about
e potential jurors' convictions is not unlawful (see p 783 *j* to p 784 *c*, post).

R v Crown Court at Sheffield, ex parte Brownlow [1980] 2 All ER 444 not followed.

In a criminal trial, prosecuting counsel has a right to request that a member of the jury panel shall stand by for the Crown, and that right may be exercised without a valid objection having to be proved until such time as the panel is exhausted. Thereafter, if the Crown still wishes to exclude a member of the jury panel, a valid objection must be
f shown (see p 783 *e f*, post).

Mansell v R (1857) 8 E & B 85 followed.

Notes

For jury panels and challenging jurors, see 11 Halsbury's Laws (4th Edn) paras 251, 255–258, and 26 ibid paras 620–629, and for cases on the subject, see 30 Digest (Reissue) 304–
g 313, *92–250*.

Cases referred to in judgment

Anon (1607) 1 Brownl 41, 123 ER 652, 30 Digest (Reissue) 297, *14*.

Mansell v R (1857) 8 E & B 85, Dears & B 375, 8 State Tr NS 831, 27 LJMC 4, 22 JP 19, 4 Jur NS 432, 120 ER 32, Ex Ch; *affg* 8 E & B 54, Dears & B 375, 8 State Tr NS 831, 26
h LJMC 137, 21 JP 309, 3 Jur NS 558, 120 ER 20, 30 Digest (Reissue) 313, *240*.

R v Chandler [1964] 1 All ER 761, [1964] 2 QB 322, [1964] 2 WLR 689, 128 JP 244, 48 Cr App R 143, CCA, 30 Digest (Reissue) 309, *173*.

R v Christ [1951] 2 All ER 254, 115 JP 410, 35 Cr App R 76, 49 LGR 547, CCA, 14(1) Digest (Reissue) 393, *3344*.

R v Crown Court at Sheffield, ex parte Brownlow [1980] 2 All ER 444, [1980] 2 WLR 892,
j 71 Cr App R 19, CA.

Cases also cited

Boardman v Director of Public Prosecutions [1974] 3 All ER 887, [1975] AC 421, HL.

Lavinger v R (1870) LR 3 PC 282.

R v Chapman, R v Lauday (1976) 63 Cr App R 75, CA.

R v Inder (1978) 67 Cr App R 143, CA.

R v Mansfield [1978] 1 All ER 134, [1977] 1 WLR 1102, CA.
R v Novac (1976) 65 Cr App R 107, CA.
R v O'Coigly (1798) 26 State Tr 1191.
R v Rance, R v Herron (1975) 62 Cr App R 118, CA.
R v Scarrott [1978] 1 All ER 672, [1978] QB 1016, CA.
R v Sims [1946] 1 All ER 697, [1946] KB 531, CCA.

Application for leave to appeal

Vincent Mason applied for leave to appeal against his conviction in the Crown Court at Northampton before his Honour Judge Macgregor and a jury on two counts of burglary and two counts of handling stolen goods. The facts are set out in the judgment of the court.

R B Martin QC and *Charles Garside* for the applicant.
David Barker QC and *D W Brunning* for the Crown.
Simon D Brown and *John Laws* as amici curiae.

Cur adv vult

3rd June. **LAWTON LJ** read the following judgment of the court: The applicant on 30th April and 1st May 1979 was convicted in the Crown Court at Northampton before his Honour Judge Macgregor, after a trial lasting five weeks, on two counts of burglary (counts 3 and 6) and two counts of handling stolen goods (counts 2 and 5). The handling counts were alternatives to counts of burglary (counts 1 and 4), and the property mentioned in them consisted of articles stolen in the course of the burglaries which had been committed. He was sentenced to concurrent terms of five years' imprisonment on each of the burglary counts and to two years' imprisonment on each of the handling counts. He now applies for leave to appeal against his convictions.

The four burglaries charged in the indictment were of country houses situated within 20 miles of one another in Derbyshire, and all within a night's operating distance for a burglar from Salford, where the applicant lived. They were committed within a period of $7\frac{1}{2}$ months. On each occasion valuable antiques were stolen. On three of the four occasions the burglar or burglars hid the stolen articles near the house, the inference being that whoever was taking part would be travelling from the houses to base by road at night and did not wish to be found by the police in possession of stolen articles. On two occasions the burglar or burglars carried with them gas cylinders which, when attached to cutting appliances, could be used for gaining entry. Similar cylinders of identical make, one with a blowlamp attachment, were found in the applicant's house when it was searched. Antiques from three of the houses either were or had been in the applicant's possession. A pair of Georgian silver wine coasters, stolen from Ashford Hall during the night of 10th–11th September 1976, were entered by him for an auction which took place in London on 29th April 1977. An eighteenth-century French mantel clock, stolen from Windley Hall in the early hours of 11th March 1977, was found in his possession on 5th May 1977, as were a gold key and a lump of gold which came from Kedleston Hall, which was burgled during the night of 22nd–23rd April 1977. Scientific examination revealed that the gold had come from gold leaf stripped from an ornamental pagoda which had been stolen from Kedleston Hall during the burglary and which had been recovered by the police on 27th April 1977.

When interviewed by the police the applicant made a number of oral statements which were consistent with his knowing that the burglaries had taken place and his being in close touch with the burglars. At his trial he put forward alibi defences in respect of two of the burglaries, those at Tissington Hall and Kedleston Hall. The jury rejected both alibi defences. The one relating to Kedleston Hall had clearly been fabricated and involved the production of a forged hotel register. The evidence of the applicant's participation in the Tissington Hall burglary was very strong. Part of the

property stolen from that house had been hidden nearby in cushion covers and half a
a curtain. Cushion covers having a similar stitching and the other half of the curtain were found in the applicant's house.

The applicant handed in a notice of appeal at the prison on 31st May 1979. He was three days out of time, but we have granted an extension. He stated that his grounds of appeal were being prepared by counsel. On 4th July 1979 grounds of appeal settled by counsel were received by the registrar. They were lengthy and related mainly to alleged
b misdirection about the evidence. After they had been submitted a journalist, so counsel for the applicant informed us, told someone representing the applicant that at his trial the jury had been empanelled in breach of the guidelines issued by the Attorney General, Mr S C Silkin QC, and communicated to chief constables, including the Chief Constable of Northamptonshire, by Home Office circular 165/1975, dated 10th October 1975. Inquiries on behalf of the applicant showed that this was so. As a result further grounds
c of appeal were submitted on 13th February 1980. They can be summarised in the terms in which counsel for the applicant made his submissions to the court, namely that before the applicant's trial the police in Northamptonshire had checked the names of those summoned to attend the Crown Court to form a jury panel against the criminal records kept locally. They had supplied prosecuting counsel in this case (Mr David Barker QC) with particulars of the convictions of those on the panel, which he had wrongly used for
d the purpose of asking some members of the panel, not disqualified by their convictions from serving, but whose names were called to serve on the jury to try the applicant, to stand by for the Crown.

As there was no report of what had happened when the jury were empanelled, I asked counsel and those instructing them to attend a pre-appeal review. Counsel were able to agree that Mr Barker had asked four members of the jury panel to stand by for the
e Crown. His recollection was that he had asked one to do so because the officer in charge of the prosecution's case had told him that this member was known to him. The probabilities were that he had asked the others to stand by because, on the information supplied to him through the instructing solicitor, they had previous convictions. He could not remember whether they were convictions which would have disqualified them from service on a jury. As a result of further inquiries which were made following
f the directions which I gave, it was discovered that at least one of the three asked to stand by because of convictions was not disqualified thereby from jury service.

It is pertinent to record what was discovered when the jury panel was scrutinised by the police against the criminal records. Of the 100 persons believed by the jury officer of the Crown Court to be qualified for jury service and summoned to attend the Crown Court at the relevant time, the police on searching the local criminal records found that
g ten appeared to have previous convictions. Of these, two had convictions for road traffic offences, but in one of these cases there was a conviction for driving with excess alcohol. In six cases, however, the convictions were not positively linked with members of the panel; there was nothing more than a similarity of names. Of those who were positively linked two were disqualified from service; and of these two one had served a sentence of five years' imprisonment for buggery; the other had numerous findings of guilt as a
h juvenile for a variety of offences, including burglary and indecent assault, and four years before the start of the trial, when he was about 17, he had been sent to a detention centre for six months for eight offences of criminal damage. The probabilities are that the member of the jury who was not disqualified, but who was asked to stand by for the Crown, had been found guilty as a juvenile in 1974 for two cases of burglary and two cases of theft. He had been made the subject of a supervision order.

j We found these facts disturbing. The inference which we draw is that persons who are disqualified from jury service are not disclosing that they are so disqualified and that they are sitting on juries. We were told by counsel who appeared as amicus curiae that since 1974, when the present qualifications for jury service were fixed by the Juries Act 1974, there have been only two prosecutions for serving on a jury whilst disqualified, which is an offence under s 20(5) of the 1974 Act. In one of these two cases there was an acquittal; in the other the penalty imposed was a fine of £10. If two disqualified jurors can turn up in Northamptonshire out of a hundred summoned, the number is likely to be much greater when a panel is summoned from an urban area with a high level of crime. This case reveals how over-optimistic Lord Denning MR was when he said, obiter, in *R v Crown Court at Sheffield, ex parte Brownlow* [1980] 2 All ER 444 at 453, [1980] 2 WLR 892 at 900:

> '... as a matter of practical politics, even if jury vetting were allowed, the chances are a thousand to one against any juror being found unsuitable; and, if he should be, the chances of his being on any particular jury of 12, so as to influence the result, are minimal, especially in these days of majority verdicts.'

In this case had not counsel for the Crown asked three jurors to stand by for the Crown there might have been two disqualified jurors and one with findings of guilt for burglary and theft on the jury which tried the applicant. As a result of what he did the members of the jury which was empanelled had no convictions. That at least is certain.

Counsel for the applicant in the course of his submissions accepted that he had to satisfy this court that there had been a material irregularity *in the course of the trial.* This was because we exercise a statutory jurisdiction under which we can allow an appeal against conviction only if we think that one or more of three grounds for doing so have been established: see s 2(1) of the Criminal Appeal Act 1968. The only relevant ground in this case was that relied on by counsel for the applicant. He agreed that he could not rely on what happened before the trial started as a material irregularity. Prosecuting counsel had knowledge about the previous convictions of members of the jury panel which had come from a police search of the local criminal records, but it might have come from some other source. Both counsel for the applicant and counsel for the Crown accepted that the police had not acted unlawfully in disclosing to prosecuting counsel the information about the jury panel which they did. It is not too fanciful, we think, to envisage the case of an experienced prosecuting counsel recognising a member of the jury panel as being someone whom he had prosecuted to conviction.

The problem in this case is the use to which prosecuting counsel can put such information when a jury is empanelled. Counsel for the applicant submitted that he can only use it, when exercising the unquestionable common law right of prosecuting counsel to ask a member of the panel to stand by for the Crown, if on the information which he has there are reasonable grounds for thinking that he could show cause if he were called on to do so. To show cause he would have to be able to satisfy the court that the member of the panel was biased towards either the Crown or the accused: see 26 Halsbury's Laws (4th Edn) para 627, and the cases referred to in note 4. The bare fact that a member of the panel has a conviction recorded against him does not by itself prove bias. Further, submitted counsel for the applicant, on its true construction the 1974 Act envisages that all who are qualified to serve as jurors in the Crown Court shall be allowed to do so unless they are ineligible or disqualified or excused under Sch 1 to that Act.

The argument based on the construction of the 1974 Act is misconceived. The Act, as is shown by its long title, was one to consolidate certain enactments relating to juries, jurors and jury service, with corrections and improvements coming within the provisions of the Consolidation of Enactments (Procedure) Act 1949. Save in relation to the statutory qualifications for jury service, it did not make any fundamental changes in the law relating to juries and jurors. Save as altered by the Act—

> 'all enactments and rules of law relating to trials by jury, juries and jurors shall continue in force and, in criminal cases, continue to apply to proceedings in the Crown Court as they applied to proceedings before a court of oyer and terminer or gaol delivery.'

See s 21(5). Before 1974 prosecuting counsel, without showing cause, could ask a member of the jury panel to stand by for the Crown, and the trial judge could refuse to allow a member of the panel to be sworn, even though there had been no challenge by either party. Counsel for the applicant accepted that this was the law before 1974.

In our judgment, the 1974 Act, far from altering the old law, has by s 21(5) confirmed it. For centuries the law has provided by enactment who are qualified to serve as jurors, and has left the judges and the parties to criminal cases to decide which members of a jury panel were suitable to serve on a jury to try a particular case. To this extent the random selection of jurors has always been subject to qualification. Defendants have long had rights to peremptory challenges and to challenges for cause; prosecuting counsel for centuries have had the right to ask that a member of the panel should stand by for the Crown *and* to show cause why someone should not serve on a jury; and trial judges, as an aspect of their duty to see that there is a fair trial, have had a right to intervene to ensure that a competent jury is empanelled. The most common form of judicial intervention is when a judge notices that a member of the panel is infirm or has difficulty in reading or hearing; and nowadays jurors for whom taking part in a long trial would be unusually burdensome are often excluded from the jury by the judge.

In our judgment, the practice of the past is founded on common sense. A juror may be qualified to sit on juries generally but may not be suitable to try a particular case. An example put to counsel for the applicant during argument shows this. X is charged with unlawfully wounding a gamekeeper whilst out poaching. The prosecution's case is that he was a member of a gang at the material time. When the jury comes to be empanelled one member of the panel is found to have a number of convictions for poaching (not amounting to disqualifications) all in the petty sessional division where the gamekeeper worked. In our judgment, to allow such a man to serve on that jury would be an affront to justice. He would be unlikely to be impartial; and, although he would be only one of twelve, he could be expected to press his point of view; and its effect on his fellow-jurors would depend on his persuasive powers and their receptiveness to suggestion. The prospect of the case being tried according to the evidence would, in our judgment, be materially reduced. Counsel accepted that this would be so; but he used this example to support his submission that prosecuting counsel should ask members of the panel to stand by for the Crown only if there are reasonable grounds for thinking that there might be bias. In the example put to him there would be such grounds.

Counsel supported his submission in this respect by inviting our attention to the history of challenges to a jury panel made on behalf of the Crown. This history is long. We shall give it only in bare outline in this judgment, as it was reviewed in the case which we consider binds us, namely *Mansell v R* (1857) 8 E & B 54, 120 ER 20. More recent statements of the historical details are to be found in the argument of the Solicitor General in *R v Chandler* [1964] 2 QB 322 at 328–330, and in Mr J F McEldowney's article 'Stand by for the Crown: an Historical Analysis' [1979] Crim LR 272.

Before 1305 the Crown at common law had the right to challenge peremptorily an unlimited number of jurors. This led to abuse in that by exhausting the panel with peremptory challenges the Crown was able to ensure that the defendant was kept without trial and in custody until the next sessions. This abuse was put an end to by the Ordinance for Inquests 1305 (33 Edw 1 stat 4), the material parts of which are as follows:

> '. . . but if they that sue for the King will challenge any of those jurors, they shall assign of their challenge a cause certain, and the truth of the same challenge shall be enquired of according to the custom of the court . . .'

That statute was repealed by s 62 of the Juries Act 1825 and replaced by s 29 of that Act. This section, which is still in force with minor amendments (see s 12(5) of the 1974 Act), provides as follows:

> '. . . That in all Inquests to be taken before any of the Courts herein-before mentioned, wherein the King is a Party, howsoever it be, notwithstanding it be alleged by them that sue for the King, that the Jurors of those Inquests, or some of them, be not indifferent for the King, yet such Inquests shall not remain untaken

> for that Cause; but if they that sue for the King will challenge any of those Jurors, they shall assign of their Challenge a Cause certain, and the Truth of the same *a* Challenge shall be inquired of according to the Custom of the Court; and it shall be proceeded to the taking of the same Inquisitions, as it shall be found, if the Challenges be true or not, after the Discretion of the Court; and that no Person arraigned for Murder or Felony shall be admitted to any peremptory Challenge above the Number of Twenty.'

b

This section had to be construed in *Mansell v R*. The defendant was indicted for murder. When the panel of jurors was called several were challenged peremptorily for the prisoner, and several at the request of counsel for the Crown were ordered to 'stand by'. By this time only nine jurors had been sworn, and no more members of the panel were in court, although other members were out of court considering their verdict in another case. When the names of those ordered to stand by were called again counsel for *c* the Crown once more asked that they should stand by. Counsel for the prisoner submitted that the Crown should now show cause. Prosecuting counsel replied that there was no need for him to show cause, as the full panel had not been exhausted, and that he was obliged to show cause only when it had been. The trial judge ruled in favour of the Crown. The record was removed by writ of error into the Queen's Bench before Lord Campbell CJ, Wightman, Erle and Crompton JJ. *d*

The judgment of the court was delivered by Lord Campbell CJ. He started by saying (8 E & B 54 at 70–72, 120 ER 20 at 27):

> 'Our judgment chiefly expands upon the right construction of the ancient statute, 4 stat. 33 Ed. 1, entitled "An ordinance for inquests" which was reenacted by 6 G. 4, c. 50, s. 29 [ie the Juries Act 1825] . . . But there was no intention of taking away *e* all power of peremptory challenge from the Crown, while that power, to the number of thirty five, was left to the prisoner. Indeed, unless this power were given under certain restrictions to both sides, it is quite obvious that justice could not be satisfactorily administered; for it must often happen that a juror is returned on the panel who does not stand indifferent, and who is not fit to serve upon the trial, although no legal evidence could be adduced to prove his unfitness. The object of *f* the statute is fully attained if the Crown be prevented from exercising its power of peremptory challenge, so as to make the trial go off while there are twelve of those returned upon the panel who cannot be proved to be liable to a valid objection. Accordingly, the course has invariably been, from the passing of the statute to the present time, to permit the Crown to challenge without cause till the panel has been called over and exhausted, and then to call over the names of the jurors peremptorily *g* challenged by the Crown, and to put the Crown to assign cause, so that, if twelve of those upon the panel remain as to whom no just cause of objection can be assigned, the trial may proceed. In our books of authority, the rule is laid down that the King need not shew any cause of his challenge till the whole panel be gone through, and it appear that there will not be a full jury without the person so challenged.'

h

It is clear from this passage that Lord Campbell CJ regarded prosecuting counsel's request that a member of the panel should stand by for the Crown as being the equivalent of a peremptory challenge which could be exercised until the whole panel had been called. It was then, and only then, that prosecuting counsel had to show cause if he still wanted to exclude from the jury any of those ordered to stand by. He referred to requests to stand by as 'the peremptory challenges of the Crown' (see 8 E & B 54 at 76, *j* 120 ER 20 at 29).

Later in his judgment Lord Campbell CJ dealt with a point which had arisen because the trial judge had suggested that a member of the panel should withdraw because, before being sworn, he had said that he had conscientious scruples against capital punishment (8 E & B 54 at 80–81, 120 ER 20 at 30);

> 'But we wish it to be understood that we by no means acquiesce in the doctrine
> a boldly contended for at the bar, on the authority of Brownlow in an *Anonymous case* ((1607) 1 Brownl 41, 123 ER 652), that a Judge, on the trial of a criminal case, has no authority, if there be no challenge either by the Crown or by the prisoner, to excuse a juryman on the panel when he is called, or to order him to withdraw, although he is palpably unfit by physical or mental infirmity to do his duty in the jury box. We are not now to define the limits of this authority; but we cannot
> b doubt that there may be cases, as if a juryman were completely deaf, or blind, or afflicted with bodily disease which rendered it impossible to continue in the jury box without danger to his life, or were insane, or drunk, or with his mind so occupied by the impending death of a near relation that he could not duly attend to the evidence, in which, although from there being no counsel employed on either side, or for some reason, there is no objection made to the juryman being sworn, it
> c would be the duty of the Judge to prevent the scandal and the perversion of justice which would arise from compelling or permitting such a juryman to be sworn, and to join in a verdict on the life or death of a fellow creature.'

This judgment was taken into the Exchequer Chamber by means of a second writ of error. The appeal was heard by Cockburn CJ, Williams, Willes JJ, and Bramwell, Watson and Channell BB. The judgment of Lord Campbell CJ was affirmed. In the course of his
d judgment Channel B said (8 E & B 85 at 115, 120 ER 32 at 42):

> 'We are to construe this old Act by the aid of the decisions, reading it with the assistance of what has been done since in course of law. It is clear, then, that till the panel is exhausted, and it is seen that a full jury cannot be obtained, the Crown has a right to ask to have a juror to stand by: and, whether this is properly called a
> e challenge or not, the course said on the record to have been adopted at the trial was right.'

In our judgment, *Mansell v R* established beyond argument that prosecuting counsel have a right to request that a member of the jury panel shall stand by, and that this right can be exercised without there being a provable valid objection, until such time as the
f panel is exhausted; and when it is, if the Crown still wants to exclude a member of the jury from the panel, a valid objection must be shown. It follows that what prosecuting counsel did in this case, by requesting that a member of the panel should stand by because he had a conviction, was not a material, or indeed any, irregularity in the course of the trial.

Complaint was made in the grounds of appeal that counsel for the Crown had not
g supplied the defence with the information which he had about members of the panel. In the circumstances of this case there was no reason why he should have done so. In general, the fewer people who know about any conviction which a member of a jury panel may have the better. This is probably why, when prosecuting counsel do exercise the Crown's right of stand by, they are never asked why they are doing so. We would expect them to act responsibly and not to request a stand by unnecessarily. In general,
h for example, a conviction for reckless driving ought not to provide a reason for a request to stand by when the indictment charges burglary; but it might if causing death by reckless driving were charged. Cases may occur when it would be fair for prosecuting counsel to disclose his information to the defence, as, for example, if it were known to him that a member of the panel was a relative of the principal police witness. What should be done must be left to the discretion of prosecuting counsel.

j Before leaving this part of the case we wish to stress that this judgment is concerned solely with what happened in the course of the applicant's trial. The facts which have been revealed show that some scrutiny of jury panels is necessary if disqualified persons are to be excluded from juries. The police are the only authority able to do this. Since it is a criminal offence for a person to serve on a jury knowing that he is disqualified, for the police to scrutinise the list of potential jurors to see if any are disqualified is to do no more than to perform their usual function of preventing the commission of offences. In the course of looking at criminal records convictions are likely to be revealed which do *a* not amount to disqualifications. We can see no reason why information about such convictions should not be passed on to prosecuting counsel. He may consider that a juror with a conviction for burglary would be unsuitable to sit on a jury trying a burglar; and if he does so he can exercise the Crown's rights. Many persons, but not burglars, would probably think that he should.

The practice of supplying prosecuting counsel with information about potential jurors' *b* convictions has been followed during the whole of our professional lives, and almost certainly for generations before us. It is not unlawful, and has not until recently been thought to be unsatisfactory. We have not been concerned in any way with, and make no comment on, the giving to prosecution counsel of information other than that relating to convictions, or with the desirability of making other inquiries about members of a jury panel. In so far as the obiter dicta of this court in *R v Crown Court at Sheffied, ex* *c* *parte Brownlow* [1980] 2 All ER 444 at 453, [1980] 2 WLR 892 at 900 differ from what we have decided in this case we justify our presumption by the knowledge that we have been able to examine the issues raised in greater depth than our brethren were able to do. Further, it is no part of our function to criticise either the contents of Home Office circular 165/1975 or the Attorney-General's statement entitled 'Checks on Potential Jurors', which he issued in October 1978. Both the circular and the statement contain *d* advice; they were not directions having the force of law, as counsel as amicus curiae accepted. Whether the advice should be changed in the light of this judgment is for the Home Secretary and the Attorney General to consider.

The submissions of counsel for the applicant about the trial judge's rulings and directions can be summarised as follows: first, that he should have withdrawn the two handling counts from the jury, and, second, that he misdirected the jury by inviting *e* them to consider the evidence on one burglary count when considering that on another.

The complaint in relation to the handling counts had two facets. First, counsel submitted that, as the prosecution were alleging that the applicant had been the burglar at all four country houses, they should not have been allowed to continue with the alternative handling charges. He invited our attention to the case of *R v Christ* [1951] 2 All ER 254. In our judgment, there is nothing in this complaint. Although the *f* prosecution invited the jury to return verdicts of guilty to burglary, there was evidence, other than that relating to burglary, on which the jury could return verdicts of guilty of handling. This case was very different from *R v Christ*. In that case when the jury rejected, as they did, the evidence relating to larceny there was no evidence left relating to receiving.

Counsel's second submission about the handling counts had more substance. At the *g* end of the prosecution's evidence relating to the applicant's possession of the two Georgian coasters stolen from Ashford Hall during the night of 10th–11th September 1976 the only evidence of possession of recently stolen property was his assertion to the police that he had bought them in February 1977, that is, five months later, from a dealer about whom he gave no particulars. The judge must have thought that this was capable of being evidence of recent possession. In his direction to the jury he explained correctly *h* what was meant by recent possession and left them to decide, having regard to the nature and quality of the articles, whether there was evidence of recent possession. They must have decided that there was, and drew inferences of guilt. In our judgment, they were entitled to do so. The evidence relating to the eighteenth-century clock stolen from Windley Hall during the early hours of 11th March 1977, and found in the applicant's house at the beginning of May 1977, was clearly evidence of recent possession. The jury *j* were correctly directed as to it.

In his directions to the jury about how they were to approach the evidence the trial judge told them that they were to consider the evidence on each count separately, but that when doing so they could consider the evidence on other counts for the purpose of identifying the applicant as the burglar on a particular count. This was because of the

similarities between the burglaries. Counsel accepted that this direction was correct,
a provided that there were similarities. He submitted that there were not. In our judgment, there were. On the evidence the jury could reasonably have inferred that all four burglaries were committed by the same man operating from a base not too far away. The burglar had left his 'hallmark' on three of them, including that at Tissington Hall, by the kind of articles that he had stolen and the way in which he had hidden the stolen property near the scenes of his crimes. The evidence relating to Tissington Hall
b identified him as the man who had burgled that house. His 'hallmark' left at Windley Hall and Kedleston Hall, together with his possession of property stolen from those houses, was capable of identifying him with those burglaries; and his possession of gas cylinders when carrying out the Tissington Hall burglary, coupled with the finding of similar gas cylinders in his house, was capable of linking him with the Ashford Hall burglary. He was fortunate that the jury acquitted him of the Ashford Hall and Windley
c Hall burglaries. In our judgment, there was nothing wrong with the judge's directions to the jury about the evidence.

The application for leave to appeal is refused.

Application refused.

d Solicitors: *John Bentham & Co*, Manchester (for the applicant); *R C Beadon*, Northampton (for the Crown); *Director of Public Prosecutions.*

N P Metcalfe Esq Barrister.

e

Note

STATEMENT BY THE ATTORNEY GENERAL

JURY CHECKS

1. I have now completed the review, which I have been carrying out over recent
f months in consultation with the Home Secretary, the Lord Chancellor and the Director of Public Prosecutions, of the arrangements whereby jury checks are carried out in a limited number of cases under the guidelines laid down by my predecessor [see the note appended to *R v Crown Court at Sheffield, ex parte Brownlow* [1980] 2 All ER 444 at 457]. In reaching my conclusions I have taken account of the recent judgments of the Court of Appeal particularly that in the case of *R v Mason* [see p 777, ante]. A copy of the revised
g guidelines which I propose to issue has been placed in the House of Commons Library.

2. The existing law provides, as it has for over six hundred years and rightly in my view, that the parties to any jury trial may inspect a copy of the panel from which the jury in their trial will be chosen, and there is no legal restriction on the use which may be made of this information. It has been accepted by the courts that the objects of this provision were to enable the parties to inquire about the members of the panel and to
h decide whether any should be challenged. I have also taken into account that, although the selection of those who are summoned for jury service from amongst those qualified and the final selection of those who are called to serve on a particular jury must be random, both parties to criminal proceedings have the right to object to a juror called to serve, the exercise of which inevitably limits the truly random nature of the jury which eventually tries the case.

j 3. A distinction must be drawn between checks to which my guidelines refer, namely checks on the records of police Special Branches, and checks of criminal records which may be made for the primary purpose of preventing persons who are disqualified by reason of their previous convictions from sitting on a jury. It is a criminal offence for a disqualified person knowingly to serve on a jury, and a check of criminal records of the members of a panel is a matter for the police. That was recognised by the Court of

Appeal in *R v Mason* as a proper thing to be done. The Association of Chief Officers of Police, after discussions with the Home Office, is making recommendations to its members as to the circumstances and procedures relating to checks on criminal records and these will be annexed to my guidelines.

4. The checks, which for convenience I shall refer to as 'authorised checks', and to which my guidelines refer are checks which go beyond criminal records and for purposes wider than the mere discovery of previous convictions. I consider that it is in the public interest that the prosecution should continue to make use of its right to make inquiries about a jury panel with a view to exercising its right to stand by a potential juror. The practice, however, should not be unlimited, and I therefore indorse the general principles of the previous guidelines which were self-imposed restraints on the part of the Director of Public Prosecutions as the prosecutor. Experience, recent observations of the Court of Appeal and a keen public interest in the subject have nevertheless caused me to make some revisions to the guidelines. The most significant are as follows:

(i) no check on the records of police Special Branches will be made except on my authority following a recommendation from the Director of Public Prosecutions;

(ii) except in terrorist cases such checks will not be authorised in cases involving so-called strong political motives;

(iii) in cases involving security, such as under the Official Secrets Act 1911 to 1939, such checks will only be authorised when national security is involved and it is expected that the court will be asked to sit in camera;

(iv) in no other type of case will such checks be authorised;

(v) except where and in so far as it may be necessary to confirm the identity of a member of the panel against whom the initial checks had raised doubts, checks will not be made which go beyond checks on criminal records or those of police Special Branches.

(vi) all parties to proceedings have a statutory right to access to inspect the jury panel under a s 5(2) of the Juries Act 1974; therefore the judge's authority for access is not required and will not be sought. However, the judge and defence counsel will be informed when a check has been authorised;

(vii) the result of an authorised check will be sent to the Director of Public Prosecutions. The Director will then decide, having regard to the provisions of the guidelines, what information ought to be brought to the attention of prosecuting counsel;

(viii) records will be kept by the Director of Public Prosecutions which I will see and thus be able to monitor the operation of the guidelines.

5. I have recognised that the defence may have a particular reason to wish to have the panel checked for disqualified persons or to seek assistance in obtaining information relative to its right of peremptory challenge but has no access to the information available to the Crown. It is also my view that the courts have no jurisdiction to order the police to reveal information on their records relating to jurors. Accordingly, in cases which would fall within my guidelines I will be prepared to consider a request made by defence counsel through the Director for assistance in obtaining information. I understand that chief constables, on the general recommendation of their association, will be prepared to consider a request relating to checks on criminal records if approved by the Director. In both cases the results of any check undertaken will be sent to the Director of Public Prosecutions who will treat them in accordance with my guidelines. The intention of this proposal is merely to assist the defence and not in any way to restrict the right of the defendant to inspect the panel and to take such action as is lawful.

ATTORNEY GENERAL'S GUIDELINES ON JURY CHECKS

(Amended, July 1980)

1. The principles which are generally to be observed are (a) that members of a jury should be selected at random from the panel, (b) the Juries Act 1974 identified those classes of persons who alone are either disqualified from or ineligible for service on a

jury; no other class of person may be treated as disqualified or ineligible, and (c) the correct way for the Crown to seek to exclude a member of the panel from sitting as a juror is by the exercise in open court of the right to request a stand by or, if necessary, to challenge for cause.

2. Parliament has provided safeguards against jurors who may be corrupt or biased. In addition to the provision for majority verdicts, there is the sanction of a criminal offence for a disqualified person to serve on a jury. The removal of a disqualified person from the panel is a matter for court officials, but any search of criminal records for the purpose of ascertaining whether or not a jury panel includes any disqualified person is a matter for the police as the only authority able to carry out such a search and as part of their usual function of preventing the commission of offences. The recommendations of the Association of Chief Police Officers respecting checks on criminal records for disqualified persons are annexed to these guidelines.

3. There are, however, certain exceptional types of case of public importance for which the provisions as to majority verdicts and the disqualification of jurors may not be sufficient to ensure the proper administration of justice. In such cases it is in the interests both of justice and the public that there should be further safeguards against the possibility of bias and in such cases checks which go beyond the investigation of criminal records may be necessary.

4. These classes of case may be defined broadly as (a) cases in which national security is involved and part of the evidence is likely to be heard in camera, and (b) terrorist cases.

5. The particular aspects of these cases which may make it desirable to seek extra precautions are (a) in security cases a danger that a juror, either voluntarily or under pressure, may make an improper use of evidence which, because of its sensitivity, has been given in camera, (b) in both security and terrorist cases the danger that a juror's political beliefs are so biased as to go beyond normally reflecting the broad spectrum of views and interests in the community to reflect the extreme views of sectarian interest or pressure group to a degree which might interfere with his fair assessment of the facts of the case or lead him to exert improper pressure on his fellow jurors.

6. In order to ascertain whether in exceptional cases of the above nature either of these factors might seriously influence a potential juror's impartial performance of his duties, it may be necessary to conduct a limited investigation of the panel. Such further investigation beyond one on criminal records made for disqualifications may only be made with records of police Special Branches. No checks other than on these sources and no general inquiries are to be made save to the limited extent that they may be needed to confirm the identity of a juror about whom the initial check has raised serious doubts.

7. No investigation of the records of police Special Branches should be made save with the personal authority of the Attorney General on the application of the Director of Public Prosecutions and such checks are hereafter referred to as 'authorised checks'. When a chief officer of police has reason to believe that it is likely that an authorised check may be desirable and proper in accordance with these guidelines he should refer to matter to the Director of Public Prosecutions with a view to his having the conduct of the prosecution from an early stage. The Director will make any appropriate application to the Attorney General.

8. The result of any authorised check will be sent to the Director of Public Prosecutions. The Director will then decide, having regard to the matters set out in para 5 above, what information ought to be brought to the attention of prosecuting counsel.

9. No right of stand by should be exercised by counsel for the Crown on the basis of information obtained as a result of an authorised check unless the information is such as, having regard to the facts of the case and the offences charged, to afford strong reason for believing that a particular juror might be a security risk, be susceptible to improper approaches or be influenced in arriving at a verdict for the reasons given above.

10. Where a potential juror is asked to stand by for the Crown, there is no duty to disclose to the defence the information on which it was founded; but counsel may use his discretion to disclose it if its nature and source permit it.

11. When information revealed in the course of an authorised check is not such as to cause counsel for the Crown to ask for a juror to stand by but does give reason to believe that he may be biased against the accused, the defence should be given, at least, an indication of why that potential juror may be inimical to their interests; but because of its nature and source it may not be possible to give the defence more than a general indication.

12. A record is to be kept by the Director of Public Prosecutions of the use made by counsel of the information passed to him and of the jurors stood by or challenged by the parties to the proceedings. A copy of this record is to be forwarded to the Attorney General for the sole purpose of enabling him to monitor the operation of these guidelines.

13. No use of the information obtained as a result of an authorised check is to be made except as may be necessary in direct relation to or arising out of the trial for which the check was authorised.

Law Officers' Department
31st July 1980.

ANNEX TO THE ATTORNEY GENERAL'S GUIDELINES ON JURY CHECKS

RECOMMENDATIONS OF THE ASSOCIATION OF CHIEF POLICE OFFICERS

1. The Association of Chief Police Officers recommends that in the light of observations made in *R v Mason* (see p 777, ante) the police should undertake a check of the names of potential jurors against records of previous convictions in any case when the Director of Public Prosecutions or a chief constable considers that in all the circumstances it would be in the interests of justice so to do, namely (i) in any case in which there is reason to believe that attempts are being made to circumvent the statutory provisions excluding disqualified persons from service on a jury, including any case when there is reason to believe that a particular juror may be disqualified, (ii) in any case in which it is believed that in a previous related abortive trial an attempt was made to interfere with a juror or jurors, and (iii) in any other case in which in the opinion of the Director of Public Prosecutions or the chief constable it is particularly important to ensure that no disqualified person serves on the jury.

2. The association also recommends that no further checks should be made unless authorised by the Attorney General under his guidelines and no inquiries carried out save to the limited extent that they may be needed to confirm the identity of a juror about whom the initial check has raised serious doubts.

3. The association further recommends that chief constables should agree to undertake checks of jurors on behalf of the defence only if requested to do so by the Director of Public Prosecutions acting on behalf of the Attorney General. Accordingly if the police are approached directly with such a request they will refer it to the Director.

4. When, as a result of any checks of criminal records information is obtained which suggests that, although not disqualified under the terms of the Juries Act 1974, a person may be unsuitable to sit as a member of a particular jury the police or the Director may pass the relevant information to prosecuting counsel, who will decide what use to make of it.

a Wadham Stringer Finance Ltd v Meaney

QUEEN'S BENCH DIVISION
WOOLF J
30th JUNE, 1st, 18th JULY 1980

b *Sale of goods – Conditional sale agreement – Statutory right to terminate agreement – Effect of clause entitling seller to elect for accelerated payment on buyer's default – Accelerated payment comprising unpaid balance of purchase price plus certain fees and charges – Whether accelerated payment clause void – Whether accelerated payment clause restricting buyer's right to terminate agreement 'at any time before the final payment ... falls due' – Whether accelerated payment when due the final payment due under agreement – Whether accelerated payment when due*
c *terminating agreement – Whether liability under clause exceeding statutory liability imposed 'by reason of termination of' agreement – Whether clause a penalty or genuine pre-estimate of seller's loss on early termination of agreement – Hire-Purchase Act 1965, ss 27(1), 28(1)(b), 29(2)(b)(c).*

The defendant ('the buyer') entered into a conditional sale agreement with the plaintiffs ('the sellers') in order to finance the purchase of a car. The agreement was subject to the
d Hire-Purchase Act 1965, but expressly gave the buyer the right to terminate the agreement on the terms of the statutory notice under the Act regarding a buyer's right to terminate, the notice being deemed to form part of the agreement. Under the agreement the buyer was required to pay the purchase price of £2,145 by a deposit and 36 monthly instalments. The agreement also included an 'accelerated payment clause' which provided that if the buyer defaulted in the punctual payment of two or more of
e the instalments the sellers could elect to call on the buyer for accelerated payment, comprising the unpaid balance of the purchase price and certain fees and charges and interest thereon, on giving the buyer written notice to pay the amount outstanding within ten days. The clause also provided for interest at the rate of $1\frac{1}{2}\%$ per month to be charged on the amount of the accelerated payment if it was not paid within the ten days. On expiry of the ten-day period title to the car would pass to the buyer. The buyer
f paid the deposit but failed to pay any of the instalments. The sellers elected to call for accelerated payment and when the buyer failed to pay the outstanding amount within the ten-day period, brought an action against her claiming £1,386 being the amount of the accelerated payment. At the trial of the action the buyer contended that the accelerated payment restricted her statutory right under s 27(1)[a] of the 1965 Act to terminate the agreement 'at any time before the final payment under [the] agreement
g falls due' and was therefore void under s 29(2)(*b*)[b] of that Act. The buyer submitted (i) that the final payment did not fall due until the last of the 36 instalments became payable and the accelerated payment clause was thus an attempt to interfere with her right under

a Section 27(1), so far as material, is set out at p 794 *e f*, post
h *b* Section 29, so far as material, provides:
'(1) Any provision to which this subsection applies shall be void.
'(2) The preceding subsection applies to any provision in any ... conditional sale agreement ... (*b*) whereby the right conferred by section 27 of this Act to terminate a ... conditional sale agreement is excluded or restricted, or whereby any liability, in addition to the liability imposed by section 28 of this Act, is imposed on a ... buyer by reason of the termination of a ...
j conditional sale agreement under the said section 27, or (*c*) whereby a ... buyer, after the termination in any manner whatsoever of a ... conditional sale agreement ... is (apart from any liability which has accrued before the termination) subject to a liability to pay an amount which exceeds whichever is the lesser of the two following amounts, that is to say—(i) the amount mentioned in paragraph (*a*) or (as the case may be) in paragraph (*b*) of section 28(1) of this Act, and (ii) an amount equal to the loss sustained by the ... seller in consequence of the termination of the agreement ...'

s 27(1) to terminate the agreement at any time until then, or (ii) alternatively, that the provision in the clause for payment of interest on non-payment of the accelerated a payment within the prescribed period prevented the accelerated payment, when due, from being final payment under the agreement. The buyer further contended that if the clause was not void by virtue of s 27(1) it was nevertheless void under s 29(2)(*b*) because, if the buyer were to exercise her statutory right to terminate the agreement after she became liable to pay the accelerated payment, she would be under a liability exceeding that imposed by s 28(1)(*b*)[c] of the 1965 Act on termination of the agreement; and if it was b not void under s 29(2)(*b*) it was nevertheless void by virtue of s 29(2)(*c*) because, although exercise by the sellers of their rights under the clause terminated the agreement, the amount payable by the buyer under the clause exceeded the amount she was required by s 29(2)(*c*) to pay on termination of the agreement. Finally, the buyer contended that the accelerated payment clause was a penalty clause and not a genuine pre-estimate of the sellers' loss on early termination of the agreement. c

Held – The buyer was liable to the sellers for the accelerated payment claimed, for the following reasons—

(1) The accelerated payment clause was not void by virtue of s 29(2)(*b*) of the 1965 Act because when it fell due on the expiry of ten days from the date of the notice to pay it became the 'final payment' under the agreement for the purposes of s 27(1) of that Act, d and thereafter the buyer's right under s 27(1) to terminate the agreement was lost. The buyer retained, by the express terms of the agreement, the right to terminate the agreement up to the date when the accelerated payment became due. It followed that the accelerated payment clause did not exclude or restrict the buyer's right under s 27(1) to terminate so as to be void under s 29(2)(*b*). Furthermore the provision in the clause for payment of interest, thereby imposing on the buyer a liability additional to that imposed e on her under s 28(1)(*b*) of the 1965 Act, was not void under s 29(2)(*b*) because the additional liability for interest was imposed not 'by reason of the termination of . . . [the] agreement' for the purposes of s 29(2)(*b*) but by the sellers' exercise of their rights under the clause, and it was in any event a liability which had 'accrued before the termination' for the purposes of s 28(1) (see p 795 *b* to *j*, post).

(2) The accelerated payment clause was not void under s 29(2)(*c*) since the fact that an f accelerated payment had fallen due under the clause did not terminate the agreement, which remained in force until the buyer and the seller had performed their obligations under the clause; and therefore the buyer's liability under the clause, though exceeding the amount specified in s 29(2)(*c*), was not a liability which arose after the termination of the agreement within s 29(2)(*c*) (see p 796 *e f*, post).

(3) The accelerated payment clause was in the circumstances a genuine pre-estimate g of what the sellers would lose because of the early termination of the agreement and accordingly was not void as being a penalty (see p 797 *d* to *f*, post).

Notes

For the statutory right to terminate a conditional sale agreement, and for the debtor's liability on termination of the agreement, see 22 Halsbury's Laws (4th Edn) para 262. h

For the Hire-Purchase Act 1965, ss 27, 28, 29, see 30 Halsbury's Statutes (3rd Edn) 85, 86, 87.

As from a day to be appointed the 1965 Act is to be repealed by the Consumer Credit Act 1974, s 192(3)(*b*) and Sch 5, Part I.

c Section 28(1), so far as material, provides: 'Where . . . the buyer under a conditional sale agreement, terminates the agreement by virtue of the last preceding section, then, subject to the following j provisions of this section, and without prejudice to any liability which has accrued before the termination, he shall be liable . . . (*b*) in the case of a conditional sale agreement, to pay the amount (if any) by which one-half of the total purchase price exceeds the total of the sums paid and the sums due in respect of the total purchase price immediately before the termination, or if . . . the agreement specifies a lesser amount, he shall be liable to pay the amount so specified.'

Cases referred to in judgment

Bridge v Campbell Discount Co Ltd [1962] 1 All ER 385, [1962] AC 600, [1962] 2 WLR 439, HL, Digest (Cont Vol A) 648, *39a*.
Dunlop Pneumatic Tyre Co Ltd v New Garage and Motor Co Ltd [1915] AC 79, [1914–15] All ER Rep 739, 83 LJKB 1574, 111 LT 862, HL, 17 Digest (Reissue) 178, *551*.
Glasgow Navigation Co v Iron Ore Co [1910] AC 293, 79 LJPC 83, 102 LT 435, 11 Asp MLC 387, HL, 16 Digest (Repl) 119, *42*.
Protector Endowment Loan and Annuity Co v Grice (1880) 5 QBD 592, 49 LJQB 812, 43 LT 564, 45 JP 172, CA, 7 Digest (Reissue) 214, *1426*.
Sun Life Assurance Co of Canada v Jervis [1944] 1 All ER 469, [1944] AC 111, 113 LJKB 174, 170 LT 345, HL, 36(1) Digest (Reissue) 548, *41*.
Wallingford v Mutual Society (1880) 5 App Cas 685, 50 LJQB 49, 43 LT 258, HL, 7 Digest (Reissue) 214, *1427*.

Action

By a writ dated 27th November 1979 the plaintiffs, Wadham Stringer Finance Ltd, claimed against the defendant, Christine Anne Meaney, the sum of £1,386 being the accelerated sum due from the defendant under a conditional sale agreement dated 12th July 1979 made between her and the plaintiffs in respect of the sale of a Triumph motor car. The facts are set out in the judgment.

Richard Southwell QC and *Richard Mawrey* for the plaintiffs.
Michael Hutchison QC and *Simon Tuckey* for the defendant.

Cur adv vult

18th July. **WOOLF J** read the following judgment: This is an action by the plaintiffs, a company which is jointly owned by Wadham Stringer Ltd and United Dominion Trust Ltd, for a sum of money alleged to be due under the terms of a conditional sale agreement.

At the outset of the case, counsel for the plaintiffs explained that the action is a test action to ascertain the effect of the Hire-Purchase Act 1965 and the law as to penalties on certain clauses in the plaintiffs' standard conditional sale agreement. The points raised are of general application on which, surprisingly, there is no previous authority which is directly applicable.

Counsel for the plaintiffs placed before me a bundle of correspondence which showed that an agreement had been reached between the parties, the effect of which can be summarised by saying that the liability of the defendant would be the same whatever the outcome of the action. She would only have to pay the balance of the cash price, and not the charges, by instalments which were not to exceed the amount of the contractual instalments of £50·98. She was also to have an indemnity as to her costs.

After counsel for the plaintiffs had referred me to the relevant authorities, I intimated that my view was that it would be wrong as a matter of principle for me to proceed with an action which was so clearly academic, particularly as the plaintiffs regarded the case as involving an important point of law which could well result in an appeal whatever the outcome.

Having made known my views, the parties asked for an adjournment, which I granted. When the hearing resumed I was informed that the agreement had been varied so that if the defendant succeeded in the action the plaintiffs would waive all further rights against her. This, in my view, made a real difference to the situation. Both the plaintiffs and the defendant now had a real interest in succeeding in the action and I no longer regarded the case as being academic and covered by the principles laid down in the authorities to which I have been referred, including *Glasgow Navigation Co v Iron Ore Co* [1910] AC 293 and *Sun Life Assurance Co of Canada v Jervis* [1944] 1 All ER 469, [1944] AC 111. Accordingly I continued with the hearing; the facts of the case being as follows.

The defendant entered into the conditional sale agreement on 12th July 1979 in respect of a Triumph motor car. Under the agreement, which was subject to the 1965 Act, the total purchase price of £2,145·63 was payable by a deposit of £307·35 and one instalment of £53·98 and 35 consecutive monthly instalments of £50·98. The defendant, having paid the deposit, made no further payments and in these proceedings the plaintiffs claim £1,386 under what has been described as 'the accelerated payment clause' of the agreement.

The first issue in this case is whether that clause is void because it contravenes the provisions of the 1965 Act. The second issue is whether, assuming the clause is valid, it provides for the recovery of a penalty which is unenforceable in law.

In order to consider these issues it is necessary to set out the relevant terms of the agreement. The agreement begins with a schedule which sets out the name of the buyer, the make and description of the goods, details of insurance and the relevant figures. This is followed by a statement:

> 'The statutory notices set out below are to be deemed to form part of this agreement only if the transaction evidenced by the agreement is one to which the provisions of the Hire Purchase Act 1965 as from time to time amended apply.'

The notice as to the right of the buyer to terminate the agreement, in the standard form required by the 1965 Act, is duly set out. Below this there is a heading 'TERMS' which is followed by the various clauses of the agreement, the majority appearing overleaf. It is not necessary to refer to all the terms but I am afraid I must refer to some:

> 'TERMS OF PAYMENT 1. On or before the making of this agreement the buyer shall pay to the seller the deposit specified in the schedule and shall punctually pay the several instalments of the balance of the total purchase price as set out in the schedule on the dates therein specified. Punctual payment of the said instalments shall be of the essence of this agreement and the buyer agrees to pay interest at the rate of 1½% per month on any overdue instalment until payment thereof such interest to accrue on a daily basis as well after as before judgment. The rights of the seller hereunder shall not be affected by any time or other indulgence that the seller may see fit to grant to the buyer . . .
>
> 'EARLY SETTLEMENT 10. The buyer may settle this transaction early (provided each previous instalment of the balance of the total purchase price has been paid when due) by paying to the seller a sum comprising such of the balance financed as remains unpaid any unpaid acceptance fee and such percentage of the charges specified in the schedule as remains unpaid and will accrue down to a date three months after the date of the instalment which would have next followed the date of early settlement (instalments being appropriated first to charges by the rule of 78 and then to part payment of the balance financed): the resulting total is then rounded off upwards if ending in 50p or more or downwards if less to the nearest whole £1.
>
> 'DEFAULT IN PAYMENT 11. Should the buyer fail to pay the deposit in full at the time when this agreement is made or make default in the punctual payment of two or more monthly instalments of the balance of the total purchase price or where instalments fall due at intervals of more than a month in the punctual payment of such an instalment for 32 days or more the seller may if it elects to do so call upon the buyer for an acceleration in payment of monies payable under this agreement in preference to pursuing its rights under the Termination Clause hereof. In the event that the seller elects to call for an acceleration in payment hereunder the seller shall (a) by written notice to the buyer (either served personally on the buyer or sent to the buyer by post to the buyer's usual or last-known address) call upon the buyer within a period of ten days from the date of such notice to pay to the seller a sum comprising such of the balance financed as remains unpaid at the date of notice, any unpaid deposit and/or acceptance fee and such percentage of the charges specified in

the schedule as will accrue down to a date three months after the date of the instalment which would next have followed the date of notice (instalments being appropriated first to charges by the rule of 78) and also to pay interest on such sum from the expiration of the said period of ten days until payment thereof at the rate of 1½ per centum per month and on the expiration of the said period of ten days title to and property in the goods shall pass to the buyer notwithstanding the provisions of the Title to the Goods Clause hereof save that should the buyer have paid the arrears within the period of ten days from the date of such notice the agreement shall continue in full force and effect unless the transaction evidenced by this agreement is one to which the provisions of the Act apply and the buyer shall have exercised the buyer's right of termination set out in the Statutory Notice overleaf (b) not be entitled after service of the notice referred to in paragraph (a) above to terminate this agreement under the Termination Clause hereof unless the buyer shall have paid the arrears under paragraph (a) hereof and subsequently makes further default in payment. But should the agreement terminate automatically under the provisions of the Termination Clause hereof during the currency of any acceleration notice served under paragraph (a) above the said notice shall cease to have any effect.

'TERMINATION 12. (a) Should the buyer fail to pay the deposit in full at the time when this agreement is made or make default in the punctual payment of two or more monthly instalments of the balance of the total purchase price or where the instalments fall due at intervals of more than a month in the punctual payment of such an instalment for 32 days or more and fail to pay the same within ten days of the seller having demanded the same or, where the transaction evidenced by this agreement is one to which the provisions of the Act apply, within ten days after the service upon the buyer of a notice of default as prescribed by s. 25 of the Act or if the buyer does or suffers anything whatsoever which in the seller's opinion bona fide formed upon reasonable grounds will or may have the effect of jeopardising the seller's right of property in the goods (if any) then in each and every such case the seller may by written notice (either served personally on the buyer or sent to the buyer by post to the buyer's usual or last known address) forthwith and for all purposes terminate this agreement and thereupon the buyer shall no longer be in possession of the goods with the seller's consent. Should the buyer or anyone included in the expression "the buyer" have a receiving order made or be made bankrupt or if any body corporate included in the expression "the buyer" calls a meeting of or makes any arrangement or composition with its creditors is wound up compulsorily goes into liquidation or is otherwise dissolved or has a receiver of any of its assets appointed or if the goods or any part thereof are seized under any execution or legal process or under any distress for rent then this agreement shall forthwith and without any notice determine and thereafter the buyer shall no longer be in possession of the goods with the seller's consent. Should the agreement be terminated by the seller or determine under this clause after one-third of the total purchase price has been paid and the transaction evidenced by this agreement is one to which the provisions of the Act apply then unless the buyer has put an end to the agreement the seller may not take back the goods from the buyer without the buyer's consent unless the seller obtains an Order of the Court in accordance with the Statutory Notice overleaf. Should the agreement be terminated by the seller or determine under this clause in any circumstances other than those set out in the last preceding sentence the seller may without notice retake possession of the goods and for this purpose shall be entitled freely to enter into and upon any premises occupied by or under the control of the buyer. (b) Where the transaction evidenced by this agreement is one to which the provisions of the Act apply the buyer shall have a statutory right to terminate this agreement and such right and the buyer's liability upon exercise of such right are set out in the Statutory Notice overleaf.

'PAYMENT ON TERMINATION OR DETERMINATION 13. Should this agreement be

> terminated by the seller or determine under the Termination Clause hereof the buyer shall forthwith pay to the seller the amount of any deposit and/or acceptance fee due but unpaid together with any instalments which are in arrear at the time of such termination or determination and, on demand, shall pay to the seller any expenses reasonably incurred by the seller in tracing and/or recovering possession of the goods (if title to and property in the goods remains vested in the seller at the date of such termination or determination) together with an amount representing the seller's loss on the transaction. It is hereby agreed that for the purpose of this clause the seller's loss shall be an amount equal to the amount by which the total purchase price set out in the schedule exceeds the aggregate of (a) any payments made by the buyer by way of deposit, acceptance fee and instalments of the balance of the total purchase price; (b) a sum representing the rebate of charges which would have been allowed in respect of the accelerated payment of all or part of the total purchase price had the transaction been settled under the provisions of the Early Settlement Clause hereof at the date of such termination or determination; and (c) if title to and property in the goods remains vested in the seller at the date of termination or determination the "net" proceeds of sale of the goods after allowing for any sums reasonably expended by the seller in putting the goods into good order and repair for the purpose of sale. Provided always that where the transaction evidenced by this agreement is one to which the provisions of the Act apply the amount payable by the buyer in respect of such loss shall not exceed the amount by which one half of the total purchase price exceeds the total of the amount paid and the amount due by way of instalments of the total purchase price immediately before such termination or determination but without prejudice to Paragraph 3 of the Statutory Notice overleaf.'

The first contention made on behalf of the defendant turns on the interpretation of s 27 of the 1965 Act. The relevant parts of that section read as follows:

> '(1) At any time before the final payment under a . . . conditional sale agreement falls due, the . . . buyer shall (subject to the next following subsection) be entitled to terminate the agreement by giving notice of termination in writing to any person entitled or authorised to receive the sums payable under the agreement.
>
> '(2) In the case of a conditional sale agreement, where the property in the goods, having become vested in the buyer, is transferred to a person who does not become the buyer under the agreement, the buyer shall not thereafter be entitled to terminate the agreement under this section.
>
> '(3) Subject to the last preceding subsection, where a buyer under a conditional sale agreement terminates the agreement under this section after the property in the goods has become vested in him, the property in the goods shall thereupon vest in the person (in this subsection referred to as "the previous owner") in whom it was vested immediately before it became vested in the buyer: Provided that if the previous owner has died, or any other event has occurred whereby that property, if vested in him immediately before that event, would thereupon have vested in some other person, the property shall be treated as having devolved as if it had been vested in the previous owner immediately before his death or immediately before that event, as the case may be.
>
> '(4) Nothing in this section shall prejudice any right of a . . . buyer to terminate a . . . conditional sale agreement otherwise than by virtue of this section.'

What the defendant says is that cl 11 of the agreement interferes with the right to terminate contained in s 27(1) and as such, it is void under s 29(2)(*b*) which provides that any provision in a conditional sale agreement is void 'whereby the right conferred by section 27 of this Act to terminate . . . a conditional sale agreement is excluded or restricted . . .' Whether the defendant's contention is correct depends on the meaning of the words 'At any time before the final payment under a . . . conditional sale agreement falls due' in s 27(1).

Counsel for the defendant says the effect of those words is that the right of termination a only comes to an end on the date when the thirty-sixth of the monthly instalments would become payable under the agreement, and that date is not affected by the fact that the plaintiffs choose to activate their rights to accelerate the time for payment under cl 11 of the agreement.

On the other hand, the plaintiffs contend that if the seller elects to call for accelerated payment and gives the necessary notice, and the ten days thereafter expires without the b buyer having paid off the arrears, the accelerated payment, which is the final payment under the conditional sale agreement, falls due for the purposes of s 27(1); so the right to terminate under s 27(1) comes to an end. On the plaintiffs' interpretation there is no interference with the buyer's right to terminate under the 1965 Act, because up until the sum under cl 11 falls due the right to terminate is expressly recognised and, whereas the right to terminate is lost thereafter, the loss occurs after the time specified, on this c interpretation, in s 27(1).

Although I recognise that the plaintiffs' interpretation can substantially restrict the protection given to a hirer or buyer by s 27, I am forced to the conclusion that it is the right interpretation. The result of the rival contention is that because under the agreement there is a provision for instalments continuing for three years, the right to terminate must continue for a like period. This is irrespective of whether the seller has d exercised his rights under cl 11 at an early stage of the agreement, which could lead to the right to terminate continuing for a period of many months after the buyer acquired title to the vehicle. Although I accept that because of the terms of s 27(2) and (3) the date on which title passes cannot be conclusive, it still seems remarkable that there should be a right to terminate under s 27 long after any payment in fact falls due and after title has passed.

e The plaintiffs being correct on their interpretation, cl 11 does not restrict the defendant's rights to terminate. The concluding words of cl 11(a) make it clear that during the period of ten days following the service of the notice under cl 11, the buyer can still exercise his statutory right, so there is no restriction during that period. As the right to terminate has thereafter ceased to exist it cannot be cut down.

The remaining points taken by the defendant do not assist her in view of my decision f on the interpretation of s 27(1). However, it is desirable that I should deal with them in case this case goes further as they have been fully argued.

The first is that the sum specified in cl 11(a) could not be the final payment because of the provisions as to interest on failure to pay the accelerated payment. However I cannot accept that the right to terminate can be extended by failing to make the accelerated payment as s 27(1) specifies the limit for termination as being when the payment 'falls g due', not when it is paid; and the liability for interest only arises after the accelerated payment has fallen due.

The defendant's next argument turns on the wording of s 28(1)(*b*) combined with the second half of s 29(2)(*b*). It is argued that cl 11 is void because if a buyer exercises his statutory right to terminate after he has become liable to pay an accelerated payment under cl 11, the buyer will be under a liability in excess of that referred to in s 28. Once h again I accept the plaintiffs' arguments. The second half of s 29(2)(*b*) only applies to a liability imposed on the buyer 'by reason of the termination of a . . . conditional sale agreement'. The liability under cl 11 does not arise by reason of such termination but because the plaintiffs exercise their rights under the clause. Furthermore, the liability under cl 11 would be one which falls within the words 'without prejudice to any liability which has accrued before the termination' in s 28(1) if those words are given their literal j meaning. The only argument to support a contrary interpretation depends on the surprising fact that the statutory notice which purports to set out the buyer's liability on termination sets out a liability which does not accord with s 28. In particular it makes no reference to the 'without prejudice to any liability which has accrued before termination' in s 28, and because of this counsel for the defendant says those words must, when the 1965 Act is read as a whole, mean no more than the instalments which are in arrear, because this is what is stated in the statutory notice. Were there no other conflicts between what is said in the statutory notice and s 28, the argument in favour of the buyer would be much stronger. However this is not the case. It is to be observed that the statutory notice makes no reference to the provisions of s 28(4) and the limits on the court's powers not to order the return of the goods to the seller after a buyer's termination. Accordingly I do not consider that the statutory notice can be regarded as the key to the meaning of s 28 and I reject the defendant's argument.

There is an additional reason why the buyer cannot rely on s 28 to render cl 11 void. The statement that the statutory notice shall 'be deemed to form part of this agreement' together with the wording of cl 12(b) is to make the statutory notice one of the terms of the agreement. Accordingly, in addition to the statutory right to terminate, the buyer has a contractual right to terminate on the terms set out in the statutory notice, and if he exercises that right his liability cannot exceed that provided for in the agreement. So that on his exercising that right to terminate, the liability specified in the statutory notice must supersede his liability, if any, under cl 11.

That brings me conveniently to the defendant's last argument on the statutory provisions. This turns on the wording of s 29(2)(*c*). Initially counsel for the defendant described this as an esoteric argument but later rather regretted using that adjective in case it should be thought to detract from it. He says that although cl 11 of the agreement is not headed 'Termination', when the seller exercises his right under cl 11 he, in effect, is terminating the agreement and should be treated as such. Accordingly, as the amount payable under cl 11 is in excess of that provided for in s 29(2)(*c*) it is void. I am not sure whether it was because of its esoteric qualities, but initially I was attracted by this argument. It did seem to me that to regard the conditional sale agreement as still being in existence after cl 11 had been activated, the property in the goods had passed to the buyer and all the buyer was left to do was to make the accelerated payment was unreal. However, quite clearly the fact that the goods had become vested in the buyer was not intended to mean that the right to terminate could not be exercised because otherwise s 27(2) and (3) would be unnecessary. It therefore seems that the legislature intended an agreement to continue even though the property had passed from the seller and because of this, with some reservations, I have come to the conclusion that the fact that an accelerated payment has fallen due under cl 11 does not terminate the agreement. The agreement remains in force not only until the seller has played his part but until the buyer has also played his part, even though that is confined to making an accelerated payment.

In expressing the view which I have about the statutory provisions, I am conscious that in the majority of cases they must apply to hire-purchase agreements as well as conditional sale agreements, and this could have an adverse effect not only on buyers under conditional sale agreements but also hirers under hire-purchase agreements. By skilful drafting of agreements it could well be possible to deprive hirers and purchasers of the protection Parliament intended them to have. While recognising this, it is also necessary to take into account the very drastic effect on the supplier of the goods were the interpretation to be otherwise than that which I have adopted. If the defendant was right in her contentions, it would be virtually impossible to design an accelerated payment provision which did not contravene the sections of the Act under consideration. As there is a special limitation, inter alia, on accelerated payments in the case of the death of a buyer in s 30(1), Parliament did not intend that there should never be an accelerated payment provision and accordingly I regard the conclusions to which I have come as being in accord with the literal terms of ss 27 and 28 and the 1965 Act as a whole.

The defendant's remaining argument does not turn on the provisions of the Act. It is a contention that cl 11 is penal in effect. Counsel for the plaintiffs' initial argument was that it was wrong to regard the payment under cl 11 as being capable of being a penalty. It did not fall within the classic statement in *Dunlop Pneumatic Tyre Co Ltd v New Garage and Motor Co Ltd* [1915] AC 79, [1914–15] All ER Rep 739. He contended that the

correct approach was that indicated in *Wallingford v Mutual Society* (1880) 5 App Cas 685
a and *Protector Endowment Loan and Annuity Co v Grice* (1880) 5 QBD 592, which cases were
not considered by the House of Lords in the *Dunlop* case or in *Bridge v Campbell Discount Co Ltd* [1962] 1 All ER 385, [1962] AC 600. If this be the position a buyer under a conditional sale agreement would be in a much worse position than he would be if he had entered into a hire-purchase agreement. Such an outcome would be highly undesirable. However, it is clear that the seller's right to serve a notice under cl 11 arises
b because of the buyer's breach of the agreement in failing to pay instalments and as the
right to call for accelerated payment only arises on such a breach I would apply the principles as to penalties to the seller's right to recover accelerated payments under a conditional sale agreement in the same way as they apply to hire-purchase agreements. It is accordingly necessary to consider whether the provisions of cl 11 are penal in effect.

In considering this it is important to bear in mind that under cl 11 the title in the
c goods vests in the buyer. Furthermore, there is an allowance because the obligation of
the buyer is only to pay a proportion of the charges calculated at a date three months after the date of the instalment which would next have followed the date of notice, the instalment being appropriated first to charges by the 'rule of 78'. Until this case I had not heard of the 'rule of 78' and I am sure that in this regard I am in the same position as many purchasers who enter into credit sale agreements with the plaintiffs. However the
d rule is well recognised in the trade and now has considerable respectability because it is
adopted, as being the appropriate formula to apply, in the White Paper on the reform of the law on consumer credit (Cmnd 5427 (1973) p 17). The only difference between the recommendations and the formula used in cl 11 is that the proposals in the White Paper take a date three to 3½ months, while in cl 11 a date is taken which is four months after the date of the notice. Counsel for the defendant conceded that were it not for this
e difference the penalty argument would fail because to have adopted the proposals in the
White Paper could not be said to be unreasonable. I have no hesitation in saying that while the difference between the two is not de minimis, it is not sufficient to prevent cl 11 containing a genuine pre-estimate of the plaintiffs' loss. Clearly the charges were not confined to interest so far as the plaintiffs are concerned and while the four-month period could in some cases bear heavily on the buyer, this does not mean that the
f accelerated payment is penal. It can still be a genuine pre-estimate of what the plaintiffs
will lose because of the early termination of the agreement.

It follows that notwithstanding the arguments advanced so skilfully by counsel for the defendant, the defendant is liable to the plaintiffs for the claim under cl 11 and I will therefore give judgment for the plaintiffs in the sum of £1,086 which, as I understand it, is the maximum amount of the defendant's liability.

g

Judgment for the plaintiffs in the sum of £1,086.

Solicitors: *M J Sechiari* for the plaintiffs; *Graham & Graham*, St Austell (for the defendant).

K Mydeen Esq Barrister.

Berry v Warnett (Inspector of Taxes) *a*

COURT OF APPEAL, CIVIL DIVISION
BUCKLEY, OLIVER AND ACKNER LJJ
20th, 21st MAY, 15th JULY 1980

Capital gains tax – Settlement – Settled property – Gift in settlement – Transfer of fund to *b* *trustees – Settlement whereby beneficial interest in fund assigned to trustees on trust for settlor for life with remainder to company – Consideration paid by company to settlor equal to market value of interest in remainder – Whether fund acquired by trustees by way of gift – Whether transfer a 'gift in settlement' – Whether settlement effected only part disposal of fund – Finance Act 1965, ss 22(2)(4), 25(2).* *c*

In March 1972 the taxpayer and his wife transferred the whole of their holding of stock and shares in R Ltd ('the fund') to a Guernsey company. On 4th April the taxpayer executed a deed of settlement between himself as vendor, a Jersey company as purchaser and the Guernsey company as trustees, whereby, in consideration of the full market value of £14,500 paid to him by the Jersey company, he assigned his beneficial interest in the fund to the Guernsey company on trust to pay the income of the fund to himself *d* for life with remainder to the Jersey company absolutely. On the same day the taxpayer's wife executed a similar settlement in consideration of £7,650 paid to her by the Jersey company. The taxpayer was assessed to capital gains tax for the year 1971–72 in the sum of £150,483 on the basis that the transfer of the fund to the trustees was a 'gift in settlement' within s 25(2)[a] of the Finance Act 1965 and that under s 22(4)[b] of that Act it was deemed to have been disposed of for a consideration equal to its full market value. *e* The taxpayer appealed contending that, since the creation of the interest in remainder under the settlement in favour of the Jersey company had been for full consideration, there was no 'gift in settlement' of the fund within s 25(2) and that, since on the making of the settlement the taxpayer's life interest in the fund remained undisposed of, there was only a part disposal of his beneficial interest in the fund within s 22(2)(*b*)[c] of the Act and that accordingly the assessment should be reduced to the sum of £14,839. The *f* Special Commissioners held that the transfer of the fund to the trustees was a disposal of the whole fund and confirmed the assessment. The judge[d] allowed an appeal by the taxpayer ([1978] 3 All ER 267), holding that the transfer of the fund was not a 'gift in settlement' within s 25(2) and, further, that the taxpayer and the trustees were not connected persons as defined by para 21 of Sch 7[d] to the 1965 Act and, therefore, the trustees did not acquire the fund otherwise than by way of a bargain at arm's length *g* within para 17(2) of that schedule. The Crown appealed.

Held (Buckley LJ dissenting) The appeal would be dismissed for the following reasons—

(1) The transfer of the fund to the trustees did not constitute a 'gift in settlement' within s 25(2) of the 1965 Act since the expression 'gift in settlement' in that section was clearly directed to the relationship between the disponor and the beneficiaries and could *h* only refer to the creation of a beneficial interest in settled property for which no consideration was given (see p 802 *f g*, p 804 *c* to *f*, p 807 *g* to *j* and p 809 *a* to *c* and *h*, post); *Inland Revenue Comrs v Plummer* [1979] 3 All ER 775 applied.

(2) The effect of the settlement was to reserve in favour of the taxpayer a life interest in the fund beneficially owned by him and to dispose of his reversionary interest in the *j*

a Section 25(2) is set out at p 802 *e*, post
b Section 22(4), so far as material, is set out at p 802 *h*, post
c Section 22(2) is set out at p 803 *f*, post
d Schedule 7, so far as material, is set out at p 807 *e f*, post

remainder to the purchaser for full consideration. In the circumstances, there was only a part disposal of the beneficial interest in the fund owned by the taxpayer within s 22(2). It followed, therefore, that the taxpayer was liable to capital gains tax only in respect of the gains arising on the disposal of the reversionary interest (see p 806 *d* to *f*, p 807 *j* and p 809 *f* to *h*, post).

Decision of Goulding J [1978] 3 All ER 267 affirmed.

Notes

For gifts in settlement, see 5 Halsbury's Laws (4th Edn) para 50, and for the distinction between disposal and part disposal for the purposes of capital gains taxation, see ibid para 36.

For the Finance Act 1965, ss 22, 25, Sch 7, paras 17, 21, see 34 Halsbury's Statutes (3rd Edn) 877, 884, 959, 962.

With effect from 6th April 1979, ss 22(2) and (4) and 25(2) of, and paras 17 and 21 of Sch 7 to, the 1965 Act have been replaced by the Capital Gains Tax Act 1979, ss 19(2) and (3), 53, 62 and 63.

Cases referred to in judgments

Attorney General v Beech [1899] AC 53, HL, 44 Digest (Repl) 332, *1658*.

Attorney General v Milne [1914] AC 765, [1914–15] All ER Rep 1061, 83 LJKB 1083, 111 LT 343, HL, 44 Digest (Repl) 210, *245*.

Canadian Eagle Oil Co Ltd v R, Selection Trust Ltd v Devitt (Inspector of Taxes) [1945] 2 All ER 499, [1946] AC 119, 27 Tax Cas 205, 114 LJKB 451, 173 LT 234, HL, 28(1) Digest (Reissue) 299, *1026*.

Cape Brandy Syndicate v Inland Revenue Comrs [1921] 1 KB 64, 12 Tax Cas 358, 90 LJKB 113; *affd* [1921] 2 KB 403, 12 Tax Cas 358, 90 LJKB 461, 125 LT 108, CA, 28(1) Digest (Reissue) 255, *798*.

Fitzwilliam's (Earl) Agreement, Re [1950] 1 All ER 191, [1950] Ch 448, 21 Digest (Repl) 30, *112*.

Greenberg v Inland Revenue Comrs, Tunnicliffe v Inland Revenue Comrs [1971] 3 All ER 136, [1972] AC 109, [1971] 3 WLR 386, 47 Tax Cas 240, 50 ATC 259, [1971] TR 233, HL, Digest (Cont Vol D) 494, *1759*.

Inland Revenue Comrs v Gribble [1913] 3 KB 212, 82 LJKB 900, 108 LT 887, CA, 44 Digest (Repl) 331, *1653*.

Inland Revenue Comrs v Joiner [1975] 3 All ER 1050, [1975] 1 WLR 1701, [1975] STC 657, [1975] TR 257, HL, Digest (Cont Vol D) 496, *1759c*.

Inland Revenue Comrs v Plummer [1979] 3 All ER 775, [1979] 3 WLR 689, [1979] STC 793, HL, Digest (Cont Vol E) 290, *866d*.

Ransom (Inspector of Taxes) v Higgs [1974] 3 All ER 949, [1974] 1 WLR 1594, [1974] STC 539, 50 Tax Cas 1, 53 ATC 285, [1974] TR 281, HL, Digest (Cont Vol D) 444, *295a*.

Rose, Re, Midland Bank Executor and Trustee Co Ltd [1948] 2 All ER 971, [1949] Ch 78, [1949] LJR 208, 24 Digest (Reissue) 579, *2442*.

Tennant v Smith [1892] AC 150, 3 Tax Cas 158, 61 LJPC 11, 66 LT 327, 56 JP 596, HL, 28(1) Digest (Reissue) 312, *1086*.

Appeal

The Crown appealed against an order of Goulding J ([1978] 3 All ER 267, [1978] 1 WLR 957) made on 22nd March 1978, reversing a decision of the Commissioners for the Special Purposes of the Income Tax Acts on an appeal by way of case stated by Norman Charles Berry ('the taxpayer'), reducing an assessment to capital gains tax in the sum of £150,483 for the year 1971–72 to £14,839. The facts are set out in the judgment of Oliver LJ.

Andrew Morritt QC and *C H McCall* for the Crown.

D C Potter QC and *David Braham QC* for the taxpayer.

Cur adv vult

15th July. The following judgments were read.

OLIVER LJ (delivering the first judgment at the invitation of Buckley LJ). This is an appeal by the Crown from a judgment of Goulding J ([1978] 3 All ER 267, [1978] 1 WLR 957) delivered on 22nd March 1978, in which he reversed the decision of the Special Commissioners.

The facts fall within a fairly short compass. The appellants from the Special Commissioners, Mr Berry ('the taxpayer') and his wife, were the beneficial owners of certain shares and units of convertible unsecured loan stock of Rothschild Investment Trust Ltd, which were either registered in their respective names or were held on their behalf by Lloyds Bank (Branches) Nominees Ltd. The question on this appeal arises out of settlements made by the taxpayer and his wife respectively of their holdings. The settlements are identical except for the settlors and the amounts of their respective holdings, and there is no question but that the same legal consequences attend the transactions carried out by the taxpayer's wife as attend those carried out by her husband. Nor is there any question but that, if a liability to tax arises from her dealings, he as her husband is responsible for discharging it. The total market value of the shares and stock at the date of the settlements was £219,880.

Since the question in each case is the same, I can confine myself to the transactions carried out by the taxpayer himself. On 15th March 1972 he transferred, or caused to be transferred, the whole of his holdings of shares and stock (consisting of 10,854 shares and a sum of £49,931 stock) to a Guernsey company, Investors Trustees Ltd. That company was not, as a matter of machinery, actually registered as the holder of the stock transferred until 28th April 1972, and did not become the registered holder of the shares until 12th May 1972, but nothing turns on the date of registration save this, so far as it is material, that at the end of the financial year 1971–72 the taxpayer or his nominee was still the registered holder.

In the meantime two documents were executed. On 4th April 1972 (that is, in the financial year 1971–72) a settlement was executed to which the parties were the taxpayer (described as 'the vendor'), First Investors & Savers (Jersey) Ltd (a Jersey company described as 'the purchaser') and Investors Trustees Ltd (described as 'the trustees'). It recited the beneficial ownership of the stock and shares to which I have referred as being in the vendor, and continued as follows:

> 'AND WHEREAS the Vendor and the Purchaser have bargained and agreed for the consideration hereinafter mentioned that the same shall be settled in manner hereinafter appearing NOW THIS DEED WITNESSETH as follows:—
>
> '1. "THE Trust Fund" means the said property specified in the Schedule hereto and the property for the time being representing the same.
>
> '2. IN pursuance of the said agreement and in consideration of the sum of £14,500 now paid by the Purchaser to the Vendor (the receipt whereof the Vendor hereby acknowledges) the Vendor as Beneficial Owner HEREBY ASSIGNS unto the Trustees ALL THAT the Trust Fund and the income thereof TO HOLD the same unto the Trustees absolutely and the Vendor hereby directs and declares that the Trust Fund and the income thereof shall henceforth be held after the death of the Vendor and subject in the meantime to the life interest of the Vendor and the powers and provisions hereinafter reserved and contained UPON TRUST for the Purchaser absolutely.
>
> '3. PROVIDED ALWAYS that during the life of the Vendor the Trustees shall pay the income of the Trust Fund to the Vendor for his own use and benefit absolutely.'

There followed a trust for sale or retention at the discretion of the trustees, which I do not think I need read, an unrestricted investment clause, a power in the vendor to appoint new trustees (but excluding the vendor himself) and a charging clause enabling

trustees to charge for work done in the execution of the trusts and entitling a trust
a corporation to remuneration in accordance with its scale of fees in force at the date of appointment. Finally the shares and stock were described in the schedule.

On 6th April 1972 (that is, in the financial year 1972–73) a further document was executed. That was an assignment, made between the taxpayer of the one part and First Investors International Ltd (a Bahamas company) of the second part. It recited the settlement and the composition of the trust fund and it continued, in recital (C), as
b follows: 'The Vendor has agreed with the Purchaser for the sale to it at the price of £130,753·72 of the said life interest of the Vendor in the Trust Fund', and the operative part was in these terms:

> 'NOW THIS DEED WITNESSETH that in pursuance of the said Agreement and in consideration of the sum of £130,753·72 paid by the Purchaser to the Vendor (who acknowledges the receipt thereof) the Vendor as beneficial owner assigns to the
> c Purchaser all the dividends interest and income to become payable or accrue henceforth during the remainder of the life of the Vendor from or in respect of the Trust Fund and the investments and property from time to time and for the time being representing the same TO HOLD the same unto the Purchaser absolutely.'

As I have said, the taxpayer's wife executed identical documents relating to her
d holdings, so the effect was that between 3rd and 7th April 1972 the taxpayer and his wife had effectively divested themselves of their entire beneficial interests in the shares and stock concerned in favour of companies which, being resident abroad, would not be liable for any capital gains tax on the distribution of the trust funds or on any subsequent disposals. It is accepted, of course, that there was a disposal by the taxpayer and his wife of their reversionary interests in favour of the Jersey company and that capital gains tax
e is payable on the gain made out of the consideration received from that disposal, calculated on the basis that this was a partial disposal only. It is agreed that on this basis the chargeable gains amount to £14,839.

It is not in issue that there is no chargeable gain in respect of the subsequent assignment of the life interest reserved to the vendor, having regard to the provisions of para 13 of Sch 7 to the Finance Act 1965, but the Crown contends that there was, on the execution
f of the settlement, a complete disposition of the shares which results in a chargeable gain of £150,483. The Special Commissioners upheld that contention. They said ([1978] 3 All ER 267 at 273):

> '... the scheme of the tax appears to be that a taxpayer who declares himself to be a trustee of property, or transfers property to a trustee other than a bare trustee for himself, makes a disposal for a consideration equal to the market value of the
> g property in respect of which trusts are declared or which is transferred to the trustees. Assets which previously belonged to the taxpayer cease so to belong: prima facie there is a disposal of the whole of the assets. Does it affect this conclusion that the transaction here in question appears to fall within the description of a part disposal in section 22(2)(*b*) Finance Act 1965? We think not: what matters is that in relation to the shares and loan stock there was a disposal. Whether that disposal was
> h a "gift in settlement" within the meaning of section 25(2) is similarly not the decisive question: as between [the taxpayer] and the trustee there was a disposal of the shares and loan stock. Sale of an asset to the trustee of a settlement would be a disposal of the asset notwithstanding that the seller was interested under the settlement. It seems possible that section 25(2) is intended to do no more than make clear that a gratuitous transfer to the trustee of a settlement is in no different
> j category.'

Goulding J felt unable to accept the reasoning of the commissioners and he allowed the taxpayer's appeal. From that decision the Crown now appeals. The point is ultimately a fairly narrow one and it turns on the provisions of ss 22 and 25 of the Finance Act 1965, which are not altogether easy to follow.

There is no doubt that, on the execution of the settlement, the shares and stock settled became settled property as defined in s 45(1) of the 1965 Act. That is not in dispute. *a* That subsection defines 'settled property' as follows: '"settled property" means, subject to subsection (8) below [which does not matter for present purposes], any property held in trust other than property to which section 22(5) of this Act applies.' Settled property is regulated by s 25 of the Act, sub-s (1) of which provides that in relation to such property the trustees of the settlement shall be treated as a single and continuing body of persons (distinct from the persons who may from time to time be the trustees) and that body is *b* to be treated as being resident and ordinarily resident in the United Kingdom except in certain circumstances which do not matter for present purposes.

It is pointed out by the Crown that the section goes on to recognise that the interest arising under the settlement is something quite different from the settled property. Thus when the beneficiary becomes absolutely entitled to the settled property as against the trustee, s 25(3) provides that the assets to which he becomes entitled are deemed to *c* have been disposed of by the trustee and immediately reacquired by him in his capacity as trustee for a consideration equal to their market value. So it is the trustee who makes the notional gain, if any. A similar result ensues on the termination of a life interest in the settled property under sub-s (4). These provisions are prayed in aid in support of what is the mainspring of the Crown's case, namely the contention that whenever property becomes settled property, the entire property in settlement is disposed of, with *d* the result that any increase which has at that point arisen over the appropriate base value of the settled property becomes a chargeable gain. That contention is based on the provisions of s 25(2) which is in the following terms:

> 'A gift in settlement, whether revocable or irrevocable, is a disposal of the entire property thereby becoming settled property notwithstanding that the donor has some interest as a beneficiary under the settlement and notwithstanding that he is *e* a trustee, or the sole trustee, of the settlement.'

The submission, then, may be summarised thus: (1) The expression 'a gift in settlement' is not referring simply to a voluntary settlement. It is looking, not at the position as between the settlor and the beneficiaries, but at the position as between the settlor and the trustees and it means merely the transfer of the settled property to the *f* trustees, for which the trustees give no consideration and which can therefore properly be described as 'a gift'. In the instant case, therefore, there was a transfer of the entirety of the settled property, notwithstanding that the taxpayer retained an interest, and the fact that he received consideration from the purchaser for making the settlement which created the purchased reversion does not prevent the transfer to the trustees from being a 'gift in settlement'. (2) The second stage, it is submitted, is then to find out what is the *g* consideration deemed to be paid by the trustees on this acquisition by them, because unless one can do that there is no machinery for ascertaining what is the chargeable gain. That, it is submitted, is found in s 22(4), which is in these terms:

> 'Subject to the provisions of this Part of this Act, a person's acquisition of an asset and the disposal of it to him shall for the purposes of this Part of this Act be deemed to be for a consideration equal to the market value of the asset—(*a*) where he *h* acquires the asset otherwise than by way of a bargain made at arm's length and in particular where he acquires it by way of gift or by way of distribution from a company in respect of shares in the company ...'

Paragraphs (*b*) and (*c*) are immaterial.

Hence the Crown's contention that the chargeable gain here is the sum of £150,483, *j* the difference between the market value of the settled property and the amount for which it was acquired by the taxpayer and his wife.

Goulding J indicated that he would have felt himself able to accept the first of these submissions, but he did not feel able to accept the second. He said ([1978] 3 All ER 267 at 278, [1978] 1 WLR 957 at 963–964):

> '. . . I have to take the deed of 4th April 1972 as showing the true situation. It recites a preliminary agreement between two parties, the taxpayer and the purchaser, and goes on to effect a single and indivisible transaction between three persons. The taxpayer assigns the fund to the trustees, grants a beneficial remainder to the purchaser, receives £14,500, and retains a beneficial life interest. The purchaser pays £14,500 and receives the beneficial remainder. The trustees accept the fund, undertake the duty of holding it as trustees, and receive a right to remuneration. On the evidence there was one arrangement between all three parties, and the taxpayer was at arm's length vis-à-vis both the purchaser and the trustees. In my judgment, s 22(4) clearly does not catch the present case even if, as counsel for the Crown asked me to do, I alter the expression "a bargain made at arm's length" to read "a bargain made by him at arm's length". In relation to s 22(4), it seems to me that I am invited, not so much to strain the language of the Act as to distort the facts of the case. Therefore, I reject the Crown's main argument.'

For the taxpayer, it is submitted in the first place that, since there is no equity about a taxing statute, the Special Commissioners were wrong to seek to find the intendment of the Act. They should, it is submitted, have been looking to see whether there were clear words which resulted in the instant case in tax becoming payable. It is not disputed for one moment that the taxpayer's purpose in making the elaborate arrangements which I have described was to make a non-taxable profit on his holding of the stock and shares. That, it is submitted, is his privilege. He is not obliged to arrange his affairs for the benefit of the fisc and equally he is entitled so to arrange them as to benefit himself if the words which the legislative draftsmen have chosen to employ fairly enable him to do so.

That leads, then, to the attack on the Crown's central proposition. Section 25(2), on which the Crown's case rests is, it is submitted, expressed in terms which make it applicable only to a settlement by way of gift, and not one executed for consideration in money or money's worth. The appropriate section to apply to the instant transaction is therefore, it is submitted, s 22(2), and that is in the following terms:

> 'For the purposes of this Part of this Act—(*a*) references to a disposal of an asset include, except where the context otherwise requires, references to a part disposal of an asset, and (*b*) there is a part disposal of an asset where an interest or right in or over the asset is created by the disposal, as well as where it subsists before the disposal, and generally, there is a part disposal of an asset where, on a person making a disposal, any description of property derived from the asset remains undisposed of.'

The very words 'any description of property derived from the asset' are clearly, it is submitted, apt to refer to the equitable life interest retained under the settlement and therefore, it is argued, all that was disposed of here was the reversionary interest sold to the purchaser under the deed and it was on that disposition that the real gain arose in the year in question.

If there is to be superimposed some notional gain, that can only be done by finding clear words in the statute imposing such a charge, and the submission is that s 25(2), which, it is conceded, overrides s 22(2) in cases to which it applies, does not contain such clear words. It applies in terms only to a 'gift in settlement', which this is not. Attention is drawn to other provisions in the Act in which references to 'gifts' appear (see for instance ss 22(4)(*a*), 27(2), 31(1) and (7), 32(1) and 34(1)). Particular attention is directed to s 31(3)(*a*), where there is a significant reference to the concession which is to be allowed in certain circumstances on a disposal of an object of national, scientific, historical or artistic interest 'by way of gift, including a gift in settlement'. Counsel for the Crown has argued that this express reference supports the construction for which he contends, because it demonstrates that 'gift in settlement' means something more than merely a voluntary settlement. I find that difficult to accept. It seems to me that what the draftsman was seeking to do was to ensure that the concession was available whether the

disposal was by way of outright gift or of a settled gift, but that in either case what the
subsection is referring to is a gift, 'a gift in settlement' being merely a particular type of a
gift. I find it difficult here to give any secondary meaning to the expression and there is
no readily explicable reason why the same expression should have different meanings in
separate sections of the same Act.

The other provision to which counsel for the taxpayer draws attention is in para 19 of
Sch 7. The paragraph is concerned with the recovery of tax from the donee in cases of
gifts. Sub-paragraph (4) is in these terms: b

> 'In this paragraph references to a gift include references to any transaction
> otherwise than by way of a bargain made at arm's length so far as money or money's
> worth passes under the transaction without full consideration in money or money's
> worth, and "donor" and "donee" shall be construed accordingly . . .'

The only significance of this is that it can be said to demonstrate that, where the c
legislature wishes to bring under the umbrella of gifts transactions which are not in fact
gratuitous, it does so in express terms.

I confess that, for my part, I find considerable difficulty in giving to the expression 'gift
in settlement' the meaning sought to be attached to it by the Crown. It is true that, as
mentioned by the learned judge, a citation from Sheppard's Touchstone of Common
Assurance (8th Edn, 1826, vol 1, p 227) might indicate that 'gift' has the rather wide d
connotation simply of a transfer of property, but I entertain some little doubt whether
that work (which originated in 1641 and the last edition of which was in 1826) formed
part of the staple reading of our parliamentary draftsmen in 1965 and, furthermore, if
it did, they must presumably also have had in mind that the extended meaning there
suggested was decisively rejected by Danckwerts J in *Re Earl Fitzwilliam's Agreement*
[1950] 1 All ER 191, [1950] Ch 448 as the touchstone for the construction, in previous e
fiscal legislation, of the words 'immediate gift inter vivos'. Not only does the construction
urged by the Crown put a strained meaning on the word 'gift', but if, as counsel for the
Crown suggests, it is really looking at the position vis-à-vis the settlor and the trustees
alone and means simply a transfer to trustees, it is impossible to fit that concept with the
case which the section itself envisages of the settlor being the sole trustee of the
settlement. Here there is clearly contemplated the case where there never was a transfer f
but merely a unilateral declaration of trust, and in that context 'gift in settlement' can
only be referring to the creation, as against the trustee, of the beneficial interests under
the settlement.

To give effect to the scheme and intendment of the Act counsel for the Crown must
therefore read the expression simply as meaning 'a settlement' or 'the making of a
settlement'. That, I agree, would make much more sense if one has regard to what the g
legislation was trying to achieve, but it is not what the Act says, and unless the court is
entitled to put a gloss on the term in order to bring within the subsection a transaction
of a type which the draftsman almost certainly did not contemplate, I do not think either
that the reference to a gift can be simply ignored or that the word can be given a meaning
which it does not naturally bear. That approach to construction is not, as I understand
the authorities, permissible in the case of a taxing statute (see *Canadian Eagle Oil Co Ltd v* h
R [1945] 2 All ER 499 at 507, [1946] AC 119 at 140 and *Ransom (Inspector of Taxes) v Higgs*
[1974] 3 All ER 949 at 969, [1974] 1 WLR 1594 at 1616).

Thus, to take a simple example, if A, the tenant under a 99-year lease, grants a sublease
to B for 20 years at a premium equal to the value of the sublease, he has clearly made a
part disposal of the lease as defined in s 22(2). If he achieves the same result, in
consideration of the same premium and of a covenant by B to observe the covenants in j
the lease, by declaring himself a trustee of the lease for B for a term of 20 years and
thereafter for himself, he has equally clearly converted the lease into settled property
within s 45(1) of the Act, since it is now property held in trust, but property to which
s 22(5) does not apply. But to describe that transaction as a 'gift in settlement' seems to
me at any rate to strain the meaning of that expression beyond the limits both of possible

construction and of common sense. The judicial conscience may sometimes be required to display a certain flexibility in questions of construction where the context is clear, but I do not think that it should be, or can be, stretched beyond the point of credibility simply because of an uneasy suspicion that the legislature, if it had given more thought to the matter, would have done more effectively what it seems to have set out to do.

As counsel for the taxpayer submits, it is a dangerous guide to seek to construe a taxing statute by looking for logic. To read the section as he would read it, that is to say, as meaning no more than it says in terms and as confined to cases of gift, does, it is true, lead to the strange result that, unless s 22(4)(*a*) applies, there is no ascertainable base value on which to assess the gain on any subsequent disposition by the trustees of the settled property, a result which might be highly disadvantageous to the taxpayer on any initial change of investment by the trustees. That subsection is in the following terms, so far as material for present purposes:

> 'Subject to the provisions of this Part of this Act, a person's acquisition of an asset and the disposal of it to him shall for the purposes of this Part of this Act be deemed to be for a consideration equal to the market value of the asset—(*a*) where he acquires the asset otherwise than by way of a bargain made at arm's length . . .'

I have already read that subsection. But, if that result follows, it indicates in my judgment no more than that there is a casus omissus for which the legislature has failed to provide. It does not fit comfortably with the logic of the scheme and intendment of the Act, but for my part I do not feel justified, as a result, in giving to the words 'gift in settlement' in s 25(2) a meaning which they do not naturally bear. I would therefore reject the Crown's primary contention based on that subsection.

That, however, is not necessarily the end of the matter. Merely because a disposal to, and an acquisition by, trustees does not fall within s 25(2) it does not follow that there is no disposal and acquisition. The only consequence is, so far as I can see, that such a disposal and acquisition does not oust the provisions of s 22(2) where those provisions apply. Under s 22(9) the amount of gain accruing on the disposal of assets is to be computed in accordance with the provisions of Schs 6, 7 and 8, and s 22(4)(*a*) contains the important 'deeming provision' in relation to acquisitions otherwise than by way of arm's length bargain, to which I have already referred. One has, therefore, as it seems to me, still got to look to see whether there has been a disposal and acquisition and to compute by reference to the statutory formulae whether there has been a chargeable gain.

A transfer to the trustees of a settlement, whether voluntary or not, is clearly a disposal by the settlor of the legal interest in the property which is transferred to the trustees and an acquisition by the trustees of that legal interest. Whether and to what extent it gives rise to a chargeable gain depends on whether apt words can be found in the Act to produce that result.

The Crown's contention is that, looked at realistically, the settlement constituted a transfer to the trustees of the stock and shares and that that transfer, being a disposal which, vis-à-vis the trustees, was not the result of an arm's length bargain, is deemed by s 22(4)(*a*) to be a transfer for a consideration equal to the value of the stock and shares. This seems to me unanswerable if, but only if, (i) the disposal can be said to have been otherwise than by way of a bargain at arm's length and (ii) it does not fall to be treated only as a part disposal under s 22(2)(*b*). Goulding J felt himself unable to accept the Crown's contention that condition (i) was satisfied, and I shall return to that point a little later; but the first and anterior question seems to me to be whether the disposal falls within the statutory definition of a part disposal only, and thus subject only to the limited charge on a gain calculated in accordance with the statutory provisions relating to such a disposal.

Counsel for the Crown contends that it cannot fairly fall within the definition of a part disposal. The property disposed of consisted of the stock and shares. What was created in the taxpayer and in the purchaser consisted of interests in 'the trust fund' which simply happened, perhaps even momentarily, to be represented by the stock and shares but which might equally well have been a fund of gilt-edged stock if the trustees had sold under their trust for sale and reinvested. There was thus, he argues, no interest or right created in or over 'the asset' within s 22(2)(*b*) because 'the asset' was the stock and shares and the right or interest created was in 'the trust fund'. Equally there was no species of property remaining 'undisposed of', but the creation of some quite different property, an equitable interest in a trust fund. This argument has an attraction, particularly if, as the Special Commissioners held, one is to look at the scheme and intendment of the Act. But I do not feel able to accept it, having regard to the actual terms of the settlement and the proprietary interests which existed prior to it and were created by it. At the date of the settlement the taxpayer had already set in train the necessary steps to transfer the legal title in the shares and stock to the trustees, although those steps had not been completed. He retained the beneficial interest and this is reflected in the form of the settlement. It begins by reciting the taxpayer's beneficial ownership of the property described in the schedule which (in cl 1) is included in the definition of the trust fund; it then recites a bargain between the taxpayer and the purchaser for the settlement for the consideration stated below; and then, in cl 2 the taxpayer, as beneficial owner, assigns 'the Trust Fund and the income thereof' to the trustees absolutely and directs that the trustees hold it after the vendor's death and meanwhile subject to his life interest on trust for the purchaser. There follows, in cl 3, the proviso that the trustees shall pay the income of the trust fund to the vendor for his own use and benefit absolutely.

When I look at this in the light of the express provisions of s 22(2), I am bound to say that I find it very difficult to escape from the conclusion that it amounts to a part disposal. All that could be transferred to the trustees by this document was the vendor's beneficial interest in the trust fund. Quite apart from the fact that transfers to the trustees had already been executed, the document itself was inappropriate to transfer the shares and stock which, under the articles and terms of issue, require instruments of transfer in the usual common form or, in the case of the stock, in the form authorised by the Stock Transfer Act 1963. What the settlement did was to create out of the beneficial interest assigned a right in the purchaser in reversion and to reserve from the beneficial interest the absolute right to payment of income during the vendor's life. That life interest clearly, in my view, remained undisposed of. Equally clearly it seems to me that it was property derived from the asset which was assigned, namely the beneficial interest in the stock and shares.

Counsel for the Crown argues that the proper analysis is that the taxpayer disposed of his whole interest in the shares and then got something different back, and that therefore his life interest, albeit derived from the asset, did not 'remain undisposed of'. This seems to me to be unreal, if I may say so respectfully. There was no moment of time under this document when the vendor did not have the absolute right to receive the income from the trust fund. The effect of the settlement was to cut that right down to a life interest only, by creating a reversionary interest in the capital in favour of the purchaser. The income arising during the vendor's life therefore seems to me to be properly and literally described as 'undisposed of' by the settlement.

Now if this is right, then the Crown's claim must, as I see it, fail, for there cannot be, by the same instrument, both a total disposition and a partial disposition, nor is it argued that there can be.

One cannot, as counsel for the taxpayer submits, overcome the effect of s 22(2) by praying in aid the provisions of s 22(4), for that subsection applies only 'Subject to the provisions of this Part of this Act', which includes s 22(2) itself and the related s 22(9) and Sch 6 which lays down (in para 7) how gains on part disposals are to be computed.

That would be sufficient to dispose of the case, but I turn to consider the ground on which the learned judge decided the case in the taxpayer's favour. He would, as I read his judgment, have felt disposed to read the expression 'gift in settlement' in s 25(2) in the sense for which the Crown contends, notwithstanding the difficulties which he saw in reconciling the word 'gift' in that section with the context in which, in other parts of the Act, the word is clearly used. The difficulty, however, which he found, and which

he felt was insurmountable, was in ascertaining, on the assumption that s 25(2) applied,
a any provision for ascertaining the amount of the gain on which tax could be charged.
The deeming provisions of s 22(4) apply only where the acquirer of the asset acquires it
'otherwise than by way of a bargain made at arm's length', and this was, as he held,
indeed such a bargain as between the vendor and the purchaser. For my part, I do not
feel the same difficulty as that felt by the learned judge. Granted that this was one
document and that the trustee was party to it, there was not in any real sense any bargain
b between the trustee and the vendor for the acquisition of the property. I cannot regard
the inclusion in the document of a charging clause, as seems to be suggested in the
learned judge's judgment, as part of a bargain made at arm's length for the acquisition
of the trust property. The trustees were parties merely as a piece of necessary machinery
and I find some difficulty in reading 'by way of a bargain made at arm's length' as
comprehending an acquisition resulting from a bargain made between two other
c persons. On that analysis if A transfers property to trustees for B's children in
consideration of B transferring property of equivalent value to trustees for A's children,
the subsection would apply to neither set of trustees because each would acquire the
property by way of the bargain made between A and B. It does not seem to me to be
necessary, even allowing for the strict construction of taxing statutes, to construe the
subsection so as to produce so bizarre a result and I do not myself feel inhibited from
d accepting counsel's submission for the Crown that the section is referring to a bargain for
the acquisition of the property made at arm's length between disponor and acquirer.

It is, on the view which I take, strictly unnecessary to consider the alternative route
which the Crown sought to take by way of paras 17 and 21 of Sch 7, but put shortly the
submission is that the settlement here is a settlement as defined in para 21 (which
incorporates the definition of 'settlement' in s 454 of the Income and Corporation Taxes
e Act 1970). The result of that is, it is submitted, that the settlor and the trustees then
became 'connected persons' as defined in para 21(3) and accordingly para 17(1) and (2)
applies.

Referring briefly to these, para 21(3) provides as follows, so far as is material: 'A person,
in his capacity as trustee of a settlement, is connected with any individual who in relation
to the settlement is a settlor . . .' and para 17(1) and (2) is as follows: 'This paragraph shall
f apply where a person acquires an asset and the person making the disposal is connected
with him' and—

> 'Without prejudice to the generality of section 22(4) of this Act the person acquiring the asset and the person making the disposal shall be treated as parties to a transaction otherwise than by way of a bargain made at arm's length.'

The difficulty here is that in *Inland Revenue Comrs v Plummer* [1979] 3 All ER 775,
g [1979] 3 WLR 689 the House of Lords has clearly stated the limitations on the definition
of 'a settlement' in s 454. That definition clearly involves the concept of bounty, which
is not present in the instant case, and I feel the same difficulty as that felt by the learned
judge in accepting the submission that the definition, having been expressly incorporated
into the 1965 Act, can nevertheless be treated as modified by its application in this
different context. It seems to me that if a definition from one statute is incorporated in
h another, it must be subject to the same limitations in both, in the absence of some clear
contrary intention or express modification.

However, for the reasons which I have given, I would not feel the same difficulty
about the application of s 22(4)(*a*) if I could once accept either that the settlement
constitutes a 'gift in settlement' within s 25(2) or if I could accept the Crown's submission
that the transaction was not, apart from that provision, a part disposal under s 22(2)(*b*).

j For the reasons which I have endeavoured to state, I feel unable to accept that
submission and I would, therefore, although for reasons rather different from those
given by the learned judge, dismiss the appeal.

ACKNER LJ. The dispute in this case, although narrow, is one I have found difficult
to resolve. It is accepted that on the execution of the settlement made on 4th April 1972

the shares and stock referred to in the schedule, and which had previously belonged to the taxpayer, became 'settled property' as defined by s 45(1) of the Finance Act 1965. The *a* contest is whether s 25(2) or s 22(2) applies to the circumstances of this case.

Section 25(2) provides:

> 'A gift in settlement, whether revocable or irrevocable, is a disposal of the entire property thereby becoming settled property notwithstanding that the donor has some interest as a beneficiary under the settlement and notwithstanding that he is a trustee, or the sole trustee, of the settlement.' *b*

Section 22(2) provides:

> 'For the purposes of this Part of this Act—(*a*) references to a disposal of an asset include, except where the context otherwise requires, references to a part disposal of an asset, and (*b*) there is a part disposal of an asset where an interest or right in or over the asset is created by the disposal, as well as where it subsists before the disposal, and *c* generally, there is a part disposal of an asset where, on a person making a disposal, any description of property derived from the asset remains undisposed of.'

It is common ground that if s 25(2) applies, then it must exclude s 22(2), because it expressly provides that a settlement to which it applies is 'a disposal of the entire property thereby becoming settled property'. Again it is common ground that the crucial words *d* in s 25(2) are 'gift in settlement', and in s 22(2) 'there is a part disposal of an asset where, on a person making a disposal, any description of property derived from the asset remains undisposed of'.

It is well established that in a taxing Act clear words are necessary in order to tax the subject. This means that in a taxing Act one has to look merely at what is clearly said. There is no room for any intendment. There is no equity about a tax. There is no *e* presumption as to a tax. Nothing is to be read in, nothing is to be implied. One can only look fairly at the language used. (See *Cape Brandy Syndicate v Inland Revenue Comrs* [1921] 1 KB 64 at 71 per Rowlatt J; approved in *Canadian Eagle Oil Co Ltd v R* [1945] 2 All ER 499 at 507, [1946] AC 119 at 140.) Therefore if the Crown claims duty under a statute it must show that the duty is imposed by clear and unambiguous words (see *Tennant v Smith* [1892] AC 150 at 154, *Attorney General v Beech* (1899] AC 53 at 59, *Inland Revenue* *f* *Comrs v Gribble* [1913] 3 KB 212 at 219 and *Attorney General v Milne* [1914] AC 765 at 781, [1914–15] All ER Rep 1061 at 1068, to quote but a few of the cases). Although it may now be questionable whether this strict rule of construction still applies where the legislation is specifically designed to prevent varying forms of tax avoidance devices (see *Greenberg v Inland Revenue Comrs* [1971] 3 All ER 136 at 149, [1972] AC 109 at 137 per Lord Reid and *Inland Revenue Comrs v Joiner* [1975] 3 All ER 1050 at 1055, [1975] 1 WLR *g* 1701 at 1705–1706 per Lord Wilberforce) the legislation with which we are here concerned is not of such a character.

I agree with Buckley LJ, whose judgment I have had the much appreciated advantage of reading in advance, that the ordinary primary meaning of 'gift' is a voluntary transfer of property made without consideration. It cannot thus, on the ordinary use of language, be made to cover a transaction for full consideration in money or money's worth. It is *h* not contended that the sum of £14,500 paid for the reversionary interest was other than its market value. The taxpayer himself retained the rest of the beneficial interest, so that there was no act of bounty involved. Since Parliament has chosen, in s 25(2), by express words, to limit the transaction to one in which a gift is made, how then, applying the proper approach to the construction of the words 'gift in settlement', can s 25(2) be said to apply here? *j*

The Crown contends that in relation to any disposal of assets the Act looks primarily at the relations between the disponor and the disponee of the trust property. It is therefore contended that, as in the present case the trustees gave no consideration for the transfers of the shares and stock, then as between the taxpayer and the trustees the transfers were voluntary. But, as Oliver LJ in his judgment, which I have also had the

benefit of studying prior to writing this judgment, points out, the final words in s 25(2)
a '... notwithstanding that he is ... sole trustee of the settlement' must contemplate the creation of a settlement by an owner merely declaring that he holds the property on trust. Since the section applies to this method of creating a settlement, it must do so on the footing that the words 'gift in settlement' are directed at the relationship between the disponor and the *beneficiaries* and *not* the trustees.

Thus when the draftsman speaks of 'gift in settlement' he is in fact, as one would
b normally expect, looking not at the transfer of the legal estate to the trustee (which he recognised may not occur at all because the trustee may have it already) but to the creation of beneficial interests. If this was not the case then 'gift in settlement' would have two different meanings in the same Act.

I accept that if the facts of this case do not come within s 25(2), then there is no method provided by the Act for fixing the base value of the trust securities in the hands of the
c trustees, since there has not been a disposition of the shares as such, and therefore there is no value at which they can be disposed of. Accordingly the consequences of adopting the natural and ordinary meaning of the word 'gift' may well produce an unforeseen result. However, as counsel for the taxpayer submitted, it is rarely profitable to look for logic in a taxing statute, and in particular one where the legislature takes on itself the burden of taxing not only real gains but deemed gains on deemed disposals. That the
d draftsman has left a lacuna in the Act is to me more acceptable than that, when he used the word 'gift' to qualify 'settlement', he intended to mean a settlement whether by way of gift or for full consideration or valuable consideration. I therefore take the view that the Crown's contention, based on the meaning of the words 'gift in settlement', fails.

However, the Crown further contends that, when a settlor disposes of property to trustees so as to become settled property, there is for the purpose of the Act a complete
e disposal of that property. It is contended that, since the trustees had power to vary the investment of the fund, interests created by or arising under the settlement are not to be regarded as interests in the specific assets held for the time being by the trustees on the trusts of the settlement but only as interests in the trust fund. Thus, the Crown contends, there was no interest or right created in or over 'the asset' within s 22(2)(*b*) because 'the asset' was the stock and shares and the right or interest created was in, and
f only in, 'the trust fund'.

I accept that there were two quite distinct disposals in this case: first, the transfer of the shares and the stock to the trustees. By that transfer the taxpayer transferred the legal ownership of those assets to the trustees. However, he retained the beneficial ownership as distinct from the legal ownership. Accordingly the second transfer was the disposal in favour of the purchaser of the settlor's beneficial interest subject to his retaining a life
g interest in the same property.

Section 22(2)(*b*) provides that there is a part disposal of an asset where an interest or right in or over the asset is created by the disposal. I can find no justification in confining the interest or right to a legal interest or right. To my mind the life interest comes within the words 'any description of property'. Further, it was 'derived' from the settlor's beneficial interests and it remained under the settlement 'undisposed of'. Accordingly
h there was a 'part disposal' of the asset, namely the beneficial interest in the stock and shares.

I too would accordingly dismiss this appeal.

BUCKLEY LJ. This case raises, in my view, difficult questions on the construction and effect of certain sections contained in Part III of the Finance Act 1965, which created the
j capital gains tax. With regret, I have reached a different conclusion from that of Ackner and Oliver LJJ on these questions. Like Oliver LJ I shall confine my observations to the settlement made by the taxpayer. Precisely the same considerations apply to the settlement made by his wife and exactly the same conclusions must follow.

It is common ground that by virtue of the settlement executed by the taxpayer on 4th April 1972 the ordinary shares and loan stock of Rothschild Investment Trust Ltd referred to in the schedule to that settlement (which I shall call 'the shares and stock') became 'settled property' as defined by s 45(1) of the 1965 Act. The section of the Act which relates to settled property is s 25. The crucial question in the present case is, in my view, whether s 25(2) applies in the circumstances of the case. If it does, the claim of the Crown in this appeal must succeed, but if it does not, the Crown's claim must fail.

In the case of an ordinary voluntary settlement, where a settlor transfers property of his to trustees to be held on the trusts of the settlement, he makes a disposal to the trustees of the settled property which for the purposes of the 1965 Act is a disposal of the entire property, notwithstanding that the settlor may have some beneficial interest under the settlement (see s 25(2)). Since the trustees acquire the settled property otherwise than by way of a bargain at arm's length, (a) the disposal by the settlor and (b) the acquisition by the trustees are to be deemed to be for a consideration equal to the market value of the settled property (see s 22(4)(*a*)). The price so deemed to have been paid by the trustees applies for the purposes of (a) calculating what capital gain or allowable loss is to be treated as having accrued to the settlor on the disposal and (b) ascertaining the amount or value of the consideration which the trustees are to be treated as having given for the acquisition of the settled property for the purposes of calculating any capital gain or allowable loss which the trustees may later realise on a subsequent actual or notional disposal by them of the settled property or any part of it. For this latter purpose the trustees of the settlement are given what can appropriately be called a quasi-corporate character by s 25(1), so that changes in the personal identities of the trustees shall not complicate the ascertainment of capital gains liabilities in respect of dealings with the corpus of the trust property. If during the continuance of the trust the trustees sell a trust asset which was part of the property initially settled by the settlor, the trustees will realise a chargeable gain or an allowable loss by reference to a notional cost of acquisition (or 'base value') equal to the market value of that asset at the date of the settlement, and the base value to the trustees for capital gains tax purposes of the newly acquired asset will be the price paid for it by the trustees. When anybody becomes absolutely entitled to the settled property or any part of it as against the trustees, the trustees are to be deemed to have disposed of that property under s 25(3). Under s 22(4) this deemed disposal is to be deemed to be for a consideration equal to the then market value of the property. So the trustees must be treated as having made a capital gain or sustained an allowable loss by reference to whatever may then be historically the notional or actual base value of that property to the trustees. A similar situation will arise under s 25(4) on the termination of a life interest in possession in all or any part of the settled property. In this way, so long as the settled property remains in settlement and on the occasion of its ceasing to be settled by reason of some person becoming absolutely entitled to the property as against the trustees, the trustees are the persons chargeable to capital gains tax in respect of all disposals, whether actual or notional, of the settled property or any part of it. They are, of course, entitled under the general law to pay the tax out of the settled property, so that the burden falls on the beneficiaries in accordance with their several interests under the settlement.

No chargeable gain arises on the disposal by a beneficiary of any beneficial interest created by or arising under a settlement, whether it is made for a consideration or voluntarily, but, if the disposal is for a consideration in money or money's worth, the acquirer will be liable to capital gains tax on any subsequent disposal of that interest by him in just the same way as anyone else who realises an investment which he has made (see Sch 7, para 13(1)) or on his becoming absolutely entitled to the property as against the trustees (see Sch 7, para 13(2)).

I have thus set out the effect of the sections in relation to an ordinary voluntary settlement at some length because it seems to me that it affords a helpful background to the consideration of the contentions in this case.

The Crown contends that, when a settlor disposes of property to trustees so as to become settled property, there is for the purposes of the Act a complete disposal of that property, and that, where the trustees have power to vary the investment of the fund, interests created by or arising under the settlement are not to be regarded as interests in the specific assets held for the time being by the trustees on the trusts of the settlement but as interests in the trust fund of whatever assets it may consist from time to time. The Crown contends that interests arising under the settlement are not, for the purposes of s 22(2)(*b*), property 'derived from' specific assets.

The Crown further submits that in relation to any disposal of assets the Act looks primarily at the relations between the disponor and the disponee, any bargain made between them and any consideration moving from one of them to the other. In the present case the trustees gave no consideration for the transfers of the shares and stock. As between the taxpayer and the trustees the transfers were voluntary.

In any event, the Crown says, the expression 'a gift in settlement' used in s 25(2) means no more than a transfer whereby property becomes settled property. In the further alternative the Crown contends that the taxpayer as settlor and the trustees were, when the settlement was made, 'connected persons' within Sch 7, para 21, so that under para 17 of that schedule the settlement must be treated as a transaction otherwise than by way of a bargain at arm's length, with the consequence that under s 22(4) the disposal of the shares and stock must be deemed to have been made for a full market value consideration.

Counsel for the Crown submits that the assets comprised in the trust and the interests under the trust should be regarded as distinct items of property. He says that there are two quite distinct disposals in this case, viz, first, the transfers of the shares and stock to the trustees and, second, a sale by the taxpayer, as settlor, of a reversionary beneficial interest in the trust fund to First Investors and Savers (Jersey) Ltd ('the Jersey company'). The first of these is a disposal of the whole property in the shares and stock. The fact that the second does not extend to the whole beneficial interest in the trust fund but only to a reversionary interest does not, counsel for the Crown submits, mean that the disposal of the shares and stock left any property in the shares and stock undisposed of. Moreover, the price paid for the reversion was not given for the acquisition of the shares and stock by the trustees.

Counsel for the taxpayer, on the other hand, submits that the taxpayer made an actual capital gain of £14,839 in the year of assessment by reason of the sale of the reversionary interest, but that no disposal of the corpus of the trust fund for a notional consideration equal to its market value should be treated as having taken place. According to this argument there was no 'gift in settlement' (s 25(2)) because the transaction was not a gratuitous one: there was no more than a 'part disposal' of the shares and stock, because a life interest in the fund remained undisposed of (s 22(2)(*b*)). The true nature of the transaction, it is said, was the sale of a reversionary interest in the settled property, not a 'gift in settlement' of anything, since that expression imports an act of bounty and there was no bounty involved here.

The contest is between s 22(2) and s 25(2). The latter, if it applies to the facts of the present case, must exclude the former because it expressly provides that a settlement to which it applies is a disposal of the entire settled property and so excludes the possibility of its being a part disposal only of that property. The answer must depend, I think, on the meaning in s 25(2) of the expression 'gift in settlement'. This is not defined in the 1965 Act. The word 'gift' is used in a number of other places in the Act in contexts which do not suggest that it is there used in any but its ordinary primary sense. Notwithstanding the passage to which we were referred in Sheppard's Touchstone of Common Assurance (8th Edn, 1826, vol 1, p 227), I think that the ordinary primary meaning of 'gift' is now a voluntary transfer of property made without consideration. There is, so far as I am aware, only one other place in the Act where the expression 'gift in settlement' is used; that is s 31(3)(*a*). That subsection provides for a concession to be made, as specified in that section, in respect of a disposal of a work of art or other object of national, scientific, historic or artistic interest in circumstances prescribed in the subsection. I do not gain much help from this. The inclusive words may, it is true, have been inserted because the draftsman considered that without them the word 'gift' would not have covered a 'gift in settlement'; but they may, as it seems to me, equally well have been inserted ex majori cautela to make clear that the word 'gift' is apt to cover not only an immediate out and out voluntary transfer to a single individual or a group of *a* individuals but also whatever is meant by a 'gift in settlement'. The expression 'gift in settlement' sounds somewhat strangely in a lawyer's ear, at any rate in the ear of a conveyancer. One thing is, I think, clear, that the expression does not mean a disposition in consequence of which the disponor ceases to have any beneficial interest in the subject matter, for s 25(2) makes clear that the settlor may retain some beneficial interest under the settlement. It also makes clear that the settlor may be the sole trustee of the *b* settlement; so a settlor may by declaring himself a trustee of property for beneficiaries, who may include himself, effect a 'gift in settlement' without disposing of any part of the legal ownership in the property.

One wonders why the draftsman selected the expression 'gift in settlement'. Two possible explanations suggest themselves to me and no more: first, that he used the expression to describe a purely voluntary settlement, made without any consideration *c* being given for it, or at any rate without any consideration in money or money's worth; and, second, that he used the expression to distinguish a disposal of an asset to trustees of a settlement by a settlor, for which the trustees gave no consideration, from a disposal of an asset to trustees of a settlement by a vendor on a purchase by the trustees out of their trust fund.

Property may become settled property in either of two ways: (a) by the settlor *d* transferring it to trustees on trust, or (b) by the trustees investing their settled fund or some part of it in the purchase of that property. In either case the property equally becomes settled property held on the trusts of the settlement. In the former case the transaction can, in my view, not inappropriately be described as 'a gift in settlement', and I think that it would not be an abuse of language so to describe it even in a case in which the settlor receives some personal advantage from making the settlement or some *e* consideration for doing so, so long as the transaction does not amount in substance to a sale of the subject matter to the trustees.

Counsel for the taxpayer have contended that the settlement of the shares and stock contained no element of gift: the party who became entitled to the reversionary interest paid £14,500 for it (which I will assume to have been its market value) and the taxpayer himself retained the rest of the beneficial interest, so that there was no act of bounty *f* involved. There was, according to the taxpayer's argument, merely a part disposal of the shares and stock, the life interest therein remaining undisposed of in the taxpayer. This argument looks exclusively at the beneficial interests in the subject matter and ignores the transfer of the legal ownership to the trustees, for, if there was a part disposal, it was not a part disposal of the legal ownership, but a disposal of part of the beneficial interest. This appears to me to fit very awkwardly, if it can be said to fit at all, with the *g* scheme of the Act as a whole. As I hope I have demonstrated, normally in the case of settled property, so long as the property remains vested in the trustees of the settlement, they are treated as the owners of the capital assets comprised in the settlement and it is on actual or notional disposal by them of any of those assets that chargeable gains or allowable losses arise. The liability to the tax follows the legal ownership of the corpus of the trust fund. For the purpose of calculating such gains or losses it is necessary to *h* discover what it notionally or actually cost the trustees to acquire each asset of the trust. This is achieved initially by the trustees being treated as if they had bought the original assets of the trust fund from the settlor at their market value. Dealings by beneficiaries with their beneficial interests may render those beneficiaries liable to tax at some stage, but such dealings have no effect on the liability of the trustees.

If in the present case there was no 'gift in settlement' within s 25(2), no disposition by *j* the taxpayer of the entire ownership of the shares and stock to the trustees, and no acquisition of that entire ownership by the trustees for a deemed consideration equal to the market value, there would be no way, so far as I can see, of fixing any notional cost of acquisition which the trustees would be entitled to deduct in computing what gain or loss, if any, had accrued to them on a subsequent sale by them of any of the settled shares or stock, or on any notional disposal by them of the corpus of the settled property. The

price paid by the purchasers for the reversionary interest would be irrelevant in this
a respect because it was not paid by the trustees and, moreover, was not a price paid, or to be deemed to have been paid, by anyone for the shares and stock, but a price paid for something else, viz a limited equitable interest in the settled fund, which would not be the asset of which the trustees would be disposing. It would follow that, if the trustees were to sell any part of the settled shares and stock, they would only be entitled to deduct incidental expenses for the purposes of calculating the notional capital gain on which
b they would be taxable. They would be taxable on the entire net proceeds of sale, notwithstanding that the sale might in fact be at a loss in relation to the taxpayer's expenditure in acquiring it, or to its market value at the date of the settlement. This surely could not be a consequence which Parliament intended.

On the other hand, if there was in the present case a 'gift in settlement' within s 25(2), the liability to tax would follow the ownership of the corpus of the settled property in the
c manner I have indicated, accompanied by a right for the trustees to deduct appropriate actual or notional base values whenever liability to tax should arise during the subsistence of the settlement. This would be a result which would conform to the apparent design and policy of the statute.

Counsel for the taxpayer has submitted that we should not concern ourselves with what the apparent design or policy of the statute is. He has reminded us of Rowlatt J's
d dictum in *Cape Brandy Syndicate v Inland Revenue Comrs* [1921] 1 KB 64 at 71 that in construing a taxing statute one has to look merely at what is clearly said without regard to intendment. When what is said is clearly said, this is no doubt so; but I do not think that the expression 'a gift in settlement' is a clear one. One must first construe the Act in order to discover what it says in this respect, and for that exercise the context of the enactment as a whole is, in my opinion, clearly not only a legitimate aid but one to which
e the court is bound to have regard.

These considerations dispose me strongly to construe 'gift in settlement' in the second of the two senses which I have indicated earlier. But let me test the position further by a consideration of s 22(2). It cannot, in my view, be disputed that when the taxpayer transferred the shares and stock to the trustees he transferred the whole legal ownership in the shares and stock. Indeed I did not understand counsel for the taxpayer to suggest
f otherwise. What is said is that for the purposes of the statute he must be treated as having made only a part disposal of the subject matter.

It must be borne in mind that the tax is a tax on capital gains (see s 19(1)), that is to say, gains accruing on the disposal of assets. The expression 'assets' comprises in this context all forms of property (see s 22(1)). The shares and stock were, immediately before the settlement, undoubtedly assets of the taxpayer. After the settlement the reversionary
g interest in the settled fund then represented by the shares and stock was undoubtedly an asset of the purchasers. The shares and stock were equally undoubtedly assets held by the trustees on the trusts of the settlement. There was no direct disposal of any asset by the taxpayer to the purchasers. In law the taxpayer disposed of his entire ownership in the shares and stock to the trustees. He did so on terms which resulted in the purchasers' becoming entitled to a reversionary interest in the property so transferred, expectant on
h his own death, and in himself becoming entitled to an immediate life interest in the same property. The taxpayer had, however, no proprietorial rights or interests specifically in the shares and stock once the settlement took effect. He could neither require nor forbid the sale of any part of them. He could not control the trustees in the exercise of their powers as holders of the shares and stock in any way. He became entitled to a life interest in the income of the settled property, however it might be
j invested from time to time.

It is contended that in these circumstances the taxpayer made a part disposal of the shares and stock within s 22(2). The words relied on are 'there is a part disposal of an asset where, on a person making a disposal, any description of property derived from the asset remains undisposed of'. These words might well be held to fit the present case if it had taken the form of a grant by the taxpayer to the purchasers of a reversionary interest expectant on his own death specifically in the shares and stock, the taxpayer reserving to

himself a life interest in them, thus constituting himself a trustee of the shares and
stock. In such circumstances the only disposal would have been of the reversionary *a*
interest, and the life interest might be accurately described as having 'remained
undisposed of'. But that was not the form of the transaction. The property disposed of
was the shares and stock. The property in which the purchasers acquired a reversionary
interest was not specifically the shares and stock, but a fund which, for the time being
only, was represented by the shares and stock. Strictly speaking, nothing, in my view,
remained undisposed of. The taxpayer acquired a new asset consisting of a life interest *b*
under the settlement, not specifically in the shares and stock, but in the fund for the time
being represented by the shares and stock. Counsel for the taxpayer contends that the
life interest was 'property derived from' the shares and stock. I see the force of that
argument, but I find difficulty in regarding the taxpayer's life interest as being accurately
described as 'derived from' specific investments which might only transiently represent
the fund in which the life interest existed. *c*

What principally weighs with me is that the assets of which the taxpayer disposed
were, as it seems to me, indisputably the shares and stock. He must either have made an
entire disposal of them or a part disposal. The disponees were the trustees. In ordinary
terms it cannot be denied that the disposal of them was entire, nothing remaining
undisposed of. One can only discover possible grounds for the view that there was no
more than a part disposal by considering the beneficial ownership distinct from the legal *d*
ownership. As I have endeavoured to show, in this Act capital gains tax on property held
in trust, except in the case of property held in the name of a nominee or vested in a bare
trustee (s 22(5)), is exacted from the trustees as the legal owners of the corpus of the
settled property, and disregards beneficial interests except in the case of a beneficiary who
has bought his interest. In these circumstances, reading ss 22(2) and 25(2) together, I
reach the conclusion that on the true construction of the Act there was not merely a part *e*
disposal of the shares and stock in the present case but an entire disposal of them to the
trustees.

Counsel for the taxpayer submits that the trustees acquired the shares and stock by
way of a bargain made at arm's length for the purposes of s 22(4), for he says that the
shares and stock were transferred to the trustees as the result of the bargain between the
taxpayer and the purchasers, which was a bargain made at arm's length. That the *f*
purchasers acquired the reversionary interest by way of a bargain at arm's length cannot,
I think, be doubted. The reversionary interest did not exist as such before the settlement
took effect. It seems to me reasonable to regard the settlement as a consequence of that
bargain. But can it sensibly and accurately be said that the trustees acquired the shares
and stock by way of that bargain? It seems to me that the language of s 22(4)(*a*) poses the
question whether the acquisition of the asset (in this case the shares and stock) was the *g*
subject matter of a bargain between the disponor and the disponee (in this case the
taxpayer and the trustees) which was at arm's length. The object of this provision is
surely to ensure that market value is treated as the consideration actually given for the
disposal of the asset where the circumstances are not such as to demonstrate that a full
and fair price was paid for it. The fact that someone other than the disponee can be taken
to have paid a full and fair price for something other than the subject matter of the *h*
disposal under consideration has no bearing on this. The learned judge regarded the
taxpayer's settlement of 4th April 1972 as a tripartite bargain in respect of which the
settlor was at arm's length with both the purchasers of the reversionary interest and the
trustees. With deference to Goulding J I feel unable to regard the taxpayer as having
made a bargain at arm's length with the trustees, although I accept that he did so with the
purchaser. Accordingly, in my judgment, s 22(4)(*a*) applies to the present case on the *j*
footing that the acquisition of the shares and stock by the trustees was otherwise than by
way of a bargain made at arm's length, so that the trustees must be deemed to have paid
market value for the shares and stock, unless the words 'Subject to the provisions of this
Part of this Act' produce a contrary result. It is said that they do so, because, by reason of
s 22(2), there was only a part disposal of the shares and stock. I have already given my
reasons for thinking that this was not the case.

For these reasons I have, with diffidence, reached a different conclusion from that reached by the learned judge in his exceptionally clear and careful judgment.

This makes it strictly unnecessary for me to consider the 'connected persons' argument, but I should perhaps state my opinion about this. This argument depends on para 21(3) of Sch 7 to the Act. As Goulding J pointed out, the word 'settlement' does not have the same meaning in that sub-paragraph as it has elsewhere in the Act, because the definition of 'settlement' which is to be found in s 454 of the Income and Corporation Taxes Act 1970 is imported into para 21(3) of the schedule but does not apply elsewhere in the Act. The House of Lords has held that bounty is an essential element of a settlement within that definition (see *Inland Revenue Comrs v Plummer* [1979] 3 All ER 775, [1979] 3 WLR 689), with the consequence that the taxpayer's settlement would not, as it seems to me, fall within the terms of the sub-paragraph. For this reason I agree with the learned judge that the sub-paragraph cannot apply to the present case.

I have not so far found it necessary to mention the fact that the transfers of the shares and stock were not registered until 12th May 1972 and 28th April 1972 respectively. It is true that until that occurred the trustees were not, vis-à-vis Rothschild Investment Trust Ltd, the holders of the shares and stock, but at 4th April 1972 the trustees had in their possession executed transfers of all the shares and stock registered in the names of the taxpayer and his wife as well as the relative certificates. As regards the shares and stock owned by the taxpayer but registered in the name of Lloyds Bank (Branches) Nominees Ltd, the transfers were signed on 21st March 1972. They and the relative certificates were received by the trustees' agents 'on or shortly after 6th April 1972'. There is no finding about precisely when they were dispatched by the nominee company to the trustees' agents, nor is there any finding that the taxpayer was in any way responsible for any delay there may have been between 21st March and 6th April or that he was even aware of it. I should be very unwilling to hold that the fiscal consequences of the transaction depended on the degree of diligence with which the nominee company or the trustees carried out the purely ministerial steps of transmitting or registering the transfers or handing over the certificates. On the findings of the commissioners I for my part think that the taxpayer and his wife should be regarded as having done all that lay in their power to transfer the shares and stock to the trustees before the date of the settlements and that the ownership of the shares and stock must be treated as having passed to the trustees at the latest when the taxpayer and his wife executed the settlements. From that time, as it seems to me, neither the taxpayer nor his wife could have asserted an equitable interest in any of the shares and stock otherwise than under and by virtue of the settlements (see in this connection the decision of Jenkins J in *Re Rose, Midland Bank Executor and Trustee Co Ltd v Rose* [1948] 2 All ER 971 at 978–979, [1949] Ch 78 at 88–90).

For these reasons I for my part would allow this appeal. The Crown does not seek to levy tax on both the £14,500 paid for the reversionary interest and the market value of the shares and stock, but on the latter only. I would restore the decision of the commissioners and the assessment to tax on a capital gain of £150,483. The learned judge thought that no chargeable gain or allowable loss would have accrued if the purchasers had subsequently disposed of the reversionary interest, because that interest was created by the settlement for the benefit of the purchaser. I should not be taken as agreeing with this view, for it seems to me that the purchaser (if otherwise amenable to a charge to tax) would not have been entitled to exemption under Sch 7, para 13. The purchaser would, it seems to me, have been a beneficiary who acquired his interest under the settlement for a consideration in money and so would have been disentitled to exemption.

Appeal dismissed. Leave to appeal to the House of Lords granted.

Solicitors: *Solicitor of Inland Revenue*; *Norton Rose, Botterell & Roche* (for the taxpayer).

Edwina Epstein Barrister.

Attorney General's Reference (No 5 of 1980) a

COURT OF APPEAL, CRIMINAL DIVISION
LAWTON LJ, CHAPMAN AND BOREHAM JJ
1st SEPTEMBER 1980 b

Criminal law – Obscene publications – Article – Film or other record of a picture or pictures – Video cassette used to show obscene film – Whether video cassette an article capable of being published – Obscene Publications Act 1959, s 1(2)(3)(b).

The respondents operated two cinemas at which they showed obscene films to paying c customers. Instead of using a conventional film projector to show the films the respondents used a video cassette player containing video tape, the image from the tape being displayed on a screen so that the effect was indistinguishable from a conventional film show. The respondents were charged with publishing an obscene article contrary to s 2 of the Obscene Publications Act 1959. The trial judge directed the jury to acquit the respondents on the ground that s 1(2)[a] of the 1959 Act defined an 'article', when d referring to the display of images on a screen, as 'any film or other record of a picture or pictures' and, construed ejusdem generis, a video tape was not of the same genus as a film and therefore there had not been publication of an obscene article. On a reference by the Attorney General on the question whether a video cassette was an article within s 1(2),

Held – Having regard to the fact that the object of s 1(2) of the 1959 Act was to bring all e articles which produced words, pictures or sounds within the compass of the Act (with two exceptions not material in the circumstances), the words 'film or other record' in s 1(2) were to be construed in the context of the subsection as a whole and were apt to cover the use of a video cassette to produce pictures, since the publication envisaged by the Act and referred to in s 1(3)(*b*)[b], namely the showing, playing or projecting of an article, covered pictures produced by a video cassette. Accordingly a video cassette was f an article within the meaning of s 1(2) (see p 819 *h j* and p 821 *g* to p 822 *b*, post).

Notes
For publishing an obscene article or having obscene articles for publication for gain, see 11 Halsbury's Laws (4th Edn) para 1016.
For the Obscene Publications Act 1959, ss 1, 2, see 8 Halsbury's Statutes (3rd Edn) 479, g 480.

Case referred to in judgment
Derrick v Customs and Excise Comrs [1972] 1 All ER 993, [1972] 2 QB 28, [1972] 2 WLR 359, 136 JP 294, DC, Digest (Cont Vol D) 774, *885a*.

h

Cases also cited
Barker v Wilson [1980] 2 All ER 81, [1980] 1 WLR 884, DC.
Cox v Stinton [1951] 2 All ER 637, [1951] 2 KB 1021, DC.
Straker v Director of Public Prosecutions [1963] 1 All ER 697, [1963] 1 QB 926, DC.

Reference j
The respondents were tried on 3rd July 1980 at the Crown Court at Knightsbridge before his Honour Judge Lewisohn and a jury on charges of publishing an obscene article,

---

a Section 1(2) is set out at p. 818 *f*, post
b Section 1(3), so far as material, is set out at p. 818 *g*, post

namely a video cassette, contrary to s 2 of the Obscene Publications Act 1959 and were
a acquitted by the jury on the direction of the judge. The Attorney General referred, under s 36 of the Criminal Justice Act 1972, for the opinion of the Court of Appeal the question whether a person who provided an obscene display of images on a screen to persons who were likely to be depraved or corrupted by that display published an obscene article contrary to s 2 of the 1959 Act where the images were derived from video tape. The alleged offences took place before the coming into force of s 53 of the Criminal
b Law Act 1977. The facts are set out in the judgment of the court.

David Tudor Price for the Attorney General.
Stuart Shields QC and *Geoffrey Robertson* for the first two respondents.
Geoffrey Robertson for the third and fourth respondents.

c

LAWTON LJ delivered the following judgment of the court: In this matter the Attorney General, acting under s 36 of the Criminal Justice Act 1972, has asked this court to give its opinion on the following point of law:

> 'Does a person who provides an obscene display of images on a screen to persons who are likely to be depraved or corrupted by that display publish an obscene
> d Article contrary to Section 2 of the Obscene Publications Act, 1959 in a case where the images are derived from Video Tape?'

The material facts which give rise to this reference are as follows. Police officers in possession of a warrant to search premises issued under the 1959 Act visited basement premises in London. These premises were set out as two small cinemas to which persons
e were admitted on payment of money. In each of the cinemas obscene displays with sound, indistinguishable to the watcher from conventional film shows, were being shown on screens to audiences who were present.

Three persons admitted responsibility for these activities and admissions of responsibility for the shows were made on behalf of the company which received the profits thereof.

f The displays were not conventional film shows but were derived from video cassettes. A video cassette contains video tape. When a video tape is played electric signals from it are fed by way of cable to a conventional television receiver containing a cathode ray display tube. This display tube within the display screen provides the means by which the images derived from the video tape are displayed on the screen. The electric signals are fired down the display tube to produce the images. The system used in this case did
g not involve the projection of light on to a screen. The light to provide the images was emitted from the cathode ray display tube.

The indictment charged three persons and a company with publishing an obscene article, namely a video cassette, contrary to s 2 of the 1959 Act, at a date prior to the coming into force of the provisions of s 53 of the Criminal Law Act 1977.

At the end of the case for the Crown the judge (his Honour Judge Lewisohn) directed
h the jury to return a verdict of not guilty against all the defendants on the ground that a video cassette was not an obscene 'article' as defined by s 1(2) of the 1959 Act, and thus there was no publication of an obscene article as alleged.

Three submissions were made to the judge at the end of the Crown's case. First, a video cassette was not an 'article' as defined by s 1(2) of the 1959 Act. The words 'any film or other record of a picture or pictures' should be construed ejusdem generis and a
j video tape was not of the same genus as a film. Secondly, that because the process by which a video tape was made in the first instance included the projection of light, the showing of a video tape was a cinematograph exhibition, and therefore exempted from the provisions of s 1(3)(*b*) of the Act by the relevant words of the proviso to the subsection which were in force at the time of the offence charged. Thirdly, in the alternative, because the Crown expert had agreed that the process of display could be described as

'television', that the display was one shown in the course of television and was therefore exempted by that part of the proviso to s 1(3)(*b*) which was then and is now in force. a

The judge, as I have indicated, ruled in favour of the defence submission on the first point. As to the second submission, he ruled that if the evidence at the end of the case showed merely that the video tape was initially recorded by means of the projection of light, then its showing would not be a cinematograph exhibition. But the judge stated that he would have left as a question of fact for the jury to determine whether the process of showing it did include the projection of light so as to make it a cinematograph b exhibition. Thirdly, he ruled that even if the process of showing the video cassette was something done in the course of television, its showing to an audience in one set of premises did not amount to broadcasting so as to bring the activity within the exemption conferred by the proviso to s 1(3)(*b*) of the 1959 Act.

We have not been concerned with the second submission made to the judge. Whether the judge was right or wrong on the evidence which was before him is of no interest now c because, as a result of the provisions of s 53 of the Criminal Law Act 1977, that which took place, even if it had been a cinematograph exhibition, would now be an unlawful publication of an obscene article.

As to the third submission, counsel for the Attorney General has been content that the law should be as the trial judge ruled it was and he has not asked us to deal with the element of television. Counsel has said on behalf of the first two respondents to this d reference that whether a particular display via a video cassette was or was not a television broadcast would depend on the evidence. He has not asked us to deal with the third of the submissions made to the judge.

It follows therefore that the sole issue before us has been whether a video cassette is an article within the definition of an obscene article in s 1(2) of the 1959 Act.

In so far as that Act provides a definition of an obscene article, it has not been affected e by subsequent legislation amending the 1959 Act, but nevertheless, because of a point taken by counsel for the first two respondents, it may be necessary to look at some of the amending legislation.

Counsel for the Attorney General puts his submissions succinctly. He says that s 1(2) was intended to embrace any article whatsoever that could be used to show images. This, he submitted, was demonstrated by the words of sub-s (2) itself and by the wide terms of f s 1(3)(*b*). The definition of an 'article' contained in s 1(2) is as follows:

> 'In this Act "article" means any description of article containing or embodying matter to be read or looked at or both, any sound record, and any film or other record of a picture or pictures.'

Subsection (3), in its relevant parts, is as follows: g

> 'For the purposes of this Act a person publishes an article who . . . (*b*) in the case of an article containing or embodying matter to be looked at or a record, shows, plays or projects it . . .'

There then follow two provisos: one relating to a cinematograph exhibition and the other to television or sound broadcasting. h

Counsel for the Attorney General submitted that the wide words of sub-s (2) indicate that any article which brought about the reproduction of an obscene image was within the contemplation of the Act and that the only kinds of reproduction of obscene images which were outside the Act were the two exemptions set out in the provisos. He went on to point out that in sub-s (3) publication embraces a person who publishes, in the case of an article containing or embodying matter to be looked at, or a record, shows, plays or j projects it. He went on to remind the court that in sub-s (2) the word 'record' occurs twice. One one occasion it has the adjective 'sound' in front of it and in the other case the adjectival phrase 'any film or other' comes before the word 'record'. It followed, so submitted counsel for the Attorney General, that an accused publishes an obscene article if it is in the form of a record and he shows, plays or projects it. The record may be either of sound or of pictures. A video tape does in fact constitute a record of pictures, albeit that it is a record which is made up of electrical impulses recorded on a video tape. As neither of the exemptions apply, so says counsel, it follows that a video cassette, being a record of pictures, does constitute an article within the meaning of s 1(2). As in this case there was clearly a publication of the video cassette, it follows that the judge ought not to have ruled as he did.

To that submission, counsel for the first two respondents, whose argument has been adopted by counsel on behalf of the other respondents, has made the following answer. He has reminded the court that in 1959, when the Obscene Publications Act was passed, video tapes had not got much beyond the experimental stage. They were probably used by broadcasting bodies (such as the British Broadcasting Corporation) but they were not on sale to the public as they are now. It follows, he says, that it is inconceivable that Parliament had video tapes in mind when it was deciding what articles should come within the description 'obscene articles' for the purposes of the 1959 Act. He says that this court should be slow to apply the words to a piece of electronic equipment which probably had not been within the contemplation of Parliament. We have kept in mind that particular admonition made by counsel, but if the clear words of the statute are sufficiently wide to cover the kind of electronic device with which we are concerned in this case the fact that that particular form of electronic device was not in the contemplation of Parliament in 1959 is an immaterial consideration. In any event in 1959 Parliament would almost certainly have had in mind the fact that electronic equipment for reproducing words and pictures was something likely to come about in the near future. In those circumstances it is not all that improbable that words were chosen which were wide enough to embrace any developments in the electronic field. But speculation as to what Parliament had in mind and what it probably had not got in mind is neither here nor there. It is the duty of this court to consider the wording of the Act and to construe the words in it (if they are words of ordinary English usage) in the ways in which they would have been understood by ordinary literate persons at the material time, namely 1959.

Counsel for the first two respondents has submitted that even when that test is applied the words are not apt to embrace what happens when a video cassette is played. He points out that sub-s (2) embraces three different situations. One is an 'article containing or embodying matter to be read or looked at or both', secondly, a 'sound record' and, thirdly, 'any film or other record of a picture or pictures'. He did not seek to say (as counsel who appeared on behalf of his client at the trial sought to do) that the ejusdem generis rule applied. The judge thought it did. He put the matter in this way in his ruling:

> 'Does a video cassette fall within the words "or other record of a picture or pictures"? Let me start this consideration by saying that I accept the submission that these words form part of one phrase or division, starting with the words "any film". Therefore the other record of picture has to have some kinship with film.'

He was wrong in that approach because what he had to do was to construe the words 'film or any other record' in the context of sub-s (2). It is clear that sub-s (2) embraced a number of articles, starting with those which contained or embodied obscene matter, those which were in the form of a soundtrack and those which were a film or other record of pictures. The judge did not have the advantage of having cited to him the decision of the Divisional Court in *Derrick v Customs and Excise Comrs* [1972] 1 All ER 993, [1972] 2 QB 28. Had he had the benefit of having that decision referred to him, he would have appreciated that he had to look at the subsection as a whole and not to pick out any particular group of words in the subsection. But the fact that he was mistaken in applying the ejusdem generis rule does not mean that there is not force in what counsel for the first two respondents has submitted to this court, because his submission has proceeded as follows. There being three types of article, each of them was dealt with, so he submits, specifically in sub-s (3)(*b*). That, he says, is shown by the way in which that paragraph is worded, because under it—

> 'a person publishes an article who . . . (*b*) in the case of an article containing or embodying matter to be looked at [that is the first category of obscene article] or a record [which could cover both the second and third categories], shows, plays or projects it.'

Counsel submitted that a video cassette shows nothing. Anyone looking at it merely sees a piece of magnetised tape. There is nothing on that tape to indicate the presence of electrical impulses and certainly nothing on the tape to show pictures. So, so he submits, the word 'shows' is inapplicable. He went on to submit that the word 'plays', bearing in mind the year in which this statute was passed (1959) clearly applied to a sound record mentioned in sub-s (2). A video tape is not played in any sort of way that a sound record would have been played in 1959. For myself I am not all that certain of that because in 1959 there were many tape recorders and, in ordinary English, those who use tape recorders play them. But be that as it may, assuming for the moment that the word 'plays' is inappropriate to a video cassette, counsel went on to submit that the word 'projects' is inapplicable to a video cassette. He submitted, again bearing in mind that the statute was passed in 1959, that the word 'projects' envisaged the kind of projection which there is for films, namely by projecting light behind the film and producing an image on a screen. That, he submitted, was not a concept which could be applicable to a video cassette.

He went on to point out that if video cassettes were to be distinguished from films (and he was submitting that the words 'other record of a picture or pictures' meant something in the nature of a film, if not a film) then anomalies would arise in the administration of the law relating to obscene publications. Those anomalies come about (so counsel submitted) in this way. After 1959, as is common knowledge, video cassettes became freely available to the public and in recent years they have been the vehicle for the publication of obscene pictures. The 1959 Act, as I have already said, exempted cinematograph exhibitions from its application. Counsel for the Attorney General has told us (and we accept) that the reason was that in 1959 it was thought that the controls which existed under the Cinematograph Acts 1909 and 1952, together with the existence of the British Board of Film Censors, provided adequate protection to the public from the showing of obscene films in what, for want of a better term, I am going to call the commercial cinema. But for various reasons, with which we are not concerned, that protection turned out to be inadequate. As a result a difficulty arose (some might describe it as a nuisance) as a result of private persons prosecuting the owners of commercial cinemas for publishing obscene films. It was thought that this was undesirable. As a result, by s 53 of the Criminal Law Act 1977, which in its material part came into operation on 1st December 1977, no prosecution of anyone for showing films in commercial cinemas could be undertaken without the consent of the Director of Public Prosecutions.

The way the provisions was enacted was this (I quote from s 53(2) of the Criminal Law Act 1977):

> 'In section 2 of that Act [that is the 1959 Act] at the end of subsection (3) there shall be inserted the following subsection:—"(3A) Proceedings for an offence under this section shall not be instituted except by or with the consent of the Director of Public Prosecutions in any case where the article in question is a moving picture film of a width of not less than sixteen millimetres . . . ".'

Commercial films are always of not less than 16 mm. It follows, said counsel for the first two respondents, that although the consent of the Director is required for a prosecution in respect of the showing of indecent films of a size of 16 mm and over, it would not be required for the showing in cinemas of video cassettes. The consequence would be that private prosecutions could be started in respect of such shows, although had they been on

16 mm film in commercial cinemas they could not have been shown. There is a difference there.

The next difference arises in this way. Under s 4 of the 1959 Act, there was a defence of public good. That defence was in these terms:

> '(1) A person shall not be convicted of an offence against section two of this Act ... if it is proved that publication of the article in question is justified as being for the public good on the ground that it is in the interests of science, literature, art or learning, or of other objects of general concern ...'

In 1968 Parliament decided to free theatres from the control of the Lord Chamberlain. That was done by the Theatres Act 1968. Section 3 of that Act provided as follows:

> '(1) A person shall not be convicted of an offence under section 2 of this Act if it is proved that the giving of the performance in question was justified as being for the public good on the ground that it was in the interests of drama, opera, ballet or any other art, or of literature or learning ...'

When Parliament decided to amend the 1959 Act in relation to (I use a wide term) the interests of the commercial cinema, it provided by s 53(6) of the 1977 Act that there should be no prosecution of such a performance in a commercial cinema—

> 'if it is proved that publication of the film or soundtrack is justified as being for the public good on the ground that it is in the interests of drama, opera, ballet or any other art, or of literature or learning.'

In other words, in relation to films, there was to be the same test of public good as there was in relation to the theatre. But that test was in different words from the general defence of public good provided by s 4 of the 1959 Act.

It followed, submitted counsel for the first two respondents, that if there was a showing in a commercial cinema of a film which was alleged to be obscene the test would be different from that which there would be if there was a showing by means of a video cassette in a cinema of the type found to exist in this case. There is something in that argument, but not much. It seems to us that what the Theatres Act 1968 and the Criminal Law Act 1977 were doing was making it clear what the word 'art' in s 4 of the 1959 Act embraced, namely drama, opera and ballet. That, in our judgment, is shown by the use of the additional words 'or any other art'. Quite clearly Parliament regarded drama, opera and ballet as being a form of art. It would have been surprising if they had not taken that view.

So although there is a very slight difference between the tests to be applied in the different cases, in our judgment, it is not sufficient to make any difference to the construction of sub-ss (2) and (3) of s 1.

The basic question is whether there is any substance in the submission of counsel for the first two respondents that the words in sub-ss (2) and (3) are not apt to cover a video cassette. In our judgment they are. As counsel for the Attorney General rightly submitted, the object of sub-s (2) was to bring all articles which produced words or pictures or sounds within the embrace of the Act. There were to be only two exceptions.

In our judgment the words 'shows, plays or projects' in sub-s (3)(*b*) are sufficiently wide to cover what happens when pictures are produced by way of a video cassette. It may be that counsel for the first two respondents was right in his submission that the word 'show', in the context of sub-s (3)(*b*), implies looking at, but the words 'play or project' cover, in our judgment, what happens when a video tape is used in such a way as to produce pictures. As I have already indicated in ordinary parlance (this would have been the same in 1959 as it is today) when a tape recorder is used it is talked about as being played. We see no reason why the same sort of language should not apply to a video cassette which produces not sounds but pictures. Even if that is not right (and we think it is right) the word 'project' would be apt to cover what happens when a video cassette is brought into use, because what is happening is that the electrical impulses recorded on the video tape are thrown onto the television screen by means of the use of an electric current. In ordinary parlance, they are projected onto the television screen.

Accordingly we find that the question posed to us by the Attorney General in this reference is to the effect that a video cassette is an article within the meaning of s 1(2) of the 1959 Act.

Determination accordingly. Leave to appeal to the House of Lords refused.

Solicitors: *Director of Public Prosecutions*; *Cowan, Lipson & Rumney* (for the respondents).

Mary Rose Plummer Barrister.

Practice Direction

QUEEN'S BENCH DIVISION

Practice – Writ – New form of writ of summons – Consequential changes in Central Office practice – RSC App A – RSC (Writ and Appearance) 1979 (SI 1979 No 1716), r 49(1).

The Masters' Practice Directions (see the Supreme Court Practice 1979, vol 2, paras 901ff, pp 195ff) regulating the practice to be followed in the Central Office of the Supreme Court shall, with effect from 3rd June 1980, be amended as follows.

1 General

1. This direction shall be amended by adding the following sub-paragraphs:

'(3) Practice directions 9, 9A, 10, 11 and 12 shall be revoked and there shall be substituted therefor the following practice directions 9, 9A, 9B, 10, 11 and 12.

'(4) In relation to any cause or matter begun on or after 3rd June 1980, unless the context otherwise requires, any reference in these directions, the extra-jurisdiction table, the judgment table and the execution table and the masters' practice forms, or elsewhere, to the words "appearance" and "entry of appearance", wherever occurring, shall be substituted by a reference to the words "acknowledgment of service" or, as the case may be, a "notice of intention to defend".'

2 Forms (see RSC Ord 1, r 9)

1. This direction shall be amended by adding the following paragraphs:

'In relation to any cause or matter begun on or after 3rd June 1980, the following practice forms shall be used for the particular case to which each of these forms applies.

'Note: Practice forms 131, 135, 138, 139, 140 and 142 have been left unchanged because they are applicable to matters that were commenced either before or after 3rd June 1980.

'The practice forms which apply to causes or matters begun before 3rd June 1980 will be prefixed by the letter "O" to stand for the description "Old", e g "OPF" followed by a number so as to distinguish such practice forms from those which will apply to causes or matters begun after 3rd June 1980 but which bear the same PF number.'

9 Issue of writ of summons (see RSC Ord 6)

a 1. *Preparation of writ of summons for issue* The responsibility for preparing for issue the new form of writ of summons (RSC App A, form 1) (see RSC (Writ and Appearance) 1979, SI 1979 No 1716, r 49(1)) rests on the solicitor acting for the plaintiff or on the plaintiff himself if he is acting in person. The new form is different from the old, but the general duty on the person preparing it for issue remains substantially the same as before. Since the new form is a single, composite, multi-purpose form, special care and
b attention must be taken in completing it. In accordance with RSC Ord 1, r 9, it may be adapted or varied to serve the particular purpose for which it is issued and it must be completed in such a way as to make it clear (i) whether the writ is to be issued in the Queen's Bench Division or in the Chancery Division, (ii) whether the writ is to be issued out of the Central Office or out of a specified district registry, (iii) whether the writ is to be indorsed with a statement of claim or with a general indorsement, (iv) whether the
c claim made by the plaintiff is for a debt or liquidated demand only, in which case the indorsement relating to the 14-day costs should be retained, (v) where the writ is issued out of a district registry, whether the indorsement as to the place where the cause of action arose should be retained or deleted.

In addition, the person preparing the form should ensure that the other necessary indorsements on the writ as required by RSC Ord 6 are fully and accurately made.

d The officer of the court should check that the necessary indorsements and variations in the prescribed form have been made to make it suitable for the particular purpose for which the writ is to be issued.

2. *Acceptance of prescribed forms already adapted* Where the prescribed form of writ of summons has already been prepared and adapted with such variations as the circumstances may require to make it suitable for the particular purpose for which it is
e to be used, the officer of the court will accept it for issue, provided of course that all the necessary indorsements are fully and accurately made.

3. *Number of copies of writ to be prepared* Copies of the writ should be prepared as follows: (i) one copy which will be treated as the original; after issue it will be returned to and retained by the issuing party; (ii) one copy which will be retained and filed by the court office out of which the writ is issued; this is the copy on which the appropriate fee
f will have been paid; and (iii) one copy for each defendant.

4. *Signing court copy of writ* The court copy of the writ of summons shall be signed with the name of the solicitor or solicitor's clerk suing it out thus: 'CD & Co' *or* 'AB for CD & Co'.

Note. The signature to a statement of claim indorsed on the writ, as required by RSC Ord 18, r 5(5), is not to be taken as a sufficient compliance with the rule requiring the
g copy writ to be signed (see RSC Ord 6, r 7(5)).

5. *Preparation of forms of acknowledgment of service*

(a) It is the duty of the issuing party to prepare a sufficient number of copies of the prescribed form of acknowledgment of service, namely RSC App A, form 14, for each defendant.

(b) The issuing party must complete the formal parts of each such acknowledgment
h of service, i e he must fill in the division of the High Court and, if it be the case, the district registry out of which the writ is to be issued, and the names of the parties exactly as they appear on the writ.

(c) The court officer, having assigned the number of the action, will insert that number on the acknowledgment of service or check that that number has been so inserted so that there will be a true correspondence between the writ and the
j acknowledgment of service.

(d) Finally, the issuing party must complete the fourth page of the acknowledgment of service by inserting his address for service in the top 'box' provided for this purpose, so that when the acknowledgment of service is returned by the defendant a copy of it may be sent on to the plaintiff in a 'window' envelope.

6. *Numerous parties*

(a) Where the parties to an action are numerous, whether as plaintiffs or defendants, so that it is not practicable to include all their names and addresses on the prescribed form of writ of summons, the issuing party may prepare and annex a schedule setting out in full detail the parties in question and their addresses. The writ will be accepted for issue in this form so long as there is a reference to the schedule on the face of the writ, eg 'AB and the other Plaintiffs [*or* CD and the other Defendants] set out in the schedule annexed hereto', and the schedule is securely annexed.

(b) As an alternative to using a schedule, the plaintiff, or his solicitor, may prepare the form of writ in typescript, with the names and addresses appearing in their proper place and, so long as an embossing machine is available for the purpose, the court officer will use it to imprint the Royal Arms on the writ. *No writ may be issued that does not bear the Royal Arms.*

7. *Tendering the writ of summons for issue* For the writ of summons to be issued the plaintiff, or his solicitor, must produce (i) a signed copy of the writ (see para 4 above) on which the appropriate fee has been paid, and this will be the court copy and will be retained and filed by the court officer, (ii) a copy which will be treated for all purposes as the original writ, (iii) one copy for each defendant named in the writ, and (iv) one copy of the form of acknowledgment of service for each defendant with the appropriate information entered on it.

8. *Issue of writ of summons* On presentation of the appropriate forms, duly completed, the court officer will (i) check the documents tendered to ensure due compliance with the applicable rules and with these directions, (ii) assign the action number, (iii) seal in red indorsing ink all the copies of the writ and the first page of the form of acknowledgment of service, (iv) seal the first page of the form of acknowledgment of service to show that it has been produced to the court officer, (v) seal the copy to be treated as the original with the word 'Original' immediately above or below the seal of the issuing court, and (vi) retain and file the court copy, i e the signed copy of the writ, and return all the other documents to the issuing party.

9. The issue of the writ takes place at the time when the issuing officer places the red indorsing seal on the writ, sealed with the word 'Original', and the writ so sealed must be produced at the court office whenever required, eg for amendment of the writ, for the addition, substitution or striking out of a party, for its renewal, for the issue of a concurrent writ, and for any like requirement.

10. *Concurrent writs*

(a) If for good reason shown the plaintiff desires to issue a concurrent writ of summons he should complete a praecipe for a concurrent writ in form PF 4A and state the reasons for his request.

(b) If the request is for a concurrent 'original' then the concurrent writ shall be so marked.

9A Postal facilities for issue of writs etc (see RSC Ord 1, r 10)

1. Subject to the following provisions, the solicitor acting for the plaintiff, or the plaintiff if he is acting in person, may tender a writ of summons or an originating summons to be issued out of the Central Office or a district registry by making application for such issue by post, instead of by personal attendance at the court office.

2. The application must be made by posting the requisite documents as defined in para 3 hereof in a prepaid envelope addressed to—

(a) in the case of the Central Office:

The Action Department, Postal Section
Central Office
Royal Courts of Justice
Strand
LONDON
WC2A 2LL

and (b) in the case of a district registry:

a

District Registrar
High Court of Justice
[*insert address of district registry*]

3. The requisite documents are the following:

b (i) an application by letter or otherwise requesting the issue by post of the writ or the originating summons, as the case may be;

(ii) a copy of the writ or originating summons for each defendant plus two further copies, one of which will be treated as the court copy and the other as the original;

(iii) each copy of the writ or originating summons must be duly completed to make it suitable for the particular purpose for which it is being issued; in the case of a writ of c summons it must contain all necessary indorsements properly made as required by RSC Ord 6 and in the case of an originating summons it must comply with the requirements of RSC Ord 7;

(iv) one copy of the writ or originating summons must be signed by the person requesting its issue, as directed by direction 9(4) above of the Masters' Practice Directions;

(v) payment of the proper amount of the court fees payable on the issue of the writ or d originating summons, which must be made (a) in the case of a solicitor, by a cheque drawn by him or by a postal order crossed and made payable to HM Paymaster General or by a banker's draft, and (b) in the case of a plaintiff acting in person, by a postal order crossed and made payable to HM Paymaster General or by a banker's draft. A cheque drawn by the plaintiff acting in person will not be accepted;

(vi) a sufficient number of copies of the appropriate acknowledgment of service, e which in the case of a writ is RSC App A, form 14 and in the case of an originating summons, App A, form 15. Each copy of such acknowledgment must be duly completed by the issuing party with the title of the action as it appears on the writ or originating summons, and the solicitor for the plaintiff, or the plaintiff if acting in person, must insert his address for service in the top 'box' provided for the purpose on the back of the form of acknowledgment;

f (vii) an envelope which must be properly addressed to the solicitor acting for the plaintiff, or the plaintiff if he is acting in person, and sufficiently stamped for the return of the relevant documents to him.

4. Where an application is made for the issue of more than one writ or originating summons by post, it is advisable to make a *separate payment for each such writ or originating summons*, as in the event of underpayment for the total number of writs or originating g summonses required the application is liable to be returned for the correct amount to be given.

5. An application for the issue of a writ or an originating summons, as the case may be, made by post will be treated as having been made *at the date and time of the actual receipt and acceptance of the requisite documents in the court office out of which it is to be issued*, and for this purpose the date or time of dispatch of the requisite documents will be h wholly disregarded.

6. On receiving the requisite documents and the appropriate payments, the court officer will affix to the application an official stamp showing the date and time on which he received the requisite documents, and if the requisite documents are in proper form and order, he will (a) seal in red indorsing ink every copy of the writ or originating summons with the seal of the court office, (b) further seal in red indorsing ink one copy j of the writ or originating summons with the word 'Original', and that copy writ or the originating summons will be treated as the original writ or originating summons for all purposes, and (c) further seal in read indorsing ink the first page of each copy of the acknowledgment of service to show that it has been produced to the court officer.

7. The court officer will retain for filing the court copy of the writ or originating summons, but he will return all the other documents by post to the solicitor for the

plaintiff, or the plaintiff if he is acting in person, in the envelope sent by him for the purpose.

8. If the requisite documents for any reason appear to the court officer not to comply with the foregoing requirements, he will not issue the writ or originating summons, but will return by post all such documents as were sent by the applicant in the envelope sent by him for the purpose.

9. No responsibility will be accepted for the non-delivery to the party making the application of the writ or originating summons duly sealed, or of the documents sent by him returned to him under para 4, 7 or 8 as the case may be.

10. It is the duty of the party making use of these postal facilities for the issue of a writ or an originating summons to ensure due compliance with the conditions for the proper operation of this procedure.

11. The use of these facilities is at the risk of the party concerned. The solicitor for the plaintiff, or the plaintiff if he is acting in person, should be particularly careful in the use of these postal facilities where time, for any reason, is material and, particularly so, when any period of limitation may be involved.

12. Any queries relating to the fact that the writ or originating summons has not been issued or is defective may more conveniently be dealt with by personal attendance at the Action Department of the Central Office of the Supreme Court or the appropriate district registry.

9B Issue of originating summons

1. Subject to the following provisions, and unless the context otherwise requires, the practice regulating the issue of the writ of summons under direction 9 of the Masters' Practice Directions shall apply to the issue of an originating summons whether it be in the general form or the expedited form, RSC App A, form 8 or form 10 respectively.

2. At the time of tendering the originating summons for issue, the issuing party must produce an acknowledgment of service in RSC App A, form 15 for each defendant named on the originating summons, except that no acknowledgment of service is required in the case of an ex parte originating summons or an originating summons under RSC Ord 113.

10 Substituted service (see RSC Ord 65, r 4)

Unless the court otherwise directs, a copy of the order allowing substituted service on a defendant by pre-paid letter and a copy of the writ accompanied by an acknowledgment of service shall be deemed to have been served on the day following the day on which a prepaid letter containing such copies shall have been posted. (See also Masters' Practice Direction 26A ([1968] 3 All ER 319, [1968] 1 WLR 1489) as to the service of documents by first and second class mail.)

11 Service out of the jurisdiction (see RSC Ord 11)

1. A writ of summons or originating summons against defendants one or some of whom appear to be out of the jurisdiction may be issued without an order for service having been first obtained, but such writ must be specially sealed with a notification that it is 'Not for service out of the jurisdiction'.

2. An order giving leave to issue a writ or a concurrent writ of summons or an originating summons for service out of the jurisdiction or to serve the writ or notice thereof or such originating summons out of the jurisdiction shall specify the country or place where service is to be effected and limit the number of days allowed for the defendant to acknowledge service thereof, and such order shall in the Queen's Bench Division be drawn up and in the Chancery Division shall be indorsed on the writ or originating summons sealed as the original.

3. Unless the court otherwise orders, the times specified in the extra-jurisdiction table shall be followed (a) for limiting the number of days to be allowed to a defendant to acknowledge service thereof when served out of the jurisdiction with a writ or notice thereof or an originating summons, (b) for providing the number of days for the service on a defendant out of the jurisdiction of a four-day summons, and (c) for providing the return day to a four-day summons served on a defendant out of the jurisdiction.

12 Acknowledgment of service (see RSC Ord 12)

1. *Completion of acknowledgment of service* The responsibility for completing the prescribed forms of acknowledgment of service (RSC App A, form 14, in the case of a writ of summons, and form 15, in the case of an originating summons) rests on the solicitor acting for the defendant, or on the defendant if he is acting in person. It is essential that the acknowledgment should be completed fully, clearly and accurately; the directions and notes for guidance should be carefully read and followed. If any information which is required to be given in the acknowledgment is omitted or given wrongly, the form may have to be returned by the court office to which it is delivered or sent, and the consequent delay may result in judgment being entered against the defendant, as a result of which he or his solicitor may have to pay the costs of setting it aside. If no acknowledgment of service is returned to the court office, the plaintiff in the Chancery Division may be required to make a certificate as in practice form PF 9 (certificate of no acknowledgment of service).

2. *Requirements for due acknowledgment of service* The information which is required to be given by or on behalf of the defendant in his acknowledgment of service includes the following: (1) the full name of the defendant must be stated; and if he was sued in a different name this must be shown by adding 'sued as' and stating the name set out in the writ or originating summons; (2) a statement whether or not the defendant intends to contest the proceedings; (3) a statement, where this is applicable, whether the defendant intends to apply for a stay of execution against any judgment entered by the plaintiff; (4) a statement, in a district registry action, applying for its transfer to the Royal Courts of Justice in London or to another, and if so which, district registry; (5) the signature of the solicitor for the defendant or of the defendant if acting in person; and (6) the address for service of the defendant, which should also be inserted in the lower box of the back page provided for the purpose.

3. *Acknowledgment by a limited company or other body corporate* Where the defendant is a limited company or other body corporate the acknowledgment of service need not necessarily be completed by a solicitor, although this will no doubt be usual. As an alternative, the acknowledgment may be completed by a person duly authorised to act on the company's behalf, in which case the acknowledgment must show, on its face, that the person who completed and signed it was so duly authorised, that is to say, the person completing the acknowledgment on the company's behalf must state, after his name, that he is the managing director, director, secretary or other officer of the defendant company, or the mayor, chairman or president of the body corporate or the town clerk, clerk, secretary, treasurer or other similar officer of such body. In the absence of such statement, the acknowledgment of service will not be accepted but will be returned by the court office to the sender. In addition he must state, as the address for service, the address of the registered office if it is a limited company, otherwise the address of the principal office of the defendant. In completing the acknowledgment the authorised person may include a statement of the defendant's intention whether or not to contest the proceedings, but the company or body corporate may not take any other step in the proceedings other than by a solicitor (see RSC Ord 5, r 6(2)).

4. *Acknowledgment on one form by two or more defendants* Where two or more defendants are represented by the same solicitor, that solicitor may acknowledge service for those defendants at the same time by one acknowledgment of service only, but he must clearly identify in this single acknowledgment the defendants for whom he is

acting and he must further make it clear what is the intention of each individual defendant, e g that one specified defendant does, or that another specified defendant does not, intend to contest the proceedings or to apply for a stay of execution or to apply for an order for the transfer of a district registry action. Effect will be given to the intentions of each defendant, even though one acknowledgment of service is completed and lodged in respect of several defendants by the same solicitor.

5. *Statement of intention whether or not to contest the proceedings* A basic requirement of the acknowledgment of service is that the defendant must state whether or not he intends to contest the proceedings.

(a) If a defendant omits to state such intention he will be taken to have expressed the intention not to contest the proceedings and the plaintiff will then be able to enter judgment against him.

(b) If he states his intention ambiguously, e g by ticking both boxes 'Yes' and 'No' or by qualifying his intention whether 'Yes' or 'No' in an unacceptable way, the acknowledgment of service will be rendered nugatory and will be returned to the sender, who will remain at the risk of *not* having acknowledged service.

(c) If the defendant states his intention to contest the proceedings, the plaintiff will not be entitled to enter judgment against him. The action will proceed as usual: the plaintiff may apply for summary judgment under RSC Ord 14 or he may serve his statement of claim if it is not indorsed on the writ and the defendant must serve his defence in due time.

(d) If on the other hand the defendant states his intention not to contest the proceedings, the plaintiff is entitled, under RSC Ord 13, as amended, to enter judgment against him forthwith.

6. *Statement of intention to apply for a stay of execution*

(a) In an action for a debt or liquidated demand only, the defendant, who has stated his intention not to contest the proceedings, may also state his intention to apply for a stay of execution by writ of fi fa against any judgment entered by the plaintiff.

(b) If the defendant should omit to state such intention, the acknowledgment of service will be accepted but the defendant will not be entitled to the automatic stay of execution for 14 days from the date of acknowledgment which is provided by RSC Ord 13, r 8, as amended.

(c) Where, however, the defendant has stated in his acknowledgment his intention to apply for such a stay, the plaintiff may enter final judgment forthwith, but may not issue a writ of execution for a period of 14 days from the date on which the acknowledgment was received at the appropriate court office. Any such writ issued during such period will be irregular and will be set aside as of right. The duty to refrain from issuing such writ of fi fa during such period is that of the plaintiff alone, and it is not the responsibility of any court officer to prevent him from doing so, though wherever possible the attention of the plaintiff may be drawn to the fact that the issue of the writ of fi fa during such period is premature.

(d) If, within the period of 14 days, the defendant issues and serves on the plaintiff a summons for an order that the stay of execution be continued supported by an affidavit in accordance with RSC Ord 41, r 1, the stay will continue in operation until the summons is heard, or disposed of, unless the court otherwise directs. The summons may be issued without waiting for the judgment to be entered.

7. *Statement of application for transfer of district registry action*

(a) In an action begun in a district registry, where in the case of a sole defendant or one of several defendants his residence, place of business or registered office, if a limited company, is *not* within the district of that registry *and* there is no indorsement on the writ that the plaintiff's cause of action arose wholly or in part within that district, that defendant may state in his acknowledgment of service that he applies for the transfer of the action either to the Royal Courts of Justice, London or to another specified district registry. Otherwise, the action will continue in the district registry in which it began.

(b) If any defendant applies in his acknowledgment for such a transfer, and the

plaintiff gives no notice of objection, the district registrar will make an order
a accordingly. See practice form PF 195.

(c) Where, however, the plaintiff gives the district registrar notice of objection within eight days of the defendant's acknowledgment being received at the court office, the district registrar will fix a time and place for the hearing of the defendant's application and will give notice thereof to every party to the proceedings. See practice form PF 196.

8. *Inserting address for service on back page of form of acknowledgment of service* The
b solicitor for the defendant, or the defendant if acting in person, must insert his address for service in the 'box' provided for this purpose on the back page of the acknowledgment of service. This is of great practical importance, for it will enable the copy acknowledgment of service to be returned by post to the solicitor or the defendant, as the case may be, with greater speed and convenience by the use of a 'window' envelope.

9. *Court procedure on receipt of acknowledgment of service* On receiving the
c acknowledgment of service, the court officer should take the following steps:

(1) he must stamp the acknowledgment with the date on which he received it;

(2) he must enter the acknowledgment in the Central Office in the Cause Book, and in district registries on the Cause Index Cards, and *record specifically* (i) whether the defendant has indicated an intention to contest the proceedings, the answer 'Yes' or if not 'No', and (ii) whether the defendant has indicated an intention to apply for a stay of
d execution in respect of any judgment obtained against him in the proceedings, the answer 'Yes' or if not 'No';

(3) he must make two copies of the acknowledgment showing the stamped date of receipt, one for the plaintiff and one for the defendant who submitted it;

(4) he must post one copy of the acknowledgment to the plaintiff or his solicitor and the other to the defendant who submitted that acknowledgment.

e 10. *Amendment of acknowledgment of service* An acknowledgment of service may be amended without the leave of the court in the circumstances provided in RSC Ord 20, r 2(2). Otherwise leave is required, which may be obtained ex parte unless the court directs the issue of a summons.

In any case the praecipe for the amendment of the acknowledgment of service should be in practice form PF 42; and the amended acknowledgment of service will be sealed
f with the seal of the court in which the amendment is made.

11. *Acknowledgment of service of third party notice or other originating process* Where an acknowledgment of service is required to accompany any originating process, other than a writ of summons or an originating summons, as, for example, a third party notice, a counterclaim served on an added party, a claim for indemnity or contribution against a co-defendant who has not acknowledged service, the prescribed form of acknowledg-
g ment of service (RSC App A, form 14) should be adapted to meet the requirements of the particular case. This should be done by the party issuing such originating process.

Thus, in the case of a third party notice, the following modifications will be necessary:

(1) the title of the acknowledgment should be made to correspond with the title in the third party notice;

(2) after the words 'Acknowledgment of Service of' the words 'Writ of Summons'
h should be deleted and substituted by the words 'Third Party Notice';

(3) paras 2, 3 and 4 of the direction for acknowledgment of service should be deleted; and

(4) either the words 'Plaintiff' and 'Defendant' wherever they occur should be deleted and replaced by the words 'Defendant' and 'Third Party' respectively *or* a general formula to the following effect should be added, namely, that the references in the prescribed
j form to 'Plaintiff' and 'Defendant' wherever they occur should be deleted and substituted by the references to 'Defendant' and 'Third Party' respectively.

In the case of other originating processes variations and modifications should be made to the prescribed form of acknowledgment of service on lines similar to those described above in relation to a third party notice as will meet the requirements of the particular case.

[The Practice Direction then sets out a number of practice forms, the text of which is not set out herein. The form numbers and titles are as follows: *a*

PF 4A	Praecipe for concurrent writ
PF 9	Certificate of no acknowledgment of service
PF 42	Praecipe for amended acknowledgment of service
PF 120 (B 35)	Affidavit on application for substituted service
PF 121 (H 19)	Order for substituted service
PF 122 (B 36)	Affidavit of service of writ (personal) *b*
PF 122A	Affidavit of service of writ on individual by post
PF 122B	Affidavit of service of writ on individual by insertion through letter-box
PF 122C	Affidavit of service of writ of summons on partnership firm by post
PF 122D	Affidavit of service of writ on body corporate by post *c*
PF 122E	Affidavit of service of writ on body corporate by insertion through letter-box
PF 123	Affidavit of service on a partner in a firm
PF 124 (B 36A)	Affidavit of service on manager of partnership firm
PF 125	Affidavit of service on officer of corporation (personal)
PF 126 (B 36C)	Affidavit of service on English limited company *d*
PF 127	Affidavit of service on foreign company registered in England
PF 128	Affidavit of service of notice of writ on foreigner abroad
PF 129 (B 36B)	Affidavit of substituted service by post
PF 130 (B 36a(1))	Affidavit of substituted service by post at two addresses
PF 132	Form of advertisement
PF 133 (B 36E)	Affidavit of service of originating summons (general form) *e*
PF 134 (B 36F)	Affidavit of service of originating summons (expedited form)
PF 136	Affidavit of service of summons or notice by post
PF 137 (B 24)	Affidavit of service of summons or notice otherwise than by post
PF 141	Affidavit of service of notice of judgment or order
PF 142A	Affidavit of service of summons or notice where defendant has no address for service *f*
PF 195	Order for transfer of district registry action to the Royal Courts of Justice or another district registry
PF 196	Notice by district registrar to parties fixing time and place for hearing of application for transfer.]

These practice directions will, of course, pursuant to RSC Ord 63, r 11, be followed in *g* the district registries.

SIR JACK I H JACOB QC
Senior Master of the Supreme Court.

12th June 1980

Practice Direction

CHANCERY DIVISION AT MANCHESTER
HIS HONOUR JUDGE BLACKETT-ORD V-C SITTING AS A JUDGE OF THE HIGH COURT
14th JULY 1980

Practice – Estimate of length of trial – Certificate of counsel – Northern area listing of Chancery cases – Necessity for case to be ready for date fixed – Procedure for vacating allotted dates.

HIS HONOUR JUDGE BLACKETT-ORD V-C gave the following direction at the sitting of the court:

1. The present practice of allotting fixed dates for all cases expected to last for a day or more depends for its working on the best possible estimates of length being supplied promptly to the court and on the cases being ready on the day. Attention is drawn to para 2 of the Practice Direction of 5th May 1972 ([1972] 2 All ER 599, [1972] 1 WLR 723).

2. Delays are caused if one or more parties neglects to join in lodging a counsel's certificate of estimated length of trial. In this case any party who desires a hearing date may lodge his own certificate and apply by summons to the district registrar to arrange a date for trial. The district registrar will have authority to deal with the costs of the summons.

3. Solicitors are reminded that they are expected to make every effort to have cases ready by the dates fixed for trial. Dates once allotted will not be vacated unless (a) the case is settled or (b) the leave of the Vice-Chancellor or his Honour Judge FitzHugh QC has been obtained.

4. If it becomes necessary to seek leave under para 3(b) above, the solicitor for the party seeking leave should forthwith apply (normally in writing) giving reasons to the Chief Chancery Clerk at the registry at which the case is listed to be heard. The clerk will then get in touch with the Vice-Chancellor or Judge FitzHugh, who will either consent or direct the application (if it is to be pursued) to be made to him personally in chambers by counsel. The consent of all parties will not of itself be a sufficient reason for an application.

5. When a case is settled, the court should be informed as soon as possible, but no leave to vacate the date is needed, even if a consent order is sought. If a consent order is required, the case will be listed for a convenient motion day.

M Denise Chorlton Barrister.

Practice Direction a

FAMILY DIVISION

Minor – Maintenance – Education or training – Maintenance order including element in respect of school fees – Amount paid direct to school – Tax relief – Form of order – Contract for child's education to be between child and school – Form of contract. b

Where a maintenance order to a child includes an element in respect of school fees, which is paid direct to the school (because, for example, it is feared that the other spouse might dissipate it), the Inland Revenue has agreed, subject to the condition hereafter set out, that tax relief will be given on that element. The wording of the order should be:

> 'That that part of the order which reflects the school fees shall be paid to the c
> headmaster [*or* bursar *or* school secretary] as agent for the said child and the receipt of that payee shall be sufficient discharge.'

The school fees should be paid *in full* and should be paid out of the net amount under the maintenance order after deduction of tax. Certificates for the full tax deduction should continue to be provided to the other spouse (or other person referred to in r 69 of d
the Matrimonial Causes Rules 1977, SI 1977 No 344) in the normal way.

It is a condition of such an order being acceptable for tax purposes that the contract for the child's education (which should preferably be in writing) should be between the child (whose income is being used) and the school and that the fees are received by the officer of the school as the appointed agent for the child.

A form of contract which is acceptable to the Inland Revenue is as follows: e

> 'THIS AGREEMENT is made between THE GOVERNORS OF........ .... by their duly authorised officer .... (hereinafter called "the school") of the first part, ... and the headmaster [*or* bursar *or* school secretary] of the second part, and .... (hereinafter called "the child") of the third part. f
>
> 'WHEREAS it is proposed to ask the ....Court to make an order [*or* the .... Court has made an order] in cause number .... that the father do make periodical payments to the child at the rate of £.......... per annum less tax until the child completes full-time education [*or as the case may be*] and that that part of the order which reflects the school fees shall be paid to the headmaster [*or* bursar *or* school secretary] as agent for the said child g
> and the receipt of that agent shall be a sufficient discharge
>
> '1. The child hereby constitutes the headmaster [*or* bursar *or* school secretary] to be his agent for the purpose of receiving the said fees and the child agrees to pay the said fees to the said school in consideration of being educated there.
>
> '2. In consideration of the said covenant the headmaster [*or* bursar *or* school secretary] agrees to accept the said payments by the father as payments on behalf of h
> the child and the school agrees to educate the child during such time as the said school fees are paid.'

Issued with the concurrence of the Lord Chancellor.

R L BAYNE-POWELL
Senior Registrar.

10th November 1980

a # Armour Hick Northern Ltd and others v Armour Trust Ltd and others

CHANCERY DIVISION

HIS HONOUR JUDGE MERVYN DAVIES QC SITTING AS A JUDGE OF THE HIGH COURT

14th, 22nd FEBRUARY 1980

b

Company – Shares – Purchase of shares with financial assistance of company – Financial assistance – Assistance given by subsidiary company – Subsidiary discharging debt owed by holding company to vendor of shares in return for vendor selling shares in holding company to directors of holding company and subsidiary – Whether subsidiary merely repaying debt owed by holding company – Whether subsidiary providing financial assistance to vendor to enable vendor
c *to sell shares – Whether subsidiary providing financial assistance for purpose of or in connection with share purchase – Companies Act 1948, s 54(1).*

A Ltd was a subsidiary of B Ltd. The shareholders of B Ltd were C Ltd which owned 7,000 shares, and W and H who owned the remaining 3,000 shares and were directors of A Ltd and B Ltd. B Ltd owed the sum of £93,000 to C Ltd and in return for C Ltd selling
d to W and H at par its holding of 7,000 shares in B Ltd W and H arranged for A Ltd to pay £93,000 to C Ltd in satisfaction of the debt owed by B Ltd. As a result W and H became the sole shareholders of B Ltd. A Ltd and B Ltd subsequently went into liquidation and the liquidators brought an action against C Ltd, W and H, claiming, inter alia, on behalf of A Ltd the return of the £93,000. It was alleged that A Ltd had given W and H 'financial assistance for the purpose of or in connection with' the purchase by W and H
e of shares in A Ltd's holding company (ie B Ltd) contrary to s 54(1)[a] of the Companies Act 1948. The question arose whether the payment by a subsidiary of a debt owed by the subsidiary's holding company to the vendor of the holding company's shares was capable in law of constituting 'financial assistance' for the purposes of s 54(1). The defendants contended (i) that if B Ltd had paid the £93,000 to C Ltd it would not have been providing financial assistance for the share purchase but merely paying off its own debt
f and that it made no difference that the debt was paid off by a subsidiary rather than the holding company since A Ltd could have paid the money to B Ltd to enable it to discharge the debt rather than pay it direct to C Ltd, and (ii) that any assistance given by A Ltd was not financial assistance 'for the purpose of or in connection with' the share purchase but assistance to B Ltd to enable it to repay the debt owed to C Ltd.

g **Held** – On the true construction of s 54(1) of the 1948 Act the prohibition against the provision of financial assistance for the purchase of shares was not confined to assistance given to a purchaser but extended to assistance given to the vendor of the shares. Thus, although a repayment of the debt of £93,000 by the holding company, B Ltd, to the vendor of the shares, C Ltd, would not have amounted to 'financial assistance' because it would not have altered the financial position except to the extent that a due debt was
h repaid, the same payment when made by the subsidiary, A Ltd, would amount to financial assistance to C Ltd for the purpose of or in connection with the share purchase by W and H because it was a voluntary payment without which C Ltd would not have proceeded with the sale. The payment of the £93,000 by A Ltd to C Ltd was therefore capable in law of constituting 'financial assistance' within s 54 (see p 837 *e f* and *h* to p 838 *b*, post).

j Dicta of Schreiner JA in *Gradwell (Pty) Ltd v Rostra Printers Ltd* 1959 (4) SA at 426 and of McInerny J in *E H Dey Pty Ltd v Dey* [1966] VR at 470 applied.

Notes

For the provision of financial assistance by a company for the purchase of its own shares,

a Section 54(1), so far as material, is set out at p 836 *c*, post see 7 Halsbury's Laws (4th Edn) para 208, and for cases on the subject, see 9 Digest (Reissue) 403–405, *2378–2379*. a

For the Companies Act 1948, s 54, see 5 Halsbury's Statutes (3rd Edn) 163.

Cases referred to in judgment

Belmont Finance Corpn v Williams Furniture Ltd (No 2) [1980] 1 All ER 393, CA.
Dey (EH) Pty Ltd v Dey [1966] VR 464.
Gradwell (Pty) Ltd v Rostra Printers Ltd 1959 (4) SA 419, AD. b
Wallersteiner v Moir [1974] 3 All ER 217, [1974] 1 WLR 991, CA, Digest (Cont Vol D) 254, *204e*.

Preliminary issue

By a writ issued on 27th July 1979 the plaintiffs, Armour Hick Northern Ltd, Armour Hick Parker Ltd and Armour Hick & Partners Ltd, claimed against the defendants, c David Stuart Whitehouse, Robert Michael Hick, Armour Trust Ltd ('Armour Trust'), E C Parker & Co Ltd and Valerie Diane Whitehouse, the return of various sums for which the defendants were alleged to be liable to account to the plaintiffs together with damages. In particular the writ included a claim by the first plaintiff that the first, second and third defendants were liable to account to the first plaintiff for the sum of £93,000. By an order dated 17th October 1979 on the summons for directions Master d Gowers ordered that there be tried as a preliminary issue between the first and third plaintiffs and the first, second and third defendants the question whether the payment by the first plaintiff, a subsidiary of the third plaintiff, of £93,000 to the third defendant in discharge of indebtedness due by the third plaintiff was capable in law of constituting financial assistance within s 54 of the Companies Act 1948 for the purpose of or in connection with the purchase of 7,000 shares in the third plaintiff purchased by the first e and second defendants as directors of the first and third plaintiffs. The facts are set out in the judgment.

Richard Sykes for Armour Trust
Alan Steinfield for the first and third plaintiffs.

f

The first and second defendants did not appear.

Cur adv vult

22nd February. **HIS HONOUR JUDGE MERVYN DAVIES QC** read the following judgment: This is a preliminary issue. In the action the three plaintiffs sue g the five defendants alleging various money claims. The writ, with the statement of claim indorsed, is dated 27th July 1979. Defences have been served, including the defence of the third defendant, Armour Trust Ltd.

By an order of the master dated 17th October 1979 made on the summons for directions, it was ordered that one of the questions raised by the pleadings be tried as a preliminary issue between the first and third plaintiffs on the one hand and the first, h second and third defendants on the other hand, that is to say, between the plaintiffs Armour Hick Northern Ltd ('Hick Northern') and Armour Hick & Partners Ltd ('Hick Partners') and the defendants, David Stuart Whitehouse, Robert Michael Hick and Armour Trust Ltd ('Armour Trust'). The first and second defendants did not attend this hearing.

The issue to be tried as a preliminary issue is set out in the master's order as follows: j

> 'Whether the payment by the Plaintiffs Armour Hick Northern Limited a subsidiary of the Plaintiffs Armour Hick & Partners Limited of sums totalling £93,000 to the Defendants Armour Trust Limited in discharge of indebtedness due and payable by the Plaintiffs Armour Hick & Partners Limited to the Defendants

Armour Trust Limited as alleged in paragraph 4 of the Statement of Claim was capable in law of constituting financial assistance within the meaning of Section 54 of the Companies Act 1948 for the purpose of or in connection with the purchase of the 7,000 shares in the Plaintiffs Armour Hick & Partners Limited purchased by the Defendants David Stuart Whitehouse and Robert Michael Hick at par and being the sales mentioned in paragraph 5 of the Statement of Claim. For the purpose of this preliminary issue it is agreed that the Defendants Armour Trust Limited were willing (and only willing) to sell their shares in the Plaintiffs Armour Hick & Partners Limited if the indebtedness to them of the Plaintiffs Armour Hick & Partners Limited were discharged in full.'

I will now read paras 1 to 6 of the statement of claim:

'1 The First and Second Plaintiffs were at all material times subsidiary companies of the Third Plaintiff within the meaning of s. 154 of the Companies Act 1948. Each of the Plaintiffs is in liquidation.

'2 At all material times the First and Second Defendants were directors of each of the Plaintiffs, and employed by the Third Plaintiff (and/or the Second Plaintiff) as, respectively, Deputy Chairman/Financial Director and Chairman. At all material times prior to 26th September 1975 the Third Defendant owned the majority of the issued shares in the Third Plaintiff. The First Defendant was also at the material times a director of the Fourth Defendant . . .

'3 In the premises the First and Second Defendants and each of them were at all material times under a fiduciary duty or duties to the Plaintiffs and each of them to act lawfully and bona fide in the interests of the Plaintiffs and to discharge their duties as directors with reasonable skill and diligence.

'4 Between about 26th September 1975 and 31st March 1976 the First and Second Defendants and each of them procured the payment by the First Plaintiff of sums totalling £93,000 to the Third Defendant. The said sums were paid by the First Plaintiff in discharge of the indebtedness of the Third Plaintiff to the Third Defendant.

'5 In consideration for the payment of the said sums by the First Plaintiff, the Third Defendant agreed to, and did, transfer its shareholding in the Third Plaintiff (7,000 out of the 10,000 issued £1 shares) to the First and Second Defendants at par. As a result of the said transfers the First and Second Defendants (who already owned shares in the Third Plaintiff) held 3,750 and 6,250 of the said shares respectively.

'6 In the premises, by the said transaction, the First Plaintiff gave to the First and Second Defendants financial assistance for the purpose of and/or in connection with their purchase of the said shares in the Third Plaintiff, and thereby acted unlawfully and in breach of the provisions of s. 54 of the Companies Act 1948.'

I need read no further. I now read para 8 of the defence of Armour Trust:

'The Third Defendant denies each of the allegations in paragraph 6 of the Amended Statement of Claim. The Third Defendant will contend that, as a matter of law, the application by a company of its funds in the repayment of indebtedness due from itself or its holding company to a vendor of shares of itself or its holding company is not capable in law of constituting financial assistance for the purpose of or in connection with the purchase of the shares to be sold by that vendor within the meaning of Section 54 of the Companies Act 1948.'

For the purpose of the preliminary issue I must assume the truth of the allegations in the statement of claim. It was accepted that it was for counsel for Armour Trust to begin before me. With the help of a most useful chart counsel summarised the material facts as at 25th September 1975. Hick Partners was the holding company of Hick Northern. Hick Partners owed Armour Trust £93,000. Armour Trust owned 7,000 shares in Hick

Partners. Mr Whitehouse and Mr Hick were directors of Hick Northern and of Hick Partners. Counsel went on to explain the position reached by 31st March 1976. By that a time Mr Whitehouse and Mr Hick had acquired at par the 7,000 shares in Hick Partners, previously owned by Armour Trust, for £7,000 cash paid to Armour Trust. As well, the £93,000 owed by Hick Partners to Armour Trust had been paid off in full. The £93,000 was paid by Hick Northern direct to Armour Trust.

It is against those facts that one must consider the questions set out in the master's order, bearing in mind the agreement recorded in the order, which in effect was that b Armour Trust was willing to sell the 7,000 shares only if the £93,000 owing to it by Hick Partners was discharged.

I now set out s 54(1) of the Companies Act 1948, omitting the proviso:

> 'Subject as provided in this section, it shall not be lawful for a company to give, whether directly or indirectly, and whether by means of a loan, guarantee, the provision of security or otherwise, any financial assistance for the purpose of or in c connection with a purchase or subscription made or to be made by any person of or for any shares in the company, or, where the company is a subsidiary company, in its holding company . . .'

I need not read the rest of the section.

Counsel for the plaintiffs conceded that, if the events had been that Hick Partners had d itself paid its debt to Armour Trust, then Hick Partners would not have given financial assistance in connection with the share purchase. Hick Partners would have been paying off its own debt. Counsel for Armour Trust then went on to contend that, if the repayment of a debt owed by a holding company is not financial assistance when made by itself, then a repayment of that debt is no more so when it is made by a subsidiary of the holding company. I do not see that that proposition necessarily follows, because it is e one thing for a company to pay its own debt and another for a subsidiary company to pay the debt of its holding company. However, counsel suggested that any financial assistance given by Hick Northern in paying off Armour Trust was given solely to Hick Partners whose debt was discharged. Section 54 cannot, so the argument goes, be intended to stop the giving of financial assistance to the company whose shares are being purchased, ie Hick Partners, particularly since the penal provision in sub-s (2) of the f section indicates that the section is to be restrictively construed. He said that all would have been well if Hick Northern had paid Hick Partners and if Hick Partners had then paid Armour Trust. To short-circuit the matter by making the payment direct to Armour Trust, he said, made no difference.

Another approach to the argument that the transaction was outside s 54 was that any assistance which Hick Northern gave was not financial assistance in connection with the g purchase of shares. Rather was it assistance in connection with the repayment of the indebtedness of Hick Partners to Armour Trust. It was accepted that Hick Northern's creditors might well have been (we do not know) prejudiced by the payment made to Armour Trust. That might have been a matter for misfeasance proceedings, but did not mean that the payment constituted conduct within s 54.

Finally, counsel for Armour Trust said that subsidiary companies are mentioned in h s 54 to stop the doing by a subsidiary company of acts which if done by the holding company would be a breach of the section. In short, as I understand, he says that an act outside s 54 which is done by a holding company is also outside s 54 if the act is done by the holding company's subsidiary. Counsel for the plaintiffs said, and I agree with him, that there is nothing in the wording of s 54 to justify the final point of counsel for Armour Trust. j

Counsel's argument for the plaintiffs in summary was (i) that s 54 is to be construed widely and liberally (he referred to *Wallersteiner v Moir* [1974] 3 All ER 217 at 239, 254, [1974] 1 WLR 991 at 1014, 1032), (ii) that the section prohibits the giving of any financial assistance by a subsidiary in connection with the purchase of shares in a holding company, and (iii) that, for a subsidiary company to discharge its holding company's indebtedness to a shareholder, to enable the sale of that shareholder's shares in the holding company to a purchaser to go forward, plainly constitutes the giving of financial assistance not only to the vendor shareholder but also to the purchaser of the shares.

If Hick Partners had paid its own debt with its own money, there would have been no giving of financial assistance for the purpose of or in connection with the share purchase.

In *Gradwell (Pty) Ltd v Rostra Printers Ltd* 1959 (4) SA 419, Schreiner JA had under consideration s 86(bis)(2) of the South African Companies Act 1926. That section is for present purposes identical with s 54. Referring to the payment of a debt comparable with the Hick Partners debt to Armour Trust, he said (at 426):

> 'But whatever may be the position in such a case the paying off of an existing debt seems to be decidedly more difficult to bring within the notion of giving financial assistance. The payer's assets and liabilities are put into a different form but the balance is unchanged. And the same applies to the financial position of the payee. Here the company would have no more and no less after the completion of the transaction than before . . . Where there is an anticipation of the date when a debt becomes due and payable the position may possibly be different, but where the debt is presently due and payable and the debtor can have no answer to the creditor's demand for payment, it would be straining the language to hold that by paying his debt the debtor gives the creditor financial assistance.'

As I understand, those observations were noted without disapproval by Buckley LJ in *Belmont Finance Corpn v Williams Furniture Ltd (No 2)* [1980] 1 All ER 393 at 401–402. Thus, if Hick Partners had paid its own debt to Armour Trust, it would have given no financial assistance within s 54, the reason being, as I understand, that such a payment does not alter the financial position, save to the extent that a debt due from the debtor is paid by the debtor, so that no help or assistance is given. There is merely a due discharge of a debt. But Hick Northern paying the Hick Partners debt is a horse of another colour. Hick Northern was not paying off its own debt. It may have been making merely a voluntary payment. Accordingly, the payment may have been financial assistance within s 54.

It follows that I must apply the words of s 54(1) to the facts. I do so reading the words neither widely nor restrictively, but in their plain ordinary meaning. I see that it was not lawful for Hick Northern, a subsidiary of Hick Partners, to give any financial assistance 'for the purpose of or in connection with' a purchase by any person of any shares in Hick Partners. The section does not say that the assistance is not to be given to the purchaser. It simply says that assistance is not to be given. In fact, no financial assistance, at any rate no direct financial assistance, was given to the purchasers because the £93,000 was paid to the vendors, and the purchasers themselves paid the £7,000 for the shares.

But is it the position that financial assistance is not to be given to the vendor? In *E H Dey Pty Ltd v Dey* [1966] VR 464 at 470 McInerny J had to deal with the Victorian equivalent of s 54:

> 'In my view, the prohibition is not confined to financial assistance to the purchaser: it is directed to financial assistance to whomsoever given, provided that it be for the purpose of a purchase of shares or in connexion with a purchase of shares.'

I agree with those remarks. So the question here is: did Hick Northern, on the assumed facts, give financial assistance to Armour Trust in connection with the Whitehouse/Hick share purchase? I have no doubt that Hick Northern gave assistance, leaving aside for the moment whether such assistance was financial assistance. Hick Northern paid Armour Trust £93,000 and, with Messrs Whitehouse and Hick as directors of Hick Northern, Hick Northern must have known that if Hick Northern had not made that payment, then the share transaction between Armour Trust and Whitehouse/Hick would not have gone forward. Thus, Hick Northern gave help to Armour Trust in connection with the share purchase.

That leaves the question whether the assistance was financial assistance. The answer is in the affirmative when one sees that the assistance was a payment of £93,000. I do not *a* see how the assistance can be described as otherwise than financial. If the payment had not been made, the share transfer would not have gone through. It appears to have been financial assistance within the phrase 'or otherwise' in s 54(1) and, as well, financial assistance 'for the purpose of or in connection with' a purchase of shares.

Accordingly, in my opinion the payment referred to in the master's order was capable in law of constituting financial assistance within s 54 for the purpose of or in connection *b* with the purchase of the 7,000 shares.

I desire to add that at the trial it may, of course, emerge, when all the facts are examined, that the payment in question did not, in fact, breach s 54.

Order accordingly.

c

Solicitors: *Clifford-Turner* (for Armour Trust); *Herbert Oppenheimer, Nathan & Vandyk* (for the first and third plaintiffs).

Frances Rustin Barrister.

d

Re Furse (deceased)
Furse v Inland Revenue Commissioners

CHANCERY DIVISION

FOX J *e*

12th, 13th, 14th, 15th MAY, 7th JULY 1980

Domicile – Acquisition of domicile of choice – Intention – Intention to return to country of domicile of origin on happening of future uncertain event – Testator born in United States – Testator resident at his farm in England for most of his life – Testator intending to return to United States only when not able to lead an active life on his farm – Testator dying in England aged 80 – *f* *Whether testator's intention sufficiently definite for acquisition of domicile of choice in England – Whether testator dying domiciled in England.*

The testator was born in Rhode Island in 1883. At the time of his birth his father, F, was domiciled in Rhode Island. In 1885 the testator's mother died. Two years later, F, with a view to bringing up his children apart from his wife's family, came to England with all *g* his children. In 1899 F and his children moved to a house which was built with funds provided by the family trust of his wife's family. A year or two after the testator had attained the age of 21, the house was sold and thereafter F no longer owned any residence in England. In 1913 F died in New York. Meanwhile the testator, after completing his education in England, took up employment with a company in New York in 1907, married a girl born and brought up in New York in 1913 and remained in the United *h* States until 1916 when he joined the British army in the 1914–18 war. In the same year his wife purchased a house in New York. The testator returned to the United States as soon as he was demobilised in 1919 or 1920. From then until 1923 he was employed by a company in New York. In 1923 the testator together with his wife and his surviving children came to England. In the next year his wife bought a farm of about 250 acres in England where the testator lived for the rest of his life. From time to time the testator *j* and his wife considered whether they should return to live in the United States. Their alternatives to living in England were to live in the house in New York or to buy a farm in Maryland or Virginia. In the late 1940s they inspected properties in Maryland. After the early 1950s, however, the testator abandoned his searches in the United States. Thereafter, there was evidence that the testator had finally decided not to return to the

United States so long as he was capable of leading an active life on the farm in England.
a In 1963 the testator died in England at the age of 80. The plaintiff, as executor of the testator's will, applied to the court to determine whether, for the purposes of estate duty, the testator had died domiciled in the State of New York or in England.

Held – (1) On the evidence, it was not possible to conclude that by the time the testator
b attained the age of 21 years F had acquired a domicile of choice in England. Accordingly the testator had not by the time he reached the age of 21 acquired an English domicile of dependency (see p 845 *c d*, post).

(2) In view of the fact that the testator's intention was to go on living his accustomed life on the farm in England and only to leave when he was no longer able to lead an active physical life there, it was clear that he had no intention, save on a vague and indefinite
c contingency, of leaving England. It followed that at the time of his death the testator had acquired a domicile of choice in England (see p 846 *c* to *j*, p 848 *c d* and *g* to *j* and p 847 *a b d* to *f* and *h j*, post); dictum of Buckley LJ in *Inland Revenue Comrs v Bullock* [1976] 3 All ER at 360 applied.

d **Notes**

For change of domicile, see 8 Halsbury's Laws (4th Edn) paras 427–441, and for cases on the subject, see 11 Digest (Reissue) 353–380, *62–241*.

Cases referred to in judgment

Aikman v Aikman (1861) 4 LT 374, 7 Jur NS 1017, 3 Macq 854, HL, 11 Digest (Reissue)
e 350, *43*.

Bell v Kennedy (1868) LR 1 Sc & Div 307, 6 Macq 69, 5 SLR 566, HL, 11 Digest (Reissue) 350, *45*.

Bowie (or Ramsay) v Liverpool Royal Infirmary [1930] AC 588, [1930] All ER Rep 127, 99 LJPC 134, 143 LT 388, HL, 11 Digest (Reissue) 364, *122*.

Doucet v Geoghegan (1878) 9 Ch D 441, CA, 11 Digest (Reissue) 361, *104*.

f *Fuld (deceased), Re (No 3), Hartley v Fuld* [1965] 3 All ER 776, [1968] P 675, [1966] 2 WLR 717, 11 Digest (Reissue) 445, *697*.

Inland Revenue Comrs v Bullock [1976] 3 All ER 353, [1976] 1 WLR 1178, [1976] STC 409, [1976] TR 179, CA, Digest (Cont Vol E) 90, *157a*.

Qureshi v Qureshi [1971] 1 All ER 325, [1972] Fam 173, [1971] 2 WLR 518, 11 Digest (Reissue) 565, *1275*.

g *Whicker v Hume* (1858) 7 HL Cas 124, [1843–60] All ER Rep 450, 28 LJ Ch 396, 31 LTOS 319, HL, 11 Digest (Reissue) 360, *96*.

Winans v Attorney General [1904] AC 287, [1904–7] All ER Rep 410, 73 LJKB 613, 90 LT 721, 11 ER 50, HL, 11 Digest (Reissue) 351, *47*.

h **Cases also cited**

Buswell v Inland Revenue Comrs [1974] 2 All ER 520, [1974] 1 WLR 1631, [1974] STC 266, CA.

Flynn (deceased), Re, Flynn v Flynn [1968] 1 All ER 49, [1969] 1 WLR 103.

Henderson v Henderson [1965] 1 All ER 179, [1967] P 77.

Jopp v Wood (1865) 4 De GJ & Sm 616, 46 ER 1057.

j *Ramsay v Liverpool Royal Infirmary* [1930] AC 588, HL.

Adjourned summons

By an originating summons dated 8th March 1976, the plaintiff, George Reginald Furse, as executor of the will of William King Furse deceased, applied for the determination of the question whether he was accountable for estate duty on the footing that the deceased died domiciled in (i) the State of New York, (ii) England or (iii) some other, if so, what, country. The facts are set out in the judgment.

Gerald Godfrey QC and *Benjamin Levy* for the plaintiff.
David Unwin for the Crown.

Cur adv vult

7th July. **FOX J** read the following judgment: This is an application by originating summons to determine whether the plaintiff, Mr George Ronald Furse, as executor of the will of his father, William King Furse ('the testator'), is accountable for estate duty on the death of the testator on the footing that the testator died domiciled in (i) the State of New York, or (ii) England or (iii) some other country.

The testator was the son of E W Furse. E W Furse was born in Italy in 1841. He came of an English family which had emigrated to Leghorn in the 1780s and there established themselves as merchant bankers. The family, which moved in both Florentine and Roman societies, later acquired a residence at Frascati, near Rome. E W Furse was brought up in Italy and, throughout his life, spoke Italian as his native language.

In 1870 E W Furse married an American girl, Lydia King, whom he had met when she was on a visit to Italy in 1869. The King family had been settled in Providence, Rhode Island since the middle of the seventeenth century. They had a controlling interest in the Rhode Island Tool Co and the Ponema Mill Co (a textile company based on Rhode Island). They had a family grave at Swan Point, Rhode Island, and it was in this grave that E W Furse was buried on his death in 1913.

On their marriage E W Furse and his wife settled in Rhode Island. Their family of eight children were born in Rhode Island and brought up there until 1887. The testator was born in Rhode Island in 1883. By then, the family seems to have been established in Rhode Island though E W Furse continued to make visits to Italy during the rest of his life.

Mrs E W Furse died in 1885, leaving her husband with a young family. The plaintiff's understanding from conversations with his father and his father's sister was that E W Furse was concerned about the mode of life of the rest of the King family who, after the death of a dominant father, had embarked on a free-spending and free-living way of life. E W Furse, therefore, decided that he wanted his children brought up apart from the King family and brought them to England for that purpose. He wanted them kept apart from the King family while they were being brought up. He had a bachelor brother in England, who was in the Black Watch and, it seems, subsequently became a British military attaché in the Far East. He died in 1906. It was with this brother that the family first stayed on arrival in England. They then moved to a house in Aldershot for some years. Then, in 1899, E W Furse and his family moved to a house at Alphington, Frimley, which was built with funds provided from a family trust of the King family.

The six living children of E W Furse were absolutely entitled under the trust on the attainment of the age of 21 by the youngest of them. The youngest was, in fact, the testator. He attained 21 in 1904. He was then at Cambridge, reading modern languages. A year or two after the testator attained 21, E W Furse ceased to live in the house at Alphington. The house was vested absolutely in the children under the provisions of the trust and it was sold. Thereafter, E W Furse no longer owned any residence in England.

The plaintiff's evidence, based on conversations in the family, is that, from the time E W Furse gave up the Alphington house until he died, he made extensive trips abroad, particularly to Italy and the United States of America. When he was in England he lived with his unmarried daughter in her house in Elm Park Gardens, London. There is no evidence as to the periods which he spent in England and in other countries respectively. He appears never to have worked for his living. He lived on his wife's income, and then on income from the King family trust and, finally, on financial assistance from his children.

E W Furse died in May 1913 at Irvington on Hudson, New York, where he had gone to attend the marriage of the testator. He was buried in the King family grave in Rhode

Island. At his death, his estate in England was worth about £2,000 and his estate in
a America was worth about £4,600. His English estate included some furniture at his daughter's residence worth about £800. The Inland Revenue affidavit in respect of the application for probate of the will of E W Furse was sworn by the testator, who deposed that E W Furse died domiciled in England.

The testator came down from Cambridge in 1905 when he was 22 years old. He then travelled on the continent for a year or two, where he took jobs as a private tutor. In
b 1907 the testator took up employment in New York with the Knickerbocker Trust Co; but, shortly after he joined the firm, it collapsed in the Wall Street slump of 1907. The testator then joined Kinnell Kinnicutt & Co, a New York firm of merchant bankers. In 1913 he married. There is no evidence as to where the testator actually lived between 1907 and his marriage.

His wife, the plaintiff's mother ('Mrs Furse'), was a citizen of the United States, who
c had been born and brought up at Irvington on Hudson, New York. After their marriage they rented a house for a time and then, in 1916, Mrs Furse purchased a house called The Pines at Irvington on Hudson as the family home. In 1916, after The Pines had been purchased, the testator left the United States to serve with the British army in the 1914–18 war. The United States had not then entered the war. The plaintiff's evidence, which is not challenged, is that he was informed by Mrs Furse that the testator's reasons for
d joining the British army were, first, that there was a strong anti-German feeling in the United States which he shared and, second, a number of his friends had already left to serve in the British army. His brother George had been killed in action in 1914.

The testator returned to the United States as soon as he was demobilised in 1919 or 1920. From then until 1923 he was employed by the Guaranty Trust Co of New York and lived at The Pines. Between 1920 and 1923 Mrs Furse's parents, and also the young
e daughter of the testator and Mrs Furse, died. In 1923 the testator and Mrs Furse and their two surviving children came to England.

The plaintiff's evidence is that the testator told him that his (the testator's) reason for coming to England was that Mrs Furse was not in a good frame of mind following on the death of her young daughter and her parents, and that her doctor recommended a change for her. They went originally for a year and took a rented house at Englefield
f Green. The testator's original intention was to continue to work in England for the Guaranty Trust Co of New York; but he abandoned that because it involved leaving his wife alone all day in a country which was quite strange to her.

It was in these circumstances that Mrs Furse bought a farm of about 250 acres at West Hoathly in Sussex. That purchase was in 1924. I should mention here that, in January 1925, the testator applied to the United States State Department for a new passport. The
g application form stated that he was residing in England 'for purposes of temporary residence'. The testator, in fact, lived at West Hoathly for the rest of his life. He died in 1963 aged 80. He was for the whole of his life a United States citizen. Apart from the daughter who died, the testator and his wife had two children, namely the plaintiff who was born in 1921 and his elder brother who was born in 1916 and died in 1943. The latter was educated at Marlborough and Oxford, and the plaintiff at Eton and
h Cambridge. Both served in the British army in the last war.

The testator and Mrs Furse, both before and after the last war, made visits to the United States. Before the war the plaintiff thinks that the visits were, at any rate, every other year. After the war they visited every year from 1946 to 1963. In 1946 they spent about eight months there. In the years from 1947 to 1963 (the year of the testator's death), the shortest period that they spent on such visits in any year was 31 days (in 1947
j and 1949). In ten of the years they spent over 60 days in the United States. From 1946 to 1964 the plaintiff was working in New York, and one of the objects of the visits was to see the plaintiff and his family. The visits were not, however, restricted to New York where the plaintiff lived; they extended to other places in the United States where the testator and his wife had friends.

During the early post-war period the testator and Mrs Furse from time to time considered whether they should return to live in the United States. The plaintiff says, and I accept it, that they were much in doubt at that time about what they wanted to do. In 1946 and 1952, when considering whether to sell the farm and return to the *a* United States, the testator and Mrs Furse took professional advice and came to the conclusion that farm prices were then too low in England and that it would be financially unwise to sell. Mrs Furse was, however, a wealthy woman, and the plaintiff, in his oral evidence, agreed that financial considerations in relation to the farm would not have been the sole factor in his parents' minds. The alternatives to living in England were to live at The Pines or to buy a farm in Maryland or Virginia. In the late 1940s they *b* inspected properties in Maryland. I think, however, that, after the early 1950s at any rate, the testator abandoned his searches in the United States and decided to remain at West Hoathly, save in the contingency which I will mention later.

Mrs Furse retained The Pines during the whole of the testator's lifetime. Until the outbreak of the 1939–45 war, the property was let to two successive tenants. During most of the war the property was left vacant. After the war it was let on short *c* tenancies. From 1948 to 1950 it was let to a Mr Sutphen and from 1952 to 1969 it was let to a Dr Sandvoss on a monthly tenancy. The rent was low to compensate the tenant for the insecurity of tenure.

On his visits to the United States after the war the testator visited The Pines regularly in order to inspect its condition. The plaintiff in his oral evidence said that the testator made such a visit every year and he (the plaintiff) went with him. Dr Sandvoss, whose *d* evidence was taken on commission, says that there was no inspection by the testator on those visits. The plaintiff, however, is quite clear that that is wrong. He says they went over the whole house. Dr Sandvoss was some 80 years of age when he gave his evidence, and I think it may be that his memory was defective. I accept the plaintiff's evidence on this matter.

The plaintiff was quite clear, and I accept it, that the purpose of granting short leases *e* of The Pines was to enable his parents to resume occupation of the house at short notice if they wished to return to the United States. This was a matter which the plaintiff discussed with the testator. Dr Sandvoss, in his evidence on commission, said that it was his (Dr Sandvoss's) understanding that the testator would not want to sell the house because he wanted to keep it for himself. He wanted to keep it 'so that any time he wanted to come back to the United States the house would be available'. Dr Sandvoss did *f* not know whether the Furses would or would not return. He could only say that, if they did want to return, they wanted the house in good shape. The house had three or four living rooms and five or six bedrooms. It was somewhat smaller, the plaintiff told me, than the house at West Hoathly. Dr Sandvoss had no living-in help in The Pines. He thought it would be an easy house for the Furses to run.

In 1963, when the testator and the plaintiff were driving away from The Pines after *g* inspecting it, the testator said that, when they came back and lived in the house, they would have to instal a new central heating system as the existing one was too expensive.

Evidence was also taken on commission from Mr Besemer, who had been an employee of the First National City Bank of New York. That bank handled the trust affairs of the family trust of which Mrs Furse was the life tenant. Mr Besemer was in charge of the 'unit' of the bank which had particular responsibility for the trust. In that capacity he *h* met the testator who, on his visits or some of his visits to the United States, came to see him to discuss the trust affairs. Mr Besemer's recollection is that he first met the testator in about 1950 and saw him every two or three years thereafter. Mr Besemer was asked whether he had formed any view as to the testator's intentions. He replied: 'Yes. I personally was convinced that he was coming back to the United States ultimately and I, as a matter of fact, would always ask him, "When are you coming back?" and he always *j* wanted to stay a little bit longer. He liked his farm very much, but he did talk about coming back to the United States to live here until he died.'

Mr Besemer was then asked: 'Do those remarks form the main basis of the view you formed that he intended to return to the United States?' He answered: 'I was convinced that he was planning on returning to this country, but there was no firm time ever mentioned.' Then Mr Besemer said: 'I think I mentioned earlier that I was convinced

that he was coming back. Personally, I thought he was postponing it too long, but there
a was no doubt in my mind that his intention was to return.'

After a meeting with the testator in February 1963 Mr Besemer made the following entry in the diary of the bank:

> 'The senior Mr. Furse [that is to say, the testator] is a citizen of the United States domiciled in the United States, but now residing in England where he is operating a farm. He is in his late 70's. He and Mrs. Furse own a house in the United States
> b and eventually expect to return here.'

Mrs Furse died in February 1977. In August 1976 Mr Lock, a partner in Coward Chance & Co (the solicitors acting for the plaintiff in these proceedings), discussed with Mrs Furse what evidence she would give regarding the testator's domicile. On the statements made to him by Mrs Furse a draft affidavit was prepared by Mr Lock, which
c was subsequently read over to her by the plaintiff. Mrs Furse was then nearly blind; she confirmed that it correctly stated her views. Mrs Furse died without swearing the affidavit. The draft had been sent to the Inland Revenue for their comments, which had not been received before her death. The draft affidavit states, inter alia, that—

> 'the property [that is to say, The Pines] was retained with the intention that my husband and I should return to live there; and that always remained my husband's
> d intention. I believe that my husband would have gone to live permanently in that house had he lived. Both my husband and myself have always considered ourselves as Americans and looked on the State of New York as our permanent home.'

I do not feel able to give weight to that document. The statement was made for the purpose of these proceedings. Mrs Furse was of very advanced age when she was
e interviewed, and I do not know to what extent she was suggestible or to what extent information was obtained by leading questions. She died before the statement was sworn, and I have not had the advantage of hearing cross-examination on it.

I now come to certain evidence of the plaintiff, which is as follows. Some seven or eight men were employed on the farm at West Hoathly, including a manager, though the testator took some hand in the management himself. The testator lived an active life
f on the farm. He depended on physical exercise and enjoyed it. The sort of work which he did was clearing woods, scything and repairing fences and gates. He remained active almost to the last. He had a prostate operation and died unexpectedly about two weeks later. There is, I think, no doubt at all that the testator greatly enjoyed his life at West Hoathly; he was essentially a countryman and the life appealed to him the plaintiff told me.

g From his conversations with the testator over the period from about the late 1940s or early 1950s onwards, the plaintiff understood that the testator's intentions as to residence were as follows. The testator had finally decided that he did not want to return to the United States so long as he was physically capable of living an active life on the farm at West Hoathly but, if he was no longer able to live such a life, he would return to the United States and live at Irvington. The plaintiff put the matter in various ways in the
h course of his evidence. Thus, he said, the testator only intended to return to the United States when he was physically unable to take an active interest in the farm and enjoy it, that the testator would continue to live at West Hoathly as long as he was physically capable of carrying on, and that, when he was unable to continue an active physical life at West Hoathly, he would return to the United States and live at Irvington.

I think that all these formulations of the contingency come to much the same thing
j and were the expressed intentions of the testator.

I should mention that it appears from the plaintiff's evidence that, in the latter part of his life, the testator was aware of the concept of domicile, and that a question had been raised relating to his domicile by the United Kingdom Revenue authorities. It does not appear from the evidence at precisely what time any question of domicile was first raised in the context of Revenue matters. The plaintiff's awareness that the testator had any concern about questions of domicile must, I think, have been during some part of the period after the war. The plaintiff did not discuss questions of residence with him before that.

The testator's estate in England was sworn for probate at about £21,000. His taxable estate at his death in the United States amounted to about $363,000. His investments at his death appear to have been almost entirely in United States companies and amounted in value to about $380,000.

Mrs Furse continued to live in England until her death in 1977 at the age of 90. After the testator's death she gave the farm to the plaintiff and moved to another house nearby.

The testator had two sisters and three brothers. The two sisters remained in England all their lives and died here in 1960 and 1963 respectively. Two of his brothers were killed in action while serving in the British army in the 1914 war. The third brother lived in New York in 1910; he then removed to Canada, where he lived until his death in 1966.

The Crown concedes that, at the birth of the testator, E W Furse was domiciled in Rhode Island and that, accordingly, the testator had a domicile of origin in Rhode Island. The Crown contends, however, that, by the time the testator attained the age of 21 in 1904, E W Furse had acquired a domicile of choice in England, with the result that the testator, at the time he attained 21, had an English domicile of dependency.

I take the test for the establishment of a domicile of choice as that propounded by Lord Macnaghten in *Winans v Attorney General* [1904] AC 287 at 291, [1904–7] All ER Rep 410 at 413, where he said, referring to Lord Cairns LC's speech in *Bell v Kennedy* (1868) LR 1 Sc & Div 307 at 311:

> 'Whether the person whose domicil was in question had determined to make, and had, in fact, made the alleged domicil of choice "his home with the intention of establishing himself and his family there, and ending his days in that country"?'

That was adopted by the Court of Appeal in *Inland Revenue Comrs v Bullock* [1976] 3 All ER 353 at 359, [1976] 1 WLR 1178 at 1185.

The evidence as to the circumstances in which E W Furse brought his family to England after his wife's death do not suggest that he was then contemplating the establishment of any permanent home in England. The plaintiff's information, obtained from the testator and the testator's sister, is that E W Furse came here for the limited purpose of keeping his children separate from the King family while they were being brought up. The house in Alphington (which belonged to the children's trust and not to E W Furse himself) was sold in about 1906. Thereafter, it does not appear that E W Furse owned any house or had any establishment of his own in England. While in England he lived with his daughter in London. The evidence as to the extent of his residence in England after about 1906 is sketchy. It is based on conversations in the family to the effect that he made extensive visits abroad, particularly to Italy and the United States.

The onus of proving that E W Furse intended to acquire a domicile of choice in England is on the Crown. I do not think that it can be said that, on the evidence to which I have referred, the balance of probability is that E W Furse intended to establish himself here and to end his days in this country. He came to England for a limited purpose. When that purpose had been achieved, the children having grown up, it is far from clear to what extent he lived in England. There is no evidence as to his intentions in this later period.

Thus far, therefore, I would not conclude that the Crown had discharged the onus of proof. The Crown, however, relies on two further circumstances: first, the fact that, in the Inland Revenue affidavit sworn by the testator in respect of the estate of E W Furse, it is stated that E W Furse died domiciled in England. The estate of E W Furse was small (the duty was under £300) and I do not know what, if any, consideration was given to the question of his domicile. It seems to me that there are considerable dangers in giving decisive weight to depositions as to law when one has no information as to what the deponent knew as to the constituents of the legal status in question.

At a much later stage in his life, after the 1939–45 war, the testator appears to have been aware of the doctrine of domicile in relation to Revenue matters, but what, if anything, he knew in 1913 is a matter on which I have no evidence.

Be that as it may, the affidavit relates only to E W Furse's domicile at the time of his death. I am still left in doubt as to what his intentions were as to residence up to the time the testator attained 21 in 1904. I am dealing with events of 75 years and more ago. I think it would be unsafe to conclude that E W Furse had reached any determination as to permanent residence in England.

Second, I am referred to an answer given by the plaintiff's solicitors in 1964 to an inquiry made by the Estate Duty Office in relation to the estate of the testator. The answer is as follows: 'The only change of domicile of the deceased's father during deceased's minority was in 1887 when he changed his domicile from Rhode Island to England.' In my view, that does not advance matters. As I have indicated, it seems to me that the evidence does not indicate that in 1887 E W Furse came to England with the determination to establish a home and end his days here. The evidence indicates residence for a limited purpose only.

In the circumstances, I take the view that it is not established that, when the testator attained full age in 1904, E W Furse had acquired a domicile of choice in England, and that, accordingly, the testator's last domicile of dependency was in Rhode Island.

I come then to the second question: whether the testator had acquired (as the Crown contends) a domicile of choice in England by the time of his death. The plaintiff's case is that by 1923 the testator had acquired a domicile of choice in the State of New York, which was where he had his matrimonial home, and that he never lost that domicile. The evidence does not suggest that when the testator came to England in 1923 he had resolved to settle here permanently. He came because of medical advice that Mrs Furse needed a change for a time. He came, initially, for a year and rented a house.

A substantial degree of stability must, I think, have been introduced by the purchase of the farm in 1924, but there is no evidence as to the testator's intentions during the years until the end of the war. The plaintiff was still at school during most of the time until the beginning of the war and did not discuss the matter with the testator. After the war there was a period up to the early 1950s when the testator was evidently uncertain whether to remain in England or not. Down to this period I do not think that there is evidence of any firm intention by the testator to settle permanently in England.

The core of the matter, I think, is the evidence given by the plaintiff as to the testator's ultimate intentions expressed to him from about the early 1950s as to the duration of his residence at West Hoathly.

Before I consider that I should refer to certain aspects of the law. In *Inland Revenue Comrs v Bullock* [1976] 3 All ER 353, [1976] 1 WLR 1178 the propositus, Group Captain Bullock, came to England from Canada, which was his domicile of origin, in 1932. He had been in England some 40 years when the case was heard. He was then aged about 63. On retiring from the Royal Air Force in 1953 he wished to return permanently to Canada. He did not do so because his wife did not wish to live in Canada. It was found as a fact that he himself would return immediately to Canada if his wife should predecease him. It was held by the Court of Appeal that Group Captain Bullock had never abandoned his intention of returning to Canada if he survived his wife, which was not an unreal possibility in view of their respective ages, and that, accordingly, he had never abandoned his Canadian domicile. Buckley LJ said ([1976] 3 All ER 353 at 360, [1976] 1 WLR 1178 at 1186):

> 'No doubt, if a man who has made his home in a country other than his domicile of origin has expressed an intention to return to his domicile of origin or to remove to some third country on an event or condition of an indefinite kind (for example, "if I make a fortune" or "when I've had enough of it"), it might be hard, if not impossible, to conclude that he retained any real intention of so returning or removing. Such a man, in the graphic language of James LJ in *Doucet v Geoghegan* (1878) 9 Ch D 441 at 457, is like a man who expects to reach the horizon; he finds it at last no nearer than it was at the beginning of his journey. In *Aikman v Aikman*

> (1861) 4 LT 374 at 376 Lord Campbell LC said that a mere intention to return to a man's native country on a doubtful contingency would not prevent residence in a foreign country putting an end to his domicile of origin. [Later Buckley LJ said:] The question can perhaps be formulated in this way where the contingency is not itself of a doubtful or indefinite character: is there a sufficiently substantial possibility of the contingency happening to justify regarding the intention to return as a real determination to do so on the contingency occurring rather than a vague hope or aspiration?'

In *Inland Revenue Comrs v Bullock* both the requirements referred to by Buckley LJ were satisfied. The contingency was a wholly clear and well-defined contingency, namely whether the propositus survived his wife; and there was a substantial possibility that the contingency might occur, having regard to the respective ages of the propositus and his wife.

The present case, it seems to me, is very different. The fundamental difference in outlook between Group Captain Bullock and the testator was that, while Group Captain Bullock had every wish to leave England, the testator was entirely happy here.

Counsel for the plaintiff says that there are two possible ways of interpreting the testator's expressed intention. First, he wanted to remain in England to the end of his days unless his physical decline was such as to prevent him going on with his usual life at West Hoathly. Second, he did not want to remain here to the end of his days. He wanted to return to the United States but, nevertheless, felt that, while he had a farm and staff and could manage, he should continue to discharge his responsibilities as a farmer.

The latter, counsel for the plaintiff submits, is correct. I do not agree with that. It seems to me that, from the manner in which he expressed his intentions, the testator's hope was that he could go on living his accustomed and very pleasant life at West Hoathly to the end of his days. It was his good fortune to achieve that. The only circumstance on the happening of which he expressed any intention of leaving England was if he was no longer able to live an active physical life on the farm. Apart from that, he intended to remain in England all his life.

But that contingency is altogether indefinite. It has no precision at all. A man's idea of an active physical life is likely to contract with the years. At the age of 80, after 40 years in England, the testator was still living at West Hoathly and, although he had been ill, he had no firm plans at all for leaving England.

The testator's expressed intention, it seems to me, depended entirely on his own assessment of whether an ill-defined event had occurred. I think it really amounted to no more than saying, 'I will leave England when I feel I want to leave England'. That is substantially the same as Buckley LJ's example of the man who says he will leave 'when I've had enough of it'.

In a significant piece of evidence Mr Besemer said that the testator always wanted to stay in England a bit longer. That, I think, is only a variant of James LJ's example of the man who expects to reach the horizon. At the end he finds himself no nearer.

If one looks at the other limb of Buckley LJ's formulation, namely, 'is there a sufficiently substantial possibility of the contingency happening to justify regarding the intention to return as a real determination to do so on the contingency occurring rather than a vague hope or aspiration?', that does not arise unless the court concludes that the contingency itself is sufficiently clear to be identified. But it seems to me that the vagueness of the notion, coupled with the fact that the testator's mode of life was wholly congenial to him, is such that one must be left in the greatest doubt whether, in the end, it had any reality in the testator's mind at all. The possibility of leaving West Hoathly was not, indeed, even a hope or an aspiration. As I interpret his outlook, it was something that the testator cannot have wished for.

Having regard to the way in which the testator expressed his intentions, one cannot, I think, conclude that there was a substantial possibility of the contingency happening. One does not really know with any certainty what the contingency was. The testator himself was the only interpreter.

In *Re Fuld (deceased) (No 3)* [1968] P 675 at 684–685 Scarman J, after referring to the need in establishing the existence of a domicile of choice to show that the propositus intended to reside indefinitely in the country in question, said:

> 'If a man intends to return to the land of his birth upon a clearly foreseen and reasonably anticipated contingency, e.g. the end of his job, the intention required by law is lacking; but, if he has in mind only a vague possibility, such as making a fortune (a modern example might be winning a football pool) or some sentiment about dying in the land of his fathers, such a state of mind is consistent with the intention required by law.'

I do not think that the testator can be described as having in mind any clearly foreseen contingency. The contingency which he expressed was vague and permitted of almost infinite adjustment to meet his own wishes.

It is said on behalf of the plaintiff that the testator's intention was simply to return to the United States on his retirement from farming. The case is thus similar to a man returning to his native country at the end of his job. I think that is unreal. Farming was not really the testator's job; rather it was an agreeable adjunct to his mode of life. He was not employed by anybody and there was a manager to run the farm. His intention was not expressed in terms of retirement from farming, but of having to give up an active physical life which he enjoyed.

The examination of the nature of the contingency on which a propositus expresses an intention to leave his place of residence is, of course, only an aid in ascertaining intention. One cannot, I think, apply tests of certainty too mechanically or in too refined a way. The question in the end is whether, on the balance of probabilities, the testator intended to end his days here.

Now, there is no doubt that the testator had substantial links with the United States. He was born there. He remained a United States citizen all his life. He married an American girl. Apart from the farm, most of the assets of himself and his wife were in the United States. His wife owned The Pines and, for many years prior to the testator's death, it was let on a monthly tenancy so that the testator and his wife could reoccupy it quickly if they wanted to. Dr Sandvoss was unable to say whether the testator and Mrs Furse actually intended to return to The Pines; he could only say that, if they did want to return, they wanted the house to be in good condition. Mr Besemer believed that the testator would return to live in the United States, though he thought that the testator was postponing it too long. The plaintiff believed that he would return.

The onus of proof of a change of domicile is, of course, on the Crown. But the facts do show a man deeply settled in England. He came to England at the age of 4; he died in England at the age of 80. Of the intervening 76 years he spent 58 in England (in the sense that England was his normal place of abode in those years) and three or four in the British army. He was educated in England. Both his sons were educated in England and served in the British army. Although Mrs Furse was an American, she does not appear to have had any particular wish to return there to live permanently and, in fact, did not do so though she survived the testator by some 14 years. It may be that, during the 1920s and 1930s, having embarked on an English education for his sons, it was convenient for him to stay here. But, from the end of the war onwards, there was no pressure on him, either domestic or external, to remain here. Indeed, from 1946, his only surviving child, the plaintiff, was actually living in New York, a fact, incidentally, which has to be borne in mind when considering the regularity of the visits paid by the testator to the United States in those years. The testator was wholly integrated into the English community in which he lived. There is no doubt at all, as I see it, that the life which he was living in England was the life he wanted to go on living to the end of his life. It is, indeed, the plaintiff's evidence in re-examination that, from about the early 1950s, the testator decided to stay in Sussex except in the contingency which I have mentioned.

The plaintiff said he doubted whether the testator could have gone on at West Hoathly for many more years. But he might well have done so; and the likelihood that, at 84 say, he (a countryman) was going to remove himself, in poor health, to Irvington (which the plaintiff described as suburbia) is, in my view, remote. I think that Mr Besemer was quite right. The testator had postponed his departure for too long. In my view, by the time of his death, the balance of probabilities is that he can have had no real intention of leaving, a fact which is emphasised by the vagueness of his expressed intentions and his obvious inclination to postpone departure.

I do not at all discount the circumstance that Mr Besemer and the plaintiff thought that the testator would return to New York. But I have the expressed intentions of the testator himself and I have to consider the evidence and the law in the light of that. Mr Besemer says that he was convinced that the testator would return. I think that evidence needs to be received with some caution. The testator's own statements do not really go that far. I do not see any indication of certainty in his own mind that he would return. It seems to me that what actually happened was what was likely to happen: namely the testator would remain in England. It has to be remembered that the testator seems to have given Mr Besemer no indication at all of *when* he would return.

In *Re Fuld (deceased) (No 3)* [1968] P 675 at 682 Scarman J said: '. . . a domicile of choice is acquired when a man fixes voluntarily his sole or chief residence in a particular place with an intention of continuing to reside there for an unlimited time.' That statement was approved by the Court of Appeal in *Inland Revenue Comrs v Bullock* [1976] 3 All ER 353 at 358, [1976] 1 WLR 1178 at 1184.

It seems to me that the intention of the testator was indeed to continue to reside in England for an unlimited period. His intention was to continue to live here for the rest of his life, save on the contingency which he expressed. That contingency is so vague that I do not think it can be regarded as imposing any clear limitation on the period of his residence. I do not believe that he was ever prepared to face up to such a limitation. The contingency is of the sort which Simon P in *Qureshi v Qureshi* [1971] 1 All ER 325 at 340, [1972] Fam 173 at 193 described as 'open-ended'. One comes back at the last, it seems to me, to the fact that the testator was determined to live in England for a quite unlimited period.

The evidence leaves on me the strong impression that he was a man very content in England and, whatever generalities that he may have talked, deeply reluctant to commit himself to any plan for leaving. It is not a case like *Bowie (or Ramsay) v Liverpool Royal Infirmary* [1930] AC 588, [1930] All ER Rep 127 where nothing at all was known of the intentions of the propositus. Nor is it like *Winans v Attorney General* [1904] AC 287, [1904–7] All ER Rep 410, the case of a man whose outlook was wholly anti-English and who lived a life withdrawn from the English community.

The authorities emphasise, of course, that a man cannot acquire a domicile of choice in a country if his intention is merely to reside there for a limited time, or for some temporary or special purpose (see, for example, *Inland Revenue Comrs v Bullock* [1976] 3 All ER 353 at 358, [1976] 1 WLR 1178 at 1184). I do not see how the testator's residence in England can, by the time of his death, be described as for some temporary or special purpose. Nor, for the reasons which I have given, was it for a limited time. 'By domicile', said Lord Cranworth in *Whicker v Hume* (1858) 7 HL Cas 124 at 160, [1843–60] All ER Rep 450 at 458, 'we mean home, the permanent home.' I think that, when the testator died in his 81st year, still in England and still with no arrangements made for leaving England, one could not realistically regard his permanent home as other than in England. He intended to live out his days here, save on a contingency so vaguely expressed that I do not think, against the history of his life, it could be regarded for practical purposes as limiting that intention.

In the circumstances I will declare the testator died domiciled in England.

Order accordingly.

Solicitors: *Coward Chance* (for the plaintiff); *Solicitors of Inland Revenue.*

Edwina Epstein Barrister.

Safeguard Industrial Investments Ltd v National Westminster Bank Ltd and another

CHANCERY DIVISION
VINELOTT J
15th, 16th APRIL, 23rd MAY 1980

Company – Transfer of shares – Restriction imposed by articles of association – Notice to be given by member wishing to transfer shares – Bank appointed as executor of member's will – Bank requested in will to transfer testator's shares to named person – Equitable interest in shares vested in bank – Bank registered as holder of shares – Whether bank having sufficient interest to be a 'member' of the company – Whether transfer of equitable or beneficial interest in shares caught by restriction on transfer of shares – Whether notice of transfer required.

The plaintiff and P each held one-sixth of the issued shares in a private company. The remaining two-thirds of the shares were held by P's cousins, M and X, and X's two children, Y and Z. Differences of opinion arose between M on the one hand, and X and his children on the other, so that at meetings of the company the plaintiff and P held the balance of power. Subsequently P died, leaving a will in which he named the defendant bank as his executor and bequeathed all his shares in the company to Z. By a deed of family arrangement, to which the bank was a party, it was declared that P's will was to take effect as if the shares had been left to Y and Z equally. During the course of the administration of the estate, the bank was registered as the holder of P's shares and as such exercised its voting rights in a manner that preserved the status quo at meetings of the company. The plaintiff feared that once the administration of the estate was completed the position might be altered by the bank then exercising its voting rights in accordance with the directions of Y and Z, with the result that X, Y and Z would secure control of the company. On the completion of the administration of the estate, the bank informed the plaintiff (i) that it regarded itself as holding P's shares on trust for Y and Z absolutely, (ii) that Y and Z had made it clear to the bank that they did not want the bank to transfer the shares to them, and (iii) that the bank was not proposing to transfer the shares unless directed to do so. Article 7B of the company's articles of association provided that a member wishing to transfer shares was, except in the case of a transfer under art 8 to certain close relatives, required to give notice of transfer to the company and was then required to offer the shares to the other members pro rata, and could not transfer them to a non-member if a member was willing to purchase them at a fair value. Article 8 provided that shares could be transferred by a member during his lifetime, or on his death, by his personal representative to certain close relatives or to trustees for the benefit of such relatives without the transfer being subject to the restrictions contained in art 7B. The plaintiff, who wished to acquire a proportion of P's shares under art 7B, applied to the court for the determination of the question whether the bank, on completion of the administration of the estate and having assented or purported to assent to the vesting of the beneficial interest in P's shares in Y and Z pursuant to the joint effect of the will and the deed of family arrangement, was bound to give notice of transfer.

Held – (1) The bank could not claim that when it was registered as the holder of P's shares it became a 'member' of the company as if it were registered as a transferee and that therefore under art 8 it could only transfer the shares to its own close relatives (if any) and not to a close relative of the deceased because on a sensible rather than literal construction of art 8 the bank did not fall to be treated as a 'member' when it was registered as the holder of P's shares but fell to be treated as P's representative and as having P's right to transfer shares to his close relatives without regard to the restrictions on transfer imposed by art 7B (see p 854 *d* to *h*, post).

(2) But, since, on the evidence, Y and Z were not close relatives of P for the purposes of art 8, the bank was not on that account exempted from the restrictions imposed by art a
7B on the transfer of shares (see p 854 *j*, post).

(3) The bank however was not obliged to give notice of transfer pursuant to art 7B on completion of the administration of the estate because—

(a) on the true construction of art 7B, the expression 'transfer of a share' covered only the transfer of the legal title to a share with the rights and liabilities attaching to it and did not include the transfer of a beneficial interest in a share; accordingly, as there was b
merely evidence of a desire to dispose of an equitable interest in P's shares, art 7B did not apply (see p 858 *f* to *j*, post); *Hunter v Hunter* [1936] AC 222 and *Lyle & Scott Ltd v Scott's Trustees* [1959] 2 All ER 661 considered;

(b) in any event, art 7B would not have been brought into operation by the bank informing Y and Z that the administration of the estate was complete and that it would deal with the shares at their direction, since P's desire to make a future and conditional c
transfer did not take effect through the bank as his personal representative as a desire to make an immediate and unconditional transfer to Z and through Z to Y (p 859 *g*, post);

(c) art 7B applied to any person who was entitled to transfer a share whether as a member or as personal representative or as trustee in bankruptcy of a member, and the desire giving rise to the obligation to give a transfer notice was a desire expressed or implemented only by such a person, and the desire of a member as expressed in his will d
that his shares should be transferred to a person who was not a close relative within art 8 could not be attributed to the bank as his personal representative (see p 860 *a* to *c*, post).

Notes

For restriction on transfer of shares, see 7 Halsbury's Laws (4th Edn) para 397, and for cases on the transfer of shares, see 9 Digest (Reissue) 372–380, *2201–2262*. e

Cases referred to in judgment

Greenhalgh v Mallard [1943] 2 All ER 234, CA, 9 Digest (Reissue) 356, *2108*.

Hunter v Hunter [1936] AC 222, 105 LJ Ch 97, 154 LT 513, HL, 9 Digest (Reissue) 223, *1344*. f

Lyle & Scott Ltd v Scott's Trustees, Lyle & Scott Ltd v British Investment Trust Ltd 1958 SC 230; *rvsd* [1959] 2 All ER 661, [1959] AC 763, [1959] 3 WLR 133, 1959 SC (HL) 64, HL, 9 Digest (Reissue) 373, *2216*.

Scott v Frank F Scott (London) Ltd [1940] 3 All ER 508, [1940] Ch 794, 163 LT 140, CA, 9 Digest (Reissue) 424, *2505*.

Yates, Re, Batcheldor v Yates (1888) 38 Ch D 112, 57 LJ Ch 697, 59 LT 47, CA, 35 Digest g
(Repl) 564, *2397*.

Cases also cited

Delavenne v Broadhurst [1931] 1 Ch 234.

Hawks v McArthur [1951] 1 All ER 22.

Inland Revenue Comrs v Hawley [1928] 1 KB 578. h

Moodie v W & J Shepherd (Bookbinders) Ltd [1949] 2 All ER 1044, HL.

Roberts v Letter 'T' Estates Ltd [1961] AC 795, PC.

Smith & Fawcett Ltd, Re [1942] 1 All ER 542, [1942] Ch 304, CA.

Adjourned summons

By an originating summons dated 26th July 1979 and subsequently amended, the j
plaintiff, Safeguard Industrial Investments Ltd ('Safeguard'), a shareholder in the second defendant, M Wright & Sons Ltd ('the company'), sought the following relief: that it might be determined whether, on the true construction of the company's articles of association, the first defendant, the National Westminster Bank Ltd, as executor of Philip James Rhodes Wright, deceased, on completion of administration of his estate and

having assented or purported to assent to the vesting of the beneficial interest in certain shares in Georgina Maltby and Michael Pochin Marius Wright pursuant to the joint effect of the will of the deceased and a deed of family arrangement, dated 10th April 1978, should (i) give to the company a transfer notice pursuant to para 7B of the company's articles of association in respect of all the ordinary shares in the company of which the deceased was the registered holder at his death or (ii) take some other (and if so, what) course of action in regard to those shares. The facts are set out in the judgment.

Gerald Godfrey QC and *Elizabeth Gloster* for Safeguard.
Oliver Weaver for the bank.
The company was not represented.

Cur adv vult

23rd May. **VINELOTT J** read the following judgment: M Wright & Sons Ltd (which I shall call 'the company') is a private company. It was incorporated in 1950. Its share capital is now £200,000 divided into 200,000 shares of £1 each of which 132,003 have been issued and are fully paid or credited as fully paid. The plaintiff, Safeguard Industrial Investments Ltd (which I shall call 'Safeguard'), is a public investment company. It specialises in acquiring strategic stakes in private companies, that is, blocks of shares which are of a size which would normally give the holder some influence over the way in which the company's affairs are conducted but which are not large enough to carry voting control. In 1961 or thereabouts Safeguard acquired approximately one-sixth of the issued shares of the company. The business was then run by two brothers Mr Michael Wright senior and Mr Marius Wright. They continued to run the business until 1971. The brothers, together with Mr Marius Wright's children, Mr Michael Pochin Marius Wright (whom I shall call 'Mr Michael Wright junior') and Mrs Georgina Maltby, together held approximately two-thirds of the shares of the company. A block of shares, 22,254 in number (approximately one-sixth of the total issued shares), was held by one Philip James Rhodes Wright, who died on 25th July 1976, and to whom I shall refer as 'the deceased'. He was the son of one Walter Wright, the brother of Sidney James Wright, who was the father of Mr Marius Wright and Mr Michael Wright senior. In 1970 there were differences of opinion between Mr Michael Wright senior and Mr Marius Wright as to the way in which the company's business should be conducted. The company suffered in consequence. Neither Mr Michael Wright senior on the one hand nor Mr Marius Wright and his two children on the other hand held a sufficient number of shares to command a majority of votes at general meetings. The votes attaching to the shares held by the deceased and by Safeguard were thus of crucial importance. In 1971 there was a change in the constitution of the board. A Mr King joined the board and became chairman. He is still the chairman. He is a director of a company associated with Safeguard and was, I assume, introduced by Safeguard. Mr Michael Wright senior and Mr Marius Wright ceased to be directors. Since 1971 the business of the company has been conducted by a board consisting of Mr King, Mr Michael Wright junior and two directors who are not connected with either side of the family. It is said by Safeguard that since this change the business of the company has prospered. Safeguard also claim that while the deceased was alive they effectively held the balance of power between the two warring factions and were able to ensure that the company did not come under the control of either of them. The details of the family shareholdings are not set out in the evidence but, as I understand the position, Safeguard held the balance of power in this way only so long as the deceased also sat on the fence and supported neither side. As I have said he died on 25th July 1976. His will, which was dated 25th March 1966, was proved on 4th October 1976 by National Westminster Bank Ltd as successor of Westminster Bank Ltd, the sole executor in the will. The National Westminster Bank (which I shall call 'the bank') was registered as the holder of the deceased's shares on or about 30th March 1977. It is said by Safeguard that the bank, since it was registered as

the holder of the deceased's shares, has exercised its voting rights 'in accordance with its
judgment of the best interests of the deceased's estate' and, as I understand it, the bank, a
in turn, has not supported either faction so that Safeguard has continued to exercise the
same degree of practical control which it was able to exercise during the lifetime of the
deceased. The position of Safeguard is now threatened by the events to which I now
turn.

By his will the deceased left his shares in the company to Mrs Maltby (then and therein
described as Miss Georgina Wright). Shortly before his death, on 27th May 1976, he b
wrote to Mr Michael Wright junior inquiring whether he would be willing to act as his
executor. In that letter he expressed his wish that his shares should go to Mr Michael
Wright junior and Mrs Maltby equally. He also expressed uncertainty whether under
his existing will the shares went to them both equally or to one or other of them. After
the death of the deceased Mrs Maltby decided to give effect to the deceased's wishes as
expressed in that letter and by a deed of family arrangement dated 10th April 1978 to c
which she, Mr Michael Wright junior and the bank were parties, it was declared that the
deceased's will should be read and take effect as if his shares in the company had been left
to Mr Michael Wright junior and Mrs Maltby equally. Safeguard feared that on
completion of administration of the estate the bank's practice with regard to the exercise
of the voting rights attached to the shares would change, that the bank would exercise its
rights in accordance with the directions of Mr Michael Wright junior and Mrs Maltby d
and that Mr Marius Wright and his children would secure control of the company. That
would deprive Safeguard of the influence over the company's affairs which their strategic
stake had previously secured. Safeguard also claimed that under certain pre-emption
provisions in the articles of association of the company the bank would be bound on
completion of the administration of the estate to offer the deceased's shares to the other
members of the company pro rata to their shareholdings. That claim having been e
disputed by Mrs Maltby and by Mr Michael Wright junior Safeguard took out the
originating summons which is now before me joining the bank and the company as
defendants. The originating summons as originally framed asked that it be determined
whether on completion of administration of the estate the bank will be bound to give a
transfer notice in respect of the deceased's shares pursuant to the pre-emption
provisions. In the course of these proceedings evidence has been filed on behalf of the f
bank in which it is said that administration of the deceased's estate is complete and that
the bank regards itself as holding 11,127 of the deceased's shares on trust for each of Mrs
Maltby and Mr Michael Wright junior absolutely. It is said by the bank that Mrs Maltby
and Mr Michael Wright junior have made it clear that they do not want the bank to
transfer the shares to them, that the bank do not propose to transfer the shares unless
directed so to do and that accordingly 'the Bank as registered holder of the said shares g
neither proposes nor desires to transfer all or any of the said shares or any interest in
them'. The significance of this last statement will appear from the pre-emption
provisions. In the light of that evidence by the bank Safeguard now ask that it be
determined whether 'on completion of administration of the deceased's estate and having
assented or purported to assent to the vesting of the beneficial interest' in the deceased's
shares in Mrs Maltby and Mr Michael Wright junior pursuant to the joint effect of the h
will and the deed of family arrangement the bank is bound to give a transfer notice
pursuant to the pre-emption provisions.

Article 1 of the articles of association of the company provides that the regulations in
Table A of Sch 1 to the Companies Act 1948—

> 'shall apply to the Company save in so far as they are excluded or varied hereby: j
> that is to say, the Clauses in Part 1 of Table A numbered 24, 30, 31, 53, 75, 77 and
> 136 shall not apply to this Company; but in lieu thereof, and in addition to the
> remaining Clauses in Part 1 of Table A, the following shall be the Regulations of the
> Company.'

Article 2 provides:

> *a* 'The Company is a Private Company, and accordingly Clauses 2, 3, 4, 5 and 6 in Part II of Table A shall apply to the Company.'

Articles 7 and 8 are headed 'Transfer of Shares'. Article 7A deals with a class of preference shares which no longer exist. The first two paragraphs of art 7B read as follows:

> 'A member shall not be entitled to transfer an Ordinary Share except subject to *b* clause 3 of Part II of Table A and in accordance with the following provisions: (a) An Ordinary Share may be transferred by a member or other person entitled to transfer to the other members in the proportions between them (if more than one) as nearly as may be to the number of Ordinary Shares held by them respectively, but no Ordinary Share shall be transferred to a person who is not a member as long as any member is willing to purchase the same at the fair value. (b) Except where the *c* transfer made is pursuant to Article 8 hereof, in order to ascertain whether any member is willing to purchase an Ordinary Share, the proposing transferor shall give notice in writing (hereinafter called "the transfer notice") to the Company that he desires to transfer the same. Such notice shall constitute the Company his agent for the sale of such share to any member of the Company at the fair value.'

d Paragraphs (c), (d), (e) and (f) provide for shares specified in a transfer notice to be offered by the directors at fair value to the other members pro rata, for the machinery for acceptance of such offers, for the execution of transfers on behalf of a proposing transferor who makes default in transferring shares specified in a transfer notice and for the ascertainment of the fair value of the shares. Paragraph (g) provides that if no member is willing to purchase shares comprised in a transfer notice within a specified period the *e* proposing transferor is to be free to sell them to a non-member but at not less than a fair value. Paragraph (h) contains special provisions concerning shares held by employees, including those departmental directors who are not directors of the company. These special provisions are not relevant to the questions I have to decide.

Article 8 I must read in full. It reads as follows:

> 'Any share in the Company may be transferred by a member (other than a *f* Departmental Director) during his life or by his legal personal representatives on his death, as the case may be, to any husband, wife, son, daughter or other lineal descendant, son-in-law, daughter-in-law, father, mother, brother, sister, nephew, niece, widow or widower of any such member or to any trustees appointed by deed or will upon trusts for the benefit of any such person or by such trustees to new trustees or by any such trustees on the termination of the said trusts to any such *g* person as aforesaid and the restrictions contained in Article 7 and in Clause 3 of Part II of Table A shall not apply to any transfer authorised by this Article.'

Article 8A contains special provisions relating to Safeguard's shares. It restricts the directors' power to refuse to register transfers to certain companies associated with Safeguard and modifies the pre-emption provisions in art 7 in effect by giving Safeguard *h* the right to specify the price at which shares it wishes to transfer are to be offered to other members.

These articles contain at least two unusual provisions which I should mention before turning to the main arguments which have been addressed to me. First, art 1 adopts Table A except certain specified clauses. The excepted clauses include cll 30 and 31. Clause 30, so far as material, provides that a person becoming entitled to a share in *j* consequence of the death of a member may be required by the directors to elect to be registered himself or to have some person nominated by him registered as transferee so that in either case the directors are to have the same power to decline or suspend registration as they would have had in the case of a transfer by a deceased member. Clause 31 provides that if a person becoming so entitled shall elect to be registered he shall send to the company a notice stating that he so elects and if he elects to have another person registered shall testify his election by executing a transfer to him. In either case—

> 'all the limitations, restrictions and provisions of these regulations relating to the right to transfer and the registration of transfers of shares shall be applicable to any such notice or transfer as aforesaid as if the death or bankruptcy of a member had not occurred and the notice or transfer were a transfer signed by that member.'

The effect of the words which I have cited is that on a personal representative electing either to be himself registered or to have another person registered any pre-emption provisions in the articles come into operation in just the same way as if the deceased member had signed a transfer. It is common ground that in the present case, cll 30 and 31 having been excluded, the bank as personal representative of the deceased was entitled to be registered as the holder of the shares registered in his name (see *Scott v Frank F Scott (London) Ltd* [1940] 3 All ER 508, [1940] Ch 794). The second and related point is that on registration as the holder of the deceased's shares the bank became a member of the company. Article 8 permits a share to be transferred by a member or by the personal representatives of a deceased member to a class of close relatives of the member or deceased member. Literally construed art 8 would permit a personal representative who became registered as the holder of the deceased's shares to transfer the shares to his close relatives. Counsel for the bank went further. He said that once the personal representative had been registered he was bound by the article in the same way as if he had been registered as transferee and could no longer transfer the deceased's shares to a close relative of the deceased. He said that the fact that the personal representative once registered would not be entitled to transfer to the close relatives of the deceased (unless they also happened to be close relatives of his) was a matter to be taken into account by the personal representative in deciding whether or not to apply for registration. While that conclusion follows from a literal construction of art 8 the article is, I think, capable of another construction which produces a more sensible result. The second part of art 8 permits a transfer to be made 'to any trustees appointed by deed or will upon trusts for the benefit of any' close relatives of a member 'or by such trustees to new trustees or by any such trustees on the termination of the said trusts' to any such close relative. These words by expressly permitting the transfer of a share by a trustee to a beneficiary (being a close relative of the settlor member) impliedly prohibit a transfer by the trustee to his own close relatives. The same restriction must, in my opinion, be read into the first part of art 8. It cannot have been intended that a personal representative who becomes registered as the holder of a share should be in any different position from that of a trustee for a close relative of a deceased member to whom the same personal representative might subsequently transfer the share pursuant to directions in the will and who, in turn, might be registered as the holder of the share. If art 8 is read as a whole it is, I think, clear that the draftsman intended that a personal representative or a trustee who became registered as the holder of a share devolving on death or transferred inter vivos though becoming a member would not fall to be treated as a member for the purposes of art 8 but would stand in the shoes and be treated as a representative of the deceased member or settlor from whom the shares were derived and that in the case of a personal representative as in the case of a trustee he would be entitled to transfer the shares to the close relatives of the deceased member even though he had himself become registered as the holder of the shares.

The bank, of course, has no relatives. And Mrs Maltby and Mr Michael Wright junior are not close relatives of the deceased; they are children of a cousin of his. Thus the fact that the bank is registered as the holder of the deceased's shares is irrelevant. The question whether the bank is bound to give a transfer notice would have arisen even if the shares had remained registered in the name of the deceased. Counsel for Safeguard did not contend that the bank became bound to give a transfer notice as regards Mr Michael Wright junior's shares when the deed of family arrangement was executed. He argued that the bank became bound to give a transfer notice as regards all the deceased's

22,254 shares as soon as it had completed administration and had informed Mrs Maltby and Mr Michael Wright junior that it held 11,127 shares as her or his nominee and would transfer them to her or him as she or he might direct. Counsel based this argument on two grounds. First, he submitted that the reference in art 7B to the transfer of a share should be construed as extending to a disposition of the entire beneficial interest in a share, that on completion of administration of the estate the deceased's beneficial interest, which was in suspense during the period of administration, vested in Mrs Maltby and in Mr Michael Wright junior and that the bank became bound to give a transfer notice at the moment when the bank first informed Mrs Maltby and Mr Michael Wright junior that administration of the estate was complete and that the bank would deal with the shares as directed by them, that being, it is said, an assent by the bank to the vesting of the beneficial interest in Mrs Maltby and Mr Michael Wright junior. The second and alternative submission is that the deceased by his will evinced a desire to transfer his shares to a person who was not a permitted transferee of his entire holding (Mrs Maltby has, of course, been a member at all material times but a transfer to a member can be made under para (a) of art 7B only if the shares are offered pro rata to all members) and that that expression of his desire to transfer his shares became on his death an irrevocable direction to his executor to transfer the shares to Mrs Maltby subject only to the bank's power as executor to sell the shares or some of them if such a sale should become necessary in the course of administration. The deceased's expressed desire to transfer his shares, it is said, must be treated as one expressed on his death. But it was not then such an expression of his desire to transfer his shares as required the bank as his representative to give a transfer notice under art 7B; the reason is that the desire evinced by the will was a desire to transfer his shares in the future (that is, on completion of administration of the estate) and was conditional in that the legatee's right to a transfer would be subject to the executor's power to sell the shares if necessary in the course of administration. But, it is said, on communication by the bank to Mrs Maltby and Mr Michael Wright junior that administration had been completed and that the bank would deal with the shares at their direction, the deceased's expressed desire to make a future and conditional transfer took effect, through the executor as his representative, as an expressed desire to make an immediate and unconditional transfer to Mrs Maltby and, in effect, through her to Mr Michael Wright junior. At that stage, it is said, para (b) of art 7B operated in just the same way as if the bank had, at the deceased's direction, entered into a contract to sell the shares to them for a nominal consideration.

In support of his first submission counsel for Safeguard relied on the decision of the Court of Session in *Lyle & Scott v Scott's Trustees* 1958 SC 230 and on certain observations in the House of Lords in the subsequent appeal from that decision ([1959] 2 All ER 661, [1959] AC 763). In that case the articles of association of Lyle & Scott Ltd prohibited any transfer by a shareholder holding more than 1% of the shares of the company for a nominal consideration or by way of security and provided that 'no transfer of ordinary shares . . . shall take place for an onerous consideration so long as any other ordinary shareholder is willing to purchase the same', either at a price to be ascertained by agreement between the transferor and the directors or failing agreement to be fixed by the auditors. That was the first and prohibitive part of the article. The article then provided that—

> 'any such ordinary shareholder who is desirous of transferring his ordinary shares shall inform the secretary in writing of the number of ordinary shares which he desires to transfer, and the price shall immediately be fixed as aforesaid.'

There followed the usual provisions for the shares to be offered by the company to the other shareholders. An offer was made by a non-member, Mr Hugh Fraser, for all the shares of the company which offer was accepted by certain of the shareholders. The offer was initially conditional on acceptance by 75% of the members and was to be completed by payment against executed transfers in the usual way. Subsequently the condition was waived. The shareholders who had accepted were paid the agreed price (which had been increased since the original offer) and each delivered a share certificate and a form of general proxy. The shareholders concerned claimed in their evidence that it had also *a* been agreed by Mr Fraser at the time of payment of the consideration for the shares that no instruments of transfer would be executed and delivered unless and until requested by him. Mr Fraser accordingly did not apply for registration. It was argued on behalf of the shareholders at first instance (1958 SC 230 at 233) that all they had done was 'to sell the beneficial interest in their shares retaining the legal title and membership of the company in themselves'. That argument was rejected by the Lord Ordinary (Lord *b* Strachan) on the ground that it had not been averred in the evidence that the sale was a sale of the beneficial interest alone. He held that the contract for the sale of the shares was a breach of the first or prohibitive part of the article. But he refused to order that the shareholders were bound to give notice to the secretary of their desire to transfer their shares, on the ground that the second part of the article prescribed the provisions by which alone a member's shares could be transferred but did not give the other members *c* the right to compel a member desirous of transferring his shares to offer them to the other members. The Lord Ordinary said (at 235) that—

> 'even if the defenders in this case do desire to transfer shares, they would be entitled to change their mind after sending the prescribed notification to the secretary, and *a fortiori* they would be entitled to do so before they had taken the *d* first step under article 9. To find that they are now bound to implement article 9, or to ordain them to do so, would be to deprive them of their right to change their mind . . .'

That decision was upheld by the Court of Session on the same ground. In the Court of Session the company sought to uphold the Lord Ordinary's judgment on the ground that the shareholders had sold and transferred the beneficial interest in the shares and that the *e* second part of the article accordingly applied. It was said in argument (at 235) that 'The term "desirous of transferring" struck at all transfers, not merely technical transfers of shares'. As to that argument the Lord President (Lord Clyde) said (at 243):

> 'An attempt was made to contend that although the legal title to the shares remained with the defenders they had competently disposed of some equitable or beneficial right in the shares. But whatever may be the validity in Scotland of such *f* a distinction—and upon that matter I reserve my opinion—the contract averred by the pursuers is, by Scots law, either a contract of sale of the shares or nothing. For the essence of the contract in question is that the price is payable against delivery of an effective transfer. As such a transfer cannot be given, no obligation has been incurred to convey an interest in the property. No question therefore arises, in my opinion, in the case as presented to us, on the pursuers' averments regarding *g* equitable or beneficial interests.'

But Lord Sorn accepted the argument. He said (at 250–251):

> 'The language of the article thus seems to me to make it clear that what it purports to prohibit is a sale of the shares, and that this includes a prohibition of the sale of the beneficial interest in them. Indeed, when the purpose of the article is *h* regarded, it would be strange if the language did not have this meaning. The article is plainly designed to give members of the company *some* kind of opportunity of keeping the share capital and control of the business in the hands of the existing members. If it is read in the way I have suggested, it purports to do this effectively. If it is read in the opposite way, it would purport to achieve little or nothing, because it would be left open to a shareholder, prepared to let himself remain on the register *j* as a bare trustee, to sell his shares to an outsider and give him a general proxy. It is difficult to think that the article intended to leave this obvious manoeuvre unprohibited.' (Lord Sorn's emphasis.)

In the House of Lords the late Sir Milner Holland QC similarly argued ([1959] AC 763 at 768) that the article prohibited 'transfers of shares, including transfers of the beneficial interest . . .' It was held in the House of Lords that the shareholders were bound to give notice to the secretary in accordance with the second part of the article. But the majority based this conclusion on the ground that the shareholders who accepted the offer had by contracting to sell their shares shown that they desired to transfer them and that they could not be heard to say that they did not desire to transfer them so long as the contract remained on foot. Viscount Simonds, after referring to this distinction which had been made in the court below between the first or prohibitive and the second part of the article, said, as regards this first part of the article ([1959] 2 All ER 661 at 664, [1959] AC 763 at 773):

> 'I do not dissent, my Lords, from the opinion expressed by the Lord Ordinary, the Lord President (LORD CLYDE) and LORD RUSSELL in the First Division that Scott's trustees had been guilty of a breach of this part of the article. The determination of this question rests on the meaning to be assigned to the word "transfer" where it there occurs. But I do not think it necessary to express a final opinion on it, for, as I have said, the question is not whether what has been done is a breach of the first part of the article, but whether it demonstrates with sufficient clearness that Scott's trustees are persons desirous of transferring their ordinary shares.'

As I read that passage the question on which Viscount Simonds refrained from expressing a final opinion was whether there had been a breach of the first or prohibitive part of the article and not the question whether the article applied to the sale of a beneficial interest in a share. But Lord Keith did deal with this question. He said ([1959] 2 All ER 661 at 672, [1959] AC 763 at 785):

> 'If I may express my view of the article in the most general sense, I think the prohibitory part of the article is the sanction which prevents a shareholder from carrying through a transfer of shares without complying with the machinery of transfer set out in the second part of the article. And I think that a shareholder who has transferred, or pretended to transfer, the beneficial interest in a share to a purchaser for value is merely endeavouring by a subterfuge to escape from the peremptory provisions of the article. A share is of no value to anyone without the benefits it confers. A sale of a share is a sale of the beneficial rights that it confers, and to sell or purport to sell the beneficial rights without the title to the shares is, in my opinion, a plain breach of the provisions of art. 9. This, I think, is the view which commended itself to LORD SORN and I think that he is right.'

The observations of Lord Keith, of course, lend powerful support to counsel for Safeguard's first argument but they do not stand alone. In the earlier case of *Hunter v Hunter* [1936] AC 222 (which was referred to by Lord Sorn) Viscount Hailsham LC expressed the contrary opinion. In *Hunter v Hunter* the main question was whether a mortgagee bank's power of sale over shares of a private company had become exercisable and, if it had, whether a purported sale by the bank was in breach of pre-emption provisions. The first part of the relevant article provided that—

> 'No member shall be entitled to transfer any shares otherwise than in accordance with the following provisions: (a) A member desirous of selling his shares (hereinafter called "the selling member") shall give a notice (hereinafter called "the notice of sale") to the secretary of the Company containing an offer to sell the same, and stating the number of the shares which he desires to sell and the price which he is willing to accept for such shares, which price shall be a price to be fixed and certified by the auditors or auditor of the Company for the time being, and which price when so fixed shall be deemed to be the fair price and final and binding . . .'

There followed provision for the secretary to give notice of the offer to the other shareholders and a right for one of the shareholders in certain circumstances to accept the offer in priority to the other shareholders.

The bank had apparently procured its nominees to be registered as the holders of the shares in question, in breach of art 17, before it purported to exercise its power of sale. a

It was held by the majority in the House of Lords that the power of sale had not become exercisable and by all their Lordships that the purported sale infringed the article. It had been argued by the bank that the sale was a sale of an equitable interest only and that the article did not apply to it. All their Lordships held that the sale was not a sale of an equitable interest divorced from the legal interest. But Viscount Hailsham LC, after making it clear that his observations on this latter point were not intended to b be binding authority, said (at 248–249):

> 'I cannot accept the view of the Court of Appeal that the transaction between the Bank and Harry Hunter operated as a valid sale of the equitable interest in the shares. A mortgagee of shares cannot split up the interest of the mortgagor and sell the mortgagor's beneficial interest while retaining for himself the legal title, any more than a mortgagee of a house can sell the fixtures in the house leaving the c mortgagor the equitable owner of what is left: *In re Yates* ((1888) 38 Ch D 112). If the Bank had been selling the equitable interest of the plaintiff in the shares, none of the provisions of article 17 as to the restriction on the possible purchasers, or as to the method of fixing a price, would have been effective; it would have been quite a different transaction from a sale of the shares.'

d

As I read the speech of Lord Russell he agreed with Viscount Hailsham LC on this point though, again, he made it clear that he was not to be taken as expressing any concluded opinion. He said (at 264):

> 'Neither am I able to justify to myself the way in which the Court of Appeal have upheld what purported to be a sale of the legal and equitable interest in the shares at the restricted price enforced by the articles (and necessarily at that price) as a sale e of the equitable interest only which, if permissible, would not be in any way subject to those restrictions but open to free competition.'

The references to the judgments in the Court of Appeal suggest that the Court of Appeal may have decided that the sale was a sale of the equitable interest and that the sale did not infringe art 17 (see also the first six lines on p 231). However, this decision of the f Court of Appeal is not reported and the record in the House has not been obtained so that this must remain at present a matter of speculation.

Faced with these conflicting observations in the House of Lords I must decide which to follow. Although it may seem at first sight unduly restrictive to read the word 'transfer' as referring only to a transfer of the legal interest in a share leaving, as Lord Sorn put it, the 'obvious manoeuvre' of a sale of the beneficial interest unprohibited, art 7 g seems to me wholly inapt to 'catch' transfers of beneficial interests. A 'transfer of a share' in the ordinary sense of that expression is a transfer of the legal title to the share with the rights and liabilities attaching to it; on registration of the transfer the transferor ceases to be, and the transferee becomes, a member of the company in right of that share. A member who desires to transfer a share will carry his intention into effect by executing a transfer and lodging it for registration. At that stage the restrictions in the pre-emption h provisions come into operation. To treat the references to the transfer of a share as comprehending a transfer or disposition of a beneficial interest in a share is to give the expression 'transfer of a share' a meaning wider than it would ordinarily bear. No doubt there are contexts in which that extension would readily be made. But this context of art 7 and 8 points, if anything, in the opposite direction. Any number of equitable interests can be carved out of the equitable ownership of a share. But it is impossible to construe j art 7 as applying to any disposition of a beneficial interest in a share however small. And if the article is construed as applying to a disposition of the entire beneficial interest in a share but not to a disposition of part of the beneficial interest it may operate in a way that is both capricious and which in practice would afford little protection against the 'obvious manoeuvre' of a shareholder determined to defeat the pre-emption provisions. A shareholder is entitled to transfer a share to trustees on trust for his infant son contingently on attaining 21 with remainder to himself or to another close relative if the son dies under 21. Article 8 clearly permits such a transfer and is not restricted to a transfer to trustees as bare trustees for a close relative absolutely entitled; for it contemplates a transfer to the beneficiary for whose benefit the trust was created on termination of the trust. On the wider construction of the word 'transfer' a sale by the son after attaining 21 would be a 'transfer' of the share bringing the pre-emption provisions into operation. But a sale by the son immediately before attaining 21 would not pass the entire beneficial interest and would not therefore bring the pre-emption provisions into operation. Similarly, a shareholder might declare himself a trustee for a purchaser who is not a close relative contingently on the happening of some future event, for instance his survival to a stated date. The declaration of trust again would not operate as a transfer of the entire beneficial interest even though it might be practically certain that the event would happen. Again, a shareholder might vest a reversionary interest expectant on his own death in a purchaser by a declaration of trust constituting himself a trustee for himself for life with remainder to the purchaser. The declaration of trust would not amount to a transfer of the share even on the wider construction. The shareholder might subsequently sell his life interest to the same purchaser. He would then have divested himself of the entire beneficial interest in the share in favour of the purchaser but without at either stage executing a transfer of the entire beneficial interest. Weighing anomalies may be an uncertain guide to construction. But it is, I think, legitimate to take into account the anomalies which result from giving an extended meaning to an expression as a ground for not departing from its ordinary meaning.

It is possible that if a shareholder were to declare himself a trustee of a share for a purchaser and were to hand over an irrevocable proxy to vote the share the court might draw the inference that the parties intended that the transaction should take effect as a contract for the sale of the share and that the owner had sufficiently evinced a desire to transfer the legal interest in the share. That, as I see it, is the ground of the opinions expressed in *Lyle & Scott Ltd v Scott's Trustees* by Lord Sorn (1958 SC 230 at 250) and by Lord Keith ([1959] 2 All ER 661 at 672, [1959] AC 763 at 785) (though it should be noted that it is inherent in the view of the majority in the House of Lords that the operation of the article could be avoided by a consensual cancellation of the contract, and that the passing of the equitable interest which resulted from the arrangements made when the purchase price was paid did not of itself bring the second part of the article into operation). However in my judgment it cannot be said that a member has transferred a share or desires to transfer a share if all that is shown is that he has disposed of or agreed to dispose of an equitable interest in it.

Counsel for Safeguard's second argument is at first sight a more formidable one. He stressed that during the period of administration the beneficial ownership of the deceased's shares was in suspense and that on completion of administration Mrs Maltby's and Mr Michael Wright junior's title to the shares related back to the date of the testator's death. Thus, said counsel, the transfer must be treated as having been made on the testator's death when his desire to transfer his shares to a person who was not a close relative was first expressed in a document containing directions as to the disposition of his shares which was the precise equivalent of a contract for the sale of the shares albeit subject to the condition that the executor was to have power to sell the shares if necessary for the purpose of administration. But the argument, though persuasively presented, leads again to anomalous results. If a testator gives his shares in the company by will to a person who is not a close relative then on completion of administration, if the argument is well founded, his executor is bound to give a transfer notice. But if he dies intestate and his sole next of kin is a person who is not a close relative this result does not follow; the deceased cannot be said to have expressed the desire that his shares should be transferred on completion of administration to his next of kin. Indeed it is not easy to see how the argument would apply to a testator's shares in the present case. The testator

did not by his will give any of his shares to Mr Michael Wright junior. Mr Michael
Wright junior became entitled only under the deed of family arrangement. The a
argument, if well founded, would seem to lead to the conclusion that on completion of
administration the executor would be bound to give a transfer notice in respect of Mrs
Maltby's 11,127 shares but not in respect of Mr Michael Wright junior's 11,127 shares.
The answer to the argument is, I think, that art 7B applies to any person who is entitled
to transfer a share whether as a member or as personal representative or trustee in
bankruptcy of a member. The desire to transfer a share, the expression or implementation b
of which gives rise to the obligation to give a transfer notice, is a desire expressed or
implemented by such a person. Article 8 excepts the case of a transfer by a member or
the personal representative of a member to, or to trustees for, a close relative of such a
member. The desire of a member as expressed in his will that his shares shall be
transferred to a person who is not a close relative cannot be attributed to his personal
representatives. c

I reach this conclusion with some regret. I have no doubt that if the draftsman had
foreseen this situation he would have found some means of extending the pre-emption
provisions in such a way as to impose on the legatee an obligation to serve a transfer
notice. But the gap cannot, in my judgment, be filled by construction. It requires a
radical redrafting of the article. And I must bear in mind the observations of Lord
Greene MR in *Greenhalgh v Mallard* [1943] 2 All ER 234 at 237 where he said: d

> 'Questions of construction of this kind are always difficult, but in the case of the restriction of transfer of shares I think it is right for the Court to remember that a share, being personal property, is *prima facie* transferable, although the conditions of the transfer are to be found in the terms laid down in the articles. If the right of transfer, which is inherent in property of this kind, is to be taken away or cut down, e it seems to me that it should be done by language of sufficient clarity to make it apparent that that was the intention.'

Declaration accordingly.

Solicitors: *McKenna & Co* (for the plaintiff); *Harvey Ingram*, Leicester (for the first defendant).

Jacqueline Metcalfe Barrister.

London and County Securities Ltd and others v Nicholson and others

CHANCERY DIVISION

BROWNE-WILKINSON J

22nd, 23rd, 24th, 25th, 28th JANUARY 1980

Company – Investigation by Board of Trade – Evidence before inspectors – Evidence given by company's auditors – Admissibility in subsequent legal proceedings – Proceedings by company in liquidation against auditors for alleged negligence in conducting audit – Whether evidence admissible in civil proceedings – Whether public interest in availability of relevant evidence to court outweighing public interest in maintaining confidentiality of evidence given to inspectors – Companies Act 1967, s 50.

In 1974 the Department of Trade and Industry appointed inspectors under s 165 of the Companies Act 1948 to investigate the affairs of the first plaintiff, which was in liquidation. In the course of the investigation the inspectors, pursuant to s 167(2) of the 1948 Act, took oral evidence on oath from four partners and an employee in the firm of accountants which had audited the accounts for the year ending March 1973 of the first plaintiff and its parent company, the second plaintiff, which was also in liquidation. Transcripts were made of that evidence and the evidence was amplified in correspondence between the inspectors and the solicitors for the firm of accountants. No express assurance was given to the witnesses that their evidence would be treated as confidential. At the conclusion of the investigation the material gathered by the inspectors was lodged with the department. On 29th October 1975 the Registrar of the Companies Court, on an application by the first plaintiff's liquidator to which the accountants were not a party, directed the department to hand over to the liquidator, inter alia, the transcripts of the evidence and the correspondence, on terms which permitted their use by the liquidator in legal proceedings, subject to the department notifying the witnesses or their solicitors that it was proposed to hand over the documents to the liquidator and subject to the liquidator undertaking to the court to treat the documents as confidential. The accountants' solicitors, by letter dated 25th November 1975, agreed to the documents being handed over provided the liquidator treated them as confidential. In due course the documents were handed to the liquidator. The inspectors' report was published in March 1977. In May 1977 the first and second plaintiff's and other companies in the group brought an action against the firm of accountants alleging negligence in the conduct of the audits for the year ending March 1973. The plaintiffs sought to adduce as evidence in the action the transcripts of the evidence given to the inspectors and the correspondence amplifying it, on the ground that those documents were admissible under the general law and under s 50[a] of the Companies Act 1967. The defendants contended that on the true construction of s 50 the documents were not admissible and that because evidence given to inspectors under the 1948 Act was confidential it was in the public interest that such confidential evidence should be protected from disclosure.

Held – (1) In general, evidence given by a person to inspectors appointed under the 1948 Act was admissible against him subsequently in both criminal and civil proceedings. Accordingly, unless the documents in question were excluded from disclosure on the ground that they were confidential documents which the public interest required to be protected from disclosure they would, under the general law, be admissible in evidence (see p 865 *h* to p 866 *c*, post); *R v Scott* (1856) Dears & B 47 and *Re Rolls Razor Ltd* [1968] 3 All ER 698 applied; *Karak Rubber Co Ltd v Burden* [1971] 3 All ER 1118 considered.

a Section 50 is set out at p 864 *c d*, post

(2) There was a presumption that the public interest that all relevant evidence be made available to the court should prevail, and it was not to be assumed in construing a
s 50 of the 1967 Act that it was intended to give as much confidentiality as possible to evidence given to inspectors under s 167 of the 1948 Act. Moreover, having regard, in particular, to the general wording of s 50 that answers given to questions put in exercise of the powers under s 167 might be 'used in evidence' against the witness, and to the other types of information which s 50 made admissible in subsequent proceedings, s 50 properly construed did not restrict the types of proceedings in which evidence given b
under s 167 was admissible to proceedings brought by a public authority in the public interest. It followed that s 50 permitted evidence which had been given under s 167 to be used in subsequent proceedings which were brought by a company or its liquidator to right wrongs allegedly done to the company, unless there was some other public interest which outweighed the presumed public interest in admitting the evidence, and that required the court to balance the public interest in having all the relevant evidence c
before the court against the public interest in maintaining the confidentiality of evidence given to inspectors to ensure that witnesses gave full and frank evidence to the inspectors. Having regard to the fact that evidence given under s 167 was not given in complete confidence because it could be put by the inspectors to other witnesses who were before them, could be incorporated in the inspectors' report and, under the general law, could be used against the witness in subsequent criminal or civil proceedings, in all d
the circumstances the public interest in admitting the documents in question outweighed the impairment of the public interest in the confidentiality of the documents involved in admitting them. Accordingly, the documents in question were admissible in the plaintiffs' action (see p 866 *f* to *j* and p 867 *b* to *e* and *g* to p 869 *a* and *d* to *f*, post); *D v National Society for the Prevention of Cruelty to Children* [1977] 1 All ER 589 applied; *Re Pergamon Press Ltd* [1970] 3 All ER 535 and *R v Cheltenham Justices, ex parte Secretary of State for Trade* [1977] 1 All ER 460 distinguished. e

Notes

For use in evidence against a witness of answers given by him to inspectors appointed under the Companies Act 1948, see 7 Halsbury's Laws (4th Edn) para 973.

For the Companies Act 1948, ss 165, 167, see 5 Halsbury's Statutes (3rd Edn) 243, 244. f

For the Companies Act 1967, s 50, see ibid 586.

Cases referred to in judgment

D v National Society for the Prevention of Cruelty to Children [1977] 1 All ER 589, [1978] AC 171, [1977] 2 WLR 201, HL, Digest (Cont Vol E) 185, *1301b*.

Karak Rubber Co Ltd v Burden [1971] 3 All ER 1118, [1971] 1 WLR 1748, 9 Digest g
(Reissue) 650, *3902*.

Pergamon Press Ltd, Re [1970] 3 All ER 535, [1971] Ch 388, [1970] 2 WLR 792, CA, 9 Digest (Reissue) 651, *3904*.

R v Cheltenham Justices, ex parte Secretary of State for Trade [1977] 1 All ER 460, [1977] 1 WLR 95, 141 JP 175, DC, Digest (Cont Vol E) 57, *3903a*.

R v Richard Harris [1970] 3 All ER 746, [1970] 1 WLR 1252, 9 Digest (Reissue) 650, *3903*. h

R v Scott (1856) Dears & B 47, 169 ER 909.

Rolls Razor Ltd, Re [1968] 3 All ER 698, 10 Digest (Reissue) 1021, *6225*.

Rogers v Secretary of State for the Home Department, Gaming Board for Great Britain v Rogers [1972] 2 All ER 1057, [1973] AC 388, [1972] 3 WLR 279, 136 JP 574, HL, Digest (Cont Vol D) 267, *2835c*.

j

Cases also cited

Ashburton (Lord) v Pape [1913] 2 Ch 469, [1911–13] All ER Rep 708.

Butler v Board of Trade [1970] 3 All ER 593, [1971] Ch 680.

Calcraft v Guest [1898] 1 QB 759, CA.

Grosvenor and West-End Railway Terminus Hotel Co Ltd, Re (1879) 76 LT 337, CA.
a *Medway v Doublelock Ltd* [1978] 1 All ER 1261, [1978] 1 WLR 710.
S B A Properties Ltd, Re [1967] 2 All ER 615, [1967] 1 WLR 799.
Selangor United Rubber Estates Ltd v Cradock (No 2) [1968] 1 All ER 567, [1968] 1 WLR 319.

Application

b By a writ dated 4th May 1977 and an amended statement of claim the first plaintiff, London and County Securities Ltd, a subsidiary of the second plaintiff, London and County Securities Group Ltd, and nine other subsidiaries of the second plaintiff brought an action against the defendants, Hugh Thayer Nicholson and 28 other former partners in Harmood Banner, a firm of accountants, seeking damages for negligence in conducting the audits for the first and second plaintiffs for the year ended 31st March 1973. At the
c hearing of the action the plaintiffs applied to the court to adduce in evidence the published report of inspectors appointed in 1974 under s 165 of the Companies Act 1948 to investigate the affairs of the first plaintiff and also transcripts of the oral evidence given on oath by four of the partners and an employee in Harmood Banner at the investigation and the correspondence passing between the inspectors and the solicitors for Harmood Banner which amplified their evidence. The parties agreed that the inspectors' report
d was inadmissible on the issues which were before the court in the action but agreed that passages in it could be put to witnesses in cross-examination and if agreed would become part of the witness's evidence; but, whereas the defendants contended that the transcripts of the partners' evidence and the correspondence amplifying that evidence were also inadmissible, the plaintiffs contended that those documents were admissible under the general law and by reason of s 50 of the Companies Act 1967. The facts are set out in the
e judgment.

Donald Nicholls QC, *Andrew Morritt QC* and *David Oliver* for the plaintiffs.
Adrian Hamilton QC and *Patrick Phillips* for the defendants.

Cur adv vult

f

28th January. **BROWNE-WILKINSON J** read the following judgment: In this action the plaintiffs, 11 companies, are suing the defendants, who are partners in Messrs Harmood Banner, accountants, for alleged negligence in conducting the audits for the first and second plaintiff companies for the year ending 31st March 1973. Both those companies are in liquidation: Mr Langdon is the liquidator of the first; the official
g receiver is the liquidator of the second. I have now to decide difficult questions on admissibility of documents which have been elaborately and exceptionally well argued.

In January 1974, the Board of Trade, acting under s 165 of the Companies Act 1948, appointed inspectors to investigate the affairs of the first plaintiff. In the course of the investigation the inspectors took oral evidence on oath from four of the defendants, partners in Harmood Banner, and from an employee of that firm. There are transcripts
h of that evidence, and that oral evidence was later amplified in correspondence passing between the inspectors on the one hand and solicitors, Linklaters & Paines, acting for the defendants on the other hand. No express assurance was given to the witnesses that their evidence would be treated as confidential. The inspectors signed their report on 7th March 1976, and it was published by HM Stationery Office one year later.

The plaintiffs in opening the case asked me to look at three separate categories of
j documents arising from the investigation. Those have been prepared in three bundles: bundle A which contains the inspectors' report; bundle B which contains transcripts of the oral evidence given on oath to the inspectors by the four defendants and the employee of the defendants; and bundle C which contains the correspondence to which I have referred. The defendants object that none of these documents is admissible, and I have not yet looked at any of them.

In the course of the argument, it emerged that there was in fact no immediate point for me to decide on the inspectors' report. It is agreed that the report as such is not *a* admissible evidence on the issues I have to decide. References to the report in the experts' proofs of evidence are to be deleted. It is agreed that passages in the report can be put to witnesses in cross-examination and that if a witness agrees with those passages they become part of that witness's evidence. The parties are not agreed as to the position which will arise if the witness does not agree with the passage put to him. I shall have to decide that point when and if it arises in the light of the actual circumstances. *b*

As to the transcripts of evidence and written replies, s 167(2) of the Companies Act 1948 confers on inspectors power to examine on oath officers and agents of the company; 'agents' includes the auditors. The 1948 Act did not in terms provide that such evidence could be used in subsequent legal proceedings, although s 167(4) provided that evidence given by persons other than officers or agents could be so used. However, s 50 of the Companies Act 1967 provides: *c*

> 'An answer given by a person to a question put to him in exercise of powers conferred by—(*a*) section 167 of the [1948] Act (as originally enacted or as applied by section 172 of that Act or section 32 of this Act); or (*b*) general rules made under section 365(1) of the [1948] Act for carrying into effect the objects of that Act so far as relates to the winding up of companies; may be used in evidence against him, and a statement required by section 235 of the [1948] Act (statement of company's *d* affairs to be made to official receiver) may be used in evidence against any person making or concurring in making it.'

The plaintiffs say that these documents are admissible both under the general law and by reason of the express statutory enactment in s 50. The defendants contend, however, that they are not admissible notwithstanding s 50. Shortly, the steps in the defendants' *e* argument are as follows. First, that evidence given to the inspectors appointed under the Companies Act 1948 is given in confidence; second, that the plaintiffs have obtained the evidence in breach of that confidence; and third, that the court should therefore not admit such evidence since confidential information of this type is not admissible on the principles recently expounded by the House of Lords in *D v National Society for the Prevention of Cruelty to Children* [1977] 1 All ER 589, [1978] AC 171. The defendants do *f* not seek to distinguish between the evidence of the four defendants themselves and the evidence given by their employee.

Before considering these arguments I must state further facts. It appears that after the conclusion of the investigation the material gathered by the inspectors was lodged with the Department of Trade and Industry. In October 1975, the liquidator obtained an order of the Companies Court for the private examination of a Mr Osborne, an officer of *g* the Department of Trade and Industry. On 29th October 1975, on an application to which the defendants were not parties, the Registrar of the Companies Court ordered:

> '(1) the Department of Trade is directed by the court that before there is handed over to the said liquidator (a) any transcript of the hearing before the inspectors appointed by the Department of Trade, and (b) any statements made by witnesses, *h* letters written by them or documents produced by them to the said inspectors otherwise than with the agreement of the witness who gave evidence at that hearing or the witnesses who made such statements or wrote such letters or produced such documents to notify such witness by writing to him at his last known address or to the solicitors who represented him at that hearing that it is proposed to hand over a copy of such transcript, letters, statements or documents in accordance with the *j* undertaking hereinafter given, unless within 14 days the witness applies to the court to discharge such undertaking.
>
> '(2) the said Michael Charles Anthony Osborne "undertakes to the court that subject to the advice of counsel he will hand over to the liquidator copies of the transcripts of hearings before the said inspectors and such further or other

documents requested by the said liquidator as the Department of Trade releases to
a him, and

'(3) the liquidator [who is named] by his counsel undertakes to the court to treat
the contents of all documents which the said Michael Charles Anthony Osborne
may disclose to him pursuant to the undertaking given by him to the court in the
course of the said examination as confidential and not to disclose their contents to
any person other than the legal advisers and accountants to [the liquidator] as such
b liquidator except to the extent that such disclosure shall be necessary for the
performance of his duties in conducting litigation as liquidator of the above-named
company and upon the footing that any such disclosure (other than in the course of
litigation) is confidential.'

That order was plainly made in reliance on the decision of Buckley J in *Re Rolls Razor Ltd*
[1968] 3 All ER 698. Pursuant to that order on 4th November 1975, the Treasury
c Solicitor wrote to Linklaters & Paines giving them notice that the department was
considering handing over the documents and inviting them to make representations to
the department within ten days. The letter stated that the department would consider
any representations so made but if, notwithstanding those representations, they decided
to release the documents it would defer such release for 14 days to enable the defendants
to apply to the court. A reminder was sent to Linklaters & Paines on 24th November and
d on 25th November there was a telephone call between Mr Pickthorn of Linklaters &
Paines and Mr Dean of the Treasury Solicitor's office. Mr Dean made a note of that
telephone call which reads, so far as material, as follows:

'Pickthorn of Linklaters & Paines 'phoned. 1. Would we keep a note of what
handed over? Would do so but might have difficulty in identifying the documents
e from Harmood Banner. But would keep a note. 2. Why does liquidator want
documents? Says don't know. Section 268 application ex parte but investigate
company. Could be claim against auditors. 3. Would documents be kept
confidential? Yes. Gave him particulars of the undertaking to the court given by
the liquidator. Pickthorn will write confirming above and that no objection to
production.'

f As that attendance note forecasts, on the same day Mr Pickthorn wrote a letter in these
terms:

'Thank you for your letters of November 4 and 24. As discussed on the telephone
our clients have no objection to the release to Mr. Osborne for production to the
liquidator of the documents to which you refer on the understanding that the
g liquidator gave an undertaking to the court that he would treat the contents
confidentially and that a record will be kept (which will be made available to us if
requested) of what documents have been handed over.'

The evidence of Mr Pickthorn and the defendants is that they did not by that letter
intend to waive any right they had to object to the use of such evidence in subsequent
h proceedings against them. In due course the documents were handed over to the
liquidator.

It is convenient, before turning to the submissions on the public interest point, first to
consider whether the sworn and unsworn evidence given to the inspectors is otherwise
admissible in evidence in subsequent proceedings. There are two decisions directly in
point, and one, *Re Rolls Razor Ltd* [1968] 3 All ER 698, in which the admissibility of such
j evidence is a tacit assumption underlying the actual decision. In *R v Harris* [1970] 3 All
ER 746, [1970] 1 WLR 1252 MacKenna J held that, quite apart from s 50 of the 1967 Act,
sworn evidence given by a witness to inspectors appointed under the 1948 Act was
admissible against that witness in subsequent criminal proceedings. He relied largely on
the decision of the Court of Criminal Appeal in *R v Scott* (1856) Dears & B 47, 169 ER
909, which held that unsworn evidence given by a bankrupt on his examination was

admissible against him on a subsequent criminal charge. In my judgment these cases establish that, even without s 50, both sworn and unsworn evidence given to inspectors is admissible against the witnesses in subsequent criminal proceedings.

Counsel for the defendants urged that the decisions were only dealing with evidence in criminal cases. But in my judgment if such evidence is admissible against a man to incriminate himself in criminal proceedings it must, a fortiori, be admissible against him in civil proceedings. Unfortunately *R v Harris* and *R v Scott* were not cited to Brightman J in *Karak Rubber Co Ltd v Burden* [1971] 3 All ER 1118, [1971] 1 WLR 1748. In that case Brightman J decided in similar litigation brought by the Board of Trade in the name of the company under its statutory powers, that only sworn evidence given to inspectors was admissible and he excluded unsworn evidence. It is clear that the only argument addressed to Brightman J was on the construction of s 50 of the 1967 Act and s 167 of the 1948 Act. As the point decided in *R v Harris* and *R v Scott* was not before him I cannot regard Brightman J's decision as impairing those earlier decisions in any way. I therefore approach the question of confidentiality on the basis that both the sworn and unsworn evidence given to the inspectors would otherwise be admissible.

In none of the cases I have so far referred to was any point taken that the evidence was inadmissible on the grounds that it was given to the inspectors in confidence. The submission of counsel for the defendants is that the evidence was given by the witnesses to the inspectors in confidence and that it is therefore not admissible. He accepts that for relevant evidence to be excluded on these grounds communication in confidence by itself is not enough; it has also to be shown that the confidence is of a kind which the public interest requires to be protected: see *D v National Society for the Prevention of Cruelty to Children* [1977] 1 All ER 589 at 594, [1978] AC 171 at 218. There is considerable authority supporting the broad proposition that evidence given to inspectors appointed under the 1948 Act is given in confidence, and that the public interest requires that confidence to be protected: see *R v Cheltenham Justices, ex parte Secretary of State for Trade* [1977] 1 All ER 460, [1977] 1 WLR 95 and *Re Pergamon Press Ltd* [1970] 3 All ER 535, [1971] Ch 388. As those cases show, the public interest is to ensure that so far as possible people will give information and evidence frankly to inspectors without fear that by so doing they will expose themselves to subsequent actions by other persons who are or may be adversely affected by their evidence.

However, it is of fundamental importance that, unlike any other instance cited to me in which evidence was excluded on this ground, it is clear that in the case of evidence given to inspectors the confidentiality of the evidence is not complete. The potential witness will, on any footing, know that his evidence and identity may be disclosed in any of the following ways: (1) by his evidence being put by the inspectors to other witnesses; (2) by being incorporated in the inspectors' report, which under s 168 of the 1948 Act is or may be distributed to the company, to members and creditors of the company, and to persons who applied for the investigation; it may be published by HM Stationery Office; (3) in criminal or civil proceedings against him.

Therefore the public interest in this case is not the same as that which protects the confidentiality of police and other informers. In the case of informers, the public interest is to provide the informant with *total* confidentiality, which apparently cannot be waived, so as to ensure that informers as a class will know that they cannot be identified. In the present case, express statutory provisions show that in the view of Parliament there are other interests which outweigh the public interest in giving potential witnesses the assurance of complete confidentiality.

The argument of counsel for the defendants runs as follows. He says first, that the authorities show that there is a public interest in preserving the confidentiality of evidence given to inspectors, and that accordingly Parliament must be taken not to have intended to breach such confidentiality, save to the extent that statutory provisions expressly authorise such breach. Then he says that although s 50 of the 1967 Act plainly envisages disclosure in some legal proceedings, properly construed the only proceedings referred to in s 50 are proceedings brought in the public interest, i e criminal proceedings, winding up proceedings brought by the department under s 35 of the 1967 Act, and proceedings brought by the department under s 37 in the name of the company. On this construction Parliament has not shown any intention that such evidence can be used in proceedings such as these brought by a company or by a liquidator of a company.

I will for the moment assume counsel for the defendants is correct in his primary submission that Parliament is to be presumed to prefer the public interest in preserving confidentiality to the public interest in all relevant evidence being available to the court. Even on that assumption I cannot accept counsel's submission, for the following reasons.

First, under the general law, evidence given to inspectors would be admissible. If Parliament intended a different result I would have expected it expressly so to have provided. See, for example, the express restrictions on disclosure of information legislated for in a similar field by s 111 of the 1967 Act, but which do not preclude the use of such information in litigation: see s 109(5) of the 1967 Act.

Secondly, the words of s 50 of the 1967 Act are entirely general. Any restriction as to the type of proceedings in which the evidence is to be admitted has to be by way of implied restriction on the generality of those words. On ordinary principles such an implication is not to be made unless the circumstances make such restriction a necessity.

Thirdly, the assurance of confidentiality is admittedly breached by the fact that the evidence can be admitted in proceedings brought by the department under s 37 of the 1967 Act in the name of the company. How will the public interest in preserving confidentiality be preserved by drawing a distinction between such proceedings and proceedings brought by the company itself or by the liquidator? In terms of a potential witness's confidence that his evidence will not be disclosed or used against him, it does not matter who brings the proceedings. Once a potential witness knows that his evidence may be used against him in any proceedings brought by anyone his assurance is gone.

Counsel for the defendants says correctly that, by the express terms of ss 35 and 37 of the 1967 Act, the department can only bring proceedings 'in the public interest,' and from this deduces that Parliament only intended company investigations, and the evidence gathered under compulsion during its conduct, to be used when a public body considers it in the public interest to take proceedings. But at least part of the purpose of company investigations is to protect the individual rights of members and creditors of the company. Under s 165 of the 1948 Act the department is bound to appoint inspectors if the company so resolves by special resolution, and may do so if one-tenth of the members request it to. In the latter case such members may be required to bear at least part of the cost. Again, the department has power to appoint inspectors of its own motion if it considers that there are circumstances suggesting that the company is being conducted in fraud of its creditors or there is misfeasance. All this suggests that Parliament was having regard not solely to the public interest in discovering criminal conduct but also to enabling members and creditors of the company to protect their individual rights. I can see no reason why Parliament should not have intended the fruits of such investigation to be available for use by the company in redressing the wrongs which such investigation has disclosed.

Fourthly, s 50 of the 1967 Act makes admissible not only evidence given to inspectors but also the statement of affairs required under s 235 of the 1948 Act and the observations of the official receiver on it, provided for by r 126 of the Companies (Winding-up) Rules 1949, SI 1949 No 330. The official receiver's observations can, and frequently do, refer to information given to him in personal interviews conducted under r 52 of the 1949 rules which the officers of the company are under a statutory duty to give. As I understand it, counsel for the defendants accepts that s 50 applies to these other types of information so as to make them admissible in any proceedings, whether or not brought by a public authority, since there is no element of confidentiality in such information. But he contends that s 50 must be construed so as to make the words 'used in evidence against him' have a different effect according to the type of information it is dealing with. I think this is too subtle and prefer the view that Parliament in enacting s 50 of the

1967 Act considered that all information of the various kinds referred to in the section was to be treated on the same footing. a

So far I have accepted counsel for the defendants' fundamental submission that Parliament is to be taken to have intended to prefer the confidentiality of evidence given to inspectors to be public interest in having all available evidence before the court. But I do not think such submission is correct. The decision of the House of Lords in *D v National Society for the Prevention of Cruelty to Children* establishes that there is a presumption that the public interest in all relevant evidence being available to the court b ought to prevail: see for example, per Lord Hailsham and per Lord Edmund-Davies ([1977] 1 All ER 589 at 599, 600, 615, [1978] AC 171 at 223, 225, 242); see also *Rogers v Secretary of State for the Home Department* [1972] 2 All ER 1057 at 1060, [1973] AC 388 at 400. If such evidence is to be excluded it must be shown that there is another countervailing public interest which necessitates the exclusion of the evidence and that such countervailing public interest outweighs the public interest in admitting it. For c this reason I do not accept that the court should first assume that Parliament intended to assure as much confidentiality as possible and that such confidentiality should only be impaired to the extent that Parliament has expressly so provided.

In my judgment, *D v National Society for the Prevention of Cruelty to Children* requires me to balance the two public interests against each other; but unless the public interest in excluding the evidence clearly outweighs the public interest in admitting it, the latter is d to prevail. On this basis, even if, contrary to my view, counsel for the defendants is correct that, on its true construction, s 50 of the 1967 Act only expressly applies to proceedings brought by a public authority, I am left with the question how to balance the two public interests. For this purpose I must identify what those interests are. In my judgment they are (1) the public interest in having all relevant evidence before the court, and (2) the loss of confidence which potential witnesses will feel if they know that their e evidence can be used in proceedings brought against them by the company or its liquidator, and not only in proceedings brought by the department under the power of s 37 of the 1967 Act.

If I have rightly identified the public interests to be balanced I have little doubt that the impairment of the public interest involved in disclosing the evidence to the liquidator and allowing it to be used by him in proceedings does not outweigh the other public f interest. There is no evidence from any minister or public servant that the public interest would be harmed; indeed the fact that the department released the evidence to the liquidator without protest on terms which permitted its use by the liquidator in legal proceedings indicates that no injury to the public interest was then foreseen.

In the absence of such evidence I must use my own judgment on the point guided by such authority as there is. For myself I cannot see that any potential witness who knows g that his evidence may be used against him in proceedings brought in the name of the company under s 37 of the 1967 Act is going to be appreciably further deterred from giving full and frank evidence to the inspectors by knowing that such proceedings might be brought by the company itself without the assistance of the department. As I have said, it is not the identity of the bringer of the subsequent proceedings but the fact that his evidence may be used against him in any proceedings which will deter the potential h witness.

There are two decisions which deal directly with the public interest in maintaining the confidentiality of evidence given to inspectors. In *Re Pergamon Press Ltd* [1970] 3 All ER 589, [1971] Ch 388 the Court of Appeal undoubtedly relied on there being a public interest in maintaining such confidentiality. But the court was there dealing with a case in which, unlike the present, the inspectors had given to the witnesses an express j assurance that their evidence would be treated as confidential. Different considerations may apply to such a case. More importantly, the Court of Appeal was not dealing with the admissibility of such evidence in subsequent proceedings; indeed Sachs LJ in terms referred to the public interest being to preserve confidentiality 'unless and until court proceedings eventuate' (see [1970] 3 All ER 589 at 543, [1971] Ch 388 at 404). In my

judgment that decision establishes that there is a public interest in preserving
a confidentiality but provides no support for the proposition that such public interest is to outweigh the public interest that all relevant evidence should be before the court.

In *R v Cheltenham Justices, ex parte Secretary of State for Trade* [1977] 1 All ER 460, [1977] 1 WLR 95 there had been an investigation under s 167(2) of the 1948 Act. Subsequently criminal proceedings were brought against one of the witnesses. He obtained a witness summons requiring one of the inspectors to produce transcripts of the
b other witnesses' evidence to the inspectors and certain other documents. The Department of Trade and Industry applied to quash the summons on two grounds: first, that the evidence given by the other witnesses would not be admissible at the trial, and second, that the production of such evidence would be contrary to the public interest. The second contention was supported by a certificate from the Secretary of State. The Divisional Court quashed the witness summons on the first ground but indicated that it
c would also have upheld the department's contention on the second ground. In that case there was evidence of the public interest since the department was itself asserting it with support of a certificate from the minister. Moreover the court was having to weigh the public interest in maintaining confidentiality against depriving a litigant not of relevant admissible evidence but of material for cross-examination. I can well understand that the balance in such a case might produce a different result from the one I have reached
d in this case.

For these reasons I hold that there is no sufficient public interest to exclude the relevant evidence contained in bundles B and C. It is therefore unnecessary for me to consider the plaintiffs' alternative submission that, if in the ordinary case such evidence would have been excluded, the fact that the defendants did not object to the evidence being released by the department to the liquidator alters the position.

e I would add two points. First, I have only considered the admissibility of this evidence in relation to proceedings brought by a company or its liquidator to right wrongs allegedly done to the company; I am not deciding whether such evidence is admissible in proceedings, such as defamation proceedings, brought by a private individual to right a wrong done to him individually. It may well be that different considerations would apply to such a case. Secondly, although I have decided that the evidence is admissible,
f the weight to be attached to it will depend on what the evidence is, bearing in mind that it was given under compulsion, or threat of compulsion, at a time when no claim had been formulated against the defendants.

Order accordingly.

Solicitors: *Herbert Smith & Co* (for the plaintiffs); *Barlow, Lyde & Gilbert* (for the defendants).

Azza M Abdallah Barrister.

Ashton v Turner and another a

QUEEN'S BENCH DIVISION AT LIVERPOOL
EWBANK J
18th MARCH 1980

Negligence – Duty to take care – Criminal activities – Duty owed by criminal to fellow participant in crime – Plaintiff injured while a passenger in get-away car fleeing from scene of b *crime – Whether driver of get-away car owing a duty of care to plaintiff – Whether public policy requiring that no duty of care be recognised as being owed to plaintiff.*

Negligence – Volenti non fit injuria – Knowledge of risk – Passenger in car – Intoxicated driver – Car being used to escape from scene of crime – Car crashing with resultant injury to passenger – Whether defence of volenti available to driver. c

After the plaintiff and two friends had spent the evening together drinking heavily the plaintiff persuaded one of the others to participate in a burglary with him. They then took a car belonging to the third and drove to a shop which they broke into. As they were leaving the shop they were disturbed and chased. They attempted to escape in the car, the friend being the driver at the time, but they crashed while travelling at high d speed and the plaintiff sustained serious injuries. The driver was later convicted of burglary, dangerous driving and driving with more than the permitted amount of alcohol in his blood. The plaintiff sued both the driver and the owner in negligence. The defence was raised that as a matter of public policy the plaintiff had no right of action, or, alternatively, that the maxim volenti non fit injuria applied, and that in any e event the plaintiff was contributorily negligent.

Held – The plaintiff's claim would be dismissed for the following reasons—

(1) As a matter of public policy, English law would, in certain circumstances, refuse to recognise the existence of a duty of care owed by one participant in a crime to another participant in the same crime in respect of an act done in connection with the commission f of that crime. On the facts, that policy applied to the plaintiff's claim, so that the driver did not owe him a duty of care during the course of the burglary or the subsequent flight in the get-away car (see p 877 *e f*, post); dictum of Sugerman J in *Godbolt v Fittock* (1963) 63 SR (NSW) at 624 and *Smith v Jenkins* [1970] ALR 519 considered.

(2) In any event, having regard to the fact that the plaintiff knew that the driver and the owner had been drinking heavily and to the fact that the plaintiff and the driver were g engaged in the intrinsically and obviously dangerous act of fleeing in a get-away car at the time the plaintiff was injured, the maxim volenti non fit injuria applied and afforded the defendants a complete defence (see p 879 *d e*, post); dictum of Sugerman J in *Godbolt v Fittock* (1963) 63 SR (NSW) at 620 considered.

(3) If, however, the defendants or either of them were in breach of a duty of care owed to the plaintiff, then, having regard to the whole of the facts, including the fact that the h plaintiff and the driver were in a get-away car which might have to be driven recklessly and dangerously and the fact that the plaintiff was not wearing a seat belt, the plaintiff and the driver were equally to blame for the accident and therefore the plaintiff would be assessed as being 50% contributorily negligent (see p 879 *h*, post); dictum of Tasker Watkins J in *Owens v Brimmell* [1976] 3 All ER at 772 considered.

j

Notes

For the application of the maxim ex turpi causa non oritur actio, see 12 Halsbury's Laws (4th Edn) para 1136, and for cases on the subject, see 1(1) Digest (Reissue) 45–46, 310–315.

For the defence of volenti non fit injuria, see 28 Halsbury's Laws (3rd Edn) 82, paras
a 87–89, and for cases on the subject, see 36(1) Digest (Reissue) 242–257, *934–1009*.
For the Road Traffic Act 1972, s 148, see 42 Halsbury's Statutes (3rd Edn) 1792.

Cases referred to in judgment

Adamson v Jarvis (1827) 4 Bing 66, [1824–34] All ER Rep 120, 12 Moore CP 241, 5 LJOSCP 68, 130 ER 693, 45 Digest (Repl) 288, *110*.
b *Colburn v Patmore* (1834) 1 Cr M & R 73, 4 Tyr 677, 3 LJ Ex 317, 149 ER 999, 45 Digest (Repl) 296, *135*.
Dann v Hamilton [1939] 1 All ER 59, [1939] 1 KB 509, 108 LJKB 255, 160 LT 433, 36(1) Digest (Reissue) 250, *976*.
Godbolt v Fittock (1963) 63 SR (NSW) 617, [1964] NSWR 22, 1(1) Digest (Reissue) 47, **171*.
c *Gregory v Kelly* [1978] RTR 426.
Hardy v Motor Insurers' Bureau [1964] 2 All ER 742, [1964] 2 QB 745, [1964] 3 WLR 433, [1964] 1 Lloyd's Rep 397, CA, Digest (Cont Vol B) 462, *3703a*.
Hillen and Pettigrew v ICI (Alkali) Ltd [1936] AC 65, [1935] All ER Rep 555, 104 LJKB 473, 153 LT 403, 41 Com Cas 29, HL; *affg* [1934] 1 KB 455, 36(1) Digest (Reissue) 120, *460*.
M'Alister (or Donoghue) v Stevenson [1932] AC 562, 101 LJPC 119, 37 Com Cas 350, 1932
d SC(HL) 31, sub nom *McAlister (or Donoghue) v Stevenson* 147 LT 281, sub nom *Donoghue (or McAlister) v Stevenson* [1932] All ER Rep 1, 1932 SLT 317, HL, 36(1) Digest (Reissue) 144, *562*.
Murphy v Culhane [1976] 3 All ER 533, [1977] QB 94, [1976] 3 WLR 458, CA, Digest (Cont Vol E) 590, *250a*.
National Coal Board v England [1954] 1 All ER 546, [1954] AC 403, [1954] 2 WLR 400,
e HL, 34 Digest (Repl) 293, *2097*.
Nettleship v Weston [1971] 3 All ER 581, [1971] 2 QB 691, [1971] 3 WLR 370, [1971] RTR 425, CA, 36(1) Digest (Reissue) 245, *952*.
Owens v Brimmell [1976] 3 All ER 765, [1977] QB 859, [1977] 2 WLR 943, [1977] RTR 82, Digest (Cont Vol E) 456, *1196a*.
Slater v Clay Cross Co Ltd [1956] 2 All ER 625, [1956] 2 QB 264, [1956] 3 WLR 232, CA,
f 36(1) Digest (Reissue) 23, *81*.
Smith v Jenkins (1970) 44 ALJR 78, [1970] ALR 519, Digest (Cont Vol D) 1, **169c*.

Action

The plaintiff, Philip Ashton, by a statement of claim dated 13th September 1978 brought an action seeking damages against the first defendant, Kevin Turner, and the second
g defendant, Peter McLune, for injuries sustained by the first defendant's negligence while driving a car owned by the second defendant and in which the plaintiff was a passenger. The facts are set out in the judgment.

G P Crowe QC and *David Lynch* for the plaintiff.
Michael Morland QC and *R J D Livesey* for the second defendant.
h The first defendant did not appear.

EWBANK J. The plaintiff, Philip Ashton, is now aged 24. On 18th December 1976, when he was 20, in the early hours of the morning he was a passenger in a car being driven by his friend Kevin Turner, the first defendant. The car was owned by another friend of theirs, Peter McLune, who is the second defendant. There was a serious
j accident with the car and Philip Ashton now claims against Kevin Turner and Peter McLune. Philip Ashton was badly hurt in the accident and the damages have been agreed, subject to liability, at £70,000.

The issue before me has been the liability of the first or second defendant to pay damages to the plaintiff. The first defendant has taken no part in the action; he entered no appearance and has not been represented. The second defendant has filed a defence.

The case against the first defendant made by the plaintiff is one of negligence. The plaintiff relies on, among other things, two convictions recorded against the first *a* defendant: on 28th January 1977 (although it is pleaded as 27th January), the defendant was charged before a magistrates' court with driving dangerously and with driving over the limit of alcohol; he pleaded guilty to both these offences and was sentenced.

The case against the second defendant is that the second defendant consented to or permitted the use of the car by the first defendant. The second defendant, in his defence, asserts that he gave no such consent or permission. He relies, among other things, on *b* another conviction recorded against the first defendant, also on 28th January, for taking a car without the consent of the owner, for which he was also sentenced. Secondly, the second defendant says that the plaintiff and the first defendant were burglars and that the car was used by them as a get-away car. As against the first defendant, he relies on a further conviction of the same date (although the memorandum is wrongly dated) for burglary, for which he was also sentenced. The second defendant asserts that the *c* plaintiff, as a matter of public policy, has no right of action against him. As an alternative, he asserts that the maxim volenti non fit injuria applies, and, in any event, he says that if he fails on these points the plaintiff was guilty of contributory negligence.

The plaintiff was badly hurt in this accident. He is partly crippled; he has a defect of speech; he has loss of memory for many of the relevant matters. I heard him in the witness box and I found myself unable to rely on his evidence. Several witnesses saw the *d* first defendant drive the second defendant's car on other occasions and it is accepted by the first defendant that he had done so. The plaintiff told me that on the night in question the first defendant had asked the second defendant if he could drive the car home, and the second defendant had replied: 'If you get caught say you pinched it', meaning that the second defendant was not insured and that the first defendant should say that if he got caught. I find myself unable to accept that that was said by these two *e* on that occasion.

I have allowed, during the course of the trial, several written statements to be put in, on the ground that the witnesses were missing, and, in particular, statements of Mr Fenelly and Mr McQueen, who were two taxi drivers. I have no particular reason to doubt what they say in their statements, but in view of the other evidence which I have had I do not attach any particular weight to their evidence. I have also had a statement *f* from the owner of the shop, and from the police, and basically the same considerations apply. I allowed in evidence also two statements by the second defendant (they are contradictory as to times). He asserts in both statements that he gave no permission to the first defendant. The plaintiff has not had an opportunity of cross-examining him and I attach no weight to these two statements. I was asked to allow in a statement by the first defendant. The application was made by the second defendant on the basis that the *g* first defendant was an opposing party. I refused that application and the first defendant was accordingly called by the second defendant, and I have seen him in the witness box. I have heard his evidence and I accept his evidence as a true account of what happened that night.

A summary of his evidence is as follows. The three men all live fairly close together. The first defendant knows the second defendant and he knows the plaintiff because they *h* went to school together. On the night before the accident he met them. The three of them were in the Railway Hotel, where they were drinking. They were drinking 'brown' and 'bitter' and might have had some whisky as well. Then they went to the Kirklands Wine Bar in the second defendant's car which the second defendant drove. There they drank sangría. They had one or two jugs of that. Then they went on to the Hanover, where they were drinking pints and shorts, buying rounds for each other. And *j* then to the Flintlock Club, where they were drinking the same. The first defendant told me he had no check on what they had. The bar closed at two o'clock in the morning. By the time the bar closed the second defendant was drunk and staggering and said to the first defendant: 'You drive the car.' This is the car which, as I said, the first defendant had driven on other occasions. The plaintiff sat in the front and they drove to the second defendant's home. They sat down. The second defendant was standing by the stairs.

The plaintiff said: 'I have just come back from Jersey and I'm skint.' He then suggested
a that they break into a shop; he suggested a jewellers in the Old Swan. The first defendant said he first of all said No, but in the end said Yes. The second defendant said, according to the first defendant, 'I want nothing to do with it', and went to bed. He was asked in cross-examination whether it was not a fact that the second defendant had said on that occasion that if he was caught he was to say that he had pinched the car, but the first defendant told me that he could not say that he had said that. The first time he borrowed
b it, he had said that he must say that he had stolen it. He said that the second defendant said that he wanted no part of it. The keys were on the mantlepiece. The first defendant says: 'We [that is the plaintiff and himself] just took the keys and went.' The plaintiff had said: 'Get the keys', and the first defendant took them, and he, the first defendant, drove. He was not certain whether they went to the Old Swan first, or to the petrol station. At some stage they bought a pound's worth of petrol. They drove around, the
c shops were shuttered and the first defendant suggested they drive down Penny Lane, four or five miles away. They saw a radio shop and he said: 'Here we are.' The plaintiff said: 'Yes, fair enough.' He parked the car in a side street, came out by a bus shelter, and the first defendant told the plaintiff to find a brick to smash the window. He said he would get the car running and ran around the corner. When he came back the plaintiff had a brick in his hand. He said: 'Yes', and the plaintiff threw the brick through the
d window. 'We both went in the window, took the radios out, the alarm went off. We reached through and took two or three radios, and started running.' The first defendant said to the plaintiff: 'You drive.' The plaintiff said: 'No, you know the car better, you drive it.' At that moment a taxi pulled across the side of the bonnet. The plaintiff said: 'Reverse', and the first defendant reversed back to Penny Lane. The plaintiff said: 'Go through the gears.' By this time there were two taxis, one was at the back. I have seen
e a plan of the place where the accident happened. He took the corner. He said the taxi was at the back of him. The car skidded. He was travelling at more than 60 miles per hour in order to get away from the taxi drivers. That is how the accident occurred.

It is clear to me that the plaintiff and the first defendant were jointly participating in a burglary. This burglary involved the use of a get-away car. It was being driven by the first defendant in order to avoid the arrest of the two of them. The question arises: what
f effect does that have on the claim made by the plaintiff? There are no direct authorities in English law. There are a number of obiter dicta, and I have been warned by counsel for the plaintiff to be cautious in considering these dicta, and must remember that in many cases they were casual observations about other matters.

The first case I refer to is *National Coal Board v England* [1954] 1 All ER 546, [1954] AC 403. This was a case about mineworkers. The facts are very far away from the facts of
g the present case. Lord Asquith said ([1954] 1 All ER 546 at 558, [1954] AC 403 at 428–429):

> 'The appellants relied on the maxim "ex turpi causa non oritur actio" as absolving them of liability . . . Cases where an action in tort has been defeated by the maxim
> h are exceedingly rare. Possibly a party to an illegal prize fight who is damaged in the conflict cannot sue for assault . . . But it seems to me in principle that the plaintiff cannot be precluded from suing simply because the wrongful act is committed after the illegal agreement is made and during the period involved in its execution. The act must, I should have supposed, at least be a step in the execution of the common illegal purpose. If two burglars, A and B, agree to open a safe by means of explosives,
> j and A so negligently handles the explosive charge as to injure B, B might find some difficulty in maintaining an action for negligence against A. But if A and B are proceeding to the premises which they intend burglariously to enter, and before they enter them, B picks A's pocket and steals his watch, I cannot prevail on myself to believe that A could not sue in tort (provided he had first prosecuted B for larceny). The theft is totally unconnected with the burglary. There is, however, a surprising dearth of authority on this point.'

On behalf of the second defendant it is suggested that this case is closer to the case of the safe-breakers than the pickpocket described in Lord Asquith's judgment. *a*

The next case is *Hardy v Motor Insurers' Bureau* [1964] 2 All ER 742 at 746, [1964] 2 QB 745 at 760. This was a case where a security officer was dragged along when he tried to stop a car. Lord Denning MR said:

> '... no person can claim reparation or indemnity for the consequences of a criminal offence where his own wicked and deliberate intent is an essential ingredient in it ... This rule is not rested on an implied exception in the policy of *b* insurance. It is based on the broad rule of public policy that no person can claim indemnity or reparation for his own wilful and culpable crime. He is under a disability precluding him from imposing a claim.'

Then I was referred to *Murphy v Culhane* [1976] 3 All ER 533, [1977] QB 94. In that case there had been an affray. This was an action by the widow of one of the participants, *c* and I have been referred to a passage in the judgment of Lord Denning MR where he said ([1976] 3 All ER 533 at 535–536, [1977] QB 94 at 98):

> 'Apart altogether from damages, however, I think there may well be a defence on liability. If Murphy was one of a gang which set out to beat up Culhane, it may well be that he could not sue for damages if he got more than he bargained for. A man *d* who takes part in a criminal affray may well be said to have been guilty of such a wicked act as to deprive himself of a cause of action, or, alternatively, to have had taken on himself the risk. I put the case in the course of argument: suppose that a burglar breaks into a house and the householder, finding him there, picks up a gun and shoots him, using more force maybe than is reasonably necessary. The householder may be guilty of manslaughter and liable to be brought before the *e* criminal courts. But I doubt very much whether the burglar's widow could have an action for damages. The householder might well have a defence either on the ground of ex turpi causa non oritur actio or volenti non fit injuria. So in the present case it is open to the defendant to raise both those defences. Such defences would go to the whole claim.'

Counsel for the second defendant has addressed me on the question of the applicability *f* of the maxim ex turpi causa non oritur actio to cases of tort, and has suggested that in a number of cases the maxim is used loosely, when the proper approach should be to look at the matter from the point of view of public policy. I come to a case in due course where the matter has been very carefully considered by an Australian judge.

Those are the obiter dicta in English cases to which I have referred, and the general trend of those dicta is that a criminal, for one reason or another, cannot bring a claim for *g* negligence for incidents which have occurred during his participation in a crime.

There have been two Australian cases where the matter has gone a good deal further, and I am asked to follow these Australian cases. The first is *Godbolt v Fittock* (1963) 63 SR (NSW) 617. This was a case of two rustlers who were driving along in a truck with some stolen cattle. The driver fell asleep. The truck ran off the road. The passenger was injured. There was no question of pursuit in that case. Sugerman J, in the leading *h* judgment, said (at 624):

> 'In my opinion, when co-adventurers in a joint criminal venture of a nature comparable with that in question in the present appeal use a motor vehicle in the pursuit of their common purpose, damages are not recoverable by one, being a passenger, against another, being the driver, in respect of injuries suffered as a result *j* of want of due care in driving on a journey which is directly connected with the execution of the criminal purpose. I use "directly" in a relative rather than in any absolute, sense. The question is one of the sufficiency of the connection to require a conclusion that it would be contrary to public policy that damages should be awarded for the injury or that the injury had its origin in a turpis causa. The

> directness of the connection between the criminal purpose and the journey in whose course the injury occurred, rather than a causal association of the injury with the specifically criminal character of the joint venture, is, in my opinion, the true criterion in these cases of mutual criminality. The latter—causal association is lacking in the present case. But the former is clearly present, the accident having occurred in the course of one continuous journey which included in uninterrupted sequence the stealing of the calves and their transportation to market.'

Counsel for the plaintiff says that this is a very hard and harsh case, and asks me not to follow it.

The other Australian case is *Smith v Jenkins* (1970) 44 ALJR 78. This is an appeal from the Supreme Court of Victoria to the High Court of Australia, with five judges, including the Chief Justice. The case involved a driver driving a stolen car with a passenger being carried, the driver and passenger being involved in the joint enterprise of stealing, and the passenger was injured. Barwick CJ, in considering that the action ought to be dismissed, said (at 78–79):

> 'The choice it seems to me is between a refusal of the law to erect a duty of care as between persons jointly participating in the performance of an act contrary to the provisions of a statute making their act a crime punishable by imprisonment and a refusal of the courts, upon grounds of public policy, to lend their assistance to the recovery of damages for breach in those circumstances of a duty of care owed by the one to the other, because of the criminally illegal nature of the act out of which the harm arose. I have come to the conclusion that the former is the proper basis. The duty of care, which is the prerequisite to success in an action of negligence to recover damages for personal injuries, is a duty which the law imposes upon a party by reason of his relationship to another in the circumstances of the case. No doubt considerations of public policy have their place in the decision in the particular case to impose or erect such a duty. But basically it is the relationship of the parties which gives rise to the duty. Here the respondent and the appellant, in my opinion, did not relevantly stand in the relationship of passenger and driver. Their relationship was that of joint participants in the very act, itself unlawful in the sense I have mentioned, out of which the mischief to the respondent arose. In my opinion, the law will not hold that a duty of care arose out of that relationship.'

The second judgment was given by Kitto J. He referred to a decision of Scrutton LJ (*Hiller and Pettigrew v ICI (Alkali) Ltd* [1934] 1 KB 455) and said (at 80):

> '... it seems equally clear that Scrutton L.J. perceived a general principle of law and thought it apposite to his illustration, namely that persons who join in committing an illegal act which they know to be unlawful (or, I should add in the language of the judgment in *Adamson* v. *Jarvis* ((1827) 4 Bing 66 at 73, [1824–34] All ER Rep 120 at 122) which they must be presumed to know to be unlawful) have no legal rights inter se by reason of their respective participations in that act. In my opinion that is the principle that governs the present case. The underlying reason of it, I think, is that in such a case the law regards the joint illegal conduct as the commission of a single wrong of which, as a whole, each participant is guilty.'

The third judgment was given by Windeyer J, and is of considerable length, and contains a valuable discussion on the application of the maxim ex turpi causa. He said (at 85–86):

> 'The question here is not: Is the plaintiff precluded from recovering because he was a wrongdoer? It is: Had the defendant a duty to the plaintiff to carry out carefully the unlawful enterprise on which they were jointly engaged? The problem is circumscribed by the facts. It is not a wide-ranging general question of the bearing that unlawful conduct has on liability in tort. It is whether when two persons are jointly engaged in a particular criminal enterprise—unlawfully taking

> or using a motor car—one can sue the other because he has been negligent in the
> course of carrying out his part in their unlawful undertaking . . . It seems to me a a
> mistake to approach the case by asking whether the plaintiff is precluded by
> considerations of public policy from asserting a right of action for negligence. The
> proper inquiry seems to me to be simply is there for him a right of action. That
> depends upon whether in the circumstances the law imposed a duty of care; for a
> right of action and a duty of care are inseparable. The one predicates the other.
> Duty here does not mean an abstract and general rule of conduct. It is not the duty b
> to God and neighbour of the catechist's question. It is a concept of the law, a duty
> to a person, which he can enforce by remedy at law. Lord Atkin's famous
> generalisations need some qualifications and require some exceptions. For instance,
> negligent misstatements are now actionable, but the duty of care in that field
> depends, it has been held, not simply on foreseeability of harm but on a special
> relationship between the parties. If a special relationship be in some cases a c
> prerequisite of a duty of care, it seems to me that in other cases a special relationship
> can exclude a duty of care. It is as well to remember, when *Donoghue* v. *Stevenson* is
> invoked, that Lord Atkin there said ([1932] AC 562 at 580, [1932] All ER Rep 1 at
> 11): "But acts or omissions which any moral code would censure cannot in a
> practical world be treated so as to give a right to every person injured by them to
> demand relief. In this way rules of law arise which limit the range of complainants d
> and the extent of their remedy." I add to that two sentences from *Salmond on Torts*
> (15th Edn, 1969, p 257) which I think correctly reflect the present state of the law:
> "The courts are still free to hold that the plaintiff's interests are not in all the
> circumstances of the case entitled to be protected against the defendant's conduct.
> For reasons of policy there are limits to the actions of negligence." The appellant
> and the respondent were companions in crime. Were they "neighbours" in Lord e
> Atkin's sense? Put in that way the question is: Was the one under a duty,
> enforceable at law, to take care not to harm the other? I prefer to ask was there a
> right then to ask whether public policy has intervened to deprive the would-be
> plaintiff of a remedy.'

Windeyer J also said (at 87–88): f

> 'It may be accepted that whether an action for negligence can be brought by one
> criminal against another depends upon whether the negligence was so related to
> their unlawful conduct that the tort can be said to arise out of the crime—but only
> in a general sense, not in the special causal sense that the peculiar phrase "an accident
> arising out of and in the course of employment" has gained by the cartload of cases
> under workmen's compensation statutes. The question is whether the harm arose g
> from the manner in which the criminal act was done. That question is not one of
> cause and consequence which can be answered in the old jargon of scholastic logic.
> Rather it is one of connection and relationship and involvement. For that the
> modern jargon of remoteness and proximity is more useful. At one end of the scale
> are cases when the same facts constitute both a crime and the tort. This is not that
> case. At the other end of the scale are cases when the tort is not related except in h
> point of time to the crime. This is not that case. Here the harm done was not
> remote from the carrying out of the illegal enterprise. It resulted from the careless
> manner in which the defendant carried out his part in it. Lord Lyndhurst expressed
> basic doctrine when, speaking as Chief Baron, he said in *Colburn* v. *Patmore* ((1834)
> 1 Cr M & R 73 at 83, 149 ER 999 at 1003): "I know of no case in which a person who
> has committed an act, declared by the law to be criminal, has been permitted to j
> recover compensation against a person who has acted jointly with him in the
> commission of the crime. It is not necessary to give any opinion upon this point;
> but I may say, that I entertain little doubt that a person who is declared by the law
> to be guilty of a crime cannot be allowed to recover damages against another who
> has participated in its commission." That doctrine, given more particularity for the
> present case, can I think be formulated as a rule as follows: If two or more persons

participate in the commission of a crime, each takes the risk of the negligence of the
a other or others in the actual performance of the criminal act. That formulation can be regarded as founded on the negation of duty, or on some extension of the rule volenti non fit injuria, or simply on the refusal of the courts to aid wrongdoers.'

The fourth judgment was given by Owen J, and he said (at 89):

'... the law does not recognise the relationship between two criminals who are
b jointly engaged in carrying out a criminal venture as being one which gives rise to a duty of care owed by the one to the other in the execution of the crime.'

His conclusion is expressed in these words:

'The answer to the plaintiff's claim is, I think, that the law does not recognise that those who are taking part in a joint criminal venture are "neighbours" . . .'

c

The last judgment was given by Walsh J. He said (at 92):

'I have come to the conclusion that upon the facts found by the learned trial judge the respondent had no right of action in negligence against the appellant. I think that the rule to which I have referred applies to those facts to produce that result.
d The relationship of the parties and the act of which the respondent complains were such that no right of action based upon the manner in which that act was performed could arise ... In my opinion, no right of action in negligence is given by the law in respect of the carrying out by one of the participants in a joint criminal enterprise of the particular criminal act in the commission of which they are engaged.'

I found the Australian authorities which I have quoted of considerable assistance in
e coming to a decision. The conclusion I have come to is that the law of England may in certain circumstances not recognise the existence of a duty of care by one participant in a crime to another participant in the same crime, in relation to an act done in connection with the commission of that crime. That law is based on public policy, and the application of the law depends on a consideration of all the facts. Having regard to all the facts in this case I have come to the conclusion that a duty of care did not exist between
f the first defendant and the plaintiff during the course of the burglary and during the course of the subsequent flight in the get-away car.

If I am wrong about the lack of a duty of care, I have to go on to consider the question whether the doctrine volenti non fit injuria could apply to this case. The point of departure is *Dann v Hamilton* [1939] 1 All ER 59, [1939] 1 KB 509. A passenger in the car was injured in an accident caused by the drunkenness of the driver. The passenger knew
g the driver might have been drinking. It was held that the maxim did not apply in that case. The way it was put by Asquith J was as follows ([1939] 1 All ER 59 at 64, [1939] 1 KB 509 at 518):

'... the plaintiff, by embarking in the car, or re-entering it, with knowledge that through drink the driver had materially reduced his capacity for driving safely, did
h not impliedly consent to, or absolve the driver from liability for, any subsequent negligence on his part whereby she might suffer harm. There may be cases in which the drunkenness of the driver at the material time is so extreme and so glaring that to accept a lift from him is like engaging in an intrinsically and obviously dangerous occupation, inter-meddling with an unexploded bomb or walking on the edge of an unfenced cliff. It is not necessary to decide whether in
j such a case the maxim *volenti non fit injuria* would apply, for in the present case I find as a fact that the driver's degree of intoxication fell short of this degree.'

It is said in the present case that the drunkenness was extreme. It is said and conceded that the concentration of alcohol in the blood was 138 mg. It is also said that two burglars fleeing from arrest in a get-away car are engaging in an intrinsically and obviously dangerous occupation.

The next case is *Slater v Clay Cross Co Ltd* [1956] 2 All ER 625 at 628, [1956] 2 QB 264 at 270–271, where Denning LJ, in relation to the judgment that I have just dealt with of *a*
Asquith J in *Dann v Hamilton*, said:

> 'In so far as he decided that the doctrine of volenti did not apply, I think the decision was quite correct. In so far as he suggested that the plea of contributory negligence might have been available, I agree with him.'

The next case is *Nettleship v Weston* [1971] 3 All ER 581, [1971] 2 QB 691. This was a *b*
case of a driver giving instruction to a learner driver, and Lord Denning MR said ([1971] 3 All ER 581 at 587, [1971] 2 QB 691 at 701):

> 'This brings me to the defence of volenti non fit injuria. Does it apply to the instructor? In former times this defence was used almost as an alternative defence to contributory negligence. Either defence defeated the action. Now that contributory negligence is not a complete defence, but only a ground for reducing *c*
> the damages, the defence of volenti non fit injuria has been closely considered, and, in consequence, it has been severely limited. Knowledge of the risk of injury is not enough. Nor is a willingness to take the risk of injury. Nothing will suffice short of an agreement to waive any claim for negligence. The plaintiff must agree, expressly or impliedly, to waive any claim for any injury that may befall him due to the lack of reasonable care by the defendant . . .' *d*

Salmon LJ drew attention to the question of drunkenness. He said ([1971] 3 All ER 581 at 589, [1971] 2 QB 691 at 704):

> 'The position, however, is totally different when, to the knowledge of the passenger, the driver is so drunk as to be incapable of driving safely. Quite apart from being negligent, a passenger who accepts a lift in such circumstances clearly *e*
> cannot expect the driver to drive other than dangerously.'

Megaw LJ said ([1971] 3 All ER 581 at 594–595, [1971] 2 QB 691 at 710):

> 'Different considerations may, indeed, exist when a passenger has accepted a lift from a driver whom the passenger knows to be likely, through drink or drugs, to drive unsafely. There may in such cases sometimes be an element of aiding and *f*
> abetting a criminal offence; or, if the facts fall short of aiding and abetting, the passsenger's mere assent to benefit from the commission of a criminal offence may involve questions of turpis causa. With great respect, I doubt the correctness on its facts of the decision in *Dann v Hamilton*. The present case involves no such problem.'

My attention was drawn to s 148(3) of the Road Traffic Act 1972. I will not read the *g*
whole section but the part with particular relevance:

> '. . . the fact that a person so carried has willingly accepted as his the risk of negligence on the part of the user shall not be treated as negativing any such liability of the user.'

The words 'such liability' have been repeated in an earlier part of that section and relate *h*
back to s 145 of the Act which makes various requirements on a policy of insurance.

That section was considered by Kenneth Jones J in *Gregory v Kelly* [1978] RTR 426 at 430 where he said:

> 'On the basis that the plaintiff did have knowledge of that defect in the Mini, [counsel] on behalf of the defendant sought to raise the defence of volenti non fit injuria. I can deal with that very shortly because it is now agreed between counsel, *j*
> as I understand it, and I certainly so judge that section 148(3) of the Road Traffic Act 1972 has the effect of depriving the defendant of that defence.'

That decision was based on a concession by counsel. In this case, the matter has been argued, the facts are entirely different and I do not find that s 148(3) of the 1972 Act of itself deprives the second defendant of this defence.

In the first of the two Australian cases that I cited, *Godbolt v Fittock*, Sugerman J, dealing with that case (and I have already recited some of the facts in it) said (at 620):

> '. . . there is, in my opinion, no question of the application in the present case of volenti non fit injuria. It was not, for example, a case of driving at a dangerously high speed for some reason associated with the commission of the crime—to escape detection or arrest or as an incident of the criminal plan. There was no peculiar causal connection linking the accident with the criminal venture The accident was attributable apparently to the dozing of a tired driver, and was such as was equally likely to have happened even had the journey been an innocent one and the load a consignment for marketing at Wingham of the parties' own calves. Putting the matter in another way, what happened was outside the scope of any consent which could be taken as having been given by the plaintiff's participation . . . different as the situation may have been, as regards volenti non fit injuria, had the collision occurred while, for example, the truck was travelling at a high speed to escape a pursuing police vehicle. Viewing the matter, as I have throughout this portion of the discussion, purely from the standpoint of voluntary assumption of risk, the risks assumed might well be regarded as including such reckless modes of driving as might be adopted in, for example, an endeavour to escape capture, but not a risk of a character so lacking in any special relationship to the criminal venture as that of the driver dozing at the wheel.'

In the circumstances of the present case of two burglars who had been drinking and were fleeing in a get-away car, I am of the view that the maxim can apply and, if I were wrong on the first point of my judgment, the maxim would apply and the defendants would be entitled to judgment on that ground.

If I am wrong on both of these points, I have to consider the question of contributory negligence. It has been agreed that the plaintiff is 15% to blame for his injuries as a result of not wearing his seat belt. I have been referred to *Owens v Brimmell* [1976] 3 All ER 765 at 772, [1977] QB 859 at 867, a case before Tasker Watkins J, where the passenger and the driver had been drinking, and the judge said:

> 'I think this is a clear case on the facts of contributory negligence, either on the basis that the minds of the plaintiff and the defendant, behaving recklessly, were equally befuddled by drink so as to rid them of clear thought and perception, or, as seems less likely, the plaintiff remained able to, and should have if he actually did not, foresee the risk of being hurt by riding with the defendant as passenger. In such a case as this the degree of blameworthiness is not, in my opinion, equal. The driver, who alone controls the car and has it in him, therefore, to do whilst in drink great damage, must bear by far the greater responsibility. I, therefore, adjudge the plaintiff's contribution to be 20 per cent.'

However, in the present case, looking at the whole of the facts, and the fact that this was a get-away car, which might have to be driven recklessly and dangerously, and the fact that the plaintiff was not wearing a seat belt, I conclude that these two, the driver and the passenger, were equally to blame for the accident, and if I had to assess the degree of contributory negligence I would set it at 50%.

Judgment for defendants.

Solicitors: *Neville, Piercy & Calverley*, Liverpool (for the plaintiff); *Rutherfords*, Liverpool (for the second defendant).

William Hoskins Esq Barrister.

R v Nazari and other cases a

COURT OF APPEAL, CRIMINAL DIVISION
LAWTON LJ, BOREHAM AND COMYN JJ
14th MARCH 1980

b

Sentence – Deportation – Recommendation – Guidelines for making orders recommending deportation.

The defendants were three immigrants who had been recommended for deportation following their conviction of, or plea of guilty to, various offences. The defendant N was an Iranian student who pleaded guilty of smuggling opium into the United Kingdom. c
He was sentenced to four years' imprisonment and recommended to be deported. He applied for leave to appeal against the recommendation on the ground that if he was sent back to Iran he faced the possibility of being executed for his actions. It was suggested in evidence on his behalf that the Iranian government took a serious view of drug smuggling and that serious consequences would befall him if he was deported. No evidence was given that an Iranian court would assume jurisdiction in relation to d
smuggling drugs into the United Kingdom. The defendant D, a Sri Lankan national, killed his wife by hitting her over the head with a heavy ornament. At his trial for murder the judge accepted a plea of manslaughter on the ground of diminished responsibility and sentenced him to five years' imprisonment. The judge also recommended that he be deported. D appealed against the recommendation, stating that he intended in any event to return to Sri Lanka voluntarily. The defendant F, a e
Spanish citizen, was convicted of conspiracy to rob and aggravated burglary. He was sentenced to 18 months' imprisonment and recommended for deportation. He appealed against the recommendation on the grounds that he was settled in England with a wife and family, that his two children were born in England and were attending school there, and that his wife would suffer hardship by having to choose between returning to Spain with her husband or remaining in England with the children. f

Held – (1) In considering whether to make an order recommending deportation the court had first to consider whether the offender's continued presence in the United Kingdom would be detrimental to the country (see p 885 *d*, post); dictum of Sachs LJ in *R v Caird* (1970) 54 Cr App R at 510 applied.

(2) In considering other matters which could be relevant, the court was not concerned g
with the political system of the country to which the offender would be deported or whether in consequence deportation to that country would be unduly harsh, since those were matters for the Home Secretary and would be considered by him at the time of the offender's release. The defendant N's appeal would accordingly be dismissed (see p 885 *f* to *j* and p 886 *h*, post).

(3) However the court ought to take into consideration the effect a deportation order h
would have on innocent persons such as the offender's family. Because of the hardship that would be suffered by his wife if he were deported, the defendant F's appeal would be allowed (see p 885 *j* to p 886 *b* and *j*, post).

(4) A statement by an offender that he intended to return voluntarily to his own country at the end of his sentence ought not to carry much weight with the court. Furthermore, where there was evidence of mental instability connected with or resulting j
in the commission of a serious crime that in itself was a good reason for making an order recommending deportation. The defendant D's appeal would accordingly be dismissed (see p 886 *d* to *f* and *h*, post).

Per Curiam. A recommendation for deportation should normally be made where an offender has been proved to be an illegal immigrant (see p 886 *h*, post).

Notes

For deportation of non-patrials, see 4 Halsbury's Laws (4th Edn) para 1011 and 11 ibid para 566, and for cases on the subject, see 2 Digest (Reissue) 208–214, *1177–1224*.

Case referred to in judgment

R v Caird (1970) 54 Cr App R 499, CA, 2 Digest (Reissue) 213, *1219*.

Case also cited

R v Thoseby CA, (30th July 1979, unreported).

Appeals and applications

R v Nazari

Fazlollah Nazari, an Iranian citizen, applied for leave to appeal against the order recommending that he be deported made by the recorder (John Alliott QC) in the Crown Court at Reading on 7th September 1979 when sentencing him to four years' imprisonment for the fraudulent evasion of the prohibition on the importation of a controlled drug, contrary to s 3(1) of the Misuse of Drugs Act 1971.

R v Dissanayake

Rohan Shivantha Dissanayake, a Sri Lankan national, appealed against the sentence of five years' imprisonment imposed on him on 12th March 1979 and the order recommending that he be deported made against him on 23rd March 1979 by Melford Stevenson J in the Central Criminal Court following his plea of guilty to a charge of manslaughter.

R v Anyanwu

Ebenezer Chukwuma Anyanwu applied for an extension of time in which to apply for leave to appeal against the sentence of a fine of £50 or two months' imprisonment in default imposed on him and the order recommending that he be deported made against him by his Honour Judge Figgis in the Crown Court at Kingston upon Thames on 22nd October 1979 following his conviction on a charge of remaining in the United Kingdom beyond the time limited by his leave to enter, contrary to s 24(1)(*b*) of the Immigration Act 1971.

R v Fernandez and another

Joseph Fernandez, a Spanish citizen, applied for leave to appeal against the order recommending that he be deported made by his Honour Judge Argyle QC in the Central Criminal Court on 9th October 1979 when sentencing him to 18 months' imprisonment for conspiracy to rob and aggravated burglary. His co-accused, Michael Joseph Adamson, was sentenced to 15 months' imprisonment and appealed against sentence.

Richard J Harvey for the applicant Nazari.
Simeon Hopkins for the appellant Dissanayake.
C A I Ginikanwa for the applicant Anyanwu.
John Laws for the Crown.
The applicants Fernandez and Adamson did not appear.

LAWTON LJ delivered the following judgment of the court: These three applicants and one appellant either appeal or apply for leave to appeal against sentence, which in each case included a recommendation for deportation.

During the last decade this court has from time to time indicated the principles on which orders recommending deportation should be made. It has been suggested that some of the decisions are conflicting. As a result it was decided that four cases raising different matters for consideration should be heard one after the other so that the court would have an opportunity of reviewing the principles which are applicable. It is first necessary to set out the facts of each case so far as they are relevant. a

R v Nazari

On 7th September 1979 in the Crown Court at Reading the applicant, Fazlollah Nazari, pleaded guilty to being knowingly concerned in the fraudulent evasion of the prohibition on the importation of a controlled drug. He was sentenced to four years' imprisonment and recommended for deportation. b

He is a young man of Iranian citizenship. In the summer of 1979 he was studying at a polytechnic in the London area. He arrived at Heathrow Airport on 19th June 1979 carrying a black suitcase. Customs officers were suspicious about the suitcase. He was allowed to pass through the customs but was kept under observation in case he met somebody and handed over the suitcase. He did not meet anybody. Before he left the airport he was detained. The suitcase was opened and found to contain 1·95 kg of opium c
in the form of sticks. It was accepted by the prosecution that opium in that form could not be converted into heroin.

There is no application for leave to appeal against the sentence of four years' imprisonment, which was in line with the kind of sentences which are passed on those who try to smuggle dangerous drugs into the United Kingdom.

Complaint is made about the recommendation for deportation. Counsel for Nazari d
has called attention to what might be called the general compassionate grounds relating to this young man. It is said that if he is deported he will not be able to continue his studies in England, that he will probably be separated from the English girl whom he hopes to marry, and that he is not likely to commit this kind of offence again. But the major part of counsel's submission was directed to the proposition that if the applicant is deported he will be sent back to Iran, where the present government is likely to take e
a very serious view of his activities and he may face a court which will have jurisdiction to pass, and may pass, sentence of death on him.

The evidence relating to what is likely to happen to the applicant if and when he returns to Iran is unsatisfactory. So far as the recorder was concerned, a statement to the effect stated above was set out in the social inquiry report. The probation officer who made it said that at some date which he did not specify he had spoken on the telephone f
to somebody at the Iranian Embassy who had confirmed that very serious consequences would befall the applicant if he returns to Iran. Before this court today counsel informed us that he personally had spoken to Professor Coulson of the School of Oriental Studies of London University who had told him that the type of consequences which have been indicated might befall the applicant. In addition counsel put in an affidavit sworn by an Iranian holding a degree in law who is at present an articled clerk with a firm of g
solicitors. He deposed that under Iranian law serious consequences, including the death penalty, could fall on anyone who imported dangerous drugs. What he meant by importing dangerous drugs was not clear. We do not know whether the deponent was talking about importation into Iran or into the United Kingdom. It seems odd that any Iranian court would have jurisdiction over somebody who was arrested for importing dangerous drugs into the United Kingdom. h

In this class of case, when it is suggested that unpleasant consequences are likely to follow for anyone recommended for deportation if the Home Secretary makes an order of deportation, it is essential that proper evidence should be before the court; the court cannot act on the kind of evidence which has been put before it in this case.

R v Dissanayake j

We turn to the next case, that of the appellant Rohan Shivantha Dissanayake. Leave to appeal against sentence has been granted to him by the single judge. Counsel for Dissanayake has urged on us that the sentence of imprisonment as well as the order recommending deportation was wrong.

On 12th March 1979 in the Central Criminal Court before Melford Stevenson J the appellant, who had been indicted for murder, pleaded guilty to manslaughter, the basis

of his plea being diminished responsibility. There was in addition a suggestion, but no
a more than a suggestion, that he had been provoked into doing that which he did. He
was sentenced to five years' imprisonment and recommended for deportation.

[His Lordship, having described the circumstances in which the appellant killed his
wife by striking her on the head with a heavy wooden ornament, continued:] In our
judgment men who batter their wives to death should consider themselves fortunate to
receive a sentence as light as five years. It could have been much longer without in any
b way being excessive.

In our judgment there is nothing in that part of the appeal which relates to the
sentence of imprisonment. We will consider the recommendation for deportation in the
light of the observations that we propose making after we have recounted the facts of the
two other cases.

c *R v Anyanwu*

[Having stated the facts his Lordship concluded that the applicant had abandoned his
application for leave to appeal against sentence and that accordingly there was nothing
for the court to consider.]

R v Fernandez

d We come now to the case of the applicants Fernandez and Adamson. Adamson
defended himself at the trial. That was by his own choice. He has had legal aid for the
purpose of advising him about the procedure to be adopted for appealing against
sentence. He now asks for an adjournment so that he can have more advice as to his
grounds of appeal. We feel impelled, albeit with some reluctance, to agree to his
application for leave to appeal against conviction being adjourned. It will be
e adjourned. He will be granted legal aid for the purpose of getting advice about his
grounds of appeal. But he should clearly understand that he must get the advice as
quickly as he can, and once he has got it the case will be restored to the list as soon as
possible thereafter. There will be no further adjournments.

Turning now to the case of Fernandez, on 25th September 1979 at the Central
Criminal Court he and Adamson were convicted of conspiracy to rob and aggravated
f burglary. On 9th October 1979 Fernandez was sentenced to 18 months' imprisonment
on each count of the indictment on which he was convicted and, in addition, sentences
of three months and three months consecutive, suspended for two years on 10th June
1977, were ordered to take effect, varied to a total of three months' imprisonment
concurrent. He was also recommended for deportation.

Fernandez applied for leave to appeal against his sentence. The single judge referred
g his application to the full court, and we grant him leave to appeal against sentence. He
himself is not present today, but we have had the benefit (and it has been a great benefit
to the court, and indeed to him) to have his wife here to speak for him. He has a
statutory right to appear himself; but, having regard to what we propose to say about the
recommendation for deportation, he will probably not want to come back to this court,
though he is at liberty to do if he wishes.

h Fernandez comes from Galicia, in north-west Spain, and has been in this country many
years. During most of the time that he has been here he has been a waiter. In June 1977
when he was working in a night club he and others decided to rob his employer of the
club takings while he was on his way home with them. He and his co-conspirators (there
were four of them altogether) met at a public house and made plans. They reconnoitred
the employer's house and agreed to break into it and to overpower anyone who might be
j there. They were to lie in wait for the employer to come home. They anticipated that
he would be carrying takings amounting to about £600. On the night of 15th–16th July
1977 Fernandez and one of his co-conspirators purchased some sticky tape. Fernandez
made a hood from a pillowcase with holes cut for the eyes so that the employer would
not recognise him. Later that night the conspirators met at the house of the employer,
Mr Leigh, and succeeded in opening a window. They carried with them knives, rope
and the tape. A cassette player, radio and silver lighter were removed from the window

sill to facilitate entry, and those items were later found in the house of one of the conspirators. They were, however, disturbed by neighbours, who saw lights on, and a
they left, intending to return later. Fortunately for justice, a police patrol car saw Fernandez walking around, and as a result of their stopping and questioning him the plot came to light.

Fernandez has not got a clean record in this country but all his offences to date have kept him out of prison, although in 1977, as we have already recounted, he received a suspended sentence for driving whilst disqualified. His appearance before the courts b
started in 1972 with two offences, one of attempted deception and the other of theft. Later that year he was convicted of assault occasioning actual bodily harm. Three years later he was again convicted of assault occasioning actual bodily harm. Then he had a few comparatively minor motoring offences. His record is not good. On the other hand, it cannot be said that he has shown by his record that he is a member of the criminal class in this country. He seems generally to be a hard-working man. His family c
situation is as follows. He has a Spanish wife who came to this country about ten years ago. She is a devoted wife. They have two children, the elder of whom is now nine, both born in this country. They are buying their own house, which is in their joint names. Spanish is the language of the home, but, although the children can understand Spanish and can say a few sentences in that language, they are more English-speaking than Spanish-speaking; and, of course, they go to English schools. d

We are satisfied, having heard Mrs Fernandez, that if the recommendation for deportation is accepted and if her husband is sent back to Spain, she is going to face a grave dilemma. She feels as a wife that she ought to go back with her husband, but as a mother she feels that she ought to stay in England with her children because she is convinced that there is a better future for them here than there would be in Spain. Clearly she and the children will suffer hardship. On the other hand, if the only matter e
which the court should take into consideration is the crime and the circumstances of the crime which Fernandez himself committed, then there are indications that there should be a recommendation for deportation.

It is against that background of facts that we come to consider the principles which should be applied in this class of case. The leading authority is *R v Caird* (1970) 54 Cr App R 499 at 510. The facts are irrelevant for the purposes of this judgment; we refer f
to it because a recommendation for deportation had been made in that case, and the court, which was presided over by Sachs LJ, set out the principles which should apply:

> 'So far as Bodea, however, is concerned, there was also a recommendation for deportation. In a case such as is under consideration the question for the Court is whether the potential detriment to this country of Bodea remaining here has been shown to be such as to justify the recommendation. This Court is of the clear g
> opinion that upon that basis the recommendation based on this particular isolated offence cannot be supported and should be cancelled.'

As we are referring to this case I go on to read the paragraph following which is relevant to a matter which arises in the case of the appellant Nazari:

> 'It desires to emphasise that the courts when considering a recommendation for h
> deportation are normally concerned simply with the crime committed and the individual's past record and the question as to what is their effect on the question of potential detriment just mentioned. It does not embark, and indeed is in no position to embark, upon the issue as to what is likely to be his life if he goes back to the country of his origin. That is a matter for the Home Secretary.'

It is relevant to point out that the power of a court to make a recommendation for j
deportation is derived from s 6 of the Immigration Act 1971 which reads:

> '(1) Where under section 3(6) above a person convicted of an offence is liable to deportation on the recommendation of a court, he may be recommended for deportation by any court having power to sentence him for the offence unless the court commits him to be sentenced or further dealt with for that offence by another court . . .

> '(2) A court shall not recommend a person for deportation unless he has been given not less than seven days notice in writing stating that a person is not liable to deportation if he is patrial, describing the persons who are patrial and stating (so far as material) the effect of section 3(8) above and section 7 below . . .'

Then there are other matters relating to adjournments and the like.

In our judgment it is clear that Parliament in 1971 intended that there should be full inquiry into a case before any order recommending deportation is made. A person who is likely to be the subject of an order must be given seven clear days' notice of what may happen to him. The object of that is to enable him to prepare his answer to a suggestion that he should be recommended for deportation. It follows that no court should make an order recommending deportation without full inquiry into all the circumstances. It should not be done, as has sometimes happened in the past, by adding a sentence as if by an afterthought at the end of observations about any sentence of imprisonment. It would be advisable for judges to invite counsel to address them specifically on the possibility of a recommendation for deportation being made.

We now indicate some guidelines which courts should keep in mind when considering whether to make an order recommending deportation. But we stress that these are guidelines, not rigid rules. There may well be considerations which take a particular case out of the guidelines; that is a matter which will depend on the evidence.

First, the court must consider, as was said by Sachs LJ in *R v Caird* (1970) 54 Cr App R 499 at 510, whether the accused's continued presence in the United Kingdom is to its detriment. This country has no use for criminals of other nationalities, particularly if they have committed serious crimes or have long criminal records. That is self-evident. The more serious the crime and the longer the record the more obvious it is that there should be an order recommending deportation. On the other hand, a minor offence would not merit an order recommending deportation. In the Greater London area, for example, shoplifting is an offence which is frequently committed by visitors to this country. Normally an arrest for shoplifting followed by conviction, even if there were more than one offence being dealt with, would not merit a recommendation for deportation. But a series of shoplifting offences on different occasions may justify a recommendation for deportation. Even a first offence of shoplifting might merit a recommendation if the offender were a member of a gang carrying out a planned raid on a departmental store.

Second, the courts are not concerned with the political systems which operate in other countries. They may be harsh; they may be soft; they may be oppressive; they may be the quintessence of democracy. The court has no knowledge of those matters over and above that which is common knowledge, and that may be wrong. In our judgment it would be undesirable for this court or any other court to express views about regimes which exist outside the United Kingdom of Great Britain and Northern Ireland. It is for the Home Secretary to decide in each case whether an offender's return to his country of origin would have consequences which would make his compulsory return unduly harsh. The Home Secretary has opportunities of informing himself about what is happening in other countries which the courts do not have. The sort of argument which was put up in Nazari's case is one which we did not find attractive. It may well be that the regime in Iran at the present time is likely to be unfavourable from his point of view. Whether and how long it will continue to be so we do not know. Whether it will be so by the end of this man's sentence of imprisonment must be a matter of speculation. When the time comes for him to be released from prison the Home Secretary, we are sure, will bear in mind the very matters which we have been urged to consider, namely whether it would be unduly harsh to send him back to his country of origin.

The next matter to which we invite attention by way of guidelines is the effect that an order recommending deportation will have on others who are not before the court and who are innocent persons. This court and all other courts would have no wish to break up families or impose hardship on innocent people. The case of Fernandez illustrates this very clearly indeed. Mrs Fernandez is an admirable person, a good wife and mother, and a credit to herself and someone whom most of us would want to have in this country. As we have already indicated, if her husband is deported she will have a heartrending choice to make; whether she should go with her husband or leave him and look after the interests of the children. That is the kind of situation which should be considered very carefully before a recommendation for deportation is made.

We have considered the case of Fernandez in the light of those considerations and have come to the conclusion that the recommendation for deportation should be quashed. We can see no reason for interfering with the sentences of imprisonment. We had to grant him leave to appeal in order to quash the recommendation for deportation. He may if he so wishes exercise his statutory right to be present, but we hold out no hope that it will do him any good; and we should be grateful if his wife would make that clear to him.

That concludes all the cases except to say a word in relation to deportation in the case of Dissanayake. He wants to go back to Sri Lanka, but says that he does not want to go back under an order of deportation. It is possible in his case (we make no finding about it) that even if we were to quash the recommendation for deportation the Secretary of State, under the powers which he has under the 1971 Act could deport him in any case, because apparently his stay here is subject to the limitations which were imposed on him when he first came to this country. His wife, whom it is said he married for reasons of convenience, is now dead; but that is not a matter into which we intend to go. It is often said in this class of case that there is no need to recommend deportation, because the accused is willing to go back of his own free will when he has served his sentence of imprisonment. We are not impressed with that argument. Assertions of intention made in this court are often forgotten on leaving the court and even more frequently forgotten once the prison gates have opened and the appellant is at large once again.

In our judgment there were very good grounds in the case of Dissanayake for making a recommendation. He had committed a serious offence, and he committed it, according to the case put forward on his behalf, when he was in a state of diminished responsibility by reason of what in his case must be inherent causes. Where there is evidence of mental instability connected with or resulting in the commission of a serious criminal offence it seems to us, again as a matter of guidelines, that that in itself is a good reason why a recommendation for deportation should be made. Whether it is carried out is entirely a matter for the Home Secretary.

We wish to state clearly and firmly that all a court does when it makes a recommendation for deportation is to indicate to the Secretary of State that in the opinion of the court it is to the detriment of this country that the accused should remain here. The final decision is for the Secretary of State. No doubt he will take into account the personal circumstances of each person whose case he is considering, and that will include the political situation in the country to which he will have to go if an order of deportation is made. These are matters solely for the Secretary of State, and not for the courts.

It follows from what we have said that in the case of Nazari the application will be dismissed. The appeal will be dismissed in all its aspects in the case of Dissanayake. In the case of Anyanwu there is now no appeal before the court; but if there had been one we should have upheld the recommendation because he was proved to have been an illegal immigrant. In such cases a recommendation should normally be made. In the case of Fernandez, as has already been indicated, the order recommending deportation will be quashed.

Orders accordingly.

Solicitors: *Offenbach & Co* (for the applicant Nazari); *Philip Kossoff & Co* (for the appellant Dissanayake); *Stuart A West & Co* (for the applicant Anyanwu); *Treasury Solicitor*.

N P Metcalfe Esq Barrister.

Edgar v Edgar

COURT OF APPEAL, CIVIL DIVISION
ORMROD AND OLIVER LJJ
2nd, 3rd, 23rd JULY 1980

Divorce – Financial provision – Lump sum order – Matters to be considered – Conduct of parties – Prior agreement by wife not to claim lump sum payment in event of divorce – Agreement in deed of separation between the parties under which wealthy husband conferred on wife substantial capital provision – Whether agreement precluding court from making order for lump sum payment – Whether any weight should be given to agreement if court not precluded from making lump sum order – Matrimonial Causes Act 1973, ss 23(1), 25(1).

The husband and wife were married in 1967 and had four young children. The husband was very wealthy. The marriage ran into difficulties and by October 1975 the wife decided to leave the husband as soon as arrangements could be made for her to do so. She was anxious to retain care and control of the children but needed her husband's co-operation to provide them with an alternative home. The husband wished to preserve the marriage and made it clear he would only agree to the wife leaving with the children if there was a suitable alternative home for them. Negotiations took place over several months between the parties' solicitors as to the terms of a separation. Because the wife was anxious to get away from the husband she pressed for a concluded separation deed, even though her lawyers advised her she could obtain a better settlement in divorce proceedings. On 1st April 1976 the husband and wife executed a deed of separation under which the husband agreed to purchase a house for the wife in her name and to confer other capital benefits on her which in total had a present value of approximately £100,000, and also to pay her £16,000 per annum less tax and to make periodical payments for the children. In accordance with the negotiated agreement between the parties the deed contained a clause whereby the wife agreed that if she obtained a divorce she would not claim lump sum or property transfer orders. The husband did not put pressure on the wife to accept the terms of the deed and in no way exploited his position as a wealthy man. He fully carried out his obligations under the deed. On 3rd November 1978 the wife presented a divorce petition which contained the usual prayer for full ancillary relief. A decree nisi was pronounced on 24th January 1979. The wife then proceeded with an application for ancillary relief in which she applied for, inter alia, a lump sum payment under s 23(1)[a] of the Matrimonial Causes Act 1973. On the hearing of the application the husband contended that the court was required to give effect to the wife's agreement in the deed not to apply after divorce for additional capital provision to that provided by the deed and should, therefore, refuse to order a lump sum payment. The judge declined to give effect to the agreement and ordered the husband to pay the wife a lump sum of £670,000. The husband appealed.

Held – The court, when exercising the discretion given to it by s 23(1) of the 1973 Act to order a lump sum payment, was required to give effect to a prior agreement by the wife not to claim a lump sum by treating that agreement as conduct of the parties which was to be taken into account when considering under s 25(1)[b] of that Act what was just

a Section 23(1), so far as material, provides: 'On granting a decree of divorce . . . or at any time thereafter . . . the court may make any one or more of the following orders, that is to say . . . (*c*) an order that either party to the marriage shall pay to the other such lump sum or sums as may be so specified . . .'

b Section 25(1), so far as material, provides: 'It shall be the duty of the court in deciding whether to exercise its powers under section 23(1)(*a*), (*b*) or (*c*) . . . in relation to a party to the marriage and if so, in what manner, to have regard to all the circumstances of the case . . . and so to exercise those powers as to place the parties, so far as it is practicable and, having regard to their conduct, just to do so, in the financial position in which they would have been if the marriage had not broken down and each had properly discharged his or her financial obligations and responsibilities towards the other.'

between the parties in all the circumstances. In deciding the weight to be given to the prior agreement in order to do justice between the parties, the court had to take into account, inter alia, the parties' conduct leading up to the agreement, their subsequent conduct, and the circumstances surrounding the making of the agreement such as undue pressure by one party on the other, exploitation by one party of a dominant position, the inadequate knowledge of one party, and any unforeseen or overlooked change in the circumstances existing at the date of the agreement. Furthermore, disparity of bargaining power between the parties was not enough of itself to justify the court in ignoring the terms of the deed and the crucial question was not, therefore, whether the husband by reason of his wealth had superior bargaining power, but whether he had exploited that power unfairly to induce the wife to act to her disadvantage. The existence of a prior agreement by the wife not to claim a lump sum required her to adduce prima facie evidence that justice required the court to relieve her from the effect of the agreement and to award her further capital provision. Since there was no evidence of adverse conduct by the husband during the negotiations leading to the agreement and no adequate explanation of the wife's conduct in agreeing, against the advice of her lawyers, not to claim a lump sum on divorce and then going back on the agreement and claiming a lump sum, and since it had not been shown that justice required the court to relieve her from the agreement, she had not established that the court was justified in going behind the agreement. Accordingly, the wife's application for a lump sum would be dismissed and the husband's appeal allowed (see p 892 *j* to p 894 *e*, p 895 *a b* and *f* to p 896 *f*, p 898 *h j* and p 899 *a* to *c*, post).

Hyman v Hyman [1929] All ER Rep 245 and *Wright v Wright* [1970] 3 All ER 209 applied.

Notes

For the effect of a covenant in a deed of separation not to claim financial provision, see 13 Halsbury's Laws (4th Edn) para 695.

For the Matrimonial Causes Act 1973, ss 23, 25, see 43 Halsbury's Statutes (3rd Edn) 564, 567.

Cases referred to in judgments

Brockwell v Brockwell [1975] Court of Appeal Transcript 468.
Dipper v Dipper [1980] 2 All ER 722, [1980] 3 WLR 626, CA.
Hyman v Hyman [1929] AC 601, [1929] All ER Rep 245, 98 LJP 81, 141 LT 329, 93 JP 209, 27 LGR 379, HL, 27(1) Digest (Reissue) 274, *2030*.
O'Donnell v O'Donnell [1975] 2 All ER 993, sub nom *O'D v O'D* [1976] Fam 83, [1975] 3 WLR 308, CA, Digest (Cont Vol D) 428, *6962Af*.
Wright v Wright [1970] 3 All ER 209, [1970] 1 WLR 1219, CA, 27(1) Digest (Reissue) 518, *3727*.

Interlocutory appeal

This was an appeal by the husband, Anthony Samuel Edgar, from the order of Eastham J made on 27th March 1980 whereby he ordered, inter alia, the husband to pay the wife, Roberta Hilary Ann Edgar, a lump sum of £670,000 within four months. The facts are set out in the judgment of Ormrod LJ.

Joseph Jackson QC and *Nicholas Wall* for the husband.
Robert Johnson QC and *Nicholas Wilson* for the wife.

Cur adv vult

23rd July. The following judgments were read.

ORMROD LJ. This is an appeal by a husband from an order made on 27th March 1980 by Eastham J in proceedings for financial provision following a divorce. It is a wholly exceptional case on the facts, and this judgment must be read in the light of the strange *a* and, in some ways, unsatisfactory state of the evidence.

The judge was dealing with applications under ss 22 and 23 of the Matrimonial Causes Act 1973 by the wife of an extremely rich husband for a lump sum and periodical payments for herself and four children, of whom she has the custody. The husband is a multi-millionaire, who is in a position to make a very large payment without liquidity problems. The main issue at the hearing was the husband's contention that the court *b* should give effect to an undertaking by the wife contained in a deed of separation, not to apply, after divorce, for additional capital provision beyond that provided by the deed, which had been fully complied with by the husband.

After hearing the evidence and argument at length the judge decided that he could properly ignore the wife's undertaking, and so proceeded to assess the lump sum under the provisions of s 25 of the 1973 Act. He ordered the husband to pay the sum of *c* £670,000 by 28th July 1980 and on payment of this sum—

> '(a) The existing order for periodical payments to [the wife] and the children of the family be discharged. (b) All other financial claims of [the wife] be dismissed. (c) The deed entered into between [the wife] and [the husband], on the 1st day of April 1976 be discharged.'

d The order was made in this form with a view to producing a 'clean break' between the parties notwithstanding that they have four children in whose lives both are playing, and intend to play, as full a part as they can in the circumstances. The consent of the wife to the dismissal of her claim to periodical payments was not obtained. (The case of *Dipper v Dipper* [1980] 2 All ER 722, [1980] 3 WLR 626, decided by this court on 5th March 1980, was not brought to the attention of the judge.) Nor, apparently, had she consented *e* to the discharge of the order for periodical payments to the children, a very unusual, if not unprecedented, order in such circumstances.

The marriage took place on 23rd August 1967 and the four children are aged 12, 9, 8 and 6. The marriage had run into serious difficulties by the summer of 1975, and by October 1975 the wife had made up her mind to leave her husband as soon as arrangements could be made for her to do so. She was extremely anxious to retain the *f* care and control of the children, but had no alternative accommodation and, without her husband's co-operation, had no means of providing an alternative home for herself and the children. The husband wished to keep the marriage going and the family together, and had made it clear to her that he would not agree to her leaving with the children unless she had a proper and suitable home for them.

The wife consulted solicitors and on 6th October 1975 they spoke on the telephone to *g* the husband's solicitors saying she wanted to leave and wanted a divorce. On 15th October 1975 she had a conference with counsel, and on 16th October her solicitors wrote to the husband's solicitors confirming her decision and setting out her requirements in detail. I will return to this and other letters at a later stage in this judgment. This letter, however, expressly stated that the wife was not asking for a full capital settlement at that stage. However, by 25th November 1975, at the latest, the wife seems to have *h* agreed that she would not ask for any further capital provision in the event of a divorce, and confirmed this in an interview with her husband's solicitor and her own solicitor on that date. On 5th December the husband's solicitors wrote a letter setting out in full proposed heads of agreement, including the following:

> 'Your client agrees that she will not ask for, now or in the future, any capital or *j* lump sum payment or provision pending, during or following any divorce proceedings nor during the subsistence of the Deed of Separation.'

The wife's solicitors sent a long, detailed letter on 15th December dealing with many points in the proposed terms, and in particular in reply to the paragraph quoted above, they wrote:

> 'As you know our client has been advised not to agree this, but she has instructed us that she is prepared subject to what we write in the final paragraph of this letter not to claim now or in the future any capital or lump sum provision with the exception that should legislation change the tax position regarding husbands paying wives maintenance as referred by you in your point 9 our client must reserve the right to claim a capital or lump sum provision to compensate her and this must be clearly accepted by your client.'

The final paragraph referred to, read thus:

> 'Finally, and this is not intended in any way to be a threat, our client is not prepared to go on bargaining about the position. She has made her situation quite clear. As you will appreciate, if the matters do proceed in accordance with our client's wishes, she is giving up a very sizeable capital payment which she would otherwise, in both Counsel's and our view receive. She has instructed us that if your client is not prepared to agree the points we have raised in this letter then we are to proceed . . . with the divorce as a matter of urgency.'

By the time this stage in the marriage had been reached the wife was emotionally involved with another man, possibly with two other men, with one of whom she had admittedly committed adultery; the husband had committed adultery on many occasions with a number of women. Both of them were, therefore, in a position to file a petition immediately.

Negotiations, mainly involving details, continued between solicitors until the deed of separation was agreed and executed by both parties on 1st April 1976. They were still living together, and continued to do so until November of that year, when the wife moved into her own house. Under the deed, the husband agreed to purchase in the name of the wife a named house, or some commensurate alternative, to pay for alterations, to provide accommodation for the wife's mother, to buy the wife a motor car, and to pay £16,000 per annum less tax to the wife, and £5,000 per annum less tax to each of the four children. These were, substantially, the provisions for which the wife had originally asked in her solicitor's letter of 16th October 1975. We were told by counsel that the present value of the capital provisions made for the wife, is approximately £100,000. In addition, the deed contained a clause in these terms:

> '8. The Wife ACKNOWLEDGES that on transfer to her of the said property referred to in paragraph 2 hereof and on payment of the sums referred to therein and in paragraph 4 hereof and always provided that no reconciliation between the Wife and Husband is effected she does not intend to seek any further capital or property provision from the Husband whether by way of ancillary relief in divorce proceedings or otherwise and in the event of a decree of divorce being granted she hereby agrees not to proceed with her claims for lump sum and property adjustment orders subject only to her right to make application to the Court for lump sum or property provision in accordance with paragraph 7 hereof if in the circumstances referred to therein the parties cannot reach agreement regarding alternative financial provision.'

This clause, of course, represented the arrangements made between the solicitors in the relevant extracts from their letters, which have already been quoted.

It was subsequently discovered that the provision in the deed for payment direct to the children of £5,000 per annum each was not effective for tax purposes. Accordingly, arrangements were made (to use neutral language) to replace this provision in the deed by consent orders under s 27 of the 1973 Act (the wilful neglect to maintain section), which were effective for tax purposes.

On 3rd November 1978 the wife presented a petition for divorce relying on two years' separation and consent. The prayer was in the usual form, asking for all forms of ancillary relief. Decree nisi was pronounced on 24th January 1979. Notice of intention to proceed with the application for all forms of ancillary relief was given on 7th March 1979 and it was supported by an affidavit of the wife which made it clear that she was claiming a 'substantial capital sum'. The affidavit referred to the contents of cl 8 of the deed and gave some explanation, but in very general terms, of the wife's change of mind in relation to claiming further capital provision. I will refer later to this part of the affidavit in greater detail.

Turning now to the law, it is common ground that the principle laid down by the House of Lords in *Hyman v Hyman* still applies. Lord Hailsham LC said ([1929] AC 601 at 614, [1929] All ER Rep 245 at 251):

> 'However, this may be, it is sufficient for the decision of the present case to hold, as I do, that the power of the court to make provision for a wife on the dissolution of her marriage is a necessary incident of the power to decree such a dissolution, conferred not merely in the interests of the wife, but of the public, and that the wife cannot by her own covenant preclude herself from invoking the jurisdiction of the court or preclude the court from the exercise of that jurisdiction.'

The judge, therefore, had jurisdiction to entertain the wife's application for a lump sum, and to make the order which he did, notwithstanding the provision of cl 8 of the deed under which the wife covenanted not to proceed with a claim for a lump sum. The real question, and it is a difficult one, is to determine the effect, if any, to be given to such a covenant when exercising the statutory discretion under s 23 of the 1973 Act to order the husband to pay a lump sum to the wife.

In *Hyman v Hyman* Lord Hailsham LC, having held that the existence of the covenant did not preclude the wife from making an application to the court, went on to say ([1929] AC 601 at 609, [1929] All ER Rep 245 at 249):

> '. . . this by no means implies that, when this application is made, the existence of the deed or its terms are not the most relevant factors for consideration by the Court in reaching a decision.'

This problem was considered in this court in *Wright v Wright* [1970] 3 All ER 209, [1970] 1 WLR 1219. In giving the leading judgment, Sir Gordon Willmer accepted that the principle of *Hyman v Hyman* applied, notwithstanding that the agreement between the parties had been approved by the court, under what was then s 5 of the Matrimonial Causes Act 1963. He said ([1970] 3 All ER 209 at 213–214, [1970] 1 WLR 1219 at 223–224):

> 'There is, of course, no doubt but that no agreement made inter partes can ever deprive the court of its right to review the question of maintenance for a wife, as was decided by the House of Lords in *Hyman v Hyman*. I do not think that anything contained in the new provisions of the Matrimonial Causes Act 1965, giving the court the power to approve reasonable arrangements between the parties, is such as to cast any doubt at all on the continuance in force of the doctrine enunciated by the House of Lords in *Hyman v Hyman*. There is, therefore, scope for two diametrically opposite views. On the one hand it may be said that the court has an absolute right to go behind an agreement between the parties so far as the question of maintenance for a wife is concerned. On the other hand, there is the learned judge's approach to the problem, ie that where there is an agreement between the parties approved by the court effect must be given to it. Under the one view, the right to award maintenance would be completely uninhibited, whereas under the other it would be strictly curtailed by the arrangement made between the parties and approved by the court at the time of the trial. Counsel for the wife, as I understood his argument, contended for an intermediate position between those two extremes. As I followed him, he said that the fact of this arrangement having been made and having been approved by the court is merely one factor amongst the numerous factors that have to be taken into consideration when the court is called on to award maintenance to

> a wife following a divorce case. I suppose that the result of this argument would be to limit or inhibit to some extent the generosity of the registrar or judge in making an award of maintenance; that is to say, supposing he would, without any such arrangement having been made, have been disposed to award X per week, he must now in deference to the arrangement made between the parties, to which some effect must be given, award only X minus Y. The difference between that and the learned judge's view is that the learned judge held that it would not be right, in the absence of proof of any unforeseen circumstances of the kind envisaged by the arrangement, to make any award of maintenance at all. The learned judge's conclusion was vigorously defended by counsel for the husband who said, and said very forcibly, that this was a perfectly valid agreement between two parties, both sui juris, arrived at with the assistance they got from their legal advisers and approved by the court. It was, therefore, something to which effect ought to be given unless compelling reasons to the contrary were shown. He added (I think with a good deal of force) that the fact that the court had given its approval to the proposed arrangement had put the stamp of reasonableness on the arrangement which was then being made, viz that there should be no maintenance. That leads me to mention a further argument put on behalf of the wife, arising from what I may describe as the tailpiece of the learned judge's judgment, in which, having decided that it would be contrary both to the letter and to the spirit of the arrangement made to award maintenance now, he in effect went on to express regret that he had to reach that conclusion, and suggested for the consideration of the husband and his legal advisers that, as a matter of humanity, they might think well of making some ex gratia payment for the maintenance of the wife. That was fastened on by counsel for the wife as affording evidence to show that the conclusion at which the learned judge actually arrived was in his own view an unreasonable result, in that it denied the wife the money which she ought reasonably to receive by way of maintenance. . . I think for my part, approaching it de novo and in the absence of authorities, that the proper view is to say that this was an agreement entered into with full knowledge of all the circumstances and with the advice of both parties' legal advisers. It is, therefore, something to which considerable attention must be paid. I accept that it would not be right to say that it has to be construed like a statute, or that it absolutely forbids any possible award of maintenance, except on the strictest proof of the existence of the circumstances mentioned. If and insofar as the learned judge so decided I would not agree wholly with his conclusion; but I do not think that he did go so far as that. I think that he was thinking along the same lines as I myself think, namely, that the existence of this agreement, having regard to the circumstances in which it was arrived at, at least makes it necessary for the wife, if she wants to justify an award of maintenance, to offer prima facie proof that there have been unforeseen circumstances, in the true sense, which make it impossible for her to work or otherwise maintain herself. If that be right, then I think that it is quite plain that the wife here did not ever give such prima facie proof.'

In *Brockwell v Brockwell* [1975] Court of Appeal Transcipt 468, Stamp LJ, having cited these passages from Sir Gordon Willmer's judgment in *Wright v Wright*, said:

> 'Nevertheless, the wife ought, in my judgment, to have the opportunity of showing that in all the circumstances, and notwithstanding the agreement, the court should exercise in her favour this discretion to award her some lump sum payment.'

That case, of course, arose under the current Matrimonial Causes Act 1973 and, in an attempt to integrate the *Hyman v Hyman* principle with the new provisions relating to the exercise of the discretion in financial matters set out in s 25 of the Act, I suggested in my judgment in that case that an agreement not to claim a lump sum should be taken into account under the heading of conduct and added: '. . . when people make an

agreement like this it is a very important factor in considering what is the just outcome
a of the proceedings.' I see no reason to resile from that statement.

Under s 25(1) it is the duty of the court to have regard to all the circumstances of the case and, in particular, to the matters detailed in paras (*a*) to (*g*), and to exercise its powers so as 'to place the parties, so far as it is practicable and, having regard to their conduct, just to do so, in the financial position in which they would have been if the marriage had not broken down'. The ideal, of course, is rarely, if ever, attainable; so, inevitably, in most
b cases, the phrase 'so far as it is practicable' dominates the issue, modified, where relevant, by conduct.

To decide what weight should be given, in order to reach a just result, to a prior agreement not to claim a lump sum, regard must be had to the conduct of both parties leading up to the prior agreement, and to their subsequent conduct in consequence of it. It is not necessary in this connection to think in formal legal terms, such as
c misrepresentation or estoppel; *all* the circumstances as they affect each of two human beings must be considered in the complex relationship of marriage. So the circumstances surrounding the making of the agreement are relevant. Undue pressure by one side, exploitation of a dominant position to secure an unreasonable advantage, inadequate knowledge, possibly bad legal advice, an important change of circumstances, unforeseen or overlooked at the time of making the agreement, are all relevant to the question of
d justice between the parties. Important too is the general proposition that, formal agreements, properly and fairly arrived at with competent legal advice, should not be displaced unless there are good and substantial grounds for concluding that an injustice will be done by holding the parties to the terms of their agreement. There may well be other considerations which affect the justice of this case; the above list is not intended to be an exclusive catalogue.

e I agree with Sir Gordon Willmer in *Wright v Wright* [1970] 3 All ER 209 at 214, [1970] 1 WLR 1219 at 1224 that the existence of an agreement—

> '... at least makes it necessary for the wife, if she is to justify an award of maintenance, to offer prima facie proof that there have been unforeseen circumstances in the true sense, which make it impossible for her to work or otherwise maintain herself.'

f

Adapting that statement to the present case, it means that the wife here must offer prima facie evidence of material facts which show that justice requires that she should be relieved from the effects of her covenant in cl 8 of the deed of separation, and awarded further capital provision.

Eastham J in the present case, approached the problem on these lines. In his judgment
g he summarised the law in five propositions as follows:

> '(1) (and this is not contested) Notwithstanding the deed of 1st April, the wife is entitled to pursue a claim under s 23 of the Act.
>
> '(2) If she does pursue such a claim, the court not only has jurisdiction to entertain it but is bound to take into account all the considerations listed in s 25 of
> h the Act.
>
> '(3) The existence of an agreement is a very relevant circumstance under s 25 and in the case of an arm's length agreement based on legal advice between parties of equal bargaining power, is a most important piece of conduct to be considered under s 25 of the Act.
>
> '(4) Providing that there is equality stated above, the mere fact that the wife
> j would have done better by going to the court, will not generally be a ground for giving her more as, in addition to its duty under s 25, the court has a duty also to uphold agreements which do not offend public policy.
>
> '(5) If the court, on the evidence, takes the view that having regard to the disparity of bargaining power, it would be unjust not to exercise its powers under s 23 (having regard to the considerations under s 25), it should exercise such powers

> even if no fraud, misrepresentation or duress is established which, at common law, would entitle a wife to avoid the deed.' a

I agree with these propositions, subject to two reservations. First, as to proposition (4), I am not sure that it is helpful to speak of the court having 'a duty' to uphold agreements, although I understand the sense in which the word is used. Secondly, the reference to 'disparity of bargaining power' in proposition (5) is incomplete. It is derived from a phrase taken from *Brockwell v Brockwell* [1975] Court of Appeal Transcript 468 and for which I must accept ultimate responsibility. I used it as a shorthand way of describing b
a situation with which all experienced practitioners are familiar, where one spouse takes an unfair advantage of the other in the throes of marital breakdown, a time when emotional pressures are high, and judgment apt to be clouded. It is unfortunate, because the judge has based his decision solely on this notion of disparity of bargaining power as such, and not on the use, if any, made of it by the husband. The wife, herself, in her affidavit in support of her application, gave as her reasons for disregarding the advice of c
her counsel and solicitors and entering into the covenant not to claim a lump sum, the fact that she felt overpowered by her husband's enormous wealth and position, coupled with her fears of losing the children. There can be no doubt that in this case, as in so many, there is a disparity of bargaining power. The crucial question, however, for present purposes is not whether the husband had a superior bargaining power, but whether he exploited it in a way which was unfair to the wife, so as to induce her to act d
to her disadvantage.

It is at this point that this case becomes so puzzling. At no time has the wife alleged that the husband put pressure on her to accept his terms during the negotiations which led up to the deed, and the judge expressly found as a fact that the husband 'did not make threats with the intention of forcing his wife to take far less than a court would award her after a divorce'. e

The course of the negotiations for the deed of separation were not gone into in any detail at the hearing, although both parties gave oral evidence. Much time was taken up in investigating the wife's emotional involvements in the summer and autumn of 1975, to show that she might have been disposed to agree to almost any terms to get away from her husband, but there was no evidence that the husband was stipulating for an abandonment by her of her claim to a lump sum as a condition precedent to arrangements f
which would enable her to leave. All we know is that the wife put forward at the outset, in the letter of 16th October 1975, her detailed demands for a house, a home for her mother, an allowance totalling £36,000 a year for herself and the children, and expressly reserved her right to claim a lump sum after divorce. There is a forthrightness and a sense of urgency about this letter which does not suggest that she was conscious of much disparity in bargaining power. Three weeks later there is a letter from the husband's g
solicitor, dated 7th November, saying that an agreement had apparently been reached by the parties themselves on the basis of the letter of 16th October with 'appropriate amendments'. Then comes the meeting on 25th November 1975 at the wife's solicitor's office, between the husband's solicitor and the wife's solicitor, at which the wife insisted on being present. She again stated her terms. The husband's solicitor, according to his note of the meeting— h

> '... asked it to be made clear that [the wife] would not ask for any further capital or lump sum payments to be made by her husband once the financial arrangements which were now being discussed had been set out in a Deed of Separation, and in fact implemented. [The wife] said she agreed to this but she was not prepared to wait on indefinitely whilst her husband made up his mind before taking any j
> further steps.'

In a revised version of the note he put it more neutrally: 'I ... asked if it was quite clear that ... she would not ask for any further capital etc.'

These notes were agreed as a fair record of the interview. There is nothing to suggest any pressure on, or exploitation of, the wife by the husband or his solicitor. So the mystery remains unsolved as to why the wife so determinedly rejected the wise advice of her counsel and solicitors not to enter into an agreement to forgo her further claim for a lump sum.

In my judgment, therefore, there is no evidence which reflects adversely on the husband's conduct in the negotiations, and no, or no adequate, explanation of the wife's conduct, and no grounds are shown for holding that justice requires the court to relieve her from the effects of the covenant.

Counsel for the wife in this court has accepted that he cannot point to any evidence of pressure from the husband on the wife to act as she did, and he has not submitted that the disparity in bargaining power is enough by itself to justify this court in ignoring the deed. Instead he has relied on a line of argument foreshadowed by Sir Gordon Willmer in *Wright v Wright* [1970] 3 All ER 209 at 213, [1970] 1 WLR 1219 at 1224 that the court in carrying out its duty under s 25 of the 1973 Act should look at the facts and decide, disregarding the deed at this stage, what provision is required to put the wife into the position she would have been in had the marriage continued, and then take into account the financial provisions of the deed. If this is done he submits that the shortfall is obvious; the provision in the deed is plainly inadequate; and, therefore, the inference must be that it would be unjust to hold the wife to her agreement not to claim a lump sum.

This argument gives no weight at all to the wife's covenant and tacitly assumes that a wife in the position of this wife would be likely to receive a much larger capital provision than that already provided for under the deed, but with no periodical payments, instead of a large order for periodical payments and a relatively small capital sum. This court has not yet had occasion to consider the application of the principles of s 25 to cases involving very rich people although a little assistance may perhaps be had from *O'Donnell v O'Donnell* [1975] 2 All ER 993, [1976] Fam 83, a case involving a rich, but not extremely rich, husband. The point does not arise directly for decision in the present case, so I shall not say any more about it on this occasion.

In the result, I have come to the conclusion that the wife has failed to show sufficient grounds to justify the court in going behind the arrangements made in April 1976 and embodied in the deed. No reasons have been given for the complete change in attidude between the letter of 16th October 1975 reserving her position in regard to capital provision, and her acceptance at the meeting on 25th November 1975, in spite of the advice of her lawyers, that she would make no further claim; there is no evidence of undue pressure by the husband or of any other circumstances that led her to act in a way apparently so contrary to her interests. Similarly, there is no evidence to explain or justify her later decision in March 1979 to go back on her undertaking and claim a further lump sum, or any suggestion that her circumstances had changed in some significant way between April 1976 and March 1979.

At one stage during the argument I thought that it might be appropriate to send the case back to give the wife an opportunity to adduce further evidence on these lines but, on reflection, I do not think that any useful purpose will be served and further costs would be involved.

I can see, therefore, no alternative but to allow the appeal and dismiss the wife's applications under ss 23 and 24. We shall have to send the case back for determination, in default of agreement, of the amounts to be paid to the wife and the children by way of periodical payments.

OLIVER LJ. I agree fully with the judgment of Ormrod LJ and I add some observations of my own only in the light of the fact that we are differing from the judge and in deference to the sustained arguments which have been advanced by counsel for the wife in seeking to uphold his decision in this court.

The principles to be applied are not seriously in dispute. After a review of the relevant authorities the judge stated them in the five propositions which have already been referred to in the judgment of Ormrod LJ and I accept them subject to the same

reservations as those which he has stated and in particular as regards the reference which
the judge made to 'equal bargaining power' and 'disparity of bargaining power'. If, by a
those references, the judge meant no more than that one must look in every case at all the
circumstances to see whether there was some unfair or unconscionable advantage taken
of some factor or of some relationship between the parties which enables the court to say
that an agreement was not truly entered into by one party or the other as a free agent,
then I have no quarrel with them. If however he meant that the court must engage in
an exercise of dissecting the contract and weighing the relative advantages and bargaining b
position on each side in order to ascertain whether there is some precise or approximate
equilibrium, then I respectfully disagree. Men and women of full age, education and
understanding, acting with competent advice available to them, must be assumed to
know and appreciate what they are doing and their actual respective bargaining strengths
will in fact depend in every case on a subjective evaluation of their motives for doing
it. One may, of course, find that some unfair advantage has been taken of a judgment c
impaired by emotion, or that one party is motivated by fear induced by some conduct of
the other or by some misapprehension of a factual or legal position, but in the absence of
some such consideration as that, and these are examples only, the mere strength of one
party's desire for a particular result or the mere fact that one party has greater wealth than
the other cannot, I think, affect the weight to be attributed to a freely negotiated bargain.

Having said that, I do not, of course, quarrel for one moment with the proposition that d
the court in every case must, indeed is enjoined by statute to, look at all the circumstances
in exercising its powers under s 25(1) of the 1973 Act to produce the result directed by
that section. That is not in issue here, but the extent to which the court is directed and
is able to produce the result of placing all the parties in the financial position in which
they would have been if the marriage had not broken down is controlled first by
practicability and secondly by the consideration of what is just having regard to their e
conduct. In that consideration the existence of a freely negotiated bargain entered into
at the instance of one of the parties and affording to him or her everything for which he
or she has stipulated must be a most important element of conduct which cannot be
lightly ignored. Essentially therefore what is in issue in the instant case is whether, in
exercising the jurisdiction which the statute required him to exercise, the judge was
right to decline to hold the wife to a particular term of the agreement into which she had f
entered four years earlier. I say 'a particular term' because there is really no dispute
between the parties that, if the wife makes out a proper case for additional income
payments beyond those specified in the agreement, the husband is willing to provide
them. There may be a lively dispute both about the necessity and the quantum, but
there is, if I understand counsel for the husband right, no dispute in principle. What is
in dispute is whether, having regard to cl 8 of the agreement, to which Ormrod LJ has g
already referred, the judge was right to award to the wife the very large capital sum
which he did award.

Substantially, the only evidence about how that clause came to be in the agreement is
provided by the agreed note of the meeting between the solicitors for the husband and
the wife on 25th November 1975 at which the wife (who is evidently a lady of some
strength of character) insisted on being present and in which she took an active part. I h
will not repeat the relevant parts of this note which have already been quoted by Ormrod
LJ. Now it seems clear that this was the first occasion on which this particular matter was
mentioned, and whether it was put forward as this note suggests as a simple inquiry by
the husband's solicitor or (as seems to be suggested by the earlier version of the note) as
a positive stipulation, seems to me to be largely immaterial. Up to this point the
negotiations between the solicitors had, as the correspondence shows, been on the basis j
that, on the marriage being dissolved, the wife would retain her liberty to claim that
provision should be made for her by way of lump sum payment. A letter of 7th
November 1975 seems to indicate that the question of the provision to be made for the
wife had been discussed between her husband and herself personally and that they had
reached broad agreement on the basis of the earlier correspondence in which this term

appeared, and nowhere in her evidence does the wife suggest that her forgoing this right
a was, up to this point, something which was insisted on by her husband or which she was
under any pressure to accept. The note of the meeting shows that when it was mentioned
she immediately agreed to it and indeed that it was she who was pressing for an
agreement to be concluded and threatening proceedings if it was not. Now she could not
have been under any misapprehension at all about what she was agreeing to. She had, on
15th October 1975, been taken by her solicitors to a conference with leading counsel and
b had been clearly advised that in any divorce proceedings she could expect to receive sums
very substantially in excess of those which she was then contemplating as acceptable to
her and that the provision made by the court would be likely to include an extremely
large capital provision, having regard to her husband's financial position. Whether the
underlying assumption that the court would necessarily be inclined to award a capital
sum of the magnitude which she was advised that she might achieve was correct is not
c something on which we are called on to express an opinion and I do not do so. I observe
only that, whilst the statute casts on the court the burden of forming a view about what
the financial position of each of the parties would have been if the marriage had not
broken down, I do not find in it anything which necessarily compels a hypothesis of such
continued affection, contentment or open-handed generosity as to lead either party to
make a gift to the other of a substantial part of his or her fortune.

d Now there was never any secret of the fact that she entered into the agreement in
deliberate defiance of the advice of her solicitors and counsel and with a full appreciation
that she had the possibility of achieving a very much more substantial settlement from
her husband if she was prepared to bargain for it.

Nor was it simply a snap decision made in a moment of rashness. The negotiation of
the terms of the agreement continued for a full four months after this meeting and
e indeed there was specific negotiation about the terms of cl 8 having regard to the
possibility, then foreseen by the parties' advisers, that changes in fiscal legislation might
require the arrangements to be reviewed. So it is really difficult to imagine a clearer case
of knowledge, understanding and assent. Furthermore, although, as counsel for the wife
has not been slow to point out, the agreement represented for a husband as wealthy as
this husband was (and is) a very cheap bargain if one assumes the inevitability of a
f divorce, the fact is (and the evidence is really indisputable) that he was in fact a very
reluctant party to it because what he really wanted was to try to preserve the marriage.
This was not a case of a disillusioned husband seeking to rid himself cheaply of a tiresome
wife. It was, throughout, she who was keeping up the pressure for an agreement which
would enable her to clear out with her children and live her own life independently of
him. I say that in no spirit of criticism. No doubt she did find that living with him was
g intolerable to her, and it is profitless to inquire whether her reasons for so feeling were
objectively justified, but it does mean that one must examine with great care the reasons
which she now advances for having entered into the bargain of which she has since
repented and which she asks the court to ignore.

In her affidavit of 28th February 1979 she said that she was adamant that she did not
feel able to claim the large capital sum which she was advised that she would achieve and
h wanted simply a house and income which, she says, she knew the husband was only
prepared to offer. And the reason for disregarding the advice which she was given was,
she said, that she felt overpowered by his enormous wealth and position. She said that
her husband had told her that unless there was agreement he would contest the custody
of the children, and although she was assured about the likely result of custody
proceedings, she was frightened that she might lose. She also said that she was concerned
j to avoid a bitter matrimonial struggle.

In the light of the correspondence which passed between the parties' advisers, to some
of which Ormrod LJ has already referred, this account of her motives is, to say the least,
lacking in conviction although her insistence on the agreement, as it appears from the
correspondence, certainly bears out her frank admission that she was desperate to leave.
She was cross-examined at length and really substantially nothing emerged from her

evidence which gave any clue to her ready acceptance of cl 8 in defiance of the advice which she had received. Her own account of the matter was that there were three motivating factors which, in descending order of priority, she stated as being (1) her fears about the custody of the children (2) her desire to get away and (3) her desire to avoid a messy divorce.

As to the first, the judge found as a fact that the husband did not make any threats with the intention of forcing his wife to accept less than the court would order. He made it plain that he would fight for the children if agreement was not reached, but there was no finding by the judge, and indeed no evidence to justify any finding, that he ever stipulated what ultimately became enshrined in cl 8 as a sine qua non of the agreement. As regards the fear of a scandalous divorce, it is quite evident from the correspondence that that had very little influence on her; indeed she was herself, through her solicitors, using it as a weapon to force agreement. I need only refer to her solicitor's letter of 31st October 1975 in which they say: 'Whilst our client does not court publicity, please be under no illusion that she fears it and it may however be that the contrary is the case.'

Having read and reread the evidence I am driven irresistibly to the conclusion that what motivated the wife was her urgent desire to disencumber herself of the company of a husband with whom, for reasons good or bad, she found it uncomfortable to live. No doubt her love for her children and her sense of responsibility for them tempered her impatience to get away but, in the ultimate analysis, what shines through her evidence (and she was devastatingly frank about it) is that her driving force was her urgent impulse to leave her husband on terms which would give her the independence which she sought.

The learned judge clearly appreciated this. He said:

> 'The husband's stance relating to the children was, in fact, I find, prompted by his concern for them, but it did have the effect of facing the lady with the choice of leaving them behind, which she was not prepared to do, or accepting terms which were dictated in the husband's interests by [his solicitor] at the meeting which took place in [the wife's solicitor's] office, the attendance note of which I have read in full.'

That the suggestion of what finally emerged as cl 8 emanated from the husband's solicitor appears from the note itself, but if by 'dictated in the husband's interest' the judge intended to draw the inference that he was placing the wife under any pressure to accept, then that inference appears to me not only to be unsupported by the evidence but indeed to have been contradicted by the wife herself. She was asked, in terms, whether any undue pressure was put on her at this meeting and her answer was that certainly none was put on her by the husband's solicitor. The undue pressure, she asserted, came from living in a house with a man she did not want to live with and the threat of having her children taken away, and the threat of a messy divorce. Indeed counsel for the wife was, I think, constrained to admit that he really could not point to any unfair advantage taken by the husband or even to any insistence on his part on cl 8 as a term of the agreement. The nearest one came to it was an admission by the husband in cross-examination that the provision was 'of the very greatest importance'.

In the last analysis the attack on the agreement centres, as the judge recognised, not on any unfair pressure or leverage, but simply on the disparity in bargaining power between the parties, that is to say, the inequality in the weapons which were available to them if they chose to use them and not in the use of them or even threats of use of them which they actually made. That does not, in my judgment, constitute any ground for going behind this agreement in the circumstances of this case where it was throughout the wife who, for her own convenience, was pressing for it and threatening proceedings if it was not concluded and implemented. By its terms she achieved the independence she desired, she obtained the home of her own choosing, and she obtained a not insubstantial income for the support of herself and her children. It was a result which commended itself to her at the time and it does not become an unjust result merely because she could

have done better if she had taken the professional advice which she was given. Clearly
a it did not give her the standard of life which she had enjoyed in the company of a
husband with whom she was no longer prepared to live, but in a consideration of what
is just to be done in the exercise of the court's powers under the 1973 Act in the light of
the conduct of the parties, the court must, I think, start from the position that a solemn
and freely negotiated bargain by which a party defines her own requirements ought to
be adhered to unless some clear and compelling reason, such, for instance, as a drastic
b change of circumstances, is shown to the contrary. No such compelling reason has been
demonstrated in the evidence placed before this court. The wife's reasons for seeking to
resile from the agreement, as they emerge from her affidavit, appear to be that she feels
unable to offer her children amenities comparable to those which her husband is able to
offer and that she would like to buy a farm and to have a house in London. I find myself
wholly unpersuaded that such considerations furnish any ground for relieving her of the
c bargain into which she freely entered and I would hold her to that bargain. I agree
therefore that the appeal should be allowed and I concur in the course proposed by
Ormrod LJ.

Appeal allowed.

d Solicitors: *Raymond Tooth & Co* (for the wife); *Sharpe Pritchard & Co* (for the husband).

Avtar S Virdi Esq Barrister.

e

R v Sheppard and another

HOUSE OF LORDS

LORD DIPLOCK, LORD EDMUND-DAVIES, LORD FRASER OF TULLYBELTON, LORD KEITH OF KINKEL AND LORD SCARMAN

6th, 7th OCTOBER, 27th NOVEMBER 1980

f

Criminal law – Child – Wilful neglect of child – Ingredients of offence – Mens rea – Wilful neglect causing unnecessary suffering or injury to health – Accused genuinely failing to realise child needed medical care – Whether simple failure to provide medical care amounting to 'wilful' neglect – Whether offence of strict liability – Children and Young Persons Act 1933, s 1(1).

The appellants were a young couple of low intelligence living in deprived conditions.
g Following the death of their 16-month old son from hypothermia and malnutrition,
they were charged under s 1(1)[a] of the Children and Young Persons Act 1933 with
wilfully neglecting the child in a manner likely to cause it unnecessary suffering or
injury to its health. At the trial it was alleged that the appellants had failed to provide the
child with adequate medical aid on several occasions, especially during the week
h immediately preceding his death. The appellants' defence was, in effect, that they had
not realised that the child was ill enough to see a doctor, and that although they had
observed his loss of appetite and failure to ingest food they had genuinely thought that
that was due to some minor upset which would cure itself. The trial judge applying
previous authority treated the offence as one of strict liability and directed the jury that
the test of the appellants' guilt was to be judged objectively by whether a reasonable
parent, with knowledge of the facts that were known to the appellants, would have
j appreciated that failure to have the child examined was likely to cause unnecessary
suffering or injury to health. The appellants were convicted and appealed unsuccessfully
against their convictions to the Court of Appeal. On appeal to the House of Lords,

a Section 1, so far as material, is set out at p 912 *d* to *g*, post

Held – (1) (Lord Fraser and Lord Scarman dissenting) The offence of wilfully neglecting a child contrary to s 1(1) of the 1933 Act was not an offence of strict liability to be judged by the objective test of what a reasonable parent would have done, since the civil law concept of negligence was not to be imported into the offence. The actus reus of the offence was simply the failure for whatever reason to provide the child whenever it was necessary with the medical care needed while the mens rea was described in the word 'wilfully'. Furthermore, although failure to provide adequate medical care was deemed by s 1(2)(*a*) to amount to 'neglect' it was not deemed to amount to 'wilful' neglect, and therefore the prosecution was required to prove not only that the child did in fact need adequate medical care at the relevant time but also that the parents had deliberately or recklessly failed to provide that care. It followed that a genuine lack of appreciation that the child needed medical care or failure through stupidity, ignorance or personal inadequacy to provide that care were both good defences to the offence (see p 902 *j* to p 903 *f* and *j* to p 904 *a* and *d* to *f*, p 906 *h j*, p 908 *h* to p 909 *a* and *h j* and p 914 *c* to *e* and *j* to p 915 *a*, post); *R v Senior* [1895–9] All ER Rep 511 explained; *R v Lowe* [1973] 1 All ER 805 overruled.

(2) Accordingly (per Lord Diplock, Lord Edmund-Davies and Lord Keith), the proper direction to be given to a jury on a charge of wilful neglect of a child under s 1 of the 1933 Act by failing to provide adequate medical aid was that the jury had to be satisfied (a) that the child did in fact need medical aid at the time of the accused's alleged failure to provide it and (b) either that the accused was aware at the time that the child's health might be at risk if medical aid was not provided or that the accused's unawareness of that fact was due to his not caring whether the child's health was at risk. Since it was not possible to say with certainty that the jury would have convicted the appellants had they been properly directed the appeal would be allowed (see p 906 *j* to p 907 *b*, p 910 *b* to *f* and p 915 *a b*, post).

Notes

For cruelty to persons under 16, see 11 Halsbury's Laws (4th Edn) para 1252, for the meaning of neglect, see ibid para 1254, and for cases on the subject, see 15 Digest (Reissue) 1147–1149, *9700–9726*.

For the Children and Young Persons Act 1933, s 1, see 17 Halsbury's Statutes (3rd Edn) 438.

Cases referred to in opinions

Andrews v Director of Public Prosecutions [1937] 2 All ER 552, [1937] AC 576, 106 LJKB 370, 101 JP 386, 26 Cr App R 34, 35 LGR 429, sub nom *R v Andrews* 156 LT 464, 30 Cox CC 576, HL, 45 Digest (Repl) 85, *281*.

Attorney General v Bradlaugh (1885) 14 QBD 667, 54 LJQB 205, 52 LT 589, 49 JP 500, CA, 14(1) Digest (Reissue) 12, *16*.

Barras v Aberdeen Steam Trawling and Fishing Co [1933] AC 402, [1933] All ER Rep 52, 102 LJPC 33, 149 LT 169, 18 Asp MLC 384, 38 Com Cas 279, HL, 42 Digest (Repl) 696, *4468*.

Black-Clawson International Ltd v Papierwerke Waldhof-Aschaffenburg AG [1975] 1 All ER 810, [1975] AC 591, [1975] 2 WLR 513, [1975] 2 Lloyd's Rep 11, HL, Digest (Cont Vol D) 858, *460b*.

Clark v H M Advocate 1968 JC 53.

Heydon's Case (1584) 3 Co Rep 7a, 76 ER 637, 44 Digest (Repl) 203, *149*.

R v Downes (1875) 1 QBD 25, 45 LJMC 8, 33 LT 675, 40 JP 438, 13 Cox CC 111, CCR, 14(1) Digest (Reissue) 24, *69*.

R v Lowe [1973] 1 All ER 805, [1973] QB 702, [1973] 2 WLR 481, 137 JP 334, 57 Cr App R 365, CA, 15 Digest (Reissue) 1148, *9725*.

R v Petch (1909) 2 Cr App R 71, CCA, 14(1) Digest (Reissue) 412, *3489*.

R v Senior [1899] 1 QB 283, [1895–9] All ER Rep 511, 68 LJQB 175, 79 LT 562, 63 JP 8, 19 Cox CC 219, CCR, 14(1) Digest (Reissue) 25, *70*.

R v Wagstaffe (1868) 10 Cox CC 530, 32 JP 215, 15 Digest (Reissue) 1148, *9720*.

R v Walker (1934) 24 Cr App R 117, CCA, 14(1) Digest (Reissue) 275, *2077*.

Sweet v Parsley [1969] 1 All ER 347, [1970] AC 132, [1969] 2 WLR 470, 133 JP 188, 53
a Cr App R 221, HL, 15 Digest (Reissue) 1084, 9179.

Consolidated appeal

James Martin Sheppard and Jennifer Christine Sheppard appealed against the decision of the Court of Appeal, Criminal Division (Lord Widgery CJ, Bridge LJ and Woolf J) dated 15th January 1980 dismissing their appeals against their conviction on 13th November
b 1979 in the Crown Court at Northampton before his Honour Judge Gosling and a jury on a charge of wilfully neglecting their infant child, Martin James Sheppard, contrary to s 1(1) of the Children and Young Persons Act 1933. The Court of Appeal adjourned their appeals against sentence and granted leave to appeal to the House of Lords, certifying that the following point of law of general public importance was involved in the decision to dismiss the appeal against conviction: what was the proper direction to be given to a jury
c on a charge of wilful neglect of a child under s 1 of the 1933 Act as to what constituted the necessary mens rea of the offence. On 14th April 1980 the House of Lords ordered that the appeals be consolidated. The facts are set out in the opinion of Lord Diplock.

Anthony Smith QC and *J M Cartwright* for the appellants.
Anthony Palmer QC and *John Reddihough* for the Crown.

d Their Lordships took time for consideration.

27th November. The following opinions were delivered.

LORD DIPLOCK. My Lords, the appellants ('the parents') were convicted in the Crown Court at Northampton of an offence under s 1(1) of the Children and Young
e Persons Act 1933 of wilfully neglecting their infant child, Martin, between 1st July 1978 and 29th January 1979 in a manner likely to cause him unnecessary suffering or injury to health.

The child, who had been a slow developer, died, at the age of 16 months, on 28th January 1979 of hypothermia associated with malnutrition, a condition which increases the susceptibility of infants to hypothermia. If Martin had received timely medical
f attention his life might well have been saved. For five days or more before his death he had probably suffered from gastro-enteritis which had caused him to vomit up and so fail to ingest the food that had been offered to him; but the details of such symptoms of serious illness as were apparent during the period before his death do not affect the question which falls to be decided by your Lordships in this appeal and is a question of law alone.

g The gravamen of the charge against the parents was that they had failed to provide Martin with adequate medical aid on several occasions during the seven months to which the charge related and, in particular, during the week immediately preceding his death. In the light of the trial judge's instructions given to the jury as to the law applicable to the offence charged, it can safely be inferred from the verdicts of guilty that the jury found (1) that injury to Martin's health had in fact been caused by the failure by each of the
h parents to have him examined by a doctor in the period prior to his death and (2) that any reasonable parents, i e parents endowed with ordinary intelligence and not indifferent to the welfare of their child, would have recognised from the manifest symptoms of serious illness in Martin during that period that a failure to have him examined by a doctor might well result in unnecessary suffering or injury to his health.

The parents, a young couple aged 20 and 22 respectively, occupied poor accommoda-
j tion, particularly as respects heating, where the family, which included another (older) child, subsisted on a meagre income. They would appear, on the evidence, to have been of low intelligence. Their real defence, if it were capable of amounting to a defence in law, was that they did not realise that the child was ill enough to need a doctor; they had observed his loss of appetite and failure to keep down his food, but had genuinely thought that this was due to some passing minor upset to which babies are prone, from which they recover naturally without medical aid and which medical treatment can do nothing to alleviate or to hasten recovery.

We do not know whether the jury would have thought that this explanation of the parents' failure to have Martin examined by a doctor might be true. In his instructions *a* the judge had told the jury that to constitute the statutory offence with which the parents were charged it was unnecessary for the Crown to prove that at the time when it was alleged the parents should have had the child seen by a doctor either they in fact knew that their failure to do so involved a risk of causing him unnecessary suffering or injury to health or they did not care whether this was so or not. Following a line of authority by appellate courts that was binding on him, the trial judge treated the offence as one of *b* strict liability and told the jury that the test of the parents' guilt was objective only: 'Would a reasonable parent, with knowledge of the facts that were known to the accused, appreciate that failure to have the child examined was likely to cause him unnecessary suffering or injury to health?' That was the question that the jury by their verdict answered Yes, not any question as to the parents' own state of mind.

The Court of Appeal, regarding themselves as bound by the same line of authority, felt *c* compelled to dismiss the parents' appeal, but expressed their opinion that the law on this subject was worthy of review by your Lordships' House and gave the parents leave to appeal. They certified as the point of law of general public importance involved in their decision to dismiss the appeal:

> 'What is the proper direction to be given to a jury on a charge of wilful neglect of a child under s. 1 of the Children and Young Persons Act 1933 as to what constitutes *d* the necessary mens rea of the offence?'

The relevant provisions of s 1 are in the following terms:

> '(1) If any person who has attained the age of sixteen years and has the custody, charge, or care of any child or young person under that age, wilfully assaults, ill-treats, neglects, abandons, or exposes him, or causes or procures him to be assaulted, *e* ill-treated, neglected, abandoned, or exposed, in a manner likely to cause him unnecessary suffering or injury to health (including injury to or loss of sight, or hearing, or limb, or organ of the body, and any mental derangement), that person shall be guilty of a misdemeanour, and shall be liable—(*a*) on conviction on indictment, to a fine, or alternatively, or in addition thereto, to imprisonment for *f* any term not exceeding two years . . .
>
> '(2) For the purposes of this section—(*a*) a parent or other person legally liable to maintain a child or young person shall be deemed to have neglected him in a manner likely to cause injury to his health if he has failed to provide adequate food, clothing, medical aid or lodging for him, or if, having been unable otherwise to provide such food, clothing, medical aid or lodging, he has failed to take steps to procure it to be provided under enactments applicable in that behalf . . .' *g*

A provision in the same terms as s 1(1) has been on the statute book since the Prevention of Cruelty to, and Protection of, Children Act 1889. It was re-enacted successively in the Prevention of Cruelty to Children Acts 1894 and 1904, the former of which was in force when *R v Senior* [1899] 1 QB 283, [1895–9] All ER Rep 511 was decided and the latter when *R v Petch* (1909) 2 Cr App R 71 was decided. It was again re- *h* enacted in the Children Act 1908. A statutory offence defined in these terms has thus been in existence for more than ninety years.

Section 1(2)(*a*) on the other hand has its legislative origin in s 37 of the Poor Law Amendment Act 1868. This made it a summary offence for a parent to 'wilfully neglect to provide adequate Food, Clothing, Medical Aid or Lodging for his Child . . . whereby the Health of such Child shall have been or shall be likely to be seriously injured'. It was *j* the only relevant provision that was in force when *R v Downes* (1875) 1 QBD 25 was decided. It was repealed by the Prevention of Cruelty to, and Protection of, Children Act 1889 and for nineteen years, which covered the date when *R v Senior* was decided, there was no corresponding provision on the statute book until its reappearance in its present form but without the adverb 'seriously' as a 'deeming' provision in the Children Act 1908.

My Lords, the language in which the relevant provisions of the 1933 Act are drafted consists of ordinary words in common use in the English language. If I were to approach the question of their construction untrammelled (as this House is) by authority I should have little hesitation in saying that where the charge is one of wilfully neglecting to provide a child with adequate medical aid, which in appropriate cases will include precautionary medical examination, the prosecution must prove (1) that the child did in fact need medical aid at the time at which the parent is charged with having failed to provide it and (2) either that the parent was aware at that time that the child's health might be at risk if it were not provided with medical aid or that the parent's unawareness of this fact was due to his not caring whether the child's health were at risk or not.

In view of the previous authorities, however, which reach a different conclusion, it becomes necessary to analyse more closely the wording and structure of s 1(1) and (2)(*a*). This I propose to do first, then to proceed to examine the authorities themselves and finally to consider what weight should be given to the subsequent re-enactments by Parliament of the selfsame provisions.

The presence of the adverb 'wilfully' qualifying all five verbs, 'assaults, ill-treats, neglects, abandons, or exposes', makes it clear that any offence under s 1 requires mens rea, a state of mind on the part of the offender directed to the particular act or failure to act that constitutes the actus reus and warrants the description 'wilful'. The other four verbs refer to positive acts, 'neglect' refers to failure to act, and the judicial explanation of the state of mind denoted by the statutory expression 'wilfully' in relation to the doing of a positive act is not necessarily wholly apt in relation to a failure to act at all. The instant case is in the latter category, so I will confine myself to considering what is meant by wilfully neglecting a child in a manner likely to cause him unnecessary suffering or injury to health.

In construing the statutory language it is not always appropriate and may often be misleading to dissect a compound phrase and to treat a particular word or words as intended to be descriptive only of the mens rea of the offence and the remainder as defining only the actus reus. But s 1 of the 1933 Act contains in sub-s (2)(*a*) a clear indication of a dichotomy between 'wilfully' and the compound phrase 'neglected him [sc the child] in a manner likely to cause injury to his health'. When the fact of failure to provide adequate food, clothing, medical aid or lodging has been established, the deeming provision applies only to that compound phrase; it still leaves the prosecution with the burden of proving the required mens rea, the mental element of 'wilfulness' on the part of the accused.

The actus reus of the offence with which the accused were charged in the instant case does not involve construing the verb 'neglect' for the offence fell within the deeming provision; and the only question as respects the actus reus was: did the parents fail to provide for Martin in the period before his death medical aid that was in fact adequate in view of his actual state of health at the relevant time? This, as it seems to me, is a pure question of objective fact to be determined in the light of what has become known *by the date of the trial* to have been the child's actual state of health at the relevant time. It does not depend on whether a reasonably careful parent, with knowledge of those facts only which such a parent might reasonably be expected to observe for himself, would have thought it prudent to have recourse to medical aid. The concept of the reasonable man as providing the standard by which the liability of real persons for their actual conduct is to be determined is a concept of civil law, particularly in relation to the tort of negligence; the obtrusion into criminal law of conformity with the notional conduct of the reasonable man as relevant to criminal liability, though not unknown (eg in relation to provocation sufficient to reduce murder to manslaughter), is exceptional, and should not lightly be extended: see *Andrews v Director of Public Prosecutions* [1937] 2 All ER 552 at 556, [1937] AC 576 at 582–533. If failure to use the hypothetical powers of observation, ratiocination and foresight of consequences possessed by this admirable but purely notional exemplar is to constitute an ingredient of a criminal offence it must surely form part not of the actus reus but of the mens rea.

It does not, however, seem to me that the concept of the reasonable parent, what he would observe, what he would understand from what he had observed and what he would do about it, has any part to play in the mens rea of an offence in which the description of the mens rea is contained in the single adverb 'wilfully'. In the context of doing to a child a positive act (assault, ill-treat, abandon or expose) that is likely to have a specified consequences (to cause him unnecessary suffering or injury to health), 'wilfully', which must describe the state of mind of the actual doer of the act, may be capable of bearing the narrow meaning that the wilfulness required extends only to the doing of the physical act itself which in fact results in the consequences described, even though the doer thought that it would not and would not have acted as he did had he foreseen a risk that those consequences might follow. Although this is a possible meaning of b 'wilfully', it is not the natural meaning even in relation to positive acts defined by reference to the consequences to which they are likely to give rise; and, in the context of the section, if this is all the adverb 'wilfully' meant it would be otiose. Section 1(1) would have the same effect if it were omitted; for even in absolute offences (unless vicarious liability is involved) the physical act relied on as constituting the offence must be wilful in the limited sense, for which the synonym in the field of criminal liability that has now c become the common term of legal art is 'voluntary'.

So much for 'wilfully' in the context of a positive act. To 'neglect' a child is to omit to act, to fail to provide adequately for its needs, and, in the context of s 1 of the 1933 Act, its physical needs rather than its spiritual, educational, moral or emotional needs. These are dealt with by other legislation. For reasons already given the use of the verb 'neglect' cannot, in my view, of itself import into the criminal law the civil law concept of d negligence. The actus reus in a case of wilful neglect is simply a failure, for whatever reason, to provide the child whenever it in fact needs medical aid with the medical aid it needs. Such a failure as it seems to me could not be properly described as 'wilful' unless the parent *either* (1) had directed his mind to the question whether there was some risk (though it might fall far short of a probability) that the child's health might suffer unless he were examined by a doctor and provided with such curative treatment as the e examination might reveal as necessary, and had made a conscious decision, for whatever reason, to refrain from arranging for such medical examination, *or* (2) had so refrained because he did not care whether the child might be in need of medical treatment or not.

As regards the second state of mind, this imports the concept of recklessness which is a common concept in mens rea in criminal law. It is not to be confused with negligence in the civil law of tort (see *Andrews v Director of Public Prosecutions* [1937] 2 All ER 552 at f 556, [1937] AC 576 at 582–583). In speaking of the first state of mind I have referred to the parent's knowledge of the existence of some risk of injury to health rather than of a probability. The section speaks of an act or omission that is 'likely' to cause unnecessary suffering or injury to health. This word is imprecise. It is capable of covering a whole range of possibilities from 'it's on the cards' to 'it's more probable than not'; but, having regard to the ordinary parent's lack of skill in diagnosis and to the very serious g consequences which may result from failure to provide a child with timely medical attention, it should in my view be understood as excluding only what would fairly be described as highly unlikely.

I turn now to the authorities. I do not find the first of them, *R v Downes* (1875) 1 QBD 25, very helpful. The charge was one of manslaughter and involved the religious beliefs of the sect known as 'the Peculiar People' who believed that all resort to medical as h opposed to spiritual aid in illness was sinful. The statute referred to was s 37 of the Poor Law Amendment Act 1868 which has long been repealed. I pause on this case only to observe that it was decided at a period when judicial opinion was less hesitant than it has since become to accept that Parliament intended to create absolute offences which required no mens rea on the part of the accused.

To the judgment of Lord Russell CJ in *R v Senior* [1899] 1 QB 283, [1895–9] All ER j Rep 511 may be ascribed the origin of the construction of s 1(1) of the Children and Young Persons Act 1933 that has since been followed. This case also was one of failure by a member of the sect of Peculiar People to provide medical attention for his infant child. In considering this judgment it is important to remember (1) that the section of the 1894 Act that Lord Russell CJ was construing did not contain the deeming provisions that are to be found in s 1(2)(*a*) of the 1933 Act and (2) that the parent knew that the child's physical suffering might be alleviated by medical treatment but had deliberately

refrained from having recourse to it because he thought to do so would be sinful as
a showing unwillingness to accept God's will in relation to the child.

So here there was not any question of the accused parent being unaware that risk to the child's health might be involved in his failure to provide it with medical aid. He deliberately refrained from having recourse to medical aid with his eyes open to the possible consequences to the child's physical health. He broke the law because he sincerely believed that to comply with its command would be sinful and would be
b against the interests of the child's spiritual welfare. In an extempore judgment directed only to a deliberate breach of the law on conscientious grounds, it is not surprising that Lord Russell CJ felt able to deal with the construction of the statute shortly. He said ([1899] 1 QB 283 at 290–291, [1895–9] All ER Rep 511 at 514):

> '"Wilfully" means that the act is done deliberately and intentionally, not by accident or inadvertence, but so that the mind of the person who does the act goes
> c with it. Neglect is the want of reasonable care—that is, the omission of such steps as a reasonable parent would take, such as are usually taken in the ordinary experience of mankind . . .'

My Lords, there was at that time no specific reference in the statute to the provision of adequate food, clothing, medical aid or lodging. The word 'neglects' was quite
d general, qualified only by the requirement that it must be in such a manner as to be likely to cause the child unnecessary suffering or injury to health. One cannot quarrel with Lord Russell CJ's statement that 'neglect is want of reasonable care' if all that that means is that a reasonable parent who was mindful of the physical welfare of his child and *possessed of knowledge of all the relevant facts* would have taken steps that the accused omitted to take to avoid the risk of unnecessary suffering by the child or injury to his
e health. The danger of the statement is that it invites confusion between, on the one hand, neglect and, on the other hand, negligence, which calls for consideration not of what steps should have been taken for that purpose in the light of the facts as they actually were but of what steps would have been appropriate in the light of those facts only which the accused parent either knew at the time of his omission to take them or would have ascertained if he had been as mindful of the welfare of his child as a
f reasonable parent would have been.

Lord Russell CJ's brief explanation of the meaning of 'wilfully' is confined to positive physical acts. In relation to these he equiparates wilful acts with acts that would now be described as 'voluntary'. I do not myself think that this was right even in relation to positive physical acts of which the statutory definition included the characteristic that they were likely to have certain consequences; but its meaning in relation to positive acts
g is clear. I find its meaning obscure, however, in relation to a failure to do a physical act where the failure is not deliberate or intentional in the sense that consideration has been given whether or not to do it and a conscious choice made not to do it. To speak of the mind going with the act is inappropriate to omissions, but the contrast drawn between 'deliberately and intentionally' and 'by inadvertence' is at least susceptible of the meaning that if the accused has not addressed his mind to the question whether or not to do the
h physical act he is accused of omitting to do his failure to do the act is not to be treated as 'wilful'.

R v Senior, however, appears to have been treated as having decided that if the child did in fact need medical treatment it did not matter whether the accused parent actually knew or ought to have known that medical treatment was needed; he was nonetheless guilty of the offence of wilfully neglecting the child if all that he knew was that the child
j had not been seen by a doctor. This appears from the judgment of the Court of Appeal in *R v Lowe* [1973] 1 All ER 805 at 807, [1973] QB 702 at 707. So *R v Senior* has been regarded as deciding that the offence under s 1(1) of the 1933 Act is an absolute offence.

My Lords, I have already said why I do not think that *R v Senior* did so decide, even in respect of the offence created by the 1894 Act which did not contain the deeming provisions that were included for the first time in the 1908 Act. Senior did know that some risk to the child's physical health was involved in refraining from allowing his child to have medical treatment and he deliberately decided to take it. It is true that in

R v Petch (1909) a prosecution under the 1904 Act, briefly reported in 2 Cr App R 71, where the jury had brought in a verdict that the accused was 'guilty of wilful neglect through ignorance' it was held that the words 'through ignorance' did not negative the wilfulness required by the section, but no reason for this holding was given by the court.

So, up to the passing of the 1908 Act, I find nothing in the nature of a clear judicial interpretation of the words 'wilfully neglects' in what then became part of s 12 of that Act and later became s 1(1) of the 1933 Act which would justify the application of the principle laid down by this House in *Barras v Aberdeen Steam Trawling and Fishing Co Ltd* [1933] AC 402, [1933] All ER Rep 52 that where words used in a statute have received a clear judicial interpretation they are presumed to bear the same meaning when used in the same context in a subsequent Act unless a contrary meaning is indicated. Furthermore, while the *immediate* context was the same in the 1908 and 1933 Acts as it had been in the 1894 and 1904 Acts, the addition of the deeming provisions in the later Acts in my view and for reasons that I have already stated casts a light on the parliamentary intention at that time which shows it to have been inconsistent with what in subsequent cases has been treated as having been held in *R v Senior* to be the meaning of 'wilfully neglects'.

So what your Lordships are faced with is a consistent practice of the courts, extending over many years without any reported exceptions, of treating *R v Senior* as if it were a binding authority for the proposition that the statutory offence of wilfully neglecting a child by failing to provide him with adequate medical aid is an absolute offence.

In many fields of law I should hesitate long before recommending this House to overturn a long-standing judicial acceptance of a particular meaning for a statutory provision. Communis error facit lex is often a good maxim in promoting legal certainty in matters in which people arrange their affairs in reliance on the accepted meaning of a law. But three reasons persuade me not to apply the maxim in the instant case. The climate of both parliamentary and judicial opinion has been growing less favourable to the recognition of absolute offences over the last few decades, a trend to which s 1 of the Homicide Act 1957 and s 8 of the Criminal Justice Act 1967 bear witness in the case of Parliament, and in the case of the judiciary is illustrated by the speeches in this House in *Sweet v Parsley* [1969] 1 All ER 347, [1970] AC 132. Secondly, the Court of Appeal in the instant case has expressed its own feeling of unease about the present state of the authorities by which it regards itself as bound and has granted leave to appeal in order that those authorities may be reviewed by your Lordship's House. Thirdly, and most importantly, the common error, as I believe it to have been, has operated to the disadvantage of the accused and to correct it will spare from criminal conviction those only who are free from any moral guilt.

To give to s 1(1) of the 1933 Act the meaning which I suggest it bears would not encourage parents to neglect their children nor would it reduce the deterrent to child neglect provided by the section. It would afford no defence to parents who do not bother to observe their children's health or, having done so, do not care whether their children are receiving the medical examination and treatment that they need or not; it would involve the acquittal of those parents only who through ignorance or lack of intelligence are genuinely unaware that their child's health may be at risk if it is not examined by a doctor to see if it needs medical treatment. And, in view of the abhorrence which magistrates and juries feel for cruelty to helpless children, I have every confidence that they would not readily be hoodwinked by false claims by parents that it did not occur to them that an evidently sick child might need medical care.

In the instant case it seems likely that on the evidence the jury, if given the direction which I have suggested as correct, would have convicted one or both of the accused; but I do not think it possible to say with certainty that they would. It follows that in my opinion these appeals must be allowed and that the certified question should be answered: 'The proper direction to be given to a jury on a charge of wilful neglect of a child under s 1 of the Children and Young Persons Act 1933 by failing to provide adequate medical aid is that the jury must be satisfied (1) that the child did in fact need medical aid at the time at which the parent is charged with failing to provide it (the actus reus) and (2) either that the parent was aware at that time that the child's health might be at risk if it

was not provided with medical aid or that the parent's unawareness of this fact was due
a to his not caring whether his child's health was at risk or not (the mens rea).'

LORD EDMUND-DAVIES. My Lords, in November 1979 the appellants were convicted in the Crown Court at Northampton of cruelty to their son Martin between 1st July 1978 and 29th January 1979, contrary to s 1(1) of the Children and Young Persons Act 1933. By leave of the single judge, they appealed to the Court of Appeal, Criminal
b Division, which dismissed their appeals and, in granting them leave to come to this House, certified the following to be a point of law of general importance:

> 'What is the proper direction to be given to a jury on a charge of wilful neglect of a child under s. 1 of the Children and Young Persons Act 1933 as to what constitutes the necessary mens rea of the offence?'

c These are the relevant parts of s 1:

> '(1) If any person who has attained the age of 16 years and has the custody, charge, or care of any child or young person under that age, wilfully assaults, ill-treats, neglects, abandons, or exposes him ... in a manner likely to cause him unnecessary suffering or injury to health ... that person shall be guilty of a misdemeanour ...
>
> d '(2) For the purposes of this section—(*a*) a parent or other person legally liable to maintain a child or young person shall be deemed to have neglected him in a manner likely to cause injury to his health if he has failed to provide adequate food, clothing, medical aid or lodging for him ...'

Martin Sheppard, who died at the age of 16 months on 28th January 1979 of
e hypothermia associated with malnutrition, was the youngest of the appellants' three children. He had seemingly taken no solid food for about five days before death, and no milk for two days, and the complete absence of subcutaneous fat indicated that he had lacked sufficient food for a substantial period. For several days before death he had suffered from gastro-enteritis and this had rendered him incapable of ingesting nourishment. The home was poor and the main room lacked a power point. And the
f appellants had failed to keep three appointments made by the health visitor over a period of months for Martin to see a paediatrician.

The evidence fully entitled the jury to find that the child might well have been saved had he timeously received proper medical attention, and that the manifest symptoms of illness had been such that reasonable parents would have concluded that failure to secure medical aid for the child might well result in 'unnecessary suffering or injury to
g health'. But the appellants seemed to be of low intelligence, and in summary form their case was (1) that, while they appreciated that Martin's physical development had been slow, this did not alarm them as so also had been his father's, (2) that, although they were aware that he had lately been vomiting back his food, they thought that this was due to no more than a passing upset which would soon disappear of itself, and (3) that they had accordingly not realised that he needed a doctor's attention. Directing the jury, the
h learned judge said:

> 'In addressing you [defence counsel] put forward this proposition. He said that if the defendants, either of them, do not know any better, how can they be guilty of neglect? If they do not know they are neglecting the child, how can they be guilty of neglect? I hope it is quite clear on what I have told you that in my
> j judgment that is not the law ... You ask yourself what a reasonable parent would have done in the circumstances. Would he or she have behaved in this way? Did the defendants or either of them fail to do that, for whatever reasons? If they did, it is objectively neglect by that parent, and the question remains: is it wilful? As I say, so far as "wilful" is concerned, there is *no* requirement that the parent who deliberately neglects should be found to have foreseen the consequences ... The question is: is it deliberate?'

My Lords, the learned judge doubtless based his direction on the well-known decision of the Court for Crown Cases Reserved in *R v Senior* [1899] 1 QB 283, [1895–9] All ER Rep 511. There the accused, charged with the manslaughter of his son, belonged to a sect who objected on religious grounds to calling in the medical aid which would have prolonged (and probably saved) the child's life. The accused's failure in that respect was alleged to constitute a breach of s 1 of the Prevention of Cruelty to Children Act 1894, the material parts of which were basically similar to those of s 1(1) of the 1933 Act. The decision has ever since been cited on numerous occasions as authority for the proposition that, on charges of cruelty to children, it is sufficient for the prosecution to establish that the child had in fact been neglected in a manner likely to cause him unnecessary suffering or injury to health, and that the state of mind of the parent or other custodian of the child is irrelevant. So to hold is to ignore the adverb 'wilfully' qualifying the allegation of neglect, and to make the charge one of absolute liability. But whether *R v Senior* decided anything of the sort is, in my judgment, questionable, for Wills J, whose direction was upheld on appeal, had told the jury ([1899] 1 QB 283 at 286, [1895–9] All ER Rep 511 at 513):

> '... there could be no doubt that the prisoner had wilfully and deliberately abstained from calling in medical assistance, *though he and those about the child were aware for some considerable period before its death that it was in a state of great danger*, and that therefore the question was narrowed down to whether his failure to procure medical aid could be "called neglecting the child so as to cause serious injury to its health."' (Emphasis mine.)

In the light of the accused's established knowledge of the precarious state of his child's health, the jury could have been in no doubt that he foresaw the probable consequences of failure to summon medical aid. The element of wilfulness was accordingly clear, and it is against that background that one should read the extemporary holding of Lord Russell CJ ([1899] 1 QB 283 at 290–291, [1895–9] All ER Rep 511 at 514) that '"Wilfully" means that the act is done deliberately and intentionally, not by accident or inadvertence, but so that the mind of the person who does the act goes with it'.

Be that as it may, *R v Senior* was the starting point of a long series of cases culminating in the Court of Appeal, Criminal Division, judgment in *R v Lowe* [1973] 1 All ER 805 at 807, [1973] QB 702 at 707 that, in the words of Phillimore LJ:

> 'It did not matter what [the father of the deceased child] ought to have realised as the possible consequences of his failure to call a doctor—the sole question was whether his failure to do so was deliberate and thereby occasioned the results referred to in [s 1 of the 1933 Act].'

By attaching no importance to the mental ingredient of wilfulness, *R v Lowe* and all similar decisions must, in my respectful judgment, be regarded as wrongly decided. 'Neglect' is doubtless a state of fact to be objectively determined, and in the circumstances of the present case it was 'deemed' by s 1(2)(*a*) to be established by the unchallenged fact that in truth the accused had 'failed to provide adequate medical aid' for their son. But there was no 'deeming' provision in the Prevention of Cruelty to Children Act 1894 which was under consideration in *R v Senior*; it made its debut in s 12(1) of the Children Act 1908. Worthy of note is the fact that there is no statutory 'deeming' about the *wilfulness* of the neglect. Yet the essence of the prosecutor's case against these appellants was that their wilfulness followed automatically from their undoubted failure to summon medical aid. In the result, on the authority of a line of cases beginning with *R v Senior* (which related to a statute containing no 'deeming' provision), it is said that at common law wilfulness is itself to be deemed whenever neglect has been established, whether by 'deeming' or otherwise. That surely cannot be right.

But this consolidated appeal raises an issue more important than the significance of the limited operation of the 'deeming' provision in s 1(2)(*a*) of the 1933 Act. Yet again it involves consideration of the acceptability in social terms of imposing strict liability in charges laid under that section. Recognition that the necessity of establishing mens rea may (in some types of cases) be properly dispensed with does not lessen the cogency of

the oft-ignored warning of Brett MR in *Attorney General v Bradlaugh* (1885) 14 QBD 667
a at 689 that—

> 'it is contrary to the whole established law of England (unless the legislation on the subject has clearly enacted it), to say that a person can be guilty of a crime in England without a wrongful intent—without an attempt to do that which the law has forbidden.'

b It has sadly to be said that the law reports are scattered with illustrations of departures from that salutary approach. But the tide has at last, fortunately turned, a fact amply recognised by your Lordships' House in *Sweet v Parsley* [1969] 1 All ER 347 at 349, [1970] AC 132 at 148, where Lord Reid said:

> 'Our first duty is to consider the words of the Act; if they show a clear intention to create an absolute offence, that is an end of the matter. But such cases are very
> *c* rare. Sometimes the words of the section which creates a particular offence make it clear that mens rea is required in one form or another. Such cases are quite frequent. But in a very large number of cases there is no clear indication either way. In such cases there has for centuries been a presumption that Parliament did not intend to make criminals of persons who were in no way blameworthy in what they did. That means that, whenever a section is silent as to mens rea, there is a
> *d* presumption that, in order to give effect to the will of Parliament, we must read in words appropriate to require mens rea.'

It is not, I think, open to doubt that s 1 of the 1933 Act falls into the third of the categories dealt with by Lord Reid, and, that being so, 'the mere fact that Parliament has made the conduct a criminal offence gives rise to *some* implication about the mental
e element of the conduct proscribed' (See [1969] 1 All ER 347 at 361, [1970] AC 132 at 162 per Lord Diplock). So regard must always be had to the state of mind of persons charged with wilful neglect. As to this, s 8 of the Criminal Justice Act 1967 requires that the state of mind is to be ascertained by a subjective investigation into the mind of the person charged, an investigation taking into account all the established facts of the case. And its aim is to enable the magistrate or jury to answer the question: what in fact did the
f *defendant* think the position was regarding his child's health at the relevant time, that is, if he gave the matter any thought at all?

The justice (and, with respect, the common sense) of the matter is surely that, as Professor Glanville Williams has put it in his Textbook of Criminal Law (1978, p 88):

> 'We do not run to a doctor whenever a child is a little unwell. We invoke medical aid only when we think that a doctor is reasonably necessary and may do some
> *g* good. The requirement of wilfulness means, or should mean, that a parent who omits to call in the doctor to his child is not guilty of the offence if he does not know that the child needs this assistance.'

But to that must be added that a parent reckless about the state of his child's health, not caring whether or not he is at risk, cannot be heard to say that he never gave the matter
h a thought and was therefore not wilful in not calling in a doctor. In such circumstances recklessness constitutes mens rea no less than positive awareness of the risk involved in failure to act.

My Lords, the supremacy of this House in its unprecedented task of interpreting s 1 of the 1933 Act should not be regarded as fettered by its legislative ancestry or its judicial history in subordinate courts, as to which the Court of Appeal, Criminal Division, in the
j present case obviously felt some disquiet. That is understandable, for the extensive interpretation hitherto accepted involves rejection of the presumption in favour of a strict construction of criminal statutes which grew up in the eighteenth century and has persisted to this day. That interpretation has again found favour, this time with some of your Lordships, but I respectfully find it unacceptable. And, notwithstanding its conformity to that given in countless cases over the last eighty years, the direction to the jury in the present case cannot in my judgment be upheld.

Nor do I consider that to depart from it would lessen the law's protection of the welfare of children. For my part, I have confidence in the vigilance and ability of magistrates and *a* juries to detect cases of wilful neglect. The stronger the objective indications of neglect, the more difficult for defendants to repel the conclusion that they *must* have known of the plight of the children in their charge, or, at least, that they had been recklessly regardless of their welfare. And, as my noble and learned friend Lord Keith, has said, feckless parents who fall into neither of those categories are not (and, in the nature of things, cannot be) deterred by the law as hitherto understood from neglecting their *b* children. To perpetuate the prevailing approach cannot therefore be said to be either in the children's interest or in accordance with justice to those having children in their charge.

What verdicts the jury would have returned had they been directed substantially in the terms indicated in the speech of my noble and learned friend Lord Diplock (which I respectfully adopt) must remain a matter of conjecture. In sentencing the accused the *c* trial judge said that it was 'a bad case of child neglect'. But he added that the evidence did not show that the parents had been persistently and deliberately cruel, that neither of them had foreseen the child's death, and that 'you simply failed during the last month to obtain the necessary and available medical assistance'.

In my judgment, the possibility that a miscarriage of justice has occurred cannot be eliminated, and I would therefore allow this consolidated appeal. *d*

LORD FRASER OF TULLYBELTON. My Lords, the appellants were convicted of having wilfully neglected their child, Martin, in a manner likely to cause unnecessary suffering to the child, or injury to its health, contrary to the Children and Young Persons Act 1933, s 1, as amended. Martin died on 29th January 1979 aged 16 months and a post-mortem examination showed that he had not retained any solid food for five days or any *e* liquid for about two days immediately before he died. The defence was that the appellants had not appreciated that there was anything seriously the matter with him or that he required treatment by a doctor during the last two or three months of his life, and particularly during the last week of his life.

An offence under s 1(1) is committed by a parent who 'wilfully assaults, ill-treats, neglects, abandons, or exposes' a child in his care in 'a manner likely to cause him *f* unnecessary suffering or injury to health.' By sub-s (2)(*a*) a parent is deemed to have neglected his child in such a manner 'if he has failed to provide adequate food, clothing, medical care or lodging for him.' In the present case it is clear that the accused failed to provide adequate, or any, medical care for Martin during the last weeks of his life and there is therefore no doubt that they did neglect him. The question is whether they did so wilfully or not. The word 'wilfully' in this context is ambiguous. It may mean that *g* the parent neglects his child intending, or at least foreseeing, that the probable consequence of neglect is that the child will suffer injury to his health. Or it may have the more restricted meaning that the parents' neglect was conduct which was deliberate, in the sense of being conscious and free from outside pressure, without necessarily intending or foreseeing the consequences. If I had to approach the question afresh without reference to authority or to the history of the legislation, my inclination would *h* be to prefer the former, and wider, meaning of the expression. Even so I would regard the answer as doubtful.

In fact authority is not lacking and the learned judge evidently had regard to it, as he was bound to do in directing the jury. He directed them that 'neglect' was not a state of mind but was conduct, and that it was to be judged by the objective standard of what a reasonable parent would have done in the circumstances (as known to the appellants at *j* the time). The words in brackets are my own, but I think they are implied in what the judge said. He directed them further that neglect was 'wilful' if it was 'deliberate', and said: 'There is no requirement that the parent who deliberately neglects should be found to have foreseen the consequences.'

I do not think it would be right to consider the effect of the words 'wilfully neglect' in the 1933 Act without having regard to authority and to the way the legislation on this matter was developed. It is convenient to begin with *R v Wagstaffe* (1868) 10 Cox CC 530 where parents were prosecuted for manslaughter of their child by neglecting to provide proper medical attention for it. The accused belonged to the 'Peculiar People' sect, who believed that medical aid for the sick was unnecessary because they believed in the healing power of God. Their faith was based on a text of the General Epistle of James as follows (5:14–15): 'Is any sick among you? let him call for the elders of the church; and let them pray over him, anointing him with oil in the name of the Lord: and the prayer of faith shall save the sick, and the Lord shall raise him up . . .' Willes J directed the jury that if the parents had acted in what they honestly believed was the child's best interest they should be acquitted. The accused were acquitted.

Just six months after that case the Poor Law Amendment Act 1868 was passed, in July 1868, and by s 37 it created an offence 'When any Parent shall wilfully neglect to provide adequate Food, Clothing, Medical Aid, or Lodging for his Child . . . whereby the Health of such Child shall have been or shall be likely to be seriously injured . . .' There seems little doubt, as Lord Russell CJ said in *R v Senior* [1899] 1 QB 283 at 289, [1895–9] All ER Rep 511 at 514, that that section was passed because the legislature was of opinion that circumstances such as had existed in *R v Wagstaffe* were not adequately provided for by the existing law. The purpose of s 37 evidently was, in my opinion, to provide that an honest but mistaken belief that medical aid was unnecessary would not be a defence, and thus in effect to reverse the direction given by Willes J in *R v Wagstaffe*. That is how the provision was construed in *R v Downes* (1875) 1 QBD 25 where the accused was another of the Peculiar People. He was held to have been rightly convicted of manslaughter notwithstanding an express finding by the jury that he bona fide, though erroneously, believed that medical advice was not required for the child. Lord Coleridge CJ said (at 29) that, had it not been for s 37 of the 1868 Act, he would have entertained 'great doubt' on the case for the reasons stated by Willes J in *R v Wagstaffe*. Referring to s 37 he said (at 30): 'By wilfully neglecting, I understand an intentional and deliberate abstaining from providing the medical aid, knowing it to be obtainable.' He said that the motives of the accused were irrelevant, and that if he had been proceeded against summarily under the statute he would clearly have been liable. His neglect was therefore culpable and to cause death by culpable neglect was manslaughter.

The Prevention of Cruelty to, and Protection of, Children Act 1889 repealed s 37 of the 1868 Act and replaced it with a provision (in s 1) that any person who wilfully 'ill-treats, neglects, abandons, or exposes such child . . . in a manner likely etc' will be guilty of an offence. That provision was repealed and substantially re-enacted by the Prevention of Cruelty to Children Act 1894, s 1, which, apart from inserting 'assaults' immediately after 'wilfully', made no other material alteration in the provision.

Under the 1894 Act there occurred the case which has generally been regarded as the most important authority on this point, *R v Senior*, where again the accused was one of the Peculiar People. He was convicted of manslaughter and the conviction was upheld on appeal. The judge, Wills J, directed the jury ([1899] 1 QB 283 at 295, [1895–9] All ER Rep 511 at 513) that they must be satisfied first that the death of the child had been caused or accelerated by the want of medical assistance and second, that medical aid and medicine were such essential things for the child that *reasonably careful parents* in general would have provided them (my emphasis). He then directed them that the accused could not be convicted of manslaughter at common law because he had been a kind and affectionate parent in all respects except the failure to provide medical aid, but that if he had done anything which was expressly forbidden by the 1894 Act, and had thereby caused the child's death, he would be guilty 'no matter what his motive or state of mind'. The accused was well aware that the child was in a state of great danger, but the prosecution conceded that he was acting bona fide and according to his conception of duty. The evidence was that the accused believed the use of medical aid to be wrong because 'to make use of it is to indicate a want of faith in the Lord'. The report does not state whether he believed that medical aid was unnecessary for the physical needs of the child, but, having regard to his faith in the efficacy of prayer which is entirely consistent with a literal reading of the text in the Epistle of James, and also to the findings in *R v*

Downes, I think he must have believed that medical aid was both wrong *and unnecessary*. Accordingly, *R v Senior* is not, in my opinion, a case where the accused a
foresaw the probable consequences of his neglect. Lord Russell CJ said ([1899] 1 QB 283 at 290–291, [1895–9] All ER Rep 511 at 514):

> '"Wilfully" means that the act is done deliberately and intentionally, not by accident or inadvertence, but so that the mind of the person who does the act goes with it. Neglect is the want of reasonable care—that is, the omission of such steps as a reasonable parent would take, such as are usually taken in the ordinary b
> experience of mankind—that is, in such a case as the present, provided the parent had such means as would enable him to take the necessary steps.'

The next significant stage in the history comes with the Children Act 1908 which repealed earlier legislation and re-enacted the provision against neglecting a child in a manner likely to cause unnecessary suffering or injury to health etc and added a deeming c
proviso in terms substantially identical with those of s 1(2)(*a*) of the 1933 Act. Since 1908 there has been no change in the legislation which is relevant for present purposes. The effect of the deeming proviso introduced in 1908 is in my opinion merely to provide that failure to provide adequate food, medical aid etc shall constitute neglect contrary to the Act, and to leave the meaning of the word 'wilfully' unaffected. As to what is meant by 'adequate' medical aid in sub-s (2)(*a*), one asks: 'adequate for what?' It cannot mean d
adequate to prevent the likelihood of injury to the child's health, or adequate in the light of what is known at the date of the trial to have prevented injury to health, because in some cases no amount of medical aid would prevent injury to health, which is defined in sub-s (1) as 'including injury to or loss of sight, or hearing, or limb, or organ of the body, and any mental derangement'. To read 'adequate' in such an absolute sense would mean that every parent whose child died would be guilty of neglect, though not e
necessarily of wilful neglect. That cannot be right. Neglect must convey some implication of omission to perform a duty. In a case where in spite of the best medical aid the child suffered injury to health, or death, it would surely be an abuse of language to say that the parent had behaved with (non-wilful) neglect. Moreover, it would throw an unduly heavy burden on the word 'wilfully' in the context. In my opinion 'adequate' medical aid (or food, clothing or lodging) means such as ordinary reasonably careful f
parents would have provided in the circumstances as known to the accused. That agrees with the explanation of the word in the 1894 Act given by Lord Russell CJ in *R v Senior* and I see nothing in subsequent legislation to change the meaning of 'wilfully' or 'neglect' there explained. Quite the contrary. If Parliament had wished to alter or correct those meanings, that could easily have been done in the 1933 Act, but it was not.

Lord Russell CJ's explanation has been followed in many cases since *R v Senior*. For g
example, in *R v Petch* (1909) 2 Cr App R 71, where a child had died of malnutrition, the parents were convicted of 'wilful neglect through ignorance', and that was held to be a good verdict of guilty. In *R v Walker* (1934) 24 Cr App R 117 Avory J adopted the explanation from *R v Senior*. In the Scottish case of *Clark v HM Advocate* 1968 JC 53 at 57 the Lord Justice-Clerk (Grant) quoted Lord Russell CJ's explanation of 'wilfully' with approval, and treated a defence that the consequences of the failure to provide medical h
aid were not intended *or foreseen* (emphasis mine) as irrelevant. In *R v Lowe* [1973] 1 All ER 805 at 807, [1973] QB 702 at 707 Phillimore LJ, delivering the judgment of the Court of Appeal, Criminal Division, consisting of himself, Cusack and Mars-Jones JJ, summarised with approval the argument for the Crown thus:

> 'It did not matter what [the accused] ought to have realised as the possible consequences of his failure to call a doctor—the sole question was whether his j
> failure to do so was deliberate and thereby occasioned the results referred to in the section.'

My Lords, in view of the long period for which the explanation in *R v Senior* has been accepted and the large number of cases in which it has been applied, apparently with approval, by many learned judges, I would be very hesitant about overruling it now even if I thought it wrong. But I do not. The provisions of what is now s 1 of the 1933 Act are intended by Parliament for the protection of children who are unable to look after themselves and are in the care of older people. There is nothing unreasonable in their being stringent and objective. If the offence required proof that the particular parents were aware of the probable consequences of neglect, then the difficulty of proof against stupid or feckless parents would certainly be increased and so I fear might the danger to their children. Such parents would not necessarily be unaffected by the existence of an absolute offence; they might not be able to appreciate when their child needed medical care whenever the child showed any signs of ill-health, even though the signs might seem to them to be trivial. I recognise that the climate of opinion has recently become less favourable than it once was to the recognition of absolute offences, but I do not think that such change of climate as has taken place justifies us in departing from a construction of this provision which has been consistently followed by the courts since 1899, and which is, at the very least, not manifestly wrong. Especially in these times when parental responsibility for children tends to be taken all too lightly, such a sharp change towards relaxation of the law on the subject seems to me appropriate only for the legislature and not for the courts.

In these circumstances I regret that I am unable to agree with the direction which has commended itself to the majority of my noble and learned friends as being appropriate for this type of case. I would dismiss the appeal.

LORD KEITH OF KINKEL. My Lords, neglect of a child means, according to the ordinary use of language, a failure to bestow proper care and attention on the child. In my opinion that is what the word means in s 1(1) of the Children and Young Persons Act 1933, where, however, the reference to unnecessary suffering or injury to health shows that its ambit is limited to the physical needs of the child and does not cover other aspects such as the moral and educational. Parents no doubt take widely varying views about what constitutes proper care and attention for their children. It is not possible to set any absolute standard, though it might not be difficult to recognise a certain minimum below which no reasonably conscientious parent would fall. By s 1(2)(*a*), however, it is deemed to constitute neglect of a child in the relevant manner that the parent 'has failed to provide adequate food, clothing, medical care or lodging for him'. In my opinion this deeming provision sets certain objective standards which certainly cover the largest part of the field of neglect. It is unnecessary to consider how much further the field may extend. The test stated, in relation to each type of provision mentioned, is that of adequacy, a word which itself conveys the idea of a minimum standard. It is necessarily to be implied that the child had need of the provision in question.

This appeal is concerned solely with a failure to provide adequate medical care. The word 'adequate', as applied to medical care, may mean no more than 'ordinarily competent'. If it is related to anything, I think it is related to the prevention of unnecessary suffering or injury to health, as mentioned in s 1(1), where in my view the adjective 'unnecessary' qualifies both 'suffering' and 'injury to health'. There could be no question of a finding of neglect against a parent who provided ordinarily competent medical care, but whose child nevertheless suffered further injury to its health, for example paralysis in a case of poliomyelitis, because the injury to health would not in the circumstances have been unnecessary, in the sense that it could have been prevented through the provision by the parent of adequate medical care. Failure to provide adequate medical care may be deliberate, as when the child's need for it is perceived yet nothing is done, negligent, as when the need ought reasonably to have been perceived but was not, or entirely blameless, as when the need was not perceived but was not such as ought to have been perceived by an ordinary reasonable parent. I would say that in all three cases the parent has neglected the child in the sense of the statute, since I am of opinion that in a proper construction of s 1(2)(*a*) it is to be ascertained objectively and in the light of events whether the parent failed to provide ordinarily competent medical care which as a matter of fact the child needed in order to prevent unnecessary suffering or injury to its health.

I turn now to consider the meaning of the adverb 'wilfully' which governs and
qualifies 'neglects' and all the other verbs in s 1(1). This is a word which ordinarily carries *a*
a pejorative sense. It is used here to describe the mental element, which, in addition to
the fact of neglect, must be proved in order to establish an offence under the
subsection. The primary meaning of 'wilful' is 'deliberate'. So a parent who knows that
his child needs medical care and deliberately, that is by conscious decision, refrains from
calling a doctor, is guilty under the subsection. As a matter of general principle,
recklessness is to be equiparated with deliberation. A parent who fails to provide *b*
medical care which his child needs because he does not care whether it is needed or not
is reckless of his child's welfare. He too is guilty of an offence. But a parent who has
genuinely failed to appreciate that his child needs medical care, through personal
inadequacy or stupidity or both, is not guilty.

A study of the nineteenth century decisions under the statutory predecessors of s 1 of
the 1933 Act, of which the most important is *R v Senior* [1899] 1 QB 283, [1895–9] All *c*
ER Rep 511, shows that none of them was concerned with the situation where a parent
was genuinely unaware that his child needed medical care. They were concerned with
quite a different problem, namely that of parent who had failed to provide medical care
because, under the influence of a religious belief which most people would regard as
quite unreasonable, he believed that it was sinful to do so. In *R v Senior* it is clear that the
accused, under the influence of this belief, had wifully shut his eyes to the need for *d*
medical care. In the circumstances it was natural to take the view that the motive for
failing to provide it merely emphasised the deliberate nature of the failure. It is true that
in *R v Downes* (1875) 1 QBD 25 the jury found that the accused, a member of the sect who
held the religious belief I have mentioned, bona fide though erroneously believed that
medical aid was not required for the child. But none of the judgments in the case
adverted to that aspect. Lord Coleridge CJ said (at 30): 'By wilfully neglecting, I *e*
understand an intentional and deliberate abstaining from providing the medical aid,
knowing it to be obtainable.' I have difficulty in understanding how the abstention
could be intentional and deliberate if the accused did not appreciate that medical aid was
needed. It seems clear that the court proceeded wholly on the irrelevance of the accused's
motive for not providing medical aid. None of these cases show any trace of an attempt
to face up to the proper application of the law to the situation where no question of *f*
motive is in issue, but where the accused's failure to provide medical care is due to
inability, through stupidity or ignorance, to appreciate the need for it. So in my opinion
it is an error to treat anything decided or said in these cases as authoritative in that
situation. I consider that the Court of Appeal fell into that error in *R v Lowe* [1973] 1 All
ER 805, [1973] QB 702.

It is suggested that, by holding the offence created by s 1(1) of the 1933 Act not to be *g*
an absolute one but as requiring proof of the type of mens rea which I have described, the
degree of protection against neglect which is thereby afforded to children would be
unacceptably diminished. In my opinion there is no substance in that consideration. If
a parent genuinely does not appreciate that his child has need of medical care, then the
existence of an absolute offence could have no effect on his conduct, and it would not
accord with ordinary concepts of justice to hold him blameworthy. I am confident that *h*
juries and summary courts can be trusted to scrutinise most carefully the genuineness of
a claim by an accused parent that he or she did not realise that their child's condition was
such as to require medical care.

My Lords, I agree that the question certified by the Court of Appeal, Criminal
Division, should be answered as proposed by my noble and learned friend Lord Diplock,
and that the appeal should be allowed. *j*

LORD SCARMAN. My Lords, agreeing as I do with the speech delivered by my noble
and learned friend Lord Fraser, I burden your Lordships with a speech only because the
question in the appeal is of considerable social importance.

The conduct charged against the two appellants was, as the trial judge put it to the jury, that 'the parents failed, each of them, to provide adequate medical care for their infant son, Martin'. The parents knew that a doctor was available and would come, if called. They also knew that their child was ill, off his food, and that he was totally rejecting food for the two days before his death. Failure in such circumstances to obtain any medical aid was clearly a neglect of the child. The live issue in the appeal is whether the neglect was 'wilful'.

The trial judge directed the jury as to the law as follows. He said that 'a person for the purposes of this charge neglects a child if he omits to take such steps in all the circumstances of the case as a reasonable parent would take'. He then put two questions to the jury:

> 'Did this [ie the conduct of the parents] amount to neglect, objectively speaking? Was it deliberate neglect? I said "deliberate" because that is what "wilful" means ... The prosecution do not have to prove that the defendants foresaw any result from neglect.'

This direction, as the trial judge recognised, put out of court the defence, which had been urged on the jury, that whatever, in the circumstances known to the appellants, a reasonable parent might have thought or done, these parents honestly believed that medical aid was unnecessary. He dealt with the defence in perfectly clear language, which I now quote:

> 'In addressing you [defence counsel] put forward this proposition. He said that if the defendants, either of them, do not know any better, how can they be guilty of neglect? If they do not know they are neglecting the child how can they be guilty of neglect? Members of the jury, I hope it is quite clear on what I have told you that in my judgment that is not the law. You ask yourselves whether this particular behaviour that you are at the time considering amounts to neglect. That is to say, you ask yourself what a reasonable parent would have done in the circumstances. Would he or she have behaved in this way? Did the defendants or either of them fail to do that for whatever reasons? If they did, it is objectively neglect by that parent, and the question remains: is it wilful? As I say, so far as "wilful" is concerned, there is no requirement that the parent who deliberately neglects should be found to have foreseen the consequences.'

Notwithstanding the attractive invocation of general principle to be found in the speeches of my noble and learned friends Lord Diplock and Lord Edmund-Davies, I have come to the conclusion that on the true construction of s 1 of the Children and Young Persons Act 1933 the trial judge's direction was correct in law. In my judgment, the conduct must be intentional. But the word does not impart into the statutory offence the requirement of foresight or recklessness as to the consequences of what was done or not done (as the case may be).

The section has a long history. It was drafted in the nineteenth century. No doubt its language is today a little old-fashioned. The section has been frequently considered by courts, which have, since 1898, consistently construed it in the sense of the trial judge's direction in this case. Can so strong and clear a current of judicial interpretation have escaped the notice of Parliament on the occasions since 1898 on which it has had under consideration the law relating to the protection and welfare of children? The most notable of these occasions, so far as concerns the statutory offence which the House now has under consideration, were when Parliament passed into law the Children Act 1908 and the Children and Young Persons Act 1932, which together with the 1908 Act and certain other enactments were consolidated into the Children and Young Persons Act 1933.

It is not possible, in my judgment, to achieve a true interpretation of the section without a knowledge of the circumstances in which it entered the law or the history of its judicial treatment thereafter. I am content on this aspect of the matter to adopt

gratefully what my noble and learned friend Lord Fraser has said, adding only a few
comments of my own. a

First, what was the mischief which the section, when first enacted, was intended to
remedy? This has always been an important consideration in construing a statute: see
Heydon's Case (1584) 3 Co Rep 7a, 76 ER 637. A modern affirmation of the principle is
to be found in the decision of this House in *Black-Clawson International Ltd v Papierwerke
Waldhof-Aschaffenburg AG* [1975] 1 All ER 810 at 814, [1975] AC 591 at 614. I quote the
words of Lord Reid: b

> 'It has always been said to be important to consider the "mischief" which the Act
> was apparently intended to remedy. The word "mischief" is traditional. I would
> expand it in this way. In addition to reading the Act you look at the facts presumed
> to be known to Parliament when the Bill which became the Act in question was
> before it, and you consider whether there is disclosed some unsatisfactory state of
> affairs which Parliament can properly be supposed to have intended to remedy by c
> the Act.'

An indictment lay (and still lies) at common law for neglecting to provide sufficient
food, medical aid or other necessaries for a person unable to provide for himself, and for
whom the defendant was obliged by duty or contract to provide, where such neglect
injured the health of that person: see Archbold's Pleading, Evidence and Practice in d
Criminal Cases (40th Edn, 1979, p 2, para 3 and the cases there cited). Neglect of a child
was, of course, within the ambit of the offence; and, if in consequence of the neglect the
child died, an indictment lay for manslaughter. The summing up of Willes J in *R v
Wagstaffe* (1868) 10 Cox CC 530 illustrates the nature of the offence at common law as it
was understood to be before the first intervention of Parliament in this field. The
defendants in that case belonged to a sect calling themselves 'Peculiar People', one of e
whose tenets was not to call in a surgeon in cases of illness, but to trust in Providence.
They knew their child was very ill. They called in the elders of the sect, and offered up
prayers to the Lord. The child died. No doctor had been called in; but both parents had
been very kind, affectionate and attentive. In directing the jury Willes J said that to
make out the offence 'gross and culpable negligence' had to be proved; and he left to the
jury the defence that these affectionate parents had done what they honestly believed was f
best for the child. The jury acquitted.

The case was decided on 29th January 1868. A few months later Parliament enacted
the Poor Law Amendment Act 1868 (royal assent, 31st July). Section 37 provided:

> 'When any Parent shall wilfully neglect to provide adequate Food, Clothing,
> Medical Aid, or Lodging for his Child ... whereby the Health of such Child shall g
> have been or shall be likely to be seriously injured, he shall be guilty of an Offence
> punishable on summary Conviction ...'

Lord Russell CJ was surely right when he commented in *R v Senior* [1899] 1 QB 283
at 289, [1895–9] All ER Rep 511 at 514 that there could be very little doubt that the
section was enacted in consequence of the decision in *Wagstaffe's* case because the
legislature was of the opinion that circumstances such as existed in that case were not h
adequately provided for by the law.

Section 37 was considered in *R v Downes* (1875) 1 QBD 25. It was another 'Peculiar
People' case in which the child had not been given medical aid. His father was indicted
for manslaughter. He, bona fide though erroneously, believed that medical advice was
not required. He also believed that it was wrong to call in medical aid. He was
convicted. His appeal against conviction was dismissed. Lord Coleridge CJ said (at 29) j
that, apart from the statute, he would have paid the greatest consideration to the
observations of Willes J in *Wagstaffe's* case but (at 30) he interpreted the statutory words
'wilfully neglect' in the sense of 'an intentional and deliberate abstaining from providing
the medical aid, knowing it to be obtainable', and added: 'If he had been proceeded
against summarily under the statute, he would clearly have been liable.' Bramwell B's

short judgment (at 30) is so revealing as to the meaning put on the word 'wilfully' by the nineteenth century judges and legislators that I quote it in full:

> 'I am of the same opinion. I agree with my Lord Coleridge as to the difficulty which would have existed had it not been for the statute. But the statute imposes an absolute duty upon parents, whatever their conscientious scruples may be. The prisoner, therefore, wilfully—not maliciously, but intentionally, disobeyed the law, and death ensued in consequence. It is, therefore, manslaughter.'

This decision is a clear indication that s 37 was interpreted by the judges as being intended to strengthen the law protecting children by introducing a statutory offence to which, if the need for medical aid were proved, it would be no defence that the parent honestly believed it was not.

The range of conduct covered by the statutory offence was widened by the Prevention of Cruelty to, and Protection of, Children Act 1889. That Act made no reference to adequate food, clothing, medical aid or lodging, but by s 1 formulated the offence in wide terms which have not since been substantially changed. The offence remained one of wilfulness. The 1889 Act was followed by a re-enactment in s 1 of the Prevention of Cruelty to Children Act 1894. In *Senior's* case, which was decided under the 1894 Act, two points were taken by the defence: first that, owing to the changed wording of the offence, mere omission to provide medical aid was not neglect, and second, that the offence required an intention to neglect the child, or, in other words, that an honest belief by the defendant that he was not neglecting the child constituted a defence. The defendant was convicted and appealed in a Crown case reserved to a Divisional Court presided over by Lord Russell CJ. The court had no difficulty in construing the new offence so as to include within it the omission to provide medical aid. The issue, on which the court's decision has ever since been treated as authoritative, was as to the meaning of 'wilfully neglects'. Lord Russell CJ put it thus ([1899] 1 QB 283 at 290–291, [1895–9] All ER Rep 511 at 514):

> '"Wilfully" means that the act is done deliberately and intentionally, not by accident or inadvertence, but so that the mind of the person who does the act goes with it. Neglect is the want of reasonable care—that is, the omission of such steps as a reasonable parent would take, such as are usually taken in the ordinary experience of mankind—that is, in such a case as the present, provided the parent had such means as would enable him to take the necessary steps.'

The five other members of the court concurred and the appeal was dismissed.

In 1908 Parliament amended the law so as to put beyond doubt that a failure to provide adequate medical aid constituted neglect. It reintroduced the 1868 formulation while retaining the broad range of the 1889 and 1894 formulation, and did so by a 'deeming' provision which has been retained in the subsequent enactment of 1933. The relevant words of s 12(1) of the 1908 Act were:

> '... and for the purposes of this section a parent or other person ... shall be deemed to have neglected [the child] in a manner likely to cause injury to his health if he fails to provide adequate food, clothing, medical aid, or lodging for the child ...'

Parliament did not, however, enact any provision modifying or extending the meaning that the judges had put on 'wilfully'.

In 1932 Parliament reviewed the law relating to the protection and welfare of children. The Children and Young Persons Act of that year left untouched s 12 of the 1908 Act. In 1933 Parliament passed the consolidating statute, the Children and Young Persons Act 1933, s 1 of which, with minor drafting changes, re-enacted s 12 of the 1908 Act.

As my noble and learned friend Lord Fraser has shown, the case law has ever since 1899 followed what has been generally considered to be the interpretation put on the section in its 1894 enactment by the court in *Senior's* case. I would not disturb this view of the law. The purpose of Parliamentary intervention from its inception in 1868 has been to strengthen the law's protection of children. In 1875 the court in *Downes's* case interpreted the wilful neglect which Parliament that year made a statutory offence as excluding the 'honest belief' defence. Foresight of consequences was not a requirement of the offence. The courts adopted the same interpretation of wilful neglect after the offence had been broadened and reformulated in 1889 and 1908. I do not accept that, had the courts misunderstood the intention of Parliament, the law would not have been amended. The reasons which could lead Parliament in this field to accept a measure of strict criminal liability are not far to seek. It is an area where the welfare of the child may well justify an exception from the general principle of criminal responsibility.

I do not share the view expressed by my noble and learned friends Lord Edmund-Davies and Lord Keith that parents who though not reckless or indifferent to their child's welfare yet fail through stupidity or immaturity to appreciate the need for medical aid will not be deterred by a criminal sanction. They underrate, with respect, the deterrent power of the law. The existence of a penalty can concentrate and sharpen the minds of men and women. It is for this reason that in some exceptional areas the law accepts strict liability.

To conclude, the view of the law which I have reached is that the statutory offence is committed (1) if the defendant knew that the child was sick and that medical aid was available or could be obtained and (2) if a reasonable parent, having the knowledge of the circumstances which the defendant had, would not have failed to provide medical aid. I would, therefore, dismiss the appeal.

Appeal allowed.

Solicitors: *Burnhams*, Wellingborough (for the appellants); *Director of Public Prosecutions.*

Mary Rose Plummer Barrister.

Barralet and others v Attorney General and others

CHANCERY DIVISION

DILLON J

3rd, 4th, 5th, 6th, 9th, 10th, 11th JUNE 1980

Charity – Religion – Society for study and dissemination of ethical principles – Whether ethics same as religion – Whether objects of society the advancement of religion.

Charity – Benefit to the community – Society for study and dissemination of ethical principles and cultivation of rational belief – Correct approach for deciding whether a trust for purposes beneficial to community – Whether objects of society beneficial to community.

Charity – Education – Society for study and dissemination of ethical principles and cultivation of rational belief – Whether objects of society the advancement of education.

The objects of a learned society were (i) 'the study and dissemination of ethical principles', those being the belief that the object of human existence was the discovery of truth by reason and not by revelation by supernatural power, and belief in the excellence of truth,

love and beauty as opposed to belief in any supernatural power, and (ii) 'the cultivation
a of a rational religious sentiment'. Cultivation of that sentiment extended to cultivation
among members of the public. The word 'religious' in the second part of the objects was
used in a sense which eschewed all supernatural belief. Although the society's beliefs
were non-theistic, it was agnostic rather than atheistic regarding belief in God.
Dissemination of ethical principles was carried out by the society by holding lectures and
musical concerts by persons of high repute which were open to the public, by publishing
b a monthly magazine and the text of some of the lectures which were available to the
public, and by other social activities. Since there was an element of public benefit in the
society's objects and activities, it was not merely a members' club devoted to members'
self improvement. By an originating summons the society asked the court to declare
whether or not its objects were charitable. The society contended, primarily, that its
objects were charitable as being for the advancement of religion because a sincere belief
c in ethical qualities was a religious belief and the advancement of such belief was the
advancement of religion. Alternatively, the society contended that its objects were
charitable as being for purposes beneficial to the community or for the advancement of
education.

Held – (1) The word 'religion', in its natural and accustomed sense, was concerned with
d man's relations with God whereas ethics was concerned with man's relations with man
and the two concepts were therefore different and were not made the same merely
because ethics involved a sincere inquiry into the nature of God. Although a sincere
belief might fill in the possessor's life a place parallel to that occupied by belief in God in
the minds of theists, that did not make the belief a religion. Furthermore, faith in a god
and worship of that god by submission, veneration, praise, thanksgiving or prayer were
e essential attributes of religion, and there could be no worship in that sense of an ethical
or philosophical ideal. It followed that the society's objects were not for the advancement
of religion and were not charitable on that ground (see p 924 *b c* and *h*, p 926 *a* and p 928
h, post); dicta of Lord Parker in *Bowman v Secular Society Ltd* [1916–17] All ER Rep at 19–
20, of Donovan J in *United Grand Lodge of Ancient Free and Accepted Masons of England v
Holborn Borough Council* [1957] 3 All ER at 285 and of Buckley LJ in *R v Registrar General,
f ex parte Segerdal* [1970] 3 All ER at 892 applied; *United States v Seeger* (1965) 380 US 163
not followed.

(2) The correct approach in deciding whether a trust fell within the charitable category
of being for purposes beneficial to the community was to determine, by analogy with the
preamble to the Charitable Uses Act 1601 and by analogy with decided cases, whether the
trust in question was within the spirit and intendment of the preamble. Since the whole
g of the society's objects were for the mental and moral improvement of man they were,
by analogy with decided cases, charitable objects as being for purposes beneficial to the
community (see p 926 *j* to p 927 *a* and p 928 *h*, post); *Re Scowcroft* [1895–9] All ER Rep
274, *Re Hood* [1930] All ER Rep 215 and dicta of Cohen J in *Re Price* [1943] 2 All ER at
510–511 and of Lord Simonds in *Williams' Trustees v Inland Revenue Comrs* [1947] 1 All
ER at 518–519 applied; dictum of Russell LJ in *Incorporated Council of Law Reporting for
h England and Wales v Attorney General* [1971] 3 All ER at 1036 considered.

(3) The whole of the society's objects were also charitable as being for the advancement
of education, a term which was to be construed widely. The dissemination of ethical
principles in the first part of the objects included dissemination of the fruits of the study
of those principles, and those objects were therefore for the advancement of education.
The cultivation of a rational religious sentiment in the second part of the objects was also
j for the advancement of education, for a 'rational' sentiment or state of mind could be
cultivated only by educational methods. The fact that in the second part of the objects
the word 'religious' was incorrectly used would not prevent the court from controlling
the administration of the society's trusts and ensuring that the society's funds were
applied for the purposes of the society (see p 927 *j* and p 928 *b* to *e* and *g h*, post); dictum
of Lord Loreburn LC in *Weir v Crum-Brown* [1908] AC at 167 applied.

Notes

For charitable religious purposes, see 5 Halsbury's Laws (4th Edn) paras 528–530 and for cases on the subject see 8(1) Digest (Reissue), 266–267, *159–163*.

For charitable educational purposes, see 5 Halsbury's Laws (4th Edn) paras 522–526, and for cases on the subject, see 8(1) Digest (Reissue) 256–266, *112–157*.

For purposes beneficial to the community, see 5 Halsbury's Laws (4th Edn) paras 535–538, and for cases on the subject, see 8(1) Digest (Reissue) 288–292, *334–359*.

Cases referred to in judgment

Attorney General v National Provincial & Union Bank of England [1924] AC 262, [1923] All ER Rep 123, sub nom *Re Tetley, Attorney General v National Provincial & Union Bank of England* 93 LJ Ch 231, 131 LT 34, HL, 8(1) Digest (Reissue) 324, *612*.

Bowman v Secular Society Ltd [1917] AC 406, [1916–17] All ER Rep 1, 86 LJ Ch 568, 117 LT 161, HL, 8(1) Digest (Reissue 302, *427*.

Brisbane City Council v Attorney General for Queensland [1978] 3 All ER 30, [1979] AC 411, [1978] 3 WLR 299, 19 ALR 681, PC Digest (Cont Vol E) 38, **154a*.

Hood, Re, Public Trustee v Hood [1931] 1 Ch 240, [1930] All ER Rep 215, 143 LT 691, CA, 8(1) Digest (Reissue) 259, *133*.

Hopkins' Will Trusts Re, Naish v Francis Bacon Society Inc [1964] 3 All ER 46, [1965] Ch 669, [1964] 3 WLR 840, 8(1) Digest (Reissue) 257, *120*.

Income Tax Special Purposes Comrs v Pemsel [1891] AC 531, [1891–4] All ER Rep 28, 61 LJQB 265, 65 LT 621, 55 JP 805, 3 Tax Cas 53, HL, 8(1) Digest (Reissue) 236, *1*.

Incorporated Council of Law Reporting for England and Wales v Attorney General [1971] 3 All ER 1029, [1972] Ch 73, [1971] 3 WLR 853, 47 Tax Cas 321, CA, 8(1) Digest (Reissue) 260, *137*.

Inland Revenue Comrs v McMullen [1980] 1 All ER 884, [1980] 2 WLR 416, HL; *rvsg* [1979] 1 All ER 588, [1979] 1 WLR 130, CA, Digest (Cont Vol E) 37, *119a*.

Inland Revenue Comrs v Yorkshire Agricultural Society [1928] 1 QB 611, [1927] All ER Rep 536, 97 LJKB 100, 138 LT 192, 13 Tax Cas 58, CA, 28(1) Digest (Reissue) 475, *1705*.

Macduff, Re, Macduff v Macduff [1896] 2 Ch 451, [1895–9] All ER Rep 154, 65 LJ Ch 700, 74 LT 706, CA, 8(1) Digest (Reissue) 322, *599*.

Price, Re, Midland Bank Executor and Trustee Co Ltd v Harwood [1943] 2 All ER 505, [1943] Ch 422, 112 LJ Ch 273, 169 LT 121, 8(1) Digest (Reissue) 260, *135*.

R v Registrar General, ex parte Segerdal [1970] 3 All ER 886, [1970] 2 QB 697, [1970] 3 WLR 479, [1970] RA 439, CA, Digest (Cont Vol C) 308, *4096a*.

Scottish Burial Reform and Cremation Society Ltd v Glasgow City Corpn [1967] 3 All ER 215, [1968] AC 138, [1967] 3 WLR 1132, 132 JP 30 [1967] RA 272, 1967 SC (HL) 116, HL, 8(1) Digest (Reissue) 301, *424*.

Scowcroft, Re, Ormrod v Wilkinson [1898] 2 Ch 638, [1895–9] All ER Rep 274, 67 LJ Ch 697, 79 LT 342, 8(1) Digest (Reissue) 259, *132*.

United Grand Lodge of Ancient Free and Accepted Masons of England v Holborn Borough Council [1957] 3 All ER 281, [1957] 1 WLR 1080, 121 JP 595, 56 LGR 68, 50 R & IT 709, 2 RRC 190, CA, 38 Digest (Repl) 535, *343*.

United States v Seeger (1965) 380 US 163, 85 S Ct 850.

Washington Ethical Society v District of Columbia (1957) 249 F 2d 127.

Weir v Crum-Brown [1908] AC 162, 77 LJPC 41, 98 LT 325, HL, 8(1) Digest (Reissue) 315, *549*.

Williams' (Sir Howell Jones) Trustees v Inland Revenue Comrs [1947] 1 All ER 513, [1947] AC 447, [1948] LJR 644, 176 LT 462, 27 Tax Cas 409, HL, 28(1) Digest (Reissue) 17, *54*.

Cases also cited

Bawden's Settlement, Re, Besant v London Hospital Board of Governors [1953] 2 All ER 1235, [1954] 1 WLR 33.

Berry v St Marylebone Corpn [1957] 3 All ER 677, [1958] Ch 406, CA.

Chartered Insurance Institute v London Corpn [1957] 2 All ER 638, [1957] 1 WLR 867.

Coates' Will Trusts, Re, Re Byng's Will Trusts [1959] 2 All ER 51, [1959] 1 WLR 375.

Hummeltenberg Re, Beatty v London Spiritualistic Alliance [1923] 1 Ch 237, [1923] All ER Rep 49.
Keren Kayemeth Le Jisroel Ltd v Inland Revenue Comrs [1931] 2 KB 465, CA.
National Anti-Vivisection Society v Inland Revenue Comrs [1947] 2 All ER 217, [1948] AC 31, HL.
Oxford Group v Inland Revenue Comrs [1949] 2 All ER 537, 31 Tax Cas 221, CA.
Pinion, Re, Westminster Bank Ltd v Pinion [1964] 1 All ER 890, [1965] Ch 85, CA.
Shaw, Re, Public Trustee v Day [1957] 1 All ER 745, [1957] 1 WLR 729.
Shaw's Will Trusts, Re, National Provincial Bank Ltd v National City Bank Ltd [1952] 1 All ER 49, [1952] Ch 163.
Thackrah, Re, Thakrah v Wilson [1939] 2 All ER 4.
Thornton v Howe (1861) 31 Beav 14, 54 ER 1042.
Tuck's Settlement Trusts, Re [1978] 1 All ER 1047, [1978] Ch 49, CA.
Watson, Re, Hobbs v Smith [1973] 3 All ER 678, [1973] 1 WLR 1472.
Wedgwood, Re, Allen v Wedgwood [1915] 1 Ch 113, CA.

Originating summons

By an originating summons dated 17th April 1978 the plaintiffs, Colin Eustace Barralet, Lily Louisa Booker and Benjamin Oliver Warwick, three of the trustees of a deed of declaration of trusts executed by Henry Sandford and others and dated 1st February 1825, suing as such and on behalf of the members of the South Place Ethical Society ('the society'), an unincorporated association whose address was Conway Hall, 25 Red Lion Square, London, sought, inter alia, by para 3 of the summons, a declaration whether the objects of the society (i) were for the advancement of religion or otherwise charitable, or (ii) were not charitable. The defendants to the summons were the Attorney General, the Treasury Solicitor and the Inland Revenue Commissioners. The facts are set out in the judgment.

Owen Swingland QC and *David Ritchie* for the society.
John Mummery for the Attorney General.
John L Knox QC and *R W Ham* for the Inland Revenue Comrs.

DILLON J. I have been asked to hear argument on question 3 raised by this originating summons, and to give judgment on that question before hearing argument on the other questions raised in the summons. Question 3 seeks a declaration whether the objects of the South Place Ethical Society (i) are for the advancement of religion or otherwise charitable or (ii) are not charitable.

The society started as the congregation of a chapel at South Place in Finsbury which was opened in 1824. It adopted the name 'South Place Religious Society' in the 1860s, and changed that name to 'South Place Ethical Society' in 1887. The name 'South Place Ethical Society' has been retained ever since. The chapel was closed in 1927 and sold, and a site in Red Lion Square was acquired, on which the present and well-known Conway Hall was built. It is named after Moncure Conway, who was minister at the chapel for a long time in the last century, and has been the society's base since 1930.

The present objects of the society are stated in r 2 of its rules as follows:

> 'The Objects of the Society are the study and dissemination of ethical principles and the cultivation of a rational religious sentiment.'

These objects have been among the objects of the society since around the turn of the century, but before 1930 there was an additional and plainly non-charitable object, namely the promotion of human welfare in harmony with advancing knowledge. The fact that there was at that time this additional object, and that it was dropped without any apparent change in the substance of the actual activities of the society, emphasises that the basic question in deciding whether or not the society's objects are charitable is a question of construction of those objects as set out in the society's rules, and then a question of assessing the objects as so construed against the yardstick of what the law regards as charitable.

The rules contain, in r 22, reference to possible alteration of the objects of the society, but it is common ground that any power to alter the rules should be ignored until it is exercised. The question whether the society is now a charity has to be decided on its objects as they now are. This is in line with the observations of Atkin LJ in *Inland Revenue Comrs v Yorkshire Agricultural Society* [1928] 1 KB 611 at 633, [1927] All ER Rep 536 at 542.

There is no doubt at all that the members of the society are sincere people of the highest integrity. Counsel for the society described it as being at the least a wholly learned society with a deep and thoughtful philosophy. They are not atheists, opposed to all belief in any god. They are agnostic about the existence of any god. The society is non-theistic, like all other ethical movements. The existence of God is neither affirmed nor denied. In the objects, in the phrase 'cultivation of a rational religious sentiment', the word 'religious' is used in a sense which eschews all supernatural belief. I shall return to this later.

Ethical principles mean, in brief summary, the belief in the excellence of truth, love and beauty, but not belief in anything supernatural. The society's beliefs are an aspect of humanism and in the tradition of Platonism, and its ideal really represents a philosophical concept. The society further believes that the great object of human existence is the discovery of truth by, as I understand it, intellectual appreciation or reason and not revelation.

The objects refer to the dissemination as well as the study of ethical principles, and I should briefly mention the activities of the society.

It holds Sunday meetings, which are open to the public. At these meetings lectures are given, often by visiting lecturers, who may be persons of very considerable distinction, on subjects of serious and mainly intellectual interest, and the lectures are followed by discussions. There are other lectures on special occasions, such as the Conway Memorial Lectures, in memory of Moncure Conway. These are also open to the public. The society publishes a monthly magazine called the Ethical Record, which is available to the public, and others of its lectures are published and widely disseminated. In addition, in pursuit of the ideal of beauty and the appreciation of it, since the turn of the century, chamber-music concerts have been given on Sunday nights in winter, first at the South Place chapel, and, since 1930, in the Conway Hall. These are open to the public. Performers of high repute and quality take part and the performances at these concerts are regarded by music experts as of a very high standard indeed. There are also, and not unexpectedly, social activities, which are broadly similar to the social activities of the congregation of a parish church, but these social activities are, in my judgment, ancillary to the other activities of the society. At the highest it can be said that they serve, as with the parish church, to further the esprit de corps of the congregation, and this in turn helps to further the cultivation of the rational religious sentiment.

However high-minded the members are, the question for decision is whether the objects of the society are charitable. It is well known that the development of the English law as to what is or is not a charity has been empirical, but Lord Macnaghten's division of charitable objects into four classes in his speech in *Income Tax Special Purposes Comrs v Pemsel* [1891] AC 531, [1891–4] All ER Rep 28 has always been found convenient and been followed.

In the present case counsel for the society contends primarily that the society is charitable because its objects are for the advancement of religion, but he says, alternatively, that it is charitable because its objects are for other purposes beneficial to the community within the fourth of Lord Macnaghten's categories, or are for the advancement of education. Counsel for the Attorney General neither supports nor opposes the society in its claim that its objects are for the advancement of religion, but he does support the society in claiming to be charitable on the ground that its objects are for the advancement of education or other purposes beneficial to the community within the fourth category. The Inland Revenue Commissioners oppose the society's claims root and branch. They have been joined in these proceedings because the Treasury Solicitor intimated that there was no claim to the society's assets as bona vacantia, and there was therefore no one else who opposed the arguments that the society is a charity.

One of the requirements of a charity is that there should be some element of public benefit in the sense that it must not be merely a members' club or devoted to the self-improvement of its own members. In the case of this society I have no doubt that it is not just a members club and that it is not merely concerned with the self-improvement of its members. In its objects there is reference to the cultivation of a rational religious sentiment; that in my judgment means cultivation wherever it can be cultivated and not merely cultivation among the members themselves.

I propose therefore to consider first the claim that the society is charitable because its objects are for the advancement of religion. In considering this, as in considering the other claims, I keep very much in mind the observation of Lord Wilberforce in the *Scottish Burial Reform and Cremation Society Ltd v Glasgow City Corpn* [1967] 3 All ER 215 at 223, [1968] AC 138 at 154, that the law of charity is a moving subject which may well have evolved even since 1891. The submissions of counsel for the society seek to establish that this is indeed so, having regard to current thinking in the field of religion.

Of course it has long been established that a trust can be valid and charitable as for the advancement of religion although the religion which is sought to be advanced is not the Christian religion. In *Bowman v Secular Society Ltd* [1917] AC 406 at 448–450, [1916–17] All ER Rep 1 at 21–22 Lord Parker of Waddington gave a very clear and valuable summary of the history of the approach of the law to religious charitable trusts. He said ([1917] AC 406 at 449, [1916–17] All ER Rep 1 at 22):

> 'It would seem to follow that a trust for the purpose of any kind of monotheistic theism would be a good charitable trust.'

Counsel for the society accepts that, so far as it goes, but he submits that Lord Parker should have gone further, even in 1917 (because the society's beliefs go back before that date) and the court should go further now. The society says that religion does not have to be theist or dependent on a god; any sincere belief in ethical qualities is religious, because such qualities as truth, love and beauty are sacred, and the advancement of any such belief is the advancement of religion.

I have been referred to certain decisions in the United States, which suggest that the arguments of counsel for the society on this point would be likely to be accepted in the United States, and the society would there be regarded as a body established for the advancement of religion. One decision is the decision of the Supreme Court of the United States in *United States v Seeger* (1965) 380 US 163. That was concerned with the exemption of a conscientious objector from conscription on grounds of religion. The decision is not of course binding on me but the reasoning merits serious consideration, not least because it really states the substance of much of the argument that counsel for the society is putting forward, and states it with great clarity. The judgment of the court (delivered by Clark J) gives as the ratio (at 176) that in the opinion of the court—

> 'A sincere and meaningful belief, which occupies in the life of its possessor a place parallel to that filled by the God of those admittedly qualifying for the exemption on the grounds of religion comes within the statutory definition.'

In his separate opinion, concurring with the opinion of the court, Douglas J said (at 193):

> '... a sincere belief which in his life fills the same place as a belief in God fills in the life of an orthodox religionist is entitled to exemption ...'

There is also a decision of the United States Court of Appeals for the District of Columbia in *Washington Ethical Society v District of Columbia* (1957) 249 F 2d 127 in which it was held that the Washington Ethical Society was entitled to exemption from local taxes or rates in respect of its premises under an exemption accorded for buildings belonging to religious corporations or societies and used for religious worship. The report of the judgment of the court is brief. It seems, however, to have adopted a definition of the verb 'to worship' as meaning to perform religious services, and to have adopted a dictionary definition of religion as 'devotion to some principle; strict fidelity or faithfulness; conscientiousness; pious affection or attachment'. In the *Washington Ethical Society* case the context of the Act undoubtedly weighed with the court. In *United States v Seeger* the judgments and the reasoning are much more thorough, and a great deal of weight has been placed on the views of modern theologians, including Bishop John Robinson and the views that he expressed in his book 'Honest to God'.

In a free country, and I have no reason to suppose that this country is less free than the United States, it is natural that the court should desire not to discriminate between beliefs deeply and sincerely held, whether they are beliefs in a god or in the excellence of man or in ethical principles or in Platonism or some other scheme of philosophy. But I do not see that that warrants extending the meaning of the word 'religion' so as to embrace all other beliefs and philosophies. Religion, as I see it, is concerned with man's relations with God, and ethics are concerned with man's relations with man. The two are not the same, and are not made the same by sincere inquiry into the question, what is God. If reason leads people not to accept Christianity or any known religion, but they do believe in the excellence of qualities such as truth, beauty and love, or believe in the Platonic concept of the ideal, their beliefs may be to them the equivalent of a religion, but viewed objectively they are not religion. The ground of the opinion of the Supreme Court in *Seeger's* case, that any belief occupying in the life of its possessor a place parallel to that occupied by belief in God in the minds of theists is religion, prompts the comment that parallels, by definition, never meet.

In *Bowman v Secular Society Ltd* [1917] AC 406 at 445, [1916–17] All ER Rep 1 at 19–20, Lord Parker, in commenting on one of the objects of the society in that case, namely to promote the principle that human conduct should be based upon natural knowledge and not on supernatural belief, and that human welfare in this world is the proper end of all thought and action, said of that object:

> 'It is not a religious trust, for it relegates religion to a region in which it is to have no influence on human conduct.'

That comment seems to me to be equally applicable to the objects of the society in the present case, and it is not to be answered in my judgment by attempting to extend the meaning of religion. Lord Parker has used the word 'in its natural and accustomed sense'.

Again, in *United Grand Lodge of Ancient, Free and Accepted Masons of England v Holborn Borough Council* [1957] 3 All ER 281 at 285, [1957] 1 WLR at 1080 at 1090 Donovan J, delivering the judgment of the Divisional Court, after commenting that freemasonry held out certain standards of truth and justice by which masons were urged to regulate their conduct, and commenting that, in particular, masons were urged to be reverent, honest, compassionate, loyal, temperate, benevolent and chaste, said:

> 'Admirable though these objects are, it seems to us impossible to say that they add up to the advancement of religion.'

Therefore I take the view that the objects of this society are not for the advancement of religion.

There is a further point. It seems to me that two of the essential attributes of religion are faith and worship; faith in a god and worship of that god. This is supported by the definitions of religion given in the Oxford English Dictionary, although I appreciate that there are other definitions in other dictionaries and books. The Oxford Dictionary gives as one of the definitions of religion:

> 'a particular system of faith and worship ... recognition on the part of man of some higher, unseen power as having control of his destiny and as being entitled to obedience, reverence and worship.'

In *R v Registrar General, ex parte Segerdal* [1970] 3 All ER 886 at 892 [1970] 2 QB 697 at 709, which was concerned with the so-called Church of Scientology, Buckley LJ in his judgment said this:

> 'Worship I take to be something which must have some, at least, of the following
> a characteristics: submission to the object worshipped, veneration of that object, praise, thanksgiving, prayer or intercession.'

He went on to say that, looking at the wedding ceremony of the scientologists, he could find nothing in the form of ceremony which would not be appropriate in a purely civil, non-religious ceremony such as is conducted in a registry office, and that it contained none of the elements which he had suggested were necessary elements of worship. He
b then said ([1970] 3 All ER 886 at 892, [1970] 2 QB 697 at 709):

> 'I do not say that you would need to find every element in every act which could properly be described as worship, but when you find an act which contains none of those elements, in my judgment, it cannot answer to the description of an act of worship.'

c The society really accepts that worship by that definition, which in my view is the correct definition in considering whether a body is charitable for the advancement of religion, is not practised by the society because, indeed, it is not possible to worship in that way a mere ethical or philosophical ideal. I have been referred, as setting out the views of the society, to a pamphlet issued in 1979 by Mr Cadogan, the secretary of the
d society. It is headed 'The Two Meanings of Worship'. After referring to the fact that the society had abandoned prayer in 1869, that is to say, in Mr Cadogan's words, that particular form of worship that is addressed to a personal god, a supreme being, a deity, Mr Cadogan went on to say that there are two kinds of worship, natural and supernatural:

> 'It is worship of the supernatural that we have transcended. For further guidance we should look to our Appointed Lecturers. The one who very specifically addressed
> e himself to the subject of worship was the late Lord Sorenson.'

He then quotes from an article of Lord Sorenson's, published in the 'Ethical Record' in 1971, where Lord Sorenson said:

> 'Worship is not necessarily theological, for the word is a contraction of "worth-ship", which means appreciation, and notwithstanding understandable prejudice,
> f itself a feeling by any humanists, in fact they too, engage in worship. They do so when, like myself, they sit in their garden and not argue with the flowers, but simply absorb their delight, and thus find benediction. They do so when for a while they allow music to nourish their hearts, when they have any kind of aesthetic experience, when in fellowship they possess a sense of profound kinship of hearts in communion, and when they find emotional satisfaction in devoted service to an
> g ideal or a great cause or when they see an infant gazing into its mother's eyes. This "appreciation" others call worship. It is an emotional response to something or someone beyond yet related to oneself...'

It seems to me that that is not worship in the sense in which worship is an attribute of religion.

h One of the matters that has been pressed in argument and which weighed with Douglas J in *Seeger's* case is the position of Buddhism, which is accepted by everyone as being a religion. It is said that religion cannot be necessarily theist or dependent on belief in a god, a supernatural or supreme being, because Buddhism does not have any such belief. I do not think it is necessary to explore that further in this judgment, because I do not know enough about Buddhism. It may be that the answer in respect of
j Buddhism is to treat it as an exception, as Lord Denning MR did in his judgment in *R v Registrar General* [1970] 3 All ER 886 at 890, [1970] 2 QB 697 at 707. Alternatively, it may be that Buddhism is not an exception, because I have been supplied with an affidavit by his Honour Judge Christmas Humphreys QC, an eminent English Buddhist, where he says that he does not accept the suggestion that 'Buddhism denies a supreme being'. I would not wish to suggest in any way that Buddhism is not a religion.

The society therefore fails in my judgment to make out its case to be charitable on the ground that its objects are for the advancement of religion. I turn therefore to the two *a* other heads, the fourth category of other purposes beneficial to the community and the category of trusts for the advancement of education.

The fourth category developed from the matters specified in the preamble to the Statute of Elizabeth (43 Eliz 1 c 4, the Charitable Uses Act 1601), but it has long been recognised that it is not limited to those matters actually listed in the preamble which do not fall within Lord Macnaghten's other three categories of the relief of poverty, the *b* advancement of education and the advancement of religion. It is also clear, as stated in Tudor on Charities (6th Edn, 1967, pp 85, 120) that the fourth category can include trusts for certain purposes tending to promote the mental or moral improvement of the community. It is on the basis of mental or moral improvement of the community that animal welfare trusts have been supported. But it is plain that not all objects which tend to promote the moral improvement of the community are charitable. *c*

Again, as Wilberforce J pointed out in *Re Hopkins' Will Trusts* [1964] 3 All ER 46 at 52, [1965] Ch 669 at 680–681, beneficial in the fourth category is not limited to the production of material benefit, but includes at least benefit in the intellectual or artistic fields.

In *Incorporated Council of Law Reporting for England and Wales v Attorney General* [1971] 3 All ER 1029 at 1036, [1972] Ch 73 at 88–89 Russell LJ seems to have taken the view *d* that the court can hold that there are some purposes 'so beneficial or of such utility' to the community that they ought prima facie to be accepted as charitable. With deference, I find it difficult to adopt that approach in view of the comments of Lord Simonds in *Williams' Trustees v Inland Revenue Commissioners* [1947] 1 All ER 513 at 518–519, [1947] AC 447 at 455 where, in holding that the promotion of the moral, social, spiritual and educational welfare of the Welsh people was not charitable, he pointed out that it was *e* really turning the question upside down to start with considering whether something was for the benefit of the community. He said:

> 'My Lords, there are, I think, two propositions which must ever be borne in mind in any case in which the question is whether a trust is charitable. The first is that it is still the general law that a trust is not charitable and entitled to the privileges which charity confers unless it is within the spirit and intendment of the preamble *f* to 43 Eliz c. 4, which is expressly preserved by s. 13(2) of the Mortmain and Charitable Uses Act, 1888. The second is that the classification of charity in its legal sense into four principal divisions by LORD MACNAGHTEN in *Pemsel's* case ([1891] AC 583, [1891–4] All ER Rep 286) must always be read subject to the qualification appearing in the judgment of LINDLEY, L.J. in *Re Macduff* ([1896] 2 Ch 466, [1895–9] All ER Rep 184): "Now SIR SAMUEL ROMILLY did not mean, and I am certain that *g* LORD MACNAGHTEN did not mean to say, that every object of public general utility must necessarily be a charity. Some may be and some may not be." This observation has been expanded by VISCOUNT CAVE, L.C. in this House in *A.G. v National Provincial Bank* ([1924] AC 265, [1923] All ER Rep 123) in these words: "LORD MACNAGHTEN did not mean that all trusts beneficial to the community are charitable, but that there were certain beneficial trusts which fall within that *h* category: and accordingly to argue that because a trust is for a purpose beneficial to the community it is therefore a charitable trust is to turn round his sentence and to give it a different meaning. So here it is not enough to say that the trust in question is for public purposes beneficial to the community or is for the public welfare; you must also show it to be a charitable trust."' *j*

Therefore it seems to me that the approach to be adopted in considering whether something is within the fourth category is the approach of analogy from what is stated in the preamble to the Statute of Elizabeth or from what has already been held to be charitable within the fourth category.

The question is whether the trust is within the spirit and intendment of the preamble, and the route that the courts have traditionally adopted is the route of precedent and

analogy, as stated by Lord Wilberforce in *Brisbane City Council v Attorney General* [1978]
a 3 All ER 30 at 33, [1979] AC 411 at 422. One of the difficulties of this approach is that it is often difficult to say which of Lord Macnaghten's categories has been held to cover some particular decided case. Many cases, such as *Re Hopkins' Will Trust* and, in the view of the majority of the court, the *Incorporated Council of Law Reporting* case have been held to be charitable under two categories: advancement of education and the fourth category of other purposes beneficial to the community. The argument often puts the claim to
b charitable status, as in the present case, on two or three of the four headings, and the judgments have not differentiated.

There are three cases which are put before me as analogies in the present case. The earliest is *Re Scowcroft* [1898] 2 Ch 638, [1895–9] All ER Rep 274. In that case there was a devise of a village club and reading room to be maintained for the religious and mental improvement of people in the neighbourhood, and there was an additional reference
c that it was to be kept free from intoxicants and dancing and to be used for the furtherance of conservative principles. Stirling J regarded this as being a valid charitable trust because it was for religious and mental improvement, and he held that the reference to conservative principles was ancillary and not a sufficient limitation to prevent it from being a perfectly good charitable gift, as he clearly thought it would be if it were for the furtherance of religious and mental improvement alone.

d Then in *Re Hood* [1931] 1 Ch 240, [1930] All ER Rep 215 there was a trust for the application of Christian principles to all human relationships, and this was linked to the reduction and ultimate extinguishment of the drink traffic. It was held that the trust for the application of Christian principles to all human relationships was a good charitable trust. The trust was put forward in the lower court by Mr Crossman for the Attorney General as being charitable for three reasons: for the advancement of religion, for the
e advancement of education and for the benefit of the community as being calculated to promote public morality.

Then there is *Re Price* [1943] 2 All ER 505, [1943] Ch 422. Here what Cohen J said about the bequest being charitable was obiter because, even if it was not charitable, it was nonetheless a valid gift to a particular society which the society was at liberty to spend. But Cohen J's views are expressed at some length in a considered judgment, and I find
f them helpful. Counsel for the Inland Revenue Commissioners has reserved to a higher court, should this case go there, the submission that Cohen J was not only obiter but wrong. The trust there was a trust of a fund to be used for carrying on the teachings of Dr Rudolph Steiner and according to the evidence set out ([1943] 2 All ER 505 at 509, [1943] Ch 422 at 431)—

> *g* 'The teachings of Steiner are directed to the extension of knowledge of the spiritual in man and in the universe generally and of the interaction of the spiritual and the physical.'

The deponent went on to say that Rudolph Steiner sought to show both how this knowledge could be acquired and how it could be applied for the benefit of man in a wide range of activities. Cohen J accepted the submission that the teachings of Rudolph
h Steiner were directed to the mental or moral improvement of man, and he would have held, if he had not held the gift otherwise valid, that a trust carrying on those teachings was a charitable trust. The submission had been that the trust was charitable as being for mental, moral or religious improvement. Those therefore are the available analogies.

On the question of trusts for the advancement of education, the authorities show that the term 'education' is to be construed very widely. In the *Incorporated Council of Law*
j *Reporting* case, Buckley LJ in his judgment said ([1971] 3 All ER 1029 at 1046 [1972] Ch 73 at 102) that this head 'should be regarded as extending to the improvement of a useful branch of human knowledge and its public dissemination'. In *Re Hopkins' Will Trust* Wilberforce J said ([1964] 3 All ER 46 at 52, [1965] Ch 669 at 680):

> '... that the word "education" ... must be used in a wide sense, certainly extending beyond teaching, and that the requirement is that, in order to be

> charitable, research must either be of educational value to the researcher or must be so directed as to lead to something which will pass into the store of educational *a* material, or so as to improve the sum of communicable knowledge in an area which education may cover—education in this last context extending to the formation of literary taste and appreciation.'

The context indicates that literary taste and appreciation did not exclude musical taste and appreciation.

I turn therefore to the objects of this society, as set out in its rules. The first part of the *b* objects is the study and dissemination of ethical principles. Dissemination, I think, includes dissemination of the fruits of the study, and I have no doubt that that part of the objects satisfies the criterion of charity as being for the advancement of education. The second part, the cultivation of a rational religious sentiment, is considerably more difficult. As I have already said, I do not think that the cultivation is limited to cultivation of the requisite sentiment in the members of the society and in no one else. *c* In the context the society is outward looking, and the cultivation would extend to all members of the public whom the society's teachings may reach. The sentiment or state of mind is to be rational, that is to say founded in reason. As I see it, a sentiment or attitude of mind founded in reason can only be cultivated or encouraged to grow by educational methods, including music, and the development of the appreciation of music by performance of high quality. The difficulty in this part of the society's objects *d* lies in expressing a very lofty and possibly unattainable ideal in a very few words, and the difficulty is compounded by the choice of the word 'religious', which, while giving the flavour of what is in mind, is not in my view used in its correct sense. Despite this, however, I do not see that the court would have any difficulty in controlling the administration of the society's assets.

It is well established that a trust cannot be charitable if its objects are too vague to be *e* carried into effect or controlled by the court. In *Weir v Crum-Brown* [1908] AC 162 at 167 however, Lord Loreburn LC in discussing the kind and degree of certainty required, said:

> 'All that can be required is that the description of the class to be benefited shall be sufficiently certain to enable men of common sense to carry out the expressed *f* wishes of the testator.'

He said that he was satisfied that the trustees, or, failing them, the court, would find no difficulty in giving effect to the bequest. Those observations were approved and applied by Lord Hailsham LC in *Inland Revenue Comrs v McMullen* [1980] 1 All ER 884 at 890, 893, [1980] 2 WLR 416 at 422, 426 where he also referred to Lord Loreburn's doctrine of the benignant approach to charitable trusts. It seems to me that these objects are *g* objects which the court could control and the court could see that the purposes of the funds of the society were not misapplied. In my judgment the second part of the society's objects is also charitable as being for the advancement of education. Alternatively, by analogy to *Re Price*, *Re Hood* and *Re Scowcroft*, the whole of the objects of the society are charitable within the fourth class. I propose therefore to declare that the objects of the society are charitable, but not for the advancement of religion. *h*

Declaration accordingly.

Solicitors: *Jaques & Co* (for the society); *Treasury Solicitor*; *Solicitor of Inland Revenue.*

Evelyn M C Budd Barrister.

End of Volume 3